The Golden Age Of Radio

SPIRIT OF COMMUNICATION

RADIO YESTERYEAR®

PRESENTS

THE GOLDEN AGE OF RADIO

by J. David Goldin

The Standard
Reference Work
Of Radio Programs and
Radio Performers
Of The Past

THE COLONIAL NETWORK
21 BROOKLINE AVENUE
BOSTON
START INSIDE
33⅓ R.P.M.
RECORDED IN THE STUDIOS OF WAAB
FEDERAL
RADIO EDUCATION COMMITTEE
U. S. Office of Education
Federal Security Agency
G-3014
INSIDE START
33 1/3 RPM
"WE HOLD THESE TRUTHS"
By Norman Corwin
Original Musical Score by Bernard Hermann
With an Address by
President Franklin D. Roosevelt
Broadcast on December 15, 1941, on the NBC, CBS and Mutual networks, featuring Lieutenant James Stewart, Orson Welles, and Dr. Leopold Stokowski.
Permission for the distribution of this recording for STRICTLY EDUCATIONAL PURPOSES has been granted by the AFM, AFRA, AGMA, and Equity.
Mfg. by
Allied Record Mfg. Co.
Hollywood, Calif.
California
Inside
Start
33.3 R.P.M.
Min.
Sec.
"SI AND ELMER"
Copyright 1933 by PERRY CRANDALL
AMERICAN
BROADCASTING
COMPANY
TYPE LAT SPEED 33⅓
Start Outside
THE VOICE OF AMERICA
Lateral Cut ★ 33⅓ R. P. M. ★ Outside Start
This transcription is the property of the UNITED STATES GOVERNMENT and is subject to recall on demand. For OFFICIAL USE only. Reproduction or use for commercial purposes is prohibited.
UNITED STATES INFORMATION AGENCY
DIVISION OF INFORMATION
OFFICE FOR EMERGENCY
Episode 14
"THE NEW SLAVERY"
Time 14:45
YOU CAN'T DO BUSINESS WITH HITLER
This recording contains only music that may be performed in U. S. A. without any further license.
OUTSIDE START
ORTHOTONE
RECORDING
Manufactured By
ALLIED RECORD MFG. CO.
Hollywood, Calif.
INT-148
RADIO SECTION

Library of Congress Cataloging in Publication Data
Goldin, J. David
The Golden Age Of Radio
Reference
1. Radio programs of the past
2. Radio performers of the past
Library Of Congress Catalog Card Number: 98-85541
ISBN 0-929541-93-6

Published in the United States by
Yesteryear Press
Box C
Sandy Hook, CT 06482

BUSINESSMAN'S VOICE (PAUL FREES):	Radio? Why should I advertise on radio? There's nothing to look at... no pictures!
FREBERG:	Listen. You can do things on radio you couldn't possibly do on TV.
BUSINESSMAN'S VOICE:	That'll be the day!
FREBERG:	All right. Watch this. Ahem (with reverb) Okay people. Now, when I give you the cue, I want the 700 foot mountain of whipped cream to roll into Lake Michigan which has been drained and filled with hot chocolate. Then the Royal Canadian Air Force will fly overhead towing a 10-ton Marischino cherry which will be dropped into the whipped cream to the cheering of 25,000 extras. All right...cue the mountain!

Sound Effects: huge rumbling sound, creaking timbers, enormous splash

FREBERG:	Cue the Air Force!

Sound Effects: squadron of planes droning overhead

FREBERG:	Cue the cherry!

Sound Effects: a bomb, whistling as it falls through the air, landing with a huge splat!

FREBERG:	Okay, 25,000 cheering extras!

Sound Effects: crowd cheering...builds and cuts off

FREBERG:	Now, you want to try that on television?
BUSINESSMAN'S VOICE:	Well...
FREBERG:	You see radio's a very special medium because it stretches the imagination.
BUSINESSMAN'S VOICE:	Doesn't television stretch the imagination?
FREBERG:	Up to 21 inches, yes!

SARAH VAUGHAN (singing with orchestra)

Who listens to radio?
That go-where-you-go medium called radio!
That's with you every night...
through the long commuter fight
and in the morning with your toast and marm-a-ladio!
Who listens to radio?
No matter if it's summer, winter, spring or fall.
Who listens to radio?
Only 150 million people...that's all!*

A promotional announcement made for the S.R.A. (Station Representatives Association), 1965.
*Written and produced, *words and music by Stan Freberg.* *© Freberg Music Corp. Property of Freberg Ltd.*

Contents

Between The Bookends *(with Ted Malone) (7/26/34 - 6/3/55) 15m; (originally broadcast in Kansas City in 1929) various days and times including: 7/26/34 - 9/27/34, CBS, Thu, 5:15 pm (first network show); 5/13/35 - 10/2/36, CBS, 5t, 15m; 10/5/36 - 4/2/37, Hinds, CBS, 5t, 15m, 12:15 pm; 7/5/37 - 7/16/37, CBS, 5t, 12:45 pm 1937 - 9/9/38, CBS, 2t, 15m; 9/12/38 - 4/21/39; 7/3/39 - 45, Sus, Bl/ABC, 5t, 15m; 1945 - 49, Westinghouse, ABC, 5t/3t, 15m also 3/9/46 - 5/25/46, ABC, Sat, 11:30 am;1949 - 6/3/55, various sponsors, ABC, 15m, various days*

Foreword

ENG. 183 9-36
Property of
NATIONAL BROADCASTING COMPANY, INC.
Made for Reference Purposes Only
NOT TO BE USED FOR ANY PURPOSE EXCEPT WITH WRITTEN CONSENT OF VICE-PRESIDENT IN CHARGE OF PROGRAMS
33⅓ R. P. M.
START INSIDE
PROGRAM
DATE
TIME
NETWORK
PART
OF
T. T. #
USE ONLY NEEDLES DESIGNED FOR ACETATE

Recollections At Thirty (with Ed Herlihy and Fred Collins) (6/11/56 - 5/8/57) NBC, Wed, 8:30 pm

When Dave Goldin was six, his parents, desiring to reward him for some precocity or other, asked him what he'd like to have. Young Dave cupped his hand behind his ear and replied, "WOR, New York...or an older brother." For the past thirty-five years Dave has been a kind of brother to me. And since I'm a year his senior, he got some of his wish. WOR remains unscathed.

When Dave was in third grade, his teacher yelled at her noisy class to settle down. "I don't want to hear even a peep!" she warned. You guessed it! The almost inaudible "peep!" came from a dark haired nine-year-old boy in jeans, a t-shirt and with the faint beginnings of a handlebar mustache under his nose. Even then Dave was a rebel. (Historians may wish to tie this event to Dave's later distinction of being the only student ever thrown out of one of NYU Professor Irving Falk's classes during Falk's academic career of nearly four decades. Are you beginning to get the picture?)

I first encountered Dave in August, 1963 in a New York University radio studio (the one in which the painters filled all the little holes in the acoustic wall tile with putty). It was my first day there and I entered the control room to find another student at the board. Several students and the professor were sitting along the back wall. The students were rolling their eyes and the professor - Bob Emerson - was trying to pull out what little hair remained on his head. "Why did I ever leave CBS?" he groaned in agony. "Doesn't he have another pair of jeans?" asked one student.

Looking through the control room glass, I saw a tall, dark haired fellow with a handlebar mustache standing by an RCA 44. "KNX, Los Angeles," he intoned, more groans from near the back wall. "This is the Don Lee Network...America is sold on ABC...It's 8 pm, B-U-L-0-V-A, Bulova watch time...Sunday is funday on NBC...." Right then I should've known.

After NYU, I ran into Dave in the prep class for the FCC license at Announcer Training Studios. Dave got his First Phone and became an instructor there. Later, he became an engineer at Mutual, NBC radio and CBS. The people at ABC breathed a sigh of relief. Then, like in an old Warner Brothers movie script where two pals take different paths (one becomes a priest, the other goes into the lingerie business), Dave and I went our separate ways, me into academia. But along his circuitous route to a job where he didn't have to wear a necktie, Dave founded Radio Yesteryear, (item #23 in the Radio Yesteryear archive is an updating of Lucille Fletcher's "The Hitchhiker," with Dave playing the Orson Welles part and me doing the engineering, music and sound effects. May Lucille and Orson forgive us!)

I could go on sharing anecdotes about Dave Goldin for a hundred pages and not scratch the surface. But what's important is that Dave is the man most responsible for unearthing, organizing, restoring and disseminating vintage radio programming to a worldwide audience. Virtually all other collectors and collections owe Dave a huge debt, as do many thousands of people born after creative radio's demise. Through Dave's effort, they've learned that well done radio production can be far more entertaining than video or film. Most people today have lost the art of listening, of using their imaginations. Dave's work has remedied that for many. And historians and researchers have long benefited from the Radio Yesteryear archive for scholarly and documentary work.

When Dave started Radio Yesteryear, the networks - if they hadn't already discarded their archival material - didn't care about it; yet, they wouldn't let anyone hear it. Collectors, then, had limited material and poor communication with non-collectors. Dissemination was almost non-existant. It was Goldin's gregariousness that made collecting old radio shows a part of our popular culture.

Were it not for Radio Yesteryear, so much great STUFF would be lost forever. The other night, watching some newsmagazine on tv, I was struck by how awful the announcer was. Where are the Glenn Riggses, the Arthur Garys, the Truman Bradleys, the Jack Costellos, the Fred Foys, the Jackson Becks? Today, they're found mostly in the Radio Yesteryear archive, the world's most comprehensive radio collection, and essentially the work of one man, J. David Goldin. Dave, thousands thank you for being the man who "saved radio." This book is only a part of that.

- Eli Segal
April, 1998

Eli Segal, an award-winning writer/producer/director, is a communication consultant and Professor of Media Communication at Governors State University, near Chicago. He resides in Kalamazoo, Michigan with his wife Connie and their cat, Splice.

Dedications and Acknowledgments

A Helping Hand (with John J. Anthony) (10/13/41 - 1/30/42) Ironized Yeast, CBS, 5t, 15m

This book, like most of radio, is a collaborative effort. I couldn't have done it alone.

It is dedicated to the memory of my parents, Buddy and Alberta Goldin, who with love and understanding endured a son interested in radio and recordings to the exclusion of much else. They seldom said "make it lower"... except when it really was too loud. It is also dedicated with all my love to my daughter Rachel Goldin and to Suzy Lamson who carry on a tradition of putting up with a guy whose passion for radio extends to having over 300 of them around the house. Doesn't everyone have 300 radios at home? I dedicate this effort as well to my fellow broadcasters, who made it all happen.

I'd like to thank Blaine Kruger, the Art Director of Radio Yesteryear and Dorothy Hill-Barnes and Victoria Drought of the Radio Yesteryear art department for taking my rough sketches, trying to teach me what good design was all about, and putting my scribbled notes into readable form. I owe much to Craig Gallichotte and all the other Radio Yesteryear employees who kept the place in business while I was off remembering "the good old days."

My thanks are also for John Gallichotte of the TLC Lotus Company for writing, re-writing and re-re-writing the custom software programs that brought the Radio Yesteryear archive out of the carbon-paper-and-index-card era and into the 20th century. Without John's software, this book would have taken not years, but decades.

I am especially obligated to Professor Eli Segal who was kind enough to write a flattering (if somewhat embellished) foreword to this book. His knowledge and proof-reading of proper names is as encyclopedic as is his ability to identify radio actors by their voices alone. He is also the world's second best tape editor. By the way Eli, ABC Radio offered me a job twice, but I was happily employed elsewhere both times.

Those who have written histories of various aspects of our business have also contributed much. Erik Barnouw, Frank Buxton, Tom DeLong, John Dunning, Ron Lackmann, Bill Owen, B. Eric Rhoads, Milo Ryan, Irving Settel, Harrison Summers, Vincent Terrace and many others.

And last, but not least, a tip of the Rophone windscreen to the many amateur audio archeologists who actually do this kind of research for the fun of it. I'm delighted to take advantage of their efforts and organize the fruits of their labors. The following people, some of whom I've never met, some now deceased, are from a list that's far from comprehensive. My apologies to those omitted. I thank you all and invite those readers who can point out the many errors in this volume to join this list of immortals in future editions:

Jerry Appleman, Richard Arnold, Don Aston, Jerry Austin, Dick Ayers, Bob Axley, John Barker, Ron Barnett, Marvin Bensman, Frank Bequaert, Peter Bernstock, Bill Blalock, Andy Blatt, Jim Blythe, Frank Bresee, Josh Bray, Bill Bright, Dr. Barry Brooks, Bill Brooks, Bob Burnham, Don Brush, Dominick Cancilla, Hugh Carlson, Ed Carr, Jerry Chapman, Phil Chavin, Barbara Davies, Tom DeLong, Fred E. Dickey, Gary Dudash, Doug Due, John Eccles, Phil Esser, Gene Ewan, John Edwards, Randy Eidemiller, Phil Evans, Mel Fischer, Robert Flatter, John Gassman, Larry Gassman, Vic Gerard, Gerald Gibson, Frank Gilmore, Ken Greenwald, Chuck Haddix, Miller Hahn, Martin Halperin, Donald Hansen, Richard Hayes, Henry Hinkel, Richard Hill, Roger Hill, Roy Hooper, Robert Imes, Chuck Juzek, Walter Keepers, Jr., Steve Kelez, Gordon Kelley, Rodney Kennedy, Larry Kiner, Fred King, Roger Kobzina, Doug Kosmonek, Nat Kruskol, Ron Lackmann, Steve Lewis, Bob Marquette, Pat McCoy, John McDonough, Louis McMahon, Marc Michaud, Aaron Mintz, Gerry Monaghan, Tom Monroe, Lee Munsick, Ken Neal, Todd Nebel, Mike Ogden, John Olsen, Jr., Cortlandt Parent, Don Pellow, Jerry Perchesky, E. M. Pienkos, Richard Pirodsky, Michael Pitts, Tom Price, Bruce Ruggles, Joseph Russell, Bill Sabis, Tom Salome, Terry Salomonson, Ted Serrill, Dejay Shriner, Dave Siegel, Al Sikora,Walter Smith, Steven Smolian, Eugene Soucek, Ray Stanich, Andrew Steinberg, Frank Swayze, Tom van der Voort, Les Waffen, George Wagner, Joe Webb, Harold Widdison, Les Zeiger and many others.

Introduction

DON LEE PRODUCTION
RECORDED BY
DON LEE BROADCASTING SYSTEM
KHJ, LOS ANGELES
PLAY 33⅓ REV.
START OUTSIDE

True Confessions (with Bess Johnson) (1944 - 1958) True Confessions Magazine, NBC, 5t (1946) Mut

This reference work must begin with two admissions, either of which usually dooms a book's usefulness

1. It is out of date.

2. It is inaccurate.

Having said this, I hasten to add that as of this writing, it is the best of its kind. The study of radio programming from the start of the "broadcast era" (generally considered the November 2, 1920 election eve coverage by KDKA in Pittsburgh) to the end of the so-called "Golden Age" (I declare that to be September 30, 1962 when CBS radio ended the last two dramatic shows still on the air) is similar to the science of archeology. The researcher is forced to draw conclusions about a great many things from very little evidence. Radio existed long before those sporadic election results came from Pittsburgh. (Guglielmo Marconi is said to have made the first successful radio transmission in 1895). WHA in Madison, Wisconsin was among the several stations broadcasting before KDKA. Radio existed long after "Suspense" and "Yours Truly, Johnny Dollar" went off the air. (Rumor has it there are still a few radio stations broadcasting even today.)

We are therefore, dealing with a continuum; a gradual evolution from a scientific experiment, to a practical means of point to point communication, to an amusing novelty, to a creative source of evening entertainment in the living room, to the news/information/recorded music service that has evolved today. As the audio archeologist digs through the sounds of radio's past, it becomes apparent how little we know. I admit that I've turned up recordings of less than a dozen broadcasts that I can date before 1930. That's a whole decade of programming by hundreds of different stations, networks and performers of which little or nothing can be heard or is even known! Obviously this situation will improve as the study continues, but I suspect that decades from now, it will still be accurate to say, "how little we know!"

This knowledge vacuum leads to an attempt to organize what we do know and to standardize the way we know it. This is the first book of its kind, but it will not be the last. Previous efforts have been in several other categories;

1. Histories of broadcasting. The best example being Erik Barnouw's trilogy beginning with "A Tower In Babel."

2. Picture books about radio. These are essentially photo collections, such as "The Pictorial History Of Radio" by Irving Settel.

3. Program rosters and cast lists, These attempt to list the better known network shows and those who participated in them. "The Big Broadcast" by Frank Buxton and Bill Owen was the first and is still one of the best of this type.

4. Program essay collections. The exhaustive "Tune In Yesterday" by John Dunning goes beyond cast lists, giving anecdotal histories of the better known shows.

There are other types of books and hybrids, all of which add to our knowledge of the subject. Most are genuine works of scholarship, involving considerable research and effort. Believe me, I know. This work is an attempt to fill two specific gaps in radio knowledge. 1. It tries to be a compilation of all network programs, plus significant local and regional broadcasts, listing facts about when the programs began, when they ended, where - as well as when - they were found on the radio dial. 2. It's a list of the people who were involved in putting these programs on the air. I define "people" as those who received air credits (or should have received air credits) which were usually heard at the end of the show. To list the names of the station management, sales and engineering staff and all the other behind the scenes personnel at the larger stations and networks is beyond the scope of any book. Before the war, it was not uncommon for some stations in larger cities to have hundreds of employees. On the other hand, the entire Mutual network had about 75 people in 1967, including secretaries and mailroom personnel.

So why then, is this book both out of date and inaccurate? It's out of date because the information comes from two sources. 1. An analysis of programs that are in the Radio Yesteryear archive. 2. The study of information researched about programs that are not yet in the Radio Yesteryear archive (and may never be). There are today 61,160 programs that have been located, sonically improved, recorded, catalogued and available for study from Radio Yesteryear. This reflects an arbitrary limit I imposed so that I could conclude this research. The acquisition, recording and cataloguing has continued far beyond this number, but information from these newly discovered programs is not integrated into this book. I had to stop somewhere. Outside of the Radio Yesteryear archive, discovery continues, books are being written and then revised, in fact, a whole army of amateur archeologists (don't they have anything better to do?) supplies us with new information continuously. This, therefore is a work in progress. It was out of date the day it went to the printers.

Stay tuned for the second edition.

The information is inaccurate not because I want it to be, nor because of sloppy scholarship, but because the information is still coming in, and some of it is going to be wrong. How do you determine when a network program started or stopped? You can check the newspapers and Radio Guide-type publications as a start. How do you handle that information when you find an original recording of a program clearly labeled as being broadcast a year after the show supposedly went off the air? What do you do when the program was heard locally in New York or Cleveland before it became a network show heard all over the country? What's the date of the show's last broadcast if it went off the network, ran just in Chicago for two years and then went into syndication around the country and was offered for sale to other radio stations for the next ten years (and then perhaps revived and resold a decade after that)? How do you determine the day of the week a show was on if it was heard on different days in different parts of the country! How can you tell its time of broadcast with four time zones, plus the delayed and repeat broadcasts? Who is the sponsor of the show if the product being advertised was different in varying parts of the country or changed from week to week! How do you spell the name of a performer whose name is mentioned on a program's closing credits, but who wasn't important enough to be mentioned in print anywhere? Is his name spelled Steven? Stephen? Stefan? Alan or Allen or Allan? William or Bill? Robert or Bob? Richard or Dick? What should Ira Grossel's listing be since he was called Jeff Chandler for most of his career, except that one western series when he was billed as "Tex" Chandler? How do you handle Myron Wallace when he starts calling himself Mike Wallace, or when Connee Boswell becomes Connie Boswell? Is an actress' name spelled Ann or Anne, is Gil Stratton the same actor as Gil Stratton, Jr.? And was Michael Ann Barrett a man or a woman?

It's easy to ask the above questions; it's a lot harder to answer them. Obviously, I've made decisions and compromises. Much time consuming research was necessary, some of it is bound to be wrong. That's why this work contains inaccuracies. There's a misspelled name on one of the labels on the copyright page and another name wrong on one of the tickets on the back cover. Can you spot them? One final question: how do you spell a name or describe a program when two trusted sources disagree?

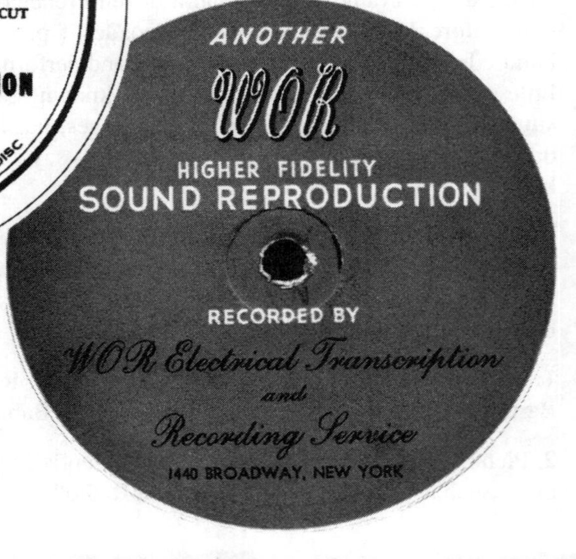

His name was Ed. His job was to stand guard just outside Jack Benny's vault, Ed hadn't seen the light of day for many years (he wasn't even sure who won the war...the Civil War!). Whenever Jack would need 50¢ to pay Professor LeBlanc for a violin lesson, or for some other worthy cause, he would descend to the basement, go past the alligator pit, set off the bells and whistles (and even a fog horn that would remind one of a Lifebuoy soap commercial) and go past the clanking chains to where Ed waited to lower the drawbridge over the moat. The security surrounding the Radio Yesteryear archive is not quite that severe...but the tapes are kept in an underground vault. We'll visit that tape vault a bit later.

If you're going to start preserving sound recordings, you might as well do it the right way. Of course, there is no one "right way," and most of us listen to and collect radio programs for the fun of it, not to preserve an art form for future generations. Nevertheless, certain standards have evolved in the radio industry, the recording studio business and institutions with sound archives such as The Library Of Congress and The National Archives.

> ***Inner Sanctum** (1/7/41 - 10/5/52) host was Raymond Edward Johnson until 5/22/45; then Paul McGrath as of 9/28/45; followed by House Jameson 1/7/41 - 3/11/41, Carters, Bl, Tue, 9:30 pm; 3/16/41 - 8/29/43, Carters, Bl, Sun, 8:30 pm; 9/4/43 - 11/18/44, Colgate, CBS, Sat, 8:30 pm; 11/22/44 - 12/27/44, Colgate, CBS, Wed, 9 pm; 1/2/45 - 6/26/45; 9/28/45 - 6/18/46, Lipton, CBS, Tue, 9 pm; 7/29/46 - 4/17/50, Bromo Seltzer, CBS, Mon, 8 pm; 9/4/50 - 6/18/51, Mars, ABC, Mon, 8 pm; 6/22/52 - 10/5/52, Pearson Pharmaceutical Company, CBS, Sun, 8 pm (all shows were repeats)*

The Radio Yesteryear archive began December 16, 1957, a few months after I bought my first tape recorder. It was on that date that I recorded my first program off the air, and I did it poorly. I believed what has turned out to be one of the greatest lies ever issued by the electronics industry: "the tape speed of 3 3/4 ips is suitable for voice recording." Here are some of the standards I've set (with a firmer grasp of reality than 1957 tape recorder manufacturers) and some of the practices we follow at Radio Yesteryear. Your standards needn't be as high, but it's nice to know how you compare.

(The following is technical stuff, skip ahead if you're not interested.)

An Overview Of Radio Recording Techniques:

From the earliest broadcast recording in our archive (it was recorded December 17, 1923, although we do have cylinder recordings of code transmissions dating back to 1913) until approximately 1931, radio recordings were made on 78 rpm records, either 10" or 12" in diameter. They looked pretty much like the commercially available records of the day. There were two types of these records: 1. "Pressings" were stamped out of shellac or a hard plastic-like material from master dies and distributed in quantity. The most famous and probably the first example of these radio pressings were "Amos 'n' Andy" shows. Starting in 1928, they were sold to stations that were not affiliated with the new "network" over which Amos 'n' Andy was heard. 2. "Cuttings" were made by putting a steel or aluminum blank disc that had been coated with nitrocellulose (a black goo) on a lathe and cutting the grooves with a sharp stylus as the program was heard. This was called an "instantaneous" recording because you could take what you'd just done off the lathe, put it on a phonograph and listen to it. A pressing had to first undergo chemical and physical processing before you could hear it (therefore, it wasn't "instantaneous"). The disadvantage of "cuttings" was that you could only make one copy at a time, unlike the mass produced "pressings." Because of their far smaller number, "cuttings" are almost always scarcer and more valuable today than mass produced "pressings." By squeezing the grooves close together, you could record a half hour show on 8 sides (or 4 records). Of course, you'd better have two recording lathes to alternate the sides, or you'd miss part of the program while changing records.

By 1931, the situation had improved considerably, The "electrical transcription" (or E.T.) became popular. This was an ordinary looking phono record...except for its size. It was 16" inches in diameter. The invention was an outgrowth of the Vitaphone system of sound film recording that had come into use in 1926. The most famous film use of Vitaphone transcriptions was, of course, "The Jazz Singer." The system was impractical for sound films, but caught on for use as a radio recording medium. At the slower speed of 33 1/3 rpm, fifteen minutes of programming could be put on each side of the disc, This made recording radio programs a lot easier. As with the 78 rpm discs, electrical transcriptions could be either "pressed" (mass produced) or instantaneously "cut." Why a 16" diameter and not 12" like home entertainment discs? The reason goes back to Thomas Edison's complaint about the disc system of recording (Edison invented sound recording and was highly opinionated about discs vs. cylinders). He used cylinders because (among other reasons) as the playback stylus approached the inside of a disc record, the relative speed between stylus and groove decreased, causing a loss of the higher frequencies. Translation: as you got to a smaller diameter of grooves remaining near the end of a record, the sound noticeably got worse (Mr. Edison wisely noted that the diameter of his cylinder remained constant from beginning to end, as did its 160 rpm rotation speed, until the spring wound down, but that's another story). By starting with a larger diameter record, this sound degradation was lessened.

Other techniques were used to improve the sound quality of discs. Some discs started at the inside and played toward the outside (an advantage when playing back a recorded show on the air). The "vertical cut" was adopted by some companies (the sounds were placed on the bottom of the grooves instead of the sides of the grooves). This actually produced a "cleaner" sound that was less subject to scratches and noise. The 2.5 mil groove width was later adopted by the industry, "Orthacoustic" recordings were made popular by NBC. With the advent of tape recordings shortly after the war, the use of 16" electrical transcriptions decreased. However, I was still cutting 16" discs on the Scully lathes at NBC's Radio Recording Division (in New York) as late as October, 1965.

Playing the discs:

Obviously, a turntable capable of playing both 16" diameter records as well as 78 rpm discs is essential. This is not an easy device to find today, but it's not impossible. Since 1969, I've been lucky to own an RCA Model 70-D turntable, made in 1947. It's given me nearly three decades of faithful service with no more than an occasional oil change. It has no speed adjustment, but it's never needed one. One thousand cycle tone test records play back at 999 to 1003 cps (cycles per second). It has two tone arms. An RCA "Universal" arm for "vertical" discs," and an aftermarket "Gray Transcription" arm for laterally cut discs. It happens to be the size of a small refrigerator and looks definitely out of place in a "media" room. I've always preferred a General Electric VR-II phono cartridge (popular at radio stations since the mid-1950s). It happily tracks at 3 grams when necessary and can press your pants while you wait! The special 2.5 mil stylii are custom made by a British company. For one brief shining moment in 1976, Panasonic sold a "Technics" turntable capable of playing 16" transcriptions. If you ever see a model SL-1100A for sale, grab it. Today, Esoteric Sound in Downers Grove, Illinois, still manufactures turntables for those with the 16" blues.

Sound processing:

I feel the less the better. We use a Urei 565 notch filter ("The Little Dipper") to remove hum, rumble and high frequency noise. A Urei 537 graphic equalizer acts as tone control during the recording process. We have an SAE Impulse Noise Reduction unit, the KLH-Burwen Transient Noise Eliminator and a Symetrix SG-200 signal gate. These are basic analogue devices that work well with certain kinds of problems, but not nearly as well as the new digital computer programs. The best sound processing still remains the least. Start with a decent source recording for decent results.

Recording medium:

I started with reel-to-reel recorders when that's all there were. I still use the reel-to-reel format for mastering. Back in the late 50s, I standardized the archive at 7 1/2 ips (inches per second), with 15 ips used only when the sound quality of the source was near perfect. There's not much difference in capability between 7 1/2 and 15 ips. There's a big difference between 7 1/2 and 3 3/4 ips. My advice: forget that 3 3/4 ips exists. Not only does a higher tape speed increase the recordable frequency range (and there are indeed sounds on a transcription beyond 10 kc.), but you can achieve a higher signal-to-noise ratio, lower wow and flutter readings and a greater timing accuracy. If you're not sure what any of this means, it can be summed up in one sentence. If you can't hear what you're losing at 3 3/4 ips, someday you will be able to; don't do it!

I've always used dual channel recording (recording on both side "A and side "B" of a tape), except for those tapes recorded at 15 ips. For those, I use two channel mono, which is equivalent to what is called "full track." I feel four channel recordings should be avoided. The only reason for four channel (sometimes called "quarter track") recordings is to save tape. Don't be so cheap! The decrease in sound quality when using four tracks on a 1/4" tape is audible, as is the increase in something called "cross-talk."

Almost as bad is the use of 1 mil tape (1800' on a 7" reel). Using a tape 1 1/2 mils in thickness (1200' on a 7" reel) eliminates many problems caused by stretching, print-through, layer-to-layer adhesion and cupping, to say nothing of fallen arches, dropsy and tennis elbow. If you're not sure what these terms mean, they too can be summed up in one sentence. "Don't do it." Dual track, 7 1/2 ips, 1 1/2 mil tape recordings are still a viable standard. There are very few brands of reel-to-reel machines still being made today. I love my Ampex 440C (all red-blooded sound engineers from the Bronx in 1957 wanted a 1956 Jaguar and an Ampex tape recorder, but for different reasons), but they're not being made any more. All the decks made by Otari today are better than any Ampex ever made (and I'll never own another Jaguar), The Studers are even better, but their cost is prohibitive. There are other brands and bargains are to be had with used gear, but condition is important. Shop around.

What about audio cassettes? Glad you asked. I remember when the first cassette machine was offered to the public in the early 60s. It was called the "Norelco Carry-Corder" and it was a good machine for taking dictation. I wouldn't try to record a flute solo with one (it sold for $29.95 and was well worth it, I had several). You've come a long way, baby! Today's more expensive cassette decks (Nakamichi, Tascam, etc.) are another story entirely. When I lived in Croton-On-Hudson, New York, I met a friend named Richard Nowak who swore his Nakamichi cassette deck sounded better than any reel-to-reel deck I owned. You know, with Dolby B and chrome tape, he was right! There was however one problem. Richard was an audio repairman by profession who knew Nakamichi decks inside and out (literally). He was known in Mt. Kisco as "Richard The Fix." It takes someone with Richard's skill and "Phillips head fingers" to allow you to put in a 40 hour week on a cassette deck and keep it up to manufacturer's specs.

This might be a good time to mention that no recorder, of any kind, will give consistently good results without proper maintenance. They are all complex electromechanical devices to which you must pay attention. If you can't remember when you last cleaned the heads, if you've never adjusted the bias nor set the record and playback level and equalization, if you don't know how to do an azimuth alignment for goodness sakes, hire someone on a regular basis who does know how! My personal opinion: cassettes are a good medium for listening in the home or (especially) in a car, but for archiving sound for the next generation, stay with reel-to-reel.

Hey Dave, haven't you heard about digital audio? As a matter of fact, I have, and I think it's a great idea...if they ever get it perfected! (I used to say the same thing about color television.) I'm the proud owner of two D.A.T. machines ("Digital Audio Tape") and I think they do a great job. A recording made on them makes my Otaris hide their (record) heads in shame! With a frequency range to please any passing bat; no audible hiss or noise, no degradation of sound no matter how many generations you make (a copy from a copy from a copy), what more could you want? Only two things: 1. The knowledge that the D.A.T. format will still be around in 10 years, in 20 years, in 50 years (we're an archive, remember). 2. The assurance that because it's a helical wrap system (technical stuff), tracking problems or dropouts won't render the entire recording inaudible. Well, O.K., how about the new recordable compact discs? As a matter of fact, I have two of those machines too and I think I they're pretty nifty (if you can ever figure out what the instruction manual is trying to tell you). I think that there are enough compact disc machines around so that compact disc players will always be available. Since it's not a helical system, if the disc plays well just after it's been recorded it will probably continue to play well indefinitely. So, I am tempted. However, there are now two competing formats of D.V.D. (Digital Video Disc) which combine compact disc audio with picture capability, so I have my suspicions about the format's longevity, Goldin's theorem; the time to switch to a digital system is when a format is introduced that meets these three criteria:

1. There are no moving parts (like a video game cartridge).

2. The format has been available for at least three years without any non-compatible changes

3. The machines are advertised at stores like Circuit City (or whatever is close to you) at sale prices, indicating consumer acceptance.

Until then, stick to analogue.

Keeper Of The Vault: a corner of the Radio Yesteryear archive, 1970.

The above recording techniques and specifications are meaningless if you have no space to keep the stuff. All those who live in apartments or who have more than 2.7 children please leave now. The three main requirements for the storing of any magnetic recordings are:

1. Low humidity. You know the humidity's right when the cacti bloom and the mushrooms wither.

2. Temperature stability. Tapes like an ambient temperature slightly below room normal, and they like it to stay that way. As little temperature variation as possible please.

3. Freedom from strong magnetic fields. Don't use steel shelving, don't locate your archive below high voltage power transmission lines or downwind from a nuclear reactor. Do not visit your archive carrying strong magnets in your pocket. The Radio Yesteryear archive is located below ground in rural Connecticut. It stays cool in the summer (without air conditioning) and mild in the winter (without heating). Although it's dry down there, there are dehumidifiers in three of the four corners of every room, They are "on" 24 hours a day...every day of the year. The tapes are stored vertically on wooden shelves, built two inches above a poured concrete floor on a plywood base.

Radio Yesteryear tapes are all stored on 10 1/2" reels, not 7" reels. The same objection Tom Edison had against small diameter disc records is valid for tapes as well. The smaller the diameter of the reel hub, the tighter the tape is curled around that hub, causing a physical deformation of the plastic backing. Not good. It doesn't matter whether you use metal or plastic reels, large center hole N.A.B. hubs or small hole N.A.R.T.B. hubs. Use whatever is cheaper. Avoid back-coated tape like the plague and be sure the tape on each reel is wrapped smoothly (no rough edges). "Exercise" each reel every ten years, whether it needs it or not. All Radio Yesteryear tapes recorded between 1957 and 1970 are on acetate tape (Scotch 111). These tapes have aged almost as well as the more modern "Mylar" reels and sound just as good (or just as bad) as they did 40+ years ago. Magnetic tape made today has a far greater life expectancy.

If all this sounds a bit much, remember, we are an archive and do consider ourselves to be the best at what we do. If your only goal is to enjoy the radio broadcasts you like to hear and care nothing for posterity, just keep your cassettes out of the direct sunlight while they're in your car and you're home free.

As we leave the elevator at ground level, please turn to your left and pause just a moment to remember our friend Ed, still standing on guard down there by the moat.

On The Cover:

This illustration will seem vaguely familiar to those over a certain age. At one time, there was only one long distance phone company in this country. It was called A.T. and T. (American Telephone and Telegraph). Many local phone companies were united in "The Bell System" and all was well. One phone book was published for each city or region and this was the illustration on many of the covers of those telephone directories during the 1930s and 1940s. The covers of these books were often a dull gray. The drawing is an accurate (with one minor change) reproduction of a real statue called "Electricity." For many years, the statue and this drawing of it were corporate symbols of A.T. and T.

The statue has an interesting history. It was commissioned in 1914 by the president of A.T. and T. for the roof of the new corporate headquarters at 195 Broadway in New York City. Created by Evelyn Beatrice Longman and placed 26 stories above the streets of Manhattan in 1916, "Electricity" was an appropriate image for the company and its new technology. The sculptor said the "work expressed the power of electricity, it's service to mankind and the intangibility and mystery of its nature." This book is about radio of course, not telephones. Commercial broadcasting, however, began shortly after the statue was created and the symbolism applies equally to radio. A.T. and T. soon became heavily involved in broadcasting. Their station (WEAF) is credited with airing the first radio commercial in 1922. Without A.T. and T. long lines, network broadcasting would not have been possible.

When the company moved to 550 Madison Avenue in 1983, the statue was taken down from the the roof of the Broadway building and placed in the six story high lobby of the new headquarters building. In October 1992, realizing the realities of the telephone business after "de-regulation" and the company's decreased dominance, the statue was moved outdoors again to an A.T. and T. building in Basking Ridge, New Jersey. The drawing hasn't been on the cover of a phone book for decades.

The statue became known as "The Spirit Of Communications" from the slogan printed on the base of its drawing on the covers of millions of those telephone directories. A.T. and T. people referred to it affectionately as "Golden Boy" (its 24 foot height was covered with 12,500 pieces of gold leaf). I feel it's an appropriate symbol for this research.

***Design For Listening** (10/12/35 - 3/29/36 with Olga Vernon) Bl, Sun, 4:30 pm; developed into Senator Fishface (with Joseph Gallichio Orchestra) (6/19/49 - 9/18/49) NBC, Sun, 60m, 2:30 pm; (1950, 1953) NBC, WMAQ origination*

Throughout The Book:

The circular designs are reproductions of actual labels that were applied to the centers of 16" electrical transcriptions (or "E.T.s"). At one time, the only practical way to preserve recordings of radio broadcasts, these large records are the way most of our audible radio history has been preserved. They were found at large stations (and small ones as well) throughout the country. A disc recorder (also known as a cutting lathe) was essential to preserve a show for sales, reference, rebroadcast or legal reasons. The blank discs were first manufactured by "Presto," but were soon made by Transco, Allied, Audiodisc, Capitol, Pyral and others. The grooves were "cut" into nitrocellulose lacquer on a metal base (or glass during the war) and a label applied to the center. Ordinary glue was used before the war and for some time afterwards. Self-stick labels became popular in the last years before the whole practice was made obsolete by magnetic recording tape.

Most Radio Yesteryear recordings were taken directly from these discs (and from "pressed" discs, which were mass produced). It is, therefore, fitting that at the beginning of this book are labels from some of the major networks and recording studios that preserved most of the programs that exist today. Throughout the alphabetical listings of people and programs are labels used by the individual stations and studios in both big cities and small towns. All these labels are unique mementos of a method used to record radio programs long ago...the "electrical transcription." These kinds of labels are seldom seen except by those who record radio programs directly from disc.

I've also used reproductions of some labels from "pressings," or mass-produced transcriptions, as a design element throughout the book. The transcriptions from which these labels were reproduced were all donated to a university sound library in 1997.

On The Back Cover:

Although I had the pleasure of attending only one "live" radio show as a kid (it was one of Arthur Godfrey's morning programs during the summer of 1949), studio audiences were common since the earliest days of broadcasting. The first studio audience was reported in a contemporary issue of "Radio Broadcast" magazine to have been assembled on February 19, 1922. During a WJZ broadcast, Ed Wynn was disconcerted when his best jokes produced no laughter from a microphone and four bare walls. Needing the reaction of real people for the timing of his giggly brand of humor, Ed asked the announcer to round up electricians, scrub women, telephone operators and others scheduled to appear later in the program. Their laughter and applause was all the encouragement that Wynn, a veteran stage entertainer, needed to make his radio debut a success. I suspect this story may be somewhat apocryphal, but whoever invented the idea of a radio studio audience, it was an institution that thrived throughout "The Golden Age."

Listeners to broadcasts that were aired before television producers came up with the idea of "canned" laughter sometimes forget that the applause and audience reaction came from real people in a theatre-like setting. Tradition called for no charge to be made for these tickets (some of the earliest shows were so bad, producers might well have bribed listeners to enter and stay). This practice continues even today for "The Tonight Show" and other television programs with an audience. Being made up of real people, these audiences needed tickets to get in (even if they were free). I've never met another collector of radio show admittance tickets, and so the back cover represents an artifact from radio's past that will be new to most.

The ticket in the lower right represents a personal triumph of sorts. Issued long after the era of creative radio (within the context of this book), the 60th Anniversary WOR broadcast was the one time in my life when I was asked to stand up in Carnegie Hall, take a bow and receive a round of applause. As a short-term employee of WOR-TV, I was eligible to join hundreds of others honored as former WOR employees during this program. I thus joined J.R. Poppele (WOR's first chief engineer, who was sitting nearby) and many other more deserving radio operators, in a memorable evening. My mother was very proud, I got to Carnegie Hall...and I didn't even have to practice!

Where Do Old Radio Shows Come From?

When you drop an audio cassette of "The Fred Allen Show" or "The Lux Radio Theatre" or any old radio show into your "Walkman" or car stereo, have you ever asked yourself where the recording came from? I don't mean whether you bought the tape from Radio Yesteryear or some other company, or got it from a friend or library. Have you ever considered how a radio broadcast, heard once some fifty or more years ago and sent out into the airwaves, never to return, wound up on your tape deck?

Somebody at the network, or at one of the network's affiliated stations, or at a recording studio or in somebody's home, took the trouble to record the program on discs (before the war) or on magnetic tape (after the war). Who made these recordings...and why? Were they made for fun or profit? Were they done well by sound engineers or recorded poorly by amateurs? Please permit us to pause just a moment and trace that great band remote or "The Adventures Of Sam Spade" you're listening to from the microphone to your tape machine.

The Answer Man (1937 - 56) Trommer's Beer; also Van Dyck cigars; mostly syndicated; carried by WOR, 5t, 15m

Most vintage radio broadcasts were saved on the 16" electrical transcriptions I've described elswhere. They may have been recorded for the performers to hear, for the ad agency and the sponsor, for the network legal department, for rebroadcast, for audition purposes or for many other reasons. But just like that one dinosaur bone that's dug up after millenia underground while thousands of bones from many other dinosaurs are never seen again, these recordings were among the few that were saved from the past.

Today, radio hobbyists thoughtlessly ask, "how many of a particular broadcast series are in circulation?" Radio shows in circulation? What a dumb idea! My dictionary has eight definitions of "circulation." Let's look at just the first two: "movement in a circle or circuit" and "the movement of blood as a result of the heart's pumping action." Perhaps what the questioner really means to ask is "how many examples of a given program have been found and how can I hear them?" Usually however, to "circulate" a radio recording means to copy it. Unlike a library, where a book can be "circulated" to many people with no degradation in quality beyond an occasional gravy stain, circulating a radio show often means making a copy of a copy of a copy. Each copy generation increases the recording's faults until a "circulated" recording has as many errors as does the message in the kid's game we used to play called "Telephone." Like our second definition of "circulation" ("the movement of blood"), the further a recording is from its "source recording" (the "heart") the more waste products the "circulated" recording will have.

If there's noise, distortion, a limited frequency range, off-pitch music and pieces missing, your enjoyment of the program is bound to suffer. It is for similar reasons that many people visit museums and art galleries to view works of art, while others are satisfied with reproductions in picture books. There is a difference...a big difference. It is this difference that's been a guiding principle of the Radio Yesteryear archive since its founding.

I would love to claim that all the recordings in the Radio Yesteryear collection originally came from discs, but that wouldn't be true. It is accurate to say that most of them did. This is a statement that few collectors of radio recordings can make...or would want to. Recording radio programs from discs is a lot more difficult, more time consuming and more needful of arcane skills than merely playing back a tape while hitting the "record" button on a second machine. I've described some of the exotic equipment we use to record these discs elsewhere. A good question to ask any potential source of radio recordings is, "do you have transcription disc transfer capability?" If the answer is "no," look back at the name of this essay and ask, "well then, from where did you get these programs?" Somebody must have made the master tapes. At Radio Yesteryear, the buck starts here!

Now that I've gotten that off my chest, I must admit that there are many broadcasts that we did obtain from tapes that others recorded from discs. It's at this point that a professional attitude makes another big difference. Every radio program we have has been listened to, timed, described and evaluated. Several decades ago, an official at the National Archives asked me for a copy of a program from the wartime series "The Man Behind The Gun." Eager to impress, I made what I thought was a first-rate copy, only to have it criticized because the recording ran almost 32 minutes. It was then I learned about the importance of "timing accuracy."

You should be aware that every "half hour" network show only ran 29:30 from the first sound to the end of the system cue. "Fifteen minute" programs ran exactly 14:30. That's a fortunate thing, for without having these reference points, the only way one could tell a program was "on-speed" would be to have perfect pitch and some musical content with which to establish a reference. Without music on the program, having an "ear" for the voices of certain actors and the ability to recognize that his or her voice was pitched too high or too low would be required to detect a speed variance. I've only met one person who could do that, Professor Eli Segal of Governors State University.

Syndicated programs, non-network programs and programs without system cues cannot be timed using my "29:30" method. Every program that comes to us on tape is auditioned and timed before being mastered. By using a variable speed playback deck, a stopwatch, a 1000 cps reference tone, a frequency counter and a simple mathematical ratio, every network show can be brought back to its correct speed as it is mastered. We always do this to ensure the performer's voices aren't pitched too high or low and the music is "on key."

Sound processing, such as re-equalization or notch-filtering is used where necessary but as sparingly as possible. I feel that whatever can be done today, probably can be done better tomorrow, so the preservation of sound in as original a condition as possible is the goal. Of course, the upper limit of sound quality is the recording equipment chosen and its state of maintenance.

So, where do old radio shows come from? A former reporter for the Boston Globe did a story about me once in a trade publication. Describing me as "a young man (who) worked weekends at an important New York radio station," he quoted me as saying that I "showed up at the rear of the radio station...loaded (transcriptions of) old shows into the back of a truck" and made a small fortune by "pilfering" those great old shows. Before calling my lawyers, I tracked the writer to his retirement home in Florida and gave him a call. We had a pleasant chat and he later admitted (in writing) that his "facts" were based on an interview he did with me "20 or 25 years ago" and that "I was relying on my memory (of that interview). There may have been some minor errors." There have been other stories about the source of many of these recordings over the years. As much as I enjoy this reputation (like "The Saint") of being "The Robin Hood Of Modern Crime" (stealing from the "rich" networks and giving to the "poor" collectors), I'm afraid these legends are just that...myths.

The truth doesn't make nearly the same kind of good copy, but let me try. Most of the transcriptions over the years have been bought, usually ten or twenty at a time, from record stores, radio stations, syndicators, advertising agencies, the performers who were on the programs and some special situations as well. Many people involved with these programs have allowed me access to personal collections. Here are just a few stories about some of my more interesting sources over the years.

A number of Mutual net broadcasts were obtained with the help of George Brown, the former news director of WOR (a warm human being and a gentleman). WOR had sold the Mutual Broadcasting System years before I ever met George. RKO-General, like most station owners, had no interest at all in the history of their industry or even of their own property. A group of discs was being stored in a closet on the 14th floor of the office building in which the station was located. Also in that closet were many paper rolls for the station's teletype machines. More space was needed for storage and the discs were in the way. With the help of Chris Steinbrunner, then a film buyer and producer for WOR-TV (also a one-time script-writer for "The Shadow" and vice president of The Mystery Writers Of America), the discs were rescued from the garbage. Alas, there were not enough discs to make "backing up a truck" worthwhile. Not even a small truck.

When Charles Michelson, a syndicator of "The Shadow" and many other programs was living in New York City, he apparently made a decision during the early 1960s to switch from 16" transcriptions to tape for the distribution of his broadcasts. Charlie had been involved in radio program sales since the 1930s, and was in fact responsible for bringing many famous series from England and Australia to American listeners. Being of a thrifty nature, to put it mildly, he sold those transcriptions to an old man named Alan Eichler who ran a used record shop on 12th Street and Broadway. There were, at the time, few people with any interest in 16" records or the ability to play them. Significant portions of my income were to be found on checks made payable to "Eichler Records." I took great pleasure in later years selling recordings of these programs back to Charlie, who should have kept them in the first place.

When I was still a young man, the largest collection of 78 rpm records (which I also collected) in the world was owned by a guy named Jake Schneider. He had a huge quantity of radio transcriptions as well. Jake was notoriously difficult to deal with, an attempt I never made. But Jake had two weaknesses; he was a great fan of James Melton records and broadcasts and he took a liking to a dentist from Boston. Dr. Barry Brooks, acknowledged and thanked elsewhere in this book, had a rare ability. He could get along with many different types of people and he could borrow 16" transcriptions from Jake. Schneider wanted to hear his Melton broadcasts (and others) and so Dr. Brooks would travel from Boston to New York regularly, load his car with transcriptions and visit with me for several days on his way home. We called these visits "Blitz Trades," as I was fortunate even then to have commercial quality sound equipment and the ability to record radio transcriptions as well. Barry and I kept many turntables and tape recorders going simultaneously for days at a time. I was happy, Barry was happy and Jake was very happy.

In the mid-1960s, NBC made a deal with a company called SCANFAX to transcribe and make available radio recordings from the NBC collection. A separate room was set up at the NBC studios, an NBC engineer was assigned the task of transferring the discs to tape. Guess who? Some very interesting recordings were saved in this way, but a great deal of junk was preserved as well. I haven't yet gotten around to adding all these programs into our archives, they are a very low priority, but there sure are a lot of 'em! All the discs were later returned to a bonded warehouse and were subsequently given away by NBC to the Library Of Congress. No trucks were backed up.

My favorite anecdote about the acquisition of radio recordings took place in 1969 and 1970, while I was still at CBS radio. William Paley was still the boss then. He had the idea to establish a Museum Of Broadcasting. The nucleus of the museum's collection of radio recordings was to be taken from CBS transcriptions which were in wooden crates, stored in a warehouse in Fort Lee, New Jersey. At the time, I was the only CBS radio night engineer, until about two in the morning (I often fantasized about war breaking out some night, sending out a code 10 "Netalert" to the CBS affiliates and...well, you get the idea). This was real radio and I had the whole damn network to play with!! However, the most exciting thing that ever happened was the occasional "First Line Report" being recorded by a grouchy Dan Rather, or a circuit from Saigon. Having little to do after the 11 pm newscast (remember, this is a network, not a radio station), after which the hourly newscasts would originate from California, I was given the job of transferring the old radio shows for Paley's museum to tape. This is, of course, like hiring a cat to guard your cream! Problems soon developed. For one thing, the studios had no turntables. When the maintenance department installed two "modern" turntables for the museum project, the equipment selected turned out to be poorly suited to the task. The network had no phono cartridges intended for use with radio transcriptions and certainly no 2.5 mil stylii. In addition, the museum specified that the recordings were to be made on cassettes. The only cassette recorders CBS then owned were the ubiquitous "Norelco Carry-Corders." These were the only machines radio reporters were allowed to operate because of union jurisdiction considerations. They weren't an ideal choice for sound archiving.

I brought my own blank tape, cartridges and stylii to CBS (coals to Newcastle, anyone?) to record the discs. If the museum wanted audio cassettes recorded on a cheap cassette recorder, made in a studio filled with full track Ampex 354s, who am I to say no? The base collection of radio recordings at this museum remains these audio cassettes, while the "back-up" full track Ampex tapes went elsewhere. What happened to the discs? Most of them were thrown out.

While I love the story about "backing up a truck" to a "large New York radio station," it's a legend that I regret has no basis in reality. Most of the programs were obtained the hard way...one at a time.

Where do old radio shows go? This is the obvious question to ask after "where do they come from?" Recordings (tape, record and otherwise) of these programs accumulate in archives such as Radio Yesteryear's, and in the hands of individual collectors and hobbyists. The actual discs themselves have a different destiny. After making a tape master, and having no further use for the transcriptions themselves (you can't collect everything!), I have, since 1976, personally given over 46,700 transcriptions to the National Archives, the Library Of Congress and other sound libraries. I'd like to think they'll stay there forever, but I doubt it. Even though the Library Of Congress has standards equal to or better than Radio Yesteryear's, and being the government, also has the advantage of being able to print enough money to pay for state-of-the-art equipment and lots of people, the story has a grim ending. The storage requirements for "instantaneous" cuttings (the most important kind of transcription) are even more stringent than for magnetic tape. The slightest moisture starts a chemical/biological process that eventually results in the acetate flaking off the base aluminum disc, making the grooves unplayable. Many other ills can befall a transcription in its old age, especially the glass discs made during the war (in case you've forgotten, metals of all kinds were needed for guns and tanks, radio transcriptions were not considered as vital in the fight against the Nazis and Japs). Glass made an excellent substitute. Today, these glass-based transcriptions (used from approximately 1942 to 1946) still sound well, but are very, very fragile. I've thought about some day writing a monograph about glass record recording and preservation, but it's an art that will soon have no value. Radio transcriptions, like nitrate film stocks, have built-in clocks ticking off limited lifespans. When last I checked, most of the discs I gave to the Library Of Congress hadn't been catalogued and the National Archives considers the Nixon tapes to be far more important than H.V. Kaltenborn.

How many radio programs, of all the hundreds of thousands that were broadcast during the so-called "Golden Age" have been found to date? What percentage of what was broadcast will ever be found? The answers to both questions is, unfortunately, "not many" and "not much." I've tried very hard to avoid locker-room comparisons. "How many shows do you have" is a question that I feel is as irrelevent as asking a museum curator, "how many paintings do you have?" Quality is far more important than quantity. I've spoken with several hobbyists who brag about the number of shows in their collection, but readily admit they haven't listened to many of them. What a waste! Youthful beginning collectors of stamps and coins often buy them by the pound or "on approval." The stamps and coins acquired this way are certainly fun when you're just starting out, but it's unlikely to generate a "find" of value. Despite being told "size doesn't count," I owe it to the reader to reveal that just over 61,000 broadcasts have been catalogued and added to our Radio Yesteryear database. The unrecorded transcriptions awaiting processing and the recorded-but-not-yet-catalogued programs we have would add many thousands to this total. The search for other recordings continues by myself and those who will come after me. It's impossible to predict how many programs will eventually turn up, any more than we can say how many more fossils or buried temples will be found. I can predict that no matter the current or future total, it will represent only the smallest percentage of what was broadcast during the "Golden Age."

How To Use This Book

The Blue Network
AMERICAN BROADCASTING COMPANY, INC.
How To Use This Book
TYPE
SPEED
USE STYLUS PRESSURE NOT IN EXCESS OF TWO OUNCES
RR-30

Assuming your plans are more ambitious than fixing a table with a short leg, a guide to some of my intentions is required. You've already glanced through the two sections that take up the most pages, "The Programs" and "The People." There's more to both sections than meets the eye. Please allow me to explain.

"The Programs" section:

To understand the symbols and abbreviations used, it helps if you're a professional broadcaster who's been in the business several decades, or a vintage radio hobbyist who pauses every half hour during the day for a station I.D. or "signs off," sings the national anthem and kills the plate voltage before kissing his wife goodnight and turning off the light. Assuming you're neither, let's briefly go through some terms and definitions you'll need to know.

> ***Author Meets the Critics*** *(6/12/46 - 4/22/51) originally a local New York show, on as early as 1/16/43; 6/12/46 - 4/2/47, Mut, Wed, 10:30 pm; continued on WQXR until 5/18/47; 5/25/47 - 2/22/48, NBC, Sun, 4:30 pm; 7/4/48 - 10/3/48, NBC, Sun, 5 pm; 11/24/49 - 9/28/50, ABC, Thu, 10 pm; 10/1/50 - 4/22/51, ABC, Sun, 11:30 am*

A. Networks and stations.

In the beginning, there were only radio stations located in cities and towns around the country. Most used the same frequency (a concept similar to quantum theory in that it defies logic and common sense). For years afterward, shared frequencies were common ("you transmit Monday through Friday, I've got the weekends"). Enlisting the aid of the the phone company (there was only one at the time), a series of "ad hoc" networks were put together for special occasions. One of the earliest broadcasts in our archive is a September 12, 1924 "National Defense Day Ceremonies" broadcast. Originating at WCAP in Washington D.C., the program was also heard over WEAF, WOAW, WFAA, KLZ and KGO. If you're a radio fanatic, you can name the cities just by these call letters. If you're normal, take my word that General Pershing was heard that day from sea to shining sea, two years before there was an NBC.

NBC (The National Broadcasting Company) formalized the concept of "chain broadcasting" on November 1, 1926 when it started two different networks, the Red and the Blue. There are several legends as to how these two strange names came to be, but please accept that research as a homework assignment. The New York station owned and operated by the Blue Net was WJZ. The New York station owned and operated by the Red Net was WEAF (both were NBC). This is important to know as much early programming came from New York. WEAF turned into WNBC on November 2, 1946. WJZ turned into WABC March 8, 1953.

The **ABC (The American Broadcasting Company)** network should be mentioned here because it was merely the Blue Network changing its name and ownership on June 14, 1945. The government forced NBC to sell off one of its two networks, so on this date (please make a note), the Blue Net became ABC. Just to make life interesting, for a considerable period of time before this date, Blue Net programs identified themselves as being on the "Blue Network of the American Broadcasting Company." After this date, some system cues (system cues are the last words on a radio show that identify the network of origination) on the new network were "this is the ABC Blue Network." There were many variations on this theme, but it is important to remember that no matter what the announcer said, before June 14, 1945, it was the Blue Net of NBC, on/after June 14, 1945, it was ABC. Any reference (in the "Programs" section of this book) to just "NBC" before this important date is an admission that I haven't information as to whether the show was on the "Red" or the "Blue" Network.

CBS (The Columbia Broadcasting System) started programming September 18, 1927, the New York "O & O" (owned and operated station) was WABC. Trying to drive fewer listeners nuts, WABC changed its call letters to WCBS on November 2, 1946, so people wouldn't think they were listening to the ABC network. I choose to not go into the locations of all these stations on the radio dial, as they shifted frequency frequently and therein lies madness.

The Mutual Broadcasting System started September 30, 1934. It's main reason for existence was "The Lone Ranger," which was then a very popular program being heard over WXYZ in Detroit. Mutual was always the poorest of the four networks, both in revenues and programming. The big name comedians, the prestige dramatic programs and the wealthy sponsors were all to be found elsewhere. One significant problem Mutual never overcame was that it had no "O&O." It didn't own a radio station. The other networks owned several. In fact, Mutual came to be owned by WOR in New York. This is the best known (perhaps the only) example of a station owning a network instead of the other way around. When WLW in Cincinnati was allowed to begin transmissions with 500,000 watts (ten times maximum normal power), it called itself a "one station network," but that's not the same thing (even though its programs could be heard all over the country).

There were other networks as well. The **Don Lee** Network consisted of Pacific coast stations. Don Lee was part of the CBS network as of July 16, 1929, but switched to Mutual on December 29, 1936, and did a lot of its own programming as well. It's beyond the scope of this book to discuss all the many local and regional networks. You should however, leave with the clear understanding of the difference between a network and a radio station. A radio station has a definite location and is authorized to transmit by the FCC with a certain amount of power in a well defined way. It originates many of its own programs. A network is a "chain" or group of radio stations, all carrying the same program at the same time (or almost the same time). It's all over the place, not just in one city. It only originates programming and does not own a transmitter. A radio network can own a radio station, but they're not the same thing. For example, programs heard on WOR might come from the Mutual network, or originate just at WOR to be heard only in New York. Mutual programs were not always heard on WOR. The situation was confused further by the use of the phrase "WOR-Mutual" for both local WOR program "station identifications" and Mutual net system cues.

B. Some of my favorite abbreviations:

Bl is the Blue Network.

ABC is the American Broadcasting Company.

Mut is the Mutual Broadcasting System.

CBS is the Columbia Broadcasting System.

WEAF, etc. represents the call letters of individual radio stations. I do not identify what city each station is licensed to. Broadcasters and radio show enthusiasts usually know the location of a station by its call letters. Those who do not can easily find this information elsewhere.

BBC is the British Broadcasting Corporation.

CBC is the Canadian Broadcasting Corporation.

NPR is National Public Radio.

AFRS is the Armed Forces Radio Service (and includes some "Special Services Division Of The War Department" programs that were heard before the AFRS formally began). The operation later became the AFRTS with the addition of television.

Syn means the program was "syndicated." You'll see this abbreviation a lot, as syndication was a popular method of program distribution. Today we would call these shows "off-line." Syndicated programs were not sent to radio stations by a network, but were recorded (on discs at first, later on tape) and mailed to stations around the country. Syndicators also used something called "Railway Express," but that was before your time. Syndicated programs might have been network shows being re-sold after their network run ended (we now call them "re-runs"). More usually, they were programs recorded just for syndication. Syndicated shows could have sponsors just like network shows (in which case, the sponsor paid the syndicator who paid the stations to run the program), or a syndicated show could be "sustaining" (see below). In this case, the station would buy the show (or get it free) to present to its listeners. Recruiting and public service shows, as well as charity fund appeals were often syndicated. The syndicated program could also be intended for local commercial sponsorship (by the station buying the series). The station theoretically sold the program to a local merchant. The syndicator would leave a "hole" in the program by having the announcer say, "we'll be back with more in just a moment, after this important message," followed by a minute of silent grooves on the record while the station engineer would add the commercial. There were many variations on this theme.

PBS-TV is the Public Broadcasting Service.

C-SPAN is the Cable Satellite Public Affairs Network.

Sus means "sustaining" which meant that the program was not intended to be sponsored. If the sponsor of a program is known, I identify it as much as possible. It's easy to do when the sponsor is something like "Lucky Strike." But what happens if the sponsor is a company with many products, one who advertises more than one of them on the program? Instead of cluttering up the listing with the names of multiple products, I've sometimes just listed the manufacturer and let the reader sort out the greater detail by listening to the program. The phrase **"air trailer"** refers to a program-length advertisement for a movie, usually with the stars from the film and scenes from it as well. Some program types are gray areas. Paid political announcements are one long commercial, but the product is a person. Religious, charity and recruiting broadcasts can't really be called "sponsored," but it's not correct to call them "sustaining" either. I deal with this problem by ignoring it.

Multi means the program is sponsored by more than one non-related product. The term "participating sponsors" is sometimes used.

2t, 3t, 5t and **6t** is the number of "times" per week the show was on the air.

2t is Tuesday and Thursday.

3t is Monday, Wednesday and Friday.

5t is Monday through Friday.

6t is Monday through Saturday.

Variations from the above are noted where necessary, no mention of any "t" means the program was on just once a week.

C. Times and dates.

The times listed are East Coast times unless otherwise noted (or a West coast only program). The length of the program is indicated by a number and an "m" (for minutes). "25m" would mean the program ran 25 minutes (actually 24:30, but don't get me started on that). The dates at the beginning of a listing ideally should be the date the show first went on the air to when the show last was heard. Most do, in fact, mean just that. However, some date listings are merely the first evidence I have that the show existed and the last time I know the show was still on. In these cases, I have no idea when the show began or when it ended. The dates and times within a show's listing refers to changes that happened to the show during its run. If only one date is indicated (as opposed to two dates connected by a dash), it means the program was heard only once, or that we have one dated example of this program in the archives with no further information available.

D. Non-radio programs.

Since this book is about "The Golden Age Of Radio," when is a radio program not a radio program?

When it's a radio transcription. These 16" discs were the stuff from which radio programs were made, but they were not complete shows by themselves. They were usually music selections or dramatic vignettes recorded on records that radio stations could play as part of their own local programming. In short, they were the phonograph record albums of their day. They contained (with few exceptions), no voice announcements to tell the listener what was to come. That was done by the local announcer. The main transcription manufacturers listed in this book are: World, Thesaurus, Standard, Capitol, Lang-Worth, SESAC, MacGregor, BMI and Muzak. There are others.

When it's a television program. The following listings contain many programs that were the sound portion of television shows. Therefore, a listing that says "CBS-TV" indicates television audio.

When it's a film soundtrack or strip film audio, it is so indicated.

So, why have non-radio material listed in a book about radio programming? Good question! It's because many of these non-radio recording are about radio, or contain people who were often heard on radio, or just because I think they're a valuable part of the Radio Yesteryear archive. Don't give me a hard time. There are many recordings listed of a political nature as well as those dealing with space exploration because I consider them both to be an outgrowth and continuation of program types that started with those election results broadcast on November 2, 1920.

The "People" Section:

This section is a lot easier to explain. It's simply an alphabetical list of every person who received air credit (or should have received air credit) on every program in the Radio Yesteryear archive. Alphabetizing a list of names would be easy if everyone had a first and a last name. But they don't and one has to start making decisions. Alphabetized by first or last name? The "program names" are alphabetized by the actual name of the program, not a person. "The Jack Benny Show" is therefore listed under "Jack" and not "Benny." I ignore "The," "A" and "An" for greater clarity. In the "people" section, I've had to deal with those with three (or more names) like "Adam Clayton Powell," those who usually use only initials ("H.V. Kaltenborn") or a combination (like "J. David Goldin") and other variations. "Benny Goodman and His Orchestra" is filed under "Goodman," as is his trio, his quartet, etc. Caution: many names look like they are spelled incorrectly, but they may not be (then again, some of them probably are). This apparent error may in fact be a reference to someone you never heard of who spells his name differently. Steven Allen is not the same person as Steve Allen, the comedian/musician/author. John Kennedy was both a NBC announcer in the mid-30s and a president. They were not the same guy.

I've tried to eliminate all titles. Therefore, unless I didn't know the first name, you'll see no "Generals," "Doctors," "Governors," "Bishops" or other honorifics. Hyphenated names, those that end with "Jr." and those with lineage descriptors (John Jones III) were invented just to make life difficult. I couldn't bring myself to list the king of England as "Windsor, George." You will probably agree with some of my decisions and disagree with others. At least I tried to be consistent.

I encourage readers to help me correct the many errors to be found in this book, both with "program" information and with "people" spelling. Please have some form of documentation beyond "I've always spelled it that way," or "the show is dated differently in the XYZ catalogue." My fellow collectors may be as perplexed, stubborn and wrong as I am. I would be most appreciative of those with definite information, and offer them immortality in the "acknowledgments" section of future editions, as well as my gratitude.

What can you do with this book?

C'mon, are you really asking me that question? Seriously, here are the uses that can be made of this research, with varying degrees of success.

Determine what programs were on network radio (and significant local programming).

Research what the exact names of these programs were and what were the alternative names used. What you call "The Jack Benny Show" was actually ten different program names (starting with "The Canada Dry Program." The most famous of them was "The Lucky Strike Program Starring Jack Benny").

Find out broadcast data about these programs (when they first went on the air, when they went off the air), the changes they went through while they were on the air.

Get information about sponsors, networks, stations, program length, frequency of broadcast, program time/day of the week, etc.

Discover who were major contributors to some of the more well known programs (other books address this area far better).

Learn how many examples of any given program are currently in the Radio Yesteryear archive (see "Where Do Old Radio Shows Come From?" and allow me to vent my spleen).

Obtain a list of major (and minor) "people" who contributed to these broadcasts, and (hopefully) how to spell their names correctly.

Learn how many examples of the work of these people are in the Radio Yesteryear archive.

Trace the broadcast career of people like Frank Sinatra. Paul Whiteman or Red Skelton.

What this book won't tell you:

You can't find out many specific details about the shows that are archived at Radio Yesteryear. Examples of information not to be found in this book are: Which Jack Benny Shows we do have. What details do we know about the programs on which all these people appeared. Which 230 Fred Allen appearances have we found. What are the dates, story titles, program numbers, plot descriptions, cast lists for each show. What about program length, audio condition, degree of completeness, etc.

Answers to all these questions (and more) are surprisingly all available from our database, but could not be included in this work for obvious reasons of space. It would take many times the number of pages in this book to present all the information we already have, or a CD-ROM. Hey! That's an idea...stay tuned! In the meantime, the information you want is probably obtainable through a "Radio Yesteryear Research Report." Follow the instructions and ye shall know.

RADIO RECORDERS
7000 SANTA MONICA BLVD.
HOLLYWOOD, CALIFORNIA
HOllywood 3917
33⅓—OUTSIDE START
DATE
PART
Radio Yestersearch™ Research Reports™

As helpful as this book may be, it is not faster than a speeding bullet, nor is it more powerful than a locomotive. It can, however, leap tall buildings in a single bound...with the help of our "Radio Yestersearch" Research Reports!

What's a Research Report? It's a list of the radio shows that we have in our archives OR it's a list of the shows on which a particular performer appears. We call them "show reports" or "people reports" for short. We CANNOT research programs by date, or by the titles of songs, or any other way. Just "name of program" or "name of person."

We believe this to be the best way available to get information from the most complete database of the world's best radio archive. There **<u>are</u>** limitations, however, as to what it can do.

Often, your research request will come back marked "none available" because we simply don't have every radio show that was ever broadcast, nor do we have examples of every actor, musician, writer, etc. that ever performed on radio. The "Program" and "People" sections can help you frame better "Research Report" requests. If the "program" part of this book shows no numbers next to the program listing (or if there is no program listing for the show in which you're interested), the chances are: 1. We just haven't found any yet. 2. We found what you're looking for after this book was published. 3. You're not using the correct name of the program or are spelling it incorrectly. The same is true for the "People" section, but with one added twist...you may be spelling the name correctly and <u>we're</u> wrong. Be creative and think of alternatives.

Sometimes we can't give you what you asked for because you've asked the wrong question, or you've asked a valid question that our database isn't prepared to handle. Some examples of "bad" questions are:

"Do a Research Report on World War II programs (or sports broadcasts or soap operas)."

Sorry, but we have to have the exact name of the program to research, not a general topic.

"Do a Research Report on Benny Goodman, but only from 1937 to 1944."

Sorry, we can't limit the report to a specific time. We have to send you a list of all the programs we have on which Benny Goodman appeared. Our computer will have to work just a little harder for you.

"Do a Research Report on the song 'Stardust,' sung by Hoagy Carmichael."

Sorry, we can't research song titles (no matter who sang it). We can do a "Hoagy Carmichael" report for you, but it wouldn't tell you which tunes he sang.

"Do a Research Report on the story, 'A Farewell to Arms' by Ernest Hemingway."

Sorry, the name of the individual drama cannot be researched, only the name of the dramatic series on which the story appeared can be researched.

Suggestion: you might try asking for a Research Report on Ernest Hemingway and see what turns up or, even better, ask us to research the drama series on which the story appeared.

We can **<u>ONLY</u>** research the name of the program series or the name of a person who received credit for performing or contributing to the show. We can't research programs sponsored by Jello, band remotes that originated from The Cafe Rouge of the Hotel Pennsylvania or programs broadcast on October 20, 1942. Maybe someday.

Some other common problems:

If you don't give us the exact name of the program, or spell the name of the performer correctly, you may get an incomplete or a "none available" response. If we can guess what you really have in mind, we'll research what we think you want, but you'll make life easier for both of us if you double check what you're asking.

I think Type #2 and Type #4 (short form) Research Reports don't give you enough information. They're intended to give you an overview of "what's available." A Type #1, #3 or #5 report gives you a lot more information. The short form reports, for example, don't tell you if the program is complete. On some shows, you can deduce the information if you know, for example, that all "Inner Sanctum" shows run 1/2 hour (except those that run 25 minutes!). The short forms also omit plot descriptions and details of other cast members.

"Good Condition": It really means "bad" condition. No, we're not nuts. The four terms we use to describe audio condition ("excellent," "very good," "good" and "fair") are based on a 30 year old tradition. It would make more sense if we called them "A, B, C and D" or "1, 2, 3 and 4." But we don't, so be aware that "Good" really means 3rd best (out of 4 grades). I urge you to read the "Important Note" at the bottom of the next page.

For a few programs and people, we return your Research Report marked, "Not For Sale." We're not trying to tease you. Some recordings in our archives are not available for sale to the public for various reasons. The data is sent for informational purposes only. I hope this answers some of the questions most commonly asked. Doubtless you can come up with a few original questions of your own. Please ask us! When all is said and done, we still have a few humans around running the database.

RESEARCH REPORT

Type #2: Program Listings Short Form. These are listings of the availability of a program by its title. It shows the catalogue number, the broadcast date, program number (when known), story title (if applicable), audio condition and duration. Type #2 reports are available for $1.00 each. An example of a Type #2 report:

"The Lux Radio Theatre"

Cat.#	Date	Program #	Title	Audio Condition	Duration
39897.	June 1, 1936		"The Legionaire and The Lady"	Excellent	60:08
23453.	June 8, 1936		"The Thin Man"	Very good to excellent	1 hour
39898.	June 15,1936		"Burlesque"	Excellent	57:28

(627 MORE "LUX" PROGRAMS ARE PART OF THIS REPORT)

Type #3: Program Listings Long Form. These are expanded descriptions of each program, showing the source, plot description, cast members and all other information known. These reports are available for $2 each. An example of a Type #3 report for the same three Lux programs:

"The Lux Radio Theatre"

39897. The Lux Radio Theatre. June 1, 1936. CBS net. Sponsored by: Lux. "The Legionaire and The Lady." First Lux broadcast from Hollywood. First show hosted by Cecil B. De Mille. A love story between a Legionaire in the desert and a night club singer. C. B. interviews Jesse Lasky about the good old days in Hollywood when they filmed "The Squaw Man" together. Clark Gable and Marlene Dietrich are interviewed. Marlene sings "Falling In Love Again," accompanied by the composer. Cecil B. DeMille, Jesse Lasky, Clark Gable, Marlene Dietrich, Louis Silvers (music), Wally Maher, Lou Merrill, Melville Ruick (announcer). 60:08. Audio condition: Excellent. Complete.

23453. The Lux Radio Theatre. June 8, 1936. CBS net. Sponsored by: Lux. "The Thin Man." The classic about the urbane and witty New York detective who solves a missing persons murder. Introduced by the director of the original film: W.S. Van Dyke. Theda Bara appears after the story and discusses her planned "comeback." William Powell, Myrna Loy, Porter Hall, Barbara Luddy, Bret Morrison, Wally Maher. 1 hour. Audio condition: Very good to excellent. Complete.

39898. The Lux Radio Theatre. June 15, 1936. CBS net. Sponsored by: Lux. "Burlesque." Well done story of backstage love and heartbreak. Eighty five year old Daniel Frohman (famous producer) is interviewed. Al Jolson and Ruby Keeler are interviewed after the story. Jolson sings "A Pretty Girl Is Like A Melody." Al Jolson, Ruby Keeler, Cecil B. DeMille (host), Daniel Frohman, Melville Ruick (announcer), Wally Maher, Frank Nelson, Lou Merrill, Louis Silvers (music). 57:28. Audio condition: Excellent. Apparently complete.

(627 MORE "LUX" PROGRAMS ARE PART OF THIS REPORT)

Type #4: People Listings Short Form. These are listings of the availability of a person (or a group) such as actors, writers, announcers, musicians, orchestras, etc. It shows the catalogue number, broadcast date, name of the program, audio condition and duration. Type #4 reports are available for $1.00 each. An example of a Type #4 request to research "William Powell" would include listings such as:

"William Powell"

Cat. #	Date	Program #	Name	Audio Condition	Duration
23453.	June 8, 1936		The Lux Radio Theatre	Very good to excellent	1 hour
37449.	May 9, 1938		The Lux Radio Theatre	Excellent	59:52
38760.	January 28, 1940		The Campbell Playhouse	Excellent	58:29

(35 MORE LISTINGS ARE PART OF THIS REPORT)

Type #5: People Listings Long Form. These are expanded descriptions similar to Type #3 above, but researched for performers, writers, announcers, etc. These reports are available for $2 each. An example of a Type #5 request to research "William Powell" would include listings such as:

23453. The Lux Radio Theatre. June 8, 1936. CBS net. Sponsored by: Lux. "The Thin Man." The classic about the urbane and witty New York detective who solves a missing persons murder. Introduced by the director of the original film: W.S. Van Dyke. Theda Bara appears after the story and discusses her planned "comeback." **WILLIAM POWELL**, Myrna Loy, Porter Hall, Barbara Luddy, Bret Morrison, Wally Maher. 1 hour. Audio condition: Very good to excellent. Complete.

(35 OTHER "WILLIAM POWELL" LISTINGS ARE PART OF THIS REPORT)

Type #1: Catalogue Listings. These listings are chosen in sequence from our database. Use a Type #1 report if you want an overall view of the Radio Yesteryear archive. There's no way to tell which programs are in any given Type #1 report. Groups of 100 listings are available on request for $1.00 per group. An example of a Type #1 report:

926. CBS Radio Workshop. November 11, 1956. CBS net. "Report on The We'ans." Daws Butler, Hans Conried, Robert Nathan (author), William N. Robson (producer). 1/2 hour. Audio Condition: Excellent. Complete.

927. The Jimmy Durante-Garry Moore Show. May 23, 1947. CBS net. Sponsored by: Rexall Drugs. The Garry Moore Travel Bureau is offering trips around the world by blimp. Jimmy Durante, Garry Moore. 1/2 hour. Audio condition: Very good. Complete.

(98 OTHER LISTINGS ARE PART OF THIS REPORT)

(Note that catalogue #926 is followed by catalogue #927 and that the two shows are not related. Our catalogue numbers are assigned to programs in the sequence of acquisition.)

Important Note:

Of course, we do not have every radio show that was ever broadcast, nor examples of every actor or musician that performed before a microphone. Therefore, please be prepared for some reports to come back marked, "None Available." Grading the audio condition of old radio broadcast recordings is very subjective, we try to be as conservative as possible to avoid disappointment. In descending order, we use the following terms:

1. Excellent 2. Very good 3. Good 4. Fair

I don't recommend requesting any program below "very good" audio condition unless you've GOT to have it, no matter what it sounds like. List below the research reports (either "show reports" or "people reports") you'd like and the type of report you'd like for each. Be sure to include the correct amount.

1.____ Type # ________

2.____ Type # ________

3.____ Type # ________

Please read the preceding three pages so you can determine which type Research Report to order. Please don't try to be "helpful." Do not tell us the plot, give the year of broadcast or fill in ***anything*** other than "name of program" or "name of person."

Please send this research to:

(Please use a photocopy of this page, don't tear it out!)

Name____

Address____

City/State/Zip____

AMOUNT ENCLOSED: $________________________

Send Research request to: Research Reports
Radio Yesteryear
Box C, Sandy Hook, CT 06482

No
33⅓ R.P.M.
RADIO UNESCO RADIO
Radio Programs
U.N.E.S.C.O. 19 AV. KLEBER . PARIS 16e . FRANCE
Use of recording is subject to conditions of A. F. M. and A. F. R. A. licenses.
GENERAL SOUND CORPORATION
"BRINCKERHOFF STUDIOS"
29 WEST 57th ST. NEW YORK, PLAZA 3-3015
33⅓ R. P. M.
No. 471
Start Outside
Purdue University
W B A A
LAFAYETTE, IND.
SERIAL No.
START INSIDE
R.P.M. 33 1/3
SUBJECT
CINEMART RECORDING STUDIOS 101
CINEMART
FILMONIC RECORD
for refere
NBC
Reference Recording
INSTANTANEOUS
Radio Performers
START
SPEED
RADIO-RECORDING DIVISION
NATIONAL BROADCASTING CO., INC.
RCA Building, Radio City, New York
THIS RECORDING IS NOT TO BE USED FOR BROADCAST PURPOSES OR FOR PUBLIC PERFORMANCE FOR PROFIT
ET-10-N
USE STYLUS PRESSURE NOT IN EXCESS OF 2 OUNCES
THIS TRANSCRIPTION CONTAINS COPYRIGHT MATTER

Radio Programs

A listing of all the "Golden Age" network radio programs known to date. Selected non-network programs, some TV audio and film sound tracks are included as well. The number to the left of each listing indicates the number of examples of that program in the Radio Yesteryear archive. Programs with no numbers listed have not yet been located. Program titles containing a performer's name are listed alphabetically as the name is written. For example, "The Jack Benny Show" is listed under "J," not "B." Check alternate titles carefully, many programs were referred to by several different names.

The Big Show (with Tallulah Bankhead and Meredith Willson Orchestra) (11/5/50 - 5/6/51; 9/30/51 - 4/20/52) Multi, NBC, Sun, 90m, 6:00 pm

A & P Gypsies (with Harry Horlick Orchestra)
(3/3/24 - 9/7/36) A & P; began on WEAF in New York until 1/3/27 when it went on the network
1/3/27 - 6/6/27; 9/12/27 - 9/7/36, NBC, Mon, 8:30 pm, 60m; 9 pm, 30m as of 9/7/31
also 9/3/31 - 6/16/32, Bl, Thu, 10 pm

1 **A-Bomb Detonation** (KRAM)

2 **A. B. Alexander** (1940, 1942) BBC

1 **A. E. F. Landing In Ireland** (1/27/42) Mut

5 **A. L. Alexander's Mediation Board**
(1/11/43 - 4/11/52) Mut; see also (Goodwill Court)
1/11/43 - 2/8/43, Mon, 45m, 9:15 pm
2/15/43 - 7/5/43, Mon, 30m, 9:15 pm
7/11/43 - 9/13/45, Serutan, Sun, 45m, 8 pm
9/20/45 - 3/31/46, Serutan, Sun, 30m, 8:15 pm; 8 pm as of 10/11/45
4/7/46 - 7/30/50, Sus, Sun, 8 pm
1/7/51 - 7/15/51, Sun, 8 pm
also 3/5/51 - 10/21/51, 3t, 15m, 9:30 pm
9/24/51 - 4/11/52, 5t, 2:30 pm

15 **Abbott and Costello Show, The**
(7/3/40 - 6/9/49)
7/3/40 - 9/25/40, Sal Hepatica, NBC, Wed, 9 pm (summer replacements for Fred Allen "Time To Smile")
10/8/42 - 3/18/43; 11/4/43 - 6/8/44; 10/5/44 - 6/28/45; 10/4/45 - 6/27/46; 10/3/46 6/27/47, Camel, NBC, Thu, 7:30 pm; 10 pm as of 1/7/43
10/1/47 - 7/21/48, Sus, ABC, Wed, 9 pm
9/23/48 - 6/9/49, Sus, ABC, Thu, 8 pm

1 **Abbott and Costello Kid's Show, The**
(12/6/47 - 3/26/49) Sus, ABC, Sat, 11 am

Abbott Mysteries, The
(6/10/45 - 8/31/47) Helbros, Mut, Sun (summer replacements for Quick As A Flash)
6/10/45 - 9/2/45, 6 pm
6/9/46 - 9/1/46 (with Les Tremayne and Alice Reinheart), 5:30 pm
6/8/47 - 8/31/47 (with Julie Stevens and Chuck Webster), 5:30 pm

Abbotts, The (see Adventures Of The Abbotts)

1 **ABC Coverage Of Roosevelt's Death**
(4/12/45) ABC

ABC Dancing Party (8/18/51 - 4/14/56) Sus, ABC, Sat, 75m - 120m

3 **ABC Mystery Time** (also called Mystery Time Classics) ABC, Fri

ABC Of Radio Broadcasting
(3/31/39 - 8/4/39) Bl, Fri, 15m

ABC Radio Workshop (see Think)

2 **ABC Scope** (1966, Jan, 1968) ABC-TV

ABC World Security Workshop (see World Security Workshop)

ABC's Of Music, The (see Robert Q. Lewis)

1 **ABC's Silver Anniversary Celebration**
(2/5/78) ABC-TV

15 **Abe Burrows Show, The**
(7/26/47 - 10/28/49) CBS
7/26/47 - 6/26/48, Listerine, Sat, 15m, 7:30 pm
7/4/49 - 10/28/49 (Breakfast With Burrows) Mon, 9:30 pm (partial summer replacement of Lux Radio Theater); Fri, 9:30 pm as of 9/9/49

1 **Abe Lincoln's Story** (12/5/43 - 5/28/44) Small Business, Mut, Sun, 4:30 pm

2 **Abe Lyman and His Californians** (1942) CBS, Standard transcription

1 **Abe Lyman and His Orchestra**
(9/1/31 - 9/1/34) (see also Melodiana, Waltz Time)
9/1/31 - 9/8/32, CBS, 3t (Tue, Thu, Sat), 15m, 8:15 pm; 2t as of 6/28/32
9/27/32 - 7/4/33, Phillips, CBS, 3t, 15m, 8:45 pm
9/24/33 - 4/21/34, Phillips, CBS, Sun, 2:30 pm
5/1/34 - 9/1/34 (Accordiana) Phillips, CBS, Tue, 8:30 pm

4 **Abie's Irish Rose** (1/24/42 - 6/27/42; 9/12/42 -6/26/43; 8/28/43 - 9/2/44) Drene, NBC, Sat, 8 pm

Abram Ruvinsky (6/5/39 - 10/2/39) Mut, Mon, 15m, 3:45 pm (not always in New York)

9 **Abroad With The Lockharts** (1932) (15m) Syn

1 **ABSIE Program** (4/30/44) ABSIE

3 **Absorbine Jr. Footnotes** (6/32 - 9/8/32) Absorbine Jr., Bl, 3t (Mon, Wed, Thu), 15m, 10:15 pm

38 **Academy Award Theater**
(3/30/46 - 12/18/46) Squibb, CBS
3/30/46 - 6/29/46, Sat, 7 pm
7/3/46 - 12/18/46, Wed, 10 pm
also 4/30/44 - 8/28/44 (different series) Bl, Mon. 10:30 pm

2 **Academy Awards Program** (3/2/44) CBS, KFWB, Los Angeles

Academy Of Medicine (3/17/37 - 9/29/37) CBS, Wed, 15m, 4:45 pm

13 **Academy Of Music** (1949 - 50) (with Alfred Wallenstein and The Los Angeles Philharmonic Orchestra)

1 **Accent** (6/15/71) WKZO-TV

1 **Accent On Music** (2/9/42) CBS

1 **Access** (9/22/90) CBS

Ace Brigade

Acousticon Hour (1927 - 28) Dictaphone, NBC, Sun, 5:30 pm

Acousticon Program (1929 - 30) Dictograph, CBS, Sun, 6:30 pm

1 **Across The River** (3/29/84) WPBH-FM

Across the Board (Mut)

1 **ACS Jamboree** (4/30/51) Syn

Action Eighty (with William Conrad) CBS

Action Theater (with William Gargan)

1 **Actual Dropping Of The Atom Bomb** (6/30/46) CBS

1 **Ad Libbers Club** (3/20/38) CBS

1 **Adam Hat Sports Parade** (12/8/41) Bl

Add A Line (7/4/49 - 9/26/49) ABC, 5t, 3:30 pm (summer replacement of House Party)

Adela Rogers St. John (1936 - 1937) NBC, 4t (Mon - Thu)

1 **Adelaide Hawley Program, The**
(9/25/39 - 11/12/43) CBS, 5t- 6t, 15m; Krug Baking Co.
(11/1/43 - 4/12/46) NBC, 6t, 9:30 am

Adele Clark (8/10/45 - 9/21/46 ABC, Sat, 15m, 11:45 am

1 **Adlai** (7/14/65)

2 **Adlai Stevenson** (9/14/48, 10/52)

1 **Adlai Stevenson Memorial** (7/14/65) CBS

1 **Adlai Stevenson Remembered** (7/14/65) CBS

1 **Admiral Blandy** (7/24/46) ABC

1 **Admiral Byrd Expedition, The** (1/18/47) CBS

1 **Admiral Harold Stark** (10/28/40) WFBR

1 **Admiral Nimitz** (4/1/45) Mut

1 **Adoan Program, The** (10/26/36) WMBQ

22 **Adolf Hitler** (3/12/38 - 1/30/45) Mut

1 **Adolf Hitler's Arrival In Vienna** (3/15/38) Mut

1 **Adolf Hitler's Mock Birthday Party** (4/20/42) Mut

5 **Adopted Daughter** (4/39 - 1941) NBC (Regional), 5t, 15m

1 **Adrian Rollini** (World transcription)

1 **Adrian Rollini and His Ensemble** (World transcription)

1 **Adrian Rollini Quartet** (World transcription)

Adrian Rollini Trio (10/15/38 - 3/8/40) Mut
10/15/38 - 1/10/39, Bl, 2t (Mon & Tue), 6:30 pm, 15m
1/17/39 - 5/9/39, Bl, Tue, 15m
also 1/19/39 - 5/25/39 (Swing To Chiclets), Chiclets, Bl, Thu, 30m, 7:30 pm
6/26/39 - 8/21/39, Bl, Mon, 5:45 pm
12/25/39 - 3/8/40, Mut, 5t, 6:30 pm

1 **Adrian Rollini Trio/The Lenny Herman Quintet, The** (6/25/48)

1 **Adrian Skill** (1/11/37) WCNW

1 **Adventure** (6/24/56), CBS-TV

10 **Adventure Ahead** (8/5/44 - 11/18/44) NBC, Sat

Adventure Bound

1 **Adventure In Sound** (pre-war) NBC

3 **Adventure In Travel** (Syn)

Adventure Into Fear (1940s)

20 **Adventure Is Your Heritage** (1950 - 1951) Syn

1 **Adventure Island** (1946) air trailer

3 **Adventure Parade** (1946 - 49) Sus, Mut, 5t. 15m (not in New York except for 2/17/47 - 9/26/47 and 2/9/48)

1 **Adventure Story** (9/29/41 - 4/3/42) Bl, 5t, 15m, 5 pm

1 **Adventure Time** (5/41) WEAF

Adventure Trails

36 **Adventurer's Club** (also called World Adventurer's Club; Strange Adventures, Strange Adventures In Strange Lands) (1932) 15m
(1/11/47 - 1/3/48) Sheaffer Pens, CBS, Sat, 11:30 am

Adventurer, The (1/25/55 - 3/29/55) ABC, Sun, 9:30 pm

52 **Adventures By Morse** (10/26/44 - 10/18/45) Syn

Adventures In Exploration (7/6/37 - 7/20/37) CBS, Tue, 15m, 5:45 pm

13 **Adventures In Folk Song** (1950) Syn

Adventures In Health (2/5/32 - 3/29/34) Horlick Malt, Bl, 2t (Wed & Fri), 15m; Fri as of 8/5/32; then 2t

1 **Adventures In Judaism** (9/67) CBS

1 **Adventures In Melody**

Adventures In Music (4/15/55 - 6/17/55) ABC, Fri, 9:30 pm

1 **Adventures In Photography** (11/8/39 - 2/28/40) Bl, Wed, 10:30 pm

Adventures In Reading (5/2/38 - 10/7/40) Bl, Mon, 2 pm

598 **Adventures In Research** (1946 - 50) Westinghouse, syndicated

9 **Adventures In Rhythm** (1/6/46 - 3/3/46) Mut-Don Lee

Adventures In Science
(3/17/38 - 8/18/57) Sus, CBS, 15m; also called Science Service Series
3/17/38 - 3/9/39, Thu, 7:15 pm
3/18/39 - 4/29/39, Sat, 6:15 pm
5/1/39 - 9/4/39, Mon, 5:45 pm
1/4/40 - 4/11/40, Thu, 4:15 pm
10/10/40 - 12/4/41, Thu, 3:45 pm
12/13/41 - 3/31/56, Sat
3/31/57 - 8/18/57, Sun

Adventures In Sound (Syn)

Adventures Of A Modern Mother
(1/20/40 - 7/7/41) Bl, Mon, 15m, 2 pm; 11:30 am as of 5/19/41

2 **Adventures Of Ace Williams, The** Recorded (1938) WOWO, Syn

Adventures Of Admiral Byrd, The (also Byrd Expedition Broadcasts)
(11/18/33 - 1/6/35)
11/18/33 - 5/19/34, Grape Nuts, CBS, Sat, 10 pm
5/30/34 - 1/6/35, Grape Nuts, CBS, Wed, 10 pm

Adventures Of Ali Oop, The

19 **Adventures Of Archie Andrews, The**
(5/31/43 - 9/12/53)
5/31/43 - 9/24/43, Bl, 5t, 15m
10/1/43 - 1/7/44, Bl, Fri, 25m, 7:05 pm
1/17/44 - 6/2/44, Mut, 5t, 15m, 5:15 pm
6/2/45 - 8/2/47, Sus, NBC, Sat, 10:30 am
8/9/47 - 10/30/48, Swift, NBC, Sat, 10:30 am
11/6/48 - 9/12/53, Sus, NBC, Sat. morning
also on 6/8/49 - 9/14/49, Kraft, NBC, Wed, 8:30 pm (summer replacement of The Great Gildersleeve)
also on 5/13/51 - 9/27/51, NBC, Sun, 6:30 pm (partial summer replacement of The Big Show)
also on 10/6/51 - 1/19/52, NBC, Sat, 7:30 pm

16 **Adventures Of Babe Ruth, The** (Syn)

1 **Adventures Of Barnaby, The**

2 **Adventures Of Bill Lance, The**
(4/23/44 - 1/4/48) West Coast , sponsored by Planters
4/23/44 - 9/9/45, CBS, Sun
1946 - 47, CBS, Sat
6/14/47 - 8/9/47, ABC, Sat
9/15/47 - 9/22/47, ABC, Mon, 9 pm
9/28/47 - 1/4/48, ABC, Sun, 5 pm

Adventures Of Captain Diamond, The (see Captain Diamond's Adventures)

Adventures Of Casanova, The (see The Modern Adventures Of Casanova)

2 **Adventures Of Champion, The** (1949) (Mut) (not in New York)

Adventures Of Charlie Chan, The (see Charlie Chan)

2 **Adventures Of Charlie Lung, The** (1948) NBC - Pacific

1 **Adventures Of Chester and Millicent, The** (Syn)

1 **Adventures Of Christopher London, The**
(1/22/50 - 4/30/50) NBC, Sun, 7 pm
(5/8/50 - 6/5/50) NBC, Mon, 10:30 pm

Adventures Of Christopher Wells, The
(9/28/47 - 6/22/48) DeSoto, CBS
9/28/47 - 1/25/48 (with Myron McCormick), Sun, 10 pm
2/3/48 - 6/22/48 (with Les Damon), Tue, 9:30 pm

Adventures Of Danny Marsden, The (1930s)

Adventures Of Dari-Dan, The
(3/1/36 - 10/29/37) Dari-Rich, NBC, Sun; Sun and Wed as of 9/3/36, 15m

4 **Adventures Of Detectives Black and Blue, The** (10/24/32 - 2/6/34) Syn, (KHJ) 3t, 15m

Adventures Of Dick Cole, The (see Dick Cole)

12 **Adventures Of Doc Savage, The** (1985) NPR

12 **Adventures Of Ellery Queen, The** (6/18/39 - 5/27/48)

1 **Adventures Of Father Brown, The** (6/10/45 - 7/29/45) Mut, 5 pm (see Father Brown)

2 **Adventures Of Frank Farrell, The** (Syn) 15m

53 **Adventures Of Frank Merriwell, The**
(3/26/34 - 6/22/34) Dr. West's Toothpaste, NBC, 3t, 15m, 5:30 pm
(10/5/46 - 6/4/49) Sus, NBC, Sat, 10 am; 11 am as of 1949

21 **Adventures Of Frank Race, The** (Syn)
(5/1/49 - 2/19/50) East Coast
(6/5/51 - 3/25/52) West Coast, Second syn

Adventures Of Hap Hazard, The (see Hap Hazard)

Adventures Of Harry Nile, The (11/22/77 - 5/30/78) still on KVI

Adventures Of Helen and Mary, The (9/27/29 - 3/17/34) CBS, Sat. (see also Let's Pretend)

Adventures Of Jack Masters, The (9/28/36 - 12/25/36) Maltex Co., CBS, 3t, 15m, 5:30 pm

Adventures Of Johnny Lujak, The (see Johnny Lujak)

Adventures Of Jungle Jim, The (see Jungle Jim)

Adventures Of Leonidas Witherall, The (see Leonidas Witherall)

Adventures Of Maisie, The (see Maisie)

12 **Adventures Of Marco Paolo, The** (Syn-1930s)

5 **Adventures Of Mark Twain, The**

Adventures Of Mr. Meek, The (see Meet Mr. Meek)

25 **Adventures Of Nero Wolfe, The** (4/7/43 - 4/27/51)
4/7/43 - 6/30/43, ABC (New England network), Wed (with J. B. Williams)
7/5/43 - 9/27/43, ABC, Mon, 8:30 pm (with Santos Ortega)
1/21/44 - 7/14/44, Sus, ABC, Fri, 7 pm (Santos Ortega; then Luis van Rooten)
1945 - 12/15/46 (New Adventures Of Nero Wolfe; with Francis X. Bushman) Jergens, Mut, Sun (not in New York)
10/20/50 - 4/27/51 (New Adventures Of Nero Wolfe) Plymouth, NBC, Fri, 8 pm (with Sydney Greenstreet)

36 **Adventures Of Ozzie and Harriet, The** (10/8/44 - 6/18/54)
10/8/44 - 6/10/45; 8/12/45 - 6/16/46; 9/1/46 - 6/1/47; 8/31/47 - 12/28/47, International Silver, CBS, Sun, 6 pm
1/2/48 - 6/11/48, International Silver, CBS, Fri, 9:30 pm
10/3/48 - 3/27/49, International Silver, NBC, Sun, 6:30 pm
4/3/49 - 7/10/49, International Silver, CBS, Sun, 6:30 pm
10/14/49 - 6/16/50; 9/8/50 - 6/22/51; 9/28/51 - 6/20/52, Heinz, ABC, Fri, 9 pm
10/3/52 - 7/3/53; 9/18/53 - 6/18/54, Lambert and GE, ABC, Fri, 9 pm

94 **Adventures Of Philip Marlowe, The** (6/17/47 - 9/15/51)

2 **Adventures Of Pinnochio, The** (10/2/39 - 12/22/39) Mut, 5t, 15m, 5:45 pm; 3t as of 10/7/39

70 **Adventures Of Princess Pet** (Syn)

Adventures Of Raffles, The (see Raffles)

Adventures Of Red Ryder, The (see Red Ryder)

1 **Adventures Of Robin Hood, The** (1938) NBC

6 **Adventures Of Ruby, The** (1985) (ZBS Foundation) NPR

7 **Adventures Of Ruby II, The** (1985) NPR

52 **Adventures Of Sam Spade, The** (7/12/46 - 4/27/51)
7/12/46 - 10/4/46, Sus, ABC, Fri (Howard Duff until 9/17/50)
9/29/46 - 9/18/49, Wildroot, CBS, Sun, 8 pm
9/25/49 - 9/17/50, Wildroot, NBC, Sun, 8 pm

Adventures Of Sandra Martin, The (see Lady Of The Press)

Adventures Of Santa Claus, The (Syn)

Adventures Of Sherlock Holmes, The (see Sherlock Holmes)

Adventures Of Sky King, The (see Sky King)

Adventures Of Sonny and Buddy, The (1935)

1 **Adventures Of Sterling Holloway, The** (1948) Audition

1264 **Adventures Of Superman, The** (1940 - 3/1/51) Mut until 1949
2/12/40 - 3/9/42, Sus, 3t, 15m (Bud Collyer as Superman until 1949)
8/31/42 - 1/1/43, Sus, 5t, 15m, 5:30 pm
1/4/43 - 3/3/44, Pep, 5t, 15m, 5:15 pm
3/6/44 - 6/30/44, Pep, 5t, 15m, 5:45 pm
7/4/44 - 9/28/44, Pep, 2t, 15m, 5:45 pm
1/15/44 - 6/27/47, Pep, 5t, 15m, 5:15 pm
9/29/47 - 12/26/47, Pep, Mut; 5t, 15m, 5:15 pm
12/29/47 - 1/28/49, Sus, 5t, 15m, 5:15 pm
1/31/49 - 6/17/49, Mut, 3t, 30m, 5 pm
11/5/49 - 2/4/50, Sus, ABC, Sat, 30m, 8:30 pm; 8 pm as of 12/17/49 (Michael Fitzmaurice as Superman for duration)
6/5/50 - 3/1/51, Sus, ABC, various days, 5:30 pm

Adventures Of Terry and Ted (12/9/35 - 2/28/36) Bond, CBS, 5t, 15m, 5 pm

Adventures Of The Abbotts, The (not the same as Abbott Mysteries) (1/2/55 - 6/12/55) Sus, NBC, Sun, 8:30 pm

Adventures Of The Lone Wolf, The (see The Lone Wolf)

13 **Adventures Of The Red Feather Man** (1946) Syn

Adventures Of The Safety Soldiers, The (11/2/32 - 3/10/33) Maltex, NBC, 2t (Wed & Fri), 15m, 5:45 pm

Adventures Of The Saint, The (see The Saint)

Adventures Of The Scarlet Pimpernel, The (see The Scarlet Pimpernel)

5 **Adventures Of The Thin Man, The** (7/2/41 - 9/1/50)
7/2/41 - 12/23/42, Woodbury, NBC, Wed, 8 pm (with Les Damon until 9/24/43)
1/8/43 - 9/24/43, Post, CBS, Fri
10/3/43 - 12/29/44, Post, CBS, Sun; NBC, Fri, 8:30 pm as of 6/22/44; CBS, Fri, 8:30 pm as of 9/15/44 (with Les Tremayne until 2/44; David Gothard until 1/26/45)
1/5/45 - 9/7/45, Post, CBS, Fri (Les Tremayne from 2/2/45 - 4/28/46)
9/16/45 - 6/9/46, Post, CBS, Sun
8/9/46 - 5/30/47; 8/1/47 - 12/26/47 (Les Damon from 5/5/46 - 12/26/47) Sanka, CBS, Fri, 8:30 pm

1 **Adventures Of Tom Sawyer, The** (1938) Air trailer

4 **Adventures Of Topper, The** (6/7/45 - 9/13/45) Post, NBC, Thu, 8:30 pm; 8 pm as of 9/6/45

3 **Adventures Of Zorro, The** (1957)

Adventuring With Count von Luckner (12/20/31 - 9/8/32) Scott's Emulsion, CBS, Sun, 9:30 pm

1 **AEF In Australia, The** (1942) Syn

16 **Aeronautics and Space Report** (1965 - 1970) Syn

Affairs Of Ann Scotland, The (10/30/46 - 10/22/47) Hudnut, ABC, Wed, 9 pm; continued on NBC - West coast

Affairs Of Anthony, The (5/29/39 - 6/4/40) Bl, 5t, 15m

1 **Affairs Of Dr. Gentry, The** (1/24/57 - 3/25/59) Multi, NBC, 5t, 15m

Affairs Of Peter Salem, The (5/7/49 - 4/18/53) Mut
5/7/49 - 6/4/49, Fri, 2:30 pm
6/13/49 - 4/17/50, Mon, 8:30 pm
4/23/50 - 3/25/51, Sus, Sun, 7 pm
4/15/41 - 6/17/51, Sun, 8:30 pm
1/6/52 - 10/5/52; 12/28/52 - 1/18/53, Sun, 7 pm
1/24/53 - 4/18/53, Sat, 1 pm

1 **Affairs Of State 4248** (Audition)

Affairs Of Tom, Dick and Harry (6/30/41 - 42) Mut, Mon, 10:30 pm (Regional)

51 **Afloat With Henry Morgan** (Syn)

African Trek (10/13/39 - 3/15/47) 15m - 30m (various days and times including:)
10/13/39 - 11/20/40, Bl, Fri
12/1/40 - 10/17/43, Sus, Bl, Sun, 30m
7/13/46 - 3/15/47, ABC, Sat, 15m, 10:15 am (music by Josef Marais) also on WOR, New York in the 40s

4 **AFRS Basic Music Library**

1 **AFRS Story, The** (1/1/53) AFRS

1 **After Dark** (8/27/53) CBS

1 **After The Thin Man** (12/31/36) Air trailer

15 **Against The Storm** (10/16/39 - 6/27/52) 5t, 15m
10/16/39 - 12/25/42, Ivory, NBC, 5t, 15m
4/25/49 - 10/21/49, Philip Morris, Mut, 11:30 pm, 30m
10/1/51 - 6/27/52, Philip Morris, ABC, 10:45 am

4 **Age Of The Atom, The** (1955) CBS

Aggie Horn (see In Care Of Aggie Horn)

1 **Agnew Steps Down** (10/10/73) PBS-TV

1 **Agronsky and Company** (1/1/77) PBS-TV

1 **Ahead Of the Headlines** (9/29/40 - 11/26/41) Newsweek, Bl, 15m
9/29/40 - 12/15/40) Sun, 11:45 pm
1/2/41 - 9/25/41, Thu, 10:30 pm
10/1/41 - 11/26/41, Wed, 10:30 pm

1 **Aileen Stanley** (Thesaurus transcription)

33 **Air Adventures Of Jimmy Allen, The** Syndicated by World Broadcasting from 1933 - 34 and 1935 - 36. In 1946 a new cast did new productions of revised scripts.
1933 - 36, Syn (Richfield), WOR, 3t, 15m
1942, 1943 (summers) transcriptions re-released

1 **Air Attack On U. S. Warships** (6/6/44) Pool feed

Air Brakes (1/13/37 - 3/24/37) Bl, Wed, 5 pm

Air Force Hour (AFRS) Mut, Sat

1 **Air Mail Mystery** (Syn)

2 **Air Power** (1942)

1 **Air Raid Warning Instructions** (Syn)

1 **Air Raid Warning System** (10/31/41) Mut

1 **Air Rescue: Vietnam** (1967) AFRTS, Syn

Air Youth For Victory
(1/25/42 - 6/13/42) NBC, Sat, 15m, 3:15 pm

Air Youth Of America (5/27/40 - 7/1/40)
Bl, Mon, 15m, 7 pm
(1/10/42 - 4/18/42) NBC, Sat, 15m, 4:30 pm

1 **Airplane Survivors Interview** (1/25/38)
WJSV

13 **Airtime** (1956) Syn

Airy Fairy Singer (5/21/32 - 7/21/32)
Airy Fairy Krik Flour, CBS - Midwest),
3t (Tue, Thu, Sat), 15m

Al and Lee Reiser (1/9/35 - 10/24/42)
various days and times, 15m; some
include:
1/9/35 - 3/27/35, NBC, Wed, 2:45 pm
8/8/35 - 5/7/36 (Fountain Of Song) NBC,
Thu. 11:30 am
1937 - 38, Sus, NBC, Sun/Thu
12/30/39 - 6/1/40, Bl, Sat
also 2/18/40 - 9/22/40, Bl, Sun, 1:30 pm
6/7/40 - 3/28/41, Bl, Fri
also 12/20/40 - 3/1/41, Bl, Sat, 10 am
7/14/41 - 9/12/41, Bl, 3t, 10m, 1:50 pm
12/25/41 - 3/29/42, Bl, Sun, 15m, 11:15 am
9/5/42 - 10/24/42, Bl, Sat, 1:30 pm

2 **Al Avilla, Pipe Organist** (Syn)

Al Bernard's Merry Minstrel Men
(1/17/35 - 10/3/39)
1/17/35 - 7/18/35, Molle, NBC, Thu,
7:30 pm
5/6/38 - 6/10/38, CBS, Fri, 15m, 3:45 pm
6/15/38 - 7/27/38, CBS, Wed, 15m,
3:45 pm
3/14/39 - 10/3/39, Tue, 15m, 4:15 pm

1 **Al Capp** (9/1/49)

2 **Al Donahue and His Orchestra** (NBC)
(5/15/39 - 10/2/39) NBC, Mon, 10:30 pm

1 **Al Gayle and His Biltmore Orchestra**
(10/12/46) NBC

1 **Al Golden and His Monarchs Of Rhythm** (D & S transcription)

2 **Al Goodman's Musical Album**
(7/14/51 - 2/18/53) Sus, NBC
7/14/51 - 9/8/51, Sat, 9 pm
9/14/51 - 9/28/51, Fri, 10 pm
12/29/51 - 2/2/52, Sat, 10:30 pm
1/28/52 - 3/24/52, Mon, 10 pm
10/15/52 - 2/18/53, Wed, 25m, 10:35 pm

Al Hefler (11/12/39 - 2/11/40) Mut, Sun,
15m, 11 am

89 **Al Jolson** (11/18/32 - 5/26/49)
11/18/32 - 2/24/33 (Presenting Al Jolson),
Chevrolet, NBC, Fri, 10 pm
8/3/33 - 10/12/33; 2/22/34 - 4/26/34;
7/12/34 - 8/16/34, Kraft, NBC, Thu (Kraft
Music Hall with Paul Whiteman) all
Kraft shows were 60m; Jolson was a
guest on 6/26/33 (Paul Whiteman)
1/4/36 - 3/28/36 (Shell Chateau) Shell,
NBC, Sat, 60m, 9:30 pm
12/22/36 - 6/29/37; 9/7/37 - 7/12/38;
9/20/38 - 7/18/39; 9/19/39 - 12/12/39
(Lifebuoy Program; Rinso Program;
also called Tuesday Night Party as of
3/21/39) Rinso-Lifebuoy, CBS, Tue,
8:30 pm, 60m on 7/11 and 7/18/39 (Dick

Al Jolson (continued)

Powell replaced Jolson on 3/21/39;
Walter O'Keefe as of 9/19/39)
10/6/42 - 6/29/43, Colgate, CBS, Tue,
25m, 8:30 pm
10/2/47 - 6/10/48; 9/30/48 - 5/26/49 (Kraft
Music Hall) Kraft, NBC, Thu, 9 pm
(see individual shows)

1 **Al Jolson Centenary** (5/26/86) BBC

1 **Al Jolson Memorial** (10/23/51) Liberty net

2 **Al Jolson Program, The** (1953) CBS

Al Kavelin 15m (12/30/39 - 2/17/40) Bl,
Sat, 25m, 1:30 pm

1 **Al Kavelin and His Cascading Chords**
(NBC)

2 **Al Lyons Orchestra** (1935)

12 **Al Pearce and His Gang**
(1/13/34 - 10/25/47)
1/13/34 - 9/1/34, Sus, Bl, Sat, 6 pm
9/3/34 - 3/29/35, Bl, 2t (Mon & Fri), 15m,
5 pm
5/13/35 - 9/27/35, NBC, Mon, Thu, Sat,
1:30 pm; then just Mon, Fri & Sat on
7/15/35
10/7/35 - 3/30/36, Pepsodent, NBC, Fri,
5 pm
also 1/10/36 - 4/3/36, Pepsodent, Bl, Fri,
9 pm
1/5/37 - 6/28/38 (Watch The Fun Go By)
Ford, CBS, Tue, 9 pm
10/10/38 - 7/31/39, Grape Nuts, NBC,
Mon, 8 pm
10/11/39 - 4/3/40, Dole, CBS, Wed, 8 pm
5/3/40 - 5/30/41; 10/3/41 - 1/2/42, Camel,
CBS, Fri, 7:30 pm
1/8/42 - 7/2/42, Camel, NBC, Thu, 7:30 pm
5/14/44 - 7/30/44 (Fun Valley) Dr. Pepper,
ABC, Sun, 4 pm
12/9/44 - 6/30/45 (Here Comes Elmer)
Lewis Howe, CBS, Sat, 10:15 pm
12/3/45 - 9/6/46, Sus, ABC, 5t, 3 pm
7/26/47 - 10/25/47, ABC, Sat, 60m, 9 am

1 **Al Roth and His Orchestra**
(1936) RCA transcription (see Roth
Orchestra)

1 **Al Schacht Sports Show**
(11/1/47 - 4/10/48) Mut, Sat, 8:30 pm;
9 pm as of 3/6/48

1 **Al Serafini and His Orchestra** (10/30/65)
CBS

1 **Al Smith Memorial** (10/4/44) Mut

5 **Alan Freed's Rock 'N Roll Dance Party**
(WINS)

Alan Gerard (1938 - 3/20/39) Mut, Mon,
9:30 am (9:45 am - 1938)

1 **Alan Horn's Contribution To Civilization** (1964)

4 **Alan Jones-Woody Herman Show, The**
(see The Old Gold Program)

Alan Lomax (1947 - 49) Sus, Sun
(Regional)
1947 - 48, CBS
1948 - 49, Mut

56 **Alan Young Show, The** (6/28/44 - 7/5/49)
6/28/44 - 9/20/44, Sal Hepatica, NBC,
Wed, 9 pm (summer replacement for
Eddie Cantor)
10/3/44 - 1/29/46. Ipana, ABC, Tue,
8:30 pm
2/8/46 - 6/28/46, Ipana, ABC, Fri, 9 pm
9/20/46 - 5/30/47, Ipana, NBC, Fri,
8:30 pm
1/11/49 - 7/5/49, Tums, NBC, Tue,
8:30 pm

1 **Albert Ammons and Pete Johnson**
(wartime rehearsal)

Albert Brooks Show, The (1943)

Albert E. Wiggam: Your Mind
(1928 - 29) Sus, NBC, Fri, 15m, 4 pm

Albert Payson Terhune's Dog Dramas
(1/21/34 - 3/29/36) Spratt, Bl, Sun, 15m,
5:45; program off the air 3/31/35 -
9/22/35 due to accident to Terhune

Albert Warner (5/20/39 - 40) CBS
1949 - 1950) ABC
(2/14/55 - 4/8/55) ABC, 5t, 10:15 pm

1 **Album Of Enchantment, The** (4/15/46)
AFRS

1 **Album Of Justice** (1936) Syn

21 **Album Of Life** (1936) Syn

1 **Album Of Manhattan** (2/21/40 - 3/27/40)
Mut, Wed, 15m, 9:15 pm

1 **Albuquerque** (1947) Air trailer

1 **Alcatraz Uprising** (5/3/46) Mut

50 **Aldrich Family, The** (7/2/39 - 4/19/53)
7/2/39 - 10/1/39, Jell-O, NBC, Sun, 7 pm
(summer replacement for Jack Benny)
10/10/39 - 5/28/40, Jell-O, Bl, Tue, 8 pm
7/4/40 - 7/24/41; 8/21/41- 7/9/42; 8/13/42 -
7/8/43; 9/2/43 - 7/20/44 (with Dickie
Jones; Norman Tokar from 6/42 -
7/8/43), Jell-O, NBC, Thu, 8:30 pm
6/29/44 - 8/30/46, Jell-O and Grape Nuts,
CBS, Fri, 8 pm (with Raymond Ives as
of 6/22/45; Ezra Stone as of 11/2/45
until 6/28/51)
3/8/46 - 6/26/47; 9/25/47 - 6/24/48;
9/30/48 - 6/16/49; 10/13/49 - 6/29/50;
8/31/50; 6/28/51, Jell-O and Grape Nuts,
NBC, Thu, 8 pm
9/21/52 - 4/19/53 (with Bobby Ellis), Sus,
NBC, Sun, 7:30 pm

1 **Alec Templeton Time** (7/4/39 - 8/31/47)
7/4/39 - 8/29/39, Johnson, NBC, Tue,
9:30 pm (summer replacement for
Fibber McGee & Molly)
9/25/39 - 6/24/40, Alka-Seltzer, NBC,
Mon, 9:30 pm
9/6/40 - 4/25/41, Alka-Seltzer, NBC, Fri,
7:30 pm
3/1/43 - 8/27/43, Dubonnet Wine, Bl, 3t,
5m, 10:30 pm
6/2/46 - 8/25/46; 6/1/47 - 8/31/47, NBC,
Sun, 8 pm (summer replacement of
Charlie McCarthy)

Alemite Half-hour (see Horace Heidt)

1 **Alex Dreier News** (1942 - 46) Red Heart
until 1944, NBC
(1951 - 56+) Skelly Oil, NBC

Alexander Semmler (1938) CBS, Thu, 7:30 pm

Alexander Woollcott (see The Town Crier)

1 **Alexander's Ragtime Band** (1938) Air trailer

1 **Alf Landon** (6/28/44) CBS

2 **Alfred Duff Cooper** (1940) BBC

1 **Alfred E. Smith Memorial Dinner** (10/25/60)

1 **Algiers** (1937) Air trailer

1 **Ali Baba Goes To Town** (1937) Air trailer

Alias Jane Doe (4/7/51 - 9/22/51) NBC, Sat, 1:30 pm

Alias Jimmy Valentine
(1/18/38 - 2/27/39) Bl
1/18/38 - 4/12/38 (with Bert Lytell), Edgeworth Tobacco, Tue, 9:30 pm
6/6/38 - 2/27/39, Dr. Lyons, Mon, 7 pm

Alias John Freedom (4/19/42 - 11/27/43) Bl
4/19/42 - 7/12/42, Sun, 7:30 pm; last show 5:30 pm
7/20/42 - 7/27/42, Tue, 10:15 pm
1/6/43 - 9/8/43, Wed, 9 pm
9/18/43 - 11/27/43, Sat, 10:30 am

Alias Romeo Syn; sponsored by Multi-Facet Diamond Corporation, 15m

1 **Alibi Club, The** (7/9/39 - 9/10/39) CBS, Sun, 7 pm; 10 pm as of 8/13/39

Alice Adams (see Wheatena Playhouse)

1 **Alice Cornell Show, The** (6/7/44) WEAF

Alice In Orchestralia (4/13/34 - 9/21/34) NBC, Fri, 15m, 5:45 pm

1 **Alice In Wonderland** (12/17/33) Air trailer

Alice Joy, the Dream Singer
(10/26/31 - 2/25/38) various times including:
10/26/31 - 4/30/32, Prince Albert, NBC, 6t, 15m, 7:30 pm (also called Prince Albert Quartet Hour)
1/2/33 - 2/3/33, Bl, 3t, 10 pm
1/31/34 - 5/16/34, Bl, 3t, 15m, 4:15 pm; Mon & Wed as of 3/16/34
1/10/38 - 2/25/38, NBC, 3t, 15m, 9:30 am

1 **Alice Reinheart** (8/3/76)

Alice Remson's Land Of Make Believe (also see Turn Back The Clock)
(12/29/35 - 1/7/40) Bl, Sun, 10m, 11:05 am (started and continued regionally)

1 **Alice's Adventures In Wonderland** (12/4/66) BBC

9 **Alien Worlds** (1979) Syn

Alistair Cooke (8/17/52 - 1/18/53) ABC, Sun, 15m, 9:45 pm

Alka-Seltzer Comedy Stars Of Hollywood (also called Comedy Stars Of Hollywood) Alka-Seltzer
5/31/32 - 8/21/34 at least, Syn, 2t, 15m

20 **Alka-Seltzer Time** (1952 - 1953) CBS and Mut (see Herb Shriner, Curt Massey)

All Aboard For Adventure
(3/8/47 - 6/26/48) NBC, Sat, 15m, 9:30 am

1 **All About Anne** (3/30/51) CBS

All About Stamps (1/32/48 - 4/24/48) Mut, Sat, 15m, 10:15 am

All Country Jamboree (1947 - 48) Sat

2 **All Girl Orchestra, Phil Spitalny, Conductor** (Syn)

All Hands On Deck (7/2/35 - 10/15/35) CBS, Tue, 9 pm
(10/24/35 - 10/14/36) CBS, Thu, 4 pm
(10/19/36 - 3/6/38) CBS, Tue, 15m
(3/16/38 - 6/17/39) CBS, Wed, 3 pm; Sat, 1 pm as of 10/22/38; 6:30 pm as of 4/1/39

All Of Us (3/10/40 - 7/7/40) NBC, Sun, 15m, 12 noon

1 **All On A Summer's Day** (1948) Syn

All Sergeant Jazz Band (7/14/51 - 10/4/51) ABC, Thu, 10 pm

1 **All Star Baseball Preview** (7/7/47) Mut

1 **All Star Cancer Show** (5/5/50) Mut

All Star Cycle Program (see Ridin' High)

1 **All Star Game** (7/11/50) Mut

All Star Parade Of Bands (1953 - 1958), NBC, various days

1 **All Star Revue** (1958) Syn

6 **All Star Revue, The** (3/4/48 - 10/28/48) Mut, Thu, 15m, 8 pm; 9:30 pm as of 5/13/48
(1951 - 1952) NBC-TV

All Star Revue (see Kate Smith)

1 **All Star Revue For 1953, The** (4/53) Syn

1 **All Star Revue For 1956, The** (4/56) Syn

2 **All Star Salute, The National Guard Summer Show** (Syn)

2 **All Star Sextette** (Standard transcription)

All Star Sports (see Harry Wismer)

1 **All Star Swing Festival** (3/19/77) PBS

1 **All Things Considered** (1971 - present), NPR, 7t, 5 - 7 pm; 4 pm as of 1995

All-American Football Show
(9/23/32 - 12/16/32) CBS, Fri, 9 pm

All-American Sports Show
(7/10/53 - 10/2/53) NBC, Fri, 10 pm

All-American Women (10/10/39 - 5/7/40) NBC, Tue, 2 pm

All-Colored Revue (see Harlem Revue)

1 **All-Star Swing Re-Union, The** (8/25/83) PBS-TV

1 **All-Star Variety Show** (1/22/38) CBS

93 **All-Star Western Theater**
(8/11/46 - 8/14/48) CBS - Pacific and Mut-Don Lee, Sun; Sat as of 5/3/47

1 **All-Time All-Star Baseball Team, The** (1953) Syn

All-Wite Melody Revue (see Time To Shine)

Alladdin Kerosene Mantle Lamp Program (1936) 15m

Alladdin Lamp Program (with Smilin' Ed McConnell) Syn (see Smilin' Ed McConnell)

Allan Jackson (4/2/50 - 56+) Met. Life, CBS, 5t

4 **Allan Jones** (4/5/44 - 10/18/44) Old Gold, CBS, Wed, 8 pm (see The Old Gold Show)

4 **Allegheny Metal Announcements** (Syn)

Allegheny Metal Show, The
(11/27/36 - 5/21/37) Allegheny Steel, Bl, Fri, 15m, 7:15 pm

Allen and Jean (Allen Prescott; Joe Bolton replaced Prescott in 9/28/46)
(4/20/46 - 10/19/46) Mild Maid, ABC, Sat. 8:30 am

5 **Allen Prescott, The Wife Saver**
(1946 - 1948) Syn

Allie Lowe Miles (1935 - 38) Mut; limited network
1935 - 36, 2t, 3:30 pm
1936 - 37, 3t, 3:30 pm 1937 - 38, Fri, 10:30 am (also see Husbands and Wives)

Allis Chalmers Pioneer Stories (1936) 15m

Alma Kitchell (8/10/35 - 5/16/42) see also Come and Get It; (also called Alma Kitchell's Brief Case; Alma Kitchell's Journal; Streamline Journal)
8/10/35 - 7/18/36, Sus, NBC, Sat, 10m, 6:35 pm
1937 - 38 (see June Hynd's Guest Book)
12/24/38 - 4/24/39, Sus, Bl, Mon, 15m, 2:30 pm
12/4/39 - 1/8/40, NBC, Mon, 1:30 pm
1/17/40 - 5/1/40, Sus, Bl, Wed, 30m
5/14/40 - 3/17/42, Sus, Bl, Tue, 30m, 2 pm
also 12/16/40 - 5/16/42, Sus, Bl, Mon, 15m

Almanac (4/4/48 - 7/3/49) ABC, Sun, 15m, 3:15 pm, 1 pm as of 10/17/48

Along Gypsy Trails (6/25/38 - 7/8/39) NBC, Sat, 15m, 12:30 pm

5 **Along The Boulevard** (1942) Bl

1 **Aluminum Scrap Drive** (7/23/41) WOR

Alvin Helfer (1947 - 1949) Mut, Appalachian Coal

3 **Alvino Rey, His Singing Guitar and Orchestra** (Standard transcription)

1 **Always Leave Them Laughing** (1948) film sound track

AMA Health Dramas (see also Doctors At Work; Doctors At War; Doctors Look Ahead) (10/13/36 - 5/16/40)
10/13/36 - 6/8/37, Bl, Tue, 5 pm; 4 pm as of 3/30/37
10/13/37 - 6/15/38, NBC, Wed, 15m, 2 pm; 1:30 pm as of 6/1/38
10/5/38 - 5/9/39, Bl, Wed, 30m, 2 pm
10/9/39 - 5/16/40, Bl, Thu, 15m, 4:30 pm

1 **Amalgamated Broadcasting System Inaugural Program** (9/25/33) Amalgamated Broadcasting System

3 **Amanda Of Honeymoon Hill**
(2/5/40 - 4/26/46) 5t, 15m
2/5/40 - 7/31/42, Cal Aspirin and Haley's M-O, Bl
8/3/42 - 4/26/46, Cal Aspirin, CBS

Amanda Snow (11/27/37 - 11/4/39) (also called Amanda's Party)
1/27/37 - 11/4/39, NBC, Sat, 15m
also 11/20/38 - 1/22/39, Sus, Bl, Sun, 30m
also 5/3/39 - 6/14/39, Bl, Wed, 15m, 3:45 pm

Amateur Gentleman (see Leslie Howard Theater)

11 **Amazing Interplanetary Adventures Of Flash Gordon, The** (1935) Syn

Amazing Mr. Malone, The (see Murder and Mr. Malone)

Amazing Mr. Smith, The
(4/7/41 - 6/30/41) American Can, Mut, Mon, 8 pm

3 **Amazing Mr. Tutt, The** (7/5/48 - 8/23/48, 1950) CBS, Mon, 9:30 pm

Amazing Mrs. Danbury
(4/21/46 - 6/16/46) CBS, Sun, 8 pm

Amazing Nero Wolfe, The (see The Adventures Of Nero Wolfe)

2 **Amazing Randi Show, The** (1965) WOR

2 **Ambassador Joseph Kennedy**
(1938, 1940) Bl, CBS

1 **America and The World** (1/68) CBS-TV

1 **America At The Ramparts** (2/12/42) Mut

1 **America At War** (1942) Syn

1 **America Calling** (2/8/41) pool feed
(1938 - 39)(also see Trans-Atlantic Call) Wed, 60m

2 **America Dances** (1938, 1939) CBS, NBC, Sat, 60m, 9 pm

6 **America First Committee** (2/41) Syn

2 **America First Rally** (1941) Mut

1 **America Goes Back To School** (9/27/38) Mut

1 **America Goes Christmas Shopping**
(12/13/48) Mut

1 **America Held Hostage: The Secret Negotiations** (1/28/81) ABC-TV

America In Music (10/15/34 - 1/7/35) Bl, Mon, 10 pm
(4/8/35 - 5/15/35) Bl, Mon; Wed as of 5/8/35

America In The Air (8/8/43 - 10/13/45) Wrigley, CBS
8/8/43 - 9/10/44, Sun, 6:30 pm
10/14/44 - 10/13/45, Sat, 7:30 pm

America In Transition
(1/11/41 - 10/21/41) CBS, Tue, 15m, 3:45 pm

3 **America Looks Ahead** (Aug, Sept/39) Mut

America On Stage (1957)

20 **America On The March** (1952, 1953) Syn

America Preferred (Treasury Dept.)
(7/13/41 - 1/24/42) Mut
7/13/41 - 7/27/41, Sun, 12 noon
9/6/41 - 10/25/41, Sat, 9:30 pm
11/3/41 - 1/24/42, Thu, 9:30 pm
1/10/42 - 1/24/42 on Sat, 8 pm

2 **America Salutes The President's Birthday** (1/30/43, 1/29/44) pool feed

2 **America Sends Greetings** (1938, 1940) Mut, WRUL (shortwave)

10 **America Sings** (1956, 1957) Syn

1 **America Today** (1942) Mut

America Tomorrow (11/23/43 - 2/15/44) Chamber Of Commerce, Bl, Tue, 10:30 pm

America United (1/7/45 - 12/16/51) NBC, Sun
1/7/45 - 7/28/46, 15m, 1:15 pm
8/4/46 - 5/18/47, 30m, 4:30 pm
5/25/47 - 8/28/49, 1 pm
9/9/51 - 12/16/51, Sun, 11:30 pm

America Unlimited (8/11/39 - 9/22/39) NBC, Fri, 15m, 10:30 pm (with David Brinkley)
(1949 - 52) NBC

America's Answer

1 **America's Choice For '39** (1939) film strip audio

1 **America's Christmas Windows**
(12/20/47) Mut

America's Famous Fathers
(10/17/41 - 1/9/42) Mut, Fri, 15m, 9:15 pm

1 **America's Fight Against 1948's Epidemic**
(1/14/49) Syn

America's First Rhythm Symphony
(12/2/34 - 9/22/35) Rexall, NBC, Sun

America's Folklore (Syn)

America's Front Door (7/18/55 - 1/20/56) Mut, 5t, 2:30 pm, 1:30 pm as of 11/14/55

America's Greatest Sports Thrills (see Greatest Sports Thrills)

America's Hour (7/14/35 - 9/35) CBS, Sun, 60m

America's Lost Plays (7/6/39 - 8/31/39) Maxwell House, NBC, Thu, 60m, 9 pm (summer replacement of Baby Snooks)

1 **America's Most Interesting People**
(12/5/38) Mut

2 **America's Music** (Syn)

1 **Americas Speak, The** (4/45)

18 **America's Town Meeting Of The Air**
(5/30/35 - 7/1/56)
5/30/35 - 5/11/39; 10/5/39 - 4/25/40; 10/31/40 - 5/29/41; 10/9/41 - 44, Sus, Bl, Thu, 60m, 9:30 pm; 9 pm, 10/9/41 - 9/24/42; 8:30 from 10/1/42 - 44
1944 - 11/30/45, Reader's Digest, Bl/ABC, Thu, 60m, 8:30 pm
12/6/45 - 12/27/49, Sus, ABC, Thu, 60m, 8:30 pm; Tue, 8:30 pm as of 9/2/47
1/3/50 - 1/2/51, Sus, ABC, Tue, 30m, 9 pm
1/9/51 - 12/28/54, Sus, ABC, Tue, 45m, 9 pm
1/2/55 - 7/1/56, Sus, ABC, Sun, 60m, 8 pm

America, The Free (6/21/41 - 1/3/42) NBC, Sat, 10:30 am

5 **America: Where Do We Go From Here?**
(1/28 - 2/1/80) CBS-TV

American Abroad, An (7/29/48 - 11/4/48) CBS, Thu, 15m, 6:15 pm

American Ace Coffee Time (1948 - 49) WSM

1 **American Action Inc. Program** (11/2/44) WFBR

American Adventure Series, The
(7/28/55 - 7/5/56) NBC, 25m
8/18/55 - 10/13/55, Thu, 8:30 pm
11/17/55 - 7/5/56, Thu, 9:05 pm

American Adventure, The
(5/6/35 - 7/22/35) Bl, Mon

American Agent (Bob Barcley, American Agent)
(12/6/50 - 9/26/51) Mars, ABC, Wed, 8 pm

27 **American Album Of Familiar Music, The**
(10/11/31 - 6/17/51) Bayer, Sun (often off in the summer)
10/11/31 - 6/25/50, NBC, 9 pm until 1933; 9:30 pm thereafter
9/3/50 - 11/19/50, NBC, 9:30 pm
11/26/50 - 6/17/51, ABC, 9:30 pm

1 **American Ambassador Orchestra** (Syn)

1 **American Artists, The** (1931) Syn

1 **American Broadcasting Symphony Orchestra, The** (11/9/46) ABC

1 **American Campus Speaks, The**
(4/20/41) Mut

14 **American Cancer Society** (1948 - 1962) Syn

1 **American Cancer Society 1954 Cancer Crusade** (1954) Syn

1 **American Cancer Society Jamboree**
(1952) Syn

2 **American Cancer Society Presents** (Syn)

1 **American Cancer Society Special**
(4/23/49) NBC

1 **American Cancer Society...Tommy Dorsey and His Orchestra** (Syn)

4 **American Challenge, The** (1939 - 40)
(1950) Syn, KFI

American Choral Festival
(7/6/40 - 9/21/40) Mut, Sat, 9:30 pm

1 **American Comedy Theatre Of The Air**
(5/28/43) CBS

American Cruise (see Summer Cruise)

2 **American Dream, American Nightmare... The Seventies** (12/28, 12/29/79) CBS-TV

American Eagle Club (12/5/42 - 3/17/43) Mut, Sat, 8 pm

American Education Forum
(11/19/38 - 3/31/41)
11/19/38 - 5/17/40, Bl, Sat, 12 noon
12/30/40 - 3/31/41, NBC, Mon, 6 pm

118 **American Family Robinson, The**
(1935 - 1/19/40, 1941) (National Industrial Council)

American Family Saga, An (8/13/44 -?)

American Farmer (3/25/45 - 56) Sus, ABC, Sat, 12:30 pm (often not in New York)

American Fireside, An
(10/14/34 - 5/19/35) Bl, Sun, 10:30 pm

1 **American Folk Singers Of Boston** (1939) Syn

1 **American Foreign Policy: Informal Discussion** (4/43) Syn

15 **American Forum Of The Air, The** (12/26/37 - 3/11/56) originally The Mutual Forum Hour starting in 1934

American Gallery (Syn)

2 **American Girls In Action** (1945) Syn

1 **American Heart Association** (2/7/49) Syn

10 **American Jazz** (Voice Of America Syn)

American Jazz Concert (11/6/48 - 5/7/49; 12/3/49 - 2/18/50; 9/9/50 - 3/31/51) Sus, ABC, Sat (also called Concert Of American Jazz)

1 **American Labor Hour, The** (1943) Mut

1 **American Legion Anniversary Show, The** (3/49) ABC

6 **American Legion Asks: How Good Is American Air Power?, The** (1953) Syn

1 **American Legion Jamboree** (9/22/37) WOR

3 **American Legion Junior Baseball** (1948) Syn

4 **American Legion Presents, The** (1947, 1948) Syn

6 **American Legion Presents: "Air Power In An Age Of Peril", The** (1953) Syn

2 **American Legion: Special Presentation, The** (10/4/46) Syn

2 **American Melody Hour, The** (10/22/41 - 7/7/48) Bayer
10/22/41 - 4/15/42, Bl, Wed, 10 pm
4/21/42 - 6/24/47, CBS, Tue, 7:30 pm
7/2/47 - 7/7/48, CBS, Wed, 8 pm

American Museum of Natural History (10/27/32 - 3/16/33) CBS, Thu, 15m, 2:15 pm

1 **American Music Festival** (2/17/48) WNYC

American Music Hall (8/17/52 - 12/13/54) Sus, ABC
8/17/52 - 6/13/54 (with Paul Whiteman), Sun, 30m, 8 pm; 60m as of 1/5/53
6/28/54 - 6/13/55 (with Glenn Osser) Mon, 8:30 pm, 15m, 8:15 pm
(4/16/56 - 2/1/57) (with Tommy Furtado and Peggy Ann Ellis) 5t, 8 pm, 30 - 60m

14 **American Novels** (3/1/46 - 12/26/47) NBC, Fri/Sat/Fri

American Opera Festival (5/7/42 - 6/13/42) Mut, Thu, 60m, 8 pm

American Panorama

1 **American Parade, The** (4/10/84) CBS-TV

1 **American Pilgrimage** (11/24/40 - 5/11/41) Bl, Sun, 15m, 2 pm
(1944) CBS

5 **American Portrait** (3/16/46 - 9/14/46) CBS, Sat, 6:15 pm

7 **American Portraits** (2/5/38 - 4/30/38) NBC, Sat, 9:30 pm
(7/10/51 - 8/28/51)
NBC, Tue, 8 pm (summer replacement of Cavalcade Of America)
(1985) NPR

American Radio Newsreel (1939)

American Radio Warblers (also Radio Canaries, Singing Canaries and Canary Pet Show)
(10/10/37 - 4/26/56) Hartz, Mut, Sun, 15m

1 **American Red Cross** (1948 - 56) Syn, 15m

2 **American Red Cross 1940 Roll Call** (Syn)

American Revue, The (10/22/33 - 2/25/34) American Oil. CBS. Sun. 7 pm

1 **American Rhapsody** (4/8/45)

2 **American Scene, The** (1983) NPR

4 **American School Of The Air, The** (2/4/30 - 4/30/48) Sus, CBS, 5t (started Tue and Thu), 2:30 pm until 4/28/39; 9:15 am from 10/9/39 - 4/27/45; 5 pm as of 10/1/45; (from 5/11/42 -10/9/42 see Radio Reader) (usually on during school year)

1 **American Security and European Recovery** (post-war) Syn

American Showcase (ABC)

American Side Show (11/13/44 - 12/17/44) Bl, Tue, 7 pm

1 **American Soap Box Derby, The** (4/18/46) CBS

American Story Teller, The (2/5/44 - 7/22/44) NBC, Sat, 7 pm
(7/6/45 - 9/7/45) (10 weeks of repeat shows) NBC, Fri, 11:30 pm

American Story, The (see The American Story Teller)

2 **American Trail, The** (1953) Syn, 15m

American Travel Guide (1/8/55 - 3/26/55) Mut, Sat, 15m, 11 am

American Viewpoints (3/16/38 - 9/20/39) CBS, 15m
3/16/38 - 9/23/38, 2t (Wed & Fri), 10:45 pm

American Weekly Program, The (see Front Page Drama)

American Wildlife (7/29/39 - 9/22/40) Mut, Sun (not in New York)

American Woman's Jury (5/15/44 - 3/16/45) Mut, Tums, 5t, 1:45 pm, 15m

1 **American Women** (8/2/43 - 6/23/44) Wrigley, CBS, 5t, 15m

30 **Americana** (1953 - 1955) NBC

1 **Americans Abroad** (7/9/49 - 9/24/49) NBC, ABC, Sat. 15m, 12:15 pm

5 **Americans All** (1984 - 1985) NPR

23 **Americans All - Immigrants All** (11/13/38 - 5/7/39) Sus, CBS, Sun, 2 pm

1 **Americans At Thanksgiving** (11/22/45) CBS

1 **Americans At Work** (4/28/38 - 4/23/40) CBS, Thu
4/28/38 - 1/4/39, Thu
1/7/39 - 9/26/39, Sat, 7 pm
9/21/39 - 11/16/39, Thu, 15m, 10:30 pm
1/9/40 - 4/23/40, Tue

1 **Americas Speak, The** (1/4/42 - 5/10/42) (1945) Mut, Sun, 3 pm

Amident Show, The (see Burns and Allen)

Amoco Program (9/22/32 - 12/17/32) CBS (Midwest), Thu, 15m, 8:30 pm; Sat as of 10/29/32)

2 **Among The Immortals** (Syn)

236 **Amos 'n' Andy** (1/12/26 - 11/25/60)
1/12/26 - 12/18/27 (Sam and Henry) WGN, 5t, 15m
3/19/28 - 8/16/29, WMAQ, 5t, 15m
8/19/29 - 7/13/34; 9/17/34 -12/31/37, Pepsodent, NBC, 15m, 6t until 1932; 5t afterwards, 7 pm
1/3/38 - 3/31/39, Campbell, NBC, 5t, 15m, 7 pm
4/3/39 - 2/19/43, Campbell, CBS, 5t, 15m, 7 pm
10/8/43 - 6/16/44; 9/22/44 - 6/1/45, Rinso, NBC, Fri, 30m, 10 pm
10/2/45 - 5/28/46; 10/1/46 - 5/27/47; 9/30/47 - 5/25/48, Rinso, NBC, Tue, 9 pm
10/10/48 - 5/8/49, Rinso, CBS, Sun, 7:30 pm
10/9/49 - 5/21/50; 9/24/50 - 6/10/51; 10/7/51 - 5/28/52; 9/28/52 - 5/24/53; 9/27/53 - 5/23/54, Rexall, CBS, Sun, 7:30 pm
9/26/54 - 5/22/55, CBS, Sun, 7:30 pm
also 9/13/54 - 11/25/60 (Amos 'n' Andy Music Hall) Multi, CBS, 5t, 9:30 pm; 7:05 pm, 25m as of 3/26/56

Ampico Hour Of Music (1927 - 28) Ampico, Bl, Thu, 8:30 pm

1 **An Accounting** (1948) Syn

1 **An Act Of Peace** (3/26/79) CBS-TV

1 **An Address On The United Nations** (Syn)

5 **An American In England** (8/3/42 - 12/22/42) CBS; see also Columbia Workshop
8/3/42 - 9/7/42, Mon, 10 pm
12/1/42 - 12/22/42, Tue

1 **An American Rhapsody** (3/5/45) Union Ice, CBS - Pacific

1 **An American With A Mission** (post-war) Syn

1 **An Army Of Stars Salutes The Salvation Army** (12/50) Syn

1 **An English Reporter In Berlin** (Germany) (8/30/39)

1 **An Evening At Crosley Square** (11/5/44) WLW

1 **An Evening At Pops** (8/17/85)

4 **An Evening With Romberg** (1945) NBC

1 **An Interview With President Clinton** (2/20/95)

1 **An Unsafe Day In The Life Of Dennis Day** (Syn)

3 **Anacin Hollywood Star Theatre, The** (1948 - 1949) NBC

1 **Anatomy Of Pop: The Music Explosion** (2/15/66) ABC-TV

Anchors Away (12/13/41 - 3/7/43) Sus, Mut
12/13/41 - 1/3/42, Sat, 5:30 pm
1/11/42 - 3/29/42, Sun, 2 pm
5/9/42 - 5/30/42, Sat, 8 pm
9/27/42 - 12/6/42, Sun, 6:30 pm
12/20/42 - 3/7/43, Sun, 9 pm

1 **And Beautiful II** (9/13/70) Syn

1 **And Bravely Walk** (5/16/52) CBS

1 **And Not Yet Free** (1949) Syn

1 **And Now: A Word From Our Sponsor** (1967) Syn

1 **And Sudden Death** (12/16/46) Mut

1 **And Ye Shall Find** (3/23/48) Mut

Anderson Family, The (1947) (Syn)

1 **Anderson Polish-American Program** (10/13/36) WMBQ

Andersons, The (4/6/42 - 7/10/42) NBC, 5t, 15m, 5:30 pm

26 **Andre Kostelanetz** (2/8/31 - 5/30/46) CBS
2/8/31 - 11/5/31, Sun, 5:30 pm; Tue and Fri as of 5/12, 15m; Tue as of 7/31, 15m
11/11/31 - 2/3/32, American Chain and Cable, Wed, 15m, 10:15 pm
12/31/31 - 2/11/32, Southern Cotton Oil, Thu 9 pm
9/6/32 - 6/6/33, Spool Cotton Co., Tue, 15m, 9:15 pm
also 12/16/33 - 2/7/34, Pontiac, Wed, and Sat, 15m, 9:15 pm
also 1932 - 7/2/33 (with Mary Eastman, Evan Evans) Sun, 8:15 pm
12/25/33 - 2/22/34 (Buick Presents; also with Robert Benchley) 2t (Mon & Thu), 15m, 9:15 pm
4/2/34 - 7/14/34; 10/1/34 - 4/20/35, Chesterfield, CBS, 3t (Mon, Wed, Sat), 9 pm (many of the shows called The Chesterfield Show)
10/2/35 - 7/29/36, Chesterfield, CBS, 2t (Wed & Sat), 9 pm; Wed & Fri as of 5/1/36
8/28/36 - 6/22/38 (Chesterfield Presents), Chesterfield, CBS, Wed & Fri; Wed, 9 pm as of 1/1/37
1/12/39 - 7/3/39; 8/21/39 - 6/24/40 (Tune-up Time) (with Tony Martin as of 8/21/39) Ethyl, CBS, Thu, 45m, 10 pm; Mon, 30m, 8 pm as of 6/5/39
12/1/40 - 12/10/44 (The Pause That Refreshes) Coca-Cola, CBS, Sun, 4:30 pm; 45m from 4/6/41 - 6/22/41; 30m, 8 pm as of 6/29/41; 4:30 pm as of 10/5/41 during 6/29/41 - 9/28/41 summer replacement for Helen Hayes, CBS, Sun, 30m, 8 pm
9/6/45 - 5/30/46 (Music Millions Love), Chrysler, CBS, Thu, 9 pm

1 **Andrea Doria Sinking, The** (7/26/56) CBS

Andrew Kelly: Philosopher (4/23/33 - 12/10/36)
4/23/33 -10/8/33 (Horse Sense Philosophy) NBC, Sun, 15m, 7:15 pm
10/16/33 - 8/6/34, Sus, NBC, Mon, 15m, 6:45 pm
1935 - 36, Sus, Mut, 3t, 15m
9/17/36 - 12/10/36, The Crusaders, Mut, 2t (Thu & Sun), 15m

Andrew Sumers (12/1/40 - 1/12/41) NBC, Sun, 15m, 3:30 pm

12 **Andrews Sisters, The** (1939 - 42) (12/31/44 - 3/27/46) Nash-Kelvinator, ABC
1939 - 42 (see Glenn Miller)
12/31/44 - 6/24/45; 8/26/45 - 9/23/45 (Eight-To-The-Bar Ranch) Norge, Sun, 4:30 pm
10/3/45 - 3/27/46 (N-K Music Showroom) Wed, 10:30 pm

Andrini Continentals (3/31/41 - 9/29/44) Bl, 15m; various times including:
3/31/41 - 4/18/41, 5t, 12 noon
5/10/41 - 7/12/41, 4t (includes Sat)
7/18/41 - 3/20/42, Fri
10/12/42 - 11/9/42, Bl, Mon, 15m, 7 pm
8/6/44 - 9/3/44, Sun, 12:45 pm
9/18/43 - 10/23/43, Sat, 10:15 am
8/18/44 - 9/29/44, Fri, 15m

Andy Devine (Syn)

4 **Andy Griffith** (1960, 1961) AFRS

1 **Andy Hardy's Private Secretary** (1940) Air trailer

2 **Andy Kirk and His Clouds Of Joy** (1937)

1 **Andy Kirk and His Orchestra** (1937)

4 **Andy Powell and His Orchestra** (1970) CBS

1 **Andy Russell** (1944)

1 **Andy Russell Show, The** (1/27/45 - 6/9/45) ABC, Sat, 10 pm

4 **Andy Williams Sings**

1 **Angel With The Cold Nose, The** (Syn)

Angelo Patri: Your Child (8/31/31 - 6/4/33) Cream Of Wheat, CBS, 15m (see also Dramas Of Childhood; Your Child)
8/31/31- 5/26/32, Thu
9/11/32 - 6/4/33, 2t, (Sun & Wed); Sun from 1/1/33

Angler and Hunter (5/30/38 - 9/26/38) NBC, Mon, 15m, 7:30 pm

Angostura Time (see Jean Tighe)

1 **Angry** (1929) Syn

Animal Closeups (7/14/36 - 9/22/36) Bl, Tue, 15m, 5:15 pm

Ann Leaf (1929 - 8/30/36) CBS; various times, often regional, including:
1929 - 30, 3t
1930 - 31, Wed
1931 - 32, 5t, 15m
1933 - 9/9/34, 2t (Mon & Thu) 15m, 2 pm
also 7/1/34 - 9/9/34, Sun, 1 pm also
8/29/34 - 9/5/34, Wed, 3 pm
5/24/36 - 8/30/36, Sun, 4 pm
5/8/37 - 2/5/38, CBS, Sat, 15m, 1:15 pm
also 7/28/37 - 9/15/37, CBS, Wed, 15m, 4 pm

Ann Of The Airlanes (1930s) 15m

1 **Ann Vickers** (1937) Syn

1 **Anne Seymour Interview** (8/3/76)

Annette Hastings (8/28/39 - 12/11/39) Bl, Mon, 15m, 6:15 pm

Anniversary Club, The

1 **Anniversary Night With Horace Heidt** (1945) Audition

1 **Anniversary Of World War II** (9/1/41) CBS

1 **Announcement Of Hitler's Death** (5/1/45) CBS

1 **Announcement Of The First Earth Satellite** (10/4/57) Radio Moscow

11 **Anson Weeks and His Orchestra** (1931- 32) (1937 - 1967) McGregor Syn; 15m

10 **Answer Man, The** (1937 - 56) Trommer's Beer; also Van Dyck cigars; mostly syndicated; carried by WOR, 5t, 15m

Answer Me This (3/30/36 - 8/27/36) NBC
3/30/36 - 6/29/36, Mon, 10m; 15m as of 6/4/36
7/9/36 - 8/27/36, Thu, 15m, 5:30 pm

2 **Answer Please** (1958) CBS

1 **Answering You** (12/25/44) Mut

Answers By The Dancers (see Horace Heidt)

ANTA Show (see Theater USA)

Anthony Candolari Orchestra (1/2/39 - 2/25/39; 6/17/39 - 7/8/39) Mut, Sat, 2:30 pm; 2 pm as of 2/4/39

3 **Anthony Eden** (1938 - 1942) BBC, WFBR

Anthony Frome (10/14/34 - 4/7/35) Bl, Sun, 15m, 2 pm

1 **Anthony Witkowski and The Brooklyn Knights** (10/20/36) WMBQ

Antonini Concert Series (11/7/39 - 5/7/40; 11/12/40 - 5/13/41) Mut, Tue, 8 pm; 8:30 pm as of 11/12/40

4 **Any Bonds Today?** (1940) Syn

1 **Anything Can Happen** (4/26/47) Mut

1 **ANZACS In New Guinea** (1942) Australia

2 **Apollo 7** (10/10 - 22/68)

2 **Apollo 8** (1/21 - 27/68)

1 **Apollo 9** (3/3/69)

1 **Apollo 10** (5/18/69)

4 **Apollo 11** (7/16 - 24/69) (8/13/69)

1 **Apollo 11 Press Conference** (7/5/69)

1 **Apollo 12** (12/14/69)

4 **Apollo 13** (4/11 - 18/70)

1 **Apollo 13 and The Future Of The Space Program** (7/26/95) C-Span

1 **Apollo 14** (7/31/71)

2 **Apollo 15** (7/23 - 8/12/71)

1 **Apollo 16** (4/16 - 28/72)

1 **Apollo 17** (12/6 - 19/72)

2 **Apollo** (5/8/76, 6/19/76)

1 **Apollo Concerts, The**

1 **Apollo Space Launches** (1967 - 1969)

3 **Apollo-Soyuz** (7/14/75) NBC-TV, CBS-TV

1 **Apollo: A Journey To The Moon, The Threshold** (7/15/69) NBC-TV

1 **Appeal For Jews and Non Ayran Christians** (12/12/38) BBC

Appointment With Life
(4/17/44 - 6/7/45) Bl, 5t

Appointment With Music (1948) NBC

1 **Appreciation Of Poetry, The**

Arabesque (1/24/29 - 3/2/33) CBS, various days and times including:
1/24/29 - 3/30/29, Thu/Sat, 10 pm
4/4/29 - 12/26/29, Thu, 8 pm
1/5/30 - 4/27/30, Sun, 10:30 pm
5/22/30 - 7/24/30, Thu, 9 pm
7/28/30 - 9/1/30, Mon, 9 pm
9/7/30 - 10/12/30, Sun, 10 pm
10/20/30 - 12/29/30. Mon, 8:30 pm
1/5/31 - 12/29/31, various days and times
1/3/32 - 3/2/33, Dixie network, various days and times

1 **Aragon Dance Time** (1955) WBBM

1 **Arch Oboler Drama**

1 **Arch Oboler Interview** (8/5/76)

34 **Arch Oboler's Plays** (3/25/39 - 3/30/40) NBC, Sat
(4/5/45 - 10/11/45) Mut, Thu, 10 pm
(1964 - 65)
(12/16; 12/30/40)

Arch Ward (1/5/44 - 4/23/44) Mut, Wed, 15m, 10:15 pm, sponsored by Wilson

1 **Archibald Cox Press Conference** (10/23/73)

1 **Archibald MacLeish's Address To Radio Stations** (2/28/42)

1 **Archie Bleyer and His Orchestra** (6/6/44) CBS

Arco Birthday Party (1930 - 1/21/32) ARCO, NBC, Thu, 9 pm

1 **Arctic Ribbon, The** (12/9/44) Mut

Arden Hour Of Charm (see Eddy Duchin)

Are These Our Children?
(9/29/46 - 1/19/48) Sus, ABC, Sun

9 **Are You A Genius?** (4/20/42 - 1/18/43) CBS, 5t, 30m; 15m, 5 pm as of 8/17/42, also an AFRS series

Are You A Missing Heir? (see Court Of Missing Heirs)

Are You Bluffing? ABC, Mon

1 **Argentina Independence Day** (7/9/40) NBC

1 **Argentina Takes The Stand**

Argive Soliloquies (see NPR Earplay)

2 **Aristocrats, The** (1934) 15m
(7/19/41 - 8/9/41) NBC, Sat, 15m, 7:30 pm, also Syn

Arkansas Traveler (see Bob Burns)

1 **Arlene Francis Show, The** (8/26/70) WOR

18 **Arm Chair Romance** (Syn)

2 **Arm-Chair Traveler, The** (1935) Syn

2 **Armand Dance, The** (4/33) (see Charles Agnew)

2 **Armchair Adventures** (7/23/39 - 9/7/39) CBS, 4t (Sun, Tue - Thu), 15m, 10:45 pm
(1952- 53) CBS, 15m
(11/57) AFRS

Armchair Quartet (3/18/39 - 1/27/40) NBC, Sat, 15m

Armco Iron Master (11/10/33 - 4/9/39) American Rolling Mills
11/10/33 - 2/2/34, Bl, Fri
9/30/34 - 3/24/35, NBC, Sun
10/28/35 - 3/25/36, Bl, Mon; Wed as of 1/8/36
12/22/36 - 2/23/37; 1/15/39 - 4/9/39, Bl, Tue, 10 pm; Sun, 3 pm as of 1/15/39

Armed Forces Radio Theatre (1946) AFRS

Armed Forces Review
(12/14/51 - 2/29/52) Mut, Fri, 9:30 pm

1 **Armed Forces VJ Program** (9/2/45) pool feed

1 **Armistice Day Prayer** (11/11/43) WLAV

3 **Armistice Day Program**
(11/11/39, 11/11/45) Mut, Syn

Armour Orchestra (with Irvin S. Cobb from 1930 - 4/22/32; Roy Shields Orchestra from 1932 - 33; East and Dumke from 9/30/32)
(1929 - 3/10/33) Armour, Bl, Fri, 60m; 30m, 9:30 pm as of 1930 (led to Phil Baker)

Armour Star Jester (see Phil Baker)

1 **Armstrong Of The SBI** (9/5/50 - 6/28/51) General Mills, ABC, 2t, 7:30 pm

Armstrong Quaker's Orchestra
(1928 - 6/12/31) Armstrong Rugs, Bl, Fri, 8:30 pm; 10 pm as of 1929

2 **Armstrong Theater Of Today**
(10/4/41 - 5/1/54) CBS, Sat, 12 noon
10/4/41 - 9/12/53, Armstrong Cork Co.
9/17/53 - 5/1/54, Cream Of Wheat

1 **Army Air Forces** (9/10/44)

1 **Army Air Forces, The** (1943) Mut

1 **Army and Navy "E" Award** (7/28/44) Mut

49 **Army Bandstand** (1958) Syn

1 **Army Day Program** (4/6/42) Syn

22 **Army Hour, The** (4/5/42 - 11/11/45) NBC, Sun afternoon, 60m; 30m as of 7/15/45
(1940 - 1960) Mut, Syn

Army Nurse (2/9/45 - 3/9/45) Bl, Fri, 8:30 pm

1 **Army Nurse Corps Spot Announcements** (Syn)

5 **Army Of Stars** (Salvation Army)
(1955 - 1967) Syn

1 **Army Of Stars Salutes The Salvation Army** (12/57) Syn

1 **Army Ordnance Program** (4/30/41) WFBR

Army Service Forces Presents
(9/4/43 - 4/29/44) Bl, Sat, 10:15 pm

Army Show, The (12/20/40 - 3/26/42) D. L. Clark Co.
12/20/40 - 3/14/41, Bl, Fri, 8 pm
10/2/41 - 3/26/42 (also called Service With A Smile; Army Camp Program), Bl, Thu, 8:30 pm; led to The Army Hour

3 **Army-McCarthy Hearings, The**
(1954, 1968) ABC-TV, Dumont

1 **Army-Navy Game, The** (6/14/42 - 4/8/44) Bl
6/14/42 - 9/20/42, Sun, 4:30 pm; 5:30 pm as of 8/16/42
10/29/42 - 1/28/43, Thu, 25m, 7:05 pm
4/24/43 - 10/23/43 (Army-Navy House Party), Mut, Sat, 12 noon
1/8/44 - 4/8/44, Mut, Sat, 3:30 pm

2 **Arnie Barnett and His Orchestra** (3/47)

2 **Arnold Grimm's Daughter**
(7/5/37 - 6/26/42)
7/5/37 - 5/27/38, Softasilk, CBS, 5t, 15m, 1:30 pm
5/30/38 - 6/26/42, Kix, NBC, 5t, 15m, 2:15 pm; 2:45 pm as of 3/24/41

1 **Arnold Johnson and His Orchestra**
(1/4/32) Syn

Around New York (9/20/38 - 5/14/41) Sus
9/20/38 - 6/11/40, NBC, Tue, 7:30 pm
9/18/40 - 5/14/41, Bl, Wed, 7:30 pm

Around The World (1929 - 30) Armstrong Rugs, Bl, Tue, 8:30 pm

1 **Around The World In Eighty Days**
(3/348) CBC

1 **Around The World With Howard Hughes and His Crew In Thirty Days**
(7/15/38) Mut

Around The World With Santa Claus
(Syn) 15m

1 **Arrival Of Deladier At Croyden Aerodrome** (9/25/38) BBC

1 **Arrival Of Delayed Pilgrims, The** (1949) Syn

1 **Arrival Of General Eisenhower**
(6/18/45) Mut

1 **Arrival Of Prisoners Of War** (9/7/45) Mut

1 **Arrival Of The Canarvan Castle In Montevideo** (12/10/40)

1 **Arrival Of The Clipper Plane "Cavalier"** (5/25/37) WOR

1 **Arrival Of The First Air France Flight At La Guardia Airport** (6/46) Mut

1 **Arrival Of The Ile De France** (7/29/49) WOR

1 **Arrival Of The King and Queen At Red Bank, New Jersey** (6/10/39) Mut

1 **Arrival Of The King and Queen At The New York World's Fair** (6/10/39) Mut

2 **Arrival Of The King and Queen In Montreal** (5/17-18/39) CBC

1 **Arrival Of The King and Queen In New York** (6/10/39) Mut

1 **Arrival Of The King and Queen In Ottawa** (5/19/39) CBC, Mut

1 **Arrival Of The King and Queen In The United States** (6/7/39) CBC

1 **Arrival Of The King and Queen In Washington, D. C.** (6/8/39) Mut

1 **Arrival Of The King and Queen Of England To Montreal** (5/17/39) NBC

1 **Arrival Of The Roosevelt Train** (4/15/45) Mut

2 **Arrival Of The S. S. New Amsterdam** (5/16/38) WOR

1 **Arrival Of The U. S. S. America** (11/11/46) Mut

1 **Arrivederci: A Tribute to Lanza** (10/7/59) WERE

4 **Arrow News Reporter** (9/21/39) WJSV

1 **Arrows In The Dust** (5/22/48) CBS

2 **Art Baker and His Notebook** (Syn)

2 **Art Baker's Notebook** (9/8/38 - 58)
KFI - Los Angeles; mostly west coast
1/9/50 - 3/31/50, ABC, 5t, 15m, 1:45 pm, sponsored by White King Soap

1 **Art Education and The Creative Process** (1950)

Art For Your Sake (10/7/39 - 4/27/40) NBC, Sat, 7:30 pm

Art In America (10/20/34 - 1/26/35) Bl, Sat, 15m, 8 pm

Art In The News (7/12/39 - 10/4/39) NBC, Wed, 15m, 6 pm

Art Jarrett (1931 - 6/14/32) CBS, 2t, 15m, 6:45/6 pm; also CBS, Fri, 15m

3 **Art Kassell and His Kassells In The Air** (Mar, Apr, 1940) Mut

1 **Art Linkletter Show, The** (4/5/42) KQW

Art Linkletter's House Party (see House Party)

4 **Art Mooney and His Orchestra** (1945 - 1968) CBS, NBC

Art Of Conversation, The

4 **Art Of Living, The** (1935 - 1958+) NBC, 15m (various days and times including:
1935
7/11/36 - 10/31/36, Sat, 6:45 pm (summer replacement for Religion In The News)
3/2/39 - 5/25/39, Thu, 12:30 pm
6/3/39 - 10/7/39, Sat, 6:30 pm
5/27/40 - 9/28/40, Sat, 6:30 pm
6/7/41 - 9/27/41, Sat, 6:30 pm
12/24/50 - 9/2/51, Sun, 11:30 pm
1/5/55 - 12/30/55, Doeskin Products, 5t, 10m, 10:15 am
1/9/56 - 2/3/56, 5t and 9/26/54 - 58+, Sun, 9:45/9:15 am

Art Of Song (8/30/36 - 10/11/36) Mut Sun, 8 pm

1 **Art Tatum** (Standard transcription)

1 **Art Tatum and His Orchestra** (2/27/34) NBC

2 **Art Tatum Trio** (World transcriptions)

Art Van Damme (1940 - 52) (Regional)
1940 - 41 (with Louise Carlyle) 15m
12/16/45 - 3/29/46; 4/28/46 - 8/30/46, NBC, 5t, 15m, 12:30 pm; Mon as of 8/2/46
1948 - 49 (Predict A Hit) (with Bob Morris), Coca-Cola, 15m

2 **Art Van Damme Quintet** (Thesaurus transcriptions)

14 **Art Van Damme Quintet with Louise Carlyle, The** (NBC) Syn

4 **Art Van Damme Quintet, The** (NBC) Syn

1 **Arthritis and Rheumatism Fund** (11/15/48) Syn

Arthur (Bugs) Baer (see Bugs Baer)

Arthur C. Clarke's World Of Science Fiction

2 **Arthur Fiedler and His Orchestra** (Associated transcriptions)

3 **Arthur Gaeth News** (1944 - 48) Mut
(4/19/48 - 50) ABC, sponsored by United Electrical Workers

Arthur Gary (1948)

10 **Arthur Godfrey** (1933 - 4/27/45) preceded Arthur Godfrey Time
1933 - 41, Washington D. C., WJSV (later WTOP)
also 12/17/37 - 1/21/38 (from New York), Barbasol, Mut, Fri, 15m, 7:45 pm
also 1/24/38 - 9/38 (from New York), Barbasol, CBS, 2t (Mon & Fri), 15m
also 4/3/39 - 9/3/41, Mut, 3t; 15m; finally Wed, 9 am as of 4/9/41
4/28/41 - 4/27/45, Washington (piped to New York), CBS, 5t, 30m - 75m; sometimes on twice a day
also 9/9/41 - 4/16/42, Mut, 2t, 15m, 12:15 pm
also 2/23/42 - 6/5/42 (Victory Begins At Home) CBS, 3t, 15m, 11:15 am

Arthur Godfrey Roundtable (taped repeats of daily show)
(2/11/50 - 9/30/55) CBS, various days and times

Arthur Godfrey Show, The (see Arthur Godfrey)

1 **Arthur Godfrey Special, The** (8/18/79) TV, Syn

74 **Arthur Godfrey Talent Scouts** (7/2/46 - 10/1/56) Lipton, CBS
7/2/46 - 4/22/47, Tue, 9 pm; 10 pm as of 8/27/46; 9:30 pm as of 12/24/46
5/27/47 - 6/17/47, Tue, 9 pm
7/4/47 - 8/1/47, Fri, 9:30 pm
8/4/47 - 6/27/49; 8/29/49 - 10/1/56, Mon, 8:30 pm; on TV from 1948

35 **Arthur Godfrey Time** (4/30/45 - 4/30/72) New York, CBS, Sus until 1947; Multi after that; mornings, 5t, 30m; 45m as of 8/27/45; 30m - 60m as of 4/29/46; also early morning local show (New York); replaced by Jack Sterling on this show 11/1/48

1 **Arthur Godfrey With Archie Bleyer and His Orchestra** (AFRS transcription)

Arthur Hale (1939 - 47) (Confidentially Yours) Richfield, Mut

50 **Arthur Holtzman** (12/48 - 11/49) WMCA

6 **Arthur Hopkins Presents**
(4/19/44 - 1/3/45) NBC, Wed, 60m, 11:30 pm

6 **Arthur Mann** (11/11/39 - 5/6/45) Mut

1 **Arthur Primm** (2/20/45) Mut

2 **Arthur Smith and The Cracker Jacks**
(1948 - 52) (also called Arthur Smith's Carolina Corner from 1950 - 51; Arthur Smith's Corner Store from 1951 - 52) see also Carolina Hayride
(also 7/2/56 - 12/28/56) American Home Foods, CBS, 5t, 5m, 4 pm, also Syn

Arthur Tracy (7/17/31 - 7/3/42) various days and times including:
7/17/31 - 4/8/32 (Pillsbury Pageant), CBS, Fri, 30m, 10 pm; 9 pm as of 1/8/32
4/11/32 - 7/4/32, CBS, Mon, 15m, 9:15 pm
1932 - 33, CBS, Sat, 15m
2/3/33 - 5/19/33, CBS, Fri, 15m, 10:30 pm
6/5/33 - 7/26/33, Non-Spi Company, CBS, 3t, 15m, 9:15 pm; Mon and Wed as of 7/1/33
2/5/35 - 6/27/35, Mut, 2t, 15m
2/18/40 - 4/21/40, Mut, Sun, 15m
1/5/42 - 7/3/42, Ex-lax, Bl, 3t, 15m, 4 pm

Arthur's Place (6/20/47 - 9/12/47)) CBS, Fri, 9 pm, sponsored by Borden

1 **Artie Arnell and His Orchestra** (3/20/66) CBS

Artie Shaw (11/20/38 - 11/14/39) (Melody and Madness) see Robert Benchley

4 **Artie Shaw and His Orchestra** (1938) NBC

4 **Artie Shaw Orchestra** (Thesaurus transcriptions)

1 **Artie Shaw's Class In Swing** (1939) film sound track

1 **Artist Recital Bureau** (Syn)

1 **Artistry and Rhythm Of Stan Kenton** (1951) Syn

1 **Artistry In Rhythm** (Syn)

2 **Artists and Models** (8/37) Air trailers

2 **Artists and Models Abroad** (1938, 1939) Air trailer, sound track

Artists In America

Arturo Toscanini (see NBC Symphony)

Arvin Dale

1 **As Europe Sees The Marshall Plan** (9/11/48) CBS

As Others See It (3/2/47 - 11/9/47) CBS, Sun, 12:30 pm

3 **As Others See Us** (Feb, 1947, 1948) CBS

As The Twig Is Bent (see We Love and Learn)

3 **As We See It** (5/9/50 - 1/3/50) ABC, Tue, 15m, 10:30 pm

Asa Martin Show

1 **ASCAP Carnegie Hall Concert** (10/2/39)

1 **ASCAP On Parade** (1942) Syn

1 **ASCAP World's Fair Concert** (10/24/40) WNYC

Asher and Little Jimmy (1931- 40s) Syndicated from WSM, Nashville

1 **Asia-Pacific Economic Co-operation Meeting** (11/20/93) C-Span

1 **Asian Flu, The** (9/19/57) CBS

Ask Eddie Cantor (1961 - 1963) Syn (see Eddie Cantor)

Ask Eleanor Nash (see Eleanor Nash)

Ask Me Another (6/16/46 - 9/22/46) NBC, Sun, 6:30 pm

1 **Ask President Carter** (3/5/77) CBS

Ask Young America (12/13/41 - 3/28/42) Bl, Sat, 15m, 11:30 am

1 **Askit Basket** (10/5/38 - 4/17/41) Colgate, CBS
10/5/38 - 6/28/39 (with Jim McWilliams), Wed, 7: 30 pm
8/17/39 - 4/17/41 (with Jim McWilliams; then Ed East as of 10/17/40), Thu, 8 pm

1 **Assassination Of Lee Harvey Oswald, The** (11/24/63) NBC-TV

1 **Assassination Round-up** (11/1/50) Mut

7 **Assignment Home** (12/9/44 - 9/15/46) Sus, CBS
2/9/44 - 6/30/45, Sat, 4:30 pm
7/7/45 - 9/8/45, Sat, 10:15 pm
12/8/45 - 7/13/46, Sat, 3 pm
7/21/46 - 9/15/46, Sun, 2 pm

1 **Associated Dance Orchestra** (Muzak transcription)

1 **Associated Press: One Hundred Years Of News** (5/23/48) NBC

1 **Associated Salutes WFBR** (6/12/39) WFBR

1 **Astaire Time** (9/28/60) NBC-TV

62 **At Ease** (AFRS) 15m

At Home With Faye and Elliott (Syn) 15m

2 **At Home With Lionel Barrymore** (1949 - 50) Syn, 5m, 3t

At Home With Music (1/26/52 - 6/21/52) ABC, Sat, 15m, 5:30 pm

At Home With The Kirkwoods (9/11/47) Audition (see Jack Kirkwood)

1 **At The Circus** (1939) Air trailer

4 **At The Crossroads** (Syn)

2 **At The Ringside Of History** (11/10 & 20/48) Mut

1 **At The Top** (9/12/76) PBS

At The U.N. (with Pauline Fredericks) (8/28/57 - 1958) NBC, Wed, 10:05 pm, 25m

At This Hour

At This Point In Time (see The Last Nixon Show)

1 **At Your Service** (4/28/71) WKZO

Atlantic Family (see Bob Hope)

2 **Atlantic Spotlight** (1/1/44 - 2/2/46) NBC, Sat, 12:30 pm

Atom and You, The (9/27/48 - 10/11/48) Mut, Mon, 9:30 pm

1 **Atom Bomb Discussion** (8/6/45) Mut

1 **Atom Bomb Spy, The** (2/20/48) Mut

4 **Atom Bomb Test** (June, July, 1946, Mar, 1953) Mut, ABC

1 **Atom Bomb Test Preview** (6/26/46) CBS

1 **Atomic Bomb Accounts** (7/24/46) ABC

1 **Atomic Bomb Explosion**

1 **Atomic City, U. S. A.** (2/25/50) CBS

1 **Atomic Energy For Peace** (8/14/48) CBS

1 **Attack At Sea** (1940) BBC

1 **Attacks On Liberty** (3/22/38) Mut

1 **Attempted Assassination Of President Ford** (9/5/75)

1 **Attempted Broadcast Of Adolf Hitler's Speech From Wilhelmshaven** (4/1/39) Germany

2 **Attorney At Law** (1/3/38 - 8/30/38) Johnson Wax
1/3/38 - 6/29/38 (with Jim Ameche and Fran Carlon), Bl, 5t, 15m, 10:30 am; 3 pm as of 5/30/38
7/5/38 - 8/30/38 (with Henry Hunter and Betty Winkler) NBC, Tue, 30m, 9:30 pm (summer replacement for Fibber McGee & Molly;)
(6/9/46 - 7/28/46) (with Al Hodge) Mut, Sun, 5 pm (partial summer replacement for The Shadow) (see The Story Of Terry Reagan, Attorney At Law)

1 **Attorney For The Defense** (12/19/44) Audition (see Jonathan Brixton)

1 **Attorney General Richardson Press Conference** (10/11/73) pool feed

1 **Attorney General Robert F. Kennedy** (8/64) pool feed

Atwater Kent Dance Orchestra (1929 - 30) Atwater Kent, Bl, Thu, 60m, 10:00 pm

1 **Atwater Kent Demonstration Record** (1932) Syn

Atwater Kent Hour (1926 - 6/28/31; 9/27/31-10/4/31) Atwater Kent, NBC, Sun, 60m (started on WEAF on 10/4/25)
(9/24/34 - 12/24/34) (with Josef Pasternack Orchestra) Atwater Kent, CBS, Mon, 8:30 pm

1 **Atwater Kents and Iconoscopes** (1965)

Aubade For Strings (10/9/38 - 9/17/39) CBS, Sun

Auction Bridge Game (1926 - 2/10/31) Work-Whitehead, NBC, Tue, 10 pm; 4:30 pm as of 1928

Auction Gallery (5/22/45 - 3/13/46) Mut
5/22/45 - 6/26/45, Tue, 8:30 pm
8/6/45 - 12/24/45 (Victory Auction then Radio Auction) Rensie, Mon, 10 pm
12/26/45 - 3/13/46 (Radio Auction) Rensie, Wed, 10 pm

Auction Quiz (6/27/41- 42) Esso, Bl (Central time zone only), Fri, 7 pm

1 **Audie Murphy Inserts** (1946) WOR

1 **Audition Of The New York Philharmonic For Thursday Night** (10/21/38) CBS

Audrey Marsh (11/21/38 - 2/10/39) CBS, Mon & Fri, 15m, 8:30 am

Aunt Fanny (see Sunday Dinner At Aunt Fanny's)

1 **Aunt Jemima Show, The** (1/17/29 - 6/5/53)
1/17/29 - 4/4/29, Quaker, CBS, Thu, 9 pm
1929 - 30 (Aunt Jemima Man), Bl, 6t, 15m
11/24/31 - 7/14/32, Jad Salts, CBS, 3t (Tue - Thu), 15m, 2 pm
9/13/32 - 3/2/33, Jad Salts, CBS, 3t; 2t as of 12/12/32, 2 pm
8/31/37 - 5/20/38 (Cabin At The Crossroads), Quaker, Bl, 5t (Tue - Sat), 15m
1/31/43 - 10/31/43, Quaker, CBS, 5m, 2:55 pm
11/6/43 - 1/22/44, Quaker, CBS, Sat, 15m, 1:30 pm
6/19/44 - 6/15/45, Quaker, Bl, 5t, 5m
9/8/52 - 6/5/53, Quaker, CBS, 10m, 3t - 5t, 3:45 pm

11 **Aunt Jenny's Real Life Stories** (1/18/37 - 9/28/56) CBS, 5t, 15m
1/18/37 - 3/18/55, Spry, 1:45 pm; 11:45 am as of 7/8/37; 12:15 pm as of 6/24/46
1/2/56 - 9/28/56, Spry; Campbell cosponsor from 1/3/56 - 3/29/56, 2:45 pm

Aunt Lulu's Adventures (1930 - 1/27/31) Bl, Tue, 15m

5 **Aunt Mary** (1942 - 50s) NBC - West, at different times, Albers Oats, Ben Hur Coffee, Kitchen Craft Flour, 5t, 15m
also 1/21/46 - 1/17/47, Mut, 5t, 15m, 9:15 am (also see The Story Of Aunt Mary)

Aurant, Dick (1951 - 53) West Coast

1 **Australia's Road To Victory** (1942) Syn

2 **Australian News** (2/21/41, 8/14/42) Australia

Author Meets the Critics (6/12/46 - 4/22/51) originally a local New York show, on as early as 1/16/43
6/12/46 - 4/2/47, Mut, Wed, 10:30 pm; continued on WQXR until 5/18/47
5/25/47 - 2/22/48, NBC, Sun, 4:30 pm
7/4/48 - 10/3/48, NBC, Sun, 5 pm
11/24/49 - 9/28/50, ABC, Thu, 10 pm
10/1/50 - 4/22/51 , ABC, Sun, 11:30 am

Author Speaks, The (5/17/52 - 8/30/52) NBC, Sat, 15m, 5:30 pm

38 **Author's Playhouse** (3/5/41- 5/8/45)
3/5/41 - 10/21/41, Sus, Bl, Wed, 10 pm
10/26/41 - 2/8/42; 7/12/42 - 9/20/42, Red, Sun, 11:30 pm
9/30/42 - 4/5/44, Philip Morris, NBC, Wed, 11:30 pm
4/14/44 - 9/29/44, NBC, Fri, 11;30 pm
also 7/8/44 - 9/2/44 (summer replacement for Truth Or Consequences) Duz, NBC. Sat, 8:30 pm
10/16/44 - 5/8/45, NBC, Mon, 11:30 pm

Author's Quiz (see Author, Author)

68 **Author's Studio, The** (8/3/75 - 11/5/78) Syn

2 **Author! Author!** (1/11/39 - 2/12/40) B. F. Goodrich, Mut, Fri; then Mon, 9:30 pm as of 6/12/39; then Mon, 8 pm as of 11/6/39 (also called Author's Quiz)

3 **Autumn In New York** (10/10/56 - 11/56) CBS, Fri

1 **Autumn Journey** (5/9/52) CBS

1 **Autumn Rhythms** (9/56) CBS

1 **Auxilliary To The Hebrew Home and Hospital For The Aged, The** (1/16/37) WCNW

1 **Avalon Showboat** (6/21/40) NBC

34 **Avalon Time** (10/1/38 - 5/1/40) Avalon cigarettes
10/1/38 - 12/31/38 (with Red Foley) NBC, Sat
1/7/39 - 12/20/39 (see Red Skelton)
1/3/40 - 5/1/40 (with Cliff Arquette) NBC, Wed, 8:30 pm

29 **Ave Maria Hour, The** (1935 -1968) WOR for first 12 shows; then WMCA - New York; broadcast from Greymoor Monastary at Garrison, NY, then syndicated

26 **Avenger, The** (10/25/45 - 4/18/46) Syn

Avenger, The (7/18/41 - 11/3/42) WHN - New York, Friday for the first 7 weeks; then Tuesday

Aviation and Civilization

1 **Axis Payday** (9/9/43) Syn

1 **Axis Sally** (1944)

B & D Chucklewagon (with Bruce Elliot and Dan Macullough)
(1949 - 50) Mut, 15m

1 **B and M Cold Storage Vaults**

B M Triangle Club (see Betty Moore)

1 **B-29 On Iwo Jima** (3/5/45) Mut

1 **B-36 Crash Report** (Mut)

1 **B. A. Rolfe and His Orchestra** (see also Lucky Strike Dance Orchestra; Saturday Night Party); also broadcast as Goodrich Silvertown Orchestra
(2/18/33 - 1/2/34) NBC, Sat
(4/5/34)

Bab-O Bright Spot (2/6/32 - 8/12/32) Bab-O, CBS, 15m
2/6/32 - 4/30/32 (with Guy Lombardo Orchestra) Sat, 7:30 pm
5/20/32 - 8/12/32) (with Irving Kaufman and Sidney Brown Orchestra) Fri, 11 am

1 **Babe Didrikson Zaharias Sports Show** (1954) Syn

1 **Babe Ruth** (4/16/34 - 10/21/44)
4/16/34 - 7/13/34 (Play Ball - with Steve Martin; Adventures Of Babe Ruth), Quaker, Bl, Mon, 3t, 8:45 pm
1936, Mut, Tue
4/14/37 - 7/9/37 (Sinclair Babe Ruth Program), Sinclair, CBS, 2t (Wed & Fri), 15m, 10:30 pm
6/5/43 - 7/10/43 (Here's Babe Ruth) NBC, Sat, 15m, 10:45 am
8/28/43 - 11/20/43; 7/8/44 - 10/21/44 (Baseball Quiz) Spaulding, NBC, Sat, 15m, 10:30 am

1 **Babe Ruth Report** (8/19/48) WOR

1 **Babe Ruth Requiem Mass** (8/19/48) WOR

1 **Babe Ruth Show, The**

1 **Babe Ruth Tribute** (8/17/48) WOR

1 **Babes In Arms** (6/39) Air trailer

Babes In Hollywood (10/16/33 - 2/16/34) Bl, 5t/4t (Mon-Wed, Fri), 15m, 5:15 pm

1 **Babes On Broadway** (1941) Air trailer

1 **Babies C. O. D.** (11/8/54) CBS

Baby Rose Marie (12/25/32 - 2/20/39) Bl, 15m
12/25/32 - 7/9/33, Julius Grossman Shoes, Sun, 12 noon
1933 - 34, Tasty Yeast, 2t
3/21/38 - 1/25/39, 2t (Mon & Wed, 7:30 pm)
1/30/39 - 2/20/39, Mon

14 **Baby Snooks Show, The** (with Fanny Brice and Hanley Stafford)
(11/4/37 - 5/29/51)
11/4/37 - 6/30/38; 9/1/38 - 6/29/39; 9/7/39 - 2/29/40 (Good News until 10/10/40) Maxwell House, NBC, Thu, 60m, 9 pm
3/7/40 - 7/25/40 (Good News) Maxwell House, NBC, Thu, 30m, 9 pm; 8 pm as of 7/4/40
9/5/40 - 7/10/41; 9/4/41 - 7/23/42; 9/3/42 - 6/17/43; 9/2/43 - 6/15/44 (Maxwell House Coffee Time as of 10/17/40) Maxwell House, NBC, Thu, 30m, 8 pm
9/17/44 - 6/10/45 (Post Toasties Time), Post Toasties, CBS, Sun, 6:30 pm
9/16/45 - 6/9/46, Sanka, CBS, Sun, 6:30 pm
9/6/46 - 5/30/47; 9/5/47 - 5/28/48, Jell-O, CBS, Fri, 8 pm
11/8/49 - 5/2/50; 10/10/50 - 5/29/51, Tums, NBC, Tue, 8:30 pm
see other listings by title

1 **Baby Snooks Promos** (CBS)

1 **Bach Aria Group** (1/16/49) NBC

Bach Cantata Series (with Alfred Wallenstein)
(1938 - 5/28/39; 10/22/39 - 5/5/40; 1/5/41 - 3/23/41) Mut, Sun, 7 pm

Bachelor Mother (1/26/42 - 2/6/42) Mut, 5t, 15m, 4:15 pm

11 **Bachelor's Children** (9/28/36 - 9/27/46) Old Dutch Cleanser, Wonder Bread, Colgate, CBS, 5t, 15m; NBC replaced CBS from 3/24/41 - 9/25/42; originally on WGN locally from 9/9/35 - 9/25/36
also 9/28/36 - 4/23/37; 9/27/37 - 9/23/38; 4/1/40 - 3/28/41, Old Dutch Cleanser, Mut, 5t, 15m

Back Of The News In Washington (with William Hard) (1930 - 7/29/31) NBC, Wed, 15m, 7:45 pm

2 **Back To Bataan** (1945) Air trailers

Back Where I Come From
(9/30/40 - 2/28/41) CBS, 10:30 pm, 15m
9/30/40 - 11/11/40, Mon
also 10/4/40 - 2/28/41, Fri

139 **Backstage Wife** (4/1/35 - 1/2/59) 5t, 15m
4/1/35 - 3/27/36, Sterling products, Mut, 9:45 am
3/30/36 - 6/26/36, Dr. Lyons, Bl, 4:15 pm
9/16/36 - 6/8/51, Dr. Lyons, NBC, 4 pm
6/11/51- 7/1/55, Procter & Gamble, NBC, 4 pm
11/56 - 1/2/59, Multi, CBS, 5t, 15m

Bailey Axton (9/28/37 - 2/7/39) Bl, Tue, 15m, 12:15 pm
also 7/16/38 - 9/17/38, NBC, Sat, 15m, 11 am

1 **Baker's Broadcast, The** (with Feg Murray, Ozzie and Harriet) (10/3/37 - 6/26/38) Fleischmann, Bl, Sun; (see also Joe Penner and Believe It Or Not)

Baker's Theater Of Stars (10/2/48 - 5/17/53) American Baker's Association
10/2/48 - 4/1/50; see Hollywood Star Theater
4/24/50 - 7/16/51; 2/24/52 - 2/15/53; see Hollywood Star Playhouse
2/22/53 - 5/17/53, CBS, Sun, 8 pm

1 **Balalaika** (1939) Air trailer

Balalaika Orchestra (at times with Peter Biljo) (also see Samovar Serenade) (7/2/34 - 8/27/34) CBS, Mon, 6 pm

1 **Ball Of Fire** (1941) film sound track

Ballad Hunter, The (with Alan Lomax) (1941)

1 **Ballad Of James Otis, The** (7/15/49) CBS

6 **Ballad Time** (Syn)

Balladeers (with Irving Miller Orch) (8/2/41 - 8/30/41) NBC, Sat, 15m, 10 am

9 **Ballads and Ballots** (10/8 - 11/1/48) WNEB

1 **Ballance 'N Records** (1951) KOA

Ballard's Oven Ready Biscuit Time (see Smilin' Ed McConnell)

1 **Baltimore Harbor Tunnel Ground Breaking Ceremonies** (4/21/55) WFBR

2 **Band Box Revue** (Pre-war) Audition

1 **Band Concert, The** (Audition)

1 **Band Goes To Town, The** (10/20/35) NBC

1 **Band Goes To Town, The** (with Jerry Sears Orchestra; with Irving Miller Orchestra as of 5/15/39)
(9/20/38 - 2/4/41) NBC, 15m
9/20/38 - 3/10/39, 5t, 9:30 am/9 am
3/13/39 - 5/10/40, 5t, 9:15 am
5/13/40 - 2/4/41, 3t (Mon - Wed) 9:15 am

Band Of The AAF Training Command, The (1944) see Glenn Miller

Band Played On, The (see Rex Maupin)

1 **Band That Jack Built, The**

1 **Band Wagon, The** (1953) film sound track

3 **Bands For Bonds** (Sept, Nov, 1947) Mut

3 **Bandstand U.S.A.** (1949 - 59) Sus, Mut (often not in New York)
1949 - 51, Fri
1951- 57, Sun
also 1952 - 59, Mut, Sat, 30m/60m

Bandwagon Mysteries (6/24/45 - 9/16/45) (with Dick Powell; beginning of Rogue's Gallery) Fitch, NBC, Sun, 7:30 pm (summer replacement for Fitch Bandwagon)
(10/2/49 - 6/25/50) ABC, Sun, 3:30 pm

Banjo Bill (with Artells Dickson) (6/8/32 - 11/30/32) Diplomat Product Corp., CBS, 15m, 8:45 am

6 **Baptist Hour, The** (10/2/49 - 1952) ABC, Sun, 3:30 pm

Bar X Days (also Bar X Days and Nights) (with Carson Robison as of 7/26/34) (6/30/33 - 9/27/34) Feen-a-Mint (as of 11/19/33), Bl
6/30/33 - 8/11/33, Bl, Fri, 8:30 pm
8/13/33 - 11/12/33, Bl, Sun, 9 pm
11/5/33 - 7/15/34, Bl, Sun, 2 pm
7/26/34 - 9/27/34, CBS, Thu, 9 pm (see Carson Robison)

3 **Barbara Bush** (1991, 1992) C-SPAN

Barbara Gould (1929 - 8/18/32) CBS, Thu, 15m (also see Have You Heard?)

2 **Barbara Walters Special, The** (1976, 1978) ABC-TV

Barbara Welles Show, The (5/19/47 - 12/7/51) Mut, 5t

Barber Shop Quartet (7/3/41 - 7/31/41) CBS, Thu, 8:30 pm

1 **Barleban On Photography** (8/20/40) WEVD

46 **Barnaby Rudge** (Syn)

Barnacle Bill (with Cliff Soubier)

Barnacle Bill, Jr. (with Ken Murray)

Barney Grant Show (4/4/45 - 5/9/45) Mut. Wed, 8:30 pm

1 **Barney Rapp and His New Englanders** (6/17/39 - 10/7/39) Bl, Sat, 10 pm

Barnsdall Musical Memories (1931 - 4/17/32) CBS - Midwest, Sun, 6:30 pm

3 **Barnyard Follies** (6/16/45 - 52) Sus (usually not in New York)
6/16/45 - 9/8/45, (with Buddy Weed) CBS, Sat, 2:30 pm
1946 - 48, Mut, Sat (10 am)?
1948 - 52, CBS, 45m, 5t

2 **Barnyard Jamboree** (1947) with Jimmie Jeffries, (Syn)

Baron and The Bee, The (Jack Pearl and Cliff Hall) (7/21/53 - 9/8/53) NBC, Tue, 9 pm
(11/14/53 - 1/16/54) NBC, Sat, 7 pm

Baron Elliott Orchestra (from Pittsburgh) (7/11/39 - 6/22/40) CBS, 15m
7/11/39 - 6/4/40, Tue, 4 pm; 2:30 pm as of 8/29/39; 4 pm as of 3/5/40
also 5/4/40 - 6/22/40, Sat, 2 pm

Barrel Of Fun (8/7/41 - 10/9/41) Mut, Thu, 8:30 pm

6 **Barrel Of Fun** (Syn) (with Charles Ruggles and Veola Vonn)

1 **Barretts Of Wimpole Street, The** (1934) Air trailer

15 **Barrie Craig: Confidential Investigator** (10/3/51 - 6/30/55)
10/3/51 - 4/2/52, Sus, NBC, Wed, 10 pm
3/18/52 - 9/9/52, Sus, NBC, Tue, 8:30 pm; sponsored by Lewis-Howe from 3/18/52 - 6/10/52
9/24/52 - 10/15/52, NBC, Wed
10/19/52 - 9/6/53, NBC, Sun, 10:30 pm; sponsored by Knomark from 3/13/53 - 5/17/53
9/15/53 - 9/7/54, NBC, Tue, 8:30 pm; sponsored by Coleman Co., 9/15/53 - 10/16/53
10/3/54 - 6/30/55, NBC, Sun, 8:30 pm; Wed, 8:30 pm as of 1/5/55; Thu, 9 pm as of 5/5/55

1 **Barron Elliot and His Stardust Melodies** (1/5/42) Mut

4 **Barry and Betty** (Syn)

1 **Barry Cameron** (4/6/45 - 10/11/46) Sweetheart Soap, NBC, 5t, 15m (8/10/48)

2 **Barry Goldwater** (1964) Mut, CBS-TV

2 **Barry Gray Show, The** (1945 - 90s) Mut

1 **Barry Gray's Nightclub** (3/5/46) Mut

Barry McKinley (1/6/39 - 11/19/39) 15m; various days and times including:
9/26/37 - 12/19/37 (see Romantic Rhythms)
1/8/39 - 3/26/39, NBC, Sun, 2:30 pm also
1/6/39 - 4/28/39, Bl, Fri, 5 pm
4/8/39 - 11/4/39, Bl, Sat, 10:30 am
11/5/39 - 11/19/39, Bl, Sat, 3 pm

Barry Sisters, The (10/26/42 - 11/13/42) Mut, 3t, 15m, 8:15 pm

Barry Valentino (5/12/52 - 8/14/55) ABC, various days and times, 25m

Barry Winton Orchestra (10/16/39 - 12/9/40) Old Gold, NBC, Mon, 10:30 pm

13 **Barry Wood Show, The** (9/9/36 - 4/11/47) 15m; many overlapping shows; various days and times including:
9/9/36 - 6/23/37, Drene, NBC, Wed, 7:45 pm; Barry Wood joined the show on 5/6/37 following Frank Parker and Jerry Cooper
also 9/10/36 - 6/24/37, Drene, Bl, Thu, 7:45 pm
1937 - 38, CBS, 5t, (on 6/38 & 9/38, CBS, Wed, 7:45 and Thu, 6:45)
1938 - 1/7/39, Sus, CBS, Sun, 10:45 am
1938 - 2/21/39, CBS, Tue, 6:45 pm
4/16/39 - 5/7/39, CBS, Sun, 10:45 pm
5/20/39 - 6/24/39, CBS, Sat, 10:45 pm
5/28/39 - 7/9/39 (with Ruth Carhart), CBS, Sun, 2:30 pm
7/10/39 - 9/18/39, CBS, Mon, 5:30 pm
5/29/43 - 3/25/44 (see Million-Dollar Band)
4/1/44 - 1/6/45 (Barry Wood - Patsy Kelly Show) Palmolive, NBC, Sat, 30m, 10 pm
1945 - 46 (see Johnny Presents)
10/21/46 - 4/11/47, NBC, 3t, 7:30 pm
Syn - ZIV; 182 shows broadcast, 15m

1 **Bartons, The** (Dick Holland) (12/25/39 - 9/11/42)
12/25/39 - 10/31/41 (The Story Of Bud Barton; Bud Barton) Bl, Sus, 5t, 15m
11/3/41 - 9/11/42, Red, Duz (until 6/26/42), 5t, 15m

5 **Baseball Game** (1939, 1950) CBS, WHN, WJSV

Baseball Quiz (see Babe Ruth)

1 **Baseball Round Table** (1956) Syn

Basil Heatter (2/13/55 - 9/11/55) Mut, Sun, 15m, 4 pm

4 **Basil Rathbone Presents** (Thesaurus transcriptions)

1 **Basil Rathbone Presents Gallant American Women** (Thesaurus transcription)

Basin Street (see Louis Armstrong)

1 **Bataan Prisoners Homecoming** (3/8/45) Mut

1 **Battle For Peace, The** (1939) Syn

1 **Battle Of Cassino, The** (3/17/44) Mut

1 **Battle Of The Ages** (8/15/43) CBS

Battle Of The Sexes (hosts were Crumit and Sanderson from 9/20/38 - 7/21/42)
(9/20/38 - 8/31/43) Molle, NBC, Tue
(9/8/43 - 2/2/44) Energine, Bl, Wed, 8:30 pm

1 **Battle Stations** (8/5/43 - 8/26/43) Jell-O, NBC, Thu, 8:30 pm (partial summer replacement for Aldrich Family)

3 **Battleship Maryland** (Mut)

1 **Baukhage Talking** (Bl)

Bavarian Band (with Billy Hillpot and Scrappy Lambert)
(10/3/33 - 2/13/34) Bl, Tue, 15m, 8:45 pm

Baxter Keating

Baxters, The (with Arthur Peterson)
(11/13/43 - 5/27/44; 9/30/44 - 9/27/47) Sus, NBC, Sat, 15m; 30m from 1946 - 47

5 **Bay Area Radio Drama** (5/28 - 7/2/85) Syn

1 **Bay Bridge Story** (7/30/52) WFBR

Bayuk Stag Party (5/10/31 - 6/26/32) Bayuk Cigars, Bl, Sun, 9:15 pm

1 **BBC Commentary** (4/28/39)

1 **BBC Jam Session** (11/5/38)

1 **BBC Memorial Program** (5/30/45)

92 **BBC News** (9/28/38 - 6/8/44)

1 **BBC News and Commentary** (8/24/39)

1 **BBC News and Fulton Lewis Jr.** (9/3/39) BBC/Mut

1 **BBC News Review and Late Bulletins** (4/9/40) BBC

44 **BBC Radio Newsreel** (1/28/41 - 6/28/50)

1 **BBC Salute To CBS** (9/20/57) BBC/CBS

Bea Wain and Andre Baruch
(2/5/56 - 4/26/57) ABC, 5t, 60m; as of 1/28/57, 1:30 pm, 30m

Beal-Taylor Orchestra (Bob Beal and Herb Taylor) 15m

7 **Beat The Band** (1/28/40 - 9/6/44)
1/28/40 - 2/23/41 (with Ted Weems) Kix, NBC, Sun, 6:30 pm
6/15/43 - 6/7/44 (with Hildegarde) Raleigh, NBC, Tue, 10:30 pm (summer replacement for Red Skelton)
9/15/43 - 6/7/44, Raleigh, NBC, Wed, 8:30 pm
6/14/44 - 9/6/44 (with Eddie Mayehoff) NBC, Wed, 8:30 pm

1 **Beat The Clock** (1/5/49 - 5/4/49) CBS, Wed, 10 pm (8/23/49)

1 **Beat Your Wife** (4/11/50) KMOX

Beatrice Fairfax (3/10/34 - 6/30/34) General Foods, NBC, Sat
(5/1/36 - 5/29/36) CBS, Fri, 15m
(8/31/37 - 2/25/38) Silver Dust, Mut, 3t (Tue - Thu), 15m

6 **Beatrice Kay** (8/14/46 - 9/4/46) Mut, Wed, 10 pm (also see Gay Nineties Revue) Thesaurus transcription

1 **Beatrice Kay Show, The** (7/3/46) Mut

1 **Beatrice Kay's Capers** (11/8/43) Audition

1 **Beatrice Lillie** (1/4/35 - 7/28/37)
1/4/35 - 6/28/35, Borden, Bl, Fri, 9 pm
2/7/36 - 5/22/36, Socony, CBS, Fri, 8 pm
1/6/37 - 7/28/37, Sterling Products, Bl, Wed, 8 pm
Jan, 1965, WQXR

Beatrice Mabie (2/17/32 - 7/27/32) Neet Inc., Bl, Wed, 15m, 10 am

Beau Bachelor (with Don Ameche, Irene Wicker) (3/4/32 - 5/27/32) Allen-A Company, CBS, Fri, 15m, 10 pm

1 **Beau Brummel** (Pre-war) Audition

Beau Brummel Of Song
(3/13/32 - 5/1/32) Howard Clothes, CBS, Sun, 6:30 pm

Beau Geste

Beautiful Thoughts (with Joan Blaine)
(7/20/31- 7/9/32) Montgomery Ward, Bl, 5t, 9:30 am
7/20/31 - 5/30/32 (also with Chuck Haynes, Ray Ferris and Gene Arnold) (also called Chuck, Ray and Gene)
5/31/32 - 7/9/32 (also with Jimmy Kemper)

1 **Beauty and Glasses** (1932) Syn

Beauty School Of The Air (with V. E. Meadows) (8/25/32 - 11/7/32) Le Gerardine, CBS, Thu, 15m, 11:45 am

3 **Beauty That Endures** (Pre-war) Syn

1 **Beauty vs. Brains** (9/2/47) Mut

Bebe Daniels (1933) 15m

1 **Bedtime Stories** (3/10/46) CBS

2 **Bedtime Story, A** (1933) film sound track and air trailer

Beechnut Hour (with Phil Baker) (1932)

1 **Before Their Time** (9/15/47) CBS

1 **Before You Buy That Farm - Stop, Look, and Figure** (1944) Syn

1 **Begue Awhile** (7/26/52) WMAQ

Behavior Of Animals (Syn)

Behind (Beyond) The Green Door (with Basil Rathbone) (Syn) 5m

Behind Prison Bars (see Twenty-thousand Years In Sing Sing)

1 **Behind The Front Page** (with Gabriel Heatter)
(9/7/47 - 1/2/49) Mutual of Omaha, Mut, Sun, 10 pm; 7:30 pm as of 8/1/48

Behind The Headlines (see Real Silk Program)

Behind The Iron Curtain
(10/31/55 - 7/2/56) Mut, Mon, 15m, 9:15 pm

2 **Behind The Mike** (stories of "Behind The Scenes In Broadcasting;" with Graham McNamee)
(9/15/40 - 4/12/42) Sus, Bl, Sun, 30m; changed to Nothing But The Truth from 4/19/42 - 6/7/42 (see)

4 **Behind The Scenes At The United Nations** (Syn)

1 **Behind The Scenes With Knox Manning** (Syn)

Behind The Story (with Marvin Miller)
(1949 - 57) Mut, 5t, 15m; mostly West Coast

1 **Behold A Woman** (4/28/50) Audition,by Carlton E. Morse, 15m

1 **Belgian Congo At War** (1943) Syn

1 **Belgium Unvanquished** (7/21/43) Syn

23 **Believe It Or Not** (Robert Ripley)
(4/14/30 - 9/3/48)
4/14/30 - 1/26/31, Colonial Oil, NBC, Mon, 30m, 7:30 pm
5/20/31 - 2/12/32; 5/11/32 - 6/3/32, Esso, Bl, 2t (Wed & Fri), 15m, 7:15 pm (also listed under Esso Hour)
1/9/34 - 3/24/34 (Saturday Night Party; also with B. A. Rolfe Orchestra), Hudson, NBC, Sat, 60m, 10 pm
10/6/35 - 6/21/36; 10/4/36 - 6/27/37 (Baker's Broadcast) Fleischmann, Bl, Sun, 7:30 pm; Joe Penner for first season; also with Ozzie Nelson, Harriet Hilliard, Feg Murray
7/16/37 - 10/1/37, General Foods (often Post Bran Flakes), Bl, Fri, 9 pm
10/9/37 - 4/16/38, General Foods, NBC, Sat, 8 pm
4/26/38 - 7/26/38, General Foods, NBC, Tue, 10 pm
8/8/38 -10/3/38, General Foods, NBC, Mon, 8 pm
3/31/39 - 9/22/39; 2/16/40 - 5/31/40; 9/13/40 - 12/6/40, Royal Crown Cola, CBS, Fri, 10:30; 10 pm from 9/13/40 - 12/6/40
1/17/42 - 7/25/42, Bl, Sat, 10 pm
1/17/44 - 4/14/44, Pall Mall, Mut, 5t, 15m, 9:15 pm
4/12/45 - 10/4/45 (Romance, Rhythm and Ripley) Bourjois, CBS, Thu, 30m, 10:30 pm
5/12/47 - 9/3/48, NBC, 5t, 15m, 1:45 pm
(10/26/57 - 11/17/57) Multi, ABC, 5m

Believe It Or Not Radio Odditorium (see Believe It Or Not)

108 **Bell Telephone Hour, The** (Donald Voorhees and The Bell Telephone Orchestra)
(4/29/40 - 6/30/58) NBC, Mon, 30m; AFRS version called Music From America
4/29/40 - 3/30/42, 8 pm
4/6/42 - 6/30/58, 9 pm
9/15/68 - 6/8/69, (Encores)

1 **Bell Telephone Jubilee, The** (9/9/76) NBC-TV

1 **Belle Of The Nineties** (1934) film sound track

1 **Bells Of Christmas, The** (1951) Syn

3 **Bells Of St. Mary's, The** (1945) Air trailers

1 **Belmont Races** (5/12/41) Mut

1 **Beloved Enemy** (1936) Air trailer

1 **Ben Adams Family Party** (Syn)

Ben Alley (11/23/31 - 1/21/34) CBS, 15m, various days

12 **Ben Bernie Show, The** (with Ben Bernie and All The Lads)
(1/24/30 - 2/19/43)
1/24/30 - ?, Mennen, Bl, Fri
6/2/31 - 7/26/32, Pabst, CBS, Tue, 9 pm
9/13/32 - 7/17/34; 10/2/34 - 10/22/35, Pabst, NBC, Tue, 9 pm
10/29/35 - 10/19/37, American Can, Bl, Tue, 9 pm
also 8/3/36 - 8/24/36, Lady Esther, CBS, Mon, 10 pm (summer replacement for Wayne King)
1/12/38 - 7/6/38 (also with Lew Lehr, Buddy Clark, Jane Pickens), U. S. Rubber, CBS, Wed, 8:30 pm
10/2/38 - 6/25/39; 10/8/39 - 7/3/40 (also called Musical Mock Trial), Half and Half Smoking Tobacco, CBS, Sun, 5:30 pm; Wed, 8 pm as of 4/10/40
also 4/1/40 - 6/21/40, NBC, 5t, 15m, 1:15 pm; 3t as of 4/20/40
also 4/20/40 - 6/22/40, NBC, Sat, 15m, 1 pm
10/1/40 - 4/1/41, Bromo Seltzer, Bl, Tue, 8 pm
4/11/41 - 8/1/41 (The New Army Game) Bl, Fri, 9 pm
6/22/41 - 11/28/41; 6/15/42 - 2/19/43, Wrigley, CBS, 5t, 15m, 5:45 pm (Ben Bernie did not appear after 1/15/43

2 **Ben Bernie's Orchestra** (Pre-war) Syn

Ben Cutler Orchestra (1/21/39 - 3/11/39) Bl, Sat, 8 pm

Ben Grauer

5 **Ben Pollack and His Pick-A-Rib Boys** (World transcriptions)

2 **Ben Pollack Dixieland Band** (World transcriptions)

Ben Selvin (1932) CBS, 15m

4 **Ben Selvin and His Cocktail Orchestra** (Associated transcriptions)

2 **Ben Selvin and His Orchestra** (Muzak transcriptions)

Benay Venuta's Variety Program (also see Freddie Rich Entertains)
(3/15/35 - 2/9/40) Sus; on various days and times including:
3/15/35 - 6/14/35, CBS, Fri, 15m, 3 pm
6/23/35 - 4/26/36 (Freddie Rich's Penthouse Party as of 9/15/35), CBS, Sun
1936 - 6/20/37, Mut, Sun
1937 - 38, Mut, Sat, 60m
10/9/38 - 2/19/39, Mut, Sun, 30m, 4 pm
2/26/39 - 7/2/39; 10/9/39 -11/19/39, Sun, 9 pm also 6/26/39 - 9/18/39 (also with Ernie Fio Rito Orchestra), Mon, 8:30 pm
12/1/39 - 2/9/40, Fri, 9:30 pm

Beneath The Surface (9/20/36 - 4/4/37) Hudson Coal, NBC, Sun, 2 pm

5 **Benito Mussolini** (1939, 1940) Italy

Bennett Sisters, The (Betty, Ruth and Helen)
(2/4/35 - 4/12/35) Bl, 3t, 15m, 12:15 pm (Mon & Wed) 4:30 pm (Fri)

Bennetts, The (by Carlton E. Morse; with Dean Jagger)

1 **Bennetts: 1946, The** (1/20/46)

Benno Rabinof (5/3/36 - ?) Bl, Sun, 4:30 pm
(2/28/39 - 9/5/39) Mut, Tue, 9:30 pm; 8:30 pm as of 5/30/39 (partial summer replacement for Morton Gould as of 5/30/39)

1 **Benny Carter and His Orchestra** (5/20/39)

Benny Fields (Your Minstrel Man)
(6/20/36 - 9/17/36) CBS, 15m; various days and times including:
6/20/36 - 6/27/36, Sat, 6:30 pm
7/1/36 - 7/17/36, 2t (Wed & Fri), 7:30 pm
7/21/36 - 9/17/36 2t (Tue & Wed) 7:15 pm; Wed & Fri as of 8/19/36

2 **Benny Goodman** (12/1/34 - 6/30/47)
12/1/34 - 6/8/35 (Let's Dance) National Biscuit, NBC, Sat, 3 hours, 10:30 pm; also with Ken Murray and Xavier Cugat
6/30/36 - 6/20/39 (Camel Caravan - Swing School) Camel, CBS, Tue, 60m until 6/22/37; Jack Oakie's College was part of the 60m show from 12/29/36 - 6/22/37; Oakie had own show starting 6/29/37 but was on vacation until 9/28/37; Goodman hosted until then (see Jack Oakie)
7/8/39 - 1/6/40, NBC, Sat, 10 pm
2/17/41 - 5/5/41 (What's New Program), Old Gold, Bl, Mon, 7:30 pm
7/17/41 - 8/28/41 (The Housewarming; host Don McNeill) NBC, Maxwell House, Thu, 8 pm (summer replacement for Baby Snooks)
1/10/42 - 2/21/42, Mut, Sat, 2 pm
7/17/43 - 8/14/43, CBS, Sat, 7:30 pm
1944 (Benny Goodman - Oscar Levant)
7/1/46 - 9/2/46, (Music Festival) NBC, Mon, 9:30 pm
9/9/46 - 6/30/47 (see Victor Borge)
1950, 1968, WNEW

31 **Benny Goodman and His Orchestra** (8/22/35 - 2/14/80)

2 **Benny Goodman and His Sextet** (12/31/66) CBS, NBC

1 **Benny Goodman Carnegie Hall Jazz Concert** (1/16/38)

6 **Benny Goodman Music Festival, The** (7/1/46 - 8/5/46) NBC

1 **Benny Goodman Presents...Fletcher Henderson Benefit Concert** (4/1/51) WNEW

1 **Benny Goodman Quintet** (5/19/66) WNEW

4 **Benny Goodman Recording Session** (1940, 1941)

1 **Benny Goodman Rehearsal Session** (10/28/40)

1 **Benny Goodman Second Carnegie Hall Concert, The** (10/6/39)

1 **Benny Goodman Sextet, The** (8/20/52) NBC

1 **Benny Goodman Special, The** (8/6/78) ABC-TV

1 **Benny Goodman: Let's Dance. A Musical Tribute** (3/8/86) PBS-TV

Benny Krueger Orchestra
(6/1/40 - 8/31/40) Mut, Sat, 11:15 am

1 **Benny Lewis and His Orchestra** (7/13/47) CJAD

Benny Meroff's Revue (see Musical Cruise)

3 **Benny Rubin Show, The** (with Mary Small)
(1/19/43 - 4/11/43) CBS
1/19/43 - 2/9/43, Tue, 10 pm
2/14/43 - 4/11/43, Sun, 8 pm
1950, 1951, ABC

1 **Benny Strong and His Orchestra**

Benrus Orchestra (1930 - 2/10/31) Benrus, Bl, Tue, 15m, 7:15 pm

1 **Bentleys At Home, The** (1930) Syn

1 **Berkshire Christmas** (12/21/48) BBC/Mut

Berkshire Festival (7/24/44 - 8/10/46) Allis Chalmers, Bl, Sat; off and on into the 1950s

1 **Berlin Air Supply** (7/28/48) CBS

Bernadine Flynn (see Crisco Radio News Program)
(9/27/43 - 6/29/45) Crisco, CBS

1 **Bernard Baruch** (6/14/46) Mut

1 **Bernardo De Pace (Thais)** (11/7/28) Synchro-disc

Bernarr MacFadden (8/26/36 - 11/17/36) MacFadden Publications, Mut, Tue, 15m, 10 pm

2 **Bernhard Levitow's Salon Orchestra** (Syn)

Bernie Cummins Orchestra
(1/31/39 - 6/10/39) Mut,
1/31/39 - 3/7/39, Tue, 15m, 1:15 pm
2/18/39 - 5/20/39, Sat, 15m, 7 pm
also 3/18/39 - 6/10/39, Sat, 1:30 pm

Berries, The (created by Carlton E. Morse) (3/11/54 - ?) 15m

Bert Andrews (1/1/49 - 12/29/51) ABC, Sat, 15m, 7:15 pm

1 **Bert Hirsch and His Orchestra** (1934)

10 **Bert Hirsch's Novelty Dance Orchestra** (Lang-Worth tancriptions)

Bert Lahr (with Rubinoff)
(4/30/33 - 11/12/33) Chase and Sanborn, NBC, Sun, 60m, 8 pm (summer replacement for Eddie Cantor)

Bert Lytell's Adventures
(1/3/39 - 2/10/39) 15m
1/3/39 - 1/19/39, Mut, 2t, 9:15 am
1/20/39 - 2/10/39, Bl, Fri, 7:30 pm

Bert Wheeler (see Fresh-up Show)

1 **Berth Mark** (1929) Synchro-disc

Beryl Davis (9/14/47 - 12/7/47) ABC, Sun, 15m, 10:45 pm

1 **Bess Johnson** (3/31/41 - 9/25/42) Kleenex, NBC, 5t, 15m
also 3/31/41 - 6/27/41, CBS, 5t, 4:30 pm

1 **Best America, The** (11/7/88) pool feed

Best Bands (4/16/56 - 1/14/57) ABC, 5t, 25m, 9:30 pm

11 **Best Bands In The Land, The** (1948) U. S. Savings Bonds, ABC, 15m

1 **Best Foot Forward** (1943) film sound track

Best Girl (1/3/49 - 9/9/49) Mut, 5t, 3:30 pm

Best Of All (with Skitch Henderson)
(6/14/54 - 7/19/54) 8 pm
(9/27/55 - 5/16/55) Sus, NBC, Mon, 45m, 8:15 pm

Best Of Benny, The (see Jack Benny)

1 **Best Of Broadway, The** (11/10/54) CBS-TV

1 **Best Of Chickenman, The** (1966)

1 **Best Of The Fourth, The** (7/4/76) NBC-TV

Best Of The Week (10/17/37 - 38) (with Clinton Twiss and Joe Parker), Globe Grain, NBC - West, 15m, 2t, Wed & Fri
(8/4/41 - 10/27/41) Bl, Mon, 7 pm
(9/25/45 - 12/11/45) (Choice Of The Week; with Bert Bachrach) ABC, Tue, 15m, 10:30 pm

2 **Best Plays** (6/8/52 - 10/4/53 (with John Chapman) Sus, NBC
6/8/52 - 2/13/53, Sun, 60m; (summer replacement of Theater Guild from 6/8/52 - 9/7/52); changed to Friday as of 10/3/52; many shows available reflect Sunday date (11/9/52 - 1/11/53)
4/17/53 - 6/12/53, Fri, 8:30 pm, 60m
6/14/53 - 10/4/53, Sun, 8:30 pm, 60m

1 **Best Radio Commercials Of The Year** (1967)

3 **Best Seller** (6/27/60 - 12/2/60) CBS, 5t, 15m

Best Sellers (with Bret Morrison)
(6/4/45 - 11/30/45) ABC, 5t, 3 pm

Best Things In Life (with Ed Begley and Arthur Kennedy)
(5/11/47 - 6/8/47, AF of L, Sun

1 **Best Things In Life Are $19.95, The** (10/65) NPR

1 **Best Things In Life Are Free, The** (1956) film sound track

3 **Better Half, The** (with Tom Slater)
(3/22/42 - 1/19/50) Sus, Mut (some overlapping)
3/22/42 - 4/26/42, Sun, 9 pm
5/4/42 - 1/4/43, Mon, 9:30 pm
1/10/43 - 2/21/43, Sun, 9 pm
3/3/43 - 4/21/43, Wed, 8:30 pm
4/26/43 - 8/8/43, Consolidated Razor, Mon, 8:30 pm
10/28/43 - 11/18/43, Thu, 8 pm
5/18/44 - 9/14/44 (with Tiny Ruffner) Thu, 8:30 pm
9/26/44 - 11/14/44, Tue, 8:30 pm
1/10/45 - 3/28/45, Wed, 9:30pm/8:30 pm
4/2/45 - 6/18/45 (with Tiny Ruffner) Mon, 9:30 pm
9/10/45 - 10/15/45, Mon, 10:30 pm
10/18/45 - 11/8/45, Thu, 10 pm
11/12/45 - 10/1/46, 5t, 4 pm
11/22/45 - 1/17/46 (Raising A Husband) Thu, 8 pm
10/7/46 - 5/9/47, 5t, 1 pm
5/17/47 - 9/6/47, Sat, 8:30 pm
9/13/47 - 10/18/47, Sat, 9:30 pm
10/26/47 - 5/30/48, Sun, 3 pm
8/12/48 - 1/20/49, Volupte Inc., Thu, 25m
1/26/49 - 4/27/49, Wed, 9:30 pm
5/6/49 - 10/7/49, Fri
10/13/49 - 12/1/49, Thu, 10 pm
12/8/49 - 1/19/50, Thu, 8 pm

Better Living Radio Theater (Electric Companies) 15m

37 **Betty and Bob** (10/10/32 - 3/15/40) 5t, 15m
10/10/32 - 5/29/36, General Mills, Bl
6/1/36 - 5/27/38, General Mills, CBS; started off as part of the Gold Medal Hour
5/30/38 - 3/15/40, General Mills, NBC (Syn) (with Arlene Francis and Carl Frank) General Mills
1947, Syn

Betty and Buddy (7/23/39 - 12/10/40) Mut, 15m
7/23/39 - 10/29/39, Sun, 12:30 pm
12/12/39 - 4/16/40, 2t, 9:15 am
10/29/40 - 12/10/40, Tue

Betty Barthell (1/29/34 - 2/11/35) CBS, various days and times, 15m

Betty Boop Fables (with Mae Questel)
(11/15/32 - 1/27/33) NBC, Tue, 7 pm; then Fri, 15m
(7/14/33 - 10/27/33) NBC, Fri, 15m, 7:15 pm

Betty Clark Sings (1/16/49 - 6/19/49; 9/25/49 - 1/15/50) ABC, Sun, 15m, 1:15 pm

1 **Betty Crocker** (Betty Bucholz)
(1926 - 11/6/53) General Mills, 15m
1926 - 5/29/36, NBC, 2t (Wed & Fri)
6/3/36 - 5/27/37, CBS, 2t (Wed & Fri), 1:15 pm
6/1/37 - 3/28/41, NBC, 2t (Wed & Fri), 10:45 am
4/2/41 - 8/1/41, CBS, 2t (Wed & Fri) 9:45 am
10/1/41 - 11/6/53, CBS, various days, 15m
5/54, ABC

1 **Betty Crocker Magazine Of The Air** (5/11/49) ABC

1 **Betty Crocker Service Program, The** (8/10/45) NBC

1 **Betty Grable-Harry James Show, The** (1953) Audition

1 **Betty Jane Rhodes Show, The** (5/5/39) Mut - Don Lee

Betty Moore (5/8/29 - 5/27/44) (also called B M Triangle Club) Benjamin Moore Paints, 15m, various days including:
10/16/31 - 7/22/32, NBC, Fri, 4 pm
10/24/34 - 5/29/35, CBS, Wed
1/8/36 - 5/27/36, NBC, Wed, 11:30 am
1/7/39 - 4/1/39, NBC, Sat, 11 am
2/24/40 - 5/25/40, NBC, Sat
3/11/44 - 5/27/44, NBC, Sat, 10:30 am

Betty Randall (12/30/40 - 3/24/41; 7/1/41-10/23/41) Bl, 15m, Mon; 2t as of 7/1/41

Betty Russell (7/12/47 - 9/6/47) ABC, Sat, 15m, 7:15 pm

3 **Between The Bookends** (with Ted Malone)
(7/26/34 - 6/3/55) 15m; (originally broadcast in Kansas City in 1929) various days and times including:
7/26/34 - 9/27/34, CBS, Thu, 5:15 pm (first network show)
5/13/35 - 10/2/36, CBS, 5t, 15m
10/5/36 - 4/2/37, Hinds, CBS, 5t, 15m, 12:15 pm
7/5/37 - 7/16/37, CBS, 5t, 12:45 pm
1937 - 9/9/38, CBS, 2t, 15m
9/12/38 - 4/21/39; 7/3/39 - 45, Sus, Bl/ABC, 5t, 15m
1945 - 49, Westinghouse, ABC, 5t/3t, 15m
also 3/9/46 - 5/25/46, ABC, Sat, 11:30 am
1949 - 6/3/55, various sponsors, ABC, 15m, various days

1 **Between The Dark and The Daylight** (5/30/48) CBS

13 **Beulah** (7/2/45 - 4/2/54)
7/2/45 - 3/17/46 (with Marlin Hurt), Tums, CBS, Mon, 9 pm (partial summer replacement of Lux); Sun, 8 pm as of 8/26/45
2/24/47 - 8/20/47 (with Bob Corley), ABC, Mon, 9 pm; Wed, 9:30 pm as of 4/2/47; Wed, 9 pm as of 6/25/47
11/24/47 - 7/2/48; 8/23/48 - 7/1/49; 8/22/49 -6/30/50; 8/28/50- 6/29/51; 8/27/51 - 12/26/52 (with Hattie McDaniel), Procter and Gamble, CBS, 5t, 15m, 7 pm
9/28/53 - 4/2/54, General Foods, Buick, Murine (depending on day), CBS, 5t, 15m, 7:15 pm

Beulah Show, The (see Beulah)

1 **Beverly Alber Audition** (4/29/49) CBS

Bewley's Chuckwagon Gang (1951- 52)

3 **Beyond Reasonable Doubt** (1939) 15m

1 **Beyond The Threshold** (1/5/62) NBC-TV

Beyond These Valleys (with Gertrude Warner and Shirling Oliver)
(10/9/39 - 9/27/40) General Mills (from 7/22/40), CBS, 5t, 15m

1 **Beyond This World** (2/23/50) CBS

3 **Beyond Tomorrow** (2/23/50 - 4/13/50) CBS

126 **Beyond Victory** (5/43 - 1947) Syn

Bible Message (1/5/46 - 7/20/46) ABC, Sat, 15m, 11:15 am

1 **Bicentennial History Of Communications, The** (1976) Syn

40 **Bickersons, The** (9/8/46 - 8/28/51)
9/8/46 - 6/1/47 (with Don Ameche and Frances Langford), Drene, NBC, Sun, 10 pm
9/24/47 - 6/25/48 (with Frank Morgan), Old Gold, CBS, Wed; Fri as of 1/2/48
6/5/51 - 8/28/51 (with Lew Parker), Philip Morris, CBS, Tue

Bicycle Party (with Bill Slater)
(9/26/37 - 12/19/37) Cycle Trades, NBC, Sun

Bid For Victor (5/7/44 - 6/29/44) CBS, Sun, 2 pm

Bide Dudley, Theater Club
(1933 - 4/10/39) Mut, 15m; various days and times, usually in the East, including:
1933 - 34, 2t, 15m
1936 - 37, Sun, 15m
1937 - 38, 2t (Mon & Fri), 15m
9/19/38 - 4/10/39, Mon, 15m

Big 'n' Little Club, The (with Dick Collier)
(1/15/49 - 4/9/49) Dr. A. Posner's Shoes, ABC, Sat, 10:30 am

Big and Little Club (1/8/49 - 5/6/49; 9/17/49 - 12/10/49) ABC, Sat, 10:30 am

1 **Big Band Bash** (3/18/78) PBS-TV

1 **Big Band Beat** (9/16/72) WQRS-FM

1 **Big Bands, The** (1968) Syn

Big Ben Dream Dramas
(1/5/32 - 1/26/36) Westclox, NBC
1/5/32 - 3/31/32 (with Westbrook van Voorhees and Virginia Gardiner, 2t, 15m, 10:45 am
9/25/32 - 1/26/36 (with Georgia Backus and Joseph Bell; Arthur Allen and Parker Fennelly from 7/7/35), Sun, 15m, 5:30 pm

Big Break, The (with Eddie Dowling)
(7/20/47 - 11/30/47) Adam Hats, NBC, Sun, 10:30 pm

1 **Big Broadcast Of 1936, The** (1935) film sound track

1 **Big Broadcast Of 1937** (7/36) Air trailer

2 **Big Broadcast Of 1938** (1938) Air trailers

1 **Big Broadcast Of 1965, The** (11/25/65) KNX

1 **Big Broadcast, The** (1932) Air trailer

Big City (7/24/56 - 2/26/57) Mut, Tue, 8:30 pm

63 **Big City Serenade** (with Bill Grisky) (1951 - 53) NBC

1 **Big Event, The** (10/23/77) NBC-TV

Big Freddy Miller (5/12/33 - 1/26/34) Admiration, CBS, Fri, 15m, 11:15 am

Big Guy, The (with John Henry Calvin) (5/7/50 - 11/5/50) NBC, Sun, 5 pm

Big Hand, The (with Rex Maupin) (10/8/51 - 12/7/51) Sus, ABC, Mon. 8:30 pm

1 **Big Joe** (11/3/49)

Big Jon and Sparkie (with Jon Arthur) (2/1/50 - 58) ABC, 60m/30m/15m; 5t; originated in Cincinnati in 1948; see also No School Today
(1962 - 82) Family Radio Network

2 **Big Lie, The** (1961, 1968) Mut

8 **Big Moments In Sports** (with Harry Wismer)
(4/29/55 - 7/22/55) Fri, 15m (Syn)

1 **Big News Of '59, The** (1/60) CBS-TV

1 **Big News Of 1957, The** (12/57) CBS-TV

1 **Big News Of 1958, The** (1/9/59) CBS-TV

Big Preview, The (12/23/54 - 9/25/54) NBC, Sat, 2 hours, 7:30 pm

1 **Big Search, The** (8/21/51) Audition

24 **Big Show, The** (with Tallulah Bankhead and Meredith Willson Orchestra)
(11/5/50 - 5/6/51; 9/30/51 - 4/20/52) Multi, NBC, Sun, 90m, 6:00 pm

11 **Big Sister** (9/14/36 - 12/26/52) CBS, 5t, 15m
9/14/36 - 6/21/46, Rinso
6/24/46 - 12/26/52, Procter and Gamble

Big Six Of The Air (with Frank Black Orchestra, Welcome Lewis, Phil Ohman and Vic Arden, Lewis James)
(2/4/32 - 7/28/32) Chevrolet, NBC, Thu, 9 pm

18 **Big Story, The** (4/2/47 - 3/16/55) NBC, Wed
4/2/47 - 7/2/52; 8/27/52 - 6/17/53; 9/23/53 - 6/2/54, Pall Mall
9/8/54 - 3/16/55, Lucky Strikes, 9:30 pm

Big Talent Hunt, The (with Jim Backus) (3/25/48 - 5/27/48) Mut, Thu, 8:30 pm

Big Time (with Johnny Hart)
(12/23/31 - 9/28/32) Flit and Mistol, NBC, Wed, 8 pm

Big Time, The (with Georgie Price)
(10/12/51 - 11/23/51; 6/6/52 - 9/26/52) CBS, Fri, 9 pm

1 **Big Tiny Little and His Orchestra** (3/21/69) CBS

23 **Big Town** (10/19/37 - 6/25/52
10/19/37 - 7/12/38; 9/29/38 - 7/18/39: 9/19/39 - 6/11/40, Rinso, CBS, Tue, 8 pm; Edward G. Robinson starred until 1942
10/9/40 - 7/2/41; 10/8/41 - 7/2/42, Rinso, CBS, Wed, 8 pm; Thu, 9:30 pm as of 1/22/42
10/5/43 - 6/22/48, Ironized Yeast or Bayer, CBS, Tue, 8 pm; Edward Pawley starred for duration
9/14/48 - 12/25/51, Lifebuoy, NBC, Tue, 10 pm
12/12/51 - 6/25/52, Lifebuoy, CBS, Wed, 8 pm

Biggest Heart, The (10/20/50 - 4/13/51)

1 **Bikini Atom Bomb Test** (6/30/46) Mut

Bill and Ginger (Lyn Murray and Virginia Baker)
(5/32 - 3/23/36) CBS
5/32 - 6/13/33, 2t, 15m 8:45 pm
6/14/33 - 4/19/35, Mueller, 15m, 5t
12/9/35 - 3/23/36, Mueller, 3t, 15m

Bill Brandt (called Inside Of Sports as of 12/6/48)
(9/24/45 - 9/2/49) Mut, 5t, 15m, 7:45 pm

2 **Bill Clifford and His Orchestra** (12/8/41) NBC

Bill Clinton (see Clinton, Bill, President)

Bill Costello (1/27/52 - 7/5/53) CBS, Sun, 15m, 12:45 pm

Bill Cullen (8/3/53 - 10/5/53) CBS, Mon, 10 pm

Bill Cunningham (1944 - 56+) Mut

1 **Bill Downs Reporting From Europe** (6/14/44)

5 **Bill Elliot, The Singing Cop** (12/40)

2 **Bill Goodwin Show, The**
(4/26/47 - 12/13/48) CBS, Sat, 9 pm; 8:30 pm as of 10/11/47 (also called Leave It To Bill)
(1/14/57 - 5/3/57) NBC, 5t, 55m, 4:05 pm

Bill Grey Show, The (also with Paul Winchell)
(11/29/43 - 7/17/44) Mut. Mon, 9:30

1 **Bill Harrington Sings** (6/25/48) Mut

1 **Bill Hay Reads The Bible** (1942) Audition

Bill Henry (1944 - 1947) CBS, sponsored by Johns Manville, Servel (on earlier on Pacific stations)

Bill Johnson (10/9/39 - 4/7/40) 15m (not in New York)
10/9/39 - 12/4/39, Bl, Mon, 1:30 pm
12/12/39 - 4/7/40, NBC, Sun, 10:30 am

Bill Kemp Show, The (with Neil Hefti Orchestra)
(10/14/57 - 12/27/57) ABC, 5t, 60m, 8 pm

Bill Lance (see Adventures Of Bill Lance)

1 **Bill McCune and His Orchestra** (10/30/40) CBS

Bill Moshier

4 **Bill Moyer's Journal** (1978 - 1982) PBS-TV

Bill Ring Show (6/30/52 - 5/28/54)
6/30/52 - 5/28/54, General Mills, ABC, 5t, 15m

Bill Slater (Sports For All)
(1/19/50 - 4/11/50) Mut, Thu, 8:30 pm

3 **Bill Snyder and His Orchestra** (1944, 1951) CBS, NBC

Bill Squirrel (1940)

Bill Stern Colgate Sports Newsreel, The (see Colgate Sports Newsreel)

17 **Bill Stern Show, The** (1964 - 1969) Mut

1 **Bill Stern Sportsreel** (1971) Mut

1 **Bill Thompson Show, The**
(3/4/46 - 6/3/46) ABC, Mon, 10 pm

1 **Bill Williams Show, The**
(12/30/48 - 3/22/49) Mut
12/30/48 - 1/20/49, Thu, 8 pm
1/25/49 - 3/22/49, Tue, 9:30 pm

2 **Bill, Mack and Jimmie, Round The World Club** (1937) Syn

3 **Billie Burke Show, The** (4/3/43 - 9/21/46) CBS, Listerine, Fashion In Rations until 10/14/44)

1 **Billion Dollar Show, The** (8/28/52) NBC

Billy and Betty (with Jimmy McCallion and Audrey Egan)
(3/25/35 - 4/19/40) 5t, 15m
3/25/35 - 12/17/37, Sheffield Farms, NBC 6:45 pm
4/25/38 - 9/23/38 (summer replacement of Jack Armstrong) Wheaties NBC, 5:30 pm
5/1/39 - 7/31/39, Kix, NBC
10/23/39 - 4/19/40, Kix, CBS

Billy Batchelor (9/25/33 - 4/20/34; 8/27/34 - 3/22/35) Wheatena, NBC, 5t, 15m

1 **Billy Graham** (6/10/51 - 3/17/57) CBS, Sun, 15m, 11:30 pm (often twice a day)

Billy Grant (6/21/41 - 9/13/41) NBC, Sat, 15m, 1:15 pm

Billy Jones and Ernie Hare (1933) (see The Happiness Boys)

15 **Billy Maxted and His Orchestra** (1969, 1970) CBS

4 **Billy Maxted Band, The** (1969) CBS

2 **Billy May and His Orchestra** (NBC) Standard transcriptions

5 **Billy May Show, The** (1956) Syn

5 **Billy Mills and His Orchestra** (Standard transcriptions)

Billy Moore Trio, The (2/28/42 - 9/12/42) Bl, Sat, 15m, 10:30 am

Billy Sawyer

Billy Swift, Boy Detective (1938 - 39) Sat, regional

2 **Billy Taylor Trio** (1955) NBC

1 **Billy Taylor Trio, The** (World transcription)

1 **Billy Van Dyk Show, The** (6/27/30) Syn

Biltmore Orchestra (1/17/39 - 5/9/39) Bl, Tue, 15m, 5 pm

Bing Crosby (5-minute shows) (1956 - 57) Ford, CBS

Bing Crosby (9/2/31 - 12/28/56)
9/2/31 - 10/31/31 (Fifteen Minutes With Crosby; also called Presenting Bing Crosby) CBS, 5t, 15m; 6t as of 9/7/31
11/2/31 - 2/27/32 (Bing Crosby - The Cremo Singer), Cremo CBS, 6t, 15m, 7:15 pm
2/29/32 - 7/27/32; 1/4/33 - 4/15/33 (Music That Satisfies), Chesterfield, CBS, 2t (Wed & Sat), 15m, 9 pm; various times as of 1/4/33
10/16/33 - 5/28/34, Woodbury, CBS, Mon, 30m, 8:30 pm
9/18/34 - 6/11/35 (with Georgie Stoll Orchestra), Woodbury, CBS, Tue, 9 pm

Bing Crosby (continued)
12/5/35 - 8/20/36; 10/15/36 - 7/1/37; 10/7/37 - 7/21/38; 10/20/38 - 6/15/39; 9/28/39 - 8/8/40 (Kraft Music Hall until 5/9/46), NBC, Thu, 60m, 10 pm; 9 pm as of 7/4/40
11/14/40 - 7/31/41; 10/30/41 - 6/25/42, Kraft, NBC, Thu, 60m, 9 pm
10/1/42 - 4/15/43; 6/17/43 - 7/27/44; 11/9/44 - 5/17/45; 2/7/46 - 5/9/46, Kraft, NBC, Thu, 60m, 9 pm; 30m, 9 pm as of 1/7/43; Bob Burns often filled in for Bing from 1935 -1941 during the summer breaks; others were Don Ameche, Edward Everett Horton, Frank Morgan
10/16/46 - 6/18/47; 10/1/47 - 6/2/48; 9/29/48 - 6/1/49 (Philco Radio Time), ABC, Wed, 10 pm
9/21/49 - 5/24/50; 10/11/50 - 6/27/51; 10/3/51 - 6/25/52, Chesterfield, CBS, Wed, 9:30 pm
10/9/52 - 7/2/53, GE, CBS, Thu, 9:30 pm
9/27/53 - 5/30/54, GE, CBS, Sun, 8 pm
11/22/54 - 12/28/56, Multi, CBS, 5t, 15m see individual program titles

Bing Crosby (This Is Bing Crosby) (11/29/48 - 1/21/49) Minute Maid, CBS, 5t, 15m, 9:45 am

Bing Crosby and Rosemary Clooney (2/28/60 - 9/28/62) Multi, CBS, 5t, 15m

1 **Bing Crosby For The Red Cross** (5/51) Syn

1 **Bing Crosby Presents** (8/16/40) Bl

153 **Bing Crosby Show, The** (see Bing Crosby)

1 **Bing Crosby Sings For Safety** (5/48) Syn

1 **Bing Crosby's Merry Olde Christmas Special** (11/30/77) CBS-TV

1 **Bing Crosby's Program** (8/18/48) WNBC

1 **Bing Crosby: His Life and Legend** (5/25/78) ABC-TV

1 **Bing: A Fiftieth Anniversary Gala** (10/25/77) NBC-TV

Binnie and Mike

39 **Biography In Sound** (2/20/55 - 59) NBC, Tue, 60m

Bird and Vash (7/6/31 - 11/6/31) CBS, 6t, 15m, 6:45 pm

Birds Eye Open House (see Dinah Shore)

1 **Birds Of A Feather** (1935) Syn

1 **Birth Of The Atom Bomb, The** (7/46) ABC

1 **Birth Of The British Nation, The** (Syn)

1 **Birthday Story, The** (10/24/49) Syn

Bishop and The Gargoyle, The
(9/30/36 - 1/3/42)
9/30/36 - 12/2/36, Sus, Bl, Wed, 9:30 pm
1/11/37 - 2/22/37, Sus, Bl, Mon, 9 pm
7/7/40 - 8/25/40, Chase and Sanborn, NBC, Sun, 8 pm (summer replacement for Charlie McCarthy)
9/6/40 - 10/4/40, Bl, Fri, 8 pm
10/8/40 - 12/31/40, Sus, Bl, Tue, 9:30 pm
1/18/41 - 1/3/42 (with Richard Gordon and Ken Lynch), Sus, Bl, Sat, 8:30 pm

50 **Bits Of Life** (1935) Syn

1 **Bitter Herb, The** (4/2/47) Mut

1 **Bittersweet** (1940) Air trailer

Bix Beiderbecke (This Is Bix; The Bix Beiderbecke Story)

4 **Black Arrow, The** (Syn)

Black Book, The (with Paul Frees)
(2/17/52 - 3/2/52) CBS, Sun, 15m, 4:15 pm

2 **Black Castle, The** (with Don Douglas)
(1942 - 6/23/44) Sus, Mut, 5t/Sat. 15m, 8 pm; New York broadcasts include:
2/7/44 - 6/23/44, Mut, 5t, 15m, 3 pm also;
2/8/44 - 3/23/44, Mut, 15m, Tue & Thu, 8 pm

4 **Black Cat, The** (Syn)

Black Chamber, The (1/21/35 - 7/12/35) written by Major Herbert Lordley, Zonite Products, NBC, 3t, 15m, 7:15 pm

1 **Black Chapel, The** (with Ted Osborne)
(8/19/37 - 7/21/39) CBS, Thu, 15m, 11:45 pm; Fri as of 10/7/38

27 **Black Flame Of The Amazon, The** (with Harold Noyce)
(1938) Mut, 5t, 15m (Midwest)

1 **Black Ghost, The** (with Barton Yarborough) (Pre-war) Syn, 15m

1 **Black Hood, The** (with Scott Douglas)
(7/3/43 - 1/14/44) Mut, 5t, 15m, 5:15 pm

4 **Black Lightning** (Syn)

2 **Black Magic** (Syn)

Black Mark

1 **Black Market, The** (7/12/43) WOR

Black Mass: Program broadcast on KPFA, Berkeley,California; 1960-1963
1 hour or less; mostly readings

38 **Black Museum, The** (with Orson Welles)
1/1/52 - 12/30/52, Sus (except F. Savor Company from 9/30/52 - 12/23/52) Mut, 8 pm
1/1/52 - 6/24/52; 9/30/52 -10/21/52, Tue
10/29/52, Wed
11/11/52 - 12/30/52, Tue
Syn, afterwards

Black Night (with Don Dowd)
(8/21/51 - 9/25/51) ABC, Tue, 8:30 pm

Black Velvet (with Ernest Gill Orchestra from San Francisco) (15m)

Blackhawk (9/20/50 - 1/3/51) ABC, Wed, 5:30 pm

Blackstone Plantation (with Frank Crumit and Julia Sanderson)
(1929 - 1/2/34) Blackstone Cigars, Tue
1929 - 30, CBS
1930 - 1/2/34, NBC, 8 pm

53 **Blackstone The Magic Detective** (with Ed Jerome)
(10/3/48 - 4/3/49) Mut, Sun, 15m, 2:45 pm

22 **Blair Of The Mounties** (Syn) 15m

22 **Bleak House** (3/2/55 - 9/4/55) Mut, Wed, 9:30 pm; also pre-war syndicated series

Blind Date (with Arlene Francis)
(7/8/43 - 1/18/46)
7/8/43 - 8/26/43, Maxwell House, NBC, Thu (summer replacement for Baby Snooks)
10/25/43 - 8/6/45, Lehn and Fink, ABC, Mon, 8:30 pm
8/17/45 - 1/18/46, Hinds Cream, ABC, Fri, 8 pm

10 **Blind Love** (Soap opera in Yiddish)

Blind Spot, The

1 **Blitzkrieg!** (9/1/59) CBS-TV

Bloch Party (with Ray Bloch)
(6/29/51 - 7/21/51) CBS, Fri, 60m, 8 pm

1 **Blockade** (1938) Air trailer

20 **Blondie** (with Arthur Lake)
(7/3/39 - 4/20/50) (started as summer replacement for Eddie Cantor)
7/3/39 - 6/22/42; 9/28/42 - 6/26/44, Camel, CBS, Mon, 7:30 pm
7/21/44 - 9/1/44, Bl, Fri, 7 pm
8/13/44 - 9/26/48, Super Suds, CBS, Sun, 8 pm (program overlapped); 7:30 pm as of 8/26/45
10/6/48 - 6/29/49, Super Suds, NBC, Wed, 8 pm
10/6/49 - 4/20/50, Sus, ABC, Thu, 8 pm

1 **Blue Barron and His Orchestra**
(4/26/41 - 7/12/41) Bl, Sat, 10:30 pm and Sun, 6 pm; also Lang-Worth transcription

48 **Blue Beetle, The** (with Frank Lovejoy, for first 10 episodes)
(5/15/40 - 9/13/40) Syn, 2t (Wed & Fri) 30m; 15m as of 6/26/40
also 1938, Syn

5 **Blue Coal Minstrels** (Syn)

Blue Coal Musical Review
(10/2/32 - 4/30/33) Blue Coal, CBS, Sun, 5:30 pm

Blue Coal Radio Revue (see The Shadow)

Blue Frolics (7/12/43 - 5/26/44) Bl, 5t, 4 pm

Blue Grass Brevities (with Chuck Horton)
(1939) CBS, 15m
(11/30/40 - 1/18/41) Bl, Sat, 1:30 pm

Blue Grass Roy (1931)

Blue Jack Choir (with Danny O'Neil)
(10/10/43 - 3/10/46) CBS, Honeywell, Sun, 25m, 11:05 - 11:30 am

Blue Monday - Jamboree (with Harrison Holliway and Juliette Dunne)
(1927 - 6/3/35) KERC in San Francisco until 4/1/35; Full CBS network after that, Mon, 12 mid, 60m

Blue Playhouse (11/13/43 - 9/9/44) Bl, Sat

1 **Blue Ribbon Guest Night** (6/13/42) WMCA

Blue Ribbon Music Time (with Georgia Gibbs and David Rose Orchestra)
(6/26/47 - 9/18/47) Pabst, NBC, Thu, 10:30 pm (summer replacement for Eddie Cantor)

4 **Blue Ribbon Town** (3/27/43 - 8/5/44)
Pabst, CBS, Sat, 10:15 pm; 8 pm as of 10/9/43; Groucho Marx host until 6/17/44; Kenny Baker host from then on; show then became The Kenny Baker Show as of 8/19/44 (See); also see Danny Kaye

1 **Blue Ridge Mountain Boys, The**
(6/12/54) WLOS

Blue Ridge Mountaineers
(7/24/34 - 9/6/34) CBS, 2t, 15m, 5:45 pm

1 **Blue Ridge Rangers, The** (WESD)

1 **Blue Skies** (1946) Air trailer

Blue Theater Plays (previously was Famous Fireside Plays and Great Plays)
(4/5/42 - 9/6/42) Bl, Sun, 2 pm

Blueberry Hill (with Ernie Whitman and Hattie McDaniel; Benny Carter Orchestra) (CBS)

1 **Blueprint For Survival** (10/12/51) WMAQ

Blue Velvet Music (Mark Warnow Orchestra, Hollis Shaw) CBS, Tue, 7 pm

2 **BMI Pin Up Platter** (World transcriptions)

Boake Carter (1/2/33 - 11/24/44)
1/2/33 - 2/18/38, Philco, CBS, 15m, 3t
2/28/38 - 8/26/38, General Foods, CBS, 5t, 15m
11/16/40 - 41, United, Mut
1941 - 43, Land O' Lakes, Mut
1943 - 11/24/44, Chef Boy-Ar-Dee, Mut

311 **Bob and Ray** (with Bob Elliott and Ray Goulding) (1946 - 1984)
1946 - 6/30/51 (Matinee with Bob and Ray) WHDH, Boston
7/7/51 - 9/26/53, NBC and local New York; various times and lengths including:
7/7/51 - 9/26/53, NBC, Sat, 9:30 pm; 8:30 pm as of 10/13/51; Fri, 8:30 pm as of 5/2/52; Sat, 8 pm as of 10/4/52; Fri, 8:30 pm as of 6/27/53
7/9/51 - 2/29/52, NBC, 5t, 15m, 5:45 pm
3/3/52 - 3/27/53, Colgate, NBC, 5t, 15m, 11:30 am
9/15/52 - 6/12/53, NBC, 5t, 15m, 6:30 pm
5/4/53 - 10/9/53, NBC, 5t, 25m, 12:05 am
6/12/55 - ?, Monitor
10/3/55 - 9/20/57, Multi, Mut, 45m, 5t
6/29/59 - 6/60, CBS, 5t, 15m
1960 - 1984; various New York stations, PBS

1 **Bob and Ray Ask "What Ever Happened To The Hard Sell?"**

18 **Bob and Ray Public Radio Show, The**
(1983 - 1984) NPR

8 **Bob and Ray Radio Show, The**
(1986, 1987) NPR

1 **Bob and Ray Routine For Radio** (1967) CBS

2 **Bob and Ray Show, The** (1951) NBC

Bob and Victoria (1/27/47 - 6/27/47)
Dutch Mill Cheese, CBS, 5t, 15m

Bob Arbogast (NBC)

1 **Bob Arbogast Interview** (8/2/76)

Bob Armstrong Orchestra
(1/30/39 - 4/10/39) Bl, Mon, 15m, 6 pm

1 **Bob Arthur Show, The** (1952) Audition

Bob Atcher (see Faultless Starch Time)

Bob Barclay, American Agent (see American Agent)

1 **Bob Becker Show, The** (3/6/32 - 7/8/44)
3/6/32 - 5/29/32 (Bob Becker's Outdoor Talks), Atlas Brewing Co., CBS (Midwest), Sun, 15m, 5:45 pm
10/21/34 - 4/23/39; 10/1/39 - 3/23/41; 12/7/41 - 4/12/42, Morrell - Red Heart, NBC, Sun, 15m
10/2/43 - 7/8/44, Morrell - Red Heart, NBC, Sat, 15m, 10:45 am

11 **Bob Burns** (also with Ann Thomas)
(9/16/41 - 5/25/47)
9/16/41 - 6/9/42, Campbell, CBS, Tue, 8:30 pm; originally called The Arkansas Traveler
10/7/42 - 12/20/42, Lever Bros., NBC, Wed, 9 pm
1/7/43 - 7/1/43; 10/7/43 - 6/29/44, Lever Bros, NBC, Thu, 7:30 pm
10/5/44 - 6/28/45; 10/4/45 - 6/27/46, Lifebuoy, NBC, Thu, 7:30 pm
9/29/46 - 5/25/47, American Foods, NBC, Sun, 6:30 pm
1949, Dreft, Fri

Bob Byron (9/26/38 - 7/8/39) CBS, 15m
9/26/38 - 2/3/39, 5t, 8 am
2/6/39 - 7/8/39, 6t, 8:15 am/8:30 am

Bob Carleton Show, The (15m)

Bob Carroll (1/4/39 - 3/31/39) Bl, 2t (Wed & Fri), 15m, 10:30 am
(10/12/41 - 11/30/41) NBC, Sun, 15m, 3 pm

7 **Bob Chester and His Orchestra**
(1939, 1941, 1942) CBS, Mut, film sound track, Standard transcriptions

Bob Considine (On the Line) (also see Headline Hunters)

Bob Crane Show, The

1 **Bob Crosby and Company** (1/22/46)

26 **Bob Crosby and His All-Stars** (Syn)

8 **Bob Crosby and His Orchestra**
1938, film sound track
1940, Mut, Standard transcriptions

4 **Bob Crosby Ford V-8 Revue, The** (with Bob Crosby and/or Ferde Grofe) (1936)

18 **Bob Crosby Show, The**
(10/25/35 - 7/16/50) (see also Club Fifteen and Ford V-8 Revue)
10/25/35 - 1/3/36, Roger and Gallet Perfume, NBC, Fri, 15m, 8:15 pm
6/27/39 - 12/26/39 (Camel Caravan) CBS, Tue, 9:30 pm
1/6/40 - 7/13/40 (Camel Caravan) NBC, Sat, 30m, 10 pm
also 4/19/40 - 6/7/40, Mut, Fri, 15m, 10:30 pm
also 7/11/40 - 7/25/40, NBC, Thu, 9 pm
8/1/40 - 9/19/40 (Camel Caravan) Bl, Thu, 7:30 pm
9/26/40 - 1/2/41 (Camel Caravan) NBC, Thu, 7:30 pm

Bob Crosby Show, The (continued)
7/18/43 - 6/25/44, Old Gold, NBC, Sun, 10:30 pm
1/1/46 - 7/17/46, Ford, CBS, Tue, 10 pm; Wed, 9:30 pm as of 3/6/46
10/13/49 - 7/16/50, NBC, Sun, 10:30 pm also Standard transcriptions

1 **Bob Crosby's Bobcats** (Standard transcription)

Bob Eberly Show, The (3/25/57 - 8/23/57) ABC, 5t, 60m, 2 pm; 1:15 as of 5/13/57, 1 hour and 45 min.

Bob Edge (see Outdoors With Bob Edge)

1 **Bob Elson Aboard The Century** (3/4/46 - 6/4/51) Mut, 5t, 15m, 6:15 pm

Bob Elson Sports (1948)

Bob Feller

Bob Finnigan (7/12/52 - 3/7/53) ABC, Sat, 15m, 6:30 pm

1 **Bob Grant Show, The** (9/4/72) WOR

Bob Hannon (12/30/40 - 6/27/41) 15m
12/30/40 - 2/10/41, Bl, Mon, 10:15 pm
5/5/41 - 6/27/41) CBS, 2t (Wed & Fri) 4 pm

1 **Bob Hawk Show, The** (7/9/43 - 7/27/53) (See also Thanks To The Yanks)
7/9/43 - 10/1/43, CBS, Fri, 10 pm
7/3/44 - 9/29/47, Camel, CBS, Mon, 7:30 pm; 10:30 pm as of 4/28/47
10/2/47 - 9/30/48, Camel, NBC, Thu, 10 pm
10/4/48 - 6/27/49; 8/29/49 - 7/2/51; 8/27/51- 7/27/53, Camel, CBS, Mon

Bob Hite (5/3/47 - 48)

1 **Bob Hite Interview** (3/1/65)

82 **Bob Hope Show, The** (1/4/35 - 4/21/55)
1/4/35 - 4/5/35 (Intimate Revue) Bromo Seltzer, Bl, Fri, 8:30 pm
9/14/35 - 9/5/36 (Atlantic Family; with Red Nichols Orchestra), Atlantic, CBS, Sat, 7 pm; Thu, 7 pm as of 6/11/36
5/9/37 - 9/26/37 (Rippling Rhythm Revue; with Shep Fields Orchestra) Woodbury, Bl, Sun, 9 pm
9/27/38 - 6/20/39; 9/26/39 - 6/18/40; 9/24/40- 6/17/41; 9/23/41 - 6/16/42; 9/22/42 - 6/15/43; 9/21/43 - 5/30/44; 9/12/44 - 6/5/45; 9/11/45 - 6/11/46; 9/24/46 - 6/10/47; 9/16/47 - 6/8/48, Pepsodent, NBC, Tue, 10 pm
9/14/48 - 6/14/49; 9/20/49 - 6/13/50, Swan, NBC, Tue, 9 pm
10/3/50 - 6/26/51, Chesterfield, NBC, Tue, 9 pm
10/2/51 - 6/24/52, Chesterfield, NBC, Tue, 9 pm
11/10/52 - 7/10/53; 9/21/53 - 7/9/54, General Foods (Jell-O), NBC, Wed, 10 pm also on for General Foods from 11/10/52 - 7/9/54, NBC, 5t, 15m, 9:30 am
9/25/53 - 6/18/54, American Dairy, NBC, Fri, 8:30 pm
10/28/54 - 4/21/55, American Dairy, NBC, Thu, 8:30 pm
(9/28/56 - 3/21/58) (Repeats)

1 **Bob Hope All Star Show - "A Dream Comes True", The** (1949) Syn

1 **Bob Hope For The Red Cross** (1951) Syn

1 **Bob Hope March Of Dimes Tour** (1/28/49) KYW

1 **Bob Hope On The Road With Bing** (10/28/77) NBC-TV

1 **Bob Hope Salutes NASA (Twenty Years Of Reaching For The Stars)** (9/19/83) NBC-TV

1 **Bob Hope Special Sendoff Show** (6/21/45) NBC

Bob Hope Swan Show, The (see Bob Hope)

1 **Bob Hope: "I Never Left Home"** (1946)

Bob Howard (NBC) 15m

Bob Johnson and Vera Massey (8/18/45 - 1/26/46) ABC, Sat, 10 pm; 15m, 10:15 am as of 9/15/45; 30m, 10:30 am as of 11/24/45

Bob Poole Show (see Poole's Paradise)

4 **Bob Scobey and His Frisco Jazz Band Featuring Clancy Hayes** (SESAC transcriptions)

Bob Smith Show (8/5/46 - 6/12/50) Multi, NBC, 5t, 8 am

1 **Bob Sterling, American Ranger**

3 **Bob Wills and the Texas Playboys** (1945 - 1953) KXLA

4 **Bobby Benson** (also called B-Bar-B Ranch; B-Bar-B Songs; Songs Of The B-Bar-B; Bobby Benson and Sunny Jim) (11/14/32 - 6/17/55) various days and times including:
11/14/32 - 3/24/33; 10/5/33 - 12/11/36, H-O Oats, CBS, 3t; 5t as of 9/18/33, 15m (developed from H-Bar-O Rangers) (originated in Buffalo; network as of 10/5/33; starred Richard Wanemaker; Billy Halop as of 10/5/33)
6/21/49 - 1/27/50, Sus, Mut, 2t; 3t as of 9/19/49; 30m from now on (with Ivan Cury)
2/6/50 - 12/18/50, Mut, Mon, 8 pm
3/25/50 - 5/13/50, Mut, Sat, 3 pm
4/2/50 - 1/28/51, Sus, Mut, Sun
1/2/51 - 6/7/51, Kraft, Mut, 2t (with Clive Rice as of 4/51)
5/19/51 - 7/21/51, Mut, Sat, 5 pm
7/8/51 - 3/9/52, Mut, Sun, 4 pm
12/28/51 - 6/29/52, Chiclets and Dentine, Mut, Sun
6/9/52 - 9/12/52, Mut, 5t, 25m, 5:30 pm (summer replacement for Sky King and Wild Bill Hickok)
11/17/52 - 6/4/54, Kraft, Mut, 3t
6/14/54 - 6/17/55, Sus, Mut, 5t, 55m; 30m as of 9/13/54

Bobby Byrne Orchestra (6/22/40 - 8/17/40, NBC, Sat, 8 pm also 6/23/40 - 9/8/40, Bl, Sun, 5 pm

Bobby Doyle Show, The (1947) ABC, 3t, 15m

2 **Bobby Hackett** (World transcriptions)

4 **Bobby Hackett and His Orchestra** (1967) CBS, World transcriptions

5 **Bobby Hackett Quartet Plus Vic Dickenson** (1969) CBS

3 **Bobby Hackett With Chuck Slate and His Orchestra** (1972, 1973)

1 **Bobby Hackett With Jack Six and Friends** (11/7/73)

1 **Bobby Hackett With Vic Dickenson** (11/10/74)

1 **Bobby Hammock Show, The** (AFRS) (1955 - 58)

Bobby Jones (Golf Talk) (1930 - 7/1/31) Listerine, NBC, Wed, 15m, 8 pm

1 **Bobby Thomson At The Plate** (8/51) WMGM

1 **Bobby Troup** (World transcription)

2 **Bobby Troup Trio** (World transcriptions)

1 **Bohemian Nights** (1932) Syn

17 **Bold Venture** (with Humphrey Bogart and Lauren Bacall) (1951 - 52) Syn (ZIV)

1 **Bolero** (2/18/34)

1 **Bomb Target U. S. A.** (3/20/53) CBS

1 **Bombadier, The** (1942) Syn

1 **Bombing Of Bougainville** (3/4/44) Mut

1 **Bombs Away**

Bon Soir Paris (2/25/56 - 6/23/56) Mut, Sat, 8:30 pm

1 **Bond Bread Commercials** (1933) Syn

1 **Bond Drive From Central Park** (6/17/45) Mut

1 **Bond Sign Unveiling** (6/17/48) WOR

1 **Bond Store Opening** (1949) WOR

Bonnie Baker Show, The

Bonnie Stewart (7/14/40 - 9/27/41) NBC, 15m; various days and times including:
7/14/40 - 10/20/40, Sun, 12 noon
1/3/41 - 2/7/41, Fri, 1 pm
2/13/41 - 3/27/41, 2t (Thu & Fri) 1 pm
4/26/41 - 5/31/41, Sat, 7:30 pm
also 5/7/41 - 6/25/41, Wed, 1 pm
6/21/41 - 9/27/41, Sat, 12:15 pm

Book Hunter (6/26/55 - 2/16/56) Mut, 15m
6/26/55 - 9/11/55, Sun, 4:15 pm
9/18/55 - 10/9/55, Sun, 9:15 pm
12/1/55 - 2/16/56, Thu, 9:15 pm

Book Of Memories (with Franklyn MacCormack (15m)

1 **Book Of The Month Club** (10/16/46) Mut

Book Reviews (10/10/39 - 12/26/39) CBS, Tue, 25m, 4:30 pm

1 **Booknotes** (8/20/89) C-SPAN

Books (Review by T. V. Smith) (6/7/39 - 10/4/39) CBS. Wed, 15m, 5:15 pm

2 **Books Bring Adventure** (1946) Syn

Bookshelf Of The World (1948 - 49) Sun

Boomerang Parade (1934) Bl, 2t

Boone County Jamboree (4/14/39 - 4/28/39) Mut, Fri, 10 pm

1 **Boone-Erickson Show, The** (5/3/71) WCCO

Boot Camp Parade (from Sampson Naval Base, New York)
(7/22/44 - 9/9/44) CBS, Sat, 4 pm

Borden Program (see The New Borden Program)

Border Patrol, The (2/6/41 - ?) Mut, Thu, 15m, 8:15 (not in New York)

6 **Boris Karloff** (1961)

Boris Karloff's Treasure Chest
(9/17/50 - 12/17/50) Sun, 7 pm; on locally WNEW, New York

1 **Born In A Merry Hour** (2/27/47) CBS

1 **Born To Dance** (1936) Air trailer

1 **Born To Sing** (1941) Air trailer

Boscul All-Star Orchestra (with Frances Alda, Andy Sannella conducting)
(1/23/31 - 4/22/32) Boscul Coffee, Bl, Fri, 15m, 7:15 pm

101 **Boston Blackie** (6/23/44 - 10/25/50)
6/23/44 - 9/15/44 (with Chester Morris), Rinso, NBC, Fri, 10 pm (summer replacement for Amos 'n' Andy)
4/11/45 - 10/25/50 (with Richard Kollmar) Syn (ZIV) 220 episodes broadcast
4/11/45 - 6/6/45, Mut, Wed, 10 pm
6/11/45 - 9/3/45, Mut, Mon, 8:30 pm
9/13/45 - 9/20/45, Mut, Thu, 8:30 pm
10/4/45 - 1/3/46, Bl, Thu, 7:30 pm
1/8/46 - 4/29/47, Bl, Tue, 7:30 pm
5/7/47 - 10/25/50, Mut, Wed, 8:30 pm
9/11/49 - 9/3/50, Lucerna Milk, CBS, Sun, 7:30 pm

1 **Boston Gardens Interviews** (1/5/46) Mut

1 **Boston Pops Concert** (7/21/44)

Boston Pops Orchestra, The (with Arthur Fiedler; usually filled in summers for the Boston Symphony)
also (1/29/51 - 9/24/51) RCA and Whitehall Pharmacy, NBC, Mon

1 **Boston Symphony** (1/7/33 - 57) broadcast most years; sponsored by Allis Chalmers (1943 - 46); John Hancock
(1/21/47 - 47); mostly on Bl/ABC; Sat until 1946 - 47 season; then days varied; mostly 60m

1 **Boston Symphony Rehearsal** (11/11/50)

4 **Boswell Sisters, The** (10/16/31 - 32) Baker, CBS, 3t, 7:30 pm; Syn, film sound tracks

Botany Song Shop (see Ginny Simms)

1 **Bougainville Engagement** (3/17/44)

1 **Bouquet For You, A** (with Patti Clayton and Bill Williams)
(12/16/46 - 6/27/47) CBS, 5t, 5:30 pm; 3 pm as of 1/13/47

Bovril Show (with Oscar Peterson) (1944 - 45)

4 **Bowl Of Rice For China, A** (1938 or 1940)

1 **Bowman Musical Milkman** (8/27/46) WMAQ

4 **Box Score Review** (1947 - 1948) also see Play Ball

52 **Box Thirteen** (with Alan Ladd)
(8/22/48 - 8/14/49) Syn (Mayfair)

1 **Boxing: Joe Frazier Vs. Jimmy Ellis** (2/15/70) Mut

Boy and Girl Next Door (with Edith Dick and Jack Shannon; Audrey Marsh as of 2/14/39)
(8/20/38 - 9/23/39) CBS
8/20/38 - 9/23/39, Sat, 8:45 am
also 8/16/38 - 4/11/39, 3t (Tue, Thu, Fri), 8:15 pm

Boy Meets Band (see Ted Steele Orch)

Boy Scout Reporter (with Dr. George J. Fisher)
(7/22/31 - 8/26/31) NBC, Wed, 15m, 4:45 pm

1 **Boy, A Girl and A Band, A**
(4/13/40 - 9/28/40) NBC, Sat
(5/5/41 - 7/26/41) CBS, Mon, 15m
(1946) WGY

1 **Boyd Raeburn and His Orchestra** (1944) KQW

1 **Boys Club Week Program** (4/2/49) NBC

1 **Boystown** (11/34) Air trailer

2 **Brace Beemer Interview** (2/28/65) WKBD-TV

1 **Brace Beemer Memorial Program** (3/65) WJR

1 **Brad and Al** (Bradford Browne and Al Llewelyn)
(4/5/32 - 11/17/32) Int. Silver, CBS, 2t, 15m
(2/19/35 - 11/14/35) Fels & Co., CBS, 2t, 15m

Brad Reynolds (6/5/41 - 3/29/42) NBC
6/5/41 - 8/28/41, Thu, 15m, 1 pm
11/23/41 - 3/29/42, Sun, 10m, 11:50 am

13 **Bradbury 13** (1984) NPR

Bradley Kincaid (1931)
(12/16/34 - 2/16/35) NBC, 4t (Sun, Mon, Fri, Sat), 15m, 8 am

Brady Kaye (8/18/55 - 12/22/55) Mut, Thu, 8:30 pm

1 **Brain Train** (7/24/47) Mut

1 **Brain Trust** (7/14/47) Mut

1 **Brave Men Are Afraid** (2/10/45) Mut

Brave New World (11/1/37 - 5/2/38) Sus, CBS, Mon, 10:30 pm

2 **Brave Tomorrow** (with Jeannette Dowling) (10/11/43 - 6/30/44) Ivory, NBC, 15m

Bravest Of The Brave, The
(5/2/37 - 10/17/37) NBC, Sun, 11:15 am

3 **Break The Bank** (10/20/45 - 7/15/55)
10/24/45 - 4/13/46, Vick Chemicals, Mut, Sat, 9:30 pm
7/5/46 - 9/23/49, Vitalis, ABC, Fri, 9 pm
10/5/49 - 9/13/50, Vitalis, NBC, Wed, 9 pm
9/25/50 - 9/21/51, Vitalis, NBC, 5t, 11:30 am
9/24/51- 3/23/53, Multi, ABC, 5t, 11 :30 am
9/15/53 - 7/15/55, Miles, NBC, 5t, 15m, 10:45 am
also 10/11/54 - 4/8/55, Miles, Mut, 5t, 15m, 12 noon

Breakfast At Sardi's (with Tom Breneman)
(8/3/42 - 2/26/43) Bl, 5t; changed to Breakfast In Hollywood (started in Los Angeles on 1/13/41)

7 **Breakfast Club, The** (with Don McNeill)
(10/24/32 - 12/27/68) known as The Pepper Pot when the show began
6/23/33 - 2/7/41, Sus, Bl, 60m, 6t, 9 am; aired different lengths of time (30m - 60m)
2/8/41 - 12/27/68, Multi (Swift was first sponsor), Bl/ABC, 30m - 60m, 6t, 9 am

2 **Breakfast In Bedlam** (12/8/41) WJZ

1 **Breakfast In Hollywood** (with Tom Breneman) (originally called Breakfast With Breneman; changed to Welcome To Hollywood)
(3/1/43 - 1/13/50) Multi, ABC, 5t, (including 1/15/45 - 8/13/48, Kelloggs); Garry Moore took over on 4/27/48

2 **Breakfast In The Blue Ridge** (Syn)

Breakfast Show (with Bea Wain and Andre Baruch)

5 **Breakfast With Burrows**

Breakfast With Dorothy and Dick (with Dorothy Kilgallen and husband Richard Kollmar) see The Dorothy and Dick Show
(4/14/45 - 60) WOR

1 **Breakfast With Sophie and Sam** (1947) WOR

1 **Breck Sunday Showcase, The** (4/3/60) NBC-TV

Breen and DeRose (with Peter DeRose and wife May Singhi Breen)
(1927 - 9/4/39) Bl; (began on WJZ in 6/1923) various days and times including:
1927 - 30, Tue, 10:30 pm
1930 - 31, 4t, 15m
1931 - 32, Knox Gelatin, 5t, 15m
1932 - 34, Sus, 5t, 15m
12/2/34 - 3/4/37 (Calling All Sweethearts; Sweethearts Of The Air), Humphrey's Remedies and Witch Hazel, various days and times, 15m
also 1/2/39 - 9/4/39, 4 - 5t, 15m, 10:45 am

Breezin' Along (with Johnny Green Orchestra, Jack Smith and Beverly Freeland)
(5/19/39 - 7/28/40) Philip Morris; (also called Singo; Rhymo; also see Johnny Green)
5/19/39 - 8/4/39, Mut, Fri, 8 pm
8/7/39 - 10/30/39, Mut, Mon, 8:30 pm
11/8/39 - 5/1/40, Bl, Wed, 8 pm (Jingo as of 4/17/40)
11/8/39 - 11/22/39; 5/5/40 - 7/28/40 (Jingo) CBS, Sun, 8:30 pm

1 **Brenda Curtis** (with Vicki Vola)
(9/11/39 - 1/19/40) Campbell, CBS, 5t, 15m

Brenthouse (Brent House) (with Hedda Hopper)
(1/21/39 - 6/4/40) Bl,
1/21/39 -10/21/39, Sat, 30m, 8:30 pm
11/28/39 - 6/4/40, Tue, 10:30 pm

2 **Brian Sisters, The** (D & S transcriptions)

3 **Bride and Groom** (with John Nelson)
11/26/45 - 6/30/50) Energine (as of 1/7/46), ABC, 5t, 4:15 pm; 2:30 pm as of 12/31/45

1 **Brigadier General James Doolittle** (5/20/42) Mut

1 **Bright Eyes** (1934) film sound track

3 **Bright Horizon** (8/25/41 - 7/6/45) Swan, CBS, 5t, 15m, 1:30 pm

Bright Idea Club (7/15/39 - 9/27/41) Sus, NBC, Sat

1 **Bright Lights** (12/12/34 - 1/23/35) CBS, Wed, 15m, 10:30 am
1935, film sound track

24 **Bright Star** (with Irene Dunne and Fred MacMurray)
(1952 - 53) Syn (ZIV) 52 episodes broadcast; NBC

5 **Brighter Day, The** (10/11/48 - 5/28/56) Dreft (until last season), 5t, 15m (developed from Joyce Jordan)
10/11/48 - 7/8/49, NBC
7/11/49 - 7/1/55, CBS
8/1/55 - 5/28/56, Multi, CBS

3 **Brighter Tomorrow, A** (with Gabriel Heatter) see The Gabriel Heatter Show
(10/13/46 - 9/7/47) Mutual of Omaha, Mut, Sun, 10 pm; 8:30 pm as of 7/20/47

Brighter World, A (1940) WBBM (Chicago)

2 **Bring 'Em Back Alive** (see Frank Buck)
1932, Syn

94 **Bring Back The Bands** (1966) Syn

1 **Bring On The Girls** (1944) Air trailer

Bringing Up Father (with Agnes Moorehead and Mark Smith)
(7/1/41 - 9/30/41) Lever Brothers, Bl, Tue, 9 pm

2 **Britain Speaks** (also see J. B. Priestley)
1941, BBC

Britain To America (7/26/42 - 9/29/42) NBC, Sun, 5:30 pm

1 **Britain Today** (9/17/40) BBC

1 **British Garden Party In Washington** (6/8/39) NBC

1 **British Pirate Radio...Dead Issue** (1967) WNYW

1 **British Royal Birth** (11/14/48) BBC

1 **British War Brides** (2/4/46) WOR

1 **Broadcast** (11/29/39) Audition

Broadcast From Berlin
(5/20/39 - 8/12/39) NBC, Sat, 4 pm

1 **Broadcast From China** (1/28/45)

1 **Broadcast From Luzon** (1/9/45) Mut

1 **Broadcast On The Eclipse** (6/7/37) NBC

Broadway (see Twin Views Of The News)

2 **Broadway and Vine** (5/14/48, 9/6/48) CBS

Broadway Bandbox (with Frank Sinatra)
(6/11/43 - 10/10/43) CBS
6/11/43 - 7/15/43, Fri
7/25/43 - 9/6/43 (partial summer replacement for Lux Radio Theater) Lux, Mon, 9:30 pm
10/3/43 - 10/10/43, Sun, 8 pm

Broadway Cinderella (see Modern Cinderella)

Broadway Cop (10/11/54 - 1/3/56) Mut
10/11/54 - 10/10/55, Mon, 8:30 pm
10/18/55 - 1/3/56, Tue, 8:30 pm

1 **Broadway Gondolier** (1935) Air trailer

2 **Broadway Hits** (with Ray Morton Orchestra) (5/4/35 - ?) Syn, 15m

26 **Broadway In Review** (with Russ Case Orchestra) Syn, 15m

119 **Broadway Is My Beat** (with Anthony Ross; Larry Thor as of 7/3/50)
(2/27/49 - 8/1/54) Sus (occasionally sponsored by Lux and Wrigley), CBS; various days and times (212 shows broadcast)
2/27/49 - 6/12/49, Sun, 5:30 pm
7/7/49 - 8/25/49, Thu, 8 pm
11/5/49 - 1/21/50, Sat, 9:30 pm
1/31/50, Tue
2/3/50 - 6/23/50, Fri, 9:30 pm
7/3/50 - 8/21/50, Mon, 8:30 pm (summer replacement of Arthur Godfrey's Talent Scouts)
10/13/50 - 12/8/50, Fri, 9:30 pm
4/7/51 - 6/30/51, Sat, 9:30 pm
7/8/51 - 8/26/51 , Sun, 9 pm (summer replacement of Meet Corliss Archer)
9/15/51 - 5/24/52, Sat, 9:30 pm
6/2/52 - 7/26/52, Mon, 9:30 pm
8/2/52 - 9/27/52, Sat, 9:30 pm
10/4/52 - 10/3/53, Sat
10/7/53 - 11/4/53, Wed, 9:30 pm
11/13/53 - 11/27/53, Fri
7/11/54 - 8/1/54, Sun, 6:30 pm

1 **Broadway Matinee** (with Jim Ameche)
(11/29/43 - 8/4/44) Owens Glass, CBS, 5t, 25m, 4pm

Broadway Melodies (Called Broadway Varieties as of 8/11/34) (with Elizabeth Lennox, Victor Arden Orchestra)
(9/24/33 - 7/30/37) BiSoDol, CBS
9/24/33 - 4/22/34 (with Helen Morgan), Sun, 2 pm
5/2/34 - 7/30/37 (with Willie and Eugene Howard, Fifi D'orsay, Wed; Fri as of 10/4/35

1 **Broadway Melody Of 1936** (1935) Air trailer

2 **Broadway Melody Of 1938** (Aug, 1937) Air trailer

Broadway Merry-Go-Round (also called Folies Bergere Of The Air; Folies de Paree; Revue de Paree) (with Fanny Brice as of 9/30/36; Beatrice Lillie as of 1/6/37)
(4/15/36 - 7/28/37) Dr. Lyons, Bl, Wed, 8 pm

1 **Broadway Open House** (5/11/51) NBC-TV

Broadway Playhouse (1949 - 50)

1 **Broadway Serenade** (1938) Air trailer

Broadway Showtime (with William Gaxton) (12/27/43 - 6/26/44) Ballantine, CBS, Mon, 10:30 pm

12 **Broadway Talks Back** (with Barrett H. Clark)
(10/7/46 - 1/13/47) Mut, Mon, 10 pm

1 **Broadway Thru A Keyhole** (1933) film sound track

Broadway To Hollywood (NBC)

Broadway Varieties (see Broadway Melodies)

1 **Brokaw Report, The** (9/6/92) NBC-TV

1 **Broken Pledge, The** (5/43) Syn

2 **Brooding With Brady** (5/7/48, 6/4/48) KNX

1 **Brooklyn Dodgers Locker Room Interviews** (10/2/51) Mut

1 **Brooklyn Symphony Orchestra** (Syn)

1 **Brotherhood Week** (2/16/46) Syn

1 **Brown Derby** (1931) Synchro-disc

12 **Brownstone Theater, The** (with Jackson Beck and Gertrude Warner until 6/13/45; then Les Tremayne)
(2/21/45 - 6/13/45; 7/8/45 - 9/30/45) Mut, Wed, 9:30 pm

Bruce Baker Orchestra (7/11/39 - 8/8/39) NBC, Tue, 15m, 5:15 pm

Brunswick Brevities

Brush Creek Follies (12/16/39 - 9/27/41) CBS, Sat,
12/16/39, 8/26/39, 2 pm; 2:30 pm as of 7/15/39
12/7/40 - 9/27/41, CBS. Sat. 2 pm; 1:30 pm as of 6/7/41

Buccaneers and Dolly (from WLW)

4 **Buccaneers, The** (1930s) Imperial Tobacco, Syn, 15m

1 **Buck Benny Rides Again** (1940) Air trailer

10 **Buck Jones In "Hoofbeats"**
(6/25/37 - 3/18/38) Syn, Grape-Nuts

Buck Private and His Girl (with Myron McCormick, Anne Seymour)
(5/26/41 - 8/23/41) Bl, 5t, 15m

19 **Buck Rogers In The 25th Century** (with Adele Ronson)
(11/7/32 - 4/14/47)
11/7/32 - 6/17/33 (with Matt Crowley; then Curtis Arnall from 12/26/35), Kellogg, CBS, 5t, 15m, 7:15 pm
10/2/33 - 6/29/34; 9/3/34 -12/26/35, Cocomalt, CBS, 4t (Mon - Thu), 15m, 6 pm
12/30/35 - 5/22/36 (with Matt Crowley) Cream Of Wheat, CBS, 3t, 15m, 6 pm
4/5/39 - 7/31/39, Popsicle, Mut, 3t, 15m
5/18/40 - 7/27/40, Mut, Sat, 30m, 12 noon
9/30/46 - 4/14/47 (with John Larkin), General Foods, Mut, 5t, 4:45 pm

Buckeye Four (4/10/39 - 6/11/39) Mut, Mon, 15m, 10 am (not in New York)

Bud Barton (see The Bartons)

1 **Bud Freeman and His Summa Cum Laude Orchestra** (5/20/40)

208 **Bud's Bandwagon** (1953, 1954) AFRS

Budapest String Quartet
(8/31/41 - 11/16/41) CBS, Sun, 55m, 11:15 am

Budd Hulick (12/19/38 - 1/23/39) Bl, Mon, 9 pm
(1/26/43 - 4/16/43) Mut, 5t, 15m (took over for Henry Morgan)

1 **Buddies** (1935) Syn

2 **Buddy Baer and His Orchestra** (1961) CBS

4 **Buddy Bear** (Syn)

Buddy Clark (see also Treet Time; Musical Toast) (4/11/38 - 9/12/40)
4/11/38 - 7/8/38, Lucky Strike, Mut, 3t, 15m, 6:45 pm (also called Design For Happiness)
12/21/38 - 2/15/39, CBS, Wed, 10:30 pm
2/21/39 - 3/28/39, CBS, Tue, 15m, 10:30 pm
4/14/39 - 5/26/39 (Buddy Clark's Musical Weekly), CBS, Fri, 7:30 pm
7/25/40 - 9/12/40, CBS, Thu, 15m, 10:45 pm

Buddy Clark's Summer Colony (7/6/39 - 8/10/39) CBS, Thu, 8 pm

1 **Buddy Kirk and His Orchestra** (5/23/65) CBS

3 **Buddy Moreno and His Orchestra** (NBC) 1949, Lang-Worth transcriptions

2 **Buddy Morrow and His Orchestra** (Lang-Worth , World transcriptions)

1 **Buddy Poppy...American Flower Of Remembrance, The** (1932)

1 **Buddy Rich Quartet, The** (3/53)

1 **Buddy Rogers Show, The** (with Fifi D'Orsay)
(8/12/34 - 10/7/34) (with Jeanie Lang) Ward Baking Co., CBS, Sun, 9 pm
(7/3/50 - 9/12/51) Mut, 5t

4 **Buddy Weed Quartet, The** (SESAC transcriptions)

4 **Buddy Weed Septet, The** (SESAC transcriptions)

1 **Buddy Weed Trio, The** (6/15/46 - 3/1/47) ABC, Sat, 10 am; on locally in New York through the 50s including:
12/14/47 - 7/18/48, ABC, Sun, 15m, 10:45 pm
7/31/48 - 10/23/48, ABC, Sat, 15m
10/31/49 - 4/10/50, ABC, Mon, 15m also known as Museum Of Modern Music

Buffalo Musicale (6/29/46 - 3/1/47) NBC, Sat, 2 pm

Buffalo Presents (10/19/35 - 4/29/39) CBS, Sat, 2:30 pm
(12/16/39 - 10/25/41) CBS, Sat afternoon

Buffalo Summer Theater (5/13/38 - 9/9/38) CBS, Fri, 3 pm

1 **Bughouse Rhythm** (with Milton Cross) (9/4/36 - 4/26/37) 15m
9/4/36 - 10/9/36, NBC, Fri, 5 pm
11/2/36 - 4/26/37, Bl, Mon, 7:15 pm

2 **Bugs Baer** (1931) Syn

Buick Presents (see Andre Kostelanetz)

Buick Revelers (with James Melton, Olga Albani, Phil Dewey)
(11/8/31 - 5/8/32) Buick, NBC, Sun, 9:45 pm

10 **Buick Berle Show, The** (1953, 1954) NBC-TV

2 **Builder Of Dreams, The** (4/2/41, 4/9/41) WCNW

1 **Builders Of Victory** (4/7/45 - 7/7/45) CBS, Sat, 15m, 3:45 pm

56 **Building For Defense** (6/41) Syn

6 **Building For Peace** (1947) Syn

6 **Building The Peace** (1945) NBC

1 **Bull Session** (5/6/39 - 4/13/40) CBS, Sat, various times; post-war, Syn

18 **Bulldog Drummond** (4/13/41 - 3/14/54) Mut
4/13/41 - 6/22/41 (with George Coulouris; located in England) Howard Clothes, Mut, Sun, 6:30 pm; (summer replacement of Show Of The Week)
9/28/41 - 3/22/42 (with George Coulouris; located in America), Howard Clothes, Sun, 6:30 pm
5/25/42 - 4/19/43 (with Santos Ortega; Ned Wever as of 3/15/43), Sus, Mon, 8:30 pm
9/26/43 - 9/17/45, Sus, Sun, 3:30 pm; 5:30 pm as of 4/30/44; Mon, 7:30 pm as of 9/4/44
9/24/45 - 10/14/46, Tums, Mon, 8 pm
12/6/46 - 9/19/47, Fri, 9:30 pm
2/28/47 - 7/11/47, American Transit, Fri, 9:30 pm
12/31/47 - 1/12/49, Wed, 10 pm
10/14/53 - 12/23/53, Wed, 9:30 pm
1/3/54 - 4/4/54, Sus (Dodge from 2/7/54 - 3/14/54), Sun, 6 pm

1 **Bulletin Of Luna Probe #4** (12/58) NBC

1 **Bulletin Of The Atlas (Talking) Satellite** (12/21/58) WQXR

1 **Bullock's Show, The** (7/3/45) with Harry Bartell; Pat McGeehan; with Claude Sweeten Orchestra

Bulova Minutemen (with Eddie Dowling) 15m

1 **Bundles For Britain** (1940 - 41) Mut, Syn, Sun, 3 pm

1 **Bunk Johnson** (World transcription)

Bunkhouse Follies (see Carson Robison)

Bunny Berigan (1937) Norge, 15m

Burbig's Syncopated History (with Henry Burbig) (1930) CBS, Mon, 8 pm

1 **Burial Of A King** (2/15/52) ABC

1 **Burial Of The Time Capsule** (9/23/38) WOR

35 **Burl Ives Show, The** (6/24/40 - 9/4/49) the program was known by different titles; various days and times including:
6/24/40 - 7/15/40, NBC, Mon, 15m, 9:45 am
8/2/40 - 9/27/40, NBC, Fri, mostly 1:15 pm
9/15/40 - 4/20/41 NBC, Sun, 15m, 11 am (not in New York)
also 1/4/41 - 4/19/41, CBS, Sat, 15m, 9:15 am
4/26/41 - 6/28/41, CBS, Sat, 15m, 11:45 am
also 5/6/41 - 5/27/41, CBS, Tue, 15m, 4 pm
also 6/3/41 - 6/26/41, CBS, 2t, 15m, 4:45 pm
6/30/41 - 7/25/41, CBS, 5t, 15m, 5:45 pm

Burl Ives Show, The (continued)
7/5/41 - 1/24/42 (The Burl Ives Coffee Club) CBS, Sat, 10 pm; 11 pm as of 9/20/41
also 8/6/41 - 10/8/41, CBS, Wed, 15m, 4:45 pm
1/31/42 - 6/27/42, CBS, Sat, 15m, 11:15 am (also called God's Country)
also 1941 - 42 (Wayfaring Stranger) CBS, Fri, 5m
7/28/42 - 10/4/42, CBS, Sun, 15m, 8:45 am
5/4/44 - 6/22/44, CBS, Thu, 15m, 5:30 pm
10/18/46 - 4/8/48, Philco, Mut, Fri, 15m, 8 pm
7/24/49 - 9/4/49, Kaiser, ABC, Sun, 15m, 9 pm (summer replacement of Walter Winchell)

211 **Burns and Allen** (2/22/32 - 5/17/50)
2/22/32 - 5/17/33 (Robert Burns Panatela Program), Robert Burns, CBS, Mon, 10 pm; Wed, 9 pm as of 5/25/32; Wed, 9:30 pm as of 1/4/33 see also Guy Lombardo
5/24/33 - 6/13/34 (White Owl Program), White Owl, CBS, Wed, 9:30 pm
9/19/34 - 9/25/35 (Adventures Of Gracie) White Owl, CBS, Wed, 9:30 pm; 10 pm as of 5/29/35
10/2/35 - 3/24/37, Campbell, CBS, Wed, 8:30 pm; called Campbell's Tomoato Juice Program until 9/23/36; called Burns and Allen (also known as "the sponsor's" show) from then on
4/12/37 - 8/1/38, Grape-Nuts, NBC, Mon, 8 pm
9/30/38 - 6/23/39, Chesterfield, CBS, Fri, 8:30 pm
10/4/39 - 6/26/40, Hinds, CBS, Wed, 7:30 pm; 6:30 pm as of 5/1/40
7/1/40 - 3/24/41, Hormel, NBC, Mon, 7:30 pm
10/7/41 - 6/30/42; 10/6/42 - 6/29/43; 8/31/43 - 6/13/44; 8/15/44 - 12/26/44, Swan, CBS, Tue, 7:30 pm; 9 pm as of 10/6/42
1/1/45 - 6/25/45, Swan, CBS, Mon, 8:30 pm
9/20/45 - 5/30/46; 9/5/46 - 5/29/47; 9/4/47 - 6/10/48; 9/30/48 - 6/23/49, Maxwell House, NBC, Thu, 8 pm from 9/20/45 - 5/30/46; 8:30 pm from 9/5/46 - 6/23/49; 12/20/45 was 60m show combining with Dinah Shore
9/21/49 - 5/17/50, Amm-I-Dent Toothpaste, CBS, Wed, 10 pm
(11/18/59 - 12/29/59) CBS, 5m see individual program names

Burns and Allen Show, The (see Burns and Allen)

Burnt Cork Dandies (with Al Bernard; developed into Al Bernard's Merry Minstrel Men)
(10/4/34 - 1/10/35) NBC, Thu, 7:30 pm

1 **Business Of Sex, The** (1/16/59) CBS

13 **Businessmen Look To The Future** (1944, 1945) Syn

Buster Brown Gang (see Smilin' Ed's Buster Brown Gang)

1 **Busy Mr. Bingle, The** (with John Brown and Jackson Beck)
(3/18/43 - 6/10/43) Mut, Thu, 8:30 pm

1 **But For Their Grace** (2/3/45) Bl

Buzz Adlam's Playroom
(1946 - 10/14/51) (also see Music By Adlam) 1946, ABC, Wed,
8/7/49 - 10/14/51, ABC, various days

By Kathleen Norris (with Ethel Everett)
(10/9/39 - 9/26/41, Wheaties, CBS, 5t, 15m

1 **By Popular Demand** (1/15/38 - 4/19/38) Conti, CBS, Sat
(1945, 6/27/46 - 11/14/46) (with Bud Collyer, Mary Small and Harry Babbitt) Mut, Thu, 9:30 pm (summer replacement of Treasure Hour Of Song)

By Request

18 **By The People** (12/11/55 - 59) Sus, Mut, Syn, Sun

Byrd Expedition Broadcasts (see Adventures Of Admiral Byrd)

1 **Byron Price** (1942) pool feed

1 **C. A. P. and The Air Age Citizen** (3/58) Syn

1 **C. P. MacGregor Show, The** (Syn)

C.M.H. Drama (The Congressional Medal Of Honor)
(7/2/45 - 8/20/45) NBC, Mon, 8 pm (summer replacement of Cavalcade Of America)

4 **Cab Calloway and His Orchestra**
(1940, 1945) NBC, Mut

Cab Calloway's Quizzicale
(7/6/41 - 6/24/42)
7/6/41 - 10/5/41, Mut, Sun, 9:30 pm; 10:30 pm as of 7/27/41
2/18/42 - 6/24/42, Bl, Wed, 9:30 pm

Cabin At The Crossroads
(see Aunt Jemima)

3 **Cabin B - 13** (with Arnold Moss)
(7/5/48 - 1/2/49) Sus, CBS
7/5/48 - 8/23/48, Mon, 8:30 pm
8/31/48 - 9/14/48, Tue, 10:30 pm
10/3/48 - 1/2/49, Sun, 8:30 pm; 10:30 pm as of 10/31/48

10 **Cabinet Of Dr. Fritz, The** (1984) NPR

Cactus Island (with Kev Golsky)
(1985 - 91)

Cadet's Quartet (8/3/34 - 4/7/42) 15m; various days and times including:
8/3/34 - 11/9/34, J. W. Marrow Company, CBS, 2t (Mon & Fri) 11:45 am
2/4/41 - 3/25/41, NBC, Tue, 10:15 am
5/24/41 - 4/7/42, Bl, Sat, 10:15 am

1 **Cadillac 1953 New Car Announcements**
(1953) Syn

1 **Cadillac Sunday Spectrum**

Cadillac Symphony Orchestra
(12/24/33 - 4/8/34; 10/14/35 - 5/5/35) Cadillac, Bl, Sun, 60m

Caesar Giovanini Trio (NBC) 15m

Cafe Istanbul (with Marlene Dietrich)
(1/6/52 - 12/18/52) ABC
1/6/52 - 4/61/52, Sus, Sun, 9:15 pm
4/17/52 - 7/3/52, Thu, 8 pm
10/12/52 - 12/28/52, Buick, Sun, 8:30 pm

1 **Cain and Mabel** (1936) film sound track

1 **Cairo** (1942) Air trailer

Cal Stewart (as Uncle Josh Weathersby)

Cal Tinney (Sizing Up The News)
(8/4/41 - 3/8/46)
8/4/41 - 42, Mut, Phillies
1942 - 44, Mut, Bayuk Cigars
12/3/45 - 3/8/46, ABC, 6:45 pm
(7/7/52 - 5/29/53) ABC, 5t, 4 pm

Calahan's Castle (with Charles Winninger and Sarah Allgood) (sponsored by Williams Cottage Cheese)

1 **Calamity Jane** (with Agnes Moorehead)
(3/31/46 - 4/14/46) CBS, Sun, 8 pm; also 1953 film sound track

Calendar Melody (with Rae Giersdorf and Leonard Joy Orchestra)
(7/3/36 - 12/9/36) Squibb, Mut, 3t, 15m, 10:30 am; Mon and Wed as of 9/2/36

2 **Calibama Co-eds, The** (1932) Syn

1 **California** (1947) Air trailer

2 **California Caravan** (1947 - 50) Sus, Mut, ABC, sponsored by California Medical Insurance (mostly regional) Sun/Sat/Tue including: 1/28/50 - 3/18/50, Sat, 3 pm

108 **California Civil Defense** (1951 - 1953) Syn

98 **California Melodies** (the CBS and Mutual Series were two different programs; Raymond Paige was band leader on CBS
1932 - 34, CBS, Tue, 9:30 pm
4/29/34 - 6/10/34, CBS, Sun, 8:30 pm
6/27/34 - 7/25/34, CBS, Wed, 10:30 pm
8/3/34 - 10/6/34, CBS, Fri, 9 pm
10/14/34 - 12/30/34, CBS, Sun, 7 pm
1/6/35 - 1/27/35, CBS, Sun, 8:30 pm

California Melodies (continued)
2/16/35 - 2/8/36, CBS, Sat, 11 pm; 9:30 pm as of 4/12/35; 10 pm as of 12/7/35
(4/18/40 - 1947), Mutual with David Rose; then Leo Arneaux and Frank DeVol.
4/18/40 - 8/1/40, Thu on Saturdays and Fridays until 10/11/40
10/19/40 - 10/31/42, Sat
11/11/42 - 9/24/44, Wed
4/29/45 - 12/29/46, Sun
1947, various days

2 **California National Guard Show, The** (Syn)

2 **California Stepping Stones** (Syn)

1 **California Tonight** (8/13/77) PBS-TV

Call For Music (with Dinah Shore, Harry James) (see The Dinah Shore Show)
(1/12/48 - 6/29/48) Philip Morris
1/12/48 - 2/23/48,CBS, Mon
4/20/48 - 6/29/48, NBC, Tue, 8 pm

Call Me Freedom (with Nelson Olmsted)
(7/26/53 - 2/7/54) ABC, Sun, 9:30 pm

1 **Call Me Madam** (1953) film sound track

1 **Call Me Mister**(1951) film sound track

Call Of The Cross (Mississippi Tabernacle)
(7/18/48 - 12/5/48) Mut, Sun, 10 am

Call Of The Range (with The Plainsmen) CBS Pacific, sponsored by Grove Laboratories

2 **Call The Police** (6/3/47 - 9/25/49)
6/3/47 - 9/23/47 (with Joseph Julian and Joan Tompkins), Rinso, NBC, Tue, 9 pm (summer replacement for Amos 'n' Andy)
6/1/48, Rinso, NBC, Tue, 9 pm
6/8/48 - 9/28/48 Johnson Wax, NBC, Tue, 9:30 pm (summer replacement for Fibber McGee & Molly)
6/5/49 - 9/25/49, Rinso, CBS, Sun, 7:30 pm

1 **Call To Arms** (3/22/40) BBC

Call To Youth (11/7/36 - 1/3/42) Bl, Sat, 15m

Callahans, The (with Arthur Kohl and Elsa Mae Gordon) (Syn)
(7/20/44 - 10/29/44) WMCA, New York

Calling Alaska

42 **Calling All Cars** (11/29/33 - 9/8/39) Rio Grande Oil, CBS - West coast, various days

195 **Calling All Detectives** (with Vincent Pelletier) (4/7/45 - 1950) Syn
4/7/45 - 8/25/45 on WOR, Sat, 9:30 pm; no details
1946 - 49
1950, Mut, 5t, 15m

2 **Calling All Girls** (1947 - 48) 15m, Syn

6 **Calling All Hearts** (1957) Syn

Calling All Stamp Collectors (see Captain Tim Healy)

Calling All Sweethearts (see Breen and DeRose)

13 **Calling All Veterans** (1946) Syn

1 **Calling America** (1939) (see Listen America) also (with Robert Trout and Walter Cassel)
(6/13/43 - 10/3/43) Squibb, Sun, 8 pm

1 **Calling America For Peace** (5/13/39) Mut

Calling Dr. Kildare (see Dr. Kildare)

Calling Pan-America (6/7/41 - 8/30/41) CBS, Sat, 4 pm

1 **Cambridge Forum** (6/7/84) WPKT-FM

10 **Camel Caravan, The** (see also Bob Crosby, Benny Goodman, Herb Shriner, Jimmy Durante, Vaughn Monroe)
(12/7/33 - 1954)
12/7/33 - 6/7/34; 10/2/34 - 6/27/35; 10/1/35 - 6/25/36 (with Glen Gray) CBS, Thu, 30m, 10 pm; Tue and Thu as of 2/13/34 (with Stoopnagle and Budd to 6/7/34); 9 or 10 pm as of 10/2/34 (with Walter O'Keefe as of 10/1/35)
6/27/39 - 1/2/41 (see Bob Crosby)
1/9/41 - 1/1/42 (see Xavier Cugat)
7/10/42 - 7/2/43 (with Connie Boswell, Lanny Ross, Herb Shriner, Xavier Cugat Orchestra) CBS, Fri, 60m, 10 pm; 45m, 10 pm as of 1/8/43
also 3/25/43 - 3/20/45 (see Jimmy Durante)
1946 - 54 (see Vaughn Monroe)
also 1948 - 50 (see Jimmy Durante)

Camel Caravan: Benny Goodman's Swing School, The (see Benny Goodman)

27 **Camel Comedy Caravan, The** (with Jack Carson)
(3/25/43 - 9/23/43) (also see Jimmy Durante)

Camel Pleasure Hour (with Mary McCoy)
(1930 - 6/3/31) Bl, Wed, 60m, 9:30 pm

Camel Presents Harry Savoy (see Harry Savoy)

Camel Quarter Hour (see Morton Downey)

Camel Rock and Roll Dance Party, The (see Rock 'n' Roll Dance Party)

Camel Screen Guild Players (see Screen Guild Theater)

Cameos Of New Orleans
(11/3/40 - 3/9/41) Illinois Central Railroad, Sun, 15m, 3:30 pm (not in New York)

1 **Camera Club Of The Air, The** (2/15/37) Mut

1 **Camera Club, The** (6/14/39) Mut

1 **Camera Three** (3/1/80) PBS-TV

Cameron Andrews Show, The
(3/19/45 - 6/4/45) CBS, Mon, 10:30 pm, Camille (Syn)

1 **Camille** (1936) Air trailer

1 **Camp McAllister Bunter Abend** (12/15/43)

Camp Meeting Choir (12/21/46 - 3/1/47) NBC, Sat, 15m, 9:30 am

1 **Campaign Countdown** (10/28/80) CBS-TV

1 **Campana Serenade** (with Dick Powell)
(10/10/42 - 2/26/44) Campana
10/10/42 - 4/10/43, NBC, Sat, 15m, 10:15 pm
9/4/43 - 2/26/44, CBS, Sat, 25m, 1 pm

Campbell Martin

Campbell Orchestra (with Robert Simmons, Howard Lanin Orchestra)
(12/7/31 - 4/22/32), Campbell, NBC, 5t, 15m, 7:15 pm

48 **Campbell Playhouse, The** (with Orson Welles)
(12/9/38 - 3/31/40) Campbell, CBS, Fri, 60m; break between 6/2/39 and 9/10/39
(11/29/40 - 6/13/41) Campbell, CBS, Fri, 9:30 pm

Campbell's Short, Short Story (see Short, Short Story)

1 **Campbell's Soups Lunch Counter Revue** (Syn)

Campus Capers
(9/3/38 - 7/25/42) NBC, Sat
9/3/38 - 7/22/39 (Campus Notes) 25m, 2:30 pm
7/29/39 - 7/25/42) 3 pm (not always in New York)

1 **Campus Correspondent** (11/29/56) WMAQ

Campus Kids, The (6/7/38 - 5/23/39) Bl, Tue, 15m, 12 noon; 12:15 pm as of 3/14/39

3 **Campus Salute** (1948, 1949) Mut

1 **Can Baseball Be Made An Even Better Game?** (1952) Syn

Can Freedom Win? (7/12/56 - 11/8/56) NBC, Thu, 25m. 9:05 pm

1 **Can You Imagine That?** (with Lindsay MacHarrie) Syn, 15m

Can You Recognize The Tune
(3/4/40 - 4/22/40) CBS, Mon, 10m, 3:35 pm

Can You Tie That? (1946) KLAC, 60m

32 **Can You Top This?** (with Peter Donald, Senator Ford, Harry Hershfield, Joe Laurie, Jr.) (12/9/40 - 7/9/54)
12/9/40 - 5/12/41, Sus, Mut, Mon, 9:30 pm
5/20/41 - 1/22/43, Sus, Mut, Tue, 8:00 pm
2/3/43 - 9/19/45, Mut, Wed, 7:30 pm
10/3/42 - 9/27/47, Colgate, NBC, Sat, 9:30 pm (started while Mutual show was on)
10/3/47 - 6/25/48, Colgate, NBC, Fri, 8:30 pm
7/2/48 - 9/25/48, NBC, Sat, 9:30 pm (summer replacement for Judy Canova)
9/29/48 - 5/24/50, Sus (occasionally Ford), Mut, Wed, 8 pm
9/23/50 - 11/25/50, ABC, Sat, 9:30 pm
1/2/51 - 6/26/51, Mars, ABC, Tue, 8 pm
10/5/53 - 3/26/54, Sus, NBC, 3t, 15m, 10:15 pm
4/2/54 - 7/9/54, NBC, Fri, 25m, 9:35 pm

2 **Can You Write A Song?** (California Radio System)

1 **Can-Can** (1960) film sound track

Canada Dry (Ginger Ale) Program, The (see Jack Benny)

Canadian Grenadier Guards (see Grenadiers)

1 **Canadian Holidays** (8/1/40)

Canadian Music In Wartime
(8/17/44 - 10/5/44) NBC, Thu, 11:30 pm

Canadian Musicale (2/26/42 - 9/24/42) Bl, Thu, 8:30 pm

1 **Canadian Red Cross Emergency Appeal** (9/29/40) Mut

1 **Canadian Scene - Ribbon Of Destiny** (4/29/56) CBC

Canadian Travelogue (with Malcolm La Prade)
(7/18/40 - 10/10/40) Bl, Thu, 8 pm; 8:30 pm as of 9/26/40

Canadians in Hollywood

6 **Canary Pet Shop (Show), The** (11/5/44) Mut
(1944, 1945, 1955) Mut, Syn (see American Radio Warblers)

1 **Cancer** (4/46) Syn

1 **Cancer Can Be Conquered** (1956) Syn

1 **Cancer Quack, The** (1956) Syn

6 **Candid Microphone, The** (with Allen Funt) (6/28/47 - 8/29/50)
6/28/47, ABC, Sat, 7:30 pm
7/6/47 - 9/21/47, Sus, ABC, Sun, 7 pm
9/29/47 - 10/20/47, ABC, Mon, 9 pm
10/30/47 - 9/23/48, ABC, Thu, 8 pm; 9:30 pm as of 5/6/48
6/6/50 - 8/29/50, Philip Morris, CBS, Tue, 9:30 pm

Candid Woman (Lady) (with Ann Stone, Fred Shields, Vema Felton and Cliff Arquette)
(3/21/38 - 9/39) Pepsodent, NBC - West coast, 5t, 15m, 2:15 pm

Candy Matson (with Natalie Masters)
(6/29/49 - 5/20/51) NBC - West coast, various days (see below as Candy changed her phone number)

1 **Candy Matson, EXbrook 2-9994**

10 **Candy Matson, YUkon 2-8209**

1 **Candy Matson, YUkon 3-8309**

Canning Time (6/20/32 - 8/25/32) Ball Brothers, Bl, 2t, 15m, 3 pm

Canovas, The

Canteen Girl (with Phyllis Jeanne Creore)
(8/28/42 - 12/29/42) NBC, Fri, 15m, 6:15 pm; Tue as of 10/20/42

2 **Canterbury Chorus, The** (Syn)

15 **Canticle For Liebowitz, A** (1981) 90m, WHA origination, NPR

1 **Cape Cod Mystery Theater, The** (1983 -1986) (NPR)

1 **Capitol Cloakroom** (2/10/50 - 8/19/57, 1967) CBS
2/10/50 - 9/1/50, Fri, 10:30 pm
9/5/50 - 10/2/51, Tue, 10:30 pm; 10 pm as of 7/10/51
10/12/51 - 8/19/57, Mon and/or Fri, 10 pm

Capitol Opinions (1/14/39 - 4/29/39) CBS, Sat, 15m, 10:45 pm
also (1/29/39 - 4/9/39) CBS, Sun, 15m, 10:45 pm

1 **Capitol Records Ground-Breaking Ceremony and Luncheon** (9/27/54)

Capitol Theater Family Show (see Roxy and Major Bowes)

1 **Capitol Transcriptions Program Service Demonstration Program** (Syn)

1 **Captain Ahrens Of The Bremen** (12/17/39) Mut

1 **Captain Clark Gable** (8/12/43) NBC

2 **Captain Courage** (1955) Auditions

Captain Diamond's Adventures (with Al Swenson and Edmund "Tiny" Ruffner)
(10/5/32 - 4/18/37) Diamond Salt, Bl
10/5/32 - 3/29/34, Wed, 8 pm; Thu, 8 pm as of 1/5/33
11/15/36 - 4/18/37 (with Alfred Swenson), Sun, 3 pm

Captain E. D. C. Herne (5/39 - 7/3/42) broadcast regionally
5/39 - 9/40, Axton Fisher Tobacco Co., Mut, 5t, 15m
also 7/29/40 - 7/3/42, Skelly Oil, NBC, 5t, 15m

1 **Captain Eddie Rickenbacker** (12/20/42) Mut

1 **Captain Eddie Rickenbacker Interview** (8/24/39) WOR

2 **Captain Flagg and Sergeant Quirt** (with Victor McLaglen and Edmund Lowe; based on "What Price Glory."
(9/28/41 - 4/3/42)
9/28/41 - 1/25/42, Mennen, Bl, Sun, 7:30 pm
2/13/42 - 4/3/42, Brown and Williamson, NBC, Fri, 10 pm

Captain Jack (with Don Ameche and Carl Boyer)
(10/24/32 - 12/23/32) Good Luck Margarine, CBS, 5t, 15m, 5:15 pm

1 **Captain James Archibald** (Audition) Syn

1 **Captain January** (1936) film sound track

1 **Captain Joseph Clark** (1942) Mut

Captain Kid (11/1/37 - 12/2/37) Cambridge Rubber Company, CBS, Fri

111 **Captain Midnight** (10/17/39 - 12/15/49) (started about 10/17/38 in the Midwest, 5t a week)
10/17/39 - 3/27/40, Skelly Oil, WGN (Midwest area)
9/30/40 - 7/3/42, Ovaltine, Mut, 5t, 15m, 5:45 pm
9/28/42 - 6/25/43; 9/27/43 - 6/23/44; 9/25/44 - 6/22/45, Ovaltine, Bl, 5t, 15m, 5:45 pm
9/24/45 - 6/20/47; 9/29/47 - 6/17/49, Ovaltine, Mut, 5t, 15m, 5:30 pm
9/20/49 - 12/15/49, Ovaltine, Mut, 2t, 5:30 pm

1 **Captain Patrick Smith** (7/15/39) Mut

1 **Captain Samuel Grashio** (1/29/44) Mut

Captain Silver and The Sea

5 **Captain Starr Of Space** (with John Larch) (6/2/53 - 5/27/54) ABC, 2t, 7:30 pm (replacement of Silver Eagle)

7 **Captain Stubby and The Buccaneers** (with Tony Walberg) (1946 - 48) Syn

Captain Tim Healy (10/1/34 - 9/21/45)
10/1/34 - 4/26/35 (Stamp Club) Ivory, NBC, 3t, 15m
9/30/35 - 6/28/36 (Captain Tim's Adventures also called Ivory Stamp Club) Ivory, Bl, 3t (Mon, Wed & Fri), 15m
9/28/36 - 6/1/37, Ivory, Bl, 5t, 15m
1/8/38 - 2/15/41 (Stamp Club; originally Calling All Stamp Collectors), Sus, NBC, Sat, 15m, 1:15 pm
also 9/12/38 - 12/9/38, Pep, Mut, 3t, 15m, 6:45 pm
also 6/19/39 - 6/13/41, NBC, 4t/3t, 15m, 6:30 pm
9/29/41 - 4/3/42 (Captain Tim Healy's Adventure Stories) Sus, Bl, 5t, 15m
8/27/45 - 9/21/45, Mut, 5t, 15m, 5:30 pm

15 **Captain Video** (1951) film sound tracks

1 **Captains Courageous** (1937) Air trailer

3 **Captains Of Industry** (1938) Syn

Captivators, The (4/1/33 - 1937) CBS, various days and times

Capture Of Lizzie Stone

1 **Captured Voices** (7/8/89) WNYC

Caravan (with John Reed King) (2/18/52 - 5/23/52) ABC, 5t, 12:30 pm

Caravan (with Lucille Wall and Alfred Shirley) (also called Desert Caravan)
(1931 - 1/23/33) Dromedary Dates, 15m
1931 - 4/22/32, NBC (Midwest), 4t (Mon, Wed, Thu, Fri)
9/26/32 - 1/23/33, Bl, 3t, 5:15 pm

Carborundum Band (11/5/29 - 2/29/36) Carborundum Abrasives, CBS, Sat (except for first few months)
11/5/29 - 3/4/30, Tue, 60m, 7 pm
11/8/30 - 2/28/31; 10/31/31 - 3/26/32, 9 pm, 30m
11/12/32 - 2/25/33, 9:30 pm
10/24/34 - 1/12/35, 10 pm
10/19/35 - 2/29/36, 7:30 pm; then called Voice Of Niagara (see)

1 **Cardinal Mindszenty Case, The** (2/13/49) Mut

Cardinet Show (15m)

Career (with Alice Eden and John Archer)
(7/9/39 - 10/4/39) Wrigley, CBS, Sun, 6:30 pm (summer replacement of Gateway To Hollywood)

4 **Career Of Alice Blair, The** (1935) CBS, Syn
(7/3/39 - 12/20/40) Syn, 130 15-minute episodes; WOR, 5t, 15m

Career Wife (with Ann Thomas) (11/13/39 - 12/22/39) Bl, 5t, 15m, 3:30 pm

1 **Carefree Carnival** (6/11/33 - 11/2/36)
6/11/33 - 9/2/34 (with Gene Arnold and The Commodores), Crazy Water Crystals, Sun, NBC, 2 pm
12/10/34 - 4/22/35 (with Meredith Willson as of 4/8/35, Crazy Water Crystals, Bl, Mon, 8:30 pm
4/28/35 - 5/12/35, Blue Jay Corn Plasters, Bl, Sun, 2:30 pm
5/18/35 - 5/9/36, Bl, Sat
5/11/36 - 11/2/36, Bl, Mon, 10 pm

Careless Love (1930 - 32) NBC, Sun, 15m

Caribbean Nights (NBC) 15m

Caricatures In Rhythm (with Harry Reser Orchestra) (1938) NBC

1 **Carl Fischer and His Orchestra** (Standard transcription)

Carl Hohengarten's Orchestra (also with Tommy Bartlett)
(12/16/39 - 4/27/40) CBS, Sat, 9:30 am

1 **Carl Kress and Tony Mottola** (Thesaurus transcription)

4 **Carl Ravazza and His Orchestra** (Standard transcriptions)

1 **Carl Sandburg** (1952) WMAQ

1 **Carl Sandburg At Gettysburg** (4/13/61) CBS-TV

1 **Carl Smith Show** (1956) Syn

1 **Carl Van Doren** (4/26/39) Audition

2 **Carlton E. Morse Interview** (4/62) KNBC

Carlton Fredericks (see Living Should Be Fun)

1 **Carlton Green and Patrick Maitland** (9/4/39) Mut

1 **Carlyle Steven's Sketch Book** (9/11/38) CBS, 15m

Carmen Cavallaro (1/10/42 - 9/21/48)
1/10/42 - 4/4/42, Sus, Bl, Sat, 10:30 pm
12/16/45 - 9/7/47 (The Sheaffer Parade), Sheaffer Pens, NBC, Sun, 3 pm
6/29/48 - 9/21/48, Tums, NBC, Tue, 8:30 pm (summer replacement for A Date With Judy)

1 **Carmen Cavallaro and His Orchestra** (12/8/41) Bl

Carmen Dragon Show, The
(6/5/51 - 9/11/51) Tums, NBC, Tue, 8:30 pm

Carmen Miranda Show, The (1939) NBC, 60m

48 **Carnation Bouquet** (1942) Syn

26 **Carnation Contented Hour, The** (with Percy Faith Orchestra; Buddy Clark as of 10/31/32)
(1/4/32 - 12/30/51) Carnation Milk (AFRS called Melody Hour)
1/4/32 - 10/24/32 (with Gene Arnold and Herman Larson), Bl, Mon, 8 pm
10/31/32 - 9/26/49, NBC, Mon, 8, pm; 10 pm as of 11/21/32
10/2/49 - 12/30/51 (with Dick Haymes), CBS, Sun, 10 pm; 9:30 pm as of 7/8/51

Carnation Family Party, The (3/12/38 - 3/24/51) Carnation
3/12/38 - 7/2/38, Bl, Sat
1/10/42 - 5/30/42, NBC, Sat
7/1/50 - 3/24/51 (with Jay Stewart), CBS, Sat

1 **Carnegie Hall** (9/26/48 - 6/20/50) American Oil, ABC
9/26/48 - 9/18/49, Sun
9/27/49 - 6/20/50, Tue, 8 pm

Carnival Of Books (2/22/53 - 6/12/55) NBC, Sun, 15m, 3:15 pm; 9:30 am as of 4/18/54

1 **Carnival Of Fun, The** (1940) WFBR

Carnival Of Music (see Cresta Blanca Carnival)

Carnival With Bernie West (also with Henry Levine Orchestra) (7/7/46 - 8/31/46) NBC, Sat, 8 pm (summer replacement for Life Of Riley)

Carol Brice (10/23/45 - 1/1/46) CBS, Tue, 15m, 6:30 pm

1 **Carol Burnett Show, The** (2/68) CBS-TV

Carol Channing (see Music You Can't Forget)

Carol Kennedy's Romance (with Gretchen Davidson) (8/31/37 - 7/30/38) Heinz,CBS, 5t, 15m, 11:15am; part of Heinz Magazine Of The Air until 11/26/37

Carolina Calling (with Grady Cole) (3/23/46 - 5/11/46) CBS, Sat, 9:30 am

2 **Carolina Cotton Calls** (AFRS origination)

Carolina Hayride (with Arthur Smith) (12/16/44 - 6/9/45) CBS, Sat, 2:30pm

Caroline's Golden Store (with Caroline Ellis) (6/5/39 - 7/19/40) General Mills
6/5/39 - 8/31/39, NBC, 5t, 15m, 1:30 pm
10/9/39 - 7/19/40, CBS, 5t, 15m, 5:15 pm (not in New York)

Carolyn Day, Detective (Syn)

1 **Carriage Trade Story, The** (film strip audio)

Carrington Playhouse (2/21/46 - 9/19/46) Mut, Thu, 8 pm

Carson Robison (with Carson Robison's Buckaroos) (11/29/32 - 4/5/40)
11/29/32 - 3/9/33, Barbasol, Bl, Fri, 15m
10/10/33 - 34, CBS, 4t (Tue, Thu, Fri. Sun), 15m, 10:30 am
7/26/34 - 9/27/34 (Bar X Days), Feen-a-Mint, CBS, Thu, 30m, 9 pm
10/1/34 - 12/24/34, Feen-A-Mint, CBS, Mon, 15m, 8 pm
6/18/35 - 9/12/35 (Bunkhouse Follies), Hecker H-O, CBS, 2t, 15m, 6:15 pm
10/4/37 - 4/1/38, Musterole, Mut, 3t, 15m, 11:30 am
10/10/38 - 4/3/39, Musterole, Bl, Mon, 30m, 8 pm
10/13/39 - 4/5/40, Musterole, Bl, Fri, 8:30 pm

4 **Carson Robison and His Buckaroos** (Syn)

1 **Carson Robison and His C. R. Ranch Boys** (Syn)

1 **Carson Robison Solos** (Thesaurus transcription)

Carter Family, The (1/9/50 - 3/3/50) ABC, 5t, 15m, 4 pm

Carter Sisters, The (Country) Syn

2 **Carters Of Elm Street, The** (with Virginia Payne and Viv Smith) (2/13/39 - 7/17/40) (locally broadcast for several months in Chicago)
2/13/39 - 6/23/39; 9/25/39 - 1/19/40, Ovaltine, NBC, 5t, 15m
1/22/40 - 7/17/40, Mut, 5t, 15m

Carton Of Cheer (see Henny Youngman)

Cary Longmire (8/31/42 - 3/31/44) NBC, 5t

1 **Casa Loma Orchestra, The** (1935) Associated transcription

1 **Case Against Cancer, The** (4/26/47) CBS

3 **Case Dismissed** (1/30/54 - 4/24/54) WMAQ/NBC, Sat

1 **Case Of Serge Rubenstein, The** (2/6/55) NBC

1 **Case Of The Elderly Cupid, The** (1946) Syn

1 **Case Of The Flying Saucer, The** (4/7/50) CBS

2 **Casebook Of Gregory Hood, The** (6/3/46 - 10/10/51)
6/3/46 - 5/26/47 (with Gale Gordon) (started as summer replacement of Sherlock Holmes); then George Petrie, Mut, Mon, 8:30 pm
3/1/48 - 6/22/48, Mut, Tue, 9:30 pm
6/28/48 - 1/31/49, Mut, Mon, 8:30 pm
6/1/49 - 10/11/49, Mut, Tue, 8 pm
10/15/49 - 10/29/49, Mut, Sat, 8:30 pm
11/13/49 - 12/25/49, Mut, Sun, 5 pm
1/25/50 - 5/3/50, Sus, ABC, Wed, 8:30 pm
5/4/50 - 9/31/50, ABC, Tue, 8 pm
10/3/51 - 10/10/51, American Chicle, ABC, Wed, 8:30 pm

2 **Cases Of Mr. Ace, The** (with George Raft) (1945, 1947) ABC, Syn

1 **Casey Stengel Announcement** (10/12/48) Mut

66 **Casey, Crime Photographer** (with Staats Cotsworth) (7/7/43 - 4/22/55) CBS
7/7/43 - 8/4/43, Sus, Wed, 11:30 pm (Flashgun Casey)
8/12/43 - 10/21/43, Sus, Thu, 11:30 pm (Flashgun Casey)
10/30/43 - 4/1/44, Sus, Sat, 11:30 pm (Flashgun Casey)
4/8/44 - 9/9/44, Sus, Sat, 11:30 pm; 5 pm as of 7/15/44 (Casey - Press Photographer)
9/12/44 - 6/26/45, Sus, Tue, 11:30 pm (Casey - Press Photographer)
7/11/45 - 9/5/45, Sus, Wed, 9 pm (Crime Photographer)
9/12/45 - 9/26/45, Sus, Wed, 10:30 pm
10/20/45 - 3/4/46, Sus, Sat, 1:30 pm; Mon, 10:30 pm as of 12/3/45 (Crime Photographer)

Casey, Crime Photographer (continued)
3/12/46 - 5/28/46, Sus, Tue, 10 pm (Crime Photographer)
6/3/46 - 7/22/46, Mon, 8:30 pm (Crime Photographer) (partial summer replacement of Joan Davis)
8/8/46 - 3/13/47, American Hocking Glass, Thu, 9:30 pm (Crime Photographer)
3/20/47 - 3/25/48, American Hocking Glass, Thu, 9:30 pm (Casey, Crime Photographer)
4/1/48 - 7/28/49, Toni Company, Thu, 9:30 pm (Casey, Crime Photographer)
8/4/49 - 10/19/50, Philip Morris, Thu, 9:30 pm, (Casey, Crime Photographer)
10/26/50 - 11/16/50, Sus, Thu, 9:30 pm (Casey, Crime Photographer)
1/13/54 - 9/29/54, Sus, Wed, 9 pm (Crime Photographer)
10/8/54 - 4/22/55, Sus, Fri, 8 pm (Crime Photographer)

Casey, Press Photographer (see Casey, Crime Photographer)

1 **Casper Citron Show** (8/21/74) (Syn)

Cass County Boys, The (with Cottonseed Clark) 15m

Cass Daley (see Fitch Bandwagon) 1945 - 46

3 **Cass Daley Show, The** (1946) (9/30/50 - 11/11/50) NBC, Sat, 8 pm

1 **Cass Daley With The Al Sack Orchestra** (Standard transcription)

1 **Cass Daley, With Orchestra Under The Direction Of Claude Sweeten** (Standard transcription)

Castillions (1938 - 10/9/39) CBS, various days, 15m

Castle Village (6/2/39 - 7/7/39) CBS, Fri, 7:30 pm

Castles In The Air (with Alice Remson, Ray Heatherton, Al and Lee Reiser) (4/3/44 - 11/13/44) NBC, 2t, 15m, 10:15 am

Castoria Program (with Albert Spalding and Conrad Thibault) (10/4/33 - 6/27/34) CBS, Wed

1 **Cat and The Fiddle, The** (1934) film sound track

1 **Cat, The** (10/21/46) Audition, with Marvin Miller and Lurene Tuttle) 15m

Catalina Islander (5/23/38 - 7/29/38) Wilmington Transportation, CBS, 5t, 15m, 2:15 pm; then local on KNH, Hollywood

Catch Me If You Can (with Bill Cullen) (5/9/48 - 6/13/48) CBS, Sun, 9 pm

Cathedral Hour (1928 - 12/27/31, Sus, CBS, Sun, 60m

1 **Catherine Cravens** (4/2/45) Mut

1 **Catholic Charity Program with Sammy Kaye and His Orchestra** (4/11/50) WOR

1 **Catholic Hour, The** (1941, 5/5/30 - 58+) NBC, Sun, varies between 30 and 60 m

Cathy and Elliott Lewis (see On Stage)

1 **Cats N' Jammers** (7/1/39 - 7/20/41) Mut
7/1/39 - 11/4/39, Sat, 15m, 7:30 pm
1/20/40 - 4/6/40, Sat, 15m, 7:15 pm
4/30/40 - 8/27/40, Tue, 8:30 pm
5/11/41
6/15/41 - 7/20/41, Sun, 6 pm

1 **Cats `N Jammers** (Swing Seven) Standard transcription

1 **Cavalcade Of 1947** (1947) Syn

1 **Cavalcade Of 1949** (1949) CBS

1 **Cavalcade Of 1950** (1950) Syn

1 **Cavalcade Of 1951** (1951) Syn

1 **Cavalcade Of 1955** (1955) Syn

1 **Cavalcade Of 1956** (1956) Syn

562 **Cavalcade Of America, The** (10/10/35 - 3/31/53) Dupont; 781 shows broadcast
10/9/35 - 6/29/38, CBS, Wed, 8 pm
12/5/38 - 5/29/39, CBS, Mon, 8 pm
1/2/40 - 6/25/40, Bl, Tue, 9 pm
10/2/40 - 3/26/41, NBC, Wed, 7:30 pm
3/31/41 - 6/25/45; 8/27/45 - 6/24/46; 8/26/46 - 6/16/47; 8/18/47 - 7/12/48; 9/13/48 - 6/27/49, NBC, Mon, 8 pm

1 **Cavalcade Of Chicago** (9/40) Mut

2 **Cavalcade Of Drama, The** (Syn)

Cavalcade Of Hits (1/12/40 - 7/28/40)
1/12/40 - 3/1/40, NBC, Fri, 9:30 pm
3/24/40 - 7/28/40, Bl, Sun, 6:30 pm

Cavalcade Of Laughter

1 **Cavalcade Of Music** (4/7/51 - 6/21/52)
4/7/51 - 8/11/51, ABC, Sat, 3 hours, 7:30 pm
3/8/52 - 6/21/52, Mut, Sat, 7:30 pm

1 **Cavalcade Of Music, The** (Syn) Audition

1 **Cavalcade Of Stars, A** (3/27/55) NBC

1 **CBC Star Time** (9/8/46) Mut

1 **CBC String Orchestra, The** (1942) CBS

1 **CBC Wednesday Night** (1/28/53) CBC

1 **CBS Church Of The Air** (9/13/31 - 58+) CBS, Sun; 2t on Sunday during 1939 - 46

41 **CBS D-Day Coverage** (6/6/44, 6/7/44) CBS

1 **CBS Editorial Time** (1/28/47) CBS

2 **CBS Evening News** (4/29/75, 10/26/83) CBS-TV

1 **CBS Evening News With Walter Cronkite, The** (3/6/81) CBS-TV

CBS Is There (see You Are There)

CBS Looks At Hollywood (with Hedda Hopper and Edward Arnold)
(1941- 42) Lucky Strike

1 **CBS Morning News Roundup, The** (5/1/46) CBS

1 **CBS New Year's Eve Dancing Party** (12/31/54) CBS

2 **CBS News 1966** (12/66) CBS-TV

2 **CBS News** (9/3/39, 11/9/65) CBS

1 **CBS News Correspondent's Report** (12/29/70) CBS-TV

2 **CBS News Retrospective** (9/60, 4/4/63) CBS-TV

1 **CBS News Retrospective: Resources For Freedom** (1/54) CBS-TV

1 **CBS News Special** (10/16/64) CBS-TV

3 **CBS News Special Report** (1/27/67, 10/6/76, 10/22/76) CBS-TV

1 **CBS News Special Report: "The Vice President Resigns"** (10/10/73) CBS-TV

1 **CBS News Special Report: "Watergate and The President"** (8/16/73) CBS-TV

1 **CBS News Summary** (6/6/44)

7 **CBS On The Air: A Celebration Of Fifty Years** (3/27/78 - 4/2/78) CBS-TV

CBS Radio Adventure Theater (see General Mills Radio Adventure Theater)

1 **CBS Radio At Fifty: An Autobiography In Sound** (9/18/77) CBS

804 **CBS Radio Mystery Theater, The** (1/6/74 - 12/31/82) CBS, 60m, 7t; 5t as of 1/1/80

2 **CBS Radio News Mementos In Sound**

81 **CBS Radio Workshop, The** (1/27/56 - 9/22/57) Sus, CBS. Fri, 8:30 pm; Sun, 4 pm as of 11/4/56

3 **CBS Report On The Murder Of George Polk** (6/19/48, 9/9/48, 4/27/49) CBS

1 **CBS Reports** (2/19/64) CBS-TV

1 **CBS Reports: Teddy** (11/4/79) CBS-TV

1 **CBS Special Report** (12/29/70) CBS-TV

1 **CBS Special Report: The Flight Of Apollo Seven** (10/11/68) CBS-TV

3 **CBS Symphony Orchestra, The** (8/4/46, 8/18/46, 8/25/46) CBS

2 **CBS This Morning** (7/1/92, 5/27/93) CBS-TV

1 **CBS Views The Press** (1/29/49) CBS

CBS Was There (see You Are There)

CBS World News Round Up (see News Of The World) (1942 - 45) CBS, 15m

1 **CBS World News - 10 O'Clock Wire** (6/6/44) CBS

2 **Cecil and Sally** (15m) Syn

1 **Cecil B. De Mille Interview** (10/12/47) WFBR

1 **Cecil Brower and His Kilocycle Cowboys** (6/25/48) KECK

1 **Cecil Brown** (Sizing Up The News) (2/7/44 - 9/14/45) Bayuk Cigars, Murine, Mut (1945 - 56+) Mut

1 **Cecil Brown's Report From The Repulse** (12/11/41)

1 **Cecil Brown, News and Commentary** (4/12/45) Mut

Cecil Golly Orchestra (4/20/40 - 9/28/40) Bl, Sat, 15m

Ceco Couriers (9/17/28 - 6/30/30) CBS, Mon

1 **Cedric Adams** (8/10/41) Mut

Cedric Foster (1/6/40 - 56+) Mut; sponsored by Employers Insurance, Grove Laboratories
1944 - 47

2 **Ceiling Unlimited** (11/9/42 - 4/30/44, 5/11/58) CBS
11/9/42 - 2/1/43 (with Orson Welles), Mon, 15m, 7:15 pm
2/8/43 - 6/21/43, Lockheed, Mon, 15m, 7:15 pm
8/8/43 - 4/30/44 (with Nan Wynn), Lockheed, Sun, 30m, 2 pm
5/11/58 (Audition) CBS-TV

14 **Celanese Hour, The** (1/7/42 - 6/26/46) Celanese Corporation, CBS, Wed, 10 pm

Celebrity Club (12/8/45 - 6/29/46) Continental Can, CBS, Sat, 10:15 pm

Celebrity Minstrels (with Jay C. Flippen) (3/12/40 - 4/2/40) Bl, Tue, 9:30 pm

Celebrity Night (with George Olsen and Ethel Shutta)
(2/22/36 - 5/23/36) NBC, Sat, 10:30 pm

Celebrity Party (1967 - 68) 60m

Celebrity Room (with Ona Munson)

Celebrity Theater (with Tom Powers)
(4/10/42 - 5/21/42) Bl
4/10/42 - 4/24/42, Fri, 9:30 pm
5/7/42 - 5/21/42, Thu, 8 pm

Cellophane Program (with Emily Post and Edward Nell)
(11/28/32 - 5/22/33) Dupont, Bl, 2t (Mon & Thu), 15m, 10:45 am

Centauri Express (Atlanta Radio Theater Company) (1987 - 1990; 1994 - present)

Central City (with Tom Powers)
11/21/38 - 4/25/41) Oxydol, Bl; NBC as of 1/2/39, 5t, 15m

1 **Centre Theatre Lobby Program** (2/1/39) WFBR

1 **Centre Theatre Opening** (2/1/39) WFBR

Century Clock (with Marvin Miller)
(7/23/39) Horlick's Malted Milk

1 **Century Federal Savings** (11/77) Syn

1 **Ceremony Of The Presentation Of The Black Beaver** (5/24/39) CBC

1 **Certified Magic Carpet** (9/21/39) WJSV

Cesar Saerchinger (3/4/38 - 7/8/44) NBC

Challenge (with Walter and Peg McGraw)
(2/20/53 - 4/17/53) NBC, Fri, 60m, 9 pm (summer replacement for Best Plays)

1 **Challenge Of Nutrition, The**

Challenge Of The Yukon (see Sergeant Preston Of The Yukon)

2 **Challenge Of Youth, The** (Syn)

1 **Challenge, The** (10/41) Syn

1 **Challenge: Election '84, The** (5/27/84) WNET-TV

1 **Challenger Has Landed: The Adventures Of Apollo Seventeen, The**
(12/23/72) CBS-TV

1 **Challenges To Democracy** (10/5/39) Mut

25 **Chamber Music Society Of Lower Basin Street, The** (2/11/40 - 8/2/52)
2/11/40 - 9/22/41, Sus, Bl, Sun; Mon, 9:30 pm as of 8/26/40; 9 pm as of 4/28/41
10/1/41 - 12/30/42, Sus, Bl, Wed, 9 pm; on at 10 pm from 2/25/42 - 4/15/42
1/4/43 - 2/8/43, Sus, ABC, Mon, 10:30 pm
4/4/43 - 10/8/44, Woodbury, Bl, Sun, 15m, 30m as of 7/18/43, 9:15 pm
7/8/50 - 9/30/50, NBC, Sat, 10 pm (summer replacement for Judy Canova)
4/12/52 - 8/2/52, Army Reserve, NBC, Sat, 10:30 pm

1 **Chamberlain's Arrival At 10 Downing Street** (9/30/38) BBC

2 **Champagne Waltz** (1937) Air trailer, film sound track

Champion (see Adventures Of Champion)

Champion Roll Call (with Harry Wismer) 1947, ABC, Champion Spark Plugs

Champions Of The Keyboard
(11/16/38 - 1/11/39) Bl, Wed, 15m

Chance Of A Lifetime (with John Reed King) (9/4/49 - 1/19/52) ABC
9/4/49 - 5/28/50, Ritter, Sun, 9:30 pm
5/29/50 - 1/5/51, Toni, 5t, 15m
7/3/51 - 10/23/51, Tue, 8 pm
10/30/51 - 12/18/51, Tue, 8:30 pm
12/22/51 - 1/19/52, Sus, Sat, 7:30 pm

2 **Chandor and His Gypsy Orchestra**
(8/13/45, 8/14/45) Mut

117 **Chandu The Magician** (10/8/32 - 6/10/50) appeared on WOR on 2/32, Syn
10/8/32 - 36 (with Gayne Whitman; also Howard Hoffman), White King Soap (West coast), Beech Nut (East), Mut and Independent, 5t, 15m; originated at KHJ in Los Angeles (1931- 32)
6/28/48 - 1/28/49 (original scripts redone) (with Tom Collins) White King Soap, Mut, 5t, 15m
11/19/49 - 6/10/50, Sus, ABC, Sat, 30m

1 **Change Your Mind** (11/25/46) CBS

Changes In Harmony (1947) Mon, 15m

1 **Changing Times** (1/19/55, 10/16/55 - 58+) Kiplinger, various networks, days and times, mostly Sat and/or Sun, Syn

1 **Changing Times Program** (8/15/69) Syn

Chanticleers (3/3/41 - 5/26/41) NBC, 2t (Mon & Thu) 8:30 am
(9/1/41 - 10/7/41) NBC, 5t, 15m, 8:30 am

1 **Chanukah Program** (12/6/64) WINS

2 **Chapel By The Side Of The Road**
(World syndication)

1 **Chapel In The Sky** (1949) Syn

1 **Chaplain Jim, U.S.A.** (4/20/42 - 6/30/46)
4/20/42 - 9/4/42, ABC, 5t, 15m, 10:45 am
9/13/42 - 4/22/45, ABC, Sun, 2 pm
4/29/45 - 12/9/45, Mut, Sun, 2 pm
2/3/46 - 6/30/46, Mut, Sun, 10:30 am

Chappel Brothers Present Little Jackie Heller (also with Harry Kogen Orchestra) (1/14/35 - 4/30/35)

Chappel Brothers (Bl) Mon, 10 pm

1 **Chariot Wheels** (4/1/51) CBS

5 **Charioteers, The** (1935 - 12/21/41)
15m (many overlapping networks, days and times) Standard transcriptions
1935 - 36, Mut, Sun
1/6/36 - 12/31/36 (with Judy Starr and Ted Husing), Wildroot, CBS, Mon; Thu as of 10/1/36
7/11/36 - 2/11/39, NBC, Sat
12/13/38 - 8/1/39, Bl, Tue, 8:15 am
2/13/39 - 10/2/39, Bl, Mon, 1:45 pm
7/13/39 - 10/5/39, Bl, Thu, 7:30 pm
7/15/39 - 9/23/39, NBC, Sat, 12:45 pm
9/30/39 - 1/20/40, Bl, Sat, 10:30 am
3/4/39 - 9/20/41, Mut, Sat
10/12/40 - 12/6/41, NBC, Sat
12/29/40 - 5/11/41, Mut, Sun, 12:30 pm
11/9/41 - 12/21/41, Mut, Sun, 7:45 pm

Charis Program (with Dorothy Chase, Ann Leaf, Ben Alley)
(2/24/32 - 11/29/32) Charis Corp., CBS, 15m
2/24/32 - 5/18/32, Wed, 3:15 pm
9/6/32 - 11/29/32, Tue, 2:15 pm

Charles Agnew and His Orchestra
(Armand Dance) (1933 - 34) Tue

Charles Boyer (see Presenting Charles Boyer)

Charles Collingwood (4/6/46 - 9/21/46) CBS, Sat, 15m
(1947) CBS Pacific, Houshold Finance
(3/6/49 - 1/20/52) CBS, Sun, 15m

Charles Courboin, Dr. (9/25/38 - 6/18/39) Mut, Sun, 12 noon

Charles Dant Orchestra
(1/28/40 - 9/13/42) CBS, Sat, 15m - 30m
(7/7/40 - 9/7/41) (with Martha Tilton) NBC, Sun
(7/3/43 - 8/21/43) Drene, NBC, Sat, 8 pm (summer replacement for Abie's Irish Rose)

Charles E. McCarthy (12/29/52 - 2/26/54) ABC, 5t, 15m, 12:45 pm

Charles Fleischer (1930 - 4/19/31) CBS, Sun, 15m, 10:45 am

3 **Charles Frederick Lindsley** (1932- 33) Syn

Charles Leland (9/25/33 - 10/23/33) NBC, Mon, 7 pm

4 **Charles Lindbergh** (1939 - 1941) Mut

1 **Charles Lyon Interview** (8/5/76)

Charles Paul (5/8/38 - 2/19/39), CBS, Sun, 11 am
(12/3/38 - 8/5/39) CBS, Sat, 3:30 pm

1 **Charles Van Doren Press Conference**
(10/14/59)

1 **Charlie and His Orchestra** (1940 - 1942)

Charlie and Jessie (with Donald Cook and Florence Cooke)
(12/16/40 - 1/10/41) Campbell, CBS, 3t, 15m

5 **Charlie Barnet and His Orchestra**
(1939, 1945) NBC, Standard transcriptions

1 **Charlie Barnet Orchestra**

Charlie Barnet Show, The

18 **Charlie Chan** (12/2/32 - 6/21/48)
12/2/32 - 5/20/33 (with Walter Connolly), Esso, Bl, Fri, 7:30 pm
9/17/36 - 4/22/38, Sus, Mut, 5t, 15m, 5:15 pm
7/6/44 - 9/28/44 (with Ed Begley until 11/30/45), Lifebuoy, NBC, Thu, 30m, 7:30 pm (summer replacement for Bob Burns)
10/5/44 - 4/5/45, Bl, Thu, 7:30 pm
6/18/45 - 11/30/45, ABC, 5t, 15m, 6:45 pm
8/18/47 - 6/21/48 (with Santos Ortega) Pharmaco, Mut, Mon, 30m, 8:30 pm

1 **Charlie Chaplin** (1952) BBC

1 **Charlie Drew** (3/20/44) WOR

122 **Charlie McCarthy Show, The** (with Edgar Bergen and Charlie McCarthy) Effie Clinker debuted on 9/3/44
(5/9/37 - 7/1/56) Sun; called The Chase and Sanborn Hour until 12/29/39; after that often called the Chase and Sanborn Program until 12/26/48
5/9/37 - 6/30/40; 9/1/40 - 6/29/41; 9/7/41 - 6/28/42; 9/23/42 - 5/30/43; 9/5/43 - 6/4/44; 9/3/44 - 5/27/45; 9/2/45 - 5/26/46; 9/1/46 - 5/25/47; 9/7/47; 5/30/48; 10/3/48 - 12/26/48, Chase and Sanborn, NBC, 60m, 8 pm; 30m as of 1/7/40
10/2/49 - 5/28/50; 11/5/50 - 6/3/51; 10/7/51 - 6/1/52, Coca-Cola, CBS, 8 pm
10/5/52 - 5/31/53, Hudnut, CBS, 8 pm
10/11/53 - 6/20/54, Multi, CBS, 9:30 pm
9/12/54 - 2/20/55, Kraft, CBS, 60m, 9 pm
10/2/55 - 7/1/56, Multi, CBS, 55m, 7 pm

1 **Charlie Parker** (8/27/54) NBC

1 **Charlie Ruggles Show, The** (also with Mischa Auer (until 3/12/39) and Mary Astor)
(6/3/43 - 11/25/43, 6/16/44 - 9/10/44) CBS
6/3/43 -11/25/43 (called Roma Wine Show), Roma Wines, Thu, 8:30 pm
6/16/44 - 9/10/44, Sanka, Fri, 8 pm (summer replacement for Kate Smith)

1 **Charlie Shavers** (World transcription)

Charlie Spivak (11/19/40 - 3/8/41) NBC, 1t - 5t, 15m - 30m, 6 pm

9 **Charlie Spivak and His Orchestra**
(World transcriptions)

2 **Charlie Spivak Orchestra** (World transcriptions)

Charlie Wild, Private Detective
(9/24/50 - 7/1/51)
9/24/50 - 12/17/50 (with George Petrie), Wildroot, NBC, Sun
1/7/51 - 7/1/51 (with K. O'Morrison; then John McQuade from 3/25/51), Sus, CBS, Sun, 6 pm

1 **Charlie's Aunt** (1952) film sound track

Charlotte Greenwood Show
(6/13/44 - 1/6/46)
6/13/44 - 9/5/44, Pepsodent, NBC, Tue, 10 pm (summer replacement for Bob Hope)
10/15/44 - 1/6/46, Hallmark, ABC, Sun, 3 pm; 5:30 pm as of 4/8/45

Charm Secrets (1/9/34 - 4/5/34) Lavoris, CBS, 2t, 15m

1 **Charmer and The Dell, The** (7/10/49) with Louise Carlyle, Mut

Chase and Sanborn Anniversary Show, The (see The Charlie McCarthy Show)

Chase and Sanborn Hour, The (also see Spike Jones, Charlie McCarthy, Eddie Cantor and Rubinoff)
1/11/31 - 9/6/31 (see Rubinoff)
9/13/32 - 11/25/34 (see Eddie Cantor)
5/9/37 - 12/26/48 (see Charlie McCarthy)
also 6/3/45 - 8/26/45 (see Spike Jones)

9 **Chase and Sanborn Program, The** (6/10/45 - 8/19/45) NBC

Chase and Sanborn's Tea Program (with Georgie Price) (6/2/32 - 12/29/32) Chase and Sanborn, CBS, 2t, 15m, 7:45 pm

Chase Twins, The (10/9/39 - 2/2/40) Bl, 5t, 15m, 3:15 pm

54 **Chase, The** (4/27/52 - 6/28/53) Sus, NBC (59 shows broadcast)
4/27/52 - 6/29/52, Sun, 6:30 pm
7/3/52 - 8/28/52, Thu, 8:30 pm
9/28/52 - 6/28/53, Sun, 4 pm

Chasin's Music Series (with Abram Chasins)
(9/5/36 - 1/9/37) NBC, Sat, 11 am

Chautauqua Symphony Orchestra (1932 - 1958+) NBC, Summers, Sun, 60m, usually 4 pm

1 **Check and Double Check** (1930) Synchro-discs

Checkerboard Fun Festival (with Eddy Arnold) (1952 - 53)

1 **Checkerboard Jamboree** (6/29/46 - 9/22/50) Ralston, Mut
7/6/46 - 12/28/46, Sat, 30m
1/6/47 - 9/22/50 (with Eddy Arnold), 5t, 15m, 12 noon

Checkerboard Square (with Ernest Tubb)

Checkerboard Time (with Chick Martin or Pappy Hal Horton) (1930s)

Cheer Up (12/15/34 - 2/16/35) CBS, Sat, 45m, 9 am

Cheer Up America (with Henry Burbig) (1/19/38 - 4/13/38) Mennen, NBC, Wed, 15m, 7.45 pm

1 **Cheer-Up Gang, The** (with Smilin' Bob Smith) (10/40- ?) Mut, 3t, 15m, 1:45 pm (not always in New York)
(5/9/41 - 6/27/41) Mut, Fri, 15m, 10:45 am

Cheerio (with Charles K. Field)
(3/14/27 - 4/14/40) NBC
3/14/27 - 6/14/37, 6t
9/29/36 - 12/29/36 (Cheerio's Musical Mosaics) Sonotone Hearing Aid, NBC, Tue, 15m
9/26/37 - 4/14/40 (Cheerio's Musical Mosaics) Bl, Sun, 10:30 pm

Cheers From The Camps (6/9/42 - 9/22/42) General Motors, CBS, Tue, 9:30 pm

3 **Cheloni Skin Program** (1932) 15m; see Eddie South and His International Orchestra

1 **Chesapeake Bay Bridge** (1/12/49) WFBR

Chester Bowles (12/8/45 - 3/2/46) ABC, Sat, 15m, 11:30 am

Chesterfield Half Hour (see the Boswell Sisters)

Chesterfield Music Shop (see Johnny Mercer)

Chesterfield Presents (see Paul Whiteman; Andre Kostelanetz)

Chesterfield Show, The (see Andre Kostelanetz)

Chesterfield Sports Show (with Paul Douglas) (4/19/37 - 9/30/38) Chesterfield, NBC, 6t, 15m, 6:30 pm

35 **Chesterfield Supper Club, The** (12/11/44 - 55) Chesterfield, NBC, CBS
12/11/44 - 9/2/49 (with Perry Como and Jo Stafford; also with Bill Lawrence and others; Johnny Johnston for a while as of 7/19/45) 5t, 15m, 7:00 pm
9/8/49 - 6/1/50 (with Peggy Lee), Thu, 30m, 10 pm
1954 - 55 (with Jo Stafford)

28 **Chesterfield Time** (1937 - 1945) some with Paul Baron Orchestra, Martin Bloch (see also Fred Waring; Hal Kemp)

Chesterfield's ABC Of Music (see Robert Q. Lewis)

Chet Huntley (4/2/56 - 9/7/56) NBC, 4t (Mon - Thu), 15m, 10 pm

Chevrolet Program, The (see Jack Benny)

Chevrolet Program...Musical Moments, The (with Rubinoff and Hugh Conrad) (1935 - 36) 5t, 15m; see Rubinoff

Chevrolet Spotlights The News

1 **Chevy Show, The** (3/30/58)

1 **Chez Show, The** (with Mike Wallace and Bubb Cobb) (NBC - Chicago)
5/14/52 (WMAQ) Jack Eigen

Chicago A Capella Choir (directed by Noble Cain) (1932 - 10/8/33) Bl, Sun; NBC as of 4/9/33

1 **Chicago Dynamic** (10/29/57) WTTW-TV

Chicago Jazz (NBC) 15m

Chicago Radio Theater

1 **Chicago Railroad Fair** (7/48)

1 **Chicago Symphony Orchestra,The** (Syn)

55 **Chicago Theater Of The Air, The** (10/5/40 - 2/22/41; 10/4/41 -2/28/42; 10/3/42 - 3/27/43; 6/5/43 - 4/29/44; 7/1/44 - 10/28/44; 11/11/44 - 5/26/45; 7/28/45 - 5/25/46; 12/14/46 - 5/31/47; 11/1/47 - 6/20/48; 10/9/48 - 5/28/49; 10/1/49 - 5/27/50; 6/16/50 - 4/28/51; 10/6/51 - 5/17/52; 10/4/52 - 5/2/53; 10/10/53 - 3/13/54; 7/3/54 - 5/7/55) Sus, Mut, Sat, 60m; started on WGN on 5/9/40

Chicago Varieties (7/16/34 - 3/25/35) CBS, Mon, 4:30 pm
(3/25/38 - 7/8/38), CBS, Fri, 4 pm)

Chicago Women's Symphony (see Design For Happiness)

1 **Chicago, Germany** (1945) WTRY

1 **Chicagoans The** (10/1/46 - 12/28/46) CBS
10/1/46 - 12/17/46, Tue, 5:30 pm
also 10/12/46 - 12/28/46, Sat, 4:30 pm
1950

Chicagoland Concert Hour (with Henry Weber Orchestra, Marion Claire)
(1/22/41 - 2/26/41) Mut, Wed, 9:30 pm (on before on Mon?)
(3/1/41 - 9/27/41) Mut, Sat, 10 am (summer replacement of Chicago Theater Of The Air)

2 **Chick Carter, Boy Detective** (with Bill Lipton; Leon Janney as of 7/3/44
(7/5/43 - 7/6/45) Mut, 5t, 15m

3 **Chick Chick Fun (Program)** (3/22/32 - 3/24/32; 4/6/33 - 4/13/33) CBS, 2t, 15m

1 **Chick Webb and His Orchestra** (5/4/39) NBC

Chicken Every Sunday (with Billie Burke and Harry von Zell)
(7/6/49 - 8/24/49) NBC, Wed, 8 pm

130 **Chickenman** (1966) (created by Dick Orkin on WCFL - Chicago) Syn

Chico Devirdi and The California Gypsies (15m)

Child Grows Up (with Katherine Lenroot, Dept. Of Labor)
(1/1/38 - 4/20/40) Sus, Bl, Sat, 15m

1 **Child's Wish, A** (1/9/47) AFRS origination

Child's World (with Helen Parkhurst)
(10/26/47 - 6/27/49) Sus, ABC
10/26/47 - 3/14/48, Sun, 7 pm
3/25/48 - 3/10/49, Tue, 10 pm
3/21/49 - 6/27/49, Mon, 9:30 pm

Children Also Are People, Too (12/2/40 - 11/5/41) CBS, 2t (Mon & Wed), 15m, 3:45 pm; Wed as of 1/29/41

Children and The War (with Mrs. Clifton Fadiman)
(1/4/43 - 2/22/43) CBS, Mon, 4:30 pm

Children In Wartime (1/5/42 - 3/16/42) Bl, Mon, 15m, 11 am

1 **Children Should Be Heard** (5/7/52) Audition

2 **Children's Chapel** (1948) Syn

1 **Children's Christmas Fund Party** (12/22/47) WOR

Children's Crusade For Children

Children's Favorite Pieces (with Paul Wing, Josef Stopak Orchestra)
(10/4/36 - 10/3/37) NBC, Sun, 8:30 am

Children's Follies (with Nick Kenny)

6 **Children's Hour** (see also Coast To Coast On A Bus)
(4/26/31 - 9/27/57) Horn and Hardart, WABC; WEAF - New York as of 6/4/39, Sun, between 30m and 60m (started on Feb. 1927 on WCAU, Philadelphia

Children's Hour (with Ethel Park Richardson) (7/28/34 - 3/2/35) Mut, Sat, 10 am

Children's Museum Of The Air (15m)

2 **Children's Orchestra** (1938) Syn

Children's Sick-Abed Program (3/25/35 - 4/19/35) NBC, 5t, 9:30 am

1 **Children's Stories As Told By The Great Gildersleeve**

Chimney House (1/1/39 - 5/7/39) NBC, Sun, 15m, 11:15 am

11 **China and India Speak To America** (1943) Syn

1 **Chinatown and The Bowery** (6/29/47) WOR

1 **Chips Davis, Commando** (called Commando until 3/28/43) (7/18/42 - 10/9/43) CBS
7/18/42 - 9/26/42, Sat, 8:30 pm
10/4/42 - 7/18/43, Sun, 7 pm
7/24/43 - 10/9/43, Sat, 5:30 pm

1 **Chocolate Soldier** (1941) Air trailer

Choose A Song, Partner (with Beryl Vaughn) (1948) ABC, 15m

1 **Choose Or Lose** (6/16/92) MTV

Choose Up Sides (with Henry McLemore) (4/14/40 - 3/27/41) CBS
4/14/40 - 6/30/40, Sun, 5 pm
7/12/40 - 9/27/49, Fri, 8:30 pm (partial summer replacement of Kate Smith)
10/24/40 - 3/27/41, Thu, 10:15 pm

Choraliers, The (with Eugene Lowell) (3/13/49 - 4/22/55) Longine, CBS (developed from Festival Of Song)
3/13/49 - 12/18/49; 4/16/50 - 6/25/50; 9/3/50 - 6/10/51; 9/16/51 - 12/28/52, Sun
9/29/53 - 6/1/54, 2t, 15m, 7:30 pm
9/6/54 - 4/22/55, 5t, 15m, 7:30 pm

1 **Christ In Exile** (1941) Syn

1 **Christening Ceremonies Of The John F. Kennedy** (5/27/67) Mut

1 **Christening Of "America" Exhibit At The New York World's Fair** (1939) NBC

1 **Christening Of The Mobile Studio** (4/5/47) WOR

1 **Christian Science Commentary** (1/7/37) WCNW

Christian Science Monitor (see Edwin Canham)

1 **Christian Science Program** (1/7/37) WCNW

1 **Christmas Air Trailer** (1939) Syn

1 **Christmas Card...From Harry's Cadillac-Pontiac Co., A** (12/24/49) WLOS

7 **Christmas Carol, A** (with Lionel Barrymore) performed 12/25/34 - 12/22/55, once a year around Christmas except on 1936 (with John Barrymore) and 1938 (with Orson Welles)

1 **Christmas Day In America** (12/25/46) NBC

1 **Christmas Eve With Marc Connelly** (12/24/63) CBS

1 **Christmas For Eve, A** (12/48) Syn

1 **Christmas Greetings From Lenox Lohr** (12/25/36)

2 **Christmas Holiday Songs** (Syn)

1 **Christmas In London** (12/21/48) BBC/WSM

1 **Christmas In New York** (12/49) Syn

1 **Christmas Lane** (Syn)

1 **Christmas Miracle Of Jasper Crown, The** (Syn)

4 **Christmas Music...Spots For The National Guard** (1966, 1970) Syn

1 **Christmas Seal Campaign 1960** (Syn)

2 **Christmas Seal Campaign** (1939, 1952) Syn

3 **Christmas Seal Campaign, 1948** (Syn)

1 **Christmas Seal Campaign, 1949** (Syn)

3 **Christmas Seal Campaign, 1951** (Syn)

2 **Christmas Seal Campaign, 1952** (Syn)

1 **Christmas Seal Campaign, 1953** (Syn)

3 **Christmas Seal Campaign, 1954** (Syn)

1 **Christmas Seal Campaign, 1964** (Syn)

2 **Christmas Seal Sale 1953** (Syn)

2 **Christmas Seal Sale** (1952) Syn

1 **Christmas Seal Sale Campaign 1948** (Syn)

1 **Christmas Seal Sale Campaign 1950** (Syn)

2 **Christmas Seal Sale, 1949** (Syn)

2 **Christmas Seal Sale, 1951** (Syn)

3 **Christmas Seal Sale, 1952** (Syn)

1 **Christmas Seal Sale, 1953** (Syn)

3 **Christmas Seal Sale, 1954** (Syn)

1 **Christmas Seal Show** (1952) Syn

1 **Christmas Sing With Bing, A** (12/24/55) CBS

1 **Christmas Stocking 1944** (AFRS origination)

1 **Christmas Story: 1947** (AFRS origination)

1 **Christmas That Almost Never Was, The** (1950) Syn

1 **Christmas Under Fire** (12/25/40) BBC

1 **Christmas Visit With Ted Malone, A** (Syn)

1 **Christmas With Love** (Syn)

1 **Christmas With The Antarctic Expedition** (12/25/46)

Christopher Lynch Show, The (1953) Mut, 15m

1 **Christopher Program, The** (12/54) Syn

1 **Christopher St. James Sports Program** (1/22/37) WCNW

Christopher Wells (9/28/47 - 6/22/48) DeSoto, CBS
9/28/47 - 1/27/48, Sun, 10 pm
2/3/48 - 6/22/48, Tue, 9:30 pm

Chrysler Air Show (with Alexander Gray, Mark Warnow Orchestra)
(3/12/36 - 6/4/36) CBS, Thu. 8 pm

Chrysler Bandstand (with Benny Goodman)

2 **Chrysler Corporation-Dodge Division** (1951, 1953) Syn

1 **Chuck Blore Creative Services** (1974) Syn

15 **Chuck Foster and His Orchestra** (1947 - 1964) CBS, WGN, Standard and Lang-Worth transcriptions

1 **Chuck Slate and His Orchestra** (4/8/73)

Chuck Wagon Jamboree (1950) (11/29/51 - 1/3/52) Mut, Thu, 8 pm

Chuck Wagon Troubadours

Chuckles In The News (with Don Dowd)

Chucklewagon (11/29/51 - 1/3/52) Mut, Thu, 8 pm

1 **Church In The Wildwood** (Syn)

1 **Church Of The Air** (see CBS Church Of The Air) Syn

2 **Church On The Air, The** (10/25/36) WMBQ

1 **Church World News** (10/54)

4 **Church World Service** (Post-war) Syn

1 **Churchill Speaking On The Fall Of France** (6/16/40) BBC

1 **Cimarron Tavern** (with Paul Conrad) (4/9/45 - 9/27/46) CBS, 5t, 15m, 5:30 pm

Cincinnati Conservatory Symphony (10/12/35 - 8/9/46) Sus, CBS; various days and times; also sometimes part of Columbia Concert Hall; some dates included:
10/12/35 - 5/16/36, Sat, 60m
10/10/36 - 2/12/37, Fri, 90m
10/9/37 - 6/4/38; 10/1/38 - 6/3/39, Sat, 60m, 11 am
10/14/39 - 3/29/41(Cincinnati Conservatory Recitals), Sat, 60m, 11 am (sometimes other orchestras)
4/6/41 - 5/25/41, Sun, 10:30 am
10/16/41 - 12/25/41, Thu, 4 pm
4/1/46 - 8/9/46, 5t, 3:30 pm

Cincinnati Music Festival

4 **Cincinnati Radio: The War Years 1941-1944**

Cincinnati Zoo Opera (7/2/38 - 8/6/38) (on other summers besides 1938; also on Blue network) NBC, Sat, 60m, 11 pm

Cinderella, Inc. (with Bob Dixon) (8/12/46 - 1/3/47) Sus, CBS, 3t, 3 pm

Cindy and Sam (with Anne Elstner and John Tucker Battle) (10/13/31 - 7/19/32) Socony, NBC, 2t, 15m, 10:30 am

26 **Cinnamon Bear, The** (11/29/37 - 12/24/37) Syn

10 **Circle Arrow Show, The** (with Jimmy Leonard) (10/7/45 - 6/26/49) Western Auto, NBC, Sun, 10:30 pm

Circle Eight Cowboys

Circle, The (with Ronald Colman, Marx Brothers, others) (1/15/39 - 7/9/39) Kellogg, NBC, Sun, 60m, 10 pm

Circus Days (with Jack Roseleigh and Walter Kinsella)
(10/20/33 - 2/10/34) Scott's Emulsion, NBC, 2t (Fri & Sat), 15m, 7:30 pm

Circus Night In Silvertown (with Joe Cook; also Tim and Irene)
(3/8/35 - 8/2/35) B.F.Goodrich, Fri
3/8/35 - 5/3/35, Bl, 45m
5/10/35 - 8/2/35, NBC, 30m

108 **Cisco Kid, The** (10/2/42 - 56)
10/2/42 - 4/23/43 (with Jackson Beck through 1945) Sus, Mut, Fri, 8:30 pm
5/4/43 - 7/6/43, Mut, Tue, 8 pm
10/8/43 - 12/17/43, Mut, Fri, 8:30 pm
1/22/44 - 10/8/44, Sus, Mut, Sat, 8:30 pm
11/1/44 - 2/14/45, Sus, Mut, Wed, 9:30 pm
1947 - 56 (with Jack Mather) Syn

12 **Citadel, The** (Syn)

Cities Service Band Of America (see Cities Service Concerts)

2 **Cities Service Concert, The**
(2/18/27 - 1/16/56) NBC, Cities Service (Edwin Franko Goldman, conductor; then Rosario Bourdon; then Frank Black as of 2/5/38)
2/18/27 - 8/2/40, Fri, 60m, 8 pm
8/9/40 - 5/28/48 (Highways In Melody with Paul La Valle from 10/27/44) Fri, 30m, 8 pm
6/4/48 - 9/19/49 (Cities Service Band Of America), Fri, 30m
9/26/49 - 1/16/56, Multi, Mon, 30m; 15m from 1/4/54

1 **Citizen Of The World** (7/10/49) CBS

1 **Citizens Committee Against Proposition #12** (10/13/44)

1 **City Club Forum** (7/27/81) NPR

City Desk (1/2/41 - 9/27/41) Palmolive, CBS
1/2/41 - 6/26/41, Thu, 8:30 pm
7/5/41 - 9/27/41, Sat, 8:30 pm

City Editor (5/27/55 - 2/8/57) Sus, Mut, Fri

9 **City Hospital** (with Santos Ortega)
(10/6/51 - 11/8/58) CBS, Sat
10/6/51 - 9/26/53, Carter, 1:30 pm
1/9/54 - 11/27/54, Carter, 15m
12/4/54 - 11/8/58, Multi

1 **City That Would Not Die, The** (4/20/56) CBS

2 **City, The** (narrated by Frank Goss)
(2/2/47 - 8/3/47) Sus, CBS - West, Syn

Civilian Defense Talks
(12/29/41 - 3/6/42) Bl, 5t, 15m, 12:15 pm

Claims Agent (7/22/46 - 10/4/46) NBC, 3t, 15m, 7:30 pm new listing;

3 **Clara, Lu and Em** (with Louise Starkey, Isabel Carothers, Helen King; later by Fran Harris, Dorothy Day and Harriet Allyn) (1930 - 12/4/42)
1930 - 31, WGN, Chicago
1/27/31 - 3/23/24, Super Suds, Bl, 5t, 15m
3/26/34 - 7/1/35, Super Suds, NBC, 5t, 15m
10/14/35 - 1/10/36, Super Suds, NBC, 5t, 15m
6/26/36 - 9/4/36, Frigidaire, Bl, Fri, 30m, 9:30 pm
6/8/42 - 12/4/42, Pillsbury, CBS, 3t, 11 am (not in New York)

1 **Clarence Furman and His Orchestra** (12/8/41) Red

1 **Clark Dennis Sings** (1/3/36 - 2/6/42) Sus, Bl, 15m; on various days and times including:
1/3/36 - 3/28/36, Fri, 2:30 pm
5/6/36 - 9/23/36, Wed, 5:15 pm
11/7/36 - 4/24/37 (called at times Originalities) Sat, 15m
4/29/40 - 2/6/42, 5t, 15m

1 **Class Of '53, The** (5/29/53) CBS

Classical Music For People Who Hate Classical Music (with George Marck, conductor)
(1/14/57 - 1958) NBC, Mon, 9:30 pm

1 **Classics In Miniature** (Syn)

1 **Claude Gordon and The Gordon Clan** (KFI)

Claude Hopkins (see Let's Go Night Clubbing)

1 **Claude Sweeten and His Orchestra** (Syn)

8 **Claude Thornhill and His Orchestra**
(9/22/48) ABC, Lang-Worth transcriptions

6 **Claude Thornhill Orchestra** (Thesaurus transcriptions)

1 **Claude Wickard and Elmer Davis** (12/31/42) CBS

179 **Claudia** (10/47 - 11/48) 15m, Syn

Claudia and David (7/4/41 - 9/26/41) CBS, Sat, 8 pm; (summer replacement of Kate Smith; heard as part of the show for several weeks before) sponsored by Grape Nuts

Clem and Maggie

1 **Clem McCarthy, The Voice Of American Sports**

3 **Clement Atlee**

Cleo Brown (4/2/35 - 5/21/35) CBS, Tue, 15m, 4:45 pm

Clete Roberts

Cleveland Calling (5/24/41 - 8/30/41) Bl, Sat, 1:30 pm

Cleveland Entertains (3/17/35 - 3/31/35) CBS, Sun, 15m, 1:30 pm

Cleveland Pops Concert (Walter Logan, director) (1932 - 10/8/33) NBC, Sun, 60m, 1:30 pm

8 **Cleveland Symphony Orchestra**
(1935 - at least 1946) Sus, various networks and days, 30m to 2 hours; including:
1/29/39 - 3/19/39, Bl, Sun, 60m, 8 pm
12/13/41 - 4/18/42, CBS, Sat, 60m, 5 pm
10/10/43 - 4/23/44, Mut, Sun, 60m, 9 pm
1946 (Mut)
1959 (CBS)

Clevelanders, The (with Walberg Brown Orchestra; vocalist Ken Ward)

Cliche Club, The (with Walter Kiernan)
(5/10/50 - 11/19/50) ABC
5/10/50 - 9/27/50, Wed, 8:30 pm
10/1/50 - 11/19/50, Sun, 7:30 pm

Clicquot Club Eskimos (with The Harry Reser Orchestra)
(1926 - 4/12/36) Clicquot Club
1926 - 1/14/33, NBC, Fri, 90m
1/23/33 - 7/24/33, Bl, Mon
12/21/35 - 1/4/36, CBS, Sat, 8 pm
1/12/36 - 4/12/36, NBC, Sun, 3 pm

2 **Cliff and Lolly** (with Cliff Arquette and Lolly Gookins) (1930) Sun, 15m

Cliff Arquette (see Avalon Variety Time, Glamour Manor)

3 **Cliff Edwards** (8/16/34 - 7/4/47)
8/16/34 - 9/6/34, CBS, Thu, 15m, 7:30 pm
6/26/44 - 6/29/45, Sus, Bl, 5t, 15m, 10:30 am
7/2/45 - 12/28/45, Grove Labs, Mut, 3t, 5m, 11:55 am
3/17/46 - 9/15/46, Harvel Watch, ABC, Sun, 15m, 1 pm
9/16/46 - 11/1/46, ABC, 5t, 15m, 4:45 pm
11/4/46 - 7/4/47, ABC, 5t, 15m, 4:30 pm
1950

1 **Cliff Edwards** ("Ukulele Ike") Lang-Worth transcription

Cliff Edwards Singing (1945) see Cliff Edwards, see Ukulele Ike

1 **Climalene Carnival, The**
(9/5/33 - 4/30/36) Climalene, NBC, Syn
9/5/33 - 11/30/33, 2t, 15m
12/5/33 - 4/5/34, 2t, 30m
4/9/34 - 4/30/36, Thu, 30m

1 **Clinton Asks The President** (3/16/77) ABC-TV

1 **Clipper Cavalier** (1/24/39) Mut

Cloak and Dagger (with Joseph Julian; based on files of the OSS)
(5/7/50 - 10/22/50) NBC, Sun (Fri, 8 pm from 9/8/50 - 10/13/50)

39 **Clock, The** (with Gene Kirby - announcer)
(11/3/46 - 5/23/48) Sus, ABC, Syn
11/3/46 - 12/29/46, Sun, 8:30 pm
1/5/47 - 7/6/47, Sun, 7:30 pm
7/14/47 - 9/1/47, Mon, 9 pm
9/4/47 - 1/29/48, Thu, 8:30 pm
2/5/48 - 4/22/48, Thu, 9:30 pm
4/25/48 - 5/23/48, Sun, 7:30 pm

2 **Close To Your Heart** (2/56) Syn

1 **Close Ups** (3/3/55) WBQT-TV

2 **Closed Circuit** (8/8/50, 12/5/56) NBC, CBS

1 **Closed Circuit: NBC's Parade Of Stars Weekly Preview** (3/18/49) NBC

3 **Closed Circuit: Parade Of Stars Weekly Preview** (12/22/49, 3/7/50, 3/30/50) NBC

3 **Closing Of The United Nations General Assembly, The** (12/15/46) WNYC

1 **Closing The New York World's Fair** (10/31/39) Mut

2 **Cloud Nine** (with Hal Stark, Art Peterson, Larry Alexander)
(7/7/50 - 7/21/50) Wrigley, CBS, Fri, 8 pm; local WBBM show goes network for 3 broadcasts

Club Car Special (3/29/34 - 6/15/34) Hearst, Syn, 15m

13 **Club Fifteen** (with Bob Crosby; often Margaret Whiting; Dick Haymes from 8/29/49 - 6/30/50)
(6/30/47 - 6/4/48; 8/2/48 - 7/1/49; 8/29/49 - 6/30/50; 8/28/50 - 6/29/51; 8/27/51 - 1/16/53) Campbell, CBS, 5t, 15m, 7:30 pm; 3t as of 12/24/51

1 **Club Good Cheer** (8/10/44) sponsored by Ranier Beer

Club Hollywood (with Rose Marie) KFWB

1 **Club Matinee** (with Ransom Sherman and Garry Moore)
(4/14/37 - 7/5/43) Sus, Bl, 30 - 60m, 4 - 6t, 4:15 pm

1 **Club Moderne** (KGER)

Club Romance (with Conrad Thibault and Lois Bennett)
(1/6/35 - 3/31/35) Hinds Cream, CBS, Sun, 8 pm; 8:30 pm as of 2/3/35

1 **Club Time** (10/20/45 - 1/23/54) Club Aluminum (often not in New York)
10/20/45 - 6/22/46, ABC, Sat, 15m, 10:15 am
6/26/46 - 7/28/47 (Club Choral Singers), CBS, Mon, 15m, 10:45 am
8/5/47 - 50, CBS, Tue, 15m
1/13/51 - 1/23/54, CBS, Sat, 15m

Club Valspar (with William Wirges Orchestra)
(6/13/31 - 6/11/32) Valspar Paints, NBC, Sat, 9:30 pm

Clyde Barrie (8/20/35 - 4/13/41) CBS, 15m; on various days and times including:
8/20/35 - 11/7/35, 2t, 10:30 am
11/11/35 - 2/10/36, Mon
2/5/36 - 10/7/36, Wed, 4:45 pm
3/12/39 - 5/14/39, 11 am
6/11/39 -7/2/39, 1:30 pm
7/23/39 - 10/1/39, 2:30pm
5/12/40 - 6/23/40; 9/29/40 - 4/13/41, 9:15 am

11 **Clyde Beatty Show, The** (Syn)
also (12/25/50 - 6/8/51; 9/10/51 - 1/18/52) Kellogg, Mut, 3t, 5:30 pm

1 **Clyde McCoy Interview**

1 **Clyde Trask and His Orchestra** (WLW)

Coast Guard Academy Band
(9/19/42 - 11/27/43)
9/19/42 - 11/27/43, NBC, Sat, 11:30 am
also 5/3/43 - 8/9/43 (Coast Guard Dance Band) Bl, Mon, 25m, 7:05 pm

1 **Coast Guard Memorial** (8/4/48)

5 **Coast To Coast On A Bus** (also called Children's Hour and White Rabbit Line) (with Milton Cross) (1924 - 11/6/48) WJZ/Bl/ABC, Sun
1924 - 27, WJZ - New York
1927 - 6/16/40, Bl, 60m, 9 am
6/23/40 - 9/8/40, 30m, 9:30 am
9/15/40 - 2/24/46, 45m, 9:15 am; 30m, 10 am from 5/21/42 - 9/20/42
3/2/46 - 4/7/46, 60m, 9 am
4/14/46 - 11/6/48, 30m, 9:30 am

2 **Cobbs, The** (with William Demarest and Hope Emerson) (6/3/54 - 9/5/54) CBS, Sun, 9 pm

Cobina Wright (12/17/34 - 8/5/35) CBS, Mon, 45m, 3 pm

Cobwebs and Cadenzas
(7/25/38 - 2/12/40) NBC, Mon, 15m

Coca - Cola Hour (see The Pause That Refreshes with Percy Faith)

Coca-Cola Program (with Gus Haenschen Orchestra)
(1930 - 6/1/32) NBC, Wed, 10:30 pm; 10 pm as of 12/23/31

Coca-Cola Summer Show, The (with Roger Pryor) (1948) Coca Cola, CBS

1 **Cocoanut Grove** (1938) Air trailer

2 **Cocoanut Grove Ambassadors** (1932) Syn

1 **Cocoanuts, The** (1929) film sound track

Coffee and Doughnuts (with "Doc" George Rockwell) (3/4/35 - 4/20/35) CBS, 6t, 15m, 9 am

1 **Coffee and...** (9/4/52) WMBQ-TV

Coffee Club (with Richard Himber Orchestra) (2/5/37 - 6/25/37) Owen's Illinois Glass, Mut, Fri, 8 pm

Coffee Matinee (1930 - 4/9/31) Brazilian-American Coffee, Bl, Thu, 5 pm (with Scrappy Lambert)
(1/7/32 - 3/17/32; 4/28/32 - 7/14/32) Coffee, Bl, Thu, 5 pm

Cohen The Detective (8/17/43 - 10/18/43) Bl
8/17/43 - 9/21/43, Wed
9/27/43 -10/18/43, Tue

Coin Of Happiness

Coke Club, The (see Morton Downey)

Coke Coke Time (with Felix Knight; Bob Hannon) (2/5/45 - 9/45) Coca-Cola, 5t, 15m (see also Eddie Fisher; Mario Lanza)

Coleman Cox, Morning Philosopher
(10/7/35 - 11/16/35) Bl, 3t (Mon, Wed, Sat), 11:15 am

1 **Coleman Hawkins** (7/9/69) WNDT-TV

2 **Coleman Hawkins and His Orchestra**
(8/14/40, 8/25/40) NBC

2 **Colgate Comedy Hour, The**
(5/20/51, 2/24/54) NBC-TV

Colgate House Party (3/3/34 - 2/25/35) Colgate, NBC
3/3/34 - 6/23/34, Sat, 9 pm
7/2/34 - 2/25/35, Mon, 9:30 pm

166 **Colgate Sports Newsreel** (with Bill Stern)
(12/5/37 - 6/22/56)
12/5/37 - 9/18/38 (called Bill Stern Review until 1939), Sus, Bl, Sun, 15m
9/22/38 - 10/5/39, Sus, Bl, Thu, 15m
10/8/39 - 9/28/41, Colgate, Bl, Sun, 15m, 9:45 pm
10/4/41 - 5/22/43, Colgate, NBC, Sat, 15m, 10 pm
5/28/43 - 6/29/51, Colgate, NBC, Fri, 15m, 10:30 pm (end of Colgate sponsorship)
11/30/51 - 9/26/52 (again called Bill Stern Sports), Sus, NBC, Fri, 15m, 6:15 pm
4/20/53 - 8/14/53, NBC, 5t, 6:15 pm
9/14/53 - 12/10/54, Budweiser, ABC, 5t, 15m, 6:30 pm

Colgate Sports Newsreel (continued)
12/13/54 - 6/22/56 (also called Sports Today With Bill Stern), All-State, others, ABC, 5t, 15m

Colgate Spotlight (with Ed East) (1941) Colgate, CBS

College Choirs (1949 - 54) Sus, Mut, Sun or Sat (often not in New York)

1 **College Holiday** (1936) Air trailer

College Humor (with Tom Wallace and Marlin Hurt) (4/29/41 - 9/30/41) Raleigh, NBC, Tue, 10:30 pm

College Prom (with Red Nichols and Ruth Etting) (1/24/35 - 4/17/36) Kellogg, Bl, Thu, 15m, 7:45 pm; Fri, 30m, 9:30 pm as of 4/12/345

College Quiz Bowl (with Allen Ludden)
(1/23/54 - 12/14/55) Sus, NBC, Sat; Wed, 8:30 pm as of 5/11/55

3 **College Swing** (1938) Air trailers, film sound track

1 **Collegiate** (1936) film sound track

Collier Hour, The (weekly Fu Manchu dramas) (1927 - 4/17/32) Bl, Sun, 60m

2 **Collins Driggs At The Hammond Novachord** (Thesaurus transcriptions)

6 **Collins Driggs At The Hammond Organ** (Standard transcriptions)

3 **Colonel Charles Lindbergh** (1939 - 1941) NBC, Mut

Colonel Humphrey Flack (with Wendell Holmes and Frank Maxwell)
(7/3/47 - 9/18/47) NBC, Thu, 8 pm (summer replacement for The Aldrich Family)

7 **Colonel Jack and Shorty's Hillbillies** (4/34) Syn, Crazy Water Crystals, 15m

1 **Colonel Josef Beck Of Poland** (5/5/39) Poland

2 **Colonel Robert McCormick**
(9/3/39, 2/19/46) Mut

1 **Colonel Stoopnagle** (with F. Chase Taylor) (often called Quixie-Doodles) (see also Stoopnagle and Budd; Town Hall Varieties) (4/10/38 - 9/13/44)
4/10/38 - 6/16/38 (with Donald Dickson), Emerson Drug, Mut, Sun, 15m, 6:45 pm
10/20/39 - 4/12/40 (Quixie-Doodles), Mennen, Mut, Fri, 8 pm
9/29/40 - 3/23/41 (Quixie-Doodles), Mennen, CBS, Sun, 5:30 pm
5/25/41- 7/13/41, Ontario Travel, CBS, Sun, 5:30 pm
11/30/42 - 3/5/43, Bl, 5t, 5m, 7 pm
also 1/10/43 - 7/4/43 (Stoopnagle's Schutter) Schutter Candy, CBS, Sun, 15m,
7/6/43 - 8/24/43, Swan, CBS, Tue, 9 pm (summer replacement for Burns and Allen)
9/4/43 - 10/9/43, CBS, Sat, 7:30 pm
10/26/43 - 11/23/43, CBS, Tue, 11:30 pm
1/15/44 - 7/15/44, CBS, Sat, 4:30 pm; 4 pm as of 6/17/44
7/26/44 - 9/13/44, CBS, Wed, 10:30 pm

Columbia Chamber Orchestra
(1/6/40 - 5/18/40) CBS, Sat, 3 pm

Columbia Concert Hall (with Howard Barlow) (2/20/35 - 6/3/40) CBS; on various days and times including:
2/20/35 - 6/19/35, Wed, 10:30 pm
7/13/35 - 9/25/35, Sat, 9 pm
10/22/36 - 2/4/37 (Story Of A Song) Thu, 4 pm
2/19/37 - 12/31/37, Fri, 3 pm
6/17/39 - 10/21/39, Sat, 11:30 am
1/8/40 - 6/3/40, Mon, 10:30 pm

1 **Columbia Electrical Transcription Demonstration Program** (Syn)

Columbia Mystery Guild
(11/30/33 - 12/14/33) CBS; Thu

Columbia Phonograph Hour
(12/9/27 - 5/23/38) CBS, Wed, 60m

26 **Columbia Presents Corwin** (see also Columbia Workshop)
(3/7/44 - 8/15/44) CBS, Tue
(7/3/45 - 8/21/45) CBS, Tue, 9 pm (summer replacement of Inner Sanctum)

Columbia Presents Perry Como (see Perry Como)

1 **Columbia Record Shop** (Syn)

Columbia Shakespeare Cycle, The (see Streamlined Shakespeare)

Columbia Square (with Lud Gluskin Orchestra) (6/10/38 - 7/8/38), CBS, Fri, 45m, 10 pm

1 **Columbia Syndication Service** (Syn)

Columbia Variety Hour
(7/22/34 - 10/14/34) CBS, Sun, 8 pm
(10/23/24 - 12/11/34) CBS, Tue, 3 pm
(5/28/35 - 6/11/35) CBS, Tue, 60m, 3 pm

333 **Columbia Workshop, The**
(7/18/36 - 1/25/47) CBS
7/18/36 - 2/13/37, Sat
2/28/37 - 11/28/37, Sun
12/9/37 - 12/30/37, Thu, 10:30 pm
1/8/38 - 8/6/38, Sat, 7:30 pm
9/15/38 - 1/5/39, Thu, 10 pm
1/9/39 - 6/26/39, Mon, 10:30 pm
7/6/39 - 4/25/40, Thu
5/5/40 - 4/27/41, Sun
5/4/41 - 11/9/41 (26 by Corwin) Sun
11/16/41 - 6/7/42, Sun
6/12/42 - 7/3/42, Fri, 10:30 pm
7/13/42 - 10/19/42; (see also American In England) Mon, 10:30 pm
11/8/42, Sun, 8 pm
12/1/42 - 12/22/42; see American In England
3/7/44 - 8/15/44; see Columbia Presents Corwin
7/3/45 - 8/21/45; see Columbia Presents Corwin
2/2/46 - 4/13/46, Sat, 2:30 pm
4/21/46 - 9/15/46, Sun, 4 pm
9/21/46 - 1/25/47, Sat, 6:15 pm

1 **Columbia's Country Caravan**

Columbia's Gay Nineties Revue (see The Gay Nineties Review)

1 **Columbia's Stage Door** (11/12/47) Audition

Columbians, The (with Freddie Rich Orchestra)
(7/20/34 - 8/31/34) CBS, Fri, 15m, 8:15 pm
(7/19/35 - 7/26/35) CBS, Fri, 10:30 pm

1 **Columbus Day Addresses** (10/12/40)

1 **Columbus Day Program** (10/12/48) Mut

1 **Columbus, World Benefactor** (10/12/49) Mut

1 **Combined Jewish Appeal** (9/17/44) WEEI

1 **Combined Wild West Rodeo and Hollywood Daredevil Thrill Circus** (9/24/46) WWNC

6 **Come and Get It** (1948) with Bob Russell and Alma Kitchell, Syn,15m

Come On, Let's Sing (with Jack Arthur)
(7/15/36 - 1/6/37) Palmolive, CBS, Wed, 8:30 pm

Comedy By - (with George Byron, Tom Howard and George Shelton)
(2/23/40 - 4/5/40) Mut, Fri, 9:30 pm

20 **Comedy Capers** (1933, 1935, 1945) Mon Syn (see also Komedie Kapers)

1 **Comedy Classics** (5/88) Syn

Comedy Kingdom (1930s)

1 **Comedy Of Ernie Kovacs, The** (4/9/68) ABC-TV

2 **Comedy Of Errors** (with Jack Bailey) (12/24/49 - 2/2/52) Sus, Mut, Sat, 7:30 pm

1 **Comedy Playhouse** (1/19/49 - 2/2/50) Sus, Mut
1/19/49 - 9/14/49, Wed, 10 pm
9/22/49 - 2/2/50, Thu, 9 pm

Comedy Stars Of Broadway (with Frank Crumit) (1932 - 1933) Alka-Seltzer, Syn, 2t 15m

Comedy Theater Of The Air (with Harold Lloyd and Jimmy Wallington)
(10/29/44 - 6/10/45) Old Gold, NBC. Sun, 10:30 pm (see The Harold Lloyd Comedy Theatre)

3 **Comedy Writers Show, The** (with Ben Bradley) (6/6/48 - 9/5/48) ABC, Sun, 10 pm (partial summer replacement of Theater Guild)

Comic Weekly (see The Adventures Of Jungle Jim)

8 **Comic Weekly Man, The** (11/21/54 - 58) Mut or Syn, Sun morning, 15m

1 **Coming Out Of The Great Depression** (Syn)

Command Performance
(3/29/40 - 10/11/40) Mut, Fri, 9:30 pm

113 **Command Performance**
(3/8/42 - 2/21/50) (AFRS)

Command Performance (see Dale Carnegie)

Commando, Mary (6/21/42 - 9/6/42) NBC, Sun, 15m, 11:45 am

Commandos (see Chips Davis, Commando)

1 **Comment By Clifton Utley** (12/10/50) NBC

1 **Commentary On King Farouk's Wedding** (1/30/38) NBC

Commentator's Forum (with Charles Payson) (9/17/37 - 12/19/37) Life Magazine, CBS, Sun, 15m, 9:30 pm; and Thu, 15m, 10 pm

Commissioner Of Police (with Lloyd Nolan and Cathy Lewis) NBC

1 **Commitment '80** (9/13/80) CBS-TV

Commodores Quartet (with Gene Arnold) (also see Carefree Carnival)
(6/12/33 - 2/10/35)
6/12/33 - 3/8/34, Crazy Water Hotel Company, Bl, 2t, 12 noon
9/16/34 - 2/10/35, Crazy Water, NBC, Sun, 2:30 pm

1 **Commonwealth Symphony and State Chorus Of Boston** (1939) Syn

1 **Communist Party Convention** (1940) Mut

1 **Communist Party Of Maryland** (2/8/49) WFBR

1 **Communist Party Paid Politial Talk** (10/20/36) WMBQ

1 **Community Chest Program** (9/26/54) pool feed

1 **Community Chest - Mobilization For Human Needs** (10/13/40) pool feed

1 **Community Forums** (Syn)

1 **Community Forums Presents Lewis L. Gough** (1953) Syn

1 **Community Resources** (Syn)

1 **Community Sing** (called Summer Hotel from 6/6/37 - 8/29/37) (with Milton Berle; Wendell Hall)
(9/6/36 - 8/29/37) Gillette, CBS, Sun, 45m; 30m as of 4/25/37 (see also Jack Barclay's Community Sing and The Gillette Community Sing)

Companion (12/19/54 - 12/16/55) ABC, 5t, 15m, 11:15 am; 11 am as of 2/28/55

1 **Complete Life Of General Douglas A. MacArthur...Through His Own Words, The** (1964)

Composer's Series (4/30/40 - 6/11/40) Mut, Tue, 10:30 pm (not in New York)

Conan, The Barbarian (15m)

78 **Concert Hall** (1946 - 1949) AFRS (with Lionel Barrymore) (see also Columbia Concert Hall)

1 **Concert Hall Of The Air** (1/11/37) WCNW

Concert Hour (with Cesare Sodero)
(1/8/36 - 4/8/36) Bl, Wed, 5 pm

1 **Concert Hour, The** (with Mary Henderson and Hugh Thompson)
(9/25/46 - 1/22/47) Mut, Wed, 10 pm

4 **Concert In Miniature** (8/22/40 - 10/3/40) Bl, Thu, 9:30 pm
also 1952, 1953 (NBC)

Concert In Rhythm (with Raymond Scott Orchestra)
(1/9/40 - 4/23/40) CBS, Tue, 9:30 pm

Concert Miniatures (3/30/36 - 2/1/37) CBS, Mon, 3:30 pm

Concert Of American Jazz (see American Jazz Concert)

Concert Of Europe (4/29/51 - 8/4/51) ABC, Sun, 5 pm

Concert Of Nations (6/6/46 - 10/31/46; 6/12/47 - 10/9/47) NBC, Thu, 11:30 pm

2 **Concert Time** (AFRS) Syn

Condido Botelho (7/26/40 - 8/30/40) Bl, Fri, 15m, 10:45 pm

1 **Coney Island** (1943) film sound track

1 **Coney Island Fire** (5/17/47) WOR

1 **Coney Island: 1946** (9/20/46) Mut/BBC

Confession (with Paul Frees)
(7/5/53 - 9/13/53) NBC, Sun, 9:30 pm

Confession Stories (1/28/57 - 58+) NBC, 5t, 25m, 2:05 pm

1 **Confessions Of A Racketeer** (1932) Syn

Confidence Man, The (3/26/34 - 4/9/34) Bl, Mon, 10 pm

Confidential Closeups (9/10/49 - 6/3/50) Animal Foundation, NBC, Sat, 15m

3 **Confidentially Yours** (see also Arthur Hale) (with Jack Lait)
(1939 - 1944)
(7/7/50 - 10/27/50) NBC, Fri, 9:30 pm

Conflict (4/17/34 - 7/19/34) CBS, 2t, 15m

1 **Congress Of American Industry** (12/9/39) Mut

Congress Speaks (4/20/43 - 5/4/45; 7/24/45 - 3/5/46) CBS, Tue, 10:30 pm

Congressional Opinion (3/24/35 - 6/23/35) CBS, Sun, 11 pm

1 **Congressional Remote** (9/21/39) CBS

1 **Congressional Tribute To General Norman Schwarzkopf** (5/8/91)

1 **Congressman Emanuel Celler** (3/5/48) Mut

1 **Congressman Fred A. Hartley** (2/28/48) Mut

2 **Connecticut Yankee In King Arthur's Court, A** (1949) Air trailer, film sound track

3 **Connee Boswell Show, The** (see also Camel Caravan and Tonight On Broadway)
(1/12/44 - 7/19/44) ABC, Wed, 7 pm

Connie Gates (7/16/35 - 12/12/35) NBC, Tue, 15m, 4:45 pm; 2t, 10m, 6:35 pm as of 11/12/35

Connie Haines (see Rhapsody In Rhythm)

1 **Connie Haines** (with Page Cavanaugh Trio) Standard transcription

1 **Connie Haines** (with orchestra under direction of Stan Myers) Standard transcription

1 **Connie Haines** (with Rhythm Accompaniment) Standard transcription

Conoco Tourist Adventures (with Carveth Wells) (1930 - 5/29/32) Continental Oil, CBS (Midwest), NBC, Thu, 11 pm; then Sun, 11 am
(1/18/33 - 4/5/33) (Exploring America) NBC, Wed, 10:30pm
(2/14/34 - 1/23/35) Continental Oil, NBC, Wed

2 **Conquest** (1937) Air trailer
(12/3/47) KFI

Console Meditation (Halo Shampoo)

Console Reflections (CBS) 15m

1 **Constance Bennett Calls On You** (5/21/45 - 3/15/46) Sus, ABC, 5t, 15m, 1:15 pm

Constance Parker Young
(10/5/31 - 12/30/31) Kenton Pharmacal, CBS, 2t (Mon & Wed) 15m, 1 pm

57 **Constant Invader, The** (1945 - 1950) Syn

3 **Constitution Day Program** (1950 - 1952) WFBR

1 **Consumer Closeups** (Syn)

Consumer Time (6/7/41 - 8/16/47) Sus, NBC, Sat, 15m

Consumer's Quiz (9/16/40 - 6/6/41; 10/13/41 - 2/6/42) Mut, 5t, 15m

1 **Contact Dave Elman** (see Dave Elman)
(10/19/40 - 9/1/41) Sus, Mut
10/19/40 - 7/5/41, Sat, 9:30 pm
7/7/41 - 9/1/41, Mon

Contemporary Composers (see Paul Whiteman)

Contented Hour, The (see Carnation Contented Hour)

Conti Castille Show (see Yours For A Song)

7 **Continental Celebrity Club, The** (with Jackie Kelk and John Daly)
(12/8/45 - 6/29/46) Continental Can, CBS, Sat, 10:15 pm

3 **Continental Trio, The** (1931) Syn

Continental Varieties (with Hugo Mariani Orchestra)
(3/31/35 - 8/18/35) NBC, Sun, 6:30 pm
(7/23/39 - 10/15/39) Bl, Sun, 1:30 pm; 2 pm as of 8/27/39

1 **Continental, The**

Contraband (Syn)

4 **Contrasts** (1948 - 1951) NBC

1 **Control Of Man Made Static, The** (4/6/39) CBS

1 **Convention Fever** (12/21/56) CBS

2 **Conversation** (with Clifton Fadiman and Bennett Cerf)
(10/14/54 - 7/19/56) Sus, NBC
10/14/54 - 6/18/55, Sat, 8:30 pm
12/1/55 - 7/19/56, Thu, 9:30 pm
1963, Mut

1 **Conversation Carte Blanche** (8/21/63) WDSU

2 **Conversation With Ross Perot, A** (10/17/92, 10/22/92) ABC-TV

13 **Conversation With..., A** (1958 - 1992) various sources

1 **Conversations On Universal Military Training** (Syn)

Cook's Travelog (with Malcolm La Prade) (1926 - 3/19/39) sponsored by Thomas Cook and Son
1926 - 5/5/35, Bl, Sun, 15m
3/8/36 - 4/26/36, Bl, Sun
12/6/36 - 4/18/37, CBS, Sun, 15m, 2:45 pm
12/12/37 - 3/6/38, NBC, Sun, 15m, 2:15 pm
12/18/38 - 3/19/39, Bl, Sun, 15m, 5:30 pm

Cooking School For Children (with George Rector) (1/22/33 - 4/27/33) A & P, Bl, Thu, 15m, 6 pm

Coon-Sanders Nighthawks (Maytag Frolic Radio Program) 1929

Cooper Clan, The (1944 - 45) Sat, 15m

1 **Copacabana** (1947) film sound track

Corn Cob Pipe Club (with Pat Binford of Virginia) (6/15/32 - 4/22/36) Edgeworth Tobacco
6/15/32 - 6/27/34, NBC, Wed, 10 pm
11/23/35 - 1/25/36, NBC, Sat
1/29/36 - 4/22/36, Bl, Wed, 9 pm

Cornelius Otis Skinner (7/5/36 - 9/6/36) Bl, Sun, 15m, 9 pm (summer replacement for Walter Winchell)

Corner Drug Store (with Rosaline Greene, Percy Harris)
(8/18/31 - 10/6/31) NBC, Tue, 7:30 pm

Corns' A Poppin' (see The Spike Jones Show)

1 **Coronado** (1935) film sound track

1 **Coronation Broadcast** (5/12/37) BBC

1 **Coronation Broadcast Tabloid Version** (5/12/37) BBC

1 **Coronation Of King George VI** (5/12/37)

1 **Coronation Of Pope Pius XII** (3/12/39) Italy

1 **Coronation Proclamation** (7/6/52) BBC

5 **Coronation Week Broadcast Series** (6/52) Syn

Coronet Cigarette Program (with Alex Cooper and Tom Brennan) (3/12/50 - ?) Mut, Sun

Coronet On The Air (with Deems Taylor, Robert Armbruster Orchestra)
(4/2/37 - 6/25/37) Bl, Fri, 9:30 pm

Coronet Quick Quiz (1/29/44 - 9/29/45) Coronet, Bl, 5m, 9:55 pm

Coronet Storyteller (with Charles Irving)
(1/24/44 - 11/2/45) Coronet, Bl/ABC, 5t, 15m, 9:55 pm

Correction Please (with Jack Shilkret; Jay C. Flippen as of 3/11/44)
(9/25/43 - 9/14/45)
9/25/43 - 12/2/44, Tums, CBS, Sat, 8 pm
6/15/45 - 9/14/45, Ipana, NBC, Fri, 10 pm (summer replacement for Duffy's Tavern)

4 **Correspondent's Report, The** (12/28/69, 12/30/71) CBS-TV

Correspondents Abroad (with Creighton Scott and Alvin West)
(6/26/44 - 9/21/46) Bl/ABC, 5t, 15m; Sat only as of 4/7/45

3 **Corsican Brothers, The** (1941) Air trailer, Syn

Cosmo Tune Time (with Alan Kent)
(3/29/45 - 10/13/45) Reichold Chemical, Mut, Sat, 60m

1 **Cosmopolitan Playhouse** (8/27/48) Mut

Cosmopolitan Rhythms
(12/10/38 - 6/17/39) NBC, Sat

3 **Cosmopolitan Rhythms By Harry Breuer and The Clefdwellers** (SESAC transcriptions)

Coty Playgirl, The (with Irene Bordoni and Adele Ronson) (3/8/31 - 5/31/31) Coty, CBS, Sun

Coty Salute To Youth (see Ray Noble)

1 **Could Be** (10/19/49) United Nations Radio

Could This Be You (Syn) 15m

3 **Counselor At Large** (12/28/46) Auditions

4 **Count Basie** (12/13/40, 7/8/66) BBC

20 **Count Basie and His Orchestra**
(1937 - 1968) various sources

1 **Count Basie Recording Session** (1/10/44)

3 **Count Of Monte Cristo, The** (with Carleton Young) (12/19/46 - 4/29/52) Mut (heard earlier on the west Coast) (various days and times including:
12/19/46 - 6/26/47, Sus, Thu, 8:30 pm
1947 - summer, Sun
1948 - summer, Sun
6/12/49 - 9/18/49, Sun, 9 pm
10/18/49 - 4/29/52, Sus, Tue (off and on), 8 pm; (on West coast 1945 - 53; mostly Tue) Syn

Count Your Blessings (5/15/50) audition

1 **Countdown To 2001** (12/4/72) ABC-TV

1 **Countdown To Discovery** (9/27/88) Fox TV

1 **Counterpoint** (9/21/58) WNEW

18 **Counterspy** (with Don MacLaughlin)
(5/18/42 - 11/29/57)
5/18/42 - 7/27/42; 8/31/42 - 1/8/45, Mail Pouch as of 9/28/42, ABC, Mon, 10 pm; 9 pm as of 8/31/42
1/17/45 - 6/20/45, Mail Pouch, ABC, Wed, 8:30 pm
6/27/45 - 12/19/45, Pharmacraft, ABC, Wed, 10 pm
2/3/46 - 12/5/48, Schutter Candy, ABC, Sun, 5:30 pm
1/11/49 - 10/20/49; 1/3/50 - 8/31/50, Pepsi, ABC, 2t, 7:30 pm; from 12/1/49 - 12/29/49 sponsored by Anahist, Thu
10/13/50 - 10/27/50, NBC, Fri
11/3/50, Sus, NBC, Fri, 9:30 pm (one show)
11/12/50 - 1/21/51, Sus, NBC, Sun, 5 pm
2/1/51 - 9/25/52, Gulf, NBC, Thu, 9:30 pm
10/5/52 - 6/28/53, Gulf, NBC, Sun, 5:30 pm
7/2/53 - 9/24/53, Gulf, NBC, Thu, 9 pm

Counterspy (continued)
10/5/53 - 12/28/53, Mut, Mon, 8:30 pm
1/3/54 - 3/14/54, Multi, Mut, Sun, 4 pm
4/2/54 - 11/29/57, Multi, Mut, Fri, 8 pm

1 **Countess Of Monte Cristo, The** (1935) Air trailer

3 **Country Church Of Hollywood**
(4/7/35 - 6/30/35) CBS, Sun, 4 pm also (Syn) (1930s) 15m

Country Club Of The Air (with Morton Gould and Don Novis (1936) Kelvinator, 15m

Country Cooking (with host Lee Arnold) (AFRS)

Country Crossroads (with Bill Mack and Leroy Van Dyke) (1973 - 75)

Country Doctor (with Phillips H. Lord)
(6/20/32 - 3/15/33) Listerine, Bl, 3t (Mon - Wed); 5t as of 7/25/32; 3t as of 12/12/32, 15m

91 **Country Hoedown** (1956 - 57) Syn, 15m

Country Journal (10/14/39 - 3/16/46) CBS
10/14/39 - 9/27/41; 12/13/41 - 5/2/42, Sat, 12 noon; 3 pm as of 12/13/41
8/1/42 - 8/28/43, Sat, 1 pm
also 1/6/43 - 2/10/43, Wed, 15m, 4:30 pm
1/29/44 - 3/16/46, Sat, 9:30 am

1 **Country Journal Digest** (1956) KMOX

123 **Country Music Time** (1952 - 1962) Syn

36 **Country Style U. S. A.** (also called Country Music Style and Country Music, U. S. A.) (1956 - 59)

Country Style (see Saturday Night Country Style)

Country Willie (with Bill Idelson)
(7/7/53 - 9/29/53) NBC, Tue, 9:30 pm (summer replacement for Fibber McGee & Molly)

County Fair (with Jack Bailey; then Peter Donald; Win Elliot as of 2/23/46)
(7/10/45 - 4/1/50) Borden
7/10/45 - 11/27/45, Bl, Tue, 7:30 pm
12/8/45 - 7/18/48, CBS, Sat, 1:30 pm
7/21/48 - 9/8/48, CBS, Wed
9/18/48 - 12/25/48, CBS, Sat
1/5/49 - 6/29/49, CBS, Wed, 9 pm
7/9/49 - 4/1/50, CBS, Sat

1 **County Seat** (with Ray Collins)
(10/27/38 - 8/26/39) CBS
10/27/38 - 3/31/39, 5t, 15m, 7 pm
4/8/39 - 8/26/39, Sat, 30m, 7:30 pm

County Sheriff (see The Sheriff)

14 **Couple Next Door, The**
(1935 - 9/16/37) Procter and Gamble, Mut, 5t, 15m; started in 1935 on WGN with Olan Soulé and Elinor Harriott for Holland Fumace
also (12/30/57 -11/25/60) (with Peg Lynch and Alan Bunce) CBS, 5t, 15m

1 **Court Is In Session** (Farrel, Block and Co.) Syn

Court Of Human Relations (with Percy Hemus) (1/1/34 - 1/1/39) True Story Magazine
1/1/34 - 4/29/34, NBC, Mon/Sun, 45m, 7 pm
5/4/34 - 8/30/35, CBS, Fri, 30m, 8:30 pm
9/6/35 - 5/26/38, NBC, Fri, 9:30 pm
10/9/38 - 1/1/39, Mut, Sun, 4:30 pm

Court Of Missing Heirs (also called Are You A Missing Heir? as of 8/19/41) (with Jim Waters) (10/11/37 - 7/10/38 in Midwest, Skelly Oil, CBS, Mon; Sun as of 12/5/37)
(12/19/39 - 4/6/47)
12/19/39 - 9/29/42, Ironized Yeast, CBS, Tue, 8:30 pm; 8 pm as of 7/9/40
3/31/46 - 6/9/46, ABC, Sun, 5 pm; 4 pm as of 4/28/46
1/26/47 - 4/6/47, Sun, 6 pm. 7 pm as of 2/9/47

Court Of The Air (1930s)

Courteous Colonels (1/2/37 - 2/6/37) Barnsdall Refining, CBS (Midwest), Sat, 10:30 pm

2 **Courtship and Marriage** (Syn)

1 **Courtship Of Andy Hardy** (1941) Air trailer

Cousin Bob Nickelson (15m)

1 **Cover Girl** (1944) film sound track

1 **Cover Story** (5/26/80) PBS-TV

1 **Coverage Of The Shooting Down Of Korean Airlines Flight #007** (9/1/83)

Crackerjack Quartet (4/22/39 - 8/17/40) NBC, Sat, 15m, 9:45 am

Cracraft Electric Orchestra (with Andre Monici) (1939) NBC

1 **Craig Worthing Show, The** (1/2/78) WKAT

Crawford Caravan (with Jesse Crawford)
(1/29/39 - 7/16/39) NBC, Sun, 9:30 am, 4:30 pm; 9:30 am as of 5/14/39

1 **Crazy About Women** (Syn)

Crazy Hillbillies (1930s) see Colonel Jack and Shorty's Hillbillies

3 **Crazy Quilt** (with Elvia Allman and Benny Light) (1933) Fri, 15m, Syn

Crazy Quilt In Rhythm (7/1/39 - 9/23/39) Bl, Sat, 3:30 pm

1 **Creeps By Night** (2/15/44 - 6/20/44) Bl, Tue, 10:30 pm

Creightons, The (with John Griggs)
(6/13/42 - 1/16/43) NBC, Sat, 11 am

1 **Cremo Singer, The** (10/7/37)

1 **Crepitation Contest, The** (Syn)

8 **Cresta Blanca Carnival, The** (also called Carnival Of Music) (with Jack Pearl until 1/6/43, Cliff Hall, Morton Gould Orchestra
(10/14/42 - 5/30/44)
10/14/42 - 4/7/43, Mut, Wed, 45m, 9:15 pm
4/14/43 - 4/26/44, CBS, Wed, 30m, 10:30 pm
5/2/44 - 5/30/44 (with Alec Templeton from 9/1/43) CBS, Tue, 30m, 9:30 pm

3 **Cresta Blanca Hollywood Players** (9/3/46 - 2/26/47) Cresta Blanca, CBS, Tue, 9:30 pm; Wed, 10 pm as of 12/25/46

Crime and Death Take No Holiday (6/20/39) Texas State network

1 **Crime and Peter Chambers** (with Dane Clark) (4/6/54 - 9/7/54) NBC, Tue, 9:30 pm

Crime Cases Of Warden Lawes (see also Twenty-thousand Years In Sing Sing)
(10/26/46 - 9/23/47) Trimount, Mut
10/20/46 - 3/30/47, Sun, 15m, 1 pm; 2 pm as of 1/19/47
4/8/47 - 9/23/47, Tue, 15m, 8 pm

29 **Crime Classics** (with Lou Merrill) (6/15/53 - 6/30/54) Sus, CBS
6/15/53 - 9/7/53, Mon, 8 pm

31 **Crime Club** (12/2/46 - 10/23/47) Sus, Mut (also see Eno Crime Club)
12/2/46 - 12/30/46, Mon, 8 pm
1/2/47 - 10/23/47, Thu, 10 pm

1 **Crime Correspondent** (1/4/49) CBS

1 **Crime Doctor** (8/4/40 - 10/19/47) Philip Morris, CBS, Sun, 8:30 pm, Syn

17 **Crime Does Not Pay** (with Don Buka) (10/10/49 - 4/11/51) WMGM, New York, Mon; Wed from 11/8/50 (78 shows in series)
(4/18/51 - 10/10/51) first repeats of show; Wed on WMGM
(1/7/52 - 12/22/52) second repeats of WMGM shows) Sus, Mut, Mon; 8:30 pm

1 **Crime Fighters** (produced and directed by Wynn Wright)
(11/7/49 - 8/2/56) Sus, Mut (off and on various days and times including:)
11/7/49 - 11/28/49, Mon, 9:30 pm
4/24/50 - 9/22/52, various days and times
1/7/53 - 9/30/53, Wed, 8:30 pm
2/4/54 - 8/2/56, Thu, 8:30 pm

1 **Crime Files Of Flammond, The** (with Everett Clark) (1/7/53 - 2/27/57) Mut, Wed. 8 pm, Syn
1/7/53 - 4/1/53, General Mills
5/20/53 - 6/3/53, Lever Brothers
6/10/53 - 7/1/53, Multi
4/4/56 - 2/27/57, Sus, 8:30 pm; 8 pm as of 10/10/56

Crime Is My Pastime (7/15/45 - 9/2/45) Knox Co., Mut, Sun, 15m, 4:30 pm

Crime Letter From Dan Dodge (with Myron McCormick)
(10/31/52 - 2/27/53) Gillette - Toni, ABC, Fri, 8 pm

Crime On The Waterfront

Crime Reporter (Syn)

Crimes (see A Nation's Nightmare)

Crimes Of Carelessness (with Luis Van Rooten) sponsored by National Board Of Underwriters
(11/3/46 - 4/27/47) Mut, Sun, 3:30 pm

Criminal Case Histories Of Warden Lewis E. Lawes (see Twenty-thousand Years In Sing Sing)

Criminal Casebook (6/3/48 - 9/9/48) ABC, Thu, 8:30 pm

2 **Crisco's Radio Newspaper** (6/6/44, 6/7/44) NBC

Crisis (11/22/73 - 12/29/77) Syn, KVI

1 **Crisis In Iran - Where Do We Go From Here?** (12/3/79) NBC-TV

13 **Crisis In War Town** (15m) Syn

Criss Cross

Critic At Large (with Leon Pearson) (8/3/52 - 2/15/53) NBC, Sun, 15m 3:45 pm

Critic's Award Theater (see Drama Critic's Award)

11 **Critic's Toscanini, A** (1970, 1971) WRVR

Crook's Cruise (with Frank Graham)

Crooked Square (see Mysteries Of The Crooked Square)

1 **Croonaders, The** (1930) 15m, Syn

1 **Crosley Follies, The** (1935) WLW

1 **Cross My Heart** (1946) Air trailer

1 **Cross Section U. S. A.** (1/4/47 - 4/26/47) CBS, Sat, 3 pm

Crossfire (4/2/52 - 10/7/53) ABC, Wed, 9:30 pm

Crossroads (with Doris Kenyon; called Saturday's Child at first)
(1/28/40 - 4/14/40) NBC, Sun, 5:30 pm also with Ted Malone
(5/1/50 - 11/19/50) ABC, Mon, 10 pm; Sun, 9:30 pm as of 6/11/50

2 **Crossroads At Geneva** (7/17/55, 7/21/55) CBS

Crossroads Hall (5/28/38 - 7/15/38) CBS, Fri, 5 pm

Crossword Quiz (with Allen Prescott) (7/6/47 - 9/21/47) ABC, Sun, 5 pm; also on with David Gilmore in 1948

1 **Croupier, The** (9/21/49 - 11/16/49) ABC, Wed, 9:30 pm

1 **Crown Princess Martha** (1/2/41) Mut

Cruise Of The Poll Parrot, The

Crumit and Sanderson (see Frank Crumit)

6 **Crusade For A New World Order, The** (1944) Syn

1 **Crusade For Freedom** (Syn)

Crusaders For Freedom (with Henry Steele Commager)

Cuckoo Hour, The (with Raymond Knight) (1/1/30 - 3/9/36) Bl
1/1/30 - 1/27/31, Wed/Tue, 30m, 10:30 pm
2/7/31 - 4/30/32, Sat, 10 pm; 15m, 10:15 pm as of 12/5/32
5/6/35 - 3/9/36, Mon, 10 pm

1 **Cugat Rhythm Revue, The** (6/2/42) Bl

Culbertson Bridge Club (10/4/32 - 12/27/32) Wrigley, NBC, Tue, 4 pm

1 **Culligan Clambake - Nickel A Name, The** (KQV)

1 **Curley Bradley - The Singing Marshall** (7/2/50 - 7/1/51) Mut
7/2/50 - 7/30/50, Sun, 6 pm (summer replacement of Roy Rogers)
8/6/50 - 12/17/50, Sun, 8 pm

2 **Curley Fox and Texas Ruby** (MacGregor transcriptions)

1 **Curly Top** (1935) film sound track

1 **Curt Massey Show, The** (KNX)

14 **Curtain Time** (1938 - 1948) Mut, NBC

6 **Cy Coleman At The Piano** (Standard transcriptions)

2 **Cypress Serenade, The** (WJR)

1 **Czech News and Bulletins In English** (9/24/38) Czechoslovakia

29 **Czech News In English** (March - September, 1938) Czechoslovakia

D - 24 (8/2/54 - 1/10/55) Mut, Mon, 9:30 pm

1 **D-Day Plus 25** (6/6/69) CBS

1 **D-Day** (6/6/44) NBC

1 **D-Day Anniversary Ceremonies** (6/6/94) pool feed

1 **D-Day Anniversary Program** (6/6/48) BBC

2 **D-Day Official Invasion Circuit** (6/6/44) pool feed

1 **D-Day Plus Twenty Years** (6/5/79) CBS-TV

1 **D. P.'s Return Home, The** (Syn)

D. W. Griffith's Hollywood Sketch (1932 - 4/5/33) Bl,Wed, 15m, 10 pm

Dad and Dave (1937 - 1960) 12m

Dad and Junior (also Ford Rush and His Tinkle Toy Band) (with Ford Rush)
(9/16/38 - 12/14/38) Wheatena, Mut, 3t, 15m, 5:45 pm

1 **Daddy and Rollo** (2/3/31 - 9/10/31) CBS, 15m
(with Craig McDonnell; then Nick Dawson; also with Georgie Ward)
(11/16/42 - 2/25/43) Mut, 15m; local and regional show during 30s and 40s
11/16/42 - 12/11/42, 3t, 8:15 pm
12/12/42 - 2/25/43, 3t (Mon, Tue, Thu) 10:45 pm

1 **Dag Hammarskjold** (6/55)

1 **Daily Dilemma** (with Jack Barry)
(4/1/46 - 12/31/48) Mut, 5t, 2 pm; 2:30 pm as of 3/31/47; 3:30 pm as of 2/2/48

1 **Daily Pasqueman Radio Minstrels** (1931)

2 **Dairy Drama** (1940) Syn

1 **Daisy Discovers America** (5/26/50) with Ella Logan) NBC audition

1 **Dal Richards and His Orchestra**

2 **Dale Carnegie** (10/15/33 - 11/25/45)
10/15/33 - 3/24/35 (Little Known Facts About Well-Known People) Maltex NBC, Sun
9/15/35 - 12/8/35, Maltex Cereal, CBS, Sun
1937 - 38, Mut, Fri, 15m
1/11/38 - 7/9/38 (How To Win Friends and Influence People), Colgate, NBC, Tue, 15m, 10:45 pm; Sat, 15m, 8:30 pm as of 6/4/38
9/2/43 - 2/1/45 (Interesting People) Lee Hats, Mut, Thu, 15m, 10:15 pm
2/7/45 - 4/4/45, Lee Hats, Mut, Wed, 15m
4/15/45 - 6/10/45, Mut, Sun, 15m, 2:45 pm
8/26/45 - 11/25/45 (Little Known Facts About Well-Known People), Lee Hats. Mut, Sun, 15m, 2:45 pm

1 **Dale Evans & Larry Stewart** with Mahlon Merrick and His Orchestra, MacGregor transcription

Dale Evans (see News and Rhythm)

2 **Dale Evans** with Eddie Skrivanek and His Orchestra, MacGregor, BMI transcriptions

2 **Dale Jones and Company** (1944) CBS

Dalton Brothers, The (6/25/35 - 9/5/35) CBS, 2t, 15m

Dameron (9/26/72 - 9/18/73) KVI

1 **Dames** (1934) Air trailer

1 **Damn Yankees** (1958) film sound track

1 **Damon Runyon Memorial Concert** (12/11/48) ABC

1 **Damon Runyon Says** (CBS) Audition

52 **Damon Runyon Theater, The** (with John Brown)
(6/22/50 - 6/7/51) Syn (Mayfair) on many Mutual stations; dates are for WOR

2 **Dan Dunn, Secret Operative #48** (Syn - 1937) 78 15-minute episodes

Dan Harding's Wife (with Isabel Randolph)
(1/20/36 - 2/10/39) NBC, 5t, 15m; sponsored by Nabisco from 1/3/38 - 9/30/38

1 **Dan Quayle Center and Museum: Dedication Ceremonies, The** (10/16/93) C-SPAN

1 **Dan Rather** (4/6/90) C-SPAN

1 **Dan Seymour Tribute**

Dance Hour (3/26/39 - 6/11/39) CBS, Sun, 60m, 8 pm

2 **Dance Orchestra** (Lang-Worth transcriptions)

Dance Quiz (with Henry Morgan)
(7/1/40 - 8/26/40) Mut, Mon, 8:30 pm

Dance With Countess D'Orsay (with Audrey Marsh, Ben Selvin Orchestra)
(9/5/31 - 8/27/32) D'Orsay Perfumes, Bl, Sat, 8:30 pm

Dancepators Orchestra (7/9/38 - 8/5/39) CBS, Sat, 4:30 pm

Dancetime USA (Voice Of America; bands)

1 **Dancin' With Anson Weeks and His Orchestra** (Standard transcription)

2 **Dancing Co-Ed** (10/39) Air trailer

1 **Dancing On A Dime** (1940) Air trailer

Danger Fighters (with Tim Frawley)
(1/2/32 - 8/18/32) Feen-a-mint, Bl, Sat, 8 pm; Thu, 9:30 pm as of 6/30/32

Danger Is My Business (with Jay Simms)
(6/2/41 - 11/26/41) Mut, 2t (Mon &Wed), 15m; Wed, 9:15 pm as of 11/12/41, sponsored by Twenty Grand, Spud Cigarettes

Danger Point (Syn)

1 **Danger Signal** (3/25/49) NBC, Audition

Danger With Granger (7/23/56 - 2/25/57) Mut, Mon, 8:30 pm

26 **Danger, Dr. Danfield** (with Michael "Steve" Dunne)
(8/18/46 - 51) Knox. Co., ABC (Regional)
8/18/46 - 4/13/47, Sun, 3 pm; 2 pm as of 2/16/47
1947 - 51, Thu/Wed and Syn

39 **Dangerous Assignment** (with Brian Donlevy until 1953)
(7/9/49 - 54) Sus, NBC except where noted (on various days and times including:)
7/9/49 - 8/20/49, Sat, 9:30 pm
2/6/50 - 4/24/50, Mon, 10:30 pm
5/3/50 - 6/7/50; 7/19/50 - 9/27/50, General Mills, Wed
11/18/50 - 5/5/51, Sat, 8 pm
5/11/51 - 5/18/51, Fri, 9 pm
6/26/51 - 9/18/51, Tue, 8:30 pm
10/13/51 - 12/22/51, Sat, 10 pm
12/31/51 - 2/13/53, Mon, 10:30 pm; 25m, 10:35 pm as of 2/4/52
2/15/53 - 7/8/53, CBS, Wed, 15m, 10:35 pm
1953 - 54, Syn (with Lloyd Burell)

1 **Dangerous Nan McGrew** (1930) film sound track

Dangerous Paradise (with Elsie Hitz and Nick Dawson)
(10/25/33 - 12/31/35) Woodbury, Bl, 2t (Wed, Fri); 3t as of 9/17/34, 15m

13 **Dangerously Yours** (with Victor Jory)
(7/2/44 - 10/15/44) Vicks, CBS, Sun, 2 pm; then changed to Matinee Theater

1 **Daniel Boone, Indian Scout** (8/16/48) Audition, 15m

1 **Danny Cool and His Velvet Rhythm** (D&S transcription)

42 **Danny Kaye Show, The** (also called Pabst Blue Ribbon Town) (Danny Kaye was absent from 10/5/45 - 11/9/45)
(1/6/45 - 6/1/45; 9/28/45 - 5/31/46) Pabst, CBS, Sat, 8 pm; Fri, 10:30 pm as of 4/27/45; 10 pm as of 3/8/46
12/4/63, CBS-TV

1 **Danny Kaye Singing "The Fairy Piper"**

1 **Danny O'Neil Show, The** (sometimes called This Is New York)
(3/19/45 - 8/31/46) CBS; continued locally for many years; various days and times including:
3/19/45 - 6/22/45, 5t, 15m, 4:45 pm
6/25/45 - 8/17/45, 4t (Tue - Fri), 15m, 7:15 pm
8/29/45 - 9/27/45, 4t, 15m, 4:45 pm
12/31/45 - 3/29/46, 5t, 30m, 3:15 pm
4/29/46 - 12/17/54, 5t, 45m, 9:15 am
also 5/18/46 - 2/13/54, Sat, 15m, 9:15 am
also 7/6/46 - 8/31/46, Sat, 8:30 pm (summer replacement for Mayor Of The Town)

Danny Thomas Show, The
(12/19/42 - 6/25/48)
12/19/42 - 5/1/43, Sus, ABC, Sat, 10 pm
1/2/48 - 6/25/48, General Foods, CBS, Fri, 25m, 8:30 pm

Danton Walker (5/16/48 - 7/25/48) Mut, Sun, 15m, 8:45 pm

26 **Daredevils Of Hollywood, The** (Syn with Frank Nelson and Earle Ross)
(4/25/38 - 7/22/38) 2t (Mon & Fri)

Dark Corridor (NBC)

Dark Destiny (8/26/42 - 3/11/43) Mut
8/26/42 - 10/7/42, Wed, 9:30 pm
10/17/42 - 11/28/45, Sat, 8 pm
12/3/42 - 3/11/43, Thu, 8:30 pm

1 **Dark Fantasy** (with Keith Painton)
(11/14/41 - 6/19/42) broadcast locally, WKY - Oklahoma city until 1/2/42; Sus, NBC, Fri; 31 episodes broadcast

4 **Dark Venture** (2/19/46 - 2/10/47) ABC, sponsored occasionally by Wildroot
2/19/46 - 6/11/46, Tue, 8:30 pm
6/15/46 - 9/14/46, Sat, 8 pm
9/29/46 - 10/13/46, Sun, 7:30 pm
10/21/46 - 2/10/47, Mon, 9 pm

2 **Darrell Calker and His Swing-Phonics** (D&S transcriptions)

2 **Darrow Of The Diamond X**
(9/29/50, 10/20/50) NBC

Darts For Dough (8/6/44 - 12/25/47) Dr. Pepper, ABC, Sun; Thu from 10/2/47 - 10/25/47 (not in NY)

1 **Date In Hollywood** (Syn)

1 **Date Night** (2/8/47) Mut

Date With Disaster (1951 - 1952)

Date With Duchin, A (see Eddie Duchin)

6 **Date With Judy, A** (6/24/41 - 4/20/50)
6/24/41 - 9/16/41, Pepsodent, NBC, Tue, 10 pm (summer replacement for Bob Hope; with Ann Gillis)
6/23/42 - 9/15/42, Pepsodent, NBC, Tue, 10 pm (summer replacement for Bob Hope; with Debbie Ellis)
6/30/43 - 9/22/43, Sal Hepatica, NBC, Wed, 9 pm (summer replacement for Eddie Cantor; with Louise Erickson)
1/18/44 - 6/22/48; 9/28/48 - 1/4/49 (with Louise Erickson), Tums, NBC, Tue, 8:30 pm
11/3/49 - 2/2/50, Revere Cameras, ABC, Thu, 8:30 pm;
11/3/49, 4/20/50, Ford, ABC, Thu, 8:30 pm

17 **Date With Music, A** (with Sammy Liver, Phil Brito) (Syn)
1945, 1946, 15m

9 **Date With The Duke, A** (with Duke Ellington)
(3/31/45 - 1/19/46) ABC - AFRS, Sat, 30m - 60m, 5 pm; full 60m version called Saturday Date With The Duke;
(4/13/46 - 9/21/46) ABC, Sat, 60m/30m, 4 pm

8 **Date With The Navy, A** (Syn)

Dateline (with Robert Trout)
(10/15/43 - 3/17/44) Philco, CBS, Fri 15m. 7:15 pm
(6/12/44 - 9/25/44) Armour, CBS, 15m, Mon (not in NY)

1 **Dateline 1954** (1/27/54)

Dateline Defense (11/1/55 - 6/19/56) Mut, Tue, 15m, 9:15 pm

Dateline For Danger

Dateline, Headline, Byline (ABC)

1 **Dateline: New Jersey** (10/26/79) WNET-TV

Daughters Of Uncle Sam, The (with B. A. Rolfe and All Girl Band, Mary Small) (2/22/42 - 4/26/42) Bl, Sun

2 **Dave Brubeck Quartet** (1954) NBC

1 **Dave Brubeck With The Paul Desmond Quartet** (1954) NBC

Dave Elman (see Contact Dave Elman, Hobby Lobby)

1 **Dave Elman's Auction Gallery** (9/14/45) Mut

3 **Dave Garroway** (1951)

1 **Dave Garroway Interview** (5/12/76)

6 **Dave Garroway Show, The** (Dial Dave Garroway) (7/1/48, 11/21/49 - 6/17/55)
NBC 11/21/49 - 6/23/50, Sus, 5t, 15m
also 11/21/49 - 12/18/50, Mon, 10:30 pm
9/4/50 - 10/30/53, Armour, 5t, 15m
4/18/54 - 6/17/55 (Sunday; then Friday With Dave Garroway) Multi Sun, 90m - 2 hours; Fri as of 10/8/54

Dave Willock and Cliff Arquette Show (NBC)

Davey Tree Hour (with Muriel Wilson)
(1929 - 4/17/32) Davey Tree Surgery, NBC, Sun; 60m from 1931 - 32

1 **David Adams, Son Of The Sea** (with Franklin Adams) (1938) Syn, possible audition

David Amity (with Joseph Bell, Mary Patton) (12/25/50 - 9/28/51) ABC, 5t, 15m

1 **David Ben Gurion** (3/6/48) Mut

1 **David Brinkley At The National Archives** (1/76)

1 **David Copperfield** (1935) film sound track

2 **David Frost Show, The** (1/71, 7/7/71) Syn

David Gilmore, The Friendly Philosopher (1947)

David Harding (see Counterspy)

17 **David Harum** (1/27/36 - 1/5/51) Bab-O, 5t, 15m
1/27/36 - 1/10/47, NBC, 11 am; 11:45 am as of 9/30/40; occasionally on Mut
also 2/2/42 - 5/14/43, CBS, 3 pm
1/13/47 - 1/6/50, CBS
1/9/50 - 1/5/51, NBC

David Lawrence (4/1/51 - 12/30/51) ABC, Sun, 15m, 3:30 pm

David Rose Show, The
(4/11/40 - 9/24/50) (also see California Melodies)
4/11/40 - 8/1/40 (with Maxine Gray and Art Tatum), Mut, Thu, 8:30 pm; 9 pm as of 4/11/40
5/7/41 - 6/11/41, Mut, Wed, 9:30 pm
8/20/41- 2/4/42, Mut, Wed, 9:30 pm
6/26/47 - 9/18/47, Pabst, NBC, Thu, 10:30 pm (summer replacement for Eddie Cantor)
8/27/50 - 9/24/50, Tide, CBS, Sun (summer replacement for Red Skelton)

David Street Show, The (1947) Fri

1 **Davie Burns Show, The** (11/15/48) Mut

Dawn's Early Light

1 **Day At La Guardia Field, A** (6/19/47) WOR

1 **Day At The Beach, A** (8/2/47) WOR

1 **Day At The Races, A** (1937) Air trailer

1 **Day Churchill Died, The** (1/24/65) CBS

58 **Day In The Life Of Dennis Day, A**
(4/18/46, 10/3/46 - 6/23/47; 8/27/47 - 6/30/51) Colgate, NBC, CBS, Syn
10/3/46 - 6/25/47; 8/27/47 - 6/30/48, Thu, 7:30 pm; Wed, 8 pm as of 12/25/46

1 **Day In The Life Of The White House, A** (2/28/90) NBC-TV

1 **Day Of Crisis** (11/21/79) CBS-TV

Day Of Reckoning (2/27/43 - 4/17/43) NBC, Sat, 7 pm

1 **Day They Landed: July 20, 1969, The** (7/20/79) NBC-TV

1 **Day With President Carter, A** (4/14/77) NBC-TV

2 **Deacon Brown and His Peacemakers** (1933) 5t, 15m, Syn

1 **Dead End** (1937) Air trailer

1 **Dead Stop** (12/23/54) CBS

Deadline (1/6/54 -1/27/54) Mut, Wed, 8:30 pm

Deadline Dramas (with Ireene Wicker) (1/5/41 - 7/20/41) Bl, Sun, 10:30 pm

1 **Deadline For Danger** (Syn)

Deadline For Murder (Syn)

2 **Deadline Mystery** (with Steve Dunne) (4/20/47 - 8/31/47, 1952) Knox Co., ABC, Sun, 2 pm

2 **Dean Acheson** (11/21/41, 6/29/50) Bl/ABC

Dean Dickerson (1943 - 1944) CBS Pacific, sponsored by Barbasol

1 **Dean Hudson and His Orchestra** (8/1/58) CBS

1 **Dean Martin and Jerry Lewis Christmas Seal Show** (1952) Syn

1 **Dean Martin Celebrity Roast, The** (2/7/78) NBC-TV

1 **Dean Martin Comedy Hour, The** (2/22/74) NBC-TV

Dean Martin Show (15m)

2 **Dean Of Commentators, The** (6/16/65) NBC

2 **Dean Ross Piano Course** (Syn)

Dear Adolf (written by Stephen Vincent Benet) (6/21/42 - 8/2/42) Council For Democracy, NBC, Sun, 5 pm

Dear Audience (see Dear Columbia)

Dear Columbia (7/10/35 - 6/20/38) CBS, various mornings

Dear John (see Irene Rich)

1 **Dear Leo** (5/8/48) Mut

2 **Dear Listener** (12/8/48) CBS

Dear Margie, It's Murder (with Mason Adams) (1/11/53 - 10/4/53) Mut, Sun, 25m, 4:30 pm

Dear Mom (with John Walsh) (2/9/41 - 12/7/41) Wrigley, CBS, Sun, 20m, 6:55 pm

2 **Dear Mr. President** (5/13/49, 6/5/83) WTOP, NBC-TV

Dear Teacher (11/4/37 - 1/13/38) CBS, Thu, 5:30 pm
1/19/38 - 3/2/38, CBS, Wed, 15m, 6 pm

2 **Dearest Mother** (with Judith March) (Syn - ZIV)
(1940 - 41) 143 15-minute episodes

1 **Death Of A King** (2/15/52) BBC/ABC

1 **Death Of Bing Crosby, The** (10/14/77) CBS

1 **Death Of Chairman Mao, The** (9/7/76) NBC-TV

1 **Death Of Flight #007, The** (9/1/83) CBS-TV

1 **Death Of President Roosevelt, The** (4/12/45) Mut

1 **Death Of The Shah, The** (7/27/80) NBC-TV

1 **Death On Wheels** (1/18/43) WOR

1 **Death Penalty and Caryl Chessman, The** (4/28/60) CBS

1 **Death Takes A Holiday** (2/25/34) Air trailer

3 **Death Valley Days** (9/30/30 - 6/21/45) Twenty Mule Team Borax
9/30/30 - 8/11/31, NBC, Tue, 9:30 pm
8/17/31 - 8/8/32, Bl, Mon, 8/8:30 pm
10/6/32 - 8/27/36, Bl, Thu, 9 pm
9/4/36 - 6/3/38, Bl, Fri, 8:30 pm
6/10/38 - 9/22/39, NBC, Fri, 9:30 pm
10/7/39 - 4/27/40, NBC, Sat, 9:30 pm
5/3/40 - 6/27/41, NBC, Fri, 8:30 pm
7/3/41 - 8/3/44, CBS, Thu, 8/8:30 pm
8/10/44 - 6/21/45 (Death Valley Sheriff CBS, Thu, 8:30 pm; from 1945 - 51 called The Sheriff

3 **December Bride** (Hal March and Spring Byington)
(6/8/52 - 5/27/53) Sus, CBS
6/8/52 - 9/7/52, Sus, Sun, 7 pm (summer replacement for Jack Benny)
10/12/52 - 2/15/53, Sun, 6 pm
2/25/53 - 5/27/53, Wed, 10 pm

Decision (1/11/54 - 4/19/54) ABC, Mon, 9:30 pm

1 **Decision For Tommy, A** (Syn)

110 **Decision Now!** (American Legion) (1947 - 49) Syn

1 **Declaration Of War Against Germany and Italy** (12/11/41) Mut

1 **Declaration Of War Against Japan By The Russians** (8/8/45) CBS

1 **Dedication Ceremonies Of The "New" WFBR** (6/19/39) WFBR

1 **Dedication Of The Fifty Kilowatt Transmitter** (3/4/35) WOR

1 **Dedication Of The Johnson Library** (5/22/71)

1 **Dedication Of The World Freedom Hall** (10/24/50) ABC

1 **Dedication Of W71NY** (11/30/41) WOR

1 **Dedication Program Of The Network Of The Americas** (5/19/42) CBS

Deeds Without Words (15m)

13 **Deems Taylor At Napoleon's Retreat** (Syn)

1 **Deems Taylor Concert** (1948 - 55) Sus, Mut
1948 - 49, Sun
1953 - 55, 3t, 30m

Deep River Boys (1/7/38 - 6/12/42) 15m; on various days and times, many overlapping, including:
1/7/38 - 3/14/38, CBS, Fri, 3:45 pm
10/6/38 - 2/9/39, CBS, 4t (Mon - Thu), 8:15 am
12/10/38 - 2/26/39, CBS, Sat, 9:45 am
2/13/39 - 6/5/39, CBS, Mon, 8:30 am
7/23139 - 10/1/39, CBS, Sun, 2:30 pm
8/12/39 - 9/23/39, CBS, Sat, 12 noon
8/22/39 - 10/24/39, CBS, Tue, 4 pm
1/3/40 - 1/17/40, CBS, Wed, 2:15 pm
1/20/40 - 3/27/41, NBC, 2t, 15m
8/6/40 - 1/14/41 , Bl, Tue, 15m, 12:15 pm
7/27/40 - 1/18/41, Bl, Sat, 15m, 11 am

Deep River Boys (continued)
1/19/41 - 2/21/43, NBC, Sun, 15m, 9:15 am
3/22/41 - 10/11/41, NBC, Sat, 8:45 am; 9 am as of 9/6/41
12/28/41 - 6/12/42, NBC, 5t, 15m, 12:30 pm

11 **Deerslayer, The** (1932) Syn

Defense and Your Dollar
(12/6/41 - 1/10/42) NBC, Sat, 15m, 3 pm

Defense Attorney (with Mercedes McCambridge)
(8/31/51 - 12/30/52) Clorets; also with Kix
(2/21/52 - 6/26/52) and Goodyear
(4/24/52 - 5/15/52) ABC
10/11/51 - 10/30/52, Thu, 8 pm
11/18/52 - 12/30/52, Tue, 8 pm; 8:30 pm as of 12/27/51

Defense For America (National Association Of Manufacturers; with Milo Boulton)
(3/1/41 - 11/1/41) NBC, Sat, 7 pm

4 **Defense In Action** (1940, 1941) Mut

5 **Defense Of The United States (CBS Reports), The** (6/14 - 18/81) CBS-TV

Defense Rests, The

2 **Defense Savings Bonds** (Syn)

DeForest Auditions (9/16/28 - 6/16/29) DeForest Radio, CBS, Sun

Del Casino (9/9/37 - 9/8/38) CBS, Thu, 6 pm

Del Courtney (1/21/39 - 5/13/39) Bl, Sat, 2:30 pm

1 **Del Courtney and His Orchestra** (10/31/38) NBC

2 **Del Courtney Orchestra** (4/1/41) Lang-Worth Syn

Del Sharbutt (The Lighter Side)

Delayed Action

Deliberate Reflections (with Hendrik Willem van Loon)
(2/19/39 - 4/23/39) NBC, Sun, 15m, 4:15 pm

2 **Delta Rhythm Boys, The** (World transcriptions)

1 **Democracy Bank, The** (11/49) Syn

13 **Democracy In Action** (5/14/39 - 6/9/40) Sus, CBS, Sun, 2 pm

Democracy In America (Syn)

1 **Democratic (Party) Presidential Debate** (2/18/88) PBS

5 **Democratic Convention Coverage** (7/12 - 14/48) Mut

2 **Democratic Debate, The** (3/28/84, 6/3/84) CBS-TV, NBC-TV

1 **Democratic National Committee** (10/24/44)

2 **Democratic National Committee Program** (11/6/44) CBS

2 **Democratic National Convention** (7/17/40, 1960) Mut

1 **Democratic Paid Political Announcement** (11/70)

1 **Democratic Paid Political Program** (11/3/52) NBC

1 **Democratic Party National Convention** (8/28/68)

1 **Democratic Party Response To The Address Of Newt Gingrich** (4/7/95) pool feed

1 **Democratic Presidential Candidate Debate: Nuclear Arms Control** (10/13/83) Special network

3 **Democratic Presidential Debate** (1/18/84, 3/11/84, 2/13/88) WNET-TV, CNN

1 **Democratic Rally At The New York Hippodrome** (10/28/37) WOR

1 **Democratic Reaction To President Reagan's Address To The Nation** (7/27/81) ABC-TV

1 **Democratic Rebuttal To President Reagan's Address To The Nation** (8/10/82) CBS-TV

1 **Democratic Response To President Reagan** (3/30/83) CBS-TV

1 **Democratic Response To President Reagan's Economic Program, A** (2/27/81) PBS-TV

1 **Democrats Respond, Part I, The** (5/70) CBS

Dennis Day (see A Day In The Life Of Dennis Day)

Dennis Day Show, The (see A Day In The Life Of Dennis Day)

2 **Dennis Day With Orchestra** (Standard transcriptions)

1 **Dennis Day With Orchestra Under The Direction Of Claude Sweeten** (Standard transcription)

Dennis The Menace (Syn)

2 **Denny Vaughn and His Orchestra** (8/11/58, 5/23/65) CBS

2 **Dental Clinic Of The Air, The** (1929, 1931) Syn

1 **Department Store and Radio Advertising, The** (1951) Associated transcription)

1 **Departure Of King George and Queen Elizabeth** (5/6/39) BBC

1 **Departure Of The Royal Party For The United States** (6/7/39) CBS

2 **Description Of Hiroshima** (9/3/45, 8/6/47) Mut

1 **Description Of President Roosevelt's Funeral Services** (8/14/45)

1 **Description Of President Truman's Meeting With King George** (8/2/45) BBC

2 **Description Of Surrender Ceremonies At Compiegne** (6/21/40, 6/22/40) CBS

1 **Description Of The Burial Of President Roosevelt** (4/15/45) Mut

1 **Description Of The Collyer Home, A** (3/25/47) WOR

1 **Description Of The Commissioning Of The U. S. S. North Carolina** (4/9/41) WOR

1 **Description Of The San Francisco Airplane Crash** (11/29/38) Mut

1 **Description Of The Ventilation Equipment At Lincoln Tunnel** (1/28/38) WOR

1 **Description Of The World's Largest Airway Beacon, A** (11/28/39) WOR

Desert Caravan (see Caravan)

1 **Desert Fury** (1947) Air trailer

Desert Kid, The (with The Ranch Boys and Burton Eisner)
(3/25/35 - 9/9/35) NBC, 3t, 15m, 6:45 pm; on previously in the Midwest

1 **Desert Song** (1929) Synchro-discs

1 **Desi Arnaz and His Orchestra** (12/6/47) CBS

1 **Desi Arnaz Tropical Trip**
(1/21/51 - 10/6/51) Sus, CBS
1/21/51 - 6/3/51, Sun, 3:30 pm
6/23/51 - 8/25/51, Sat, 7 pm
9/1/51 - 10/6/51, Sat, 7:30 pm (summer replacement for Vaughn Monroe)

3 **Design For Dancing** (7/8/38 - 12/16/38) CBS, Fri, 9 pm
(1950 - 1951) NBC, WMAQ origination

Design For Happiness (with Chicago Women's Symphony)
(9/29/40 - 3/23/41) Libby-Owen, CBS, Sun, 5 pm; also see Buddy Clark

5 **Design For Listening** (with Joseph Gallichio Orchestra)
(6/19/49 - 9/18/49) NBC, Sun, 60m, 2:30 pm
(also 10/12/35 - 3/29/36 with Olga Vernon) Bl, Sun, 4:30 pm; developed into Senator Fishface
(1950, 1953) NBC, WMAQ origination

1 **Design For Living** (12/24/33) Air trailer

Design For Melody (with Willie Morris, Raoul Nadear, Alfred Wallenstein conducting)
(6/4/39 - 10/1/39) Mut, Sun, 7 pm

37 **Destination Freedom** (1948 - 11/19/51) (WMAQ, Chicago)

1 **Destination Space** (1947 - 49) ABC, NBC various days

15 **Destination Tomorrow**
(12/16/44 - 3/24/45) CBS

1 **Destination: Blood Center** (1953) Syn

30 **Destiny Trails** (1945 - 1947) NBC Syn

Detect and Collect (6/13/45 - 9/28/46)
6/13/45 - 9/5/45 (with Lew Lehr), Lorillard, CBS, Wed, 9:30 pm
10/4/45 - 9/28/46, Goodrich, ABC, Thu, 9:30 pm; Sat, 8:30 pm as of 8/17/46

2 **Detect-A-Tune** (11/19/45 - 2/25/46) Mut, Mon, 10:30 pm

Detective Drama (4/13/55 - 9/28/55) Mut, Wed, 15m, 8 pm

Detective Stories (1/2/38 - 3/20/38) CBS, Sun, 8 pm

Detective Story Hour (see The Shadow)

Detectives Black and Blue (see The Adventures Of Detectives Black and Blue)

Detectives Dalt and Zumba (1938)

Detour (6/21/50 - 11/8/50) ABC, Wed, 9 pm (first episodes until 9/13/50 from The Clock)

Detroit Musicale (12/13/41 - 9/19/42) CBS, Sat, 3:30 pm
(4/3/43 - 11/12/44) CBS, Sat

Detroit Symphony Orchestra
(1/4/31 - 3/22/49) on various days and times including:
1/4/31 - 6/28/31, CBS, Sun
10/21/44 - 4/7/45, Reichold Chemical, Mut, Sat, 8:30 pm; 60m as of 1/6/44
7/21/45 - 9/22/45, Reichold Chemical, Mut, Sat
1/19/47 - 6/1/47, Reichold Chemical, ABC, Sun, 60m
11/2/47 - 1/25/48, Musical Digest, ABC, Sun, 60m
2/1/48 - 4/18/48, Sus, ABC, Sun, 60m
11/9/48 - 3/22/49, Sus, ABC, Tue, 45m

Devil's Holiday

2 **Devil and Mr. O, The** (see Lights Out)

Devil Bird, The (8/10/32 - 6/9/33) Horlicks, CBS, 15m
8/10/32 - 9/21/32, Wed
2/6/33 - 6/9/33, 5t

1 **Devil Who Walks Like A Man, The** (6/7/47) Mut

Devil's Scrapbook

Devil's, Drugs and Doctors
(1/25/31 - 1/17/32) Kodak, CBS, Sun, 15m

1 **Dewey Train** (10/8/48) Mut

1 **Dexter Randolph** (10/1/36) WJR, audition

1 **Di Maggio Farewell** (12/11/51) CBS

Dial Dave Garroway (see Dave Garroway)

1 **Dial David Valentine** (Syn)

2 **Dial M For Music** (1967, 1968) CBS-TV

Diamond Dramas (From Freeman Lang) (Syn; 1933)

1 **Diamond Horseshoe, The** (1945) film sound track

Diane and Her Life Saver (with Alfred Drake and Lucille Wall; also with Rhoda Amold and John Griggs)
(1/7/35 - 4/3/35) Life Savers, CBS, 2t (Mon & Wed) 15m

8 **Diary Of Fate, The** (1948) Mon/Tue, Syn

1 **Diary, The** (Syn)

5 **Dick and Jeannie** (Syn)

6 **Dick Aurandt Show, The** (1950 - 1953) CBS Pacific net

1 **Dick Brown, The Smoothest In Music**
(7/9/44 - 7/1/45) Formfit Company, Mut, Sun, 15m, 6:45 pm

1 **Dick Carlson** (Mut)

1 **Dick Carlton and His Orchestra**

3 **Dick Cavett Show, The**
(3/15/78, 6/79, 1/28/81) PBS-TV

20 **Dick Cole** (with Leon Janney) (Syn)
(1942, 1946) Blue Bolt and Foremost Comics

Dick Daring's Adventures (with Merrill Fugit)
(3/12/33 - 4/30/33) Bl, Sun, 15m, 4 pm
(3/13/33 - 6/9/33) Bl, 5t, 15m, 5:15 pm
5t, 15m, 10 am

1 **Dick Gasparre and His Orchestra**
(12/30/38) NBC

2 **Dick Gates and His Orchestra**
(11/9/36, 12/21/36) WCNW

2 **Dick Gates and His Polish Orchestra**
(11/9/36, 12/21/36) WCNW

2 **Dick Haymes** (World transcriptions)

6 **Dick Haymes Show, The**
(7/18/43 - 6/29/51)
7/18/43 - 10/10/43, Bourjois, ABC, Sun, 6 pm
10/14/43 - 3/2/44, Bourjois, CBS, Thu, 10:30 pm
6/27/44 - 10/9/45 (see Everything For The Boys until 6/25/45), Autolite, NBC, Tue, 7:30 pm
10/13/45 - 6/1/46, Autolite, CBS, Sat, 8 pm
6/6/46 - 6/5/47; 9/11/47 - 7/1/48, Autolite, CBS, Thu, 9 pm
8/29/49 - 3/24/50, (see Club Fifteen); also 10/9/49 - 10/1/50, (see Carnation Contented Hour)
4/16/51 - 6/29/51, Procter & Gamble, ABC, 5t, 5m

3 **Dick Jurgen's Orchestra** (Standard transcriptions)

Dick Jurgens (Summer Spotlight Review; with Margaret Whiting)
(7/2/48 - 9/24/48) Coca-Cola, CBS, Fri, 10:30 pm

10 **Dick Jurgens and His Orchestra** (7/9/49) Associated transcriptions

2 **Dick Jurgens Orchestra** (6/21/42, 7/27/42) Thesaurus transcriptions

1 **Dick Kuhn and His Orchestra** (5/4/49) Mut

Dick Lawrence Review (60m)

14 **Dick Leibert** (11/2/34 - 5/28/43) 15m; on various days and times including:
11/2/34 - 3/1/35, Bl, Ludens, Fri, 7:15 pm
8/26/35 - 1/27/36 (Dinner Concert) Bl, various days, 7 pm
9/27/38 - 3/25/41, Bl, Tue, 8:30 am; 2t as of 1/7/41
10/1/38 - 10/11/41, Bl, Sat; NBC as of 5/24/41
5/12/42 - 8/14/42; 10/1/42 - 5/28/43, NBC, 2t (Thu, Fri) 9:45 am
Thesaurus transcriptions

Dick Powell (see Campana Serenade)

1 **Dick Powell Program, The** (3/6/43) NBC

Dick Robertson Show, The
(2/9/40 - 4/26/40) Mut, Fri, 15m, 10:30 pm

Dick Stabile Orchestra (4/1/40 - 5/20/40) Bl, Mon, 15m, 7 pm

Dick Steele, Boy Reporter (with Merrill Fugit)
(10/1/34 - 11/30/34) Educator Biscuit, NBC, 5t, 15m

35 **Dick Tracy** (2/4/35 - 7/16/48)
2/4/35 - 7/11/35, Sterling Products,CBS, 4t, 15m, 5:45 pm
9/30/35 - 37, Sus, Mut, 5t, 15m, 5 pm
1/3/38 - 6/3/38; 9/26/38 - 4/28/39, Quaker, NBC; 5t, 15m, 5 pm
4/29/39 - 7/29/39, Quaker, NBC, Sat, 30m, 7 pm; 8 pm as of 6/3/39
8/7/39 - 8/28/39, Quaker, NBC, Mon, 30m, 8 pm
9/9/39 - 9/30/39, Quaker, NBC, Sat, 30m, 7 pm
9/13/43 - 10/1/43, Sweets Company, ABC, 3t, 15m, 5:15 pm
10/4/43 - 10/25/46, Sweets Company, ABC, 5t, 15m, 5:15 pm
also 9/13/45 - 6/1/46, Sweets Company, ABC, Sat, 30m;
also 10/28/46 - 7/16/48, ABC, 5t, 15m, 4:45 pm; 5 pm as of 11/17/47

13 **Dick Wickman and His Orchestra**
(7/27/69 - 7/19/70) CBS

Dick Workman (9/3/41 - 10/1/41) CBS, Wed, 15m, 9:30 am

2 **Dickies Hometowners** (1953) Syn

Dictators, The (1/4/37 - 5/30/38) CBS, Mon 4 pm
(6/6/38 - 6/21/38) CBS, Mon & Thu, 2 pm

15 **Did Justice Triumph?** (1/27/47 - 11/3/47) Mut, Wed, 10 pm; Mon as of 6/9/47

1 **Diet** (4/6/50) Syn

1 **Different Story, A** (Syn)

Dime A Month Club (1938)

1 **Dimension** (1963) CBS

Dimension Of Imagination

50 **Dimension X** (4/8/50 - 9/29/51) NBC, sponsored by General Mills from 7/7/50 - 9/29/50
4/8/50 - 7/1/50, Sat, 8 pm
7/7/50 - 9/29/50, Fri, 9 pm
10/29/50 - 11/26/50, Sun
12/24/50 - 1/7/51, Sun
6/3/51 - 6/24/51, Sun, 6:30 pm
7/12/51 - 8/30/51, Thu
9/8/51 - 9/29/51, Sat, 8 pm

Dimension Y (AFRS Japan) (1950s)

1 **Dinah Shore Chevy Show, The** (4/2/60) NBC-TV

1 **Dinah Shore Christmas Card** (12/44) AFRS

Dinah Shore Program, The (see The Dinah Shore Show)

132 **Dinah Shore Show, The** (8/6/39 - 7/1/55)
8/6/39 - 1/14/40 (with Paul La Valle Orchestra as of 10/15/39), Bl, Sun
6/14/40 - 9/27/40 (with Irving Miller Orchestra) Bl, Fri, 15m, 10:15 pm
11/2/41 - 4/24/42, Bristol Myers, Bl, Sun, 15m, 9:45 pm (Songs By Dinah Shore)
5/1/42 - 4/23/43, Bristol Myers, ABC, Fri,

Dinah Shore Show, The (continued)
15m (In Person, Dinah Shore)
9/30/43 - 6/29/44 (CBS, 9:30 pm);
10/5/44 - 5/31/45 (NBC, 8:30 pm);
9/6/45 - 5/30/46 (CBS), Birdseye, Thu, 30m, 8:30 pm (Birdseye Open House through 1946) 12/20/45 was 60m program combined with Burns and Allen
9/18/46 - 6/11/47, Ford, NBC, Wed, 9:30 pm (Ford Show)
2/13/48 - 4/16/48, Philip Morris, CBS, Fri, 10 pm
4/20/48 - 6/29/48, Pabst, NBC, Tue, 8 pm
4/20/50 - 6/29/50; 8/28/50 - 6/30/51; 8/27/51- 6/27/52; 8/25/52 -12/16/5 (see Jack Smith)
3/23/53 - 6/29/53; 10/6/53 - 7/9/54, Chevrolet, NBC, 2t (Tue & Fri), 15m, 8 pm; 8:15 pm as of 10/6/53
10/6/54 - 7/1/55, Chevrolet, NBC, 2t, 15m, 7:30 pm (TV simulcast)

Dining With George Rector
(2/17/37 - 2/11/38) Phillips Packing, CBS, 3t, 15m

1 **Dinner At Howard K. Smith's** (1/8/70) ABC-TV

Dinner Date (1949 - 10/27/55) Sus, Mut, 5t, 15m (often not in New York)

1 **Dinner For Edward R. Murrow** (12/2/41) CBS

1 **Dinner In Honor Of General Eisenhower** (6/19/45) Mut

1 **Dinner Rhythms** (10/11/39) WFBR

1 **Dinning Sisters, Acc.: George Barnes Guitar and Qtte., The** (Standard transcription)

2 **Dinning Sisters, The** (6/24/40 - 9/12/40) Bl, 4t (Mon - Thu), 15m, 6 pm, Syn, Standard transcription

1 **Disability Freeze** (1954) Syn

1 **Disabled American Veterans** (Syn)

1 **Disabled Veterans Make Good** (1948) Syn

Disaster (5/22/55 - 9/4/55; 6/3/56 - 8/26/56) ABC, Sun, 15m, 5:05 pm

4 **Disc Derby, The** (1/26/55 - 6/3/55) CBS

2 **Disciples Of Christ, Brotherhood Dinner** (Syn)

2 **Discoparade** (Syn)

1 **Discoverer Satellite Launching** (4/13/59)

Discoveries of '41 (1/3/41 - 3/28/41) Bl, Fri, 7:30 pm

1 **Discussion At The Jet Propulsion Labs** (7/31/69)

1 **Discussion Between H. G. Wells and Orson Welles, A** (11/7/40) KTSA

1 **Displaced** (Syn)

Distinctive Furniture Dramas (15 minute syn. show from the 1930s)

1 **District Roundtable** (12/17/50) WWDC

2 **Dithering With Davey** (1940) Syn

Diversion Without Exertion (see Norman Cloutier)

1 **Divine Lady** (Synchro-discs)

Dixie Circus (1929 - 30) Bl, Fri, 7:30 pm
(1930 - 4/11/31 (Dixie Spiritual Singers) CBS, Sat, 8 pm
(5/14/34 - 9/10/34) (with "Uncle" Dixie Bob Sherwood)

Dixie Cup, (CBS) Mon

Dixie Four, The

1 **Dixie Handicap, The** (5/7/41) WFBR

1 **Dixie Memories** (1934) Syn

2 **Dixieland Club** (4/23/52, 4/24/52) AFRS, 15m

Dixieland Jambake (5/6/50 - 9/8/51) ABC, Sat, 8 pm; 10:30 pm as of 9/23/50

1 **Dixielanders, The** (Associated transcription)

13 **Dizzy Dean Show, The** (7/3/48 - 9/18/48) Johnson Wax, NBC, Sat, 15m

1 **Dizzy Gillespie and His Group** (NBC)

1 **Dizzy Gillespie and His Orchestra** (1954) NBC

1 **Django Reinhardt and The Quintet Of The Hot Club Of France** (1948) Belgium

1 **Do It On Radio** (1/70)

Do It Yourself Club (1/24/49 - 9/4/49) 15m
1/24/49 - 4/1/49, NBC, 5t
6/12/49 - 9/4/49, Mut, Sun

1 **Do It Yourself Show** (5/21/55) KNX

Do Re Mi Program, The (with Ann Balthy and Mabel & Evelyn Ross)
(5/21/33 - 10/1/33) CBS, Sun, 2:30 pm
(7/23/34 - 8/27/34) CBS, Mon, 11:30 am
(7/17/36 - 9/11/36) CBS, Fri, 15m, 1:45 pm

1 **Do W.P.A. Workers Reject Jobs In Private Industry?** (6/2/39) Mut

2 **Do You Know** (1956) CBS

1 **Do You Need Advice?** (1/1/45) Mut

Do You Remember? (6/18/35 - 11/25/37) CBS, various days
(11/21/38 - 41), NBC, 5t, 15m

Do You Want To Be An Actor? (with Haven MacQuarrie)
(1/3/37 - 5/2/37) Chase and Sanborn, NBC, Sun, 8 pm; show replaced by Charlie McCarthy Show
(12/5/37 - 2/20/38) NBC, Sun, 10:30 pm also on in 1946

Do You Want To Write?
(2/17/37 - 6/9/37) Bl, Wed, 15m, 3 pm

Doc Barclay's Daughters (with Bennett Kilpack)
(1/16/39 - 1/19/40) Personal Finance, CBS, 5t, 15m

Doc Hopkins and His Country Boys (1945) Syn, 15m

Doc Pearson's Drug Store (with The Landt Trio and White)
(10/5/36 - 12/23/36) Omega Oil, NBC, 2t (Mon & Wed) 15m, 7:45 pm

Doc Savage (written by Lester Dent)
(2/34 - 9/34) Cystex, Don Lee, 15m, 9 pm
(10/34 - 35) same episodes syndicated (Doc Savage, Man Of Bronze) (written by Edward Gruskin with Bernard Lenrow, Earl George)
(1/6/43 - 6/9/43) WMCA, New York, Wed, 30m; 3 episodes rerun
6/17/43 - 7/1/43, Thu
(NPR) (1985) (see The Adventures Of Doc Savage)

Doc Schneider's Yodeling Cowboys
(1/6/36 - 7/16/36) Bl, Mon, 15m; Thu as of 4/23/36

2 **Doc Sellers' True Stories** (1938) Syn

Doc, Duke and The Colonel (with Jess Pugh) (1945) NBC

2 **Docking Of The Queen Mary** (10/18/38) WOR

Doctor Alfred C. Walton
(1/10/42 - 2/7/42) NBC, Sat, 15m, 1:30pm

Doctor Allen Roy Dafoe (10/5/36 - 4/1/38) Lysol, CBS, 3t, 15m

Doctor Arthur J. Payne (1935 - 37) Mut, 15m, 3t/2t

Doctor Barclay's Daughters (see Doc Barclay's Daughters)

71 **Doctor Bob Jones** (Syn)

10 **Doctor Bob Jones Chapel Talk** (Syn)

1 **Doctor Buffalo's Chickens** (7/1/47) WRVA (Syn)

6 **Doctor Christian** (with Jean Hersholt)
(11/7/37 - 1/6/54) Vaseline, CBS
11/7/37 - 4/24/38, Sun, 2:30 pm
10/18/38 - 4/11/39, Tue, 10 pm
11/1/39 - 1/6/54, Wed, 10 pm; 8:30 pm as of 1/3/40

1 **Doctor Copeland Talks About Unpleasant Breath** (Syn)

1 **Doctor Copeland's Health Talks** (Syn)

Doctor Dana (see The Private Practice Of Dr. Dana)

Doctor Danfield (see Danger, Dr. Danfield)

Doctor Dolittle (based on stories by Hugh Lofting) (1/10/33 - 1/25/34) Bl, 2t, 15m

11 **Doctor Fights, The** (with Raymond Massey)
(6/6/44 - 8/29/44; 6/5/45 - 9/11/45) Schenley Laboratories, CBS, Tue, 9:30 pm; (summer replacement of This Is My Best in 1945)

1 **Doctor Fretz** (Syn)

Doctor Gino's Musicale (with Gene Hamilton) (6/30/51 - 4/10/54) ABC
6/30/51 - 7/7/51, Sat, 11:30 am
10/21/51 - 5/4/52, Sun, 10:45 pm
5/9/53 - 4/10/54, Sat, 1:30 pm

1 **Doctor Gradenwitz Interview** (1948)

1 **Doctor Hans Thompson** (9/12/39) Mut

Doctor Howard W. Haggard
(12/4/32 - 6/4/33) Sharp and Dome Pharmaceuticals, Bl, Sun, 15m, 7:15 pm

2 **Doctor I.Q.** (4/10/39 - 11/29/50)
4/10/39 - 7/3/39, Mars, Bl, Mon, 10:30 pm
7/10/39 - 3/30/42, Mars, NBC, Mon, 9 pm
4/6/42 - 3/27/44, Vick Chemical, NBC, Mon, 9:30 pm
4/3/44 - 10/28/49, Mars, NBC, Mon; Fri as of 7/1/49
1/4/50 - 11/29/50, Embassy Cigarettes, ABC, Wed, 8 pm

3 **Doctor I.Q. Jr.** (with Lew Valentine)
(5/11/41 - 4/2/49) Mars, NBC
5/11/41 - 8/24/41 (with Jimmy McClain), Sun, 6:30 pm
3/6/48 - 4/2/49 (with Lew Valentine), Sat

Doctor Jekyll and Mr. Hyde (Syn; with George Edwards)

1 **Doctor Jekyll and Mr. Hyde** (1932) film sound track

3 **Doctor John R. Brinkley** (1933, 1941)

Doctor Joseph Jastrow (Your Mind)
(1/9/35 - 4/24/35) NBC, Wed, 15m, 3:45 pm

Doctor Karl Reiland (How To Live)
(11/5/37 - 1/28/38) Pepperell Mfg. Co., Bl, Fri, 15m, 7:15 pm

Doctor Kate (with Comelia Burdick)
(1/31/38 - 9/38) Sperry Flour, NBC - West coast. 5t, 15m

Doctor Kenrad's Unsolved Mysteries (see Unsolved Mysteries)

15 **Doctor Kildare** (with Lew Ayres and Lionel Barrymore) (2/1/50 - 52) Syn; originated on WMGM, NY; on Mut, Tue, 8:30 pm

2 **Doctor LeGear's Pioneers** (Syn)

1 **Doctor Lisa Meitner** (8/11/45) Mut

Doctor Manning, Professional Witness (Herbert Rawlinston) (Syn)

Doctor Morelle (see Case For Doctor Morelle)

4 **Doctor Norman Vincent Peale** (6/15/54) Auditions

8 **Doctor Oral Roberts** (10/4/53 - 1958+) Healing Waters of Sus, ABC, Sun

16 **Doctor Paul** (1940 - 45) mostly regional; Jack Moyles announcer on 1945 shows (announcer is Vincent Pelletier)
(9/3/51 - 8/28/53) Wesson, Safeway, NBC, 5t, 15m

2 **Doctor Rhythm** (7/38) film sound track, Air trailer

Doctor Rockwell's Brain Trust (with Allen Roth Orchestra)
(2/21/39 - 5/23/39) Bl, Tue, 9:30 pm

Doctor Royal S. Copeland
(1927 - 6/2/32) 1927 - 30, Bl, 5t
1930 - 31, Ceresota Flour, NBC, Thu, 15m
9/23/31 - 12/16/31, Ceresota Flour, CBS, Wed, 15m
1931 - 4/8/32, Ceresota Flour, NBC, 3t, 15m
also 9/17/31 - 6/2/32, Ceresota Flour, CBS, Thu, 15m

Doctor Ruth Wadsworth
(1930 - 4/22/31) NBC, Wed, 15m, 11 am

Doctor Satan (Syn) (1936 - 37)

1 **Doctor Secaucus** (10/20/36) WMBQ

43 **Doctor Sixgun** (with Karl Weber)
(9/2/54 - 10/13/55) Sus, NBC
9/2/54 - 10/21/54, Thu, 8:30 pm
10/10/54 - 4/21/55, Sun, 8 pm
4/28/55 - 8/11/55, Thu, 8:30 pm
8/18/55 - 10/13/55, Thu, 8 pm

3 **Doctor Standish, Medical Examiner** (with Gary Merrill, Audrey Christie and Eric Dressler)
(7/1/48 - 8/19/48) CBS, Thu, 8 pm (summer replacement of FBI In Peace and War)

Doctor Tim, Detective (1940s) 15m

Doctor Tweedy (see The Fabulous Dr. Tweedy)

Doctor West's Celebrity Night (with Ethel Shutta and George Olsen)
(2/22/36 - 5/16/36) Dr. West's Tooth Powder, NBC, Sat, 10:30 pm

Doctor's Courage (Syn) (1936)

2 **Doctor's Orders** (Syn)

Doctor's Story (Syn)

Doctor's Wife, The (with Dan Curtis and Patricia Wheel)
(3/3/52 - 4/13/56) NBC, 5t, 15m
3/3/52 - 8/28/53, Ex-lax
1/3/55 - 4/13/56, Sus

Doctors At Home (AMA Health Series)
(12/22/45 - 6/8/46) NBC, Sat, 4 pm

Doctors At War (AMA Health series)
(12/26/42 - 6/26/43; 1/15/44 - 6/24/44) NBC, Sat, 5 pm for first series; 4:30 pm for second series

Doctors At Work (AMA Health Series)
(11/13/40 - 6/13/42)
11/13/40 - 6/4/41, Bl, Wed, 10:30 pm
12/13/42 - 6/13/42, NBC, Sat, 5 pm

10 **Doctors Courageous** (1941) Syn

Doctors Look Ahead (AMA Health Series) (1/6/45 - 6/9/45) NBC, Sat, 4 pm

1 **Doctors Talk It Over, The** (sponsored by American Cyanamid
(10/6/44 - 11/3/47) Bl/ABC, 15m
10/6/44 - 8/31/45, Fri
9/4/45 - 9/23/46, Tue, 9:30 pm
9/30/46 - 11/3/47, Mon, 10 pm

Doctors Today (AMA Health Series)
(12/13/47 - 6/26/48) NBC, Sat, 4 pm

Doctors, Then and Now (AMA Health Series) (12/7/46 - 6/21/47) NBC, Sat, 4 pm

1 **Document A/777** (4/17/50) Syn

1 **Dodge Division Spot Announcements** (c. 1950) Syn

1 **Dodge Motor Economy Day** (7/15/35) CBS

1 **Dodge Program, The** (1936) Syn

Dodge Show (see Harry Richman)

1 **Dodge Truck Radio Spots** (2/26/53) Syn

1 **Dodo Marmarosa Trio** (MacGregor transcription)

Dodsworth

Dog Heroes (with Harry Swan)
(10/6/36 - 4/23/39) Thrivo, Bl, 15m
10/6/36 - 5/25/37, Tue
10/17/37 - 4/10/38, Sun
10/16/38 - 4/23/39, Sun

Dol Brissett Orchestra
(3/18/39 - 5/13/39; 9/30/39 - 11/4/39; 12/9/39 - 6/29/40) NBC, Sat,

Dollar A Minute Show (with Bill Goodwin) (10/4/50 - 5/20/51) Sus, CBS
10/4/50 - 10/11/50, Wed, 10 pm
10/17/50 - 1/9/51, Tue, 10 pm
2/11/51 - 5/20/51, Sun, 4 pm; 4:30 pm as of 2/12/51

1 **Dollar Derby** (WLOS)

2 **Dollars For Breakfast** (1940s) Mut

1 **Dolly Dawn** (Thesaurus transcription)

Dolly Dawn and Her Dawn Patrol (Easy To Remember) 15m

1 **Dolly Dawn and The Manhattan Nighthawks** (Thesaurus transcription)

1 **Dolly Dawn With Manhattan Nighthawks** (Thesaurus transcription)

2 **Dolly Dawn With The Manhattan Nighthawks** (Thesaurus transcription)

1 **Dolly Sisters, The** (1945) film sound track

1 **Dominican Day Broadcast** (1946) CBS International

2 **Don Allen and His Music, Featuring Martha Tilton** (Standard transcriptions)

1 **Don Allen and His Orchestra, Featuring Martha Tilton**

Don Amaizo (9/15/30 - 4/6/31) American Maize Products, CBS, Mon

1 **Don Ameche and Edgar Bergen Interviews** (1969) WRC

1 **Don Ameche Show, The**
(6/24/46) Audition
(1/3/49 - 2/25/49) CBS, 5t, 3:30 pm (also see The Bickersons)

Don Ameche Variety Show, The (also with Claire Trevor)
(4/5/40 - 9/27/40) Old Gold, NBC, Fri, 10 pm

Don and Betty (with Vinton Haworth and Betty McLean)
(9/5/30 - 7/3/31; 9/4/31 - 5/27/32) Martin Senour Paint Co., CBS, Fri, 15m, 10:45 am

Don Arres (often called Tropical Serenade)
(11/15/38 - 9/22/40) Mut
11/15/38 - 2/21/39, Tue, 15m, 1:30 pm
4/16/39 - 4/21/40, Sun, 15m, 1 pm. 1:15 pm as of 3/3/40
also 10/28/39 - 5/4/40, Sat, 10 pm
5/12/40 - 7/14/40, Sun, 7 pm
also 6/11/40 - 10/12/40, Sat, 1 pm
8/3/40 - 9/22/40, Sun, 30m, 6 pm

2 **Don Bell** (7/1/46) Mut

1 **Don Bell Reporting From Bikini** (6/9/46) Mut

1 **Don Budge - Fred Perry Tennis Match** (3/10/39) Mut

Don Carney's Dog Chats
(1/30/33 - 4/24/33) Spratts, Bl, Mon, 8:30 pm (9/12/33 - 12/5/33) Spratts, Bl, Tue, 7:45 pm

Don Cornell (4/5/53 - 5/30/54) ABC, Sun, 15m, 6:15 pm; 6:45 pm as of 4/5/53

Don Drysdale's Bullpen (1/13/75 - 1976)

Don Gardiner (6/28/44 - 46) Serutan, Bl (1946 - 56+) Air Wick, ABC

16 **Don Glasser and His Orchestra** (10/16/60 - 6/21/70) CBS

1 **Don Goddard News** (6/7/44) NBC

1 **Don Hollenbeck News** (6/7/44) NBC

Don Jose (6/25/36 - 7/9/36) NBC, Thu, 15m, 10:15 am

Don Lang - True Animal Stories (original title was The Junket Folks)
(11/15/32 - 4/6/33) CBS, 2t, 15m, 5:45 pm

1 **Don Leary Show (Open House), The** (8/16/47) WDGY

1 **Don Lee New Year's Party** (12/31/29) Don Lee

Don Mosley

1 **Don Pryor** (6/23/45)

1 **Don Pryor Broadcast From Admiral Turner's Flagship** (4/2/45)

1 **Don Quixote** (1935) Syn

4 **Don Redman and His Orchestra, Featuring Coleman Hawkins** (SESAC transcriptions)

1 **Don Reid and His Orchestra** (CBS)

Don Ross, Pontiac Minstrel
(8/1/33 - 9/21/33) Pontiac, CBS, 2t, 15m, 2:30 pm

1 **Don Thomas and His Symphonic Swing Orchestra** (MacGregor transcription)

2 **Don Winslow Of The Navy**
(10/19/37 - 1/1/43) on regionally on WMAQ, Chicago from 3/29/37: maybe earlier
10/19/37 - 6/17/38, Sus, Bl, 5t, 15m
5/2/38 - 3/24/39 (with Bob Guilbert), Kelloggs, NBC, 5t, 15m, 7 pm; Bl as of 8/15/38
3/27/39 - 5/26/39, Ipana, Bl, 5t, 15m, 5:30 pm
10/5/42 - 1/1/43, Post, ABC, 5t, 15m, 6:15 pm

Don Wright Chorus (Mut, Sun)

1 **Don't Be A Sucker** (11/18/45 - 5/12/46) Mut, Sun, 15m, 8:30 pm

Don't Forget (with Allen Prescott)
(5/5/39 - 2/16/40) Bl
5/5/39 - 10/6/39, Fri, 8:30 pm
10/12/39 - 11/9/39, Thu, 8 pm
11/17/39 - 2/16/40, Fri, 8 pm

1 **Don't Let's Be Beastly To The Germans** (11/23/43) Mut

Don't You Believe It (7/26/38 - 47) (often not in New York)
7/26/38 - 4/20/39 (with Alan Kent and Tom Slater), Sensation Cigarettes, Mut, 2t, 15m, 7:30
1944, Bl, Tue, 15m
1946 - 47 (with Toby Reid) CBS Pacific, sponsored by Solitare Cake Make-Up, 15m
1947, ABC Pacific, sponsored by Forty Two Shampoo

Donald Dame and Louise Carlyle (7/29/45 - 8/19/45) ABC, Sun, 6:30 pm

1 **Donald Day** (4/14/40) Mut

2 **Donald Novis** (Standard transcriptions)

3 **Donald Novis Sings** (Radio Features transcriptions)

Donna Fargo Show (Social Security) (1974)

8 **Doorway To Life** (5/9/47 - 6/20/48) CBS, Sun, 1:30 pm; 1 pm as of 1/18/48

Dorian String Quartet (7/29/39 - 10/7/39; 7/13/40 - 10/5/40; 6/7/41 - 9/27/41 CBS, Sat,

6 **Doris Day Show, The** (1/11/52 - 5/26/53) Columbia Records, CBS
1/11/52 - 5/30/52, Fri
6/1/52 - 9/21/52, Sun, 7:30 pm (summer replacement for Amos 'n' Andy)
10/9/52 - 10/30/52, Thu
11/4/52 - 5/26/53, Tue, 10:05 pm
Standard transcriptions

2 **Doris Day With Les Brown and His Orchestra** (World transcriptions)

1 **Doris Day With Page Cavanaugh Trio** (Standard transcription)

Doris Kerr (7/16/36 - 10/15/36) CBS, Thu, 15m, 12:45 pm
(12/28/36 - 10/27/37) CBS, 2t (Mon & Wed) 15m, 5:30 pm

Doris Rhodes (1/24/38 - 10/3/39) CBS, 5t, 15m
(1/24/38 - 3/10/38) CBS, Mon, Thu, 15m, 6:45 pm
(12/3/38 - 2/11/39) CBS, Sat, 9:30 pm
(4/4/39 - 10/3/39) CBS, Tue, 15m, 10:30 pm

Dorothy and Dick (see Breakfast With Dorothy and Dick)

1 **Dorothy and Dick Show, The** (5/7/45) WOR

Dorothy Claire (12/30/45 - 3/24/46) ABC, Sun, 2 pm

Dorothy Dix (1947) ABC Pacific, Union Pharmaceuticals
(1/3/49 - 3/31/50) Sealtest. 5t, 15m
1/3/49 - 9/30/49, ABC
10/3/49 - 3/31/50, NBC

Dorothy Dreslin (9/5/38 -12/4/39) Bl, Mon, 15m, 12 noon

Dorothy Gordon (also called The Children's Corner)
(1/11/37 - 4/23/37, 9/29/37 - 1/14/38) CBS, 3t 15m, late afternoon
(12/16/38 - 3/17/39) Wheatena, Mut, 3t, 15m

Dorothy Kilgallen (9/18/47 - 7/28/49)
Drakett Co., ABC, Thu, 15m

2 **Dorothy Kilgallen's Diary** (1945) Syn

Dorothy Kirsten (see Vacation Serenade)

1 **Dorothy Lamour** (12/30/35 - 7/7/49)
12/30/35 - 2/26/36, Sus, Bl, 10m, 3t, 11:05 pm
7/6/47 - 9/28/47 (see Front and Center)
9/2/48 - 7/7/49 (Sealtest Variety Show as of 11/48), Sealtest, NBC, Thu, 9:30 pm

Dorothy Thompson (People In The News) (8/6/37 - 6/17/45)
8/6/37 - 5/27/38, Pall Mall, NBC, Fri, 15m, 10:45 pm
also 1/4/38 - 5/24/38, Bl, Tue, 15m, 7:30 pm
10/3/38 - 5/29/39, GE, NBC, Mon, 30m, 9 pm
8/30/38 - 3/30/41, Mut
3/19/42 - 6/11/42, Trimount, Bl, Thu, 15m, 8:45 pm
9/20/42 - 12/13/42; 3/28/43 - 6/20/43, Trimount, Bl, Sun, 15m, 9:45 pm
9/19/43 - 12/19/43; 3/19/44 - 6/11/44; 9/24/44 - 12/17/44; 3/25/45 - 6/17/45, Trimount, Bl, Sun; Mut as of 3/25/34

5 **Dorsey Brothers Orchestra, The** (stage show from the Statler Hotel, NY)
(1953 - 3/57) NBC

2 **Dorsey Brothers Show, The**
(3/14/56, 11/25/56) NBC, CBS

2 **Dossier On Demetrius** (Australian; with Bruce Stewart and Guy Doleman) 15m, Syn

Dot and Will (with Florence Freeman and James Meighan)
(7/22/35 - 1/29/37) Bl, various days, 15m

Dotto (1/6/58 - 8/15/58) CBS, 5t

Double Date (2/10/56 - 4/27/56) Mut, Fri, 9:30 pm

Double Everything (with Carl Hohengarten Orchestra, Al Shaw and Stan Lee)
(12/26/37 - 3/20/38) Wrigley, CBS, Sun, 6:30 pm

2 **Double Feature** (with Alfred Drake until 8/6; Jackie Gleason from 8/13; and Les Tremayne)
(7/2/44 - 10/22/44) NBC, Sun, 10:30 pm
(6/15/46 - 9/14/46) Mut, Sat, 3 pm

17 **Double Or Nothing** (1937) Air trailer
(9/29/40 - 1/15/54) 9/29/40 - 5/11/41 (Walter Compton first host until 2/7/43), Feen-A-Mint, Mut, Sun, 6 pm
5/23/41 - 9/26/41, Feen-A-Mint, Mut, Fri, 8 pm
9/28/41 - 5/10/42, Feen-A-Mint, Mut, Sun, 6 pm
5/22/42 - 7/13/45 (John Reed King host from 2/14/43),
7/15/45 - 6/15/47 (host is Todd Russell), Feen A-Mint, Mut, Sun, 9:30 pm
6/30/47 - 6/25/48 (Walter O'Keefe host for duration) Campbell, CBS, 5t, 3 pm
5/31/48 - 6/19/53, Campbell, NBC, 5t
6/22/53 - 1/15/54, Campbell, ABC, 5t, 11:30 am

Double Play (with Leo Durocher and Laraine Day) 15m

Doubleday Quiz Show
(3/28/49 - 2/17/50) Doubleday, Mut, 15m
3/28/49 - 4/22/49, 5t 11/6/49 - 11/27/49; 1/8/50 - 2/12/50,Sun
also 1/13/50 - 2/17/50, Fri

Dough Re Mi (with Hope Emerson, Radcliffe Hall, Paul La Valle Orchestra)
(7/15/42 - 9/9/42) NBC, Wed, 8:30 pm

1 **Douglas Corrigan Dinner At The Advertising Club** (8/5/38) Mut

1 **Douglas Corrigan Parade** (8/5/38) Mut

Douglas Edwards

Douglas Of The World (with Jack Moyles) (1950s)

1 **Dowery, The** (10/18/54) CBS

Down At Holmesy's (4/12/55 - 6/17/55) Mut, 5t, 15m, 12:15 pm

Down Mexico Way (also called Pan-American Holiday) (with Mitzi Gould and Richard Kollmar)
(3/14/42 - 9/26/42) NBC, Sat, 4 pm

Down Our Way (Syn)

1 **Down South** (1931) Synchro-disc, also see Fisk Jubilee Singers

1 **Down To Earth** (1947) Air trailer

Down You Go (with Dr. Bergen Evans) (3/22/52 - 8/15/53) Sus, Mut, Sat

37 **Downbeat** (AFRS) (1944 - 45)

2 **Downhomers, The** (AFRS)

2 **Dr. Pepper Parade, The** (with Pick Malone and Pat Padgett) CBS, Syn

Dr. Pepper's Treasure Hunt (1939)

296 **Dragnet** (with Jack Webb)
(6/3/49 - 2/26/57) NBC
6/3/49 - 6/24/49, Fri
7/7/49 - 9/1/49, Thu
9/3/49 - 10/1/49, Sat
10/6/49 - 9/11/52, Fatima, Thu
9/14/52 - 6/28/53, Chesterfield, Sun, 9:30 pm
9/1/53 - 9/20/55, Chesterfield, Tue
9/27/55 - 6/26/56; 9/18/56 - 2/26/57, Multi, Tue (repeats)

Drama Behind the News
(2/10/41 - 8/15/41) American Chicle Co., Bl, 5t, 5:15 pm

1 **Drama Critics Award** (4/4/48) Mut

2 **Drama Of Food** (1940) Syn

2 **Drama Of Medicine** (Syn)

Drama Of The Skies (12/5/36 - 7/24/37) Sat, 15m, 5:30 pm
(7/27/37 - 9/30/37) CBS, Tue, 15m, 5:45 pm; Thu, 5:30 pm as of 9/16/37

Drama With Bert Lytel (No Talent Wanted) (11/14/38 - 2/20/39) Bl, Mon, 15m, 7:30 pm

Dramas Of Childhood (with Angelo Patri)
(10/8/33 - 4/29/34) Cream Of Wheat, CBS, Sun, 10 pm; 9 pm as of 4/8/34

3 **Dramas Of The Courts** (Syn)

Dramas Of Youth (1933 - 40s) Mut (1940) not in NY; some dates are: 5/11/40 - 6/9/40, Sat, 8 pm

Dramatic Interlude (with Jeanette Nolan) (7/16/35 - 9/24/35) CBS, Tue, 8:30 pm

1 **Dramatization Of The Life and Death Of George Gershwin, A** (1937) WJR

4 **Dramatizations From Redbook Magazine** (Syn)

2 **Dramatized Defense Programs** (Syn)

Dramatized Fan Mail (see Dear Columbia and Dear Audience)

1 **Dreadful John At Midnight** (15m)

1 **Dream Come True, A** (1948) Syn

Dream Drama (see Big Ben Dream Dramas)

Dream Harbor (see Mary Lou Harp)

1 **Dream Of Baltimore: 1958** (1948)

Dream Singer, The (1/36 - 11/5/36) 15m
1/36 - 2/27/36, Piso Co., Mut, 2t
5/14/36 - 11/5/36, Lipton Tea, NBC, Thu

1 **Dream Time** (with Jeanie Taylor) Syn

2 **Dream Weaver, The** (Syn)

Dreamboat (with Doris Drew)
(4/9/51 - 6/18/51) ABC, Mon, 9:30 pm

Dreamer, The (9/24/39 - 12/17/39; 1/14/40 - 4/7/40; 9/29/40 - 12/22/40) Fendrich, NBC, Sun

Dreams Come True (with Barry McKinley) (7/16/34 - 4/11/35) Camay, NBC, 3t, 15m, 3 pm

Dreams Of Long Ago (see Heartthrobs Of The Hills)

Dreft Star Playhouse (6/28/43 - 3/30/45) Dreft, NBC, 5t, 15m; started off as Hollywood Theater Of The Air (6/28/43 - 10/1/43)

1 **Drene Program** (Syn)

Drene Show, The (see The Bickersons)

Dress Parade (3/9/36 - 7/13/36) (with Anthony Candelori Orchestra) NBC, Mon, 1:30 pm
(7/17/49 - 10/16/49) CBS, Sun, 10 pm

Dress Rehearsal (see Joe Rines)

3 **Drew Pearson** (often with Robert Allen) (1939 - 3/29/53)
1939 - 1940 (see Listen America)
2/9/41 - 11/25/45, Serutan, Bl, Sun, 15m (called News For The Americas from 2/9/41 - 4/27/41)
12/2/45 - 8/28/49, Lee Hats, ABC, Sun, 15m
9/4/49 - 2/18/51, Adam Hats, ABC, Sun, 15m
4/29/51 - 3/29/53, Serutan, ABC, Sun, 15m

Drowsy Rhythm (with Eva Taylor and Clarence Williams) (5/8/36 - 6/12/36) NBC, Fri, 15m, 7:15 pm

1 **Drums** (7/38) Mut

Duart Fair Show (1931) 15m

DuBarry Beauty Talk (5/23/29 - 5/15/30) Hudnut, CBS, Thu, 15m

1 **Dubarry Success Stories** (6/44) WOR

3 **Duck Soup** (11/33) Air trailers

1 **Dude Martin's Radio Ranch** (also with Rusty Draper's Orchestra) (1947) ABC

1 **Dude Martin's Sunrise Roundup** (2/11/48) KGO

Dude Ranch (with Jackie Coogan and Louise Massey) (9/29/36 - 3/23/37) Log Cabin, Bl, Tue, 8 pm

Dude Ranch Jamboree (10/18/52 - 2/7/53), NBC, Sat, 8:30 pm; 10 pm as of 12/6/52

1 **Duel Of Destiny** (Mut) Audition

104 **Duffy's Tavern** (with Ed Gardner) (3/1/41 - 1/18/52) from 10/6/42 - 3/5/44 show was called Duffy's or Duffy's Variety
3/1/41 - 6/14/41, Schick, CBS, Sat, 8:30 pm
9/18/41 - 3/12/42, Schick, CBS, Thu, 8:30 pm
3/17/42 - 6/30/42, Sanka, CBS, Tue, 9 pm
10/6/42 - 6/29/43; 10/5/43 - 6/27/44, Ipana, Bl, Tue, 8:30 pm
9/15/44 - 6/8/45; 9/21/45 - 6/14/46, Ipana, NBC, Fri, 8:30 pm
10/2/46 - 6/25/47; 10/1/47 - 6/23/48; 10/6/48 - 6/29/49, Ipana, NBC, Wed, 9 pm
9/29/49 - 9/21/50, Blatz, NBC, Thu, 9:30 pm
11/10/50 - 5/4/51; 10/5/51 - 1/18/52, Multi, NBC, Fri, 9:30; 9 pm as of 10/5/51

2 **Duke Ellington** (12/11/43, 1/66) CBS-TV

9 **Duke Ellington and His Famous Orchestra** (World transcriptions)

25 **Duke Ellington and His Orchestra** (3/18/37 - 1974) CBS, NBC, Mut, film sound track, KVOX, ABC/Bl, Standard and World transcriptions

1 **Duke Ellington Broadcast Of The Annual Gridiron Ball** (11/6/48) NBC

Duke Ellington Show (see also A Date With The Duke)
(5/5/43 - 7/22/43) Mut, Thu, 5t, 15m, 10:15 pm
also (5/16/43 - 9/19/43) Mut, Sun, 7 pm
(1952) Wed 48 Syndicated shows; 15m

Duke Of Paducah and Opry Songs (with Whitey Ford) (8/16/52 - 11/6/53) see also Plantation Party
8/16/52 - 11/8/52, NBC, Sat
8/14/53 - 11/6/53, Locke Stove, CBS, Fri

1 **Duke Of Windsor, The** (5/8/39) NBC

1 **Duke University Glee Club, The** (5/29/50) NBC

1 **Dumont Network Closed Circuit Telecast** (11/1/50) Dumont-TV

8 **Dunninger The Mentalist** (with Joseph Dunninger) (9/12/43 - 6/25/46) (also known as "The Kemtone Hour")
9/12/43 - 11/28/43, ABC, Sun
1/5/44 - 12/27/44, Sherwin Williams, ABC, Wed, 9 pm
6/8/45 - 9/28/45, Rinso, NBC, Fri, 10 pm (summer replacement of Amos 'n' Andy)
6/4/46 - 6/25/46, Rinso, NC, Tue, 9 pm (partial summer replacement of Amos 'n' Andy)

Dupont Speed Blenders (with Don Voorhees) (1931)

1 **Dupont Zerone Jesters** (with Irene Beasley and Paul Douglas) (10/13/36)

1 **Dutch Light Music** (Syn)

Dutch Masters (2/27/31 - 10/25/31) Consolidated Cigars, CBS, Fri

1 **Dwight Eisenhower** (9/23/52) ABC

1 **Dyke Easter, Detective** (3/13/39) NBC, Audition

Eagle and The Bear, The (1964) ABC

3 **Eagle Club, The** (1943) BBC/Mut

1 **Eagle's Brood, The** (3/5/47) CBS

Earbenders (with Irving Miller Orchestra) (9/19/38 - 4/26/40) Bl, 5t, 15m, 8 am

1 **Earl "Fatha" Hines** (7/4/77) PBS-TV

1 **Earl "Fatha" Hines and His Orchestra** (8/3/38) NBC

Earl Godwin (also called Watch The World Go By)
(1942 - 49) Bl/ABC
6/30/42 - 44, Ford
1944 - 45, Hastings
1945 - 7/18/46, North West Insurance
1946 - 49, Sus

1 **Earl H. Graser Obituary** (4/10/41) Mut

1 **Earl Hines and His Orchestra** (1/11/37) WCNW

3 **Earl Sheldon and His Orchestra** (Standard transcriptions)

1 **Earl Warren For Governor Committee** (5/46)

Earl Wilson's Broadway Column (1/7/45 - 7/1/45) General Cigar, Mut, Sun, 15m, 10 pm

Earl Wrightson (12/28/42 - 4/11/48)
12/28/42 - 1/29/43, Bl, 5t, 15m, 1:15 pm
1/5/48 - 4/11/48 (with Eileen Farrell), Sus, CBS, Sun, 4:30 pm

Early American Dance Music (1/8/44 - 7/7/45) Ford, Bl, Sat, 15m, 8 pm; 30m as of 5/20/44

Early Morning Report (CBS)

3 **Earn Your Vacation** (with Jay C. Flippen) (3/7/49 - 7/2/50) Sus, CBS, Sun

4 **Earnshaw Radio Short Story** (1938) Syn

69 **Earplay** (1971- Present) NPR; from University of Wisconsin

34 **Earplay Weekday Theatre** (1975 - 1981) NPR

East and Dumke (Sisters Of The Skillet; Quality Twins) (with Ed East and Ralph Dumke)
(1930 - 38) started in Chicago in 1928; on various days and times including:
1930 - 2/12/31, NBC, various days, 15m
7/7/31 - 7/1/32, Crisco, Bl, 3t (Tue, Thu, Fri), 15m, 8:45 pm
9/30/32 - 3/10/33, (see Armour Orchestra)
7/9/34 - 7/13/34, NBC, 5t, 15m, 12:15 pm
1/1/35 - 1/24/35 (with B.A. Rolfe) NBC, 3t (Tue - Thu), 45m, 8 am
4/30/35 - 6/4/35, Norsec Co., CBS, 3t, 15m, 11:45 am
9/15/35 - 12/8/35, CBS, Sun, 15m, 1:45 pm
9/29/36 - 9/23/37, Knox, CBS, 2t, 15m, 11:15 am
1937 - summer, Bl, Fri, 15m
1937 - 38 (Quality Twins) Kellogg, CBS, 15m

East Of Cairo (with Sven and Gene von Hallberg, musical directors)
(2/5/30 - 10/15/30) NBC, Wed, 8 pm

1 **East Side Of Heaven** (1939) film sound track

1 **Easter Parade For Crippled Children By Bing Crosby** (Syn)

1 **Easter Seal Campaign Disk Jockey Interviews** (1958) Syn

1 **Easter Seal Campaign Five Minute Musical Spots** (1958) Syn

1 **Easter Seal Concert** (1958) Syn

1 **Easter Seal Party** (1958) Syn

1 **Easter Seal Society** (1956) Syn

1 **Easter Seal Society, The** (1956) Syn

1 **Easter Show** (Syn)

Eastman Program (4/29/32 - 9/9/32) Kodak, CBS, Fri, 9 pm

Eastman School Of Music (1932 - 4/5/41) often listed under Rochester Philharmonic; on during the school year
1932 - 4/11/35, Sus, Bl, Thu, 45m
11/4/37 - 4/7/38, Bl, Thu, 30m
10/22/38 - 4/5/41, NBC, Sat
10/28/41 - 12/21/41, CBS, Tue, 4 pm (sometimes called Milestones In Music)

145 **Easy Aces** (with Jane and Goodman Ace) (3/1/32 - 1/17/45) on from 1930- 32 in KMBC, Kansas City
3/1/32 - 7/1/32; 9/26/32 - 5/30/33, Lavoris, CBS, 3t, 15m; Tue, Thu, Sat except for 3/14/32 - 1/25/33 when it was on Mon, Wed, Fri
10/10/33 - 4/27/34, Jad Salts, CBS, 4t (Tue - Fri), 15m, 1:30 pm
5/2/34 - 12/14/34, Jad Salts, CBS, 3t (Mon, Wed, Fri), 15m
1/7/35 - 1/31/35, Jad Salts, CBS, 4t (Mon - Thu), 15m
2/4/35 - 5/29/35, Anacin, NBC, 3t (Mon, Tue, Wed), 15m, 7:30 pm
6/4/35 - 10/22/42, Anacin, Bl, 3t (Tue, Wed, Thu), 15m, 4:15 pm; 7 pm from 10/1/35
10/28/42 - 11/26/43, Anacin, CBS, 3t (Wed, Thu, Fri), 15m, 7:30 pm
12/1/43 - 1/17/45, Anacin, CBS, Wed, 30m, 7:30 pm
(1945 - 46) Syndicated, 5t, 15m

Easy Does It (5/15/40 - 9/11/40) (with Paul La Valle Orchestra) Bl, Wed, 7:30 pm
(1/6/47 - 9/4/47) California Fruit, Mut, 3t, 15m, 11:30 am
(12/13/54 - 11/4/55) Mut, 5t, 15m, 2:15 pm

Easy Money (1/12/46 - 9/13/46) NBC
1/12/46 - 1/26/46, Sat, 7:30 pm
2/23/46 - 3/23/46, Sat, 5 pm
5/18/46 - 6/8/46, Sat, 4:30 pm
6/21/46 - 9/13/46, Fri, 8:30 pm
(10/3/54 - 6/5/55) (Mystery) NBC, Sun, 9:30 pm

Easy To Remember (see Dolly Dawn)

Eb and Zeb (1930s)

Ebony and Ivory (with Johnny Duffy) ABC, 15m

10 **Echoes Of A Century** (1947) Syn

Echoes Of History (12/13/39 - 10/2/40) Women's Clubs, Bl, Wed, 15m, 2:15 pm; every other week until 4/17/40
(5/21/41 - 7/9/41) Bl, Wed, 15m, 11:45 am

1 **Echoes Of New York** (1935 - 4/10/47) often a local program; with Josef Bonime Orchestra
1935 - 3/8/36, NBC, Sun, 60m
3/15/36 - 5/31/36, Consolidated Gas, NBC, Sun, 60m, 6:30 pm
9/19/39 - 6/18/40, NBC, Tue, 7:30 pm
9/18/40 - 6/11/41 (with Kay Lorraine and Jack Arthur) Bl, Wed, 7:30 pm
10/8/46 - 12/24/46, ABC, Tue, 9 pm
1/9/47 - 4/10/47, ABC, Thu, 9:30 pm

Echoes Of The Opera (1930 - 4/23/31) Bl, Thu, 10 pm

Echoes Of The Orchestra Pit (with Emil Polak Orchestra) (5/3/36 - 6/14/36) NBC, Sun, 7 pm

Echoes Of The Orient (with George Hicks, announcer; music by Sven and Gene Hallberg)
(6/30/29 - 11/29/31) NBC, Sun, 15m

1 **Economist National Committee Of Monetary Policy, The** (10/19/36) WMBQ

Ed East (see New York Town)

Ed East - Jingles (3/18/40 - 6/7/40) NBC, 5t, 5m, 6:25 pm

Ed East and Polly (with Ed and Polly East) (6/4/43 - 6/23/44) Sus, Bl, 5t
(2/19/45 - 12/28/45) NBC, 5t, 9 am

1 **Ed Fitzgerald** (10/17/38 - 8/2/41) later on locally on WOR, New York
10/17/38 - 3/24/39, Mut, 3t, 15m, 2:45 pm
1/10/39 - 3/23/39, Mut, 2t, 30m, 2:15 pm
12/30/39 - 5/25/40, Mut, Sat, 1 pm
3/22/41 - 8/2/41 (Ed Fitzgerald Revue) Mut, Sat, 15m, 2 pm

Ed Herlihy (4/15/45 - 5/18/47) NBC, Sun, 15m, 1 pm

1 **Ed Paul and His Orchestra** (1936) film sound track

1 **Ed Schwartz Show, The** (12/28/77) WIND

2 **Ed Sullivan Show, The** (1/12/32 - 9/30/46)
1/12/32 - 4/26/32; 6/30/32 - 8/18/32, La Gerardine, CBS, Tue, 15m, 8:45 pm; 8:30 pm as of 6/30/32
6/5/32 - 9/11/32, American Safety Razor, CBS, Sun, 10 pm
4/27/41 - 9/28/41 (Ed Sullivan Variety) International Silver, CBS, Sun, 30m, 6 pm (summer replacement of Silver Theater)
9/13/43 - 6/5/44 (Ed Sullivan Entertains), Mennen, CBS, Mon, 15m, 7:15 pm
4/2/46 - 9/30/46 (Ed Sullivan's Pipelines) Larus, Bl, Tue, 9 pm; Mon, 15m, 8:15 pm as of 6/10/46
12/25/55, 2/10/57(CBS-TV)

1 **Ed Sullivan's Diary** (1945) Syn

Ed Thorgersen (9/30/39 - 12/9/39) Congress Cigars, Mut, Sat, 15m, 5:45 pm

23 **Ed Wynn** (4/26/32 - 2/26/45) see also James Melton for Texaco shows in 1946
4/26/32 - 7/4/33; 10/31/33 - 5/29/34; 10/2/34 - 6/4/35 (The Fire Chief) Texaco, NBC. Tue, 9:30 pm; first performed on WJZ, New York on 2/19/22
2/13/36 - 5/7/36, (Gulliver) Plymouth, CBS, Thu
5/12/36 - 8/4/36 (Ed Wynn and His Grab Bag) Plymouth, NBC, Tue, 9:30 pm
11/14/36 - 5/8/37 (The Perfect Fool) Spud, Twenty Grand Cigarettes, Bl, Sat, 8 pm
9/8/44 - 1/12/45 (Happy Island) Borden, ABC, Fri, 9 pm
1/15/45 - 2/26/45 (with Minerva Pious), Borden, Bl, Mon 9 pm

Ed Wynn Show, The (see Ed Wynn)

Ed Wynn Texaco Show, The (see Ed Wynn)

1 **Eddie Albert Show, The** (6/25/47 - 9/24/47) ABC, Wed, 9:30 pm
(1949 - 50) Sus, NBC, 30m, 5t

Eddie Bergman

3 **Eddie Bracken Show, The** (1/28/45 - 3/23/47)
1/28/45 - 5/27/45, NBC, Sun, 8:30 pm
9/29146 - 3/23/47, Texaco, CBS, Sun, 9:30 pm

1 **Eddie Cantor** (7/3/50) NBC

1 **Eddie Cantor Christmas Show** (12/48)

24 **Eddie Cantor Pabst Blue Ribbon Show, The** (see The Eddie Cantor Show)

103 **Eddie Cantor Show** (9/13/31 - 10/8/53)
9/13/31 - 1/31/32; 10/30/32 - 4/23/33; 11/19/33 - 4/15/44; 10/7/34 - 11/25/34 (called Chase and Sanborn Hour), Chase and Sanborn, NBC, Sun, 60m, 8 pm (guest artists during breaks)
2/3/35 - 4/28/35; 9/29/35 - 5/10/36, Pebeco Toothpaste, CBS, Sun, 30m, 8 pm; 7 pm as of 1/5/36
9/20/36 - 5/30/37 (Texaco Town), Texaco, CBS, Sun, 8:30 pm
9/29/37 - 3/23/38 (Texaco Town), Texaco, CBS, Wed, 8:30 pm
3/28/38 - 6/27/38; 10/3/38 - 6/26/39, Camel, CBS, Mon, 7:30 pm
10/2/40 - 6/25/41; 9/3/41 - 6/24/42; 9/30/42 - 6/23/43; 9/29/43 - 6/21/44; 9/27/44 - 6/20/45; 9/26/45 - 6/19/46 (Time To Smile) Sal Hepatica, NBC, Wed, 9 pm; replaced Town Hall Tonight
9/26/46 - 6/19/47; 9/25/47 - 6/15/48, Pabst, NBC, Tue, 10:30 pm; 9 pm as of 6/8/48
10/1/48 - 6/24/49, Pabst, NBC, Fri, 9 pm
10/14/51 - 5/13/52 (as a DJ), Philip Morris, NBC, Sun, 9:30 pm; Tue, 10 pm as of 1/15/52
10/2/52 - 7/1/54, NBC, Thu, 9:30 pm (called Show Business Old and New from 1951 - 1954)
(1956) Syndicated -ZIV;
(1961 - 1963) (Ask Eddie Cantor) 5m each sponsored by Copper-Glo and Alumi-Glo

Eddie Cantor Show Business Show (Philip Morris) 15m

1 **Eddie Cantor Speaks For Youth Alijah** (1/9/43) CBS

1 **Eddie Cantor Story, The** (1953) film sound track

1 **Eddie Cantor Traffic Safety Programs** (Syn)

1 **Eddie Cantor's March Of Dimes Special** (1/23/44) Mut

6 **Eddie Cantor's Show Business** (1959)

3 **Eddie Condon** (World transcriptions)

2 **Eddie Condon and His Orchestra** (World transcriptions)

3 **Eddie Condon Program, The** (1949) NBC-TV

41 **Eddie Condon's Jazz Concert** (5/20/44 - 4/7/45) Sus, Bl, Sat, 1 pm

Eddie Dooley Sports Review (12/29/34 - 3/9/35) CBS, Sat, 15m, 6:30 pm

Eddie Dooley's Football Dope (9/29/32 - 12/3/32) Shell, CBS, 3t (Thu - Sat) 15m, 6:30 pm

Eddie Dowling's Revue (see Elgin Campus Revue)

Eddie Duchin (1/2/34 - 10/6/47)
1/2/34 - 6/23/34, Pepsodent, Bl, 3t, 9:30 pm
11/5/36 - 1/28/37 (also with Charles Le Maire), La Salle, NBC, Thu, 4 pm (La Salle Style Show)
9/29/37 - 12/22/37 (also with Lisa Sergio), Elizabeth Arden, Bl, Wed, 8 pm (Arden Hour Of Charm)
also 9/24/37 - 12/17/37, Koppers Coke, NBC, Fri, 7 pm
12/28/37 - 3/22/38 (Hour Of Romance), Elizabeth Arden, Mut, Tue, 10 pm
9/5/38 - 5/29/39, Pall Mall, NBC, Mon, 9:30 pm
10/8/38 - 1/28/39, CBS, Sat, 5:30 pm
5/6/39 - 5/11/40, Mut, Thu, 10 pm
12/2/39 - 5/4/40, CBS, Sat, 5:30 pm
9/16/40 - 11/25/40, Mut, Mon, 9:30 pm
also 10/26/40 - 2/1/41, Sus, CBS, Sat, 5:30 pm
7/14/47 - 10/6/47 (A Date With Duchin) Kre-mel Shampoo, ABC, 3t, 15m, 4:30 pm

3 **Eddie Duchin and His Orchestra** (10/30/40) CBS, Standard transcriptions

2 **Eddie Duchin Show, The** (1949) Syn

1 **Eddie Duchin Story, The** (1956) film sound track

Eddie Dunn Show, The
(10/22/43 - 10/6/44) CBS, 5t, 5 pm
(8/4/52 - 8/14/53) ABC, 5t, 25m, 2:35 pm

5 **Eddie Dunstedter** (4/7/35 - 1/16/37) various days and times, United transcriptions

8 **Eddie Dunstedter At The Organ** (MacGregor transcriptions)

120 **Eddie Fisher** (9/15/51 - 10/27/55)
9/15/51 - 4/4/53, Sus, ABC, Sat, 15m, 11:30 am
12/6/52 - 9/26/53, CBS, Sat
5/5/53 - 10/30/53 (also with Don Ameche), Coca-Cola, NBC, 2t (Tue, Fri), 15m (also TV simulcast)
5/12/53 - 11/5/53, Coca-Cola, Mut, 2t (Mon, Thu), 15m, 10:30 pm (TV simulcast) (also called Coke Time)
1/5/54 - 10/27/55 (Coke Time; TV simulcast), Coca-Cola, Mut, 2t, 15m, 7:45 pm

2 **Eddie Fisher Show, The** (1955) AFRS

Eddie Fitzpatrick (Music For Moderns)

2 **Eddie Fitzpatrick and His Orchestra** (4/40, 6/7/40) Mut

Eddie Garr Revue (also with Joan Brooks) (6/18/44 - 9/10/44) CBS, Sun, 7:30 pm

Eddie Mayehoff (9/5/40 - 10/31/40) (with Bob Stanley Orchestra) Mut, Thu, 9:30 pm (also see Eddie Mayehoff On The Town)

2 **Eddie Mayehoff "On The Town"** (11/19/40 - 2/12/41) Mut, 2t, 15m

13 **Eddie McGinnis and His Orchestra**
(1969) CBS, Syn
(2/27/70, 3/13/70) CBS

1 **Eddie Oliver and His Orchestra** (7/29/45) Mut

1 **Eddie Rickenbacker** (6/19/50) WFBR

1 **Eddie Rodgers and His Orchestra** (1939) WFBR

1 **Eddie Safranski Orchestra Featuring Jack Haskell, The** (SESAC transcription)

16 **Eddie Safranski Orchestra, The** (SESAC transcriptions)

2 **Eddie Safranski Quintet, The** (SESAC transcriptions)

1 **Eddie Sauter and His Orchestra** (1/1/58) NBC

4 **Eddie Skrivanek and His Orchestra** (MacGregor transcriptions)

Eddie South and His International Orchestra (see Cheloni Skin Program)

1 **Eddie South and His Orchestra** (8/19/35) NBC

Eddy Arnold (1940s) (see also Checkerboard Fun Festival)
(7/9/56 - 9/7/56) CBS, 5t, 8 pm

6 **Eddy Arnold Five Minute Shows** (5/54 - 9/54) Syn

17 **Eddy Arnold Show, The** (Syn)

Eddy Howard (1941 - 9/5/48)
1941, Land-O-Lakes, 15m
8/31/47 - 9/5/48 (Sheaffer Parade) Sheaffer Pens, NBC, Sun, 3 pm

6 **Eddy Howard and His Orchestra** (1945, 1960) Mut, CBS

Edgar Bergen (see Charlie McCarthy)

Edgar Bergen and Charlie McCarthy (see Charlie McCarthy)

Edgar Bergen and Charlie McCarthy Show, The (see Charlie McCarthy)

1 **Edgar Bergen Audition** (5/5/59) CBS

1 **Edgar Bergen Interview**

Edgar Bergen Show With Charlie McCarthy, The (see Charlie McCarthy)

Edgar Bergen Show, The (see Charlie McCarthy)

Edgeworth Program (with George Chappel; Dixie Spiritual Singers)
(6/25/31 - 6/9/32) Edgeworth Tobacco, Bl, Thu, 15m, 8 pm

Edith Adams (with Della Louise Orton)
(3/3/41 - 6/27/41) Mut, 6t, 15m, 1:15 pm; continued on West coast for a while

1 **Edith Adams' Future** (7/21/41) Mut

Edith Hendrick Orchestra
(4/12/40 - 5/20/40) CBS, Mon, 15m, 4:30 pm

1 **Editor's Daughter** (with Joan Banks)
(2/14/38 - 6/30/50+) Regional; starring Joan Banks until 1/10/47; Parker Fennelly on most shows; usually not in the east; sponsored by Kroger's Markets

Editor's Diary (1946 - 49) Sus, Mut, 5t, 15m

1 **Editorial Comments About The Pearl Harbor Attack** (12/7/41) CBS

8 **Editorial Opinion Of The Carolinas** (11/39) Syn

1 **Editors Of America Report, The** (Syn)

Editors Speak, The (8/29/43 - 10/3/43) NBC, Sun, 4:30 pm

Edna O'Dell and Dave Bacal
(5/17/38 - 6/7/38) CBS, Tue, 15m, 12:15 pm

Edna Wallace Hopper Program (with E.W. Hopper and Harry von Zell)
(9/17/31 - 3/23/32) E.W. Hopper, CBS, Wed, 15m, 3 pm

Edna Wallace Hopper Variety Show (with E.W. Hopper) (3/13/32 - 5/15/32) E.W. Hopper, CBS, Sun, 10 pm

1 **Edouard Daladier** (9/3/39) France/NBC

1 **Edsel Show, The** (10/57)

1 **Educated Woman, The** (4/30/59) CBS

Education and Radio (see National PTA Congress)

1 **Education Democracy Needs, The** (1939) Syn

1 **Education In The News** (5/2/34 - 5/27/38) NBC, 15m, various days and times

Edward Everett Horton Show, The (see Bing Crosby; 1945 - 46)

2 **Edward McHugh** (10/31/33 - 6/25/43)
10/31/33 - 7/3/36, Bl, 3t/5t, 15m
7/6/36 - 7/1/39, Ivory, Bl, 5t, 15m
also 5/28/38 - 7/1/39, Ivory, NBC, 6t, 15m, 9:45 am
also 5/30/38 - 11/4/38, Ivory, CBS, 5t, 15m
12/18/39 - 2/6/42, NBC, 3t- 5t, 15m
3/23/42 - 12/21/42, Bl, 5t, 15m, 1:15 pm
also 8/9/42 - 12/13/42 ((Toastchee Time; with Paul La Valle Orchestra and Will Donaldson Quartet) Lance Inc., Bl, Sun, 4:30 pm
2/1/43 - 6/25/43, Bl, 5t, 15m, 1:15 pm

Edward P. Morgan (1/17/55 - 12/30/55) ABC, 5t, 15m, 10 pm

12 **Edward R. Murrow** (9/3/39 - 9/17/44) CBS, NBC, BBC

1 **Edward R. Murrow Memorial** (4/30/65) CBS

6 **Edward R. Murrow News**
(1948, 1954, 1957) CBS, sponsored by International Silver, Amoco, Campbell Soup

1 **Edward R. Murrow: A Reporter Remembers**

1 **Edward R. Murrow: A Reporter Remembers Vol. II**

3 **Edward Tomlinson** (9/7/39 - 2/28/48)
(April, May, 1949) Bl (also see The Other Americas)
9/7/39 - 46, Bl/ABC
1946 - 2/28/48, NBC

Edward Weeks (also see Meet Edward Weeks)
(2/8/48 - 6/19/49) ABC, Sun, 15m, 1:15 pm

5 **Edwin C. Hill** (1932 - 2/10/52) often called The Human Side Of The News starting in 1933
1932 - 33, CBS
6/19/33 - 35, Barbasol, CBS
1/27/36 - 38, NBC
5/9/38 - 39, Campbell, NBC
1939 - 42, American Oil, CBS
1942 - 45, Johnson & Johnson, CBS
1946 - 47, Wesson, ABC
1/22/50 - 4/9/50, NBC, Sun
1951 - 2/10/52, Beltone, NBC, Sun

Edwin C. Hill News (see Edwin C. Hill)

Edwin D. Canham (1945 - 58+) ABC

6 **Edwin La Mar (Le Mar)** (Standard transcriptions)

1 **Eerie Stories** (Syn)

Egbert and Ummly Show, The (with Herb Shelton) (10/11/53 - 12/26/54) NBC, Sun, 15m, 8:30 am

1 **Egg Frying** (8/27/48) WOR

1 **Egyptian Problem Before The United Nations, The** (Syn)

1 **Eichmann Trial** (4/12/61) CBS

Eight Sons Of Eli (2/28/32 - 5/22/32) R. Wallace and Sons, CBS, Sun, 2 pm

Eight-To-The-Bar Ranch (see The Andrews Sisters)

Eileen and Bill (with Eileen Douglass and Robert Griffin)
(5/23/32 - 8/19/32) Nivea Cream, NBC, Mon, 15m, 12:15 pm

13 **Eileen Barton Show, The** (1954) CBS, Syn, 15m

Eileen Christie (with Robert Armbruster Orchestra) (1/20/52 - 3/23/52) NBC, Sun, 10:30 pm

Eileen Farrell (6/5/42 - 12/24/47)
6/5/42 - 7/24/42, CBS, Fri, 7:30 pm
8/10/43 - 11/19/43, CBS, Fri, 11:30 pm
1/23/44 - 11/12/44, CBS, Sun, 15m, 11:15 pm
2/28/45 - 5/23/45, CBS, Wed, 15m, 6:30 pm
6/1/45 - 8/24/45, CBS, Fri, 15m, 6:30 pm
7/10/45 - 8/21/45, CBS, Tue, 15m, 6:30 pm, co-star with Sally Moore
8/27/45 - 3/6/46, CBS, 3t, 15m, 6:30 pm
3/5/46 - 5/6/46; 7/8/46 - 12/23/46, CBS, Mon, 11:30 pm
10/7/47 - 12/24/47, CBS, Wed, 11:30 pm

1 **Eisenhower 1890 - 1969** (3/28/69) NBC

1 **El Alamein Re-union** (10/23/48) BBC

El Chico (5/30/36 - 12/28/40) 15m, on various days and times
5/30/36 - 10/24/36, Bl, Sat, 7 pm
6/26/37 - 11/4/39, NBC, Sat, 10m, 6:05 pm
12/11/39 - 2/12/40, Mon, 15m, 6 pm
5/18/40 - 12/28/40, Sat, 15m, 6 pm

El Lobo Rides Again

El Paseo Troubadours (intermittently during 1940 and 1941; not always in New York) including:
6/2/40 - 9/22/40, Mut, Sun, 4 pm
2/2/41 - 7/7/41) Mut, Sun, 15m, 3:45 pm

1 **El Radioteatro De America** (6/2/43) Syn

El Toro Weekend Revue (with Gus Van, Pickens Sisters, Vic Arden Orchestra)
(7/30/32 - 1/9/33) El Toro Cigars, Bl
7/30/32 - 11/19/32, Sat, 9 pm
11/21/32 - 1/9/33, Mon, 8 pm

Elder Michaux Congregation
(1/27/34 - 5/19/34) CBS, Sat, 7 pm

Eleanor Lane (8/7/39 - 1/15/40) Bl, Mon, 15m, 8:45 am

Eleanor Nash (5/21/41 - 3/18/42) Sus, Bl, Wed, 15m

3 **Eleanor Roosevelt** (11/11/34 - 9/7/51)
11/11/34 - 12/16/34, CBS, Sun, 15m
2/15/35 - 4/19/35 (It's A Women's World) Selby Shoe Co., CBS, Fri
4/21/37 - 7/14/37, L. Corliss, Bl, Wed
4/30/40 - 7/25/40, Sweetheart Soap, NBC, 2t, 15m
9/28/41 - 4/12/42 (Over Our Coffee Cups; Current Events), Pan Am Coffee, Bl, Sun, 15m, 6:45 pm
11/8/48 - 9/2/49 (also with daughter, Anna Boettiger), Sus, ABC, 3t, 15m
10/11/50 - 9/7/51, NBC, 5t, 45m

1 **Eleanor Roosevelt Diamond Jubilee** (10/25/59) NBC-TV

1 **Eleanor Roosevelt Recalls Her Years With F. D. R.**

3 **Eleanor Roosevelt Speech** (10/23/39, 10/17/44, 1/26/47) Mut

1 **Election Night Concession Speeches** (11/4/80)

2 **Election Night Coverage** (11/3/48, 11/4/52) NBC-TV, ABC-TV

1 **Election Night Preview** (11/2/48) CBS

2 **Election Night Speeches** (11/7/72, 11/3/76) pool feeds

2 **Election Night Statements** (11/3/76, 11/4/88) NBC-TV, CBS-TV

1 **Election Night Victory** (11/4/80) pool feed

2 **Election Returns** (11/8/44, 11/8/60) Mut, WQXR

9 **Electric Hour, The** (with Nelson Eddy until 6/9/46) (9/20/44 - 9/8/46) Electric Companies, CBS; during the summer program was called The Electric Summer Hour
9/20/44 - 12/13/44, Wed, 10:30 pm
12/17/44 - 9/8/46, Sun, 4:30 pm

1 **Electric Summer Hour, The** (7/22/45 - 9/9/45; 6/16/46 - 9/8/46; 7/13/47 - 8/31/47) CBS, Sun, 4:30 pm

2 **Electric Theater, The** (with Helen Hayes) (10/3/48 - 5/29/49) Electric Companies, CBS, Sun, 9 pm

Electronic Band (with Raymond Scott) (8/26/39 - 9/17/39) NBC, Sun, 3 pm

15 **Eleventh Hour, The** (1941) CBS, Syn (also known as At The Eleventh Hour)

Elgin Adventurer's Club (see Floyd Gibbons)

Elgin Campus Revue (with Art Kassel Orchestra, Mills Brothers)
(10/4/35 - 12/27/35) Elgin Watch, NBC, Fri, 10:30 pm (also Eddie Dowling Revue with Eddie Dowling, Benny Goodman, Helen Ward)
(3/17/36 - 6/9/36) Elgin, NBC, Tue, 10 pm

Elgin Football Revue (with Kay Kyser) (10/3/36 - 5/28/37) Elgin, CBS, Sat, 8:30 pm

2 **Elgin Holiday Programs** (Thanksgiving and Christmas from 4 pm - 6 pm, CBS, 1942 - 1947; NBC, 1948)

Elinor Sherry (12/19/38 - 3/20/39) Mut, Mon, 15m, 2 pm

Elizabeth Bemis (9/27/43 - 4/7/44) CBS, 5t

1 **Elizabeth Hart Presents** (5/24/43) WMAQ

1 **Elizabeth Has A Baby** (11/15/48) BBC

1 **Elizabeth Is Queen** (1953) Air trailer

Elizabeth Rethberg (with Alfred Wallenstein) (7/11/41 - 9/12/41) Mut, Fri, 9:30 pm

1 **Elizabeth Wayne** (12/9/41) Mut

1 **Ella Fitzgerald** (8/1/39 - 6/8/43, 1955)
8/1/39 - 9/19/39, NBC, Tue, 15m, 5:15 pm
8/24/42 - 11/17/42 (Ella Fitzgerald and The Four Keys) Bl, 2t (Mon, Wed) 7:15 pm
12/27/42 - 2/7/43, Sus, Bl, Sun, 15m, 8:15 pm
3/30/43 - 6/8/43, Bl, Tue, 10m, 7:05 pm

4 **Ella Fitzgerald and Her Orchestra** (Jan, Mar, 1940) NBC

1 **Ella Fitzgerald With The Song Spinners** (World transcription)

Ellen Randolph (with Elsie Hitz) (10/9/39 - 9/22/41) Super Suds, NBC, 5t, 15m

Ellery Queen (see The Adventures Of Ellery Queen)

Elliot Lawrence Orchestra (6/16/45 - 3/30/46) CBS, Sat, 4:30 pm

1 **Elliot Richardson Press Conference** (10/23/73) pool feed

Elliott Roosevelt (4/3/39 - 11/30/39) Mut, Tue, 15m, 7:15 pm

1 **Elmer Davis and George Fielding Eliot** (11/30/39) CBS

80 **Elmer Davis and The News** (10/23/39 - 42) CBS, sponsored by Chrysler, Palmolive, Post Toasties, Gillette
(1945 - 6/26/55) ABC

Elmo Roper (9/19/48 - 8/27/50) CBS, Sun, 15m, 1:15 pm

2 **Elsa Maxwell's Party Line** (1938 - 46)
1938 - 39, NBC
1/2/42 - 6/26/42, Ry-Krisp, Bl, Fri, 15m, 10 pm
1943 - 45, Sus, Mut, 5t, 15m
1945 - 46, Mut, 5t, 11:15 am

Elsie MacGordon (11/7/32 - 4/17/33) Bl, Mon, 15m, 11:15 am

Elton Britt Show (2/23/53 - 7/10/53) Mut, 5t, 15m, 10:15 pm

Elvera (5/6/41 - 10/7/41) CBS, Tue, 15m, 9:15 am

1 **Elvis In Concert** (5/7/78) CBS-TV

1 **Elvis Presley Story, The** (10/24/71) Syn

1 **Elvis Presley's First Appearances On The Ed Sullivan Show** (10/56) CBS-TV

Elwyn Owen (7/14/41 - 9/12/41) Bl, 5t, 15m, 8:45 am

Ely Culbertson (4/11/32 - 6/25/32) Wrigley, NBC, 3t (Mon, Wed, Sat) 15m

Elza Schallert Interviews
(10/16/36 - 9/22/37) Bl, 15m
10/16/36 - 8/20/37, Fri, 10:45 pm
8/25/37 - 9/22/37, Wed, 10 pm

1 **Emerald Isle**

1 **Emergency March Of Dimes Presents Freddy Martin, The** (8/16/54) Syn

Emerson Buckley Orchestra
(9/11/46 - 10/2/46) Mut, Wed, 10 pm

Emery Deutsch Orchestra
(5/7/34 - 8/24/41) (also called Poetic Strings) on various days and times including:
5/7/34 - 10/8/34, CBS, Mon, 30m, 2:30 pm
7/4/34 - 9/19/34, CBS, Wed, 15m
8/7/35 - 9/25/35 (with Connie Gates) CBS, Wed, 9 pm; 15m, 8:15 pm as of 8/7/35
6/23/36 - 9/7/36, CBS, Mon, 15m, 12:15 pm
9/16/36 - 2/24/37, CBS, Wed, 3:30 pm
12/24/38 - 2/11/39, CBS, Sat, 3:30 pm
4/3/41 - 8/15/41, CBS, Thu, 15m, 8:30 am
4/12/41 - 8/16/41, CBS, Sat, 15m, 8:30 am
7/27/41 - 8/24/41, CBS, Sun, 15m, 11:15 am

1 **Emil Coleman and His Orchestra** (7/53) Mut

1 **Emil Vandis and His Orchestra** (4/28/45) Bl

Emily Post (6/27/30 - 4/25/39)
6/27/30 - 6/26/31, Camay, CBS, Fri, 15m, 11 am
1931- 32, Bl, Mon, 15m, 4 pm
12/15/32 - 5/18/33, Dupont, Bl, 2t, 15m, 6:45 pm
10/28/34 - 11/25/34 (with Roger Whitman) Bl, Sun, 15m, 12 noon
10/21/37 - 4/19/38 (How To Get The Most Out Of Life), Florida Citrus, CBS, 15m, 2t, 10:30 am
10/3/38 - 12/26/38, G. W. Loft, NBC, Mon, 30m
1/3/39 - 4/25/39, NBC, Tue, 15m

Emma Otero (12/15/40 - 1/3/42) NBC
12/15/40 - 8/24/41, Sun, 12 noon
2/4/41 - 8/26/41, Tue, 15m, 1 pm
10/18/41 - 1/3/42, Sat, 15m, 7:30 pm

1 **Emotion** (7/6/49) NBC

2 **Emperor Waltz** (1948) Air trailer, film sound track

Empire Builders, The (with Harvey Hays and Don Ameche; many with Bernadine Flynn)
(9/30/29 - 6/22/31) Great Northern Railroads, Bl, Mon, 9:30 pm

1 **Empire Day Broadcast** (5/24/39) CBC

1 **Empire Of The Air** (2/92) American Public Radio

2 **Empire State Building Plane Crash** (7/28/45) Mut

10 **Empire Strikes Back, The** (2/16/83 - 4/20/83) NPR

1 **Empire's Answer, The** (10/6/39) BBC

Empires Of The Moon (compiled by H. Bedford Jones) (4/10/38 - 7/3/38) Bl, Sun, 1:30 pm

1 **Empty Chair, The** (2/4/47) Syn

1 **Empty Noose, The** (10/16/46) CBS

1 **Empty Sleeve, The** (8/15/41) CBS

23 **Enchanted Hour, The** (with Nancy Carr and Henry Weber Orchestra)
(5/7/49 - 9/4/49) Sus, Mut
5/7/49 - 5/28/49, Sat, 11:30 am
6/26/49 - 9/4/49, Sun, 1 pm
11/12/50

Enchanted Room, The (with Dorothy McGuire)

Encore (with Robert Merrill and Meredith Willson) (12/8/52 - 3/16/53) Sus, NBC, Mon, 10 pm

Encore Appearance (11/29/44 - 46) CBS, Wed, 15m

13 **Encore Theater, The** (6/4/46 - 49)
6/4/46 - 8/27/46, Schenley, CBS, Tue, 9:30 pm

Encores From The Bell Telephone Hour (see The Bell Telephone Hour)

1 **End Of An Era** (1/16/53) NBC

5 **Endless Frontier, The** (Jan, Feb, 1952) NBC, Syn

8 **Endorsed By Dorsey** (3/27/46 - 10/18/46) Mut

1 **Energy Program: Other Views, The** (7/20/79) CBS-TV

1 **Energy: A Light At The End Of The Tunnel** (1/10/80) Capitol Cities-TV

1 **Energy: Other Views** (4/9/79) CBS-TV

1 **Energy: Republican Reponse** (7/20/79) ABC-TV

1 **Energy: The Facts, The Fears, The Future** (8/31/77) CBS-TV

Engineer At War, The (7/16/42 - 9/24/42) NBC, Thu, 15m, 6:30 pm

1 **English Resume Of Hitler's Speech** (3/18/38) Mut

1 **English Summary Of Adolf Hitler's Address** (12/10/40) Mut

1 **English Summary Of Adolf Hitler's Address To The Reichstag** (5/18/38) Mut

1 **English Summary Of Adolf Hitler's Nuremberg Speech** (9/12/38) Mut

5 **English Summary Of Adolf Hitler's Speech** (1/30/39 - 10/6/39)

1 **English Summary Of Mussolini's Speech** (3/30/38)

Enna Jettick Melodies (Mixed quartet)
(1928 - 1/23/33) Enna Jettick Shoes, Bl, 15m
1928 - 1/15/33 (with Robert Armbruster Orchestra), Sun, 8 pm; 9 pm as of 5/8/32
1932 - 1/23/33 (with Ramona), Mon, 6:30 pm
(8/20/39 - 11/19/39) (with Jim Shields, D'Artega Orchestra) NBC, Sun, 5 pm

Enna Jettick Songbird (1930 - 4/24/31) NBC, Fri, 15m, 9:30 pm

6 **Eno Crime Club** ((2/9/31 - 6/30/36) Eno Fruit Salts
2/9/31 - 7/4/31, CBS, 6t, 15m, 6:45 pm
7/6/31- 9/30/31, CBS, 2t (Mon & Wed), 30m
10/7/31 - 12/30/31, CBS, Wed, 30m
1/5/32 - 10/26/32, CBS, 2t (Tue, Wed), 9:30 pm
11/9/32 - 12/21/32, CBS, Wed
1/3/33 - 7/24/34 (called Eno Crime Clues), Eno Salts, Bl, 2t (Tue & Wed), 30m
9/4/34 - 6/30/36, Eno Salts, Bl, Tue, 8 pm

Eno Penthouse (see Hal Kemp)

Enoch Light Orchestra (5/18/38 - 3/2/40) on various days and times, many overlapping
5/14/38 - 6/28/38, CBS, 2t (Wed and Sat), 15m
5/27/38 - 1/26/39, CBS, 2t (Mon & Thu), 15m, 2 pm
1/30/39 - 7/3/39, CBS, Mon, 15m, 6:45 pm
4/22/39 - 10/28/39, CBS, Sat, 1 pm
8/7/39 - 10/6/39, CBS, 3t, 15m, 2:45 pm
8/20/39 - 11/19/39 (with Jimmy Shields, Rosamond Ames), NBC, Sun, 5 pm
11/14/39 - 1/30/40, Mut, Tue, 1:30 pm
1/13/40 - 3/2/40, Mut, Sat, 15m, 12:45 pm

Enough and On Time (6/5/43 - 8/28/43) Bl, Sat, 7:30 pm

1 **Epic Journey Of Apollo 11, The** (7/14/69) CBS-TV

1 **Epic Of America, The** (1/9/38 - 2/13/38) Mut, Sun, 8 pm

Eric Hodgins (Minority Of One) (1/7/54 - 2/11/54) CBS, Thu, 15m, 10 pm

2 **Eric Sevareid** (1940s) including 6/17/40, 3/77, CBS
(2/17/47 - 1/14/51) Metropolitan Life, CBS

5 **Eric Sevareid Reports From Paris** (CBS)

1 **Ernest Chappell** (1947) Audition

Ernest Gill's California Concerts (see Songs We Remember)

Ernest Hutcheson (9/27/31 - 3/19/33) CBS, Sun

4 **Ernest Tubb** (World transcriptions)

1 **Ernie Fiorito's Studies In Contrast** (12/19/38 - 11/3/39)
12/19/38 - 6/12/39, Mut, Mon, 8 pm; 8:30 pm as of 4/17/39
6/16/39 - 11/3/39 (with Jimmie Shields), Mut, Fri, 9:30 pm; Benay Venuta; also called Take A Note

1 **Ernie Kovacs Show, The**
(6/4/55 - 8/25/56) ABC, 5t, 60m, 8 am
(12/23/62) ABC-TV

Ernie Lee's Omega Show
(10/5/47 - 6/27/48; 9/26/48 - 6/19/49) H.C. Cole Milling Co., Mut, Sun, 3 pm

1 **Ernie Pyle Funeral** (4/22/45)

E. Robert Schmitz (see Columbia Concert Hall)

78 **Errand Of Mercy** (11/16/47 - 9/20/53) Syn

Erroll Garner

Erskine Butterfield (8/29/39 - 2/27/40) Mut, Tue, 15m, 11:45 am

2 **Erskine Hawkins and His Orchestra** (3/20/40) NBC

Erskine Johnson's Hollywood
(1944) CBS Pacific, sponsored by Jergens
(1945 - 49) Mut, 5t, 15m (Regional)
(11/14/49 - 2/10/50) Ry-Krisp, Mut, 3t, 5m

1 **Erskine Johnson's Hollywood Story** (8/25/48) Mut

1 **Eruption Of Vesuvius** (3/23/44) Mut

Erwin Of The Arctic (Dave Erwin) 15m

2 **Erwin Yeo** (Pipe Organ) Standard transcriptions

4 **Erwin Yeo At The Organ** (D&S transcriptions)

187 **Escape** (1944, 7/7/47 - 9/25/54) CBS

Escape With Me (with Kathleen Norris)
(3/20/52 - 9/23/52) ABC, Tue, 8 pm; 8:30 pm as of 4/15/52

Escorts and Betty (1937) Bl, 15m, 4:15 pm
(1/14/38 - 6/12/38) NBC, various days, 15m, 1:15 pm
(4/1/40 - 12/9/40) NBC, Mon, 15m, 9:30 am; 6 pm as of 9/30

Eskimo Pie Program (with Harold Stokes Orchestra) 15m

2 **Esquire Jazz Concert** (various dates from 1938 - 1946)

Essays In Music (with Victor Bay Orchestra) (10/10/37 - 9/8/38) CBS, Thu

Esso Program (with Harry Salter, Edwin Whitney and Robert Ripley)
(5/20/31 - 6/3/32) Esso, Bl, 2t (Wed & Fri) 15m, 7:45 pm; 7:15 pm as of 3/16/32 (also listed under Esso Hour)

Esso Theater (11/30/32 - 2/22/33) Esso, Bl, Wed, 7:30 pm

1 **Estampas Musicales** (12/45) CBS International

1 **Etchings In Jazz** (1930) Syn

Etchings in Music (15m)

74 **Eternal Light, The** (10/8/44 - 92+) Jewish Theological Seminary, NBC, Sun

2 **Ethel and Albert** (with Peg Lynch and Alan Bunce)
(5/29/44 - 8/28/50) Sus, ABC
5/29/44 - 8/11/44, Bl, 5t, 15m, 4 pm
8/14/44 - 6/24/49, 5t, 15m (6:15 pm)
1/16/49 - 8/28/50, Mon, 30m, 8 pm
1973 (Earplay - with Peg Lynch) NPR

Ethel Barrymore Theater, The (Famous Actor's Guild) (9/30/36 - 7/28/37) Bayer, Bl, Wed, 8:30 pm

1 **Ethel Merman** (1931) film sound track

1 **Ethel Merman and Polly** (3/30/58)

Ethel Merman Show, The
(7/31/49 - 11/14/49) NBC
7/31/49 - 9/11/49, Sun, 9:30 pm
10/24/49 - 11/14/49, Mon, 10:30 pm

1 **Ethel Waters** (1958)

Eton Boys, The (5/27/36 - 6/24/39) CBS, 15m
5/27/36 - 8/12/36, Wed, 5 pm
9/30/37 - 12/9/37, Thu, 6:15 pm
12/11/37 - 6/24/39, Sat morning

Eugene Conley (7/11/39 - 9/19/39) NBC, Tue, 8:30 pm

Eugene International Revue (with Al Shirley, Alice Remson and Sam Lanin Orchestra)
(3/6/32 - 6/13/32) Eugene Hair Wave Lotion, CBS, Sun; Mon & Thu as of 4/4/32; Mon as of 5/16/32

Eugene O'Neill Cycle (8/2/37 - 8/23/37) Bl, Mon, 9:30 pm

Eugenia Baird Show (7/7/46 - 10/13/46) Mut, Sun, 6:30 pm
(9/29/52 - 9/11/53) Mut, 5t, 9:30 pm

Europe Calling (3/13/38 - 12/11/38) CBS, Sun, 15m, 11:30 pm

Europe Confidential (Syn)

European News Roundup

1 **European Radio** (5/28/38) WOR

1 **European Situation** (3/14/38) Mut

18 **European War Crisis** (8/27/39 - 10/6/39) CBS

Evangeline Adams (1930 - 7/17/31) CBS, 3t, 15m, 7:30 pm

Evangeline Baker and The News (KGO)

1 **Eve Of Christmas Eve, The** (12/23/77) ABC-TV

1 **Eve Of The Atom Bomb Test, The** (6/29/46) ABC

Eve Young Show, The (1951) NBC, 15m

Evelyn Knight (see Your Singing Secretary)

Evelyn Pasen Show, The (also with Bernard Herrmann)
(10/30/45 - 11/27/45) CBS, Tue, 15m, 6:30 pm

Evelyn Winters (see Strange Romance Of Evelyn Winters)

3 **Evening At Pops** (9/28/75, 7/15/79) PBS-TV

Evening Comes (11/29/53 - 5/23/54) Thomas Nelson & Sons, ABC, Sun
(1/2/55 - 2/6/55) ABC, Sun, 5 pm

Evening In Paris, An (1928 - 5/11/36) Bourjois
1928 - 29, NBC, Fri, 9 pm
10/7/29 - 6/16/30; 9/15/30 - 8/15/32, CBS, Mon, 9:30 pm, 30m; 15m from 6/20/32 - 8/15/32 with Frank Parker and Agnes Moorehead
9/12/32 - 10/30/33 (with Elsie Hitz, Patricia Barlow and Agnes Moorehead), CBS, Mon, 30m; 15m from 6/19/33 - 10/30/33
11/5/33 - 4/22/34, CBS, Sun, 8 pm
8/19/35 - 5/11/36 (with Odette Myrtil), Bl, Mon

Evening With Arthur Lyman, An

Evening With Romberg, An
(6/12/45 - 8/31/48) Raleigh, NBC
6/12/45 - 9/4/45, Tue, 10:30 pm (summer replacement for Hildegarde)
10/17/45 - 11/28/45, Wed, 8:30 pm
6/11/46 - 9/3/46; 6/10/47 - 9/2/47; 6/8/48 - 8/31/48, Tue, 10:30 pm (summer replacement for Red Skelton)

Ever Since Eve (with Keith Morgan)
(4/5/54 - 12/17/54) ABC, 5t, 15m, 11:15 am

Ever-Ready Radio Gaieties (with Belle Baker, Jack Denny Orchestra)
(3/13/32 - 5/29/32) Ever-Ready Razors, CBS, Sun, 9 pm

Eveready Hour, The (12/4/23 - 30) Eveready
12/4/23 - 24, WEAF - New York, irregular time; first sponsored show 1924 - 26, WEAF, 60m
1926 - 30, NBC, Tue, 60m

1 **Everett Dirksen Obituary** (9/7/69) CBS-TV

2 **Everett Hoagland and His Orchestra** (1939, 3/30/40) Mut

Eversharp Penman (9/27/29 - 3/21/30) Eversharp, CBS, Fri, 8:30 pm

2 **Every Day's A Holiday** (1938) film sound track, 1949

3 **Every Four Years** (Jan, Feb, 1980) PBS-TV

2 **Every Penny Counts** (Syn)

1 **Everybody Sing** (1/38) Air trailer

1 **Everybody Wins** (with Phil Baker)
(4/23/48 - 10/22/48) Philip Morris, CBS, Fri, 10 pm

1 **Everybody's Business** (11/22/52) Syn

1 **Everybody's Church** (10/4/42) WEEI

Everybody's Music (with Howard Barlow) also Music and The Theater
(5/3/36 - 10/17/37), CBS, Sun, 60m, 2 pm
(5/15/38 - 10/23/38) CBS, Sun, 3 pm

Everyday Beauty (with Eileen Douglass)
(1/4/32 - 10/28/32) Nivea Cream, Bl, 2t (Mon & Wed) 15m, 10 am

2 **Everyman's Theater** (written by Arch Oboler) (10/4/40 - 3/28/41) Oxydol, NBC, Fri, 9:30 pm

18 **Everything For The Boys** (with Ronald Colman; with Dick Haymes as of 6/27/44)
(1/18/44 - 6/25/45) Autolite, NBC, Tue, 7:30 pm; see Dick Haymes

Everything Goes (3/29/43 - 11/20/43) NBC, 6t, 9 am

1 **Ewing Sisters With The Van Alexander Trio, The** (Standard transcription)

Ex-lax Big Show, The (9/25/33 - 6/25/34) (with Henrietta Schumann)
(9/24/34 - 6/17/35) (with Lud Gluskin, Block and Sully, Gertrude Niesen) Ex-lax, CBS, Mon, 7:30 pm

Exciting Lives

2 **Exclusive Story** (Syn)

1 **Excursions In Modern Music** (7/2/49) Mut

536 **Excursions In Science** (1943 - 1955) Syn

1 **Exit Of The King and Queen From The Federal Building** (6/10/39) Mut

1 **Exodus Re-union** (8/9/49)

Expectant Father (with Perry Ward)

1 **Experiment In Living** (6/6/47) CBS

Experiments In Drama (1963) Sat

1 **Explorers Of The Wild** (1950) Syn

Exploring America (see Conoco Tourist Adventures)

Exploring Music (2/9/42 - 10/5/42) CBS, Mon, 3:30 pm

Exploring Space (1/3/41 - 8/8/41)
(2/13/42 - 2/12/43) CBS, Fri, 15m, 3:45 pm

Exploring Space (10/7/37 - 10/5/38) CBS, 15m
10/7/37 - 10/28/37, Thu, 5:30 pm
4/27/38 - 10/5/38, Wed, 5:45 pm

8 **Exploring The Unknown**
(12/2/45 - 3/14/48) 12/2/45 - 6/23/46; 9/15/46 - 8/31/47, Revere, Mut, Sun, 9 pm
9/2/47 - 3/14/48, Sus, ABC, Sun, 7:30 pm

26 **Exploring Tomorrow** (host, John Campbell) (12/4/57 - 6/13/58) Multi, Mut, Wed, 25m, 8:05 pm

1 **Expose** (8/63) WNOR

2 **Extemporaneous Recordings** (1939)

Eye Witness (see Dateline)

1 **Eye, The** (9/1/49) ABC

Eye-Sketch (6/16/49 - 9/22/49) ABC, Thu, 8 pm

Eyes Aloft (8/7/42 - 43) NBC - West

15 **Eyes and Ears Of The Air Force, The** (1942) Syn

1 **Eyes Of Knight** (15m) Syn

1 **Eyes Of The War** (1947)

2 **Eyes On The Future** (4/16/47) Syn

6 **Eyes On The Skies** (Syn)

13 **Eyes Wright** (with Mel Allen, Page Cavanaugh Trio) (12/6/54 - 8/23/57) Coast Guard, CBS, 5t, 9:30 am
also (1954) Syn

1 **Eyewitness '52** (1/2/53) Syn

1 **Eyewitness Account Of The German Surrender In Northern Italy** (5/2/45) Mut

5 **Eyewitness News** (Syn)

1 **Eyewitness To History: 1959** (1/1/60) CBS-TV

Ezio Pinza Show (3/7/53 - 8/15/53) NBC, Sat, 9:30 am

F. O. B. Detroit (9/12/42 - 9/26/42) CBS, Sat, 3:30 pm

Fables For Fun (12/6/41 - 3/28/42) Bl, Sat, 15m, 11:45 pm

Fables In Rhythm (8/17/39 - 11/2/39) Mut, Thu, 15m, 7:30 pm

Fables In Verse (by Alfred Kreymborg) (1/8/39 - 3/12/40) NBC, Sun, 15m, 2:45 pm

1 **Fabulous Dr. Tweedy, The** (with Frank Morgan) (6/2/46 - 3/26/47) NBC
6/2/46 - 9/22/46, Lucky Strike, Sun, 7 pm (summer replacement for Jack Benny)
10/2/46 - 3/26/47 (also called Frank Morgan Show), Pall Mall, Wed, 10 pm

1 **Fabulous Mr. Manchester, The** (5/6/50) ABC

25 **Face The Nation** (12/21/54 - 97+) CBS, Sun

68 **Faces Of Love** (8/4/75 - 11/12/75) Syn

Fact Or Fiction (10/6/46 - 12/28/47) Wings Cigarettes, ABC, Sun, 5m, 1:55 pm

2 **Fact Or Fantasy** (Syn)

14 **Factfinder, The** (1937) Syn
(12/12/38 - 4/10/39) CBS, 15m
12/12/38 - 2/24/39, 3t, 11 am
4/3/39 - 4/10/39, 2t (Mon & Wed), 4 pm

1 **Facts For Action** (1949) Syn

Facts Unlimited (1/22/50 - 4/9/50) Doubleday, NBC, Sun, 15m, 4:15 pm

FADA Hour (7/9/29 - 12/31/29) Fada Radio, CBS, Tue, 10 pm

Fairchild and Carroll

Faith and Freedom (with E. J. Mollenauer)
(4/3/39 - 6/26/39) NBC, Mon, 15m, 12:30 pm
(4/7/41 - 10/6/41) NBC, Mon, 15m, 1:30 pm

Faith For The Future (10/13/51 - 1/19/52) ABC, Sat, 15m, 6:15 pm

1 **Faith For Tomorrow** (4/16/49) NBC

4 **Faith In Our Time** (1946 - 54) Mut, 5t (not always in New York)

14 **Falcon, The** (4/10/43 - 11/27/54)
4/10/43 - 8/28/43, Sus, Bl, Sat, 7 pm (with Berry Kroeger)
9/1/43 - 12/29/43, Bl, Wed, 25m, 7:05 pm
7/3/45 - 9/23/47, Gem Blades, Mut, Tue, 8:30 pm (with James Meighan)
1/5/48 - 12/27/48 (with Les Tremayne), Sus, Mut, Mon, 8 pm
1/2/49 - 6/18/50, Sus, Mut, Sun, 7 pm; Anahist from 1/7/50 - 3/26/50, Mut, Sat; NBC, 7 pm as of 5/7/50
6/21/50 - 8/30/50, Kraft, NBC, Wed, 8:30 pm
9/3/50 - 5/27/51, Kraft, NBC, Sun, 4 pm
6/6/51 - 8/29/51, Kraft, NBC, Wed, 8:30 pm (summer replacement for The Great Gildersleeve)
10/21/51 - 6/8/52, Sus, NBC, Sun, 4 pm (with Les Damon)
6/19/52 - 8/28/52, Sus, Mut, Mon, 8 pm (broadcast Sundays in New York)
9/7/52 - 9/14/52, Sus, NBC, Sun, 4 pm
1/5/53 - 9/27/54, Multi, Mut, Mon, 8 pm
11/1/54 - 11/27/54, Multi, Mut, Mon, 8 pm

1 **Fall Of France, The** (6/12/60) CBS

1 **Falla Trio, The** (1939) WWRL

1 **Fallout: The Clouded Horizon** (1961) CBS

2 **False V-J Day Coverage** (8/10/45) NBC

Falstaff Show (with Alan Reed)
(4/3/44 - 3/30/45) Falstaff Brewing, Bl, 3t, 15m, 11 pm

Falstaff's Fables (with Alan Reed Sr. and Jr.) (9/18/50 - 12/28/50) Mars,

Fame and Fortune (see Tommy Dorsey)

6 **Families Need Parents** (Syn)

Family Circle (with Walter Kiernan) (5/14/51 - 5/9/52) ABC, 5t, 60m

4 **Family Closeup** (ABC) Syn

1 **Family Doctor, The** (1930s) 15m

Family Hotel (see Jack Pearl)

Family Hour (see Prudential Family Hour)

Family Hour Of Stars (see Prudential Family Hour Of Stars)

Family Living (1958) with Eddie Cantor

Family Man, The (9/12/38 - 12/15/39) NBC, 5t, 15m

Family Party (3/12/38 - 3/24/51) Sat
3/12/38 - 7/2/38, Allis Chalmers, Bl, 10:30 am
1/10/42 - 5/30/42 (with Joe Emerson and Betty Crocker), General Mills, NBC, 10 am
7/1/50 - 3/24/51, Carnation, CBS, Sat, 10 am

Family Quiz (1940s)

1 **Family Skeleton** (with Mercedes McCambridge; created by Carlton E. Morse) (6/8/53 - 3/5/54) Multi, CBS, 5t, 15m

Family Theatre (5/6/34 - 9/30/34) (with James Melton) Ward Baking Company, CBS, Sun, 9 pm

14 **Family Theater** (created by Rev. Patrick Peyton)
(2/13/47 - 1/31/62) Sus, Mut
2/13/47 - 11/4/48, Thu
11/10/48 - 1/31/62, Wed

Famous Actor's Guild (see The Ethel Barrymore Theater)

Famous Artists Of The Air (with Eddie Dowling) (1934) CBS, 15m

Famous Babies (with Dr. Louis I. Harris) (5/6/35 - 10/21/35) CBS, Mon, 15m, 11 am

1 **Famous Belgians** (1946) Syn

3 **Famous Comic Artists** (1934) 10m, Syn

3 **Famous Court Dramas** (Syn)

23 **Famous Escapes** (1945) Syn

1 **Famous First Facts** (with Joseph Nathan Kane) (12/22/38 - 8/27/39) Sus, Mut, Thu, 9:30 pm

Famous Fortunes (with Mark Hawley (2/8/38 - 5/10/38) Richland Shoes, Mut, Tue, 15m, 7:45 pm

Famous Furniture Stories

1 **Famous Homes Of Famous Americans** (Syn)

9 **Famous Jury Trials** (with Maurice Franklin) (1/5/36 - 6/25/49)
1/5/36 - 3/30/36, Mennen, Mut, Sun/Mon, 10 pm
9/28/36 - 5/10/37; 9/27/37 - 12/20/37, Mennen, Mut, Mon, 45m, 10 pm
11/2/38 - 3/8/39, Goodrich, Mut, Wed, 10 pm
11/11/40 - 4/21/41, O'Henry, Bl, Mon, 7 pm
4/28/41 - 9/30/41, O'Henry, Bl, Mon, 10 pm
10/7/41 - 10/31/44, Bl, Tue, 9 pm
11/10/44 - 1/5/45, O'Henry, ABC, Fri, 8:30 pm
1/12/45 - 2/1/46, O'Henry, ABC, Fri, 9 pm
2/9/46 - 5/24/47, Sus, ABC, Sat, 8:30 pm; 8 pm as of 10/19/46
6/7/47 - 12/4/48, General Mills, ABC, Sat, 8:30 pm; 7:30 pm as of 6/5/48
12/11/48 - 6/25/49, Sus, ABC, Sat, 8:30 pm

Famous Loves (11/4/32 - 7/28/33) NBC, Fri, 15m, 3:15 pm

Famous Rescues (Syn)

1 **Famous Romances** (with William Farnum and Martha Wentworth) Syn

1 **Famous Speeches In The American Tradition** (Syn)

Famous Trials In History (3/15/31 - 5/17/31) NBC, Sun, 10:15 pm

Fannie Hurst Presents (7/8/44 - 12/30/44) Borden, Bl, Sat, 10 am

1 **Fannie Hurst Reviews** (10/31/46) WJZ

Fanny Brice (see Baby Snooks)

Fanny Brice Show, The (see The Baby Snooks Show)

Fanny Brice-Frank Morgan Show, The (see The Frank Morgan Show)

Fantasies From Lights Out (see Lights Out)

Fantastic Four, The (Syn) 1975

Fantasy

Fantasy In Melody (8/17/41 - 5/27/42) (with Paul La Valle) Bl, Sun, 10 am
(3/21/42 - 10/3/42) (with Paul La Valle and Clark Dennis) Bl, Sat, 2 pm
(2/3/46 - 3/24/46) Mut, Sun, 15m, 4 pm
Farley and Riley
(6/14/36 - 8/5/36) NBC, Wed, 4:30 pm

1 **Farewell To Studio Nine** (8/16/64) CBS

1 **Farewell Visit With President and Mrs. Ford, A** (1/2/77) ABC-TV

Farm and Home Hour (see National Farm and Home Hour)

Farm Quiz (8/23/52 - 5/2/53) Mut, Sat

2 **Farmer and His Livestock, The** (Syn)

4 **Farmer and The Market Place, The** (1953) Syn

Farmer Takes The Mike, The (7/17/38 - 8/21/38) CBS, Sun, 4 pm

1 **Faron Young Show, The** (1957) Syn

1 **Farrell Dobbs** (8/6/45) NBC

Fascinating Facts (with Art Dickson and Charles Morgan) (2/9/35 - 5/4/35) Delco Appliances, CBS, Sat, 15m, 5:45 pm

1 **Fascinating Rhythm** (1948) ABC

Fashion Discoveries (with Wynn Price) (1941) NBC

Fashion Flashes By Virginia Hull (1944) 15m

Fashion Parade (1946 - 47) Esquire

Fashions and Figures (with Evelyn Tobey) (3/11/32 - 6/3/32) I. Newman and Sons, NBC, Fri, 15m, 10:30 am

Fashions In Loveliness (with Myndall Cain) (1931 - 6/24/32) Palmolive, Bl - Midwest, 5t, 15m, 2:30 pm

Fashions In Rations (see Billie Burke)

Fast Freight (1929 - 11/2/32) Gold Medal, Wheaties, CBS, various days and times

9 **Fat Man, The** (with J. Scott Smart) (1/21/46 - 9/26/51, 1952) ABC, Syn
1/21/46 - 1/6/47, Sus, Mon, 8:30 pm
1/10/47 - 2/7/47, Sus, Fri, 8 pm
2/14/47 - 8/4/50, Pepto-Bismol, Fri, 8 pm
10/6/50 - 12/29/50, R J Reynolds, ABC, Fri, 8 pm
1/10/51 - 9/26/51, American Chicle, ABC, Wed, 8:30 pm

Father Brown (see The Adventures Of Father Brown)

1 **Father Cares: The Last Of Jonestown** (4/23/81) NPR

36 **Father Coughlin** (from Shrine Of The Little Flower, Royal Oak, Michigan) began in 1926 on WJR in Detroit
(10/5/30 - 42)
10/3/30 - 4/31, Little Flower, CBS, Sun, 60m
10/4/31 - 42, bought time on various stations including
1/24/37 - 4/11/37, Sun, 3 pm

6 **Father Flanagan's Boy's Town** (1941) Syn

7 **Father Knows Best** (with Robert Young and June Whitley) (8/25/49 - 7/5/51; 9/27/51 - 7/3/52; 9/4/52 - 11/19/53) General Foods, NBC, Thu, 8:30 pm; 8 pm from 9/27/51 - 7/3/52
Audition show (12/20/48)

1 **Father O'Connor's Jazz Anthology** (12/70) WRVR

4 **Father's Day Program** (1945, 1946, 1948, 1950) Syn

1 **Fats Waller Jam School** (10/19/38)

Fats Waller Rhythm Club (4/24/34 - 3/25/35) CBS, 15m, various days and times

Faultless Starch Time (with Ernie Lee and The Pleasant Valley Boys; then Bob Atcher)
(10/10/48 - 12/27/53) Faultless Starch, NBC, Sun, 15m, 11 am

40 **Favorite Story** (with Ronald Colman) (6/18/46 - 5/27/47; 9/23/47 - 6/8/48; 9/14/48 - 4/19/49) Syn; dates are NBC - Pacific, Tue

7 **Favorites Forever** (7/13 - 17/51)

Faye Emerson (9/15/52 - 6/18/54) NBC, 5t, 40m, 12:05 pm

30 **FBI In Peace and War, The** (with Martin Blaine) (11/25/44 - 9/28/58) CBS
11/25/44 - 6/30/45, Lava, Sat, 8:30 pm
8/23/45 - 6/27/46; 8/29/46 - 6/26/47, Lava, Thu, 8:30 pm
8/22/47 - 11/21/47, Lava, Fri, 9:30 pm
11/27/47 - 6/24/48; 8/26/48 - 6/30/49; 9/1/49 - 6/29/50; 8/31/50 - 12/28/50, Lava, Thu, 8 pm
1/4/51 - 9/25/52, Multi, Thu, 8 pm; 8:30 pm as of 6/12/52
10/1/52 - 9/28/55, Wed, 8 pm
10/5/55 - 7/4/56, Wed, 8:30 pm
7/8/56 - 9/29/57, Sun, 6:05 pm
10/6/57 - 9/28/58, Sun, 5:30 pm

FDR - Sunrise Hour

1 **FDR** (1/29/82) ABC-TV

1 **Fear Begins At Forty** (10/28/47) CBS

Feature Artist (Mut) 15m

Feature Assignment (Syn)

1 **Feature Page** (11/27/47) CBS

4 **Feature Project** (1953, 1954) CBS

Feature Story (with Robert Trout) (1/1/45 - 3/29/46) CBS, 5t, 15m

Featuring Marjorie Mills
(9/21/27 -12/23/37) Maine Development Commission, Mut, 2t, 1:45 pm

2 **Federal Agent** (1947) 15m

1 **Federal Aid To Wildlife** (3/40) Syn

1 **Federal Symphony Of New York** (1939) Syn

Federal Theater Project (1936 - 39)

1 **Federal Theatre Special Broadcast** (6/26/39) NBC

Federation Of Women's Clubs
(7/6/34 - 8/31/40) Sus
7/6/34 - 9/27/35, Bl, Fri, 15m, 4:45 pm
10/1/35 - 4/20/37, NBC, Tue, 15m
12/16/37 - 1/20/38, Bl, Thu, 30m
11/1/38 - 10/17/39, NBC, Tue, 15m
6/29/40 - 8/31/40, NBC, Sat, 15m, 11:45 am

106 **Feeling Is Mutual, The** (Harry Zimmerman Orchestra; often with The Lyttle Sisters and Andy Williams) (10/24/44 - 6/27/46) Mut

Feen-A-Mint National Amateur Night (see National Amateur Night)

Feg Murray Show, The

Felix Knight (see Schaefer All-Star Parade)

Felix Mills Presents (with Otto Kruger and Martha Tilton)

1 **Fella and A Girl, A** (11/1/47) audition

Fels Naptha Show (1930)

1 **Ferde Grofe and Orchestra** (Thesaurus transcription)

5 **Ferde Grofe Orchestra** (Thesaurus transcriptions)

Ferde Grofe Show, The (11/3/31 - 4/3/32) (with Jane Froman) NBC, Sun, 4 pm
(7/29/34 - 8/26/34) (Americana) CBS, Sun, 10:30 pm

1 **Festival Of American Music** (with Alfred Drake) (6/30/46 - 9/22/46) Ford, ABC, Sun, 60m, 8pm

Festival Of Brazilian Music

Festival Of Music (with Maurice Spitalny Orchestra, Mary Briney; from Pittsburgh)
(12/11/38 - 7/2/39) Bl, Sun, 3:30 pm
(10/22/39 - 3/10/40) Bl, Sun, 8 pm
(9/26/48 - 3/6/49) (originally Festival Of Song until 12/19/4; with Mishel Piastro) Longine, CBS, Sun, 5 pm (changed to Choraliers)
(1/8/55 - 2/12/55) ABC, Sat, 5:30 pm

Festival Of Opera (11/11/51 - 7/1/56) Mut, Sun, 2 hours, 1:30 pm; 1 pm as of 12/23/51; 1:30 pm as of 3/1/53

561 **Fibber McGee and Molly** (with Marian and Jim Jordan)
(4/16/35 - 3/23/56) NBC; (see also Smackout) (739 - 30m shows broadcast)
4/16/35 - 7/2/35, Johnson Wax, NBC, Tue
7/8/35 - 3/7/38, Johnson, NBC, Mon
3/15/38 - 6/28/38; 9/6/38 - 6/27/39; 9/5/39 - 6/25/40; 10/1/40 - 6/24/41; 9/30/41 - 6/23/42; 9/29/42 - 6/22/43; 9/28/43 -

Fibber McGee and Molly (continued)
6/20/44; 10/10/44 - 6/26/45; 10/2/45 - 6/11/46; 10/1/46 - 6/17/47; 10/7/47 - 6/1/48; 10/5/48 - 5/31/49; 9/13/49 - 5/23/50, Johnson, NBC, Tue, 9:30 pm; 473 shows broadcast
9/19/50 - 6/12/51; 10/2/51 - 6/10/52, Pet, NBC, Tue, 9:30 pm
10/7/52 - 6/30/53, Reynolds, NBC, Tue, 9:30 pm

Fiddler's Fancy (1937, 1/15/38 - 4/15/39; 7/1/39 - 11/11/39) CBS, Sat, 25m, 9:30 am; 9:15 am as of 7/1/39

4 **Fidler Now Talks Music** (Nov, Dec, 1963) Syn

1 **Field Sanitation: The Fly** (8/11/43) filmstrip audio

Fields and Hall (Streamliner Show)
(8/30/33 - 6/1/35) 15m
8/30/33 - 7/25/34, NBC, Wed, 11:45 am
7/30/34 - 6/1/35, Bl, 5t

2 **Fields and Hall Mountaineers** (Thesaurus transcriptions)

Fiesta (with Harry von Zell and Olga San Juan) (8/12/51 - 9/30/51) CBS, Sun, 7:30 pm (partial summer replacement of Amos 'n' Andy)

1 **Fiesta In Nueva York** (3/30/47) CBS International

Fiesta Time (see World Dances)
(3/11/39 - 9/23/39) (from Treasure Island, San Francisco) Mut, Sat, 8:30 pm; 9 pm as of 7/1/39

1 **Fifi Dorsay, Buddy Rogers Program, The** (7/11/33) NBC

Fifteen Minutes In The Nation's Capital (1930 - 2/23/31) NBC, Mon, 15m, 8:15 pm

Fifteen Minutes With Crosby (see Bing Crosby)

1 **Fifth Anniversary Salute Of "Operation Skywatch"** (Syn)

Fifth Horsemen, The (7/4/46 - 8/22/46) NBC, Thu, 10:30 pm

2 **Fifth Row Center** (2/4/40 - 5/29/40) Mut
2/4/40 - 4/7/40, Sun, 6 pm
4/19/40 - 5/29/40, Fri, 8 pm

1 **Fifth War Loan Drive; Opening Program** (6/12/44) pool feed

Fifty One East Fifty First (see Kay Thompson)

1 **Fifty Years Of Chevrolet** (1972)

Fight Camp (Blanche Ring; then Marion Barney; also with Sam Byrd)
(6/8/41 - 8/10/41) Mut. Sun, 7 pm

1 **Fight Night** (11/26/42)

1 **Fight Of The Month** (9/16/70) TV Syn

1 **Fight Preview** (6/16/38) NBC

1 **Fighter Pilots At Work** (8/12/43) BBC

Fighting AAF, The (also called Your AAF)
(3/31/45 - 6/23/45) Bl, Sat, 1:30 pm
(7/8/45 - 9/2/45) ABC, Sun, 8:30 pm
(9/6/45 - 11/8/45) ABC, Thu, 10:30 pm

1 **Fighting In Vietnam** (4/14/61)

1 **Fighting Parson, The** (Mut) audition

Fighting Senator (Richard Coogan also with Louise Fitch) (7/29/46 - 9/23/46) CBS, Mon, 8:30 pm (partial summer replacement of Joan Davis)

Final Edition (with Dick Powell)
(9/23/48 - 10/28/48) ABC. Thu, 7:30 pm

Find That Twin (with Bill Goodwin and John Holbrook)

1 **Finders Keepers** (with Happy Felton)
(7/3/44 - 6/8/45) NBC, 5t, 10:30 am; 11 am as of 4/16/45

Finding Yourself (1/12/37 - 6/15/37) Burdett College, CBS, Tue, 15m, 6:15 pm

Fine Arts Quartet (1948 - 53) Sus, ABC, Sun (not in New York)

Finley H. Grey (Don Corday)
(7/8/38 - 8/12/38)

1 **Finnish Foreign Minister** (12/5/39) Mut

2 **Fiorello LaGuardia** (1940 - 46) locally in New York 4/12/45; 7/13/45: 7/18/45; 12/30/45
also (1/6/46 - 6/30/46) Liberty Magazine, ABC, Sun, 15m, 9:30 pm

Fire Chief, The (see Ed Wynn)

5 **Firefighters** (Syn; 1948) 15m

1 **Firefly** (11/37) Air trailer

Fires Of Men (9/16/39 - 11/7/29) Domestic Staker Co., CBS, Thu, 7:30 pm

Fireside Chats (see Franklin D. Roosevelt

1 **Fireside Family, The** (1931) Syn

Fireside Party (10/17/43 - 1/16/44) Moose Lodge, Mut, Sun, 5 pm

Fireside Recitals (with Sigurd Nilssen)
(9/16/34 - 1/2/38) American Radiator, NBC Sun, 15m, 7:30 pm

Firesided Singers, The (12/9/40 - 3/17/41) NBC, Mon, 15m, 12:30 pm

1 **Firestone Voice Of The Farm** (7/8/38)

3 **Firing Line** (1973, 1981, 1986) PBS-TV

1 **First 1946 Civilian Auto Off The Ford Assembly Line, The** (1946) WOR

1 **First American Opera Festival, The** (5/7/42) Mut

1 **First Anniversary Of The Death Of Franklin D. Roosevelt** (8/12/46) Mut

1 **First Anniversary Of The United Nations** (8/25/46) CBS

1 **First Broadcast To Russia By The U. S. State Department** (2/17/47)

1 **First Came The Word**

1 **First Comes Food** (12/14/47) WEEI

1 **First Daylight Raid On Berlin, The** (3/7/44) BBC

5 **First Fabulous Fifty, The** (10/10/76 - 11/7/76) NBC

1 **First Game Of The 1951 World Series, The** (10/4/51) Mut

First Hundred Years, The (with Sam Edwards) (7/7/49 - 9/29/49) ABC, Thu, 8:30 pm

1 **First In Peace** (4/30/39) Bl

First Ladies Of Radio (60m)

1 **First Lady: Nancy Reagan, The** (6/24/85) NBC-TV

First Line (...of Defense)
(12/2/41 - 11/1/45) Wrigley, CBS, Thu, 10 pm

1 **First Manned Space Shuttle Launch, The** (4/10/81) NBC-TV

32 **Firstnighter Program, The**
(11/27/30 - 10/20/49) Campana
1/27/30 - 3/26/31, Bl, Thu, 8:30 pm; 8 pm as of 2/5/31; started with Don Ameche and June Meredith; Betty Lou Gerson as of 11/8/35; Barbara Luddy as of 9/4/36 - 9/8/53
5/6/31 - 9/9/31, Bl, Wed, 8 pm
9/19/31 - 8/20/32, Bl, Sat, 9:30 pm
8/26/32 - 4/24/36; 9/4/36 - 2/12/37, Bl, 9 pm; NBC as of 10/6/33, Fri, 10 pm as of 8/11/33
2/19/37 - 12/21/37, CBS, Fri, 9:30 pm; Les Tremayne replaced Don Ameche on 6/4/37
1/7/38 - 8/26/38, NBC, Fri, 9:30 pm
9/2/38 - 5/24/40, CBS, Fri, 8 pm; 9:30 pm as of 6/30/39
9/3/40 - 9/9/41, CBS, Tue, 8:30 pm
9/19/41 - 5/29/42, CBS, Fri, 9:30 pm
10/4/42 - 4/25/43; 11/7/43 - 4/2/44, Mut, Sun, 6 pm; Olan Soule from 11/7/43
4/12/44 - 10/25/44, Mut, Wed, 9:30 pm
10/20/45 - 4/13/46, CBS, Sat, 7:30 pm
10/4/47 - 12/13/47, CBS, Sat, 8 pm
12/18/47 - 6/24/48, CBS, Thu, 10:30 pm
10/7/48 - 10/20/49, CBS, Thu, 10:30 pm; 10 pm from 6/9/49 - 9/1/49
(4/27/52 - 9/8/53) Repeats
4/27/52 - 8/31/52, Miller, NBC, Sun
9/9/52 - 9/8/53, NBC, Tue
(9/13/53 - 9/27/53) NBC, Sun, 7 pm

2 **First Offender, The** (7/1/39 - 7/6/41) Sus, Mut; started 3/18/39 on Colonial Network, Thu, 8:30 pm
7/1/39 - 3/1/41, Sat. 10:45 am/10 am
3/9/41 - 7/6/41, Sun, 8:30 am

First Person Singular (see Mercury Theater)

First Piano Quartet (3/30/41 - 53) various days, 15m including the following:
3/28/41 - 9/26/41, Bl, Fri, 10:30 pm
also 3/31/41 - 4/21/41, Bl, Mon, 10:15 pm
also 6/22/41 - 9/21/41, Bl, Sun, 11:15 am
10/2/41 - 1/1/42, Bl, 2t
also 11/23/41 - 12/14/41, Bl, Sun, 11:15 am
1/8/42 - 5/29/42, Bl, 2t Thu, Fri, 10:15 pm
also 3/22/42 - 7/19/42, Bl, Sun, 12:15 pm
3/11/44 - 8/26/44, NBC, Sat, 9:30 am
9/2/44 - 10/27/45, NBC, Sat, 11 am
1/5/46 - 4/13/46, Sus, NBC, Sat, 4:30 pm
5/25/47 - 7/6/47, NBC, Sun, 10:30 pm
7/1/47 - 9/29/47, NBC, Mon, 10:30 pm
10/16/47 - 2/19/48, NBC, Thu, 11:30 pm
1950 - 53, Sus, NBC, various days

1 **First Polio Vaccine** (4/18/55) WFBR

2 **First Spaceman, The** (4/12/61, 3/65) CBS, NBC-TV

2 **First Three Months, The**
(4/20/81, 4/23/81) CBS-TV

Fish and Hunt Club, The (with Sanford Bickart)

Fish Pond (with Win Elliot))
(8/13/44 - 10/1/44) ABC, Sun, 4 pm

Fish Tale (9/19/39 - 7/25/35) Booth Fisheries, CBS
9/19/39 - 12/12/39, Wed, 15m, 11:15 am
5/2/35 - 7/25/35, Thu, 15m, 11 am

2 **Fisher's Seven O'Clock News**
(10/24/50, 10/25/50) NBC Pacific, 15m

1 **Fisherman's Wharf** (4/5/46) ABC

Fishing and Hunting Club (with Jim Hurley and Dave Navell)
(6/27/45 - 1/12/50) Mail Pouch
6/27/45 - 12/18/46, ABC, Wed, 8:30 pm
12/23/46 - 1/12/50, Mut, Mon; Thu, 8:30 pm as of 5/26/49

Fisk Jubilee Choir (Magnolia Blossoms)
(10/5/38 - 5/28/41)
10/5/38 - 2/8/39, Bl, Wed, 9 pm
5/1/39 - 7/3/39, Bl, Mon, 10:30 pm
1939 - 3/31/40, Bl, Tue, 15m, 7:30 pm (not in New York)
4/7/40 - 6/30/40, Bl, Sun, 7:30 pm
10/3/40 - 12/26/40, Bl, Thu, 10:30 pm
4/2/41 - 5/28/41 (Down South) NBC, Wed, 7:30 pm

27 **Fitch Bandwagon, The** (9/4/38 - 5/23/48) Fitch Shampoo, NBC
9/4/38 - 6/17/45 (different bands) Sun, 7:30 pm; AFRS version usually 15m; Dick Powell host for 1944 - 45 season
also 9/8/43 - 12/29/43 (with Freddy Martin Orchestra) Bl, Wed, 9 pm
9/23/45 - 6/16/46 (with Cass Daley) Sun, 7:30 pm
9/29/46 - 6/1/47; 10/5/47 - 5/23/48 (with Phil Harris and Alice Faye) Sun, 7:30 pm

Fitch Jingle Show (see Morin Sisters)

Fitch Professor, The (with Carl Way and Jack Brooks)
(1/15/32 - 1/22/33) CBS, 15m
1/15/32 - 5/13/32, Fri, 11 am
11/2/32 - 1/22/33, Wed, 11:30 am

1 **Fitzgeralds, The** (Ed and Pegeen)
(1938 - 88) (started in 1927)
1938 - 84, WOR - New York; WJZ from 4/30/45 - 47
1984 - 88, WNYC - New York also network
(10/38 - 3/39) T. Leeming Co., Mut, 3t, 2:45 pm

Five After The Hour

1 **Five Cent Beer** (3/29/49) WOR

Five Men Of Fate (not in NY)
(5/13/40 - 9/2/40) Mut, Mon, 15m, 6:30 pm

2 **Five Minute Musical Programs** (1951) Syn

146 **Five Minute Mysteries** (1945 - 48) NBC, 5m; the first 6 discs were recorded on 4/20/45

2 **Five Minute Programs** (Syn)

4 **Five Minutes With Jack Baker and The Cadets** (Syn)

2 **Five Mysteries Program, The**
(8/10/47 - 8/29/48) Mut, Sun, 2 pm
(3/31/49 - 12/1/49) Mut, Thu, 8 pm
(12/12/49 - 3/27/50) Mut, Mon, 9:30 pm

2 **Five Of A Kind** (Standard transcriptions)

1 **Five Presidents On The Presidency**
(9/11/80) PBS-TV

1 **Five Star Final** (1935 - 36, 3/12/45) KOIN

11 **Five Star Matinee** (12/31/56 - 12/58) Multi, NBC, 5t, 3 pm

Five-Star Jones (with John Kane)
(2/4/35 - 2/5/37)
2/4/35 - 6/26/36, Mohawk, CBS, 5t, 15m
7/6/36 - 2/5/37, Oxydol, Bl, 5t, 15m, 10:15 am

Five-Star Revue (with Ray Sinatra Orchestra) (11/16/36 - 5/28/37) Karo and Linit, CBS, 15m, 3t, 1 pm

Five-Star Theater (15m)

Five-Star Theater (with Josef Bonime on Tue; Aborn Opera Company on Thu) (Flywheel, Shyster and Flywheel on Mon)
(12/6/32 - 5/23/33) Esso, CBS, 2t, 10 pm

1 **Flash Flood** (3/29/55) CBS

Flash Gordon (4/27/35 - 2/6/36) Sus, Mut, 15m
4/27/35 - 10/26/35, Sat (with Gale Gordon)
10/28/35 - 2/6/36, 5t

Flash Gun Casey, Press Photographer (see Casey, Crime Photographer)

1 **Flashback**

1 **Flavored With Flute** (7/3/49) CBC-Mut

1 **Fleet's In, The** (1941) Air trailer with Betty Jane Rhodes
(3/20/43 - 4/3/43) Mut, Sat, 8 pm

Fleetwood Lawton (1943 - 1947) Anacin, NBC

Fleischmann Yeast Hour, The (see Rudy Vallee)

1 **Fletcher Henderson's Sextet** (12/20/50)

Fletcher Wiley (4/29/40 - 4/3/42, 1944) Campbell, CBS, 5t, 15m, 2:30 pm; started in 1934 on West Coast in Los Angeles
(6/15/42 - 9/25/42) CBS, 5t, 15m, 11:15 am
(1944) Anacin, CBS

1 **Fletcher Wiley Of The Housewives' Protective League** (12/12/38)

1 **Flight In The Night** (Syn)

1 **Flight Of Apollo 8, The** (12/27/68) NBC-TV

1 **Flight Of Gemini 3, The** (3/21/65) NBC-TV

1 **Flight Of Gemini 5, The** (8/18/65) NBC-TV

1 **Flight Of The B-19, The** (6/27/41) Mut

1 **Flight Of The Constitution, The** (2/3/49) CBS

1 **Flight Of The Flagship** (Syn)

Flight With Music (with Johnny Desmond) (1946) 15m

1 **Flirtation Walk** (1934) Air trailer

26 **Flit Frolics** (1947) Syn

Flit Soldiers (with Harry Reser) (1929 - 30) Flit, NBC

1 **Flood Broadcast** (1/27/37) WFBR

1 **Flood Broadcast From New London** (9/24/38) Mut

Florence Hale Forum (Methods Of Teaching) (1/8/38 - 7/8/39) NBC, Sat, 15m

Florence Wyman (5/16/40 - 10/15/40) Bl
5/16/40 - 6/6/40, Thu, 45m, 10:15 pm
8/20/40 - 10/15/40, Tue, 10:30 pm

1 **Florida Calling** (1955) Mut

Florsheim Frolics (1930 - 6/2/33) Florsheim Shoes, NBC 1930 - 6/2/33, Tue, 8:30 pm
also (1930 - 1/25/31) Florsheim, Bl, Sun, 4 pm

Flow Gently Sweet Rhythm (see John Kirby)

Floyd Gibbons: World Adventures (1/24/30 - 12/23/32) 15m
1/24/30 - 9/26/30, Literary Digest, NBC, 5t, 6:45 pm
9/28/30 - 8/23/31, Bl, Sun, 9:30 pm
10/21/32 - 12/23/32 (also called Elgin Adventurer's Club), Elgin, NBC, Fri, 10:30 pm

1 **Flying Commandoes** (6/12/42)

Flying Family, The (with George Hutchinson) (12/3/32 - 4/7/33) Cocomalt, NBC, 3t, 15m, 5:30 pm

Flying For Freedom (AFRS) (1942)

Flying High (AFRS) 15m

Flying Hutchinsons, The

1 **Flying Patrol** (with Hugh Rowlands) (9/29/41 - 8/28/42) Sus, Bl, 5t, 15m

Flying Red Horse Tavern (with John March; Lennie Hayton Orchestra as of 3/27/36; also with Jim Harkins, Freddy Rich; sometimes with Willie Morris) (10/4/35 - 9/25/36) Mobil, CBS, Fri, 8 pm

Flying Time (with Colonel Roscoe Turner) (7/1/35 - 12/4/36) NBC, 5t, 15m

Flywheel, Shyster and Flywheel (with Groucho and Chico Marx) (11/28/32 - 5/22/33) Esso, Bl, Mon, 7:30 pm

1 **FM Demonstration: Music** (Syn)

1 **FM Demonstration: Sounds** (Syn)

1 **Focus** (7/28/74) WLNA

Folies Bergere Of The Air (see Broadway Merry-Go-Round)

Folies de Paree (see Broadway Merry-Go-Round)

1 **Folk Song Festival** (7/8/89) WNYC-FM

1 **Folk Songs Of Belgium** (1943) Syn

Folks From Dixie (5/7/33 - 8/6/33) NBC, Sun, 1:30 pm

1 **Follow The Crowd** (Syn)

Follow The Moon (with Nick Dawson and Elsie Hitz) (1/4/37 - 4/1/38) 5t, 15m
1/4/37 - 7/2/37, Jergens, NBC, 4:30 pm
10/4/37 - 4/1/38, Pebeco, CBS, 5 pm

1 **Fontane Sisters** (1954) World transcription

1 **Food and Defense** (5/40) Syn

1 **Food and Freedom** (11/21/41) Mut

Food For Thought (with Virginia Graham) (1955 - 56)

1 **Food Rationing** (12/27/42) Mut

1 **Foodtown Pops Revue** (Syn)

2 **Footlight Melodies** (1934 - 35) Syn

1 **Footlight Parade** (1933) film sound track

1 **For America We Sing** (7/22/41 - 5/4/42) Bl
7/22/41 - 9/23/41, Tue, 8:30 pm
9/29/41 - 5/4/42, Mon, 9:30 pm

1 **For Americans Only** (6/17/47) Mut

For Men Only (see George Jessel)

1 **For Men Only** (8/14/46) (with Nan Wynn) audition, 15m

2 **For Mercy's Sake** (Salvation Army) (1950, 1957) Syn

For The Children (not in NY) (5/4/40 - 7/40) Mut, Sat, 7 pm

1 **For The Defense** (Syn)

13 **For The Living** (1950) Syn

1 **For The Love O' Lil** (1930) Synchro-discs

1 **For The Record** (7/31/44 - 11/19/44) NBC, Mon, 11:30 pm

For This We Fight (5/22/43 - 12/25/44) NBC, Sat, 7 pm

For You Alone

4 **For Your Approval** (1946, 1947) Mut

Forbidden Cargo (Syn)

4 **Forbidden Diary** (Syn)

1 **Ford 1953 New Car Spots** (10/27/52) Syn

1 **Ford 1953 Used Car and Truck Spots** (7/17/53) Syn

Ford Bond (see Stainless Show)

1 **Ford Commercials** (1960) Syn

1 **Ford Fiftieth Anniversary Spot Announcements** (1953) Syn

Ford Rush and His Tinkle Toy Band (see Dad and Junior)

Ford Show, The (see Dinah Shore)

1 **Ford Showroom, The** (6/18/47) with Meredith Willson, CBS

1 **Ford Star Jubilee** (10/22/55) CBS-TV

6 **Ford Sunday Evening Hour, The** (10/7/34 - 6/23/46) Ford
10/7/34 - 3/1/42, CBS, Sun, 60m (called Ford Summer Hour during the summer)
9/30/45 - 6/23/46, ABC, Sun, 60m, 8 pm

15 **Ford Theater, The** (10/5/47 - 7/1/49) Ford, Fri, 60m
10/5/47 - 6/27/48, NBC
10/8/48 - 7/1/49, CBS

Ford V8 Revue (see Bob Crosby Ford V-8 Revue)

19 **Forecast** (preview of possible series) (7/15/40 - 9/2/40, 7/14/41 - 9/1/41) CBS, Mon, 60m (summer replacement for Lux in 1940); broadcast in 12 30-minute parts and 2 60-minute performances

Forecast School Of Cookery (with Mrs. A. M. Goudiss (1928 - 1/12/33) various sponsors from 1932 - 1933, Bl, various days, 15m, 11 am

2 **Foreign Assignment** (with Jay Jostyn) (7/24/43 - 1/8/44) Mut, Sat

Foreign Legion, The (3/2/33 - 5/12/33) CBS, Thu, 10 pm

1 **Foreign Minister Tariq Aziz** (1/9/91) C-SPAN

2 **Foreign News** (12/18/39, 4/11/40) WGN

Foreign Policy Association Talks (1936 - 6/19/42) Bl, Sun, 15m

1 **Forest Hills Tennis** (7/13/46) Mut

Forest Ranger Series, The

Forever Ernest (with Jackie Coogan, Lurene Tuttle) (4/29/46 - 7/22/46) Bromo-Seltzer, CBS, Mon, 8 pm

1 **Forever Susan** (2/8/48) Mut audition

Forever Tops (see Paul Whiteman)

Forever Young (1/13/36 - 6/26/36) NBC, 5t, 15m; led to Pepper Young's Family as of 6/29/36

2 **Forfeits** (4/1/47, 4/18/47) CBS audition

1 **Forgotten Children** (Syn)

Forhan's Song Shop (1928 - 1929) NBC, Mon, 8 pm; then Thu

1 **Former President Gerald Ford** (8/20/92) C-SPAN

1 **Former President Herbert Hoover** (1960) NBC-TV

3 **Former President Jimmy Carter** (7/18/88, 5/3/93, 12/1/93) C-SPAN

2 **Former President Ronald Reagan** (8/17/92, 5/15/93) C-SPAN

2 **Forrester's Wharf** (Syn)

1 **Fort Dix Army Program** (Mut)

57 **Fort Laramie** (with Raymond Burr) (1/22/56 - 10/28/56) CBS, Sun

Fortune Builders (4/12/31 - 7/12/31) Distributors Group - Inc., CBS, Sun/Thu, 15m, 10:30 pm

Fortune Stories (9/24/37 - 10/29/37) Bl, Fri, 10:30 pm

1 **Forty Eight Hours** (3/24/93) CBS-TV

Forty Fathom Travelers (11/13/29 - 11/5/30) Bay State Fishing, CBS, Wed, 8:30 pm

7 **Forty Million, The** (1952 - 53) NBC, Sat

Forty-five Minutes In Hollywood (with Cal York, Mark Warnow Orchestra) (1/27/34 - 12/27/34) Borden, CBS, Sat, 45m. Sun as of 4/8; Thu as of 7/26

Forum Of Liberty (10/18/34 - 4/11/35) MacFadden Publications, CBS, Thu, 8:30 pm

9 **Forum Of The Air, The** (1938, 1939) Syn

Forward Hour (WEVD, New York)

56 **Forward March** (1952 - 1954) Syn, 15m

2 **Foundation For Good Job Relations** (tape slide audio)

1 **Foundation For Tomorrow** (1950) Syn

Fountain Of Song (see Al and Lee Reiser)

Four Belles (9/15/39 - 6/13/42) 15m
9/15/39 - 10/6/39, Bl, Fri, 7:30 pm
11/26/39 - 8/17/40, Bl, 15m
11/26/39 - 6/2/40, Sun, 10:30 am
6/29/40 - 8/17/40, Sat, 10:15 am
11/29/41 - 6/13/42, Bl, Sat, 12 noon

Four Clubmen, The (1/22/38 - 9/27/41) 15m; various days and times including:
1/22/38 - 10/22/38, CBS, 2t (Tue and Sat)
1/2/40 - 8/20/40, CBS, Tue, 15m, 10:45 pm
8/2/41 - 9/27/41, CBS, Sat, 10:30 pm

Four Corners, USA (Four Corners Theater) (with Parker Fennelly and Arthur Allen) (7/19/38 - 4/15/39) CBS
7/19/38 - 9/22/38, Tue, 8 pm
10/22/38 - 4/15/39, Sat, 10:30 am

4 **Four For The Fifth** (written by Arch Oboler and directed by William N. Robson) (6/17/44 - 7/8/44) CBS, Sat

3 **Four Freshmen, The** (World transcriptions)

1 **Four Frightened People** (1/21/34) Air trailer

1 **Four Hundred Hour, The** (9/2/53) WMAQ

2 **Four Ink Spots, The** (8/9/35, 7/12/39) NBC

1 **Four Playboys, The** (Standard transcription)

Four Polka Dots (5/29/41 - 2/21/42) Bl, Sat, 15m, 10:30 am
(9/30/41 - 12/18/41) Bl, 2t, 10m, 1:50 pm
(5/1/42 - 5/29/42) Bl, Fri, 10m, 9:45 am

Four Showmen (8/24/34 - 2/1/41) 15m, CBS/NBC, various days and times

3 **Four Star Playhouse** (7/3/49 - 9/11/49) NBC, Sun, 8 pm

Four Story Theater

Four To Go (2/22/43 - 3/19/43) CBS, 5t, 15m, 7 pm

1 **Fourteen August, A Message For The Day Of Victory** (8/14/45) CBS

1 **Fourth Anniversary Salute To The Ground Observer Corps** (Syn)

1 **Fourth Christmas, The** (12/25/42) BBC

1 **Fourth Estate, The** (6/27/46) NBC, Syn, audition, Thu

Fourth Tower Of Inverness (The Adventures Of Jack Flanders) (1972) ZBS Media

Fox Fur Trappers Orchestra (8/4/29 - 35) I. J. Fox
8/4/29 - 7/27/30; 8/3/30 - 8/30/31, CBS, Sun, 6 pm
1933 - 34, NBC, Tue, 15m, 7:30 pm
1934 - 35, NBC, Mon, 15m, 7:30 pm

Foxes Of Flatbush (with Mignon Schreiber) (6/1/36 - 9/11/36) Bl, 6t, 15m, 3 pm

4 **Foxglove Street** (Syn)

5 **Foy Willing and The Riders Of The Purple Sage** (Syn) 15m

1 **Foy Willing Show, The**

1 **Fram Sports Thrill Of The Week** (4/2/49) Mut

Fran Hines (12/17/38 - 4/29/39) CBS, Sat, 15m, 2:45 pm

1 **Fran Warren** (Thesaurus transcription)

4 **Fran Warren Sings** (Thesaurus transcriptions)

2 **Fran Warren Sings Accompanied By The Allen Roth Orchestra** (Thesaurus transcriptions)

Frances Langford (6/5/47 - 8/28/47) Maxwell House, NBC, Thu, 8:30 pm (summer replacement for Burns and Allen)

Frances Lee Barton (9/20/32 - 9/20/35) General Foods, NBC
9/20/32 - 11/23/33, 2t, 15m, 11:15 am
11/30/33 - 1/10/35, General Foods, Thu, 15m, 11:15 am
1/18/35 - 9/20/35 (Kitchen Party; also wih Al and Lee Reiser), Fri, 30m

Frances Scully (2/5/51 - 4/13/51) ABC, 5t, 15m, 2:45 pm

1 **Frank and Ernest** (10/16/49 - 10/5/52) Sun, 11:15 am; continued throughout the 1950s at different times on Mutual
10/16/49 - 10/8/50, ABC
10/15/50 - 10/5/52, Mut

Frank and Flo Cronin (5/19/32 - 6/30/32) McLaughlin Gormley King insecticides, Bl, 2t (Thu and Sat), 15m, 7:30 am

4 **Frank Bettencourt and His Orchestra** (1970) CBS

13 **Frank Black Cadillac Show** (1953) Syn

Frank Black Presents (4/20/41 - 5/25/41) Bl, Sun, 6:30 pm

Frank Buck (see Bring 'Em Back Alive) (10/30/32 - 12/18/32) A. C. Gilbert, NBC, Sun, 15m, 5:45 pm

1 **Frank Buck Jungle Quiz, The** (7/15/41) Mut

Frank Buck, Jungle Adventures (see Bring 'Em Back Alive)
(7/16/34 - 11/16/34) Pepsodent, Bl, 5t, 15m, 7:45 pm

1 **Frank Buxton and Bill Owen Interview** (2/8/67) Mut

Frank Caniff

1 **Frank Crumit and Julia Sanderson** (see also Blackstone Plantation)
(10/1/29 - 9/6/43)
10/1/29 - 12/30/30 (Blackstone Plantation), Blackstone Cigars, CBS, Tue, 8 pm
also 1/6/31 - 12/26/33, Blackstone Cigars, NBC, Tue, 8 pm
also 1/22/31 - 6/2/32, Blackstone Cigars, Bl, Thu, 9 pm
1/11/31 - 4/28/33, Bond, CBS, Fri, 10:15 am
also 9/23/31 - 11/25/31, Bond, CBS, 2t (Mon & Wed), 6 pm
also 2/25/32 - 5/19/33, Bond, CBS, Thu, 6:15 pm
5/5/33 - 5/17/36, Bond, Sun, 5:30 pm
6/28/36 - 9/20/36 (with Hal Kemp Orchestra), Gulf, Sun, 7:30 pm (summer replacement for Phil Baker)
1936 - 37 (Norge Musical Kitchen) Sun, 15m
8/31/37 - 11/26/37, Heinz, CBS, 2t (Wed & Fri) 11 am
9/27/38 - 7/21/42 (see Battle Of The Sexes)
10/3/42 - 9/4/43 (Crumit and Sanderson Quiz; also called Mr. Adam and Mrs. Eve) Tums, Sat, 8 pm
also 3/1/43 - 9/6/43 (Swinging Sweethearts) Southern Cotton Oil Co., CBS - West, 5t, 15m, 2 pm

Frank Dailey (10/15/36 - 11/26/37) CBS, Fri, 10m, 6:35 pm

Frank Edwards (12/12/49 - 8/13/54) AFL - CIO, Mut, 5t, 15m, 10 pm

Frank Farrell (8/6/49 - 3/18/50) Mut, Sat, 15m, 7 pm
(5/18/54 - 3/15/57) ABC, 5t, 25m, 1:35 pm; 45m, 12:15 pm as of 6/6/55

Frank Fay Show, The (4/18/36 - 4/16/42)
4/18/36 - 8/28/36, Royal Gelatin, Bl, Sat, 9 pm; Fri, 8:30 pm as of 6/12/36
10/23/41 - 4/16/42 (Tums Show), Tums, NBC, Thu, 10:30 pm

1 **Frank Fontaine Show, The**
(7/48) audition
(6/8/52 - 9/28/52) CBS, Sun, 8 pm (summer replacement for Charlie McCarthy)

Frank Forrest (8/23/41 - 6/27/42) Mut, Sat, 15m

3 **Frank Froeba and His Backroom Boys** (World transcriptions)

3 **Frank Knox** (1941, 1942) Mut

Frank Leahy Show (1949 - 53)

Frank Luther (see I'll Never Forget)

1 **Frank Luther Fun Show, The** (Thesaurus syndication)

18 **Frank Morgan Show, The**
(8/31/44 - 5/31/45) Maxwell House, NBC, Thu (see also Baby Snooks, The Fabulous Dr. Tweedy and The Bickersons)

Frank Morgan-Fanny Brice Show, The

9 **Frank Parker Show, The** (1943) (with Kay Lorraine) 15m also syndicated with Andre Baruch and Paul Baron Orchestra

1 **Frank R. McNinch** (11/12/38) Mut

Frank Ross** (8/22/40 - 3/27/41) Bl, Thu, 15m, 12 noon

3 **Frank Sinatra** (6/2/62, 11/13/67) BBC, NBC-TV, AFRS

2 **Frank Sinatra and Company** (1948) Syn

72 **Frank Sinatra Show, The** (10/27/42 - 58)
10/27/42 - 6/9/43, CBS, Tue, 15m, 10:45 pm
5/14/43 - 5/28/43 (with Raymond Scott Orchestra) CBS, Fri, 45m, 11:15 pm
10/24/43 - 12/26/43, CBS, Sun, 15m, 7:15 pm
1/5/44 - 6/14/44; 8/16/44 - 11/15/44, Vimms Vitamins, CBS, Wed, 9 pm
11/20/44 - 12/25/44, Vimms, CBS, Mon, 8:30 pm
1/3/45 - 5/16/45, Sales Builders, CBS, Wed, 9 pm
9/12/45 - 5/29/46; 9/11/46 - 6/4/47 (Songs By Sinatra), Old Gold, CBS, Wed, 9 pm
9/16/47 - 5/28/49 (Light Up Time) Lucky Strike, NBC, 5t, 15m; also Sat, 9 pm, 30m
9/5/49 - 6/2/50, NBC, 5t, 15m
10/29/50 - 7/22/51 (Meet Frank Sinatra; Here's Frank Sinatra as of 6/3/51), Multi, CBS, Sun, 60m, 5 pm; 4:30 pm as of 6/3/51
11/10/53 - 7/9/54 (To Be Perfectly Frank to 1955), Sus, NBC, 2t (Tue & Fri), 15m, 8:15 pm
7/13/54 - 8/24/54, NBC, Tue, 15m, 8:15 pm
9/1/54 - 7/15/55, Multi, NBC, 2t (Wed & Fri), 15m, 8:15 pm
1956 - 58, ABC, 5t, 15m also 1 show with Axel Stordahl; 10/10/44

1 **Frank Sinatra Timex Show, The** (10/19/59) ABC-TV

1 **Frank Singiser** (9/18/40) Mut

1 **Frank Singiser News** (6/27/39) Mut

1 **Frank Stanton Talk** (10/15/50) CBS

Frank Strasik

1 **Frank Trumbauer's Orchestra** (Standard transcription)

16 **Frank Watanabe and The Honorable Archie** (1938) Syn

4 **Frank Yankovic and His Yanks** (Standard transcription)

13 **Frankenstein** (with George Edwards) (1932)

2 **Frankie Carle** (1945) Lang-Worth transcriptions)

6 **Frankie Carle and His Orchestra** (8/7/47, 7/29/50) ABC, NBC, Lang-Worth transcriptions

Frankie Carle Orchestra
(7/10/46 - 10/9/46) ABC, Wed, 9:30 pm; 10 pm as of 9/4/46
(5/9/48 - 7/11/48) CBS, Sun, 5:30 pm

1 **Frankie Carle: Piano Solos (Rhythm Background)** Lang-Worth transcription

Frankie Laine Show, The
(10/7/51 - 10/21/51) CBS, Sun, 4:30 pm

1 **Frankie Laine Sings...For The 1950 March Of Dimes** (1950) Syn

3 **Frankie Laine With Carl Fischer's Orchestra** (Standard transcriptions)

2 **Frankie Laine With Orchestra Directed By Carl Fischer** (Standard transcription)

8 **Frankie Masters and His Orchestra** (1939) film sound track, Syn, Associated and Lang-Worth transcriptions

Frankie Masters Orchestra
(9/2/40 - 1/22/41) NBC, 5t/3t, 15m
also 6/29/40 - 11/30/40) NBC, Sat, 1:30 pm
4/5/41 - 6/28/41 , NBC, Sat, 15m, 1 :30 pm

1 **Frankie Trumbauer Orchestra** (Standard transcription)

1 **Frankie Trumbauer's Swing Seven** (Standard transcription)

1 **Franklin D. Roosevelt Jr. Speech** (1/17/46) Mut

2 **Franklin Roosevelt Speech** (8/9/20, 6/26/24)

1 **Franklin Roosevelt: In Memorium** (4/12/45) WGN

1 **Franklin Stewart Entertains** (5/1/41 - 10/2/41) CBS, Thu, 15m, 9:15 am

18 **Franklyn MacCormack's Book Of Memories** (Syn)

1 **Franz Lehar Festival** (1953) Syn

1 **Franzella Quintette, The** (Lang-Worth transcription)

Fray and Baum (5/1/36 - 8/22/36) CBS, Fri

Fray and Braggiotti (Jacques Fray and Mario Braggiotti) on various days and times including:
(5/25/31 - 10/18/31) CBS, Sun, 7:30 pm
(7/24/34 - 8/28/34) CBS, Tue, 10 pm
(2/7/38 - 8/12/38) Loxol Oil Tint Shampoo, CBS - West, 15m, 2t

Frazier Hunt (1/21/41 - 4/15/41) Mut
(3/10/42 - 5/27/43) Johns Manville, CBS
(1945 - 3/29/46) Mut

1 **Freberg Stanberg: The Interview** (11/91) NPR

131 **Fred Allen** (10/23/32 - 6/26/49)
10/23/32 - 4/16/33 (Linit Bath Club Revue), Linit Bath Oil, CBS, Sun, 30m, 9 pm
8/4/33 - 12/1/33 (Salad Bowl Revue), Hellmann's Mayonnaise, NBC, Fri, 30m, 9 pm
1/3/34 - 3/14/34 (Sal Hepatica Revue), Sal Hepatica, NBC, Wed, 30m, 9:30 pm
3/21/34 - 7/4/34 (Hour Of Smiles), Ipana - Sal Hepatica, NBC, Wed, 60m, 9 pm
7/11/34 - 6/26/35; 10/2/35 - 6/24/36; 10/7/36 - 6/30/37; 11/17/37 - 6/29/38; 10/5/38 - 6/28/39 (Town Hall Tonight), Ipana- Sal Hepatica, NBC, Wed. 60m, 9 pm
10/4/39 - 6/26/40 (Fred Allen Show), Ipana - Sal Hepatica, NBC, Wed, 60m, 9 pm
10/2/40 - 6/25/41; 10/1/41 - 2/25/42 (Texaco Star Theater), Texaco, CBS, Wed, 60m, 9 pm
3/8/42 - 6/28/42 (Texaco Star Theater), Texaco, CBS, Sun, 60m, 9 pm
10/4/42 - 6/27/43; 12/12/43 - 6/25/44 (Texaco Star Theater), Texaco, CBS, Sun, 30m, 9:30 pm; first Allen's Alley was 12/13/42

Fred Allen (continued)
10/7/45 - 6/30/46; 10/6/46 - 6/29/47; 10/5/47 - 12/28/47 (Fred Allen Show), Tenderleaf Tea, NBC, Sun, 30m, 8:30 pm
1/4/48 - 6/27/48; 10/3/48 - 6/26/49 (Fred Allen Show), Ford, NBC, Sun, 30m, 8:30 pm; 8 pm as of 1/9/49

Fred Astaire Show, The (with Johnny Green Orchestra) (9/8/36 - 8/31/37) Packard, NBC, Tue, 60m, 9:30 pm

Fred Brady Show, The (That's Life)
(7/8/43 - 9/30/43) Lever Brothers, NBC, Thu, 7:30 pm (summer replacement of Bob Burns)

Fred Feibel (4/29/32 - 12/27/32) International Oil Burners, CBS, 15m
(1937 - 39) CBS, Sat or Sun, mornings

Fred Kaltenback

1 **Fred Lowery (Whistler-Organ)** United transcription

1 **Fred Lowery Show, The** (Audition)

2 **Fred Robbins Show, The**
(10/12/53 - 4/23/54) Mut, 5t, 25m, 2 pm; also on early mornings and other times for many years in New York
(7/4/55 - 12/2/55) CBS, 5t, 15m, 3:30 pm

1 **Fred Waring Christmas Album, The** (12/44) AFRS

80 **Fred Waring Show, The**
(1/4/32 - 10/4/57)
1/4/31 - 32, Sus, NBC, Mon
1932 - 33, CBS, Sun
2/8/33 - 1/31/34, Old Gold, CBS, Wed, 10 pm
2/4/34 - 9/30/34, Ford, CBS, Sun, 8:30 pm; 9:30 pm as of 4/29/34
also 2/8/34 - 6/28/34; 9/13/34 - 6/27/35, Ford, CBS, Thu, 30m, 9:30 pm; 60m as of 1/3/35
7/2/35 - 7/28/36; 9/1/36 - 12/29/36, Ford, CBS, Tue, 60, 9:30 pm; 30m as of 1/21/36; 9 pm as of 6/30/36
also 1/17/36 - 12/25/36, Ford, Bl, Fri, 30m, 9:30 pm; 9 pm as of 6/5/36
10/8/38 - 3/4/39, Bromo-Quinine, NBC, Sat, 8:30 pm
6/19/39 - 6/9/44 (Chesterfeld Time; also called Pleasure Time; Victory Tunes, Words and Music) Chesterfield, NBC, 5t, 15m, 7 pm
9/7/44 - 12/28/44, Bl, Thu, 7 pm
1/4/45 - 5/31/45, Bl, Thu, 10 pm
6/4/45 - 8/27/46, Sus, NBC, 5t, 11 am; 3t as of 1/14/46
also 1/15/46 - 7/7/49, American Meat, NBC, 2t, 30m, 11 am; 10 am as of 9/30/47, Thu, 10 am as of 1/13/49
also 6/18/46 - 9/24/46; 6/24/47 - 9/30/47, Johnson Wax, NBC, Tue, 9:30 pm (summer replacements for Fibber McGee & Molly)
8/30/46 - 11/27/46, Florida Citrus Growers, NBC, 3t, 11 am
also 3/14/47 - 4/4/47; 7/18/47 - 7/849, Minneapolis Valley Canning Company, Fri, 11 am; 10 am as of 10/3/47

Fred Waring Show, The (continued)
10/6/47 - 9/29/49, GE, NBC, Mon, 10:30 pm; Thu as of 7/29/48
also (6/7/48 - 9/29/48) Johnson, NBC, Tue, 9:30 pm (summer replacement for Fibber McGee & Molly)
7/16/49 -7/22/50, Minneapolis Valley Canning, NBC, Sat, 10 am
10/1/56 - 3/15/57, ABC, 5t, 2 pm
4/9/57 - 10/4/57, ABC, 5t, 9:30 pm; 10:30 pm as of 6/17/57 Syndicated - ZIV (156 - 30m shows broadcast)

4 **Fred Waring's "Uncle Lumpy"** (3/47 - 5/47) Syn

2 **Freddie Martin and His Orchestra**

Freddie Rich (with Mildred Bailey) (10/1/33 - 11/19/33) CBS, Sun, 60m, 8 pm

1 **Freddie Rich and His Orchestra** (Associated transcription)

1 **Freddie Rich and His Orchestra/Ben Selvin and His Orchestra** (Muzak transcription)

Freddie Rich Entertains (1932 - 1936) CBS, various days and times (also see Benay Venuta)

Freddie Rich's Penthouse Party (see Benay Venuta)

Freddie Stewart (7/13/42 - 9/11/42) Bl, 5t, 15m, 10:45 pm

1 **Freddy Archer vs. Ralph Zanelli** (1/19/45)

5 **Freddy Martin and His Orchestra** (10/52) CBS, Syn, Standard transcriptions

13 **Freddy Martin Orchestra**
(1/16/33 - 11/4/56) (see also Penthouse Serenade)
1/16/33 - 9/29/33, Tydol, CBS, 3t, 15m, 7:30 pm
1934 (Going Places) 15m
10/7/34 - ?, Vicks, CBS, Sun afternoon
1935 - 36, Eden Liquid Dry Shampoo, Mut, Sun, 15m
12/13/36 - 3/21/37 (see Penthouse Serenade)
8/4/41 - 9/8/41, CBS, Mon, 10 pm
2/9/42 - 10/12/42, Lady Esther, CBS, Mon
also 7/4/42 - 9/5/42 (summer replacement of Truth Or Consequences) Duz, NBC, Sat, 8:30 pm
4/24/43 - 5/22/43, NBC, Sat, 15m, 10:15 pm
7/8/56 - 11/4/56, CBS, Sun, 12:30 pm
Syndicated - ZIV (78 - 15m shows broadcast) (It's Showtime From Hollywood)
Thesaurus syndication

3 **Freddy Martin Show, The** (6/56, 7/19/58) CBS, Thesaurus audition

22 **Freddy Martin, His Singing Saxophone and His Orchestra** (Standard transcriptions)

5 **Freddy Nagel and His Orchestra** (1946, 1947) WGN, ABC, MacGregor transcriptions)

Frederick William Wile (1923 - 6/20/36) CBS, Sat, various days (The Political Situation In Washington)

9 **Free Company, The** (with Burgess Meredith) (2/23/41 - 5/11/41, CBS, Sun, 2 pm

Free For All (1943) Mut
(1947) Portait Cold Wave, CBS - Pacific

1 **Free Time** (12/23/70) WNET-TV

Free World Theater (produced and directed by Arch Oboler)
(2/21/43 - 6/27/43) Bl, Sun, 25m, 6:05 pm; 30m, 6:30 pm as of 4/18

12 **Freedom Forum** (also see London Forum) (12/6/44 - 3/12/47) BBC

1 **Freedom Garden Spots** (1948) Syn

1 **Freedom House: Annual Awards** (10/8/46) CBS

2 **Freedom Is Our Business** (World syndication, audition)

1 **Freedom Never Dies** (4/30/44) Syn

15 **Freedom Of Opportunity** (1/7/44 - 7/7/46) Mutual Benefit, Mut
1/7/44 - 12/28/45, Fri, 8:30 pm
1/6/46 - 7/7/46, Sun, 10 pm

1 **Freedom Of Speech** (12/2/41) CBS

82 **Freedom Story, The** (1951 - 1955) Syn

2 **Freedom Train, The** (1947, 9/24/47) CBS, Decca transcriptions)

5 **Freedom U. S. A.** (Syn - ZIV, 1952) 52 episodes broadcast

2 **Freedom's Fighting Men** (Syn)

8 **Freedom's People** (1942) Red, Sun, 12:30 pm

1 **Freedom, The Living Tradition** (12/12/39) Red

1 **French News** (12/3/38) France

31 **French News In English** (9/19/38 - 5/20/40) France

1 **French Program Of Recorded Music** (8/23/38) Paris Mondial

1 **Fresh-Up Show, The** (with Bert Wheeler; Bert Lahr as of 12/5/45)
(4/4/45 - 6/26/46) Seven-Up, Mut, Wed, 8:30 pm

1 **Friar's Club Annual Testimonial Dinner** (1/8/61) CBS

1 **Friday Is A Big Day** (12/13/50) NBC

Friday Night Camel Show, The (see Jimmy Durante)

Friday On Broadway (with Jacques Renard Orchestra)
(12/3/43 - 6/29/45) American Home Products, CBS, Fri, 7:30 pm

Friday With Dave Garroway (see Dave Garroway)

Friend In Deed (with Richard Maxwell)
(9/2/40 - 6/27/41) CBS, 5t, 15m, 3:30 pm; 3:45 pm as of 10/7

Friend In Need (Turn To A Friend as of 4/20/53)
(3/24/53 - 11/5/53) Toni, ABC, 3t (Tue, Thu, Fri) 15m, 11:30 am; Tue and Thu as of 6/23/53

1 **Friendly Five Footnotes** (with Freddie Rich Orchestra)
(8/28/30 - 4/1/32) Friendly Five Shoes, 15m
8/28/30 - 4/9/31, Bl, Thu
9/4/31 - 4/1/32, CBS, Fri, 9:45 pm
also 12/7/31 - 32, CBS, Mon

Friendly Neighbors (8/4/40 - 11/25/40) NBC, 5t, 15m, 1:30 pm

1 **Friendship Airport Opening** (6/24/50) WFBR

Friendship Circle (5/27/40 - 8/16/40) NBC, 5t, 15m, 12 noon

Friendship Ranch (6/3/45 - 11/25/45) General Baking Co., Bl, Sun, 12:30 pm

Friendship Town (with Virginia Gardiner and Don Carney) (1/1/32 - 12/21/32) Vaseline, Bl, Fri, 9 pm; Tue, 9:30 pm as of 8/23/32; Wed, 9:30 pm as of 12/7/32)

1 **Friendship Train Program** (11/7/42) CBS

Frigidaire Country Club (1930)

Frigidaire Frolics (with Ted Fio Rito) (6/26/36 - 9/18/36) Bl, Fri, 9:30 pm

Frigidairians, The (2/1/32 - 10/20/32) Frigidaire, Bl, 15m, various days and times

1 **Fritzie Zivic vs. Al Davis** (7/2/41) Mut

Fro-Joy Players (3/6/30 - 4/16/31) General Ice Cream Co., CBS, Thu, 7 pm

1 **From Headquarters** (1929) Synchro-disc

1 **From Here To The Seventies** (10/7/69) NBC-TV

From Hollywood Today
(10/22/39 - 11/1/40) NBC
10/22/39 - 4/21/40, Sun, 1:30 pm
4/28/40 - 6/30/40, Sun, 5:30 pm
8/13/40 - 11/1/40, Fri, 8:30 pm

From The Annals Of History (see Marine Corps)

3 **From The Bookshelf Of The World** (1949) AFRS

2 **From The Capitol** (1967) ABC-TV

1 **From The House Of Bondage** (CBS)

3 **From The Indianapolis Motor Speedway** (1956 - 1958) Syn

1 **From The Midway** (1966) WAIT

From The Organ Loft (with Julius Mattfield, Charles Paul, E. Power Biggs)
(4/24/38 - 9/25/56) CBS, Sun, 15m, 9 or 9:15 am

1 **Front and Center** (with Dorothy Lamour)
(7/6/47 - 9/28/47) Tenderleaf Tea, NBC, Sun, 8:30 pm (summer replacement for Fred Allen) (different series)
(9/5/53 - 10/10/53) ABC, Sat, 11 am

1 **Front Line Features** (4/23/44) Mut

10 **Front Line Theater** (AFRS) (1943 - 44)

Front Lines Of Mercy (shows functions of Red Cross) (3/23/41 - 6/15/41) Bl, Sun, 11:15 am

Front Page (with Dick Powell and William Conrad) (5/6/48 - 9/16/48) ABC, Thu, 8 pm

124 **Front Page Drama** (by The American Weekly) Syn (4/27/33 - 5/23/54) 15m

Front Page Exclusive (with John Randolph Hearst and Edwin Lee) (1953 - 56) Mut, 15m

11 **Front Page Farrell** (6/16/41 - 3/26/54) 5t, 15m
6/16/41 - 3/13/42, Anacin, Mut
9/14/42 - 3/26/54, Hills Tablets and Multi, NBC

Front Page Features (with Knox Manning) (1945 - 1947) Pacific, Bruce Floor Cleaning, Washington State Apples, CBS - Pacific

1 **Front Page Headlines** (Syn)

Front Page Parade (with Peter Grant) (2/27/39 - 5/26/39) Mut, 3t, 15m, 6:30 pm

39 **Frontier Fighters** (1930s) Syn, 15m

39 **Frontier Gentleman** (with John Dehner) (2/2/58 - 11/16/58) CBS, Sun

24 **Frontier Town** (with Jeff Chandler; then Reed Hadley as of #24; (1952 - 53)

Frontiers Of American Life (with Dr. Mark Dawber)
(6/1/39 - 9/7/39) NBC, Thu, 15m, 12:30 pm
(7/1/40 - 9/30/40) Bl, Mon, 15m, 1:30 pm

Frontiers Of Science (7/9/46 - 10/1/46) CBS, Tue, 15m, 6:15 pm
(2/18/47 - 10/26/48) Sus, CBS, Tue, 15m, 6:15 pm

3 **Frontline** (1987, 1988, 1989) PBS-TV

Frostilla Broadcast Rehearsal (with Harry Salter Orchestra)
(1/4/32 - 3/28/32) Frostilla Skin Lotion, CBS, 15m, Mon, 9:15 pm

41 **Fu Manchu** (with John C. Daly)
(9/26/32 - 4/24/33) Campana, CBS, Mon, 8:45 pm; see also Collier Hour
(5/8/39 - 11/1/39) (with Hanley Stafford) Syn, 3t, 15m; rebroadcast from 3/18/40 - 9/11/40 as The Shadow Of Fu Manchu; 77 shows broadcast

2 **Fuel Conservation Program For National Defense** (1940) Syn

3 **Full Speed Ahead** (Mitchell Field, Men Of The Air) (with Lionel Stander)
(11/3/43 - 12/29/43) Mut, Syn, Wed, 4:30 pm

Fuller Brush Man, The
(9/29/29 - 3/29/32) Fuller Brush
9/29/29 - 5/19/31, Bl, Sat, 7:30 pm/8:30 pm
5/26/31 - 3/29/32 (with Earle Spicer and Mabel Jackson), NBC, Tue, 9:30 pm

1 **Fullness Of Times, The** (Syn)

22 **Fulton Lewis Jr.** (8/15/38 - 56+) Mut

Fulton Lewis Jr. At Home

Fulton Oursler (11/22/43 - 5/12/44) Loews Inc., Mut

Fun and Fancy Free (ABC) 60m

24 **Fun At Breakfast** (with Tom Howard, Ford Bond, George Shelton)
(1946 - 48) 3m, Syn

Fun Bug, The (with Edwin Reeser) (9/2/37 - 12/26/37) Barnsdall Refining, CBS, Sun, 2 pm

Fun Canteen (4/21/45 - 8/4/45) ABC, Sat, 25m, 1:05 pm

Fun For All (with Arlene Francis and Bill Cullen) (9/27/52 - 12/26/53) Toni, CBS, Sat; except for 4/17/53 - 5/29/53, ABC, Fri, 8:30 pm

1 **Fun House (Laugh Of The Party), The** (1/16/47) CBS

Fun In Print (with Sigmund Spaeth) (5/12/40 - 9/29/40) International Silver, CBS, Sun, 6 pm (summer replacement for Silver Theater)

Fun In Swing Time (see Tim and Irene)

Fun Valley (see Al Pearce)

8 **Fun With Books** (Syn)

3 **Fun With Dunne** (1943) CBS

Fun With Music (1930s)

Fun With The Famous (with Mort Lewis) (10/17/39 - 11/21/39) Bl, Tue, 10:30 pm

1 **Funfest** (1933) 15m, Syn

1 **Funny Face** (1957) film sound track

1 **Funny Side, The** (9/28/71) NBC-TV

Funny Things (with Nora Sterling) (4/26/37 - 10/1/37) CBS, 15m, 5:45 pm

Furlough Fun (with Beryl Wallace, George Riley and Spike Jones Band) (10/1/42 - 6/23/44) Gilmore Oil, NBC - West

1 **Furniture Company Spot Announcement**

Further Interplanetary Adventures Of Flash Gordon, The (see The Amazing Interplanetary Adventures Of Flash Gordon)

1 **Future Champions Of America** (Syn)

1 **Future Forum: A World Of Competition** (1/7/90) PBS-TV

Future Of America, The (10/10/48 - 1/9/49) ABC, Sun, 15m, 3:15 pm

1 **Future Of Cancer Research, The** (1956) Syn

1 **Future Of Wildlife Conservation** (Syn)

26 **Future Tense** (9/19/73 - 7/76) WMUK

G.E. Circle (also Home Circle) (with Grace Ellis, Theodore Webb) (10/4/31 - 1/13/33)

G.E. Sunday Circle (10/25/31 - 6/12/32; 12/25/32 - 4/2/33) General Electric, NBC, Sun

90 **G. I. Jive** (1942 - 1946, 1980) (AFRS) PBS-TV, 15m

G. I. Joe (1951 - 52) NBC, Tue
(2/22/53 - 7/9/53) NBC, Sun, 4 pm

50 **G. I. Journal** (AFRS) (8/43 - 46)

G. I. Laffs (with William Gargan) (6/29/45 - 8/22/45) CBS, Thu, 8:30 pm; Wed as of 7/11/45

2 **G. I. Ambassador Of Goodwill** (AFRS)

1 **G. I. Rhythm Round-Up** (1/28/45) KONO

1 **G. I. Showcase**

G-Men (see Gangbusters)

1 **G. O. P. "Toot By Toot" Reply To Truman's Whistle Stop Speeches** (5/14/50) Mut

Gabby Hayes Show, The (1/6/51 - 5/18/52) Quaker, Mut, Sun, 6 pm

4 **Gabriel Heatter** (see also America Today; A Brighter Tomorrow) (9/21/35 - 58+) Mut; some sponsors and other networks indicated
9/21/35 - 4/19/36, Scott, Sun
1937 - 38, NBC
6/1/40 - 42, Kreml
also 4/6/41 - 6/30/46, Barbasol
1942 - 58+, Multi
1960, Syn

2 **Gabriel Heatter Commentary** (1945) Mut

1 **Gabriel Heatter News** (11/7/44) Mut

Gabriel Heatter Show, A Brighter Tomorrow, The (see A Brighter Tomorrow)

Gabriel Heatter Theater

Gabriel Heatter's Stories (10/13/46 - 7/13/47,) Mut, Sun, 10 pm

GAI Paris Music Hall (1950 - 52) 15m

1 **Gala Armed Forces Day Program** (5/20/50) Mut

1 **Gala Performance** (1/1/64) Syn

Galaxy Of Stars (10/17/33 - 7/14/35) Red Star Yeast, NBC, 3t, 15m (1957)

1 **Galen Drake** (8/14/44 - 60s) various days and times including:
8/14/44 - 3/12/45, Bl, 5t, 15m, 1:45 pm
also 9/15/45 - 6/8/46, William Wise, ABC, Sun, 15m
3/19/45 - 7/16/48, Kellogg, ABC, 5t, 15m
7/19/48 - 1/6/50, Pillsbury, ABC, 5t, 15m
also 10/1/49 - 6/24/50, Sat, 10 am
1949 - 50, Doubleday, CBS, Sun, 15m
1951 - 53, Sus, CBS, Sat, 15m
1953 - 56, Multi, CBS, Sat, 60m
2/2/53 - 58, Multi, CBS, 5t, 15m
1958 - 60s, Mut; also WOR, New York, 15m, and 45m

1 **Galindez-Murphy Case: A Chronicle Of Terror, The** (5/20/57) CBS

14 **Gallant American Women** (written by Jane Ashman) (10/17/39 - 7/1/40) Bl
10/17/39 - 5/7/40, Tue, 2 pm
5/13/40, Mon, 10 pm
5/27/40 - 7/1/40, 10:30 pm

1 **Gallant Fox Handicap** (10/25/47) Mut

1 **Game Of Baseball, The** (9/25/53)

1 **Game Parade** (with Arthur Elmer) (2/5/38) Mut
(11/21/42 - 11/6/43) Bl, Sat

1 **Gandhi Memorial** (1/30/48) Mut

76 **Gangbusters** (7/20/35 - 12/20/57) FBI cooperation starting with 1/15/36
7/20/35 - 10/19/35 (G-Men), Chevrolet, Bl, Sat, 9 pm
1/15/36 - 6/15/38; 8/17/38 - 6/28/39, Palmolive, CBS, Wed, 10 pm; 8 pm as of 8/17/38
10/21/39 - 6/15/40, Cue Magazine, CBS, Sat, 8 pm
10/11/40 - 4/4/41 ; 10/10/41 - 4/3/42, Sloans, Bl, Fri, 9 pm
5/1/42 - 9/11/42, Sus, Bl, Fri, 9 pm
9/18/42 - 4/6/45, Sloans, ABC, Fri, 8 pm; 9 pm as of 7/17/42
9/15/45 - 6/8/46, Waterman, ABC, Sat, 9 pm
6/15/46 - 9/7/46, Sus, ABC, Sat, 9 pm
9/14/46 - 8/9/47, Waterman, ABC, Sat, 9 pm
8/16/47 - 9/6/47, Sus, ABC, Sat, 9 pm
9/13/47 - 2/29/48, Waterman, ABC, Sat, 9 pm
3/13/48 - 12/25/48, Tide, ABC, Sat, 9 pm
1/8/49 - 6/12/54, Grape Nuts, CBS, Sat, 9 pm; occasionally sustained during this time, usually during the summer
7/5/54 - 6/25/55, Wrigley or Sus, CBS, Mon, 9:30 pm
10/5/55 - 11/27/57, Multi, Mut, Wed, 8 pm

1 **Garden Gate, The** (7/6/40 - 1/13/58) CBS, Sat or Sun, morning; 15m except where noted
7/6/40 - 2/19/44, Sus; called Old Dirt Dobber with Tom Williams until 1/31/42
2/26/44 - 3/18/44, Burpee, 30m,
3/25/44 - 5/5/56, Ferry-Morse Seed Co.; occasionally sustained
5/12/56 - 1/13/58, Multi and Sus

1 **Garden Of Romance** (with Theodore von Eltz) NBC, 15m (2/3/47) Syn

Garden Of Tomorrow (with E.L.D. Seymour)
(3/3/35 - 5/19/35) CBS, Sun, 15m, 12:15 pm

Garden Program (with Mario Chamlee) (2/17/35 - 4/21/35) Swift, NBC, Sun, 2:30 pm

2 **Gardeners, The** (5/44) Syn

14 **Gardens For Freedom** (1948) Syn

Gardner Benedict Orchestra
(5/4/40 - 8/3/40) NBC, Sat, 15m, 2:15 pm

1 **Garroway At Large** (3/4/51) NBC-TV

9 **Garry Moore Radio Show, The** (10/31/62 - 6/28/63) CBS

9 **Garry Moore Show, The** (see also Club Matinee) (9/12/49 - 3/24/50; 7/3/50 - 7/27/55) Sus, CBS, 5t, 60m
11/23/49; 11/25/49 also (Funny Side Up) (AFRS)

Garry Moore Variety Show
(7/1/42 - 3/26/43)
7/1/42 - 7/29/42, Bl, Wed, 10 pm
8/17/42 - 3/26/43, NBC, 6t, 30m, 9 am

1 **Garry Moore's Culture Corner** (1946) Syn

Gary Crosby Show, The
(6/6/54 - 9/19/54) CBS, Sun, 8 pm
(6/26/55 - 9/4/55) CBS, Sun, 8:30 pm

1 **Gary Powers** (1960) Radio Moscow

Gaslight Gaieties (see The Gay Nineties Revue)

Gasoline Alley (2/17/41 - 5/9/41) NBC, 5t, 15m, 6:45 pm
(7/16/48 - 1/7/49) Multi Fri, 15m

1 **Gates Of Hope: The Coming Of Tomorrow, The** (1946) Syn

1 **Gateway To Hollywood, The** (with Jesse Lasky) 1/8/39 - 7/2/39; 10/8/39 - 12/31/39) Wrigley, CBS, Sun, 6:30 pm

Gateway To Music (1946 - 47)

Gauchos, The (with Tito Guizar)
(4/23/33 - 7/2/33) CBS, Sun, 9 pm

2 **Gay Divorcee, The** (1934) Air trailer, film sound track

Gay Hedlund Players (3/28/41 - 6/28/41) NBC, Sat, 3:30 pm

Gay Mrs. Featherstone, The (see Billie Burke)

3 **Gay Nineties Revue, The** (with Beatrice Kay as of 2/14/43) (7/2/39 - 12/29/45)
7/2/39 - 9/12/39, CBS, Sun, 6 pm
10/7/39 - 12/2/39, CBS, Sat, 7:30 pm
12/9/39 - 6/8/40, CBS, Sat, 10:15 pm; 10:30 pm as of 1/7/40
6/22/40 - 2/22/41, Sus, CBS, Sat, 7:30 pm; 8:30 pm as of 2/1/41
2/24/41 - 11/6/44 (also with Joe Howard), Model Tobacco, CBS, Mon, 8:30 pm
11/11/44 - 4/28/45 (Gaslight Gaieties (Gayeties)), Procter and Gamble, NBC, Sat, 8 pm
8/11/45 - 12/29/45, WQXR (NY), Sat, 10:30 pm

Gayelord Hauser

Gem Highlights (see Ed Sullivan)

1 **Gemini 3 Coverage** (3/22/65) NBC-TV

1 **Gemini 4 Coverage** (6/4 - 6/8/65) NBC

1 **Gemini 5 Coverage** (8/19 - 21/65) NBC-TV

1 **Gemini 5 Press Coverage** (9/5/65) ABC-TV, WNDT-TV

1 **Gemini 6 Coverage** (10/25/65) NBC-TV

1 **Gemini 7-6 Coverage** (12/4/65) NBC-TV

1 **Gemini 8 Coverage** (3/16/66) NBC-TV

1 **Gemini 8 Interviews** (3/66) Syn

1 **Gemini 9 Coverage** (6/3/66) NBC-TV

1 **Gemini 10 Coverage** (7/18/66) NBC-TV

1 **Gemini 11 Coverage** (9/9/66) NBC-TV

1 **Gemini 11 Interviews** (9/66) Syn

1 **Gemini 12 Coverage** (11/11 - 15/66) NBC-TV

1 **Gemini Report** (1/1/67)

1 **Gemini Space Launches** (12/65 - 7/18/66)

1 **Gemini-Titan Five** (8/15/65) NBC

Gems For Thought (11/5/46 - 7/4/50) ABC, Tue; then 5t, 5m, 8:55 am

Gems Of Melody (10/15/33 - 4/11/35) Fox Furs
10/15/33 - 4/8/34 (with Muriel Wilson and Fred Hufsmith) NBC, Sun, 15m, 2:45 pm
10/18/33 - 4/11/34 (with John Herrick, Harold Sanford Orchestra), Fox Furs, Bl, Wed, 15m, 7:15pm
4/19/34 - 4/11/35, Bl, Thu, 15m, 7:15 pm

Gene and Glenn (with Eugene Carroll and Glenn Rowell) (9/29/30 - 8/31/41) various network and local stations including:
9/29/30 - 7/2/32; 8/30/32 - 12/31/32 (Quaker Early Bird's Program) Quaker, NBC, 6t, 15m, 8 am; 3t from 8/30/32
4/23/34 - 11/30/34, Gillette, NBC, 5t, 15m, 7:15 pm
9/26/38 - 8/31/41, Sus, NBC, 7t, 15m

1 **Gene and Kathleen Lockhart Hollywood Album, The** (audition)

Gene Archer (3/9/42 - 8/10/42) NBC, Mon, 15m, 9:45 am

Gene Arnold and The Ranch Boys
(12/17/35 - 9/18/36) Bl, 3t - 5t, 15m (also see The Commodores)

1 **Gene Austin** (Standard transcription)

1 **Gene Autry Show, The** (1944) AFRS

30 **Gene Autry's Melody Ranch**
(1/7/40 - 5/13/56) Wrigley, CBS
1/7/40 - 8/1/43, Sun, 6:30 pm, 25m as of 2/2/41; 45m as of 12/21/41; 30m as of 7/12/42
9/23/45 - 12/17/48, Sun, 15m, 5:30 pm; 30m, 7 pm as of 6/16/46
12/25/48 - 6/24/50; 7/29/50 - 6/30/51; 8/4/51 - 7/25/53, Sat, 8 pm
8/2/53 - 5/13/56, Sun, 6 pm; then 6:05 pm

Gene Erwin Orchestra (6/10/39 - 9/2/39) Mut, Sat, 15m, 6:30 pm (not in New York)

6 **Gene Krupa and His Orchestra** (1940 - 1946) NBC, CBS, Mut

1 **Gene Krupa Quartet, The** (12/31/65) NBC

1 **Gene Krupa Story, The** (1959) film sound track

1 **Gene Pope** (10/12/40) WWRL

Gene Price Country Express

1 **General Armchair, Or "How To Be A Hero With Modern Convenience"** (audition)

1 **General Charles De Gaulle** (7/10/44) WOR

8 **General Douglas MacArthur** (3/21/42 - 6/13/53) Mut, NBC-TV, AFRTS

6 **General Eisenhower** (5/8/43 - 6/5/52) Mut, ABC, CBS

1 **General Eisenhower In New York** (6/19/45) WOR

1 **General Eisenhower Luncheon** (6/12/45) BBC

1 **General Eisenhower Speech** (9/4/50)

General Electric Stereo Drama (Early 60s; 4-program series) titles were: "The Turn Of The Screw," "Billy Budd," "The Fall Of The House Of Usher" and "Visit To A Small Planet"

1 **General Electric Theater, The** (7/9/53 - 10/1/53, 11/14/54) GE, CBS, Thu, 8:30 pm General Electric, NBC, various days and times

1 **General Groves** (8/5/48) Mut

1 **General Harbord** (Syn)

2 **General Hugh Johnson** (9/27/37 - 1/6/38, 1940) Bromo Quinine, NBC, Bl, 4t (Mon - Thu), 15m

1 **General John J. Pershing**

1 **General John J. Pershing Memorial**

1 **General Joseph W. Stillwell**

1 **General MacArthur In Honolulu** (4/16/51) Mut

1 **General MacArthur Welcome** (4/18/51) Mut

1 **General MacArthur's Arrival At Idlewild Airport** (4/19/51) Mut

1 **General MacArthur's Arrival In Honolulu** (4/19/51) Mut

1 **General MacArthur's Departure From Honolulu** (4/17/51) Mut

1 **General MacArthur's Departure From Japan** (4/15/51) Mut

1 **General Marshall** (6/6/47)

1 **General Matthew Ridgeway** (5/22/52) Mut

General Mills Radio Adventure Theater (2/5/77 - 1/29/78) General Mills; Multi from 8/6/77, CBS, 2t; called CBS Radio Adventure Theater from 8/6/77

General Motors Concerts (1929 - 12/26/37) General Motors
1929 - 7/27/31, NBC, Mon
10/7/34 - 4/21/35, Bl, Sun, 60m, 8 pm
10/6/35 - 6/28/36; 9/13/36 - 3/28/37, NBC, Sun, 60m, 10 pm
4/4/37 - 6/6/37, Bl, 60m, 8 pm
10/3/37 - 12/26/37, Bl, Sun, 60m, 8 pm

1 **General Motors New Assembly Plant, The** (5/27/37) WOR

1 **General Motors Parade Of Melody, The**

General Motors Symphony Of The Air, The (see NBC Symphony Orchestra)

1 **General Norman Schwarzkopf...Talking With David Frost** (3/27/91) PBS-TV

1 **General Omar Bradley** (4/27/48) Mut

1 **General Patton** (6/7/45) Mut - Yankee

1 **General Secretary Mikhail Gorbachev** (6/1/88) pool feed

1 **General Squawks** (3/18/38) WABC

1 **General Store, The** (Syn)

1 **General Thomas Watson** (7/13/44) Mut

General Tire Revue, The (see The Jack Benny Program)

6 **General's Victory Statements**

General, The (NBC)

Genevieve Rose (7/10/40 - 8/28/40) CBS, Wed, 15m, 10:45 pm

34 **Genius Of Duke, The** (Tribute to Duke Ellington) (1974) Syn

1 **Gentleman Adventurer, The** (with James Meighan) (2/16/48) Mut

1 **Gentleman, The** (with Reginald Gardiner and Alan Reed) (7/17/50) NBC

Gentlemen Of The Press (1/24/50 - 9/26/50) ABC, Tue, 8:30 pm

Geography

George Ansbro Show (5/30/55 - 11/11/55) ABC, 5t, 15m, 2 pm

3 **George Barnes Octet** (Standard transcriptions)

3 **George Bernard Shaw** (1946) BBC, NBC

1 **George Bernard Shaw Obituary Program** (11/2/50) BBC

1 **George Bernard Shaw Speech** (1937)

1 **George Blake** (1931) Syn

1 **George Bruce's Air Stories Of The World War** (1932) Tue, 15m, Syn

George Burns and Gracie Allen (see Burns and Allen)

George Burns and Gracie Allen Show, The (see Burns and Allen)

1 **George Burns Celebrates Eighty Years In Show Business** (9/18/83) NBC-TV

1 **George Burns In Concert** (1/84) HBO

1 **George Burns "One Man Show"** (12/77) CBS-TV

1 **George Burns Sings** (7/2/69) Syn

1 **George Burns-Gracie Allen Show, The** (see Burns and Allen)

2 **George Bush** (11/28/88, 1/12/89) pool feeds

1 **George Carson Putnam News** (9/4/47) WOR

1 **George Darling** (2/21/45) BBC

6 **George Doerner and His Orchestra** (1964 - 1970) CBS

30 **George E. Sokolsky** (1940 - 1941) Syn (12/26/48 - 1/15/56) ABC, Sun

1 **George Eckhardt and His Ambassadors**

George Fisher (Hollywood Whispers; Hollywood Reporter) (1938 - 4/26/42, 1947) Mut; mainly, in the 30s and 40s, on the West Coast; some times include:
1938, Sun
3/4/39 - 8/5/39, Mut, Sat, 15m, 9 pm
1/7/40 - 4/27/40, Sat, 15m, 9 pm
also 2/19/40 - 3/15/40, 3t, 15m, 2:45 pm
also 3/28/40 - 5/3/40, 3t, 15m, 6:45 pm
9/28/41 - 4/26/42, Sun, 15m, 1:15 pm
1947, sponsored by Forty Two Oil Shampoo

15 **George Fisher Interviews The Stars** (Standard transcriptions)

13 **George Fisher's Filmtown Featurettes** (Standard transcriptions)

1 **George Gershwin Memorial Concert** (9/8/37) CBS

1 **George Gershwin Memorial Program** (7/12/37) Mut

1 **George Grim From China** (5/19/45) XGOY

1 **George Grove** (10/25/36) WBMQ

1 **George Hall and His Orchestra** (film sound track)

2 **George Hall Orchestra** (12/14/35 - 5/7/38) CBS, Sat, 11:30am Thesaurus transcription

2 **George Hamilton Combs** (1966, 1969) Mut

1 **George Hicks** (4/12/36) NBC
9/24/44 - 5/20/45) Scripto, Bl/ABC
(7/21/47 - 51) NBC

1 **George Hicks With The Normandy Invasion** (6/7/44) pool feed

George Holmes (2/21/34 - 1/3/36) NBC

1 **George Jessel**

1 **George Jessel Carnegie Hall Concert**

30 **George Jessel Show, The** (1/2/34 - 55)
1/2/34 - 2/20/34, CBS, Tue, 9:30 pm
6/17/34 - 8/26/34 (George Jessel Variety Hour) CBS, Sun, 60m, 8 pm
10/10/37 - 7/3/38 (Thirty Minutes In Hollywood; with Tommy Tucker Orchestra) Mut, Sun, 6 pm
also 1/10/38 - 6/27/38 (For Men Only) (Fred Uttal; George Jessel started on 3/21/39) Vitalis, NBC, Mon, 10:30 pm
7/6/38 - 9/28/38 (George Jessel Jamboree; with Mary Small and Ernest Chappell) (replaced second half of Town Hall Tonight) Ipana - Sal Hepatica, NBC, Wed, 30m, 9:30 pm

George Jessel Show, The (continued)
10/4/38 - 7/4/39 (For Men Only until 3/28/40) Vitalis, NBC, Tue; 8:30 pm
also 3/15/39 - 8/2/39 (George Jessel Jamboree with Mary Small) Bl, Wed, 7:30 pm
7/5/39 - 10/4/39 (George Jessel's Celebrity Program), Vitalis, NBC, Wed, 9:30 pm
10/6/39 - 1/5/40, Vitalis, NBC, Fri, 9:30 pm
1/11/40 - 3/28/40, Vitalis, NBC, Thu, 8 pm
1949 (This Is Show Business)
10/15/53 - 1/28/54 (George Jessel Salutes), Sus, ABC, Thu
1955 (George Jessel Salutes) NBC

1 **George Jessel Vaudeville Routine** (9/1/26) Synchro-disc

1 **George Lyons, The Singing Harpist** (1929) Synchro-disc

1 **George Meany** (9/56) Syn

George O'Hanlon Show (also with Lurene Tuttle) (11/2/48 - 2/26/49) Mut, Tue, 8 pm

6 **George Olsen and His Orchestra** (1945 - 1950) Mut, NBC

George Olsen Orchestra (1932) Oldsmobile, 15m

5 **George Orwell: A Radio Biography** (1/5/84 - 2/2/84) American Public Radio

George Paxton

1 **George Polk Reports** (1/3/47) CBS

George Putnam (10/27/43 - 5/24/44) NBC (1945 - 10/3/47) Mut

1 **George Putnam Audition** (12/5/45) Mut

George Rector (2/17/37 - 7/1/37) Phillips Soups, CBS, 3t (Wed - Fri), 15m, 1:30 pm (see also Our Daily Food)

George Rector's Cooking School For Children (1/9/33 - 5/4/33) Bl, Thu, 6:15 pm

George Shakley Orchestra (1935) Nehi Bottling Company

6 **George Shearing Quintet** (1953) NBC, World transcriptions

1 **George Shearing Quintet, The** (5/30/53) NBC

1 **George Shearing/Stephane Grappelly In Concert** (11/6/83) USA net - Ovation

1 **George Washington Slept Here** (1944) Syn

1 **George White's Scandals** (1945) film sound track

16 **George Wright-Hammond Organ** (4/16/48) Thesaurus transcriptions

George, The Cave Man (1930 - 7/2/31) Bl, Thu, 15m

Georgia Crackers, The (10/25/38 - 5/9/39) Mut, Tue, 15m, 11:15 am

3 **Georgia Gibbs-Paul Whiteman Show, The** (1945)

1 **Georgie Price Reynolds Pen Show, The**

2 **Gerald Ford** (11/1/76, 8/16/88) ABC-TV, C-SPAN

1 **Gerald R. Ford: Presidential Decisions** (8/26/78) NBC-TV

Gerardine Program (3/12/31 - 8/18/32) La Gerardine Inc., CBS, 15m
3/12/31 - 6/22/31, 2t (Mon & Thu), 5:45 pm
6/30/32 - 8/18/32 (with Sidney Skolsky, Jack Berger Orchestra), Thu, 8:30 pm

1 **German Announcement** (8/31/39) Germany

1 **German Declaration Of War On Yugoslavia And Greece** (8/6/41) Germany

1 **German Entertainment** (1/13/37) WCNW

9 **German Language Program** (10/7/36 - 11/3/36) WMBQ

1 **German Language School Of The Air** (10/15/36) WMBQ

73 **German News In English** (3/11/38 - 4/21/40) Germany

3 **German Overseas Service** (2/26/44 - 7/27/44) Germany

1 **German Program** (1/7/37) WCNW

1 **German Radio Announcement** (9/1/39) Germany

1 **German Submarine Surrender** (5/14/45) WIP

1 **German-American Bund Rally** (2/20/39) WOR

1 **Germany Today and 1914** (10/13/39) Germany

1 **Germany; An Inside Story** (11/30/47) CBS

Gertrude Lawrence Theater (also Revlon Theater) (also with Robert Benchley)
(9/30/43 - 3/26/44) Revlon, Bl, Thu, 10:30 pm; Sun, 10:30 pm as of 10/17/43

2 **Gertrude Niesen** (1932 - 3/10/33) CBS, Lang-Worth transcriptions, Fri, 15m, 6:30 pm

Get More Out Of Life (1/3/49 - 4/10/51) Wise, 15m
1/3/49 - 4/16/49, Mut, 5t, 9:15 am
1/14/50 - 5/13/50, CBS, Sat, 2:30 pm
11/12/50 - 1/14/51, Mut, Sun, 9:45 pm
3/6/51 - 4/10/51, Mut, Tue, 9:30 pm

1 **Get Out The Vote** (9/13/44) CBS

Get Rich Quick (with Johnny Olsen) (7/26/48 - 10/11/48) ABC, Mon, 9:30 pm

1 **Get That Story** (with Knox Manning) (5/7/46) CBS, Wed

Get Thin To Music (see Keep Fit With Music)

Get Together Program (with Jack Berch) summer replacement for Al Jolson (7/19/38 - 9/13/38) Rinso, CBS, Tue, 8:30 pm

Getting The Most Out Of Life (with Dr. William Stidger) (5/30/38 - 6/30/39; 10/2/39 - 12/29/39) Fleischmann, Bl, 5t, 15m, 11:45 am

1 **Getting The Most Out Of Life-Today** (Syn)

1 **Gettysburg: One Hundred Years Later** (11/19/63) Mut

26 **Ghost Corps, The** (1930s) Syn

Ghost Of Benjamin Sweet, The (written by Pauline Gibson and Fred Gilsdori
(3/25/38 - 8/26/38) CBS, Fri, 8 pm
(9/4/38 - 9/25/38) CBS, Sun, 10 pm

Ghost Shift (2/26/43 - 5/21/43) MacFadden Publications, CBS, Fri, Sm, 6:10 pm

Ghost Stories (1935 - 8/15/51)
1935, Bl, Sun
1935 - 36, CBS, Sun
7/16/51 - 8/15/51, ABC, Mon, 9:30 pm

Ghost Stories By Elliott O'Donnelle (3/28/34 - 5/3/34) NBC, Wed, 10:30 pm

1 **Ghosts** (Syn)

1 **Giant Quiz** (5/29/48) Mut

1 **Giant Speaks, The** (1939) Syn

Giants Of Freedom (8/3/42 - 12/28/42) CBS, Mon, 15m, 4:30 pm

Gibbs and Finney, General Delivery (with Parker Fennelly and Arthur Allen) (7/26/2 - 10/18/42) Bl, Sun, 15m, 8:15 pm

Gibson Family, The (with Loretta and Jack Clemens)
(9/15/34 - 6/30/35) Procter and Gamble, NBC
9/15/34 - 2/23/35, Sat, 30m
3/31/35 - 6/30/35, Sun, 60m

1 **Gift Of Gab** (1934) Air trailer

Gigantic Pictures (with Sam Hearn and Alice Frost; Reggie Childs Orchestra) (12/9/34 - 3/3/35) Tastyeast, Bl, Sun, 12 noon

1 **Gil Gross Show, The** (8/2/91)

2 **Gilbert and Sullivan** (9/44) AFRS

Gilbert and Sullivan Breakfast Hour (with Gene and Kathleen Lockhart) (11/12/31 - 1/28/32) Thomas A. Edison Inc., CBS, Thu, 15m 8:45 am

Gilbert and Sullivan Opera (1929 - 39) short periods of time, Bl

2 **Gilbert Highet Program, The** (1955) Syn

Gilbert Martyn (8/18/43 - 47) Kellogg, Bl

6 **Gillette Cavalcade Of Sports, The** (1945 - 1948) Mut, ABC, ABC-TV

Gillette Community Sing, The (see Community Sing)

1 **Gillette Program, The**

1 **Ginny Simms Show, The** (9/19/41 - 3/18/51)
9/19/41 - 5/29/42, Kleenex, CBS, Fri, 5m, 9:55 pm
9/8/42 - 9/4/45 (Purple Heart; with David Rose Orchestra), Philip Morris, NBC, Tue 8 pm
9/28/4 - 5/3/46, Borden CBS, Fri, 7:30 pm
9/27/46 - 6/13/47, Borden, Fri, 9 pm
9/17/50 - 3/18/51 (Botany Song Shop), Botany Mills, ABC, Sun, 15m, 10 pm

Girl Alone (with Betty Winkler) (7/8/35 - 4/25/41) NBC, 5t, 15m
7/8/35 - 7/10/36, Sus
7/13/36 - 4/22/38, Kellogg, 12 noon
5/30/38 - 9/23/38, Sus
9/26/38 - 6/2/39; 9/25/39 - 4/25/41 Quaker

Girl Back Home, The (7/9/44 - 7/30/44) Bl, Sun 15m, 12:45 pm

1 **Girl Crazy** (1943) film sound track

Girl From Maine, The (with Marjorie Mills) (10/11/38 - 1/5/39) Maine Development Commission, Mut, 2t, 2:15 pm

1 **Girl From Paradise** (9/7/55) CBS audition

Girl From Paris (with Jane Morgan) (1951) NBC, 15m

Girl Next Door, The (with Mary Smith and J. Anthony Hughes) (1/1/35 - 4/30/35) Procter and Gamble, NBC, 3t, 15m 3:30 pm

1 **Girl Of The Golden West, The** (4/38) Air trailer

1 **Girl Scout Birthday** (3/12/49) NBC

Girl Who Lives Next Door, The (with Ruth Russell, Curtis Anall) (10/3/32 - 4/4/33) 3t (Tue-Thu) 15m, 2:15 pm

1 **Girl Without A Room** (1933) Air trailer

Girls Corps (3/5/49 - 11/12/49) Hormel, ABC, Sat, 12 noon

1 **Girls Of The Golden West** (6/24/83) NPR

1 **Gisele Of Canada** (Syn) (also see A Program Of Canada)

Giselle MacKenzie (with Skitch Henderson) (3/21/56 - 6/13/56) NBC, Wed, 25m, 8:30 pm

3 **Give and Take** (with John Reed King) (8/25/45 - 12/26/53) CBS, Sat except as noted
8/25/45 - 12/28/46 Chef Boy-Ar-Dee, 10 am; 11:30 am as of 10/5/46
also 6/3/46 - 9/27/46, American Home Products, 3t, 4:30 pm; led to Hollywood Jackpot
1/4/47 - 3/31/51, 2 pm; 1:30 pm as of 7/24/48
4/2/47 - 9/26/47, 5t, 4:30 pm
10/6/51 - 12/26/53, Cannon Mills, 11:30 am

1 **Give My Regards To Broadway** (12/6/59) NBC-TV

Gladys Swarthout (2/10/37 - 5/9/37) National Ice Advertising Company, NBC, Wed, 10:30 pm; Sun as of 4/4/37

2 **Glamorous Yesterdays In Old California** (1945) Syn

1 **Glamour Girl** (4/21/46) Syn

3 **Glamour Manor** (with Cliff Arquette; Kenny Baker from 9/30/46) (7/3/44 - 6/27/47) Ivory, ABC, 5t, 12 noon; (called the Kenny Baker Show from 12/16/46 - 6/27/47)

Glen Darwin (6/13/39 - 3/25/41) Tue, 15m
6/13/39 - 9/19/39, NBC, 12:45 pm
5/14/40 - 11/12/40, Bl, 12:15 pm
12/3/40 - 3/25/41, Bl, 12 noon

Glen Gray (also see Camel Caravan (1/2/43 - 2/13/43) Mut, Sat, 60m, 5 pm

14 **Glen Gray and The Casa Loma Orchestra** (1937, 1940) NBC, CBS, World transcriptions

2 **Glen Gray's Casa Loma Orchestra** (World transcriptions)

Glen Osser Orchestra (10/10/48 - 12/6/48) ABC, Mon, 9 pm

Glenn Garr Orchestra (6/24/40 - 10/22/40) NBC, Mon, 15m, 6:15 pm; not in NY

Glenn Miller (1939 - 6/10/44)
1939, CBS, 5t, 15m
1/2/40 - 9/24/42 (often with the Andrews Sisters) Chesterfield, CBS, 5t, 15m; 3t (Tue-Thu) as of 5/4/42
also 9/6/41 - 5/30/42 (Sunset Serenade) Bl, Sat, 60m, 5 pm
5/29/43 - 6/10/44 (see I Sustain The Wings) Syn (ZIV) (Moonlight Serenade) about 1940 (Uncle Sam Presents) (Command Band)
(1944) (Mel Powell - Uptown Gang)
(1944 - 45) (AAF Band) various lengths
(1943 - 44) Sat (Swing Shift) (propaganda broadcasts)
(11/8/44 - 12/13/44) (Glenn Miller Time) (with Ray McKinley and Johnny Desmond)

Glenn Miller and His Orchestra (see Glenn Miller)

Glenn Miller From America (AFRS) (1943) 15m

Glenn Miller Orchestra, The (see Glenn Miller)

1 **Glenn Miller Story, The** (1954) film sound track

Glenn Miller's Moonlight Serenade (see Glenn Miller)

Glenn Miller's Sunset Serenade (see Glenn Miller)

12 **Globe Theater, The** (host, Herbert Marshall) (1944 - 46) rebroadcasts of Screen Guild Theater and others

Gloom Chasers, The (see also Stoopnagle and Bud) (with Allen Courtney) (9/10/38 - 12/23/39) Mut, Sat except from 3/17/39 - 3/31/39, Fri

2 **Gloom Dodgers** (1944, 1945) WHN, Mut

Gloria Carroll Entertains (Syn) 1947, 15m

Gloria Gay's Affairs (1930 - 7/1/31) Bl, Wed, 15m, 6:30 pm

2 **Gloria LaVey and Willard Amison** (Lang-Worth transcriptions)

Gloria Parker (5/13/51 - 56) Sus, ABC
5/13/51 - 54, Sun, 15m
1954 - 56, 5t, 15m

2 **Gloria Swanson** (11/5/63)

1 **Gloria Swanson Interview** (6/6/50) WOR

Gloria Swanson Show (10/13/50 - 11/30/51) Mut, 5t

Glorious One, The (see Irene Rich)

1 **Glory Of Their Times, The** (3/20/77) PBS-TV

Go For The House (with John Reed King) (5/5/4 - 2/6/49) Sus, ABC, Wed, 9:30 pm; Sun, 7 pm as of 9/19/48

2 **Go Get It** (also Treasure Hunt) (with Joe Bolton and Tom Slater) (9/10/41 - 1/27/43) Mut, Wed

1 **Go Into Your Dance** (1935) Air trailer

1 **Goal Beyond, The** (Syn)

1 **Goal Is Freedom, The** (4/4/49) CBS

1 **God and Uranium Were On Our Side** (4/19/45) CBS

God's Country (see Burl Ives)

1 **Goin' To Town** (1935) film sound track

1 **Going Hollywood** (1933) film sound track

1 **Going Places** (1/4/48) WOR (also see Freddy Martin)

Going South (see Clyde Barrie)

Gold and Silver Minstrels (with Eddie Green, Jimmy Carroll) (9/14/46 - 2/15/47) Mut, Sat, 9 pm

Gold Coast Revue (2/4/38 - 3/18/38) CBS, Fri, 4 pm

1 **Gold Diggers Of 1935** (1935) Air trailer

1 **Gold Diggers Of 1937** (1936) film sound track

1 **Gold Diggers Of Broadway** (1929) Synchro-discs

Gold Is Where You Find It (4/5/41 - 8/30/41) CBS, Sat, 10:30 am

Gold Medal Fast Freight (see Fast Freight)

Gold Medal Orchestra (with Phil Ohman and Vic Arden, piano duo) (3/30/31 - 1932) Gold Medal, Bl, Mon, 8:30 pm; 9 pm as of 7/20/31

6 **Goldbergs, The** (with Gertrude Berg) (11/20/29 - 6/24/50)
11/20/29 - 5/23/31, Bl, Fri, 15m (often called Rise Of The Goldbergs)
7/13/31 - 7/6/34, Pepsodent, NBC, 6t, 15m; 5t as of 11/12/3
1/13/36 - 4/25/36, Colgate, Mut, 5t, 15m
9/13/37 - 12/3/37, Oxydol, NBC, 5t, 15m
1/3/38 - 3/30/45, Oxydol, CBS, 5t, 15m; at times also on NBC and Mut
9/2/49 - 1/27/50, General Foods, CBS, Fri, 30m
2/11/50 - 6/24/50, CBS, Sat, 8:30 pm

Goldcrest Star Time

1 **Golden Anniversary Report** (1949) Syn

Golden Blossoms (with Maria Cardinale) (4/10/32 - 6/12/32) Golden Blossom Honey, Bl, Sun, 15m, 7 pm

1 **Golden Days Of Christmas, The** (12/24/69) AFRTS

11 **Golden Days Of Radio, The** (with Frank Bresee)
(8/5/49 - present) (Frank Bresee)
8/5/49 - 9/10/50, KSCI, 53 shows broadcast
1/6/50 - 12/28/53, Liberty Broadcasting System, 154 shows broadcast
1/54 - 12/66, various stations in southern California, over 2600 shows broadcast
also 9/66 - 3/67, Armed Forces Network in Europe, 26 shows broadcast
also 1/1/67 - 9/95, AFRTS, worldwide, 2739 shows broadcast
9/94 - present, Yesterday USA Superstation
1996, 260 Golden Days Of Radio 5-minute shows

1 **Golden Door, The** (1948) Syn

1 **Golden Earrings** (1947) Air trailer

Golden Gate Park Band Concert (4/11/37 - 7/25/37) Bl, Sun, 5:30 pm

4 **Golden Gate Quartet** (mostly CBS, 15m; on various days and times including:)
1/29/40 - 4/15/40, 3t-5t, 3:15 pm
4/22/40 - 6/10/40, Mon, 4:45 pm
also 5/4/40 - 7/6/40, Sat, 9 pm
6/14/40 - 9/13/40, Fri, 10:45 pm
10/18/40 - 12/9/40, Mon, 10:30 pm
1/25/41 - 5/17/41, Sat, 10:30 pm
4/6/42 - 4/29/42, 2t (Mon, Wed), 4:30 pm
10/9/44 - 3/30/45, NBC, 3t, 7:45 am Thesaurus transcriptions

10 **Golden Gate Quartet Sings** (Syn)

1 **Golden Glove Championships** (3/14/39) Mut

1 **Golden Hour Of Music** (1931) Syn

2 **Golden Melodies** (11/18/41, 11/19/41) WCFL

Golden Melodies Variety (5/14/38 - 9/27/41) NBC, Sat, various times

Golden Theater Group, The (with Bert Lytell) (2/17/39 - 5/12/39) Tums, Bl, Fri, 15m, 7 pm

Golden Treasury Of Song (see Squibb Golden Treasury Of Song)

Golden Voices (10/11/53 - 2/21/54) NBC, Sun, 3 pm

Goldenrod Revue (8/11/33 - 11/4/33) Hittleman Goldenrod Brewery, Inc., CBS, Fri, 8:30 pm; Sat, 8:30 pm as of 10/13/33

Goldman Band Concerts (summers; from Central Park; with Edwin Franko Goldman, conductor) (1920s and 1930s)

2 **Goldwyn Follies, The** (1938) Air trailer, film sound track

Goldy and Dusty, The Silver Dust Twins (with Harve Hindermyer and Earle Tuckerman) (12/5/32 - 10/25/33) Silver Dust, CBS, 5t, 9: 15 am

1 **Golf Doctor, The** (Audition)

1 **Gone With The Wind** (8/16/40) audition

Good Afternoon, Neighbors (with Tom Breneman) (1/26/37 - 38) Durkee, CBS, Sun

1 **Good Earth, The** (1937) Air trailer

Good Listening (with Lionel Kaye) (4/22/43 - 5/13/43) CBS, Thu, 11:30 pm

Good Morning (5/8/41 - 10/3/41) CBS, Thu, 9:30 am

1 **Good Morning 1950** (1/1/50) WOR

Good Neighbors (5/22/41 - 10/9/41) NBC, Thu, 10:30 pm

1 **Good News** (6/8/49) WOR

12 **Good News Of 1938** (see Baby Snooks)

34 **Good News Of 1939** (see Baby Snooks)

17 **Good News Of 1940** (see Baby Snooks)

Good News Program (with Kay Costello) (Pittsburgh Paints)

Good Old Days (see Those Good Old Days)

2 **Good Old Days Of Radio, The** (1976, 8/27/76) PBS-TV, NPR

Good Time Society (with Chick Webb Orchestra)
(4/23/36 - 12/31/36) NBC, Thu, 8:30 pm
(1/11/37 - 9/20/37) Bl, Mon, 10 pm; 9 pm as of 3/1/37 (with Juano Hernandez)

Good Word, The (with Tom Paxton and Herb Ellis) (1947) ABC, Wed

1 **Goodbye Mr. Chips** (1937) Air trailer

1 **Goodnight and Good Luck** (9/12/76) BBC-TV, Syn

Goodrich Silvertown Orchestra (see B. A. Rolfe)

3 **Goodrich Silvertown Time** (1936) Syn

1 **Goodrich Sports Reporter** (9/21/39) WJSV

1 **Goodwill Court, The** (with Albert L. Alexander) (9/20/36 - 3/21/37) Chase and Sanborn, NBC, Sun, 8 pm; also on The Goodwill Hour, (with John J. Anthony)
(6/7/36 - 11/26/44)
6/7/36 - 8/25/36, Mut, Sun, 10:30 pm
7/25/37 - 1/16/38, MacFadden Publishing, Mut, Sun, 10 pm
1/23/38 - 4/14/40, Ironized Yeast, Mut, Sun, 60m, 10 pm
4/21/40 - 10/10/43, Ironized Yeast, Bl, Sun, 60m, 10 pm
12/5/43 - 11/26/44, Clark Gum, Mut, Sun, 45m, 10:15 pm; 10 pm as of 9/17/44; continued on WMCA (New York) until 12/3/44

Goodwill Hour, The (see The Goodwill Court and John J. Anthony)

Goodyear Farm Radio News (with Don Goddard) (9/26/38 - 6/23/39) Goodyear, Bl, 5t, 15m

Goodyear Program (with Revelers Quartet, Grace Moore)
(10/28/31 - 11/9/32) NBC
10/28/31 - 4/23/32, Tue and Sat; Wed and Sat as of 12/23/31
4/27/32 - 11/9/32, Wed, 9 pm

Goodyear Theater (1944)

74 **Goon Show, The** (with Peter Sellers, Spike Mulligan and Harry Secombe) (BBC) (5/28/51 - 1/28/60) occasionally after that

Goose Creek Parson (3/9/36 - 6/4/36) CBS - West, 2t (Mon & Thu)
(8/30/36 - 1/1/37) Super Suds, CBS, 3t, 15m

Gordon Clifford (10/9/39 - 8/25/41) 15m
10/9/39 - 11/6/39, Bl, Mon, 3:30 pm
1/23/41 - 8/25/41, NBC, Mon, 1 pm

Gordon Jenkins Orchestra
(1/11/41 - 10/25/41)
1/11/41 - 10/25/41, NBC, Sat, 3 pm; 2 pm as of 6/28/41
also 4/8/41 - 8/12/41, Bl, Tue, 8 pm
9/6/41 - 10/25/41 (see Sweet and Rhythmic)

5 **Gordon MacRae** (10/31/45) audition
12/3/45 - 9/15/48) CBS 12/3/45 - 3/21/46, Sus, 5t, 15m, 4:30 pm
1/11/48 - 3/21/48, Texaco, CBS, Sun, 9:30 pm
3/24/48 - 9/15/48 (see Texaco Star Theater) (see also Railroad Hour)

24 **Gordon MacRae Gulfspray Show, The** (1947) Syn

1 **Gordon MacRae, Troubador** (8/1/47) CBS

1 **Gorgeous Hussey** (1936) Air trailer

Gospel Hour (see Old Fashioned Revival Hour)

2 **Gospel In Song, The** (1948) Syn

2 **Gospel Singer, The** (Syn)

Gould and Shefter (12/10/33 - 1/20/36) NBC, various days and times, 15m

Government Girl (with Nancy Ordway) (3/3/41 - 3/20/42) Mut, 6t, 15m, 1:30 pm; 1:15 pm as of 6/30/41

8 **Governor Bill Clinton** (5/1/92 - 9/3/92) C-SPAN, CNN

1 **Governor Christine Whitman** (1/24/95) C-SPAN, CNN

2 **Governor Dewey** (1948) Syn

1 **Governor Hoffman Of New Jersey** (8/17/37) Intercity Broadcasting System

3 **Governor Michael Dukakis** (7/21/88 - 10/30/88) C-SPAN, WCBS

1 **Governor Ronald Reagan** (10/19/80) CBS-TV

4 **Governor Thomas Dewey** (1940, 6/28/44, 10/7/44, 11/4/44) NBC, CBS

1 **Grab Bag Quiz** (1940) WWRL

Grace Hayes (5/1/35 - 6/18/35) Bl, Wed, 15m; Tue as of 5/21/35

Grace Morgan (4/10/43 - 11/26/43) Bl, 5t, 5m, 9:55 pm

1 **Gracie Allen Murder Case, The** (1939) Air trailer

3 **Gracie Fields Show, The**
(10/12/42 - 1/2/53)
10/12/42 - 7/9/43, Pall Mall, ABC, 5t, 5m, 9:55 pm; 15m, 10:15 pm as of 1/11/43
10/18/43 - 1/14/44 (Gracie Fields Victory Show, The), Pall Mall, Mut, 5t, 15m, 9:15pm
6/11/44 - 8/27/44 (with Lou Bring Orchestra), Chase and Sanborn, NBC, Sun, 8 pm (summer replacement for Charlie McCarthy)
11/14/44 - 2/6/45, Bristol Myers, ABC, Tue, 9 pm
1/11/52 - 1/2/53 Sus, Muto Fri, 8:30 pm also syndicated

Grady Cole and The Johnson Family
(1/15/50 - 9/25/53) CBS, l5m
1/15/50 - 6/22/51, Quaker, 3t, 2 pm
10/1/51 - 9/25/53 (Grady Cole Show) General Foods, 3t, 2 pm; 5t as of 1/3/52

Grammy Treasure Chest (with Mike Douglas) (Treasury Dept.) (1973 - 76)

Gramps (with Edgar Stehli)
(7/2/47 - 8/20/47) Colgate, NBC, Wed, 8 pm (summer replacement of A Day In The Life Of Dennis Day)

Granat Brothers, The (Bl)

5 **Granby's Green Acres** (with Gale Gordon, Bea Benadaret)
(3/30/50 - 8/21/50) CBS, Mon, 9:30 pm (half of summer replacement of Lux Radio Theater)

1 **Grand Alliance, The** (10/24/53) United Nations Radio

7 **Grand Central Station** (9/28/37 - 4/2/54)
9/28/37 - 4/15/38, Listerine, Bl, Tue, 9:30 pm
4/24/38 - 10/18/40, Listerine, CBS, Sun; Tue as of 7/5/38; Fri, 10 pm as of 9/30/38; 9:30 pm as of 5/31/40
11/12/40 - 7/1/41, Rinso, Bl, Tue, 9 pm
7/9/41 - 10/1/41, Rinso, CBS, Wed, 8 pm (summer replacement of Big Town)
10/10/41 - 7/3/42, Rinso, NBC, Fri, 7:30 pm
3/4/44 - 9/1/51, Pillsbury, CBS, Sat, 25m, 1 pm; 30m as of 6/2/45; 12:30 pm as of 9/18/48; 25m, 12:30 pm as of 5/27/50
9/21/51 - 9/20/52, Toni, CBS, Sat, 25m, 1 pm
12/13/52 - 9/5153, Cream Of Wheat, CBS, Sat, 25m, 11:05 am
1/18/54 - 4/2/54, Campbell, ABC, 5t, 15m

1 **Grand Hotel** (10/1/30 - 10/27/45)
10/1/30 - 9/24/33 (Chicago area)
10/1/33 - 4/22/34, Campana, Bl, Sun, 5:30 pm
9/23/34 - 3/15/36, Campana, Bl, Sun, 6:30 pm
10/4/36 - 4/4/37, Campana, NBC, Sun, 3:30 pm
11/8/37 - 3/28/38, Campana, Bl, Mon, 8:30 pm
1/7/40 - 3/31/40, Campana, CBS, Sun, 25m, 1:35 pm
11/4/44 - 10/27/45, Campana, NBC, Sat, 5 pm

17 **Grand Marquee** (7/9/46 - 9/11/47) NBC
7/9/46 - 9/24/46, Sus, Tue (partial summer replacement for Amos 'n' Andy)
11/17/46 - 12/15/46, Sus, Sun
12/26/46 - 9/25/47, Thu; sponsored by Rayve Shampoo from 1/23/47 - 7/17/47

1 **Grand National Race** (3/25/38) BBC/Mut

37 **Grand Ole Opry** (11/28/25 - 12/28/57)
11/28/25 - 10/7/39, WSM, Nashville (local) Sat; called WSM Barn Dance until 1928
10/14/39 - 7/25/53; 9/5/54 - 12/28/57, Prince Albert, NBC, Sat, 10:30 pm; 9:30 pm as of 10/6/51; in New York from 10/16/43; sponsored by Purina from 1/2/43 - 12/29/45 (broadcast continuously; in New York for above dates)
(1/4/58 - 92+); still on locally in Nashville

1 **Grand Opera Chorus and Orchestra Of Los Angeles** (1939) Syn

5 **Grand Slam** (with Irene Beasley and Dwight Weist) (9/30/46 - 8/14/53) Wesson Oil, CBS, 5t, 15m

Grandma Travels (with Hazel Dopheide) (Syn) Sears

Grandpa Burton (with Bill Baar) (4/1/35 - 1/22/37) NBC, 3t, 15m

1 **Grandstand Manager** (5/15/48) Mut

Grandstand Thrills (with Olan Soule')

Grant Park Concerts (from Chicago) (summers, late 30s early 40s)

1 **Grantland Rice Football Forecast, The** (9/51) CBS

1 **Grantland Rice Story, The**
(12/11/43 - 9/9/44) Sus, NBC, Sat, 15m, 2:30 pm
(11/11/44 - 5/5/45) Sus, NBC, Sat, 15m, 10 am; 2 30 pm as of 3/17/45
(9/28/51 - 11/23/51) CBS, Fri, 15m, 8 pm

Grapevine Rancho (see Ransom Sherman)

1 **Gray Gordon and His Tick Tock Rhythm** (1/18/39) NBC

1 **Gray Gordon Orchestra** (Thesaurus transcription)

Gray Wolf (Syn) 15m

Great Adventure, The (with Westbrook van Voorhis) ABC, Sun,7:30 pm

1 **Great American Broadcast** (1941) Air trailer

Great American Heroes

Great American Women (with Basil Rathbone) 5m (see Basil Rathbone Presents)

4 **Great Balls Of Fire!** (CBC Syndication)

1 **Great Caesar's Ghost** (3/8/46) ABC, audition

1 **Great Day, A** (6/14/55) United Nations Radio

Great Day, The (with John Reed King) (3/21/52 - 3/20/53) Mut, Fri, 9:30 pm; Wed, 8:30 pm as of 7/9/52; Fri, 25m, 9:05 pm as of 10/3/52

40 **Great Days We Honor** (Syn)

4 **Great Debate, The** (9/26/60 - 10/21/60) pool feed

4 **Great Expectations** (Syn)

592 **Great Gildersleeve, The**
(5/16/41) audition
(8/31/41 - 3/21/57) NBC (Hal Peary played the lead until 6/14/50; Willard Waterman from 9/6/50 - 3/21/57
8/31/41 - 7/5/42; 8/30/42 - 6/27/43; 8/29/43 - 6/25/44; 9/3/44 - 7/1/45; 9/2/45 - 6/9/46, Kraft, Sun, 6:30 pm
9/11/46 - 6/4/47; 9/10/47 - 6/2/48; 9/8/48 - 6/1/49; 9/21/49 - 6/14/50; 9/6/50 - 5/30/51; 9/5/51 - 6/2/,54, Kraft, Wed, 8:30 pm
9/27/54 - 6/30/55, Multi, 4t, (Mon-Thu) 15m
10/20/55 - 4/5/56; 10/11/56 - 3/21/57, Multi, Thu, 25m, 8 pm
1957 - 1958, Thu, 8 pm

Great Gunns, The (with Bret Morrison and Barbara Luddy) (5/8/41 - 9/25/41) Mut, Thu, 10:30 pm (not in New York)

Great Merlini, The (with Chester Morris) (1950) NBC

Great Moments From Great Plays
(3/21/41 - 8/8/41) Philip Morris, CBS, Fri, 9 pm

1 **Great Moments In Great Music**
(10/13/41) audition

Great Moments In History (written by Merrill Denison) (10/2/32 - 7/2/33) Fleischmann's Yeast, Bl, Sun, 7:30 pm

Great Moments In Music (see The Celanese Hour)

Great Moments In Sports (with Harry Wismer) (Syn) including:
4/4/56 - 7/4/56, Mut, Wed, 15m, 9:15 pm

Great Moments In The Lives Of Great Women (with Noreen Gammill) 1937

4 **Great Music** (with Walter Huston and William Moore) (AFRS origination) 15m

Great Mysteries (15m)

Great Personalities (8/18/31 - 5/31/32) New York Life Insurance, Bl, Tue, 9:30 pm

1 **Great Plays** (2/26/38 - 9/6/42) Sus, Bl, Sun, 60m
2/26/38 - 5/7/38 (first series)
10/16/38 - 5/7/39 (second series)
10/15/39 - 4/21/40 (third series)
10/13/40 - 5/4/41 (fourth series)
11/16/41 - 9/6/42 (also called Famous Fireside Plays)

4 **Great Scenes From Great Plays** (with Walter Hampden) (10/1/48 - 2/25/49) Mut, Fri, 8 pm, Syn

2 **Great Stories About Corn** (1948) Syn

1 **Great Talent Hunt, The** (3/18/48) Mut

1 **Great Waltz, The** (11/38) Air trailer)

1 **Greater New York Fund Program** (5/19/40) WOR

1 **Greatest Adventure, The** (3/8/81) PBS-TV

1 **Greatest Gift, The** (12/24/46) CBS

Greatest Of These, The (with Tom Collins) (Syn)

1 **Greatest Show On Earth, The** (1952) film sound track

34 **Greatest Sports Thrill** (Syndicated) (with Harry Wismer) (9/29/56 - 8/15/58 are one set of dates)

43 **Greatest Story Ever Told, The** (1/26/47 - 6/27/48; 9/12/48 - 6/12/49; 9/18/49 - 5/7/50; 10/1/50 - 5/20/51; 9/23/51 - 5/18/52; 9/21/52 - 5/17/53; 9/20/53 - 5/16/54; 9/19/54 - 5/15/55; 9/18/55 - 5/6/56; 9/16/56 - 12/30/56) Goodyear, ABC, Sun, 6:30 pm; 5:30 pm as of 9/18/49

1 **Greece Fights On**

2 **Greek News In English** (4/25/41, 4/26/41) Greece

1 **Greek War Relief Presents The Collegiate Chorale** (11/46) Syn

1 **Green Border** (5/8/53) CBS

1 **Green Brothers Orchestra** (Thesaurus transcription)

109 **Green Hornet, The** (1/31/36 - 12/5/52) Al Hodge (1936 - 43) A. Donovan Faust (1943) Robert Hall (1943 - 46) Jack McCarthy (1946 - 52); dates and times varied around the country
1/31/36 - 4/7/38, WXYZ, Detroit, Fri; 2t as of 2/18/36
4/12/38 - 11/9/39, Sus, Mut, 2t
11/16/39 - 1/20/40, Bl, Thu & Sat
1/24/40 & 1/25/40, Bl, Wed & Thu
1/20/40 - 8/28/40, Bl, Mon & Wed
9/2/40 - 10/23/40, Mut, 2t (Mon & Wed)
9/20/40 - 9/27/40, Bl, Fri (not in New York)
10/3/40 - 10/10/40, Bl, Thu (not in New York)
12/28/40 - 12/13/41, Sus, Mut, Sat, 8 pm
1/3/42 - 11/28/42, Sus, Bl, Sat, 8 pm; 8:30 pm as of 7/18/42
12/6/42 - 4/18/43, Sus, Bl, Sun, 4:30 pm
4/20/4 - 8/24/43, Sus, Bl, Tue, 7 pm
9/2/43 - 3/16/44, Sus, Bl, Thu, 8:30 pm
3/21/44 - 1/23/45, Sus, Bl, Tue, 7:30 pm
2/1/45 - 12/20/45, Sus, ABC, Thu, 7:30 pm
12/25/45 - 2/12/46, Sus, ABC, Tue, 7:30 pm

Green Hornet, The (continued)
2/16/46 - 10/19/46, Sus, ABC, Sat, 7:30 pm
10/27/46 - 3/2147, Sus, ABC, Sun, 4:30 pm
3/11/47 - 12/30/47, Sus, ABC, Tue
1/6/48 - 8/24/48, General Mills, ABC, Tue
9/14/48 - 6/9/49, Sus, ABC, 2t, 5 pm
6/13/49 - 9/12/49, Sus, ABC, Mon
9/20/49 - 6/6/50, Sus, ABC, Tue, 5:30 pm
6/16/50 - 9/8/50, Sus, ABC, Fri, 5:30 pm
9/10/52 - 12/5/52, Orange Crush, ABC, 2t (Wed, Fri), 5 pm

2 **Green House** (1939) Syn

1 **Green Is For Go** (10/29/54) CBS

1 **Green Joker, The** (Syn)

3 **Green Lama, The** (with Paul Frees) (6/5/49 - 8/20/49) Sus, CBS, Sun, 5:30 pm; Sat, 7 pm as of 7/9/49

Green Mr. Pepper (NBC) 15m

Green Room Club, The (with Lionel Barrymore) see Guest Night At The Green Room

26 **Green Valley Line, The** (Syn) (1930s)

1 **Green Valley U. S. A.** (7/5/42 - 8/20/44)
7/5/42 - 7/26/42 (citizens' reaction to the war), Sus, CBS, Sun, 25m, 1:35 pm
7/29/42 - 10/21/42 (with Gertrude Lawrence), Sus, CBS, Wed, 7:30 pm
1/4/43 - 5/14/43, Sus, CBS, 5t, 15m, 4:15 pm
2/27/44 - 8/20/44 (with Santos Ortega), Emerson Radio, Mut, Sun, 5 pm

Greenfield Village Chapel Choir (9/29/37 - 7/1/45) 15m, on various days and times including:
9/29/37 - 5/24/39, Sus, CBS, Wed
10/11/39 - 4/11/40, Sus, CBS, Wed, 8:45 am
5/4/40 - 6/5/40, Sus, CBS, Sat
10/6/40 - 4/27/41, Sus, CBS, Sun, 8:45 am
5/6/41 - 6/10/41, CBS, Thu, 9:30 am
10/12/41 - 7/21/42; 10/11/42 - 6/20/43, CBS, Sun, 8:45 am
10/30/43 - 1/1/44, Bl, Sat, 15m, 10:15 am
1/9/44 - 7/1/45, Ford, Bl, Sun, 5m, 8 pm

1 **Greg Garrison Interview** (8/5/76)

1 **Grenada Invasion** (10/25/83) NBC-TV

4 **Grenada Invasion Coverage** (10/25 - 28/83) CBS-TV, NBC-TV

Grenadiers, The (5/12/35 - 9/22/35) (Canadian Grenadiers) Bl, Sun, 6 pm; often not in New York
(6/11/39 - 9/17/39) Bl, Sun, 6 pm

Greyhound Highway Traveler (with Harlow Wilcox) (4/3/32 - 6/5/32) Greyhound, CBS, Sun, 15m, 8:30 pm

Gridley and The Girls (with Fran Allison)

Griff Williams (10/17/43 - 10/24/43) Mut, Sun, 5 pm

1 **Griff Williams and His Orchestra** (6/26/46)

2 **Grimm's Fairy Tales** (Syn)

6 **Grip Of Terror, The** (1978) WMUK

1 **Gripsholm Interviews** (3/16/44) WOR

Grits and Gravy (with George Gaul and Peggy Paige)
(4/12/34 - 10/11/34) Bl, Thu, 8 pm

Grouch Club, The (with Jack Lascoulie) (4/16/39 - 1/21/40) Kix, NBC, Sun; started 10/17/38 CBS - Pacific; replaced by Beat The Band (continued on West coast-CBS)

1 **Groucho Marx Audition** (1943)

1 **Ground Breaking: U. N. Site** (9/14/48) WNYC

1 **Gruen Answer Man** (1933) Syn

Grummits, The (with Senator Ed Ford) (10/29/34 - 37)
10/29/34 - 1/9/35, Sus, NBC, 2t, 15m
1936 - 37, Mut, Fri, 30m, 8:30 pm

3 **Guam Broadcast** (8/26/44, 4/2/45, 4/3/45) Mut

1 **Guam Recordings** (8/20/44)

104 **Guard Session** (National Guard) (1957 - 1969) Syn, 15m

1 **Guardian Eyes** (Syn)

1 **Guess What** (with Lindsay MacHarrie) (Syn) 15m

Guess Where (1939 - 5/12/39) (with June Walker, Budd Hulick) Philip Morris, Mut, Fri, 8 pm
(8/11/43 - 11/24/43) Mut, Wed, 9:30 pm

1 **Guess Who** (with Peter Donald; then Happy Felton as of 8/11/45)
(4/12/44 - 4/30/49) Sheffield Farms, Mut, Sat, 7 pm

6 **Guessin' Guys and Gals** (1/15/49 - 6/11/49) WMAQ

7 **Guest Critic Series** (9/45) CBS

1 **Guest Critic Series Starring Fanny Brice** (CBS)

1 **Guest Night At The Green Room** (6/1/36) audition

693 **Guest Star** (Treasury Dept.) (3/27/47 - 10/17/66) 15m

4 **Guest Star Show Of The Month** (1968, 1969) Syn

21 **Guest Star Time** (1951, 1952) Syn, 15m

1 **Guida Pastry Shop Program, The** (10/19/36) WMBQ

Guidepost's Drama (15m)

205 **Guiding Light, The** (1/25/37 - 6/29/56) 5t, 15m (called Good Samaritan for first few episodes)
1/25/37 - 12/26/41, White Naptha, NBC
3/17/42 - 11/29/46, General Mills, NBC
6/2/47 - 6/29/56, Duz, CBS, 1:45 pm

2 **Guilty Or Not Guilty** (1932) Syn, 15m

1 **Gulden Serenaders, The** (10/5/38 - 4/29/41) Gulden, Bl, 6:30 pm
10/5/38 - 5/10/40, 2t (Wed & Fri)
10/15/40 - 4/29/41, 2t

Gulf Headliners, The (see Will Rogers)

Gulf Musical Playhouse (with Jane Froman, Jan Peerce, Erno Rapee Orchestra) (6/11/39 - 9/17/39) Gulf, CBS, Sun, 7:30 pm (summer replacement for Screen Guild Players)

Gulf Screen Guild Theatre, The (see The Screen Guild Theatre)

Gulf Show, The (see Will Rogers)

Gulf Spray (see also Jack Berch)

Gulf Spray Presents (with Jerry Wayne and Dan Seymour)
(1944 - summer) 15m

Gulf Spray Show (CBS)

1 **Gulliver's Travels** (1938) Air trailer

Gumps, The (with Wilmer Walter and Agnes Moorehead) (11/5/34 - 7/2/37) originally broadcast locally over WGN, Chicago
11/5/34 - 11/1/35, Pebeco Toothpaste, CBS, 5t, 15m, 12:15 pm; 3t as of 8/5/35
10/5/36 - 7/2/37, Lehn and Fink, CBS, 5t, 15m, 12 noon

406 **Gunsmoke** (with William Conrad)
(7/13/49) audition
(4/26/52 - 6/18/61) CBS
4/26/52 - 9/26/53, Sus, Sat,
10/3/53 - 12/26/53, Post Toasties, Sat
1/2/54 - 7/3/54, Sus, Sat
7/5/54 - 9/27/54, Chesterfield, Mon
10/2/54 - 10/8/55, Liggett and Myers, Sat
10/9/55 - 4/7/57, Liggett and Myers, Sun
4/14/57 - 6/18/61, Sus/Multi, Sat
also syndicated

2 **Gus Arnheim** (Syn)

2 **Gus Arnheim and His Orchestra** (Syn)

1 **Gus Arnheim Orchestra, The**
(3/26/30 - 5/31/30) (with Bing Crosby) (various days) (from Coconut Grove, Ambassador Hotel, Los Angeles)
(1933) 15m also National Wild Life (15m) also syndicated

2 **Gus Gray, Special Correspondent**
(1930s) 15m

3 **Gus Haenschaen All-String Orchestra, The** (2/20/45 - 4/23/46) WJR

Gus Steck Orchestra (4/13/40 - 9/21/40) Bl, Sat, 5 pm

1 **Gus Van Show**

Guy Hedlund Players (3/1/41 - 6/28/41) CBS, Sat, 3:30 pm

41 **Guy Lombardo** (1927 - 67) much overlapping 1927 - 9/13/33 (Robert Burns Panatella Proram) Robert Bums, CBS, Mon; Burns and Allen were on 2/22/32 - 9/13/33 (also see Burns and Allen)
7/11/34 - 7/3/35 (Pleasure Island), Plough Inc., NBC, Wed, 10 pm
7/8/35 - 6/29/36, Esso, CBS, Mon
9/6/36 - 8/14/38, Bond, CBS, Sun, 5:30 pm
10/10/38 - 7/28/41, Lady Esther, CBS, Mon, 10 pm; 9:30 pm from 7/17/39 - 9/4/39
also 10/14/38 - 1/26/40, Lady Esther, NBC, Fri, 10 pm
also 11/20/40 - 4/30/41, Mut, Wed, 25m, 9:30 pm

Guy Lombardo (continued)
8/2/41 - 7/11/42, Colgate, CBS, Sat, 8 pm
3/8/43 - 12/20/43 (with Ogden Nash), Ballantine, CBS, Mon, 10:30 pm
also 10/19/43 - 11/23/43, CBS, Tue, 15m, 10:45 pm
1/16/44 - 4/30/44, Chelseas, Bl, Sun, 10:30 pm
5/6/44 - 12/30/44, Bl, Sat, 10 pm
1/1/45 - 5/7/45, Chelseas, Bl, Mon, 10 pm
5/15/45 - 3/26/46, Chelseas, ABC, Tue, 9 pm
7/2/48 - 7/16/48, CBS, Fri, 9 pm
10/30/48 - 12/18/48, Mut, Sun, 9:30 pm
7/3/49 - 9/11/49, NBC, Sun, 7:30 pm (summer replacement for Phil Harris)
6/4/50 - 9/3/50; 6/10/51 - 8/8/51; 6/14/53 - 9/6/53, CBS, Sun, 7 pm (summer replacement for Jack Benny)
7/13/5 - 9/11/53, NBC, 5t, 7:30 pm (summer replacement for Longine Symphonette)
11/27/55 -7/1/56, CBS, Sun, 1:30 pm
also 10/30/48 - 5/19/57 (often called Lombardoland USA) Sus, Mut, Sat or Sun (Syn - ZIV) 92 shows broadcast 1964 (from Tiparillo Band Pavilion, New York World's Fair)
1966 - 67 (from Blue Room, Hotel Tropicana, Las Vegas)
1968 - 1970, CBS, CBS-TV, World transcription

Guy Lombardo and His Musical Autographs (see Guy Lombadro)

Guy Lombardo and His Orchestra (see Guy Lombadro)

Guy Lombardo and His Royal Canadians (see Guy Lombadro)

Guy Lombardo Show, The (see Guy Lombadro)

Guy Lombardo Time (see Guy Lombadro)

Guys Next Door, The (ABC)

Gwen Williams (12/11/39 - 7/26/41) Bl, 15m
12/11/39 - 12/27/40, Mon, 12 noon
1/22/41 - 3/26/41, Wed, 12 noon
3/31/41 - 5/26/41, Mon, sometimes 2t-5t, 8:15 am
7/5/41 - 7/26/41, Sat, 8:15 am

Gypsy Caravan (6/1/41 - 10/4/42) CBS, Sun, 15m, 9:45 am

Gypsy Ensemble (10/12/41 - 3/1/42) NBC, Sun, 8:30 am

1 **Gypsy Fiddles** (12/8/41) Red net

Gypsy Joe (Syn)

Gypsy Serenade (6/27/43 - 8/8/43) Bl, Sun, 10 am

RADIO STATION
KGW
PORTLAND 5, OREGON
PROGRAM NO.
PART NUMBER
TITLE
DATE
RECORDED AT
RPM
START - OUTSIDE
INSIDE

H-Bar-O Rangers (9/26/32 - 11/11/32) Hecker H-O Oats. CBS, 15m (became Bobby Benson)

H. R. Baukhage (2/9/42 - 10/13/50) Bl/ABC
(1952 - 1953) Mut

5 **H. R. Knickerbocker** (6/18/49 - 7/16/49) Mut

1 **H. Ross Perot** (11/8/93) NBC-TV

5 **H. V. Kaltenborn** (12/7/41 - 12/45) NBC

1 **H. V. Kaltenborn With The News**
(1927 -1/15/55)
1927 - 4/15/40, CBS
4/6/40 - 1/15/55, Pure Oil and Sus, NBC

2 **Hail and Farewell** (11/2/46 - 11/23/47) NBC

1 **Hail The Champ** (11/7/46) ABC

1 **Hal Howard and His Serenade In Satin** (4/41) Mut

2 **Hal Kemp** (1934 - 10/24/39)
1934, Lavena Cosmetics
1935 (see Penthouse Party)
8/5/36 - 8/26/36 (Hal Kemp substitutes for Wayne King), Lady Esther, NBC, Wed, 8:30 pm
1/1/37 - 12/24/37 (Music From Hollywood; also called Chesterfield Time) Chesterfield, CBS, Fri, 8:30 pm
4/19/38 - 10/11/38 (Time To Shine) Griffin, CBS, Tue, 10 pm
1938, film sound track
5/2/39 - 10/24/39 (Time To Shine), Griffin, CBS, Tue, 10 pm

2 **Hal Kemp and His Orchestra**
(1936, 2/15/39) CBS

Hal McIntire Orchestra
(1/16/43 - 1/30/45)
1/16/43 - 1/8/44, Sus, Mut, Sat, 2 pm
1/2/45 - 1/30/45, Eversharp, ABC, Tue, 10:30 pm

3 **Hal McIntyre and His Orchestra**
(12/23/43 - 12/31/52) Standard transcriptions

Hal Peary Show (see Honest Harold)

Hal Willard (ABC) 15m

Hal Winters (10/22/45 - 11/30/45) CBS, 5t, 15m, 4:30 pm

2 **Haldeman: The Nixon Years** (3/23 - 30/75) CBS-TV

Half Hour To Kill, A

2 **Halfway To Heaven** (CBS)

Halicrafters Hour (with Hildegarde)

Hall and Gruen (8/13/33 - 34) NBC, Sun, 15m

2 **Hall Of Fame, The** (1/7/34 - 12/30/34) Lysol, NBC, Sun, 10:30 pm

38 **Hall Of Fantasy, The** (written and directed by Richard Thorne)
(1947) (broadcast in Utah; directed by Ray Thorne; sponsored by Granite Furniture Company)
(8/22/52 - 9/26/52) Mut, Fri, 9:30 pm
(1/5/53 - 9/28/53) Sus, Mut, Mon, 8:30 pm; originated in Chicago, WGN

Hall Of Fun (with Ernest Trex)
(12/3/38 - 12/18/39)
12/3/38 - 5/20/39, NBC, Sat, 9:30 pm
5/28/39 - 8/20/39, NBC, Sun, 5 pm
9/10/39 - 10/29/39, NBC, Sun, 4 pm
11/27/39 - 12/18/39, Bl, Mon, 10 pm

1 **Hallelujah** (1929) film sound track

2 **Hallmark Charlotte Greenwood Show, The** (11/11/45, 11/18/45) ABC

3 **Hallmark Hall Of Fame, The** (2/8/53 - 5/31/53; 9/13/53 - 6/6/54; 10/3/54 - 3/27/55) Hallmark, CBS, Sun, 9 pm; 6:30 pm as of 10/3/54

74 **Hallmark Playhouse** (narrated by James Hilton)
(12/25/47) CBS
(6/10/48 - 2/1/53) Hallmark, CBS
6/10/48 - 6/2/49; 9/8/49 - 6/1/50; 9/7/50 - 5/31/51; 9/6/51 - 5/29/52, Thu, 10 pm. 9:30 from 11/16/50 - 5/31/51; 8:30 pm as of 9/6/51
9/7/52 - 2/1/53, Sun. 9 pm; developed into Hallmark Hall Of Fame

1 **Halloween Horror** (WMUK)

Halls Of Horror

40 **Halls Of Ivy, The** (with Benita Hume and Ronald Colman)
(6/22/49) audition
(1/6/50 - 6/25/52) Schlitz, NBC
1/6/50 - 5/5/50, Fri, 8 pm
5/10/50 - 6/27/51; 9/12/51 - 6/25/52, Wed

1 **Halls Of Montezuma, The** (3/11/45) Mut, 30m

Halsey Stuart Program
(10/28/31 - 6/29/32) Halsey, Stuart & Co., NBC, Wed, 9 pm; 8:30 pm as of 4/6/32; started locally in the Midwest in 1928

Hamilton Watchman, The
(9/25/30 - 6/17/31) Hamilton Watch, CBS, Thu, 15m, 8:45 pm

1 **Hamlin's Wizard Oil Country Music Program** (Syn)

Hammerstein Music Hall (with Ted Hammerstein) (11/27/34 - 3/18/38)
11/27/34 - 3/31/35, Hill Drops, CBS, Sun, 2:30 pm
9/30/35 - 6/22/36, Kolynos, NBC, Mon, 8 pm
6/30/36 - 7/27/37, Kolynos, CBS, Tue, 8 pm
8/6/37 - 3/18/38, Kolynos, CBS, Fri, 8 pm

1 **Hammond Organ Recital** (9/21/39) WJSV

1 **Hand To A Hero** (3/20/46) WOR

1 **Hands Across The Sea** (1/27/50) Mut

1 **Handshake In Space** (7/14/75) NBC-TV

Hank D'Amico (9/20/47 - 11/1/47) ABC, Sat, 7:30 pm

Hank Lawson's Knights Of The Road
(12/16/40 - 4/10/43) 15m
12/16/40 - 1/24/41, NBC, 5t, 10:15 am
5/24/41 - 8/16/41, NBC, Sat, 8:15 am
9/6/41 - 8/15/42, NBC, 5t, 15m, 9:15 am
8/31/42 - 4/10/43, Bl, Sat, 15m, 10:30 am
also 9/3/42 - 12/11/42, Bl, 5t, 15m, 10:30 am

1 **Hank Says** (2/10/53) audition

Hank Simmons' Showboat
(1928 - 12/26/31) CBS, Sat, 60m

Hank Thompson and His Brazos Valley Boys (11/6/52 - 4/7/53) Falstaff Beer; Mut, 3t (Tue, Thu Fri), 15m, 10:15 pm

1 **Hank Thompson and His Orchestra** (World transcription)

1 **Hank Williams and His Drifting Cowboys** (1951) Syn

8 **Hank Williams Health and Happiness Show** (1949) Syn, 15m

1 **Hannibal Cobb** (with Santos Ortega) (1/9/50 - 5/11/51, Sus, ABC, 5t, 3; 30pm

2 **Hap Hazard** (with Ransom Sherman)
(7/1/41 - 9/23/41, 11/7/41) Johnson Wax, NBC, Tue, 9:30 pm (summer replacement for Fibber McGee & Molly) 32 five to eight-minute shows called The Adventures Of Hap Hazard were broadcast over WYVE, Wytheville, Virginia with Paul Dellinger

2 **Hap Miller and His Orchestra** (3/71, 10/71) CBS

5 **Happiness** (1/84 - 2/84) NPR

1 **Happiness Ahead** (1934) Air trailer

1 **Happiness Boys, The** (with Billy Jones and Ernie Hare) (1926 - 11/23/40) started locally on WJZ New York on 10/18/21 (various days and times including:)
1926 - 29, Happiness Candy, Bl, Fri, 30m
1929 - 7/10/31 Interwoven Socks, Bl, Fri
1931 - 38, Tastyeast Bakers, Bl, 3t, 15m
3/7/32 - 9/30/32, Hellmans, Bl, 5t; 3t from 7/18/32
10/3/32 - 12/9/32, Hellmans, NBC, 3t, 7:30 pm
1933
1939 - 11/23/40 (Sachs Program) WMCA New York, Sun, 3 pm; with death of Emie Hare on 3/9/39, daughter Marilyn continued until March of 1940; Jones did it alone until 11/23/40 when Billy Jones died

1 **Happiness Hotel** (4/30/46) NBC

1 **Happy Adventure, A** (Syn)

1 **Happy Birthday Bob** (3/28/78) NBC-TV

Happy Days Revue (with Jimmie Grier Orchestra) (10/23/34 - 6/25/35) CBS, Tue, 9 am

Happy Felton Show, The
(4/16/45 - 5/11/45) NBC, 5t 11 am

6 **Happy Gang, The** (CBC; with Bert Pearl) (1937 - 4/17/48) on briefly from 3/15/48 on Mut, also Syn

1 **Happy Go Lucky** (1943) film sound track

4 **Happy Hank** (1946 - 1948) Syn

Happy Hollow (written by Everett Kemp) (5/13/35 - 10/9/36) CBS, 5t, 15m (started on KMBC on 7/1/29)

Happy Homemaker, The (see Ida Bailey Allen)

Happy Island (see Ed Wynn)

Happy Jack Turner (with Irving Kaufman as of 1936) (1932 - 5/26/43) various days and times including:
1932 - 5/27/33, Sus, Bl, 6t, 15m
1935 - 5/3/41, NBC, 4 - 6t, 15m (sponsored by Lewis Howe 6/1/36 - 7/3/36)
5/3/41 - 10/11/41 Fitch, NBC, Sat, 15m
10/18/41 - 8/15/42, NBC, Sat, 9 pm
8/17/42 - 1/27/43; 5/3/43 - 5/26/43, NBC, 3t - 6t, 15m, 9:45 am

Happy Jim Parsons (1/28/40 - 6/30/40) Air Conditioning Training Corp., Bl, Sun, 15m
(6/16/41 - 9/26/41) Mut, 5t, 10:30 am
(9/27/41 - 1/15/43) Mut, 5t - 6t, 15m

1 **Happy Landing** (1938) film sound track
(2/20/50 - 7/7/50) ABC, 5t, 15m, 4:30 pm (with Bud Collyer)

Happy Rambler, The (with Irving Kaufman) (10/6/32 - 11/25/32) Swift, NBC, 2t (Thu & :Fri), 15m, 10:30 am

4 **Happy The Humbug** (Syn)

1 **Happy Valley Folks, The** (Syn)

Happy Wonder Bakers (1927 - 5/5/31) (with Frank Luther; Frank Black Orchestra) Wonder Bread, NBC, Tue, 15m
(5/8/33 - 5/4/34) Wonder Bread, CBS, 3t, 15m, 6:30 pm

Happy-Go-Lucky Hour (7/5/32 - 1933) Swift, CBS - Midwest, 2t, 15m

12 **Hardy Family, The** (with Mickey Rooney and Lewis Stone) (1/3/52 - 1/1/53) Sus, Mut, Thu, 8:30 pm, Syn

Harlem (All-Colored) Revue (with Louis Armstrong) (4/9/37 - 7/9/37) Fleischmann, Bl, Fri, 9 pm

Harlem Hospitality Club
(9/20/47 - 12/13/47) Mut, Sat, 9:30 pm

Harmonaires, The (9/24/49 - 12/31/49) ABC, Sat, 15m, 6:45 pm

1 **Harmony Hall** (8/43) Mut

1 **Harmony Hotel** (8/13/52) WMAQ

1 **Harmony Rangers** (with Mac McGuire) (6/21/51) AFRS

1 **Harold Arlen Audition** (1/14/47) CBS

1 **Harold Arlen - Sidney Skolsky** (11/19/46) CBS

4 **Harold Lloyd Comedy Theatre, The** (with Harold Lloyd and Jimmy Wallington) (10/29/44 - 6/10/45) Old Gold, NBC. Sun, 10:30 pm

Harold Nagel and His Rumba Orchestra (6/21/36 - 9/20/36) NBC, Sun, 1 pm

Harold Peary Show, The (see Honest Harold)

Harold Stokes Eskimo Pie Orchestra (see also Eskimo Pie; Melodies From The Skies)
(8/27/37 - 12/11/37) Sheaffer Pen, Mut, Fri, 15m, 8:15 pm
(6/27/40 - 8/1/40) Mut, Thu, 10:30 pm

1 **Harold Teen** (1934) film sound track (8/5/41 - 42) Mut (Midwest), Tue

Harold Turner (1940s) usually not in New York

Harriet Parsons (1/12/38 - 6/29/38) Bromo-Seltzer, Bl, Wed, 15m, 8:30 pm

Harrington and Wood

1 **Harrison Woods** (6/20/48 - 2/26/50) (8/21/50) Sus (This Changing World) Fruehauf Trailers, ABC, Sun, 15m, 3 pm

Harry Babbitt Show, The (ABC), 15m

1 **Harry Bluestone** (Standard transcription)

1 **Harry Brandon and His Orchestra** (6/15/47) ABC

1 **Harry Breuer Group** (Thesaurus transcription)

2 **Harry Breuer's Novelty Orchestra** (Lang-Worth transcriptions)

Harry Clark

Harry Cool and the Harmonettes (4/12/38 - 6/21/38) CBS, Tue, 15m, 4:30 pm

Harry Farbman (7/9/39 - 8/20/39) NBC, Sun, 12 noon

1 **Harry Hershfield Spotlighting New York** (11/1/48) WOR

1 **Harry Hopkins** (7/27/41) BBC

Harry Horlick (with Eugene Conley) (5/5/39 - 9/29/39) Bl, Fri, 9:30 pm

5 **Harry Horlick and His Orchestra** (1936) RCA, Associated, World transcriptions

2 **Harry Horlick Orchestra** (Thesaurus transcriptions)

1 **Harry Horlick's Orchestra** (Lang-Worth transcription)

Harry James (9/29/42 - 9/21/45) CBS
9/29/42 - 3/24/44, Chesterfield, 3t, 15m (replaced Glenn Miller)
6/8/45 - 9/21/45, Pabst, Fri, 10:30 pm (summer replacement for Danny Kaye)

7 **Harry James and His Music Makers** (6/7/44 - 2/7/59) CBS, NBC, KFI

29 **Harry James and His Orchestra** (1940 - 12/5/66) Mut, NBC, CBS, Syn, WNEW, World transcription

1 **Harry James "Live In London"** (10/23/71)

16 **Harry James Show, The** (Syn)

Harry Kogen Orchestra (12/7/40 - 2/15/41) Bl, Sat, 10:30 am

1 **Harry Lauder**

Harry Lime (see The Third Man)

1 **Harry Marble News** (6/7/44, 4/16/46 - 4/28/47) CBS

Harry Nile (see The Adventures Of Harry Nile)

4 **Harry Owens and His Orchestra** (3/27/43) Bl, United transcriptions

Harry Prime - Monica Lewis Show, The (10/24/44 - 6/22/45) CBS, 4t (Tue - Fri), 15m, 7:15 pm

7 **Harry Reser Orchestra** (with Ray Heatherton and Peg La Centra) (12/9/34 - 6/2/35) Wrigley, NBC, Sun, 4:30 pm, Thesaurus transcriptions

Harry Revel Show

35 **Harry Richman** (4/18/34 - 38)
4/18/34 - 3/6/35 (with Jack Denny Orchestra) Conoco Oil, Bl, Wed
1/4/36 - 37, Dodge, Syn (The Dodge Show)
1937 - 38 Syn, (Florida Treat)

Harry Richman Dodge Program (see Harry Richman)

Harry Richman Florida Show, The (see Harry Richman)

3 **Harry Roy and His Orchestra** (BBC transcriptions)

1 **Harry S. Truman Obituary** (7/66) CBS

Harry Savoy (6/15/44 - 9/28/44) Camel, NBC, Thu, 10 pm (summer replacement for Abbott and Costello)
(2/23/46 - 5/11/46) Mut, Sat, 8:30 pm

3 **Harry "The Hipster" Gibson** (BMI, MacGregor transcriptions)

1 **Harry "The Hipster" Gibson, Accompanied By "Shep" and "Tiny"** (MacGregor transcription)

1 **Harry Truman Interview** (1964)

Harry Von Zell (1937) Gulf, CBS, 7:30 pm

1 **Harry Von Zell Tells The P. B. S. Story** (1951) Syn

Harry Wismer (5/6/44 - 10/23/55) (see also Greatest Sports Thrill; Champion Roll Call; All Star Sports)
5/6/44 - 6/25/49, Sus, ABC, Sat, 15m, 6:30 pm
7/2/49 - 7/5/52, Multi, ABC, Sat, 15m
4/11/54 - 10/23/55, General Tires, Mut, Sun, 15m

Hart, Schaffner and Marx Trumpeters (with Victor Young Orchestra, Edwin C. Hill, Herman Hupfeld)
(10/15/31 - 5/19/32) Hart, Schaffner and Marx, CBS, Thu, 10 pm

Hartford Pop Concert (1932 - 11/8/33) NBC, Wed, 4 pm

Hartz Mountain Canaries (see American Radio Warblers)

1 **Hartz Mountain Spot Announcements** (Syn)

Harv and Esther (with Teddy Bergman and Audrey Marsh) (9/12/35 - 3/5/36) International Cigars, CBS, Thu, 8 pm

4 **Harvest Of Stars, The** (with Raymond Massey; James Melton from 10/6/46)
(10/7/45 - 9/17/50) International Harvester, NBC
10/7/45 - 3/28/47, Sun, 2 pm; 2:30 pm as of 7/7/46
4/7/48 - 3/30/49, Wed, 9:30 pm
4/3/49 - 6/26/49; 8/28/49 - 9/17/50, Sun, 5:30 pm

Harvey and Dell (with The Meade Family)
(8/1/39 - 7/24/42) 15m
8/1/39 - 10/11/40, Bl, 5t; 6t as of 3/18/40
10/18/40 - 5/3/41, Bl, Sat, 8:15 am
4/8/42 - 5/6/42, CBS, 3t (Mon - Wed), 9:45 am
6/1/42 - 7/24/42, CBS, 5t, 9:45 am; General Mills as of 6/30/42 (alternated with Thus We Love)

1 **Harvey Girls, The** (1945) Air trailer

Harvey Harding (10/1/40 - 7/11/41) Bl, 3t - 5t, 10m, 1:50 pm

2 **Hashknife Hartley and Sleepy Stevens** (with Frank Martin and Barton Yarborough) (7/2/50 - 12/30/51) Sus, Mut, Sun, various times

4 **Hasten The Day** (1943) Syn, Sun, 15m

1 **Haunted House, The** (1931) Syn

50 **Haunting Hour, The** (1945 - 1949) Syn

150 **Have Gun Will Travel** (with John Dehner) (11/23/58 - 11/27/60) Multi, CBS, Sun, 25m, 6:05 pm

Have You Heard? (with Barbara Gould; Patricia French)
(9/15/32 - 8/3/33), CBS, Thu, 15m, 10:45 am
(3/36 - 5/29/36), Bl, Fri, 10m, 6:35 pm)
(6/2/36 - 9/28/37) Bl, Tue, 15m, 3:45 pm

Haven Of Rest (founded by Haddox Paul Myers) (1934 - ?) Mut, Sun,

5 **Hawaii Calls** (with Webley Edwards; with Danny Kaleikin until 1975 when the show went off the air. It was revived on 10/3/92)
(7/5/35 - 92+) Mut
7/5/35 - 45, mostly West Coast network from 1/21/39 - 2/25/39, Sat, 9 pm
7/1/39 - 3/9/40, Sat, 8:30 pm
3/8/41 - 5/3/41, Sat, 15m, 8:45 pm
8/31/41 - 11/16/41, Sun, 25m, 11 am
1945 - 52, Sus, Sat, various times; often not in New York
1952 - 56, Sus, Mut, Sat and/or Sun
1956 - 1975; 10/3/92- present, Regionally

1 **Hawaii, The 50th State** (8/21/59) CBS-TV

1 **Hawaiian Fantasies** (1930s) Syn, 15m

Hawaiian Music (1939 - 3/31/40) Bl, Sun, 8:30 pm
(12/5/42 - 3/27/43) CBS, Sat, 3:30 pm (Hello From Hawaii)

6 **Hawk Larabee** (7/12/46 - 2/7/48) originally called Hawk Durango
7/12/46 - 8/16/46 (Hawk Durango; with Elliott Lewis), CBS, Fri, 10:30 pm
10/3/46 - 12/12/46 (with Barton Yarborough), CBS, Thu, 5:30 pm
5/31/47 - 6/7/47, CBS, Sat, 7 pm
6/20/47 - 8/1/47, CBS, Fri, 8 pm
8/9/47 - 2/7/48, Sus, CBS, Sat, 7 pm plus 12/28/48

1 **Hawk, The** (Syn) (1936 - 37)

Hawthorne House (with Pearl King Tanner) (10/28/35 - 40s) Wesson, NBC - West, Wed; Mon as of 4/25/38

9 **Hawthorne Thing, The** (1948)

3 **Hawthorne's Adventures** (Hawthorne Show) (with Jim Hawthorne from California)
(1940s - 1950s) KXLA; KNX, 55m; Network includes: 1949 - 50, ABC

Hayden Planetarium Talks
(12/12/36 - 4/13/41) also known as Drama Of The Skies; Men Behind The Stars; This Wonderful World
12/12/36 - 4/24/37, CBS, Sat, 15m, 5:30 pm
12/30/38 - 4/12/40, CBS, Fri, 15m, 5:30 pm
1/21/39 - 3/1/41 (This Wonderful World), Mut, Sat, 15m
3/2/41 - 4/13/41, Mut, Sun, 9:30 am; on locally in New York after that

Hayloft Hoedown (6/16/45 - 7/9/49) Sus, ABC, Sat, 30m; 15m as of 12/22/45, 10:45 pm

Hazel Markel (1951 - 55) Multi, Mut, Sun

Headin' South (11/22/36 - 2/14/37) Illinois Central Railroad, CBS, Sun, 7:30 pm

2 **Headline Edition** (with Taylor Grant and others) (4/2/45 - 12/24/54) ABC

Headline Hunters (with Bob Considine)

Headlines and By-Lines (with Mel Allen, Ken Roberts, Robert Trout, H. V. Kaltenborn, others)
(10/10/37 - 12/25/38) CBS, Sun, 10:30 pm

Headlines and History (see Robert Trout)

1 **Headlines From Washington** (1/1/42) Atlantic Coast net

Headlines In Song (with Macy and Smalle) (7/31/33 - 5/7/34) NBC, Mon, 15m, 4 pm

1 **Headlines Of Tomorrow** (2/16/45) Mut

Healani Of The South Seas
(5/19/37 - 8/18/37) Bl, Wed, 10 pm, 15m, then Thu, 7:15 pm

Healing Waters (see Doctor Oral Roberts)

Health and Happiness Show, The (see Hank Williams)

8 **Health For America** (1941, 1942) Syn

14 **Health Magazine Of The Air** (with H.V. Kaltenborn) (1958) Syn

Hear America Swingin'
(7/30/54 - 8/27/54) NBC, Fri, 15m, 8 pm

27 **Hear It Now** (with Edward R. Murrow) (12/15/50 - 10/26/51) Sus, CBS, Fri, 60m, 9 pm

5 **Heart Of America, The** (1959) Syn

1 **Heart Of Gold, The** (8/24/37)

2 **Heart Of Show Business, The** (2/58) Syn

Heart of Julia Blake, The
(10/23/39 - 9/26/41) Mut, 3t, 15m

1 **Heart Songs** (Syn)

Heart Strings (with Michael Reid and Bill Goodwin) NBC, 15m

2 **Heart Throbs** (with Maurice Gunsky) (9/34 - 36) Syn, Wed, 15m

Heart Throbs Of The Hills (also called Hillbilly Heart Throbs; also called Dreams Of Long Ago as of 11/6/35) (written by Ethel Park Richardson)
(5/22/33 - 9/27/38) mostly regional, Sus, various days, NBC, 15m
(4/17/39 - 6/30/39) NBC, 2t, 15m

6 **Heart To Heart** (2/1/55) Syn

4 **Heart's Desire** (with Ben Alexander) (9/9/46 - 1/30/48) Mut, Philip Morris, 5t
9/9/46 - 4/25/47, Sus, 3 pm (not in New York)
4/28/47 - 1/30/48, Multi, 11:30 am

4 **Heartbeat Of Broadway, The** (Heart Fund) (2/59) Syn, 15m

412 **Heartbeat Theater** (Salvation Army) (3/4/56 - 92+) Syn

3 **Hearthstone Of The Death Squad**
(8/30/51 - 9/17/52) Sus, CBS
8/30/51 - 1/10/52, Thu, 9 pm
1/13/52 - 6/1/52, Sun, 5:30/9:30 pm; 4:30 pm as of 2/17/52
6/3/52 - 9/17/52, Tue; Wed, 8 pm as of 3/2/52

Hearts In Harmony (with Jone Allison)
1941 - 4/14/50+, Kroger's Markets, Regional, 15m

1 **Heat's On, The** (1943) film sound track

Heatherton House (4/30/51 - 9/21/51) Mut, 5t, 2:30 pm

5 **Heavyweight Championship Fight** (1976 - 1978) ABC-TV, NBC-TV, CBS-TV

13 **Hebrew Christian Hour, The** (1945)

Hecker Surprise Party (with Meredith Willson Orchestra) (1/7/32 - 3/10/32) H-O Oats, CB Thu, 12 midnight

Hecker's Information Service
(9/7/37 - 3/7/38) Hecker Products, Mut, 5t, 15m, 11:45am

2 **Hedda Hopper** (often called Hedda Hopper's Hollywood) (11/15/31 - 5/20/51)
11/15/31 - 5/15/32, Edna Wallace Hopper, CBS, Sun, 10 pm
11/6/39 - 10/30/42, Sunkist, CBS, 3t, 15m, 6:15 pm
10/2/44 - 9/3/45, Armour and Company, CBS, Mon, 15m, 7:15 pm
9/10/45 - 6/3/46, Armour, ABC, Mon, 15m, 8:15 pm
10/5/46 - 6/28/47 (This Is Hollywood) Procter & Gamble, CBS, Sat, 10:15 pm; 10 pm as of 4/19/47
10/14/50 - 6/11/51, NBC, Sat, 30m, 8 pm; Sun as of 11/19/50

Hedda Hopper Show, The (see Hedda Hopper)

2 **Hedda Hopper's Diary**

Hedda Hopper's Hollywood (see Hedda Hopper)

Heel Hugger Harmonies
(9/15/31 - 4/26/32) Heel Hugger Shoes, Bl, Tue, 15m, 8:30 pm

Heidelberg Harmonaires (1950s)

Heidelberg Students (5/10/34 - 11/8/34) Blatz Beer, CBS, Thu, 15m, 10:45 pm

Heinie and His Band (2/11/50 - 4/1/50) ABC, Sat, 8 pm

Heinz Magazine Of The Air (with B. A. Rolfe Orchestra)
(9/2/36 - 4/10/38) Heinz, CBS
9/2/36 - 8/27/37, 3t, 11 am
8/31/37 - 3/21/38, 3t (Mon, Tue & Thu), 11:15 pm effective 1/2/38 - 4/10/38 (with Mark Warnow Orchestra), Sun instead of Thu, 5 pm

Heirs Of Liberty (see Speaking Of Liberty)

1 **Heisman Trophy Award** (1/6/46) Mut

2 **Helen Forrest** (World transcriptions)

3 **Helen Forrest With Carmen Dragon and His Orchestra** (World transcriptions)

6 **Helen Hayes Theater** (with Helen Hayes) (10/1/35 - 3/23/46) (see also Electric Theater)
10/1/35 - 3/24/36 (The New Penny), Sanka, Bl, Tue, 9:30 pm
9/28/36 - 3/22/37 (Helen Hayes in Bambi) Sanka, Bl, Mon, 8 pm
9/10/39; 9/24/39; 10/22/39; 12/10/39; 1/7/40; 2/4/40; Campbell, CBS, Sun, 60m, 8 pm
9/29/40 - 6/22/41; 10/5/41 - 2/1/42, Lipton, CBS, Sun, 8 pm
2/25/45 - 6/24/45 (This Is Helen Hayes), Textron, Mut, Sun, 15m, 10:15 pm
9/8/45 - 2/23/46 (Textron Theater), Textron, CBS, Sat, 7 pm
3/2/46 - 3/23/46, Sus, CBS, Sat, 7 pm
1/16/56 - 3/23/56, NBC, 5t, 15m, 3:15 pm

Helen Holden (see Government Girl)

1 **Helen Kane** (1956)

7 **Helen O'Connell** (7/15/70) CBS, World transcriptions

4 **Helen O'Connell With Irving Orton's Orchestra** (World transcriptions)

Helen Traubel (11/29/36 - 7/4/37) Bl, Sun, 7 pm
(7/11/37 - 8/22/37) NBC, Sun, 5:30 pm

Helen Trent (see The Romance Of Helen Trent)

1 **Helicopter Rescue Of Hermit** (2/12/47) WOR

1 **Hell Or High Water** (KOIN)

Hello (with Louise King) (1943) NBC, 15m

1 **Hello America, Here Are The Netherlands** (2/28/39) PCJ (Holland)

8 **Hello Americans** (see Orson Welles Theater) (11/15/42 - 1/31/43) CBS, Sun, 8 pm

Hello From Hawaii (see Hawaiian Music)

Hello Joyce (15m)

1 **Hello Latin America** (12/18/43) NBC

3 **Hello Mom** (8/1142 - 1/22/43) NBC Pacific, Red
(5/5/45 - 9/8/45) Mut, Sat, 15m, 12 noon; 1:30 pm as of 6/23/45

10 **Hello Sucker** (1951 - 1952) WMAQ

Hello Sweetheart (with Nancy Martin; Marion Mann as of 1/13/45)
(12/18/43 - 3/10/45) Ivoryne Gum, Bl, Sat, 15m, 5:45 pm

Hello, Peggy (with Eunice Howard)
(8/4/37 - 7/29/38) Drano, NBC, 2t (Wed & Fri), 15m

Help Yourself (with Clara Thompson and Margaret Wise)
(6/15/39 - 10/31/39) Mut, Tue, 9:30 pm

6 **Help Yourself To Health** (1941) Syn

2 **Helping Hand, A** (with John J. Anthony) (10/13/41 - 1/30/42) Ironized Yeast, CBS, 5t, 15m

2 **Helpmate** (9/22/41 - 6/30/44) Old Dutch Cleanser, NBC, 5t, 15m, 10:30 am

Hemisphere Revue (5/14/41 - 1/3/42) Bl
5/14/41 - 9/24/41, Wed, 9 pm
10/4/41 - 1/3/42, Sat, 10 pm

1 **Hemphill Diesel Engineering School** (1936) Syn

Henn House, The (with Mitzi Green) (1950)

Henny Youngman Show, The (also called Carton Of Cheer) (9/13/44 - 4/25/45) Raleigh, NBC, Wed, 8:30 pm

Henri Deering (4/7/35 - 6/16/35) Bl, Sun, 15m, 2:15 pm

Henrik Willem Van Loon
(12/22/36 - 3/25/38) NBC

1 **Henry A. Wallace Speech** (5/16/43) CBS

2 **Henry Brandon and His Orchestra** (7/7/47, 2/28/49) ABC, NBC

Henry Burbig (5/30/31 - 8/29/31) CBS, Sat, 15m, 8:15 pm

1 **Henry Busse and His Montmartre Orchestra** (8/35)

4 **Henry Busse and His Orchestra** (1940) film sound track
(12/8/41, 12/28/44, 8/23/49) Bl, CBS

Henry Busse Orchestra
(9/9/36 - 11/28/37) J. W. Marrow, NBC, 15m
9/9/36 - 3/3/37, Wed, 4 pm
3/10/37 - 4/21/37, Wed, 4:15 pm
4/25/37 - 11/28/37, Sun

1 **Henry Cabot Lodge** (1960) NBC

Henry George Program (with Harry Salter Orchestra)
(10/29 - 7/28/31) Henry George Cigars, CBS
10/29 - 3/28/30, Fri, 7 pm; Mon, 8 pm as of 11/25/29
1930 - 7/28/31, Tue, 9 pm

Henry Gladstone (10/11/43 - 10/28/50) Mut, White Owl, others

1 **Henry Gladstone News** (5/16/47) WOR

1 **Henry J. Song, The** (1953) Syn

2 **Henry J. Taylor** (Your Land and Mine)
(12/21/45 - 12/3/56) General Motors, 15m
12/21/45 - 12/17/48, Mut, 2t (Mon & Fri) 10 pm; 7:30 pm as of 4/1/46
12/20/48 - 12/6/54, ABC, Mon
12/13/54 - 12/3/56, NBC, Mon

3 **Henry Jerome and His Orchestra** (Lang-Worth transcriptions)

Henry Jerome Orchestra (Treasury Varieties) (10/31/42 - 6/12/43) Mut, Sat, 1:30 pm

11 **Henry King and His Orchestra** (6/7/44) CBS, MacGregor, United transcriptions

1 **Henry King Orchestra** (Standard transcription)

15 **Henry King Show, The** (1948) Syn

1 **Henry Kissinger: An Interview With David Frost** (10/11/79) NBC-TV

1 **Henry L. Stimson** (5/6/41) Mut

63 **Henry Morgan Show, The**
(10/28/40. - 6/23/50) started as early as 7/15/38 as a non-comedic announcer at WOR-Mut, local show in New York in 9/21/40, 6t (WOR) called Meet Mr. Morgan
10/28/40 - 1/25/43 (went into service) (Here's Morgan until 3/8/46) Sus, Mut, 6t, 15m
10/8/45 - 3/8/46, ABC, 6t (Mon - Fri, Sun), 15m; Sunday until 1/27/46
3/7/46 - 5/9/46, ABC, Thu, 15m, 10:30 pm
6/11/46 - 7/16/46, ABC, Tue, 15m, 9 pm
9/2/46 - 7/9/47; 9/10/47 - 12/24/47, Eversharp, ABC, Mon; Wed as of 10/30/46, 30m, 10:30 pm (New York Times listed show)
9/3/46 - 10/15/46, ABC, Tue, 8:30 pm)
1/29/48 - 6/24/48 (with Arnold Stang) ABC, Thu, 7:30 pm
3/13/49 - 5/29/49 (with Arnold Stang) NBC, Sun, 8:30 pm
7/6/49 - 12/30/49, Camel, NBC, Wed; Fri, 8 pm as of 10/14/49
1/15/50 - 6/16/50, Bristol Myers, NBC, Sun, 6:30 pm
2/6/50 - 6/23/50, NBC, 5t 15m, 6:30 pm

Henry Russell Orchestra (6/7/47 - 49) NBC, Sun/Mon

1 **Henry Wallace** (7/20/44) Mut

1 **Henry Wallace Speech** (3/27/49) CBS

Henry Weber's Concert Orchestra (3/3/38 - 5/9/40) Mut, Thu

1 **Hep Session In Holland** (11/27/45) CBC

Her Honor, Nancy James (with Barbara Weeks) (10/3/38 - 7/28/39) Kleenex CBS, 5t, 15m

Herald Of Truth (3/2/52 - 58+) ABC, Sun, 12:30 pm

Herb Anderson (with Carole Bennett) (9/2/57 - 58) ABC, 5t, 60m, 10 pm

Herb Sheldon (12/12/49 - 2/15/52) ABC, 5t, 15m, 12:45 pm/12:30 pm

3 **Herb Shriner Show, The** (1942 - 6/10/49)
1942 - 43 (see Camel Caravan)
9/27/48 - 6/10/49 (Alka-Seltzer Time; also with Raymond Scott Quintet), Alka-Seltzer, CBS, 5t, 15m, 6:30 pm

11 **Herbert Hoover** (1/16/40 - 2/9/51) Mut

1 **Herbie Kay and His Orchestra** (1939) film sound track

10 **Hercule Poirot** (with Harold Huber)
(1/45 - 10/14/45) Mut
2/22/45 - 9/6/45, Thu, 8:30 pm
10/7/45 - 10/14/45, Sun, 9 pm
possibly as late as 1947

Here's To Music (Mut - Don Lee)

Here Come The Big Bands (host-Ted Lawrence)

Here Comes Elmer (see Al Pearce)

1 **Here Comes Louis Jordan** (Syn)

1 **Here Comes McBride** (with Frank Lovejoy) (5/19/49) NBC

2 **Here Comes The Band** (1935) Air trailer, film sound track

3 **Here Is America** (Syn)

1 **Here Is Australia** (Syn)

1 **Here You Are** (see You Are There)

Here's Babe Ruth (see Babe Ruth)

2 **Here's Hollywood** (8/20/49 - 10/22/49) ABC, Sat, 15m, 7 pm
(6/20/56) Mut
(1961) AFRTS

2 **Here's Howe** (with Pete Howe)
(8/13 - 8/14/45) Mut, 15m

Here's Looking At You (with Pegeen Fitzgerald and Willard Willis)
(2/19/41 - 6/11/41) Mut, 2t (Mon & Wed), 15m, 8:45 pm

2 **Here's Mexico** (1944) XEOX (Mexico), Mut

Here's Morgan (see Henry Morgan)

3 **Here's To Music** (5/6/45 - 6/45) Mut-Don Lee

23 **Here's To Romance** (4/18/43 - 10/4/45)
4/18/43 - 10/10/43 (with Jim Ameche; then Dick Haymes as of 7/28/43) Bl, Sun, 25m, 6:05 pm
10/14/43 - 10/4/45 (with Buddy Clark) Evening In Paris Face Powder, CBS, Thu

Here's To The Family (1/16/49 - 5/29/49) NBC, Sun, 2 pm

499 **Here's To Veterans** (5/23/46 - 8/30/46) NBC, 4t (Tue - Fri) 15m, 12:30 pm
(5/23/46 - 2/23/47) NBC, Sun, 15m, 1 pm
(1947 - 1963+) Syn, 15m

Here's To You (with Phil Hanna and Phil Davis Orchestra) (1/26/47 - 7/18/48) Hires, CBS, Sun, 30m; 15m as of 7/20/47

Here's To Youth (1/8/44 - 8/26/44) NBC, Sat, 1 pm

Here's What I Saw (5m)

1 **Here's What They Said** (12/17/49) CBS

Heritage (12/11/52 - 10/8/53) Life Magazine, ABC, Thu, 8:30 pm

Heritage Over The Land (with Henry Cassidy) (1/10/54 - 4/4/54) NBC, Sun, 1 pm

Herman and Banta (with Samuel Herman and Frank Banta)
(12/19/34 - 6/9/45) Bl, 15m
12/19/34 - 1/24/36, 2t/5t
1/6/39 - 3/10/39, Fri, 9:45 am
4/7/45 - 6/9/45, Sat, 12 noon

Herman Middleman Orchestra (4/15/40 - 6/17/40) Bl, Mon, 15m, 6 pm

8 **Hermit's Cave, The** (with John Kent; Charles Penman; Clark Ryder)
(1935 - about 1947, 1950) Olga Coal (from 9/37), WJR, Detroit, Tue, 11:30 pm; then 10:30 pm as of 3/22/38 (started as 15m show, then changed to 30m)
(1940 - about 1944) (with Mel Johnson; John Dehner) KMPC, Beverly Hills (same format as Detroit series with new casts and different scripts

11 **Heroes Of The Merchant Marine** (1945) Syn, 15m

1 **Hess Bails Out** (5/16/41) CBC

Heywood Braun (1930 - 2/13/31) CBS, 5t, 15m, 6:45 pm

Hi Boys (5/1/39 - 8/12/39) NBC, 6t, 15m, 8:15 am

1 **Hi Fi Demonstration Discs and Historical Broadcasts** (1904 - 1962)

4 **Hi Forum** (1951) Syn

Hi Jinx (see Tex and Jinx)

1 **Hi Kids**

12 **Hi Neighbor** (1950) Syn, AFRS origination

Hi There Audience (with Ray Perkins) (6/27/37 - 11/27/37) Mut, Sun, 8:30 pm; 8 pm as of 9/19/37

Hicks In Hollywood (1930s)

Hidden History (5/28/41 - 9/7/41) Library Of Congress, Bl, Sun, 2 pm

1 **Hidden Million, The** (11/10/50) CBS

7 **Hidden Revolution, The** (1/29/59 - 2/2/60) CBS

Hidden Stars (with Orrin Tucker and Bonnie Baker) (12/15/40 - 3/9/41) Bl, Yeast Foam, Sun, 5:30 pm

Hidden Truth, The (with Harp McGuire) (5/31/50 - 1/2/52) Sus, Mut, various days including: (South Africa origination)
5/31/50 - 12/20/50, Wed
1/24/51 - 3/28/51, Wed, 8 pm
4/1/51 - 5/20/51, Sun, 7 pm
5/30/51 - 1/2/52, Wed, 8 pm

5 **High Adventure** (3/8/47 - 9/21/54) (various days including:)
3/8/47 - 9/6/47, Mut, Sat, 9:30 pm
9/11/47 - 9/25/47, Mut, Thu, 8 pm
12/22/47 - 1/19/48, Sus, Mut, Mon, 9:30 pm
4/17/48 - 6/19/48, Sat, 9:30 pm
8/11/48 - 9/21/48,Thu,9:30 pm
12/4/48 - 1/22/49, Sat, 2:30 pm
1/29/50 - 10/8/50, Old Spice, NBC, Sun, 4:30 pm
1/13/53 - 9/21/54, Sus, Mut, Tue, 8:30 pm

1 **High Hilarities** (1933) Syn

High Moment (Stories Of Community Service) (2/8/56 - 8/19/56) ABC
2/8/56 - 5/2/56, Wed, 8:30 pm
5/20/56 - 8/19/56, Sun, 5:30 pm

1 **High Mountain, The** (2/28/54) CBS

High Places, The (with Joan Tetzel) (7/10/44 - 1/19/45) CBS, 5t, 15m, 3:30 pm

1 **High Society** (1956) film sound track

2 **High Spots** (1931) Syn

2 **High, Wide, and Handsome** (1937) Air trailer, film sound track

Highlights In Harmony (with William Wirges and Peg La Centra) (10/18/35 - 11/8/35) Bl, Fri, 10:30 pm

1 **Highlights Of A Quarter Century Of Bob Hope On Television** (10/24/75) NBC-TV

1 **Highlights Of America's First Manned Orbital Flight** (2/20/62) Mut

Highlights Of The Bible (with Dr. Frederick K. Stamm) (1933 - 1941) NBC, Sun (usually summer replacement for National Radio Pulpit)

1 **Highlights Of The Royal Wedding** (11/20/47) CBS

1 **Highlights Of The Seagram Symposium** (3/3/55) CBS

3 **Highway Harmonies** (Mar, Apr, 1953) NBC

9 **Highway Patrol** (with Jack Kirkwood) (1938)(with Michael Fitzmaurice and John McGovern) (4/5/43 - 7/2/43) Mut, 5t, 15m

2 **Highway To Heaven, The** (Syn)

Highways In Melody (see Cities Service Concerts)

Highways To Health (3/15/38 - 5/31/41) CBS, 15m
3/15/38 - 8/1/39, Tue, 4:30 pm; 5:30 pm as of 5/16/39
1/3/40 - 4/10/40, Wed, 4:15 pm
5/18/40 - 5/31/41, Sat, 1:15 pm; 2:30 pm as of 1/25/4

1 **Highways To Safety** (Syn)

Hilda Hope, M.D. (with Selena Royle) (9/2/39 - 3/30/40) Wheatena, NBC, Sat, 15m, 11:30 am

6 **Hildegarde** (with William Wirges Orchestra) (9/29/36 - 12/15/36) Bl, Tue, 10 pm
(6/13/44 - 3/30/47) (see also Halicrafters Hour; Beat The Band)
6/13/44 - 6/5/45 (Raleigh Room), Raleigh, NBC, Tue, 10:30 pm (summer replacement for Red Skelton)
9/11/45 - 3/27/46 (Raleigh Room), Raleigh, NBC, Tue,10:30 pm; Wed, 8:30 pm as of 12/5/45
4/3/46 - 7/24/46 (The Penguin Room) Raleigh, NBC, Wed, 8:30 pm
10/6/46 - 3/30/47, Campbell, CBS, Sun, 9 pm also 13 5-minute shows sponsored by U.S. Rubber Tire Dealers
also Thesaurus transcription

2 **Hillary Rodham Clinton** (4/22/94, 5/8/94) C-SPAN

Hillbillies With Colonel Jack (see Colonel Jack)

Hillbilly Champions (usually with Pappy Cheshire) (10/29/38 - 2/27/43) CBS, Sat
10/29/38 - 10/21/39, 30m, 10 am; 9:30 am as of 7/15/39
7/13/40 - 2/27/43, 15m

Hillbilly Heart Throbs (see Heart Throbs Of The Hills)

1 **Hillbilly Roundup** (1/7/37) WCNW

16 **Hilltop House** (11/1/37 - 7/30/57) 5t, 15m (see also Bess Johnson)
11/1/37 - 3/28/41 (with Bess Johnson), Palmolive
5/17/48 - 3/24/55, Miles (with Jan Miner)
9/3/56 - 7/30/57, Multi, NBC

Hind's Hall Of Fame (1/7/34 - 12/30/34) Hind's, NBC, Sun, 10 pm

Hind's Romance Exchange (with Ray Heatherton and Beatrice Fairfax) (2/29/32 - 5/16/32)

1 **Hindenberg Airship Disaster** (5/8/37) WOR

1 **Hindenberg Disaster** (5/7/37) Bl

2 **Hinds Honey and Almond Cream Program** (Bl) 3t (Mon, Wed, Thu), 15m, 11:30 am
(1/36) WJR

Hinges Of History

Hint Hunt (2/17/47 - 5/13/49) Armour, CBS, 5t, 15m; 30m as of 4/28/47

Hires Ice Box Follies (see Ice Box Follies)

1 **Hiroshima Countdown** (8/9/85) Syn

2 **Hirsch Telephone Quiz, The** (WGN)

1 **His Honor, The Barber** (with Barry Fitzgerald) (10/16/45 - 4/9/46) Ballantine, NBC,Tue, 7:30 pm

1 **His Wonders To Perform** (Syn)

1 **History In The Making** (with Richard Tobin) (3/25/50 - 12/22/51) Mut, Sat, 15m, 7 pm
also 10/59, NBC

History Is Fun (with Ted Malone) (6/18/43 - 8/27/43) Bl, Fri, 8:30 pm

1 **History Is Made At Night** (4/14/37) Air trailer

1 **History Of Heavyweight Boxing, A** (2/15/70) Mut

History Of Medicine (see Dr. Howard W. Haggard)

1 **History Of Network Broadcasting** (1934)

1 **History Of Rock and Roll, The** (9/5 - 9/69) Syn

11 **History Of Space Flight, The** (2/10/81 - 6/21/81) PBS-TV

1 **History Of The Communist Party In The U.S.S.R.** (9/4/39) Russia

1 **History Of WFBR, The** (6/19/39) WFBR

History's Headlines (1938) CBS, Wed, 15m

Hit Makers, The (10/16/39 - 12/18/39) Mut, Mon, 15m, 1:30 pm

1 **Hit That Ball** (with Stan Lomax) (5/15/39 - 6/9/39) Mut, Fri

Hit The Jackpot (with Bill Cullen) (6/29/48 - 9/3/50) CBS
6/29/48 - 12/27/49, Chrysler, Tue, 9:30 pm; 10 pm as of 9/21/48
5/28/50 - 9/3/50, Rinso, Sun, 7:30 pm (summer replacement for Amos 'n' Andy)

12 **Hitch Hiker's Guide To The Galaxy, The** (BBC) (3/8/78 - 1/25/80)

1 **Hitch-Hiker, The** (1964)

1 **Hitler Gang, The** (5/31/44) Air trailer

1 **Hitler's Arrival At Vienna** (4/14/38) Mut

2 **Hitler's Children** (1939) Air trailer (3/4/43) WCAU

1 **Hitler's Declaration Of War Against Russia** (6/22/41) NBC

1 **Hitler's Fiftieth Birthday Celebration** (4/20/39) CBS

Hits and Bits Revue (with Madge Marley and Charles Leland) (3/26/35 - 5/21/35) (also with Hildegarde) Bl, Tue, 7:30 pm (5/29/35 - 8/7/35) Bl, Wed, 10 pm

Hits and Misses (12/30/46 - 12/21/51) CBS, 5t, (5:30 pm)

1 **Hits From "Swingtime"** (11/6/36) WCNW

Hits Of Wartime Era (with Harry Von Zell) (AFRS) 15m

8 **Hoagy Carmichael** (9/44 - 6/26/48)
9/44 - 2/45 (Tonight At Hoagy's) Nu-Made Mayonnaise
2/45 - 46 (Something New) NBC, Mon
10/26/46 - 6/15/47, Ludens, CBS, Sun, 15m, 5:30 pm
11/16/47 - 6/26/48, Sus, CBS, Sat, 15m
also 6 five-minute shows for Helbros Watches, 1951

Hoagy Carmichael Helbros Show, The (see Hoagy Carmichael)

1 **Hoagy Carmichael Sings For The 1948 March Of Dimes** (1948) Syn

1 **Hoagy Carmichael Story, The** (Syn)

Hobby Horse (WMAQ) Chicago

3 **Hobby Lobby** (with David Elman) (10/6/37 - 3/5/49)
10/6/37 - 3/30/38, Hudson, CBS, Wed, 7:15 pm
7/3/38 - 9/25/38, Jell-O, NBC, Sun, 7 pm (summer replacement for Jack Benny)
10/5/38 - 9/27/39, Fels Naphtha, Bl, Wed, 8:30 pm
10/8/39 - 3/31/40, Fels Naphtha, CBS, Sun, 5 pm
10/4/41 - 8/28/43, Colgate, CBS, Sat, 8:30 pm; Tue, 8:30 pm from 7/21/42 - 9/29/42 (partial summer replacement of Bob Burns)
8/30/45 - 8/1/46, CBS, Thu, 9:30 pm
1/15/49 - 3/5/49, Sus, Mut, Sat, 4 pm

1 **Hogan's Daughter** (with Shirley Booth) (6/21/49 - 9/14/49) Philip Morris, NBC, Tue, 8 pm; Wed as of 8/31/49

1 **Hold Back The Dawn** (1941) Air trailer

Holiday and Company (with Ray Mayer and Edith Evans) (2/1/46 - 4/26/46) CBS, Fri, 9 pm (replacement of It Pays To Be Ignorant)

Holiday For Music (see Curt Massey)

Holiday For Strings (with conductor, Arnold Eldus) (12/11/55 - 1/29/56) ABC, Sun, 25m, 5 pm

1 **Holiday Wilde** (with Gloria Blondell) (1947) Mut, audition

1 **Holing Through Ceremonies Of The Queens Midtown Tunnel** (11/8/39) WOR

Hollis Shaw (3/11/38 - 9/23/38) CBS, Fri, 15m, 7:45 pm

7 **Holland Calling** (Syn)

Holland Housewife (with Merle Oberon and Benny Goodman) (1941) Holland Furnaces, NBC

1 **Holland Shall Rise Again** (6/6/44) Syn

Holly Sloan (See The Story Of Holly Sloan)

Hollywood 10,000 (announcer - Ken Carpenter)

Hollywood Airport (with Joe Jeigesen) (2/3/54 - 6/2/54) ABC, Wed, 9 pm

Hollywood and The Stars (Syn)

Hollywood and Vine (ABC) 15m

Hollywood Barn Dance (12/4/43 - 48) CBS Pacific, Buckley's Canadiol Mixture, Sat

1 **Hollywood Becomes Wistful Vista For A Day** (3/11/52) NBC

Hollywood Bowl (1951- 52) network includes: 7/27/52 - 9/14/52, NBC, Sun, 60m, 7 pm

Hollywood Byline (1/28/50 - 9/16/50) ABC, Sat, 8:30 pm

9 **Hollywood Calling** (with George Murphy) (7/3/49 -1/8/50) Gruen, NBC, Sun, 60m; 30m as of 1/15/50; also Syn with George Fisher

9 **Hollywood Calling-George Fisher Interviews The Stars** (Syn)

15 **Hollywood Calling - George Fisher's Filmtown Featurettes** (Syn)

Hollywood Canteen (11/1/42 - 45)
11/1/42 - 43, Mut, Sun
1943 - 45, NBC, Wed

1 **Hollywood Casting Office** (Syn) 15m

Hollywood Comments (see Hollywood News Girl)

2 **Hollywood Fights Back** (10/26/47, 11/2/47) ABC, Sun

Hollywood Headlines (1/3/48 - 7/24/48) ABC Pacific, Sat, 10:30 pm

2 **Hollywood Highlights** (Syn)

1 **Hollywood Horror** (WMUK)

1 **Hollywood Hotel** (10/5/34 - 6/24/38; 9/9/38 - 12/2/38) Campbell, CBS, Fri, 60m, usually 9:30 pm; 9:00 pm from 5/3/35

Hollywood Impressions (with Lou Tobin)

Hollywood In Person (7/19/37 - 3/4/38) General Mills, CBS, 5t, 15m

Hollywood Is On The Air (see individual film titles)

Hollywood Jackpot (with Kenny Delmar) (9/30/46 - 3/28/47) Anacin, CBS, 3t, 4:30 pm

1 **Hollywood Lights** (9/6/30) Syn

Hollywood Love Story (with Alexander Scourby) (10/27/51 - 3/7/53) Sus, NBC, Sat, 11:30am

1 **Hollywood March Of Dimes Of The Air, The** (1/24/42) Bl

Hollywood Mardi Gras (see Lanny Ross)

Hollywood Music Box (1/10/52 - 4/10/52) NBC, Thu, 25m, 10:35 pm

9 **Hollywood Music Hall** (with Lucille Norman) (4/1/46 - 8/19/52) Gruen, CBS; also (1947 - 1949) ABC Pacific, Bekins Moving

1 **Hollywood Mystery Playhouse** (4/30/49) ABC

Hollywood Mystery Time (with Carleton Young; also Gloria Blondell)
(7/20/44 - 12/16/45)
7/20/44 - 9/7/44, Sus, CBS, Thu
9/15/44 - 10/13/44, Sus, CBS, Fri
10/15/44 - 12/16/45, Woodbury, ABC, Sun, 9:15 pm

Hollywood News Girl (with Stella Unger)
(6/27/38 - 9/2/38) Lydia Pinkham, Mut, 3t, 15m, 1:45 pm
(1/9/39 - 2/17/39) Clear-Again, Mut, 3t, 15m, 1:15 pm
(1/1/40 - 7/5/40) (originally called Hollywood Comments) NBC, 3t, 15m, 1:45 pm
(3/8/41 - 6/14/41) NBC, Sat, 15m, 1:15 pm

1 **Hollywood Newsreel Of The Air** (1930) Syn

Hollywood Nights (with Frank Luther)
(11/25/31 - 7/21/32) Kissproof Lipstick, Bl, 2t (Wed & Sat), 15m; Thu as of 4/28/32

1 **Hollywood Notebook** (Syn)

Hollywood Observer (with Del Casino, Ray Block Orchestra) (6/4/37 - 8/19/37) Noxema, CBS, Mon, 7:30 pm

5 **Hollywood On Parade** (10/14/33 - 1/27/34) NBC

11 **Hollywood On The Air** (many with Jimmy Fidler) (3/20/33 - 7/15/34) NBC

3 **Hollywood Palace, The** (5/30/64, 1/16/65, 7/24/65) ABC-TV

1 **Hollywood Parade, The** (1935) Syn (with Dick Powell; Bob Hope as of 12/29/37) (12/8/37 - 3/23/38) Lucky Strikes, NBC, Wed, 60m, 10 pm

1 **Hollywood Personality Parade, The** (1939) Syn

1 **Hollywood Personals**

Hollywood Picture Snatches (with Nancy Kelly and Robert Lowry)

Hollywood Players (see Cresta Blanca Hollywood Players)

Hollywood Playhouse (with Charles Boyer off and on until 1/1/39; with Jim Ameche and Gale Page during the summers of 1939 and 1940; also with Tyrone Power; Herbert Marshall; Don Ameche) (10/3/37 - 12/25/40) Woodbury, Bl
10/3/37 - 6/26/38; 10/2/38 - 9/24/39 (with Harry Sosnik Orchestra), Sun, 9 pm
10/4/39 - 12/25/40, Wed, 8 pm (from 7/3/40 -10/2/40 program called Promoting Priscilla)
also 1937, KFWB

1 **Hollywood Premier** (1937) KFWB, also (with Louella Parsons)
(3/28/41 - 11/28/41) Lifebuoy, CBS, Fri, 10 pm

1 **Hollywood Preview #17** (Syn)

1 **Hollywood Preview** (with Diane Stephanie and Paul Carson) (1945) Koret, 15m also (with Knox Manning)
(5/1/45 - 4/27/46)
Mobil, CBS - West

2 **Hollywood Profiles** (Syn)

Hollywood Quiz (12/10/49 - 3/4/50) Halicrafter Co., Mut, Sat, 15m, 5:45 pm

1 **Hollywood Radio Previews** (6/34) Syn

Hollywood Radio Theater, The
(4/1/43 - 4/24/44) Bl, 10:30 pm
4/1/43 - 8/25/43, Thu
8/30/43 - 4/24/44, Mon

72 **Hollywood Radio Theater** (Rod Serling - host)
(9/10/73 - 12/7/73) Mut, 5t, 30m, 13 stories, each in five parts
(4/29/74 - 7/26/74) Mut

1 **Hollywood Rendezvous** (6/12/38) CBS (with Connie Boswell and Johnny Mercer)

Hollywood Reporter (see Erskine Johnson)

Hollywood Review (with Gene and Kathleen Lockhart) (1935, 15m)

Hollywood Review (with Al Pearce and Cass Daley)
(5/1/45 - 4/27/46) Rexall, CBS
5/1/45 - 12/4/45, Tue, 10:30 pm
12/15/45 - 4/27/46, Sat, 9 pm

Hollywood Rodeo (with Tex Ritter)

4 **Hollywood Room Recipes** (3/37, 4/37) Syn

Hollywood Roundup (with Redd Harper) (1950 - 51)

1 **Hollywood Salutes The National Guard** (2/2/59) Syn

Hollywood Screen Scoops (with George McCall) (11/16/37 - 11/10/38) Old Gold, CBS. 2t, 15m, 7:15 pm

Hollywood Searchlight
(7/13/53 - 9/28/53) NBC, Mon, 10 pm

Hollywood Show Time
(9/11/44 - 10/15/45) Bl, Mon, 10:30 pm

1 **Hollywood Showcase** (7/24/37 - 9/12/48) CBS - often West
7/24/37 - 11/28/37, Sus, Sat, 10 pm; Sun as of 10/3
1/13/38 - 3/17/38, Thu
4/10/38 - 4/17/38, Sun
7/1/38 - 9/2/38, Fri, 9 pm (summer replacement of Hollywood Hotel)
10/2/38 - 10/8/38,Sun,10 pm
4/1/41 - 9/9/41, Hudnut, Tue, 9:30 pm; 8:30 pm as of 4/29/41
9/15/41 - 9/21/42, Hudnut, Mon, 9:30 pm
(6/15/48 - 9/12/48) CBS Pacific, Sun, 10 pm

Hollywood Sound Stage
(12/13/51 - 4/3/52) CBS, Thu, 10 pm; changed to Screen Guild Theater on 3/13/52

29 **Hollywood Spotlight** (with Phil Harris, Martha Raye and Bob Burns) (1937) 15m

Hollywood Squares (with Mickey Rooney) (1948) CBS

Hollywood Stairway (10/15/53 - 4/22/54) ABC, Thu, 8:30 pm

10 **Hollywood Star Playhouse**
(4/24/50 - 2/15/53)
4/24/50 - 7/16/51, Bromo Seltzer, CBS, Mon, 8:00 pm
7/26/51 - 1/17/52, Sus, ABC, Thu, 8:30 pm
2/24/52 - 2/15/53 (also called Baker's Theater Of Stars), American Baker, NBC, Sun, 5:00 pm

Hollywood Star Preview (see Hollywood Star Theater)

Hollywood Star Showcase (with Herb Rawlinson) (1950) CBS

Hollywood Star Theater
(9/28/47 - 4/1/50) NBC
9/28/47 - 9/26/48 (Hollywood Star Preview until 8/15/48) Anacin, NBC, Sun, 6:30 pm
10/2/48 - 4/1/50 (also called Baker's Theater Of Stars), American Baker, NBC, Sat, 8 pm; Sun, 8 pm as of 8/27/49

12 **Hollywood Star Time** (5/29/44 - 3/27/47) Frigidaire
5/29/44 - 11/24/44 (Interviews), Bl, 5t, 15m, 3:15 pm
1/6/46 - 6/2/46, CBS, Sun, 2:30 pm
6/8/46 - 3/27/47, CBS, Sat, 8 pm; last show on Thu, 10:30 pm

Hollywood Stars On Stage
(10/7/51 - 12/30/51) ABC, Sun, 9:30 pm

1 **Hollywood Story** (with Charles Paul)
(12/30/46 - 6/27/47) Kellogg, ABC, 5t, 11:30 am; split network with Galen Drake

Hollywood Strikes Back (see Hollywood Fights Back)

Hollywood Sunshine Girls (with Vivian Edwards) (7/6/37 - 8/3/37) Skol, Mut, Tue, 15m, 12:15 pm

Hollywood Theater (4/22/45 - 7/15/45) Mut, Sun, 3:30 pm

Hollywood Theater Group (with Howard Culver) (1930s)

2 **Hollywood Theater Of Stars**
(10/12/48 - 4/6/51) Mut, 5t, 1:30pm

Hollywood Theater Of The Air (see Dreft Star Playhouse)

Hollywood Today (see From Hollywood Today)

Hollywood Tomorrow (with Ben Gage)
(9/21/40 - 11/23/40) Bl, Sat, 8:30 pm

3 **Hollywood Tour** (with Cal York) (1947) ABC, 15m

Hollywood Trends (with Sara Berner)

1 **Hollywood U.S.A.** (with Paula Stone) (Syn) 15m (10/12/52 - 4/12/53) (with Conrad Nagel) NBC, Sun, 12 noon

Hollywood Variety (see Little Ol' Hollywood)

1 **Hollywood Victory Show, On V-E Day** (5/8/45) CBS

Hollywood Whispers (see George Fischer)

34 **Hollywood's Open House** (with Jim Ameche, Jerry Cooper) (1946 - 6/1/48) NBC, Thu, 7:30 pm, Syn

1 **Holmes Radio Magazine** (12/22/47) Syn, also known as The Helen Holmes Show or McCall's On The Air

Home and Garden (see American Farmer)

1 **Home Base** (4/21/44) Syn

Home Edition (with Marvin Miller and Gilbert Martyn (12/30/45 - 12/27/47) Kellogg, ABC, 5t, 15m, 11:30 am

Home Folks (with Owen Bradley) (9/8/52 - 6/8/53) Quaker Oats, CBS, Mon, 10m, 3:45 pm

12 **Home Harmony Time** (1937) Syn

Home Is What You Make It (with Ben Grauer) (11/18/44 - 2/21/48) Sus, NBC, Sat

Home Of The Brave (1/6/41 - 9/19/41) Swans-Down, 5t, 15m
1/6/41 - 4/25/41 (with Tom Tully and Richard Widmark), CBS
4/28/41 - 9/19/41 (with Tom Tully) NBC

1 **Home Sweet Home** (with Cecil Secrest) (7/30/34 - 11/20/37) 15m, 5t
7/30/34 - 4/26/35, Bl, 2:30 pm
4/29/35 - 6/30/36, Chipso, NBC, 5t, 15m; Bl as of 5/25/36
7/3/36 - 11/20/37, Bl, 9:15 am; also Syn

Home Town Dramas (1/25/36 - 40)
1/25/36 - 10/3/36, Bl, Sat, 15m, 7:15 pm
10/10/36 - 6/12/37, NBC, Sat, 15m
1939 - 40, Raleigh, NBC, Sun, 30m, 10:30 pm (not in NY)

Home Town, Unincorporated (see Show Boat)

Homecoming (with Paul Douglas) (4/17/49 - 5/29/49) NBC, Sun, 2 pm

1 **Homecoming Of Generals Patton and Doolittle** (6/9/45)

Homefront - Matinee (with Alfred Drake) (5/17/43 - 8/4/44) CBS, 5t, 25m, 4 pm

Homemaker's Exchange (with Eleanor Howe)
(10/27/36 - 5/12/38) National Ice, 2t, 15m
10/27/36 - 6/1/37, CBS, 11:45 am; Tue only as of 4/27/37
11/30/37 - 5/12/38, NBC, 2t, 11:30 am

Homer Rodeheaver (1/14/31 - 3/11/31) NBC, Wed, 15m, 7 pm

8 **Homes On The Land** (1946) Syn

Homespun (with Rev. William Foulkes) (10/17/34 - 3/3/37) Wed, 15m
10/17/34 - 6/16/35, NBC
6/23/35 - 3/3/37, Bl

4 **Hometowners, The** (4/16/45 - 4/11/47) NBC, 3t, 15m, 7:45 am
also (1950) AFRS

1 **Homewood** (12/70) TV syn

Honest Abe (with Ray Middleton; then Henry Hull as of 4/5/41)
(7/13/40 - 6/28/41) CBS, Sat, 9:30 am; 11 am as of 4/5/41

5 **Honest Harold** (Hal Peary Show) (9/10/50 - 6/13/51) Sus, CBS
9/10/50 - 9/17/50, Sun, 7:30 pm
9/20/50 - 6/13/51, Wed, 9 pm

Honeyboy and Sassafras (with George Fields and Johnnie Welsh)
(7/16/34 - 5/13/37) Bl, 15m, 6t/2t

Honeymoon Hill (see Amanda Of Honeymoon Hill)

1 **Honeymoon Hotel** (1964) film sound track

1 **Honeymoon In New York** (with Durward Kirby, Joy Hodges; Ed Herlihy as of 3/10/47)
(12/31/45 - 7/28/48) Sus, NBC, 5t, 25m, 9:00 am
also 7/13/46 - 8/31/46, Duz, NBC, Sat, 8:30 pm

1 **Honeymooners Christmas Special, The** (11/28/77) ABC-TV

Honeymooners, The (with Grace and Eddie Albert) (9/25/34 - 7/17/36) Bl
9/25/34 - 10/28/35, 5t, 11 am
7/2/36 - 7/17/36, 3t (Wed - Fri), 11 am

39 **Honeymooners, The** (TV syn)

1 **Honeymooners: The Second Honeymoon, The** (2/2/76) ABC-TV

1 **Honolulu** (1939) Air trailer

1 **Honolulu Bound** (with Phil Baker) (1/14/39 - 10/4/39) Dole, CBS, Sat, 9 pm; Wed, 8 pm as of 7/5/39

1 **Honolulu Lu** (1941) film sound track

1 **Honor America Day** (7/4/70) CBS-TV

1 **Honor The Law** (39 syndicated shows; with Frank Nelson; dates on discs were 1/10/38 - 3/3/38) 15m

Honorable Archie and Frank (with Eddie Holden and Reggie Sheffield) (5/21/34 - 9/20/34) Bl, 4t (Mon - Thu), 15m

Hoofbeats (see Buck Jones)

Hoofers, The (produced by Radio Features Syndicate; with Alice Smith)

Hoofinghams, The (3/22/35 - 9/13/35) NBC, 5t, 15m, 11:45 pm

Hook and Ladder Follies (with Ralph Dumke and Carson Robison)
(11/13/43 - 5/14/44) Goodyear, NBC, Sat, 11 am

2 **Hookey Hall** (with Bobby Hookey) (6/3/44 - 12/15/45) White Labs., Mut, Sat, 11:30 am

Hoosier Editor (with Frederick Landis, Mary Miles) (10/16/32 - 1/22/33) Alka-Seltzer, CBS, Sun, 15m, 2:45 pm

Hoosier Hop (9/2/40 - 12/30/40) Bl, Mon, 15m
(7/14/45 - 1/14/46) Bl
7/14/45 - 10/6/45) Sat, 10 pm
11/12/45 - 1/14/46, Mon, 10:30 pm

2 **Hoosier Hot Shots Show, The** (with Anita Gordon)) (1950 - 1951) Mut

2 **Hoosier Hot Shots, The** (World transcriptions)

1 **Hootenanny**

Hoover Sentinel Concerts (10/8/33 - 4/28/35) Hoover, NBC, Sun

13 **Hop Harrigan** (2/19/42, 8/31/42 - 2/6/48)
8/31/42 - 9/29/44 (with Chester Stratton), Sus, Bl, 5t
10/2/44 - 6/29/45; 10/1/45 - 8/2/46, Grape Nuts Flakes, ABC, 5t, 4:45 pm
10/2/46 - 1/31/47, Mut, 5t, 15m, 5 pm
2/3/47 - 6/20/47, Taylor-Reed, Mut, 3t, 5 pm; 2t as of 5/5/47
6/23/47 - 2/6/48, Lever Brothers, Mut, 5t, 5:30 pm; 5 pm as of 9/29/47 (Matt Crowley as of 7/22/47)

98 **Hopalong Cassidy** (with William Boyd and Andy Clyde; Joe Duval replaced Andy Clyde from 7/9/50 -12/30/50)
(1/25/48 - 12/27/52)
1/1/50 - 9/24/50, General Foods, Mut, Sun, 4 pm
9/30/50 - 6/30/51; 9/22/51- 3/15/52, General Foods, CBS, Sat, 8:30 pm
4/26/52 -12/27/52 (Repeats), Cella Vineyards, CBS, Sat, 9:30 pm (Mountain States network)
also Syn

1 **Hopkinson Theatre Program, The** (1/16/37) WCNW

1 **Horace Heidt and His Brigadiers** (3/25/37)

4 **Horace Heidt and His Musical Knights** (Standard transcriptions)

3 **Horace Heidt Orchestra** (Thesaurus transcriptions)

3 **Horace Heidt Show, The** (1932 - 12/24/53)
1932 (Ship Of Joy) Shell, Bl,
also 1932 (Answers By The Dancers) Bl
2/26/35 - 4/23/35 (Captain Dobbsie's Ship Of Joy), Alemite, CBS, 2t, 15m, 10:30 pm
5/2/35 - 6/29/35, Alemite, CBS, Thu, 10:30 pm; 10 pm as of 7/18/35
7/6/36 - 12/20/37 (Alemite Half-Hour), Alemite, CBS, Mon, 8 pm
12/28/37 - 12/18/38, Alemite, Bl, Tue, 9 pm; NBC, Sun, 10 pm as of 7/17/38
12/19/38 - 3/6/39, NBC, Mon, 10:30 pm
12/21/38 - 3/8/39, Bl, Wed, 7:30 pm
6/23/39 - 9/1/39, Bl, Fri, 10:30 pm
7/17/39 - 9/18/39, Tums, NBC, Mon, 9:30 pm
9/26/39 - 6/4/40 (Pot O' Gold) NBC, Tue, 8:30 pm
6/13/40 - 6/5/41 (Pot O' Gold), Tums, Bl, Thu, 8:30 pm; 8 pm as of 10/3/40
also 6/11/40 - 1/11/44 (Tum's Treasure Chest; Musical Treasure Chest) NBC, Tue, 8:30 pm
7/5/42 - 4/25/43 (Sunday Morning Review) Bl, Sun, 55m, 11:05 am; 1 pm as of 10/11/42
5/8/43 - 9/25/43, Sus, Bl, Sat, 60m
1/24/44 - 1/15/45, Hires, Bl, Mon, 7 pm
12/7/47 - 8/28/49 (known from now on as Youth Opportunity Program) Philip Morris, NBC, Sun, 10:30 pm; 7 pm as of 1/2/49; 10:30 pm as of 4/24/49
9/4/49 - 12/16/51, Philip Morris, CBS, Sun, 9:30 pm; 8:30 pm as of 7/1/51
1/1/53 - 12/24/53, Lucky Strike, CBS, Thu, 10 pm
also Syn audition

Horace Heidt's Highlights (see The Horace Heidt Show)

Horace Heidt's Original Youth Opportunity Program (see The Horace Heidt Show)

18 **Horatio Hornblower** (with Michael Redgrave) (originally on Radio Luxembourg)
(7/7/52 - 5/22/57) Sus (various days and times including:)
7/7/52 - 9/8/52, CBS, Mon, 8 pm (summer replacement for Suspense)
10/3/52 - 10/31/52, CBS, Fri, 9 pm
11/7/52 - 12/12/52, CBS, Fri, 9:30 pm
1/22/54 - 3/26/54, ABC, Fri, 9:30 pm
3/6/57 - 5/22/57, Mut, Wed, 8:30 pm
also Syn

13 **Horizons West** (with Harry Bartell and John Anderson) (AFRTS origination)

Hormel Chili Beaners (1/20/36 - 8/11/36) Hormel, CBS, Mon, 8 pm; Tue, 10:45 pm as of 4/28

Hormel Girl's Band (12/18/49 - 2/13/54) Hormel
12/18/49 - 7/2/50, ABC, Sun, 6:30 pm
12/10/50 - 12/2/51, NBC, Sun
also 5/20/50 - 2/13/54, CBS, Sat, 2 pm

Horn and Hardart Children's Hour, The (see The Children's Hour)

1 **Horn Blows At Midnight, The** (1945) film sound track

1 **Horowitz At The White House** (3/1/78) PBS-TV

Horror Inc. (with Eve LeGallienne) (1/17/43 - 3/16/43) Bl, 15m
1/17/43 - 2/7/43, Sun, 5:15 pm
2/16/43 - 3/16/43, Tue, 7:15 pm

Horse and Buggy Days (12/23/38 - 1/31/40) Bl
12/23/38 - 2/3/39, Fri, 9:30 pm
2/15/39 - 1/31/40, Wed, 9 pm; 9:30 pm as of 12/13/39

Horse Sense Philosophy (see Andrew Kelly)

1 **Hospital On The Thames** (2/2/41) Mut

4 **Hospitality Time** (with Snooky Lanson) (1947) Syn, 15m

1 **Hostage Release Coverage** (1/18/81) CBS-TV, NBC-TV

1 **Hostages' Second Christmas, The** (12/26/80) CBS-TV

3 **Hot Copy** (10/4/41 - 11/19/44)
10/4/41 - 6/29/42, Sus, NBC, Sat, 10:30 pm
7/27/42 - 8/10/42, NBC, Mon, 11:30 pm
8/29/42 - 9/26/42, NBC, Sat, 9:30 pm
7/18/43 - 6/18/44 (with Eloise Kummer), O'Cedar Polish, Bl, Sun, 3:30 pm
6/25/44 - 11/19/44 (with Eloise Kummer), O'Cedar Polish, Bl, Sun, 5:30 pm

Hot From Hollywood (Syndicated by Major Radio Features, mid-forties; with Bob Richardson

2 **Hot Jazz Excerpts** (12/14/38, 1/11/39)

32 **Hot Off The Record Press** (AFRS origination)

1 **Hotel Dixie Re-Union** (6/26/45) WOR

Hotel For Pets (with Charlotte Manson) (9/13/54 - 3/30/56) Quaker, NBC, 3t, 15m

1 **Hottentot, The** (8/1/29) Synchro-disc

1 **Houdini Seance** (10/31/36)

Hour Glass, The (Jerry Brannon - tenor, Paul Gersman - violin)
(4/25/37 - 9/26/37) NBC, Sun, 11 am

38 **Hour Of Charm, The** (with Phil Spitalny Orchestra) (5/18/34 - 5/2/48)
5/18/34 - 9/26/34, Cheramy, CBS, Fri, 15m, 10:30 pm; Wed, 8 pm as of 6/6/34
1/3/35 - 6/25/35, Linit, CBS, Thu, 8 pm; 9:30 pm as of 4/9/35
2/23/36 - 6/21/36, Zotos, CBS, Sun, 6:30 pm
11/2/36 - 4/18/38, GE, NBC, Mon, 4 pm; 9:30 pm as of 4/26/37
4/24/38 - 7/3/38, GE, NBC, Sun, 10 pm
10/3/38 - 5/29/39, GE, NBC, Mon, 9 pm
9/17/39 - 9/1/46, GE, NBC, Sun
9/29/46 - 7/6/47; 9/7/47 - 5/2/48 (Electric Companies Adventure Program; Electric Hour as of 9/7/47, Electric Companies, CBS, Sun, 4:30 pm; 30m, 5:30 pm as of 1/4/48; also Syn

Hour Of Decision, The (with Billy Graham) NBC (see Billy Graham)

Hour Of Faith (10/24/43 - 12/31/51) Bl/ABC, Sun, 11:30 am

Hour Of Musical Fun (with David Ross and Ted Cott) (6/4/39 - ?) CBS

Hour Of Mystery (6/9/46 - 9/1/46) U.S. Steel, ABC, Sun, 60m, 10 pm (summer replacement for Theater Guild Of The Air)

2 **Hour Of Praise, The** (11/7/43) Wolverine net

Hour Of Romance (11/15/34 - 1/17/35+) Syndicated by Brunswick General Broadcasting Company sponsored by Cosmopolitan Magazine

Hour Of Romance (see Eddy Duchin)

Hour Of Smiles (see Fred Allen)

6 **Hour Of St. Francis, The** (1950) Syn, 15m

House Beside The Road, The (see The Wayside Cottage)

House By The Side Of The Road, The (with Tony Wons) (9/2/34 - 6/30/35) Johnson, NBC, Sun, 5:30 pm (also see Wayside Cottage)

4 **House In The Country, A** (with John Raby and Joan Banks)
(10/6/41 - 10/28/42) Sus, Bl, 5t, 15m, 10:15 am; 10:30 am as of 10/27/41
also Syn

10 **House Judiciary Committee Impeachment Hearings** (7/24 - 30/74) PBS-TV

1 **House Of Dreams, The** (15m) Syn

1 **House Of Glass, The** (4/17/35 - 3/12/54)
NBC 4/17/35 - 1/1/36 (with Gertrude Berg), Palmolive, Wed, 8:30 pm
10/23/53 - 3/12/54 (with Gertrude Berg, Josef Buloff), Sus, Fri

1 **House Of Hope, A** (5/3/50) CBS

1 **House Of Music, The** (6/13/51) NBC, audition

1 **House Of Musical Fun, The** (6/4/39) CBS

5 **House Of Mystery, The** (with John Griggs) (1/15/45 - 12/25/49) Mut
1/15/45 - 5/11/45, Sus, 5t, 15m
9/15/45 - 6/1/46, General Foods, Sat, 30m
10/6/46 - 12/25/49, General Foods, Sun, 30m, 4 pm

House On Q Street (with Jessie Royce Landis, Celeste Holme)
(11/4/43 - 3/9/44) Bl, Thu, 7 pm

2 **House Party** (with Art Linkletter) (1/15/45 - 10/13/67)
1/15/45 - 9/28/45, GE, CBS, 5t, 25m, 4 pm
10/1/45 - 1/10/47, GE, CBS, 3t, 25m, 4 pm
12/1/47 - 12/31/48, GE, CBS, 5t, 25m, 3:30 pm
1/3/49 - 7/1/49, GE, ABC, 5t, 30m, 3:30 pm
9/29/49 - 12/30/49, Sus, ABC, 5t, 25m, 3:30 pm
1/2/50 - 5/2/52, Pillsbury, CBS, 5t
5/5/52 - 8/24/56, Lever Brothers, CBS, 3t
8/27/56 - 10/13/67, Multi, CBS, 5t

House Party (with Donald Novis) (6/18/34 - 1/28/35) Colgate, NBC, Mon, 9:30 pm

3 **House Unamerican Activities Committee** (8/2, 3, 4/48) Mut

Houseboat Hannah (10/26/36 - 4/25/41) 5t, 15m (Regional)
10/26/36 - 38, Mut
9/26/38 - 4/25/41, Lava, Bl & NBC (not in New York)

Household Helpers (with Joe Green Orchestra) (7/21/32 - 9/29/32) Socony, NBC, 2t, 15m, 10:30 am

Household Program (with Don Ameche until 3/30, Alice Mock; Edgar Guest from 5/30/32)
(1/27/31 - 9/27/32) Household Finance, Bl, Tue, 9 pm (led to Musical Memories)

4 **Houses In Our Street** (Syn)

Housewarming, The (see Benny Goodman)

Housewives, Incorporated

1 **Housing Shortage Discussion** (8/15/46) Mut

How's The Family (with Marshall Kent) (1953) Mut

How's Your Health (3/8/47 - 5/10/47) NBC, Sat, 15m, 2 pm

2 **How About That** (1947) Syn

1 **How America Votes** (10/38/58) CBS

8 **How Can We Make The Victory Stick?** (1945) Syn

1 **How CBS Covers The War** (6/1/41) CBS

1 **How CBS Will Cover The Invasion** (5/14/44) CBS

How Did You Meet? (1/1/41 - 6/25/41) Woodbury, NBC, Wed, 15m, 8:15 pm

How Do You Know (2/1/40 - 6/20/40) Bl, Thu, 2 pm

1 **How Hungry Can You Get?** (11/27/47) CBS

How To (with Roger Price)
(10/7/51 - 12/2/51) CBS, Sun, 5:30 pm

1 **How To Be Charming** (with Beatrice Bessabera) (3/30/36 - 5/27/38) 15m
3/30/36 - 6/26/36, Bl, 3t, 4:30 pm
9/14/36 - 5/27/38, Phillips, NBC, 3t,

1 **How To Get People To Like You** (film strip audio)

How To Get The Most Out Of Life (see Emily Post)

How To Live (see Dr. Karl Reiland)

1 **How To Make People Appreciate You** (film strip audio)

1 **How To Save Money On Your Car** (1954) Syn

How'm I Doin' (1/9/42 - 10/1/42) Camel
1/9/42 - 7/3/42 (with Bob Hawk, Vaughn Monroe), CBS, Fri, 7:30 pm; 10 pm as of 5/15/42
7/9/42 - 10/1/42, NBC, Thu, 7:30 pm

Howard and Shelton (with Tom Howard and George Shelton) (Syn) Royal Crown, 5m (1/3/33 - 2/10/33) Chesterfield, CBS, 2t (Tue & Fri), 15m, 9 pm (Music That Satisfies)

1 **Howard Barnes** (4/13/45) Mut

Howard Dandies (4/27/29 - 12/13/31) Howard Clothes, CBS
4/27/29 - 4/13/30, Fri, 7 pm
9/14/30 - 12/13/31, Sun, 6:30 pm

1 **Howard Fogarty and His Orchestra** (1964) CBS

1 **Howard Hughes** (8/6/47) Mut

1 **Howard Hughes Airplane** (11/2/47) Mut

39 **Howard Hughes Flight** (7/9 - 14/38) Mut

3 **Howard K. Smith News** (1945 - 46) (5/9/45)
(7/9/50 - 9/21/52) CBS, Sun, 15m, 12:30 pm
(1/25/53 - 5/16/54; 6/5/55 - 7/10/55) CBS, Sun, 12:30 pm

Howard Miller Show, The
(7/18/55 - 1/9/59) CBS, 5t, 15m

1 **Howard Miller's Chicago** (12/71) WLS-TV

Howard Ropa (5/11/40 - 9/28/40) NBC, Sat, 15m, 2:30 pm; 1 pm as of 7/13/40
(8/23/41 - 11/15/41) Bl, Sat, 15m

Howard Thurston (see Thurston, The Magician)

Howard Vincent O'Brien

3 **Howdy Doody** (12/15/51 - 9/12/53) NBC, Sat, 60m, 8:30 am (sponsored in part by International Shoes)
(9/13/53 - 4/11/54) NBC, Sun, 60m, 9:30 am
also NBC-TV

Howie Wing (with William Janney)
(10/3/38 - 6/30/39) Kellogg, CBS, 5t, 15m, 6:15 pm

4 **Hubert Rostang Sextette, The** (Standard transcriptions)

1 **Hughes Newsreel, The** (with Rush Hughes) Syn

Hughesreel (with Rush Hughes)
(1/31/38 - 7/29/38) Borden, NBC, 5t, 15m, 4:30 pm

1 **Hula Heaven** (1937) film sound track

1 **Hullabaloo** (10/1/40) Air trailer

1 **Human Adventure, The**
(7/25/39 - 9/28/40) CBS
7/25/39 - 9/12/39, Tue, 60m, 8 pm (summer replacement for Big Town and Al Jolson)
2/3/40 - 4/13/40, Sat, 5 pm
5/11/40 - 6/15/40, Sat, 5:30 pm
6/22/40 - 9/28/40, Sat 8:30 pm (summer replacement of Wayne King)

5 **Human Adventure, The**
(9/30/43 - 11/25/45) Sus, Mut; on locally in late 30s to 40s
9/30/43 - 5/11/44, Thu, 8:30 pm
6/4/44 - 7/9/44, Sun, 4:30 pm
7/16/44 - 9/3/44, Sun, 4 pm
12/13/44 - 1/17/45, Wed, 8:30 pm
4/7/45 - 6/2/45, Sat
6/3/45 - 10/17/45, Wed, 10 pm
10/21/45 - 11/25/45, Sun, 9 pm; remained on WGN (regionally)

1 **Human Heritage** (1951) U.N. Radio

Human Nature In Action (with Dr. Harold D. Lasswell)
(1/12/40 - 12/24/40) NBC, 15m
1/12/40 - 6/21/40, Fri, 10:45 pm
6/30/40 - 9/29/40, Sun, 10:30 pm
11/29/40 - 12/24/40, Tue, 1:15 pm

Human Side Of Literature (see Meet Edward Weeks)

Human Side Of The News, The (see Edwin C. Hill)

Human Side Of The Record (see Paul Whiteman's Record Programs)

1 **Humphrey Bogart Audition**

Humphrey Bogart Presents (also Humphrey Bogart Theater)

Hunchback Of Notre Dame (1930s)

4 **Hungarian News In English**
(3/15 - 21/39) Hungary

1 **Hungarian Program** (12/21/36) WWRL

1 **Hunted, The** (Syn)

2 **Huntley-Brinkley Report, The**
(5/3/66, 7/31/70) NBC-TV

Hurtado Brothers Orchestra
(La Marimba Club Orchestra)
(1/25/41 - 4/19/41) Bl, Sat, 15m, 8 pm

Husbands and Wives (with Alice Lowe Miles and Sedley Brown)
(1935 - 12/28/37)
1935 - 36, WOR, New York; then Mut
7/5/36 - 10/4/36, Sus, Bl, Sun, 7:30 pm (summer replacement for Believe It Or Not)
10/6/36 - 12/28/37, Ponds, Bl, Tue, 9:30 pm; 8 pm as of 4/6/37

1 **Hy Gardner** (3/65) WOR-TV

Hy Gardner Calling (5/30/52 - 2/6/53) NBC, Fri, 15m, 10 pm

1 **Hy Gardner Show, The** (8/22/63) WOR-TV

1 **Hyde Park Burial Ceremony** (4/15/45) Mut

1 **Hyde Park Memorial Ceremony** (3/17/50) Mut

1 **Hyde Park Service For President Roosevelt** (4/15/45) Mut

2 **Hymn Sing** (1/4/44, 1/11/44) WLAV

12 **Hymn Time** (with Smilin' Ed McConnell)
(6/25/51 - 12/21/51) General Mills, NBC, 5t, 15m
also Syn and
(1954) ABC (with Joe Emerson)

1 **Hymns** (Lang-Worth transcription)

Hymns From Home (AFRS) 15m

1 **Hymns Of All Churches** (with Joe Emerson) (8/29/35 - 3/28/47)
8/29/35 - 5/29/36, Mut, 5t, 15m
6/1/36 - 5/26/38, General Mills, CBS, 3-5t (Mon, Tue & Thu), 15m
5/30/38 - 1/11/46, General Mills, NBC, 2-5t, 15m; CBS from 3/31/41- 3/19/42
also 7/9/45 - 3/28/47, General Mills, ABC, 5t, 15m

Hymns You Love (see Richard Maxwell)

2 **Hymns (Keith McLeod, Godfrey Ludlow and Male Trio)** (Lang-Worth transcriptions)

1 **I Am A Displaced Person** (1948) Syn

2 **I Am An Alcoholic** (11/8/52, 7/55) WFBR

I Am An American (see I'm An American)

I Ask You (1/22/55 - 7/7/56) Mut, Sat
1/22/55 - 3/12/55, 12 noon
3/17/55 - 10/15/55, 3 pm
10/22/55 - 7/7/56, 9 pm

1 **I Confess** (10/17/52) (Audition) with Paul Frees

I Cover The Waterfront (2 part audition) 8/29/55, CBS, 15m (TS)

1 **I Deal In Crime** (with William Gargan) (1/21/46 - 10/18/47) ABC
1/21/46 - 10/14/46, Sus, Mon, 9 pm
10/19/46 - 10/18/47, Hastings, Sat, 8:30 pm; 8 pm as of 5/31/47

1 **I Devise and Bequeath** (also see Strange Wills)

1 **I Fly Anything** (with Dick Haymes) 11/29/50 - 7/19/51) Sus, ABC, 8:30 pm
11/29/50 - 1/3/51, Wed
1/23/51 - 5/22/51, Tue
6/7/51 - 7/19/51, Thu

I Give You My Life (with Molly Picon) (1938 - 42) Maxwell House, WMCA, WHN - New York, Tue

1 **I Have No Prayer** (Bl)

I Hear America Singing (6/7/41 - 1/3/42) Mut, Sat, 15m

1 **I Knew A Woman** (1940s) Syn

115 **I Love A Mystery** (originally called I Loved An Adventure)
(1/16/39 - 12/26/52)
1/16/39 - 9/29/39, NBC-West Coast, 5t, 15m, 3:15 PST
10/2/39 - 3/29/40, Fleischmann, NBC, 5t, 15m, 7:15 pm
4/4/40 - 6/27/40, NBC, Thu, 30m, 8:30 pm
9/30/40 - 6/30/41; 10/6/41 - 6/29/42, Fleischmann, Bl, Mon, 30m, 8 pm
3/22/43 - 12/29/44, Ivory, CBS, 5t, 15m, 7 pm
10/3/49 - 12/26/52, Sus, Mut, 5t, 15m

13 **I Love Adventure** (used I Love A Mystery stories)
(4/25/48 - 7/18/48) ABC, Sun, 30m

I Love Linda Dale (see Linda Dale)

1 **I Love Lucy** (with Lucille Ball) CBS 2/27/51 (Wed; show not listed in New York Times); TV show was on Monday nights

1 **I Married An Angel** (1942) Air Trailer

1 **I Met Him In Paris** (1937) Air Trailer

1 **I Packed My Trunk** (3/15/47) Mut

1 **I Pledge Allegiance** (1947) Syn

1 **I Remember** (3/28/44) Mut

1 **I Remember Kaltenborn** (4/4/52) NBC

I Sat in Judgment (15m)

1 **I See America** (Syn)

1 **I Shall Not Want** (11/28/46) Syn

1 **I Speak For Democracy** (1947) Syn

I Spy (15m)

8 **I Sustain The Wings** (with Glenn Miller's Orchestra until 6/10/44)
(5/29/43 - 11/24/45) first 6 broadcasts just over WEEI (CBS), Boston
7/10/43 - 9/4/43, CBS, Sat, 25m, 2:05 pm
9/18/43 - 6/30/45, NBC, Sat, 11:30 pm
7/7/45 - 8/25/45, NBC, Sat, 10 pm
9/1/45 - 11/24/45 (Glenn Miller Orchestra led by Jerry Gray), NBC, Sat, 11:30 pm
also 11/30/43 - 6/1/45 (Strings With Wings) NBC, Tue/Fri, 15m

1 **I Took It Lying Down** (1951) Syn

1 **I Walk Alone** (1947) Syn

1 **I Want A Baby** (8/3/43) Audition

3 **I Want A Divorce** (10/22/39 - 5/26/40) Glass Jar, NBC, Sun, 3 pm
(10/18/40 - 4/18/41) (with Joan Blondell) Mut, Fri, 9:30 pm also on regionally for S & W Foods
10/17/37 - 10/9/38, NBC - West, 2t (Sun & Wed), 15m (on 1/16/38, Sun)
10/16/38 - 10/13/39, S&W, CBS-West, Fri, 15m, 8 pm
also 1941, Mut

I Want To Come Back

70 **I Was A Communist For The FBI** (with Dana Andrews) (1952 - 54) Syn - ZIV; 78 episodes broadcast; on WOR in New York

4 **I Was A Convict** (1945 - 47) Sus, Mut
1945 - 46, Sat, 15m (not in NY) 7:45 pm
9/28/46 - 10/19/46, Sat, 9:30 am
1946 - 47, Thu, 30m

2 **I Was There** (with Knox Manning) (1935 - 45) Mobil, Sea Island Sugar, Hunt's, CBS- Pacific

1 **I Wonder Who's Kissing Her Now** (1947) film sound track

I'll Find My Way (with Phyllis Jeannie) (3/3/41 - 12/5/41; 3/16/42 - 5/1/42) Multi, 6t, 15m; 5t as of 9/15/41

I'll Never Forget (Songs by Frank Luther) (8/5/40 - 11/1/40) Mut, 5t, 15m, 1 pm

1 **I'll See You In My Dreams** (1952) film sound track

1 **I'll Take The Machine Age** (KDKA) Syn

9 **I'm An American** (5/11/40 - 9/28/40) NBC, Sat, 2 pm
(10/20/40 - 3/1/42) Bl, Sun, 15m, 1 pm; 12:15 pm as of 12/15/40, also syndicated

1 **I'm Too Busy To Talk Now** (2/18/85) NPR

3 **Ian Ross MacFarlane** (1942, 1944) Mut

Ice Box Follies (with Wendell Niles) (1/24/45 - 7/22/45) Hires, ABC
1/24/45 - 6/6/45, Wed, 10 pm
6/17/45 - 7/22/45, Sun, 6:30 pm

1 **Ice Skooting On Great South Bay** (2/11/40) Mut

Ida Bailey Allen (1928 - 3/26/36) also called The Happy Homemaker
1928 - 4/20/31 (Radio Homemaker's Club) Multi, CBS, 3t, 30m - 2 hours
10/26/31 - 32, Multi, CBS, various days and times
1932 - 33, Best Foods, CBS, 2t, 15m
1933 - 1/31/35, Sus, CBS, Thu, 15m
10/8/35 - 3/26/36, Sus, NBC, 2t, 15m

1 **Ida Bailey Allen and The Chef** (Syn)

1 **Ida James With The King Cole Trio** (MacGregor transcription)

Idea Mart (5/31/39 - 8/9/39) Bl, Wed, 9:30 pm

Ideas That Come True (with Dr. R. G. Reynolds) (10/27/38 - 1/18/40) Bl, Thu, 2 pm

1 **Idlewild Air Show** (7/31/48) WOR

1 **Idlewild Airport Dedication** (7/31/48) WOR

If I Could Live It Over (with Walter Pitkin) (5/2/39 - 7/25/39) Gruen, 15m

If I Had The Chance (with Cal Tinney, Al Roth Orchestra)
(8/19/38 - 11/18/38) Bl, Fri, 8:30 pm
(11/29/38 - 10/10/39) Bl, Tue, 10 pm; 10:30 pm as of 9/26/39

If You Had A Million (11/12/39)

1 **If You Think It Was Tough Making Ends Meet In 1974, Wait 'Til You Hear About 1975** (1/1/75) NBC-TV

1 **Ignace Paderewski**

2 **Ike Carpenter and His Orchestra** (Standard transcription)

1 **Ike Williams vs. Beau Jack** (7/12/48) Mut

1 **Ike Williams vs. Willie Joyce** (3/3/45) Mut

Ilka Chase (2/24/40 - 9/11/46) 15m (see also Penthouse Party)
2/24/40 - 5/17/41 (Luncheon At The Waldorf) (with Paul Baron's Orchestra), Camel, Bl, Sat, 1:30 pm
1/10/42 - 7/25/42, Sus, NBC, Sat
9/9/45 - 9/1/46, Berkshire, Mut, Sun, 15m, 1:15 pm

6 **Illinois March Of Health, The** (1940) Syn

Immortal Dramas (with Roy Shields Orchestra) (1/13/35 - 4/7/35) Montgomery-Ward, NBC, Sun, 2 pm

2 **Immortal Stories From The Book Of Books** (Syn)

Immortal Tales

Imogene Wolcott (also see What's Your Idea) (1940 - 1941) WOR, New York

2 **Impeachment: The Committee Votes** (7/27/74) CBS-TV (7/28/74) NBC-TV

1 **Impeachment: The Court and The Committee** (7/24/74) CBS-TV

Imperial Hawaiian Band (10/23/35 - 1/15/36) CBS, Wed, 15m, 7:15 pm

Imperial Time (see Mary Small)

Impressions (with Yasha Davidoff and Hazel Hayes) (10/11/37 - 11/22/37) Mut, Mon, 11:30 pm

In A Word (see Take A Word)

1 **In Caliente** (1935) Air trailer

1 **In Care Of Aggie Horn** (with Harriet Allyn) (11/17/41 - 4/23/42) Sus, Bl, 5t, 15m

1 **In Celebration Of U. S.** (7/4/76) CBS-TV

1 **In Chicago Tonight** (with Harold Stokes Orchestra) WGN; on network (8/8/40 - 10/17/40) Mut, Thu, 8:30 pm

2 **In His Steps** (1940) Syn

1 **In Memory: Franklin Delano Roosevelt** (4/13/45) BBC

In My Opinion (4/1/46 - 10/25/48) CBS, 15m
4/1/46 - 6/6/46, 5t, 11:15 pm; Thu only as of 5/2/46
7/9/46 - 10/25/48, 2t (Mon & Thu) 6:15 pm; Mon as of 1/1/48

1 **In Old Chicago** (1938) film sound track

1 **In Performance At The White House** (12/26/82)

1 **In Performance At Wolf Trap** (12/6/77) PBS-TV

In Person (with Ron Cochran) (6/27/60 - 7/6/61) CBS, 5t, 10m, 7:35 pm

In Person, Dinah Shore (see Dinah Shore)

In The Air With Roger Gale (Syn)

1 **In The Cameo Room** (Syn)

1 **In The Good Old Summertime** (1948) film sound track

In The Modern Manner (with Johnny Green) (9/3/33 - 9/24/33) (also with Gertrude Niesen) CBS, Sun, 8:30 pm (6/8/34 - 9/28/34) General Motors, CBS, Fri, 9:30 pm; 9 pm as of 9/7/34

1 **In The Mood** (AFRS)

1 **In The Morgan Manner** (6/28/54) Syn

In The Name Of The Law (Syn)

1 **In This Case, It's George** (Syn)

2 **In Town Today** (6/2/52 - 11/28/52) CBS, 5t, 15m, 9:45 am, also syndicated

In Town Tonight (with Helen Morgan) Remote: 1/24/40 from St. Francis Hotel, San Francisco

40 **In Your Name** (1947, 1948) Syn

In Your Own Words (Story Of Ruth Kearns) NBC, 15m

Ina Claire (7/25/37 - 8/8/37) Bl, Sun, 60m, 8 pm

1 **Inaugural Gala** (1/19/41) CBS

1 **Inaugural Review** (1/20/49) CBS

1 **Inauguration Of Facsimile Service** (2/9/38) WOR

1 **Inauguration Of President Truman** (1/20/49) Mut

1 **Inauguration Of Queen Juliana** (9/6/48) BBC

1 **Inauguration Of The Sale Of Defense Bonds** (4/30/41) CBS

1 **Incendiary Blonde** (1945) Air trailer

1 **Incident Near Harper's Ferry**

Incomparable Charlie Chan, The (see Charlie Chan)

Incredible Adventures Of Jack Flanders (1981) Syn

4 **Incredible But True** (with Ken Nordine) (1950 - 51) Mut, 15m, various days and times including:
4/17/51 - 6/5/51, 2t, 9:30 pm
6/30/51 - 12/22/51, Sat, 6:15 pm, also syndicated

1 **Incredible Shrinking Gas Pump, The** (6/3/79) NBC-TV

1 **Incredible Year - 1968, The** (1968) CBS

1 **India** (11/24/55) NBC-TV

1 **Indiana Indigo** (often regional) (3/14/39 - 9/23/44) 15m
5/31/38 - 3/7/39, Bl, Tue, 5:45 pm
3/14/39 - 6/6/39 (with Gene Brown Orchestra) Bl, Tue, 3 pm
7/1/39 - 10/21/39, Bl, Tue, 2:30 pm
1/9/40 - 7/30/40, Bl, Tue, 12 noon
4/5/41 - 9/13/41, Bl, Sat, 2 pm; 3 pm as of 6/21/41
also 1/14/43, NBC
6/3/44 - 9/23/44, NBC, Sat, 15m, 1:30 pm

2 **Indiana School Of The Sky** (10/7/48, 11/5/48) Indiana University

Indianapolis Symphony Orchestra (11/23/38 - 2/19/43)
11/23/38 - 3/22/39. CBS, Wed, 60m, 3 pm
11/22/39 - 3/30/41, CBS, Wed, 30m, 10:30 pm; Sun, 10:30 am as of 1/5/41
11/5/42 - 2/19/43, CBS, Thu, 30m, 3:30 pm

4 **Indictment** (based on cases of former Assistant DA Eleazar Lipsky) (1/29/56 - 1/4/59) CBS, Sun, 25m

1 **Infinite Horizons** (7/19/79) ABC-TV

Information Central (4/26/61 - 2/8/62) CBS, 5t

66 **Information Please** (with Clifton Fadiman) (5/17/38 - 4/22/51)
5/17/38 - 11/8/38, Sus, Bl, Tue, 8:30 pm
11/15/38 - 11/5/40, Canada Dry, Bl, Tue, 8:30 pm
11/15/40 - 2/5/43, Lucky Strike, NBC, Fri
2/15/43 - 7/12/43; 9/13/43 - 7/10/44; 9/11/44 - 2/5/45, Heinz, NBC, Mon
2/12/45 - 6/24/46, Mobil, NBC, Mon
10/2/46 - 6/25/47, Parker, CBS, Wed, 10:30 pm
9/26/47 - 6/25/48, Sus, Mut, Fri, 9:30 pm
9/10/50 - 4/22/51, Sus, Mut, Sun, 10 pm

Inheritance (4/4/54 - 8/22/54, 9/26/54 - 5/1/55) NBC, Sun, 4:30 pm

2 **Ink Spots, The** (3/4/35 - 6/21/42) 15m; on various days and times including:
3/4/35 - 4/15/35, Bl, Mon, 11:30 pm
8/17/38 - 9/20/38, Bl, Tue, 15m, 7:30 pm
10/10/39 - 10/31/39, Bl, Tue, 12:15 pm
6/26/40 - 9/25/40, Bl, Wed, 10:15 pm
8/9/40 - 9/27/40, Bl, Fri, 10:30 pm
12/31/41 - 1/14/42, NBC, Wed, 7:45 pm
4/19/42 - 6/21/42, Bl, Sun, 6:45 pm
8/9/35, Bl, 15m
7/12/39, NBC, 15m

Inlaws, The (15m)

Inner Circle (with Constance Bennett) (1/26/56 - 6/21/56) ABC, Thu, 45m, 10:45 pm

98 **Inner Sanctum** (1/7/41 - 10/5/52) host was Raymond Edward Johnson until 5/22/45; then Paul McGrath as of 9/28/45; followed by House Jameson
1/7/41 - 3/11/41, Carters, Bl, Tue, 9:30 pm
3/16/41 - 8/29/43, Carters, Bl, Sun, 8:30 pm
9/4/43 - 11/18/44, Colgate, CBS, Sat, 8:30 pm
11/22/44 - 12/27/44, Colgate, CBS, Wed, 9 pm
1/2/45 - 6/26/45; 9/28/45 - 6/18/46, Lipton, CBS, Tue, 9 pm
7/29/46 - 4/17/50, Bromo Seltzer, CBS, Mon, 8 pm
9/4/50 - 6/18/51, Mars, ABC, Mon, 8 pm
6/22/52 - 10/5/52, Pearson Pharmaceutical Company, CBS, Sun, 8 pm (all shows were repeats)

16 **Inquiring Parent, The** (1948) Syn

1 **Inquiring Reporters** (6/24/39) WFBR

2 **Inside Bob and Ray** (9/8/51) NBC

Inside China (15m)

Inside MGM

1 **Inside New York** (4/8/49) WMCA

Inside News (see Drew Pearson)

2 **Inside Of Sports, The** (6/24/48, 7/14/48) Mut

1 **Inside Pop, The Rock Revolution** (6/67) CBS-TV

Inside Story (with Victor Riesel)

Inside Story, The (with Fred Sullivan) (3/14/39 - 10/3/39) Shredded Ralston, Bl, Tue, 8 pm; originally in Chicago area
12/6/38 - 3/2/39, CBS - Pacific, Thu, 8 pm

Inspector Burke (see Scotland Yard's Inspector Burke)

2 **Inspector Thorne** (with Karl Weber; Staats Cotsworth on last show)
(7/20/51 - 9/27/51) Sus, NBC, Fri, 9 pm; Thu, 9 pm as of 9/6/51

Inspector White Of Scotland Yard (1936 - 37) Mut, 2t, 15m

Inspiration Please (1/14/56 - 6/23/56) Mut, Sat, 7:30 pm

Intercollegiate Debates (2/4/39 - 4/15/39) Mut, Sat, 2:30 pm

Intercollegiate Quiz (with Ben Grauer and Maggie McNellis) 15m

Interesting Neighbors (with Jerry Belcher, Roy Shield Orchestra)
(9/26/37 - 8/28/38) Fitch, NBC, Sun, 15m, 7:45 am; 30m, 7:30 pm as of 1/9/39; as of 9/4/38 replaced by Fitch Bandwagon
also 11/3/38 - 1/12/39, Bl, Thu, 8 pm

Interesting People (see Dale Carnegie)

49 **Intermezzo** (c. 1944 - 1945) AFRS origination, Meredith Willson, conductor, Erno Neufelt, violin
(1952 - 1953) NBC, Chicago origination, NBC String Orchestra

Intermezzo For Strings (6/1/41 - 9/6/42) CBS, Sun, 8:30 am; 15m as of 10/12/41

International Airport (5/7/49 - 1/2/52) Sus, Mut (various days and times including:)
5/7/49 - 6/25/49, Sat, 5:30 pm
9/26/49 - 10/17/49, Mon, 10 pm
10/21/49 - 1/20/50, Fri, 8:30 pm
4/18/50 - 6/22/50, Thu, 8:30 pm
9/23/50 - 10/14/50, Sat, 9 pm
10/25/50 - 1/2/52, Wed, 8:30 pm

1 **International House** (1933) film sound track

International Jazz Club
(11/17/51 - 9/27/52) ABC, Sat, 10 pm; 9:30 pm as of 6/28/52

1 **International Lifeboat Races** (9/10/38) Mut

1 **International Meeting Of Film Experts At UNESCO House** (1953) U.N. Radio

1 **International Victrola Concert** (1/1/25) Special network

International Weekend (with Roy Shield's Orchestra) (2/23/35 - 5/11/35) Bl, Sat, 30m, 11:45 am

1 **Interview On Board The S. S. Argentina** (2/4/46) WOR

1 **Interview With Army Generals** (6/24/45) pool feed

1 **Interview With Clyde Beatty**

1 **Interview With Floy Margaret Hughes** (KGO-FM)

1 **Interview With Matt Cvetic** (4/30/51)

1 **Interview With Mrs. Amy Otis Earheart** (5/20/47) WOR

1 **Interview With Russell E. Singer** (1939) Syn

1 **Interview With The Parents Of The A-Bomb Test Pilots** (6/30/46) Mut

1 **Interviews With Production Credit Commissioner C. R. Arnold** (1946) Syn

Intimate Revue (see Bob Hope)

Into The Light (with Margo and Peter Donald) (8/18/41 - 3/20/42) Bl, 5t, 15m

1 **Intrigue** (with Joseph Schildkraut) (7/24/46 - 9/11/46) Sus, CBS, Wed, 9:30 pm

2 **Introducing The Hometowners** (NBC syn, Morton syn)

8 **Introducing The Peoples Of Asia** (12/18/44 - 4/23/45) WMAL origination, NBC syn

Introduction To Music (with Sigmund Spaeth) (also called At Home With Music) (10/1/49 - 2/11/50) ABC, Sat, 10 am

3 **Invasion Broadcast** (6/6/44) Mut

1 **Invasion Bulletins** (6/6/44) Mut

1 **Invasion Coverage** (7/10/43)

2 **Invasion News** (6/6/44, 6/29/44) NBC, Mut

2 **Invasion Of Guam, The** (7/21/44, 8/5/44)

1 **Invasion Of The Philippines** (10/20/44) KFRC

1 **Invasion Report** (8/15/44)

1 **Investigator, The**

1 **Invisible Walls (The Portland Story)** (2/21/50) KPOJ

1 **Invitation To Learning** (with Dr. Lyman Bryson) (5/26/40 - 12/28/64) CBS
5/26/40 - 6/24/41, Sun; Tue as of 11/26/40
6/29/41 - 12/28/64, Sun

Invitation To Music (4/6/43 - 8/10/43) CBS, Tue, 11:30 pm
(2/23/44 - 10/1/47) (with Bernard Herrmann, Donald Hansen) CBS, Wed, 11:30 am

Invitation To The Dance (with Jacques Fray) (8/25/35 - 10/14/35) NBC, Sun, 6:30 pm

2 **Invitation To The Fair** (with Lou Breese and His Orchestra) (1940) 15m

Invitation To The Waltz (5/8/41 - 7/3/41) CBS, Thu, 15m, 9:30 am

Iodent Club Of The Air (with Joe Rines Orchestra) (9/27/31 - 3/13/32)

Iodent Dress Rehearsal (with Pinky Lee) (11/1/36 - 4/25/37) Iodent, Bl, Sun, 11:30 am

Iodent Program (with Jane Froman, Roy Shields Orchestra) (4/10/32 - 2/19/33)
Iodent, NBC, Sun, 15m, 4 pm
Iodent, NBC, Sun, 7:30 pm

1 **Iowa Democratic Debate** (2/11/84) PBS-TV

1 **Iowa Presidential Debate** (1/8/88) PBS-TV

Ipana Troubadours (1926 - 3/14/34) (various days and times including:)
1926 - 28, Bl, Wed, 9 pm
1929 - 30, Bl, Mon, 8:30 pm
10/4/33 - 3/14/34, NBC, Wed, 9 pm

Ira Cook

1 **Iran: The Oil Cut-Off** (11/12/79) CBS-TV

1 **Iranian Rescue Mission** (4/25/80)

1 **Iraqi Situation Press Conference** (8/8/90) pool feed

Ireene Wicker (see The Singing Lady)

Ireene Wicker's Music Plays (see the Singing Story Lady)

Ireene Wicker, The Singing Story Lady (see The Singing Lady)

1 **Irene** (1940) Air trailer

Irene Beasley (Old Dutch Girl)
(1930 - 1/27/39)
1930 - 6/10/32, Old Dutch Cleanser, CBS, 3t, 15m
10/4/33 - 5/2/34, Old Dutch Cleanser, Bl, Wed, 15m, 6:30 pm
also 10/16/33 - 5/4/34, NBC, 2t (Mon & Fri) 15m, 6:30 pm
1936 - 37 (see Dupont Zerone Jesters)
10/10/38 - 1/27/39 (RFD#1), CBS, 5t, 15m

Irene Bordini (with Emil Coleman Orchestra) (5/2/33 - 5/27/33) Bl, 2t (Tue & Sat) 15m, 7:45 pm

Irene Castle (with Irene Rich) 15m

Irene Rich Dramas (10/4/33 - 5/28/44) Welch's, 15m
10/4/33 - 12/15/33, Bl, 2t (Wed & Fri), 7:45 pm
12/17/33 - 2/18/34, Bl, Sun, 3:15 pm
12/20/33 - 5/30/34, Bl, Wed, 7:45 pm
6/6/34 - 9/26/34, Bl, Wed, 7:30 pm
10/5/34 - 8/13/37, Bl, Fri, 8 pm
8/15/37 - 9/24139, Bl, Sun, 9:45 pm
10/1/39 - 5/31/42, Bl, Sun, 9:30 pm
6/5/42 - 8/7/42, CBS, Fri, 7:15 pm
8/16/42 - 6/27/43, CBS, Sun, 6:15 pm
7/4/43 - 5/28/44, CBS, Sun, 5:45 pm

4 **Iron Fireman Military Parade, The** (1931) Syn

1 **Iron Mask, The** (1928) Synchro-discs

2 **Irv Orton-Pop Organ** (World transcriptions)

1 **Irv Orton-Popular Organ** (World transcription)

1 **Irvin S. Cobb** (with Al Goodman Orchestra) (5/3/33 - 11/22/33) CBS, Wed, 9 pm
also 1940

1 **Irving Fields Trio, The** (3/23/65) CBS

1 **Irving Kaufman** (Thesaurus transcription)

2 **Irving Miller Orchestra** (5/29/39 - 9/1/41) on various days and times including:
5/15/39 - 8/11/41 (Rhythmic Melodies) NBC, 5t, 15m, 9:15 am
5/29/39 - 8/21/39, Bl, Mon, 15m, 10:45 am
12/29/40 - 3/15/41, Bl, Sun, 15m, 11:15 am
also 1/13/41 - 2/10/41, Bl, Mon, 15m, 2:15 pm
5/19/41 - 9/1/41, Bl, Mon, 2pm also Thesaurus transcription

Is Anybody Home? (1940) Mut, Mon, 15m, 2 pm (not in New York)

1 **Is Anybody There?** (7/20/76)

1 **Is Everybody Happy?** (1943) film sound track

1 **Is There A Santa Claus? (An Answer To Little Virginia)**

1 **Is This Peace?** (9/2/46) Mut

Isabel Manning Hewson: Market Basket (7/1/39 - 5/26/44) 15m
7/1/39 - 3/1/42, Sus, NBC, 5t; often 6t
9/14/42 - 5/26/44, Mueller, Bl, 3t, 10 am; CBS, 3t, 9:45 am as of 11/29/43
also 1/10/42 - 5/6/44, Tetley, Bl, 3t (Tue, Thu, Sat) 10 am; CBS, 9:45 am as of 11/9/43

1 **Isham Jones** (1936) film sound track

1 **Isham Jones and His Orchestra** (1934) film sound track

Isham Jones Orchestra (10/9/34 - 4/2/35) General Motors, CBS, Tue, 9:30 pm
(10/1/35 - 11/12/35) (Good Evening Serenade) (with The Eton Boys; Loretta Lee) United Cigar, Mut, Tue, 8:30 pm
(1/36 - 3/29/36) (Yours Sincerely) United Whelan Drug, Mut, Sun, 6 pm (1938) Mar-O-Oil

Island Venture (with Jerry Walter) (11/22/45 - 6/20/46) Wrigley, CBS, Thu, 10 pm

1 **Isn't It A Crime?** (12/14/45) WNEW

1 **Israel Anniversary Show** (5/6/54) CBS

1 **Israel Is Born** (5/12/53)

10 **Israel Spotlight** (1950) Syn

1 **Israel Under Fire** (5/20/48) Mut

13 **Issues and Answers** (1967 - 1981) ABC-TV

It's Up To You (host is Dale Baxter) (3/18/39 - 9/28/39) Bl
3/18/39 - 4/1/39, Sat, 3 pm
5/18/39 - 9/28/39, Thu, 8:30 pm

It Can Be Done (with Edgar Guest) (1/5/37 - 6/28/39) Household Finance
1/5/37 - 3/29/38, Bl, Tue, 8:30 pm
4/6/38 - 6/28/39, CBS, Wed, 10 pm; 10:30 pm as of 2/22/39; 10 pm as of 6/7/39

13 **It Can Happen To You** (with Eddie Cantor) (Syn)

1 **It Happened In 1955** (4/23/45 - 7/15/45) New York Stock Exchange, Mut, Tue, 15m, 10:15 pm

It Happened In Hollywood (with John Conte and Martha Mears) (4/3/39 - 7/5/40) Hormel, CBS, 3t, 15m, 5:30 pm; 8:45 am as of 5/13/40

It Happened In The Service (1942, 1943) NBC, 15m

6 **It Happened To Me** (1939) WINS (1940) WEVD

1 **It Happened Today** (5/26/55) CBS

It Happens Every Day (with Arlene Francis) (9/29/51 - 6/5/53) CBS, 5m

It Happens To You (8/3/54 - 10/5/50 NBC, Tue, 15m, 8 pm

It May Have Happened with Burr Cook (6/8/38 - 10/5/38) Bl, Wed, 9 pm

16 **It Pays To Be Ignorant** (with Tom Howard) (6/25/42 - 9/26/51)
6/25/42 - 11/26/42, Mut, Thu, 8 pm
3/29/43 - 2/28/44, Sus, Mut, Mon, 7:30 pm
2/25/44 - 1/25/46; 5/3/46 - 2/6/48, Philip Morris, CBS, Fri, 9 pm; 10 pm as of 9/20/46
2/28/48 - 7/17/49, Sus, CBS, Sat; Sun as of 1/8/49 (on 3/13/49?)
7/25/49 - 9/13/49, Sus, CBS, Tue, 9:30 pm
7/5/50 - 9/27/50, Chrysler, CBS, Wed, 9 pm
7/4/51-9/26/51, DeSoto, NBC, Wed, 9 pm (summer replacement for You Bet Your Life)

It Pays To Be Married (9/28/53 - 5/27/55) (originally West Coast show, starting on 7/20/53) Multi, NBC, 5t, 15m

It Really Happened (with Jim Ameche) (Syn)

1 **It Started In A Rowboat** (1944) Syn

8 **It Takes A Woman** (with Frankie Burke) (1945) Syn, 5m

It Was A Very Good Year (1971)

12 **It's A Crime Mr. Collins** (with Mandel Kramer) (8/9/56 - 2/28/57) Mut, Thu, 8:30 pm, also syndicated

1 **It's A Gift** (1934) film sound track

It's A Great Life (with Terrance O'Sullivan) (Wheaties and Bisquick)

1 **It's A Living** (with Ben Alexander) (6/6/48 - 7/31/48) Mut, Sun, 9:30 pm

1 **It's A Man's World** (Syn)

It's A Racket (4/3/37 - 5/22/37) also 1947, Mut, Sat, 15m, 9 pm

It's A Women's World (see Eleanor Roosevelt)

2 **It's Always Albert** (with Arnold Stang and Jan Murray) (7/2/48 - 7/23/48) CBS, Fri. 8:30 pm

1 **It's Always Sunday** (10/5/51) audition (11/11/51 - 2/10/52) CBS, Sun, 4:30 pm

1 **It's Dave Garroway** (Syn)

It's Dream Time (see Dream Time)

2 **It's Fun To Be Young** (1/21/50, 2/11/50) CBS - Pacific, sponsored by Globe A-1 Biscuit Mix

It's Harvel Music Time (see Johnny Thompson)

13 **It's Higgins, Sir** (with Harry McNaughton) (7/10/51 - 9/25/51) NBC, Tue, 9 pm (summer replacement for Bob Hope)

1 **It's In The Air** (1935) film sound track

1 **It's In The Bag** (1945) spot announcement

1 **It's Jump Time** (8/28/42) CBS

1 **It's Later Than You Think** (Syn)

It's Maritime (7/17/43 - 9/30/45) CBS
7/17/43 - 12/4/43, Sat, 5 pm
7/8/44 - 8/26/44, Sat, 7 pm
10/10/44 - 9/30/45, Tue; Mon, 5 pm as of 9/9/45

1 **It's Murder** (with Joan Alexander) (6/8/44 - 7/6/44) Bl, Thu, 15m, 11:15 pm also 8/10/44, Bl, Safety Council

It's Our Turn (with Hugh Downs) (WMAQ, Chicago) (1948)

1 **It's Pleasure Time** (1942) Syn

16 **It's Show Time From Hollywood** (Syn)

1 **It's That Time Again** (1946) Syn

It's The Barrys (with Jack Barry) (7/6/53 - 9/4/53) NBC, 5t, 15m, 9:15 pm

3 **It's The Berries** (1954) CBS

16 **It's The Tops** (1949) Syn, with Connie Haines, Kay Starr

3 **It's Time For Johnny Mercer** (1953) CBS

It's Time For Love (see Time For Love)

It's Time To Smile (see The Eddie Cantor Show)

1 **It's Up To You** (5/2/51) Syn

1 **It's Up To Youth** (6/8/46 - 3/26/47) Triangle, Mut, Seventeen Magazine
6/8/46 - 8/10/46, Sat, 12 noon
8/21/46 - 3/26/47 (with F. Chase Taylor as of 1/15/47), Wed, 8:30 pm

2 **It's Your Business** (1/5/46 - 10/20/56) Sus, ABC, 15m; also called The Voice Of Business as of 4/6/46
1/5/46 - 8/30/47, Sat, 7 pm
9/2/47 - 10/7/47, Tue, 10:45 pm
1/6/48 - 6/20/50, Tue
9/2/50 - 10/20/56, Sat

1 **It's Your Navy** (1950) Syn

9 **It's Your World and You Can Have It** (1965, 1966) WBAI-FM

7 **Italian Language Program** (10/7/36 - 10/20/36) WMBQ

43 **Italian News In English** (3/11/38 - 6/24/40) Italy

2 **Italian Program** (7/7/37, 7/31/37) WCNW

2 **Italian Propaganda Broadcast** (10/6/41, 2/19/42) Italy

7 **Ivan Ditmars** (MacGregor, United transcriptions)

Ivory Program (with B. A. Rolfe Orchestra) (4/7/32 - 7/1/32) Ivory, Bl, 2t (Thu & Fri) 15m, 8:30 pm

Ivory Reporter (3/31/36 - 6/25/36) Ivory, Bl, 2t, 15m, 6:15 pm

Ivory Stamp Club (see Captain Tim Healy)

1 **Ivory Tower, The** (Syn)

1 **I Want The Fish** (1947) NBC, Cantor Bob Segal's Country Gentlemen

1 **Iwo Jima Broadcast** (3/3/45)

1 **Iwo Jima Interviews** (2/45)

1 **Iwo Jima Marines** (2/45)

1 **J. A. Krug Press Conference** (5/21/46) Mut

J. Alden Edkins (1/31/37 - 6/6/40) Griswold Mfg. Co., 15m
1/31/37 - 4/18/37, Bl, Sun, 8:45 am
4/25/37 - 5/23/37, NBC, Sun, 9:30 am
1/30/38 - 4/17/38, NBC, Sun, 9:30 am
3/7/40 - 6/6/40, Bl, Thu, 11:30 am

J. B. Priestley (Britain Speaks) (1942) Tue

3 **J. Edgar Hoover** (9/23/40, 3/26/47, 4/10/56) Mut, CBS

1 **J. F. K. Conflict, The** (1988) The Public Interest Affiliates network

Jack and Cliff (see Jack Pearl)

Jack and Jill (1930s)

Jack and Loretta Clemens (11/27/33 - 8/22/39)
11/27/33 - 3/14/34, NBC, 3t (Mon - Wed), 15m, 4:30 pm
1/13/34 - 4/21/35, Venida, NBC, Sun, 15m
1/4/37 - 10/29/37, Kirkman Soap, CBS, 5t, 15m, 9:15 am; 2:15 pm as of 5/31/37
11/15/37 - 4/29/39, Bl, 5t-6t, 15m, 8:45 am
8/8/39 - 8/22/39, Bl, Tue, 15m, 8:15 am

1 **Jack Anderson Confidential** (9/19/82) TV syn

114 **Jack Armstrong** (7/31/33 - 6/1/50) Wheaties
7/31/33 - 4/24/36, CBS, 6t; 5t as of 11/5/34, 15m, 5:30 pm
8/31/36 - 4/23/37; 9/27/37 - 4/22/38; 9/26/38 - 4/28/39; 9/25/39 - 9/26/41, NBC, 5t, 15m, 5:30 pm; 5:45 pm as of 6/2/41
9/29/41 - 7/3/42, Mut, 5t, 15m, 5:30pm
8/31/42 - 5/31/46; 9/2/46 - 8/29/47, ABC, 5t, 15m, 5:30 pm; 3t from 5/31/43 - 8/28/43; 6/5/44 - 9/1/44 (Michael Rye lead 1944 - 46)
9/1/47 - 6/17/48; 9/6/48 - 5/30/49; 9/5/49 - 6/1/50, ABC, 3t one week; 2t next week; alternates with Sky King, 30m, 5:30 pm; changed to Armstrong Of The SBI as of 9/5/50

Jack Baker Show, The (1950 - 51) NBC, 5t, 15, 9 am (not in New York)

1 **Jack Benny** (12/28/74) NBC-TV

1 **Jack Benny Birthday Special, The** (2/17/69) NBC-TV

1 **Jack Benny Heart Fund Show** (1959) Syn

Jack Benny Program For Grape-Nuts and Grape-Nuts Flakes, The (see The Jack Benny Program)

697 **Jack Benny Program, The**
(5/2/32 - 5/22/55) 925 shows broadcast;
5/2/32 - 10/26/32 (Canada Dry Ginger Ale Program), Canada Dry, Bl, Mon & Wed, 9:30 pm
10/30/32 - 1/26/33, Canada Dry, CBS, Sun, 10 pm and Thu, 8:15 pm; 8 pm as of 1/5/33 (78 Canada Dry shows broadcast)
3/17/33 - 6/23/33 (Chevrolet Program), Chevrolet, NBC, Fri, 10 pm
10/1/33 - 4/1/34, Chevrolet, NBC, Sun, 10 pm; (43 Chevrolet shows broadcast)
4/6/34 - 9/28/34 (General Tire Show), General Tire, NBC, Fri, 10 pm; (26 General Tire shows broadcast) (The Jell-O Program), Jell-O, Bl; NBC as of 10/4/36, Sun, 7 pm; (301 Jell-O shows broadcast)
10/10/43 - 6/4/44 (The Grape-Nuts Program), Grape Nuts, NBC, Sun, 7 pm; (70 Grape Nuts shows broadcast)
10/3/48 - 12/26/48 (also called The Lucky Strike Program), Lucky Strike, NBC, Sun, 7 pm
9/14/52 - 6/7/53; 9/13/53 - 6/6/54; 9/26/54 - 5/22/55, Lucky Strike, CBS, Sun, 7 pm; (406 Lucky Strike shows broadcast)
(10/28/56 - 7/7/57; 9/29/5-6/22/58) (The Best Of Benny), Home Insurance from 9/29/57, CBS, Sun, 7 pm (Repeats)

Jack Benny Show, The (see The Jack Benny Program)

1 **Jack Benny Speaks For The NAB Code** (Syn)

2 **Jack Benny Special Christmas Show, The** (12/56) CBS

1 **Jack Benny Tenth Anniversary Testimonial** (5/9/41)

1 **Jack Benny's 20th Anniversary Special** (11/16/70) NBC-TV

1 **Jack Benny's Bag** (11/16/68) NBC-TV

1 **Jack Benny's First Farewell Special** (1/18/73) NBC-TV

1 **Jack Benny's New Look** (12/3/69) NBC-TV

1 **Jack Benny's Second Farewell Special** (1/24/74) NBC-TV

1 **Jack Benny's Tenth Anniversary In Radio** (5/10/41) KFI

7 **Jack Berch Show, The** (4/6/36 - 10/15/54) 15m
4/6/36 - 7/9/37, Wasey Products, Mut, 3t, 9:45 am
also 1/19/37 - 7/15/37, Fels Naphtha, CBS, 2t, 1 pm
7/19/37 - 10/22/37, Fels Naphtha, CBS, 3t, 9:30 am
10/4/38 - 2/21/39, CBS, Tue, 15m, 10:30 pm
1/11/39 - 5/31/40, Sweetheart Soap, NBC, 2t (Wed & Fri), 7:45 pm
also 5/1/39 - 6/7/40, Bl, 3t, 10:30 pm; 11:30 pm as of 11/6/39
also 5/16/39 - 5/30/40, Mut, 2t, 15m, 12:15pm
5/20/41 - 9/2/41, Mut, 15m, 2t 1942 (with John Reed King), Gulf Spray, 15m
9/20/43 - 10/6/44, Kellogg, Mut, 5t, 15m, 1:15 pm
10/9/44 - 12/29/44, Kellogg, ABC, 5t, 15m, 11:45 am
8/27/45 - 9/27/46, Prudential Insurance, ABC, 5t, 15m, 4 pm
9/30/46 - 9/21/51, Prudential Insurance, NBC, 5t, 15m
9/24/51 - 10/15/54, Prudential Insurance, ABC, 5t, 15m; gradually lessened to 5 minutes also 50 five-minute shows for Canada Dry

5 **Jack Berch and His Gulfspray Gang** (1940) Syn

Jack Bundy and His Jukebox (15m)

1 **Jack Bundy's Carnival** (also with Monica Lewis) (4/15/44 - 11/1/46) Mut
4/15/44 - 6/24/44, Sat, 3 pm
1/22/45 - 8/16/46; 10/7/46 - 11/1/46 (Jack Bundy's Album), 5t, 15m

9 **Jack Carson Show, The**
(6/2/43 - 12/20/56)
6/2/43 - 6/13/45; 9/19/45 - 6/26/46; 10/2/46 - 6/25/47, Campbell, CBS, Wed
1947 - 48 (see Sealtest Village Store)
10/8/48 - 7/1/49, Sealtest, CBS, Fri, 8 pm
5/11/54, Audition
7/13/54 - 9/8/54, CBS, Wed, 9:30 pm
10/3/55 - 12/20/56, Multi, CBS, 5t

Jack Coffey Show, The (with Jack Coffey Orchestra) (1941) Bl

Jack Dempsey's Sports Quiz (with Mark Goodson) (2/14/42 - 8/22/42) Mut, Sat, 8:30 pm

Jack Duggan (1/15/40 - 5/24/40) NBC, Mon, 15m, 1:30 pm

Jack Edwards (CBS)

3 **Jack Fina and His Orchestra** (1/14/47, 5/5/50, 6/4/50) ABC, NBC

Jack Frost Melody Moments (1929 - 6/25/34) Jack Frost
1929 - 7/2/31 (with Eugene Ormandy), NBC, Thu
7/8/31 - 11/3/32 (with Josef Pasternack Orchestra), Bl, Wed, 8:30 pm
11/7/32 - 6/25/34 (with Josef Pasternack Orchestra), Bl, Mon, 9:30 pm

Jack Fulton (see Poetic Melodies)

Jack Gregson Variety Show (also called Jack's Place; Just Easty) (Variety) on West Coast in the 1940s
(10/12/53 - 6/3/56) ABC
10/12/53 - 1/1/54, ABC, 5t, 85m
5/10/54 - 6/3/56 (with Peggy Ann Ellis), 3t - 5t, 45m, 8 pm

7 **Jack Haley Show, The** (10/9/37 - 4/7/39, 1945) 10/9/37 - 4/2/38 (Log Cabin Jamboree), Log Cabin, NBC, Sat, 8:30 pm
10/14/38 - 4/7/39 (The Wonder Show, Wonder Bread, CBS, Fri, 7:30 pm
also 11/29/45

Jack Haskell (1950 - 51) NBC, 15m

1 **Jack Hooley Report** (4/29/45) NBC

Jack Hylton's Continental Revue (10/13/35 - 6/28/36) Standard Oil, CBS, Sun, 10:30 pm

Jack Joy Orchestra (7/27/39 - 8/10/39) Bl, Thu, 15m, 7:30 pm

Jack Kilty Show, The (8/4/40 - 11/3/40) Mut, Sun, 1:30 pm
(3/10/47 - 10/24/47) NBC, 5t, 15m

20 **Jack Kirkwood Show, The** (5/17/43 - 2/20/53)
5/17/43 - 2/12/45 (Mirth and Madness), Sus, NBC, 5t, 12:30 pm; 9 am as of 12/3/43; Ransom Sherman replaced Jack Kirkwood
1/1/45 - 6/30/45; 9/10/45 - 3/29/46, Procter & Gamble, CBS, 5t, 15m, 7 pm
7/1/46 - 8/19/46, Lux, CBS, Mon, 9:30 pm (partial summer replacement for Lux Radio Theater)
9/1/46 - 9/29/46, CBS, Sun, 30m, 6:30 pm
1948 - 49 (At Home With The Kirkwoods) ABC
1949 - 50 (Kirkwood Corner Store) ABC
8/25/50 - 11/24/50 (Kirkwood-Goodman Show), Mut, Fri, 9:30 pm
10/13/52 - 2/20/53, Mut, 5t, 4 pm

Jack Leonard (with Marion Shaw and Walter Groves Orchestra)
(10/5/40 - 1/18/41) CBS. Sat. 15m, 10:30 pm

Jack Marshard Orchestra (2/4/39 - 6/23/39) CBS, Sat, 5:30 pm; 5 pm as of 5/6/39

Jack Miley (11/14/39 - 1/26/40) NBC, 5t, 15m, 6:15 pm

1 **Jack Mullin Interview** (9/12/73)

2 **Jack Oakie College, The** (12/29/36 - 3/22/38) Camel, CBS, Tue, 30m
12/29/36 - 6/22/37 (part of Benny Goodman's Swing School)
6/29/37 - 3/22/38 (separate show), 9:30 pm

Jack Owens (see Tin Pan Alley Of The Air)

12 **Jack Paar Program, The** (6/1/47 - 9/28/47) NBC, Sun, 7 pm (summer replacement for Jack Benny)
(10/1/47 - 12/24/47) ABC, Wed, 9:30 pm
(7/2/56 - 12/28/56) ABC, 5t, 15m, 11:15 am

Jack Pearl Show, The (also with Cliff Hall) (4/3/32 - 9/25/51) (see also Cresta Blanca Carnival)
4/3/32 - 6/26/32, Chrysler, CBS, Sun, 10:30 pm
9/8/32 - 6/29/33 (Lucky Strike Hour with Paul Whiteman), Lucky Strike, NBC, Thu, 60m, 10 pm
10/7/33 - 12/23/33, Lucky Strikes, NBC, Sat, 9 pm
1/3/34 - 9/26/34, Royal Gelatin, NC, Wed, 30m, 8 pm
2/13/35 - 5/22/35 (Family Hotel), Frigidaire, CBS, Wed, 10 pm
11/9/36 - 6/25/37, Raleigh and Kool, NBC, Mon; 9:30 pm; Fri, 10 pm as of 3/19/37
6/9/48 - 9/15/48 (Jack and Cliff Sus, NBC, Wed, 8:30 pm
6/19/51 - 9/25/51 (with Mirni Benzel), Pet Milk, NBC, Tue, 9:30 pm (summer replacement for Fibber McGee & Molly)

Jack Pepper Show, The (with Jackson Beck, Jeri Sullivan) (6/20/44 - 8/8/44) Swan, CBS, Tue, 9 pm (summer replacement for Burns and Allen)

2 **Jack Randolph and His Music** (Syn)

Jack Savage's Peaceful Valley Folks (3/26/35 - 5/18/35) Crazy Water, NBC, 4:30 pm

Jack Shannon (5/10/38 - 7/12/38) CBS, Tue, 15m, 5:15 pm)

1 **Jack Sharkey vs. Max Schmeling** (6/21/32)

38 **Jack Smith Show, The** (also called at different times; Tide Show (from 1/1/51 - 12/26/52); Oxydol Show; see also Jeri Sullivan, Three Sisters)
(8/21/45 - 6/28/46; 8/19/46 - 7/4/47; 8/25/47 - 7/2/48; 8/23/48 - 7/1/49; 8/22/49 - 6/30/50; 8/28/50 - 6/29/51; 8/27/51 - 6/27/52; 8/25/52 - 12/26/52) Tide & Oxydol, CBS, 5t, 15m, 7:15 pm; Dinah Shore on from 4/20/50 - 12/26/52
also 10/2/43 - 3/28/44, CBS, Tue, 15m, 6:30 pm

1 **Jack Sterling Money Quiz** (1/22/50)

3 **Jack Teagarden and His Orchestra** (1/23/40, 7/12/50) NBC, CBS, Standard transcription

3 **Jack Teagarden, His Trombone and Orchestra** (Standard transcriptions)

Jack Turner (see Happy Jack Turner)

2 **Jack Webb Show, The** (April, 1946) ABC, Wed

1 **Jack Wheeler Show, The** (4/13/70) KDKA

Jack's Place (see Jack Gregson)

Jack, June and Jimmie (4/25/35 - 6/6/35) H.C. Brill Co., CBS, Thu, 10m, 10:05 am

4 **Jackie Gleason Show, The** (1952 - 1967) CBS-TV

Jackie Heller (1/14/35 - 12/30/35) Bl, 3t (Mon, Tue, Fri), 15m, 5:15 pm (also see Chappel Brothers)

Jackie Hill Show, The (from St. Louis) 15m

1 **Jackie Robinson** (NBC)

Jackie Robinson Show (1/22/50 - 12/31/50) ABC, Sun, 15m, 10:30 pm

Jackson Wheeler (1941 - 1942) Curtis, CBS

Jacques Abrams (2/5/41 - 5/14/41) NBC, Wed, 15m, 1 pm

Jacques Fray and Mario Braggiotti (see Fray and Braggiotti)

Jacques Fray Show, The

1 **Jacques Jou-Jerryville** (4/30) Syn

Jacques Renard Orchestra (12/23/38 - 2/10/39) Mut, Fri, 10:30 pm

Jailbusters (1945) CBS, 15m

Jake and Lena

3 **Jam** (12/29/42)

Jamboree (AFRS)

Jamboree (from Chicago with Don McNeill) (6/6/36 - 10/3/36) NBC, Sat, 30m; 60m as of 8/22/36
(4/26/38 - 7/21/39) Bl
4/26/38 - 11/1/38, Tue, 9:30 pm
11/1/38 - 7/21/39, Fri, 8:30 pm; 8 pm as of 4/28/39

Jamboree USA (Mut; started on WWVA on 1/33) Sat; still being broadcast as of 1996

4 **James (Jimmie) Carroll** (also with Ken Christy) (3/26/45 - 3/29/46) CBS, 3t, 15m, 6:15 pm
(9/24/51 - 1/3/52) Squibb, Mut, 2t, 15m, 12:15 pm
(7/1/52 - 9/23/52) (summer replacement for The Black Museum) Mut, Tue, 8 pm
(10/24/52 - 1/9/53) CBS, Fri, 15m, 9:45 pm

James and Pamela Mason Show, The (7/14/49 - 9/8/49) NBC, Thu, 9:30pm

1 **James Baker** (1/9/91) pool feed

James Hilton (6/28/43 - 8/9/43) CBS, Mon, 15m, 7:15 pm

James J. Braddock (Unsung Champions) (12/8/36 - 1/21/37) Bl, 3t (Tue-Thu) 15m, 7:15 pm

4 **James J. Walker V-Mail Program** (8/20/43 - 12/19/43) Mut

1 **James J. Wilson** (9/18/37) WINS

46 **James Melton Show, The** (Texaco Star Theater) (7/4/43 - 9/22/46)
7/4/43 - 12/5/43, Texaco, CBS, Sun, 9:30 pm (summer replacement for Fred Allen)
7/2/44 - 9/22/46 (with Ed Wynn from 1/6/46 - 7/28/46), Texaco, CBS, Sun (see also Harvest Of Stars) (started as summer replacement for Fred Allen)

1 **James P. Johnson (Jazz Pianist)** (World transcription)

2 **James P. Johnson** (World transcriptions)

1 **James Petrillo Hearing** (1/28/48) Mut

1 **Jan August Show, The** (12/19/47 - 2/26/48) Revere, Mut, Thu, 15m, 8 pm

10 **Jan Garber and His Orchestra** (5/40 - 8/13/66) Mut, NBC, CBS, WGN, Capitol, MacGregor transcriptions

Jan Savitt (15m) (see also Rhapsody In Rhythm)
(3/26/39 - 4/7/40) Bl, Sun, 15m, 10 pm; 10:15 pm as of 4/30/39

4 **Jan Savitt and His Orchestra** (9/15/38 - 1940) NBC, KYW, Thesaurus transcriptions

3 **Jan Savitt and His Top Hatters** (10/10/38, 10/17/38, 8/15/39) KYW, NBC

1 **Jan Savitt and The Top Hatters** (9/14/37) KYW

1 **Jan Savitt Orchestra** (1937) Thesaurus transcription

Jane Ace, Disc Jockey (10/27/51 - 9/27/52) NBC, Sat, 10:30 pm; 8 pm as of 11/17/51

1 **Jane Arden** (with Ruth Yorke) (9/26/38 - 6/23/39) Ward Baking, Bl, 5t, 15m, 10:15 am; on previously in New York for 14 weeks, also syndicated

1 **Jane Cowl Show, The** (7/10/44 - 11/16/45) Mut, 5t, 15m

Jane Cozzens (3/18/40 - 4/8/40) NBC, Mon, 15m, 6 pm

Jane Ellison (see Magic Recipes)

1 **Jane Endicott, Reporter** (1/7/42) Rancho Soups, CBS, 5t, 15m

Jane Eyre (11/24/41 - 12/19/41) Mut, 5t, 15m, 4:15 pm; part of limited-run series based on books

Jane Froman - Don Ross (with D'Artega Orchestra) (7/4/37 - 9/26/37) Jell-O, NBC, Sun, 7 pm (summer replacement for Jack Benny)

Jane Froman - Jan Peerce Show, The (see Gulf Musical Playhouse)

Jane Froman Show, The
(2/21/33 - 4/14/33) Chesterfield, CBS, 2t (Tue & ?), 15m, 9 pm (Music That Satisfies)
(7/14/33 - 8/25/33) (with Jacques Renard Orchestra) CBS, Fri, 10:30 pm (also see Iodent Program)
(7/19/33 - 8/23/33) (with Ed Marsh) CBS, Wed, 10:30 pm
(1938) CBS (also see Pontiac Show)
(7/5/42 - 9/27/42) (with Al Goodman Orchestra) Texaco, CBS, Sun, 30m, 9:30 pm (summer replacement for Fred Allen)

Jane Grant's Steero Program
(9/30/31-11/30/32) Steero bouillon cubes, NBC, Wed, 15m, 10:15 am

7 **Jane Pickens Show, The**
(10/24/48 - 4/13/57) NBC (also called Picken's Party during certain years)
10/24/48 - 3/20/49 (with Norman Cloutier Orchestra), Sun, 5 pm
7/4/49 - 8/22/49 (with Bob Houston) Mon, 9:30 pm
2/5/51 - 9/12/52, Sus, 5t
10/12/52 - 5/24/53, Sun, 15m, 11:45 am
11/20/52 - 1/13/55, Sus, Thu, 15m
1/16/55 - 6/5/55, Sun, 1:30 pm
also 5/4/53 - 4/9/54, 5t, 15m, 2:45 pm
12/3/55 - 4/13/57, Sat, 15m, 6:45 pm

15 **Janet Williams Chats About Children** (1948) Syn

Janette Davis Show, The (1946) ABC
(1/5/48 - 7/4/48) (with Howard Smith Orchestra) CBS, Sun, 15m, 5 pm

3 **Jantzen Radio Program** (1931) Syn

1 **Jap Attack On The Fifth Fleet** (3/3/45) Mut

1 **Japan's Acceptance** (8/15/45) ABC

1 **Japanese Attack On The U. S. S. Franklin** (5/17/45) Mut

3 **Jason and The Golden Fleece** (with Macdonald Carey)
(10/22/52 - at least 6/17/54) NBC; in New York until 7/19/53
10/22/52 - 12/31/52, Wed, 10 pm
1/11/53 - 7/19/53, Sun, 4:30 pm
10/5/53 - 11/16/53, Tue
5/6/54 - 6/17/54, Thu

Jay Simms (1941 - 43) Mut

Jay Stewart's Fun Fair
(5/21/49 - 9/24/49; 12/16/50 - 3/17/51) ABC, Sat, 11:30 am; 9:30 pm as of 12/16/50

9 **Jazz Alive** (12/31/78 - 8/12/83) NPR

2 **Jazz Alley** (9/69) NET-TV (with Art Hodes)

1 **Jazz America** (12/31/83) NPR

Jazz Anthology (with George Mercer) 60m

1 **Jazz At The Smithsonian** (TV syn)

Jazz Band Ball (7/9/55 - 9/3/55; 1/14/56 - 2/4/56) CBS, Sat, 15m, 7 pm; 6:05 pm as of 1/14/56

1 **Jazz Casual** (5/64) WNDT-TV

1 **Jazz Concert From The Los Angeles Philharmonic Auditorium**
(1945) AFRS

1 **Jazz From Birdland** (1952)

Jazz Goes To College (WNEW-NY) (12/10/50 - 52)

Jazz Is My Beat (with Jim Lowe) (12/3/58 - 12/23/58) Scripto, 3t (Tue, Thu, Fri), 15m, 8:25 pm

Jazz Nocturne (WOR) (1930s)
(8/7/52 - 3/1/53) Mut
8/7/52 - 9/25/52, Thu, 8 pm
11/30/52 - 3/1/53, Sun, 9 pm

1 **Jean Abbey Notes** (9/21/39) WJSV

Jean Carroll (1930 - 9/7/31) NBC, Mon, 15m, 10:30 am

Jean Cavall (5/24/41 - 2/20/42) Bl, 15m
5/24/41 - 9/27/41, Sat
also 6/15/41 - 9/21/41, Sun, 7:45 pm
10/3/41 - 2/20/42, Bl, Fri, 15m, 7:30 pm

Jean Colbert (8/19/46 - 12/27/46) ABC, 5t, 15m

Jean Dickenson (7/20/36 - 9/21/36) Bl, Mon, 15m, 8 pm

Jean Ellington (4/8/39 - 10/7/39) NBC, Sat, 15m, 1 pm

1 **Jean Merrill** (1/25/41 - 8/16/41) Mut, Sat, 15m, 8:45 pm; 7:15 pm as of 3/8/41
(4/14/45) Mut

2 **Jean Sablon Show, The** (with Paul Baron's Orchestra)
(1941) Bl, Kolynos
(9/1/46 - 11/2/47) CBS, Sat, 15m
11/9/46 - 6/14/47, 7:15 pm; 7:45 pm as of 5/3/47, Richard Hudnut
6/22/47 - 11/2/47, Sun, 5:30 pm
(2/19/51 - 7/20/51) Mut, 5t, 3:30 pm

12 **Jean Shepherd Show, The**
(3/5/55 - 4/1/77) (WOR) various days and times, 45m - 55m

Jean Tighe (1/13/45 - 11/15/47) Sat, 15m
1/13/45 - 3/31/45, Bl, 12 noon
11/9/46 - 11/15/47 (with Hal Horton) Mut, 5:45 pm; 5:30 pm as of 2/15/47

1 **Jeanette Davis Show, The** (5/2/48) CBS

Jeannie Taylor (see Dream Time)

3 **Jeff and Lucky** (9/27/39, 1947) with Olan Soule) auditions

14 **Jeff Regan, Investigator** (with Jack Webb until 12/18/48; then Frank Graham)
(7/10/48 - 12/18/48) CBS, Sat;
(10/5/49 - 8/27/50) CBS, Wed; then Sun; also called Lion's Eye; mostly a West Coast show

12 **Jeffersonian Heritage, The** (with Claude Rains) 1952; 12 episodes; syndicated; by National Association Of Educational Broadcasters

Jello Program Starring Jack Benny, The (see Jack Benny)

Jelly Elliott and The Three Knotheads

Jenny Peabody (10/18/37 - 1/14/38) F & F Labs, CBS, 3t, 15m

Jeno Bartal Orchestra (5/2/39 - 10/9/41)
5/2/39 - 1/9/40, NBC, Tue, 15m, 1 pm
5/20/41 - 10/9/41, Bl, 2t, 15m, 1:50 pm

Jergen's Hollywood Playhouse (see Romance)

Jergen's Journal, The (see Walter Winchell)

1 **Jeri Sullivan** (6/14/43 - 12/21/44) CBS; often with Jack Smith
6/14/43 - 7/30/43, 3t, 15m, 6:30 pm
8/2/43 - 9/24/43, 3t, 30m, 6:15 pm
10/11/43 - 12/21/44, 4t - 2t, 15m, 6:30 pm

1 **Jeri Sullivan With The Mel-Tones and Johnny White Quintet** (Standard transcription)

Jeri Sullivan's Dream House (see Jeri Sullivan)

1 **Jerome Kern Memorial Special Show** (12/9/45) CBS

Jerry and Skye (with George Michael, announcer) Mut

59 **Jerry At Fair Oaks** (1937 - 38) Syn

Jerry Cooper Show, The
(12/4/34 - 4/2/35) CBS, Tue, 7:30 pm
(4/7/35 - 7/7/35) (with Roger Kinne and Freddie Rich Orchestra) CBS, Sun, 6 pm
(3/17/36 - 4/23/36) (with Ted Royal Orchestra) CBS, 2t, 15m, 12:15 pm
(9/9/36 - 3/3/37) Drene, NBC, Wed, 15m, 7:45 pm
(12/10/44 - 4/8/45) Mut, Sun, 15m, 9:45 pm; 2:45 pm as of 3/25/45, sponsored by Miss Swank's Slips

1 **Jerry Dean, Boy Trooper** (2/12/47) Mut

1 **Jerry Gray and His Band Of Today** (6/9/51) NBC

1 **Jerry Gray and His Orchestra (The Bob Crosby Show)** (Standard transcription)

8 **Jerry Gray and His Orchestra** (Standard transcriptions)

Jerry Gray Orchestra (1950) from Hollywood Palladium, Sun

Jerry Lester Show, The
(7/23/40 - 1/16/44)
7/23/40 - 9/17/40 (see Tommy Dorsey)
1/11/41 - 4/5/41, Lucky Strike, CBS, Sat, 45m, 9 pm
7/10/41 - 3/10/42, Kraft, NBC, Thu, 60m, 9 pm
7/25/43 - 1/16/44, CBS, Sun, 7 pm; 8 pm as of 10/24/43

1 **Jerry Livingstone and His Orchestra** (9/21/39) CBS

124 **Jerry Of The Circus** (1937) Syn

Jerry Sears Orchestra
(10/10/38 - 4/24/39) Bl, Mon, 15m, 10:30 am

3 **Jerry Wayne Show, The**
(1/5/42 - 9/21/45) (often called Memory Lane) (see also Gulf Spray Presents)
1/5/42 - 3/2/42 (with Ted Straeter Orchestra), Mut, 3t (Mon-Wed) 15m, 10:30 pm
3/27/42 - 6/12/42, CBS, Fri, 15m
3/5/45 - 3/19/45 (with Mark Warnow Orchestra), Bl, Mon, 9 pm
3/25/45 - 7/1/45, Bl also Mut, Sun, 8:30 pm (The New Borden Show)
7/13/45 - 9/21/45, CBS, Fri, 7:30 pm

2 **Jess Stacy Trio** (World transcriptions)

1 **Jesse Crawford** (1929 - 8/25/35)
1929 - 31, Royal Typewriter, CBS, Sun
1931 - 32, Sus, NBC, 3t 1932 - 33, Bl, 3t
8/26/34 - 8/25/35, NBC, 3t (Thu, Fri, Sun), 11:15 pm
also 2/9/35 - 4/6/35, Bl, Sat, 4:30 pm also World transcription

Jessel Jamboree (see George Jessel)

Jester's Trio (Red Latham, Wamp Carlson and Guy Bonham)
(8/22/34 - 9/24/44) 15m
8/22/34 - 3/27/35, Bl, 2t (Tue & Wed) 4:30 pm
also 1/20/35 - 4/14/35, Bl, Sun, 11 pm
10/5/38 - 4/28/39, Guldens, Bl, 2t (Wed & Fri), 6:30 pm
3/26/42 - 9/24/44 (with Diane Courtney), Bl, 2t, 7:45/7:30 pm
also 6/28/42 - 8/9/42, Bl, Sun, 15m, 9:45 pm

9 **Jesters, The** (1/9/42 - 7/28/42) Thesaurus transcriptions

1 **Jesus Christ and Karl Marx** (12/6/49) Mut

Jewel Cowboys (2/5/38 - 10/15/38), CBS, Sat, 10:30 am

Jewel Hour (1/1/29 - 5/28/29) Jewel Tea Co., CBS, Tue, 10:30 am

1 **Jeweler's Shop, The** (9/30/79) NBC

1 **Jewels Of Music** (4/23/53) CBS

9 **Jewish American Board For Peace and Justice, The** (1/1/45 - 5/21/45) WWRL

4 **Jewish Hour, The** (11/9/36 - 1/22/37) WCNW

1 **Jewish Services** (Syn)

11 **Jewish Show Time** (11/7/58 - 3/9/59) WEVD

1 **JFK: A Profile In Courage**

13 **Jill Corey Sings** (1957) Syn

16 **Jill's All Time Juke Box** (AFRS)

Jim Ameche Naval Air Reserve (15m)

Jim Backus (6/18/42 - 58)
6/18/42 - 7/23/42 (Jim Backus Variety (Vaudeville) Show) (also with Mary Small, Jeff Alexander) CBS, Thu, 8 pm
8/3/47 - 5/30/48, Feenamint, Mut, Sun, 9:30 pm
10/14/57 - 58, ABC, Mon, 60m

Jim Backus Vaudeville Show, The (see Jim Backus)

1 **Jim Cullum's Happy Jazz Band** (2/16/75)

Jim Hawthorne (see Hawthorne)

Jim Hawthorne Show, The (see Hawthorne's Adventure)

Jim McWilliams National Question Bee (see Uncle Jim's Question Bee)

1 **Jim Pierce Interview** (1/6/82)

1 **Jim Reeves Show, The**
(10/7/57 - 2/28/58) ABC, 5t, 5m
10/7/57 - 12/27/57, Heinz
1/6/58 - 2/28/58, Multi, also syndicated

2 **Jimmie Dean and His Trail Riders** (MacGregor transcriptions)

7 **Jimmie Grier and His Orchestra** (MacGregor, BMI transcriptions)

1 **Jimmie Lunceford and His Orchestra** (World transcription)

Jimmie Shields (8/23/41 - 10/11/41) Mut, Sat, 15m, 11:15 am

Jimmie, June and Jack
(4/25/35 - 6/20/35) E-Zee Freeze Deserts, CBS, Thu, 25m, 10:05 am

Jimmy Barrie (7/2/41 - 8/27/41) CBS, Wed, 15m, 9:30 am

1 **Jimmy Beats Rheumatic Fever** (film strip audio)

1 **Jimmy Blade and His Music** (10/18/48) WMAQ

Jimmy Blaine Show (8/29/48 - 9/20/48) ABC, Mon, 9 pm

Jimmy Carroll Show, The (see James Carroll)

Jimmy Carroll Sings (see James Carroll)

3 **Jimmy Carter** (7/15/76, 10/30/76, 7/18/84) ABC-TV, pool feed

1 **Jimmy Carter Report Card, The** (8/14/77) ABC-TV

1 **Jimmy Carter, Walter Mondale** (7/15/76) pool feed

1 **Jimmy Dean Show, The** (1/6/65) ABC-TV

Jimmy Dorsey (2/3/39 - 8/2/40)
2/3/39 - 3/10/39, Mut, Fri, 8:30 pm
5/28/39 - 10/22/39, Bl, Sun
6/14/40 - 8/2/40, Bl, Fri, 7:30 pm (Marine Corps) also Jimmy Dorsey Show (1950) CBS

9 **Jimmy Dorsey and His Orchestra** (1935, 10/20/41, 1956) Bl, CBS, Associated, World, Standard transcriptions

1 **Jimmy Dorsey Orchestra, The** (1957) CBS

1 **Jimmy Dorsey's Original Dorseyland Jazz Band** (1950) Syn

1 **Jimmy Doyle vs. Frank Terry** (1/13/45) Mut

1 **Jimmy Durante Interview** (11/8/61) WINS

85 **Jimmy Durante Show, The**
(9/10/33 - 6/30/50)
9/10/33 - 11/12/33, Chase and Sanborn, NBC, Sun, 60m, 8 pm (summer replacement for Eddie Cantor)
4/22/34 - 9/30/34, Chase and Sanborn, NBC, Sun, 60m, 8 pm (partial summer replacement of Eddie Cantor)
3/25/43 - 10/28/43 (Camel Comedy Caravan until 9/23/43), Camel, NBC, Thu, 10 pm (filled in for Abbott and Costello from 10/7 - 10/28)
10/8/43 - 3/30/45 (with Garry Moore) (Camel Caravan) Camel, CBS, Fri, 10 pm
4/6/45 - 6/29/45; 9/14/45 - 6/7/46; 9/13/46 - 6/27/47 (with Garry Moore), Rexall, CBS, Fri, 10 pm; 9:30 pm as of 3/8/46
10/1/47 - 6/23/48, Rexall, NBC, Wed, 10:30 pm
10/8/48 - 7/1/49; 10/7/49 - 6/30/50 (with Alan Young), Camel, NBC, Fri, 8:30 pm; 9:30 pm as of 10/7/49

Jimmy Durante-Garry Moore Show, The (see The Jimmy Durante Show)

Jimmy Edmondson Show, The (Edmondson talks backwards; also with Nanette Fabray and Pat Hosley) (2/2/46 - 6/8/46) NBC, Sat, 7:30 pm

7 **Jimmy Featherstone and His Orchestra** (11/23/69 - 4/26/70) CBS

2 **Jimmy Fidler** (1933 - 7/3/49)
1933 - 34 (also called Hollywood On The Air)
1/16/35 - 5/22/35, Tangee Lipstick, Bl, Wed, 15m, 10 pm
11/10/36 - 3/2/37, Ludens, NBC, Tue, 15m
3/16/37 - 11/8/38, Drene, NBC, Tue; 2t (Tue & Fri), 15m as of 5/21/37
11/11/38 - 7/21/39, Drene, NBC, Fri
also 11/15/38 - 7/18/39; 9/5/39 - 4/16/40, Drene, CBS, Tue, 15m, 7:15 pm
11/13/41 - 11/27/41, Mut, 15m
3/2/42 - 6/15/42, Arrid, Bl, Mon 15m, 7 pm
6/28/42 - 6/4/50, Arrid, Bl/ABC, Sun, 15m, 9:30 pm; 9:45 pm from 1/6/46 - 6/30/46; 10:30 pm as of 9/7/47
also 3/2/43 - 10/5/43, Mut, 2t, 15m; then Tue, 10:30 pm
9/26/48 - 7/3/49, Arrid, Mut, Sun, 15m, 9:30 pm
(5/21/51 - 7/27/51) Starlet Home Permanent, 5t, 5m (with Harry von Zell, announcer)

1 **Jimmy Fidler's Diary** (10/5/45) Syn

Jimmy Gleason's Diner (with Lucille and Jimmy Gleason) (1/26/46 - 2/25/46) ABC, Mon, 10 pm

8 **Jimmy Grier and His Orchestra** (1936, 3/40) Mut, Syn, MacGregor transcriptions)

Jimmy Grier Orchestra (with Donald Novis; from Coconut Grove, Hotel Ambassador, Los Angeles (1932-33)

1 **Jimmy Grier's Orchestra** (1935) Syn

1 **Jimmy Jones** (10/20/36) WMBQ

Jimmy Joy Orchestra Remotes: (1940) 5/16; 5/20; 5/31; all from Casino Gardens, Ocean Park, CA

Jimmy Kemper (1937) NBC, Wed, 15m
(3/13/39 - 5/22/39) Bl, Mon, 15m, 7:30 pm

2 **Jimmy Lunceford and His Band** (Lang-Worth transcriptions)

1 **Jimmy Lunceford and His Orchestra** (6/12/40)

2 **Jimmy Lytell and His Delta Eight** (Thesaurus transcriptions)

Jimmy Lytell Orchestra
(7/7/41 - 8/27/41) NBC, Wed, 15m, 1 pm
(7/8/41 - 8/26/41) (Get Goin') Bl, Tue, 7:30 pm

1 **Jimmy McDaniels vs. Ralph Zanelli** (9/8/44) Mut

1 **Jimmy McHugh** (10/2/63)

4 **Jimmy Palmer and His Orchestra** (12/31/59 - 1/24/62) CBS

Jimmy Powers (12/27/54 - 58+) NBC, 5t, 10m

1 **Jimmy Rushing** (1/3/64)

7 **Jimmy Wakely** (8/29/53 - 56+) Bristol-Myers, CBS, Sat (World, MacGregor transcriptions)

2 **Jimmy Wakely and His Rodeo Boys** (World transcriptions)

2 **Jimmy Wakely and The Sunshine Girls** (World, MacGregor transcriptions)

1 **Jimmy Walker**

1 **Jimmy Walsh and His Orchestra** (4/5/40) Mut - Don Lee

1 **Jingle Bell's Happiest Christmas** (Syn)

Jingo (see Breezin' Along)

14 **Jive Patrol** (1952) Coast Guard, Syn

Jo And Vi (see Mr. and Mrs.)

1 **Jo Stafford Show, The** (11/9/45 - 12/25/45) (also with Lawrence Brooks) CBS, Tue, 10 pm
(11/11/48 - 5/5/49) Revere Cameras, ABC, Thu, 15m, 8:30 pm; 25m, 9:30 pm as of 1/6/49 (see also Chesterfield Supper Club)
(1/19/53 - 6/12/53) CBS, 5t, 15m, 7:30 pm

3 **Joachim Von Ribbentrop** (10/24/39, 4/27/40, 6/10/40) Germany

Joan and Kermit (with Olan Soule and Fran Carlon) (4/24/38 - 7/10/38) CBS, Sun, 7 pm

Joan and The Escorts (4/29/36 - 9/21/36) NBC, various days, 15m, 12 noon

Joan Benoit Show, The (6/1/41 - 7/20/41) NBC, Sun, 15m, 4 pm

2 **Joan Brooks Show, The** (1944) CBS, 15m, 11 pm

Joan Brooks, The Girl With The Voice You Won't Forget (see The Joan Brooks Show)

15 **Joan Davis** (7/8/43 - 8/28/50)
7/8/43 - 6/28/45 (see Sealtest Village Store)
9/3/45 - 5/27/46; 9/30/46 - 6/23/47 (Joanie's Tea Room), Swan, CBS, Mon, 8:30 pm
10/4/47 - 7/3/48, Sus, CBS, Sat, 9 pm
7/4/49 - 8/22/49 (Leave It To Joan), CBS, Mon, 9 pm (half of summer replacement of Lux)
9/9/49 - 3/3/50 (Leave It To Joan), Roi-Tan, CBS, Fri, 9 pm
7/3/50 - 8/28/50, CBS, Mon, 10 pm (summer replacement for My Friend Irma)

Joan Davis Show, The (see Joan Davis)

Joan Davis Time (see Joan Davis)

Joan Edwards Show, The (3/5/41 - 12/3/54) CBS
3/5/41 - 4/30/41, Wed, 15m, 10:30 pm
also 3/7/41 - 5/2/41, Fri, 15m, 10:30 pm
5/4/41 - 5/25/41, Sun, 15m, 7:15 pm
3/3/52 - 12/3/54, CBS, 5t,

1 **Joan Fairfax and Her All Girl Orchestra** (1964) CBS

Joan Marrow (1933 - 6/7/34) Mar-O-Oil, 2t, 15m, 1:15 pm

Jobs After Victory (8/11/45 - 12/15/45) ABC, Sat, 15m, 7 pm

8 **Jobs For America** (1938) Syn

Jobs For Defense (3/22/41 - 5/17/41) CBS, Sat, 15m, 12:45 pm

Jobs For Tomorrow (1/6/45 - 3/24/45) CBS, Sat, 15m, 3:45 pm

Joe Allen (7/14/41 - 10/6/41) CBS, Mon, 15m, 9:30 am

1 **Joe and Cynthia** (Syn)

Joe and Ethel Turp (with Block and Sully in 1941; with Jackson Beck and Patsy Campbell during 1943)
(1941) (Syn)
(1/4/43 - 9/24/43) CBS, 15m
1/4/43 - 2/21/43, 3t, 11 am
2/15/43 - 4/16/43, 3t - 5t, 4:30 pm
4/19/43 - 9/24/43, 5t, 3:15 pm

Joe and Mabel (with Ted De Corsia and Ann Thomas) (2/13/41 - 9/27/42) NBC
2/13/41 - 2/20/41, Thu, 10:30 pm
3/2/41 - 10/19/41, Sun
4/5/42 - 9/27/42, Sun, 10:30 pm

Joe Cook Show, The (see Shell Chateau)

1 **Joe D'Amica, The Eastern Ranger** (11/6/36) WCNW

Joe DiMaggio Show, The (9/17/49 - 3/18/50) M & M, CBS, Sat, 10:30 am

2 **Joe E. Brown Show, The** (with Harry Sosnik's Orchestra) (10/8/38 - 9/28/39) Post Toasties, CBS, Sat, 7:30 pm; Thu, 7:30 pm as of 4/6/39

1 **Joe E. Howard** (Thesaurus transcription)

2 **Joe Emerson's Hymntime** (12/24/51 - 5/28/54) General Mills, ABC, 5t, 15m, 3 pm, also syndicated

1 **Joe Franklin Show, The** (3/16/69) WOR

Joe Gallichio Orchestra (see Joseph Gallichio)

Joe Hasel (1/13/48 - 3/16/51) ABC, 5t, 15m, 6 pm
(10/26/53 - 12/31/54) NBC, 5t, 15m, 11:15 pm

1 **Joe Louis Interview** (3/8/49) Mut

2 **Joe Louis vs. Billy Conn** (6/18/41, 6/19/41) Mut

1 **Joe Louis vs. Billy Conn Weigh-In** (1941) Mut

1 **Joe Louis vs. Paolino Uzcudun Interviews** (12/13/35) WMCA

2 **Joe Marsala** (World transcriptions)

Joe McDoaks (with George O'Hanlon, Marcie McGuire and Clifton Young) NBC

Joe Mooney (ABC) 15m

1 **Joe Mooney Quartette, The** (11/4/46) ABC

Joe Palooka (with Ted Bergman) (4/12/32 - 8/16/32) Heinz, CBS, 2t, 15m

6 **Joe Penner Show, The** (10/8/33 - 4/25/40)
10/8/33 - 7/1/34 (Baker's Broadcast), Fleischmann, Bl, Sun, 7:30 pm
10/7/34 - 6/30/35 (Baker's Broadcast) Fleischmann, Bl, Sun, 7:30 pm
1935 - 36 (see Believe It Or Not)
10/4/36 - 6/27/37; 10/3/37 - 6/26/38 (Park Avenue Penners) Cocomalt, CBS, Sun, 6 pm
10/6/38 - 3/30/39, Huskies, CBS, Thu, 7:30 pm
10/5/39 - 4/25/40 (Tip Top Show), Ward Baking, Bl, Thu, 8:30 pm

Joe Penner, The Breadwinner (see The Joe Penner Show)

Joe Powers Of Oakville
(8/26/46 - 12/13/46) CBS, 5t, 10 am

1 **Joe Pyne Show, The** (1964 - 65)

18 **Joe Reichman and His Orchestra**
(6/7/44) NBC, Standard, Lang-Worth transcriptions

5 **Joe Reichman and His Orchestra ("The Pagliacci Of The Piano")** (1964) CBS, Standard transcriptions

1 **Joe Reichman At The Piano (with Rhythm Accompaniment)** (Standard transcription)

2 **Joe Reichman At The Piano** (Standard transcriptions)

Joe Rines Dress Rehearsal (also with Mabel Albertson) (11/1/36 - 4/25/37) Iodent, Bl, Sun, 11:30 am

3 **Joe Schirmer Trio** (Standard transcriptions)

Joe Venuti (The Venutians)
(8/14/35 - 9/25/35) Bl, Wed, 10 pm

4 **Joe Venuti and The Blue Five** (SESAC transcriptions)

Joe White (3/21/34 - 1/16/35) Bl, Wed, 15m, 3 pm

1 **Joey and Chuck** (Thesaurus transcription)

Joey Kearns Orchestra (8/6/40 - 9/24/40) CBS, Tue, 15m, 7:15 pm
(1/21/47 - 3/27/47) CBS, 2t, 4:30 pm

John Agnew Orchestra
(4/4/39 - 10/10/39) Mut, Tue, 15m, 2:15 pm (not in New York)
(5/11/40 - 6/22/40) Mut, Sat, 15m, 11:15 am

John Allen Wolfe (1942)

2 **John Anderson** (7/17/80, 11/30/80) ABC-TV, CBS-TV

John B. Hughes (7/14/41 - 12/15/43) Aspertine, Mut

John B. Kennedy (11/28/33 - 3/1/51)
11/28/33 - 39, NBC
also 5/13/36 - 8/26/36 (While There's Life) Bl, Wed, 15m, 10:15 pm
1939 - 40, Mut 1942 - 43, Barbasol, CBS
1942 - 44, Bl
1945 - 3/10/46, Harvel Watch, Bl/ABC
1948 - 49, Doubleday, Mut, Sun
9/18/50 - 3/1/51, ABC, 4t (Mon - Thu), 10:30 pm

John Baker (see Steel Horizons)

John Barclay's Community Sing
(5/10/36 - 8/30/36) CBS, Sun, 9:30 pm

John Barrymore (9/6/37 - 9/13/37) Bl, Mon, 60m, 9:30 pm

John Barrymore and Shakespeare (see Streamlined Shakespeare)

3 **John Cameron Swayze News**
(4/1/57 - 5/1/53) NBC

15 **John Charles Thomas** (Westinghouse Program) (also with Ken Darby Singers) (1/10/43 - 6/30/46) Westinghouse, NBC, Sun, 2:30 pm

John Conte Show, The (also with John Magnante Trio)
(4/5/53 - 11/20/53) ABC, 5t, 45m, 5:15pm
(6/19/54 - 4/30/55) NBC, Sat, 11:30 am

1 **John Cudahy** (8/26/40) Mut

John Derr (1/24/54 - 9/19/54) CBS, Sun, 15m, 10:45 pm

1 **John Duffy At The Organ** (MacGregor transcription)

1 **John F. Kennedy Press Conference** (1/2/60)

1 **John Fitzgerald Kennedy...As We Remember Him**

1 **John Foster Dulles** (10/28/48) ABC

1 **John Gambling's Gym Classes** (12/21/37) WOR

John Gart Trio (5/17/43 - 9/10/43) CBS, 5t, 15m, 3:30 pm
(1/4/46 - 3/15/46) Mut, Fri, 15m, 10:15 pm

1 **John Glenn Flight** (2/20/62) pool feed

1 **John Glenn Press Conference** (2/23/62) CBS

1 **John Glenn Souvenir Album** (2/20/62)

John Gunther (1/15/43 - 4/14/44) General Mills, Bl, Fri, 10m

John Gurney (Metropolitan Moods)
(1/17/40 - 2/11/40) Bl, Sun, 1:30 pm

1 **John Hagelin** (10/31/92)

John Henry, Black River Giant
(1/15/33 - 9/24/33) CBS, 2t (Sun & Thu), 15m; Sunday only as of 7/16/33

John Higgins (1941) Bl, 5t, 15m

6 **John J. Anthony** (3/19/45 - 57) Mut (also see The Goodwill Hour; 1936 - 44)
3/19/45 - 12/27/46, Carter, 5t, 15m
12/9/51 - 6/29/52; 10/5/52 - 1/4/53, Sterling, Mut, Sun, 9:30 pm 1957, 5t, 15m

John J. Anthony Program, The (see John J. Anthony)

1 **John Kirby Orchestra** (also called Flow Gently, Sweet Rhythm) with Maxine Sullivan and Golden Gate Quartet)
(4/7/40 - 1/12/41) CBS. Sun
4/7/40 - 9/1/40, 5:30 pm
9/29/40 - 1/12/41, 2:30 pm

1 **John L. Lewis Speech** (10/25/40) CBS

1 **John Lennon 1940-1980** (12/80) ABC-TV

1 **John Lennon, The Man and His Music** (12/9/80) NBC-TV

John Martin Story Program
(1933 - 4/22/35) NBC, Mon, 15m

John McVane (1945 - 46) NBC

John Metcalf's Choir Loft (1938 - 41) Mut, 5t, 15m (often not in New York)

John Nesbitt (see The Passing Parade)

John O'Donnell

1 **John Paul Dixon** (4/41) Mut

1 **John Phillip Sousa Memorial Program** (10/22/38) Mut

John R. Tunis (11/21/35 - 1/23/36) Bl, Thu, 15m, 6:15 pm

John Stanley (1941 - 1942) Douglas Shoes, Mut

11 **John Steele** (2/21/38 - 4/9/40) Mut

6 **John Steele, Adventurer** (with Don Douglas) (4/26/49 - 7/16/56) Sus, Mut (on various days and times; New York often broadcast on days different than dates for available shows; some dates follow:)
4/26/49 - 10/4/49, Tue, 9 pm
12/25/49 - 3/26/50, Sun, 2:30 pm
6/11/50 - 7/30/50, Sun, 9:30 pm
9/17/50 - 10/8/50, Sun, 2:30 pm
10/17/50 - 1/2/51, Tue, 9 pm
3/6/51 - 1/1/52, Tue, 9 pm
1/10/53 - 10/1/53, Thu, 8:30 pm
9/28/54 - 10/11/55, Tue, 8:30 pm
10/17/55 - 7/16/56, Mon

16 **John T. Flynn** (10/53) Syn

1 **John Thompson** (5/4/45) Mut

1 **John W. Vandercook** (10/21/40 - 46) NBC
10/21/40 - 41, Remington
1941 - 46 (News Of The World), Alka-Seltzer

John W. Vandercook Air Age News Of The Day (Syn), 5m

John W. Vandercook News Of The World (see John W. Vandercook)

John Wingate

1 **John Wittaker** (9/24/38)

John Wyatt Sr. Stories

5 **John's Other Wife** (9/14/36 - 3/20/42) 5t, 15m
9/14/36 - 3/22/40, American Home Products, NBC
3/25/40 - 3/20/42, American Home Products, Bl

Johnny and His Foursome (with Johnny Green) (4/24/35 - 10/1/35) Philip Morris, CBS, Wed, 15m, 8 pm

Johnny Augustine's Music (with Patti Chapin) (8/11/35 - 10/25/35) CBS, Sun, 2 pm

1 **Johnny Bond and His Red River Boys** (Standard transcription)

2 **Johnny Bond and His Red River Valley Boys** (Standard transcriptions)

1 **Johnny Cash Show, The** (12/59) Syn

Johnny Cuba (with Gerald Mohr)
(3/25/57 - 6/10/57) ABC, Mon, 7:30 pm

1 **Johnny Desmond** (3/12/55 - 9/17/55) Mut, Sat, 15m, 12:15 pm, also Thesaurus transcription

1 **Johnny Desmond's Follies** (also with Margaret Whiting who took over on 7/23/46) (Philip Morris)
(1/22/46 - 9/3/46) NBC, Tue, 8 pm

1 **Johnny Desmond Goes To College** (also with Margaret Whiting)
(11/13/50 - 3/26/51) ABC, Mon, 9:30 pm

1 **Johnny Desmond With Art Van Damme Quintet** (Thesaurus transcription)

1 **Johnny Desmond With Hugo Winterhalter's Orchestra** (Thesaurus transcription)

1 **Johnny Desmond With Manhattan Nighthawks** (Thesaurus transcription)

1 **Johnny Desmond With The Manhattan Nighthawks** (Thesaurus transcription)

2 **Johnny Fletcher** (5/30/48 - 11/27/48) NBC, Sun, also syndicated
5/30/48 - 9/5/48 (with Bill Goodwin), Sus, ABC, Sun, 7:30 pm (summer replacement for The Clock)
9/11/48 - 11/27/48, ABC, Sat, 8 pm

Johnny Fletcher Mystery (see Johnny Fletcher)

Johnny Fletcher Show, The (see Johnny Fletcher)

Johnny Grant (AFRS)

1 **Johnny Greco vs. Bobby Ruffin** (2/3/45) Mut

2 **Johnny Green and His Orchestra** (World transcriptions)

Johnny Green Orchestra (also see Breezin' Along; In The Modern Manner; Socony Sketch book)
(11/8/39 - 7/28/40) Philip Morris, Bl, Wed; Sun, 8:30 pm as of 5/5/40
4/10 - 5/1 (Swing-Go as of 4/17/40)

1 **Johnny Guarnieri** (Thesaurus transcription)

2 **Johnny Guarnieri Quintet** (Thesaurus transcription)

1 **Johnny Hamilton Quintet and The Tony Scott Quartet, The** (1954) NBC

Johnny Hart In Hollywood
(10/3/32 - 1/13/33) Flit and Mistol, Bl, 15m, 5t, 6:15 pm

2 **Johnny Horton and The Four B's** (SESAC transcriptions)

Johnny Lee Willis (1945) 5m

4 **Johnny Long and His Orchestra** (8/15/58, 8/21/58) CBS, World transcriptions

1 **Johnny Long and His Orchestra With Dick Robertson** (World transcription)

Johnny Long Show, The (with Helen and Johnny Long)
(1939) NBC
(8/10/40 - 9/21/40) NBC, Sat, 3:30 pm; Bl; as of 8/31/41
(1/11/41 - 5/17/41) Bl, Sat, 6 pm
(6/28/41 - 9/27/41) Bl, Sat, 2 pm

Johnny Lujack Of Notre Dame (with Lujack and Ed Prentiss)
(6/6/49 - 9/2/49) ABC. alternating 3t/2t, 15m, 5:30 pm (summer replacement for Jack Armstrong)

Johnny Mack Brown Show, The (also called Under Western Skies)
(6/30/39 - 10/6/39) CBS, Fri, 8 pm

2 **Johnny Madero, Pier 23** (with Jack Webb) (4/24/47 - 9/4/47) Mut, Thu

Johnny Marvin (1932 - 5/17/35) NBC, 5t, 15m

Johnny Mercer (1947) Chesterfield, Thu

2 **Johnny Mercer Show, The**
(5/5/53) Audition
(6/8/53 - 9/25/53) CBS, 5t, 15m, 7:30 pm; 7:15 pm as of 6/29/53

16 **Johnny Mercer's Music Shop**
(6/22/43 - 9/14/43) Pepsodent, NBC, Tue, 10 pm (summer replacement for Bob Hope)
(6/12/44 - 12/8/44) (with Jo Stafford) Chesterfield, NBC, 5t, 15m

2 **Johnny Mercer, With Orchestra Conducted By Paul Weston** (Capitol transcriptions)

1 **Johnny Messner and His Music** (Associated transcription)

1 **Johnny Messner and His Music Box Band** (10/10/38) NBC

3 **Johnny Messner and His Orchestra**
(1940) film sound track
(12/7/41) Mut, Associated transcription

Johnny Morgan Show, The
(11/8/43 - 12/20/43) Bl, Mon, 25m, 7:05 pm
(7/10/44 - 3/12/45) Ballantine Beer, CBS, Mon, 10:30 pm
(7/4/46 - 8/29/46) NBC, Thu, 7:30 pm

3 **Johnny Mulay and His Orchestra** (5/10/70, 12/7/70, 12/13/70) CBS

2 **Johnny Murphy and His Orchestra** (7/27/70, 8/3/70) CBS

1 **Johnny Nighthawk** (with Howard Duff) TV audio

Johnny Olsen Show (6/29/46 - 5/4/57)
6/29/46 - 9/14/46 (Johnny Olsen's Rumpus Room) ABC, Sat, 1:30pm
3/28/49 - 10/21/49, Mut, 5t
also 5/13/49 - 10/24/49 (Johnny Olsen's Get-together) ABC, Sat, 10 am
7/24/50 - 7/20/51 (Johnny Olsen's Luncheon Cub), ABC, 5t, 12 noon
1/4/54 - 56, Mut, 5t, 25m
1956 - 5/4/57, Mut, Sat, 15m

1 **Johnny Presents** (2/13/37 - 1/15/46, 1959) Philip Morris; this title used for several programs sponsored by Philip Morris; also see Johnny Green
2/13/37 - 9/24/38, CBS, Sat, 8:30 pm (Russ Morgan Orchestra)
10/1/38 - 6/24/39, CBS, Sat, 8 pm (Johnny Green and Ray Bloch started 1/28/39 replacing Russ Morgan)
6/30/39 - 9/8/39 (Johnny Presents Dramatized Short Stories), CBS, Fri, 8:30 pm
9/15/39 - 3/14/41, CBS, Fri, 9 pm

Johnny Presents (continued)
also 1/2/34 - 2/9/37; 2/16/38 - 9/1/42 (with Leo Reisman; with Russ Morgan Orchestra as of 2/16/38; then Johnny Green Orchestra on 1/31/39; Ray Bloch as of 8/6/41; with Tallulah Bankhead for a while as of 2/3/42) (had a segment called The Perfect Crime as of 11/22/38), Philip Morris, NBC, Tue, 8 pm
9/8/42 - 9/4/45, NBC, Tue, 8 pm (see Ginny Simms)
9/11/45 - 1/15/46 (with Barry Wood), NBC, Tue, 8 pm

1 **Johnny Smith Quartet, The** (8/20/54) NBC

Johnny Thompson (9/29/45 - 3/28/48) ABC
9/29/45 - 11/10/45 (also with Ilene Woods) Sat, 10:30 am
11/18/45 - 4/7/46 (also with Ilene Woods), Sun, 3:30 pm
4/14/46 - 5/19/46, Sun, 15m, 3:45 pm
6/1/46 - 9/14/46 (It's Harvel Music Time) Harvel, Sat, 15m, 11:30am
9/15/46 - 5/18/47, Harvel (until 3/9/47), Sun, 15m, 1 pm
10/4/47 - 12/6/47, ABC, Sat, 15m, 12 noon
12/7/47 - 3/28/48, ABC, Sun, 15m, 3:15 pm

Johnny's Front Porch (6/16/46 - 8/11/46) CBS, Sun, 5:30 pm (not in New York)

Johnson Family Singers, The
(6/25/45 - 8/28/45) CBS, 5t, 15m, 4:45 pm

25 **Johnson Family, The** (with Jimmy Scribner) (1936 - 9/22/49) occasionally sponsored, Mut, 5t, 15m (on most years); also syndicated in the 1950s and 60s; various dates and times also
(2/18/52 - 9/12/52) CBS, 4 pm

10 **Johnson Wax Program, The**
(7/4/39 - 9/22/42) NBC

1 **Johnson Wax Show** (1934) audition

5 **Join The Navy** (Syn)

1 **Joint Session Of Congress To Honor General Eisenhower** (6/18/45) Mut

Jolly Bill and Jane (with William J. Steinke and Muriel Harbater) (4/28 - 35) Cream Of Wheat, Bl, 5t, 15m

Jolly Coburn Orchestra (2/25/3 - 5/5/35) Sparton, Bl, Sun, 4 pm, also known as The Spartan Triolians

3 **Jolson Sings Again** (1948) Air trailers, film sound track

1 **Jolson Song Parade, The** (1946) Air trailer

2 **Jolson Story, The** (1946) Air trailer, film sound track

1 **Jonah Jones and His Orchestra** (9/23/70) CBS

1 **Jonah Jones and His Quartet** (CBS)

1 **Jonah Jones Orchestra** (World transcription)

Jonathan Brixton's Murder Cases (with Michael Raffetto) (1945) Mut; see Attorney For The Defense)

Jonathan Kegg (see A Life In Your Hands)

Jonathan Trimble, Esq. (with Donald Crisp) (5/4/46 - 9/7/46) Mut, Sat, 9:30 pm

Jones And I (with Sammie Hill and Scott Farnsworth)
(9/6/41 - 4/4/42) CBS, Sat, 10 am
(9/30/45 - 3/24/46) ABC, Sun, 4:30 pm; 5 pm as of 12/2/45

Jones and Hare (see The Happiness Boys)

José Betencourt (1/13/47 - 3/28/47) NBC, 5t, 15m, 9:45 am

José Manzanares and His South Americans (12/1/35 - 4/12/36) Ford, CBS, Sun, 2:30 pm

1 **José Moran and His Orchestra** (8/14/45) Mut

José Remato (5/18/41 -7/6/41) Mut, Sun, 15m, 12:30 pm

Josef Marais (see African Trek)

Joseph C. Harsch (1944) B.F. Goodrich
(9/19/48 - 49) CBS, Sun

Joseph Enos (NBC)

Joseph Gallichio Orchestra
(1/23/32 - 1/25/33) (with Sara Ann McCabe) Bl, Wed, 5 pm
(5/31/38 - 8/11/38), NBC, Sat, 3:30 pm
(4/13/41 - 11/30/40) Bl, Sat, 11:30 am; 10:30 am as of 8/10/40

1 **Joseph In America** (Syn)

1 **Joseph Marais and Miranda** (12/7/46) Mut

Josephine Gibson (1929 - 3/20/36) Heinz, 15m
1929 - 6/18/31, Bl, 2t
1/26/34 - 4/13/34, Bl, 3t, 10 am
10/7/35 - 3/20/36, CBS, 3t, 10 am

Josh Higgins Of Finchville (with Joe DuMond) (11/27/40 - 5/2/41) Bl, 5t, 15m, 10 am; 6t as of 3/31/41; also on regionally from 1938 - 8/4/39

1 **Journalists Remember The J. F. K. Assassination** (11/29/93) C-SPAN

1 **Journey Of The Magi, The** (12/24/47) Mut

Journey To The Center Of The Earth (Syndicated)

1 **Journey To The Moon - The Original Version**

Journeys (Audio Portrait Of America) 60m

Joy Boys, The (Ed Walker and Willard Scott) (WRC, Washington, D. C.)

20 **Joyce Jordan, M.D.** (originally Joyce Jordan, Girl Intern)
(12/18/36, 5/30/38 - 7/1/55) 5t, 15m
5/30/38 - 5/26/39, Calox Tooth Powder, CBS, 9/30 am
7/3/39 - 42, General Foods; includes La France, Satina and Minute Tapioca, CBS
1942 - 3/23/45, General Mills, CBS, 2 pm
3/26/45 - 10/8/48, Dreft, NBC (developed into A Brighter Day)
12/10/51 - 4/11/52, Lever Brothers, ABC
1/3/55 - 7/1/55, Sus, NBC, 10:15 am

Juan Arvizu (5/5/41 - 42) CBS, various days, 15m

10 **Jubalaires, The** (5/29/44 - 7/7/44) CBS, 5t, 15m, 3:45 pm
(7/10/44 - 8/4/44) CBS, 5t, 15m, 3:15 pm, also Standard, World transcriptions

108 **Jubilee** (AFRS) (10/9/42 - 50)

1 **Jubilee Time** (1946)

1 **Judge, The** (with John Dehner and Larry Dobkin) (6/5/52 - 6/26/52) CBS, Thu, 9:30 pm

1 **Judgement At Nuremberg** (10/1/46) BBC/Mut

Judith Arlen (7/10/39 - 9/18/39) CBS, Mon, 15m, 6:45 pm
(10/10/39 - 11/21/39) CBS, Tue, 15m, 10:30 pm

3 **Judy and Jane** (2/8/32 - 4/26/35) Folgers, 5t, 15m
2/8/32 - 6/17/32, CBS - Midwest
9/26/32 - 4/28/33; 9/17/33 - 4/27/34; 10/15/35 - 4/26/35, NBC-Midwest
(8/18/41 - 8/14/42) Mut, 5t, 15m
(1953 - 1954), also syndicated

Judy and Lanny (1/16/39 - 2/16/39) Bl, Mon, 15m, 1:45 pm

2 **Judy Canova Monologs** (World transcriptions)

3 **Judy Canova Monologs and Recipes** (World transcriptions)

14 **Judy Canova Show, The** (7/6/43 - 5/28/53)
7/6/43 - 6/27/44 (Rancho Canova), Colgate,CBS, Tue, 8:30 pm
1/6/45 - 6/30/45; 9/1/45 - 6/29/46; 8/31/46 - 6/28/47; 8/30/47 - 6/26/48; 10/2/48 - 6/25/49; 10/1/49 - 7/1/50; 10/7/50 - 6/30/51, Colgate, NBC, 5t, 10 pm; 9:30 pm from 10/4/47 - 6/25/49
12/29/51 - 7/5/52, Sus, NBC, Sat, 9 pm
10/23/52 - 5/28/53, Multi, NBC, Thu, 10 pm

5 **Judy Garland Show, The** (10/30/52) CBS
(1963) CBS-TV

Judy Lang (2/17/46 - 4/7/46) Mut, Sun, 15m, 2:45 pm

1 **Judy Sings** (1964) CBS-TV

Judy, Jill and Johnny (with Johnny Desmond) (10/28/46 - 1/4/47) Junior Miss Fashions, Mut, Sat, 12 noon

1 **Juke Box Saturday Night** (3/19/83) WNET-TV

Jukebox Jury (with Peter Potter)
(5/20/54 - 10/6/56)
5/20/54 - 8/22/54, Toni, CBS, Sun, 7:30 pm
10/16/54 - 4/23/55, CBS, Sat, 8:30 pm
5/29/55 - 9/25/55, CBS, Sun, 7 pm
10/8/55 - 10/6/56, ABC, Sat, 60m, 7 pm

Jukebox USA (AFRS)

6 **Jules Herman and His Orchestra**
(8/24/69 - 9/27/70) CBS

Julia Sanderson (see Let's Be Charming)

Julio Martinez Oyanguren
(12/18/38 - 2/9/41) NBC, 15m
12/18/38 - 11/30/40, Sun
also 6/25/40 - 7/16/40, Tue, 9:45 am
also 7/27/40 - 11/2/40, Sat, 12:15 pm
1/19/41 - 2/9/41, Sun, 3:30 pm

1 **Julius La Rosa** (Syn)

Julius La Rosa Show, The (also with Russ Case Orchestra)
(11/9/53 - 5/31/54) CBS, 3t, 10m, 7:35 pm; Mon, 15m, 7:30 pm as of 2/15/54

Julliard School Concert
(11/7/46 - 12/26/46) CBS, Thu, 11:30 pm

1 **Julliard School Of Music Concert** (11/28/46) CBS

1 **Jumbo** (1962) film sound track

1 **Jumbo Fire Chief Program, The** (with Jimmy Durante) (10/29/35 - 4/3/36) Texaco, NBC, Tue, 9:30 pm

33 **Jump-Jump Of Holiday House** (1948) Syn

7 **Jumpin' Jacks** (Thesaurus transcriptions)

5 **Jumpin' Jacks, The** (Thesaurus transcriptions)

1 **Junction Of Russian and American Forces** (4/27/45) CBS

3 **June Christy** (Thesaurus transcriptions)

1 **June Christy With The Johnny Guarnieri Quinte** (Thesaurus transcription)

1 **June Dairy Month** (6/53) Syn

June Hynd's Guest Book
(12/28/37 - 5/30/40) 15m
12/28/37 - 10/20/38 (Let's Talk It Over) (with Alma Kitchell, June Hynd and Lisa Sergio), Bl, 3t (Tue - Thu), 2:15 pm
10/17/38 - 10/6/39 (Let's Talk It Over) NBC, 3t, 1:15 pm
10/26/39 - 5/30/40 (Let's Talk It Over) NBC, Thu, 1:30pm
also 10/12/39 - 4/11/40, Sus, NBC, Thu, 6 pm

1 **June Valli With Art Van Damme Quintet** (Thesaurus transcription)

1 **Jungle Jazz** (1930) Synchro-disc

482 **Jungle Jim** (with Matt Crowley)
(11/2/35 - 8/1/54) (Syn) (961 episodes broadcast within one week prior to the Sunday comic page

1 **Jungle School** (1951) U.N. Radio

1 **Junior Achievement Award Program** (10/30/47) CBS

1 **Junior Brains Trust** (6/6/44) BBC/Mut

1 **Junior Celebrities** (4/17/50) Mut

Junior G-Men (see True Adventures Of Junior G-Men)

Junior Junction (6/22/46 - 7/5/52) Sus, ABC, Sat

5 **Junior Miss** (with Shirley Temple)
(3/4/42 - 8/26/42) CBS, Wed, 9 pm
(5/8/48 - 7/1/54) CBS
5/8/48 - 12/30/50, Lever Brothers, Sat, 11:30 am
10/2/52 - 12/25/52, Thu, 8:30 pm
12/29/52 - 6/5/53, Sus, 5t, 15m, 7:15 pm
6/7/53 - 9/20/53 (with Barbara Whiting), Sun, 8 pm
9/28/53 - 11/7/53, 3t, 15m, 7:30 pm
11/12/53 - 7/1/54, Sus, Thu, 30m, 8:30 pm

Junior Newscaster (with Georgie Ward) (12/28/42 - 4/2/43) Mut, 5t, 15m,5:30 pm

Junior Nurse Corps (with Sunda Love) (2/17/36 - 3/25/38) 15m
2/17/36 - 5/15/36, Swift, CBS, 3t
10/12/36 - 38, Sunbrite Cleaner, 15m
10/12/36 - 4/23/37, CBS, 3t, 5 pm
9/27/37 - 3/25/38, Bl, 5t, 5 pm

Junior Town Meeting (Syn)

1 **Just Between Ourselves** (with Brenda Adams) (11/29/39) Mut

4 **Just Between Us** (with Pat Bames) (5/2/37 - 7/25/37) Rabin Cosmetics, Mut, Sun, 15m, 11:15 pm, also AFRS origination with Knox Manning

1 **Just Call Me Maestro** (7/15/79) PBS-TV

Just Easy (see Jack Gregson)

5 **Just Entertainment** (with Jack Fulton and Carl Hohengarten Orchestra)
(3/21/38 - 7/1/38) Wrigley, CBS, 5t, 15m, 7 pm
also 1941, Wrigley
also (8/21/45 - 9/25/45) Wrigley, CBS, Tue, 10 pm
also (7/9/56 - 1959+) Wrigley, CBS, 5t, 15m; (with Pat Buttram)

1 **Just Five Lines** (12/23/42 - 2/24/43) Mut, Wed, 8:30 pm
(7/29/43 - 9/23/43) Mut, Thu, 8:30 pm

Just For You (with Eddy Howard) (from Chicago) (1954) NBC, 60m

8 **Just Jazz** (1949, 5/26/71, 6/71) AFRS, also PBS-TV

Just Mart (9/1/40 - 9/22/40) Mut, Sun, 15m, 1:15 pm

Just Neighbors (with Betty Caine) (1938) NBC

1 **Just Outside Hollywood** (c. 1948) with Hanley Stafford, Veronica Lake and Frank Nelson, audition

12 **Just Plain Bill** (with Arthur Hughes)
(9/19/32 - 8/11/55) 15m, 5t
1/16/33 - 6/12/36, Kolynos, CBS (Network)
9/14/36 - 3/25/54, Anacin/Kolynos/Bi-So-Dol, NBC until 3/18/40; Bl from 3/25/40 - 7/31/42; NBC from 9/14/42-3/25/54
9/27/54 - 8/11/55, Alka-Seltzer, NBC, 5 pm

1 **Just Relax** (1/16/46) CBS

Just Willie (with Dave Elman and Arthur Fields) (7/20/36 - 9/21/36) Bl, Mon, 15m, 8 pm

Justice Triumphs (see Did Justice Triumph?)

1 **Justice Hugo Black** (10/1/37) Mut

1 **Justice Oliver Wendell Holmes Memorial Birthday Program** (3/3/36) WEAF

3 **Juvenile Jury** (with Jack Barry)
(5/11/46 - 2/15/53) started as local show in New York over WOR for 5 weeks
6/15/46 - 9/14/46, Sus, Mut, Sat, 8:30 pm
12/8/46 - 6/1/47; 9/7/47 - 6/27/48; 10/3/48 - 6/26/49; 10/2/49 - 6/25/50; 10/8/50 - 4/1/51, Gaines, Mut, Sun
9/28/52 - 2/15/53, Sus, NBC, Sun, 6:30 pm

1 **KDKA School Of The Air, The** (1/2/47) KDKA

1 **KFI Calling** (8/18/52) KFI

1 **KFI 50th Anniversary Show** (4/16/72) KFI

3 **KIRO Mystery Playhouse, The** (1993, 1994) KIRO

1 **KITO San Bernadino, Inaugural Broadcast** (11/9/47) KITO

1 **KLX Kitchen** (KLX)

1 **KOIN - B. M. I. Program** (8/11/40) KOIN

5 **Kai Winding and His Sextet** (5/23/69 - 6/20/69) CBS

1 **Kaiser '53 Song, The** (1953) Syn

2 **Kaiser - Frazer News** (9/15/47, 9/16/47) WFBR

Kaiser Traveler, The (see Burl Ives)

1 **Kaleidoscope** (1/31/53 - 9/12/53) NBC, Sat, 3 hours, 2 pm, also 1968 NET-TV

32 **Kaltenborn Edits The News** (1/27/39 - 5/27/41) CBS, NBC, Pure Oil

Kaltenmeyer's Kindergarten (with Bruce Kamman) (10/14/32 - 9/14/40)
10/14/32 - 12/29/34, Sus, WMAQ, Chicago; NBC from 12/16/33, various days
1/5/35 - 12/25/37, Quaker, NBC, Sat, 5:30 pm
1/1/38 - 9/14/40, Sus, NBC, Sat, 6 pm; 7 pm as of 5/4/40; 15m as of 6/1/40

1 **Kangaroo, The** (1952) Syn

1 **Karl Zomar's Scrapbook** (10/30/42) Mut

1 **Kate Hopkins, Angel Of Mercy** (with Margaret MacDonald)
(10/7/40 - 4/3/42) Maxwell House, CBS, 5t, 15m; syndicated in 1939

1 **Kate Smith Calls** (8/8/49 - 1/30/50) ABC, Mon, 60m, 9 pm

1 **Kate Smith Christmas Salute To Hopitalized Children** (12/14/49) WOR

Kate Smith and Her Swanee Music (CBS) (9/14/31 - 8/22/35)
9/14/31 - 11/28/31, La Palina Cigars, 4t (Mon, Wed, Thu, Sat), 15m, 8:30 pm
12/1/31 - 6/21/32, La Palina Cigars, 4t (Mon - Thu), 15m
6/6/32 - 12/28/32, 3t (Mon - Wed), 15m
1/3/33 - 10/31/33, La Palina Cigars, 3t (Tue - Thu), 15m, 8:30 pm; Sus, Mon - Wed as of 9/18/33
7/16/34 - 9/7/34, CBS, 3t (Mon, Thu, Fri), 15m, 8 pm
9/13/34 - 11/26/34, Sus, Thu, 8 pm; Fri, 10:30 pm as of 10/5/34
12/24/34 - 5/27/35 (New-Star Revue), Hudson, CBS, Mon, 30m, 30m, 8:30 pm
also 9/12/34 - 5/22/35 (Kate Smith Matinee Hour; also with Parker Fennelly, Bob Trout), CBS, Wed, 60m, 3 pm
5/30/35 - 9/5/35, CBS, Thu, 60m, 8 pm

Kate Smith Hour, The (see The Kate Smith Show)

5 **Kate Smith Sings** (3/17/31 - 9/12/31)
3/17/31 - 4/23/31, Sus, NBC, 2t, 15m, 11:30 pm
4/26/31, CBS, Sun, 15m, 7:45 pm (one show)
4/27/31 - 9/12/31, CBS, 4t (Mon, Wed, Thu, Sat), 15m, 7:45 pm; 6t, 7 pm as of 5/24/31
10/1/35 - 9/10/36, A & P Coffee, CBS, 3t (Tue - Thu), 15m, 7:30 pm; 2t as of 6/30/56 (also known as Kate Smith Coffee Time); developed into The Kate Smith Show
(7/7/47 - 9/21/51) Philip Morris, Mut, 5t, 15m

22 **Kate Smith Show** (9/17/36 - 6/29/47) also called Kate Smith A & P Bandwagon while sponsored by A & P
9/17/36 - 6/24/37, A & P, CBS, Thu, 60m, 8 pm
9/30/37 - 6/23/38, Calumet Baking Powder & Swans Down Cake Flour, CBS, Thu, 60m, 8 pm
9/29/38 - 6/29/39, Swans Down, CBS, Thu, 60m, 8 pm
10/6/39 - 6/28/40; 9/20/40 - 6/27/41; 10/3/41 - 6/26/42, Grape-Nuts, CBS, Fri, 55m, 8 pm

Kate Smith Show (contined)
9/18/42 - 6/4/43, Jell-O, CBS, Fri, 55m, 8 pm; 30m as of 1/8/43
10/1/43 - 6/9/44, Sanka, CBS, Fri, 55m, 8 pm
9/17/44 - 6/10/45, Sanka, CBS, Sun, 60m, 7 pm
9/14/45 - 6/28/46 (called Kate Smith Sings), Postum, CBS, Fri, 25m, 8:30 pm
10/6/46 - 6/29/47 (Kate Smith Sings), Sanka, CBS, Sun, 6:30 pm

3 **Kate Smith Speaks** (4/4/38 - 9/14/51)
4/4/38 - 6/22/38 (Kate Smith's Column);
10/4/38 - 5/27/39 (Speaking Her Mind), Sus, CBS, 3t, 15m, 3:30 pm
1/10/39 - 6/7/39, Diamond Salt, CBS, Tue, 15m, 12 noon
10/9/39 - 6/28/40; 10/1/40 - 6/20/47, General Foods, CBS, 5t, 15m, 12 noon
also 3/22/47 - 7/26/47 (Kate Smith's Serenade) Mut, Sat, 15m, 10:15 am; 12 noon as of 6/14/47
6/23/47 - 9/14/51, Mut, 5t, 15m

Kate Smith Program (9/17/51 - 9/12/52) NBC, 5t, 40m, 12:05 pm

Kate Smith Show, The (1/6/58 - 1/2/59) Reader's Digest, Mut, 5t, 30m

Kathryn Cravens (News Through A Woman's Eyes) (10/19/36 - 4/8/38) Pontiac, CBS, 3t, 15m, 2 pm

Kathy Godfrey Show, The
(6/5/55 - 9/21/56) CBS
6/5/55 - 10/9/55, Sun, 25m 2:05 pm
12/17/55 - 5/26/56, Sat, 1:30 pm
5/28/56 - 9/21/56, 5t, 15m

1 **Katie's Daughter** (3/31/47 - 9/26/47, 12/29/47) Sweetheart Soap, NBC, 5t, 15m, 10 am

Katim's Orchestra (7/14/45 - 9/1/45) NBC, Sat, 8 pm

Kay Allen Interviews (1947 - 48)

Kay Armen Sings (1/26/44 - 8/19/54) Bl (except where noted), 15m
1/26/44 - 3/16/44, 2t (Wed & Thu), 10:15 pm
7/24/44 - 10/6/44, 5t, 10:30 am
12/2/44 - 1/6/45, Sat, 12 noon
4/8/45 - 4/15/45 (Kay's Canteen), Sun, 3 pm
5/1/45 - 6/5/45, Tue, 10:30 pm
also 5/14/45 - 6/15/45, 5t, 6:45pm
6/24/45 - 7/29/45, Sun, 3:30 pm
8/5/45 - 9/2/45, Sun, 2 pm
9/4/49 - 10/23/40; 7/23/50 - 9/10/50, NBC, Sun, 10:30 pm
11/26/53 - 8/19/54, (also called Meet Me At Kay's) NBC, Thu, 8 pm
(2/6/56 - 7/27/56) NBC, 5t, 9:30 am

Kaye Brinker (see also True To Life) (10/13/41 - 1/8/42) Mut, 2t-4t, 15m, 10:30 pm

3 **Kay Fairchild, Stepmother**
(1/17/38 - 7/10/42) Colgate, CBS, 5t, 15m

2 **Kay Kyser and His Band From The Carolines** (6/12/34) Syn

1 **Kay Kyser and His Southern Gentlemen** (1934) Syn

27 **Kay Kyser's Kollege Of Musical Knowledge** (3/30/38 - 7/29/49) started on 2/1/38 in Chicago
3/30/38 - 12/20/44, Lucky Strike, NBC, Wed, 60m, 10 pm
also 6/29/39 - 5/9/40, Mut, Thu, 8 pm
12/27/44 - 9/11/46, Colgate, NBC, Wed, 60m, 10 pm
9/18/46 - 7/2/47, Colgate, NBC, Wed, 30m, 10 pm; 10:30 pm as of 10/2/46
10/4/47 - 6/26/48, Colgate, NBC, Sat, 10 pm
11/4/48 - 7/29/49, Pillsbury, ABC, 5t, 11 am; 4 pm as of 1/10/49

2 **Kay Kyser's Orchestra** (1934) Syn
(5/2/37 - 7/25/37) Willys, Mut, Sun, 10 pm

1 **Kay Kyser Show, The** (1948) Syn

Kay Parker In Hollywood (1933) Tangee Lipstick, 5m

Kay's Canteen (see Kay Armen)

Kay Starr Show, The
(10/4/48 - 11/15/48) ABC, Mon, 10:30 pm

Kay Starr and Larry Stewart
(6/16/45 - 7/7/45) Bl, Sat, 10:30 pm

1 **Kay Starr with Dave Matthew's Orchestra** (Standard transcription)

1 **Kay Starr with Eddie Pripps' Orchestra** (Standard transcription)

1 **Kay Starr with Novelty Orchestra** (Standard transcription)

1 **Kay Starr with orchestra directed by Buzz Adlam** (Standard transcription)

1 **Kay Starr with The Billy Butterfield Quintet** (Standard transcription)

1 **Kay Thompson Show, The**
(9/3/41- 3/4/42) CBS
9/3/41 - 10/1/41, Wed, 7:30 pm (summer replacement of Meet Mr. Meek)
10/1/41 - 1/24/42, Sat, 25m, 11:05 am
1/28/42 - 3/4/42, Wed, 7:30 pm

1 **Keel Laying Of The U.S.S. North Carolina** (10/27/37) Mut

1 **Keep Ahead Program, The** (Lynn Gardner)
(6/25/43 - 9/21/45) Mut, Fri, 7:30 pm

3 **Keep 'Em Rolling** (with Morton Gould and Clifton Fadiman)
(11/9/41 - 5/17/42) Mut, Sun, 10:30 pm

Keeper Of The Coffin (Chicago; nine 15m horror stories told on Oct 30, 1970)

1 **Keep Fit To Music With Wallace** (Get Thin With Music) (Beatrice Creameries)
(8/15/38 - 9/13/40) Mut, 5t, 15m, 11:30 am

Keep Healthy (3/20/54 - 9/2/56) Mut, Sat or Sun, 15m - 45m

1 **Keep It Dark** (9/28/41) Mut

Keepin' Company (7/4/55 - 8/5/55) Mut, 5t, 11 am

Keeping Up With Daughter (with Nan Dorland) (9/30/31 - 6/22/32) Sherwin Williams, NBC, Wed, 11 am

Keeping Up With Rosemary (with Fay Wray) (7/4/42 - 9/12/42) NBC, Sat, 8 pm (summer replacement of Abie's Irish Rose)

Keeping Up With The World
(7/23/44 - 4/22/45) Bl, Sun, 10:30 pm; Wed, 9 pm as of 1/3/45

2 **Keeping Up With The Wigglesworths** (with Jack Ayres)
(1/20/46 - 9/29/46) Mut, Sun, 5m
1/20/46 - 4/21/46, 12:30 pm
8/4/46 - 9/29/46, 1 pm
also syndicated

Keep It In The Family (with Harry Babbitt)

Keepsakes (with Dorothy Kirsten, Mack Harrell) (9/5/43 - 10/1/44) Carter, Bl, Sun, 8:30 pm

Keep Working, (Keep Singing) America (Squibb programs such as Walter Cassell; Squibb Golden Treasury Of Song)

4 **Keep Your Guard Up** (11/7 - 28/53) Syn

1 **Keep Your Powder Dry** (1/7/45) Syn

1 **Kellogg's Pep and Kellogg's Cocoa-Marsh Announcement** (Mut)

Kellogg Slumber (1930 - 7/26/31) Kellogg, Bl, Sun, 10:30 pm

Kelly's Courthouse (with Fred Uttal)
(4/20/44 - 6/8/44) Bl, Thu, 7 pm

3 **Kelvinator Club, The** (1936)

Kelvinator Country Club (see Country Club Of The Air)

Kemtone Hour, The (see Dunninger The Mentalist)

Ken Banghart Show, The (with Arthur Gray) (1947) NBC, 15m

16 **Ken Carson Show, The** (5/20/45 - 9/9/45) Mut , Don Lee, Sun (also known as Music With The Accent On Romance)

12 **Ken Griffin At The Hammond Organ** (World transcriptions)

1 **Ken Murray** (1/4/33 - 6/26/40) (see also Let's Have Fun; Which Is Which?)
1/4/33 - 3/8/33, Royal Gelatin, NBC, Wed, 8 pm
3/24/36 - 12/15/36 (Laugh With Ken) Rinso and Lifebuoy, CBS, Tue, 8:30 pm replaced by Al Jolson (see)
3/31/37 - 9/22/37 (with Shirley Ross, Lud Gluskin Orchestra), Campbell, CBS Wed 8:30 pm
9/13/39 - 6/26/40 (see also Texaco Star Theater) Texaco, CBS, Wed, 60m, 9 pm

Ken Murray Lifebuoy-Rinso Program, The (see Ken Murray)

10 **Ken Nordine's Word Jazz**
(10/31/81 - 12/29/81) NPR

3 **Ken Wright At The WKY Organ** (Standard transcriptions)

3 **Kennedy Assassination, The** (11/22/63) CBS, ABC, NBC-TV

1 **Kennedy Center Tonight** (1/31/82) PBS-TV

1 **Kennedy Wit, The**

4 **Kenny Baker Program, The**
8/19/44 - 12/23/44, Pabst, CBS, Sat, 8 pm
11/18/45 - 12/23/45, Mut Sun, 15m, 8:30 pm
4/28/46 - 7/28/46, Mut, Sun, 15m, 2:45 pm
9/30/46 - 6/27/47, (see Glamour Manor) (Sincerely, Kenny Baker) (Syn)

1 **Kentucky Derby Report** (5/7/50) CFCN

Keyboard and Console (8/31/40 - 11/30/40) CBS, Sat, 15m

Keyboard Capers (6/29/40 - 9/28/40) CBS, Sat, 15m, 1 pm

Keynote Ranch (6/15/53 - 9/11/53) Mut, 5t, 25m, (summer replacement for Sky King and Wild Bill Hickok)

Keys To The Capital (with David Brinkley) (1955 - 56) NBC

Key, The (1956)

1 **Khruschev and Castro In New York** (9/21/60) NBC-TV

1 **Khruschev and The U.S.A.** (9/27/59) CBS

1 **Kid From Brooklyn, The** (1946) Air trailer

1 **Kid From Spain, The** (1932) film sound track

Kid On The Corner, The (with Walter Tetley) NBC

1 **Kidoodlers, The** (Thesaurus transcription)

Kidoodlers Novelty Quartet (10/24/38 - 6/16/40) 15m; various days and times including:
10/24/38 - 11/22/39, Bl, 2t (Mon & Wed), 12:15 pm; in New York as of 3/13/39
also 11/4/38 - 1/27/39, Bl, Fri, 9:30 am
also 3/19/39 - 6/4/39, NBC, Sun, 2:45 pm
4/1/40 - 6/3/40, Bl, Mon, 12:15 pm
also 5/12/40 - 6/16/40, Bl, Sun, 3 pm

1 **Kieren Guilfoyle** (10/20/36) WMBQ

Kilmer Family, The (7/9/35 - 10/4/35) Bl, 5t, 15m, 1:15 pm

1 **Kilroy and Prickley Pete** (4/23/47)

1 **Kindled Spark, The** (Syn)

1 **King and Queen Depart From Halifax, The** (6/15/39) CBS

1 **King and Queen In New York, The** (6/10/39) BBC/CBC

6 **King and Queen In The U.S.A., The** (6/8/39 - 6/11/39) NBC

1 **King and Queen Leave Washington, The** (6/9/39) Bl

King Arthur, Jr. with Jerry Tucker (11/25/40 - 2/14/41) Sus, Bl, 5t, 15m, 5 pm

13 **King Cole Trio** (with Nat King Cole) (late 1938) Bl - West, Mon, 5 pm (PT)
(1/15/39 - 4/23/39) (Swing Soiree) Bl - West, Sun, 8:30 pm (PT)
(10/19/46 - 4/10/48) Wildroot, NBC, Sat, 15m, 5:45 pm also (King and His Court) also Capitol, Standard and MacGregor transcriptions

1 **King Cole Trio with Ida James** (MacGregor transcription)

1 **King Cole and His Swing Trio** (Standard transcription)

12 **King For A Night** (6/7/49 - 10/49) (with The King's Men) Johnson's Wax, NBC, Tue, 9:30 pm (summer replacement for Fibber McGee & Molly)

19 **King George VI** (5/12/37 - 12/25/51) BBC/CBC/Mut

1 **King Haakon Of Norway** (4/3/42) BBC

King Kong (3/18/33 - 4/22/33) NBC, Sat, 15m, 6:30 pm

1 **King Leopold (of Belgium)** (8/23/39)

2 **King Of The Royal Mounted** (Zane Grey) (1943) Syn

King Of The Royal Mounties (with Richard Dix) (1930s)

King's Guard, The (with Ken Darby) (NBC) 15m,

King's Jesters (6/25/37 - 8/37) NBC, Fri (1/18/36 - 6/6/36) Bl, Sat, 7 pm

16 **King's Men, The** (1933) Syn, Standard transcriptions
also 1947, NBC Almond Roca Candy

1 **King's Men accompanied by Perry Botkin and Trio, The** (Standard transcription)

1 **King Of Jazz, The** (1930) Synchro-discs

King's Row (with Francis DeSales) (2/26/51- 2/29/52) Colgate, CBS, 5t, 15m; NBC as of 10/22/51

Kirkwood Corner Store (see Jack Kirkwood)

2 **Kiss and Make Up** (see Milton Berle)

1 **Kiss The Boys Goodbye** (1941) Air trailer

Kitchen Cavalcade (with Crosby Gaige) (2/22/37 - 5/27/38) Mueller, Bl, 5t, 15m, 10:45 am

Kitty Foyle (with Julie Stevens) (10/28/42 - 6/9/44) General Mills, CBS, 5t, 15m, 10:15 am (developed from Stories America Loved Best)

1 **Kitty Keene, Inc.** (9/13/37 - 4/25/41) 5t, 15m
9/13/37 - 12/31/37, Dreft, CBS
5/30/38 - 5/31/40, Dreft, Mut, 8:30 am
10/28/40 - 4/25/41, Dreft, Mut, 8:45 am

5 **Klondike** (CBC)

1 **Klondike Annie** (1936) film sound track

16 **Knickerbocker Four** (Thesaurus transcriptions)

1 **Knickerbocker Little Symphony** (Syn)

1 **Knickerbocker Playhouse** (with Elliott Lewis) (5/21/39 - 1/17/42) (started on 4/30/39 on WBBM, Chicago)
5/21/39 - 7/9/39, CBS, Sun, 10 pm
7/12/39 - 8/8/39, Wed, 9 pm
9/21/40 - 5/31/41; 9/6/41 - 1/17/42, Drene, NBC, Sat, 8 pm; Abie's Irish Rose starts on 1/24/42

4 **Knights Of The Round Table, The** (Syn)

1 **Know Your Maryland** (5/9/46) WFBR

Knox Manning Reports (1947 - 1949) (see also Front Page Features) Multi, CBS Pacific

Knox Sparkling Music (with Ed Trautman Orchestra) (1/5/32 - 6/14/32) Knox Gelatin, NBC, 3t (Tue, Thu, Sat), 15m, 9:15 am

Kodak Week-End Hour (with Nat Shilkret Orchestra) (4/29/32 - 8/8/32) Kodak, CBS, Fri, 9 pm

2 **Kol America** (WEVD)

20 **Komedie Kapers** (with Tom Post) (1936) 15m (also see Comedy Capers)

1 **Komedy Kingdom** (with Elvia Allman) 15m, Syn

2 **Kool-Aid Commercials** (1933) Syn

1 **Kopec's Dilemma, The** (Syn)

2 **Korea Story, The** (8/53) United Nations Radio

1 **Korea, Land Of The Morning Calm** (11/16/53) United Nations Radio

18 **Korn Kobblers** (11/17/42 - 47) Sus (Syndicated by ZIV; 376 broadcasts during 1946 and 1947)
11/17/42 - 3/12/43, Bl, 4t, 15m, 6:30 pm
812/43 - 12/26/43, Bl, 5t, 5m, 7 pm

1 **Korn Kobblers Kornival, The** (Syn)

1 **Kraft Family Reunion** (2/12/78)

218 **Kraft Music Hall, The** (6/26/33 - 9/22/49)
6/26/33 - 11/28/35 (see Paul Whiteman) Al Jolson co-starred from 8/3/33 - 10/19/33; 2/8/34 - 4/26/34; 7/12/34 - 8/16/34
12/5/35 - 5/9/46 (see Bing Crosby)
5/16/46 - 12/26/46 (with Edward Everett Horton) Kraft, NBC, Thu, 9 pm
1/2/47 - 6/26/47 (with Eddie Foy and Eddy Duchin Orchestra) NBC, Thu, 9 pm
7/3/47 - 9/25/47, (with Nelson Eddy) NBC, Thu, 8 pm
10/2/47 - 6/10/48 (see Al Jolson)
6/17/48 - 9/2348 (with Nelson Eddy, Dorothy Kirsten)
9/30/48 - 5/26/49 (see Al Jolson)
6/2/49 - 9/22/49, with Nelson Eddy, Dorothy Kirsten)
3/60 - 10/23/68, NBC-TV

Kraft Program, The (see The Kraft Music Hall)

4 **Krausemeyer and Cohen** (1936) Syn

1 **Kremlin Tells The Russians, The** (3/28/49) CBS

K - 7, Secret Service Spy Story (5/6/34 - 8/2/36) NBC, Sun, 7 pm

1 **Kukla, Fran and Ollie** (3/16/49) NBC-TV (8/31/52 - 5/1/53) Sus, NBC, 5t, 10m, 2:45 pm

Kup's Column Of The Air

1 **Kup's Show** (8/69) TV Syn

WSAZ
TRANSCRIPTION
HUNTINGTON, W. VA.
INSIDE OUT — OUTSIDE IN
78-33 R. P. M.
PROGRAM
DAT

1 **LBJ: Recollections Of The Kennedys and The Assassination** (5/2/70) CBS-TV

1 **LBJ: The Decision To Halt The Bombing** (2/6/70) CBS

1 **LBJ: The Last Interview** (2/1/73) CBS-TV

1 **La Guardia Memorial Program** (9/21/47) Mut

2 **La Juventud Combatiente** (Syn)

1 **La Libre Belgique** (Syn) Wartime

1 **La Rosa Hollywood Theatre Of Stars** (11/15/49)

6 **La Rosa Sings For Safety** (1954) Syn

Labor For Victory (4/18/42 - 10/3/42) NBC, Sat, 15m, 10:15 pm
(1/23/44 - 6/25/44) AFL & CIO, NBC, Sun, 15m, 1:15 pm

1 **Labor Day, 1946** (9/2/46) Syn

1 **Labor Parade, The** (1938) Syn

1 **Labor Rally** (7/17/41) Mut

1 **Labor U. S. A.** (AFL & CIO) (1/13/45 - 8/30/47) Bl, Sat, 15m, 6:45 pm

La Choy Chopsticks (with Billy Hughes) (9/13/32 - 12/8/32) La Choy, CBS, 15m, 2t, 11am

Ladies Be Seated (with Johnny Olsen; Tom Moore from 1949)
(6/26/44 - 7/20/50) Bl/ABC
6/26/44- 6/15/45, Sus, 5t
6/18/45 - 3/24/47, Quaker, 5t
3/31/47 - 10/21/49, Multi, various days
10/24/49 - 7/20/50, Philip Morris, 5t, 25m; 15m as of 2/5/51, 12 noon

Ladies Fair (with Tom Moore)
(1/23/50 - 1/1/54) Mut
1/23/50 - 2/17/50, Sus, 5t, 30m, 2 pm
2/20/50 - 9/29/50, Miles Laboratories, 5t, 15m, 2:15 pm; 3t as of 5/8/50
7/23/51 - 9/21/51, 5t, 3:30 pm
10/1/51 - 6/27/52; 9/29/52 - 1/1/54, Sterling Drugs, 5t, 25m, 11 am; except for 2 pm from 7/6/53 - 9/4/53

Ladies Man (8/4/47 - 3/25/49) Mut, 5t, 4 pm; 4:30 pm as of 2/9/48

1 **Lady Be Good** (8/5/41) Air trailer

Lady Esther Screen Guild Theatre, The (see The Screen Guild Theater)

2 **Lady Esther Serenade, The** (5/25/34, 8/26/36) CBS, NBC

Lady Go Lucky (1946 - 47)

1 **Lady In Blue** (pre-war syndicated) also (5/5/51 - 12/8/51) NBC, Sat, 8:30 am

1 **Lady In The Dark** (1944) film sound track

Lady Next Door, The (with Madge Tucker) (1930 - 1/24/35) NBC, various days, 15m

4 **Lady Of Millions** (with May Robson) (1930s) 15m, Syn

Lady Of The Press, Sandra Martin (with Janet Waldo) (6/11/44 - 45) Alka-Seltzer, CBS - West, Sun, 7 pm;
also 5/1/44 - ?, CBS - West, 5t, 15m, 4 pm (PST)

2 **Lady Skyhook Stories** (Syn) Auditions

Laff Parade (see The Laugh Parade)

1 **Lamp Is Lit, The** (12/14/52) CBS

Lamplighter, The (with Jacob Tarshish) (1/3/36 - 4/13/41) Mut, 15m; on various days and times including:
1/3/36 - 4/30/37, Wasey Products, 6t (Sun, Mon - Wed, Fri)
3/27/38 - 4/18/40, Multi, 2t (Sun & Thu)
10/20/40 - 4/13/41, Sun, 10:15 am

1 **Lana Turner Story, The** (9/27/48) Air trailer

Land Is Bright, The (12/30/44 - 9/8/45) CBS, Sat, 3 pm; 8 pm as of 7/21/45

Landmarks Of Radio (4/6/40 - 6/15/40) NBC, Sat, 8 pm

Land Of Make Believe (with Dr. Arthur Torrance)
(1930) CBS, Sun, 10 am (with Warren Scofield)
(1932) CBS, Sun, 9 am

1 **Land Of The Didjeridu, The** (UNESCO) Syn

137 **Land Of The Free, The** (1944 - 1953) Syn

6 **Land Of The Lost** (with Isabel Manning Hewson) (1/8/44 - 7/3/48) (may have started 10/9/43 locally)
1/8/44 - 9/22/45, Sus, ABC, Sat, 11 am/ 10:30 am
also 7/4/44 - 10/3/44, Bl, Tue, 7 pm
10/14/45 - 1/13/46, Sus, Mut, Sun, 3:30 pm (10:30 am in New York)
1/26/46 - 7/6/46, Mut, Sat, 11:30 am
10/11/47 - 7/3/48, Bosco, ABC, Sat, 11:30 am

1 **Landing Of Jap Planes On Ie Shima** (8/18/45) Mut

1 **Landing Of MacArthur In San Francisco** (4/17/51) Mut

1 **Landing On Luzon** (1/9/45) Mut

8 **Land's Best Bands, The** (1951) Syn

Lands Of The Free (International-American University) (7/5/42 - 8/6/44) Sus, NBC
7/5/42 - 2/1/43, Mon, 10:30 pm
2/21/43 - 8/22/43. 10/10/43 - 8/6/44, 25m, 4:30 pm

2 **Landt Trio with The Noveliers, The**

4 **Landt Trio, The** (often called Landt Trio and White until 1/18/38 when Howard White died) (1927 - 11/22/46) 15m (see also Doc Pearson's Drugstore) 1t - 6t
1927 - 31, NBC, Sat
1931- 36, NBC, 6t
1936 - 37, Hudson Coal, NBC, 3t
1937 - 10/24/38, NBC, Sat
10/13/41 - 12/11/42 (with Ken Roberts), Sus, CBS, 4t (Mon, Tue, Wed, Fri) (also called Landt Trio and Curley)
12/28/42 - 4/16/43, CBS, 5t, 3:15 pm
10/11/43 - 4/28/44, CBS, 3t, 5:30 pm
3/19/45 - 11/22/46, 3t; 5t as of 3/25/46 also Empire and Thesaurus transcriptions

Lane Reporter (with Nan Dorland) (4/1/32 - 5/20/32) Lane Cedar Chests, CBS, Fri, 15m, 11:15 am

2 **Lang - Worth Concert Orchestra** (15m) Lang-Worth transcriptions

2 **Lang - Worth Foursome, The** (Lang-Worth transcriptions)

2 **Lang - Worth Gypsy Orchestra** (Lang-Worth transcriptions)

1 **Lang - Worth Gypsy Trio, The** (Lang-Worth transcription)

1 **Lang - Worth Hillbillies** (Lang-Worth transcription)

1 **Lang - Worth Military Band** (Lang-Worth transcription)

1 **Lang - Worth Military Band (Anthems)** (Lang-Worth transcription)

1 **Lang - Worth Singing Saxophones, The** (Lang-Worth transcription)

1 **Lang - Worth Swing Orchestra** (Lang-Worth transcription)

Lanny and Ginger (10/2/44 - 6/24/45) Grove Labs, Mut, 3t, 5m, 11:55 am
(8/11/45 - 6/22/46) Mut, Sat, 15m, 5:45 pm

Lanny Corey's Rhythm (12/6/38 - 4/11/39) Bl, Tue, 15m, 10:30 pm

3 **Lanny Ross Show, The** (1929 - 52)
1929 - 31, NBC, Sun, 15m
6/1/31 - 9/16/31, Best foods, NBC, 5t, 15m, 12 noon
10/29/31 - 3/10/32, Maxwell House, NBC, Thu, 30m, 9:30 pm
7/1/32 - 9/30/32, Maxwell House, 3t, 15m, 7:30 pm
1932 - 33, Campbell Soups, NBC, Fri, 15m
9/8/34 - 4/10/35, Log Cabin, NBC, Wed, 30m, 8:30 pm
7/21/35 - 9/22/35 (Lanny Ross and His State Fair Concert) Bl, Sun, 7pm (summer replacement for Jack Benny)
9/7/37 - 3/1/38 (Mardi Gras with Walter O'Keefe) Packard, NBC, Tue, 60m, 9:30 pm

Lanny Ross Show, The (continued)
10/9/39 - 1/19/40, Franco-American, CBS, 3t, 15m, 11 am
1/22/40 - 3/29/40, Franco-American, CBS, 5t, 15m, 2 pm
4/1/40 - 4/26/40, Franco-American, CBS, 4t, 15m
4/29/40 - 5/1/42, Franco-American, CBS, 5t, 15m, 7:15 pm
1942 - 43 (see Camel Caravan)
4/1/46 - 6/28/46 (with Evelyn Knight), Procter & Gamble, CBS, 5t, 15m, 7 pm
1948 - 50, Sus, Mut, 5t, 15m
1/23/51 - 1/25/51, Dictograph, Mut, 2t, 10m, 12:15 pm
1951 - 52, Sus, Mut, 5t, 15m
8/9/54 - 8/16/57, CBS, 5t, 30 - 55m; on locally in New York into the 60s

3 **Lanny Ross with Henry Sylvern's Orchestra** (World transcriptions)

1 **Lantern In The Dark** (4/22/47) CBS

La Palina Smoker (1929 - 1930) La Palina Cigars, CBS, Wed, 9:30 pm

Larry Burke (see Melody Lane)

Larry Carr Show, The (1946) CBS, 15m

Larry Clinton (Larry Clinton's Musical Conversations; also called Sensation and Swing) (7/3/39 - 6/24/40) NBC, Mon, 7:30 pm

4 **Larry Clinton and His Orchestra** (1938) NBC

Larry Clinton and The RCA Victor Campus Club (7/2/38) NBC (see The RCA Campus Club)

1 **Larry Faith and His Orchestra** (CBS)

18 **Larry King Live** (10/23/88 - 11/6/94) CNN-TV

Larry King Show, The (see Larry King Live)

Larry Lesueur (9/28/46 - 11/28/58) Multi, CBS

1 **Larry Tighe** (1945)

La Salle Style Show, The
(11/5/36 - 1/28/37) Cadillac, NBC, Thu, 4 pm

1 **Las Vegas Nights** (1941) film sound track

8 **Lassie Show, The** (6/8/47 - 5/27/50) Red Heart, 15m
6/8/47 - 5/30/48, ABC, Sun, 3 pm
6/5/48 - 5/27/50, NBC, Sat

Last Class, The (with Nelson Olmsted)

1 **Last Man Out** (11/13/53 - 4/4/54) Sus, NBC, Sun

13 **Last Of The Mohicans, The** (Syn)

4 **Last Nixon Show, The** (11/9 - 12/75) WBAI

1 **Last Program Of ABSIE** (7/4/45) ABSIE

1 **Last Trip On The Sixth Avenue El** (12/4/38) WOR

Last Word, The (2/2/57 - 3/5/57) CBS, Sat, 8:30 pm

1 **Late Joseph Stalin, The** (3/8/53) NBC

1 **Latitude Zero** (with Lou Merrill)
(6/7/41 - 9/27/41) NBC, Sat, 8 pm; 10:30 pm as of 9/6/41 (started as summer replacement of Knickerbocker Holiday) began on West Coast on 2/11/41

1 **Laugh (Laff) 'N' Swing Club** (with Morey Amsterdam)
(11/25/36 - 4/4/41)
11/25/36 - 12/9/36, NBC, Wed, 10:30 pm
11/26/39 - 2/4/40, Mut, Sun, 9 pm
2/13/40 - 10/29/40, Mut, Tue, 9:30 pm
11/29/40 - 4/4/41 (Laugh Doctors), Mut, Fri, 8:30 pm

Laugh Clinic (with Ransom Sherman and Russell Pratt) (12/11/34 - 2/18/35) CBS
12/11/34 - 12/25/34, Tue, 10:30 am
12/31/34 - 2/18/35, Mon, 60m, 9 am

Laugh Club (with Tom Brennie)
(1931 - 6/18/32) Bl, 5t, 15m; then NBC (see also Lou Holtz)

Laugh Doctors (see Laugh Clinic)

Laugh Liner, The (with Jack Fulton, Billy House) (7/10/38 - 1/1/39) Wrigley, CBS, Sun, 6:30 pm

1 **Laugh Of The Party** (1/15/47) CBS

5 **Laugh Parade, The** (with Ken Niles) (1932 - 36; 1945) 15m, also syndicated

Laugh With Ken (see Ken Murray)

1 **Launch Of Sky-Lab III, The** (7/28/73) NBC-TV

1 **Launch Of The Sky-Lab Astronauts** (5/25/73) CBS-TV

1 **Launching Ceremonies Of The Battleship U.S.S. Iowa** (8/27/42) Mut

1 **Launching Of German Battleship** (4/1/49) Germany

2 **Launching Of The Mauretania** (7/28/38) BBC/Mut

1 **Launching Of The S.S. America, The** (8/31/39) Mut

1 **Launching Of The U.S.S. North Carolina** (6/13/40) Mut

1 **Launching The U.S.S. Roosevelt** (4/29/45) WOR

1 **Laundry Blues** (1930) Synchro-disc

1 **Laura Lofton** (6/7/48) NBC

1 **Laurel and Hardy**

Lavena Program (see Hal Kemp)

Lavender and New Lace (see Sylvia Marlowe)

Lavender and Old Lace (with Fritzi Scheff, Lucy Monroe, Frank Munn)
(6/19/34 - 9/23/36)
6/19/34 - 4/14/36, Bayer, CBS, Tue, 8 pm
4/22/36 - 9/23/36, Bl, Wed, 8:30 pm

Law and You, The (6/24/51 - 9/16/51) ABC, Sun, 15m, 9:30 pm

2 **Lawless Twenties, The** (Syn)

Lawnhurst (see Vee Lawnhurst)

2 **Lawrence Welk Show, The**
(6/1/49 - 11/16/57) ABC
6/1/49 - 5/24/50; 10/4/50 - 3/28/51 (Lawrence Welk High Life Revue), Miller, Wed, 9:30 pm; 10 pm as of 9/28/49
5/30/51 - 6/20/51, Sus, Wed, 10 pm
1952 - 53 (Treasury Hour) Mon
8/27/55 - 11/16/57, Sat, 10 or 10:30 pm

27 **Lawrence Welk and His Champagne Music** (Standard, Capitol transcriptions)

6 **Lawrence Welk and His Orchestra** (1954, 1966) ABC, NBC, World transcriptions

1 **Lawrence Welk Army Show, The** (12/2/60) AFRTS

3 **Lawrence Welk Orchestra** (Thesaurus transcriptions)

1 **Laws That Safeguard Society** (Syn)

Law West Of The Pecos (with Walter Brennan)

1 **Lawyer Q's Jury Of The Air** (with Karl Swenson)
(4/3/47 - 6/29/47) Mut
4/3/47 - 4/17/47, Thu, 8 pm
4/27/47 - 6/29/47, Sun, 3 pm

Lawyer Tucker (with Parker Fennelly) (6/12/47 - 9/4/47) Autolite, CBS, Thu, 9 pm (summer replacement of Dick Haymes)

Lazy Dan, The Minstrel Man (with Irving Kaufman)
(3/12/33 - 6/23/36) Old English Wax, CBS
3/12/33 - 6/4/33; 9/24/33 - 6/17/34; 9/30/34 - 5/26/35, Sun
6/27/35 - 8/22/35, Thu, 2:30 pm
8/30/35 - 4/10/36, Fri, 7:15 pm
4/21/36 - 6/23/36, Tue, 8 pm

1 **Le Grande Parade Du Jazz** (8/19/77) PBS-TV

Leading Question, The (1/24/54 - 9/5/54) CBS, Sun, 12 noon
(3/29/56 - 8/15/56) CBS, Thu, 25m, 9:30 pm

1 **Leap Year** (9/52) Syn

2 **Leatherneck Legends** (Syn)

Leave It To Annie (with Thelma Ritter)

Leave It To Joan (see Joan Davis)

2 **Leave It To Mike** (with Walter Kinsella; also Joan Alexander)
(6/7/45 - 2/12/46) Sus, Mut (originally called Paging Mike McNally)
6/7/45 - 7/30/45, Mon, 10 pm
8/5/45 - 9/2/45, Sun, 5 pm
9/14/45 - 11/9/45, Fri, 10 pm
11/20/45 - 2/12/46, Tue, 8 pm

1 **Leave It To Sam** (5/29/47) CBS

5 **Leave It To The Girls** (with, at different times, Constance Bennett; Vanessa Brown; Binnie Barnes; George Brent)
(10/6/45 - 1/21/49) Sus, Mut
10/6/45 - 2/15/47, Sat, 9 pm; 9:30 pm as of 9/14/46
3/7/47 -1/21/49, Fri; sponsored by Continental Parmac. Co. from 9/10/48 - 12/3/48

Lecture Hall (4/22/40 - 9/30/40; 2/3/41 - 10/6/41)) CBS, Mon, 15m, 4 pm; 3:45 pm as of 2/3/41

1 **Lee Evans and His Orchestra** (12/31/65) CBS

Lee Gordon Orchestra (2/2/41 - 10/5/41) NBC, Sun

Lee Graham (11/14/55 - 6/8/56) Mut, 5t, 25m, 2:05 pm

1 **Lee Harvey Oswald Speaks** (8/63) WDSU

Lee Sullivan's Varieties
(10/21/46 - 3/14/47) NBC, 5t, 15m, 10 am

Lee Sweetland Show, The
(7/13/44 - 8/20/44) Westinghouse, NBC, Sun, 2:30 pm (summer replacement for John Charles Thomas)
(9/21/47 - 12/7/47) ABC, Sun, 2 pm

Lee Wiley (6/24/36 - 9/2/36) CBS, Wed, 15m, 6 pm

Lefty (with Jack Albertson)
(3/11/46 - 4/15/46) CBS, Mon, 10:30 pm

1 **Legends Of The Screen** (1/1/83) TV Syn

2 **Legion Answers The Call, The** (12/7/41) Red, Bl

5 **Legion Of Safety, The** (1939, 1940) Syn

9 **Leighton Noble and His Orchestra**
(1/14/39 - 3/11/39) CBS, Sat, 15m, 6:15 pm
(5/1/40 - 9/16/40) Mut, Mon, 15m, 7:15 pm (not in NY)
also Standard transcriptions

1 **Leith Stevens Harmonies**
(12/27/34 - 4/17/35) CBS, Thu, 8 pm; Wed 9 pm as of 1/2/35
(4/18/35 - 5/2/35) CBS, Thu, 8:30 pm
also 1/26/38

Leland Stowe (7/15/44 - 7/14/45, National Underwriters, Bl
(4/23/47 - 4/21/48) (You and The News) Mut, United Electrical Radio and Machine Workers

2 **Lenny Herman Quintet, The**
(9/10/48, 6/17/60) NBC, CBS

2 **Leo and The Blonde** (with Lionel Stander and Florence Lake) 1947) 15m

Leo Cherne (1/1/44 - 7/8/44) Mut

Leo Diamond Harmonaires (1943 - 44) NBC, 15m

1 **Leo Durocher Sports** (10/13/46 - 1/26/47) ABC, Sun, 15m, 1:15 pm

Leon Henderson (8/21/43 - 8/12/44) O'Sullivan, Bl

4 **Leon Kellner and His Orchestra**
(11/8/65 - 6/27/70) CBS

18 **Leon Pearson** (Syn)

1 **Leonard Bernstein On Broadway**
(1966) Syn

7 **Leonidas Witherall** (with Walter Hampden; also Agnes Moorehead) (9/7/43) CBS
(6/4/44 - 5/6/45) Mut, Sun
6/4/44 - 10/1/44, 9 pm
10/8/44 - 11/26/44, 7 pm
12/3/44 - 5/6/45, 10 pm; 7 pm as of 1/21/45

1 **Leopold Spitalny Orchestra, H.** (Tapestry Musicale) (also with Emma Otero) (2/26/39 - 5/23/42) NBC, Sun

1 **Leo Reisman and His Orchestra**
(1931 - 2/9/37) NBC
5/29/31 - 32 (see Pond's Program)
1/9/34 - 2/9/37, Philip Morris, Tue (see Johnny Presents)
also Standard transcription

1 **Les Baxter and His Orchestra** (World transcription)

12 **Les Brown and His Orchestra**
(10/40 - 1/1/66) NBC, CBS, World transcriptions (also Melody Ballroom)
(1956 - 57)

14 **Les Brown Show, The** (1953) Syn

Les Elgart (9/18/55 - 11/20/55) CBS, Sun, 12:30 pm

Leslie Howard Theater (Amateur Gentleman) (10/6/35 - 3/29/36) Hinds, CBS, Sun, 8:30 pm; 2 pm as of 1/5/36

7 **Les Miserables** (with Orson Welles)
(7/23/37 - 9/3/37) Mut, Fri

16 **Les Paul Show, The** (with Basil Heatter)
(3/30/50 - 9/22/50) NBC
(10/30/55 - 6/3/56) Mut, Sun, 15m, 1 pm and 6:45 pm

Les Paul and Mary Ford (5/5/50 - 51) 15m
(11/28/53 - 1/9/54) CBS, Sat, 5m, 2 pm

6 **Les Paul Trio** (World, MacGregor transcriptions)

3 **Les Paul, His Guitar and Rhythm Accompaniment** (Standard transcriptions)

4 **Lester Lanin and His Orchestra** (1958) CBS

Les Tremayne (see Double Feature)

12 **Lest We Forget** (1940, 1946) NBC, 15m, also syndicated

1 **Lest We Forget Pearl Harbor** (12/7/44) WIDC

13 **Lest We Forget: A Better World For Youth** (Wartime) Syn

26 **Lest We Forget: America Determines Her Destiny** (Wartime) Syn

26 **Lest We Forget: Democracy Is Our Way Of Life** (pre-war) Syn

14 **Lest We Forget: Eternal Vigilance Is The Price Of Liberty** (1943) Syn

14 **Lest We Forget: One Nation Indivisible** (1944) Syn

26 **Lest We Forget: Our Constitution** (Syn)

13 **Lest We Forget: Our Nation's Shrines** (1944) Syn

13 **Lest We Forget: Stories To Remember** (1948) Syn

6 **Lest We Forget: The American Dream** (1947) Syn

17 **Lest We Forget: The Story Of America** and **Our Battle Won Freedom** (Syn)

26 **Lest We Forget: The Story Of Our Free America** (1946) Syn

22 **Lest We Forget: These Great Americans** (1946) Syn (also see The New Frontier)

1 **Let Freedom Ring** (10/14/47 - 6/29/48; 4/5/49 - 6/28/49; 10/4/49 - 12/26/49) Chamber of Commerce, ABC, Tue, 15m, 10:45 pm
also 1939, Air trailer

13 **Let Freedom Sing** (Syn)

55 **Let George Do It** (with Bob Bailey)
(5/14/46) Audition
(10/18/46 - 9/27/54) Standard Oil, Mut - West coast, Fri; Mon, 8 pm as of 1948 (414 shows broadcast)
1/20/54 - 1/12/55 (in New York) Wed, 9:30 pm

1 **Let Television Advance** (4/6/40) Mut

1 **Let There Be Music** (with Wilbur Hatch)
(3/26/38) CBS

1 **Let Your Hair Down** (6/21/43) Mut

Let Yourself Go (see Milton Berle)

Let's Be Charming
(with Julia Sanderson)
(12/2/43 - 5/25/44) Lewis Howe, Mut, Thu, 1:30 pm

Let's Be Lazy (with Dale Evans, Tom Moore; Cesar Petrillo Orchestra)
(7/6/40 - 9/28/40) CBS, Sat, 9:30 am

2 **Let's Dance** (1/5/35, 5/18/48) NBC

Let's Dance America (with Fred Robbins) (1948)

1 **Let's Dance...To The Recordings Of Ambrose and His Orchestra** (1/15/37) WCNW

1 **Let's Do It Again** (1937) film sound track

Let's Face The Issue (12/3/44 - 5/26/45) C & O Railroad, Mut, Sun, 5 pm

1 **Let's Fall In Love** (1934) Air trailer

Let's Find Out (2/8/53 - 6/23/57) CBS, Sun, various times

Let's Go Back To The Bible (? - 3/19/39)

5 **Let's Go Nightclubbing** (2/28/45 - 3/20/46) with Claude Hopkins Orchestra; Cootie Williams (from Club Zanzibar, NY) NBC

Let's Go To Slapsie's (with Jane Withers and Margaret Whiting)

Let's Go To The Met (12/27/48 - 3/30/50) Sus, ABC
12/27/48 - 6/27/49, Mon, 9 pm
1/26/50 - 3/30/50, Thu, 10:30 pm

Let's Go To The Movies
(2/19/47- 10/22/47) Mut, Wed, 9:30 pm

Let's Go To The Opera
(4/28/46 - 10/27/46) Mut, Sun, 7 pm

153 **Let's Go To Town** (1952 - 1954) Syn, 15m

Let's Go To Work (with Herbert Hadell)
(2/5/40 - 6/24/40) Mut, Mon, 8:30 pm (New York only)

13 **Let's Go With Music** (National Guard) (with Vaughn Monroe) Syn

1 **Let's Have Fun** (10/22/35) CBS

Let's Join The Band (with Orrin Tucker) (8/26/39 - 10/21/39) CBS, Sat, 8:30 pm

Let's Laugh (with Jack Gregson) (1946) NBC, Sat

Let's Listen To Harris (see Phil Harris Orchestra)

1 **Let's Listen To Lopez** (6/64) CBS

2 **Let's Listen To Spencer** (with Sweeney and March) CBS, Ivory, 15m

1 **Let's Make A Date** (7/18/45) Audition

Let's Meet McCoy (ABC; with Jack McCoy)

1 **Let's Play Games** (11/5/37 - 4/38) Folgers, Vapex, Mut, Fri, 15m, 8:45 pm
(3/31/49 - 4/28/49) Mut, Thu, 9:30 pm

Let's Play Reporter (with Frances Scott) (1943) NBC

22 **Let's Playwright** (6/9/40 - 5/8/41) WINS, WEVD

36 **Let's Pretend** (with Nila Mack) (3/24/34 - 10/23/54) CBS
3/24/34 - 1/15/38, Sat, 10:35 am; 10:30 am as of 5/2/36
1/25/38 - 3/31/38, 2t, 6:30 pm
4/5/38 - 10/6/38, 2t, 5:30 pm
10/10/38 - 4/13/39, 2t (Mon & Thu), 5:30 pm; 5:15 pm as of 1/5/39
4/22/39 - 9/18/43, Sus, Sat, 12:30 am; 11:30 am as of 2/7/42; 11:05 as of 4/3/43
9/25/43 - 12/6/52, Cream Of Wheat, Sat, 25m, 11:05 am
12/13/52 - 10/23/54, Sus, Sat, 10:30 am; 2:05 as of 1/2/54; 1:35 pm as of 6/12/54; 2 pm as of 9/11/54

1 **Let's Rock!** (1958) film sound track

Let's Stand By For Music (with Jerry Gray Orchestra) 15m

Let's Swing (6/21/41 - 7/26/41) NBC, Sat, 15m, 10 am

Let's Talk Hollywood (with George Murphy) (7/4/48 - 9/26/48) NBC, Sun, 7 pm

Let's Talk It Over (see June Hynd)

Let's Visit (12/15/37 - 5/11/38) Mut, Wed, 8:30 pm

1 **Letter From America** (BBC; with Alistair Cooke) (3/23/46 - present)

Letter Of Destiny (Syn)

Letters From Abroad (see Tom Terris)

Letters Home (5/7/39 - 9/24/39) Westinghouse, Bl, Sun, 15m, 5:45 pm

1 **Letter To The O.P.A.** (Syn)

Letter To Your Service Men (10/15/43 - 6/8/45) Bl, Fri, 15m

Let There Be Light (1951- 52) Mon

Lew Childre (Syn) 15m

8 **Lew Parker Show, The** (1946) Syn

1 **Lew White with Waldo Mayo and Theodore Cello** (3/19/38 - 10/15/38) CBS, Sat, 10 am also Lang-Worth transcription

2 **Libelled Lady** (1936) Syn

1 **Liberace Interview** (8/28/53) WDSU-TV

2 **Liberace Radio Program, The** (1954 - 55) Syn

2 **Liberace Show, The** (1954) TV Syn

1 **Liberation** (6/45) Syn

Liberty Magazine Hour (7/3/31 - 12/25/31) McFadden Pub., CBS, Fri, 45m, 9 pm

Liberty Magazine - Short, Short Story (1943)

1 **Liberty Production Rally** (7/3/42) WOR

Liberty Theater (1930s)

Library Of Congress Concert (11/19/38 - 3/25/39) Bl, Sat
(8/10/40 - 9/29/40) NBC, Sat
(3/8/41 - 5/3/41) CBS, Sat; also on occasionally at other times

2 **Library Of Congress Radio Ressearch Project, The** (7/41) Syn

1 **Libya Attack Coverage** (4/15/86)

2 **Lies** (2/23/84, 3/1/84) WPBH-FM

1 **Lieutenant Alder's Rescue** (11/14/44)

1 **Life and Love Of Dr. Susan, The** (with Eleanor Phelps) (2/13/39 - 12/29/39) Lux, CBS, 5t, 15m

2 **Life and Loves Of Linda Lovely, The** (1/49) WHDH auditions

2 **Life and The World** (8/24/57 - 12/58) Life Magazine, NBC, Sat, 15m, 7:45 pm

1 **Life and Times Of Robert Q. Lewis, The** (11/19/47) CBS

1 **Life At Father Flanagan's Boys' Town** (4/8/45)

Life Begins (see Martha Webster)

1 **Life Begins At Eighty** (with Jack Barry) (7/4/48 - 5/6/53)
7/4/48 - 9/26/48, Mut, Sun, 3:30 pm
10/2/48 - 9/24/49, Mut, Sat, 9 pm; 8:30 pm as of 10/16/48
10/1/52 - 5/6/53, Beltone Hearing Aid as of 1/14/53, ABC, Wed, 8:30 pm

1 **Life Begins For Andy Hardy** (6/27/41) Air trailer

2 **Life Begins In College** (1937) Air trailer, film sound track

Lifebuoy Program, The (see Al Jolson)

Lifebuoy Show, The (see Bob Burns)

10 **Life Can Be Beautiful** (9/5/38 - 6/25/54) 5t, 15m
9/5/38 - 11/4/38, Ivory, NBC
11/7/38 - 6/21/46, Ivory, CBS
also 7/3/39 - 4/25/41, NBC
also 10/9/39 - 3/28/41, Mut
6/24/46 - 6/25/54, Ivory, NBC, 3 pm

10 **Life For Wildlife** (1941) Syn

6 **Life In The Great Outdoors** (Syn)

Life In Your Hands, A (by Erle Stanley Gardner) (6/7/49 - 8/21/52) NBC
6/7/49 - 9/13/49; 6/27/50 - 9/12/50, Raleigh, Tue, 10:30 pm (summer replacement for People Are Funny)

Life In Your Hands (continued)
6/29/51 - 9/21/51 (with Lee Bowman), Heinz, ABC, Fri, 9 pm (summer replacement of The Adventures Of Ozzie and Harriet)
7/10/52 - 8/21/52, Thu, 8 pm (summer replacement for Father Knows Best)

Life Is A Song (with Countess Albani and Charles Previn Orchestra)
(10/6/35 - 3/22/36) Real Silk Hosiery, Bl, Sun, 9 pm

2 **Life Is Good** (1950) Syn

Life Is Worth Living (3/12/53 - 5/14/53) Admiral, Mut, Thu, 25m, 9:05 pm
(10/18/55 - 4/10/56) (with Bishop Fulton J. Sheen) ABC, Tue, 8:30 pm

1 **Life Of Irene Castle, The** (Syn)

Life Of Mary Sothern (11/4/35 - 4/22/38) 5t, 15m; on originally in 1930 on WLW, Cincinnati
11/4/35 - 4/30/37, Hinds, Mut
10/4/37 - 4/22/38, Hinds, CBS, 5:15 pm

125 **Life Of Riley, The** (4/26/41 - 9/13/41; with Lionel Stander)
(1/16/44 - 6/29/51; with William Bendix)
4/26/41 - 9/13/41, CBS, Sat, 10 pm
1/16/44 - 7/8/45, American Meat, ABC, Sun, 3 pm; 10 pm as of 7/9/44
9/8/45 - 7/6/46; 9/7/46 - 7/5/47; 9/6/47 - 6/26/48, Teel Dentifrice; Dreft as of 1/11/47; Prell as of 9/6/47, NBC, Sat, 8 pm
8/27/48 - 5/27/49, Prell, NBC, Fri, 10 pm
10/7/49 - 6/30/50; 10/6/50 - 6/29/51, Prell; Pabst as of 3/10/50, NBC, Fri, 9 pm; 10 pm as of 1/6/50

Life Of Uncle Ned (with Joseph R. Jones) (5/26/35 - 8/18/35) CBS, Sun, 15m, 4:30 pm; 2 pm as of 7/28/35

Life Savers Rendezvous (9/18/35 - 3/11/36) Life Savers, Bl, Wed, 8 pm

Lifetime Living (with Ted Malone) (1/22/56 - 6/3/56) ABC, Sun, 15m, 9:15 pm

Lifetime Revue (with Leo Spitalny) (2/14/32 - 12/25/32) Sheaffer Pens, Sun
2/14/32 - 5/8/32, Bl, 4:30 pm
5/15/32 - 8/21/32, NBC, 15m
8/28/32 - 12/25/32, Bl, 30m, 9:45 pm

Life With Fred Brady (7/15/43 - 9/30/43) Lever Brothers, NBC, Thu, 7:30 pm (summer replacement of Bob Burns)

35 **Life With Luigi** (with J. Carroll Naish) (5/15/47) Audition
(9/21/48 - 3/3/53) CBS
9/21/48 - 1/4/49, Sus, Tue, 9 pm
1/9/49 - 7/3/49, Sun, 10 pm
7/10/49 - 9/25/49, Sun, 8:30 pm
9/27/49 - 1/3/50, Tue, 9:30 pm
1/10/50 - 6/13/50; 8/15/50 - 7/3/51; 8/28/51 - 5/27/52, Wrigley, Tue, 9 pm
8/12/52 - 3/3/53, Tue, 9 pm
(1954) 15m

2 **Life With The Lyons** (with Ben Lyon and Bebe Daniels) (BBC) (11/5/50 - 5/19/61)

2 **Life's Fuller Measure** (1952) Syn

1 **Lifting The Berlin Blockade** (5/12/49) CBS

2 **Light Crust Doughboys, The** (with Jack Perry) (12/48 - 4/27/51) Burrus Mill and Elevator Co., Mut, 3t, 15m

3 **Light Of The World, The** (with Bret Morrison) (3/18/40 - 6/2/50) General Mills, Red, CBS

1 **Light That Was Never Seen On Land Or Sea, The** (Wartime) Syn

Lighted Windows (with Ruth Matteson) (12/4/43 - 5/27/44) Alcoa, NBC, Sat, 11:30 am

Lighter Side, The (with Del Sharbutt) Wrigley, Mut, 5m

41 **Lightning Jim** (1950s) (Syn - ZIV) 98 episodes broadcast; also on in the West Coast in the 40s

95 **Lights Out** (written by Wyllis Cooper; Arch Oboler from 6/10/36 - 6/29/38) (1/1/34 - 9/3/47)
1/1/34 - 4/10/35, WENR, Chicago, 15m; 30m as of 4/25/34
4/17/35 - 8/16/39, NBC, Wed
10/6/42 - 9/28/43, Ironized Yeast, CBS, Tue, 8 pm
7/14/45 - 9/1/45(Fantasies From Lights Out) NBC, Sat, 8:30 pm
7/6/46 - 8/24/46, NBC, Sat, 10 pm (summer replacement of Judy Canova)
7/16/47 - 9/3/47 (with Boris Karloff until 8/6/47), Eversharp, ABC, Wed, 10:30 pm (summer replacement of Henry Morgan)
(1971 - 72) (Revival) (Syn) The Devil and Mr. O

1 **Light and Cook** (1932) Syn

28 **Light-Up and Listen Club** (with Peter Donald; Milton Cross)
(1937 - 1940) Sweet Caporal Cigarettes, NBC, 15m

3 **Light and Mellow (1942 - 1947) KPO**

Light Up Time (see Frank Sinatra)

1 **Lighting Of The Holly Tree By The Tracks** (12/53)

1 **Lights Of New York** (6/27/29) Synchro-discs

1 **Lights Up** (4/23/45) BBC

1 **Like It Is** (12/68) WABC-TV

Li'l Abner (with John Hodiak) (11/20/39 - 12/6/40) NBC, 5t, 15m

Lilac Time (with Arthur Murray)
(12/1/34 - 2/23/35) Pinaud, CBS, Sat, 6 pm
(10/11/35 - 4/10/36) Pinaud, Mut, 3t, 15m, 7:15 pm

Lilac Time With The Night Singer (with Jeannie Macy, Baron Sven Von Hallberg Orchestra) (3/4/35 - 8/19/35) Pinaud, CBS, Mon, 10:30 pm; continued regionally after 1935

1 **Lillian Randolph Interview** (8/9/76)

1 **Lillian Roth and Her Piano Boys** (1929) film sound track

1 **Lillian Russell** (1940) film sound track

Limerick Show (2/9/50 - 9/14/50) Mut, Thu, 9 pm

Lincoln Cathedral Choir (3/11/38 - 4/15/38) CBS, Fri, 15m, 3:45 pm

1 **Lincoln Highway** (with John McIntire) (3/16/40 - 6/6/42) Hecker Products, NBC,

1 **Lincoln Inaugural Centennial**

Linda Dale (with Helen Shields) (4/29/40 - 2/7/41) Bl, 5t, 15m

1 **Linda's First Love** (with Arline Blackbum) (1939 - 50) (Syndicated and regional) Spotlight Coffee, Kroger Markets (two of the sponsors depending on the region) NBC, 5t, 15m

28 **Lindsay Crosby Show, The** (1958) Syn

1 **Line Is Busy, The** (Syn)

34 **Line-Up, The** (with Bill Johnstone) (7/6/50 - 2/20/53) CBS (various days and times including:)
7/6/50 - 3/1/51, Sus, Thu (except 9/9/50 - 9/23/50, Sat, 8:30 pm) (7/6/50 - 8/24/50, Thu, 8 pm, summer replacement for FBI In Peace and War))
3/6/51 - 7/3/51, Tue, 10 pm
7/12/51 - 8/23/51, Thu, 9 pm
9/5/51 - 9/26/51, Wed, 9 pm
10/4/51 - 11/29/51, Thu, 10 pm
1/8/52 - 8/5/52, Wrigley (some shows), Tue, 10 pm; 9 pm as of 6/3/52
12/26/52 - 2/20/53, Fri, 9:30 pm

Linit Bath Club Revue (also see Fred Allen) (with Margaret Santry) (1/4/32 - 7/1/32) Linit, CBS, 5t, 15m, 8 pm

Linit Orchestra (9/14/31 - 10/30/31) Corn Products, CBS, 3t, 15m, 7:15 pm

Lionel Barrymore (see At Home With Lionel Barrymore)

1 **Lionel Hampton** (World transcription)

1 **Lionel Hampton and His Orchestra** (World Transcription)

1 **Lionel Parent Chantes** (1941) CKAC

Lion's Den, The (with Marvin Miller)

Lion's Eye, The (see Jeff Regan)

Lion's Roar (MGM; with Colonel Stoopnagle until 3/5/43)
(11/30/42 - 7/2/43) Bl, 5t, 5m, 7 pm (not in NY)

Lisa Sergio (One Woman's Opinion) (10/30/44 - 4/22/46) Botany, Bl, Mon, 15m, 10:45 am

1 **Listen America** (10/22/39 - 1/14/40) (Calling America) with Drew Pearson, Erno Rapee Orchestra, Mut, Sun, 6 pm
(11/23/41 - 7/10/42) (host: John B. Kennedy) Sus
11/23/41 - 5/31/42, Red, Sun, 3:30 pm
6/12/42 - 7/10/42, Bl, Fri, 9 pm

Listen and Live (6/2/40 - 9/8/40) American Red Cross, Bl, Sun, 1 pm

Listen Carefully (with Jay Jostyn) (6/22/47 - 9/6/47) Mut, Sun, 9:30 pm; Sat, 9 pm as of 8/2/47

Listener's Club, The (1930s)

1 **Listen Darling** (11/38) Air trailer

1 **Listen, It's Summer**

1 **Listener Reports, The** (7/20/46) WOR

1 **Listener's Grandstand** (4/3/47) CBS

6 **Listener's Playhouse** (6/29/40 - 1/18/42)
6/29/40 - 9/14/40, NBC, Sat, 8:30 pm; 8 pm as of 8/24/40
9/19/40 - 10/31/40, NBC, Thu, 10:30 pm
11/9/40 - 11/23/40, Bl, Sat, 6:30 pm
11/30/40 - 1/18/41, Bl, Sat, 7:30 pm
3/6/41 - 5/1/41, NBC, Thu, 10:30 pm
12/21/41 - 1/18/42, Bl, Sat, 7:30 pm

Listener's Theater (1/2/39 - 5/1/39) Mut, Mon, 9 pm (not in New York)

1 **Listening For Signals From Mars** (7/27/39) WOR

Listening Post, The (with Bret Morrison) (2/8/44 - 10/29/48) Saturday Evening Post, Bl/ABC, 4t (Tue- Fri), 15m, 10:45 am

1 **Listening To Jazz with Ernie Kovacs** (1957) Syn

1 **Listening To Jazz with Hal March** (1956) Syn

1 **Listening To Music with Skitch Henderson** (1962) Syn

1 **Listening To Music with Tony Perkins**

1 **Listening World, The** (CBS)

Listen, The Women (with Janet Flanner; Dorothy Thompson as of 10/22/44) (4/2/44 - 3/27/45) Bl
4/2/44 - 7/2/44, Sun, 10 pm
7/9/44 - 10/8/44, Sun, 3 pm
10/15/44 - 12/24/44, Sun, 4 pm
12/31/44 - 3/27/45, Tue, 10 pm; 10:30 pm as of 2/13/45

Listen To A Love Song (see Tony Martin)

1 **Listen To The People** (7/4/41) NBC

Listen To This (with Kay St. Germain and Lew Diamond Orchestra)
(12/19/35 - 4/6/37) Murine, Mut
12/19/35 - 4/16/36, Thu, 15m, 9:30 pm
4/21/36 - 4/6/37, Tue, 30m

Listerine Program (12/8/31- 4/9/32) Listerine, Bl, 3t (Tue, Wed, Sat), 15m, 10 pm

16 **Lithuanian Language Program** (10/7/36 - 11/30/36) WMBQ

1 **Little Balsam** (1953) Syn

1 **Little Box That Talked, The** (11/2/70) KDKA

Little Betsy Ross Girl Variety Program, The (with Marion Loveridge)
(10/10/43 - 10/28/45) NBC, Sun, 15m, 11:45 am
10/10/43 - 10/29/44, Modern Food Co.
11/5/44 - 10/28/45, Campana

Little Blue Playhouse (4/4/42 - 10/2/43) Bl, Sat, 11:30 am

2 **Little Cafes** (7/29/30) Syn

1 **Little Flower - Fiorello La Guardia, The**

Little Herman (1/1/49 - 7/12/49) Cheeseborough, ABC, Sat, 9 pm; Tue, 8 pm as of 5/3/49

Little House Family (also Visiting America's Little House)
(11/26/34 - 10/28/35) CBS, Mon, 15m, 4 pm

1 **Little Immigrant, The** (6/15/48) CBS (also see Life With Luigi)

Little Italy (with Ned Wever, Himan Brown, Ruth Yorke)
(2/3/33 - 12/21/33) Del L & W Coal, Bl, various days, 15m

1 **Little Jack Little** (1930 - 8/4/44) 15m
1930 - 5/31/31, Bl, Sun
also 1930 - 3/11/31, Bl, Wed, 15m, 1:45 pm
4/18/32 - 4/22/32, P. Lorillard Co., CBS, 5t, 15m, 9 am
1932 - 33, CBS, Sun; also Bl, 3t
2/13/34 - 5/8/34, Wonder Bread, CBS, Tue, 15m, 8 pm
5/18/34 - 6/29/34, Wonder Bread, CBS, Fri, 15m, 9:15 pm
10/28/34 - 3/15/35, Pinex, CBS, Sun & Wed
4/17/44 - 8/4/44, Bl, 5t, 15m, 1:45 pm

1 **Little Jack Little and His Orchestra** (9/14/39) NBC

Little Known Facts (with Tiny Ruffner)
(9/7/44 - 5/27/45; 8/26/45 - 11/25/45) Frank W. Lee Co., Mut, Thu, 15m, 10:15 pm (not in New York)

Little Known Facts About Well Known People (see Dale Carnegie)

1 **Little Man Inside, The** (5/21/45) ABC/Bl, 15m

Little Matchmaker (with Sheldon Leonard)

1 **Little Miss Broadway** (1938) film sound track

Little Miss Bab-O's Surprise Party (see Mary Small)

1 **Little Miss Marker** (1934) film sound track

1 **Little Nellie Kelly** (11/1/40) Air trailer

Little Night Music, A (5/30/38 - 7/18/38) CBS, Mon, 10:30 pm)

Little Old Man (5/2/35 - 7/9/35) Bl, Thu, 15m, 6 pm; Fri, 6 pm as of 7/2/35

Little Old New York (with Jack Arthur)

Little Ol' Hollywood (with Ben Alexander) (mostly West Coast)
(11/21/39 - 2/7/42) Bl
11/21/39 - 12/19/39, Tue, 9 pm
12/25/39 - 1/22/40, Mon, 10 pm
3/25/40 - 9/16/40, Mon, 8 pm
9/23/40 - 10/28/40, Mon, 25m, 9:35 pm
also 9/21/40 - 2/7/42, Sat, 7:30 pm

Little Orly Stories (with "Uncle Lumpy") (see Fred Waring Shows)

6 **Little Orphan Annie** (with Shirley Bell until 12/28/34; then Bobby Dean) Started in Chicago in 1930
(1930 - 4/24/42)
4/6/31 - 10/30/36, Ovaltine, Bl, 6t/5t
11/2/36 - 7/9/37, Ovaltine, NBC, 5t
9/27/37 - 1/19/40, Ovaltine, NBC, 5t
1/22/40 - 6/28/40, Ovaltine, Mut, 5t
1/27/41 - 4/25/41, Quaker, Mut, 5t
9/29/41 - 4/24/42, Quaker, Mut, 5t
also syndicated

2 **Little Red Door, The** (Syn)

Little Show, The (7/4/43 - 2/13/44)
Esquire Polish, Mut, Sun, 15m
7/4/43 - 10/3/43, 1:45 pm
12/5/43 - 2/13/44, 6:45 pm
(5/3/47 - 6/7/47) CBS, Sat, 7:30 pm

1 **Little Story, The** (10/29/52)

Little Theater Of The Air (1947) WLWA, Sat

1 **Little Theatre Workshop Players**

68 **Little Things In Life, The**
(8/4/75 - 2/25/76) (with Peg Lynch and Bob Dryden) (Syn)

Little Variety Show (with Rakov Orchestra) (9/13/38 - 7/4/39) Bl, Tue, 2:30 pm (with Anson Weeks)
(4/22/39 - 10/7/39) Bl, Sat, 1 :30 pm

Little Women (with Elaine Kent and Pat Ryan) (2/9/42 - 3/6/42) Mut, 5t, 15m, 4:15 pm

1 **Littlest Angel, The** (World syndication)

Live and Learn (4/2/39 - 7/2/39) (with Alice Duer Miller) Mut, Sun, 15m, 2 pm
(1952 - 53) Chicago

1 **Live A New Life** (3/5/49) WOR

Live Like A Millionaire (with Jack McCoy) (6/5/50 - 8/28/53) 5t
6/5/50 - 9/12/52, General Mills, NBC, 2:30 pm
11/3/52 - 8/28/53, Sus, ABC, 11 am

1 **Lively Touch, The** (4/66)

2 **Lives In The Making** (1944) Syn

Lives Of Great Men (with Dr. E. H. Griggs) (12/24/38 - 6/10/39) NBC, Sat, 15m, 7:30 pm

Lives Of Harry Lime, The (Syn) (see The Third Man)

4 **Lives Of The Great** (1934) 15m

51 **Living** (with Ben Grauer) [date following Living changed with year such as Living 1948; Living 1949; Living 1950; Living 1951]
(2/29/48 - 3/27/49; 6/26/49 - 5/50; 10/7/50 - 1/20/51; 6/16/51 - 9/29/51) NBC, Sun; Sat as of 10/7/50

Living Art (with John D. Morse)
(7/7/42 - 2/23/43) CBS, Tue, 15m, 4:30 pm

2 **Living Bible, The** (Syn)

Living Biographies (9/7/41- 9/28/41) NBC, sun, 7 pm (partial summer replacement of Jack Benny)

Living Dangerously (see Dangerously Yours)

1 **Living Desert Suite, The** (1953)

Living Diary (10/26/4 - 11/23/41) NBC, Sun, 5:30 pm

Living Dramas Of The Bible
(5/2/37 - 10/10/37) CBS, Sun, 1:30 pm

Living Fiction (1954) Chicago

Living History (3/3/42 - 6/30/42) CBS, Tue, 15m; developed into "Living Art"

Living In An Atomic Age (with Bertrand Russell) (5/12/53 - 6/20/53)

Living Literature (7/16/41 - 3/18/42) Bl, Wed, 15m, 11:45 am

Living Should Be Fun (with Carlton Fredericks)

1 **Loan To Britain, The** (12/19/45) Mut

1 **Local Boys Club Show** (1949) Syn

Lockharts, The (11/5/31 - 1/28/32) Thomas A. Edison, Inc., CBS, Thu, 15m, 8:45 am

Log Cabin Dude Ranch, The (with The Westerners and Cameron Andrews) (9/29/36 - 3/23/37) Log Cabin, Bl, Tue, 8 pm

1 **Log Cabin Inn** (4/3/35) NBC

18 **Log Cabin Jamboree** (11/6/37 - 4/2/38) NBC

Log Cabin News (8/29/52 - 12/53) Log Cabin, NBC, Thu, 5m, 8:25 pm

Log Cabin Revue (10/2/35 - 12/25/35) Log Cabin, NBC, Wed, 10 pm

Log Cabin Show (Jamboree) (see Jack Haley; Lanny Ross)

1 **Log Of The Black Parrott, The** (5/6/50) Audition (with Elliott Lewis, CBS)

1 **Lois Long and Three Sons** (also called Shopping Talk) (12/9/44 - 6/23/45) Chatham Co., Bl, Sat, 15m

Lombardoland U.S.A. (see Guy Lombardo)

1 **London After Dark** (8/24/50) CBS

1 **London Air Raid**

1 **London Calling Europe**

3 **London Column**

10 **London Forum** (6/8/49 - 6/18/51) BBC

2 **London Playhouse** (2/23/44) BBC

1 **Lone Journey** (5/27/40 - 6/27/52) 5t, 15m (sometimes regional)
5/27/40 - 6/25/43, Dreft, NBC
4/1/46 - 9/28/46 (with Staats Cotsworth, Gladys Holland), Camation, NBC, 10 am
9/30/46 - 9/26/47 (with Staats Cotsworth, Gladys Holland), Carnation, CBS, 2:30 pm
7/2/51 - 6/27/52, Lever Bros. (as of 10/1/51), ABC, 11:30 am; 11 am as of 9/24/51

Lonely Women (with Betty Lou Gerson)
(6/29/42 - 12/10/43) General Mills, NBC, 5t, 15m; led to Today's Children

438 **Lone Ranger, The** (1/31/33 - 5/25/56) started on WXYZ, Detroit and gradually spread, 2t; George Seaton as the Lone Ranger until 5/9/33; Jack Deeds 5/11/33; James Jewell 5/13/33; Earl Graser from 5/15/33 - 4/7/41 (3374 shows broadcast)
11/21/33 - 2/10/39, Silvercup, Mut, 3t
2/13/39 - 5/1/42, Bond Bread (until 8/9/40), Mut, 3t; Brace Beemer as the Lone Ranger from 4/18/41 on
5/4/42 - 9/3/54, Cheerios, ABC, 3t, 6 pm; 7:30 pm as of 11/2/42; 25m as of 12/1/52; last live broadcast on 9/3/54
9/6/54 - 5/25/56 (rebroadcasts on ABC and NBC) Cheerios, ABC, 3t, 25m, 7:30 pm; NBC, 5t, 25m, 5:30 pm as of 5/30/55

1 **Lone Star Quartet, The** (11/14/41) WPTF, audition

12 **Lonesome Gal** (with Jean King) (10/13/47 - 51) 15m
10/13/47 - 49, WING, Dayton, Ohio (local)
1949 - 51, Syn

1 **Lonesome Train, The** (World syndication)

1 **Lone Wolf, The** (6/29/48 - 1/1/49) Sus, Mut
6/29/48 - 8/24/48, Tue, 9:30 pm
12/4/48 - 1/1/49, Sat, 2 pm

Lone Wolf Tribe (with Chief Whirling Thunder and Chief Wolf Paw) was heard regionally in the midwest before 1932
(1/4/32 - 5/5/33) Wrigley, CBS, 3t, 15m, 5:45 pm

Long John Nebel (1954 - 78) WOR, WNBC

7 **Long Night, The** (1947) Syn

1 **Longest Day That Ever Was, The** (6/30/72) WBAI

Longines Choraliers, The (see Festival Of Song; Choraliers, The Longines Symphonette)

Longines Musicale (see The Longines Symphonette)

89 **Longines Symphonette, The**
(7/5/43 - 3/11/49) (with Macklin Marrow) Mut, 5t, 15m, 10:45 pm; network on 1/14/44, 5t, 30m, 10:30 pm
(3/13/49 - 5/26/57) (with Mishel Piastro) Longine, CBS
3/13/49 - 12/18/49; 4/16/50 - 6/25/50; 9/3/50 - 6/8/52; 9/14/52 - 4/26/53; 9/27/53 - 5/30/54; 9/5/54 - 4/17/55; 10/2/55 - 4/29/56; 9/30/56 - 5/26/57, Sun, 30m
also 10/2/50 - 12/28/50, ABC, 4t (Mon - Thu), 25m, 10:35 pm
also 10/2/50 - 7/10/53; 9/3/53 - 2/12/54, NBC, 5t, 30m, 7 pm
also 3/6/54 - 6/5/54, CBS, 3t (Wed, Fri, Sat), 30 on Sat; 15m, on Wed & Fri

Longines World's Most Honored Music Program (see The Longines Symphonette)

Looking Into Space (with Willy Ley)
(10/12/52 - 1/18/53) ABC, Sun, 15m, 7:45 pm

2 **Look and Listen** (Syn)

1 **Look To The East** (5/8/45) CBS

4 **Look To The Skies** (1953) Syn

1 **Look Up and Live** (1959) CBS-TV

1 **Look Your Best** (with Richard Willis) (1947 - 48) CBS, 5t, 15m

16 **Lora Lawton** (5/31/43 - 1/6/50) Babbitt, NBC, 5t, 15m

2 **Lord Halifax** (8/24/39, 12/7/42) BBC, WFBR

4 **Lord Haw Haw** (3/22/40 - 4/30/45) Germany

4 **Lord Oakburn's Daughters** (Syn)

26 **Lord Of The Rings, The** (1980, 1986 in the U.S.A.) (NPR; originally BBC)

57 **Lord Peter Wimsey** (BBC) (with Ian Carmichael)
(1982 - 1985) NPR rebroadcast

7 **Lorenzo Jones** (with Karl Swenson) (4/26/37 - 9/30/55) NBC, 5t, 15m
4/26/37 - 12/9/49, Phillips Milk Of Magnesia and Bayer
12/12/49 - 9/30/55, Procter & Gamble and Hazel Bishop

Lorne Greene (9/11/54 - 2/19/55) Mut, Sat, 5m, 9:25 pm

1 **Lorraine Lesk Recital** (1/16/37) WCNW

1 **Los Angeles Dance Band** (1939) Syn

1 **Los Angeles Folklore Choir** (1938) Syn

1 **Los Angeles Negro Choir** (Syn)

5 **Los Angeles Symphony Orchestra** (1937) Syn

Loser, The (with Richard McGee) (5/5/55 - 8/4/55) NBC, Thu, 9:30 pm

1 **Lost Class Of '59, The** (1/59) CBS-TV

1 **Lost Colony, The** (Syn)

2 **Lost Empire** (1930s) (Syn)

Lou Breese Orchestra (5/8/36 - 6/5/36) Bl, Fri, 8:30 pm (also called Sheaffer Parade)
(3/18/45 - 12/9/45) Sheaffer Pens, NBC, Sun, 3 pm

1 **Lou Diamond and His Orchestra** (7/31/47) ABC

4 **Lou Donn and His Orchestra** (1969) CBS

Louella Palkin (11/10/41 - 1/5/42) Bl, Mon, 15m, 7:30 pm

Louella Parsons (2/28/34 - 5/23/34) CBS, Wed, 15m, 12:15 pm
(12/3/44 - 6/22/54) Jergens
12/3/44 - 12/23/51, Bl/ABC, Sun, 9:15 pm
4/1/52 - 6/22/54, CBS, Tue, 5m, 9:30 pm; 15m as of 3/31/53

1 **Lou Holtz** (5/65)

6 **Lou Holtz Laugh Club** (6/2/33 - 8/25/33) (with Grace Moore) CBS, Fri, 10 pm
(6/21/42 - 10/25/42) (Time Out For Laughs) CBS, Sun, 15m, 7:15 pm
also syndicated

Louisa (with Spring Byington)

Louis Armstrong (1937) (Norge Program) 15m (Basin Street) (1954 - 56)

1 **Louis Armstrong Yokahama Concert** (1953) NBC

1 **Louis Armstrong and Bing Crosby Live** (1949)

3 **Louis Armstrong and His All-Stars** (1954, 1/1/68) NBC

1 **Louis Armstrong and His Orchestra** (6/19/47) NBC

1 **Louis Armstrong and The Original "All-Stars"** (6/19/47) WNBC

1 **Louis Jordan** (World transcription)

2 **Louis Jordan and His Orchestra** (World transcriptions)

2 **Louise Florea with Male Choir** (Lang-Worth transcriptions)

Louise Florea Show, The (also called Song Sweets) (7/10/39 - 9/18/39) NBC, Mon, 15m, 5:15 pm

5 **Louise Massey and The Westerners** (also with Curt Massey)
(1936) Bl, Tue, 15m, 8 pm
(10/6/41 - 3/28/47) (Reveille Roundup) Grove Labs, NBC, 3t, 15m, 7:45 am also syndicated

Louise Rice (1930 - 4/23/31) Bl, Thu, 15m, 11:30 am

1 **Louise Wilcher At The Console** (5/13/38) Mut
also (9/29/40 - 42) CBS, Sun, 15m, 8:30 am; 8:15 am as of 6/1/41

Louisiana Hayride (1948 - 92+)

1 **Louisiana Purchase** (1941) Air trailer

1 **Louisville Symphony**

2 **Louis Prima and His Orchestra** (9/22/39) CBS

1 **Louis - Sharkey Fight, The** (8/18/36) CBS

Louis Sobel Show, The (also with Vincent Lopez) (3/6/44 - 9/4/44) (Mut, Mon, 7:30 pm
(1/28/57 - 10/4/57) ABC, 5t, 25m, 9:30 pm; 8 pm as of 4/15/57

Lou Lacey Show (15m)

Loulie Jean (4/20/41 - 5/25/41) NBC, Sun, 15m, 4 pm

Lou Little Football Forecast
(10/22/37 - 12/3/37) American Chicle, Mut, Fri, 15m, 7:30 pm

Love Affair (12/22/41 - 1/23/42) Mut, 5t, 15m, 4:15 pm (limited run serial)

1 **Love and Hisses** (1938) film sound track

2 **Love Finds Andy Hardy** (1938) Air trailer, film sound track

Love For A Day (15m)

Love Letters (with Franklin MacCormack)

Lovely Lady (with John Slanton) (1940) NBC

2 **Lovemaking, Inc.** (Pre-war)

1 **Love Me Tonight** (1932) film sound track

1 **Love On The Run** (1937) Air trailer

Love Notes (with Jerry Wayne) (1945) Sun, 5m

1 **Love Songs** (8/31/36 - 3/5/37) Gold Medal (as of 10/1/36), Mut, 5t, 15m, 11:30 am
also 4/3/48, WLOS

Love Songs and Waltzes (with Frank Munn) (5/16/32 - 7/25/32) Phillips, Bl, 2t (Mon & Fri), 15m, 10:30 pm

2 **Love Story** (1938) 15m

Love Story Drama Hour (see the Shadow)

Love Story Dramas (5/2/34 - 7/18/34) Bl, Wed, 9:30 am
(4/19/37 - 3/13/38) Love Story Magazine

Love Story Girl (Syn)

Love Story Theater (with Jim Ameche) (10/25/46 - 47) Mut, Fri, 8:30 pm

39 **Love Tales** (Syn)

2 **Love Thy Neighbor** (1940) Air trailers

13 **Lowell Thomas News** (9/30/30 - 5/14/76)
9/30/30 - 6/17/32, Literary Digest, Bl, 5t, 15m, 6:45 pm; also CBS for 6 months
6/20/32 - 12/18/45, Sunoco, Bl (NBC from 1932 - 33)
12/25/45 - 9/26/47, NBC, Sunoco
9/29/47 - 5/14/76, CBS, various sponsors

1 **Lowell Thomas Recalls**

1 **Loyalty Day Parade** (8/28/51) ABC

1 **Lucille Norman Program** (1/7/37) WCNW

Lucille Manners (9/27/36 - 12/6/36) NBC, Sun, 1 pm

Luck Of The Irish (with Chester Morris and Bea Benadaret)

Lucky and Lefty (1934) Mut, Mon, 15m

Lucky Girl (1937 - 38) 15m

Lucky Kids (with Hugh Aspinwall) (1/12/32 - 2/6/32) Coco Cod Liver Oil.

2 **Lucky Millender and His Orchestra** (12/41) WMCA, WNEW

Lucky Partners (with Paul Brenner) (5/13/48 - 8/5/48) Mut, Thu, 8 pm

1 **Lucky Seven Program, The** (1931)

3 **Lucky Shopper Show, The** (1944, 1946) KNX

Lucky Smith (with Max Baer and Peg La Centra) (4/29/35 - 7/22/35) Gillette, NBC, Mon, 10:30 pm

Lucky Stars (with Jack Kilty) (1946) NBC

Lucky Strike Dance Orchestra (with Walter Winchell, Jack Pearl, Bert Lahr at different times)
(9/15/28 - 1/2/34) Lucky Strike except where noted, NBC, 60m
9/15/28 - 9/6/32 (with B. A. Rolfe until 10/30/31), Sat; 3t (Tue, Thu, Sat) as of 1930
9/8/32 - 6/29/33, Thu (see Jack Pearl)

Lucky Strike Dance Orchestra (continued)

9/10/32 - 2/11/33 (with Ted Weems; Vincent Lopez), Sat
2/18/33 - 1/2/34 (with B. A. Rolfe) Sus, Sat
9/13/32 - 3/28/33 FBI cases dramatized from 10/25/32 -1/31/33; other police cases dramatized before and after those dates) (with Ferde Grofe or Ted Weems Orchestra) Tue, 10 pm

Lucky Strike Music Hall (with Milton Cross) 1934 (with Jessica Dragonette in Teresina)

Lucky Strike Program Starring Jack Benny, The (see The Jack Benny Program)

11 **Lucky U Ranch** (1952, 1953) Mut

Luden's Musical Revue (with Robert Armbruster Orchestra)
(10/27/34 - 2/23/35) Ludens, CBS, Sat, 15m, 8:45 pm

Luden's Novelty Orchestra (with Dan Rybb, Conrad Thibault)
(10/18/31 - 4/10/32) CBS Sun, 30m, 7:30 pm; 15m as of 11/1/31

Lud Gluskin Orchestra (7/2/40 - 8/27/40) CBS, Tue, 8:30 pm (also see The World Dances)

Lud Gluskin Presents (On The Air) (7/2/35 - 9/24/35) CBS, Tue, 9 pm

Luigi Romanelli Orchestra
(6/17/39 - 9/9/39) Bl, Sat, 12 noon
also 6/26/39 - 9/8/39) Bl, 5t, 15m, 12 noon

13 **Luke Slaughter Of Tombstone** (with Sam Buffington)
(2/23/58 - 6/15/58) CBS, Sun

Lullaby Lady, The

Lulu and Johnny (with Lulu Bates and Johnny Morgan)) (7/12/43 - 9/10/43) Bl, 5t, 15m, 10:15 pm

Lulu Belle and Scotty (Syn) 15m, on WLS in 1937

823 **Lum and Abner** (with Chester Lauck, Norris Goff) (4/26/31 - 5/7/54)
4/26/31 - 7/5/31, KTHS
8/24/31 - 9/25/31 , Quaker, NBC, 5t
8/28/31 - 12/26/31, Quaker, 6t
1/11/32 - 4/1/32, NBC, Sus, 5t
4/4/32 - 4/29/32, NBC, 3t
5/2/32 - 6/17/32, 5t
8/1/32 - 10/7/32, 5t
11/24/32 - 5/19/33, 5t
5/23/33 - 3/30/34, Ford, NBC, 5t, 15m
4/2/34 - 6/14/34, Horlick, Mut, 4t, Mon - Thu, 6:15 pm
6/17/34 - 12/14/34, 6t
12/17/34 - 8/30/35, 5t
9/2/35 - 11/26/37, Horlick, Bl, 5t, 15m, 7:30 pm
11/29/37 - 2/5/38, 3t
9/5/38 - 6/30/39, Postum, CBS, 3t, 15m, 6:45 pm; 7:15 pm as of 9/26/38
9/3/45 - 10/2/47, Alka-Seltzer, Bl/ABC, 4t (Mon, Tue, Thu, Fri), 15m, 6:30 pm; 4t (Mon - Thu), 8:15 pm as of 7/6/42; 8 pm as of 7/2/45

Lum and Abner (continued)

10/6/47 - 9/24/48, Alka Seltzer, CBS, 5t, 15m, 5:45 pm
9/26/48 - 6/26/49, Frigidaire, CBS, Sun, 30m, 10 pm; 8:30 pm as of 1/23/49
11/2/49 - 4/26/50, Ford (on some shows), CBS, Wed, 10:30 pm
2/16/53 - 5/15/53, ABC, 5t, 15m
11/9/53 - 5/7/54, Local sponsors, ABC, 5t, 15m

1 **Luna Probe #1** (8/17/58) NBC-TV

1 **Luna Probe #2** (10/11/58) NBC-TV

Luncheon At Sardi's (with Bill and Tom Slater) (3/22/47 - 1958) WOR, New York, 6t, mostly 45m

Luncheon At The Waldorf (see Ilka Chase)

Luncheon With Lopez (see Vincent Lopez)

1 **Lure Of Perfume, The** (10/19/36) WMBQ

3 **Lure Of The Tropics** (2/36) WMBC

4 **Lutheran Hour, The** (with Dr. Walter Maier until 1950)
(10/2/30 - 6/11/31) CBS, Thu, 10 pm
(10/20/35 - 1956) Mut, Sun
also 10/29/49 - 3/25/51, ABC, Sun, 3:30 pm
1956 - Present, NBC, syndicated

Luther-Layman Singers (with Frank Luther, Zora Layman)
(7/17/39 - 4/27/41) 15m
7/17/39 - 9/28/39, NBC, 2t (various days), 7:15 pm
10/25/39 - 12/20/39, NBC, Wed, 6 pm
3/20/40 - 4/10/40, NBC, Wed, 6 pm
5/12/40 - 4/27/41 (Sweet Land Of Liberty), Bl, Sun, 11:30 am

Lux Hour Of Romance, The (see The Lux Radio Theatre)

630 **Lux Radio Theater, The**
(10/14/34 - 6/7/55) Lux, 60m; 927 shows broadcast directors: Antony Stanford (10/14/34 - 5/25/36); Cecil B. DeMille (6/1/36 - 1/22/45); guest stars (1/29/45 - 10/29/45); William Keighley (11/5/45 - 5/12/52); guest hosts on 5/19 and 5/26; Irving Cummings
(9/8/52 - 6/7/55) except from 6/1/53 - 8/31/53 (Summer Theater); during this time guest hosts included Ken Carpenter and Don Wilson
10/14/34 - 6/30/35, NBC, Sun, 2:30 pm; from New York
7/29/35 - 7/5/37; 9/13/37 - 7/4/38; 9/12/38 - 7/10/39; 9/11/39 - 7/8/40; 9/9/40 - 7/7/41; 9/8/41 - 7/20/42; 9/14/42 - 7/12/43; 9/13/43 - 7/3/44; 9/4/44 - 6/25/45; 8/27/45 - 6/24/46; 8/26/46 - 6/23/47; 8/25/47 - 6/28/48; 8/30/48 - 6/27/49; 8/29/49 - 6/26/50; 8/28/50 - 6/25/51; 8/27/51 - 5/26/52; 9/8/52 - 6/28/54, CBS, Mon, 9 pm; from New York until 5/25/36; from Hollywood starting with 6/1/36; 6/1/53 - 8/31/53 called Summer Theater
9/14/54 - 6/7/55, NBC, Tue, 9 pm

Lux Summer Theatre, The (see The Lux Radio Theatre)

1 **Luxembourg and The United States** (8/30/39) Mut

Lydia (3/9/42 - 3/27/42) Mut, 2t - 4t, 15m

Lyle Van (10/6/48 - 1/19/51) Mut, 5t, 15m, 6 pm

9 **Lyman Bryson** (Time For Reason) (Problems Of Peace) (3/25/45 - 10/5/47) Sus, CBS, Sun, 15m, 1:30 pm

3 **Lyn Murray** (Squibb Show; To Your Good Health; Music From The House Of Squibb)
(10/11/43 - 3/23/45) Squibb, CBS, 3t, 15m

1 **Lyn Murray Show, The** (World syndication) audition

1 **Lyndon Baines Johnson 1908 - 1973** (1/22/73) CBS-TV

1 **Lyndon Baines Johnson: An Appreciation** (1/23/73) ABC-TV

1 **Lyndon LaRouche** (11/5/88) CBS-TV

Lynn Allison (3/10/42 - 8/11/42) NBC, Tue, 15m, 9:45 pm

Lynn Cole Orchestra (Grove's Bromo Quinine)
(6/27/38 - 3/1/39) (As You Like It), Mut, 15m, 3:15 pm
(1947 - 48) Grand Prize Beer

Lyrics By Liza (with Liza Morrow) (3/20/43 - 9/11/43) NBC, Sat, 25m, 3:35 pm

Lyrics By Loretta (5/21/43 - 10/8/43) Mut, 4t (Mon, Tue, Thu, Fri) 5t, 25m, 10:30 am

Ma and Pa (6/28/36 - 9/27/36) (with Parker Fennell and Effie Palmer) CBS, Sun, 6 pm
(12/29/36 - 6/25/37) (with Margaret Dee, Parker Fennelly) Atlantic, CBS, 3t (Tue, Thu, Sat), 15m, 7:15 pm; 5t as of 3/1/37

2 **MacArthur Story, The** (4/11/51) CBS

8 **Macabre** (AFRTS-FEN origination) (11/13/61 - 1/8/62)

Machine Age Housekeeping (with Ida Bailey Allen) (1/21/32 - 4/14/32) Hamilton-Beach, CBS, Thu, 15m, 10:15 am

1 **Machines Without Men** (9/7/50) NBC

1 **MacNeil-Lehrer News Hour, The** (11/21/88) PBS-TV

15 **Mac Baldy, The Tall Shooter** (Syn)

Mac McGuire Show (12/20/52 - 2/7/53) Mut, Sat, 4:30 pm

Madame Ambassador (with Rosalind Russell) NBC

6 **Madame Chiang Kai-Shek** (3/8/42 - 4/13/45) China, WOR, Mut

Madame Courageous (with Betty Caine) (9/26/38 - 12/23/38) Durkee, Bl, 5t, 15m

Madame Ernestine Schumann-Heink (Sentinels Serenade) (1/6/34 - 5/5/35) Hoover, Bl, Sun, 10 pm

1 **Madame Manhattan and Montana Slim** (1936)

1 **Madame Q** (1928) Synchro-disc

Madame Sylvia (9/26/33 - 3/27/35) Ralston Purina, 15m
9/26/33 - 3/26/34, NBC, Tue
10/3/34 - 3/27/35, Bl, Wed

Madeleine Carroll Reads (Judith Evelyn from 8/2/43 - 9/17/43)
(1/18/43 - 10/8/43) CBS, 5t, 15m, 5pm

Madison Square Garden Boxing (11/26/37 - 58+)
11/26/37 - 5/30/41, Adam Hats, Bl, Fri, 10 pm (occasionally other days depending on boxing schedule)
10/31/41 - 58+, Gillette, Mut, Fri, 10 pm; ABC as of 9/7/45 (not every Friday); NBC as of 9/17/54

1 **Mad Masters, The** (with Monte and Natalie Masters) (3/19/46) ABC
(7/12/47 - 8/31/47) NBC, Sat, 8:30 pm (summer replacement of Truth Or Consequences)

2 **Madrigal Singers Of New York** (1939) Syn

1 **Madrigal Singers, The** (12/12/37 - 4/17/38; 6/19/38 - 2/54/39; 8/25/40 - 9/22/40) NBC, Sun, also syn

1 **Mae West Interview** (2/4/49) WOR

Magazine Of The Air (see Heinz Magazine Of The Air)

Magazine Theater (2/23/51 - 9/16/51) Mut
2/23/51 - 4/13/51, Fri, 8 pm
5/6/51 - 9/16/51, Sun, 10 pm

Maggie and Jiggs (see Bringing Up Father)

Maggie McNellis (7/10/44 - 5/27/55) 5t (also called Maggie's Private World; Maggie's Magazine)
7/10/44 - 6/20/47, NBC, 15m
6/23/47 - 4/1/49, ABC, 30m
9/22/52 - 5/27/55, ABC, 5t, 15m, 12:15 pm

6 **Magic Carpet** (AFRS) (1945 - 47) 15m

1 **Magic Carpet, The** (12/17/46) WOR

4 **Magic Christmas Window, The** (Syn)

1 **Magic Curtain** (7/14/48) Mut

1 **Magic Curtain Auditions** (6/8/48, 6/22/48)

128 **Magic Island** (with Bill Johnstone) (1936) 12m

17 **Magic Key, The** (with Milton Cross) (9/29/35 - 9/18/39) RCA, Bl, Sun; Mon, 8:30 pm as of 6/26/39; 9 pm as of 8/14/39

2 **Magic and Moonlight** (Syn)

Magic Of Believing (12/24/51 - 12/21/52) Mut, Sun, 15m, 9:15 am

Magic Of Music (AFRS)

Magic Of Speech, The (with Vida Sutton) (1929 - 6/26/37)
1929 - 31, NBC, Thu, 15m
1931- 32, NBC, Tue
1932 - 36, NBC, Fri
1936 - 6/26/37, Sus, NBC, Sat

2 **Magic Of Vision, The** (1/56) Syn

Magic Piano Twins (2/26/32 - 5/27/32) (with Frank Westphal and Albert Nilsen)
(9/9//32 - 12/2/32) (with Harry Sosnik and William Moss) Dri-Brite Wax, CBS, Fri, 15m

Magic Recipes (with Jane Ellison)
(1/10/34 - 12/25/35) Borden, Wed, 15m, 11:45 am
1/10/34 - 12/26/34, CBS
1/2/35 - 12/25/35, NBC

Magic Rhythm (with the Debonaires and Betty Dorsey) (1948 - 49) Mut

Magic Sounds

Magic Voice, The (with Elsie Hitz, George Dawson) (11/15/32 - 6/27/33) Ex-Lax, CBS, 2t (Tue & Sat), 15m, 8:15 pm
(3/30/36 - 8/28/36) Chipso, Bl, 5t, 15m, 4:45 pm

Magic Waves (with Orestes Caldwell) (10/13/39 - 4/27/40) Bl, 15m (also see Radio Magic)
10/13/39 - 1/16/40, Fri, 7:45 pm
2/3/40 - 4/27/40, Sat

20 **Magnificent Montague, The** (with Monty Woolley)
(11/10/50 - 11/10/51) Multi, NBC, Fri; Sat, 8:30 pm as of 5/12/51; 8 pm as of 10/6/51

Magnolia Blossoms (see Fisk Jubilee Choir)

3 **Mahalia Jackson Show, The** (8/25/54 - 2/6/55) CBS, Sun, 25m, 10:05 pm

Mahlon Merrick Orchestra (Songs Without Words)

1 **Maiden Flight Of The B-19 (Sunrise Salute)** (6/21/41) CBS

75 **Mail Call** (AFRS) (8/11/42 - 1950)

1 **Main Attraction, The** (4/17/70) CBS

2 **Main Street Album**

7 **Main Street Music Hall** (with Earl Wrightson, Russ Emery)
(7/23/50 - 8/27/50; 7/29/51 - 9/2/51; 6/15/52 - 8/3/52) CBS, Sun, CBS

1 **Main Street Music Hall, The** (Syn)

33 **Maisie** (with Ann Sothern)
(7/5/45 - 12/26/52)
7/5/45 - 8/16/45, Eversharp, CBS, Thu, 8:30 pm
8/22/45 - 2/27/46, Eversharp, CBS, Wed, 10:30 pm; 9:30 as of 9/12/45
3/8/46 - 6/28/46; 8/16/46 - 3/28/47, Eversharp, CBS, Fri, 10:30 pm
11/24/49 - 52, Sus, Mut, Thu/Fri (not in New York)
1/11/52 - 12/26/52, Mut, Fri, 8 pm

Majestic Curiosity Shop
(10/14/28 -12/21/30) General Household Utilities, CBS, Sun, 9 pm

7 **Majestic Master Of Mystery** (with Maurice Joachim)
(12/30/33 - 2/10/34) Grigsby Grunow, (Majestic Radio) 15m, syn

Majestic Theater Hour (featuring Moran and Mack) (1927 - 30) General Utilities, CBS, 60m, 9 pm

12 **Majestic Theater Of The Air, The**
(5/10/32 - 7/26/32) 15m

Major Bowes' Capitol Family
(7/26/25 - 5/25/41) Sus, NBC, Sun (started locally 11/19/22)
7/26/25 - 3/1/31, 30m - 90m
3/6/31 - 12/21/31- 8/30/36, 60m, 11:30 am
6/9/36 - 5/25/41, CBS, 60m, 11:30 am

10 **Major Bowes' Original Amateur Hour** (with Major Edward Bowes)
(3/24/35 - 1/4/45) (started on WHN, New York in 1924) (see also Shower Of Stars)
3/24/35 - 9/13/36, Chase and Sanborn, NBC, Sun, 60m
9/17/36 - 1/15/42, Chrysler, CBS, Thu, 60m, 9 pm
1/22/42 - 1/4/45, Chrysler, CBS, Thu, 30m, 9 pm; Bowes was sick from 2/8/45 - 7/19/45; no active part from 4/27/45

1 **Major Charles De Gaulle** (6/23/40) France

1 **Major George Fielding Eliot** (7/30/50)

1 **Major Gregory "Pappy" Boyington**
(1/13/44) Mut

Major Hoople (with Arthur Q. Bryan)
(6/22/42 - 4/26/43) Bl, Mon, 25m, 7:05 pm

1 **Major Kent C. Lambert** (9/2/39) Mut

Major North (see The Man From G-2)

10 **Make Believe Ballroom** (1944, 1947) Michigan Radio Net, Voice Of America (see also Martin Block)

1 **Make Believe Town** (with Virginia Bruce)
(8/1/49 - 9/8/51) CBS
8/1/49 - 9/9/49, 5t, 3:30 pm
10/1/50 - 12/31/30, Sun, 3:30 pm
7/21/51 - 9/8/51, Sat, 11:30 am

2 **Make Mine Music** (with Connie Russell, Billy Leach) (1946) syndication
(7/11/48 - 9/19/48) CBS, Sun, 4:30 pm; 5 pm as of 9/12/48

7 **Makers Of History** (15m) Syn

Make Up Your Mind (8/17/53 - 10/2/56) Wonder Bread, CBS, 5t, 15m

1 **Make Way For Youth** (with Don Large Youth Chorus) (5/7/49 - 7/9/55) CBS, Sat, 60m, 30m

Make Yours Music (with Lyn Murray) Ivory and Oxydol, CBS

1 **Making Of "A Soldier's Story," The**
(12/12/84) NPR

1 **Making Of Star Wars For Radio: A Fable For The Mind's Eye, The**
(10/10/82) NPR

1 **Making Of The President: 1972, The**
(5/25/75) Syn

Making The Movies (with Raymond Knight) (3/20/32 - 6/12/32) Kelly-Springfield, Bl, Sun, 9:45 pm

Malcolm Claire (1931 - 9/17/40) NBC, 15m; various days and times including:
7/18/36 - 6/10/40, 6t/5t; not always in New York
6/17/40 - 9/17/40, Bl, 5t, 15m, 5:15 pm (Uncle Mal)

Malcolm LaPrade
(see Cook's Travelogue)

Malik Mystery Drama (with Stanley Andrews and Bernadine Flynn)
(1/7/32 - 9/25/32) Bl, Sun, 11 pm

Maltex Program (with Frank Pinero Orchestra; Sam Lloyd)
(9/16/31 - 3/3/32) Maltex, NBC, Wed, 15m, 5:30 pm; Thu as of 1/7/32

Maltine Story Time (1930 - 4/6/31) Maltine, Bl, Mon, 4 pm

1 **Mama Bloom's Brood** (1930s) 15m, Syn

1 **Mammy** (1930) film sound track

Man About Hollywood (with George McCall (7/17/39 - 9/4/49) Lux, CBS, Mon, 9 pm (partial summer replacement of Lux Radio Theater)
(7/12/40 - 9/27/40) Grape-Nuts, CBS, Fri, 8 pm (summer replacement for part of Kate Smith)

Man About Music (AFRS)

1 **Man About Town** (1935) 15m, also (1939) Air trailer

2 **Man Against The Crippler** (1953) Syn

1 **Man At The Moon** (12/27/69) CBS-TV

6 **Man Behind The Gun, The** (with Jackson Beck)
(10/7/42 - 3/4/44) CBS
10/7/42 - 3/3/43, Sus, Wed, 10:30 pm
3/7/43 - 6/27/43, Elgin, Sun, 10:30 pm
7/3/43 - 3/4/44, Elgin, Sat, 7 pm

2 **Man Behind The Masterpiece, The**
(12/13/46, 12/20/46) Syn

37 **Man Called X, The** (with Herbert Marshall) (7/10/44 - 5/20/52)
7/10/44 - 8/28/44, Lockheed, CBS, Mon, 9:30 pm (half of summer replacement for Lux Radio Theater)
9/9/44 - 3/3/45, Lockheed, Bl, Sat. 10:30 pm; 10 pm as of 1/6/45
6/12/45 - 9/4/45, Pepsodent, NBC, Tue, 10 pm (summer replacement for Bob Hope)
6/18/46 - 9/17/46, Pepsodent, NBC, Tue, 10 pm (summer replacement for Bob Hope)
4/3/47 - 10/16/47, General Motors, CBS, Thu, 10:30 pm
11/2/47 - 9/26/48, Frigidaire, CBS, Sun, 8:30 pm, 25m; 30m as of 6/20/48
10/13/50 - 11/3/50, Multi, NBC, Fri, 8:30 pm
11/11/50 - 4/28/51, Multi, NBC, Sat, 8 pm; 8:30 pm as of 11/18/50
5/4/51 - 7/13/51, Multi, NBC, Fri, 9:30 pm
7/20/51 - 8/31/51, NBC, Fri, 8 pm
9/7/51 - 9/28/51, NBC, Fri, 9:30 pm
10/1/51 - 12/24/51, NBC, Mon, 10:30 pm
1/1/52 - 5/20/52, Sus, NBC, Tue, 10:30 pm

2 **Mandrake The Magician** (with Raymond Edward Johnson)
(11/11/40 - 2/6/42) Mut, 5t, 15m, also syn

1 **Man and His Music, A** (10/8/44) WOR

Man (Major North) From G-2 (with Staats Cotsworth)
(4/12/45 - 2/2/46) Sus, ABC
4/12/45 - 5/24/45, Thu, 7:30 pm
6/29/45 - 8/24/45, Fri, 10pm
9/1/45 - 2/2/46, Sat, 8:30 pm

2 **Man From Homicide, The** (with Dan Duryea) (6/25/51 - 10/1/51) ABC, Mon. 8:30 pm

1 **Man From Missouri, The** (1976)

Manhattan At Midnight
(7/24/40 - 9/1/43) Energine, Bl, Wed, 8:30 pm

8 **Manhattan Concert Band** (1938) Syn

99 **Manhattan Melodies** (10/31/38 - 9/23/39) (with Norman Cloutier Orchestra
10/31/38 - 4/24/39, Bl, Mon, 15m, 2:45 pm
5/1/39 - 9/4/39, Bl, Mon, 30m, 2:30 pm
also 6/3/39 - 9/23/39, NBC, Sat, 12 noon (also with Annette Hastings; Mary McHugh as of 8/19/39)
also 1957 - 1961, Syn

11 **Manhattan Merry-Go-Round**
(11/6/32 - 4/17/49) Dr. Lyons (Sus from 3/6/49), Sun
11/6/32 - 4/2/33, Bl, 3:30 pm
4/9/33 - 4/17/49, NBC, 9 pm

1 **Manhattan Mother** (with Margaret Hillas) (3/6/39 - 4/5/40) Chipso Soap, CBS, 5t, 15m

1 **Manhattan Playhouse**
(12/4/48 - 1/8/49) Mut, Sat, 3 pm

Manhattan Serenaders (CBS)

2 **Manhattan Tower** (Syn)

Manhatters, The (1/5/39 - 6/6/39) Mut, Tue, 15m, 11:45 am

2 **Manhunt** (with Maurice Tarplin and Larry Haines) (1945 - 46) (Syn)

1 **Manitoba Flood Relief Show** (5/26/50) CBC/Mut

Man I Married, The (7/3/39 - 4/3/42) 5t, 15m
7/3/39 - 5/2/41, Oxydol, NBC
7/21/41 - 4/3/42, Campbell, CBS

1 **Man In Space** (7/66) WOR-TV

1 **Man In The Street** (11/30/45) WOR

1 **Man In The Street's Reactions To Truman's Address** (3/17/48) WOR

1 **Man In The Street, The**

Man In The Iron Mask (1930s)

4 **Man Named Jordan, A** (1/8/45 - 4/20/47) CBS Pacific network
1/8/45 - 6/29/45, Mon, 15m, 7:15 pm
also 1/9/45 - 6/25/45, Tue - Fri, 15m, 8 pm
7/2/45 - 8/17/45, Tue, 30m from now on
11/3/45 - 12/1/45, Sat
12/2/45 - 4/21/46, Sun
5/2/46 - 5/23/46, Thu
9/29/46 - 10/6/46, Sun
11/10/46 - 4/20/47, Sun; developed into Rocky Jordan

Man Next Door, The (3/28/49 - 6/23/51) U. S. Tobacco Co., Mut, Sat, 8:30 pm

1 **Man Of Magic, The** (with Felix Greenfield)
(3/16/44) Eichler's Beer, Mut

1 **Man Of The People** (4/15/45) Mut

Man Of The Week (9/3/53 - 6/13/54) CBS, Sun, 10 pm

Man On The Farm (9/30/39 - 4/13/40; 9/21/40 - 4/19/41; 10/18/41 - 4/17/43; 10/30/43 - 4/28/45; 9/7/46 - 4/16/49; 8/27/49 - 5/6/50, Quaker until 5/1/54; 8/26/50 - 5/19/51; 8/15/51 - 5/17/52; 8/23/52 - 5/16/53; 8/22/53 - 5/1/54) Mut, Sat

1 **Man On The Line, The** (Syn)

1 **Man On The Moon**

1 **Man On The Moon: The Epic Journey Of Apollo Eleven** (7/14/69) CBS-TV

Man On The Street (8/7/45 - 2/25/46) WOR, 5t, 15m, 6:15 pm

2 **Manor House Party** (with Skip Farrell)
(3/3/47 - 2/27/48) Manor House Coffee, NBC, 4t (Mon - Wed, Fri) 15m

1 **Manor House Summer Party, The** (6/20/47) WMAQ

2 **Manny Strand and His Band** (6/7/44) CBS

Man's Right To Knowledge (with Dr. Grayson Kirk)
(1/3/54 - 3/28/54) CBS, Sun, 1 pm

1 **Man Walks In Space** (3/65) NBC-TV

1 **Man With A Cause, A** (1947) Syn

Man Without A Shadow

Man With The Story (1949)

1 **Man Who Wasn't Always Wrong, The** (11/29/54) CBS

5 **Man Your Battle Stations** (1942) Syn

164 **Ma Perkins** (with Virginia Payne)
(12/4/33 - 11/25/60) Oxydol (until 11/30/56), 5t, 15m
12/4/33 - 9/30/35, NBC; started 8/14/33 on WLW, Cincinnati
10/1/35 - 7/8/49, NBC
also 2/8/37 - 12/31/37; 5/30/38 - 11/18/38, Bl
also 1/3/38 - 5/27/38, CBS
9/28/42 - 6/29/56; 10/8/56 - 11/30/56 CBS, 1:15 pm
12/3/56 - 11/25/60, Sus, CBS
also syndicated

1 **Mara Tapp Show, The** (3/23/92) WBEZ-FM

1 **March Of Dimes Is On The Air, The** (1/16/50) Syn

3 **March Of Dimes March Of Stars, The** (1/2/59) Syn

1 **March Of Dimes Time** (1948) Syn

2 **March Of Dimes Victory Program** (1/2/54) Syn

1 **March Of Faith, The** (1/15/46) Syn

1 **March Of Games** (with Arthur Ross)
(3/26/38 - 7/20/41) CBS
4/25/38 - 9/5/38, CBS, Mon, Wed, 5:30 pm
9/12/38 - 4/14/39, 2t (Mon, Wed), 2 pm
4/18/39 - 10/3/39, 2t (Tue & Thu)
10/8/39 - 7/20/41, Sun, 10:30 am; 1:30 pm as of 6/27/40

1 **March Of Stars** (1/2/59) Syn

1 **March Of Stars On The Air For The March Of Dimes, The** (1/3/59) Syn

15 **March Of Time, The** (3/6/31 - 7/26/45) Time Magazine only or partial sponsor of all shows; other sponsors listed
3/6/31 - 6/19/31; 9/11/31 - 2/26/32; 11/4/32 - 3/17/33, CBS, Fri, 10:30 pm; 8:30 pm from 9/11/31
10/13/33 - 4/13/34; 10/5/34 - 4/26/35, Remington-Rand, CBS, Fri, 8 pm; 9 pm as of 10/5/34
8/26/35 - 3/27/36, Remington-Rand, CBS, 5t, 15m, 10:30 pm
3/30/36 - 9/25/36, Wrigley, CBS, 5t, 15m, 10:30 pm
10/15/36 - 10/7/37, Electrolux Refrigerator, CBS, Thu, 30m, 10:30 pm
10/14/37 - 6/30/38, Electrolux Refrigerator, Bl, Thu, 8:30 pm, 8 pm as of 1/27/38
7/8/38 - 12/2/38; 2/10/39 - 4/28/39, Bl, Fri, 9:30 pm
10/9/41 - 2/5/42. Bl, Thu, 8 pm
2/13/42 - 6/5/42, Bl, Fri, 9:30 pm; 9 pm as of 4/10/42
7/9/42 - 7/1/43; 8/19/43 - 6/29/44; 8/3//44 - 10/26/44, NBC, Thu, 10:30 pm
11/2/44 - 7/26/45, ABC, Thu, 10:30 pm
6/25/46, 1947, film sound track

1 **Marconi Memorial Program** (7/20/37) Mut

Marco Polo (see The Adventures Of Marco Polo)

1 **Marcus O'Connor, Detective First Class** (1946) Syn

Mardi Gras (see Lanny Ross)

Margaret Brainard (with Johnny Augustine Orchestra)
(10/5/34 - 4/26/35) Wrigley, CBS, 3t, 15m, 6:45 pm

Margaret MacDonald (see Meet Margaret MacDonald)

Margo Of Castlewood (with Barbara Luddy) (1/3/38 - 5/20/38) Quaker, Bl, 5t, 15m

Marguerite Padula (with Jerry Sears Orchestra) (5/6/36 - 5/27/36) Bl, Wed, 15m, 3:45 pm

Maria Certo's Matinee (with Lanny Ross, Conrad Thibault, Gus Haenschen Orchestra)
(5/25/34 - 8/24/34) NBC, Fri, 3 pm

1 **Marie Antoinette** (1938) Air trailer

Marie, The Little French Princess (with Ruth Yorke) (3/7/33 - 4/27/34; 10/15/34 - 10/18/35) Louis Phillipe, CBS, 4t (Tue - Fri), 15m; 5t as of 10/15/34

1 **Marilyn Quayle** (8/16/92) C-SPAN audio

2 **Marine Band Symphonette** (Syn)

1 **Marine Christmas In The Pacific** (12/25/44) Mut

Marine Corps (From The Annals Of History) (1948)

1 **Marine Interviews Enroute To Guam** (7/21/44) Mut

26 **Marine Story** (1948) Syn

1 **Mariner 4 Press Conference** (7/16/65) NBC-TV

1 **Mariner 9 Reports** (11/2/71) NASA

Mario Cozzi (on several times including: 1/20/35 - 2/10/35, Bl, Sun, 11:05 pm)

21 **Mario Lanza Show, The**
(6/10/51 - 9/26/52) Coca- Cola, (also called Coke Time) many with Giselle MacKenzie
6/10/51 - 9/30/51, Sun, CBS, 8 pm (summer replacement of Charlie McCarthy)
10/8/51 - 1/21/52, Mon, NBC, 10 pm
1/25/52 - 9/26/52, Fri, NBC, 9 pm

1 **Marion and Reggie** (1935) Syn

Marion Carley (4/24/39 - 9/5/39) CBS (Regional), Tue, 15m, 9:15 am
(7/7/40 - 8/25/40) CBS, Sun, 15m, 9:15 am

Marion Mann (6/16/41 - 8/13/41) Bl, 2t (Mon & Wed), 15m, 7:30 pm

Marion Talley (also called Ry-Krisp Presents; Music All America Loves To Hear)
(4/3/36 - 6/27/37) (9/26/37 - 9/18/38) Ry-Krisp, NBC, Fri, 15m, 10:30 pm; 10 pm as of 7/6/36; Sun, 30m, 5 pm as of 9/6/36

Marion Theater (with Father Patin)

1 **Maritime Day Tribute To Men Of The Merchant Marine** (1945) Syn

4 **Marjorie Dunton's Fashion Report** (1946) Syn

Mark Hawley (1/5/42 - 43) Mueller Noodle, CBS

1 **Mark Lane - Rush To Judgement**

Mark Sabre (see Mystery Theater)

24 **Mark Trail** (1/30/50 - 6/27/52)
1/30/50 - 6/30/50; 9/18/50 - 6/8/51, Kellogg, Mut, 3t, 30m
9/10/51 - 6/27/52, Sus, ABC, 3t, 15m; 5t as of 1/7/52

Mark Warnow Orchestra
(5/2/35 - 5/23/35) CBS, Thu, 8:30 pm
(11/29/35 - 1/24/36) CBS, Fri, 4:30 pm (also see Sound Off; Presenting Mark Warnow)

Marlin Arms Show (with Kay Lorraine and Redd Evans) 15m

1 **Marlin Hurt Memorial Program** (3/24/46) CBS

Marlin Hurt and Beulah Show, The (see Beulah)

4 **Marmola Entertainers, The** (1934) 15m, Syn

Marquette, The Little French Girl (with Marian and Jim Jordan)
(7/22/31 - 6/1/32) Sus, WMAQ - CBS/NBC as of 11/31, 15m, 9:45 pm

13 **Marriage, The** (with Hume Cronyn, Jessica Tandy)
(10/21/52, 10/24/52) Auditions
(10/4/53 - 3/28/54) Sus, NBC, Sun

Marriage Clinic (1/1/38 - 6/29/40) Mut, Sat

Marriage Club (see Your Marriage Club)

Marriage For Two (with Staats Cotsworth) (7/11/49 - 1/18/52) 5t, 15m
7/11/49 - 9/13/49, Sus, NBC
10/3/49 - 3/31/50, Kraft, NBC
10/8/51 - 1/18/52, Sus, ABC, 4:15 pm

Marriage License Romances
(10/10/38 - 9/2/40) Mut, Mon, 15m, 3 pm (usually not in New York)

1 **Married For Life** (with Bill Slater)
(3/23/46 - 6/29/47) Mut
3/23/46 - 7/20/46, Sat, 9:30 am
10/20/46 - 6/29/47, Sun, 2 pm

1 **Mars Close-Up: Are We Alone?** (7/14/65) ABC-TV

1 **Mars: The First Look** (7/22/76) NBC-TV

1 **Mars: The Search For Life** (7/28/76) NBC-TV

1 **Marshall Meditations** (5/25/39) WWRL

Martha and Hal (with Martha Lawrence and Hal Bogg) (11/23/37 - 2/25/38) Humphrey's Homeopathic Medicine Mut, 3t (Sun, Mon, Wed), 15m

Martha Deane (see also Mary Margaret McBride) (8/9/37 - 4/14/56) WOR - New York, various days and times

Martha Jackson

Martha Lane's Modern Kitchen

Martha Lou Harp (9/18/50 - 7/2/56) Sus, ABC (on various days and times)

4 **Martha Meade Society Program, The** (1933) Sperry, 15m, 30m; on West Coast since 1931

Martha Mears (10/28/34 - 1/20/35) NBC, Sun, 15m, 7 pm

1 **Martha Tilton Time** (also with Charles Dant Orchestra) (12/15/40 - 3/23/41) NBC, Sun, 15m, 3 pm (see also Curt Massey)

Martha Webster (1/22/40 - 7/18/41) Campbell, CBS, 5t, 15m, 11:15 am; started as Life Begins until 7/13/40 with Bess Flynn

2 **Martha White Biscuit Time** (6/53) WSM

Martha Wright (see Eyes Wright)
(12/6/54 - 8/23/57) CBS, 5t, 9:30 am

1 **Martin Agronsky News** (7/10/44 - 56+) Bl/ABC

24 **Martin and Lewis Show, The** (with Dean Martin, Jerry Lewis)
(12/22/48)
(4/3/49 - 7/14/53) NBC
4/3/49 - 6/12/49, Sus, Sun, 6:30 pm
6/21/49 - 9/6/49, Swan Soap, NBC, Tues, 9:00 pm (summer replacement for Bob Hope)
10/7/49 - 10/28/49, Fri, 8:30 pm
11/7/49 - 1/30/50, Mon, 10 pm
10/5/51 - 4/25/52, Multi, Fri, 8:30 pm
9/16/52 - 7/14/53, Chesterfield, Tue, 9 pm

6 **Martin Block Show, The** (2/3/35 - 9/16/67)
2/3/35 - 1/1/54 (Make Believe Ballroom) WNEW, New York, 15m/90m/3 1/2 hours, 6t
1/1/54 - 61, Sus, ABC, 5t, 90m
1961 - 9/19/67 (Hall Of Fame) WOR, New York, Sat & Sun

1 **Martin Kane, Private Eye** (with William Gargan; Lee Tracy as of 6/1/52)
(8/7/49 - 12/21/52) U S Tobacco, Sun
8/7/49 - 6/24/51, Mut
7/1/51 - 12/21/52, NBC, 4:30 pm
all shows were TV simulcasts; TV shows were on Thu nights; the dates of all the radio shows are Thu

1 **Martin Luther Reformation Program** (10/31/55) CBS

Marty May Time (with Carol Dee)
(7/25/35 - 9/12/35) CBS, Thu, 9:30 pm
(10/5/35 - 12/14/35) CBS, Sat, 9:30 pm

Marvelous Margie (with William Demarest, Marjorie Reynolds)

Marvelous Melodies (The Powder Box Revue with Jack Whiting, Jack Denny Orchestra)
(2/9/34 - 6/1/34) Hudnut, CBS, Fri, 9:30 pm

1 **Marvin Ash (Honky Tonk Piano)** MacGregor transcription

9 **Marvin Miller, Storyteller** (Syn)
(1948 - 49) 260 5-minute programs
(1958) CBS, 5 minutes, also syndicated

1 **Marx Brothers, The** (1932 - 39)
1932 - 33 (see Flywheel, Shyster and Flywheel)
3/4/34 - 4/15/34 (The Marx Of Time), American Oil, CBS, Sun, 7 pm (8 wks)
1937, NBC
1938, CBS
1939 (see The Circle)

1 **Marx Brothers Go West, The** (1940) Air trailer

Mary and Bob's True Stories
(1/6/28 - 1/18/32) True Story Magazine, CBS, Fri, 60m, 9 pm; NBC, Mon, 45m, 10 pm as of 6/29/31 (also see True Story Hour with Mary and Bob)
(10/11/38 - 5/16/39) True Story Magazine, Bl, Tue, 9 pm

Mary Dietrich (with Josef Hontis Orchestra) (6/11/36 - 9/24/36) Bl, Thu, 12 noon

Mary Eastman (Melody Masterpieces)
(8/8/34 - 7/24/35) CBS, Wed, 10:30 pm
(4/7/35 - 9/23/35) (He, She and They also with Evan Evans) CBS, Sun, 12:30 pm; Wed, 10:30 pm as of 7/31/35; Sun, 10:30 pm as of 9/2/35

Mary Ellis Ames (9/11/33 - 2/14/36) Pillsbury, CBS, 15m
9/11/33 - 34, 3t, 11 am
1934 - 35, Wed
1935 - 2/14/36, 2t

Mary Foster, The Editor's Daughter (see Editor's Daughter)

Mary Jane Walsh (10/29/37 - 12/10/37) Barbasol, Mut, Fri, 15m, 7:45 pm

22 **Mary Lee Taylor Program, The**
(11/7/33 - 10/9/54) Pet Milk; originally called Pet Milky Way
11/7/33 - 11/18/43, CBS, 2t, 15m
11/7/43 - 10/16/48, CBS, Sat, 30m
10/23/48 - 10/9/54, NBC, Sat, 30m, 10 am

Mary Lou Harp (10/8/51 - 2/26/52) ABC, various days, 15m, 10:15 pm

1 **Mary Margaret McBride**
(10/4/37 - 5/21/56) also broadcast as Martha Deane on WOR, New York; first broadcast on 5/3/34, New York City; continued locally in Kingston, NY until 1976
10/4/37 - 7/1/38, Minute Tapioca, CBS, 3t; 5t as of 1/3/38, 15m
8/1/38 - 6/30/39, La France and Satina, CBS, 3t, 15m
10/7/40 - 8/21/41, Florida Citrus, CBS, 5t, 15m (ended up to be once a week)
9/2/41 - 10/6/50, NBC, 5t, 45m
10/9/50 - 5/21/56, Sus, ABC, 5t, 30m - 60m

1 **Mary Margaret McBride Interviews A Friend From Australia** (1942) Syn

1 **Mary Margaret McBride's Scrapbook**

Mary Marlin (see The Story Of Mary Marlin)

Mary Mercer (1943) CBS, 5m

Mary Noble (see Backstage Wife)

Mary Pickford Dramas (with Mary Pickford, Buddy Rogers) (also called Parties At Pickford) (10/3/34 - 6/21/36)
10/3/34 - 35, Royal, NBC, Wed, 7 pm
1935 - 6/21/36, Ice Manufacturers Of America, CBS, Tue; Sun, 9 pm on 6/21/36

Mary Quevil (5/1/39 - 7/5/39) NBC, Mon, 15m, 7:15 pm

2 **Mary Small Show, The** (10/7/33 - 3/24/46)
10/7/33 - 11/12/33, Bl, Sat, 15m, (Mary was 11 years old)
2/8/34 - 5/19/35 (also called Little Miss Bab-O's Surprise Party), Bab-O, NBC, Sun, 1:30 pm; NBC, 15m from 5/20/34 - 8/31/34
12/20/35 - 6/26/36, Sus, NBC, Fri, 15m, 6:15 pm
6/29/36 - 6/28/37, Sus, Bl, Mon, 15m, 7 pm
6/2/41 - 10/20/41 (Imperial Time), Imperial Margarine, Mut, Mon, 15m, 10:15 pm
also 6/16/42 - 10/20/42, CBS, Tue, 15m, 10:45 pm
11/10/41 - 11/31/41, Mut, Mon, 15m, 9:15 pm
8/17/42 - 10/9/42, CBS, 2t (Mon, Fri), 15m
2/27/44 - 3/24/46 (Mary Small's Revue; also with Ray Bloch Orchestra) Clark, Bl/ABC, Sun, 5 pm; 4:30 pm as of 12/2/45

1 **Maryland Hunt Cup Race** (4/30/38) NBC

1 **Masquers Club** (1953)

1 **Masquers, The** (2/9/36) WMBC

Masquerade (4/8/35 - 6/28/35; 9/10/35 - 9/27/35) (with Gale Page) NBC, 5t, 15m
(1/14/46 - 8/29/47) (with Marguerite Anderson) General Mills, NBC, 5t, 15m
3/19/49 (Audition)

Masquerader (4/17/55 - 7/10/55) Mut, Sun, 5:30 pm

1 **Mass For President Rooevelt** (4/14/45) WOR

Master Builders, The (5/1/38 - 12/4/38) Bl, Sun, 15m, 5:45 pm

Master Of Mystery (see Majestic Master Of Mystery)

1 **Master Race, The** (1948) Air trailer

Master Radio Canaries, The (see The Canary Pet Show)

1 **Master's Music Room** (Syn)

23 **Masterpiece Radio Theater**
(5/5/79 - 5/3/80) NPR

Masters Music Room (with Frankie and Phyllis Masters) (1934 - 35) 15m

Masters Of Melody (AFRS) (with Alben White Orchestra) (15m)

1 **Masters Of Mystery** (5/2/56 - 10/2/57) ABC, Wed, 7:30 pm

1 **Mastersingers Of Llangollen, The**
(2/12/54) United Nations Radio

1 **Matarie Rancourt** (7/31/41) CBC

1 **Material For The Fred Allen Obituary Program** (3/20/56) NBC

Matinee At One (1967 - 69)

1 **Matinee At Meadowbrook**
(with John Tillman as host with various orchestras) (5/24/41 - 12/6/41) CBS, Sat, 60m, 5 pm
also 9/7/46

Matinee In Rhythm (with Ruth Norcross; Ed Reimers announcing)
(3/18/39 - 5/3/41) NBC, Sat, 15m

23 **Matinee Theater** (with Victor Jory)
(10/22/44 - 4/8/45) Vicks, CBS, Sun, 2 pm

Matinee With Bob And Ray (see Bob and Ray)

Matinee With Lytell (with Jim Lytell Orchestra) (5/25/41 - 10/5/41) Bl, Sun, 1:30 pm

1 **Matter Of Cooperation, A** (UNESCO Radio)

12 **Matthew Slade, Private Investigator** (KPFA)

Mattinata Salon Orchestra
(1/19/41 - 5/25/41) CBS, Sun, 15m, 8:15 am

Matty Malneck and His Orchestra
(Music By Malneck) (6/1/39 - 8/24/39) Pall Mall, CBS, Thu, 15m, 7:15 pm
(4/12/41 - 5/31/41) NBC, Sat, 10:30 pm
Remotes: 3/7/39; 3/30/39; both from Cafe Le Mays, Hollywood

1 **Maud and Cousin Bill** (with Vivian Block and Andy Donnelly)
(9/21/32 - 10/28/32; 1/9/33 - 6/16/33) A & P, Bl, 2t, 15m (Wed & Sat); 3t; (Mon - Wed) as of 10/17/32; then Thu and Fri as of 5/4/33

Maudie's Diary (8/14/41 - 9/24/42) Wonder Bread, CBS, Thu, 7:30 pm

Maurice Gunsky (15m)

1 **Maurice Spitalny and His Orchestra**
(1/11/39 - 6/5/40) Bl
1/11/39 - 3/19/39, Sun, 10 pm
12/1/39 - 1/22/40, Mon, 1:30 pm
2/6/40 - 6/5/40, various days and times
6/45, Mut

1 **Maurie Condon With The News**
(11/18/41) WGAR

Maverick Jim (with Artells Dickson)
(1934) Mut, Mon

1 **Max Dolin and His Grenadiers** (NBC) 15m, also syndicated

Max Haines' Hall Of Fame (Syn)

1 **Max Kaminsky** (World transcription)

1 **Max Pillar and His Orchestra** (12/31/76) KIXI

1 **Maxim Litvanoff** (NBC)

Maxine Gray (see David Rose)

Maxine Sullivan (Recital In Swingtime)
(4/26/38 - 6/14/38) CBS, Tue, 15m, 6:45 pm

Max Jordan

75 **Maxwell House Coffee Time**
(11/4/37 - 6/23/49) shows are listed under other headings, usually the star
11/4/37 - 6/22/44 (see Baby Snooks)
6/16/44 - 8/25/44 (see Charles Ruggles)
8/31/44 - 5/31/45 (see Frank Morgan)
6/7/45 - 8/30/45 (see Topper)
9/20/45 - 6/23/49 (see Burns and Allen)

Maxwell House Concerts (with Donald Voorhees Orchestra) (1927 - 3/31/32) Maxwell House, Bl, Thu

Maxwell House Showboat, The (see Showboat)

Maxwell House Tune Blenders (with Lanny Ross, Donald Voorhees Orchestra) (3/7/32 - 10/3/32)

Maxwell House (CBS) 3t, 15m, 7:15 pm; 7:30 pm as of 7/1/32

1 **May Day Celebration** (5/1/40) RW96 (Moscow)

Mayfair Orchestra (12/16/39 - 1/27/40) CBS, Sat, 15m, 1:45 pm

Maynard Ferguson (U S Army Reserve)

1 **Mayo Story, The** (4/10/48) NBC

2 **Mayor Fiorello La Guardia**
(12/14/41, 2/25/45) WNYC, WOR

4 **Mayor La Guardia** (7/22/40 - 10/21/45) WNYC, WWRL, WOR

1 **Mayor La Guardia and The City Fusion Party** (10/8/41) WOR

23 **Mayor Of The Town** (with Lionel Barrymore) (9/6/42 - 7/30/49)
9/6/42 - 9/27/42, Rinso, NBC, Sun, 7 pm (partial summer replacement of Jack Benny)
10/7/42 - 12/9/42, Rinso, CBS, Wed, 9:30 pm
1/6/43 - 12/26/43, Rinso, CBS, Wed, 9 pm
3/11/44 - 7/1/44, Noxzema, CBS, Sat, 7 pm
7/10/44 - 8/28/44, Noxzema, CBS, Mon, 9 pm (half of summer replacement for Lux
9/2/44 - 7/14/45; 9/1/45 - 6/29/46; 7/13/46; 9/7/46 - 47, Noxzema, CBS, Sat, 7 pm; 8 pm as of 4/28/45; 8:30 pm as of 9/1/45
10/8/47 - 6/30/48, Noxzema, ABC, Wed, 8 pm
1/9/49 - 7/30/49, Mutual Benefits, Mut, Sun, 7:30 pm

Maytag Dance Orchestra
(1/18/31 - 4/4/32) (Clarence Wheeler, musical director) Maytag, Bl, Mon, 9 pm

Maytag Frolic Radio Program (see Coon-Sanders)

1 **Maytime** (1937) Air trailer

1 **McAlister Buick Spots** (1953)

1 **McCall's Interviews** (7/24/53) Syn

2 **McCosker-Hershfield Cardiac Foundation Dinner** (12/5/37, 12/4/38) Mut

1 **McCoy, The** (with Howard Duff) 4/22/51 (Audition)

McFarland Twins Orchestra
(5/11/40 - 9/14/40) Mut, Sat, 1:30 pm

McGarry and The Mouse
(6/26/46 - 3/31/47)
6/26/46 - 9/25/46 (with Wendell Corey, Kitty Archer), NBC, Wed, 9 pm (summer replacement for Eddie Cantor)
1/6/47 - 3/31/47, General Foods, Mut, Mon, 8 pm

McGeachy Daily News Roundup

McKesson Musical Magazine (with Erno Rapee Orchestra) (1930 - 4/19/32) McKesson and Robbins, NBC, Tue, 9 pm

McKesson Musical Novelties (with Josef Stopek Orchestra, Fred Hufsmith, J. Alden Edkins)
(5/19/32 - 9/28/32) McKesson and Robbins, Bl, Thu, 15m, 11:45 am

McLean Of The Northwest Mounted (with Monty Blue, Francis X. Bushman) 15m

Meadows Beauty Forum (with V. E. Meadows) (1/7/37 - 5/27/37) McKesson & Robbins, Mut, Thu, 15m, 9:45 am

Me and Janie (with George O'Hanlon, Lurene Tuttle) (7/12/49 - 10/4/49) NBC, Tue, 8:30 pm

Me and The Missus

1 **Meal Of Your Life, The** (Syn)

23 **Meaning Of America, The** (10/3/52 - 7/3/53) WMAQ

2 **Medicine U.S.A.** (3/29/52, 4/5/52) NBC

Meditation and Melody
(12/24/39 - 3/10/40) Mut, Sun, 3 pm

1 **Meditations** (10/36) WJR

1 **Meet America** (5/17/38) CBS

11 **Meet Corliss Archer** (1/7/43 - 9/30/56) auditioned on CBS on 11/26/42
1/7/43 - 2/25/43, CBS, Thu, 8 pm
3/10/43 - 4/7/43, CBS, Wed, 10:30 pm
4/11/43 - 6/6/43, CBS, Sun, 8 pm
6/11/43 - 9/24/43, CBS, Fri, 8 pm (summer replacement of Kate Smith)
1/8/44 - 7/1/44, Anchor Hocking Glass, CBS, Sat, 5 pm
7/6/44 - 8/23/45, Anchor Hocking Glass, CBS, Thu, 9:30 pm
4/28/46 - 9/29/46; 4/6/47 - 5/12/47, Campbell until 3/28/48, CBS, Sun, 9 pm
6/15/48 - 9/7/48, Pepsodent, NBC, Tue, 10 pm (summer replacement for Bob Hope)
7/31/49 - 6/25/50; 8/27/50 - 7/1/51, Electric Companies, CBS, Sun, 9 pm
9/9/51 - 4/6/52, Electric Companies, CBS, Sun, 9 pm
4/13/52 - 6/29/52, Electric Companies, CBS, Sun, 9:15 pm
10/3/52 - 6/26/53, Electric Companies, ABC, Fri, 9:30 pm
12/25/53 (one show), ABC, Fri, 9:30 pm
8/30/54 - 11/30/54, Toni and Carter Products, CBS, Mon, 8 pm
6/24/56 - 9/30/56, CBS, Sun, 8 pm

1 **Meet Debbie Dixon** (1958) Syn

Meet Edward Weeks (also called The Human Side Of Literature)
(11/7/39 - 3/11/41) Bl, Tue
11/7/39 - 2/20/40, 9:30 pm
11/12/40 - 3/11/41, 10:30 pm

Meet Frank Sinatra (see Frank Sinatra)

Meetin' House (with The Southernaires) (3/10/36 - 6/30/36) Bl, Tue, 5 pm

Meet Margaret MacDonald
(7/2/45 - 11/23/46) Procter&Gamble, CBS, 5t, 15m, 1:30 pm

1 **Meet Me After The Show** (1951) film sound track

Meet Me At Kay's (see Kay Armen)

4 **Meet Me At Parky's** (with Harry Einstein) (6/17/45 - 7/11/48) Sun
6/17/45 - 6/9/46; 9/15/46 - 4/6/47, Old Gold, NBC, 10:30 pm
10/26/47 - 7/11/48, Sus, Mut, 9 pm

Meet Me In Manhattan (with Walter Kiernan) (8/12/46 - 9/20/46) ABC, 5t, 4:30 pm

1 **Meet Me In St. Louis** (5/29/48) ABC (with Margaret Whiting) also (with Peggy Ann Garner) (9/17/50 - 11/5/50) NBC, Sun, 10:30 pm

19 **Meet Millie** (with Audrey Totter)
(7/2/51 - 9/23/53) CBS
7/2/51 - 8/20/51, Sus, Mon (partial summer replacement of Lux Radio Theater)
9/4/51 - 9/11/51, Tue
10/9/51 - 1/1/52, Tue, 10 pm
1/6/52 - 5/18/52, Sun, 9:30 pm
5/25/52 - 6/29/52, Sun, 6 pm
7/6/52 - 8/31/52, Sun, 9 pm
10/3/52 - 9/23/54, Multi, Thu, 8 pm

Meet Miss Julia (with Josephine Hall)
(7/10/39 - 10/4/40) Mut, 5t, 15m, 5 pm; 10:15 am as of 7/10/39

1 **Meet Miss Sherlock** (7/3/46 - 10/26/47) CBS - Pacific
7/3/46 - 9/26/46 (with Sondra Gair) Wed/Thu
9/28/46 - 10/26/47 (with Betty Moran for first episode, Monty Margetts for rest; also with William Conrad) Sat

2 **Meet Mr. America** (Syn)

Meet Mr. McNutley (with Ray Milland)
(9/17/53 - 6/10/54) General Electric, CBS, Thu, 9 pm

Meet Mr. Meek (with Frank Readick; also Jack Smart, Adelaide Klein)
(7/10/40 - 9/3/41; 10/8/41 - 4/1/42) Lifebuoy, CBS, Wed, 7:30 pm; 8 pm as of 1/28/42

1 **Meet The Band** (1949) Syn

Meet The Champ (with Ed East and Ralph Dumke) (6/29/38 - 10/5/38) CBS, Wed, 9 pm

1 **Meet The Colonel** (7/6/43) CBS

Meet The Dixons (with Richard Widmark) (7/31/39 - 10/6/39) Campbell, CBS, 5t, 15m

Meet The Family (with Babe Herman) ABC, 11/14/47 (Audition)

37 **Meet The Meeks** (with Fran Allison, Forrest Lewis) (7/14/47) Audition
(9/6/47 - 4/30/49) Swift, NBC, Sat

14 **Meet The Menjous** (with Verree Teasdale and Adolphe Menjou) (Syn - ZIV) 520 15-minute programs broadcast
(4/25/49 - 50) WOR, 5t, 15m

3 **Meet The Missus** (1944 - 50) CBS, 15m; usually on West Coast only, Multi

Meet The Morgans (15m)

Meet The Music (with Lyn Murray Orchestra) (5/18/41 - 6/8/41) CBS, Sun, 25m, 2:35 pm, Multi

1 **Meet The People** (1944) film sound track

37 **Meet The Press** (founded by Martha Roundtree and Lawrence Spivak)
(12/7/45) Mut
12/1/46 - 7/27/86) Sus; Mut, Sat, 9:30 am; broadcast off and on including:
12/1/46 - 2/23/47, Mut, Sun, 10:30 pm
3/7/47 - 8/18/50, Fri
5/11/52 - 10/12/52, Sun, 10 pm
11/2/52 - 7/27/86, NBC, Sun or Sat still on NBC-TV

2 **Meet The Stars** (with Betty Jane Rhodes and David Rose Orchestra)
(4/9/40 - 6/4/40) Mut, Tue, 9 pm
(2/10/48) Two Mut auditions

1 **Meet The WLOS Staff** (6/48) WLOS

Meet Your Lucky Partners (see Lucky Partners)

Meet Your Match (with Jan Murray)
(5/5/49 - 1/18/53) Sus
5/5/49 - 9/15/49, Mut, Thu, 9 pm
10/1/49 - 4/15/50, NBC, Sat, 9 pm
7/1/52 - 9/9/52, NBC,Tue,9 pm
9/21/52 - 1/18/53, NBC, Sun, 7 pm

1 **Meet Your Navy** (1/27/42 - 10/8/45) Bl (originally on WLS)
1/27/42 - 3/3/42, Bl, Tue, 8:30 pm
3/13/42 - 1/8/43, Hallmark from 8/21/42, Fri, 10 pm
1/15/43 - 5/28/43; 9/17/43 - 10/6/44, Hallmark, Bl, Fri, 8:30 pm
10/14/44 - 10/8/45, Raytheon Tubes, Sat, 7:30 pm; Mon, 9 pm of 7/16/45; Mon, 8:30 pm as of 8/13/45

2 **Melachrino Musicale, The** (with George Melachrino) (1954) Syn, 15m

Mel Allen (7/13/39 - 12/31/54) 15m
7/13/39 - 4/6/40, CBS, 2/3t (various days), 6:15 pm
9/15/49 - 9/30/49, Mut, 5t, 15m, 7:45 pm
1949 - 50, Sus, Mut, Sat
8/31/53 - 12/31/54 (with Russ Hodges) NBC, 6t, 6:15 pm

1 **Mel Allen Sports** (3/12/49) Mut

Mel and Jane (6/26/39 - 7/31/39) Mut, Mon, 15m, 3:30 pm

20 **Mel Blanc Show, The** (also Mr. Blanc's Fix-It Shop) (9/3/46 - 6/24/47) Colgate, CBS, Tue, 8:30 pm

1 **Mel Blanc With Billy May and His Orchestra** (AFRS Music Library)

Mel Blanc - Woody Woodpecker Program (1953 - 54) Mut, Sat, 60m

Melo-Clarions (with Lew White)
(1/6/32 - 3/23/32) Brown Show Company, Bl, Wed, 15m, 8:15 pm

Melodiana (with Abe Lyman Orchestra)
(8/20/34 - 12/28/36) Phillips
8/20/34 - 7/2/35, CBS, Tue, 8:30 pm
7/7/35 - 5/17/36, CBS, Sun, 5 pm
5/25/36 - 12/28/36, Bl, Mon, 7:0 pm

2 **Melodic Moments** (6/17/41 - 9/7/41) CBS, Tue, 15m, 9:30 am
also (7/5/41 - 1/3/42) CBS, Sat, 15m, 9:15 am
(7/27/47) WARE

Melodies From The Skies (with Harold Stokes Orchestra) (6/16/37 - 8/9/39) Mut, Wed, 10:30 pm

Melodies Of Home (11/4/43 - 6/8/44) General Mills, NBC, Thu, 15m

Melodies Organistic (KNX)

2 **Melodies That Endure** (Syn)

Melodies To Remember
(2/2/47 - 4/20/47) ABC, Sun, 15m, 1:45 pm

1 **Melody and Madness** (see Artie Shaw; Robert Benchley) (8/22/39) NBC

Melody Ballroom (see Les Brown, Jo Stafford)

Melody For Milady (6/11/39 - 10/29/39) Bl, Sun, 15m, 3:30 pm

Melody Girl (7/16/31 - 10/9/31) Coty, CBS, Thu, 15m

1 **Melody Grove** (3/6/41) WLW

Melody Hall (with Genevieve Rowe, Bob Stanley Orchestra) (8/9/42 - 10/27/42) Mut, Sun, 9:30 pm; Tue, 11:30 pm as of 10/20/42

Melody Highway (with Milton Cross, Stuart Foster) (7/6/52 - 1/18/53) ABC, Sun

Melody Hour
(see Carnation Contented Hour)

Melody House (with Lawrence Salerno and Irma Glen) (1947) CBS Pacific, Loma Linda Foods

2 **Melody In Spring** (1934) film sound track, air trailer

Melody In The Night (with Paul La Valle Orchestra) (5/11/40 - 9/28/40) Bl, Sat, 10:30 pm

13 **Melody Lane** (1932) Syn

1 **Melody Lane With Jerry Wayne**
(11/30/42) Mut

Melody Lingers On, The (with Leo Spitalny Orchestra) (1/12/36 - 4/26/36) NBC, Sun, 8 pm

Melody Madcaps (1/17/39 - 4/4/39) CBS, Tue, 15m, 4:45 pm

Melody Marathon (9/1/39 - 5/24/40) Ohio Oil, Bl, Fri, 10:30 pm

Melody Master (10/20/35 - 4/12/36) GE, NBC, Sun, 11 pm

Melody Masterpieces (see Mary Eastman)

Melody Matinee (with Muriel Dickson, Victor Arden Orchestra)
(1/12/36 - 3/15/36; 11/15/36 - 3/28/37) Smith Brothers, NBC, Sun, 2 pm; 1:30 pm as of 11/15/36

Melody Moments (with Myra Lane)
(12/26/37 - 5/7/39) NBC, Sun, 9:30 am

Melody Of Romance (with Charles Sears Orchestra; then Harry Kogen Orchestra)
(11/7/36 - 1/30/37) Maple-Mix, Bl, Sat 15m 11:15 am

Melody Parade (1/21/34 - 7/15/34) CBS, Sun 10:30 am

15 **Melody Promenade** (3/1/50 - 4/14/50) ABC

1 **Melody Puzzles** (with Fred Uttal)
(11/2/37 - 1/25/38) Lucky Strike, Mut, Tue, 8 pm
(1/10/38 - 4/4/38) Lucky Strike, Bl, Mon, 8 pm

Melody Ramblings (with Marty Dale)
(6/11/38 - 6/24/39) CBS Sat, 15m 12 noon; 9:30 am as of 4/22/39)

Melody Ranch (see Gene Autry)

62 **Melody Round-Up** (1942 - 45) (AFRS)
also 5/13/44 - 11/4/44) Goodyear, NBC Sat 11:30 am

Melody Showcase (with Sammy Kaye)
(1939)

Melody Strings (1939) Mut (Regional), Tue, 15m 10:30 am

Melody Time (3/27/39 - 7/17/39) CBS, Mon, 15m 8:45 am

Melody Treasure Hunt (see Go Get It)

Mel Torme Show, The
(8/2/47 - 10/19/48) NBC
8/2/47 - 10/25/47 Toni, Sat, 15m, 5:30 pm
7/6/48 - 10/19/48 Philip Morris, Tue, 8 pm

1 **Mel Torme** (World transcription)

2 **Mel Torme With Dave Barbour Four** (MacGregor transcriptions)

2 **Mel Torme and The Page Cavanaugh Trio** (MacGregor transcriptions)

1 **Mel Torme and The Wesson Brothers**
(4/30/47) NBC

Melvin Elliott (2/4/45 - 1/14/51) Mut, Sun

1 **Memo For Americans** (1/13/51) NBC

4 **Memo From The United Nations**
(1/15/54 - 2/12/54) United Nations Radio

Memoirs Of The Movies (narrated by Myrna Loy; KFWB) (1970)

1 **Memorial Day Program** (5/30/45) Mut

1 **Memorial Program For Colonel Jacob Ruppert** (1/15/39) WOR

1 **Memorial Program To Marconi**
(7/20/37) Red, Blue nets

1 **Memorial To James J. Walker**
(11/21/46) WOR

1 **Memorial To Raymond Clapper** (2/3/44)

3 **Memories** (Syn)

2 **Memories Of A Pioneer** (4/15/47, 1/6/48) KNBC

1 **Memories Of Hawaii** (Syn)

Memory Lane (with Jerry Wayne) (1947)

Memphis Five (1949)

8 **Men Against Death** (6/30/38 - 5/13/39) CBS, Sat (summer replacement for Kate Smith, Thu, 8 pm)
10/8/38 - 5/13/39, Sat

Men At Sea (7/4/43 - 8/22/43) Kraft, Sun, 6:30 pm (summer replacement for Great Gildersleeve)
(7/9/44 - 8/27/44) Kraft, NBC, Sun, 6:30 pm (summer replacement for The Great Gildersleeve)
(7/8/45 - 8/26/45) Kraft, NBC, Sun, 6:30 pm (summer replacement for The Great Gildersleeve)

Men Behind The Guns, The (10/14/41) Mut

Men Behind The Stars (see Hayden Planetarium Talks)

2 **Men In Scarlet** (with John Drainie)
(3/29/43 - 5/6/48) CBC, 15m

Men, Machines and Victory (National Safety Council) (6/5/42 - 9/25/42) Bl, Fri, 15m
(3/23/43 - 8/10/43) Bl, Tue, 15m, 7:15pm
(10/23/43 - 12/6/43) Bl, Mon, 15m, 10:15 pm

Mennen Program (with Freddie Rich Orchestra; Irene Beasley)
(1/28/32 - 4/21/32) Mennen, CBS, Thu, 15m, 9:15 pm

58 **Mennen Shave Time With Lew Parker**
(1946 - 47) 15m (5m) syndicated

1 **Men Of Boy's Town** (1941) Air trailer

Men Of Daring (10/31/33 - 12/26/33) Bl, Tue, 9:30 pm

Men Of Magic (1944)

Men Of Vision (1933) (1937 - 1938) Syn

3 **Men Of Vision** (1945) Sanka, CBS, Sun, 7 pm
(2/23/46) Mut

1 **Men Who Fight For Freedom** (11/11/43)

Men Who Made The Movies (Syn) 60m

Men With Wings (7/31/38 - 10/23/38) Mut, Sun, 1;30 pm

1 **Menace In White** (5/25/47) CBS

1 **Mendicant Christ, The** (1941) Syn

Menjous, The (see Meet The Menjous)

8 **Mercer McLeod, The Man With The Story** (1947, 1948) 15m, Syn

1 **Merchant Of Venice** (1939) Syn

1 **Mercury Spaceflight** (5/5/61) CBS

40 **Mercury Theater, The** (with Orson Welles) (7/11/38 - 12/4/38) Sus, CBS, 60m; led to Campbell Playhouse
7/11/38 - 9/5/38, Mon, 9 pm (First Person Singular)
9/11/38 - 12/4/38, Sun, 8 pm
(6/7/46 - 9/13/46) (Mercury Summer Theater) Pabst, CBS, Fri, 10 pm

7 **Meredith Willson's Musical Revue** (7/2/40 - 9/24/40; 6/30/42 - 9/22/42) Johnson, NBC, Tue, 9:30 pm; summer replacements for Fibber McGee & Molly; second series also called America Sings

3 **Meredith Willson** (4/29/35 - 2/12/54)
4/29/35 - 5/13/35, Bl, Mon, 8:30 pm
6/35/35 - 7/6/35, Bl, Mon, 8:30 pm
6/16/36 - 8/4/37, NBC, Tue, 9 pm; Bl, Wed, 10:30 pm as of 1/13/37
6/6/46 - 8/29/46, Maxwell House, NBC, Thu, 8:30 pm (summer replacement of Burns and Allen)
10/4/46 - 3/28/47 (Sparkle Time) Canada Dry, CBS, Fri, 7:30 pm
6/18/47 - 9/24/47, Ford, CBS, Wed, 9:30 pm
10/6/48 - 3/30/49, General Foods, ABC, Wed, 10:30 pm
8/25/49 - 9/29/49, General Foods, NBC, Thu, 8 pm (partial summer replacement for Aldrich Family)
8/8/51 - 12/26/51, RCA, NBC, Wed, 10:30 pm
6/1/52 - 9/28/52, RCA, NBC, Sun, 8 pm
8/8/51 - 5/28/52, Sus, NBC, Wed, 10:30 pm; 25m, 10:35 as of 2/6/52
6/1/52 - 9/28/52, NBC, Sun, 8 pm (summer replacement for Phil Harris - Alice Faye)
1/3/53 - 6/13/53, Sus, NBC, Sat, 10:30 pm
also 4/15/52 - 11/28/52, Multi, NBC, 5t, 15m, 2:15 pm
12/16/53 - 2/12/54, Florida Citrus, NBC, 5t, 15m, 9:45 am

1 **Meredith Willson Show** (1947) Syn

1 **Meredith Willson Show, The**

1 **Meredith Willson and His Orchestra** (1/2/52) Syn

3 **Merry Christmas Mom** (12/23 - 25/44) KGMB

Merry-Go-Round (with Jimmy Blaine) (9/23/50 - 3/31/51) ABC, Sat, 8:30 pm

2 **Merry Life Of Mary Christmas, The** (with Mary Astor, Paul Marlon)
(7/2/45 - 8/27/45) CBS, Mon, 8:30 pm (summer replacement of Joan Davis)

Merry Macs Show, The
(1/23/34 - 5/24/34) Bl, 2t, 15m, 1:45 pm
(5/3/35 -1/17/36) Bl, Fri, 15m, 12:15 pm

Merry Mailman, The (1952 - 56) Multi, Mut, Sun, 15m

Merry Makers, The (9/2/35 - 10/7/35) (with The Eton Boys) CBS, Mon, 1:30 pm
(6/1/38 - 8/5/39), CBS, Wed, 15m, 2 pm

Merry Music (4/7/39 - 12/26/39) Bl, Tue, 15m, 12:15 pm
also (7/18/39 - 10/3/39) Bl, Tue, 15m, 2 pm

2 **Merry Widow, The** (1934) Air trailer, film sound track

2 **Merv Griffin Show, The** (10/7/57 - 1958) ABC, 5t, 45m, 7:15 pm
(8/2/73, 1/28/76) TV syn

Mesa Memories (with Helen Baer and Ted Arthur)

2 **Message From William R. Hearst, A** (1935) Syn

Message To Israel (9/7/35 - 58+) Bl/ABC
9/7/35 - 8/17/43, Sat
8/25/43 - 58+, Sun

Mess Call (8/11/45 - 9/8/45) ABC, Sat, 25m, 1:05 pm

1 **Metro Goldwyn Mayer Time** (11/21/44) WLW

2 **Metropolis** (1935) Syn

Metropolitan Moods (see John Gurney)

6 **Metropolitan Opera, The** (with Milton Cross until 1974)
(12/25/31 - present) season normally from about 12/1 to 4/1
12/25/31 - 11/30/40, Sus; Lucky Strike
12/25/33 - 4/7/34, Listerine
12/25/34 - 3/23/35, RCA
12/26/36 - 3/27/37, NBC/Bl, Sat, up to 3 hours; first broadcast was "Hansel and Gretel" on Friday, Christmas Day, 1931; Saturday schedule started the following day with "Norma."
12/7/40 - present, Texaco, ABC/NPR, Sat, up to 3 hours

10 **Metropolitan Opera Auditions Of The Air, The** (with Milton Cross)
(12/22/35 - 58) usually followed Metropolitan Opera schedule
12/22/35 - 3/29/36; 10/18/36 - 3/28/37, Sherwin Williams, NBC, Sun, 3:30 pm; 3 pm as of 10/18/36
10/3/37 - 3/27/38; 10/9/38 - 4/2/39; 10/1/39 - 3/24/40, Sherwin Williams, Bl, Sun, 5 pm; 5:30 pm as of 10/1/39
10/20/40 - 3/31/41; 10/19/41 - 3/22/42, Sherwin Williams, NBC, Sun, 5 pm
11/29/42 - 3/14/43; 11/28/43 - 4/9/44; 11/26/44 - 4/1/45, Sherwin Williams, Bl, Sun
1/4/48 - 5/16/48; 11/28/48 - 3/13/49, Farnsworth, ABC, Sun, 4:30 pm
3/20/49 - 6/18/50, Sun, 4:30 pm (Milton Cross Opera Album)
11/14/50 - 3/27/51; 12/25/51 - 4/8/52, Sus, ABC, Tue, 8:30 pm; 10 pm from 1/23/51 - 3/27/51
1/12/53 - 3/26/56, Sus, ABC, Mon
1956 - 58, Sus, ABC, Sun

Metropolitan Parade (with Leith Stevens Orchestra) (5/20/35 - 6/24/38) CBS
5/20/35 - 6/22/36, Mon, 60m, 9 am
10/9/36 - 6/24/38, Fri, 9 am

Mexican Marimba (5/7/33 - 2/4/34) NBC, Sun, 10:30 pm
(3/24/35 - 9/8/35) NBC, Sun, 10:30 am

Mexican Musical Tours (Angel Mercado Orchestra) (4/6/35 - 6/13/35) Mexican Tourist Board, Bl, Thu, 15m, 9:30 pm

Meyer Davis Orchestra (host is Larry Higgin) (1954) Mut

Meyer, The Buyer (with Harry Hershfield) (Syndicated - mid 1930s)

MGM Hollywood Theater (1940)

MGM Musical Comedy Theater Of The Air (1/2/52 - 6/25/42; 10/1/52 - 12/24/52), Mut, Wed, 60m; sponsored by C. Antel Co., from 4/23/52 - 6/25/52; sponsored by R. J. Reynolds from 10/1/52 - 12/24/52; repeat broadcasts from 10/1/52 - 12/24/52

MGM Screen Test (with Dean Murphy) (1940s) 15m

MGM Theater Of The Air (with Howard Dietz; Syn) (10/14/49 - 12/7/51) Sus, WMGM (NY) Fri, 60m, 7:30 pm
(1/5/52 - 12/27/52) Mut, Sat, 8:30 pm; all programs from 5/4/51 are repeats

Michael and Kitty (also Michael Piper) (with Elizabeth Reller and John Gibson)
(10/10/41 - 2/6/42) Canada Dry, Bl, Fri, 9:30 pm

Michael Bartlett (3/12/34 - 3/26/34) Bl, Mon, 15m, 8:30 pm

Michael Duffy (8/22/48 - 10/2/49) Mut Sun 3 pm; 1 pm as of 5/1/49

1 **Michael Flagg, M.D.** (10/4/54) CBS

Michael Loring (7/3/39 - 8/21/39) CBS, Mon, 15m, 7:15 pm (partial summer replacement of Lum and Abner)
also (7/14/39 - 8/11/39) CBS, Fri, 15m, 7:30 pm

1 **Michael O'Duffy** (12/28/48) Mut

Michael Piper (see Michael and Kitty)

Michael Shayne (10/16/44 - 7/10/53) (with Wally Maher until 11/4/47)
10/16/44 - 46, Mut - West Coast Mon
10/15/46 - 11/14/47, Hastings, Mut, Tue, 8 pm
7/15/48 - 50 (New Adventures Of Michael Shayne) (with Jeff Chandler until 1950 (Syn) ABC or Mut various days including:
5/7/49 - 7/25/49, Mut, Sat, 5 pm
10/14/52 - 11/4/52 (with Donald Curtis), ABC, Tue, 8 pm
11/6/52 - 2/5/53 (with Robert Sterling) Sus, ABC, Thu, 9:30 pm
2/13/53 - 7/10/53, ABC, Fri, 8 pm

2 **Mickey Mouse Theater Of The Air** (1/2/38 - 5/21/38) Pepsodent NBC Sun

Mickey Of The Circus (with Chester Stratton) (2/2/35 - 7/5/35) CBS
2/2/35 - 4/27/35, Sat, 15m, 5 pm
5/3/35 - 7/5/35, Fri, 2:30 pm

Mickey Spillane Mystery (see That Hammer Guy)

1 **Mid-Century Broadcast** (1/1/50) CBS

2 **Mid-Century White House Conference** (12/50) Syn

Mid-Day Bath Club (with Roger White Orchestra) (3/22/32 - 5/26/32) Linit, CBS, 2t, 15m, 12:30 pm

1 **Mid-Day Review, The** (1942)

1 **Mideast Treaty: The Signing, A** (3/26/79) pool feed

1 **Middle East Peace: The Carter Gamble** (3/10/79) ABC-TV

2 **Midge At The Mike** (5/18/43, 7/23/43) Germany

1 **Midmorning Matinee** (with Hal Hodge) (Mutual - Don Lee) (5/31/39)

9 **Midnight** (NPR) (7/13/82 - 9/28/82)

1 **Midnight At V-Disc** (12/7/44)

1 **Midnight To Dawn In New York and London** (1/2/48) BBC/Mut

4 **Midstream** (5/1/39 - 11/13/41) Teel Toothpaste, NBC (until 9/27/40) & Bl (until 3/26/40) 5t, 15m; started on WLW, Cincinnati in 1938
3/4/41 - 11/13/41, Bl, 5t, 15m

Midweek Hymn Sing (1926 - 11/10/36) NBC
1926 - 31, Thu
1931 - 11/10/36, Tue, 15m

1 **Midweek Review, The** (9/21/39) CBS

3 **Miff Mole and His Orchestra** (World transcriptions)

1 **Mighty Casey, The** (with Millard Mitchell) (3/1/47 - 7/26/47) Mut, Sat, 9 pm

Mighty Memory Mobile (with Garry Moore, Bob Maxwell; broadcast from Baltimore) (1975 - 76) (Each show is a year, usually in two parts; years covered are between 1920 and 1964)

Mighty Show, The (with Agnes Moorehead) (9/12/38 - 4/28/39) My-T-Fine, CBS, 5t, 15m, 5:45 pm

1 **Mike Levine Show, The** (4/26/71) KDKA

Mike Malloy, Private Eye (with Steve Brodie) 7/16/53 - 9/24/53, ABC, Thu, 9 pm
10/12/53 - 4/23/54, ABC, 5t, 15m, 8:45 pm
4/30/56 - 3/18/57, CBS, Mon, 7:30 pm

9 **Mike Nichols and Elaine May** (1955) WFMT/NBC

1 **Mike and Buff Mailbag** (6/54) CBS

3 **Mike-ing History** (Syn)

1 **Milan Hodja** (9/18/38) Czechoslovakia

18 **Mildred Bailey Show, The** (12/16/33 - 2/9/45)
12/16/33 - 2/3/34, CBS, Sat, 15m, 6:15 pm
10/1/34 - 4/26/35 (Plantation Echoes) Vicks, Bl, 3t, 15m
6/21/44 - 8/9/44, Campbell,, CBS, Wed, 9:30 pm (summer replacement for Jack Carson)
9/1/44 - 2/9/45 (Music Till Midnight), CBS, Fri, 11:30 pm

Mildred Dilling (6/23/35 - 8/11/35) Bl, Sun, 15m, 2:15 pm

Milestones In American Music (10/28/41 - 3/25/42) CBS, Tue, 4 pm

1 **Milestones On The Road To Peace** (5/8/45) NBC

Milligan and Mulligan (with Don Ameche and Bob White)

Million - Dollar Band (5/29/43 - 3/25/44) Palmolive, NBC, Sat, 10 pm; developed into Palmolive Party (Barry Wood/Patsy Kelly Show) on 4/1/44

Millions For Defense (7/2/41 - 9/24/41) Texaco, CBS, Wed, 60m (summer replacement for Fred Allen; see also Treasury Hour

1 **Mills Brothers, The** (12/7/31 - 7/19/42) were on CBS, sustained before this
12/7/31 - 3/31/32, Vapex inhalant, CBS, 2t (Mon & Thu), 15m, 9 pm
4/12/32 - 4/10/33, Crisco and Chipso, CBS, 2t, 15m, 9:15 pm; Mon & Thu as of 7/11/32
7/4/35 - 1936, Dodge
6/28/42 - 7/19/42, Bl, Sun, 15m, 6:45 pm also Standard transcription

16 **Milt Herth Trio** (9/30/38 - 6/5/39) 15m
9/30/38 - 4/29/39, NBC, 6t, 8 am
5/1/39 - 6/5/39, Bl, Mon, 6 pm
(7/13/42 - 11/13/42) Bl, 4t (Tue - Fri), 15m, 6:30 pm
(1946) Syn, 15m
also World, Muzak transcriptions

38 **Milton Berle Show, The** (9/6/36 - 6/15/49)
9/6/36 - 8/29/37 (see Community Sing)
10/7/39 - 2/24/40 (see Stop Me If You've Heard This One)
9/12/41 - 12/5/41 (Three Ring Time) (also with Charles Laughton, Bob Crosby, Shirley Ross) Ballantine Ale, Mut, Fri, 9:30 pm
12/12/41 - 6/2/42 (Three Ring Time), Ballantine, Bl, Fri, 8:30 pm; Tue, 8:30 pm as of 3/10/42
3/3/43 - 5/26/43, Campbell Soup, CBS, Wed, 9:30 pm
3/21/44 - 6/27/45 (Let Yourself Go), Eversharp, CBS, Tue, 7 pm; 10:30 pm as of 7/4/44; Wed, 10:30 pm as of 1/3/45, 7 pm7/1/46 - 8/19/46 (Kiss and Make Up) CBS, Mon, 9 pm (partial summer replacement of Lux Radio Theater)
3/11/47 - 4/13/48 (At Home With The Berles; with Arnold Stang), Philip Morris, NBC, Tue, 8 pm
9/22/48 - 6/15/49, Texaco, ABC, Wed, 9 pm; TV show on Tue nights at 8 pm

Milton Charles (1/7/41 - 2/25/41) CBS, Tue, 15m, 8:30 am

1 **Milton DeLugg and His Swing Wing** (Standard transcription)

Milton Katims (1/7/40 - 4/7/40) Mut, Sun

Milton Kaye (11/7/39 - 8/16/41) Mut, 15m
11/7/39 - 2/27/40, Tue, 11:15 am
4/2/40 - 6/18/40, Tue, 2:30 pm
6/21/41 - 8/16/41, Sat, 11:15 am

1 **Mind In The Shadow** (2/2/49) CBS

97 **Mind's Eye, The** (1972 - present) syn

Mind Webs (4/18/75 - at least 6/29/80) WHA, Madison, WI; hosted by Michael Hansen; 167 shows made

2 **Mindy Carson Show, The** (12/12/49 - 9/22/50) NBC, different days, 15m
(11/16/52 - 1/22/53) Buick, CBS, 2t, 15m, 7:30 pm

1 **Mind Your Manners** (with Allen Ludden) (6/5/48 - 10/4/53) Sus, NBC, Sat
6/3/50 - 8/5/50, 11 am
8/12/50 - 12/8/51, 10 am
3/22/52 - 6/7/52, 7:30pm
7/12/53 - 10/4/53, Sun, 1 pm

Minneapolis Symphony Hour (with Eugene Ormandy) (2/23/35 - 3/23/35) General Household Utilities, CBS, Sat, 10 pm

Minnie and Maud (12/18/35 - 2/5/36) Pennsylvania Dutch, Bl, 3t (Wed, Thu, Sat), 15m, 10:05 am

Minstrel Melodies (3/6/43 - 10/16/43) NBC, Sat, 4:30 pm

1 **Minstrel Show, The** (1927) Syn
(4/21/37 - 5/28/40) Sus
4/21/37 - 1/11/39 (with Gene Arnod) Bl, Wed
1/19/39 - 4/14/39, Bl, Thu
12/12/39 - 5/28/40, Mut, Tue, 10:30 pm

Minstrel Train, The (see Molasses and January)

Minute Dramas (8/5/30 - 9/22/31) Consolidated Cigar, CBS, Mon; Thu as of 6/10/31

Minute Men (see Stoopnagle and Budd)

1 **Miracle In The Bronx** (11/12/45) WOR

14 **Miracles and Melodies** (Syn)

Miracles Of Magnolia (with Fanny May Baldridge) (1931) Bl

Mirth and Madness (see Jack Kirkwood)

1 **Mirth and Melody** (with Ken Christy and Buzz Adlam's Orchestra) ABC (12/2/48)

Mirth For Moderns (with Abe Burrows)

1 **Mirth Parade, The** (with Don Wilson) (1932) Syn

37 **Misadventures Of Si And Elmer, The** (1933) Syn

Mischa The Magnificent (with Mischa Auer) (7/5/42 - 9/6/42) CBS, Sun

1 **Miss Fane's Baby Is Stolen** (1/7/34) Air trailer

1 **Miss Kieffer and Her Kiddies** (10/25/36) WMBQ

Miss Hattie (with Ethel Barrymore) (9/17/44 - 6/17/45) Alcoa, ABC, Sun, 3:30 pm

Miss Information (1945)

Miss Meade's Children (with Margaret Ryan) (2/9/42 - 5/15/42) Mut, 5t, 15m, 9:45 pm

Miss My-T-Fine (1930 - 5/23/31) My-T-Fine, CBS, Sat, 15m, 8:30 am

2 **Miss Pinkerton, Inc.** (with Joan Blondell, Dick Powell) (7/12/41) CBS

Miss Switch, The Witch (with Miriam Wolfe) (Syn) 1950s, 15m

1 **Miss Tatlock's Millions** (1948) Air trailer

1 **Mission Accomplished** (AFRS)

1 **Mission Not Completed** (1947) Syn

1 **Mission Of Apollo 15: Countdown To Launch, The** (7/21/71) NBC-TV

1 **Mission Of Discovery** (9/28/88) PBS-TV

1 **Mission To Mars: The Search For Life** (7/11/65) CBS-TV

5 **Mission To The Middle East** (8/54) UNESCO Radio

1 **Mississippi** (1935) film sound track

1 **Mitch Miller Show, The** (6/26/55 - 7/29/61) CBS
6/26/55 - 60, Sus (Kraft from 6/26/55 - 9/4/55), Sun, 60m/45m
1960 - 7/29/61, Sat, 45m

MJB Coffee Demitasse Revue (with Ruth Etting, Gus Arnheim) (1934) MJB Coffee, NBC, Mon

Mobiloil Concert (with Emo Rapee Orchestra; then Nathaniel Shilkret) (1929 - 10/12/32) NBC, Wed

1 **Mobilization Story** (8/10/50) WOR-TV

1 **Mobilizing For Human Needs** (10/3/41) pool feed

Model Airplane Club (6/17/39 - 4/27/40) Mut, Sat, 15m

Model Minstrels, The (also called Pipe Smoking Time) (with Tom Howard and George Shelton) (2/27/39 - 11/18/40) Model Tobacco, CBS, Mon, 8:30 pm

1 **Modern Adventures Of Casanova, The** (with Errol Flynn)
(1/10/52 - 7/3/52; 10/2/52 - 12/25/52) Multi, Mut, Thu, 8 pm

Modern Cinderella (6/1/36 - 7/2/37) Gold Medal, CBS, 5t, 15m; started at an earlier date on WGN

3 **Modern Jazz Quartet, The** (1955, 1957, 7/8/70) CBS

Modern Living (with Dr. E. Parrish) (7/13/36 - 11/24/39) Mut, 3t, 15m, 9:15 am

2 **Modern Melody Trio, The** (Lang-Worth transcriptions)

6 **Modern Organ Rhythms. Renditions By Arlo** (SESAC transcriptions)

6 **Modern Rhythm Ensemble Of Boston** (1937 - 1939) Syn

31 **Modern Romances** (10/7/36 - 3/31/37) (11/14/49 - 2/25/55) Bl/ABC, 5t and 6t except where noted
10/7/36 - 3/31/37, Modern Romances Magazine, Bl, Wed, 2 pm
1944, Syn
4/11/49 - 8/5/50, Multi
8/8/50 - 2/2/51, Norwich
8/31/51 - 10/2/51, Sus
3/14/53 - 8/29/53, NBC, Sat, 11:30 am
10/5/53 - 7/2/54, Ex-lax, 15m
7/26/54 - 2/25/55, Multi, 15m

Modern Symphonics (with Ferde Grofe) (6/4/37 - 8/6/37) American Banks, CBS, Fri, 10 pm

Modern Touch, The (see Art Van Damme)

Modesty Blaise (Last Day In Limbo) (with Barbara Kellerman)

1 **Mohawk Treasure Chest, The** (with Harold Levey Orchestra)
(3/20/34 - 11/29/34) Mohawk Carpet, NBC, 15m
3/20/34 - 6/7/34 (with Howard Phelps) 2t, 10:30 am
9/6/34 - 11/29/34 (with Ralph Kirberry) 2t (Sun & Thu) 12 noon and 10 am

1 **Molasses and January** (with Pick Malone, Pat Padgett)
(8/17/42 - 10/9/42) Bl, 5t, 5m, 9:55 pm
(1945) (Minstrel Train)

Mollé Mystery Theater, The (see Mystery Theater)

Molly (Mollie) Of The Movies (with Gene Byron) 11/4/35 - 4/23/37) Ovaltine, Mut, 5t, 15m

Molly Picon (see I Give You My Life)

1 **Momentous Years 1927 - 1957, The** (1/57) CBC

1 **Moment For Meditation** (7/4/44) NBC

1 **Moments Make Up The Year** (12/31/46) CBS

5 **Moments Of Melody** (1936) Syn

1 **Moments Of Memory** (with Chet Gaylord) (9/9/43) WOR

Mommie and The Men (with Elspeth Eric, Lon Clark) (8/27/45 - 9/7/45) Procter & Gamble, CBS, 5t, 15m, 7 pm

1 **Monday At 8:30** (9/2/39) Mut

Monday Evening Melody (see Buddy Weed)

2 **Monday Merry-Go-Round, The** (with Victor Arden's Orchestra, Bea Wain and Phil Duey) (10/20/41 - 4/13/42) Bl, Mon, 10 pm

2 **Monday Night Show** (You Said It) (with Lou Holtz until 4/11/38; then Henny Youngman as of 9/5/38; also Richard Himber Orchestra, Ted Husing and Connie Boswell)
(2/28/38 -11/28/38) Brewer's Association, CBS, Mon, 8 pm (developed into Wednesday Night Show)

Money-Go-Round (with Benay Venuta and Fred Uttal) (4/1/44 - 4/15/44) Bl, Sat, 7 pm

1 **Money - Money - Money** (9/52) Syn

1 **Monica Lewis and Frank Farrell Show, The** (3/19/49 - 7/23/49) Mut, Sat, 1:30 pm

1 **Monitor** (6/12/55 - 1/26/74) Multi, NBC, Sunday afternoons, Saturday evenings, 60m ; 5/11/55 (Audition) also see NBC Monitor Sales Presentation

1 **Monitor Preview** (4/28/55) NBC

1 **Monitor Views The News, The** (1/13/37, 1/27/37) WCNW

1 **Monitor's Salute To Jimmy Durante** (1963) NBC

Monsanto College Concerts (1949)

1 **Monsanto Night: Benny Goodman** (3/31/74) NBC-TV

1 **Monsieur Beaucaire** (1946) Air trailer

Monsieur Le Capitaine (about Paul Maupin; by Ted Sherdeman) (6/11/40 - 8/13/40) Bl, Tue, 10:30 pm

Montana Slim (1/13/36 - 5/23/39) CBS, various days and times

Monty Woolley Program (see Sammy Kaye)

1 **Montgomery Speaks His Mind** (4/28/59) CBS

Monticello Party Live (1930s)

4 **Montmartre** (1932) Syn

Montreal Symphony Orchestra (1939 - 4/23/40) Mut, Tue (not in New York)
(7/11/40 - 8/29/40) Bl, Thu, 45m, 9:15 pm

2 **Montville and The Valley** (1949) Syn

2 **Mood Music Concert** (Lang-Worth transcriptions)

2 **Moods In Melody** (1/24/58) ABC

2 **Moody Speaking** (6/23/53)

Moonbeams (11/11/38 - 1/13/39) Swiss Colony Wine, Mut, Fri, 9:30 pm; possibly started 10/38

8 **Moon Dreams** (with Marvin Miller) (2/26/46 - 47) 15m, Syn

2 **Moon Mullins** (CBS) (15m) 3/15/40 and 1/31/47 (Auditions)

1 **Moon Over Africa** (also see Talking Drums) (1937 - 38) 15m, Syn

1 **Moon Over Miami** (1941) film sound track

13 **Moon Over Morocco** (1973) (ZBS Production) The Adventures Of Jack Flanders

44 **Moon River** (1930 - 1940s)) from WLW, Cincinnati, 15m; Midwest, also syndicated

1 **Moondial** (1946) WTOP

Moonshine and Honeysuckle (by Lulu Vollmar; with Louis Mason) (1930 - 4/23/33) Sus, NBC, Sun

Moorish Tales (10/16/36 - 1/15/37) NBC, Fri, 6 pm

1 **More Here Than Meets The Ear** (1965) Syn

5 **Morey Amsterdam Show, The** (7/10/48 - 2/15/49) Sus, CBS, Sat, 9 pm; Tue, 9:30 pm as of 10/12/48

4 **Morgan Beatty** (4/3/44 - 58+) (1946 - 58+) Miles, NBC

Morin Sisters (1932 - 1/4/39) 15m
1932 - 3/8/33, Bl, Wed
6/13/33 - 34, Sweetheart Soap, Bl, 2t (Tue & Wed)
1934 - 4/6/35, Bl, Fri
also 3/22/35 - 9/23/35, Bl, Mon, 15m, 3:45 pm
5/30/35 - 9/19/37 (Sunset Dreams; with the Ranch Boys) Fitch, CBS, Sun, 7:45 pm (often called at times Fitch Jingle show)
6/3/39 - 1/4/39, Bl, Sat, 15m, 10 am

Mormon Tabernacle Choir, The (see Salt Lake Tabernacle Choir)

1 **Morning After Creation** (5/5/49)

1 **Morning Edition** (7/4/83) NPR

2 **Morning In Manhattan** (12/8/41, 6/7/44) WEAF

Morning Matinee (9/10/36 - 3/4/37) local department stores, Mut, Thu, 15m, 9:30 am

Morning Melodies (1944 - 51) Chicago area, CBS, 15m

1 **Morning Melodies With Mary Ann** (4/25/48)

Morning News (NBC)

1 **Morning News Round-Up** (6/7/44) NBC

1 **Morning Scene** (5/4/71) WCCO-TV

6 **Morning Special** (6/11 - 28/44) BBC

5 **Morris H. Siegel, The Insurance Counselor** (1939, 1940) WOR, WINS, Syn

Mortimer Gooch (with Bob Bailey) (1/13/36 - 3/26/37) Wrigley, CBS, Fri, 15m

Mortimer Meek (see Meet Mr. Meek)

9 **Morton Downey** (1930 - 6/30/51)
1930 - 4/23/31, CBS, 4t (Tue, Wed, Fri, Sat), 15m
6/1/31 - 5/28/32 (Camel Quarter-Hour; also with Tony Wons), Camel, CBS, 6t, 15m
1932 - 33, Woodbury, Bl, Sun, 30m
1933 - 1/25/34, Sus, CBS, Thu, 15m, 8 pm
5/1/34 - 8/11/34, Woodbury, CBS, Tue, 7 pm; Sat, 45m, 7:45 pm as of 7/21/34
12/16/34 - 4/16/35, Carlsbad, Bl, Sun, 30m, 4:30 pm, also on with Ray Sinatra Orchestra,
12/18/34 - 4/22/35, Bl, Tue, 15m
4/19/35 - 6/14/35, Bl, Fri, 15m, 8:15 pm
2/8/43 - 12/1/44, Coca Cola, ABC, 5t, 15m, 3 pm; called (The Coke Club through 1951)
2/5/45 - 1/31/47, Coca-Cola, Mut, 5t, 15m
6/8/48 - 6/4/49; 10/4/49 - 7/6/50, NBC, 3t (Tue, Thu, Sat), 15m, 1:15 pm
10/7/50 - 6/30/51, Coca-Cola, CBS, Sat, 30m, 10:30 am

2 **Morton Downey Dodge Show, The** (1936) Syn

Morton Franklin's Notes Of Grace (6/3/39 - 9/23/39) Bl, Sat, 2 pm

1 **Morton Gould and His Orchestra** (often with Jack Arthur; Jimmie Shields) (12/6/36 -10/6/42) on various days and times including:
12/6/36 - 37, Mut, Sun, 8 pm
1937 - 38, Mut, Mon
1938 - 1/30/40, Sus, Mut, Tue, 8:30 pm; 10 pm from 6/6/39 - 9/29/39
2/5/40 - 5/13/40, Mut, Mon, 9:30 pm
5/16/40 - 8/29/40, Mut, Thu, 9:30 pm
9/5/40 - 10/31/40, Mut, Thu, 10:30 pm
9/19/40 - 2/3/42, Mut, Tue; Sat, 9:30 pm from 7/19/41 - 8/30/41
2/9/42 - 5/18/42, Mut, Mon, 8:30 pm; 45m, 8:15 pm as of 3/23/42
7/14/42 - 10/6/42, Mut, Tue, 8 pm also syndicated

1 **Mosquito Music** (9/7/45) Mut

1 **Most Gratefully Yours** (1949) AFRS

Mostly Music (1951) Fri

3 **Mother and Dad** (with Charme Allen and Parker Fennelly) (8/10/42 - 9/23/44) CBS
8/10/42 - 10/4/43, 5t, 15m, 5:15 pm
10/9/43 - 9/23/44, Allegheny Steel, Sat, 30m, 5:30 pm
(1948)

Mother-In-Law (3/21/38 - 5/13/38) Bl, 5t, 15m, 1:30 pm

Mother Knows Best (with Warren Hull) (1940s and 50s) mostly CBS - Pacific:
10/15/49 - 1/7/50, CBS, Sat, 5:30 pm

1 **Mother 'O Mine** (with Agnes Young) (9/30/40 - 7/11/41) Clapps, Bl, 5t, 15m, 4 pm

1 **Mother's Day Program From China** (5/12/44) XGOY

Mothers Of Men (1938)

Motor City Melody (with Cyril Wezemael) (1/29/38 - 7/16/38) CBS, Sat, 2:30 pm

2 **Mountain Music** (with Macy and Smalle) (12/29/33 - 2/16/34) NBC, Fri, 15m, 5:45 pm
also 1937, Air trailer, film sound track

1 **Mountain Music Time** (1954) WLOS

3 **Mouquin, Inc. Presents** (with Louis F. Mouquin) (1930s)

Mouth Health (with Marley Sherris) (1930 - 34) Bl, 15m (also see Preventing Mouth Trouble)
1930 - 6/30/31, Tue, 8:15 am
7/8/31 - 3/9/32, Calsodent, Wed, 5:15 pm
3/22/32 - 34, Calsodent, Tue

Movietown Radio Theater (1951- 52) Syn (ZIV)

Movie Star Revue (with Dorothea James, Syd Gary and Ted Astor Orchestra) (2/18/32 - 8/16/32) Danderine Hair Tonic, CBS, 2t, 15m

1 **Moving Earth, The** (1955) UNESCO Radio

Moving Stories Of Life (1930s) (Syn) 15m

1 **Moylan Sisters, The** (with Marianne and Peggy Joan Moylan) (10/15/39 - 6/18/44) Sun, 15m
10/15/39 - 42, Thrivo, Bl
1942 - 6/18/44, Sus, Bl

Mozart Concerto Series (11/7/39 - 4/23/40) Mut, Tue, 9:30 pm; 8:30 pm as of 2/20/40

1 **Mozart Opera Series** (5/11/40 - 7/6/40) Mut, Sat, 60m, 9:30 pm

6 **Mr. Ace and Jane** (with Jane and Goodman Ace) (1/16/48 - 12/31/48) CBS
1/16/48 - 5/29/48, Sat, 7 pm
6/4/48 - 9/3/48, Fri, 8 pm
9/10/48 - 12/31/48, Fri, 8:30 pm

Mr. Adam and Mrs. Eve (see Frank Crumit and Julia Sanderson)

Mr. Aladdin (with Paul Frees) (7/7/51 - 9/8/51) CBS, Sat, 9:30 pm (summer replacement for Broadway Is My Beat)

1 **Mr. and Mrs.** (with Jack Smart and Jane Houston) (9/27/29 - 6/2/31) Graybar Electric, CBS, Sat, 9 pm; Tue, 10 pm as of 1/7/30
(6/16/46) Sealy, WGN

1 **Mr. and Mrs. America** (8/28/45) Syn

2 **Mr. and Mrs. Blandings** (with Cary Grant and Betsy Drake) (1/21/51 - 6/17/51) TWA, NBC, Sun, 5:30 pm

Mr. and Mrs. Music (1947)

24 **Mr. and Mrs. North** (12/30/42 - 4/18/55) (with Alice Frost and Joseph Curtin; Barbara Britton and Richard Denning)
12/30/42 - 12/18/46, Woodbury, NBC, Wed, 8 pm
7/1/47 - 5/30/50, Colgate, CBS, Tue, 8:30 pm
9/5/50 - 6/22/54, Halo, CBS, Tue, 8:30 pm
9/5/54 - 9/26/54, Palmolive, CBS, Sun
10/4/54 - 11/19/54, Palmolive, CBS, 5t, 15m
11/29/54 - 4/18/55, Sus, CBS, Mon, 8 pm

Mr. Blanc's Fix-it Shop (see Mel Blanc Show)

Mr. Broadway (with Anthony Ross and Irene Manning) (8/7/52 - 9/25/48) ABC, Thu, 8 pm

1 **Mr. Bugs Goes To Town** (1942) Air trailer

2 **Mr. Chameleon** (with Karl Swenson) (7/14/48 - 1/9/53) CBS
7/21/48 - 6/20/51, Bayer, Wed, 8 pm
8/29/51 - 12/5/51, Wed, 8 pm
12/9/51 - 1/6/52, Sun, 5:30 pm
1/17/52 - 6/26/52, General Foods, Thu, 9 pm
7/3/52 - 8/28/52, Wrigley, Thu, 9 pm
10/7/52 - 10/28/52, Sus, Tue, 10:05 pm
11/7/52 - 1/9/53, Sus, Fri, 9 pm
3/13/53 - 8/7/53, Sus, Fri, 8:30 pm

Mr. Coco and Mr. Malt (with Al Cameron and Pete Bontsema) (1931- 6/30/32) Cocomalt, Bl - Midwest, 2t, 15m, 10:45 am

1 **Mr. Confusion** (Syn)

42 **Mr. District Attorney** (4/3/39 - 6/13/52)
4/3/39 - 6/16/39, NBC, 5t, 15m
6/27/39 - 9/19/39 (with Raymond Edward Johnson), Pepsodent, NBC, Tue, 30m, 10 pm; (summer replacement for Bob Hope)
10/1/39 - 4/7/40, Pepsodent, Bl, Sun, 7:30 pm
4/11/40 - 6/27/40, NBC, Thu, 8 pn
7/3/40 - 9/19/51, Vitalis, NBC, Wed, 9:30 pm
9/28/51 - 6/13/52, Vitalis, ABC, Fri, 9:30 pm
(1952 - 53) Syn - ZIV (with David Brian) 52 episodes broadcast, originally on Mutual

2 **Mr. Feathers** (with Parker Fennelly) (11/9/49 - 8/31/50) Sus, Mut
11/9/49 - 3/1/50, Wed, 9 pm
6/29/50 - 8/31/50, Thu, 8:30 pm

Mr. Fix-it (with Jim Boles) (6/5/49 - 4/1/50) 15m
6/5/49 - 8/28/49, Mut, Sun
9/11/49 - 12/4/49, NBC, Sun
1/7/50 - 4/1/50, CBS, Sat

Mr. Good (sponsored by Lydia Pinkham) 15m

6 **Mr. I. A. Moto** (with James Monks) (5/20/51 - 10/20/51) NBC (New York dates) conflicting dates are probably West Coast dates
5/20/51 - 9/23/51, Sun, 9:30 pm
9/30/51 - 10/7/51, Sun, 10 pm
10/13/51 - 10/20/51, Sat, 10:30 pm

61 **Mr. Keen, Tracer Of Lost Persons** (10/12/37 - 4/19/55)
10/12/37 - 10/22/42, Bi-So-Dol, Bl, 3t, (Tue, Wed, Thu) 15m
10/28/42 - 11/5/43, Kolynos, CBS, 3t, 15m
11/11/43 - 6/23/47; 9/11/47 - 7/12/51, White Hall (Kolynos) CBS, Thu, 30m, 7:30 pm; 25m, 8:30 pm as of 9/11/47
7/20/51 - 8/31/51, CBS, Fri, 9:30 pm
9/13/51 - 9/25/52, Chesterfield, NBC, Thu, 8:30 pm; 9:30 pm as of 5/8/52; 8 pm as of 6/5/52
10/3/52 - 10/1/54, Multi; the Procter & Gamble, CBS, Fri, 8 pm
also 5/24/54 - 1/14/55, CBS, 5t, 15m, 10 pm
2/22/55 - 4/19/55, CBS, Tue, 8:30 pm

1 **Mr. Mergenthwirker's Lobblies** (5/5/38) Mut

Mr. McNutley (see Meet Mr. McNutley)

Mr. Mercury (with John Larkin) (7/10/51 - 12/25/51) General Mills, ABC, Tue, 7:30 pm

Mr. Moonseed (with Ezio Pinza) NBC (Audition)

Mr. Mystery (1/13/53 - 2/5/53) Mut, 2t, 15m, 10:15 pm

1 **Mr. Pickwick's Christmas** (World Syn)

58 **Mr. President** (with Edward Arnold) (5/17/47) Audition
(6/26/47 - 9/23/53) Sus, ABC
6/26/47 - 12/25/47, Thu, 9:30 pm
1/11/48 - 11/19/50, Sun, 2:30 pm (New York lists all Sundays)

1 **Mr. Robert Kennedy and Congressman William Miller** (10/60)

1 **Mr. Roger Weem and Mr. Henry Haines** (1/15/37) WCNW

1 **Mr. Smith Goes To Town** (12/19/42) WSM

Mr. Twister, Mind Trickster (with Jim Jordan) (6/24/32 - 11/10/33) Borden's Ice Cream, NBC, 3t, 15m

Mrs. A. M. Goudiss (1/5/32 - 12/27/32) Bl, 15m
1/5/32 - 6/12/32) Kelvinator, Mon, 11 am
5/27/32 - 7/2/32, Kraft, Sat, 11 am
9/27/32 - 12/27/32, Kraft, Tue, 11 am

1 **Mrs. Barbara Bush** (6/1/90)

Mrs. Blake's Radio Column (7/6/31 - 4/23/32) Crisco, NBC, 6t, 15m, 10 am

1 **Mrs. Franklin Delano Roosevelt** (Syn)

1 **Mrs. Gertrude Lawrence and Mrs. Bernard Baruch** (12/29/43) Mut

2 **Mrs. Goes A'Shopping, The** (with John Reed King) (2/17/41 - 12/21/51) CBS, 3t, 15m; 5t as of 8/18/41 (often local New York from 1939)

Mrs. Julian Heath (1928 - 32) Bl, 5t, 15m

Mrs. Miniver (with Judith Evans and Karl Swenson; Gertrude Warner and John Moore as of 6/30/44)
(1/7/44 - 10/7/44) CBS
1/7/44 - 6/14/44, Fri, 11:30 pm
6/30/44 - 10/7/44, Sat, 7:30 pm

4 **Mrs. Tucker's "Smile Program"** (12/19 - 26/52) Syn

Mrs. Wiggs Of The Cabbage Patch (2/4/35 - 12/30/38) 5t, 15m
2/4/35 - 9/11/36, Jad Salts, CBS
9/14/36 - 12/30/38, Old English Wax and Hills Cold Tablets, NBC

1 **Mrs. Winston Churchill Speech** (12/22/41) BBC/Mut

1 **Much Ado About Doolittle** (with Jack Kirkwood; Hans Conreid) Audition
(7/2/50 - 8/20/50) CBS, Sun, 8:30 pm (partial summer replacement for Red Skelton)

1 **Much Ado About Music** (5/9/50) WQXR

Much - Binding - In - The - Marsh (with Richard Murdoch, Ken Horne, Sam Costa) (on first 3/31/44 - 9/28/45; every 6 weeks) then 1/2/47 - 3/23/54

3 **Muggsy Spanier** (World transcriptions)

Muggsy Spanier All-Stars (1954)

3 **Muggsy Spanier and His Dixieland Band** (World transcriptions)

1 **Muhammed Ali vs. Jean Pierre Coopman** (2/20/76) CBS-TV

Mulligan's Travels (with Sheldon Leonard)

Munros, The (with Neal Keehan and Margaret Heckle) (2/10/41 - 5/9/41) Bl, 5t, 15m

7 **Murder and Mr. Malone** (usually with Frank Lovejoy)
(1/11/47 - 7/13/51) ABC
1/11/47 - 4/17/48, Guild Wines, Sat, 9:30 pm
4/24/48 - 3/26/49 (called The Amazing Mr. Malone from now on), Guild Wines, Sat, 9:30 pm; 8:30 pm from 6/5/48 - 12/4/48
9/21/49 - 9/24/50, Sus, Wed, 8 pm; (with Gene Raymond) Sun, 7:30 pm as of 11/6/49
5/25/51 - 7/13/51, Sus, Fri, 9 pm

Murder and Mrs. Chase (9/11/56 - 6/11/57) ABC, Tue, 7:30 pm

Murder and Music (4/6/50 - 4/27/50) ABC, Thu, 10:30 pm

27 **Murder At Midnight** (with Raymond Morgan) (9/16/46 - 9/8/47) Syn; 48 shows broadcast; (dates are WJZ, New York) Mon, 10:30 pm; rebroadcast in 1950
(5/1/50 - 7/31/50) Mut, Mon, 9:30 pm

6 **Murder By Experts** (with John Dickson Carr, Brett Halliday and Alfred Hitchcock as hosts)
(6/11/49 - 12/17/51) Sus, Mut
6/11/49 - 7/30/49, Sat, 2:30 pm
7/31/49 - 9/18/49, Sun, 10 pm
9/26/49 - 12/7/51, Mon

6 **Murder Clinic** (7/21/42 - 9/5/43) Mut
7/21/42 - 3/9/43, Tue, 9:30 pm
3/14/43 - 4/18/43, Sun, 9 pm; 5:30 pm as of 4/4/43
5/2/43 - 9/5/43, Sun, 6 pm (summer replacement for First Nighter)

Murder Is My Hobby (with Glenn Langan) (10/14/45 - 7/14/46) Knox Gelatin, Mut, Sun, 4 pm
(see Mystery Is My Hobby, a similar show)

2 **Murder Will Out** (with Edmund MacDonald and Eddie Marr) (Ranier Brewing Company), ABC - Pacific (1946)

Muriel Angelus (1/18/41 - 4/19/41) NBC, 2t (Sat & Sun) 15m, 7:30 pm and 4 pm

Muriel Wilson (Songs You Love) (also with Fred Hufsmith)
(12/13/36 - 1/17/37) Smith Brothers, NBC, Sun, 1 pm (also see Gems Of Melody)

1 **Murray Arnold and His Orchestra** (6/30/47) ABC

1 **Murray The K: Live From The Brooklyn Fox** (12/63)

4 **Murrow Retrospective, A** (1/3 - 7/52) WNET-TV

Museum Of Modern Music (see Buddy Weed)

Music All America Loves To Hear, The (see Marion Talley)

2 **Music America Loves** (Syn)

37 **Music America Loves Best**
(3/4/44 - 5/22/49) RCA
3/4/44 - 8/26/44 (with Perry Como), ABC, Sat, 7:30 pm
9/3/44 - 11/25/45, NBC, Sun, 4:30 pm
12/2/45 - 5/22/49 (RCA Victor Show) NBC, Sun, 4:30 pm; with Robert Merrill as of 6/9/46; 2 pm as of 7/7/46; 2:30 pm as of 4/4/48; 5:30 pm as of 9/19/48; 5 pm as of 3/27/49

1 **Music America Loves, The** (CBS)

Music and American Youth
(1935 - 4/4/36; 1/8/39 - 5/25/41 (not always in New York) Sus, NBC, Sun

1 **Music and Comedy Excerpts** (pre-war)

1 **Music and Flowers** (1/13/37) WCNW

1 **Music and Lyrics** (1/16/45) Mut

1 **Music and Manners** (9/8/39) Mut

Music and The Muse (with Janet Logan) (1949 - 50) NBC, Sun

1 **Music and You** (6/17/37) Mut

Music Appreciation Hour (with Walter Damrosch) (10/29/29 - 5/1/42) Sus, Bl, Fri, 60m, 2 pm; usually on from October through April

9 **Music As You Like It** (1959)15m, Syn

Music At The Haydn's (with Otto Harbach, Al Goodman Orchestra; then James Melton)
(1/8/35 - 6/24/35) Colgate, NBC, Mon, 9:30 pm

1 **Music Box** (MacGregor transcription)

Music Box Review (4/29/36 - 10/21/36) Mut, Wed, 8:30 pm

3 **Music Builders, The** (3/23/46 - 6/8/46) WGY

Music By Adlam (with Buzz Adlam Orchestra) ABC (1946 - 1947)

Music By Camarata (with Tutti Camarata) (4/12/54 - 10/4/54) ABC, Mon, 9 pm

1 **Music By Faith** (9/10/50) AFRS

2 **Music By Gershwin** (with George Gershwin) (2/19/34 - 12/23/34) Feen-A-Mint, Bl, Mon, 7:30 pm; CBS, Sun, 5 pm as as of 9/30/34

Music By Goodman (with Al Goodman) (10/6/35 - 12/8/35) Ludens, NBC, Sun, 15m, 5:45 pm

Music By Mantovani (7/11/52 - 11/28/52) NBC, Fri, 9:30 pm; 8:30 pm as of 10/3/52

1 **Music By Martin** (NBC)

2 **Music By Maupin** (5/31/50, 6/14/50) ABC

Music By Meakin (with Jack Meakin) (1938) Sat

Music By Moonlight (with Howard Price; then Willie Morris and Raoul Nadeau as of 9/16/39)
(6/17/39 - 5/11/40) Mut, Sat, 10:30 pm

Music By Rex Koury (ABC)

Music By Richard Himber
(12/8/35 - 2/16/36) Ludens, NBC, Sun, 15m, 5:45 pm

1 **Music By Roth** (Thesaurus transcription)

8 **Music By Sweeten (Claude Sweeten and His Orchestra)** Standard transcriptions

2 **Music By Warrington** (1943) WCAU, CBS

2 **Music By Woodbury** (1940) NBC, KDYL origination

Music City USA (with Tommy Cutrer) (1973 - 74)

2 **Music Depreciation** (with Les Paul Trio, Frank DeVol) Mut - Pacific (10/22/44 - 4/22/45)

Music Doctors (1930 - 4/11/31) Vapex, Bl, Sat, 9:30 pm

1 **Music Every American Knows** (12/8/41) Red

Music Festival (see Benny Goodman)

5 **Music Fights For Infantile Paralysis** (1945) Syn

11 **Music Fights Infantile Paralysis** (1946, 1947) Syn

17 **Music For America** (1942) Mut (1956) Syn

Music For An Hour (with Alfred Wallenstein) (5/9/43 - 9/24/44) Mut, Sun, 9 pm; 1:30 pm as of 10/10/43

Music For Fun (10/11/38 - 3/7/39) CBS, Tue, 15m, 5:15 pm

4 **Music For Half An Hour** (with John Stanley Orchestra) (1/10/44 - 9/4/44) Mut, Mon, 4:30 pm
(with Emerson Buckley Orchestra) (1949)

Music For Listening (9/6/40 - 10/19/41) Bl, Sun
9/6/40 - 4/27/41 (with Charles Dant) 15m, 7:45 pm
6/22/41 - 10/19/41 (with Gordon Jenkins) 6:30 pm; 6 pm as of 8/31/41

Music For Meditation (1955)

32 **Music For Millions** (1945) Seventh War Loan, Victory Loan) Treasury Department, 15m, Syn

19 **Music For Moderns** (with Clarence Fuhrman) (12/17/38 - 9/27/40)
12/17/38 - 4/15/39, (with Lyn Murray) CBS, Sat, 45m, 1:30 pm
2/12/39 - 6/30/40, NBC, Sun (overlap)
8/23/40 - 9/27/40, NBC, Fri, 9:30 pm
(8/6/52 - 9/53) NBC) Sat

1 **Music For Remembrance** (8/25/45) Mut

3 **Music For Sunday** (with Art Baker) (AFRS)

1 **Music For The March Of Dimes** (1951) Syn

Music For The Shut-In (1945)

Music For Tonight (with Milton Katims Orchestra; Betty Spain, Edna Phillips) (3/7/45 - 5/23/45) NBC, Wed, 11:30 pm

6 **Music For You** (with Earl Nightingale and Cesar Petrillo Orchestra)
(7/8/51 - 10/5/52) CBS, Sun
7/8/51 - 3/9/52, 1:30 pm; 10:30 pm as of 11/11/51
8/17/52 - 10/5/52, Sun, 6 pm

Music For Your Mood (1945)

Music From America (see The Bell Telephone Hour, also see Glenn Miller)

Music From Hawaii (see Hawaii Calls)

1 **Music From Holland** (Syn)

Music From Hollywood (see Hal Kemp)

1 **Music From Hollywood** (NBC)
(1950 - 1951) (Robert Armbruster Orchestra)

1 **Music From Maryland** (6/21/39) WFBR

Music From Meadowbrook
(1/18/41 - 10/24/42) CBS, Sat, 60m

Music From Mexico (11/7/39 - 4/9/40) NBC, Tue, 15m, 6 pm

Music From Texas (9/2/36 - 3/26/37 Crazy Water Crystals, Mut, 3t, 15m, 1 pm

50 **Music From The Heart Of America**
(11/25/47 - 9/8/49) NBC - Chicago

Music From The Hometown (AFRS)

Music From The House Of Squibb (see Lyn Murray)

2 **Music From Your Hometown** (AFRS) (with Emil Petty, Wayne King)

2 **Music Goes To War** (Syn)

1 **Music Goes 'Round, The** (1936) Air trailer

Music Hall From London
(12/10/38 - 8/5/39) Mut, Sat, 60m, 3 pm

1 **Music Hall Of Fame, The** (9/22/47) Syn

Music Hall Of The Air (see Radio City Music Hall)

2 **Music Hall Theatre** (7/1/49, 7/4/49) WOR audition

1 **Music Hall Varieties** (Thesaurus transcription)

1 **Music Hall Varieties (That Snappy Saxophone Eight)** (Thesaurus transcription)

1 **Music Hall Varieties Orchestra** (Thesaurus transcription)

Music In A Mellow Mood
(9/7/40 - 3/1/41) NBC, Sat, 15m, 2 pm

Music In American Cities
(10/12/44 - 12/28/44) NBC, Thu, 11:30 pm

Music Internationale (1/21/39 - 6/10/39) Bl, Sat, 11 am

13 **Music In The Air** (1953) Syn

1 **Music In The Modern Mood** (1949) Syn

Music In The Moonlight (with Jane Grant and Lionel Reiger) (1941) NBC

2 **Music In The Morgan Manner** (8/29/59, 1/65) KFI

1 **Music In The Night** (1949) NBC

1 **Music Is Magic** (1937) film sound track

Music Is My Hobby (9/19/35 -11/28/35) NBC, Thu, 7:30 pm
(1/17/38 - 5/23/38) Bl, Mon, 15m, 7 pm
also (6/3/38 - 9/9/38) Bl, Mon, 15m, 7:15 pm

1 **Music Land U.S.A.** (with Earl Wrightson) (10/5/51 - 9/26/52) CBS, Fri, 45m, 8:15 pm; 30m, 8 pm as of 11/30/51

Music Library, The (with Buzz Adlam Orchestra and Betty Russell)
(2/8/47 - 6/21/47) ABC, Sat, 7:30 pm

Music Magic (with Ruth Lyon and Edward Davies) (1/4/34 - 10/1/34) Bl, Thu, 3:30 pm (with Roy Shield Orchestra and Joan Blaine)
(4/13/35 - 12/14/35) Bl, Sat, 2:30 pm (with Charles Sears, Joan Blaine, Harry Kogen Orchestra)
(4/9/36 - 4/30/36) Bl, Thu, 10:30 pm

1 **Music Makers** (with Skitch Henderson) also 1950 film sound track

4 **Music Master** (1949) Syn

Music Millions Love (see Andre Kostelantz)

Music Of Americas (1/2/43 - 2/13/43) NBC, Sat, 4:30 pm

2 **Music Of Belgium, The** (10/43) Syn

2 **Music Of Manhattan** (with Louise Carlyle) (1945) NBC, Sat, also Thesaurus transcriptions

2 **Music Of Manhattan, The** (Thesaurus transcriptions)

Music Of The Americas
(3/29/41 - 9/27/41) Bl, Sat, 3:30 pm

Music Of The Church (6/23/35 - 8/25/35) CBS, Sun, 10 am

Music Of The New World
(12/3/42 - 7/6/44) NBC, Thu, 11:30 pm

Music Of The Evening (7/27/44 - 9/7/44) NBC, Thu, 8:30 pm

Music Of The Restoration (then **Music Of The Georgian Period**)
(1/16/39 - 4/24/39) CBS, Mon, 15m, 5 pm

Music Of Wartime America
(6/10/42 - 9/42) with Joe King

Music Of Worship (7/24/44 - 3/26/45) Mut, Mon, 9:30 pm

93 **Music On Deck** (Navy recruiting) 15m; various bands, Pat Boone, Lawrence Welk

Music On The Air (with Jimmie Kemper)
(4/16/34 - 6/25/34) Tide Water Oil, CBS, 3t, 15m, 7:30 pm

1 **Music Out Of The Blue** (11/9/50) WNUR

2 **Music Please** (8/28/58) CBS

Music Room (see Jerry Wayne)

Music Shop (see Johnny Mercer)

1 **Music Show** (10/22/44) Mut (exact title unknown, similar to CMSOLBS)

Music Styled For You (4/8/39 - 6/10/39) NBC, Sat, 15m, 11 am
(12/2/39 - 6/8/40) NBC, Sat, 2:30 pm

1 **Music Takes A Holiday** (1/3/54) NBC

Music Tent (with Dirk Fredericks; Joyce Krause, Art Fleming, host)
(3/3/55 - 10/24/55) ABC, Thu, 9:30 pm; Mon, 9 pm as of 4/11/55

1 **Music That Satisfies** (with Nathaniel Shilkret Orchestra; Norman Brokenshire)
(1/4/32 - 12/31/32) Chesterfield, CBS, 6t, 15m
(10/19/44 - 6/21/45) (with Monica Lewis) Chesterfield, CBS, 3t (Tue - Thu), 15m, 7:15 pm; see also Bing Crosby; Boswell Sisters

Music Through The Night (with Harry Fleetwood) (8/31/53 - ?) NBC, 6t, 5 hours, 1 am

1 **Music 'Til Dawn** (with Bob Hall, Don Robertson)
(4/13/53 - 1/3/70) WCBS, New York, 6t, 6 hours, 12 midnight (sponsored by American Airlines)

Music Till Midnight (see Mildred Bailey)

1 **Music Valley** (with Merle Travis and Jimmy Wakely) (10/26/42)

2 **Music We Love, The** (Syn)

Music Without End (4/11/39 - 5/16/39) CBS, Tue, 15m, 4:45 pm

Music Without Words (1940) CBS, 15m

Music With The Accent On Romance (see The Ken Carson Show

8 **Music With The Hormel Girls**
(11/20/49 - 11/25/51) Hormel
11/20/49 - 11/26/50, ABC, Sun
also 5/20/50 - 2/13/54, CBS, Sat, 2 pm; 1:30 pm as of 10/10/53
12/3/50 - 11/25/51, NBC, Sun

1 **Music With Wings** (Voice Of America) (Sgt. Earl Hagen directing) (9/8/45)

1 **Music Workshop** (6/24/49) ABC

Music You Can't Forget (with Carol Channing) 15m

10 **Music You Like** (1948) Syn

Music You Love, The
(9/13/36 - 12/13/36) Pittsburgh Plate Glass, CBS, Sun, 45m, 2pm

Musical Almanac (with Fred Grunfeld)
(2/5/55 - 2/26/55) Mut, Sat, 4:30 pm

Musical Americana (Music Of America with Deems Taylor and Raymond Paige Orchestra)
(1/25/40 - 1/16/41) Westinghouse
1/25/40 - 6/27/40, Bl, Thu, 8 pm
7/2/40 - 10/1/40, Bl, Tue, 9 pm
10/10/40 - 1/16/41, NBC, Thu, 10:30 pm
(6/5/47 - 8/28/47) (with Carmen Dragon and Frances Langford) NBC, Thu, 8:30 pm

Musical Autographs (see Guy Lombardo)

Musical Bouquet (with Bret Morrison)
(4/22/45 - 10/14/45) ABC, Sun, 4 pm

Musical Camera, The (with Josef Cherniavsky Orchestra and Willie Morris) (10/25/36 - 4/18/37)

Musical Comedy Hour, The (with Jessica Dragonette as the Coca-Cola girl)

Musical Comedy Revue (with Leo Spitalny Orchestra and Tom Thomas)
(10/27/35 - 5/19/40) Bl, Sun
7/19/36 - 8/30/36, 7 pm; 60m as of 8/23/36
3/17/40 - 5/19/40, Bl, Sun, 8 pm

9 **Musical Comedy Theatre, The** (Syn)

Musical Cruise (also called Benny Meroff's Revue; with Vincent Lopez Orchestra, Tony Cabooch) (1933 - 34) Plough, Bl, Wed, 10 pm

Musical Crusaders (1930 - 3/8/31) Canadian Pacific Railroad, Bl, Sun, 4:15 pm

Musical Fast Freight (see Fast Freight)

Musical Footnotes (with Vivienne Della Chiesa) (9/8/35 - 4/5/36) Julian and Kokenge Co. CBS, Sun, 15m

Musical Gazette (with Lyn Murray)
(2/27/38 - 5/8/38) CBS, Sun, 8:30 pm

Musical Grab Bag (15m) (1950)

Musically Yours (AFRS) 5th Army Band, 15m

Musical Melodrama (with Lorin Baker, Jack Smart and Nora Stirling)
(9/17/29 - 30) Johnson & Johnson, Bl, Tue, 9 pm

10 **Musical Memories** (with Edgar Guest)
(10/4/32 - 12/25/35) Household Finance, Bl
10/4/32 - 33, Tue, 9 pm
also 10/9/32 - 1/1/33 (with Thora Martens, Frank Westphal Orchestra) Investors Syndicate, CBS, Sun, 15m, 7:30 pm
1933 - 12/25/35, Tue
also 1948, Loyal Order Of Moose
1957, Syn

Musical Merry-Go-Round, The
(5/12/51 - 10/6/51) NBC, Sat, 8 pm; 9 pm as of 9/15/51

Musical Millwheel (with Walter Patterson) (9/11/41 - 6/14/42) Pillsbury, NBC, 4t (Thu - Sun), 15m

Musical Mock Trial (see Ben Bernie)

Musical Moments (see Chevrolet Show)

1 **Musical Moments Of 1957** (1957) Syn

Musical Mysteries (6/15/44 - 10/5/44) Bl, Thu, 7 pm; 11:30 pm from 9/7/44

Musical Reveries (1/20/36 - 7/18/36) Corn Products, 4t (Mon, Wed, Fri, Sat), 15m, 12:15 pm

Musical Romance (with Don Mario Alvarez and Jimmy Fidler)
(9/16/34 - 12/23/34) Maybelline, NBC, Sun, 3:30 pm

1 **Musical Roundup** (1949) Syn

1 **Musical Showcase** (Syn)

Musical Showman, The (with Nat Brusiloff Orchestra; George Martin)
(9/27/31 - 1/31/32 Shur-on Eye Glasses, Bl, Sun, 4:30 pm

2 **Musical Steelmakers** (with John Winchell as host) (1/2/38 - 6/18/44) Wheeling Steel, Sun (Began on WWVA on 11/15/36)
1/2/38 - 6/25/39; 10/8/39 - 6/30/40; 10/6/40 - 6/19/41, Mut, 5 pm
10/5/41 - 7/5/42; 10/4/42 - 7/27/43; 9/26/43 - 6/18/44, Bl, 5:30 pm

Musical Story Lady (see Alice Remsen)

Musical Tete-A-Tete (8/24/40 - 10/5/40) NBC, Sat, 15m, 9:45 am

Musical Toast (8/1/35 - 3/22/37) Krueger Beer; with Buddy Clark (BC) or Jerry Cooper (JC)
8/1/35 - 5/28/36 (with BC; JC as of 1/30/36) CBS, 2t, 15m, 7:15 pm
5/1/36 - 2/12/37 (BC) CBS, Fri, 15m, 4 pm; 5 pm as of 5/29/36
6/21/36 - 9/8/36 (with JC) CBS, Tue, 30m
9/28/36 - 3/22/37 (with JC) NBC, Mon, 10:30 pm

Musical Treasure Chest (see Horace Heidt)

1 **Musical Tour For Crippled Children By Bob Hope** (1953) Syn

Musical Varieties (with Leigh Orchestra) (3/18/39 - 6/10/39) NBC, Sat, 3:30 pm

17 **Musicana** (4/15/48 - 9/15/51) NBC

1 **Musicana Workshop** (12/14/48) WMAQ

1 **Musicomedy** (Silver Summer Revue) (with Johnny Desmond, Raymond Paige Orchestra) (6/18/48 - 10/1/48) CBS, Fri, 9:30 pm (summer replacement for The Adventures Of Ozzie and Harriet)

5 **Musings** (1938) Syn

10 **Musings and Music** (post-war) Syn

1 **Mussolini Declares War** (6/10/40)

1 **Mutiny On The Bounty** (1935) Air trailer

4 **Mutual Chamber Music Concert** (Mut)

1 **Mutual Dedicatory Program** (12/29/36) Mut

Mutual Forum Hour (see American Forum Of The Air)

Mutual Matinee (with Jerry Lawrence) (10/12/42 - 5/28/43) Mut, 5t, 60m - 120m

Mutual News (1944)

1 **Mutual Pacific News** (3/31/45) Mut

1 **Mutual Presents Curt Masssey** (2/5/45) Mut

Mutual Radio Chapel (10/12/41 - 11/28/43) Mut, Sun, 11:30 am

Mutual Radio Theater (see Sears Radio Theater)

Mutual's Block Party (with Ray Bloch and Martin Block) (7/3/47 - 11/27/47) Mut, Thu, 9:30 pm

Mutual School Of The Air (1/20/39 - 4/28/39) Mut, Fri, 10 am

1 **Mutual Showcase** (8/21/47) Mut

Mutual Sports Headlines (1948)

1 **Mutual Sports Question Box, The** (6/14/46) Mut

1 **Mutual Views The Convention** (6/20/48) Mut

2 **Mutual's Melodies** (6/20/45, 7/4/45) Mut

1 **Mutual's Theatre Of Song** (2/29/48) Mut

1 **Mutual - Don Lee Dedicatory Program** (12/30/36) Mut

1 **Muzzy Marcellino and His Orchestra** (MacGregor transcription)

My Best Girls (2/9/44 - 1/10/45) ABC, Wed, 8:30 pm

My Children (with Sydney Rogers and Mary Parker) (1939) Energine, Syn, 15m

54 **My Favorite Husband** (with Lucille Ball) (7/23/48 - 3/31/51) Sus, General Foods, CBS
7/23/48 - 9/24/48, Fri, 9 pm
10/2/48 - 12/25/48, Sat, 7 pm
12/26/48, Sun, 7 pm
1/14/49 - 7/1/49, Fri. 8:30 pm
9/2/49 - 3/31/50, Fri, 8:30 pm
4/2/50 - 6/25/50, Sun, 6 pm
9/2/50 - 3/31/51, Sat, 9:30 pm

3 **My Favorite Singer** (1948) Syn

25 **My Friend Irma** (with Marie Wilson) (4/11/47 - 8/23/54) CBS
4/11/47 - 6/20/47, Pepsodent, Fri, 10:30 pm
6/30/47 - 7/28/47, Pepsodent, Mon, 8:30 pm
8/4/47 - 6/27/49; 8/29/49 - 6/26/50; 9/14/50 - 6/25/51, Pepsodent, Mon, 10 pm
10/14/51 - 6/15/52, Pearson, Sun, 6 pm; 9:30 pm as of 5/28/52
10/7/52 - 6/30/53, Camel, Tue, 9:30 pm
12/1/53 - 8/23/54, Multi, Tue, 9:30 pm

1 **My Gal Sal** (1942) Air trailer

My Good Wife (with Arlene Francis and John Conte) (5/27/49 - 9/30/49) NBC, Fri 9.30 pm

1 **My Gremlin** (1946) Syn

1 **My Home Town** (with Cliff Arquette) (4/3/49) CBS

16 **My Little Margie** (with Gale Storm) (12/7/52 - 6/26/55) Philip Morris, CBS, Sun, 8:30 pm; also on Mut from 1953 - 54

2 **My Lucky Break** (with Josef Chemiavsky Orchestra) (1/1/39 - 9/17/39) Mut, Sun, 6 pm

My Lucky Stars (with Paul Whiteman) (5/13/51 - 9/16/51) ABC, Sun, 15m, 10:45 pm

My Man Godfrey (11/10/41 - 11/21/41) Mut, 5t, 15m, 4:15 pm

My Mother's Husband (with William Powell) (7/2/50 - 7/16/50) NBC, Sun, 9:30 pm

1 **My Musical Pilgrim's Progress** (2/25/41) CBS

My Name Is Logan (3/20/49 - 4/24/49) Mut, Sun, 15m, 10:30 pm

1 **My Secret Story** (with Anne Seymour) (6/2/51 - 10/20/51) NBC, Sat, 11:30 (1/26/52 - 2/2/52) NBC, Sat (developed in Hollywood Love Story)
also (2/20/54)

My Secret Ambition (with Ted Maxwell; replaced by Tom Breneman as of 6/38) (12/26/37 - 7/1/38) Durkee, CBS, Sun, 6:30 pm; Fri as of 4/17/38

My Silent Partner (with Faye Emerson) (6/23/49 - 8/18/49) NBC, Thu, 8 pm (partial summer replacement for The Aldrich Family)

2 **My Son and I** (with Betty Garde and Kingsley Colton; also with Jackson Beck as of 9/16/40
(10/9/39 - 12/30/40) Swans-Down and Calumet, CBS, 5t, 15m
also (2/13/49)

4 **My Son Jeep** (with Donald Cook and Martin Huston)
(1/25/53 - 6/14/53) NBC, Sun
1/25/53 - 4/21/53, 7:30 pm
4/26/53 - 6/14/53, 7 pm (partial summer replacement for The Aldrich Family)
(10/3/55 - 3/30/56) Sus, CBS, 5t, 15m, 8 pm
(4/2/56 - 11/9/56) CBS, 5t, 15m, 9 pm

2 **My True Story** (with Glenn Riggs, announcer) (2/15/43 - 2/1/62)
2/15/43 - 4/14/44, Sus, ABC, 5t, 30m
4/17/44 - 49, Libby, ABC, 5t
1949 - 52, Multi, ABC, 5t
1952 - 54, Sterling Drugs, ABC, 5t
1954 - 61, Multi, ABC, 5t; also on NBC some of these years
1961- 2/1/62, Mut, 4t

My World Is Music (see Stan Kenton)

Myra Kingsley (9/7/37 - 38) H-O, Mut, 5t, 15m

Myra Lane (see Melody Moments)

39 **Myrt and Marge** (11/2/31 - 8/30/46)
11/2/31 - 5/27/32; 8/29/32 - 1/1/37, Wrigley, CBS, 5t, 15m
1/4/37 - 12/31/37, Super Suds, CBS; Mut from 3/27/39 - 10/6/39), 5t, 15m
1/3/38 - 3/27/42, Super Suds, CBS, 5t, 15m
4/1/46 - 8/30/46, Syn (WOR, New York), 5t, 15m

Mysteries In Paris (1/4/32 - 4/10/33) Bourjois, CBS, Mon, 9:30 pm

Mysteries Of Crooked Square (6/17/45 - 8/12/45) Mut, Sun, 15m

1 **Mysteries Of The Mind** (with Hugh Casey, Henry Morgan) (12/4/38 - 12/25/38) Mut, Sun, 1:30 pm

61 **Mysterious Traveler, The** (hosted by Maurice Tarplin) (12/5/43 - 9/23/52) Sus, Mut (conflict in dates with New York broadcasts)
12/5/43 - 4/23/44, Sun, 7 pm
4/30/44 - 9/24/44, Sun, 3:30 pm
10/7/44 - 3/31/45, Sat, 9:30 pm
7/14/46 - 9/29/46, Sun, 4 pm
12/1/46 - 9/28/47, Sun, 7 pm
10/7/47 - 10/26/48, Tue, 8 pm
11/11/48 - 3/24/49, Thu, 9:30 pm
3/29/49 - 2/27/51, Tue, 9:30 pm
3/6/51 - 9/2/52, Tue, 9:30 pm in New York, on Wed from 3/7/51 - 9/19/51; Fridays from 9/28/51 - 12/7/51; Tuesdays from 12/11/51 - 9/2/52

Mystery Award Theater (1949)

1 **Mystery Chef, The** (with John MacPherson) (10/6/3 - 8/4/44) Davis Co., until 12/28/34, 15m; each network listed separately
10/6/31 - 6/30/32, Bl, 2t, 10:45 am
1/3/34 - 6/22/34, Bl, 2t (Wed & Fri)
1/6/32 - 6//29/32, CBS, Wed, 11:15 am
10/3/33 - 6/28/34, CBS, 2t
10/4/32 - 12/28/34, NBC, 2t, 10 am
12/4/35 - 11/24/38, Sus, NBC, 2t (Wed & Fri)
3/19/41 - 12/5/41, NBC, 2t (Wed & Fri) 9:45 am
12/7/42 - 8/4/44, Sus, ABC, 5t
also 3/1/48, Mut audition

Mystery Classics (5/3/56 - 9/30/57) ABC
5/3/56 - 6/13/57, Thu, 7:30 pm
6/17/57 - 9/30/57, Mon, 7:30 pm

1 **Mystery Club, The** (Syn)

Mystery File (with Walter Kiernan) (11/26/50 - 4/8/51) ABC, Sun, 7:30 pm; 6:30 pm as of 3/18/51

Mystery Hall (4/22/40 - 1941) Mut, various days, 8:30 pm (not in New York)
(11/29/41 - 12/20/41) Mut, Sat, 3 pm
(11/29/42 - 5/9/43) Mut, Sun, 10:15 am
(7/3/49 - 9/18/49) Mut, Sun, 3:30 pm

Mystery History Quiz (9/30/39 - 6/9/40) Mut, Sun, 2 pm; not in New York from 3/10/40

2 **Mystery House** (1/9/51 - 1/4/52) Mut
1/9/51 - 4/10/51, Fri, 8 pm
12/14/51 - 1/4/52, Fri, 9:30 pm
(1/14/54 - 10/28/54) Mut, Thu, 9:30 pm, also syndicated

Mystery House (different series; with Bela Lugosi) NBC (1944)

8 **Mystery In The Air** (with Stephen Courtleigh) (7/5/45 - 9/27/45) NBC, Thu, 10 pm (summer replacement of Abbott and Costello)
(7/3/47 - 9/25/47) (with Peter Lorre) Camel, NBC, Thu; (summer replacement of Abbott and Costello)

Mystery Island (1934) NBC, 4t, 15m

8 **Mystery Is My Hobby** (Syn) (1949 - 1951) (see Murder Is My Hobby, a similar show)

1 **Mystery Man** (3/24/41 - 3/16/42) Wheaties, Betty Crocker Soup, Red, 5t, 15m, 2:15 pm

Mystery Of The Week (4/1/46 - 11/21/47) Ivory, CBS (not always in New York), 5t, 15m, sponsored by Dreft

18 **Mystery Playhouse** (AFRS; with Peter Lorre) (1944 - ?) many were rebroadcasts of Inner Sanctum, The Whistler, Mr. and Mrs. North (these 18 are unidentified as yet)

Mystery Serial (by Carlton E. Morse) (5/2/30 - 6/20/32) NBC (West coast), Fri; Wed as of 10/21/31; Mon as of 4/18/32

Mystery Tenor (also with news by Charles J. Gilchrest) (1/1/33 - 6/4/33) Bl, Sun, 15m, 2 pm

27 **Mystery Theater** (9/7/43 - 6/30/54)
9/7/43 - 7/3/45, Mollé, NBC, Tue, 9 pm; called Mollé Mystery Theater when sponsored by Mollé
10/5/45 - 6/25/48, Mollé, NBC, Fri, 10 pm
6/29/48 - 6/19/51, Mollé, CBS, Tue, 8 pm
10/3/51 - 6/11/52; 10/8/52 - 7/1/53; 10/7/53 - 6/30/54 (Mark Sabre) Mollé, ABC, Wed, 8 pm; 9:30 pm as of 10/7/53 (see also Hearthstone Of The Death Squad)

1 **Mystery Time** (see ABC Mystery Time) also syndicated

1 **Mystery Without Murder** (with Luther Adler) (4/26/47 - 8/23/47) NBC, Sat, 10 pm (summer replacement of Judy Canova)

1 **Mystic Knights Of The Sea Minstrel Show, The** (12/4/36) Red

1 **Mystical Body Of Christ, The** (10/25/36) WMBQ

N R Millionaires (10/3/28 - 1/2/29) Lewis Howe, CBS, Wed, 9 pm

N R Modern Love Stories (3/5/28 - 4/2/28) Lewis Howe, CBS, Mon, 9 pm

N-K Music Showroom (see Andrews Sisters)

1 **N. A. M. Summer Show, The** (7/5/47) ABC

NABC World Theater (1960s) 45 - 60m

Nadia Boulanger (4/8/37 - 4/22/37) Bl, Thu, 4 pm

Name It and It's Yours (11/3/39 - 11/17/39) Bl, Fri, 8 pm

Name It and Take It (with Ed East) (5/19/39 - 6/14/40) Bl, Fri, 5 pm

3 **Name Speaks, The** (with Quenton Reynolds) (3/30/46 - 7/10/46) Brand Names, NBC, Sat, 15m, 2 pm, also syn

Name That Tune (with Red Benson; Harry Salter Orchestra) (12/20/52 - 4/10/53) Sus, NBC, Sat, 8:30 pm; Fri, 8:30 pm as of 1/2/53

Name The Movie (with Clark Dennis) (5/12/49 - 11/3/49) Revere, ABC, Thu, 9:45 pm

Name The Place (with Ben Grauer) (2/12/39 - 7/16/39) Bl, Sun, 15m, 3:30 pm
also 2/14/39 - 4/25/39, NBC, Tue, 15m, 10:45 pm

Name Three (with Bob Hawk) (4/10/39 - 4/20/40) Philip Morris, Mut
4/10/39 - 7/31/39, Mon, 8 pm
8/9/39 - 10/18/39, Wed, 8 pm
10/28/39 - 4/20/40, Sat, 7:30
(7/7/40 - 9/29/40) Jell-O, NBC, Sun, 7 pm (summer replacement for Jack Benny)

18 **Name You Will Remember, The** (12/29/48 - 3/5/49) NBC syndication

Name Your Music (with Tommy Cauthers and Margaret Carroll) Neighbors Of Woodcraft, NBC (1946 - 1947)

1 **Name Your Poison** (12/10/49) WOR

Nan Wynn (6/6/38 - 6/22/40) CBS, 15m
6/6/38 - 5/15/39, Mon
2/1/40 - 6/6/40, Thu
also 5/11/40 - 6/22/40, Sat

Nancy Booth Craig (6/10/40 - 4/27/51)
6/10/40 - 1/3/41, Bl, 2t - 3t, 10m, 12:15 pm
10/27/41 - 10/30/42, Bl, 5t, 10m -15m, 12 noon
10/21/46 - 4/27/51, Sus, ABC, 5t, 15m; twice a day for awhile starting 4/11/47

Napoleon's Retreat (with Deems Taylor, The Memphis Five, Phil Napoleon) (Marine Corps) (1945), 15m

4 **NASA Audio News Feature** (4/70 - 4/81) NASA

9 **NASA Audio News Features** (3/72 - 6/19/76) NASA

1 **NASA Press Conference** (1/13/94) C-SPAN

1 **NASA Shuttle Program** (10/31/93) C-SPAN

38 **NASA Space Notes** (11/73 - 2/83) NASA

175 **NASA Special Report** (9/66 - 5/85) NASA

3 **Nash Announcements** (1/34) Syn

Nash Program (with Floyd Gibbons, Vincent Lopez Orchestra; Grace Moore as of 4/3/37)
(10/3/36 - 6/26/37) Nash, CBS, Sat, 9 pm (also called Speed Show)

4 **Nat and Bridget (The Natural Bridge Pair)** (1931) Natural Bridge Shoes, 15m, Syn,

1 **Nat Brandwynne** (World transcription)

2 **Nat Brandwynne and His Orchestra** (World transcriptions)

Nat Brandwynne Orchestra (7/27/40 - 9/7/40) CBS, Sat, 5:30 pm

1 **Nat Brandwynne, His Piano and Orchestra** (8/23/49) CBS

2 **Nat Brandwynne, Piano and Rhythm Section** (World transcriptions)

Nat King Cole (also see King Cole Trio) (1956)

16 **Nat King Cole Show, The** (11/5/56 - 1/28/58) NBC-TV

1 **Nation's Economy: A Democratic View, The** (2/20/81) NBC-TV

1 **Nation's Economy: Some Opposing Views, The** (4/28/81) NBC-TV

6 **Nation's Nightmare, The** (with Bill Downs) (7/19/51 - 9/27/51) CBS, Thu, 8:30 pm; 9:30 pm as of 8/30/51

Nation's Playhouse, A (7/1/38 - 39) Mut, Fri, 11:30 pm

1 **National Air Races** (1937) Mut

11 **National Air Travel Club, The** (1947) Syn

5 **National Amateur Night** (with Ray Perkins) (12/30/34 - 5/16/37) Feen-A-Mint, Sun, 6 pm
12/30/34 - 2/16/36, CBS
2/23/36 - 5/16/37, Mut

10 **National Barn Dance** (with Joe Kelly) (4/19/24 - 4/30/60)
4/19/24 - 9/23/33, WLS (local)
9/30/33 - 6/22/40, Alka Seltzer, Bl, Sat, 60m
6/29//40 - 9/28/46, Alka Seltzer, NBC, Sat, 60m; 30m, 9 pm as of 7/4/42
3/19/49 - 3/11/50, Phillips Milk Of Magnesia, ABC, Sat, 10 pm
3/18/50 - 4/30/60, WLW (local) Sat

3 **National Boys Club Week** (Syn)

1 **National Children's Week** (3/6/39) Red

1 **National Conference Of Christians and Jews** (3/1/49) ABC

National Consumer Finance Association (15m)

1 **National Defense Day Ceremonies** (9/12/24) An ad-hoc network

1 **National Defense Week** (2/22/38)

54 **National Farm and Home Hour, The** (with Everett Mitchell) (9/30/29 - 58) started locally on WENR; continued locally after 1958
9/30/29 - 2/7/42, Bl, 6t, 45 - 6m, 12:30 pm
2/9/42 - 3/17/45 (called Farm and Home Hour during this period) ABC, 6t, 30m, 12:30 pm
9/15/45 - 58, Allis Chalmers, NBC, Sat, 30m

National Federation Of Music Clubs (4/8/39 - 5/13/39) NBC, Sat, 11:30 am (5/10/41 - 7/22/41) NBC, Sat, 5:30 pm

1 **National Federation Of Small Business** (1948) Syn

1 **National Football League Championship Game, The** (12/59) NBC

1 **National Foundation For Infantile Paralysis** (1/15/43) Syn

1 **National Guard Assembly** (see Paul Whiteman) (1948) ABC

National Guard Session (see Guard Session)

37 **National Guard Show, The** (1950) 15m, Syn

1 **National Heart Week Show** (2/14/49) Mut

National Hillbilly Champions (see Hillbilly Champions)

National Hour, The (11/18/45 - 9/1/46) NBC, Sun, 4 pm

National Juke Box (10/25/55 - 8/25/56) ABC, Sat, 25m, 9:35 pm

26 **National Lampoon Radio Hour, The** (11/17/73 - 6/1/74) (Syn)

1 **National Moondial, The** (6/16/48) WWDC

National Music Camp (7/13/41 - 8/24/41) Bl, Sun, 6 pm

1 **National Negro Health Week** (Syn)

2 **National Newspaper Boy Day** (10/2/43) Syn

1 **National Nutrition Conference For Defense** (5/40) Syn

National Philharmonic Orchestra, Los Angeles (1940)

1 **National Press Club, The** (10/18/94) C-SPAN

National Radio Fan Club (with Bill Silbert) (6/24/55 - 9/21/56) ABC, Fri, almost 2 hours, 8 pm

1 **National Radio Forum, The** (originated by Oliver Owen Kuhn) (1/11/32 - 5/12/43) Sus
1/11/32 - 4/22/35, NBC, Mon
5/2/35 - 9/26/35, NBC, Thu, 11:30 pm
11/16/36 - 8/24/42, Bl, Mon
9/2/42 - 5/12/43, Bl, Wed, 10:15 pm; 10:30 pm as of 1/15/43

National Radio Pulpit (with Dr. Ralph W. Sockman, Christ Church, New York) (1925 - 60s+) NBC, Sun; usually not broadcast between April and October; Highlights Of The Bible; then Sabbath Reveries

1 **National Radio Theatre** (8/31/84) NPR

1 **National Radio Theatre Sampler** (8/27/85) NPR

1 **National Schools-At-War Presentation** (6/23/45)

2 **National Singers, The** (Syn)

National Spelling Bee (see Spelling Bee)

1 **National Sports Car Races** (7/5/56) Yankee net

National Symphony Orchestra (Bl) (1939)

1 **National Tennis Doubles Championship** (8/26/38) CBS

1 **National Vespers** (with Harry Emerson Fosdick) (2/6/27 - 5/30/54) Bl/ABC, Sun

1 **National War Fund 1943 Campaign** (1943) Syn

National War Loan Campaign (1944)

1 **National War Monument** (5/21/39) CBC

1 **National Wildlife Restoration Week** (1940) Syn

Natural Bridge Revue (with Arthur Murray) (1930 - 4/24/31) Natural Bridge Shoes, Bl, Fri, also with Ray Perkins

1 **Natural Bridge Shoe Program** (1933) also see Nat and Bridget

Nature Of The Enemy, The (6/16/42 - 7/14/42) CBS, Tue, 8:30 pm

4 **Nature Sketches** (with Raymond Gregg) (6/24/39 - 9//21/46) NBC, 15m (on various days and times including:)
6/24/39 - 9/9/39, Sat, 11:45 am (on since 1938)
4/2/40 - 5/7/40; 6/15/40 - 7/20/40, Tue
5/10/41 - 8/30/41, Sat, 3 pm
6/13/42 - 9/26/42, Sat, 3 pm
6/29/46 - 9/21/46, Sat, 2:45 pm
also 1947, 1948

26 **Naval Air Reserve Show, The** (Syn)

1 **Navy Blue and Gold** (1937) Air trailer

3 **Navy Bulletin Board** (7/44 - 10/1/44) Mut

1 **Navy Comes Through, The** (1942) Syn

1 **Navy Day Fleet Review** (10/27/45) Mut

2 **Navy Day Salute** (10/26/41, 10/27/46) Mut

1 **Navy Diving School** (10/29/42) WOR

1 **Navy Is Fit To Fight** (12/8/41) Mut

1 **Navy Relief Program** (1/7/42) Mut

26 **Navy Star Time** (1951 - 52) 15m, Syn

2 **Navy "Swing and Sway Time"** (Syn)

75 **Navy Swings, The** (15m) Syn

1 **Nazi Eyes On Canada** (CBC) (9/20/42 - 10/25/42)

NBC Bandstand (1956 - 58) Multi, NBC, 5t, 30 - 90m

NBC Comedy Theater (11/5/44 - 6/10/45) NBC, Sat

1 **NBC Concert Orchestra, The** (12/8/41) Bl

48 **NBC D-Day Coverage** (6/6/44 - 6/7/44) NBC

2 **NBC Experiment In Drama** (12/22/63 - 1/64) Syn

NBC Great Plays (see Great Plays)

NBC Little Theater (1949)

1 **NBC London and Berlin Correspondents** (6/22/41) NBC

1 **NBC Magazine: A Day With President Reagan** (2/13/81) NBC-TV

1 **NBC Monitor Sales Presentation** (4/26/55) NBC

NBC Music Guild (11/20/34 - 8/22/38) Bl, Tue
also (6/4/38 - 8/27/38) NBC, Sat, 12 pm

1 **NBC New Year (1943) Parade Of Stars** (1943) NBC

1 **NBC New Year's All Star Parade Of Bands** (12/31/70) NBC

3 **NBC News** (8/27/39, 7/16/48, 7/31/53) NBC

1 **NBC News Debate Analysis** (10/28/80) NBC

NBC News Roundup (1945)

4 **NBC News Special Report** (10/15/64, 8/16/73, 10/15/73, 10/7/76) NBC

1 **NBC Nightly News** (10/25/83) NBC-TV

1 **NBC Orchestra, The** (6/7/44) NBC

2 **NBC Parade Of Stars** (10/8/45, 10/14/46) NBC

11 **NBC Presents: Short Story**
(2/21/51 - 5/30/52) Sus, NBC
2/2 1/51 - 4/25/51 , Wed
5/4/51 - 7/13/51; 11/23/51 - 5/30/52, Fri also syndicated

3 **NBC Radio Institute, The** (1946) NBC, Sat

1 **NBC Radio Theater** (also RCA Radio Theater) (produced by Himan Brown)
(4/27/59 - 1/1/60) NBC, 5t, 55m, 11:05 am
(9/18/55 - 3/11/56) (host is Pat O'Brien) Sus, NBC, Sun, 60m

1 **NBC Salutes Your Happy Birthday** (12/13/40) NBC

NBC Short Story (see NBC Presents: Short Story)

NBC Stamp Club (3/8/47 - 6/3/50) NBC, Sat morning, 15m

1 **NBC Star Playhouse** (with John Chapman) (10/4/53 - 4/11/54) Sus, NBC, Sun, 6:30 pm; 8:30 pm as of 11/8/53

1 **NBC Story Shop, The** (with Craig McDonnell) (8/23/47) NBC

NBC String Symphony (see String Symphony)

NBC Summer Symphony (see The NBC Symphony Orchestra)

NBC Symphony Of The Air (see The NBC Symphony Orchestra)

NBC Symphony Orchestra Conductors (see The NBC Symphony Orchestra)

128 **NBC Symphony Orchestra, The** (with Arturo Toscanini; Leopold Stokowski)
(12/25/37 - 3/14/54) time fluctuates between 30 and 90 minutes.
1937 - 4/4/54, mostly sustained; occasional sponsors were General Motors (8/1/43 - 7/21/46) and Squibb; programs were more than often named after sponsor (General Motors Symphony Of The Air) Bl
(1937 - 4/28/42) NBC
(9/27/42 - 3/14/54), varied among Sat, Sun and Tue also
6/11/50 - 9/3/50 (summer replacement of Theater Guild) NBC, Sun, 60m, 8:30 pm

NBC Symphony Spring Concert (see The NBC Symphony Orchestra)

NBC Theater (see NBC University Theater, The)

118 **NBC University Theater, The**
(7/30/48 - 2/14/51) Sus, NBC; preceded by World's Greatest Novels
7/30/48 - 8/27/48, Fri, 60m, 9 pm
9/3/48 - 9/17/48, Fri, 30m, 9 pm
9/26/48 - 6/12/49, Sun, 60m, 2:30 pm
6/18/49 - 9/3/49, Sat, 60m, 6:30 pm
9/25/49 - 9/24/50, Sun, 60m, 2 pm; title changed to NBC Theater from 10/2/49 - 4/16/50
10/1/50 - 10/22/50, Sun, 30m, 3 pm
11/2/50 - 11/9/50, Thu, 60m, 10 pm
11/12/50 - 11/19/50, Sun, 30m, 10:30 pm
12/2/50 - 12/9/50, Sat, 30m, 6:30 pm
12/27/50 - 2/14/51, Wed, 30m, 10:30 pm

1 **NBC Washington Studios Dedication Program** (7/22/37) NBC

1 **NBC's Fortieth Anniversary Program** (11/13/66) NBC

1 **NBC's All Star New Year's Parade Of Bands** (12/31/71) NBC

1 **NBC's Fifteenth Anniversary Free For All** (11/15/41) NBC

1 **NBC: The First Fifty Years** (11/21/76) NBC

1 **NBC: The First Fifty Years: A Closer Look** (1/31/78) NBC-TV

1 **NCFA Public Service Dramas** (Syn)

Neal O'Hara's Radio Gazette
(6/28/37 - 12/6/37) Brown and Williamson, CBS, 3t, 15m, 7:30 pm

4 **Nebbs, The** (with Gene and Kathleen Lockhart) (9/9/45 - 1/13/46) Cystex, Mut, Sun, 4:30 pm

Necco Surprise Party (with Henry Burbig)
(9/30 - 2/28/31) Necco candy, CBS, Sat, 7:30 pm

Ned Calmer (9/2/43 - 9/7/44) CBS, Parker Pens
(2/8/45 - 1/17/46) ABC
(1947) Parker Pens, Ludens

3 **Ned Jordan, Secret Agent** (with Jack McCarthy) (1938 - 42) Mut; Midwest regional; started on WXYZ in 1938; network programs include:
11/30/39 - 12/28/39, Thu, 10 pm
1/4/40 - 6/6/40, Thu, 9:30 pm; 8:30 pm as of 5/9/40
12/28/41 - 3/15/42, Mut, Sun, 10:30 am
4/5/42 - 5/10/42, Mut, Sat, 2 pm

Ned Sparks Variety (Travel Bureau, Ontario Government)
(4/20/41 - 5/17/41) CBS, Sun, 5:30 pm

1 **Negro Art Singers** (Syn)

Negro College Choirs (4/30/50- 58) Sus, ABC, Sun

5 **Negro Melody Singers Of New York** (1938, 1942) Syn

Nehi Program (with Norman Brokenshire; George Shackley Orchestra) (1935) 15m

Neighbor Nell (see Nellie Revell Show)

15 **Neighborhood Call** (7/10/42 - 3/26/43) NBC, Syn

1 **Neighborly Songs and Poems** (Pre-war Syn)

Neighbors (2/14/43 - 9/5/43) Bl, Sun, 15m, 8:15 pm

1 **Neither Free Nor Equal** (2/20/49) CBS

1 **Nell Vinick Show, The** (1929 - 1/15/42) 15m
1929 - 7/6/32; 9/14/32 - 6/21/33, Kreml Hair Tonic as of 1/6/32, CBS, Wed
11/21/37 - 11/17/38, Mut, 2t, 11 am
10/9/39 - 6/24/40, Mut, 3t
12/17/40 - 1/15/42, Sus, CBS, 2t

1 **Nellie Revell Show, The** (originally Neighbor Nell; also called Meet The Songwriters; Strolling Songsters
(3/9/34 - 11/27/43) (overlapping shows)
3/9/34 - 10/2/36, Sus, NBC, Fri, 15m
9/15/35 - 6/14/36, Bl, Sun, 15m, 11:15 am
6/21/36 - 11/1/36, NBC, Sun, 11:15 am
11/0/36 - 2/15/37, Bl, Mon, 10:45 am
8/16/36 - 3/1/39, Bl, 3t, 15m, 12:15 pm
7/4/37 - 12/31/39, Bl, Sun, 15m, 11:15 am
3/14/39 - 5/3/40, Bl, 2t (Tue & Fri) 15m, 12 noon
1/8/41 - 9/26/42, NBC, Wed, 15m, 12:30 pm
9/5/42 - 11/27/43 (Nellie Revell Presents), NBC, Sat, 15m, 10:30 am; 10 am

1 **Nelson Eddy** (Thesaurus transcription)

1 **Nelson Eddy Show, The** (also onVick's Open House (1936 - 38); Chase and Sanborn Hour
(8/8/37 - 1/29/39; 8/13/39 - 11/15/39); Electric Hour
(1944 - 1946); Kraft Music Hall
(1947, 1948, 1949)
(2/27/31 - 1/20/43)
2/27/31 - 7/31/31, Congress Cigar, CBS, Fri, 8:30 pm
5/23/32 - 12/30/32, Hoffman Beverages, WOR - New York, Fri, 15m
1/27/33 - 6/9/33, Socony Vacuum, CBS, Fri, 9:30 pm
11/12/34 - 6/8/36 (on Voice Of Firestone most of the time)
4/29/42 - 1/20/43 Old Gold, CBS, Wed, 8 pm; many with Nadine Connor
also 7/25/52 Audition

1 **Nelson Eddy With Gale Sherwood** (Thesaurus transcription)

2 **Nelson Eddy's Penthouse Party** (Syn)

31 **Nelson Olmsted** (listed under various titles from 1939 - 4/24/57, some regional, some local; (also see Roy Shield and Company; Organ Reveries); some include:
1939 - 40 (World's Greatest Stories)
9/30/40 - 4/1/41 (Story Dramas By Olmsted) NBC, 3t (Mon, Tue, Wed), 15m
1941 (Dramas By Olmsted) NBC, 2t, 15m
1/3/44 - 4/1/44 (World's Greatest Stories) NBC, 5t, 15m, 10:15 am; 9:45 pm as of 2/7/44

Nelson Olmsted (continued)
3/9/46 - 9/21/46 (Stories By Olmsted), NBC, Sat, 15m, 2:45 pm; 4:45 pm as of 6/29/46
6/6/46 - 9/26/46, (Nelson Olmsted Playhouse) NBC, Thu, 8 pm; 7:30 pm as of 9/5/46 (Started as summer replacement for Burns and Allen)
9/30/46 - 1/10/47, NBC, 5t, 15m, 9:45 am
1/13/47 - 3/28/47, NBC, 5t, 15m, 10:15 am
11/19/46 - 3/29/47, NBC, Sat, 15m, 5 pm
6/13/47 - 6/27/47 (Stories By Olmsted) NBC, Fri, 30m, 8:30 pm
7/6/47 - 7/27/47 (Story For Tonight) NBC, Sun, 30m, 10 pm
8/6/47 - 10/47 (World's Greatest Short Stories) NBC, Wed, 15m
10/19/47 - 7/16/48 (Stories By Olmsted), NBC, 5t, 15m; not in New York in 1948
also 1946 - 48, Sus, ABC, 5t, 15m
9/13/48 - 3/4/49, ABC, 5t, 15m (Story For Today)
3/7/49 - 4/8/49, ABC, 5t, 15m, 11 am
also 1948, NBC, 5t, 15m, 9:45 am
1952 - 56 (Sleep No More) Wed, 15m
also 11/7/56 - 4/24/57 (Sleep No More) Wed, 30m, 10 pm
(1961 - 1978) Pacific Powerland, Western stations

1 **Nemesis Inc.** (Pre-war Syn)

1 **Neptune All Night** (8/25/89) PBS-TV

Nero Wolfe, Detective (see The Adventures Of Nero Wolfe)

Nestles Chocolateers (1930 - 5/26/33) Bl, Fri

1 **NET Festival** (8/66) NET-TV

1 **Netty Needle Nurt** (1935) Syn

1 **Neutrality Act Vote** (11/13/41) Mut

1 **Never Give A Sucker An Even Break** (1941) film sound track

Never Too Old (with Art Baker) (2/5/45 - 4/27/45) Mut, 5t, 15m, 2:45 pm

1 **Never Walk Alone** (1/10/54) NBC

3 **Neville Chamberlain** (11/26/39, 1/1/40, 6/30/40) BBC

26 **New Adventures Of Michael Shayne, The** (1948, 1949) Syn

New Adventures Of Nero Wolfe, The (see The Adventures Of Nero Wolfe)

New Adventures Of Perry Mason, The (see Perry Mason)

New Adventures Of Sherlock Holmes, The (see Sherlock Holmes)

New Adventures Of The Thin Man (see Adventures Of The Thin Man)

New American Music (with Frank Black) (3/18/41 - 7/22/41) Bl, Tue, 10:30 pm; 45m, 10 pm as of 5/6/41

2 **New and Original Adventures Of Robin Hood and His Merry Men, The** (Syn)

New Beulah Show, The (see Beulah)

1 **New Birth Of Freedom** (10/6/50) CBS

New Borden Program (with Mark Warnow Orchestra) (1/7/48 - 4/14/48) Borden, CBS, Wed, 9 pm

New Burns and Allen Show, The (see Burns and Allen)

New Edgar Bergen Hour, The (see The Charlie McCarthy Show)

New England Barn Dance (1/10/53 - 9/26/53) Mut, Sat, 9 pm

New England Variety (4/12/41 - 9/27/41) NBC, Sat, 15m/30m (also called New England To You)

2 **New Faces Of 1937** (1937) Air trailer, film sound track

1 **New Faces Of 1948** (with Leonard Sillman) (6/17/48 - 9/23/48) NBC, Thu, 8:30 pm (summer replacement for Burns and Allen)

New Fads Of 1948 (6/17/48 - 9/23/48) General Foods, NBC, Thu, 8:30 pm

New Fitch Bandwagon, The (see The Fitch Bandwagon)

1 **New Friends Of Music Concert** (10/16/38 - 3/17/40; 10/20/40 - 4/13/4; 10/26/41 - 12/14/41) Bl, Sun, 60m, 6 pm; 30m as of 10/26/41

13 **New Frontier, The** (1950) Syn

1 **New Hampshire Democratic Debate** (2/26/84) CNN

1 **New Hampshire Primary** (2/28/84) ABC-TV

1 **New Harry Babbitt Show, The** (7/31/52) CBS

New Hoagy Carmichael Show, The (see Hoagy Carmichael)

1 **New Hope On The Horizon, A** (1/2/53) Syn

New Horizons (American Museum Of Natural History) (4/4/38 - 9/5/380 CBS, Mon, 15m, 5:45pm)

New Junior Junction, The (see Junior Junction)

4 **New Life, The** (Syn)

1 **New Men, New Nations, A New World** (1939) Syn

27 **New National Guard Show, The** (Syn)

1 **New Orleans** (1947) film sound track

3 **New Orleans Jazz** (10/64) WNDT-TV

New Penny, The (see Helen Hayes)

New Poetry Hour (with A. M. Sullivan) (11/28/37 - 6/5/38) Mut, Sun, 2:30 pm

New Roy Rogers Radio Show, The (see The Roy Rogers Show)

1 **New Social Security For Farm People** (Syn)

New Stan Freberg Show, The (see The Stan Freberg Show)

New Swan Show, The (see The Bob Hope Show, also George Burns and Gracie Allen)

New Talent, USA (6/13/53 - 9/12/53) NBC, Sat, 2 hours, 7:30 pm

1 **New Theater, The** (6/3/51 - 9/23/51) NBC, Sun, 60m, 7:30 pm (partial summer replacement of Phil Harris and Tales Of The Texas Rangers)

1 **New Vice President, The** (12/6/73) CBS-TV

1 **New War In Vietnam, The** (7/10/65) NBC

40 **New World A' Coming** (with Canada Lee) (3/5/44 - 5/27/45) (WMCA) also syndicated from 1945 - 1952

New World Choristers (7/13/44 - 8/10/44) NBC, Thu, 11:30 pm

1 **New World: Hard Choices** (1/5/76) NBC-TV

1 **New Year and The Nation** (1/1/63) ABC-TV

1 **New Year's Dancing Party** (12/31/45) AFRS

1 **New Year's Eve** (12/31/45)

3 **New Year's Eve All-Star Parade Of Bands** (1/1/70, 12/31/70, 12/31/72) NBC

6 **New Year's Eve With Guy Lombardo** (1971 - 1976) CBS-TV, Syn

1 **New Year's Eve With Guy Lombardo's Royal Canadians** (12/31/77) CBS-TV

1 **New Years Eve All-Star Parade Of Bands Celebration** (12/31/68) NBC

1 **New York 1960** (12/60) WCBS

1 **New York At War** (6/13/42) WOR

1 **New York Blackout Coverage** (7/13/77) WCBS

1 **New York City Air Raid Drill** (11/11/51) pool feed

1 **New York City Dinner For Eisenhower** (6/19/45) Mut

1 **New York City Memorial Service For President Roosevelt** (4/14/45) WOR

1 **New York City Symphonic Orchestra** (1941) Syn

1 **New York City Symphony** (1941) Syn

1 **New York City Welcome To Howard Hughes and His Crew** (7/15/38) Mut

3 **New York Civic Orchestra** (1938) Syn

1 **New York Civic Symphony** (1939) Syn

1 **New York Curfew** (2/26/45) WOR

1 **New York Firemen Program** (10/29/36) WMBQ

1 **New York Handicap** (9/25/48) Mut

24 **New York Philharmonic Symphony Orchestra, The** (12/17/23 - 63) CBS, Sun unless indicated, 45m to 2 hours
1927 - 4/18/43 (on Thu from 6/8/39 - 6/29/39; on Wed from 7/5/39 - 8/23/39)
5/23/43 - 4/12/47, US Rubber
10/10/48 - 4/17/49, Esso
10/16/49 - 4/20/52, Sus
10/19/52 - 12/27/53, Willys Motors
1/3/54 - 63, Sus

New York Philharmonic Symphony Orchestra, The (see The New York Philharmonic Symphony Orchestra)

New York Philharmonic Symphony, The (see The New York Philharmonic Symphony Orchestra)

New York Philharmonic, The (see The New York Philharmonic Symphony Orchestra)

1 **New York Soap Box** (12/15/47) WOR

1 **New York State Symphonic Band, The** (1938) Syn

1 **New York Subway** (8/11/47) WOR/BBC

1 **New York Times Youth Forum, The** (10/28/50) WQXR

New York Tonight (with Allen Prescott) Multi, ABC (1947)

New York Town (with Ed East) (7/9/39 - 10/1/39) Sus, Mut, 9 pm

1 **New York Tribute To MacArthur** (4/20/51) Mut

1 **New York's Greatest Industry** (2/14/48) WOR

1 **New York, New York** (7/5/46) Audition

1 **New Yorkers, The** (11/7/51) ABC

11 **Newport Jazz Festival** (6/30/73 - 7/12/73) NBC

1 **Newport Jazz Festival In New York** (7/4/72) WRVR

2 **Newport Jazz Festival, The** (7/11/70) NBC

6 **News** (9/21/39 - 11/24/63) CBS, WEAF, Mut, WOR

1 **News Analysis** (12/19/39)

1 **News and Commentary** (9/4/39) Mut

1 **News and People In The News** (6/7/44) NBC

News and Rhythm (with Todd Hunter; Carl Hohengarten Orchestra; also with Dale Evans)
(6/4/39 - 5/25/41) Dari-Rich, CBS, Sun, 11 am, 10m, 11:05 as of 6/2/40; 25m, 11:05 as of 9/29/40

1 **News At Noon** (6/7/44) WEAF

1 **News Behind The News** (6/6/44) NBC

1 **News Bulletin** (4/23/44) Mut

1 **News Bulletins** (5/24/45)

1 **News Bulletins and Reports** (7/24/74) CBS-TV, NBC-TV

1 **News Comes To Life** (WJR, Detroit) (10/5/37)

1 **News Flash** (10/15/46) Mut

1 **News For Women** (11/1/45) Mut

2 **News Forum** (4/1/84, 5/11/86) WNBC-TV

72 **News From Europe, The** (6/30/40 - 9/28/40) CBS

1 **News From Rome** (4/7/39) Italy/Mut

News Game (with Kenneth Banghart) (7/7/54 - 8/25/54) NBC, Wed, 8 pm (summer replacement for Walk A Mile)

1 **News In English** (1/13/37) WCNW

1 **News In History, The** (1940) WOV

1 **News In Perspective** (12/17/69) WDNT-TV

1 **News Oddities Of The Week** (10/20/36) WMBQ

1 **News Of Public Interest** (10/15/36) WMBQ

2 **News Of The Day** (12/8/41, 5/3/46) Bl, Mut

8 **News Of The World** (1941 - 45) (CBS); was CBS World News Roundup (1941 - 43, 9/25/67, 11/27/69) CBS, Red, Mut, NBC

1 **News Of The World Today** (12/17/44) Mut

1 **News Of Tomorrow** (with Les Griffith) (1947) 15m
also 7/30/51, ABC

News Of Youth (with Laddie Seaman) (12/31/35 - 3/19/37) Wonder Bread, CBS, 3t (Tue, Thu, Sat), 15m, 6:15 pm

1 **News Reports On Vice President Agnew's Resignation** (10/10/73) CBS-TV, NBC-TV

2 **News Roundup** (12/7/41, 6/25/44) CBS

1 **News Story Of The Week** (4/23/37)

1 **News Tester** (4/10/38) Mut

News Through A Woman's Eyes (see Kathryn Cravens)

1 **Newsmaker Saturday** (9/19/92) CNN

2 **Newsmaker Sunday** (10/23/88, 11/1/92) CNN

1 **Newsmark** (3/13/88) CBS

1 **Newspaper Boy Promotion Program** (1949) Syn

Newspaper Of The Air (KOIN) (1945)

Newsreel Of The Air (9/29/29 - 4/20/30) McKesson and Robbins, CBS, Sun, 5 pm

Newsstand Theater (4/5/51 - 12/4/52) ABC
4/5/51 - 10/4/51, Thu, 10 pm; 8 pm as of 6/14/51
10/9/51 - 6/17/52, Tue, various times
7/4/52 - 9/19/52, Fri, 9 pm
9/25/52 - 12/4/52, Thu, 8:30 pm

1 **Next Door Neighbor** (1950) Syn

1 **Next President, The** (11/5/89) WWOR-TV

Next Step Forward, The (2/7/40 - 5/8/40) NBC, Wed, 15m, 11:15 pm

Niagara-Hudson Program (1930 - 7/30/31) Niagara Coal, NBC, Thu, 7:30 pm

1 **Nichols Family Of Five, The** (also How To Win $5000)
(11/30/41 - 3/29/42) Vicks, Red, Sun, 5:30 pm

358 **Nick Carter, Master Detective** (with Lon Clark) (4/11/43 - 9/25/55), 4/11/43 was audition program; all shows were on Mut except as noted
4/11/43 - 4/18/43, Sun, 5:30 pm
4/27/43 - 7/6/43, Tue, 9:30 pm (called The Return Of Nick Carter until 12/8/46)
7/12/43 - 10/25/43, Mon, 9:30 pm
11/3/43 - 11/24/43, Wed, 8:30 pm
12/4/43 - 4/15/44, Sat, 7 pm
4/17/44 - 4/21/44, 4t, 15m
4/24/44 - 6/9/44; 5t, 15m, 9:15 pm
6/12/44 - 9/1/44, 5t, 15m
10/1/44 - 4/15/45, Lin-X, Sun, 3:30 pm
4/22/45 - 2/24/46, Sus, Sun
3/5/46 - 8/13/46, Tue
8/18/46 - 9/21/52, Sun, 6:30 pm; Old Dutch Cleanser sponsor from 9/15/46 - 6/5/49
9/28/52 - 7/12/53, Libby, Sun, 6 pm
7/19/53 - 9/25/55, Sus, Sun; sponsored by Harrison Products from 6/12/55 - 8/14/55
also 6/25/94

11 **Nick Harris Program, The** (7/1/38 - 4/7/40) KECA, also known as The Detective Nick Harris

Nick Kenny (see Children's Follies)

Nick Lucas (5/28/34 - 6/16/35) CBS, 15m
5/28/34 - 10/10/34 (with Freddie Rich Orchestra) Wed, 11 pm
also 6/10/34 - 9/23/34, Sun, 6 pm
1/17/35 - 6/16/35, Thu, 7:30 pm

1 **Nick Martin and His Orchestra** (12/31/65) CBS

1 **Nick Stuart and His Orchestra** (7/4/49) CBS

Nickel Man, The (4/28/41 - 9/12/41) Pepsi Cola, Bl, 5t, 5m, 9:55 pm

Nickelodeon (with Sylvia Clark) (7/18/35 - 12/19/36) Bl
7/18/35 - 11/21/35, Thu, 8 pm
12/6/35 - 2/14/36; 5/22/36 - 6/12/36, Fri, 10 pm
9/9/36 - 10/5/36, Mon, 10:30 pm
10/10/36 - 12/19/36, Sat, 10 pm

1 **Night At The Cotton Club, A** (4/12/29)

46 **Night Beat** (with Frank Lovejoy) (2/6/50 - 9/25/52) Sus, NBC
2/6/50 - 9/25/50, Mon, 10 pm; sponsored by Wheaties from 5/1/50 - 7/31/50
10/6/50 - 11/10/50, Fri
3/4/51, Sun (one show only)
5/18/51 - 9/28/51, Fri, 8:30 pm; 9 pm as of 9/7/51
10/5/51 - 4/25/52, Fri, 10 pm
5/1/52 - 9/25/52, Thu, 8:30 pm; 10 pm as of 7/3/52; sponsored by Pabst from 7/3/52 - 9/25/52

1 **Night Before Christmas, The** (12/16/47) Mut-Don Lee

18 **Night Cap Yarns** (with Frank Graham) (1938 - 43) CBS - West, 5t, 15m (also known at times as Armchair Adventures) also syndicated

Night Club (with Morey Amsterdam) (5/20/37 - 6/10/37) Bl, Thu, 11 pm

Night Court Of The Air (6/20/36 - 7/11/36) CBS, Sat, 8:30 pm

28 **Night Editor** (with Hal Burdick)
10/16/38 - 1/22/39, CBS, Sun, 7:45 pm
also 1941, NBC - Pacific
(1945 - 48) Edwards Coffee, NBC, 15m; started 9/12/34 on NBC - Pacific for Cardinet Candy

Night Hawk, The (1930s) 15m

1 **Night In A Foxhole, A** (5/24/44) Mut

1 **Night In Italy, A** (1/16/37) WCNW

Night Life (with Willie Brandt, Teddy Wilson Orchestra)
(6/11/46 - 7/16/46) CBS, Tue, 10 pm
(1955) (with Ken Nordine and the Fred Kaz Trio) (NBC)

1 **Night Nurse** (Syn)

1 **Night Of The Auk** (WTIC)

Night Of The Witches (Boris Karloff)

1 **Night Song** (1948) Air trailer

2 **Night Surgeon** (AFRTS)

1 **Night The Martians Landed, The** (10/30/88) NPR

1 **Night Train, The** (12/29/77) WLRN-FM

2 **Night Watch** (the following dates are East Coast dates; it apparently was on the West Coast in April)
5/3/54 - 5/24/54, CBS, Mon, 10:05 pm, 25m
5/28/54 - 7/9/54, Sus CBS, Fri, 9:30 pm
7/17/54 - 9/18/54, Sus CBS, Sat, 8 30 pm
9/30/54 - 4/21/55, Sus CBS, Thu, 8 30 pm

30 **Nightfall** (on CBC 7/4/80 - 5/22/81; 11/20/81 - 6/24/83) 39 shows repeated on NPR 10/2/81- 6/25/82;

17 **Nightline** (with Walter O'Keefe)
(7/8/57 - 58+) NBC, 5t, 90m, 8 30 pm
also (11/5/80 - present) ABC-TV

Nightmare (most with Peter Lorre)
(10/8/53 - 10/6/54) Sus, Mut, Thu, 8:30 pm; Sus, Wed, 8 pm as of 1/6/54; 8:30 pm as of 3/31/54

1 **Nightmare At Noon** (5/18/41) Mut

Niles and Prindle (with Wendell Niles and Don Prindle) (1945) ABC

4 **Nill and Null** (Pre-war Syn)

1 **Nimitz Communique** (3/31/44) Mut

Nine To Five (with Lucille Wall and Parker Fennelly) (12/19/35 - 3/12/36) L. C. Smith, Bl, Thu, 15m, 7:15 pm

1 **Nineteen Forty Five** (4/26/65) CBS-TV

1 **Nineteen Sixty Eight** (8/25/78) CBS-TV

Nineteen Thirty Seven Radio Show (with Ray Knight Orchestra)
(5/24/36 - 5/16/37) Health Products, Mut, Sun, 6 pm

1 **Ninety Seven: Hear and Now** (11/30/72) WFLA

1 **Ninety Years Of News: The Story Of The Associated Press** (12/25/38) NBC

Ninety-nine Men and A Girl (with Hildegarde until 5/31/39, Raymond Paige Orchestra)
(2/22/39 - 8/18/39) US Rubber, CBS, Wed, 10 pm; Fri, 9 pm as of 6/9/39

1 **Ninety-Sixth Anniversary Of The U. S. Naval Academy, The** (10/9/41) Mut

Nitwit Court (with Ransom Sherman)
(7/4/44 - 9/26/44) Ipana, Bl, Tue, 8 30 pm (summer replacement for Duffy's Tavern)

5 **Nixon Interviews, The** (5/4/77 - 9/8/77) TV syn

1 **Nixon Interviews: Lessons Learned, The** (5/26/77) ABC-TV

1 **Nixon Obituary** (4/11/69) CBS

1 **Nixon Transcripts, The** (5/3/74) NBC-TV

1 **Nixon Years: Change Without Chaos, The** (10/19/72) CBS-TV

1 **Nixon-Khruschev Debate** (7/23/59) Mut

1 **Nixon: A Full, Free, and Absolute Pardon** (9/8/74) CBS-TV

1 **Nixon: The Next Four Years** (1/8/73)

1 **No Brass Bands** (2/22/55) CBS

1 **No Call Unanswered** (10/14/49) WOR

No Happy Ending (with Dorothea Lewis)
(6/22/46 - 8/31/46) NBC, Sat, 5 pm

1 **No Help Wanted** (1938) CBS/BBC

1 **No More Women** (2/11/34) Air trailer

1 **No Other Road** (9/5/48) BBC/U.N.

No Politics (2/8/41 - 6/28/41) CBS, Sat, 1:30 pm; 2 pm as of 6/7/41

26 **No School Today** (9/24/38 - 1/14/39)
11 am (1/21/39 - 2/17/40) (with Arthur Fields and Fred Hall) CBS, Sat, 15m, 10:15 am; 10 am as of 3/4/39
(2/18/50 - 5/22/54) (with Jon Arthur) ABC, Sat (continued, but not in New York)
2/18/50 - 9/29/51, Multi, 2 hours, 9 am
10/6/51 - 5/22/54, Sponsored and Sus at different times, 90m
also 1964 - 1970, AFRTS

5 **Noah Webster Says** (with Haven MacQuarrie) (4/4/42 - 12/1/45) (continued on a regional basis)
4/4/42 - 5/9/42, NBC - West Coast, Sat
also 7/6/43 - 9/28/43, Ipana, Bl, Tue, 8:30 pm (summer replacement for Duffy's Tavern)
5/16/42 - 2/20/43, NBC, Sat, 7 pm
7/14/45 - 12/1/45, NBC, Sat, 7:30 pm
also 9/25/47 - 12/21/50, NBC, Wesson (1947 - 1948)

1 **Noah's Ark** (1929) Synchro-disc

Noble Cain and A Capella Choir
(6/6/36 - 3/18/37)
6/6/36 - 10/3/36, NBC, Sat, 10m, 6:35 pm
10/9/36 - 9/19/37, Bl, Thu, 15m, 5 pm; Sunday, 2 pm as of 3/21/37

Nobody's Children (with Walter White, Jr.)
(7/2/39 - 9/21/40, 12/15/40 - 1/12/41) Mut, Sun; Sat as of 5/11/40; Sun, 2:30 pm as of 12/15/40

Nona From Nowhere (with Toni Damay)
(1/9/50 - 1/5/51) Bab-O, CBS, 5t, 15m

1 **None Shall Escape** (1942) Syn

1 **Nonsense and Melody** (Syndicated; with Frank Gill, Jr. and William Demling) (1930s) 15m

Nora Martin Show, The (1945)

1 **Nordic Choral Ensemble Of Duluth** (1941) WJZ

Norge Kitchen (with Tim Ryan and Irene Noblette)

2 **Norge Kitchen Committee** (Syn)

Norge Musical Kitchen, The (see Frank Crumit and Julia Sanderson)

Norge Program (see Louis Armstrong; Bunny Berigan)

Norma Young (1949) Colgate

1 **Norman Brokenshire** (Pre-war Syn)

Norman Brokenshire Show, The
(1/15/39 - 12/17/50)
1/15/39 - 2/19/39, Mut, Sat, 15m, 7:45 pm.
7/24/39 - 8/17/39, Mut, 5t, 15m, 10:30 am
1945, ABC, Sat/Sun
9/1/47 - 7/7/50, NBC, 5t, 9:30 am
7/10/50 - 10/13/50, ABC, 5t, 45m, 4 pm
also 7/15/50 - 9/16/50 (also with Bemie Green Orchestra), ABC, Sat, 9 pm
9/17/50 - 12/17/50, (also with Bemie Green Orchestra) ABC, Sun, 6:30 pm

Norman Cloutier Orchestra
(2/27/38 - 7/17/38) NBC, Sun, 10:30 pm; 10 pm as of 4/24/38
(6/25/39 - 4/6/40) Bl, various days (called Diversion Without Exercise from 6/25/39 - 10/15/39)
(1/11/39 - 2/17/40) NBC, various days; sometimes with Annette Hastings
(7/24/39 - 8/25/39) Mut, 5t, 15m, 10:30 am
(12/30/40 - 4/7/41) Bl, Mon, 15m, 12:15 pm
(2/8/41 - 3/29/41) Bl, Sat, 15m, 11 am

1 **Norman Corwin Audition** (4/24/43) CBS

1 **Norman Corwin Biography and Interviews** (KUSC, KRHN)

2 **Norman Corwin Interview** (6/15/46, 8/6/76) CBS

2 **Norman Thomas** (2/26/50, 6/3/50) Mut

Norman Vincent Peale (see The Art Of Living)

Norseman Quartet (9/26/38 - 12/18/39) Bl, Mon, 15m, 8:15 am; 8:30 am as of 8/7/39

1 **North American Guest Night** (4/21/44) BBC

1 **Northern California Committee For Stevenson** (10/20/52) KPIX-TV

1 **Northern California Symphony Orchestra** (1941) Syn

2 **Northern California WPA Symphony Orchestra** (1941, 1942) Syn

1 **Northern Life Insurance Company** (Audition)

6 **Northerners, The** (2/16/53 - 9/27/54) WMAQ

1 **Northwest Airline Route Special** (6/1/45) WOR

1 **Northwest Mounted Police** (1940) Air trailer

Northwestern Chronicles (1934 - 35) N. W. Yeast, Bl, Mon

25 **Northwestern Reviewing Stand, The** (Northwestern University Forum) (1936 - 1967) Mut, Sun;

Norton and The Neighbors (with Cliff Norton and The Hometowners) (1948)

2 **Norvell Knight and His Orchestra** (1947, 1949) NBC

18 **Norway Fights On** (12/43 - 4/9/45) Syn

1 **Nostalgia Merchants, The** (6/16/71) WMUK-FM

1 **Not For Children** (5/27/50) Mut

Not For Glory (7/3/43 - 9/11/43) NBC, Sat, 5 pm

1 **Not So Long Ago** (7/22/38 - 8/19/38) CBS. Fri, 6:30 pm
1/16/39 - 7/24/39) CBS, Mon, 4:15 pm (not always in New York)
(8/1/39 - 10/10/39) CBS, Tue, 3 pm also NBC-TV

1 **Not This NAFTA Rally** (11/7/93) C-SPAN

Notebook On... (different countries)

Notes On Jazz (with Duke Ellington)

1 **Nothing But The Truth** (with Alexander McQueen)
(1932 - 4/22/33) Bl, 5t (Mon, Wed - Sat). 15m, 9:45 am (with Graham McNamee)
(4/19/42 - 7/7/42) Bl, Sun, 4:30 pm
also 1941 Air trailer

1 **Nothing Serious** (with Caswell Adams, George Matthews and Frances Mercer)
(7/12/42 - 8/9/42) Mut, Sun, 9:30 pm
(4/23/43 - 5/28/43) Bl, Fri, 25m, 7:05 pm

1 **Notorious Tariq** (with Turhan Bey) 8/16/47 (Audition)

7 **Nova** (1/29/78 - present) PBS-TV

2 **Novatime Trio** (1/9/47) Thesaurus transcriptions

Now and Forever (10/11/43 - 7/7/44) CBS, 5t, 15m, 3:30 pm

Now and Then With Frank (with Hodak Orchestra) (7/12/38 - 10/11/38) Bl, Tue, 9 pm

Now Hear This (with Amold Robertson; then Larry Haines) (6/24/51 - 11/4/51) NBC, Sun, 5:30 pm

2 **Now It Can Be Told** (6/25/45 - 8/24/45) Mut, 5t, 15m, 8:15 pm

16 **NPR Playhouse** (5/5/83 - 2/6/85) NPR

NTG and His Girls (with Nils Thor Granlund) (7/9/35 - 1/21/36) Bromo Seltzer, NBC, Tue, 9 pm

1 **Nujol's Clinic Of The Air** (Pre-war Syn)

2 **Number Seven, Front Street** (9/25/47, 10/2/47) Mut, Thu, 8 pm

1 **Nuremberg Executions** (10/16/46) Mut

3 **Nuremberg Trial Reports** (11/22/45, 12/4/45) Mut/BBC/AP

2 **Nuremberg Report** (10/1/46, 10/15/46) Mut

1 **Nuremberg Trial Coverage** (9/30/46) BBC

1 **Nuremberg Trials** (10/1/46) BBC

1 **Nutcracker Suite, The** (12/19/38) WGN

Nuts Of Harmony (with Cliff Arquette and Lolly Gookins)

O'Cedar Melody Men (4/12/32 - 7/28/32) O'Cedar Polish, Bl, 2t; Thu as of 6/9/32

O'Cedar Time (1930 - 2/10/31) O'Cedar Polish, CBS, Tue, 15m, 10:30 am

O'Flynn, The (with Milton Watson) (12/21/34 - 3/8/35) Esso, CBS, Fri, 10:30 pm

1 **O'Hara** (with Jack Moyles)
7/2/51 (Audition)
(5/20/56 - 7/1/56) CBS, Sun, 6:05 pm
(10/8/56 - 10/29/56) CBS, Mon, 8:30 pm

O'Henry Playhouse (Syn)

O'Henry Stories (with Leigh Lovel and Joseph Bell) (5/11/32 - 6/15/32) G. Washington Coffee, Bl, Wed, 9 pm

1 **O'Hoolihans: Michael and Mary Ann, The** (1931) Syn

O'Malley Family, The (see Those O'Malleys)

O'Neills, The (with Kate McComb) (6/11/34 - 6/18/43) 15m
6/11/34 - 12/7/34, Mut, 3t
12/10/34 - 16/17/35, Gold Dust, CBS, 3t
10/1/35 - 12/31/37, Ivory, NBC, 5t, 3:45 pm
also 11/16/36 - 12/31/37 Ivory, Bl, 5t, 11 am
1/3/38 - 12/26/41, Ivory, NBC, 5t, 12:15 pm
also 1/3/38 - 5/27/38, Ivory, CBS, 5t, 2:15 pm
also 7/3/39 - 10/18/40, Ivory, NBC, at other times
10/21/40 - 3/27/42, Ivory, CBS, 5t
10/5/42 - 6/18/43, Standard Brands, NBC, 5t, 15m, 10:15 am

O'Neils, The (9/4/46 - 1/14/47) ABC
9/4/46 - 9/25/46, Wed, 9:30 pm
10/22/46 - 1/14/47, Tue, 8:30 pm

7 **Objective** (10/7/60 - 12/16/60) American Chemical Society

1 **Objective-Tokyo** (1942) Syn

8 **Obsession** (Syn)

Odd Side Of The News (11/4/38 - 12/16/39) CBS, Sat, 15m, 8 am/8:15 am

6 **Odyssey Of Homer, The** (10/18/81 - 11/24/81) NPR

1 **Of Black America**

Of Human Bondage (see Wheatena Playhouse))

1 **Of Interest To The Enemy** (1943) Syn

Of Men and Books (with John T. Frederick) (9/27/38 - 12/21/46) CBS
9/27/38 - 1/10/39, Tue, 15m, 4:45 pm
1/18/39 - 10/4/39, Wed, 4 pm; 5:15 pm as of 4/12/39
10/10/39 - 9/24/40, Tue, 15m
10/5/40 - 3/1/41, Sus, Sat, 15m
3/8/41 - 6/10/44, Sus, Sat, 30m, 2:30 pm
6/17/44 - 12/21/46, Sus, Sat, 15m; often preempted
(1/15/48 - 7/22/48) with Russell Maloney; Sterling North as of 1/22/48) Thu, 6:15 pm

13 **Of These We Sing** (15m) Syn

1 **Off The Record** (7/26/45) BBC

1 **Off The Set** (6/17/84) WNEW-TV

Offbeat (11/1/55 - 4/13/56) ABC, 4t - 5t, 25m, 9:30 pm

Offical Adventures Of The Shadow, The (see The Shadow)

1 **Office Of Price Stabilization - Radio Announcements** (In Yiddish) Syn

1 **Office Of Price Stabilization - Short Radio Talks** (In Spanish) Syn

1 **Office Of Price Stabilization - Short Radio Talks** (In Yiddish) Syn

1 **Office Of Price Stabilization: Radio Announcements** (In Italian) Syn

1 **Office Of Price Stabilization: Radio Announcements** (In Spanish) Syn

1 **Office Of Price Stabilization: Short Radio Talks** (In Italian) Syn

1 **Office Of War Information** (2/12/45) Syn

Official Adventures Of Flash Gordon, The (see The Amazing Interplanetary Adventures Of Flash Gordon)

7 **Official Detective** (1/19/47 - 3/7/57) Mut
1/19/47 - 3/30/47, Sus, Sun, 15m, 2:15 pm
6/24/47 - 9/23/47, Mut, Tue, 8:15 pm
9/30/47 - 7/13/48, Pharmaco, Tue, 25m, 8:30 pm
7/20/48 - 11/2/48, Tue, 8:30 pm
11/20/48 - 6/4/49, Sat, 1:30 pm; 2 pm as of 4/9/49
6/7/49 - 1/15/52, Tue, 8:30 pm
1/20/52 - 6/29/52, Sun, 25m, 8 pm
9/28/52 - 1/4/53, Sun, 6:30 pm
also syndicated

Og, Son Of Fire (with Alfred Brown) (11/23/34 - 6/28/35; 9/30/35 - 12/27/35) Libby, CBS, 3t, 15m

1 **Ohio Flood Broadcast** (3/6/45) WKRC

Ohio River Jamboree (7/12/52 - 8/30/52) NBC, Sat, 9 pm

Ohio School Of The Air
(12/13/39 - 1/17/40) Mut, Wed, 15m, 1:30 pm

1 **Ohman and Arden** (Phil Ohman and Vic Arden) (1931) Syn
(10/23/32 - 1/8/33) U S Industries Alcohol Company, NBC, Sun, 15m, 10 pm

Okay Speaking (1943)

1 **Oklahoma**

10 **Oklahoma City Symphony Orchestra, The** (KOCY origination)
(11/12/49 - 55) Sus, Mut (Regional)
11/12/49 - 2/4/50, Sat
2/15/50 - 50, Wed
1950 - 55, 60m, on various days and times

1 **Oklahoma Roundup** (with Hiram Higsby) (7/6/46 - 8/9/47) CBS
7/6/46 - 9/28/46, Sat, 10:15 pm
9/31/46 - 12/9/46, Mon, 5:30 pm
6/28/47 - 8/9/47, Sat, 7:30 pm

1 **Ol' Blue Eyes Is Back** (11/18/73) NBC

1 **Old Army Game, The** (4/5/51) CBS audition

1 **Old Black Joe** (1928) Synchro-disc

Old Company's Program, The (with William Wirges Orchestra; American Singers) (9/13/31 - 3/6/32) Lehigh Navigation Coal Company, NBC, Sun, 15m, 1:45 pm

2 **Old Corral, The** (with Pappy Cheshire) (1941- 42) Syn - ZIV; 143 15m shows broadcast

Old Curiosity Shop, The (with David Ross)

Old Dirt Dobber, The (see Garden Gate)

Old Dutch Girl (see Irene Beasley)

14 **Old Fashioned Revival Hour, The** (also called Gospel Hour; Pilgrim Hour; with Charles E. Fuller)
(4/4/37 - 6/12/60) Mut, Sun, 60m; ABC as of 6/19/49; 30m as of 1/19/58; started 10/28 locally in Los Angeles,
also syndicated

Old Gold Comedy Theater (see Comedy Theater)

Old Gold Hour (see Paul Whiteman)

Old Gold Program, The (with Dick Powell and Ted Fio Rito Orchestra)
(2/7/34 - 5/3/34) CBS, Wed, 10 pm; (see also Robert Benchley; The Bickersons)
(11/3/41 - 4/24/42) (New Old Gold Program) (with Herbert Marshall, Bert Wheeler, Hank Ladd) Old Gold, Bl
11/3/41 - 1/19/42, Mon, 7 pm
1/30/42 - 4/24/42, Fri, 8 pm
also see The Bickersons

4 **Old Gold Show, The** (4/5/44 - 10/18/44) CBS, Wed, 8 pm

Old Gold Time (see The Bickersons)

4 **Old Goriot** (Syn)

Old Heidelberg Orchestra (with Ernie Stemm) (7/7/36 - 10/6/36) Bl, Tue, 5 pm

Old Homestead, The (1/11/37 - 5/7/37) Bl, 3t, 15m, 5:45 pm

Old Kentucky Barn Dance (see Saturday Night Country Style)

1 **Old Observer, The** (Syn)

Old Scout Masters Series, The

Old Singing Master, The (with William Stickles Orchestra; Harry Frankel)
(1/3/32 - 12/18/32) Barbasol, Bl, Sun, 10:15 pm

Old Skipper's Gang (with Don Hix)
(10/26/35 - 11/21/36) Bl, Sat, 15 - 30m

10 **Old Sunday School Program** (15m)
Post-war Syn

Old Timers Radio Program (with Uncle Norman Edmonds)

Old Town Auction Block (with "Colonel" Robert Brown) (6/20/41 - 6/27/41) Bl, Fri, 8 pm

Old Vienna (11/18/39 - 9/14/40) CBS, Sat, 15m, different times

Old-Time Spelling Bee (1936 - 37) Mut, Sun, 8:30 pm

1 **Oldsmobile 1957 Spot Announcements** (1957) Syn

3 **Oldsmobile Headliners** (with Ed Smalle) (1936) Syn

Oldsmobile Program (with George Olsen, Ethel Shutta, Gus Van) (1/7/33 - 4/8/33) NBC Sat, 9:30pm

Olga Baclanova's Continental Revue (12/4/37 - 3/5/38) Mut, Sat, 8:30 pm

Olivio Santoro (9/15/40 - 9/26/43) Vogt Scrapple, Bl, Sun, 15m; NBC, Sun, 11:45 am as of 9/13/42

Olson and Johnson (9/22/33 - 3/30/34) (with Harry Sosnik Orchestra) Swift, CBS, Fri, 10 pm; also on West coast (1936 - 37)

13 **Olympian Quartet** (1931) Syn

1 **Olympic Team Interview** (1948)

Omar Khayam (with Stuart Buchman and Betty Webb) (10/6/32 - 12/29/32) Diamond Walnuts, CBS, Thu, 9:30 pm

Omar, The Mystic (also Omar, The Wizard) (with M. H. Joachim)
(10/7/35 - 7/10/36) Taystee Bread, Mut, 5t, 15m, 5:15 pm

1 **Omar, The Wizard Of Persia** (Syn)

1 **Omni: Visions Of Tomorrow** (8/19/85) TV syn

1 **Omnibus** (1/25/53) NBC-TV

2 **On A Note Of Triumph** (5/8/45, 5/13/45) CBS

3 **On A Sunday Afternoon**
(10/23/38 - 10/8/39) (with Harold Stokes Orchestra) Mut, Sun, 3 pm
also 1940s, CBS - Pacific
(6/14/53 - 9/6/53; 10/10/54 - 11/4/56) CBS, Sun, 30m - 60m)

On Broadway (with Alice Frost, John Brown) (10/3/37 - 4/24/38) Diamond Salt, Bl, Sun,

1 **On Record In Favor Of Radio** (Mut)

21 **On Stage** (with Cathy and Elliott Lewis)
(11/24/52) Audition
(1/1/53 - 9/30/54) Sus, CBS, Thu, 9 pm
1/1/53 - 8/27/53, CBS, Thu, 9 pm
9/9/53 - 1/6/54, CBS, Wed, 9 pm
6/17/54 - 9/30/54, CBS, Thu, 9 pm

2 **On Stage America** (with Paul Whiteman)
(1/8/44 - 10/7/44) ABC, Sat, 11 am; 7:30 pm as of 9/16/44 - 2/17/45
(9/29/47 - 5/23/48) ABC, Mon, 8 pm; 9 pm as of 10/27/47
also 6/2/48

On Stage Everybody (1/2/45 - 1/23/45) ABC, Tue, 7:30 pm

1 **On Target (V-15 Program)** War-time

2 **On The Air For The Emergency March Of Dimes** (8/16/54) Syn

1 **On The Avenue** (1937) Air trailer

2 **On The Beam With Tex Beneke** (1948) Mut

On The Front Porch (6/29/28 - 9/21/28) Kodak, CBS, Fri, 10 pm

On The Home Front (1/10/42 - 4/18/42) NBC, Sat, 15m, 3:15 pm

2 **On The Mall** (10/27/40, 9/20/41) WHN, WMCA

1 **On The Record** (6/23/51) UN Radio

3 **On The Swing Side** (1/20/46, 8/2/47) Mut

1 **On The Town** (1948) film sound track

1 **On The Way To Yorktown** (2/2/38) NBC

On Trial (2/15/48 - 1/16/51) ABC
2/15/48 - 7/4/48, Sun, 12:30 pm
11/22/48 - 8/1/49, Mon, 8:30 pm
10/3/50 - 1/16/51, Tue, 10 pm

2 **On With The Show** (1928) Synchro-disc, also syndicated

On Your Job (6/25/39 - 7/6/41) Sus, NBC, Sun, 12:30 pm; 1:30 pm as of 10/6/40

1 **On Your Mark** (with Bud Collyer) (7/12/48 - 2/18/49) Mut, 5t, 15m, 2:30 pm; 2:45 pm as of 1/10/49

1 **On Your Toes** (Audition)

Ona Munson Show, The (see The Open House)

1 **Once Over Lightly** (3/6/46) Mut

1 **Once Upon A Midnight** (1945) ABC/Bl audition

28 **Once Upon A Time** (12/10/38 - 2/25/39) Sus, Mut, Sat, 10:30 am, also syndicated

Once Upon A Tune (with Morris Surdin and Ray Darby)
(1/5/47 - 4/26/48) Sus, CBS
1/5/47 - 1/19/47, Sun, 2:30 pm
2/1/47 - 4/26/47, Sat, 6:15 pm; 8 pm as of 4/5/47

Once Upon Our Time (with Jack Hilty) 15m (1947)

3 **One Among Us** (1952, 1953) Syn

One Day Painters (1935) Pittsburgh Paints, 15m (see Pittsburgh One Day Painters)

1 **One Foot In Heaven** (with Philip Merivale; Dean Jagger as of 7/8/45)
(1/28/45 - 11/28/45) Bl
1/28/45 - 7/29/45, Sun, 10:30 pm
8/2/45 - 10/4/45, Thu, 10 pm
10/10/45 - 11/28/45, Wed, 9 pm
also 1941 Air trailer

One For The Book (see Sam Balter)

One For The Money (with Mel Allen) CBS, Sat (1947)

1 **One Great Hour** (3/26/49) CBS

1 **One Half Hour Later** (9/11/41) CBS

1 **One Heavenly Night** (1931) film sound track

4 **One I'll Never Forget** (Syn)

1 **One In A Million** (1937) Air trailer

1 **One Man Show** (10/30/69) WABC-TV

1 **One Man's Convention** (7/23/52) BBC

1 **One Man's Destiny** (8/12/45 - 1/13/46) Mut, Sun, 12:30 pm

214 **One Man's Family** (with J. Anthony Smythe) (4/29/32 - 5/8/59) 3256 shows (134 books) broadcast
4/29/32 - 7/29/32, KGO (NBC - Pacific), Fri
8/3/32 - 5/10/33, Wesson Oil, NBC - Pacific, Wed
5/17/33 - 1/30/35, Kentucky Winner, NBC - Pacific, Wed; East Coast as of 11/21/34
4/3/35 - 36, Royal Gelatin, NBC, Wed, 8 pm
1936 - 9/27/39, Tenderleaf Tea, NBC, Wed, 8 pm
10/5/39 - 12/28/39, Tenderleaf Tea, NBC, Thu, 8 pm
1/7/40 - 9/25/49, Tenderleaf Tea, NBC, Sun; Bl, Tue as of 1/30/45; NBC, Sun as of 7/15/45
10/2/49 - 6/4/50, Sus, NBC, Sun
6/5/50 - 1954, Miles Laboratory, NBC, 5t, 15m
1954 - 55, Toni, NBC, 5t, 15m
1955 - 5/8/59, Multi, NBC, 5t, 15m

One Man's Opinion (10/24/49 - 7/20/51) Philip Morris, ABC, 5t, 5m

2 **One Million B. C.** (1940) Air trailers

1 **One Million Three Hundred Thousand Men Is A Small Army Today** (Syn)

1 **One Minute Of Truth** (2/27/56) CBS

1 **One Nation Indivisible** (10/12/50) CBS

1 **One Night Stand** (3/5/35)

219 **One Night Stand** (AFRS) (9/43 - 12/65) 6560 shows broadcast

One Of The Finest (10/9/39 - 7/25/40) Silvercup, Bl, 2t (Mon & Thu), 15m; 30m as of 11/13/39

1 **One On One** (12/26/92) WPRO

One Out Of Seven (with Jack Webb) (1946) ABC - West coast, Wed, 15m

1 **One Stolen Night** (2/29) Synchro-disc

One Thousand Dollars Reward (with John Sylvester; Ken Roberts announced) (6/25/50 - 10/29/50) NBC, Sun, 7 pm

One Thousand One Wives
(5/5/39 - 9/14/39) Bl
5/5/39 - 7/7/39, Fri, 10 pm
7/13/39 - 9/14/39, Thu, 10 pm

1 **One Touch Of Venus** (1948) Air trailer

One Woman's Opinion (see Lisa Sergio)

1 **One World** (7/4/43) CBS

2 **One World Award Program** (2/18/46, 3/31/46) CBS, CBS - Pacific

13 **One World Flight** (Norman Corwin;) (1/14/47 - 4/8/47) Sus, CBS, Tue, 10 pm

1 **One World Or None** (1/10/47) WMCA

1 **One Year From Victory...A Challenge** (8/14/46) CBS

1 **One-Hundredth Anniversary Of The Philadelphia Bulletin, The** (4/10/47) CBS

Only Yesterday (see Benny Rubin)

1 **Ontario Show, The** (with Nancy Douglas and Colonel Stoopnagle)
(3/20/42 - 6/26/42) Ontario Travel, Bl, Fri, 7 pm

1 **OPA Report** (3/16/45) Bl/ABC

1 **Open Air New England** (1/10/92) WPKT

2 **Open Door, The** (with Dr. Alfred Dorf) (6/21/43 - 6/30/44) Standard Brands, 5t, 15m
6/21/43 - 12/31/43, NBC, 10:15 am
1/3/44 - 6/30/44, CBS, 10:30 am

Open Hearing (3/12/46 - 7/1/47) CBS, Tue, 10:30 pm

2 **Open House Party** (4/10/43, 4/7/46) Bl/Mut

Open House, The (7/19/41 - 4/22/46
7/19/41 - 8/30/41 (with Helen Morgan), NBC, Sat, 10:30 pm
9/2/43 - 11/25/43, CBS, Thu, 3 pm
9/6/43 - 3/25/46 (with Ona Munson), CBS, Mon, 3 pm
4/1/46 - 4/22/46, CBS, Mon, 4 pm

1 **Open Letter On Race Hatred** (7/24/43) CBS

Open Mind (1957 - 63) NBC, Sun

Open Road, The (1935 - summer) NBC

1 **Open Spaces, The** (Pre-war Syn)

1 **Open The Gates-The Vision Of Hubert Humphrey** (8/12/80) pool feed

1 **Opening Ceremonies Of The New York World's Fair** (4/3/39) Mut

1 **Opening Of The Bronx Whitestone Bridge** (4/29/39) Mut

1 **Opening Of The Fourth War Loan** (1/18/44) Mut

1 **Opening Of The Lord Baltimore Hotel Studios** (1937) WFBR

1 **Opening Of The NBC Hollywood Studios** (12/7/35) Red/Bl

1 **Opening Of The New Approach To The George Washington Bridge** (6/27/40) WOR

1 **Opening Of The New Sixth Avenue Subway** (12/14/40) WOR

1 **Opening Of The New York World's Fair, The** (4/22/64)

1 **Opening Of U. N. O.** (1/10/45)

Opera Concert (with Sylvan Levin) (9/25/49 - 11/23/52) Mut, Sun, 9 pm

1 **Opera Festival** (6/18/42) Mut

1 **Opera Forum Quiz** (War-time) NBC

Opera Guild, The (12/2/34 - 3/17/35) Chase & Sanborn, NBC, Sun, 60m, 8 pm

Operalogue (Metropolitan Opera Guild) (preview of Metropolitan broadcast) (11/10/38 - 3/9/39) NBC, Thu, 15m, 6 pm

Operation Danger (Audition), 6/25/50 with Howard Culver

1 **Operation Nightmare** (6/9/47) CBS

2 **Operation Roger**

Operation Tandem (NBC) promotional shows 12/22/49; 12/20/50

Operation Underground
(6/26/51 - 4/19/52) CBS
6/26/51 - 10/5/51, Tue, 8 pm
10/11/51 - 1/10/52, Thu, 8:30 pm
1/19/52 - 4/19/52, Sat, 7:30 pm

1 **Operation Crossroads** (6/30/46) Mut

Opie Cates (10/20/47 - 2/2/48) Sus, ABC, Mon

Opportunity Matinee (with Reggie Childs Orchestra; then Johnny Johnson as of 3/24/35)
(3/10/35 - 10/13/35) Tastyeast, Bl, Sun, 12 noon

Opportunity USA (9/8/46 - 10/13/46) Mut, Sun, 15m, 1:15 pm

1 **Opry House Matinee** (with Eddy Arnold) (12/1/45 - 6/29/46) Ralston, Mut, Sat

1 **Optimist Week** (11/7/48) Syn

Orange Blossom Quartet
(8/8/39 - 10/31/39) Mut, Tue, 15m, 11:15 am

Orange Lantern, The (with Arthur Hughes) (10/2/32 - 7/2/33) Sus, Bl, Sun, 11:30 pm

Orbit One Zero (4/21/61 - 5/26/61)

1 **Orchestra Wives** (1942) film sound track

1 **Orchestras Of The Nation** (1944 - 50) NBC, Sat, 60m, 3 pm; on for about 26 weeks each season from December of each year

1 **Orchestras Of The World** (Syn)

1 **Orchestration**

24 **Order In The Court** (1953) Syn

Order Of Adventurers (6/5/39 - 9/25/39) Bl, Mon, 8 pm
(10/13/39 - 11/3/39) Bl, Fri, 8 pm

3 **Organ Music** (1939, 1940) WWRL

Organ Reveries (with Nelson Olmsted) (with Archer Gibson from 11/9/32 - 11/30/32, Bl, Wed, 9:30 pm)

Orgets Of The Air (5/28/35 - 6/25/35) NBC, Tue, 6 pm

Orientale (6/11/38 - 10/8/38), CBS, Sat, 15m, 12:15 pm

24 **Origin Of Superstition, The** (Syn) (1933) 15m

Original Amateur Hour, The (with Ted Mack)
(9/29/48 - 9/18/52) Old Gold, ABC
9/29/48 - 7/21/49, Wed, 60m
7/28/49 - 9/18/52, Thu, 45m

2 **Original Dixieland Jazz Band** (World transcriptions)

Original Dramas (5/28/38 - 1/14/39) Bl, Sat, 8:30 pm

Original Plays (see Original Dramas)

Original Tastyeast Jesters (1933 - 37) Tastyeast, Bl, various days and personnel, 15m

Originalities (6/8/39 - 3/27/41) Bl, 15m
6/8/39 - 9/7/39, 2t, 10:30 am
1/21/41 - 3/27/41, Thu, 2 pm

Originals By Bennett (with Joan Bennett)

Orphans Of Divorce (with James Meighan) (3/6/39 - 6/26/39; 9/25/39 - 4/17/42) Dr. Lyons, Bl, 5t, 15m

5 **Orrin Tucker and His Orchestra** (2/25/41, 4/12/48, 4/19/48) NBC, Syn

Orrin Tucker Orchestra (see also Let's Go To Town) (1948)

Orson Welles' Peace Conference Forum (5/6/45 - 6/10/45) Sus, Bl, Sun, 3 pm

Orson Welles' Radio Almanac (with Agnes Moorehead and Hans Conreid) (1/26/44 - 7/19/44) Mobil, CBS - West Coast, Wed, 9:30 pm

18 **Orson Welles' Theater, The** (1/20/36 - 10/17/46) CBS (except where noted)
7/11/38 - 11/27/38 (see Mercury Theater)
12/9/38 - 3/31/40 (see Campbell Playhouse)
9/15/41 - 2/2/42, Lady Esther, Mon, 10 pm
11/9/42 - 4/30/44 (see Ceiling Unlimited)
11/15/42 - 1/31/43 (Hello Americans), Sun, 8 pm; under auspices of the CLA
1/26/44 - 7/19/44 (see Orson Welles' Radio Almanac)
3/13/45 - 4/24/45, Cresta Blanca, Tue, 9:30 pm
9/16/45 - 10/17/46 (Lear Radio Show) ABC, Sun, 1:15 pm

Orville Knapp Orchestra (CBS) 15m (1935 - 1936)

2 **Oscar Dumont and His Orchestra** (5/7/50, 1957) CBS

1 **Oscar Peterson and Art Tatum** (1953)

1 **Oscar Peterson At The Piano With Instrumental Accompaniment** (World transcription)

1 **Oscar Peterson Trio** (World transcription)

Other Americans, The (with Edward Tomlinson) (12/6/35 - 3/6/36) Bl, Fri, 10:30 pm

Other People's Lives (8/3/38) (Audition)

1 **Other Women's Children** (5/31/49) CBS

Otto Harbach Show (with Johnny Johnson Orchestra) (2/4/35 - 3/11/35) NBC, Mon, 9:30 pm (also see Music At The Haydn's)

2 **Our American Heritage** (1949) AFRS

Our American Leaders (Syn) 15m

Our American Music (John Howard, conductor) (1932 - 3/19/33) Bl, Sun, 3 pm

Our American Neighbors (6/20/37 - 9/26/37) CBS, Sun, 5 pm

Our American Schools (with Belmont Farley) (12/6/31 - 7/5/39) Sus, NBC
12/6/31 - 7/1/34, Sun, 6:30 pm
1934 - 35, Sat, 15m
1/29/36 - 7/5/39, Wed, 15m, 6 pm

Our Barn (directed by Madge Tucker) (1/28/36 - 12/6/41) Bl, Sat

1 **Our Best Girl** (12/16/48) Audition

Our Boarding House (see Major Hoople)

1 **Our Christmas Stocking** (World transcription)

4 **Our Daily Food** (with George Rector) (11/3/30 - 3/3/33) A & P, 15m
11/3/30 - 8/13/32, NBC, 6t, 9:45 am also
11/3/30 - 12/13/32, Red, Bl, 6t, 10:30 am
1/13/33 - 3/3/33, Bl, Fri, 6 pm

Our Foreign Policy (1/24/45 - 9/27/47) NBC, Sat, 7 pm

8 **Our Freedom's Blessings** (Syn)

10 **Our Gal Sunday** (3/29/37 - 1/2/59) CBS, 5t, 15m
3/29/37 - 8/26/55, Anacin, Kolynos
8/29/55 - 1/2/59, Multi

1 **Our Hearts Were Young and Gay** (7/26/50) NBC

Our Home On The Range (with John McCormack; John Charles Thomas as of 4/24/35; William Daly Orchestra) Sloan's Linament
(10/11/33 - 4/15/36) Warner, NBC, Wed
10/11/33 - 4/17/35, 30m, 9:30 pm
4/24/35 - 9/11/35, 45m, 9 pm
9/18/35 - 4/15/36, 30m, 9 pm

Our House (1945 - 46) Sears, 15m

27 **Our Land Be Bright** (1947) Syn

82 **Our Miss Brooks** (with Eve Arden) (7/19/48 - 7/7/57) CBS, Sun; Mon from 7/19/48 - 9/13/48 (376 shows broadcast)
7/19/48 - 9/13/48, Sus
9/19/48 - 8/28/49, Colgate from 10/3/48, 9:30 pm
9/11/49 - 5/28/50; 9/3/50 - 7/1/51; 10/7/51 - 6/29/52; 10/5/52 - 6/28/53; 10/4/53 - 6/27/54, Colgate, 6:30 pm
9/26/54 - 6/17/56; 1/6/57 - 7/7/57, American Home Products and Toni until 6/17/56; Multi after that

1 **Our Modern Maidens** (1929) Synchro-disc

Our Mutual Friend (10 part serial)

Our Nation's Heritage (1970) Tue

4 **Our Neighbors** (10/11/36 - 10/25/36) Bl, Sun, 3 pm, Syn

Our New American Music (directed by Frank Black) (3/11/41 - 7/15/41) Bl, Tue, 30 - 45m, 10 pm

1 **Our Present Duty** (1951) UNESCO Radio

Our Secret Weapon (8/9/42 - 10/8/43) CBS
8/9/42 - 10/18/42 (written by Paul Luther; with Rex Stout, Guy Repp, Ted Osborne), Sun, 15m, 7 pm
10/16/42 - 10/8/43 (with Rex Stout), Philco, Fri, 15m (7:15 pm)

2 **Our Secret World** (10/17/42 - 1/16/43) Mut, Sat, 8:30 pm

1 **Our Silver Jubilee Show...Of The NBC** (1951) NBC

Our Singing Land (8/5/46 - 8/9/46) ABC, 5t, 15m

Our Son (1934) Bl, Sun

Our Spiritual Life (with J. S. Bonnell) (10/1/40 - 3/25/41) Bl, Tue, 15m, 1:30 pm

1 **Our Town** (1/23/47) CBS (Audition)

1 **Out Of The Dark** (11/10/46) Mut

3 **Out Of The Deep** (with Ted Maxwell) (12/1/45 - 2/16/46) NBC, Sat, 7:30 pm Audition show (1/10/51)

1 **Out Of The Frying Pan Into The Firing Line** (8/3/42) WOR

12 **Out Of The Night** (Australian) (1946) 15m

1 **Out Of The Past** (1948) Syn

Out Of The Shadows (with Hugh James) (12/13/43 - 3/744) Bl, Mon, 15m, 10:15 pm

Out Of The Thunder (1/20/52 - 6/29/52) Mut, Sun, 10 pm

Out Of The West (with Ernie Gill Orchestra) (10/23/38 - 1/22/39) Bl, Sun, 8 pm

1 **Out Of This World** (2/28/47) CBS also (1946) Air trailer

Outdoor Girl Beauty Parade (with Gladys Baxter and Walter Preston; Vic Arden Orchestra
(5/35 - 11/22/35) American Home Products, CBS
1/5/35 - 5/18/35, Sat, 7:30 pm
5/20/35 - 11/22/35, 3t, 15m

2 **Outdoor Life Time** (Syn) Auditions

Outdoors With Bob Edge
(3/16/39 - 5/5/40) CBS, 15m
3/16/39 - 5/25/39, Thu, 7:15 pm
10/8/39 - 5/5/40, Sun, 9:15 am

1 **Outlet Radio Magazine, The** (1/2/48) WJAR audition

6 **Outpost Concert Series** (Syn)

Outstanding Figures In World History (15m)

1 **Oval Office: An Historical Perspective, The** (10/17/93) C-SPAN

5 **Over Here** (12/12/42 - 1/9/43) Bl

Over Our Coffee Cup (see Eleanor Roosevelt)

Over There (with Ronald Colman, Jane Froman, Igor Gorin)
(11/28/42 - 12/26/43) Bl, Sat, 60m, 8:30 pm, Owl-Rexall
2/14/50 (Audition) Mut; with Gene Baker

1 **Overseas Roundup** (5/2/45) Mut

Oxol Feature (1931 - 33) J. L. Prescott, Company, CBS, 15m, various days

12 **Oxydol Show, The** (1950) CBS

Ozark Jubilee (8/7/54 - 4/9/55) Sus, ABC, Sat

Ozark Mountaineers (1933 - 34) Bl, 4t, 15m

Ozark Ramblers (1/25/44 - 5/23/44) Bl, Tue, 4 pm
(4/24/44 - 8/12/44) Bl, Sat, 10:30 pm

Ozzie and Harriet (see The Adventures Of Ozzie and Harriet)

WQXR
INTERSTATE BROADCASTING COMPANY, Inc.
730 Fifth Avenue. New York 19. N. Y.
33⅓ R.P.M.
LATERAL
START
OUTSIDE
INSIDE
P

4 **P.A.L. Show, The** (12/7/46 - 6/21/47) WOR

Pabst - Ett Varieties (10/13/31 - 2/5/32) Pabst-ett cheese, CBS, 2t (Tue & Fri), 15m, 1 pm

18 **Pabst Blue Ribbon Bouts** (1955 - 71) ABC, Wed (not every Wednesday)

1 **Pabst Blue Ribbon Sport Of Kings** (7/29/50) NBC

1 **Pacific Air Front** (6/43) Syn

1 **Pacific News Broadcast** (5/19/45) Mut

1 **Pacific Pioneers Luncheon For Norman Corwin** (1974)

Pacific Serenade (8/27/45 - 1/13/46) Bl, Mon, 10 pm; 8:30 pm as of 10/22/45

1 **Pacific Story, The** (7/11/43 - 1/26/47) Sus, NBC, Sun, 11:30 pm

1 **Pack-Up Time** (6/14/50) WMAQ audition

Packard Cavalcade (9/18/34 - 12/18/34) Packard, Bl, Tue, 45m, 8:30 pm

Packard Hour, The (with Johnny Green; Fred Astaire until 6/1/37)
(9/8/36 - 7/20/37) Packard, NBC, Tue, 9:30 pm

Packard Show, The (9/18/34 - 3/19/35; 10/1/35 - 3/17/36) Packard, Bl, Tue, 8:30 pm; CBS from 10/1/35; led to The Packard Hour

Packham Inn (with Bill Packham and Rex Maupin Orchestra) (1946) NBC

1 **Paderewski's Eightieth Birthday Tribute** (4/16/40) Bl

Paducah Plantation (see Plantation Party)

1 **Pagan, The** (1929) Synchro-disc

4 **Page Cavanaugh Trio, The** (World transcriptions)

Pageant Of Art (11/3/40 - 5/25/41) NBC, Sun, 4:30 pm; 2:30 pm as of 3/2/41

4 **Pageant Of Melody** (with Henry Weber Orchestra) (6/20/37 - 4/18/41) Mut
6/20/37 - 10/30/39, Mon, 30m, 10:30 pm (10 pm 1938)
11/6/39 - 1/29/40, Mon, 15m, 10:45 pm
2/2/40 - 9/25/40, Wed, 30m, 10:30 pm
2/21/41 - 4/18/41, Fri, 10:30 am

Pageant Of Youth (with Johnny Johnson's Orchestra)
(10/20/35 - 12/6/36) Bl, Sun, 12 Noon

Pages Of Melody (6/15/45 - 1/16/46) Bl/ABC
6/15/45 - 8/10/45, Fri, 8:30 pm
12/5/45 - 1/16/46, Wed, 25m, 9:30 pm

Pages Of Romance (10/2/32 - 3/19/33) Fletcher's Castoria, NBC, Sun, 5:30 pm

Paging Mike McNally (see Leave It To Mike)

Paging The Judge (with Robert Paige) (8/31/53 - 1/15/54) ABC, 5t, 15m, 11:15 am

Paging The News (2/28/55 - 12/23/55) ABC, 5t, 15m, 11:15 am

1 **Pagliacci** (1937) film sound track

Painted Dreams (with Ireene Wicker)
(10/30 - 9/28/36) mostly regional; Midwest
10/30 - 33, WGN - local
10/10/33 - 2/2/34, Kellogg, CBS, 4t, 15m
12/30/35 - 9/28/36, Cal-Aspirin, Mut - Midwest, 3t, 15m
(4/29/40 - 11/20/40), Bl, 5t, 15m, 10 am

1 **Palace Personalities** (1949 - 50) West Coast, Wed

Palm Beach Program (with Phil Spitalny; Peg La Centra) (5/12/32 - 6/30/32) Palm Beach and Nurotex summer suits, CBS, 15m, Thu, 10:45 pm; Mon as of 6/6/32

2 **Palm Springs** (1936) Air trailer, film sound track

Palmer House (ABC) Chicago (1947)

18 **Palmolive Beauty Box Theater, The**
(4/8/34 - 10/6/37) Palmolive
4/8/34 - 7/30/35 (with Nat Shilkret Orchestra), NBC, Tue, 60m, 10 pm
8/9/35 - 12/27/35 (with Al Goodman), Bl, Fri, 60m, 9 pm
1/11/36 - 2/15/36, CBS, Sat, 60m, 8 pm
1/13/37 - 10/6/37 (with Jessica Dragonette and Al Goodman Orchestra), CBS, Wed, 30m, 9:30 pm

Palmolive Hour (1927 - 7/29/31) Palmolive, NBC, Wed, 60m

Palmolive Party (see Barry Wood - Patsy Kelly Show)

Pan-American Holiday (see Down Mexico Way)

Pan-American Music (1/23/43 - 9/11/43) CBS, Sat, 4:30 pm

2 **Pan American Day** (4/14/42, 4/14/44) Syn

1 **Pan American Way, The** (8/31/47) WHDH

1 **Panama Hattie** (1942) Air trailer

1 **Panama Invasion** (12/20/89) pool feed

1 **Pancho and His Orchestra** (6/7/44) NBC

Panorama Time (with Johnny Desmond) (1955) Mut

1 **Papal Consistory Ceremonies** (2/21/46) ABC

Pappy Cheshire and His National Hillbilly Champions (see Hillbilly Champions)

35 **Pappy Smith and His Hired Hands** (Wartime) Syn

Parade Of Melodies (with Harry Sosnik Orchestra) (2/14/32 - 2/19/33) Pennzoil, CBS, Sun, 8 pm; 9:30 pm as of 4/3/32

1 **Parade Of Musical Hits** (12/10/33)

Parade Of Progress (with Charlotte Manson) (1/19/39 - 5/11/39) International Foods, Bl, Thu, 8 pm

1 **Parade Of The News, The** (2/6/41) Mut

Parade Of The Years (8/18/40 - 11/24/40) Bl, Sun, 6:30 pm; 8 pm as of 9/29/40

Parallel (with Ken Banghart) (10/13/57 - 60) NBC, Sun, 25m

Paramount Playhouse (1930 - 6/16/31) CBS, Tue, 10:30 pm

1 **Paramount Trio** (1938) Air trailer

1 **Pardon: A New Debate, The** (9/9/74) PBS-TV

2 **Parents Club Of The Air** (10/2/37, 6/39) Mut

2 **Parents Magazine On The Air** (Syn)

1 **Paris Fashions** (7/14/45) Mut

1 **Paris Honeymoon** (2/39) Air trailer

Paris Night Life (8/3/31 - 6/5/36)
8/3/31 - 10/5/31, Bl, Mon, 15m, 7:45 pm
10/27/31 - 7/19/32 (with Bertram Hirsch Orchestra) Angelus Rouge, Bl, 2t; Tue as of 4/26/32
4/30/33 - 5/21/33, American Home Products, Sun, 15m
1/22/36 - 6/5/36, Wed; Fri as of 4/24/36

2 **Paris Star Time** (2/63) Syn

Park Avenue Penners (see Joe Penner)

2 **Parker Family, The** (with Leon Janney) (7/7/39 - 4/10/44) 15m
7/7/39 - 8/25/39, Woodbury, Fri, 7:15 pm
8/31/39 - 10/5/39, Woodbury, CBS, Thu, 7:15 pm
10/8/39 - 3/18/43, Woodbury, Bl, Sun, 9:15 pm
4/30/43 - 4/10/44, Bristol Myers, ABC, Fri, 8:15 pm

2 **Parkway Theatre Program, The** (1/15/37, 1/16/37) WCNW

1 **Parnell** (6/37) Air trailer

Parties At Pickford (see Mary Pickford Dramas)

1 **Parts Of A Pattern** (1949) Syn

Party Line (see Elsa Maxwell)

1 **Pass In Review** (5/13/42 - 8/26/42) Mut, Wed, 9:30 pm

Passage To Home, A (1950)

1 **Passing Of The Hickory Stick, The** (Syn)

17 **Passing Parade, The** (with John Nesbitt) (2/1/37 - 6/24/49)
2/1/37 - 9/6/37, Creme Of Milk Facial Creme, NBC, 2t/Mon, 15m, 7:45 pm
9/12/37 - 12/5/37, Duart, Mut, Sun, 15m, 9 pm
2/25/38, Audition
4/25/38 - 10/22/38 (Conrad Nagel from 7/25/38), Union Oil, NBC, Mon, 8 pm
also 7/3/38 - 1/1/39, Gulf, CBS, Sun, 7:30 pm; (summer replacement for Phil Baker)
1/28/40 - 1/41, Bl - Pacific, Bank Of America
6/29/43 - 9/21/43, Johnson, NBC, Tue, 9:30 pm; (summer replacement for Fibber McGee & Molly)
3/28/44 - 10/12/44, CBS, 3t (Tue, Wed, Thu), 15m, 7:15 pm
2/9/48 - 6/24/49, Sus, Mut, 5t, 15m also syndicated

1 **Passport For Adams** (with Robert Young, later Doug Adams) (8/17/43 - 10/12/43) CBS, Tue, 10 pm (summer replacement for Suspense)

1 **Passport To Daydreams** (Syn) audition

7 **Passport To Romance** (with Mitzi Green and Larry Brooks) (3/15/46 - 8/30/46) Mut, Fri, 8 pm

Past Is Dead, The (15m)

1 **Past, Present and Future Of Radio, The** (9/22/39) Mut

3 **Pastels In Rhythm** (10/1/48 - 11/5/48) NBC

1 **Pastor's Study, The** (5/6/47) WGN

Pat Barnes (also with Larry Larsen, organist) (8/3/31 - 11/23/32) Quick Arrow Soap Flakes, Bl, 6t, 15m; 2t (Mon & Tue) as of 10/3/32; 3t (Mon - Wed) as of 11/7/32

1 **Pat Barnes and His Barnstormers** (12/4/37 - 4/30/38) Mut, Sat, 8 pm

Pat Barnes In Person (also with Larry Larsen, organist) (9/2/35 - 3/27/36) Procter & Gamble, NBC, 3t, 15m, 12 noon

Pat Buttram (AFRS) on WLS pre-war

Pat Hollis (10/10/48 - 11/14/48) Mut, Sun, 15m, 10:30 pm

Pat Kennedy (with Art Kassel Orchestra) (9/30/34 - 3/24/35) Grove Labs, CBS, Sun, 15m, 1:45 pm

21 **Pat Novak For Hire** (with Ben Morris; Jack Webb as of 2/13/49) (1946 - 6/25/49) ABC (18 Jack Webb shows broadcasts)
1946 - 47, ABC - Pacific, Gallenkamp Shoes, Sun
2/13/49 - 3/27/49, Sun, 7 pm
4/2/49 - 6/18/49, Sat, 9:30 pm; 8 pm as of 5/14/49

Pat O'Brien From Inside Hollywood (12/15/48 - about 6/13/49) NBC, 5t, 15m

1 **Path Of Glory, The** (Pre-war) Syn

8 **Pathe Audio Review** (8/24/29 - 12/14/30) Synchro-discs

1 **Pathe News Of The Air** (4/8/35 - 7/10/35) Bromo-seltzer, Mut, Mon and Wed, 15m, 8:45 pm

6 **Pathfinder Playhouse** (1951) Syn

1 **Pathfinders, The** (12/31/50) UNESCO Radio

Paths To Prosperity (with Edward Tomlinson) (2/13/38 - 4/24/38) Bl, Sun, 7 pm

Patricia Gilmore (1/2/39 - 7/31/39) Bl, Mon, 15m, 6:15 pm

1 **Patricia Hearst: The End Of The Trail** (9/18/75) CBS-TV

1 **Patricia McCann Show, The** (11/22/79) WOR

1 **Patrick Henry and The Frigate's Keel** (World syndication)

5 **Patrick Maitland** (8/27/39 - 9/3/39) Mut

Patsy Montana and Slim (Syn)

2 **Patterns In Popular Culture** (5/9/73, 9/12/73) WMUK-FM

Patterns In Swing (with Carl Hohengarten Orchestra) (5/16/38 - 10/31/38) CBS, Mon, 15m, 4 pm

Patterns Of Melody (4/14/47 - 9/27/48) NBC, Mon, 15m, 7:30 pm

Patti Chapin (4/1/35 - 8/8/35) CBS, Mon, 15m, 5 pm; 7:15 pm as of 7/29/35

Patti Clayton (7/4/46 - 9/20/46) CBS, 2-5t, 15m
(12/7/46 - 4/26/47) CBS, Sat, 15m, 7 pm

Paul Allison (1939 - Regional) Mut, Tue, 15m, 9:15 pm

8 **Paul Baron Orchestra** (11/8/39 - 5/8/40) Bl, Wed, 15m, 7:30 pm, also Standard transcriptions

8 **Paul Carson, Pipe Organist** (Standard transcriptions)

2 **Paul Clifford** (Syn)

Paul Douglas (4/15/40 - 10/4/40) NBC, 6t, 15m, 6:45 pm

Paul Harvey (11/26/50 - present) ABC, various days and times

Paul Keast (7/9/34 - 12/7/34) CBS, 3t, 15m, 7:30 pm

1 **Paul Killiam Aboard The S. S. Argentina** (2/4/46) WOR

Paul La Valle Orchestra
(7/1/39 - 11/4/39) NBC, Sat, 4:30 pm
(8/17/41 - 6/20/43) Bl, Sun, 10 pm

1 **Paul Manning** (3/8/45) Mut

1 **Paul Manning and The Human News Behind The War News** (5/5/45) Mut

1 **Paul Manning Reporting From Supreme Allied Headquarters** (5/5/45) Mut

9 **Paul Martell and His Orchestra** (9/12/64 - 10/18/70) CBS

Paul Martin Orchestra (7/4/37 - 8/12/40) Bl
7/4/37 - 9/19/37, NBC, Sun, 5 pm
9/26/37 - 9/2/38, Bl
9/9/38 - 12/16/38, Fri, 9 pm
4/10/39 - 5/29/39, Mon, 8 pm
4/8/40 - 5/6/40, Mon, 10 pm
6/3/40 - 8/12/40, Mon, 9:30 pm

Paul McNutt (1941- 42) Mut

2 **Paul Neighbors and His Orchestra** (8/29/64, 9/5/64) CBS

1 **Paul "Pops" Whiteman and His Orchestra** (concert recording)

2 **Paul Revere** (9/9/41) German Overseas Service

Paul Schubert (12/27/39 - 2/14/40) Mut (2/9/42 - 3/22/45) Mut

2 **Paul Sparr and His Orchestra** (10/11/50, 10/18/50) NBC

Paul Specht (1930s) 15m

Paul Sullivan (9/24/39 - 9/18/41) Raleigh, CBS

26 **Paul Temple, Detective** (BBC) (4/8/38 - 2/26/68) (with Peter Cook) 11 serials

Paul Weston (11/30/51 - 3/21/52) CBS, Fri, 9 pm

1 **Paul Weston and His Orchestra** (Syn)

2 **Paul Whiteman** (2/5/29 - 12/28/39) first sponsored by Old Gold on WEAF, New York on 1/4/28 (see also Stairway To The Stars)
2/5/29 - 5/6/30 (Old Gold Hour) (with Bing Crosby) CBS, Tue, 60m, 9 pm
1/27/31 - 1/8/32, Allied Paints, Bl, Tue, 8 pm; Fri, 10 pm as of 6/19/31
1/15/32 - 9/30/32, Pontiac, Bl, Fri, 10 pm; NBC as of 7/8/32
10/24/32 - 3/27/33, Buick, NBC, Mon, 9:30 pm
6/26/33 - 7/31/33, NBC, Mon, 2 hours
8/3/33 - 11/28/35 (Kraft Music Hall) (with Al Jolson from 8/3/33 - 8/16/34; Jolson missed some of these dates because of movie commitments) NBC, Thu, 60m; (see also Al Jolson and Kraft Music Hall) see Bing Crosby for further Kraft
1/5/36 - 12/27/36 (with Morton Downey) Woodbury, Bl, Sun, 45m, 9:45 pm; 9:15 pm as of 8/12/36
12/31/37 - 7/8/38, Chesterfield, CBS, Fri, 8:30 pm; (replaced Hal Kemp) (Chesterfield Presents)
7/13/38 - 12/27/39 (with Joan Edwards), Chesterfield, CBS, Wed, 8:30 pm
also 11/9/39 - 12/28/39, Mut, Thu, 9:30 pm

Paul Whiteman (Forever Tops) (with Eugenie Baird) (1/21/46 - 9/23/46) Sus, ABC, Mon, 9:30 pm

Paul Whiteman (Youth Production Program) (1952)

3 **Paul Whiteman and His Orchestra** (12/8/41) Red, Bl, Syn

3 **Paul Whiteman Concerts** (Contemporary Composers)
(9/5/44 - 11/14/44) Bl, Tue, 11:30pm

1 **Paul Whiteman Hour, The** (9/29/46 - 10/27/46) ABC, Sun, 60m, 8 pm

12 **Paul Whiteman Presents**
(6/6/43 - 8/29/43) Chase & Sanborn, NBC, Sun; (summer replacement for Charlie McCarthy)
6/4/44 - 9/24/44 (see Radio Hall Of Fame)
(6/27/50 - 11/7/50) ABC, Tue, 8 pm

Paul Whiteman Program
(11/3/46 - 1/5/47) ABC, Sun, 30m, 8 pm
(1/1/47 - 9/24/47) ABC, Wed, 30m, 9 pm; 8:30 pm as of 6/25/47
(9/29/47 - 11/17/47) ABC, Mon, 30m
(1949 - 50) ABC, Sun, 30m

Paul Whiteman Record Program (Club) also called The Human Side Of The Record (6/30/47 - 6/25/48) Multi, ABC, 5t, 15m

1 **Paul Whiteman Show, The** (12/15/46)

Paul Whiteman Teen Club
(10/29/51 - 4/28/53) Sus, ABC
10/29/51 - 9/8/52, Mon, 60m, 9 pm
9/30/52 - 4/28/53, Tue, 30m, 8:30 pm

Paul Whiteman Varieties
(2/4/54 - 6/3/54) ABC, Thu, 9 pm
(7/14/54 - 10/20/54) ABC, Wed, 9:30 pm

1 **Paul Whiteman's Birthday Party** (3/27/37) NBC

Paul Whiteman's Musical Varieties (see Paul Whiteman)

1 **Paul Whiteman's Seventieth Birthday Party** (3/24/60) CBS-TV

4 **Paul Winchell** (7/5/48 - 8/27/48) WOR (7/2/48) audition

1 **Paul Winchell and Jerry Mahoney Show, The** (11/29/43 - 9/17/44) Sus
11/29/43 - 7/17/44, Mut, Mon, 9:30 pm
8/29/44 - 9/17/44, Tue, 8:30 pm

Paul Wing and His Magic Typewriter (NBC) 15m

Paul Wing, The Story Man (also with Adele Harrison) (9/26/32 - 9/22/33) Post Toasties, NBC, 3t, 15m, 5:15 pm

Paula Stone - Phil Brito Show, The (also with Doc Whipple Orchestra)
(12/5/44 - 12/27/45) R. B. Semler, Inc., Mut, 2t, 15m, 1:30 pm

Paula Stone Show (6/9/52 - 1/23/53) Mut, 5t, 15m, 2:30 pm

Paulina Carter (2/20/54 - 12/4/54) ABC, Sat, 15m

Pauline Alpert (1/2/39 - 8/16/41) Mut, 15m
1/2/39 - 3/20/39, Mon, 2:30 pm
8/7/39 - 8/21/39, Mon, 3:45 pm
7/5/41 - 8/16/41, Sat, 1:30 pm

Pauline Frederick (1949 -1953) ABC (usually not in New York)

1 **Pauline Frederick News** (12/14/52) NBC

19 **Pause That Refreshes, The** (with Frank Black)
(12/21/34 - 5/3/35) Coca-Cola, NBC, Fri, 10:30 pm; (see also Andre Kostelanetz)
(8/17/47 - 2/18/49) (also called Coca-Cola Hour; with Andre Kostelanetz; then Percy Faith) Coca-Cola, CBS Sun, 6:30 pm; Fri, 10:30 pm as of 1/7/49
(6/4/50 - 10/1/50) CBS, Sun, 8 pm

Payroll Party (with Nicholas Girrard) (11/22/52 - 12/13/52) American Labor Supply ABC, Sat, 25m

Peables Takes Charge
(10/24/38 - 9/22/39) Bl, 3t, 15m, 1:30 pm; 5t as of 3/13/39 (originally called Nora, Ned and Peables)

1 **Peabody Awards, The** (5/4/50) CBS

Peabodys, The (with Fran Allison and Norman Gottschalk) (1946 - 47) 15m

1 **Peace Begins** (1/27/73) NBC-TV

1 **Peace Is Our Business** (4/3/49) CBS

Peace Of Mind (with David Amity) (9/18/50 - 12/22/50) ABC, 5t, 15m, 2:45 pm

1 **Peace Road Is Rough, The** (9/2/47) Mut

1 **Peacock Variations** (1956) CBS

1 **Peanuts To The Presidency: The Jimmy Carter Campaign** (3/18/78) TV Syn

68 **Pearl Harbor Coverage** (12/7/41, 12/8/41) Red, Bl

1 **Pearl Harbor To Tokyo** (8/10/45) CBS

1 **Pearl Harbor: How America Dropped Her Guard** (1945) Syn

Pebeco Playboys (5/17/32 - 12/13/32) Pebeco, CBS

Pedro De Cordoba (with Will Osbourne) (4/10/33 - 7/6/34) Corn Products, CBS, 3t, 15m

Pee Wee King Orchestra (9/6/52 - 55) NBC, Sat
9/6/52 - 54, Multi
1954 - 55, Sus

3 **Pee Wee Hunt and His Orchestra** (Capitol transcriptions)

1 **Pee Wee Hunt and His Twelfth Street Rag Band** (WFMD)

Pee Wee King (9/6/52 - 6/13/53) NBC, Sat, 9 pm

5 **Pee Wee King and His Golden West Cowboys** (Standard transcriptions)

Pee Wee Reese Show (4/26/52 - 8/30/52) S. C. Johnson & Sons, Mut, Sat, 15m 5:45 pm

Peerless Trio (1/2/38 - 11/3/39) Bl, Sun, 15m, 8 am

Peewee and Windy (with Jack MacBryde and Walter Kinsella) (NBC)

Peg La Centra Show, The
(10/6/34 - 3/9/35) NBC, Sat, 15m, 6:30 pm (also with John Gart)
(1938) NBC, 15m
(10/24/40 - 5/15/41) Bl, Thu, 15m, 12:15 pm
(11/19/40 - 12/31/40) Bl, Tue, 15m, 12:15 pm

Peggy and Paul (15m)

3 **Peggy Lee** (World transcriptions)

6 **Peggy Lee Show, The** (6/17/51 - 8/5/51) CBS, Sun, 7:30 pm (partial summer replacement for Amos 'n' Andy)
also 1952

5 **Peggy Lee With Orchestra Accompaniment** (World transcriptions)

2 **Peggy Lee With Orchestral Accompaniment** (World transcriptions)

Peggy Mann (12/31/44 - 5/11/45) Bl, 5t, 15m, 6:45 pm

Peggy Wood Calling (6/9/37 - 9/15/37) Bl, Wed, 15m, 2:45 pm (every other week)

Peggy's Doctor (with James Meighan; Rosaline Greene) (10/1/34 - 3/29/35) Blue Coal, NBC, 3t, 15m

1 **Peliliu Invasion Broadcast** (9/21/44) Mut

39 **Pendleton Story, The** (4/19/51 - 8/14/52) AFRS

Penguin Room (see Hildegarde)

1 **Pennies From Heaven** (1936) film sound track

1 **Pennsylvania State Society Program** (1/19/38) Bl

Penny Singleton Show, The
(5/30/50 - 9/26/50)
5/30/50 - 6/27/50, Johnson, NBC, Tue, 9:30 pm; (summer replacement for Fibber McGee & Molly)
7/4/50 - 9/26/50, Wheaties, NBC, Tue, 9:00 pm; (summer replacement for Bob Hope)

Pennzoil Pete (1930 - 2/22/31) Pennzoil, Bl, Sun, 15m, 10:15 pm

1 **Pentagon Papers: What They Mean, The** (1971) CBS-TV

Penthouse Blues (with Judith Arlen) (1939) CBS, 15m

Penthouse Party (with Mark Hellinger; Hal Kemp as of 4/3/35)
(1/2/35 - 7/24/35) Eno Salts, Bl, Wed
(6/6/41 - 12/31/41) (with Ilka Chase, Bert Parks, Yvette Harris) Camel
6/6/41 - 9/26/41, CBS, Fri, 10:30 pm; 10 pm from 6/20/41 - 9/12/41
10/8/41 - 12/31/41, Bl, Wed, 9:30 pm

Penthouse Serenade (with Don Mario, Charles Gaylord Orchestra; Freddy Martin as of 12/13/36)
(1/6/35 - 3/21/37) Maybelline, NBC, Sun, 4 pm

People (2/6/54 - 4/24/54) NBC, Sat, 6:30 pm

16 **People Act, The** (1/6/52 - 6/29/52) Sus, CBS, Sun, 25m, 10:05 pm
also 12/50
also NBC and a syndicated series

14 **People Are Funny** (4/3/42 - 60) (on West Coast for previous three years under different titles
4/3/42 - 7/26/46 (with Art Baker and Art Linkletter), Wings, NBC, Fri
9/20/46 - 6/13/47; 9/12/47 - 6/11/48, Raleigh, NBC, Fri, 9 pm
9/7/48 - 5/30/49; 9/20/49 - 6/20/50; 9/19/50 - 5/29/51 Raleigh, NBC, Tue
also 10/7/50 - 6/2/51, NBC, Sat, 7:30 pm
10/9/51 - 3/30/54, Mars, CBS, Tue
10/12/54 - 10/4/56, Toni, NBC, Tue, 8 pm
10/10/56 - 59, NBC, Wed, 8 pm
1959 - 60, Multi, NBC, Fri

1 **People Are Like That** (7/49) Syn

People I Have Known (with Ransom Sherman) (7/7/38 - 10/27/38) Bl, Thu, 10 pm

1 **People In Love** (9/6/45)

People In The News (9/23/55 - 3/16/56) Anahist, ABC, Fri, 5m

1 **People Look To The Future** (8/5/44) Mut

4 **People Sing and Dance, The** (U.N. Syn)

People You Know and Fun Quiz (1946) (Audition)

People's Choice, The (with Earl McGill) (12/5/37 - 2/6/38) CBS, Sun, 8 pm

2 **People's Hymn Sing (Hymn Sing), The** (1/4/44 - 5/16/44) WLAV

1 **People's Platform, The** (with Lyman Bryson) (6/28/38 - 8/10/52) Sus, CBS
6/28/38 - 6/28/38, CBS, Wed, 8 pm
9/11/38 - 6/25/39, Sun, 7 pm
7/5/39 - 8/9/39, Wed, 7:30 pm
9/23/39 - 2/7/42, Sat, 7 pm
3/19/42 - 5/14/42, Thu, 8:30 pm
5/18/42 - 3/9/46, Sat, 7 pm
3/17/46 - 8/10/52, Sun

People's Playhouse (with Bob and Betty White)
(5/30/41 - 7/4/41) Mut, Fri, 9:30 pm
(7/15/41 - 9/2/41) Mut, Tue, 9:30 pm (summer replacement of Morton Gould)

People's Rally, The (with John B. Kennedy and Bob Hawk)
(10/16/38 - 4/30/39) Mennen, Mut, Sun, 3:30 pm; 9 pm as of 4/16/39

People's Reporter (11/15/43 - 5/12/44) MGM, Mut, 5t, 15m

People's Vote, The (with Sam Hayes) (10/10/38 - 39) Mennen, Mon, 15m, 8 pm; Tue, 15m, 8:15 pm as of 4/39

2 **People, Just People** (Syn)

1 **Pepe Moriale Trio, The** (7/4/65) CBS

Pepper Pot, The (see The Breakfast Club)

11 **Pepper Young's Family** (6/29/36 - 12/58) Procter & Gamble (Camay) until 1957; Multi from 1957 - 58, NBC, 5t, 15m also on Mut, Bl and CBS

2 **Pepsi Cola Concert Band, The** (8/1/42) WNYC

Pepsodent Show, The (see Bob Hope)

Percy Faith Orchestra (10/5/38 - 4/24/40) Sus, Mut, Wed, 9:30 pm (see also Coca-Cola Hour; Pause That Refreshes)

Perfect Circle Orchestra (with Charlie Davis) (1935)

1 **Perfect Husband, The** (5/6/49) CBS
(7/9/51 - 9/21/51) ABC, 5t, 15m, 2:30 pm

1 **Perfect Marriage, The** (1946) Air trailer

9 **Peril** (Syn)

Perole String Quartet (9/24/39 - 4/21/40) Mut, Sun, 12 noon
(6/29/41 - 10/5/41) Mut, Sun, 11:30 am

3 **Perry Como Show, The** (4/9/43 - 7/15/55) (see also Chesterfield Supper Club)
4/9/43 - 12/31/43, CBS, 5t, 15m
1/2/44 - 6/18/44(Columbia Presents Perry Como), Sus, CBS, Sun, 15m, 7:15 pm
9/1/53 - 3/26/54, Chesterfield, Mut, 3t, 15m, 7:45 pm, Simulcast
6/27/54 - 8/8/54, Mut, Sun, 15m, 11:15 am
10/11/54 - 7/15/55, Chesterfield, CBS, 3t, 15m, 9 pm (TV simulcast)

Perry Martin (3/11/42 - 5/13/42) NBC, Wed, 15m, 9:45 am

12 **Perry Mason** (with John Larkin from 3/31/47 - 12/30/55)
(10/18/43 - 12/30/55) Procter & Gamble (Tide, Camay), CBS, 5t, 15m

4 **Person To Person** (CBS-TV/PBS-TV)

118 **Personal Album** (1944 - 45) 15m, AFRS origination

Personal Column Of The Air
(7/1/36 - 9/10/37) Chipso, Bl, 5t, 15m; NBC. 4t (Mon - Thu) as of 11/16/36

4 **Personality Time** (1949) Syn

1 **Personally, It's Off The Record** (with Fats Waller) ABC (9/23/43)

1 **Perspective** (12/1/74) ABC

1 **Perspective '71** (1971) Westinghouse, Syn

1 **Perspective: A Conversation Between Walter Cronkite and Eric Sevareid:** (7/6/79) CBS-TV

Pertussin Playboys (with Frank Stretz Orchestra) (12/8/31 - 3/17/32) Pertussin, CBS, 2t, 15m, 6:45 pm

1 **Pet Milk Show, The** (with Vic Damone) (10/2/48 - 9/10/50) Pet Milk, NBC; see also Grand Ole Opry; Jack Pearl
10/2/48 - 8/28/49, Sat, 7:30 pm
10/24/49 - 9/10/50 (with Bob Crosby), Sun, 10:30 pm
also 10/30/50

Pet Milky Way (see Mary Lee Taylor)

6 **Pete Kelly's Blues** (with Jack Webb) (7/4/51- 9/19/51) NBC, Wed, 8 pm (summer replacement for Halls Of Ivy)
also 1955, film sound track

Pete Smythe Show, The (1947 - 1952)

1 **Pete Vantveer** (4/16/40) Mut

Pete Woolery and His Friends (7/12/35 - 8/10/35) CBS, Fri, 15m, 1:45 pm

Peter Absolute (with Arthur Anderson, Ray Collins) (2/9/36 - 9/20/36) Sus, NBC, Sun, 2:30 pm

Peter Brescia Orchestra (see Way Down South)

2 **Peter Donald Show, The** (Syn)

Peter Duchin Orchestra (1959)

3 **Peter Lind Hayes Show, The** (2/20/54 - 9/10/54) CBS
2/20/54 - 5/29/54, CBS, Sat, 1:30 pm
6/7/54 - 9/10/54, 5t, 30m, 7:15 pm

1 **Peter Potter's Juke Box Jury** (4/12/54) CBS audition

Peter Quill (with Marvin Miller; also with Ray Herbeck's Orchestra)
(4/14/40 - 3/30/41) Beich Candy, Mul, Sun, 4 pm; often pre-empted in New York

Peter Salem (see The Affairs Of Peter Salem)

Peter Zorn (8/2/31 - 10/25/31) Consolidated Cigar, CBS, Sun, 9 pm

Peter's Parade (4/30/31 - 7/23/31; 9/3/31 - 11/26/31) International Shoe, CBS, Thu, 15m

20 **Petroleum Conservation Spots** (1940) Syn

Petticoat Philosopher (with Isabel Manning Hewson) (12/1/36 - 12/9/37) 2t, 15m
12/1/36 - 4/22/37, Pure Milk Cheese, Mut, 11:45 am
9/14/37 - 12/9/37, Wyandotte Cleansing Products, CBS, 2 pm

Pfaender and Miles (5/4/40 - 9/14/40) NBC, Sat, 15m, 12:45 pm

1 **Phantom Dancer, The** (1931) Henna-Foam Shampoo, Syn, 15m

Phantom Of Crestwood, The (with Eunice Howard and Ned Wever) 8/26/32 - 10/7/32) RKO. NBC, Fri, 10:30 pm

1 **Phantom Pirate, The** (1950) Syn, audition

1 **Phantom President** (1932) film sound track

Phantom Rider (with Tex Ritter) (Syn) 1930s

Phantom Spoilers, The (see Majestic Master Of Mystery)

3 **Phil Baker Show, The** (12/6/31 - 10/4/39)
12/6/31 - 12/20/31 (with Ted Weems, Ruth Lyons), Sheaffer Pens, CBS, Sun, 9 pm
3/17/33 - 7/26/35 (Armour Star Jester) Armour, Bl, Fri, 9:30 pm
9/29/35 - 6/21/36; 9/27/36 - 6/27/37; 10/3/37 - 7/3/38, Gulf, CBS, Sun, 7:30 pm
1/14/39 - 10/4/39 (see Honolulu Bound) also 1945

Phil Bovero Orchestra (5/28/49 - 9/24/49) ABC, Sat, 9:30 pm

Phil Brestoff Orchestra (4/5/47 - 5/24/47) ABC, Sat, 3 pm
(5/28/50 - 8/27/50) ABC, Sun, 3 pm; 6:30 pm as of 7/9/50

1 **Phil Brito Show, The** (also see Paula Stone)
(12/14/38 - 9/20/39) Bl, Wed, 15m, 1:45 pm also 8/14/45, Mut

Phil Cook Show, The (1930 - 6/28/40) 15m
1930 - 6/28/32, Aunt Jemima, Bl, 6t
1/2/34 - 12/28/34 (see Silver Dust Serenaders)
also 12/21/34 - 2/1/35, NBC, Fri, 7 pm
2/23/35 - 5/11/35 (Phil Cook's Show Shop) Bl, Sat, 8 pm
2/25/35 - 7/8/35, NBC, 5t, 15m, 8 am
1935 - 36, Bl, 5t
3/27/38 - 6/28/40 (Phil Cook's Almanac) CBS, 5t-7t; also on WABC, New York in the 40s

Phil Davis Sunday Party (see Sunday Evening Party)

92 **Phil Harris - Alice Faye Show, The** (10/3/48 - 6/18/54) (for 1946 - 48 see Fitch Bandwagon) (225 shows broadcast)
10/3/48 - 6/26/49; 9/18/49 - 6/4/50, Rexall, NBC, Sun, 7:30 pm
10/1/50 - 1/28/51, Sus, NBC, Sun, 7:30 pm
2/4/51 - 5/20/51; 9/30/51 - 5/25/52; 10/5/52 - 6/28/53, RCA, NBC, Sun
9/18/53 - 6/18/54, RCA, NBC, Fri

3 **Phil Harris and His Orchestra** (1933, 1935) Syn

Phil Harris Orchestra (Let's Listen To Harris) (6/23/33 - 12/14/34) Northam-Warren Co., Bl, Fri, 9 pm

Phil Levant and His Orchestra (1940)

Phil Napoleon (also see Napoleon's Retreat)

2 **Phil Napoleon and His Memphis Five** (Mut)

Phil Ohman (15m) (1936)

2 **Phil Ohman and His Orchestra** (Standard transcriptions)

1 **Phil Regan Show, The** (Syn) 15m 1/2/51 (Audition) NBC
(9/26/35 - 10/7/35) (with Harry Jackson Orchestra) Bl, Thu, 15m, 7:45 pm
(3/4/51 - 8/26/51) Sun
3/4/51 - 5/27/51, NBC, 25m, 5 pm
6/3/51 - 8/26/51, CBS, 25m, 5:30 pm

4 **Phil Rizzuto's Sports Caravan** (1954) Syn,15m; also 1951 Audition

Phil Silvers (6/25/47 - 9/24/47) Philco, ABC, Wed, 10 pm (summer replacement for Bing Crosby)
(9/29/47 - 10/13/47) ABC, Mon, 8:30 pm

Phil Spitalny (see Hour Of Charm)

6 **Phil Spitalny All-Girl Orchestra** (Thesaurus transcriptions)

4 **Phil Spitalny All-Girl Orchestra and Choir** (Thesaurus transcriptions)

1 **Phil Spitalny and His (Hotel Pennsylvania) Orchestra** (11/11/28) Synchro-disc

1 **Phil Spitalny and His All-Girl Orchestra and Choir** (Thesaurus transcription)

1 **Philadelphia Navy Yard Band** (12/7/41) WCAU

1 **Philadelphia Orchestra, The** (1/2/52) Syn

1 **Philadelphia Reception To Generals Bradley and Spaatz** (6/4/45) Mut

1 **Philadelphia Symphony Orchestra** (9/13/31 - 57)
9/13/31 - 12/6/31, Sus, CBS, Sun, 15m
1932 - 33, Sus, CBS, Tue
11/28/33 - 3/24/34, Chesterfield, CBS, 6t, 15m
11/13/36 - 8/6/37, American Banks, CBS, Fri, 30m, 10 pm; 9 pm as of 6/4/37
10/18/37 - 4/11/38, American Banks, NBC, Mon
1/29/44 - 4/22/44, CBS, Sat, 3:30 pm
9/30/44 - 48, 1953 - 57, Sus, CBS, Sat, 60m & 30m

2 **Philco** (1931) Syn

Philco Radio Hall Of Fame (see Radio Hall Of Fame)

Philco Radio Hour (1927 - 6/30/31)
1927 - 28, Bl, Sat, 60m
1928 - 29, Bl, Fri, 30m, 9:30 pm
1929 - 30 (Philco Concert Orchestra) CBS, Thu, 10 pm
1930 - 6/30/31, CBS, Tue, 9:30 pm

Philco Radio Playhouse (4/16/53 - 1/27/54) Philco, ABC
4/16/53 - 7/9/53, Thu, 9 pm
9/30/53 - 1/27/54, Wed, 8 pm

100 **Philco Radio Time** (see Bing Crosby)

Philco Summer Hour (1927 - 6/30/31) Philco, CBS, Tue (also see Radio Hall Of Fame)

1 **Philharmonic Presentation** (5/20/49) CBS

1 **Philharmonic Symphony Orchestra Of New York** (WHN)

1 **Philip Morris Night With Horace Heidt** (5/23/48) NBC

2 **Philip Morris Playhouse On Broadway, The** (with Charles Martin) (9/11/51 - 9/2/53)
9/11/51 - 1/8/52, NBC, Tue, 10:30 pm
1/13/52 - 11/30/52, CBS, Sun, 10 pm
12/3/52 - 9/2/53, CBS, Wed, 8:30 pm

6 **Philip Morris Playhouse, The** (8/15/41 - 2/18/44) CBS, Fri, 9 pm
(10/29/48 - 7/29/49) CBS, Fri, 10 pm
(3/15/51 - 9/6/51) CBS, Thu, 10 pm; 9:30 pm as of 6/7/51

Philip Morris Program (with José Ferrer) (1942)

Philip Morris Programs (also see Johnny Presents, Great Moments From Great Plays, Philip Morris Playhouse, Philip Morris Playhouse On Broadway; Breezin' Along; Johnny Green)

1 **Philip Morris Show, The** (12/29/48) CBS, audition

1 **Phillip F. Lafollette** (10/3/39) Mut

Phillip Marlowe (see The Adventures Of Phillip Marlowe)

1 **Phillip Murray** (12/8/41) Bl

Phillips Poly Follies (with Al Cameron, Joe Karns) (10/10/36 - 5/17/38) Phillips Petroleum, CBS (Regional), Tue, 10:30 pm

51 **Philo Vance** (7/5/45 - 7/4/50)
7/5/45 - 9/27/45, Lifebuoy, NBC, Thu, 7:30 pm (summer replacement for Bob Burns)
1948 - 7/4/50 (with Jackson Beck), Syn - ZIV; 104 episodes broadcast

2 **Phone Again, Finnegan** (with Stu Ervin; Frank McHugh as of 10/10/46)
(3/30/46 - 3/20/47) Household Finance
3/30/46 - 6/22/46, NBC, Sat, 5 pm
6/27/46 - 3/20/47, CBS, Thu, 10:30 pm

1 **Photoplay Eleventh Annual Gold Medal Awards** (2/10/55) ABC

Photoplay's Life Stories Of Movie Stars (with Cal York and Ireene Wicker)
(4/16/32 - 6/13/32) Photoplay, CBS, Sat, 8:30 pm; Mon, 15m, 10:15 pm as of 5/20/32

Phrase That Pays, The (with Red Benson)
(3/30/53 - 9/30/55) Colgate, NBC, 5t, 15m

12 **Phyl Coe Mysteries** (Syn)
(1/29/36 - 5/16/36+) Philco

1 **Piano Parade** (1965) BBC

7 **Piano Playhouse** (6/16/45 - 2/24/52) sus, ABC
6/16/45 - 3/2/46, Sat, 15m, 12 noon
also 12/2/45 - 2/24/46, Sun, 30m, 12:30 pm
5/5/46 - 6/30/46, Sun, 5 pm
also 4/6/46 - 9/24/46, Sat, 3 pm
9/28/46 - 3/20/51, Sat, 30m
also 7/11/48 - 2/24/52 (with Cy Walter, Stan Freeman, Milton Cross), ABC, Sun, 12:30 pm

Piano Trio (5/4/41 - 2/1/42) Bl, Sun, 15m, 8:15 am

Pibby Houlihan (with Arthur Shields and Adrienne Marden)

Pick A Date (with Buddy Rogers)
(9/19/49 - 9/15/50) ABC, 5t

12 **Pick and Pat** (with Pick Malone and Pat Padgett) (1/27/34 - 8/30/45)
1/27/34 - 5/31/35, Dill's Best, NBC, Sat; Fri, 10:30 pm as of 3/9/34
6/3/35 - 2/20/39 (Pipe Smoking Time), U.S. Tobacco (Dill's Best, Model Tobacco), CBS, Mon, 8:30 pm
1/18/44 - 7/18/44 (Pick and Pat Time; with Mary Small), Helbros, Mut, Tue, 8:30 pm; in New York as of 3/28/44
7/23/45 - 8/30/45, ABC, Alka Seltzer, 4t (Mon - Thu) 15m, 8 pm (summer replacement of Lum and Abner)
also syndicated

Pick and Pat Time (see Pick and Pat)

Pick The Winner (8/10/52 - 11/2/52) Westinghouse, CBS, Sun, 30m, 4:30 pm

Pickard Family, The (1928 - 31) Interlwoven Socks; Billiken Shoes from 1929, Bl, Sat, 15m
7/23/31 - 34, Bl, various days and times
1935 - 4/19/36, Mut, 3t (Sun, Tue, Fri), 30m, 9 pm

Picken's Party (see Jane Pickens)

Pickens Sisters, The (1932 - 35) Sus, 15m
1932 - 2/5/33, NBC, Sun
1932 - 2/11/33, Bl, Sat
12/27/33 - 34, Bl, Wed, 11 pm
1934 - 35, Bl, 3t, various times

1 **Pigskin Parade** (1936) Air trailer

1 **Pigskin Predictions** (10/52) ABC

Pilgrim Hour, The (see The Old Fashioned Revival Hour)

1 **Pilgrim's Progress** (12/8/41) KFWB

Pilgrimage Of Poetry (with Ted Malone)
(10/1/39 - 6/2/40) Bl, Sun, 1 pm

4 **Pilgrimage To Amsterdam** (1948) Syn

Pillsbury House Party (see House Party)

Pillsbury Pageant (with San Lanin Orchestra, Arthur Tracy)
(1/29/32 - 7/4/32) Pillsbury, CBS, Fri, 9 pm; Mon, 15m, 9:15 pm as of 4/11/32

1 **Pilots Who Spotted The Altmark, The** (2/20/40) BBC

1 **Pimlico Futurity** (11/2/40) WFBR

1 **Pimlico Opening Day** (4/29/37) WFBR

1 **Pimlico Special** (11/1/39) NBC

Pin Money Party (10/30/40 - 1/13/40) NBC, Mon, 15m, 9:30 am
(4/3/41 - 8/28/41, NBC, Thu, 15m

Pine Mountain Merrymakers (with Red Foley, Lulu Belle, John Lair)
(10/20/35 - 3/1/36) Pinex, Bl, Sun, 15m, 3:15 pm

2 **Pinky Tomlin and His Orchestra** (1940) film sound track, Standard transcription

1 **Pins and Needles** (3/66) PBS-TV

1 **Pinto Pete and His Ranch Boys** (Pre-war) Syn

1 **Pinto Pete In Arizona** (Pre-war) Syn

1 **Pioneer 11 Reports** (11/29/74)

1 **Pioneer IV Satellite Launching** (3/9/59) WNEW, WCBS-TV, WQXR

1 **Pioneers Of Music** (1945 - 50) NBC, Sat, 60m, 15 - 25 weeks of the year

Pipe Dreams (with Alan Reed) (1939) NBC, 5m

1 **Pipe Organ (Ralph Waldo Emerson)** (Standard transcription)

1 **Pipe Organ Solos (Chester Gay)** (Standard transcription)

Pipe Smoking Time (with Arthur Fields and Fred Hall; Ray Bloch Orchestra)
(12/30/40 - 2/17/41) Model Tobacco, CBS, Mon, 8:30 pm; see also Pick and Pat; Model Minstrels

Pitching Horseshoes (with Billy Rose)
(1941) Mut, 60m

12 **Pittsburgh One Day Painters, The** (see One Day Painters)

Pittsburgh Symphony
(2/27/36 - 12/13/36) Pittsburgh Plate Glass
2/27/36 - 5/21/36, Bl, Thu, 30m
9/13/36 - 12/13/36, CBS, Sun, 45m

1 **Place Called Klay, A** (10/11/55) UNESCO syn

2 **Planet Man, The** (15m) Syn

149 **Planned Program Service** (Pre-war, Lang-Worth syndication)

1 **Planning Wildlife For The Future** (3/40) Syn

1 **Plantation Echoes** (1932) Syn

2 **Plantation Jubilee** (with Curt Massey)
(1/27/49 - 9/23/49) Mut
1/27/49 - 3/24/49, Thu, 8 pm
4/1/49 - 9/23/49, Fri, 8 pm

1 **Plantation Melodies** (Syn)

Plantation Party (Paducah Plantation) (often with Irvin S. Cobb and Whitey Ford as The Duke Of Paducah)
(10/17/36 - 1/22/43)
10/17/36 - 4/10/37, Oldsmobile, NBC, Sat, 10:30 pm
5/7/38 - 12/3/38 (with Whitey Ford), Bugler Tobacco, Mut, Sat, 10:30 pm; 10 pm as of 10/1/38 (with Red Foley)
12/9/38 - 5/3/40, Bugler Tobacco, Bl, Fri
5/8/40 - 2/4/42 (with Louise Massey on many shows) Buglar, NBC, Wed, 8:30 pm
2/13/42 - 1/22/43, NBC, Fri, 9:30 pm

1 **Platter Brains** (1/26/46) Mut, audition

Platter Brains, The (10/17/53 - 4/12/56) ABC
10/17/53 - 12/26/53, Sat, 11 am
1/4/55 - 10/25/55, Tue, 9:30 pm
11/3/55 - 1/19/56, Thu, 45m, 10:45 pm
1/26/56 - 4/12/56, Thu, 15m, 10:30 pm

Play At Home (11/16/47 - 4/4/48) Mut, Sun, 10:30 pm

14 **Play Ball** (see Babe Ruth, also see Box Score Review)
6/16/38, audition
4/14/41, Mut
1946, Syn
4/17/48, CBS

Play Broadcast (with Dennis Wood) (Marvin Miller; from Chicago)
(2/19/40 - 3/31/41) Broadcast Corn Beef, Mut, Mon, 8 pm

2 **Play For Tonight** (8/23/46) Auditions

Play Safe (2/2/41 - 4/27/41) Mut, Sun, 15m, 1:15 pm

Play's The Thing, The (with Betty Adler)
(1932 - 33) Bl, Sat, 8 pm

1 **Playback '66** (12/66) Syn

Playboys Trio (with Leonard Whitecup, Walter Samuels, Felix Bernard)
(10/18/33 - 4/27/34) Pepto-Magnum, CBS, 2t (Wed & Fri
also (1/7/34 - 4/22/34) M. J. Brettenbach, CBS, Sun, 15m

4 **Playboys, The** (Standard transcriptions)

6 **Player, The** (with Paul Frees) (1948 - 49) Syn, 15m

22 **Playhouse 25** (AFRS) adaptations of Hallmark Playhouse and Screen Guild Theater (see Play Is Written, A)
(1934) Mut, Sun, 10:30 pm, war-time

1 **Playhouse New York "The Forties"** (5/12/72) TV syn

Playhouse Of Favorites (4/24/45 - 4/7/46) Syn, 52 shows produced
(4/22/50 - 5/13/50) Mut, Sat, 9 pm

Playhouse Of Romance (see Romance)

Plays By Ear (6/23/47 - 8/11/47) NBC, Mon, 8 pm (summer replacement of Cavalcade Of America)

3 **Plays For Americans** (written by Arch Oboler) (2/1/42 - 6/21/42) NBC, Sun, 4:30 pm; 5:30 pm as of 4/5/42; on 7/5/42 repeated first show

Playtime Frolics (1950) 60m

3 **Playwright Theatre** (11/23/41 - 12/7/41) WEVD

Pleasant Valley Folks (with Charles Sears and the DeVore Sisters)
(2/12/36 - 7/1/37) Crown Overalls, Mut, Thu, 15m

13 **Pleasantdale Folks** (1940) Syn

Pleasure Island (see Guy Lombardo)

5 **Pleasure Parade** (with The Modernaires and Paula Kelly; also Vincent Lopez, Milton Cross or Jimmy Wallington announcing) (1945 - 47) Syn - ZIV; 138 15m shows broadcast

Pleasure Time (see Fred Waring)

1 **Pledge (Everybody's For It), The** (1949) Syn

Plot For Victory (4/3/43 - 10/9/43) NBC, Sat, 15m, 1 pm

4 **Plymouth Admirals, The** (1936) Syn

1 **Plymouth Rock 1949** (1949) Syn

1 **P.O.W....A Study In Survival** (6/9/58) CBS

Pocket Book Mystery (1946)

1 **Poem and Prayer For An Invading Army, A** (6/6/44) NBC

Poet Prince, The (with Anthony Frome, Dick Liebert) (1933 - 34) Bl, Sun, 15m, 10:30 am

Poet's Gold (with David Ross Orchestra) (1932)
(12/19/37 - 10/9/38) CBS, Sun, 15m, 1:45 pm

Poetic Melodies (with Jack Fulton and Franklyn MacCormack)
(1932 - 3/18/38)
1932 - 33, Bl, 2t, 15m
2/4/35 - 4/5/35, CBS, 5t, 15m, 10:30 am
1935 - 36, NBC, Sun, 30m
11/9/36 - 3/18/38, Wrigley, CBS, 5t, 15m

Poetic Strings (see Emery Deutsch)

Poetry and Two Pianos (8/20/33 - 7/5/34) S.C. Johnson & Son, CBS, 3t- 2t, 15m

Point Blank (1953 - 54)

1 **Point Of Order!** (4/22/54) Syn

1 **Point Ration Discharges** (5/12/45) WOR

4 **Point Sublime** (with Cliff Arquette)
(12/40 - 5/31/48)
12/40 - 42, NBC - Pacific, Union Gas, Mon
1942 - 44, Mut - Pacific, Mon
10/6/47 - 5/31/48, John Hancock, ABC, Mon, 8 pm

1 **Pokey, The Christmas Elf** (1949) Syn

18 **Poland Vs. Hitler** (9/43 - 1/44) Syn

Police Blotter (11/17/52 - 1/23/53) ABC, 5t, 5m, 7:55 pm
(5/4/56 - 10/4/57) Mut, Fri, 7:30 pm

1 **Police Department Band** (5/2/42) WNYC

2 **Police Department Program** (10/15/36) WMBQ
(1/7/37) WCNW

1 **Police Department Safety Campaign** (10/20/36) WMBQ

37 **Police Headquarters** (Syn) (1932) NBC, 15m

Police Lineup (5/27/50) Audition

Police Reporter, The (with Noreen Gamill) (1/2/35 - 2/5/35) Syn, 5t, 15m

1 **Police Safety Campaign** (10/19/36) WMBQ

1 **Police Safety Campaign Talk** (10/26/36) WMBQ

1 **Police Woman, The** (with Betty Garde) (5/6/46 - 6/29/47) ABC 15m
5/6/46 - 6/19/46, Mon, 10:45 pm
7/7/46 - 6/29/47, Carter, Sun, 9:45 pm

6 **Polish Language Program** (10/14/36 - 1/17/38) WMBQ

Polish Melodies (with Henry Morgan) (10/17/37 - 11/14/37) Katro - Lek Labs, Mut, Sun, 15m, 12:15 pm

17 **Polish News In English** (9/20/38 - 9/5/39) Poland

1 **Polish Talk** (10/15/36) WMBQ

1 **Political Future Of Indonesia, The** (1948) Syn

1 **Political Talk** (11/4/44) WFBR

1 **Political Talk By Walter Johnson** (11/7/38) NBC

1 **Political Talk By Women Who Are Voting For Thomas Dewey** (11/7/38) WJZ

1 **Politics 1952** (12/30/51) Mut

2 **Polka Holiday** (World auditions)

Polka Party (with Dick Sinclair)

Pollock and Lawnhurst (1/4/32 - 5/1/34) Bl, 5t/3t, 15m

Polly Preston's Adventures
(1929 - 6/30/31) Bl, Tue, 15m

Pollyanna, The Glad Girl (with Gertrude Hardemen, Mark Smith)
(2/26/32 - 5/20/32) Pollyanna Shoes, CBS, Fri, 15m, 5:30 pm

Pompeian Make-up Box (with Boswell Sisters) (1/4/32 - 3/11/32) Pompeian Face Cream, CBS, 2t (Mon & Wed), 15m

Pond's Players (with Maude Adams and Victor Young Orchestra)
(1/26/34 - 3/2/34) Ponds, NBC, Fri, 10:30 pm

Pond's Program (with Eleanor Roosevelt from 12/9/32 - 2/24/33; Leo Reisman Orchestra; then Victor Young)
(5/29/31 - 1/19/34) Ponds, NBC,Fri, 9:30 pm

Pond's Speaker (1930 - 6/2/31) Ponds, NBC, Tue, 5 pm

Pontiac Show (with Jane Froman, Frank Black Orchestra) (9/30/34 - 3/24/35) Pontiac, NBC, Sun

Pontiac Surprise Party (2/10/34 - 3/10/34) CBS, Sat

Pontiac Varsity Show, The
(1/22/37 - 12/31/37) Fri
1/22/37 - 5/14/37 (with John Held, Jr.), NBC, 10:30 pm
10/1/37 - 12/31/37 (with Paul Dumont), Bl, 9 pm

1 **Pontiac, Chief Of Values** (1932) Syn

1 **Pool Broadcast From Guam** (11/12/44) pool feed

1 **Pool Broadcast From London** (9/21/44) pool feed

1 **Pool Broadcast From Rome** (10/14/44) pool feed

1 **Pool News Bulletin** (8/7/44) pool feed

7 **Poole's Paradise** (with Bob Poole) (also called Presenting Poole; Poole's Parlor)
(9/28/48 - 5/26/50) Mut, various days and times, 15m

Poole's Parlor (see Poole's Paradise)

1 **Poor Little Rich Girl** (1936) film sound track

1 **Poor Richard Award To Bob Hope** (1/17/45)

Pop Concerts (12/8/35 - 1/5/36) NBC, Sun, 2 pm

1 **Pop Goes The Question** (1/20/41) WLW

1 **Pop Operetta, The** (12/10/47) NBC

Pop Revue (with Jerry Sears Orchestra) (1/3/36 - 1/24/36) NBC, Fri, 10:30 pm

Pop The Question (12/25/54 - 2/5/55; 4/9/55 - 12/8/56) Mut, Sat, 8 pm

Pop's Pirate Club (6/27/32 - 7/29/32) Wheat and Rice Pops, CBS, 6t, 15m, 5:15 pm

1 **Pope John Paul II Assassination Attempt** (5/13/81) ABC-TV, CBS-TV

1 **Pope Paul VI Obituary** (11/4/67) CBS

1 **Pope Pius XI** (12/24/36) Vatican Radio/NBC

2 **Pope Pius XII** (8/24/39, 10/19/40) Vatican Radio/NBC

4 **Popeye The Sailor** (9/3/35 - 7/29/38) 3t, 15m
9/3/35 - 3/27/36 (with Detmar Poppen), Wheatena, NBC
8/31/36 - 2/26/37 (with Floyd Buckley), Wheatena, CBS
5/2/38 - 7/29/38, Popsicle, CBS, 6:15 pm

1 **Porgy and Bess** (7/19/35) Play rehearsal

Port Of Missing Hits (with Edna Phillips) (1945) NBC

6 **Portia Faces Life** (with Lucille Wall) (10/7/40 - 6/29/51) Post Cereals, 5t, 15m; originally on KTSA
10/7/40 - 4/25/41, CBS
4/28/41 - 3/31/44, Red
4/3/44 - 9/30/44, CBS, 2 pm
10/3/44 - 6/29/51, NBC

1 **Portrait In Music, A** (9/6/64) TV syn

Portrait Of A City (6/4/52 -10/8/52) NBC, Wed, 25m, 10:35 pm

Portrait Of Freida Lawrence

Portrait Of Love (with Mary Lee Davis, Sue Stutz) Syn, 5m

1 **Portrait Of Manhattan** (10/29/48) CBS

1 **Portraits** (10/19/41) Audition

Portraits In Harmony (9/15/36 - 12/8/36) General Shoe, Bl, Tue

Portraits In Jazz (1965 - 66)

Portraits In Literature

1 **Ports Of Call** (1935 -1936) Syn

1 **Post Bikini Review** (6/30/46) Mut

1 **Post Parade** (6/5/45) Syn

Post Toasties On The Air (1939)

1 **Post Toasties Time** (7/23/42 - 8/27/42) Maxwell House, NBC, Thu (summer replacement for Baby Snooks)

Postcard Serenade (with Judy Lang) (7/8/45 - 9/30/45) Mut, Sun, 6:45 pm

Pot O' Gold (9/26/39 - 3/26/47)
9/26/39 - 6/5/41 (see Horace Heidt)
10/2/46 - 3/26/47 (with Happy Felton) Lewis-Howe, ABC, Wed, 25m, 9:30 pm

Potash and Perlmutter (6/26/33 - 2/16/34) Health Foods, Bl, 3t, 15m, 7:30 pm

Potluck Party (1944)

Powder Box Theater (with Ray Bloch, Evelyn Knight and Danny O'Neil) (10/11/45 - 4/11/46) Boujois, CBS, Thu, 10:30 pm

1 **Power For The Pacific Punch** (2/14/45) WOR

Powers Charm School (with John Powers; Pat Hosley) (12/30/46 - 4/11/47) ABC, 5t, 15m, 1:15 pm

1 **Practice Blackout** (8/24/41) KPAC

Prairie Folks (with Erik Rolf) (3/6/40 - 6/26/40) Bl, Wed
3/6/40 - 5/1/40, 10:30 pm
5/8/40 - 6/26/40, 8 pm

1 **Prairie Home Companion, A** (6/13/87) Minnesota Public Radio

3 **Preakness, The** (5/38, 5/14/39, 5/10/41) NBC, Red

Predict A Hit (see Art Van Damme)

Prelude For Strings (7/13/47 - 9/14/47) ABC, Sun, 15m, 9:45 am

Prelude To Dusk (with Joe Ennis, Dolores) NBC (1951)

1 **Prelude To Invasion** (11/43)

Prelude To Midnight (with Milton Charles) Mon (1945)

1 **Prelude To Moscow** (3/9/47) CBS

7 **Premier Edouard Daladier** (3/29/39 - 10/10/39) France, CBS, NBC

1 **Premier Hepburn** (9/21/41) WOR

1 **Premier Marshall Petain** (6/17/40) France

1 **Premier Of "The Best Years Of Our Lives"** (11/21/46) WOR

8 **Premier Paul Reynaud** (3/26/40 - 6/13/40) France

1 **Premier Playhouse** (11/6/58) Syn

Premium Salad Dressers (9/9/30 - 9/3/31) F.H. Leggett & Co., CBS, Thu, 15m

1 **Preparations For The Douglas Corrigan Welcome** (8/4/38) Mut

1 **Prepare For Winter ("And Miners Sing")** (Wartime) Syn

Presbyterian Hour, The (1946)

8 **Presbyterian Laymen Speak** (10/48) Syn

1 **Prescott Presents** (12/8/41) Bl

Prescott Robinson (11/1/42 - 2/8/43) Mut (1947 - 50) Mut

1 **Present For Sally, A** (Syn)

Present From Hollywood, A (4/7/46 - 3/30/47) William Scott Co., Boscul Tea, ABC, Sun, 15m, 3:30 pm

1 **Presentation Of The Health Care Reform Plan To Congress** (9/27/93) C-SPAN

1 **Presentation Of The "One World Awards"** (5/11/49) NBC

1 **Presenting Bing Crosby** (see Bing Crosby) (9/2/31)

Presenting Boris Karloff (9/21/49 - 12/14/49) Sus, ABC, Wed, 9 pm

Presenting Charles Boyer (7/4/50 - 9/12/50) Johnson, NBC, Tue, 9:30 pm (summer replacement for Fibber McGee & Molly)
(9/14/50 - 10/26/50) NBC, Thu, 10:30 pm

6 **Presenting Joy Nicholls** (Post-war) Syn

1 **Presenting Lily Mars** (1943) film sound track

Presenting Mark Warnow (see Mark Warnow)

Presenting Paulina Carter (1954)

1 **Presidency and The Nation, The** (12/30/81) NBC-TV

1 **President and Mrs. Bush...Talking With David Frost, The** (1/2/91) PBS-TV

1 **President and The Editors, The** (11/17/73) pool feed

1 **President Anwar Sadat Assassination** (10/6/81)

1 **President At Annapolis, The** (6/7/78) pool feed

1 **President Benes Of Czechoslovakia** (9/10/38) Czechoslovakia

175 **President Bill Clinton** (1/20/93 - 2/26/96)

1 **President Bush Speaks To The Heartland** (12/8/90) WHO

1 **President Clinton Answering Children's Questions** (2/2/93) ABC-TV

13 **President Dwight Eisenhower** (1/20/53 - 11/11/55) CBS, Mut, ABC

1 **President Eisenhower Inaugural Ceremonies** (1/21/57) NBC

1 **President Franklin Roosevelt Memorial Program** (4/9/46) Mut

140 **President George Bush** (1/20/89 - 1/13/93)

44 **President Gerald Ford** (8/12/74 - 6/6/94)

113 **President Harry Truman** (4/16/45 - 1/15/53)

1 **President Herbert Hoover** (7/28)

91 **President Jimmy Carter** (1/20/77 - 7/27/92)

2 **President John Kennedy** (1/20/61, 6/62) pool feed, ABC

1 **President Johnson** (1/22/73) CBS

1 **President Kennedy's Funeral Procession and Burial** (11/25/63) pool feed

9 **President Lyndon Johnson** (11/28/63 - 3/15/67)

1 **President Nixon and Vice President Agnew** (1/20/73) pool feed

1 **President Nixon Funeral** (4/27/94) pool feed

1 **President Nixon's Resignation** (8/8/74) CBS-TV

6 **President Nixon: Paid Political Announcement** (10/7/72 - 11/6/72) Mut, CBS, NBC-TV

1 **President Reagan and General Secretary Gorbachev** (1/1/88) pool feed

1 **President Reagan Assassination Attempt** (3/30/81)

1 **President Reagan Inauguration** (1/20/81) pool feed

1 **President Reagan's Address To The Congress: A Response** (4/30/81) ABC-TV

59 **President Richard Nixon** (1/20/69 - 3/8/90)

421 **President Ronald Reagan** (1/29/81 - 5/6/91)

145 **President Franklin Roosevelt** (3/4/33 - 3/21/45)

1 **President Roosevelt Funeral Procession** (4/14/45) NBC

1 **President Roosevelt Memorial** (4/15/45) NBC

1 **President Roosevelt Memorial Services From Washington** (4/15/45) Mut

1 **President Roosevelt's Funeral** (4/13/45) CBS

1 **President Truman and Winston Churchill** (3/5/46) Mut

1 **President Truman Bulletins and Reports** (12/72) CBS

1 **President Truman Homecoming** (6/27/45) Mut

1 **President Truman's Arrival In Union Square** (10/28/48) WOR

1 **President Wasn't Fooling, The** (Wartime)

1 **President's Lawyer: James St. Clair, The** (7/22/74) pool feed

1 **President's Tax Message: Other Views, The** (7/28/81) CBS-TV

1 **President, The** (1/6/80) ABC-TV

3 **President-Elect Bill Clinton** (11/12/92 - 1/17/93) pool feed

3 **President-Elect Carter** (12/3/76 - 12/6/76) pool feed

1 **President-Elect Ronald Reagan** (11/6/80) pool feed

1 **Presidential Assassination: Another Attempt** (9/23/75) CBS-TV

13 **Presidential Debate** (9/23/76 - 10/30/92) pool feeds

1 **Presidential Debate Analysis** (9/23/76) CBS-TV

2 **Presidential Debate, The** (10/28/80, 10/21/84) pool feed

1 **Presidential Inaugural Opening Ceremonies** (1/17/81) pool feed

1 **Presidential Pardon, The** (9/8/74) NBC-TV

1 **Press Association News** (8/27/39) CBS

Press Club (with Marvin Miller) (1939 - 40)
also 1944, Packard Bell, CBS - Pacific

1 **Press Conference** (Post-war) KECA

1 **Press Interview - Topic Polio** (1953) Syn

1 **Press Radio News Reports** (9/34) WEAF

3 **Pretty Kitty Kelly** (with Arline Blackburn) (3/8/37 - 9/27/40) Wonder Bread, CBS, 5t, 15m

Preventing Mouth Trouble (with Marley Sherris) (3/25/32 - 9/29/32) Calsodent Company NBC, Fri; Thu as of 6/9/32

1 **Preview Of "Love Thy Neighbor"** (12/17/40) Mut

1 **Preview Of The Eclipse Of The Sun** (4/6/40) Mut

1 **Preview Of The Yale - Harvard Crew Race** (6/24/37) Mut

6 **Price Of Liberty, The** (Syn)

2 **Pride Of The Outfit** (AFRS) Syn

8 **Prime Minister Chamberlain** (9/24/38 - 5/10/40)

1 **Prime Minister Daladier** (9/28/38) France/Mut

1 **Prime Minister Nehru Of India** (10/17/49) Mut

1 **Prime Minister Neville Chamberlain** (9/3/39) BBC

1 **Prime Time** (8/27/92) ABC-TV

1 **Prime Time Live** (9/21/89) ABC-TV

Primrose String Quartet (3/27/39 - 8/10/41)
3/27/39 - 5/8/39, Mut, Mon, 9 pm
5/18/39 - 6/8/39, Bl, Thu, 8 pm
6/28/39 - 7/19/39, NBC, Wed, 2 pm
10/8/39 - 5/5/40, NBC, Sun, 10:30 pm
2/2/41 - 8/10/41, Bl, Sun, 10 am

Prince Albert Quarter Hour (see Alice Joy)

1 **Prince Bernhardt** (6/25/40) BBC

1 **Prince Charming** (7/18/49) WOR

1 **Prince Of Wales, The**

2 **Princess Elizabeth** (10/13/40, 10/10/51) BBC/CBS, CBC

1 **Princess Juliana Of The Netherlands** (6/17/40) CBC

Princess Pat Players (7/31/33 - 4/9/39) Princess Pat Ltd.
7/31/33 - 6/15/36, Bl, Mon, 9:30 pm
6/21/36 - 4/9/39 (also called A Tale Of Today), NBC, Sun, 6:30 pm

1 **Priorities On Parade** (1942) film sound track

1 **Private Eye, The** (Audition)

Private Files Of Matthew Bell, The (with Joseph Cotten) (3/16/52 - 6/8/52; 9/7/52 - 12/21/52) SeabrookFarms, Mut, Sun, 4:30 pm

Private Files Of Rex Saunders, The (with Rex Harrison and Leon Janney) (5/2/51 - 8/1/51) RCA, NBC, Wed, 8:30 pm

4 **Private Practice Of Dr. Dana, The** (with Jeff Chandler) (8/10/47 - 48) CBS, Sun

2 **Private Showing** (with Walter Hampden) (5/12/46 - 10/30/46) Mut, Sun, 2 pm

5 **Private Space, A** (7/16/85 - 8/20/85) NPR

1 **Prize Songs** (6/10/48) Mut

Pro and Con (with Leif Eid) (12/5/47 - 12/12/52) NBC, Fri, 15m, 10:45 pm

1 **Pro-Arte Quartet Of The University Of Wisconsin** (12/23/45) Mut

Problem Clinic (with Tom Breneman) (1/15/39 - 39) Creme Of Milk Face Cream, Sun, CBS, 2:30 pm

Problems For Pamela (Syn) (1937) 15m

Problems Of The Peace (see Lyman Bryson)

1 **Proclamation Of Queen Elizabeth** (2/8/52) BBC

Producer's Showcase (1956)

Professional Parade (with Fred Niblo, Leo Spitalny Orchestra) (11/18/36 - 3/31/37) Bl, Wed, 9 pm

Professor and The Major (with Bradford Browne and Al Llewelyn) (3/8/32 - 6/2/32) Kolynos, CBS, 3t, 15m, 5:30 pm

1 **Professor Fiddle De Dee** (7/9/35) NBC

Professor Puzzlewit (with Larry Keating) (3/19/37 - 1942) Gallenkamp Stores, NBC - West, Fri/Sun

3 **Professor Quiz** (with Craig Earl) (5/9/36 - 7/17/48)
5/9/36 - 9/12/36, G Washington Coffee, CBS, Sat
9/18/36 - 11/1/36, CBS, Sun, 7 pm
11/9/36 - 11/23/36, CBS, Mon, 10:30 pm
11/29/36 - 2/28/37, CBS, Sun, 7 pm
3/6/37 - 9/24/38, Nash, CBS, Sat
10/1/38 - 8/19/39 (with Bob Trout), Noxzema, CBS, Sat, 8:30 pm; sustained from 7/1
8/18/39 - 4/26/40 (with Bob Trout), Teel, CBS, Fri, 7:30 pm
4/30/40 - 3/25/41, Velvet Tobacco (Chesterfield as of 10/2/40) CBS, Tue, 9:30 pm
4/3/41 - 9/25/41, CBS, Thu, 1:45 pm
1/24/46 - 2/27/47, American Oil, ABC, Thu, 7:30 pm
3/8/47 - 7/17/48, American Oil, ABC, Sat, 10 pm

1 **Program About A Lot Of Things, A** (1948) Syn

1 **Program For America, A** (4/44) Syn

2 **Program Of Canada, A** (15m) with Gisele MacKenzie; & with Leslie Bell Singers, Syn (also see Gisele Of Canada)

1 **Program Of Latin Music** (11/17/40) NBC

1 **Progressive Party Candidates** (7/52)

1 **Project '73** (9/19/73) WMUK-FM

2 **Project 20** (1954, 1955) NBC-TV

1 **Projection '59** (12/28/58) NBC-TV

1 **Projection '60** (12/27/59) NBC-TV

1 **Projection '62** (1/5/62) NBC-TV

1 **Projection '64** (12/63) NBC-TV

1 **Projection '65** (12/29/64) NBC-TV

1 **Projection '66** (12/26/65) NBC-TV

1 **Projection '68** (1/68) NBC-TV

1 **Projection '69** (12/29/68) NBC-TV

1 **Projection '70** (12/28/69) NBC-TV

1 **Projection '71** (1/10/71) NBC-TV

1 **Projection '72** (1/9/72) NBC-TV

1 **Projection '73** (1/6/73) NBC-TV

1 **Prologue 1959** (12/59) ABC-TV

1 **Prologue 1961** (1/4/61) ABC-TV

Promenade Symphony Of Toronto (with Reginald Steward, conductor) (7/6/39 - 9/28/39) Bl, Thu, 60m, 9 pm

1 **Promise Vs. The Dead, The** (8/6/44) CBS

436 **Proudly We Hail** (6/1/41 - 9/26/41) (a salute to defense workers)
6/1/41 - 6/15/41, CBS, Sun, 2 pm, 15m
6/20/41 - 9/26/41, CBS, Fri, 8:30 pm, 15m
(1947 - 8/25/57) (Army/Army Air Forces Recruiting) Syn

1 **Prowl Car** (2/3/49) Audition

Prudence Club (with Charles Hector Orchestra) (3/8/32 - 5/24/32) Prudence Corn Beef Hash, CBS, 2t, 15m, 10:30 am

36 **Prudential Family Hour, The** (with Deems Taylor until 8/30/42) (8/31/41- 9/26/48) Prudential Insurance, CBS, Sun, 45m, 5 pm; 6 pm as of 1/4/48

7 **Prudential Family Hour Of Stars, The** (10/3/48 - 2/26/50) CBS, Sun, 6 pm

Pryor's Cremo Band (with Arthur Pryor) (3/16/31 - 11/2/31) Cremo, CBS, 6t, 15m, 8 pm

Public Affairs (1/6/40 - 10/24/42) CBS, Sat, 15m, 10:15 pm

1 **Public Health Nurse** (Wartime) Syn

6 **Public Health Series** (1952) Syn

2 **Public Hearing** (10/12/83, 1/4/84) NPR

Public Hero #1 (with Sydney Ellstrom) (10/18/37 - 10/10/38) Falstaff Beer, NBC, Mon

Public Interest In Democracy (with Mark Sullivan and Jay Franklin) (12/21/38 - 8/9/39) Bl, Wed, 10:30 pm

Public Prosecutor (1/2/55 - 3/28/56) Mut
1/2/55 -10/2/55, Sun, 6 pm
10/5/55 - 3/28/56, Wed, 8 pm

1 **Publications For All** (UNESCO Radio)

Puck's Comic Weekly (see Comic Weekly)

Pueblo Serenade (with Wilbur Hatch Orchestra) (1948)

1 **Pulaski Military Memorial** (10/11/39) Mut

1 **Pulaski Parade (Poland Vs. Hitler)** (10/10/43) Syn

Pulitzer Prize Plays (6/2/38 - 8/11/38) Bl, Thu, 10 pm; 9 pm as of 7/7/38

Pull Over Neighbor (3/7/39 - 9/21/39) Wilshire Oil
3/7/39 - 6/24/39, NBC - West
7/6/39 - 9/12/39, CBS - West

1 **Punch Line** (Syn)

2 **Purdue University School Of The Air** (11/24/47) WBAA

Pure Oil Concert (with Vincent Lopez; with Wayne King as of 10/7/30) (1929 - 1/27/31) Bl, Tue, 8 pm

1 **Purely Coincidental** (UNESCO Radio)

Purple Heart (see Ginny Simms)

2 **Purple Heart Album** (AFRS)

1 **Purple Heart Program, The** (8/27/44) NBC

4 **Purple Heart Theatre** (Syn)

7 **Pursuit** (10/27/49 - 3/25/52) CBS,
10/27/49 - 1/13/50, Sus & Ford, Fri, 10 pm
1/31/50 - 5/9/50, Sus & Ford, Tue, 10:30 pm
7/1/50 - 7/22/50, Wrigley, Sat, 8 pm (summer replacement for Gene Autry)
7/10/51 - 8/21/51, Wrigley, Tue, 9 pm (summer replacement for Life With Luigi)
9/18/51 - 3/25/52, Mollé, Tue, 9:30 pm

12 **Pursuit Of Happiness, The** (with Burgess Meredith) (10/22/39 - 7/21/41) CBS, Sun, 4:30 pm

Pursuit Of Learning (8/13/44 - 10/1/44) NBC, Sun, 4:30 pm; 11 am as of 9/3/44

1 **Put Up Or Shut Up** (with Jack Barry) (1/4/46) Audition

3 **Puttin' On The Ritz** (1930) Synchro-discs, air trailer, film sound track

1 **Puzzle Boat, The**

1 **Puzzle Party** (11/1/46) Mut

1 **PX Party, The** (2/9/45) Sioux Falls

Q.E.D. Quiz (4/15/51 - 10/14/51) ABC, Sun, 6 30 pm

1 **Quail Hunt At Forked River, New Jersey** (12/10/37) Mut

Quaker Hour Serenade (1937)

Quaker Party, The (see Tommy Riggs and Betty Lou)

Quaker Variety Show (see Tommy Riggs and Betty Lou)

22 **Quality Set To Music** (3/12/53 - 1/2/54) WMAQ

Quality Twins, The (see East and Dumke)

1 **Quarter Hour Conelrad Test Program** (1/20/56)

1 **Queen Comes Calling, A** (11/5/54) CBS

4 **Queen Elizabeth** (5/20/39, 6/14/40, 4/10/41, 4/27/47) CBC, BBC

1 **Queen Elizabeth Christmas Message** (12/25/53) BBC/ABC

4 **Queen For A Day** (with Jack Bailey) (4/30/45 - 6/10/57) 5t
4/30/45 - 46, Multi, Mut, 5t
1946 - 12/1/50, Alka Seltzer, Mut, 5t
12/4/50 - 6/10/57, Multi, Mut, 5t
also on 3/8/57 - 5/24/54, Fri, 8 30 pm

1 **Queen Juliana Of The Netherlands** (4/3/52) ABC

1 **Queen Mary, Ship-To-Shore** (2/9/46) WOR

2 **Queen Wilhelmina** (8/28/39, 5/14/40) Holland/BBC

1 **Queens Marine Sales and Service** (10/12/39) WWRL

1 **Quentin Reynolds** (1/26/42) WOR, also (2/24/46 - 5/19/46) Pepsi, Mut, Sun, 15m, 6:45 pm

Quest For Happiness (4/10/43 - 9/11/43) Bl, Sat, 10:15 am

Question Bee (see Uncle Jim's Question Bee)

Question Box (9/14/50) CBS

Question For America (with Don Hollenbeck) (3/11/46 - 9/16/46) ABC, Mon, 15m, 10:30 pm; 10 pm as of 7/8/46

Question Of Pianos, A (1948)

3 **Quick and The Dead, The** (with Bob Hope) (7/6/50 - 8/17/50) NBC, Thu, 8 pm (partial summer replacement for The Aldrich Family)

1 **Quick As A Flash** (7/16/44 - 6/29/51) (Shadow segments starring John Archer; then Bret Morrison)
7/16/44 - 6/3/45; 9/9/45 - 6/2/46; 9/8/46 - 6/1/47; 9/7/47 - 5/30/48; 9/5/48 - 5/29/49, Helbros, Mut, Sun, 6 pm; 5:30 pm as of 1/20/46
9/24/49 - 12/17/49, Helbros, Mut, Sat, 25m, 7:30 pm
12/12/49 - 6/9/50, Quaker, ABC, 3t, 11:30 am
5/30/50 - 8/4/50, Toni, ABC, 5t, 15m
9/19/50 - 6/29/51, Block Drug, ABC, 5t, 25m, 11:30 am

Quicksilver (with Ransom Sherman and Bob Brown) (6/27/39 - 4/17/40) Tums
6/27/39 - 9/26/39, NBC, Tue, 15m, 7:15 pm
10/11/39 - 4/17/40, Bl, Wed, 8 30 pm

82 **Quiet Please** (with Ernest Chappell; written by Wyllis Cooper) (6/8/47 - 6/25/49) Sus, on Sundays in some parts of country
6/8/47 - 6/29/47, Mut, Sun, 3:30 pm
7/30/47 - 1/28/48, Mut, Wed; Mon in New York only 7/28/47 - 1/26/48
other dates are:
6/8/47 - 6/29/47, Sun

Quiet Please (continued)
7/20/47 - 8/31/47, Sun
9/3/47 - 5/10/47 Wed
9/15/47 - 1/26/48, Mon
2/2/48 - 9/13/48, Mut, Mon, 9:30 pm
9/19/48 - 5/15/49, ABC, Sun, 5:30 pm
5/21/49 - 6/25/49, ABC, Sat, 9 pm

Quilting Bee (with Peggy Wood)
(12/20/39 - 4/10/40) Bl, Wed, 15m, 2:15 pm (every other week)

Quincy Howe (2/17/43 - 4/13/46) CBS
(3/23/53 - 2/8/57) ABC, 5t

3 **Quincy Howe Commentary**
(9/27/38, 9/28/38) Mut

Quite By Accident (12/30 - 4/31) NBC, Tue
(10/4/38 - 12/26/38) Lamont Corliss, NBC, Tue

Quixie-Doodles (see Colonel Stoopnagle)

57 **Quiz Kids, The** (with Joe Kelly)
(6/28/40 - 7/5/53)
6/28/40 - 8/30/40, Alka-Seltzer, NBC, Fri, 10:30 pm
9/4/40 - 7/8/42, Alka Seltzer, Bl, Wed
7/12/42 - 9/22/46, Alka Seltzer, ABC, Sun
9/29/46 - 3/25/51, Alka-Seltzer, NBC, Sun
5/13/51- 9/23/51, NBC, Sun, 7 pm
4/12/52
9/14/52 - 10/12/52, Sus, CBS, Sun, 4 pm,
11/16/52 - 3/1/53, CBS, Sun, 4:30 pm
5/31/53 - 7/5/53, CBS, Sun, 6 pm

1 **Quiz Of Two Cities, The** (with Reid Kilpatrick) (9/24/44 - 4/6/47) Listerine, Mut, Sun, 3:30 pm; Mut - Pacific; originated on WTIC, 10/6/40

1 **Quiz Wizard** (9/24/43 -1/26/45) Mut, 15m
9/24/43 - 10/6/44, Fri
10/9/44 - 1/26/45, 5t

1 **Quizathon** (Mut) (3/5/49) WOR

Quizdom Class (11/10/46 - 6/25/49) ABC
11/10/46 - 6/29/47, Sun, 5 pm
9/13/47 - 7/10/48, Sat, 7 pm
9/18/48 - 6/25/49, Sat, 6:30 pm

13 **Quizpiration** (15m) Syn

Quizzer Baseball (with Budd Hulick and Harry von Zell) (7/2/41 - 8/27/41) NBC, Wed, 9 pm; (summer replacement for Eddie Cantor)

1 **Quote and Unquote** (1/28/47)

1 **R & H Boys, The**

1 **R. B. Bennett** (5/27/40) BBC

1 **R. J. Shiel Statement** (12/11/38) WEAF

1 **R.A.B. Presents Bob and Ray** (Syn)

1 **R.A.B. Sound Service** (Syn)

Racket Smashers (Racket Busters)
(10/1/47 - 12/10/47) Sus, Mut, Wed
10/1/47 - 10/22/47, 10 pm
12/3/47 - 12/10/47, 9:30 pm

1 **Racketbusters Round Table** (4/23/47) Mut

1 **Radar To The Moon** (1/27/46) Mut

Radio Almanac (see Orson Welles)

1 **Radio Almanac, The** (4/5/37) WHN

1 **Radio At Twenty Five** (3/23/47) WIP

Radio Auction (see Auction Gallery)

7 **Radio Beat** (1/13/54 - 3/22/59) CBS

1 **Radio Before Radio** (11/5/45) Mut

Radio Bible Class (1940 - 57) Mut, Sun; ABC as of 1953 (often not in New York)

Radio Canaries (see American Radio Warblers)

Radio Chapel (see Mutual Radio Chapel)

Radio City Matinee (1/9/35 - 4/10/35) RCA, Bl, Wed, 60m, 2 pm

Radio City Music Hall (Music Hall Of The Air) (with Erno Rapee)
(1932 - 9/27/42) Sus, Bl, Sun, 60m
(12/3/43 - 12/10/43) NBC, Fri, 11:30 pm

Radio City Party (9/15/34 - 7/13/35) RCA, Bl, Sat, 9 pm; NBC as of 4/20/35

10 **Radio City Playhouse** (7/3/48 - 1/1/50) Sus, NBC
7/3/48 - 8/21/48, Sat, 10 pm; 10:30 pm as of 7/31/48
8/23/48 - 9/6/48, Mon, 10:30 pm
9/11/48 - 9/25/48, Sat, 8 pm
11/8/48 - 8/29/49, Mon, 10:30 pm
10/2/49 - 1/1/50, Sun, 5 pm

1 **Radio City Revels** (1938) film sound track

Radio Comedy Theater (1946)

3 **Radio Commercials**

1 **Radio Commercials Workshop** (4/29/65) Syn

1 **Radio Crusade To End War**

1 **Radio Day 1974**

10 **Radio Edition Of The Bible, The** (10/10/45 - 1/23/46) Syn

Radio Fan Club (see National Radio Fan Club)

Radio Follies (with Guy Lombardo Orchestra) (9/26/30 - 12/19/30) Assoc. Jewelry Retailers, CBS, Fri, 10 pm

1 **Radio Forum** (8/3/50) VOA

1 **Radio Forum, The** (1948)

4 **Radio Free Europe Story** (1951) Syn

Radio Garden Club (2/9/37 - 7/7/41) Mut, 15m
2/9/37 - 7/4/39, Mut, Tue, various times, 15m
7/10/39 - 3/1/40, 2t (Mon & Fri), 11:45 am
3/8/40 - 12/20/40, 2t (Mon & Fri) 2:30 pm
12/23/40 - 7/7/41, Mon, 2:30 pm

Radio Gossip Club (with Eddie and Fannie Cavanaugh) (11/19/34 - 2/14/36) Broadcast Corn Beef Hash, CBS, 5t, 15m

Radio Guide's Court Of Honor (with Ben Grauer, Shep Fields)
(10/9/36 - 1/1/37) Radio Guide, NBC, Fri, 10 pm

23 **Radio Guild** (11/6/33 - 10/12/40) Sus, Bl, on various days and times including:
11/6/33 - 4/22/35, Mon, 3 pm
4/29/35 - 9/16/35, Mon, 4:30 pm
9/26/35 - 6/25/36, Thu, 4:30 pm
7/3/36 - 6/10/38, Fri, 1 pm
3/26/39 - 9/17/39, Sun, 7:30 pm
11/29/39 - 1/17/40, Wed, 9 pm
1/27/40 - 10/12/40, Sat

31 **Radio Hall Of Fame, The** (with Paul Whiteman)
(12/5/43 - 4/28/46) Philco, Bl/ABC, Sun; called Philco Summer Hour summers of 1944 and 1945
12/5/43 - 6/10/45, 60m
1/7 - 6/10; 6/17/45 - 4/28/46, 30m

Radio Homemaker's Club (see Ida Bailey Allen)

Radio Household Institute (1927 - 34) Multi, NBC, 5t, 15m

1 **Radio Industry Discussion** (1940) WWRL

Radio Listening Test (1/12/31 - 4/6/31) Auto Electric Washer, CBS, Mon, 15m

Radio Magic (with Orestes Caldwell)
(5/8/40 - 7/17/40) Bl, Wed, 15m, 10:30 pm (see also Magic Waves)
(7/22/40 - 11/5/40) Bl, Mon, 15m, 7:15 pm
(11/15/40 - 3/13/42) Bl, Fri, 15m, 7:30/7:15 pm

1 **Radio Net** (1/2/77) NPR

Radio Newsreel Of Hollywood (Syn)
(1932) Mobil

Radio Newsreel, The (with Wally Butterworth and Parks Johnson)
(10/24/37 - 7/24/38) Energine, NBC, Sun, 3 pm; 5:30 pm as of 5/22/38

1 **Radio Novel** (Syn)

1 **Radio Party, A**

1 **Radio Plays The Plaza** (1969) Syn

Radio Ranch House (with Ken Curtis) (1946 - 47)

Radio Reader (with Mark Van Doren) (5/11/42 - 10/9/42) CBS, 5t, 15m, 9:15 am (1/18/43 - 10/8/43) (see Madeleine Carroll)

112 **Radio Reader's Digest, The** (9/13/42 - 6/3/48) CBS
9/13/42 - 9/30/45, Campbell, Sun, 9 pm
1/13/46 - 7/14/46, Hallmark, Sun, 2 pm
9/12/46 - 6/3/48, Hallmark, Thu, 10 pm; led to Hallmark Playhouse

1 **Radio Revels** (1936) Syn

Radio Rubes (with Rube Davis, Arty Hall, John & Neal Laby) (11/7/32 - 12/29/32) Bl, Mon, 10:30 pm; Thu, 11 pm as of 12/15/32; (on at various times)
(10/31/38 - 4/28/39) NBC, 5t, 15m, 8:45 am

2 **Radio Rundfunk** (10/16/36, 1/22/37) WMBQ, WCNW

Radio Short Stories (Syn) 15m

Radio Studio Mysteries (15m)

Radio Theater Of Famous Classics (1942; 1946) Syn

3 **Radio Theatre** (11/21/47, 12/17/47, 6/2/48) VOA

1 **Radio Tribute To The King and Queen** (6/11/39) NBC

Radio Theatre Of Famous Classics (1942) Syn

3 **Radio Varieties U. S. A.** (VOA)

1 **Radio Vaudeville Theater** (6/15/42 - 11/23/42) Mut, 5t - Mon, 15m, 10:15 pm

1 **Radio Views** (1/13/47) CBS

1 **Radio Warsaw** (9/39)

1 **Radio's Biggest Show** (6/18/46) Syn

Radio's Court Of Honor (see Radio Guide's Court Of Honor)

8 **Radio's Golden Age** (7/9/76 - 8/27/76) WMUK-FM

Radiotron Varieties (1930 - 6/6/31) NBC, 2t (Wed & Sat), 15m, 8:15 pm

RAF Fighter Pilot (1941) NBC, 15m

4 **Raffles** (1942 - 45)
1942 - 43, CBS - Pacific, Wed, 5t
1945 - summer (with Horace Braham) Thu (not in New York)

Raffles, The Amateur Cracksman (with Frederick Worlock)
(3/29/34 - 10/7/34) CBS
3/29/34 - 7/5/34, Thu, 8 pm
7/30/34 - 10/7/34, Mon, 8:30 pm; Sun, 6:30 pm as of 9/9/34

1 **Raggedy Ann** (10/23/47) 15m

1 **Ragtime** (10/7/74) TV syn

3 **Ragtime Era, The** (1963) NET-TV

30 **Railroad Hour, The** (with Gordon MacRae) (10/4/48 - 6/21/54) American Railroads, Mon, 8 pm
10/4/48 - 4/25/49, ABC, 45m
5/2/49 - 9/26/49, ABC, 30m
10/3/49 - 6/21/54, NBC

Rainbow Court (see Song Of The City)

1 **Rainbow House** (with Bob Emery) (3/8/41 - 3/1/47) Sus, Mut, Sat (local show in New York since 4/11/37), later on Sun
3/8/41 - 9/22/45, 45m, 10/10:15 am
9/29/45 - 3/1/47, 30m (9:30 am)

Rains Came, The (9/29/41 - 11/7/41) Mut, 5t, 15m, 4:15 pm (part of limited run series based on books)

1 **Raintree County** (1957) Air trailer

Raising A Husband (see The Better Half)

Raising A President (9/29/41 - 12/29/41) Bl, Mon, 15m, 11:30 am; 11 am as of 12/8/41

Raising Junior (1930 - 4/21/32) (with Aline Berry and Peter Dixon) Wheatena, Bl, 6t (not Wed), 15m, 6 pm

1 **Raising The Next President** (12/8/41) Bl

Raising Your Parents (with Milton Cross) (10/17/36 - 10/16/37) NBC, Sat, 10:15 am

Rakov Orchestra (12/17/38 - 8/3/40) Bl, 15m
12/17/38 - 4/10/39, Mon, 5 pm
9/12/39 - 11/9/39, 2t, 10:30 am; 10:45 am as of 10/10/39
11/27/39 - 12/29/39, 3t, 12:15 pm
12/30/39 - 8/3/40, Sat

53 **Raleigh Cigarette Program Starring Red Skelton, The** (see Red Skelton)

Raleigh Room, The (see Hildegarde)

Raleigh Serenade (11/42 - 1/22/43) Raleigh, NBC, 7m, 9:53 pm (not in New York)

Raleigh-Kool Program (see Tommy Dorsey)

1 **Raleigh-Kool Show, The** (1938) NBC

1 **Rally For The National Foundation For Infantile Paralysis** (1/24/38) Mut

Ralph Flanagan (1/22/51 - 7/16/51) ABC, Mon, 10 pm

2 **Ralph Flanagan and His Orchestra** (8/9/52, 7/2/54) NBC, CBS

1 **Ralph Flanagan Orchestra** (Thesaurus transcription)

Ralph Ginsberg Concert Orchestra (from Chicago) (3/18/39 - 12/23/39) Mut, Sat, 15m, 2 pm

1 **Ralph Ginsburg and The Palmer House Concert Orchestra** (1/7/43) Mut

Ralph Kirbery, The Dream Singer (9/13/31 - 1/15/37) 15m, various days and times including:
9/13/31 - 32, NBC, Sun
2/2/34 - 3/9/34, NBC, Fri, 9:30 am
10/22/35 - 36, Piso Syrup, Mut, 2t
5/14/36 - 1/15/37, Lipton, Bl, 2t (Mon & Fri)

1 **Ralph Marterie and His Orchestra** (1/1/58) CBS

1 **Ralph Morrison and His Orchestra** (6/7/44) CBS

Ralph Norman Orchestra (7/4/49 - 8/1/49; 12/26/49 - 1/30/50) ABC, Mon

Ralph Slater Show, The (10/24/45 - 12/26/45) Mut, Wed, 10 pm

1 **Ram-Jet Demonstration** (4/21/47) WOR

1 **Rambling With Gambling** (5/31/89) WOR

Rameses Program (with William Wirges and Joe Kahn and John Cali) (1/5/32 -12/27/32) Rameses II and Stephano Cigarettes, Bl, Tue, 15m

2 **Ramona and Her Mighty Miniature Minstrels** (also with Don Frederick) (1/21/45 - 2/18/45) Mut, Sun, 15m, 10:15 pm

Ramona and The Tune Twisters (4/14/40 - 7/31/42) Mut
4/14/40 - 6/30/40 (also with Jimmy Shields Orchestra), Sun, 5:30 pm (part of summer replacement for The Shadow) (also called (Rendezvous With Ramona)
7/21/40 - 10/27/40 (also with Jimmy Shields Orchestra) Sun, 7 pm
11/10/40 - 6/1/41 (also with Jimmy Shields Orchestra), Sun, 1:15 pm; 1:30 pm as of 2/2/41
6/2/41 - 7/31/42, 3t - 6t, 15m; sponsored by Pepsi Cola from 5/4/42 - 7/31/42, 5m, 9:55 pm

1 **Ramsey Lewis Trio, The** (1/1/66) NBC

1 **Ranch Boys, The** (1934 - 3/17/56) (also see Gene Arnold)
1934 - 36, NBC, 3t/5t, 15m
10/27/34 - 1/19/35, Bl, Sat, 15m, 5:45 pm
11/29/37 - 4/4/38, Sus, NBC, Mon, 15m, 2:30 pm
2/18/39 - 5/27/39, Bl, Sat, 15m, 10 am
11/19/49 - 3/17/56, ABC, Sat, 15m - 30m also Thesaurus transcription

Ranch Party (with Tex Ritter) (1957)

3 **Randy Brooks and His Orchestra** (7/12/47) Lang-Worth transcriptions

2 **Ranger Bill, "Warrior Of The Woodlands"** (Post-war) Syn

1 **Ranger Seven Hits The Moon** (7/31/64) NBC-TV

Ranger's Serenade (with Men Of The West Quartet) (11/6/38 -10/29/39) NBC, Sun, 4 pm

Ransom Sherman (also see Club Matinee; Hap Hazard; Sunbrite Smile Parade)
(1/2/42 - 2/27/42) Procter & Gamble, CBS - West, Fri, 10 pm; full network as of 1/23/42
(3/4/42 - 6/24/42) Procter & Gamble, CBS, Wed, 9:30 pm
(3/4/43 - 5/27/43) (Grapevine Rancho) Roma, CBS, Thu, 8 pm (1950)

Ransom Sherman Variety
(2/1/39 - 10/4/39) Bl, Wed, 10 pm; 9 pm as of 6/28/39

5 **Rate Your Mate** (with Joey Adams)
(4/17/50 - 7/28/51) CBS
4/17/50 - 8/20/50, Sun, 9 pm
9/3/50 - 12/31/50, Sun, 6 pm
1/23/51- 2/27/51, Tue, 10 pm
7/7/51 - 7/28/51, Wrigley, Sat, 8 pm (partial summer replacement for Gene Autry)

2 **Ray Anthony and His Orchestra** (1/52) Syn, Lang-Worth transcription

Ray Bloch's Varieties (11/27/38 - 7/7/38) CBS, Tue, 15m, 3 pm

2 **Ray Bolger Show, The** (with Jeri Sullivan; Roy Bargy Orchestra)
(7/6/45 - 9/7/45) Rexall. CBS, Fri, 10 pm; (summer replacement for Jimmy Durante)

Ray Dady (10/25/43 - 45) Grove Labs, NBC; Mut from 1934 - 44

Ray Heatherton (1/1/34 - 10/20/38) 15m, on various days and times including:
1/1/34 - 3/30/34, NBC, 2t (Mon & Fri), 3:15 pm
8/23/34 - 8/30/34, NBC, Thu, 12 noon
11/8/34 - 12/9/34, Bl, Sun, 11 am
7/7/35 - 9/22/35, NBC, Sun, 5:45 pm
5/4/36 - 5/18/36, NBC, Mon, 2:15 pm
1/22/37 - 2/12/37, CBS, Fri, 7:30 pm
4/19/38 - 10/20/38, CBS, various days (often with Lucille Manners) (on in New York, locally, in the 1940s and 50s)

1 **Ray Heatherton and His Orchestra** (Muzak transcription)

2 **Ray Herbeck and His Orchestra** (4/28/45, 5/23/45) NBC

Ray Kinney Orchestra
(5/14/38 - 9/29/41) Bl
5/14/38 - 11/4/39, Sat, 1:30 pm; 2 pm as of 4/15/39
10/16/39 - 1/22/40, Mon, 7:30 pm
5/24/41 - 9/27/41, Sat, 2:30 pm
also 6/18/41 - 9/29/41, Wed, 10:30 pm

5 **Ray McKinley and His Orchestra** (12/12/69 - 1/16/70) CBS

4 **Ray McKinley Orchestra** (Thesaurus transcriptions)

Ray Miller Orchestra (Sunny Meadows Radio Show) (Meadows Speed Washer) 1929

Ray Noble (2/6/35 - 9/2/48)
2/6/35 - 10/17/35 (Coty Salute To Youth), Coty, NBC, Wed, 10:30 pm
1935 - 36, Coca-Cola, CBS, Wed (see Refreshment Time)
(1945) Max Factor, CBS
7/15/48 - 9/2/48) (see Sealtest)

2 **Ray Noble and His Orchestra** (Standard transcriptions)

3 **Ray Pearl and His Orchestra** (4/40, 10/52) Mut, Don Lee

Ray Perkins (1930 - 3/28/41) Bl (except where noted), 15m (on various days and times including:)
1930 - 12/25/31, Fri, 10 am
also 8/31/31 - 9/14/31 , NBC, 3t
12/8/31 - 5/31/32, Woodbury, 2t (Tue & Sat); Tue as of 3/1/32
5/31/32 - 11/24/32, Barbasol, NBC, 2t, 15m, 7:30 pm
5/7/39 - 9/24/39 (Letters Home for New York World's Fair) Sun, 15m, 5:45 pm
1/30/39 - 1/29/40, Mon, 6:30 pm
2/5/40 - 3/28/41, 3t, 8:30 am

1 **Rayburn and Finch Show, The**
(1/21/50 - 10/5/51)
1/21/50 - 7/8/50 (with Bob Crosby at first until 2/25/50), ABC, Sat, 60m, 9 pm; 10 pm as of 4/22/50
6/22/51 - 10/5/51, CBS, Fri, 9 pm

Raymond Clapper (9/2/42 - 1/6/44) General Cigar, Mut

22 **Raymond Gram Swing** (1936 - 2/1/48)
1936 - 38, Mut
1/17/39 - 9/19/39, Mut, Tue, 7:15 pm
9/25/39 - 9/17/42, White Owl, Mut, 4t
9/28/42 - 12/28/44, Socony Oil, Bl, 4t
1/22/45 - 1/3/47, Bl/ABC, 5t- 2t, 15m
11/30/47 - 2/1/48, ABC, Sun, 1:15 pm

2 **Raymond Knight Cuckoo Program** (2/7/37, 2/14/37) Mut

Raymond Knight's Cuckoos
(3/21/34 - 6/6/34) AC Sparkplugs, Bl, Wed, 9 pm

1 **Raymond Massey. Familiar Readings From The Bible** (World transcription)

Raymond Paige Show, The (see Musicomedy)

Raymond Scott and His Orchestra (8/27/40, 8/28/40, 10/2/40) NBC

38 **Raymond Scott Show, The**
(1/9/40 - 12/24/44) CBS
1/9/40 - 4/16/40, (see Concert In Rhythm)
4/23/40 - 5/12/40, Sun
4/8/42 - 4/22/42, CBS, Wed, 8 pm
7/16/43 - 8/13/43, CBS, Fri, 11:30 pm
8/17/43 - 10/19/43, CBS, Tue, 11:30 pm
10/28/43 - 1/6/44, CBS, Thu, 11;30 pm
1/10/44 - 12/22/44, CBS, 5t, 15m - 30m
also 8/27/44 - 11/24/44, CBS, Fri, 15m, 7:15 pm

Raymond Swing Explains The News (see Raymond Gram Swing)

RCA Magic Key (see Magic Key)

RCA Radio Matinee (1935)

RCA Radio Theater (directed by Himan Brown) (4/27/59 - 1/1/60) NBC, 5t, 60m, 11:00 am

1 **RCA Show, The** (see The Tommy Dorsey Orchestra)

RCA Victor Campus Club, The (with Larry Clinton and Bea Wain) (7/28/38) RCA, NBC, Sat, 7:30 pm

RCA Victor Radio Review (1931- 32) RCA, Sun, 15m

RCA Victor Show (see Music America Loves Best)

RCA Victor Show, The (see Music America Loves Best)

1 **Reactions To Hitler's Death** (5/1/45) Mut

Reader's Digest (with Boris Karloff) 5m (1966) see Tales From The Reader's Digest

Reader's Guide (with Joseph Henry Jackson) (4/9/39 - 6/4/39) Bl, Sun, 15m, 5:30 pm (on West Coast since 1924)

1 **Reading Of The Yamashita Verdict** (12/2/45) Mut

Reading, Writing and Rhythm (2/22/41 - 5/3/41) NBC, Sat, 3 pm

Real Folks (with George Frame Brown)
(8/6/28 - 4/3/32)
8/6/28 - 1/4/32, Vaseline, Bl, Mon; first serial broadcast
1/10/32 - 4/3/32, Log Cabin, CBS, Sun, 5 pm

Real Life Stories (1958-59) NBC, 5t, 15m

6 **Real Moments Of Romance** (with Johnny Thompson) Bendix Radio, 5m, Syn

Real Silk Program (with Edwin Hill; Harry Sosnik Orchestra)
(10/4/36 - 3/28/37) Real Silk, Bl, Sun, 9:45 pm

2 **Real Stories From Real Life** (8/8/44 - 12/31/47) Anacin, Mut, 5t, 15m

1 **Rear Admiral Richard Truly** (10/26/89) C-SPAN

1 **Rebecca Of Sunnybrook Farm** (1938) film sound track

1 **Recent Advances In Animal Science** (Syn)

Recital In Swingtime (see Maxine Sullivan)

Recital Period (6/7/41 - 11/22/41) NBC, Sat, 5:30 pm

1 **Reckless** (1934) Air trailer

Recollections (see Recollections At Thirty)

36 **Recollections At Thirty** (with Ed Herlihy and Fred Collins) (6/11/56 - 5/8/57) NBC, Wed, 8:30 pm

2 **Recorded Music** (9/21/39) WJSV

12 **Recorded Music Program** (10/13/36 - 6/7/44) WMBQ, WCNW, WNYC, WEAF

1 **Recorded Piano Music** (1/13/37) WCNW

1 **Recordings From "Lautarchiv Des Deutschen Rundfunks"** (1938 - 1940) Germany

Red Adams (10/2/32 - 1/22/33) Bl, Sun; led to Red Davis, Red Barber
(10/22/45 - 2/18/50) Sus
10/22/45 - 3/1/46 (Red Barber's Star Review) NBC, 3t, 15m, 7:30 pm
9/23/46 - 1/2/48, CBS, 5t, 15m, 6:30 pm
12/18/48 - 3/5/49, CBS, Sat, 30m, 5:30 pm
4/30/49 - 2/18/50, CBS, Sat, 15m

1 **Red Barber In The Catbird Seat** (8/17/48) CBS

2 **Red Barber Sports** (9/16/46, 8/12/47) CBS

1 **Red Barber's Clubhouse** (5/8/48) CBS

Red Barn Of Broadway (see WOR Summer Theater)

Red Benson (6/5/55 -10/28/55) ABC, 5t, 60m, 8 pm

1 **Red Benson's Movie Matinee** (3/2/49) Mut

Red Cross (see American Red Cross)

2 **Red Cross 1948 Fund Campaign** (1948) Syn

1 **Red Cross At Work** (2/22/44) WOR

1 **Red Cross Blood Bank** (2/14/42) WOR

1 **Red Cross Flood Relief Show** (6/13/48) CBS

2 **Red Cross Girls In Action** (1945) Syn

1 **Red Cross Program** (1/21/42) CBS

1 **Red Cross Rally** (2/29/44) Mut

1 **Red Cross War Fund Rally** (1/1/42) WAAT

Red Davis (with Burgess Meredith)
(10/2/33 - 4/26/34; 10/1/34 - 5/34/35) Beechnut, Bl, 3t, 15m; led to Forever Young which led to Pepper Young's Family in 1936

1 **Red Feather Round-Up** (9/3/48) CBS

Red Foley (1942) (1951 - 52) (1959 - 60) Syn

1 **Red Foley and The Cumberland Valley Boys** (1/2/52) Syn

Red Foley Variety Show, The
(1/19/57 - 61) Dow, Sat
1/19/57 - 7/6/57, ABC, 12:30 pm
11/2/57 - 61, NBC

Red Goose Adventures
(5/1/31 - 11/24/31) International Shoe, CBS, 15m
5/1/31 - 7/23/31, Fri 7:30 pm
9/1/31 - 11/24/31, Tue, 8:30 pm

Red Grange (9/4/36 - 11/28/36) Sinclair, NBC, 2t (Fri, 10:30 pm; Sat 7 pm), 15m
(9/22/38 - 11/26/38) Pure Oil Co., CBS, 2t (Thu & Sat), 15m, 6 pm
(9/28/40 - 11/30/40) Mut, Sat, 15m, 6:45 pm

Red Hook 31 (with Woody and Virginia Klose) (1947 - 48) Mut, 5t, 15m

2 **Red Horse Ranch** (1935) Syn

1 **Red McKenzie** (with Jerry Shields Orchestra) (1936) also World transcription

5 **Red Nichols and His Five Pennies** (1935) film sound track, MacGregor transcriptions

12 **Red Nichols Show, The** (1951) Syn

Red Norvo (NBC) (1935)
(5/13/39 - 7/23/39) Mut, Sat, 45m, 5 pm

1 **Red Norvo Sextet** (World transcription)

3 **Red Norvo Trio** (Standard transcriptions)

1 **Red River Dave** (12/20/38 - 4/15/44) Mut, 15m; regional; often sponsored by Bell & Co.
12/20/38 - 11/7/39, Tue, 12 noon
11/14/39 - 5/14/40, Bell Ans., 2t
1940 - 41, Sat
10/30/43 - 4/15/44, Sat, 9:30 am

15 **Red Ryder** (5/7/42 - 49) Mut
5/20/42 - 9/9/42, Wed, 30m, 8:30 pm; started in 2/3/42 on West coast (Bl; Tue, Thu, Sat) and continued through the 40s; mostly a west coast show
1948 - 49, 2t, 7:30 pm

Red Seal Program (9/4/29 - 12/17/29) McFadden Pub., CBS, Wed, 9 pm

163 **Red Skelton** (1/7/39 - 5/26/53)
1/7/39 - 12/20/39 (Avalon Time) NBC, Sat, 7 pm; 8:30 pm as of 3/11/39; Wed, 8:30 pm as of 9/27/39; also with Red Foley who was replaced by Curt Massey as of 7/1/39
9/9/47 - 6/1/48, Raleigh, NBC, Tue, 10:30 pm (in Army from 6/13/44 - 12/4/45; see Hildegarde)
9/3/48 - 5/20/49, Raleigh, NBC, Fri
10/2/49 - 6/25/50; 10/1/50 - 6/24/51, Tide, CBS, Sun, 8:30 pm
10/3/51 - 6/25/52, Norge, CBS, Wed, 9 pm
9/16/52 - 5/26/53, Multi, NBC, Tue, 8:30 pm (see individual program titles)

5 **Red Skelton Program, The** (see Red Skelton)

71 **Red Skelton Show, The** (see Red Skelton)

Red Trails (written by Stewart Sterling; with Victor McLaglen)
(2/21/35 - 7/6/35) American Tobacco Co., Bl
2/21/35 - 3/28/35, Thu, 8:30 pm
4/2/35 - 7/6/35, Tue, 9 pm

1 **Red, White and Blues** (7/8/89) WNYC-FM

Redbook Drama (5/26/32 - 11/3/32) Redbook Magazine, 15m

18 **Redd Harper's Hollywood Roundup** (1951) AFRS

Redhead, The (with Mary McCarty and Dick Van Patton) (1/24/52 - 3/13/52) ABC, Thu, 8 pm

1 **Reeducation Of Cecil Binks, The** (3/21/54) CBS

6 **Reflections** (Syn)

5 **Reflections By Starlight** (12/60 - 12/67) Syn

Reflections In Rhythm
(5/24/41 - 6/13/42) NBC, Sat

1 **Reflections On A President** (1/23/73) WNET-TV

Refreshment Time (also see Morton Downey) (10/30/35 - 4/22/36) (with Ray Noble) Coca-Cola, CBS, Wed, 9:30 pm also Coca-Cola, 5t, 30m

8 **Refreshment Time With Singin' Sam** (Syn)

Reg'lar Fellers (with Dick Van Patton and Dickie Monahan) (6/8/41 - 8/31/41) Jell-O, NBC, Sun, 7 pm (partial summer replacement for Jack Benny)

1 **Regards To America** (1945)

1 **Registration Day Program** (10/16/40) Mut

Reis and Dunn (10/6/31 - 34) CBS, 6t/3t, 15m; first 3 weeks on Tue, sponsored by Icyeast Corp.

Relaxation In Music (with Jean Tighe and Bob Barry) (1944) Mut, sponsored by Miss Swank Slips

Relay Quiz (Norge) 15m

1 **Released American Prisoners** (4/28/45) WOR

1 **Releasing Frozen Bank Deposits** (1935)

1 **Religion and The New World** (with Dr. Joseph Sisoo) (10/9/39 - 6/3/40; 10/7/40 - 3/31/41; 10/13/41- 3/30/42) Bl, Mon, 15m, 1:30 pm

Religion In Life (7/10/39 - 10/2/39) NBC, Mon, 15m, 12:30 pm

Religion In The News (with Dr. Walter W. Van Kirk) (1933 - 4/15/50) NBC, Sat, 15m (summer breaks)

Remarkable Miss Tuttle, The (with Edna May Oliver; also called The Private Life Of Josephine Tuttle) (7/5/42 - 8/30/42) Jell-O, NBC, Sun, 7 pm (partial summer replacement for Jack Benny)

1 **Rembrandt** (1936) Air trailer

33 **Remember** (with Fred MacMurray; Robert Young; Roddy McDowell) AFRS, 15m

Remember (with Ted Steele)
(2/7/43 - 5/9/43) Mut, Sun, 9:30 pm

1 **Remember December 7th** (12/7/42) Syn

Remember With Tiny Fairbanks
(11/28/53 - 3/6/54) Grand Duchess Steaks, Mut, Sat, 15m

1 **Reminiscenses Of My Career** (12/6/39) BBC

13 **Reminiscenses Of Victor Herbert**
(Pre-war) Syn

Reminiscin' With Singin' Sam (see Singin' Sam)

1 **Remodel For Veterans** (1946) Syn

1 **Remote Control** (1930) film sound track

1 **Rendezvous In Paris, A** (1947) Syn

Rendezvous Musical (with Jane Williams and Phil Duey; then Irene Beasley)
(9/18/35 - 4/8/36) Life Savers, Bl, Wed, 8 pm

1 **Rendezvous With Destiny** (NBC)

Rendezvous With Ramona (see Ramona)

Rendezvous With Romance (with D'Artega) ABC (1946)

1 **Rendezvous With Ross** (Syn)

3 **Renfrew Of The Mounted** (with House Jameson) (3/10/36 - 10/19/40)
3/10/36 - 2/26/37, Wonder Bread, CBS, 3t (Tue, Fri, Sat), 15m, 6:45 pm; 4t as of 3/30/36; 5t as of 4/13/36
1937 - 38, Wonder Bread, Bl, 5t, 15m
12/24/38 - 10/19/40, Sus, Bl, Sat, 30m, 6:30 pm

Renfro Valley Country Store (see Renfro Valley Folks)

1 **Renfro Valley Folks** (Renfro Barn Dance; Renfro Gatherin') (2/19/38 - 12/28/51) continued mostly local and regional (WLW)
2/19/38 - 9/24/38, Allis Chalmers, Mut, Sat
8/5/40 - 4/28/41, Big Ben's Tobacco, NBC, Mon
6/30/41 - 2/6/42, Sus, CBS, 5t, 15m, 3:30 pm
also 9/13/41 - 12/27/41, Brown & Williamson, Bl, Sat, 8:30 pm
2/2/43 - 7/30/44, Ballard & Ballard, CBS, 4t, 15m
8/2/44 - 1/23/49, CBS, 5t (Wed- Sun)
also 1946 - 47, Sus, Mut, Sat, 30m, 9:30 am (not in New York)
1/1/51 - 12/28/51 (Renfro Valley Country Store) General Foods, CBS, 5t, 15m

2 **Repertory Theatre Of The Air, The** (5/30/37, 4/3/38) Mut

1 **Report Card** (3/24/48) CBS

1 **Report From Guam** (2/24/45) Mut

1 **Report From Guam On The A-Bomb Drop** (8/7/45) CBS

31 **Report From Israel** (12/1/48 - 1/10/50) WMCA

2 **Report From Kwajalein** (2/23/44, 1/30/46) Mut

3 **Report From Nuremburg** (11/20/45, 11/30/45, 10/46) Mut

1 **Report From Prague** (9/23/38) Czechoslovakia

1 **Report From Rome** (1944) Mut

1 **Report From Stockholm** (5/4/45) Mut

1 **Report From The Flight Control Room Of A Typhoon Bomber Wing** (6/10/44) BBC

1 **Report From The North Pole** (12/21/58) CBS

1 **Report From The Philippines** (10/20/44) Mut

1 **Report From The San Francisco Conference** (6/26/45) Mut

1 **Report From Tokyo** (1942) Syn

Report On America (9/3/49 - 9/30/49) NBC, 15m

1 **Report On General Yamashita Interview** (12/2/45) Mut

1 **Report On Human Rights** (12/10/52) U.N. Radio/WOR

1 **Report On Hunger** (4/18/46) CBS

1 **Report On Jobs Program** (9/26/46) CBS

1 **Report On Polio** (9/30/56) Syn

Report On Rationing (2/14/43 - 2/13/44) NBC, Sun, 15m, 3 pm

1 **Report On The Death Of The Rosenbergs** (6/19/53) WOR

1 **Report On The Explosion Of The Atom Bomb** (6/30/46) CBS

1 **Report On The First Atomic Bomb Test On Bikini Atoll** (6/29/46) ABC

1 **Report On The Freedom Rally** (5/5/49) CBS

1 **Report On The Macquis** (8/44) CBS

6 **Report To The Nation, A** (12/7/40 - 12/1/45) CBS
12/7/40 - 6/28/41, Electric Companies, Sat, 6 pm
6/30/40 - 7/28/40, Electric Companies, Mon, 8 pm
8/5/41 - 6/2/42, Electric Companies, Tue, 9:30 pm
6/14/42 - 7/19/42, Sun, 10:30 pm
7/31/42 - 10/23/42, Fri, 7:30 pm
10/25/42 - 2/28/43, Electric Companies, Sun, 10:30 pm
6/15/43 - 4/26/44, Electric Companies, Tue, 9:30 pm
5/3/44 - 7/19/44, Electric Companies, Wed, 10:30 pm
9/16/44 - 6/9/45; 9/14/45 - 12/1/45, Continental Can, Sat, 1:30 pm; 1:45 pm as of 9/15/45
also 11/9/50, CBS

Report To The People (1948) ABC, 15m; with Edward Arnold

4 **Report To The People On The Race For Air Power, A** (1947) Syn

1 **Report To You, A** (1/14/49) Syn

1 **Report Uncensored** (8/11/47) WBBM

1 **Reporter Remembers, A** (2/24/46) BBC

1 **Reporter Summing Up: Debriefing, A** (11/14/77) CBS

Reporter's Roundup (9/27/51 - 58+) Mut, various days and times
also 1957, KVI

1 **Reports Of Stalin's Death** (3/6/53) CBS

1 **Representative Newt Gingrich** (4/7/95) C-SPAN

Republic Music Almanac (15m)

1 **Republican Convention Acceptance Speeches** (8/23/72) pool feed

5 **Republican Convention Coverage** (6/21/48 - 6/25/48) Mut

3 **Republican National Convention** (7/7/52, 1960, 8/23/84)

1 **Republican Paid Political Announcement** (11/70) NBC-TV

1 **Republican Party Program** (10/19/36) WMBQ

1 **Republican Party Response** (2/17/93) pool feed

1 **Republican Party Response To The State Of The Union Address** (1/15/94) pool feed

1 **Republican Presidential Candidate Forum** (2/20/80) PBS-TV

1 **Republican Presidential Candidates Debate, The** (1/5/80) PBS-TV

2 **Republican Presidential Debate** (2/14/88, 2/19/88) CNN, PBS-TV

1 **Republican Radio Rally** (1/5/48) Mut

Request Of The Troops (see Your America)

3 **Request Performance** (10/7/45 - 4/21/46) Campbell, CBS, Sun, 9 pm
(11/5/47 - 11/26/47) Mut, Wed, 9:30 pm

Reserved For Garroway (see Dave Garroway)

Reserved For You (Air Force Dance Band) 15m

2 **Results Inc.** (with Lloyd Nolan and Claire Trevor) (10/7/44 - 12/30/44) Sus, Mut, Sat

1 **Return Engagement** (7/11/48 - 9/12/48) CBS, Sun, 2 pm; 1 pm as of 8/22/48

1 **Return Of Atlantis, The** (5/8/89) CBS-TV

2 **Return Of Inspector Scott, The** (Syn)

1 **Return Of Mr. Grimsby, The** (1939) Syn

Return Of Nick Carter, The (see Nick Carter)

1 **Return To Christmas Island** (Syn)

1 **Return To Duty** (9/29/45) Mut

1 **Return To Studio 1A** (1970) ABC

1 **Return To The Moon The Flight Of Apollo 12** (11/13/69) CBS-TV

1 **Return To The Philippines** (10/20/44) CBS

Reuben, Reuben (12/6/52 - 3/21/53) NBC, Sat, 8:30 pm

Reunion (with Milo Boulton, Edwin C. Hill) (3/14/47 - 10/5/47) Mut, Sun, 3 pm

1 **Reunion Of The Crew Of The "Siberia," A** (9/27/37) WOR

Reunion, USA (5/21/45 - 8/20/45) Bl, Mon, 10:30 pm

1 **Reveille Record** (7/9/42)

Reveille Round-Up (see Louise Massey)

1 **Reveille With Beverly** (1943) film sound track

2 **Revelers, The** (4/18/38 - 8/28/40) Boned Chicken, NBC, 3t, 15m, 6:15 pm; Wed & Fri, 15m, 7:30 pm as of 7/13/38; on locally in New York earlier; also on Blue Revere All Star, also Thesaurus transcriptions

1 **Reverend Jesse Jackson** (7/19/88) C-SPAN

Reverend Matthews (15m)

1 **Review Of The War** (9/2/40) Mut

Revival Time (12/20/53 - 58+) ABC, Sun, 10:30 pm

Revlon Theater (see Gertrude Lawrence)

Revolving Stage (10/17/32 - 9/23/35) Sus, NBC, Mon, 60m, 2 pm

Revue (with Andy Russell and Marion Hutton) (3/11/48 - 11/4/48) Revere, Mut, 15m; 25m as of 8/12/48 pm (see Jo Stafford after 11/4/48)

Revue de Paree (see Broadway Merry-Go-Round)

2 **Revue Musicale (The Muriel Halle Show)** (2/12/50, 2/19/50) WHDH

Revuers, The (with Bob Schakleton; Paul La Valle Orchestra)
(4/30/40 -10/6/40) Bl
4/30/40 - 8/6/40, Tue, 9:30 pm
8/25/40 - 10/6/40, Sun, 4: 30 pm

Rex Allen (also with Mary Ellen Kaye)
(1950 - 52) Phillips, CBS (Regional)
1950 - 51, Fri, 10 pm
1951- 52, Mon, 10:30 pm

Rex Coal Mountaineers
(3/2/31 - 6/25/32) GE Refrigerators, NBC, 5t, 15m

Rex Koury (10/29/49 - 2/4/50) ABC, Sat, 15m, 7 pm

Rex Maupin's Orchestra
(1/5/41 - 9/16/48) Bl/ABC, various days and times including:
1/5/41 - 9/7/41, Sun, 15m, 12 noon
also 1/18/41 - 3/29/41, Sat, 5 pm
2/22/41 - 11/14/42 (The Band Played On), Bl, Sat, 10:30 am; 11 am as of 4/5/41
also 8/18/41 - 9/8/41, Mon, 7:30 pm
9/28/47 - 10/19/47, Sun, 7 pm
1/31/48 - 4/3/48, ABC, Sat, 9 am
7/1/48 - 9/16/48, ABC, Thu, 7:30 pm
also 8/8/48 - 9/12/48 (Rex Maupin's Musicale) ABC, Sun, 7 pm

Rex Saunders (see The Private File Of Rex Saunders)

Rex Stewart and His Orchestra (1958)

1 **Rexall Magic Hour** (with Victor Arden Orchestra, Frank Parker) (1935) Rexall, 15m

4 **Rexall One Cent Sale** (1939) Syn

Rexall Radio Party (with Andy Sannella Orchestra) (2/7/32 - 5/1/32) Rexall, NBC, Sun, 15m, 7: 15 pm

Rexall Summer Show (7/6/45 - 9/26/48) Rexall
7/6/45 - 9/7/45 (with Roy Bargy and Ray Bolger), United Drug, CBS, Fri, 10 pm
7/2/47 - 9/24/47, Rexall Drugs, NBC, Wed, 10:30 pm
5/30/48 - 9/26/48 (with Pat O'Brien and Virginia Bruce) NBC, Sun, 7:30 pm; (led to Phil Harris and Alice Faye Show)

8 **Rexall's Parade Of Stars** (with Ken Murray and/or Donald Voorhees; Glen Gray) (1936 - 42) Rexall, 15m, Syn

RFD #1 (see Irene Beasley)

24 **RFD America** (with Ed Bottcher)
(10/29/47 - 9/24/49)
10/29/47 - 11/26/47, Mut, Wed, 9:30 pm
12/4/47 - 4/22/48, Sus, Mut, Thu, 9:30 pm
7/4/48 - 9/26/48, Ford, NBC, Sun, 8:30 pm (summer replacement of Fred Allen)
1/8/49 - 9/24/49, Sus, NBC, Sat, 2:30 pm

Rhapsody For Strings (12/22/45 - 2/16/46) Mut, Sat, 8:30 pm

4 **Rhapsody In Rhythm** (with Jan Savitt and Connie Haines) (1936) with Charles W. Hamp and The Rhythm Rascals, Syn
(6/16/46 - 9/15/46) Old Gold, CBS, Sun, 10:30 pm (summer replacement of Meet Me At Parky's)
(6/11/47 - 9/17/47, (with Johnny Johnston and Peggy Lee) Old Gold, CBS, Wed

1 **Rhubarb Red and His Rubes** (MacGregor transcription)

1 **Rhumba Rhythms and Tango Tunes**

Rhyme and Rhythm Club (from Chicago; regional) (4/4/41 - 10/10/41) NBC, Fri

Rhymes and Romance with Retta Revell
(7/24/38 - 8/14/38) Bl, Syn, 11:45 am, 15m

Rhymes For Reverie (15m) (1949)

Rhyming Minstrel, The (with Don Ross)
(4/4/38 - 7/1/38) Bosco, Mut, 3t, 15m, 12 noon

Rhythm and Blues On Parade (with Willie Bryant) (4/14/55 - 10/27/55) ABC, Thu, 9:30 pm

1 **Rhythm and Rhyme** (with Jack Arthur and Pauline Alpert) (10/20/39) Mut

Rhythm At Eight (with Ethel Merman, Johnny Green Orchestra)
(5/5/35 - 9/22/35) Lysol, CBS, Sun, 8 pm (possibly Buddy Clark, CBS, Mon) (with Al Goodman)

Rhythm Boys (4/1/35 - 5/6/35) Bl, Mon, 15m, 5:15 pm
(2/18/36 - 12/3/36) Fels Naphtha, CBS, 2t, 25m

4 **Rhythm Five, The** (Lang-Worth transcriptions)

10 **Rhythm Makers Orchestra** (1935) Thesaurus transcriptions

10 **Rhythm Makers, The** (1935, 1937) Thesaurus transcriptions

1 **Rhythm On The Range** (1936) Air trailer

1 **Rhythm On The River** (1940) Air trailer

1 **Rhythm On The Road** (with Bob Dixon and Elliott Lawrence Orchestra)
(7/4/54 - 9/26/54; 6/12/55 - 9/4/55) Amoco, CBS, 60m, 4:30 pm; 4 pm as of 6/12/55

Rhythm Road (with Johnny Morgan; Ann Thomas; Jimmy Lytell Orchestra)
(4/5/43 - 8/23/43) Bl, Mon, 25m, 10:35 pm; called Johnny Morgan Show as of 8/2/43

Rhythm Romance (1939)

Rhythm Serenade (5/18/40 - 7/6/40) CBS, Sat, 10:30 am

1 **Rhythm Symphony, The** (NBC)

Rhythm Time With Rosa Rio

1 **Rhythm Workshop, The**

1 **Rhythm `N Romance**

Rhythmaires and Jimmy Farell
(8/14/36 - 10/23/36) CBS (Midwest), Fri, 15m

1 **Rhythmaires, The** (8/16/38 - 10/11/41) 15m
8/16/38 - 11/21/39, CBS, Tue, 11 am
also 5/2/39 - 7/4/39, CBS, Tue, 5:15 pm
8/9/41 - 10/11/41, NBC, Sat, 7:30 pm
(1942) NBC (KYW, Philadelphia), 15m

Rhythmic Concert (with Paul Whiteman)
(1932 - 3/5/33) Bl, Sun, 6:30 pm

1 **Rhythmic Melodies** (see Irving Miller)

Rhythms By Ricardo (5/11/40 - 9/28/40) Bl, Sat, 5:30 pm
(6/29/41 - 9/28/41) Bl, Sun, 5:30 pm

Rich Man's Darling (2/17/36 - 3/26/37) Affiliated Products, CBS, 5t, 15m, 12:45 pm; replaced by Our Gal Sunday

Richard Aurant (CBS) (1952 - 1953)

1 **Richard C. Hottelet Reporting From A Bomber Over France**

105 **Richard Diamond, Private Detective** (with Dick Powell) (4/24/49 - 9/20/53)
4/24/49 - 6/26/49, Sus, NBC, Sun, 7 pm
7/2/49 - 12/31/49, Sus, NBC, Sat
1/8/50 - 3/26/50, Sus, NBC, Sun, 5 pm
4/5/50 - 8/30/50, Rexall, NBC, Wed, 10 pm
9/6/50 - 12/6/50, Rexall, NBC, Sat, 8:30 pm
1/5/51 - 6/29/51, Camel, ABC, Fri, 8 pm
10/5/51 - 6/27/52, Rexall, ABC, Fri, 8 pm
5/31/53 - 9/20/53 (repeats of 1950 series) Rexall, ABC, Sun, 7:30 pm (summer replacement for Amos 'n' Andy)

Richard Dyer-Bennett (1941) 11/18/41, NBC, Thu, 15m, 1 pm (not in New York)

1 **Richard Farina Long Time Coming, Long Time Gone**

Richard Harkness (1944 - 53) NBC; sponsored by Pure Oil from 1948

Richard Hayes (Take 30) (1954 - 56) Sus, ABC, Tue (not in New York)
also 1955 - 56, ABC, Sun, 15m & CBS, Sat

Richard Himber (1938) NBC, 15m
(3/5/40 - 6/6/40) Bl, 2t, 15m, 6:30 pm

7 **Richard Himber and His Orchestra**

Richard Hottelet (7/7/47 - 9/26/47) CBS

Richard Kent (Traveling Chef)
(11/28/39 - 3/19/42) Sus, Bl, 15m 11/28/39 - 5/28/40, Tue
6/15/40 - 3/19/42, 2t (Thu & Fri)

Richard Lawless (with Kevin McCarthy)
(6/23/46 - 9/22/46) CBS, Sun, 8 pm

Richard Leibert (see Dick Leibert)

Richard Leibert At The Organ (see Dick Leibert)

Richard Leibert, Organist (11/18/41) (see Dick Liebert)

Richard Leibert-Pipe Organ (see Dick Leibert)

1 **Richard Maltby and His Orchestra** (12/31/58) CBS

3 **Richard Maxwell** (5/28/34 - 5/17/46) 15m (see also A Friend In Deed)
5/28/34 - 1/21/35, Bl, Mon, 2:45 pm
4/21/36 - 5/25/40, CBS, various days, early morning
6/30/41 - 10/10/41, CBS, 5t, 4 pm
9/17/45 - 5/17/46 (Hymns You Love), Serutan, Mut, 5t

1 **Richard Nixon "Checkers Speech"** (9/23/52) CBS

Richard Rendell (9/27/54 - 2/11/55) ABC, 5t, 15m, 10:15 pm

Richfield Reporter, The (8/1/32 - 5/1/47) Richfield Oil, NBC - Pacific/ABC - Pacific

Richman Brothers Program (with Louis Silvers Orchestra, Sylvia Froos and Victor Moore) (3/8/32 - 6/3/32) Richman Brothers Clothing, CBS, 2t, 15m, 7:30 pm

1 **Riding High** (with Ray Sinatra Orchestra) (4/1/37 - 6/24/37) Cycle Trades, Bl, Thu, 15m, 7:15 pm
also (1943) film sound track

Right Down Your Alley (with Bill Slater) (3/31/46 - 10/6/46) Hastings Mfg. Co. Bl, Sun, 4:30 pm

Right Thing To Do, The (with Emily Post) (10/3/38 - 4/25/39) Tangee Lipstick, NBC, Mon. 7:30 pm; Tue, 15m, 7:45 pm as of 1/3/39

7 **Right To Happiness, The** (10/16/39 - 11/25/60) Procter & Gamble (Crisco, Ivory), 5t, 15m
10/16/39 - 1/19/40, Bl, 10:15 am
1/22/40 - 12/26/41 , CBS, 1:30 pm
12/28/41 - 11/25/60, NBC, 11:15 am; Sus after 12/29/59

1 **Right To Live, The** (5/18/47) NBC

1 **Right You Are** (9/19/52) CBS

Riley and Farley (6/3/36 - 6/10/36) NBC, Wed, 15m, 2:45 pm

Rin-Tin-Tin (with Francis X. Bushman and Lee Duncan) (1930 - 12/25/55)
1930 - 3/28/31, Ken-L Ration, Bl, Sat, 15m, 8:15 pm
4/2/31 - 6/8/33, Ken-L Ration, Bl, Thu, 15m, 8:15 pm (with Junior McLain and Don Ameche)
10/15/33 - 5/20/34, Ken-L Ration, CBS, Sun, 15m
1/2/55 - 12/25/55, Milk Bone, Mut, Sun, 5 pm

Rinso Talkie Time (see Talkie Picture Time)

1 **Rio Rhythms** (1/13/51) WMAQ

1 **Rio Rita** (1941) Air trailer

1 **Riot Squad** (Post-war) Syn

2 **Rip Lawson, Adventurer** (Post-war) Syn, 15m

Rip Van Winkle (15m) with Walter Huston

Ripley's Believe It Or Not (see Believe It Or Not)

Rippling Rhythm Revue (with Shep Fields, Frank Parker and The Three Canovas; Bob Hope joined the cast in May) (1/3/37 - 9/26/37) Woodbury, Bl, Sun, 9:15 pm (see also Bob Hope)

1 **Rise and Recite** (3/29/39) Mut

1 **Rise and Shine** (1941) film sound track

1 **Rise Stevens Show, The** (7/2/45 - 9/3/45) NBC, Mon, 9:30 pm

Rising Musical Stars (with Alexander Smallens Orchestra and Richard Gordon) (10/17/37 - 4/10/38) Sealtest, NBC, Sun, 10 pm

River Boat Revels (with Kay Carlisle and Minnie Pearl) (1941) NBC

2 **Riverside Rancho** (11/50) AFRS

1 **RKO Bushwick Theatre Program** (1/7/37) WCNW

RKO Hour (with Leo Reisman) (1929 - 30) NBC, Tue, 60m, 10:30 pm

RKO Radio Pictures Presents (ABC) (1946)

RKO Theater (with William Hanley) (1930 - 4/22/32) RKO, NBC, Fri, 10:30 pm

Road Ahead, The (with Clifton Fadiman) (5/2/45 - 6/13/45) Bl, Wed, 9 pm

34 **Road Of Life, The** (9/13/37 - 1/2/59) Procter & Gamble (Chipso, Duz), 5t, 15m
9/13/37 - 6/18/54, NBC; often on CBS including:
12/29/52 - 1/2/59, CBS; last sponsored show on 11/20/58

Road Show (1/9/54 - 9/25/54) Multi, NBC, Sat, 3 hours, 2 pm

Road To Danger, The (with Curley Bradley and Clarence Hartzell) (11/6/42 - 3/4/45) Sus, NBC
11/6/42 - 11/26/43, Fri, 11:30 pm
12/4/44 - 3/4/45, Sat, 10 am

1 **Road To Glory, The** (1939) Air trailer

1 **Road To Peace, The** (10/22/51) U.N. Radio

1 **Road To Rio, The** (1947) Air trailer

Road To Romany (with Alexander Kirilloff Orchestra)
(11/12/32 - 12/31/32) NBC, Sun, 1 pm (with Genia Fonariova)
(3/4/34 - 8/26/34) NBC, Sun, 1 pm
(3/24/35 - 4/19/36) NBC, Sun, 1 pm

1 **Road To Singapore, The** (1940) Air trailer

1 **Road To The White House, The** (12/20/91) C-SPAN

2 **Road To Utopia, The** (1946) Air trailer, film sound track

2 **Road To Zanzibar, The** (1941) Air trailer, film sound track

1 **Roads Rule The World** (1939) Syn

Roadways Of Romance (see Jerry Cooper)

Robert Allen (9/19/48 - 11/20/49) Mut, Sun, 15m, 8:45 pm

Robert Arden (1940 - 1942)

Robert Benchley (also with Artie Shaw; with Jimmy Durante from 10/3/39) (11/20/38 - 11/14/39) (also called Melody and Madness; Old Gold Program) Old Gold
11/20/38 - 5/14/39, CBS, Sun, 10 pm
5/23/39 - 11/14/39, Bl, Tue, 9 pm

1 **Robert Benchley Special Audition** (KNX)

1 **Robert Best** (9/12/42) German Overseas Service

Robert Burns Panatella Program (see Burns and Allen; Guy Lombardo)

1 **Robert C. Sprague** (10/22/50)

Robert Denton (1944)

1 **Robert Francis Kennedy, A Memorial** (1968) Syn

2 **Robert F. Hurleigh News** (1949 - 56+) Sus, Miller
(11/30/50, 12/20/50)
(1951- 52), Mut

1 **Robert Kennedy**

1 **Robert Kennedy Assassination, The** (6/5/68) Mut, NBC, CBS-TV

1 **Robert MacNeil Report, The** (4/13/76) PBS-TV

2 **Robert Maxwell-Harpist** (MacGregor transcriptions)

Robert McCormick (1947 - 49) NBC

Robert Merrill Show, The (also with Leopold Spitalny Orchestra) (12/2/45 - 3/24/46) RCA, NBC, Sun, 12:30 pm (for shows starting 6/9/46 see Music America Loves Best)

2 **Robert Montgomery Dramatic Recitations** (World transcriptions)

Robert Montgomery Speaking (11/10/49 - 7/4/52) Lee Hats, 15m
11/10/49 - 6/8/50; 8/24/50 - 6/7/51, ABC, Thu, 9:45 pm
2/4/52 - 7/4/52, NBC, 5t, 10:30 pm

5 **Robert Q. Lewis Show, The** (4/7/45 - 59) various days and times, some overlapping, including:
4/7/45 - 7/7/45, NBC, Sat, 7:30 pm
8/6/45 - 12/29/45 (with Jack Arthur), NBC, 5t, 8 am
6/6/47 - 7/25/47, CBS, Fri, 8:30 pm (summer replacement of Adventures Of The Thin Man)
7/7/47 - 8/29/47, CBS, 5t, 30m, 7 pm
4/26/48 - 7/2/48, CBS, 5t, 30m, 5 pm
7/9/48 - 8/16/48, CBS, 5t, 7 pm (summer replacement for Beulah and Jack Smith)
9/26/48 - 12/12/48, CBS, Sun, 5 pm
1/10/49 - 7/29/49, CBS, 5t
1/20/50 - 7/4/50 (The Show Goes On), Sus, CBS, Fri, 60m, 8 pm
5/31/50 - 10/4/50 (ABC's Of Music) Chesterfield, CBS, Wed, 9:30 pm (summer replacement for Bing Crosby)
8/27/51 - 9/27/52 (Waxworks) CBS, 3t (Mon, Tue, Thu), 30m, 10:30 pm; 4t including Saturday as of 10/13/51
11/22/52 - 5/2/53 (Waxworks) CBS, Sat, 30m, 15m, 10:45 pm

Robert Q. Lewis Show, The (continued)
6/7/53 - 8/30/53, Webster Chicago Corp., CBS, Sun, 10 pm
1/9/54 - 59, Multi, CBS, Sat, 60m
also (1946 - 58) CBS, 5t

Robert Q. Lewis' Little Show (see The Robert Q. Lewis Show)

1 **Robert S. Henry** (1941) Syn

Robert Seagrist (1949)

Robert Shaw Chorale (6/6/48 - 4/9/50) Sun
6/6/48 - 9/26/48, NBC, 8 pm (summer replacement for Charlie McCarthy)
3/19/50 - 4/9/50, ABC, 7 pm

Robert St. John (1941; 1/4/43 - 5/28/43; 2/7/44 - 9/27/46) NBC, sponsored by American Bakeries and South Spring Bed Co.

1 **Robert Stewart** (4/14/40 - 6/9/40) NBC, Mut, Sun, 15m, 10:30 am (not in New York)

1 **Robert Taylor Story, The** (1951) Air trailer

3 **Robert Trout News** (1/23/37 - 1953) CBS, 15m; started on CBS in 1932; still active in 1992
1/17/37 - 4/18/37, Sun, 1:45 pm
9/5/38 - 5/12/39, 5t
4/10/44 -10/6/44 (Headlines and History), 5t
4/1/46 - 9/19/47, Campbell
1952 - 53 (Robert Trout and Cedric Adams), Ford, CBS

Robert Trout and The News Until Now (see Robert Trout News)

1 **Robert Trout News (Edwin C. Hill and The Human Side Of The News)** (1/23/41) CBS

Robert Trout With The News Until Now (see Robert Trout News)

1 **Robert Vogler** (6/8/51) CBS

1 **Roberta** (1935) Air trailer

Robin Hood Dell Concert (7/28/39 - 8/11/39) Bl, Fri, 9:30 pm

1 **Robin Morgan Show, The** (9/27/46; 5/3/47 - 1/3/48; 6/5/48 - 7/10/48) Mut, Sat, 15m, 10:15 am

Robinson Crusoe Jr. (with Lester Jay) (10/2/34 - 2/2/35) Bureau Of Milk, CBS, 4t, 15m

Rochester Civic Orchestra (1929 - 3/25/47) Bl
1929 - 7/13/31, Stromberg-Carlsen, Mon
10/17/33 - 4/13/42, Sus, Mon, Tue and/or Wed, 30 - 60m
1/7/47 - 3/25/47, CBS, Tue, 11:30 pm

Rochester Philharmonic Orchestra (often other orchestras connected with Eastman University)
(1935 - 2/18/42) Sus, Bl
1935 - 5/1/41, Thu, 30 - 60m
10/29/41 - 2/18/42 (with Conrad Thibault, Vivian Della Chiesa), Wed, 30m

23 **Rock 'n' Roll Dance Party** (with Joe Williams; Count Basie Orchestra) (4/7/55 - 9/18/56) CBS
4/7/55 - 7/14/55, Sat, 9 pm
3/24/56 - 7/7/56, Sat
7/17/56 - 9/18/56, Tue, 8:30 pm

Rock and Stock Audition, The (with Frances Stock and Jack Rock) 15m

Rocking Horse Rhythms (see Hookey Hall)

13 **Rocky Fortune** (with Frank Sinatra) (10/6/53 - 3/30/54) Sus, NBC, Tue, 9:30 pm

Rocky Gordon (6/17/40 -10/5/40) Bl, 5t, 15m, 5 pm

29 **Rocky Jordan** (1/8/45 - 8/22/51)
1/8/45 - 47 (see A Man Named Jordan)
10/31/48 - 9/10/50 (with Jack Moyles), Del Monte, CBS - Pacific, Sun (98 shows broadcast)
6/27/51 - 8/29/51 (with George Raft), CBS, Wed, 8 pm (summer replacement for Mr. Chameleon)

1 **Rocky Mountaineers, The** (10/25/36) WMBQ

Rod and Gun Club (9/7/50 - 2/6/55) Mut
9/7/50 - 9/25/52, Pal Blades, Thu, 25m
10/2/52 - 3/5/53, Multi, Thu, 25m
9/27/53 - 2/6/55, Multi, Sun

3 **Rod Brown Of The Rocket Rangers** (8/53) CBS-TV

Rodriguez and Sutherland (1944)

Roger Allen - Criminal Lawyer (see Attorney For The Defense)

4 **Roger Kilgore, Public Defender** (with Santos Ortega and Staats Cosworth) (4/18/48 - 10/12/48) Mut, Tue, 7 pm

1 **Roger Wolfe Kahn and His Orchestra** (1931) Vita Ray Facial Cream, 15m

Rogers Musical Trio (12/7/31 - 2/15/32) Rogers Brushing Lacquer, Bl, Mon, 15m, 11:30 am

24 **Rogers Of The Gazette** (with Will Rogers, Jr.) (5/8/53; 6/10/53 - 1/20/54) CBS, Wed (33 shows broadcast)

15 **Rogue's Gallery** (6/23/45 - 11/21/51)
6/23/45 - 9/17/45, Fitch, Sun, 7:30 pm (summer replacement for Fitch Bandwagon) (also called Bandwagon Mysteries)
9/27/45 - 6/20/46 (with Dick Powell), Fitch, Mut, Thu, 8:30 pm
6/23/46 - 9/22/46, Fitch, NBC, Sun, 7:30 pm (summer replacement for Fitch Bandwagon)
6/8/47 - 9/28/47 (with Barry Sullivan) Fitch, NBC, Sun, 7:30 pm (summer replacement for Fitch Bandwagon)
11/29/50 - 11/21/51 (with Paul Stewart), Sus, ABC, Wed, 9 pm

Roll Call (with Burgess Meredith) (7/1/48 - 7/29/48) NBC, Thu, 8 pm

1 **Roll Call Of The Nation, The** (1942) Syn

Roller Derby (11/21/49 - 12/19/49) ABC, Mon, 10:30 pm

Roma News (Mut) (1942)

Roma Wine Show (see Charles Ruggles)

130 **Romance** (4/19/43 - 1/5/57) CBS
4/19/43 - 11/22/43, Sus, Mon
11/30/43 - 6/20/44, Sus, Tue
7/4/44 - 8/27/46, Colgate, Tue (Theater Of Romance)
10/2/46 - 12/11/46 (Theater Of Romance), Sus, Wed, 5:30 pm
4/23/47 - 6/25/47, Sus, Wed, 7:30 pm
6/30/47 - 7/21/47, Sus, Mon, 10 pm
10/18/47 - 12/27/47, Sus, Sat, 7:30 pm
2/4/48 - 3/17/48, Sus, Wed, 9:30 pm
7/5/48 - 7/26/48, Sus, Mon, 10:30 pm
8/6/48 - 8/20/48, Sus, Fri, 8:30 pm
10/23/48 - 2/5/49, Sus, Sat, 10:30 pm
6/20/50 - 8/8/50, Wrigley, Tue, 9 pm (summer replacement for Life With Luigi)
1/6/51 - 1/13/51, Sat
7/2/51 - 8/20/51, Sus, Mon, 9 pm
9/8/51 - 9/29/51, Sus, Sat
12/23/51 - 1/6/52, Sus, Sun
6/2/52 - 9/1/52, Sus; Lux from
6/2/52 - 6/30/52, Mon
9/4/52 - 1/8/53, Jergens, Thu (also called Jergens Hollywood Playhouse / Playhouse Of Romance)
6/4/53 - 12/26/53; 5/22/54 - 1/5/57, Sus, Thu; Sat from 9/12/53, 9 pm

Romance and Melody (with Jules Landin) NBC, 15m

Romance In Rhythm (3/29/38 - 7/1140) Mut, 15m
3/29/38 - 7/12/38, Tue, 4:15 pm
9/13/39 - 11/1/39, Wed, 10:30 pm
5/13/40 - 7/1/40, Mon, 12:45 pm

3 **Romance In The Dark** (1938) Air trailers

Romance Of Beauty (with Mary Olds) (9/14/32 - 12/23/32) Primrose House, CBS, 2t (Wed & Fri) 15m, 9:45 am

2 **Romance Of Dan and Sylvia, The** (6/1/36 - 8/21/36) Bl, 5t, 10:45 am, 15m also wartime audition

6 **Romance Of Famous Jewels, The** (Syn) 15m

11 **Romance Of Helen Trent, The** (7/24/33 - 6/24/60)
7/24/33 - 10/27/33, regionally (started 9/32?)
10/30/33 - 6/24/60, CBS, 5t, 15m; sponsored by American Home Products, Affiliated Products, Whitehall Drugs, Pharmaco

1 **Romance Of Music** (Pre-war) Syn

35 **Romance Of The Ranchos, The** (with Howard McNear and Pat McGeehan) (9/7/41 - 5/10/42) Title Insurance and Trust Co., KNX, Sun; Wed as of 10/1/41

Romance, Rhythm and Ripley (see Believe It Or Not)

Romances Of Science (11/12/33 - 2/11/34) Notex, NBC, Sun, 15m, 5:15 pm

Romantic Bachelor (1/25/33 - 4/26/33) Vicks, CBS, Wed, 15m, 9 pm

Romantic Melodies (2/22/34 - 5/17/34) Campana, NBC, Mon, 8 pm

Romantic Rhythms (with Sally Nelson and Barry McKinley)
(9/26/37 - 12/19/37) Chevrolet, CBS, Sun, 6:30 pm

Romantic Serenaders (with Fred Jacky Orchestra) (1/10/37 - 4/4/37) Mut, Sun, 15m, 5:30 pm

Romany Trails (with Emery Deutsch)
(10/27/35 - 7/31/39) CBS
10/27/35 - 9/6/36, Sun, 12:30 pm
9/14/36 - 12/28/36, Mon, 2:15 pm
1/3/37 - 10/3/37, Sun, 10:30 pm
5/29/39 - 7/31/39, Mon, 15m, 9:15 am

1 **Romeo and Juliet** (1936) Air trailer

Ron Perry and His Orchestra (1950)

5 **Ronald Reagan** (7/6/67 - 11/3/80)

1 **Ronald Reagan and David Brinkley** (12/22/88) ABC-TV

1 **Ronald Reagan: The First One Hundred Days** (4/23/81) NBC-TV

1 **Ronald Reagan, An American Success Story** (1/18/89) NBC-TV

2 **Ronnie Kemper** (9/19/52, 10/1/52) ABC

Ronnie Mansfield (1946)

2 **Rooftops Of The City** (5/8/47) Audition (7/10/47 - 9/4/47) CBS, Thu, 8:30 pm

Rookies, The (with Jay C. Flippen and Joey Faye) (8/17/41 - 11/6/41) Mut
8/17/41 - 9/21/41, Sun, 7 pm
9/25/41 - 11/6/41, Thu, 8 pm

1 **Roomful Of Music** (7/26/65) WNDT-TV

Rooster Gazette (12/11/34 - 1/3/35) NBC, 2t, 15m, 5:30 pm

2 **Roosty Of The A. A. F.** (with William Tracy) (4/9/44 - 1/20/45) Sus, Mut
4/9/44 - 7/9/44, Sun, 6 pm
7/16/44 - 9/17/44, Sun, 4:30 pm
12/2/44 - 1/20/45, Sat, 3:30 pm

Rosa Lee (6/5/40 - 3/7/42) Bl, Sat, 15m

Rosa Rio (see also Rhythm Time With Rosa Rio)
(7/2/43 - 11/5/43) Bl, Fri, 15m 1:45 pm
(4/2/45 - 5/25/45) Bl, 5t, 15m, 1:15 pm
(11/28/49 - 2/13/50) ABC, Mon, 15m, 4:15 pm

1 **Rosalie** (1938) Air trailer

Rose Marie (see Baby Rose Marie)

Rose Of My Dreams (with Mary Rolfe) (11/25/46 - 5/14/48) Sweetheart Soap, CBS, 5t, 15m

1 **Rose Of Washington Square** (1939) film sound track

10 **Rosemary** (with Betty Winkler)
(10/2/44 - 7/1/55) Procter & Gamble, 5t, 15m
10/2/44 - 3/23/45, NBC
3/26/45 - 7/1/55, CBS

Rosemary Clooney (5/5/53 - 9/26/55) 15m
5/5/53 - 10/2/53, NBC, Tue & Fri, 8:15 pm
3/1/54 - 7/14/55, CBS, 2t, 9 pm; Thu as of 10/7/54
7/18/55 - 9/26/55, CBS, Mon, 9 pm

14 **Rosemary Clooney Sings** (1952) Syn

Roses and Drums (with Reed Brown, Jr. and John Griggs)
(4/24/32 - 3/29/36) United Central Life, Sun
4/24/32 - 6/13/33; 9/3/33 - 6/3/34, CBS
9/9/34 - 3/29/36, Bl

Ross Dolan, Detective (10/25/47 - 9/4/48) Sus, Mut, Sat, 8 pm

1 **Ross Mulholland** (5/6/42) WCAU

8 **Ross Perot** (6/8/92 - 11/1/92) C-SPAN, pool feed, CBS-TV, NBC-TV, CNN

1 **Ross Perot's Solutions** (10/16/92) NBC-TV

Ross Trio, The (6/13/39 - 2/14/41) 15m
6/13/39 - 10/3/39, Bl, Tue, 12:15 pm
also 6/17/39 - 9/23/39, Bl, Sat, 11 am
9/30/39 - 11/4/39, NBC, Sat, 11 am
10/10/39 - 11/7/39, Bl, Tue, 10:30 am
1/28/40 - 41, NBC, Sun, 10:45 am (not in New York)
also 1940 - 2/14/41, NBC, Fri, 12:30 pm

Rotary Golden Theater (3/1/55 - 3/18/55) 5t, 15m

Roth Orchestra Program (with Allen Roth) (4/27/35 - 9/27/45)
4/27/35 - 12/7/35 (Allen Roth's Syncopators) CBS, Sat, 12:30 pm
12/11/35 - 2/12/36 (Allen Roth Presents) CBS, Wed, 3 pm
1/7/39 - 5/6/39 (Al Roth and Company), Bl, Sun, 3:30 pm
5/13/39 - 6/23/39, Bl, Sat, 10 pm
7/2/39 - 10/29/39 (Al Roth Presents), Bl, Sun, 3:30 pm
9/25/39 - 10/16/39, Bl, Mon, 9 pm
1/1/42 - 1/22/42, Bl, Thu, 7:30 pm
1/28/42 - 5/13/42, NBC, Wed, 7:30 pm
5/18/42 - 8/17/45, NBC, 2t (Mon, Wed) 15m, 7:30 pm; 3t from 9/15/42 - 3/9/45
also 7/5/45 - 9/27/45, NBC, Thu, 7:30 pm (summer replacement for Bob Burns)

1 **Round Table Discussion On The Pan-American Bird Treaty** (Syn)

4 **Round The World With Father Time** (Syn)

1 **Round Up Of Invasion News** (6/6/44) CBS

1 **Roundtable Conference With Members Of The N.A.R.N.D.** (5/23/48) U.N. Radio

1 **Roundup Of Declaration Of War Against Japan By Russia** (8/8/45) CBS

Roxy and His Gang (with Samuel Rothafel) (4/5/23 - 7/19/25) (hosted Capitol Theater Family Show) first on November 1922
(3/7/27 - 7/27/31) Bl, Mon, 45m - 60m

Roxy Revue (Roxy's Gang)
(9/15/34 - 4/27/35) Castoria, CBS, Sat, 45m, 8 pm

Roxy Symphony (Theater) Concert
(1929 - 32) 1929 - 3/8/31, Bl and/or NBC, Sun, 30m
5/4/31 - 7/27/31, Bl, Mon, 45m, 7:45 pm
8/2/31 - 32, CBS, Sun, 30m, 9 pm

1 **Roy Acuff and The Cumberland Valley Boys** (Syn)

52 **Roy Acuff Show, The** (Syn) Royal Crown, 15m

Roy Campbell Royalists
(4/28/36 - 6/9/36) NBC, Tue, 15m, 9:30 pm

2 **Roy Eldridge** (7/15/39 - 9/23/39) NBC, Sat, 3:30 pm, also World transcriptions

1 **Roy Eldridge and His Orchestra** (World transcription)

1 **Roy Fox Show, The** (8/21/78) KDKA

1 **Roy Leonard Show, The** (4/30/71)WGN

Roy Porter (9/14/42 - 10/8/43) Bl

76 **Roy Rogers Show, The**
(11/21/44 - 7/21/55) (with Gabby Hayes; Pat Brady as of 10/5/51
11/21/44 - 5/15/45 (with Sons Of The Pioneers) Goodyear, Mut, Tue, 8:30 pm
10/5/46 - 3/29/47, Miles, NBC, Sat, 9 pm
8/29/48 - 6/25/50; 8/6/50 - 5/13/51 (with Dale Evans, Foy Willing and The Riders Of The Purple Sage) Quaker, Mut, Sun, 6 pm
10/5/51 - 6/27/52, Post, NBC, Fri, 8 pm
8/28/52 - 8/20/53, Post, NBC, Thu, 25m, 8 pm
8/25/53 - 9/29/53, Tue, 6 pm (not in New York Times)
10/1/53 - 12/24/53, Post, NBC, Thu, 25m, 8 pm
1/28/54 - 7/21/55, Dodge, NBC, Thu, 8 pm

1 **Roy Shield and Company** (with Nelson Olmsted) (NBC - West coast) Network includes:
6/9/51 - 9/7/51, NBC, Sat, 30m, 7:30 pm; Fri, 10 pm as of 7/6/51

1 **Roy Shield and His Orchestra** (6/6/44) NBC

2 **Roy Shield Revue, The** (with Roy Shield Orchestra) 5/7/36 - 8/22/52) Sus, Bl (except where noted)
5/7/36 - 5/14/36, Bl, Thu, 10:30 pm
5/16/35 - 5/23/35, Thu, 5:30 pm
12/16/36 - 1/6/37, NBC, Wed, 10:30 pm
5/23/37 - 9/26/37 (Roy Shield Encore Music) NBC, Sun, 5:30 pm
1/4/39 - 6/21/39, Wed, 8 pm
9/24/39 - 10/15/39, NBC, Sun, 3 pm
11/7/39 - 5/21/40, Bl, Tue, 10 pm
also 11/29/39 - 3/13/40, Bl, Wed, 10 pm
also 4/3/40 - 8/28/40, Bl, Wed, 9:30 pm
6/4/40 - 9/24/40, Tue, 8 pm (started as summer replacement for The Aldrich Family)
11/20/40 - 4/30/41, Wed, 9 pm
5/4/41- 9/7/41, NBC, Sun, 5:30 pm
9/14/41 - 2/1/42 (Blue Echoes) Sun, 8 pm
3/6/43 - 3/25/44, NBC, Sat, 45m-30m, 2 pm
3/26/44 - 3/11/45 (The Sheaffer Parade) Sheaffer Pens, NBC, Sun, 3 pm
6/4/52 - 7/30/52, NBC, Wed, 10 pm
8/8/52 - 8/22/52, NBC, Fri, 8 pm

1 **Royal Air Force Band** (10/18/41) BBC/CBS

1 **Royal Arch Gunnison**
(1/5/44 - 10/7/44; 2/14/45) Mut

Royal Crown Revue (with Tim Ryan and Irene Noblette; also George Olsen Orchestra) (3/11/38 - 9/2/38) Nehi Soft Drinks, Bl, Fri, 9 pm

Royal Football Roundup (with Eddie Dooley) (9/17/36 - 12/12/36) Royal Typewriter, CBS, Thu, 15m, 6:30 pm

Royal Gelatin Hour, The (see Rudy Vallee)

Royal Hawaiian Band (9/30/34 - 4/9/36) American Home Products, CBS
9/30/34 - 3/31/35, Sun, 2:30 pm
10/16/35 - 4/9/36, Wed, 15m, 7:5 pm

1 **Royal Party From Sandy Hook, N. J. to Pier #1 in New York, The** (6/10/39) Mut

Royal Theater (see Theater Royal)

Royal Vagabonds (with Fanny Brice) (3/15/33 - 10/4/33) Royal Gelatin, NBC, Wed, 8 pm

Royal Vagabonds (with Ward Wilson) (1/4/32 - 12/30/32) Royal Gelatin, Bl, 3t, 15m; Wed - Fri as of 6/15/32

1 **Royal Visit Of The King and Queen** (6/9/39) Mut

1 **Royal Wedding Reprise** (7/29/81) NBC-TV

1 **Royal Wedding, Edited Version** (11/20/47) BBC

1 **Royal Wedding, The** (7/29/81) NBC-TV

Rubbertown Revue (5/26/38 - 11/4/38) CBS, Thu, 5 pm; Fri, 4 pm as of 7/15/38

1 **Rube Appleberry** (11/5/37 - 11/25/37) Campbell Cereal, Mut (Midwest), various days, 15m

Rubinoff and His Musical Moments Revue (see Rubinoff Orchestra)

28 **Rubinoff Orchestra** (with Dave Rubinoff) (10/26/35 - 7/11/37) first began on Chase & Sanborn Program on 1/11/31, NBC, Sun, 8:30 pm; 60m, 8 pm as of 3/8/31 (developed into Eddie Cantor on 9/13/31) (see)
10/26/35 - 4/11/36, Chevrolet, NBC, Sat, 9 pm (Chevrolet Show) (also see Chevrolet Show)
10/18/36 - 7/11/37 (with Hugh Conrad), Chevrolet, CBS, Sun, 6:30 pm

1 **Ruble War, The** (7/23/58) CBS

1 **Ruby Keeler Interview** (9/28/63)

Ruby Mercer (1/21/55 - 7/2/56) Mut, 6t, 15m, 11:15 pm

Ruby Newman Orchestra (3/13/39 - 4/24/39) NBC, Mon, 10:30 pm

Ruby One - Four (ZBS Production) (see The Adventures Of Ruby)

4 **Rudolph Friml Jr.** (Thesaurus transcriptions)

1 **Rudolph Friml Jr. Orchestra** (Thesaurus transcription)

1 **Rudolph Valentino** (1923) record

44 **Rudy Vallee** (10/24/29 - 6/19/55)
10/24/29 - 7/16/36 (Fleischmann Hour; Sunshine Hour), Fleischmann, NBC, Thu. 60m, 8 pm
8/6/36 - 9/28/39 (Royal Gelatin Hour), Royal Gelatin, NBC, Thu, 60m, 8 pm
3/7/40 - 7/1/43, (sometimes called Vallee Varieties) Sealtest, NBC, Thu, 30m, 9:30 pm; 10 pm as of 7/4/40; 9:30 pm as of 1/7/43; developed into Sealtest Village Store
9/9/44 - 6/28/45, Drene, NBC, Sat, 8 pm; Thu, 10:30 pm as of 11/9/44
8/30/45 - 6/27/46, Drene, NBC, Thu, 10:30 pm
9/10/46 - 3/4/47 (with Ruth Etting), Philip Morris, NBC, Tue, 8 pm
2/20/50 - 4/27/51, Mut, 5t, 11:15 am; 2:30 pm as of 12/4/50
2/27/55 - 6/19/55, Kraft, CBS, Sun, 60m, 9 pm

Rudy Vallee Hour, The (see Rudy Vallee)

Rudy Vallee Sealtest Show, The (see Rudy Vallee)

Rudy Vallee Show, The (see Rudy Vallee)

1 **Rudy Wiedoeft** (1931) Syn

1 **Rudy Wissler Audition** (6/18/54) CBS

Rumpus Room (see Johnny Olsen)

Rupert Hughes (4/25/43 - 10/3/43) NBC

Russ Brown Show, The (also with The Cadets) (1945) (Syn) 15m

7 **Russ Carlisle and His Orchestra** (7/5/58 - 5/2/65) CBS

Russ Columbo (12/7/31 - 34) Listerine, NBC & Bl, various days and times

Russ David Orchestra (7/14/45 - 9/22/45) NBC, Sat, 1:15 pm

1 **Russ Hodges News**

3 **Russ Morgan and His "Music In The Morgan Manner"** (Lang-Worth transcriptions)

48 **Russ Morgan and His Orchestra** (10/14/38 - 8/9/69) NBC; CBS; Thesaurus, Lang-Worth, World and Associated transcriptions)
(3/16/36 - 5/4/36) Bl, Mon, 10 pm
(2/13/37 - 1/21/39) (see Johnny Presents) Philip Morris, CBS, Sat; Johnny Green replaced Morgan as of 1/28/39
(8/23/40 - 9/27/40) Bl, Fri, 7:30 pm (1945) (Mut) (1966 - 69) (from The Dunes Hotel and Country Club, Las Vegas) CBS, Sat

Russell Bennett's Notebook (11/17/40 - 12/29/40; 3/30/41 - 5/11/41) Mut, Sun, 7 pm
(7/14/41 - 12/1/44) Mut, Mon, 9 pm
(1/16/42 - 3/6/42) Mut, Fri, 15m, 8:30 pm

1 **Russell Thorson, Jim Boles Interview** (8/9/76)

Russian Gaieties (with Alexander Kiriloff Balalaika Orchestra)
(11/13/32 - 2/12/33) Bl, Sun, 8 pm

Russian Melodies (with Nicholas Vasilief and Alexander Kiriloff)
(3/12/39 - 9/3/39) Bl, Sun, 10:30 am

6 **Russian News In English** (9/28/38 - 9/18/93) Russia

1 **Russian River Medley**

1 **Rustco Ramblers, The** (Pre-war) Syn

Rusty Draper (with Louise O'Brien) (AFRS) (7/22/57 - 58) CBS, 5t, 25m, 8:35 pm

2 **Ruth Berman, Swing Harpist, and Her Orchestra** (Standard transcriptions)

Ruth Carhart (1/7/38 - 7/24/39) CBS, 15m (also see When We Were Young)
1938 - 1/23/39, 2t (Mon & Fri)
1/30/39 - 7/24/39) CBS, Mon, 15m, 4 pm (not always in New York)

Ruth Etting (3/16/32 - 36)
3/16/32 - 4/20/33 (called Music That Satisfies until 12/31/32, Chesterfield, CBS, 2t (Mon & Thu), 15m, 9 pm
1934 - Summer (see MJB Coffs Demitasse Revue)
1935 - 36, Dodge, NBC

Ruth Lyon (1933 - 38) Bl, various days and times, 15m
also (1937 - 38) NBC, 5t, 15m, 1:30 pm

2 **S-O-S Scouring Pads** (Pre-war) Syn

1 **S. F. '68** (South Africa) Syn

3 **S. S. City Of Flint** (1/27/40) WFBR, Mut

2 **S. S. Normendie Salvage Operations** (8/8/43) WOR

1 **S. S. Queen Elizabeth Coverage** (3/7/40) Mut

1 **S. S. Rex Broadcast** (2/11/39) Mut

1 **S. S. United States Broadcast** (7/12/52) Mut

S.R.O. (with Betty Furness) (4/14/53 - 5/5/53) ABC, Tue, 8 pm

Sabbath Reveries (with Dr. Charles Goodell) (6/2/29 - 11/1/36) NBC, Sun (summer replacement of National Radio Pulpit)

1 **Sachs Program, The** (2/12/39) Intercity Broadcasting System

5 **Sacred Heart Program, The** (1951) Syn

1 **Sacrifice Day** (9/9/43) Syn

1 **Sad Sack Show, The** (with Herb Vigran) (6/13/46 - 9/4/46) Old Gold, CBS, Wed (summer replacement for Frank Sinatra)

Saddle Rockin' Rhythm (with Shorty Thompson) (1949 - 50) ABC, Sat, 15m (Regional; network includes 11/19/49 - 12/10/49)

Safari (with Ray Milland) (Audition) 1950s

1 **Safe Driving On Safe Roads** (1939) Syn

Safety Legion Time (with Colleen Moore) (1944) Mut, 5t, 15m

Safety Songs (with Irving Caesar) (see Sing A Song Of Safety Club)

1 **Saga** (3/15/55 - 10/28/55) ABC
3/15/55 - 5/26/55, 2t, 25m, 7:30 pm
5/30/55 - 10/28/55, 5t, 15m, 7:45 pm

Saga City, USA (1938) Audition

1 **Saga Of #7, The** (7/10/45) CBS

1 **Saga Of A Sawbuck**

2 **Saga Of Davy Crockett, The** (Syn)

Saint Louis Blues (also Music From St. Louis)
(7/1/35 - 7/22/35) CBS, Mon, 9:30 pm
(2/13/38 - 4/17/38; 5/19/38 - 6/23/38 (Thu); 2/12/39 - 8/20/39) CBS, Sun (often not in New York)
(7/1/38 - 2/3/39) Fri, 9:30 pm

Saint Louis Melodies (1954)

Saint Louis Municipal Opera
(7/6/40 - 8/31/40) CBS, Sat, 7 pm
(6/5/48 - 8/28/48) CBS, Sat, 7 pm
(7/8/51 - 9/30/51) CBS, Sun, 6:30 pm (summer replacement for Our Miss Brooks) Salada Salon Orchestra
(1930 - 7/2/31) Salada Tea, Bl, Thu, 8:30 pm

8 **Saint, The** (1/6/45 - 10/21/51)
1/6/45 - 3/31/45 (with Edgar Barrier) Bromo Seltzer, NBC, Sat, 7:30 pm
6/20/45 - 9/12/45 (with Brian Aherne) Campbell, CBS, Wed, 8 pm (summer replacement of Jack Carson)
7/9/47 - 6/30/48 (with Vincent Price) CBS - Pacific, Wed
7/10/49 - 5/28/50 (with Vincent Price) Ford from 1/8/50, Mut, Sun, 7:30 pm (shows were repeats until 1/8/50)
6/11/50 - 10/21/51 (with Vincent Price; then Tom Conway as of 5/27/51; Barry Sullivan for 9/17 and 9/24/51), Sus, NBC, Sun, 7:30 pm; 4:30 pm as of 10/1/50; 4 pm as of 7/1/51

1 **Sainted Sisters, The** (1947) Air trailer

1 **Saints and The Sinners, The** (5/21/70) CBS

1 **Saipan Recordings** (7/4/44)

Sal Hepatica Revue (see Fred Allen)

4 **Sal Matthews and His Orchestra** (10/16/69 - 11/16/69) CBS

Salad Bowl Revue (see Fred Allen)

1 **Sally in Hollywood** (6/3/47) Audition

Sally Moore (11/26/44 - 8/22/45) CBS, various days, 15m, 6:30 pm

Sally Of The Talkies (see Talkie Picture Time)

2 **Sally, Irene and Mary** (1938) Air trailer, film sound track

Salon Silhouettes (5/12/40 - 8/11/40) Bl, Sun, 2:30 pm

1 **Salt II, A Great Debate Begins** (6/18/79) CBS-TV

6 **Salt Lake City Tabernacle Choir** (1929 - 71+)
1929 - 9/2/32, Bl, Fri
9/4/32 - 71+, CBS, Sun

Salty Sam, the Sailor (with Irving Kaufman) (7/6/31 - 3/1/32) Kolynos, CBS, Mon, 15m, 6:30 pm; 3t (Tue, Wed, Thu), 15m, 5:30 pm as of 9/8/31

Saludas Amigos (with Victoria Cordova)
(6/4/43 - 9/24/43) Bl, Fri, 25m, 7:05 pm
(4/16/45 - 6/4/45) Bl, Mon, 11:30 pm

1 **Salute From The Baltimore Association Of Commerce** (6/29/39) WFBR

1 **Salute From WFMD** (6/39) WFMD/WFBR

1 **Salute From WJEJ** (6/22/39) WJEJ

1 **Salute From WRC** (6/22/39) WRC/WFBR

1 **Salute From WSAL** (6/20/39) WSAL/WFBR

1 **Salute To 1776** (7/3/71) pool feed

Salute To Aviation (see Ceiling Unlimited)

1 **Salute To Bob Hope** (5/68) AFRTS

Salute To Britain (15m)

1 **Salute To Canada Lee** (6/9/41) Mut

1 **Salute To Eddie Condon** (3/65) WABC-TV

1 **Salute To Eugene O'Neil** (5/15/54) NBC

1 **Salute To Jack Benny** (11/9/51) CBS

1 **Salute To Labor** (9/1/41) NBC

1 **Salute To National Wildlife Week** (3/19/39) Mut

1 **Salute To Navy Day** (10/26/38) Mut

41 **Salute To Reservists** (1950, 1951) Syn

1 **Salute To Romance** (10/12/45) Mut

Salute To Song (1940) 15m

1 **Salute To The 1954 Easter Seal Campaign** (1954) Syn

Salute To The Americas (Celebration Of World's Fair) (4/7/40 - 6/30/40) all three networks, Sun, 2 PM

Salute To The Nation (12/20/52 - 56) Sus, Mut, Sat (off and on)

1 **Salute To The States** (with Alvino Rey) (8/16/42 - 9/3/42) Mut, Sun, 25m, 12:05 pm, also syndicated

1 **Salute To The U.S.S. Maryland** (1945) WBAL

Salute To Veterans (see Veteran's Aide)

2 **Salute To Victory** (5/8/45, 9/45) CBS, WWDC

1 **Salute To W71NY From W65H In Hartford Connecticut** (11/30/41) Yankee FM net

6 **Salute To War Workers** (Wartime) Syn

1 **Salute To WFBR From Hollywood** (6/17/39) Red net

1 **Salute To XEW** (7/18/42) NBC

1 **Salute To Your Pharmacist** (10/1/55) Syn

Salute To Youth (with Raymond Paige Orchestra) (4/20/43 - 1/11/44) Autolite, NBC, Tue, 7:30 pm

7 **Salute To..., A** (8/23/44 - 11/7/75) Mut, CBS, Syn, ABC-TV

1 **Salvation Army, The** (12/59) Syn

Salvatore Mario de Stefano (1/1/39 - 10/29/39) Mut, Sun, 15m, 2:30 pm; 1:30 pm as of 5/14/39

Sam and Henry (see Amos and Andy)

16 **Sam Balter** (Inside Of Sports) (6/14/38 - 6/27/42) Phillies Cigars, Mut, 3t (Tue, Thu, Sat), 15m (previously on the West Coast) (One For The Book) Syn - ZIV; 192 5-minute shows broadcast

Sam Donahue Orchestra

1 **Sam Donaldson** (4/1/94) C-SPAN

Sam Hayes (1947 - 1949) Wheaties, NBC, earlier on West coast

Sam Herman and Frank Banta (8/19/35 - 12/30/35) Bl, Mon, 15m, 10:45 am (continues on Tue)

Sam Pilgrim's Progress (1940s) ABC

41 **Same Time, Same Station** (12/26/71 - 10/7/73) KRLA

23 **Sammy Kaye** (12/17/38 - 2/12/56) (on Mutual off and on earlier)
11/13/37, CBS
12/17/38 - 4/29/39, Mut, Sat, 45m, 5 pm
1/1/40 - 6/24/40 (Sensation and Swing; with The Vass Family), Sensation Cigarettes, NBC, Mon, 7:30 pm
also 12/16/39 - 4/27/40, Mut, Sat, 60m, 5 pm
1/12/41 - 2/7/43, NBC, Sun
also 11/1/41 - 1/3/42, Bl, Sat, 10:30 pm
also 6/4/41 - 7/9/41, NBC, Wed, 7:30 pm
1/2/44 - 4/30/44 (on Sunday called Sunday Serenade), Sus, ABC, Sun
also 1/27/43 - 3/29/44 (with Monte Woolley) Old Gold, CBS, Wed, 8 pm
5/7/44 - 8/26/45 (Tangee Varieties), Tangee, Bl/ABC, Sun, 25m, 1:30 pm
also 8/24/44 - 2/15/45, Tangee, Mut, Thu, 8:30 pm

Sammy Kaye (continued)
also 2/23/45 - 5/18/45, Tangee, Bl, Fri, 10 pm
11/18/45 -11/10/46, Rayve, ABC, Sun, 25m, 1:30 pm
11/17/46 - 1/25/48, Richard Hudnut Dreme Shampoo, ABC, Sun, 25m, 1:30 pm
also 1/23/46 - 6/19/46, ABC, Wed, 9:30 pm
also 6/25/46 - 8/20/46, ABC, Tue, 8:30 pm
also 9/5/46 - 10/24/46 (So You Want To Lead A Band) ABC, Thu, 10 pm
also 11/7/46 - 1/2/47, ABC, Thu, 9:30 pm
1/6/47 - 6/7/48, ABC, Mon, 9:30 pm
6/7/48 - 9/24/48 (see Chesterfield Supper Club)
1948 - 49, Chrysler-Plymouth, 15m
11/13/49 - 2/26/50, Sus, CBS, Sun
4/2/50 - 9/30/51, Sus, ABC, Sun
10/7/51 - 3/30/52 (Sammy Kaye's Sylvania Serenade), Sylvania, ABC, Sun, 5 pm
4/19/53 - 10/4/53, ABC, Sun, 12 noon
7/13/53 - 5/7/54, ABC, 5t, 15m, 8:15 pm
6/7/54 - 10/28/55, ABC, 30m, 4 - 5t, 9 pm
also 1/9/55 - 2/12/56, ABC, Sun, 9:30 pm
also syndicated, Thesaurus transcriptions

Sammy Kaye and His Orchestra (see Sammy Kaye)

Sammy Kaye Orchestra (see Sammy Kaye)

Sammy Kaye's Sunday Serenade (see Sammy Kaye)

Samovar Serenade (with a Balalaika Orchestra) (7/9/33 - 6/7/36) Bl, Sun, 10:30 am

Sampler Program (with Andy Sannella Orchestra, Fred Hufsmith)
(2/2/32 - 5/6/32) Whitman's Chocolates, NBC, Fri, 10 pm
(10/26/32 - 12/22/32) (with Jack Denny Orchestra, Even Evans) (Whitman's Chocolates, NBC, Wed, 15m, 8:45 pm

1 **Samson and Delilah** (1948) Air trailer

Samsonite Travel Bureau
(9/8/55 - 12/21/55) Shwayder Brothers, NBC, Wed, 5m, 9:55 pm

2 **Samuel B. Pettengill** (5/26/46 - 10/3/48) America's Future, ABC, Sun, 15m (1 pm)

1 **Samuel Goldwyn Interview** (1955)

San Felician Serenade (with Bob Nolan)
(2/1/32 - 6/13/32) Bl, 2t (Mon & Fri), 15m; (Mon & Wed) as of 3/14/32

1 **San Francisco** (1936) Air trailer

1 **San Francisco Conference** (4/26/45) Mut

1 **San Francisco Earthquake Coverage** (10/18/89)

1 **San Francisco Giants** (1959) KSFO

San Francisco Opera (Bl)
10/30/36; 11/13/36; 10/7/38; (1939) 10/13; 10/20; 10/12/40

1 **San Francisco Opera Company On The Air, The** (9/26/43)

San Francisco Symphony Orchestra (NBC)

2 **San Quentin** (12/46) Air trailers

Sandra Martin (see Lady Of The Press)

Sandy and Lil (9/24/30 - 12/30) Eskimo Pie, CBS, Wed, 15m, 7:45 pm

Sanka Salutes With Win Elliott (see Gunsmoke)
(1/26/52 - 6/27/53; 10/3/53 - 9/22/54) General Foods, CBS, Sat, 5m

2 **Santa and His Christmas Kids** (World syn)

1 **Santa Claus In Blue** (12/25/45) WOR

1 **Santa Claus Rides Again** (Syn)

1 **Santa Flies The Airlift** (12/24/48) CBS

2 **Santa's Magic Christmas Tree** (Syn)

Sara's Private Caper (with Sara Bemer) (6/15/50 - 8/24/50) Wheaties, NBC, Thu, 10:30 pm

1 **Sardines A La Carte** (1/25/29) Synchro-disc

Satan's Waiting (with host, Frank Graham) (6/6/50 - 8/29/50) Colgate, CBS, Tue, 8:30 pm (summer replacement for Mr. and Mrs. North)

1 **Satchmo!** (3/8/80) PBS-TV

Saturday At The Chase
(11/8/52 - 12/22/56) Sus, CBS, Sat, 5:30 pm

Saturday At The Shamrock (from the Shamrock Hotel in Texas)
(7/16/49 - 6/6/53) ABC, Sat (Regional; sometimes in New York)

Saturday Morning Club
(9/17/38 - 4/15/39) NBC, Sat, 10 am; 9:15 am as of 1/21/39

Saturday Morning Serenade
(5/20/39 - 12/9/39) CBS, Sat, 10:30 am; 9:30 am as of 10/28/39

Saturday Morning Vaudeville Theater (with Charles Kemper, Dick Todd, Joan Shea, Jim Ameche) (7/12/41 - 1/3/42) Lever Brothers, NBC, Sat, 11:30 am

1 **Saturday Night Barndance**

4 **Saturday Night Bondwagon** (Treasury Department) (10/3/42 - 4/1/44) Mut, Sat, 10:15 pm

Saturday Night Country Style (with Tom George) (10/13/51 - 12/22/56) Sus, CBS, Sat, 30m - 60m

Saturday Night Dance Date
(7/1/50 - 9/16/50; 11/22/52 - 12/27/52) NBC, Sat

Saturday Night Dance Party (1952) Benrus; 15m

Saturday Night Party (with Jane Pickens; Walter O'Keefe) (10/17/36 - 10/10/37) Sealtest, NBC, Sat, 60m, 8 pm; Sun, 10 pm as of 5/23/37; changed to Sunday Night Party on 5/23/37

1 **Saturday Night Revue** (with Robert Q. Lewis) (5/11/46 - 6/8/46) Mut, Sat, 8:30 pm

9 **Saturday Night Serenade**
(10/3/36 - 9/25/48) Pet Milk, CBS, Sat, 9:30 pm; 9:45 pm as of 7/8/39; 9:30 pm as of 4/26/47; 10 pm as of 7/5/47; 7:30 pm as of 7/3/48; (starred Mary Eastman until February, 1941; Jessica Dragonette from 8/16/41 on) not always carried in New York

7 **Saturday Night Swing Club**
(6/20/36 - 4/1/39) Hormel, CBS, Sat, 7 pm; 6:30 pm as of 1/14/39

4 **Saturday Night Swing Session** (WNEW, New York) (1947)

Saturday Party (see Believe It Or Not)

Saturday Playhouse

Saturday Senior Swing (with Jill Warren, Jack Manning) (9/15/45 - 1/5/46) ABC, Sat, 1 pm

Saturday Showcase (with Snooky Lanson, Evelyn Parker)
(6/1/46 - 9/21/46) NBC, Sat, 3 pm

Saturday Showdown (with John Gibson, Ted de Corsia) (1943) NBC

1 **Saturday Symphonies** (10/17/46) Mut

1 **Saturday Theater** (with host, George Walsh) (10/2/54 - 1/8/55) CBS, Sat

Saturday's Child (see Crossroads)

1 **Saturn Watch** (11/12/80) PBS-TV

3 **Sauer Show, The** (11/3/49 - 7/6/50) WLOS

1 **Saunders Of The Circle X** (with John Cuthbertson) (10/2/41 - 42) Bl - Pacific, Thu

4 **Sauter-Finegan Orchestra** (World transcriptions)

1 **Sauter-Finegan Orchestra, The** (11/53) CBS

Savannah Liners (with Robert Armbruster Orchestra (1928 - 7/28/31) Ocean Steamship Lines, Bl, Tue, 15m, 6:30 pm
(10/11/32 - 12/27/32) Ocean Steamship Co., Bl, Tue, 15m, 6:30 pm

15 **Savings Bond Campaign** (1946) Syn

9 **Savings Bond Campaign: Fall 1946** (1946) Syn

1 **Saxophone Sextette Of Boston** (1939) Syn

4 **Say It With Music** (Mut)

1 **Say It With Songs** (1929) Synchro-disc

1 **Say It With Words** (5/24/38 - 8/17/38) Mut, Tue, 9:30 pm

Says Who (see Sez Who)

1 **Scalamandre Concert Hour, The** (11/13/46) Mut

1 **Scalf's Indian River Medicine Program** (8/20/48) WLBG

1 **Scarlet Claw, The** (1944) film sound track

1 **Scarlet Cloak, The** (with Wendell Niles) 2/15/50 (Audition)

36 **Scarlet Pimpernel, The** (with Marius Goring)
(9/21/52 - 9/20/53) Sus, NBC, Sun, 6 pm
(7/1/52 - 8/19/52) NBC, Tue, 8 pm (summer replacement for Cavalcade Of America)

Scarlet Queen, The (see Voyage Of The Scarlet Queen)

6 **Scattergood Baines** (2/22/37 - 10/26/49)
2/22/37 - 10/28/38, Wrigley, CBS - West coast, 5t, 15m
11/7/38 - 8/29/41; 12/1/41 - 6/12/42, Wrigley, CBS, 5t, 15m, 5:45 pm; with Jess Pugh on 12/1/41
2/10/49 - 4/28/49, Mut, Thu, 8:30 pm
7/2/49 - 9/17/49, Mut, Sat, 5:30 pm
9/2/49 - 10/26/49, Sus, Mut, Wed, 10 pm

1 **Scenes From The Best Selling Books Of Today** (5/25/45) Mut

Schaefer All-Star Parade (with Felix Knight, Al Roth Orchestra)
(9/29/38 - 9/19/40) Schaefer, NBC, Thu, 7:30 pm

2 **Schaeffer Parade, The** (10/3/44, 5/9/48) NBC

1 **Schaeffer Revue, The** (3/18/42)

1 **Schenectady Public School Program** (1949) WGY

2 **Schlitz Palm Garden Of The Air** (Pre-war) Syn

1 **Schlitz Playhouse Of Stars, The** (5/6/55) TV syn

1 **School Manpower Warcast** (8/20/43) Mut

Schools Are Yours, The (NEA)
(6/15/46 - 9/7/46) NBC, Sat, 4:30 pm

Schumann-Heinck (see Madame Schumann-Heinck)

2 **Schooner Conquest, The** (Syn)

1 **Schubert Group, The** (1938) Syn

1 **Schubert's Unfinished Symphony** (1929) Synchro-disc

1 **Schuster Murder, The** (3/11/52) ABC

1 **Science and Food** (11/16/53) U.N. Radio

13 **Science and Life** (1938) Syn

1 **Science and News, 1962** (1962) Syn

Science Everywhere (with Dr.Carroll Lane Fenton) (12/13/38 - 5/9/39) Bl, Tue, 2 pm

Science In The News (with Olan Soulé)
(10/13/36 - 10/2/39) Sus, NBC
10/13/36 - 9/6/38, Tue, 15 m
9/12/38 - 10/2/39, Mon, 15m, 6 pm

2 **Science In War and Peace**
(10/23/45 - 46) Mut, Mon, 15m, 7:15 pm (not in New York)

Science Magazine Of The Air

Science On The March (with C. L. Fenton)
(10/10/38 - 11/6/39) Bl, Mon, 15m, 7:45 pm (with Dr. Forest Ray Moulton)
(10/9/39 - 2/12/40) Bl, Mon, 15m, 7:15 pm

1 **Science, News, and Politics Of 1956, The** (12/16/56) CBS-TV

1 **Scientist Meets The Press A** (4/10/56) U.N. Radio

1 **Scotland Yard** (11/13/51)

Scotland Yard's Inspector Burke (with Basil Rathbone)
(1/27/47 - 12/29/47) Sus, Mut
1/21/47 - 4/1/47, Tue, 8:30 pm
4/7/47 - 12/29/47, Mon, 8 pm

11 **Scout About Town** (with hosts, Hunt Stromberg, Jr. and Annamary Dickey, Barry Gray) (10/17/45 - 10/10/47) Mut, 15m

Scramble (7/10/42 - 4/16/43) Bl, Fri, 7 pm

2 **Scramby Amby** (with Perry Ward)
(1941 - 5/10/47)
1941 - 43, WLW - Cincinnati
1943 - 44, Sweetheart Soap, Bl - Pacific
7/26/44 - 1/17/45, Sweetheart Soap, Bl, Wed, 7 pm; 10:30 pm as of 9/6/44
12/21/46 - 5/10/47, Sus, Mut, Sat, 8:30 pm

3 **Scrapbook** (Syn)

Scrappy Lambert and Billy Hillpot (also with Nat Shilkret Orchestra)
(10/3/33 - 2/13/34) CBS, Tue, 15m, 8:45 pm

95 **Screen Director's Playhouse**
(1/9/49 - 9/28/51) NBC
1/9/49 - 6/5/49 (Screen Director's Guild) Sus, Sun
7/1/49 - 9/30/49, Pabst, Fri
10/3/49 - 10/31/49, Sus, Mon
11/11/49 - 12/30/49, Sus, Fri
1/6/50 - 6/30/50, RCA, Fri
11/9/50 - 8/30/51, Multi, Thu; 60m from 11/16/50
9/7/51 - 9/28/51, Fri, 60m, 8 pm

194 **Screen Guild Theater, The**
(1/8/39 - 6/29/52) see also Stars In The Air; Hollywood Soundstage
1/8/39 - 6/4/39 (Gulf Screen Guild Show), Gulf, CBS, Sun, 60m, 7:30 pm
9/24/39 - 4/21/40; 9/29/40 - 4/20/41; 9/28/41 - 4/19/42 (Gulf Screen Theater as of 11/26/39) Gulf, CBS, Sun, 30m
10/19/42 - 7/7/47 (Lady Esther Screen Guild Theater), Lady Esther, CBS, Mon
10/6/47 - 6/28/48 (Camel Screen Guild Players until 6/29/50), Camel, CBS, Mon
10/7/48 - 6/30/49; 10/6/49 - 6/29/50, Camel, NBC, Thu
9/7/50 - 5/31/51, Sus, ABC, Thu, 60m
4/3/52 - 6/29/52, CBS, Sun, 9 pm

1 **Screen Test** (6/12/44 - 12/8/44) MGM, Mut, 5t, 15m, 9:15 pm

Sea Has A Story, The (see Story Of The Sea)

5 **Sea Hound, The** (with Ken Daigneau)
(6/29/42 - 8/7/51)
6/29/42 - 9/22/44, Sus, Bl, 5t, 15m
1946 - 47, Mut, 5t, 15m
6/21/48 - 9/2/48, ABC, Mon
6/26/51 - 8/7/51, ABC, alternates 3t/2t

1 **Sea Scouter Program, The** (12/29/35) WNYC

2 **Seal Of The Don** (1933 - 5/33) Syn, 5t, 15m

27 **Sealed Book, The** (narrated by Philip Clark; written by Robert A. Arthur and David Kogan) (3/18/45 - 9/9/45) Mut, Sun, 10:30 pm

Sealed Power Show (with Koestner Orchestra) (1932 - 4/2/33) Sealed Power, Bl, Sun, 6 pm

1 **Sealed Power Side Show**
(10/30/33 - 3/19/35) Sealed Power Corp., Bl, Mon, 8 pm

Sealtest Variety Show, The (see Dorothy Lamour)

Sealtest Variety Theater (see Dorothy Lamour)

11 **Sealtest Village Store, The**
(7/8/43 - 9/2/48) Sealtest, NBC, Thu. 9:30 pm
7/8/43 - 7/5/45 (with Joan Davis and Jack Haley)
7/12/45 - 9/20/45 (with Jack Haley)
9/27/45 - 6/26/47 (with Eve Arden and Jack Haley)
7/3/47 - 9/4/47 (with Eve Arden)
9/11/47 - 7/8/48 (with Eve Arden and Jack Carson)
7/15/48 - 9/2/48 (with Ray Noble and Ilene Woods)

1 **Search For Beauty** (1934) Air trailer

13 **Search That Never Ends, The**
(9/30/52 - 4/9/55) Sus, Mut
9/30/52 - 10/12/53, Tue, 9 pm
10/17/53 - 4/9/55, Sat, 9 pm

128 **Sears Radio Theater** (2/5/79 - 12/19/80)
2/5/79 - 8/3/79, Sears, CBS, 5t, 60m; rebroadcast 8/6/79 - 2/11/80
2/14/80 - 12/19/80, Sus, Mut, 5t, 60m

3 **Sears - Then and Now** (with Les Tremayne) (9/17/36 - 12/10/36) Sears, CBS, Thu, 10 pm

Sears Children's Theater Of The Air (1949)

5 **Second Annual American Swing Festival** (2/4/45 - 2/11/45) WNEW

1 **Second Annual International Potato Picking Contest, The** (9/30/38) Mut

Second Chance (1/25/54 - 7/1/55) Multi, NBC, 5t, 15m, 11:45 am

1 **Second Guessers** (with Paul Douglas; during 1941 with Lou Little, Henry McLemore, others) (1937 - 1941) NBC, Sun (during football season)

1 **Second Honeymoon** (with Bert Parks)
(9/20/48 - 1/16/50) 5t
9/20/48 - 1/14/49, ABC, 4 pm
6/27/49 - 11/11/49, ABC, 2:30 pm
11/14/49 - 1/16/50, Mut, 2 pm
also 5/30/50, Mut

11 **Second Husband** (with Helen Menken and Joseph Curtin) (4/26/36 - 4/26/46) (sometimes called Ethel Barrymore Theater)
4/26/36 - 4/37, Bayer, Bl, Sun
4/21/37 - 5/26/37, Bayer, Bl, Wed
6/2/37 - 7/28/37, Bayer, NBC, Wed
8/3/37 - 4/14/42, Bayer, CBS, Tue
4/20/42 - 7/31/42, Bl, 5t, 15m, 11 am
8/3/42 - 4/26/46, Dr. Lyons, CBS, 5t, 15m
1955 - 1956, CBS

4 **Second Mrs. Burton, The**
(1/7/46 - 11/25/60) CBS, 5t, 15m; started as Second Wife from
5/4/42 - 12/25/42, CBS - West coast, Postum
1/7/46 - 9/17/54, General Foods
9/20/54 - 6/17/55, Armour
6/20/55 - 11/25/60, Multi

1 **Second Seagram Symposium, The** (10/2/55) CBS

1 **Second Spring** (1948) Syn, 15m

2 **Second Sunday** (1966, 11/7/69) NBC

7 **Secret Agent K-7 Returns** (Syn) (1938) 15m

1 **Secret City** (with Bill Idelson) (11/3/41 - 9/25/42) Sus, Bl, 5t, 15m

4 **Secret Diary** (Syn - ZIV) 117 15-minute shows broadcast

8 **Secret Garden, The** (8/11/83 - 9/29/83) NPR

Secret Life Of Walter Mitty (with Eddie Albert and Margo) (1948)

56 **Secret Mission** (with Admiral Ellis M. Zacharias) (3/19/48 - 10/31/49) Mut
7/18/48 - 5/22/49, Sun, 10 pm
5/30/49 - 10/31/49, Mon, 9:30 pm

17 **Secret Mission** (1950s; Edward Arnold as host, with Hy Averback)

Secret Service Spy Stories (1932 - 1/22/33) NBC, Sun, 1 pm

Secret Three (with Murray McLean)

Secret Weapon (see Our Secret Weapon)

1 **Secretary Of State Henry Kissinger** (3/26/75) pool feed

1 **Secretary Of State Henry Kissinger Press Conference** (10/25/73) pool feed

1 **Secretary Of State Resigns, The** (6/25/82) CBS-TV

1 **Secretary Of The Navy Forrestal** (2/25/45) Mut

1 **Secretary Of War Stimson** (12/28/43) Mut

33 **Secrets Of Scotland Yard** (3/14/57 - 58) Multi, Mut, Thu, 8 pm, also syndicated

Security Agent USA (with Mike Wallace) (1949) NBC

4 **Security and Disarmament Under The United Nations** (1946, 1947) Syn

6 **See It Now** (4/6/54 - 3/58) CBS-TV

1 **Seems Radio Is Here To Stay** (11/5/45) CBS

4 **Seger Ellis' Orchestra** (Standard transcriptions)

2 **Seiberling Singers, The** (Pre-war) Syn

Sekatary Hawkins (with Robert Franc Scholkers) (10/4/32 - 4/4/33) Ralston Purina, NBC, 3t (Tue, Thu, Sat), 15m, 5:45 pm

1 **Selective Service Ends** (3/31/47) WOR

1 **Selective Service Information** (8/23/41) WOR

1 **Selective Service Lottery Drawing** (10/29/40) Mut

1 **Selling Of The Pentagon, The** (5/23/71) CBS-TV

1 **Semi-Classical Replacement** (1/13/46)

1 **Senate Investigating Committee: Alger Hiss Hearing** (8/5/48) Mut

1 **Senate Subcommittee Hearings** (3/12/52) Mut

1 **Senator Abraham Ribicoff** (3/10/73) pool feed

1 **Senator Alben Barkley** (7/17/40) NBC

1 **Senator Albert Gore** (7/16/92) pool feed

1 **Senator Barry Goldwater** (1960) NBC-TV

1 **Senator Burton K. Wheeler** (9/17/37) Mut

4 **Senator Dan Quayle** (8/18/88 - 10/24/88) C-SPAN

1 **Senator Edmund Muskie** (8/68)

1 **Senator Edward Kennedy** (8/12/80) NBC-TV
(7/19/88) C-SPAN

1 **Senator Everett Dirksen Obituary** (9/7/69) CBS

2 **Senator Fishface** (1936) Syn

Senator Fishface and Professor Figgsbottle (with Jerry Sears Orchestra, Showman Quartet) (4/5/36 - 3/13/38) Sun, Bl, 4:30 pm

2 **Senator Frankenstein Fishface** (Syn)

1 **Senator Gerald Nye** (9/23/41) Mut

1 **Senator Hubert Humphrey** (8/64)

1 **Senator Huey P. Long** (3/7/35) NBC

1 **Senator John F. Kennedy** (7/60) pool feed

3 **Senator Joseph McCarthy** (1950, 1952, 7/9/52) CBS, ABC-TV, NBC-TV

1 **Senator Joseph McCarthy Address** (11/27/53) CBS

2 **Senator Lloyd Bentsen** (7/21/88, 10/26/88) C-SPAN

1 **Senator Lyndon Johnson and Senator John F. Kennedy** (7/60)

1 **Senator Robert Wagner** (10/28/37) WOR

Sensation and Swing (see Larry Clinton)

Sensations In Swing (see Sammy Kaye)

1 **Sensations Of 1945** (1944) film sound track

1 **Sense and Nonsense** (4/40) WOR

Sentenced (10/13/54 - 9/28/55) Multi, Mut, Wed, 8:30 pm

1 **Sentiment Still Lives** (Syn)

Sentimental Bachelor (15m)

1 **Sequoia** (1935) Air trailer

Serenade For Strings (from Montreal)
(7/6/39 - 8/3/39) CBS, Thu, 8:30 pm
(5/1/40 - 8/28/40) Mut, Wed, 9:30 pm
(9/7/48 - 1/4/49, ABC, Tue, 15m, 10:45 pm

1 **Serenade In Blue** (Syn) (1951 - 1958)

2 **Serenade To America** (with H. Leopold Spitalny; then Frank Black; also Thomas Hayward) (5/28/45 - 10/2/47) NBC, various days

Serenade To Loveliness (with John Stanton, Andrew Gainey)
(11/10/40 - 41) NBC (Midwest and West), Sun, 10:30 pm
(1/24/44 - 6/13/44) (with Nora Stirling) NBC, Chamberlain Sales Corp, 5t, 15m, 6:15 pm

3 **Serenade To Romance** (Syn)

21 **Sergeant Preston Of The Yukon** (with Jay Michael) (2/3/38 - 6/9/55) (called Challenge Of The Yukon until 11/11/51. It was then officially called Sgt. Preston Of The Yukon) (dates and times varied around the country) (1260 shows broadcast)
2/3/38 - 1/30/47, Sus, WXYZ, Thu, 15m
2/4/47 - 2/11/47, Sus, WXYZ, Tue, 15m
2/22/47 - 3/6/47, Sus, WXYZ, Thu, 15m
3/12/47 - 5/28/47, Sus, WXYZ, Wed, 15m
6/12/47 - 7/3/47, Quaker, ABC, Thu, 30m (Quaker and ABC until 12/30/49)
7/12/47 - 9/6/47, Sat
9/11/47 - 10/23/47, Thu
11/1/47 - 7/24/48, Sat
7/28/48 - 9/1/48, Wed
9/6/48 - 6/10/49, Mon, Wed, Fri
9/12/49 - 12/30/49, Mon, Wed, Fri
1/2/50 - 12/15/50, Quaker, Mut (from now on), Mon, Wed, Fri
1/1/51 - 1/8/51, Mon, 5:30 pm
1/20/51, Sat
1/27/51 - 7/8/51, Sat and Sun
7/10/51 - 1/3/52, Sun, Tue, Thu
6/29/52 - 9/7/52, Sun
9/16/52 - 5/14/53, Tue and Thu
5/19/53 - 6/9/53, Tue
9/15/53 - 6/10/54, Tue and Thu
9/14/54 - 6/9/55, Tue and Thu

2 **Sermon Of The Week** (3/9/47, 10/19/47) Mut

1 **Sermons In Song** (Syn)

2 **Service Digest** (1946) AFRS

1 **Servicemen's Hop** (7/18/42) Bl

1 **Service Time (Marines In The Making)** (10/12/44) CBS

1 **Service To The Front** (6/23/44 - 8/14/45) Wrigley, CBS
6/23/44 - 9/8/44, Fri, 25m, 8:30 pm
9/12/44 - 8/14/45, Tue, 10 pm

2 **Service Unlimited** (Red Cross) (8/6/44, 8/16/44) Syn

Service With A Smile (see The Army Show)

1 **SESAC Presents Adventures In Sound** (Syn)

1 **SESAC Presents Bridges, Moods and Themes** (Syn)

Set Sail (10/7/40 - 11/22/40) Bl, 5t, 15m, 5 pm

1 **Seth Parker** (with Phillips H. Lord) (3/3/29 - 3/19/39) 3/3/29 - 12/3/33 (also called Sunday At Seth Parker; Sunday Evenings At Seth Parker), Sus, NBC, Sun
also 12/5/33 - 3/27/34 (Cruise Of The Seth Parker) Frigidaire, NBC, Tue, 10 pm
6/30/35 - 3/22/36, Bl, Sun, 10/10:30 pm
1937 - 38, Vick Chemical, NBC, Sun
9/25/38 - 3/19/39, Vick Chemical, Bl, Sun, 7:30 pm

Seven Seas (with Cameron King) (10/16/34 - 1/8/35) Bl, Tue, 10 pm

Seven Star Revue (10/1/33 - 4/1/34) Corn Products Refining, CBS, Sun, 60m, 9 pm

1 **Seven Sweethearts** (1942) Air trailer

1 **Seventh Crisis: Nixon On Nixon, The** (1/10/74) CBS-TV

Seventh Man, The (with Joseph Cotten)

2 **Seventy Fifth Anniversary Of The Battle Of Gettysburg** (6/30/38, 7/2/38) Mut

Seventy-Six Review (with Conrad Nagel) (1/26/38 - 10/22/38) Union Oil, NBC - West, Mon

7 **Sextette From Hunger** (MacGregor transcriptions)

13 **Sextette From Hunger Show, The** (1951) Syn

Sez Who? (with Henry Morgan and John Cameron Swayze) (7/14/57 - 9/29/57; 10/27/57 - 58) CBS, Sun, 7 pm; 7:30 pm as of 10/27/57 (summer replacement for Jack Benny from 7/14/57 - 9/29/57)

SF Diary (with Scott MacKenzie) 1948 (Audition) 15m

SF Unlimited (1947) (Audition) 15m

Shadow Of Fu Manchu, The (see Fu Manchu)

230 **Shadow, The** (7/31/30 - 12/26/54)
7/31/30 - 7/30/31 (Detective Story Hour; then Detective Story Program) Street & Smith, CBS, Thu, 9:30 pm; with James La Curto; then Frank Readick, Jr.
9/6/31 - 6/5/32 (Blue Coal Radio Revue) Blue Coal, CBS, Sun, 60m, 5:30 pm; with Frank Readick, Jr., Barbara Maurel, Fred Vettel, George Earle Orchestra; Ken Roberts (announcer); Tim Frawley was "John Barclay" until 3/27/35
10/1/31 - 9/22/32 (Love Story Drama; Love Story Hour as of 10/15/31) Street & Smith, CBS, Thu, 9:30 pm; with Elsie Hitz, Ned Weaver, Adele Ronson, Dick Osgood, Teddy Bergman; David Ross (announcer); Frank Readick, Jr. was The Shadow. Above had overlapping. The following are now called The Shadow
1/5/32 - 2/2/32, Perfect-o-Lite, CBS, Tue, 10 pm; with Frank Readick, Jr.; music by Eugene Ormandy
10/5/32 - 4/26/33 (called Blue Coal Mystery Revue from 10/5 - 10/12), Blue Coal (sponsored on the East Coast), NBC, Wed; with Frank Readick, Jr. with Agnes Moorehead, Ford Bond (announcer), with George Earle Orchestra
10/1/34 - 3/27/35, Blue Coal, CBS, Mon & Wed, 6:30 pm; with Frank Readick, Jr; (James La Curto was The Shadow in Nov and Dec), Bill Johnstone, Jeanette Nolan, announcers were Del Sharbutt and Ken Roberts
9/26/37 - 3/20/38, Blue Coal, Mut, Sun, 5:30 pm; with Orson Welles; also for the first time, the character Margot Lane appears (Agnes Moorehead) and Ray Collins as Commissioner Weston; The Shadow now written by Walter Gibson; announcers were Arthur Whiteside (9/26 - 11/28) and Ken Roberts; Paul Huber takes over as "John Barclay."
1938 (Syn) Goodrich; 26 shows broadcast; with Orson Welles, Margot Stevenson with Ken Roberts announcing
9/25/38 - 3/19/39, Blue Coal, Mut, Sun, 5:30 pm; with Bill Johnstone, Agnes Moorehead with Ken Roberts announcing
1939 (summer); repeats of 1938 - 1939 season (Goodrich); 26 shows broadcast
9/24/39 - 4/7/40; 9/29/40 - 4/20/41; 9/28/41 - 3/22/42; 9/27/42 - 3/21/43; Blue Coal (East) other sponsors elsewhere, Carey's Salt, Mut, Sun, 5:30 pm; with Bill Johnstone and Marjorie Anderson (Jeanette Nolan on 4/7/40), Ken Roberts announcing, Paul Huber still was "John Barclay"
9/26/43 - 4/16/44, Blue Coal, Mut, Sun, 5:30 pm; with Bret Morrison and Marjorie Anderson, Kenny Delmar, Ken Roberts announcer; Paul Huber was "John Barclay"
9/24/44 - 4/8/45, Blue Coal (28 stations) and Acme/Linex (50 stations), Mut, Sun, 5:30 pm; with John Archer and Judith Allen; announcer was Don Hancock; also see Quick As A Flash
9/9/45 - 6/2/46, Blue Coal (East); other sponsors elsewhere; Mut, Sun, 5 pm; with Steve Courdeigh and Laura Mae Carpenter until 10/14/45; with Bret Morrison and Lesley Woods after that; announcer was Don Hancock for Blue Coal
9/8/46 - 6/1/47; 9/7/47 - 5/30/48; 9/12/48 - 6/5/49, Blue Coal (East); other sponsors elsewhere, Mut, Sun, 5 pm; with Bret Morrison and Grace Matthews; announcer was Andre Baruch for Blue Coal
9/11/49 - 9/3/50, Grove Laboratories, Mut, Sun, 5 pm; with Bret Morrison and Gertrude Warner; Santos Ortega; Carl Caruso (announcer)
9/10/50 - 9/2/51, Sus; U S Army/Air Force starting 1/21/51, Mut, Sun, 5 pm; with Bret Morrison and Gertrude Warner, Santos Ortega; Carl Caruso (announcer)
9/9/51 - 8/31/52, Wildroot, Mut, Sun, 5 pm; with Bret Morrison and Gertrude Warner, Santos Ortega, Ross Martin, Sandy Becker announcer
9/7/52 - 8/30/53, Wildroot (also Sylvania), Mut, Sun, 5 pm; with Bret Morrison and Gertrude Warner, Santos Ortega, Ross Martin, Sandy Becker (announcer)
9/6/53 - 7/25/54, Carnel, Tide and No-Doz, Mut, Sun, 5 pm; with Bret Morrison and Gertrude Warner, Santos Ortega, Ted Mallie (announcer)
8/1/54 - 12/26/54, Sus, Mut, Sun, 5 pm; with Bret Morrison and Gertrude Warner, Santos Ortega, Ted Mallie (announcer). The Shadow was also broadcast in Australia (Grace Gibson Productions) with Lloyd Gamble as Lamont Cranston, South Africa, England (Radio Normandy), Brazil (over 250 episodes translated into Portuguese and Spanish
also see The Official Adventures Of The Shadow

Shadows Of The Mind (7/9/47 - 9/24/47) Mut, Wed, 10 pm

2 **Shady Valley Folks** (1942 - 47) Mut (usually regional) 1942 - 45, 5t, 30m
also 1944 - 45 (Shady Valley Jamboree) Sus, Sat, 60m
1946 - 47, Sus, 5t, 45m, 9:15 am

Shafter Parker's Circus (with Hal Berger) (1940 - 41) Southwest Tablet, Mut - Pacific

Shakespeare (see Streamlined Shakespeare)

1 **Shamrocks** (Pre-war) Syn, 15m

1 **Shangri-La** (Wartime) Syn

Shannons (with James Walle and Russell Gleason) (15m)

1 **Share The Wealth** (11/9/48 - 1/9/50)
11/9/48 - 5/31/49, Mut, Tue, 8:30 pm
10/17/49 - 1/9/50, Waltham Watch, ABC, Mon, 25m, 8 pm, also syndicated

1 **She Loves Me Not** (1934) film sound track

1 **She Made Her Bed** (3/4/34) Air trailer

1 **She Shall Have Music** (1936) Air trailer

Sheaffer Parade (see Eddy Howard; Carmen Cavallaro, Roy Shield, Lou Breese)

Sheep and Goats Club Revue (3/13/40 - 10/30/40) Mut, Wed, 8 pm; 9:30 pm as of 9/18/40

Sheer Romance (1932 - 2/22/33) Bl, Wed, 15m, 6:30 pm

Shefter and Brenner (12/5/36 - 4/20/37) Bl, Tue, 10m, 10:05 am

Sheilah Graham (7/10/49 - 5/7/50) Sus, Mut, Sun, 15m, 9:30 pm

24 **Shell Chateau** (4/6/35 - 6/26/37)
4/6/35 - 3/28/36 (see Al Jolson); Walter Winchell hosted on 10/5/35; Wallace Beery hosted 10/12/35 - 12/28/35
4/4/36 - 12/26/36 (with Smith Ballew), NBC, Sat, 60m
1/2/37 - 6/26/37 (with Joe Cook) NBC, Sat, 60m

1 **Shep Fields and His New Music** (1945) WLW

1 **Shep Fields and His Orchestra** (Thesaurus transcription)

6 **Shep Fields and His Rippling Rhythm Orchestra** (Lang-Worth transcriptions)

5 **Shep Fields Orchestra** (Thesaurus transcriptions)

Sheriff Bob (3/27/39 - 4/28/39) Bl, 5t, 15m, 5:15 pm

Sheriff, The (6/29/45 - 9/14/51) ABC, Fri, 9:30 pm
6/29/45 - 3/23/51, Pacific Borax
4/6/51 - 6/29/51, Procter & Gamble
7/13/51 - 9/14/51, American Chicle

95 **Sherlock Holmes** (10/20/30 - 7/1/69)
Often on different days and/or times in different parts of the country
10/20/30 - 6/15/31, George Washington Coffee, NBC, Mon, 10 pm; William Gillette played lead in first show; then Clive Brook; then Richard Gordon and Leigh Lovel as Dr. Watson
9/23/31 - 5/4/32, George Washington Coffee, Bl, Wed, 9 pm; with Gordon and Lovel
also 9/17/31 - 3/31/32, NBC, Thu, 9:30 pm
5/5/32 - 6/23/32, George Washington Coffee, NBC, Thu, 9:30 pm; with Gordon and Lovel
10/5/32 - 5/31/33, George Washington Coffee, Bl, Wed, 9 pm (9:30 pm); with Gordon and Lovel
11/11/34 - 12/30/34, George Washington Coffee, Bl, Sun, 4 pm; with Luis Hector and Lovel
1/6/35 - 5/26/35, George Washington Coffee, Bl, Sun, 9:45 pm; with Hector and Lovel
2/1/36 - 9/26/36, Household Finance, Mut, Sat, 10:30 pm; 7:30 pm as of 4/4/36; with Richard Gordon and Harry West
10/1/36 - 12/24/36, Household Finance, NBC, Thu, 11:15 pm; with Richard Gordon and West
10/2/39 - 3/11/40, Bromo Quinine, Bl, Mon, 8:30 pm; with Basil Rathbone and Nigel Bruce
9/29/40 - 3/9/41, Bromo Quinine, Bl, Sun, 8:30 pm; with Rathbone and Bruce
10/5/41 - 3/1/42, Bromo Quinine, NBC, Sun, 10:30 pm; with Rathbone and Bruce
5/7/43 - 10/1/43, Petri Wine, Mut, Fri, 25m, 8:30 pm; with Rathbone and Bruce
10/4/43 - 5/28/45; 9/3/45 - 5/27/46, Petri Wine, Mut, Mon, 8:30 pm; with Rathbone and Bruce

Sherlock Holmes (continued)

10/12/46 - 1/4/47, Semler Co., ABC, Sat, 9:30 pm; with Tom Conway and Nigel Bruce
1/13/47 - 7/7/47, Semler Co., ABC, Mon, 8:30 pm; with Conway and Bruce
9/28/47 - 6/20/48; 9/12/48 - 12/26/48, Trimount Clipper Craft, Mut, Sun, 7 pm; with John Stanley and Alfred Shirley until 6/20/48; Stanley and Ian Martin from 9/12/48
1/3/49 - 6/6/49, Trimount, Mut, Mon, 8:30 pm; with George Seldon
9/21/49 - 6/14/50, Petri Wine, ABC, Wed, 8:30 pm; 9 pm as of 1/25/50; with Ben Wright and Eric Snowden
1/2/55 - 6/5/55, Sus, NBC, Sun, 9 pm; with John Gielgud and Sir Ralph Richardson originally broadcast in England (10/5/54 - 12/21/54)
5/1/56 - 9/4/56 (with John Gielgud and Sir Ralph Richardson), ABC, Tue, 7:30 pm Sherlock Holmes was also broadcast in England; with Carleton Hobbs and Norman Shelley
also 5/12/59 - 7/1/69, BBC/NPR

1 **Shine Smith's Christmas Party** (12/10/49) NBC

1 **Ship Ahoy** (1941) Air trailer

Ship Of Joy (1932 - 4/23/35)
1932 (See Horace Heidt)
9/25/33 - 6/4/34 (with Captain Hugh Dobbs) Del Monte, CBS, Mon, 9:30 pm
2/26/35 - 4/23/35 (see Horace Heidt)

1 **Shipmates Forever** (1935) Air trailer

Shirley Howard (with The Jesters)
(11/27/33 - 8/9/34) Molle, NBC, 2t - 3t (Mon, Wed, Thu) 15m

2 **Shirley Temple Time** (12/5/39 - 12/26/39) CBS, Tue
(12/5/41 - 12/26/41) (Shirley Temple Variety Show) Elgin Watch Co., CBS, Fri, 10 pm

Shoot The Moon (with Bud Collyer)
(9/23/50 - 5/23/51) ABC, Sat, 8 pm; Wed, 10 pm as of 4/25/51

1 **Shoot The Works** (1934) film sound track

1 **Shooting Gallery** (12/26/51) U.N. Radio/NBC

Shopping Talk (see Lois Long)

1 **Shopping With The Missus** (3/19/52) WBBM

1 **Shopworn Angel, The** (7/38) Air trailer

1 **Short Short Stories** (1932) Syn

2 **Short Short Story From Liberty Magazine, A** (1943) Syn

Short Story (see NBC Presents Short Story)

Short, Short Story (with George Putnam)
(1/22/40 - 1/17/41) Campbell, CBS, 3t, 15m, 11 am

Shorty and Sue (5/8/43 - 9/25/43) NBC, Sat, 15m, 10:45 am

5 **Shorty Bell** (with Mickey Rooney)
(12/18/47 - 6/27/48) CBS, Sun, 9:30 pm; 10 pm as of 5/2/48

3 **Showboat** (10/6/32 - 4/21/41)
10/6/32 - 10/28/37 (with Lanny Ross until 7/1/37; then Jack Haley until 10/28/37, Maxwell House, NBC, Thu, 60m
11/26/39 - 4/28/40 (from Chicago; with Cliff Soubier (also called Home Town Unincorporated) Brown and Williamson, NBC - South, Sun, 10:30 pm
5/3/40 - 8/2/40 (with Dick Todd, Virginia Verrill and Marlin Hurt) Brown and Williamson, Bl, Fri, 9 pm
8/5/40 - 4/21/41, Avalon Cigarettes, NBC, Mon, 9:30 pm

Showboat Matinee (with Lanny Ross)
(5/18/34 - 8/24/34) NBC, Fri, 60m, 3 pm

Show Goes On, The (see Robert Q Lewis)

1 **Show Of The Week, The**
(9/25/38 - 4/27/41) Sus, Mut, Sun; local sponsors (with Vincent Lopez Orchestra, others) (1/7/40 - 4/6/41)
(11/21/43 - 2/20/44) Mut, Sun, 4 pm

1 **Show Shop, The** (with Gertrude Niesen, Ray Nelson Orchestra; later George Hicks)
(1/24/42 - 8/29/42) Bl, Sat, 1:30 pm
(11/13/50 - 11/23/51) (with Walter Preston), Mut, 5t, 10:30 pm
(12/20/52 - 2/13/54) Mut, Sat, 60m, 5 pm

26 **Show Stoppers** (1946) Syn

1 **Show That Jack Built, The** (1/30/41) WLW

Showcase (NBC)

Showcase From Hollywood (see Freddy Martin)

2 **Shower Of Stars** (with Morton Gould Orchestra; with Donald Voorhees as of 7/26/45)
(2/8/45 - 8/30/45) Chrysler, CBS, Thu, 9 pm (replaced Major Bowes Original Amateur Hour while Bowes was sick)

71 **Showtime** (1943 - 1947) (AFRS) First 140 shows are 15m; those following are 30m (see also Broadway Showtime)
(1/8/56 - 6/3/56) ABC, Sun, 10m, 7:05 pm

1 **Shuffle Rhythm Time with Henry Busse and His Orchestra** (Standard transcription)

1 **Shuffle Rhythm With Henry Busse and His Orchestra** (Standard transcription)

Shumilk Program (with Rollickers Quartet) (6/2/32 - 9/7/32) Shumilk Shoes, Bl, Wed, 15m, 8:15 pm

3 **Shuron Showmen, The** (10/31) Syn

1 **Shuttle Discovery Flight** (9/29/88) CBS-TV

1 **Shuttle Launch** (3/13/89) CNN

1 **Si Zentner and His Orchestra** (9/5/65) CBS

1 **Sid Hoff and His Orchestra** (3/12/76) National Science net

Sid Skolsky (Hollywood News) (10/6/37 - 1/5/38) Bromo-Seltzer, Bl, Wed, 15m, 8:30 pm

Side Show (with Dave Elman)

1 **Sidewalk Cafe** (10/29/40) Mut

Sidney Albright (1943 - 44) NBC; 1948, Mut

1 **Sidney Mosley News** (10/7/43)

Sidney Walton's Music (7/6/40 - 10/20/40) Air Conditioning Training Corp., Bl, Sun, 15m; Sat from 8/10/41 - 9/21/40
(9/25/49 - 2/17/50) Doubleday, Mut, Sun, 15m, 1 pm; 5t, 11:30 am as of 1/9/50

Sigmund Spaeth's Music Quiz (see Tune Detective)

Signal Carnival (with Meredith Willson) (11/20/36 - 40) Signal Oil, NBC - west, various days

1 **Signing Ceremony At The White House** (6/1/90) pool feed

1 **Signing The German-Italo-Japanese Pact** (9/20/40) Mut

6 **Sigrid Schultz** (9/29/38 - 2/25/40) Mut

2 **Sigrid Schultz Reporting From Berlin** (6/6/40, 7/14/40) Mut

1 **Silent Guest** (11/48) Syn

Silent Men, The (with Douglas Fairbanks, Jr.) (10/14/51 - 5/28/52) Sus, NBC, Sun; Wed, 10 pm as of 3/19/52

Silhouettes (1/30/39 - 3/20/39) Mut, Mon, 15m, 1:30 pm
(1/7/41 - 3/28/41) (with Paul La Valle String Ensemble) NBC, Fri, 15m, 1:15 pm

Silken Strings, The (with Charlie Previn Orchestra; often with Countess Olga Albani) (1/7/34 - 9/29/35) Realsilk, Bl, Sun

Silver Cup Royal Wheat Revue

Silver Dust Serenaders (1/2/34 - 12/28/34) (with Paul Keast) Hecker Products, CBS, 15m, 3t (Tue, Thu, Sat) until 5/19/34; Tue & Thu until 6/28/34; 3t as of 7/2/34

1 **Silver Eagle, The** (with Jim Ameche) (7/5/51 - 3/10/55) General Mills, ABC, 7:30 pm
7/5/51 - 12/27/51, Thu
1/1/52 - 5/28/53; 6/1/54 - 3/10/55, Tue & Thu

Silver Flute, The (with Helen Walpole) (12/19/37 - 6/10/38) NBC, Sun, 11 am

1 **Silver Plate, The** (8/16/54) CBS

2 **Silver Platter** (AFRS)

2 **Silver Sails** (WLS) (with Jack Brinkley) (2/13/44, 5/7/44)

Silver Strings (4/10/38 - 10/9/38; 4/28/40 - 9/29/40; 6/15/41 - 12/28/41) NBC, Sun

Silver Summer Revue (see Musicomedy)

Silver Theater Summer Show (with Ed Sullivan) (4/27/41 - 9/28/41) CBS, Sun, 6 pm

44 **Silver Theater, The** (10/3/37 - 8/17/47) International Silver, CBS
10/3/37 - 12/26/37; 10/2/38 - 5/28/39; 10/8/39 - 4/20/41, Sun, 5 pm; 6 pm as of 10/2/38
10/5/41 - 4/19/42, Thu, 6 pm
7/4/43 - 10/1/44; 6/17/45 - 8/5/45; 6/23/46 - 8/25/46; 6/15/47 - 8/17/47, Sun, 6 pm (summer replacement of Ozzie and Harriet during 1945 - 47)

1 **Simon Ackerman Audition** (11/14/44)

Simoniz Guardsman (11/8/31 - 5/15/32) Simoniz Auto Cleaner, Bl, Sun, 5:30 pm

Simpson Boys Of Sprucehead Bay, The (with Parker Fennelly and Arthur Allen) (7/9/35 - 5/1/36) Bl, 5t (Tue - Sat) 15m, 12 noon

1 **Sinatra...The Main Event** (10/13/74) ABC-TV

1 **Since You Went Away** (1944) Air trailer

Sincerely, Kenny Baker (see Kenny Baker)

3 **Sinclair Headliner, The** (1943 - 1947) Mut

Sinclair Wiener Minstrels, The (with Gene Arnold) (3/5/32 - 1/4/37) Sinclair, Bl, Sat; Mon, 9 pm as of 4/11/32 (originated on WENR, Chicago in 1930)

1 **Sinfonia India**

Sinfonietta (with Alfred Wallenstein) (7/24/35 - 8/20/44)
7/24/35 - 36, Mut, Wed, 9:30 pm
1936 - 39, Mut, Tue, 60m/30m
6/22/39 - 11/2/39, Mut, Thu, 9:30 pm
11/10/39 - 11/15/40, Sus, Mut, Fri, 8:30 pm
11/21/40 - 1/14/43, Sus, Mut, Thu
10/2/43 - 8/20/44, Sus, Mut, Tue, 11:30 pm

1 **Sinfonietta Concert** (3/16/46) Mut

Sing Along (1942) (see The Landt Trio) (1948) CBS, 5t

Sing Along Club (5/1/44 - 3/19/46) CBS
5/1/44 - 10/5/44, 5t, 45m
10/8/44 - 3/16/45) 5t
11/5/45 - 3/19/46, Tue, 15m, 3:45 pm

2 **Sing Along With Mitch** (6/64, 7/66) NBC-TV

Sing Along With The Landt Trio (see The Landt Trio)

Sing and Swing (1/17/38 - 2/28/38) CBS, Mon, 4 pm

2 **Sing Baby Sing** (1936) Air trailer, film sound track

1 **Sing Before Breakfast** (7/6/42) NBC

Sing Before Supper (with Clark Dennis) (1/18/41 - 5/17/41) Bl, Sat, 5:30 pm

Sing For Dough (with Lew Valentine) (6/23/42 - 9/29/42) Bl, Tue, 8:30 pm

21 **Sing For The Seventh** (5/45) Syn

Sing For Your Supper (with Tommy Tucker Orchestra) (5/5/49 - 9/15/49) Longine, Mut, Thu, 9:30 pm

8 **Sing It Again** (with Dan Seymour) (5/29/48 - 6/23/51) Sus and Multi, CBS, Sat, 60m, 8 pm; 10 pm as of 12/25/48

1 **Sing With Bing** (10/31/46) WOR

1 **Sing You Sinners** (1938) Air trailer

Sing-A-Song-Of-Safety Club (with Irving Caesar) (10/17/40 - 2/21/43) Mut, Sun, 15m, 12:30 pm (on locally on WOR from 1939; often on WNYC, New York)

Singin' Sam, The Barbasol Man (WELI)

22 **Singin' Sam** (with Harry Frankel) (1930 - 47) 15m
1930 - 12/5/33, Barbasol, CBS, 2t, 8:15 pm; 3t as of 7/20/31; Mon as of 4/10/33; 2t as of 9/11/33 (Midwest only until 7/20/31)
5/28/34 - 8/20/34, Atlas Brewing, CBS, Mon, 10:30 pm
also 1/18/35 - 7/19/35, Barbasol, Mut, Fri, 15m, 9:45 pm
5/14/35 - 4/20/36, Barbasol, CBS, Tue, 7:30 pm; Mon as of 9/17/35
11/2/36 - 1/4/37, Barbasol, Bl, Mon, 10 pm
also 9/4/36 - 5/28/37, Barbasol, Bl, Fri, 8:15 pm
9/11/39 - 42 (Refreshment Time) (with Victor Arden Orchestra; announcer is Del Sharbutt) Syn, Coca-Cola
1/5/43 - 6/30/43, Barbasol, Mut, 2t, 15m, 8 pm; Mon & Wed as of 5/3/43
1943 - 44, Coca-Cola, Mut, 2t, 15m
1945 - 47 (Reminiscing) Syn

2 **Singing (Story) Lady, The** (with Ireene Wicker) (5/31 - 9/7/45) 15m except where noted; broadcast to 1975 in New York
5/31, WGN
1/11/32 - 8/11/38, Kellogg, Bl, 5t; 4t (Mon - Thu) as of 12/21/36; 5t as of 7/1/37; 4t (Mon - Thu) as of 8/2/37
also 12/25/36 - 6/25/37, Bl, Fri, 30m, 5:15 pm
also 10/3/37 - 12/26/37, Mut, Sun, 30m, 5 pm
12/11/38 - 5/7/39, Sus, NBC, Sun, 30m, 11:15 am; 1 pm as of 1/1/39
1/22/40 - 9/26/41, Sus, Bl, 4t (Mon - Thu), 15m
6/25/45 - 9/7/45, ABC, 5t, 15m, 5:45 pm

Singing and Swinging (5/16/40 - 12/6/40) Bl
5/16/40 - 6/6/40, Thu, 8:30 pm
8/8/40 - 10/17/40, Thu, 9 pm
11/8/40 - 12/6/40, Fri, 8 pm

Singing Bee, The (7/5/40 - 11/19/43) (with Welcome Lewis and Art Gentry)
7/5/40 - 4/19/41, CBS, Sat, 10:30 am; 10 am as of 10/5/40
11/5/42 - 3/11/43, NBC, Thu, 15m, 4 pm
3/15/43 - 11/19/43, Bl, 3t, 10m, 6:30 pm

Singing Canaries, The (see American Radio Warblers)

Singing Chef, The (with Irving Kaufman, Arnold Moss) (2/8/32 - 5/6/32) Kreml, CBS, 3t, 15m, 12:30 pm

1 **Singing Country**

1 **Singing Kid, The** (1936) film sound track

Singing Lady, The (see The Singing Story Lady)

1 **Singing Marine, The** (1937) film sound track

Singing Marshal, The (see Curley Bradley)

Singing Strings, The (7/13/40 - 2/15/41) Mut, Sat, 10:30 am

Singing Waiters (2/27/37 - 4/24/37) CBS, Sat, 15m, 5:45 pm

Singo (with Welcome Lewis) (1/25/44 - 4/13/44) Bl, 2t, 15m, 1:45 pm

1 **Sinking Of The Jacob Jones** (10/21/42) Mut

1 **Sir Anthony Eden** (6/26/40) BBC

1 **Sir Arthur Conan Doyle** (1930)

1 **Sir Harry Lauder** (5/16/38) BBC/Mut

1 **Sir Stafford Cripps** (4/11/42) All India Radio/BBC

Sisters Of The Skillet (see East and Dumke)

16 **Sisters, The** (3/52 - 4/12/52) WEVD

3 **Sitting Pretty** (11/33, 12/33) Air trailers

6 **Six By Corwin** (1/1/83 - 11/10/83) NPR

Six Gun Justice (with W. C. Robison; written by Wilbur Hall) (4/22/35 - 10/23/35) CBS
4/22/35 - 7/22/35, Mon, 9 pm
8/7/35 - 9/25/35, Wed, 9 pm
10/2/35 - 10/23/35, Wed, 9:30 pm

1 **Six Of A Kind** (2/4/34) Air trailer

54 **Six Shooter, The** (with James Stewart) (7/15/53) Audition
(9/20/53 - 6/24/54) Sus, NBC, Sun; Thu as of 4/1/54, 8 pm (until 3/21/54)

2 **Sixteen...Growing Up!** (1955) Syn

1 **Sixth War Loan Station Break Jingles** (Syn)

1 **Sixty Hours From You** (4/14/44) Mut

8 **Sixty Minutes** (8/11/74 - 10/25/92) CBS-TV

Sixty-Four Dollar Question, The (with Jack Parr; Phil Baker as of 3/18/51; Jack Parr as of 12/23/51)
(9/10/50 - 6/1/52) NBC, Sun
9/10/50 - 5/6/51, NBC, 10 pm
5/13/51 - 9/30/51, Multi, 10 pm
12/23/51 - 6/1/52, Sus, NBC, Sun, 9:30 pm

Sizzlers Trio, The (3/4/35 - 7/22/35) NBC, Mon, 15m, 3:45 pm

Sketches From Life (8/28/49 - 9/18/49) ABC, Sun, 15m, 10:30 pm

Sketches In Melody (with Milton Shrednick Orchestra; from KOA, Denver) (1942 - 46) NBC

5 **Skinnay Ennis and His Orchestra** (9/23/47) ABC, Standard transcriptions

Skip Farrell Show, The (also with Jack Lester, The George Bames Trio) (1947) ABC, 15m

1 **Skip James** (6/65) WBAI-FM

Skipper Jim (with James Sarsfield)

Skippy (with Franklin Adams, Jr.) (1/11/32 - 3/29/35) 15m
1/11/32 - 7/9/32, Wheaties, NBC, 6t, 5:15 pm
7/11/32 - 7/7/33, Wheaties, CBS, 6t, 5:30 pm
7/31/33 - 7/20/34; 10/l1/34 - 3/29/35, Phillips, CBS, 5t, 5 pm; 5:15 pm as of 4/30/34

7 **Skippy Hollywood Theater** (12/1/49 - 9/21/50) Rosefield Packing Co., CBS, Thu; previously syndicated since 1940

4 **Skitch and Company** (5/27/73 - 12/16/73) Syn

Skitch Henderson (6/13/50 - 9/10/54)
6/13/50 - 8/15/51, NBC, 5t, 8 am
9/23/51 - 9/10/54, NBC, 5t, 45m, 12:45 pm

8 **Skitch Henderson and His Orchestra** (SESAC transcriptions)

Sky Blazers, The (written by Phillips H. Lord; with Col. Roscoe Turner)
(12/9/39 - 8/31/40) Wonder Bread, CBS, Sat; 7:30 pm; 8 pm as of 6/29/40

7 **Sky King** (10/28/46 - 6/3/54) (see The Adventures Of Sky King)
10/28/46 - 8/29/47, Swift, ABC, 5t, 15m
9/2/47 - 6/2/50, Peter Pan, ABC, 2t and 3t, alternating mostly with Jack Armstrong; sometimes Sea Hound
9/12/50 - 6/11/53; 9/14/53 - 6/3/54, Peter Pan, Mut, 2t

Sky Over Britain (6/5/41 - 11/24/41) Mut, 15m, 8:15 pm
6/5/41 - 9/4/41, Thu
9/8/41 - 11/24/41, Mon

1 **Sky Raiders** (6/18/44) Mut

1 **Sky-Lab Blastoff** (5/14/73) CBS-TV

1 **Sky-Lab Recovery** (6/22/73) NBC-TV

1 **Sky-Lab: Journey's End** (9/25/73) CBS-TV

7 **Skyline Roof** (with Gordon MacRae, Archie Bleyer Orchestra)
(5/6/46 - 9/20/46) CBS, 5t, 15m, 6:30 pm

Skyrider Quiz (1944 - 45) Sus, Mut, Sat

1 **Skyway To The Stars** (9/12/48 - 5/22/49) CBS, Sun, 4:30 pm

Slanguage Quiz (1944) ABC, Sat

1 **Slappy Birthday Adolf** (4/20/43) KIRO

Slapsie Maxie Rosenbloom Show (also with Benny Rubin and Patricia Bright) (7/23/48 - 9/29/48) NBC, Fri, 10 pm; Wed, 8 pm as of 8/25/48

Sleep No More (see Nelson Olmsted)

5 **Sleepy Joe** (Syn)

2 **Slick and His Boys** (1939) Syn

1 **Slide Music Of Will Osborne and His Orchestra, The** (10/4/48) NBC, Standard transcription

Slight Case Of Ivory, A (with Walter Gross, Anita Boyer, Bob Hanna) (1941) CBS

4 **Slim Bryant and His Wildcats** (7/19/47) Thesaurus transcriptions

1 **Slim Duncan and His Texas Tornadoes**

Slim Martin and His Transco All Americans (1931) 15m

11 **Slums Cost You Money** (1938, 1939) Syn

Smackout (with Marian and Jim Jordan) (3/2/31 - 8/3/35) Sus, 15m
3/2/31 - 10/31/31, CBS, 4t/5t
11/3/31 - 8/3/35, NBC, 2 - 6t

5 **Smart Set** (with Teddy Black Orchestra) (11/17/40 - 1/12/41) Mut, Sun, 15m, also syndicated

Smart Six (Studebaker Show) (with Jack Haskell) (15m) (1948)

Smile Awhile (10/5/42 - 5/14/43) Wilson Milk, Bl, 3t, 15m, 11:30 pm; 2t (Wed & Fri) as of 12/30/42

Smile Parade (with Ransom Sherman) (1938 - 39) NBC, Fri

2 **Smile Time** (with Steve Allen and Wendell Noble) (2/5/46 - 47) Mut - Don Lee, 5t, 15m

4 **Smiley Burnette Show, The** (1950 - 53) 15m (292 shows were syndicated)

17 **Smilin' Ed McConnell's Buster Brown Gang** (9/2/44 - 4/11/53) Buster Brown Shoes, NBC, Sat, 11:30 am

2 **Smilin' Jack** (with Frank Readick, Jr.) (2/13/39 - 5/19/39) Tootsie Rolls, Mut, 3t, 15m

1 **Smilin' Through** (1941) Air trailer

2 **Smilin'Ed McConnell** (9/20/32 - 4/5/41) Acme Quality Paints,Taystee Bread, Ovenready Biscuits or Sus; varies between NBC, CBS, Bl; sometimes all three at once; different days; some include:
9/20/32 - 11/3/32, Acme, CBS, 2t, 15m
11/6/32 - 10/7/33, Acme, CBS, Sun, 15m
10/14/34 - 6/6/36, Acme, CBS, Sun, 6:30 pm
also on 4/4/35 - 5/30/35, CBS, Thu, 15m, 1:45 pm
8/30/36 - 7/4/37, Acme, NBC, Sun, 5:30 pm
8/29/37 - 3/27/38, Acme, Bl, Sun, 5:30 pm
9/27/38 - 6/1/39, Acme, Bl, 2t, 10:30 am
9/16/39 - 5/25/40, Acme, NBC, Sat, 15m
10/16/39 - 4/12/40, Taystee Bread, CBS, 5t, 15m, 4:45 pm
also 11/5/39 - 1/21/40, Bl, Sun, 15m, 10:45 am
also 11/7/36 - 1/30/37 (see also Aladdin Lamp Program), Aladdin Kerosene Mantle Lamp Co., Mut, Sat, 30m, 9 pm
also 9/16/38 - 3/11/39 (Ballard's Oven Ready Biscuit Time), Ballard's, NBC, 15m, 2t (Fri & Sat)
9/7/40 - 4/5/41, NBC, Sat, 15m, 11:45 am

Smith Brothers Program (Trade and Mark) (with Billy Hillpot and Scrappy Lambert)
(1926 - 3/31/34) Smith Brothers Cough Drops, 15m (on various days and times including:)
1926 - 4/8/31, Bl, Wed
10/16/31 - 4/1/32, Bl, Fri, 8:30 pm
also 11/28/31 - 3/26/32, CBS, Sat, 9:30 pm
10/30/32 - 12/25/32, Bl, Sun, 9:15 pm
1/1/33 - 4/2/33, NBC, Sun, 7:45 pm
11/16/32 - 3/31/34 (also with Nat Shilkret Orchestra), CBS, Sat, 8:45 pm; 8 pm as of 12/30/32

27 **Smiths Of Hollywood, The** (with Harry von Zell and Arthur Treacher)
(1/10/47 - 7/11/47) Mut, Fri, 8 pm
(5/14/48 - 10/1/49) Mut, Fri, 8 pm

Smiths Of San Fernando (with William Holden) NBC, 1946 (Audition)

Smoke Dreams (1928 - 2/24/46) (Regional)
1928 - 1/28/31, La Palina, CBS, Wed
2/16/36 - 5/3/36, Mut, Sun, 1:30 pm
9/27/36 - 5/23/37, H Fendrich Cigars, Mut, Sun, 1:30 pm
9/26/37 - 3/30/38, H Fendrich, NBC, Sun, 1:30 pm, Virginio Marucci Orchestra, WLW origination
10/2/38 - 5/16/39, H Fendrich, NBC, Sun, 15m, 10:45 pm; Tue as of 1/2/39
9/24/39 - 40, NBC, Sun, 2 pm
9/2/45 - 2/24/46 (with Tom Moore), Chesterfield, ABC, Sun

2 **Smoke Rings** (4/13/48) CKNX, (9/11/49) Mut

1 **Smokey's Army** (Syn)

1 **Smoothies, The** (5/15/44 - 6/23/44) Mut, 5t, 15m, 8:15 pm
also 5/25/45

Sneak Previews (7/4/43 - 9/5/43) Bl, Sun, 5:30 pm; summer replacement for The Musical Steelmakers

Snooky Lanson (9/14/46 - 10/19/46) NBC, Sat, 15m, 5:45 pm

Snoop and Peep (with Charles Finan and Paul Winkopp) (5/12/31 - 12/16/31) NBC
5/12/31 - 8/11/31, Tue, 11 pm
8/19/31 - 12/16/31, Wed, various times

5 **Snow Village Sketches** (with Parker Fennelly) (10/3/36 - 6/16/46)
10/3/36 - 6/26/37, Loose Wiles Biscuit Co., NBC, Sat, 9 pm
12/28/42 - 11/11/43, Procter & Gamble, NBC, 5t, 15m, 11:30 am
1/13/46 - 6/16/46, Mut, Sun, 10:30 am; 11 am as of 2/3/46

2 **Snow White and The Seven Dwarfs** (1937) Air trailers

1 **So That They Might Walk** (12/5/45) Mut

1 **So The Story Goes** (with John Nesbitt) (Syn) (1945 - 46)

4 **So They Say** (2/27/56 - 11/56) CBS

So This Is Love (with Eddie Dunn)
(1/6/47 - 7/4/47) Mut, 5t, 15m, 12:45 pm

So, You Think You Know Music (with Ted Cott; Leonard Liebling)
(7/9/39 - 4/26/46) (sometimes New York local)
7/9/39 - 9/17/39, CBS, Sun, 4 pm
10/15/39 - 2/18/40, CBS, Sun, 2:30 pm
4/17/40 - 4/28/40, CBS, Sun, 8:30 pm
9/17/40 - 4/29/41, NBC, Tue, 9:30 pm; 7:30 pm as of 10/1/40
11/23/45 - 12/28/45, Mut, Fri, 10 pm
1/4/46 - 4/26/46, Mut, Fri, 8:30 pm

So, You Want To Be... (7/8/38 - 10/7/38) CBS, Fri, 15m, 5:45 pm
(10/12/38 - 12/21/38) CBS, Wed

So, You Want To Lead A Band (see Sammy Kaye)

1 **Socialist Convention** (4/6/40) Mut

Society Brand Program (3/8/32 - 5/31/32) Alfred Decker and Cohn, CBS, Wed, 15m

4 **Society For The Propagation Of The Faith, The** (1948) Syn

Society Girl (with Charlotte Manson)
(10/9/39 - 10/4/40) Corn Refining Company, CBS, 5t, 15m

Society Of Amateur Chefs (with Allen Prescott) (8/13/46 - 10/1/46) ABC, Tue, 9 pm

Society's Playboy Hour (with Nat Brusiloff Orchestra, Norman Brokenshire, Welcome Lewis)
(3/8/32 - 6/1/32) Society Brand Clothing, CBS, Tue, 15m; Wed as of 3/30/32

Socony Sketchbook (with Johnny Green)
(6/14/35 - 9/13/35) Socony, CBS, Fri

Soconyland Sketches (with Parker Fennelly and Arthur Allen)
(2/29/28 - 5/11/35) Socony Oil
2/29/28 - 12/30/30, NBC, Tue, 7:30 pm
1/2/31 - 7/16/34, NBC, Mon, 8 pm
7/24/34 - 9/26/34, NBC, Tue, 9:30 pm
10/6/34 - 5/11/35, CBS, Sat, 7 pm; developed into Snow Village Sketches

Soft Lights and Sweet Music (1940s) ABC, 15m, with Jeff Brook

1 **Soldier Poets** (1946)

1 **Soldiers In Greasepaint** (11/25/43) NBC

87 **Soldiers Of The Press** (with Lon Clark)
(1942 - 1945) Syn
(2/28/43 - 8/5/45) Mut, Sun, 15m, 12:30 pm

1 **Soldiers With Coupons** (5/1/45 - 7/31/45) Mut, Tue, 15m, 6:15 pm

3 **Soldiers With Wings** (7/25/42 - 9/26/42; 10/17/42 - 10/24/42) CBS, Sat
(4/14/43 - 8/11/43) (3/15/44 - 6/21/44) Mut, Wed, 9:30 pm
(8/10/44 - 8/31/44) Bl, Thu, 11:30 pm
(1/6/45 - 3/24/45) Mut, Sat, 1:30 pm

1 **Solitaire Time** (with Warde Donovan and Tex Antoine) (11/4/45 - 1/21/51) NBC, Campana, Sun, 15m, 11:45 am, also WMAQ audition

2 **Solo In Crime** (Syn)

1 **Some Friends Of Stevenson** (7/19/65) CBS

1 **Some Fundamentals For Radio Salesmen** (1951) Syn

1 **Some Like It Hot** (1938) Air trailer

1 **Some Memory Songs To Jog Yours** (1964) Syn

2 **Somebody Knows** (with Jack Johnstone)
(7/6/50 - 8/24/50) CBS, Thu, 9 pm (summer replacement for Suspense)

1 **Someone Is Crying In The Night** (Wartime) Syn

Someone You Know (9/29/49 - 1/19/50) ABC, Tue, 10:30 PM

Someplace To Go (with Charles Arlington) (15m)

Somerset Maugham Theater
(1/20/51 - 7/14/51; 10/27/51 - 1/19/52) Tintair CBS, Sat, 11:30 am; NBC, Sat, 11 am as of 10/27/51

1 **Something About Believing** (4/14/68) CBS-TV

1 **Something For The Boys** (1944) film sound track

2 **Something For The Family** (Syn)

6 **Something For The Girls** (with Jean Colbert) (Wartime) Syn
(6/21/46 - 9/46) with Morton Gould (different show) 6/1/44 (with Helen Hayes) (different show) 15m

1 **Something New** (also see Hoagy Carmichael)

Something To Talk About
(5/24/43 - 6/16/44) Cudahy, CBS, 5t, 4:30 pm

1 **Son Of Erin** (AFRS origination)

1 **Son Of Man, The** (4/48) CBS

42 **Son Of Porthos** (by Alexandre Dumas) (Pre-war) Syn

Song and A Story (with Jimmy Newall) (15m)

Song Folks (6/1/40 - 9/14/40) NBC, Sat, 15m, 11 am

4 **Song Is Born, A** (2/21/44 - 12/2/44) Langendorf Breads, NBC, Mon
also 1948 film sound track, air trailers

1 **Song Of Liberty** (4/3/51) AFRS

1 **Song Of Scheherazade** (1947) Air trailer

1 **Song Of Siam** (1/4/54) UNESCO Radio

Song Of The City (8/14/34 - 7/4/35) Dreft, NBC (Regional), 5t, 15m; 3t (Tue - Thu) as of 4/30/35; first broadcast as Rainbow Court

1 **Song Of The Growth Of Democracy, The** (NBC/Syn)

2 **Song Of The Islands** (1942) Air trailer, film sound track

1 **Song Of The Stranger** (with Bret Morrison) (9/29/47 - 3/26/48) Feen-A-Mint, Mut, 5t, 15m, 3:30 pm

Song Of Your Life (with Harry Salter)
(11/23/40 - 3/29/41) Bl, Sat, 9 pm

Song Shop, The (9/10/37 - 6/3/38) Coca-Cola, CBS, Fri, 45m; with Kitty Carlisle until 1/21/38; with Nadine Connor from 1/28/38

Song Spinners (5/4/41 - 7/20/41) Mut, Sun, 15m, 10:15 pm
(11/1/41 - 12/6/41) Mut, Sat, 15m, 8:30 pm
(1/11/47 - 7/5/47) ABC, Sat, 15m, 7:15 pm

Song Sweets (see Louise Florea)

Song Time (with Betty Grable and John Payne) (7/17/37 - 11/12/37)
(11/19/37 - 2/25/38) CBS, Fri, 15m, 6:45 pm

Song Time In Tennessee
(4/13/35 - 6/1/35) CBS, Sat, 9 pm

2 **Song Writing Machine, The**
(1/3/48 - 4/10/48) Mut, Sat, 9:30 pm

1 **Songs Along The Trail** (3/31/46) Mut

Songs America Sings (1940s) Republic Steel (Audition)

Songs By Ann Brae (6/3/36 - 7/22/36) E Z Freeze Ice Cream, Mut, Wed, 15m, 9:30 am

Songs By Dinah Shore (see The Dinah Shore Show)

1 **Songs By Don Cherry** (9/21/50) NBC

1 **Songs By Dorothy Fischer** (4/1/44) KMBC

2 **Songs By Eddie Fisher** (also with Alvy West Orchestra) (1954) NBC, 15m

Songs By George Bryan (also with Dan Seymour, Jeff Alexander Orchestra)
(1946) Syn, 15m

Songs By Great Singers
(1/16/49 - 3/6/49) Radio Art Club, Mut, Sun, 15m, 1:45 pm

1 **Songs By Jimmy Kane** (1945) WWRL

Songs By Marcia Neil (also with Irving Miller Orchestra) (1942) NBC, 15m

Songs By Morton Downey (see Morton Downey)

Songs By Sinatra (see The Frank Sinatra Show)

10 **Songs For America** (1951, 1952) Syn

1 **Songs For Sale** (with Jan Murray)
(6/30/50 - 10/6/51) Sus, CBS, Fri, 60m, 9 pm; 8 pm as of 10/6/50; Sat, 10 pm as of 6/30/51
also 3/29/52, CBS-TV

Songs For Saturday (with Brick Holton; Ralph Blane as of 6/17/39)
(11/26/38 - 11/25/39) Bl, Sat, 15m, 8 am

1 **Songs For You** (8/14/45) Mut

1 **Songs From Incendiary Blonde** (1945) Air trailer

1 **Songs From Irving Berlin's Blue Skies**
(9/9/46) Air trailer

8 **Songs From Morton Downey**
(2/5/45 - 2/16/45) Syn

2 **Songs From "The Babe Ruth Story"**
(1948) Air trailers

Songs My Mother Used to Sing
(9/24/33 - 3/25/34) American Home Products, CBS, Sun, 6 pm

Songs Of A Dreamer (with Gene Baker and Doris Rich) (Syn) (1940) WENB - local
(10/5/42 - 4/1/44) Bl, 3t, 15m

Songs Of America (NBC)

Songs Of Dick Todd (ABC) 15m

32 **Songs Of George Byron** (1946) Syn

8 **Songs Of Good Cheer** (Syn - ZIV) 117 15-minute shows broadcast

Songs Of Home Sweet Home (with Edward Davies, Lucille Long)
(1/17/32 - 7/10/32) Alka-Seltzer, Bl (WLS), Sun, 4 pm

11 **Songs Of Jack Smith, The** (Post-war) Syn

30 **Songs Of Jerry Wayne, The** (1944) Syn

1 **Songs Of Lorette Howard, The** (1/22/37) WCNW

2 **Songs Of Praise** (Syn)

Songs Of Russia (5/3/36 - 8/30/36) CBS, Sun, 3:30 pm

Songs Of The B-Bar-B (see Bobby Benson)

Songs Of The Century
(11/18/42 - 12/23/42) CBS, Wed, 3:30 pm

1 **Songs Of The Gospel** (Audition)

Songs Of The Islands (with Harry Owens) 15m

Songs Of The Shanty Boy (15m)

1 **Songs Of The Synagogue** (2/12/61) WEVD-FM

2 **Songs Of The West** (1931) Syn

2 **Songs Of Tito Guizar, The**
(5/21/39, 7/2/39) CBS

1 **Songs Of Yesteryear** (Pre-war) Syn

Songs Sweethearts Sing
(8/31/40 - 10/19/40) Mut, Sat

12 **Songs To Remember** (Wartime) Syn

Songs We Remember (with Ernie Gill Orchestra) (1/9/38 - 10/16/38) Bl, Sun, 8:30 pm (originally called Ernest Gill's California Concert until 4/3/38)

2 **Songs Without Words** (1939) Syn

Songs You Love (with Nat Shilkret Orchestra)
(1/7/34 - 3/30/35) Smith Brothers
1/7/34 - 3/25/34, Bl, Sun, 15m, 9:45 pm
10/4/34 - 3/30/35, NBC, Sat, 30m
1936 - 37 (see Muriel Wilson)

Sonny and Buddy (see The Adventures Of Sonny and Buddy)

2 **Sonny Burke and His Orchestra**
(Standard transcriptions)

Sonny Dunham (7/5/41 - 8/30/41) CBS, Sat, 55m, 5 pm

Sonora Hour (9/28/28 - 5/30/29) Acoustic Products, CBS, Thu, 60m, 9 pm; 30m, 9:30 pm as of 1/10/29

3 **Sons Of The Pioneers** (led by Bob Nolan)
(2/4/39 - 7/8/39) Mut, Sat, 15m
(1947 - 48) 15m, also auditions, Thesaurus transcriptions

4 **Sons Of The Pioneers Show, The** (Syn)

1 **Sons Of The Pioneers, The** (11/9/36) Syn, WCNW

Sophie Tucker and Her Show
(11/7/38 - 5/5/39) Roi-tan, CBS, 3t, 15m, 6:45 pm (not in New York)

Sophisticated Ladies (1/27/41 - 4/24/41) NBC, Mon, 15m, 1:30 pm

8 **Sorrel and Son** (Syn)

1 **Sorrowful Jones** (1949) Air trailer

1 **Soul** (8/19/71) WNET-TV

18 **Sound '62** (1962) Syn

Sound Mirror (10/31/55 - 4/13/56) ABC, 5t, 25m, 9 pm

1 **Sound Of 50 Years, The 1920s To The 1970s, The**

1 **Sound Of Friendship, The** (9/22/60) AFRTS

1 **Sound Of Jazz, The** (12/57) CBS-TV

1 **Sound Of Living, The** (Syn)

3 **Sound Of Selling In The 60s, The**
(1963, 1964, 1965) Syn

18 **Sound Of War, The** (1965) Westinghouse Broadcasting

43 **Sound Off** (with Harry von Zell, Mark Wamow Orchestra, Evelyn Knight)
(Wartime) Syn, AFRS, 15m
(7/4/46 - 6/21/48) Sus
7/4/46 - 8/22/46) CBS, Thu, 8:30 pm (summer replacement for FBI In Peace and War)
10/3/46 - 3/27/47, Mut, Thu, 8 pm
7/6/47 - 8/10/47, ABC, Sun, 6:30 pm
8/16/47 - 10/11/47, CBS, Sat, 7:30 pm
4/5/48 - 6/21/48, ABC, Mon, 8:30 pm

Sound Stage For Joan Crawford (ABC)
(1947) Audition

Sound Stage West

2 **Sounding Board** (10/16/72, 2/16/73) WNAB

13 **Sounds Of Freedom** (Syn)

8 **Sounds Of Tel Aviv, The**
(12/24/61 - 10/17/65) WEVD

1 **Sounds Of The City** (7/7/48)

3 **Sounds Of The World** (CBS)

1 **Sounds To Remember** (10/29/67) WRFM-FM

3 **Soundstage** (5/17/70, 12/6/75, 12/13/75) Mut

1 **South African Album Of Familiar Melodies** (Syn)

1 **South Eastern World's Fair** (9/12/40) Syn

South Sea Islanders (1927 - 6/30/36) Sus; various days and times including:
1927 - 32, Bl, Sun, 15m
10/7/35 - 6/30/36, NBC, various days

2 **Southern California Light Opera Orchestra and Chorus** (1940) Syn

1 **Southern California Mexican Typica Orchestra** (1940) Syn

1 **Southern California Symphony Orchestra** (1941) Syn

4 **Southern California WPA Symphony Orchestra** (1942) Syn

1 **Southern Corn Conference** (11/16/51)

Southern Dairies Orchestra
(9/29/31 - 3/25/32) National Dairy, CBS, 2t (Tue & Fri), 15m, 7:30 pm

Southernaires (NBC) (1938)

Southernaires Quartette, The
(1930 - 2/11/51) Sus, Sun (also see Meetin' House)
1930 - 2/5/33, NBC
1933 - 2/11/51, Bl - ABC
also 5/1/40 - 3/14/41, Bl, 2t (Wed & Fri) 15m, 12:15 pm
also 4/21/41 - 7/11/41, Bl, 3t, 15m, 12 noon

3 **Southland Harmony Quartet, The** (7/10/49, 10/16/49, 1/15/50) WLOS

1 **Southland Singers Of Boston** (1939) Syn

Southwestern Serenade (1/6/40 - 9/29/40) NBC
1/6/40 - 4/13/40, Sat, 15m, 6:45 pm
8/18/40 - 9/29/40, Sun, 2 pm

Southwestern Stars (2/4/39 - 5/27/39) Sat
2/4/39 - 3/11/39, Bl, 5:30 pm
3/18/39 - 5/27/39, NBC, 4:30 pm

Space Adventures Of Super Noodle, The (with Charles Flynn and Robert Englund) (10/11/52 - 4/4/53) I. J. Grass Noodle Company, CBS, Sat, 15m, 10:15 am

1 **Space For Man?** (7/17/75) PBS-TV

1 **Space For Women** (7/3/81) WLIW-TV

5 **Space Notes** (8/83 - 11/84) Syn

165 **Space Patrol** (with Ed Kemmer)
(9/18/50 - 3/19/55) ABC, first few shows were 15 minutes; rest were 30m (221 shows broadcast)
9/18/50 - 1/8/51, Sus, 2t (Mon & Fri), 5:30 pm
8/18/51 - 3/27/54, Ralston, Sat, 7:30 pm; 10:30 am as of 10/6/51
4/3/54 - 3/19/55, Nestles, Sat also ABC-TV

1 **Space Shuttle Challenger Coverage** (1/28/86)

1 **Space Shuttle Columbia, First Launch** (4/12/81) NBC-TV

3 **Space Shuttle Landing** (4/9/83, 6/24/83, 9/15/83)

5 **Space Shuttle Launch** (11/12/81, 3/22/82, 6/27/82, 4/4/83, 8/30/83, 2/3/84)

1 **Space Shuttle Re-Entry** (3/29/82) ABC-TV

1 **Space Shuttle Test Launch #4, Landing** (7/4/82) CBS-TV

195 **Space Story, The** (11/11/70 - 6/9/86) Syn

1 **Space: A Report To The Stockholders** (7/22/74) CBS-TV

1 **Spaceship Enterprise, The** (8/12/77) ABC-TV

1 **Spaceship Enterprise: A Crucial Test, The** (10/12/77) ABC-TV

1 **Spade Cooley and His Orchestra** (Standard transcription)

3 **Spade Cooley Show, The** (1946) (also with Tex Williams) Syn, 15m
(7/27/51 - 9/21/51) CBS, Fri, 60m, 8 pm

3 **Spade Cooley, "The King Of Western Swing" and His Dance Band** (Standard transcriptions)

6 **Spade Cooley, "The King Of Western Swing" and His Dance Gang** (Standard transcriptions)

Sparkle Time (see Meredith Willson)

Sparkling Silver Summer Revue (see Musicomedy)

Sparky and Dud (Syn - 1930s) ZIV; 66 15-minute shows broadcast

Sparring Partners (with Walter Kiernan and Eloise McEthone) (1/6/53 - 4/7/53) ABC, Tue, 8 pm

1 **Sparrow and The Hawk, The** (with Michael Fitzmaurice)
(5/14/45 - 9/27/46) Sus, CBS, 5t, 15m

Spartan Hour (with Frances Langford, Richard Himber Orchestra)
(1/7/34 - 2/11/34) Spartan Radio, NBC, Sun, 3:30 pm, also see Jolly Coburn

1 **Speak Up** (3/8/46) CBS

Speak Up America (with Vincent Pelletier)
(9/29/40 - 12/22/40) Bl, Sun, 7:30 pm
(4/4/48 - 6/27/48) (with John B. Kennedy) ABC, Sun, 15m, 4 pm

Speaking Of Liberty (with Rex Stout, M.C.)
(4/14/41 - 2/5/42) (title changed to Heirs Of Liberty on 8/28/41) NBC, Thu, 15m, 6:30 pm

1 **Speaking Of Words** (8/26/46) CBS

4 **SPEBSQSA Finals** (6/23/57, 7/5/59, 6/25/61, 6/24/62) CBS

1 **Special 1945 Christmas Program** (1945, 12/25/45) Syn

1 **Special Agent** (with James Meighan)
(4/17/48 - 8/28/48) Mut, Sat, 9 pm; 11:30 pm as of 6/26/48

2 **Special All-Star Revue** (1951, 1952) Syn

12 **Special Assignment** (11/37)
(4/28/46 - 10/19/47) Mut, Sun, 15m, 12:30 pm, also syn

1 **Special Broadcast From Cairo and London** (12/1/43) BBC

1 **Special Broadcast From Manila** (5/7/42) NBC

1 **Special Broadcast From The New England Flood Areas** (9/24/38) Mut

1 **Special Broadcast From The Philippines** (10/2/45) Mut

1 **Special Bulletin From Guam** (2/15/45) Mut

1 **Special Care Program, "Aftermath"** (4/13/49) CBS

2 **Special Chanukah Program** (12/20/62, 12/15/63) WINS

Special Delivery (with Marian Randolph) (9/4/37 - 1/22/38) NBC, Sat, 9:30 pm

1 **Special Delivery: Vietnam** (8/24/69) Mut

1 **Special Documentary Program On The Fall Of Berlin** (5/2/45) CBS

1 **Special Easter Seal Program** (1954) Syn

1 **Special Eddy Arnold Show** (1953) Syn

1 **Special Features Division Jazz Show** (3/12/36) Mut

1 **Special Friday Night Star Recording**

Special Investigator (5/19/46 - 6/17/47) Commercial Credit, Mut, 15m
5/19/46 - 3/30/47, Sun, 8:30 pm
4/8/47 - 6/17/47, Tue, 8:15 pm

1 **Special Mileage Rationing Program** (1945) Syn

1 **Special New Year's Program** (1/1/46) Syn

1 **Special News Bulletins** (3/15/38) Mut

1 **Special News Roundup** (4/13/45) Mut

1 **Special Nuremberg Broadcast** (10/15/46) pool feed

1 **Special Passover Program** (4/7/63) WINS

1 **Special Program In Memory of President Roosevelt** (4/12/45) CBS

1 **Special Space Shuttle** (6/77) Syn

1 **Special Storm Report** (2/4/61) WNBC-TV

1 **Special Victory Program, A** (1/2/54) Syn

1 **Special World Series Preview** (10/3/39) Mut

1 **Spectator, The** (3/29/79) WMUK-FM

Spectrum USA (1970 - 72)

1 **Speculations On The Next Thirty Three Years** (12/29/67) WNDT-TV

2 **Speed and Double Speed** (Pre-war) Syn, 15m

1 **Speed Demon** (9/52) Syn

176 **Speed Gibson Of The International Secret Police** (with John Gibson, Howard McNear and Hanley Stafford) (Syn) (1937 - 38) 15m; 178 episodes broadcast

1 **Speed Limit** (1931) Synchro-disc

1 **Speed Riggs** (11/7/66) Mut

Speed Show (see Nash Program)

1 **Spellbound** (1945) Air trailer

Spelling Bee (with Paul Wing)
(5/6/37 - 1/14/40) (began several months earlier but only in towns participating)
5/6/37 - 6/10/37, Bl, Thu, 10 pm
1/8/38 - 2/26/38, Bl, Sat, 8:30 pm
3/1/38 - 9/2/38, Bl, Fri, 9:30 pm
9/11/38 - 1/14/40, Energine, NBC, Sun, 5:30 pm

1 **Spencer Tracy Story, The** (1948) Air trailer

Spend A Million (with Joey Adams)
(6/9/54 - 8/25/54) NBC, Wed, 8:30 pm
(10/28/54 - 5/5/55) Sus, NBC, Thu, 9 pm

2 **Spice Of Life, The** (Syn)

Spider's Web

5 **Spike Jones and His City Slickers** (Standard transcriptions)

33 **Spike Jones Show, The** (6/3/45 - .6/25/49)
6/3/45 - 8/26/45 (with Frances Langford), Chase & Sanborn, NBC, Sun, 8 pm (summer replacement for Charlie McCarthy)
10/3/47 - 6/25/48; 10/1/48 - 12/24/48 (Spotlight Revue), Coca-Cola, CBS, Fri, 10:30 pm
1/2/49 - 3/6/49, Coca-Cola, CBS, Sun, 6:30 pm
3/12/49 - 6/25/49, Coca-Cola, CBS, Sat, 7:30 pm

1 **Spike Jones' Other Orchestra** (Standard transcription)

Spin and Win (with Warren Hull)
(12/4/40 - 4/30/41) Bl, Wed
(5/10/41 - 1/24/42) (with Jimmy Flynn) Bl, Sat, 9 pm

2 **Spin Back The Years** (Mut)

1 **Spin To Win** (6/27/49 - 9/18/49 CBS, Sat, 60m, 7 pm

1 **Spinner Of Yarns, The** (11/25/47) Mut, audition

1 **Spirit Of '43** (5/22/43) CBS

27 **Spirit Of The Vikings, The** (1943 - 1954) Syn

1 **Spirit Of '41 ('42) ('43)** (program for National Defense) (started as summer replacement for Andre Kostelanetz)
(6/29/41 - 9/11/43) CBS
6/29/41 - 10/4/42, CBS, Sun; 4:30 pm; 2 pm as of 10/5/41
12/5/42 - 9/11/43, CBS, Sat, 2:30 pm

1 **Spirituals By Madame Dujour And Her Daughter** (1/7/37) WCNW

6 **Sport Spotlight** (World syn)

2 **Sport-O-Grams** (Syn)

1 **Sports Answer Man, The** (1950) 15m

Sports Digest (with Al Helfer) Mut (1950)

Sports For All (see Bill Slater)

Sports Interviews

1 **Sports Magazine Of The Air, The** (11/6/46) CBS

1 **Sports Parade Interviews** (1949) Syn

2 **Sports Parade, The** (10/9/48, 1949) Mut, Syn

Sports Resume (with Paul Douglas) (see Chesterfield Sports Show)

1 **Sports Review 1960** (1960) ABC

Sports School (with Bill Stern)
(6/17/39 - 11/4/39) Bl, Sat, 15m, 11:15 am
(6/1/40 - 8/17/40) NBC, Sat, 15m

1 **Sports Secrets** (1934) Syn

1 **Sports Star Record** (Syn)

Sports Star Special (15m)

1 **Sports Straight From The Shoulder** (4/14/50) NBC

3 **Sports Ten** (12/23/53, 12/29/53, 12/31/53) Mut

15 **Sports Week** (10/8/56 - 1/17/60) AFRTS

16 **Sportsmen's Club** (see Grantland Rice Sports Stories) (see also Fishing and Hunting Club) (2/26/44 - 12/2/44) NBC

1 **Sportsman's Show** (2/21/38) Mut

4 **Sportsmen Quartet, The** (MacGregor, World transcriptions)

Sportsreel

1 **Spot Recordings Of The Bouganville Landing By The Marines** (1/6/44) CBS

Spotlight (4/24/41 - 6/26/41) CBS, Thu, 8 pm

145 **Spotlight Bands** (also called Victory Parade Of Spotlight Bands)
(11/3/41 - 11/22/46) Coca-Cola; about 1300 programs broadcast
11/3/41 - 5/2/42, Mut, 6t, 15m, 10:15 pm; 30m on Saturday
9/21/42 - 6/16/45, Bl, 5t - 6t, 25m, 9:30 pm
6/18/45 - 7/5/46; 9/16/46 - 11/22/46, Mut, 3t, 9:30 pm; as of 4/1/46 G Lombardo on Mon; X Cugat on Wed; H James on Fri

2 **Spotlight Champion Of Champions** (1942) Syn

1 **Spotlight On America** (with George Putnam) (7/19/46 - 2/21/47) Transit Company Of America, Mut, Fri, 10 pm

1 **Spotlight On Iran** (12/1/79) CBS-TV

4 **Spotlight On Music** (with Marion Nichols and Lud Gluskin's Orchestra; also Wilbur Hatch) CBS (1944 - 1947)

Spotlight On Paris (with Gregoire Aslan) (1954)

3 **Spotlight On Science**

2 **Spotlight Playhouse** (3/14/46, 3/21/46) ABC, Thu

Spotlight Revue (see Spike Jones; Dick Jurgens)

9 **Spotlight Story** (4/18/55 - 10/20/55) (with Brian Aherne) Mut, 4t (Mon - Thu), 15m

5 **Spotlighting New York** (10/25/48 - 12/14/48) WOR

1 **Springtime In The Rockies** (1942) Air trailer

1 **Spirit Of Christmas** (1940) Syn

Spud Murphy Orchestra
(4/13/40 - 6/1/40) Bl, Sat, 11 am

1 **Sputnik Reports** (10/7/57)

Spy At Large (written by George Ludlam) (3/27/38 - 10/9/38) Bl, Sun, 8 pm

Spy Masters

1 **Spy Ring Testimony** (7/31/48) Mut

Spy Secrets (produced by Himan Brown) (7/31/38 - 9/5/38) Energine, NBC, Sun, 5:30 pm

Spy Stories (see Ned Jordan)

Spycatcher (1960 - 1961)

Squad Car (with Peter Finch, James Van Sickle) (1954) Syn, 15m

Squad Room (1/11/53 - 7/17/56) Mut
1/11/53 - 1/24/54, Sus, Sun, 6:30 pm
2/3/54 - 4/6/55, Wed, 8 pm
1/8/56 - 7/17/56, Sus, Tue, 8:30 pm

4 **Squalus Disaster** (5/23/39, 5/24/39, 5/25/39) Mut

2 **Squalus Salvage** (8/12/39, 8/13/39) Mut

1 **Square Moons** (1948) Syn

Square With The World
(11/28/45 - 2/21/46) Household Finance, Mut, Thu, 9:30 pm

Squibb Golden Treasury Of Song
(10/7/40 - 11/27/42) Squibb, CBS, 15m
10/7/40 - 1/31/41 (with Jan Peerce) 5t, 3:15 pm
2/3/41 - 9/26/41 (with Frank Parker) 5t, 3:15 pm
9/29/41 - 11/27/42 (with Frank Parker) 3t, 6:30 pm

Squibb Program (with Revelers, Frank Black Orchestra) (1932 - 4/2/33) NBC, Sun, 4:30 pm

Squibb Show (see Lyn Murray)

SSS Music Box (1/36 - 5/19/37) SSS Co., Mut, Fri, 9:30 pm; 8:30 pm as of 5/6/36

2 **St. Louis Blues** (1/37, 1938) Air trailer, film sound track

4 **St. Ronan's Well** (Syn)

Stag Party (with Alan Young)
(4/25/42 - 9/26/42) ABC, Sat, 10:30 pm

Stage 52 (10/21/51 - 11/18/51) ABC, Sun, 60m, 6:30 pm

1 **Stage Forty Seven** (1/28/47) CBC

2 **Stagedoor Canteen** (with Raymond Paige Orchestra; Bert Lytell)
(7/30/42 - 4/20/45) Corn Products, CBS
7/30/42 - 9/23/43, Thu, 9:30 pm
10/1/43 - 4/20/45, Fri, 10:30 pm

20 **Stagestruck** (with Mike Wallace; Ben Grauer 11/13/53 - 1/1/54)
(10/2/53 - 5/2/54) CBS, Fri, 60m, 8:30 pm; 9 pm as of 11/13/53; Sun, 5 pm as of 1/8/54
also 1936, Air trailer

Stainless Show (with Ford Bond, Mario Cozzi) (11/27/36 - 5/21/37) Allegheny Steel as of 1/15/37, Bl, Fri, 15m, 7:15 pm

1 **Stairway To The Stars** (7/11/39) CBS; with Paul Whiteman (5/5/46 - 6/30/46; 8/8/47 - 8/29/47) Philco, ABC, Sun

1 **Stalin Special** (3/53) NBC

1 **Stalin Story, The** (3/4/53) CBS

Stamp Adventurer's Club
(5/5/33 - 5/10/34) Louden Packing Co., CBS, Fri, 15m; Thu as of 9/28/33

Stamp Club (see Captain Tim Healy) (also 10/18/52 - 5/16/53) CBS, Sat, 15m, 10:30 am

2 **Stamp Man, The** (Syn)

Stamp News (with Ernest Kehr)

16 **Stan Freberg Show, The**
(7/14/57 - 10/20/57) CBS, Sun, 7:30 pm (see also That's Rich)
(11/91) NPR

Stan Freeman (3/22/53 - 6/26/53) NBC, 5t, 15m, 10:30 am

6 **Stan Freeman and His Jazz Quartet** (SESAC transcriptions)

Stan Freeman Little Revue
(9/28/53 - 2/12/54) NBC, 4t (Mon - Wed, Fri), 25m, 10:35 pm Stan Getz

2 **Stan Kenton** (My World Is Music) (3/31/53, 4/7/53) NBC, Wed

11 **Stan Kenton and His Orchestra**
(12/8/41 - 1957) Bl, Red, CBS, ABC, NBC, Tempo and MacGregor transcriptions

1 **Stan Kenton Concert Encores** (9/2/52) NBC

1 **Stan Kenton Encores** (NBC)

5 **Stan Kenton Show, The** (Syn)

1 **Stan Laurel Interview**

Stan Lomax Show, The (1935 - 9/22/45) Sus, Mut, 15m; broadcast until 1977 on WOR in New York City; also syndicated; see also Hit The Ball
1935 - 45, 5t - 7t
also 1/29/44 - 9/22/45 (This Is Halloran), Mut, Sat, 3 pm

6 **Stand By For Adventure** (Syn) (1950) 15m

Stand By For Crime (with Glenn Langan and Adele Jergens) (Syn - 1953)

42 **Stand By For Music** (Navy) Syn

1 **Stand Up and Cheer** (1934) film sound track

Standard Hour, The (1925 - 56+) Standard Oil, NBC - West, Sun

1 **Standard Oil "Seventy Fifth Anniversary Entertainment"**
(10/13/57) NBC-TV

6 **Standard School Broadcast, The**
(10/1/28 - 2/1/70) (Standard Oil, NBC - West, Syn, Thu, 45m

Standard Symphony (10/23/27 - 39+) Standard Oil, NBC - West, Thu, 60m

Star and The Story, The (with Walter Pidgeon) (2/6/44 - 7/30/44) Goodyear, CBS, Sun, 8 pm

Star Carousel (1958)

Star For A Night (with Paul Douglas, Hugh James, Wendy Banie)
(12/15/43 - 3/8/44) Adam Hats, Bl, Wed, 10:30 pm

1 **Star Gazer (Are You A Poet?), The** (4/22/45) WNYC

1 **Star Kings, The** (1/30/50) NBC, audition

2 **Star Maker, The** (9/39) Air trailer, film sound track

1 **Star Parade** (Wartime) Syn

Star Performance (1944)

Star Reveries (5/3/31 - 11/24/31) International Shoe, CBS, 15m
5/3/31 - 7/26/31, Sun, 10:45 pm
9/1/31 - 11/24/31, Tue, 10:15 pm

1 **Star Spangled Rhythm** (1942) Air trailer

1 **Star Spots** (1949) Syn

2 **Star Time** (Post-war) Syn

13 **Star Wars** (1/80 - 4/80) NPR

4 **Star-Spangled Theatre** (12/1/40 - 9/7/41) Bl, Sun, 8 pm

Star-Spangled Vaudeville (with Walter O'Keefe) (7/5/42 - 9/6/42) Chase & Sanborn, NBC, Sun, 8 pm (summer replacement of Charlie McCarthy Show)

1 **Stardust Program** (12/27/36) WAAT

Starlight and Music (with Genevieve Rowe, Leonard Stokes, Bob Stanley Orchestra) (6/21/42 - 2/21/43) Mut, Sun, 9:30 pm

Starlight Concert (with Eloise Dragon, Don Wilson, Carmen Dragon Orchestra) (5/9/50 - 10/3/50) Turns, NBC, Tue, 8:30 pm (summer replacement for Baby Snooks)

1 **Starlight Operetta** (6/10/50) CBS

3 **Starlight Serenade** (with Victoria Cordova) (6/29/44 - 11/23/44; 6/7/45 - 11/15/45) Conti, Mut, Thu, 9:30 pm (summer replacements for Treasure Hour Of Song) (with Bea Wain and Nestor Nestor-Chayres in 1945)

Starlight Theater (with Madeleine Carroll) (10/16/53 - 3/26/54) Multi, Mut, Fri, 8:30 pm; 8 pm as of 1/8/54

3 **Starlite Concert** (7/4/50 - 10/3/50) NBC

Starr Of Space (see Captain Starr Of Space)

Starring Boris Karloff (see Presenting Boris Karloff)

1 **Stars About Town** (12/26/46) Mut

Stars and Starters (with Jack Barry) (5/19/50 - 8/25/50) NBC, Fri, 8 pm

Stars and Stripes (broadcast from London) (5/31/42 - 11/22/42) Mut, Sun, 9 pm

23 **Stars and Stuff** (1/13/82 - 7/8/82) ZBS Foundation, NPR

208 **Stars For Defense** (4/3/52 - 3/26/67) OPA, Civil Defense, Syn,15m

Stars From The Blue (5/16/43 - 9/12/43) Bl, Sun, 12:30 pm from Paris
(4/7/53 - 4/28/53) NBC, Tue, 8 pm

Stars In Action (National Guard)
(5/23/53 - 9/26/53) NBC, Sat, 5 pm

Stars In Khaki 'n' Blue (with Arlene Francis) (3/30/52 - 10/11/52) NBC
3/30/52 - 4/20/52, Sun, 10 pm
6/28/52 - 10/11/52, Sat, 8:30 pm

2 **Stars In The Afternoon**
(9/22/46, 9/29/46) CBS

4 **Stars In The Air** (12/13/51 - 6/30/52) CBS
12/13/51 - 4/24/52, Thu, 9:30 pm
5/3/52 - 6/14/52, Sat, 10 pm; 9:30 pm as of 5/31
6/30/52, Mon, 8 pm

Stars In The Night (6/28/48 - 1/3/49) ABC, Mon, 8:30 pm; 9:30 pm as of 10/18/48
(6/22/49 - 7/27/49) ABC, Wed, 9 pm
(8/4/52 - 9/22/52) Mut, Mon, 8 pm

Stars Of The Future (with Lawrence Brooks and Frances Greer)
(12/8/44 - 5/31/45) Ford, Bl, Fri, 8 pm

Stars Of The Milky Way
(9/27/36 - 3/31/37) Fresh Milk, Mut, Sun, 6:30 pm

1 **Stars Of Tomorrow** (3/18/34) Air trailer

80 **Stars On Parade** (8/20/50 - 3/23/56) Army, Air Force, Syn, 15m

1 **Stars On Parade For The Muscular Dystrophy Association** (Syn)

Stars Over Broadway (2/25/50 - 8/19/50) Bowey's Inc., Mut, Sat, 15m, 5:30 pm

44 **Stars Over Hollywood** (5/31/41 - 9/25/54) CBS, Sat
5/31/41 - 9/11/48, Dari-Rich, 12:30 pm
9/18/48 - 9/8/51, Armour
10/6/51 - 9/25/54, Carnation

1 **State Concert**

4 **State Department Speaks, The**
(1/8/44 - 1/29/44) NBC

1 **State Dinner At The Soviet Embassy** (6/1/90) pool feed

1 **State Fair** (1962) film sound track

1 **State Of The Union: 1982, The** (1/26/82) pool feed

2 **State Of The Union: A Democratic View, The** (2/1/74, 1/21/76) pool feed

1 **State Of The Union: A Republican Response, The** (1/30/79) CBS-TV

1 **State Of The Union: Alternate Views, The** (1/27/79) ABC-TV

1 **State Of The Union: Republican Responses** (1/28/80) ABC-TV

1 **State Symphony Of Boston, The** (1939) Syn

1 **Statement Of Polish Ambassador** (9/1/39) Mut

12 **States Of The Union, The** (1975, 1976) NPR

3 **Station Debunk** (4/29/42 - 6/22/42)

Stay Tuned For Terror (adapted by Robert Bloch) (1945; produced in Chicago) (Syn) 15m

1 **Steamboat Jamboree** (with Lanny Ross) (1940) Audition

Stebbins Boys, The (with Parker Fennelly and Arthur Allen) (6/22/31 - 10/21/32) Swift, NBC, 5t, 15m, 6:45 pm; Bl as of 3/14/32

1 **Steel Horizons** (with John Baker)
(10/1/44 - 9/9/45) Allegheny Steel, Mut, Sun, 9 pm

Steinie Bottle Boys Swing Club (5/19/38 - 6/16/38) Glass Containers Assoc., Bl, 2t (Mon & Thu) 15m, 7:45 pm

15 **Stella Dallas** (with Anne Elstner) (10/25/37 - 12/22/55) Sterling Drugs (Phillips Milk Of Magnesia), NBC, 5t, 15m; began as a local show on WEAF in New York; sponsored by Tetley; first network show on 6/6/38

1 **Step By Step** (filmstrip audio)

3 **Step Lively** (1944) Air trailer

Stepmother (see Kay Fairchild, Stepmother)

Stepping Ahead With America (with John B. Kennedy) (7/7/38 - 8/25/38) Bl, Thu, 8 pm

Stepping Along (with Budd Hulick and Jimmy Shields; Lew Parker as of 4/8/39) (2/18/39 - 7/1/39) CBS (Partial), Sat, 4:30 pm

1 **Stepping Out** (with Rosemary Clooney) (7/3/50 - 8/25/50) CBS, 5t, 7:30 pm (summer replacement of Club 15)

1 **Stepping Stones To Victory** (1945) Air trailer

Sterling Holloway (1948) (Audition)

8 **Steve Allen Show, The**
(11/10/49 - 1/24/53) Sus, CBS; started in 1947 on KNX; also on 1963 on KRHM
6/4/50 - 8/27/50, Sun, 6:30 pm (summer replacement for Our Miss Brooks)
7/11/52 - 9/25/52, Fri, 9:30 pm
8/4/52 - 9/26/52, 4t (Mon, Wed - Fri), 9:30 pm
10/4/52 - 1/24/53, Sat, 60m, 9:30 pm; 30m, 10 pm as of 11/29/52
11/30/52 - 1/18/53, Sun, 10:30 pm

2 **Steve Canyon** (with Barry Sullivan) (9/2/48) Auditions

44 **Steve Lawrence Show, The** (1960) Syn

2 **Stevie** (5/27/83, 6/3/83) NPR

Stewart Alsop (10/19/47 - 11/23/47) ABC, Sun, 15m, 1:15 pm

1 **Stick To The Facts** (10/15/48) Mut, audition

1 **Stock Market "Crash"** (10/19/87) FNN audio

Stolen Husband, The (1931)

Stoned Ranger, The (1960s) 65 2-minute episodes (KY)

1 **Stonehill Prison Mystery** (Pre-war) Syn

1 **Stones Of History** (1934, 6/23/35 - 9/25/36) Bl, Sun, 10:30 pm; Wed as of 7/10/35

2 **Stoopnagle and Bud** (with E. Chase Taylor and Budd Hulick)
(5/24/31 - 9/28/38) 5/24/31 - 12/3/31 (Gloom Chasers) CBS, 4t (Sun - Wed), 15m, 8:45 pm
2/1/32 - 8/31/32, Ivory, CBS, 2t (Mon & Wed), 15m, 8:45 pm
12/29/32 - 6/22/33 (also with Andre Kostelanetz Orchestra), Pontiac, CBS, Thu, 9:30 pm
12/16/33 - 2/7/34, Pontiac, CBS, 2t (Wed & Sat), 15m, 9:15 pm
2/12/34 - 6/7/34 (see Carefree Carnival)
6/22/34 - 9/7/34, Schlitz, CBS, Fri, 45m, 10 pm
11/18/34 - 12/16/34, Gulf, CBS, Sun, 9:30 pm
3/8/35 - 7/12/35, CBS, Fri, 10:30 pm
also 5/21/35 - 7/1/35, DeVoe and Reynolds, CBS, 2t, 15m, 6:45 pm
3/14/36 - 6/18/36, CBS, Sat, 9:30 pm; Thu, 8:30 pm as of 5/14/36
7/1/36 - 9/28/36, Ipana and Sal Hepatica, NBC, Wed, 60m, 9 pm (summer replacement for Town Hall Tonight)
10/4/36 - 5/16/37 (Minute Men) Minute Tapioca, Bl, Sun, 5:30 pm
7/6/38 - 9/28/38, Ipana and Sal Hepatica, NBC, Wed, 9 pm

Stoopnagle's Schutter (see Colonel Stoopnagle)

Stop Or Go (with Ken Murray; Joe E. Brown) (3/14/43 - 3/18/45)
3/14/43 - 9/44, Greyson's, CBS, Sun
also 3/23/44 - 10/5/44 (with Joe E. Brown) Bl, Thu, 10:30 pm
10/8/44 - 3/18/45 (with Joe E. Brown), McKesson, Bl, Sun, 8:30 pm

1 **Stop Me If You've Heard This One**
(10/7/39 - 10/9/48)
10/7/39 - 2/24/40 (with Milton Berle) Quaker, NBC, Sat, 8:30 pm
9/13/47 - 10/9/48 (with Morey Amsterdam), Sus, Mut, Sat, 9 pm; 8:30 pm as of 3/6/48

Stop That Villain (with Jack Bailey and Marvin Miller) (9/6/44 - 11/29/44) Dubonnet Wine, Mut, Wed, 8:30 pm

8 **Stop The Music** (with Bert Parks)
(3/21/48 - 2/15/55)
3/21/48 - 50, Multi, ABC, Sun, 60m, 8 pm
1950 - 8/10/52, Old Gold, ABC, Sun, 60m, 8 pm
8/10/54 - 2/15/55, sponsored for 15m, CBS, Tue, 75m

Stop, Look and Listen (with Edwin C. Hill) (5/22/39 - ?) Metropolitan Life, Mut, 5t, 15m

Stories America Loves (10/6/41 - 10/16/42) Wheaties, CBS, 5t, 15m, 9:45 am; 10:15 pm as of 3/30/42

Stories By Olmsted (see Nelson Olmsted)

1 **Stories From The Great Book** (Syn)

6 **Stories In Christian Stewardship** (Syn)

Stories In Steel (15m)

Stories Of The American Scene (Audition) 1948; with Howard Culver)

Stories Of The Black Chamber (with Jack Arthur; written by Major Herbert Yardley,) (1/21/35 - 6/28/35) Forhan's Toothpaste, NBC, 5t, 15m, 7:15 pm; 3t as of 2/11/35

Stories Of The Living Great (with Ida Bailey Allen) (2/16/32 - 6/14/32) Pebeco, CBS, Tue, 15m, 11:15 am

Stories Of Valor

3 **Stork Club, The** (1945, 1946) Air trailers, film sound track

Story Behind The Claim (10/2/34 - 11/27/34) Provident Mutual Life, Bl, Tue, 15m, 9:15 pm

1 **Story Behind The Railroads, The** (7/28/39) Bl

3 **Story Behind The Song, The**
(5/14/31 - 7/30/31) Bl, Thu, 10 pm (with Don Ameche and Bob White)
(11/19/34 - 4/1/35) Roque Cheese, CBS, 2t (Mon & Thu), 15m, 1:30 pm
also Pre-war syndication

10 **Story Behind The Story, The** (with Dick Kollmar) (1/7/52) Mut, also syndicated with Marvin Miller

Story Book Dramas (see Vernon Crane)

1 **Story Dramas** (9/30/40 - 12/8/41) Red, 2t (Mon & Wed), 15m, 10 pm

Story For Tonight (see Nelson Olmsted)

1 **Story For V-J Day, A** (7/10/46) Syn

1 **Story Of A Town** (1941) Syn

1 **Story Of A Young Man** (1941) Syn

1 **Story Of Amelia Earhart, The** (7/2/60) KCBS

1 **Story Of American Diplomacy, The** (3/21/40)

Story Of Aunt Mary, The (see Aunt Mary)

Story Of Bess Johnson, The (see Bess Johnson)

Story Of Bud Barton, The (see The Barton)

1 **Story Of Christmas, The** (12/12/45) Mut

2 **Story Of Crazy Nora, The** (6/10/83, 7/17/83) NPR

Story Of Doctor Kildare, The (see Dr. Kildare)

2 **Story Of Flight, The** (Pre-war) Syn

Story Of Food (3/10/33 - 4/28/33) A&P, Bl, Fri, 15m, 6 pm

1 **Story Of Gunsmoke, The** (4/25/76) WAMU-FM

Story Of Holly Sloan (with Gale Page) (9/1/47 - 5/28/48) General Mills, NBC, 5t, 15m

1 **Story Of Joan and Kermit, The** (7/10/38) CBS

1 **Story Of Madame Dumont, The** (1942) Syn

7 **Story Of Mary Marlin, The** (10/3/34 - 4/11/52) 5t, 15m; broadcast just on WMAQ until 12/28/34; first network show started on 1/1/35
10/3/34 - 9/24/43, Kleenex, Ivory, NBC & Bl
9/27/43 - 4/12/45, Tenderleaf Tea, CBS
9/24/51 - 4/11/52, Sus, ABC

1 **Story Of Mickey Mouse, The** (10/31/47)

Story Of Music, The (9/27/45 - 6/5/47)
9/27/45 - 5/30/46, CBS, Sat, 7 pm
10/10/46 - 6/5/47, NBC, Thu, 11:30 pm

1 **Story Of Phyllis Wheatley, The** (1/25/49) CBS

2 **Story Of Ruby Valentine, The** (with Juanita Hall) (1955 - 56)

Story Of Sandra Martin, The (with Mary Jane Croft) (1945 - 46) CBS, 5t, 15m

1 **Story Of Silent Night, Holy Night, The** (Syn)

1 **Story Of Sweeney and March, The** (9/6/44) Audition

1 **Story Of Swing, The** (5/38) Mut

Story Of Terry Reagan, Attorney At Law, The (see Attorney At Law)

1 **Story Of The Bell, The** (4/6/47) WOR

1 **Story Of The Bible, The** (9/24/46)

1 **Story Of The Big Mo, The** (10/30/45) Mut

2 **Story Of The Juggler Of Our Lady, The** (12/44) Syn

1 **Story Of The Nativity, The** (Thesaurus transcription)

Story Of The Sea, The (with Pat O'Brien and Lud Gluskin Orchestra)
(7/2/45 - 8/19/45) CBS, Mon, 9:30 pm (partial summer replacement of Lux)

Story Of The Song (12/13/38 - 10/10/39) CBS, Tue, 3:30 pm

Story Of the Month (11/14/38 - 7/21/39) Bl, 5t, 15m, 10 am

1 **Story Of Tommy Hoxie, The** (1948) Syn

1 **Story Of Will Rogers, The** (1952) film sound track

1 **Story Princess, The** 1/19/45)

Story Shop (with Craig MacDonald) (Sat)

Story Singer (12/1/33 - 1/26/34) NBC, Fri, 15m, 10:30 am

Story Teller Baron (with Jack Pearl)

Story Time (with Russell Thorson) (NBC) (with Sanford Marshall)
(8/15/55 - 11/23/56) Mut, 5t, 11 am

Story To Order (with Lydia Perera)
(3/11/45 - 12/23/45) NBC, Sun, 15m, 9:15 am

1 **Stowaway** (1936) film sound track

3 **Stradivari Orchestra, The** (with host, Paul La Valle until 12/23/45; also Jacques Gasselen)
(10/24/43 - 12/29/46) Sun (occasional single performances from 12/20/42 - 6/20/43)
10/24/43 - 4/8/45, Prince Matchabelli, NBC, Sun, 12:30 pm
4/15/45 - 12/23/45, Prince Matchabelli, CBS, 2 pm
3/3/46 - 5/26/46, ABC, 12:30 pm
10/6/46 - 12/29/46 (with Alfredo Antonini), CBS, 2:30 pm

5 **Straight Arrow** (with Howard Culver)
(5/6/48 - 6/21/51) Nabisco (sustained from 6/20/49 - 9/12/49), Mut started on the Don Lee Network - West coast; network shows started on 2/7/49
2/7/49 - 1/30/50, Mon, 8 pm
also 2/8/49 - 6/14/49; 9/15/49 - 6/22/50; 9/19/50 - 6/21/51, 2t, 5 pm

1 **Straight Arrow Pow-Wow** (2/6/49) Mut

Straight From The Shoulder (1950) (Audition) NBC

1 **Straight, Place and Show** (1938) film sound track

1 **Strand Of Thread** (Syn)

5 **Strange** (with Walter Gibson)
(5/30/55 - 10/28/55) ABC, 5t, 15m, 7:30 pm

Strange Adventure (see The Adventurers Club) 15m

Strange Adventures (see The Adventurer's Club)

Strange Adventures In A Strange Land (see The Adventurer's Club)

Strange Adventures In Strange Lands (see The Adventurers Club)

56 **Strange As It Seems** (with John Hix)
(8/17/39 - 12/26/40) Palmolive, CBS, Thu, 8:30 pm
(11/22/47 - 12/13/47) Mut, Sat, 15m, 5:30 pm
(4/3/48 - 5/23/48) Mut, Sat, 15m, 10:30 am; Sun, 10:45 pm as of 5/2/48, also syn

2 **Strange But True** (AFRTS)

Strange Dr. Karnac, The (with James Van Dyke) (2/20/43 - 4/3/43) Bl, Sat

29 **Strange Dr. Weird, The** (with Maurice Tarplin) (11/7/44 - 5/23/45) Adam Hats, Mut, Tue, 15m, 7:15 pm

Strange Facts (15m) (1952)

1 **Strange Romance Of Evelyn Winters, The** (with Toni Damay)
(11/20/44 - 11/12/48) Sweetheart Soap, CBS, 5t, 15m
(7/2/51 - 6/27/52) Sus, ABC, 5t, 15m, 11 am; Philip Morris, 3:45 pm as of 10/1/51

57 **Strange Wills** (I Devise and Bequeath) (with Warren Williams) (1946) Syn

Strangest Of All (with Frank Edwards; Robert Mahaffey) (1960s)

1 **Stratospheric Murder Mystery** (Pre-war) Syn

Straw Hat Concert (7/4/49 - 8/22/49) CBS, Mon, 10 pm (summer replacement for My Friend Irma)

1 **Strawberry Statement** (10/69) Syn

Streamline Journal (see Alma Kitchell)

2 **Streamlined Fairy Tales** (Syn)

4 **Streamlined Shakespeare** (with John Barrymore) (6/21/37 - 7/26/37) Bl, Mon, 9:30 pm; rebroadcast in 1950 (John Barrymore and Shakespeare)
also (7/12/37 - 8/30/37) CBS, Mon, 60m, 10 pm (The Shakespearian Circle)

Streamliner Show, The (see Fields and Hall)

Street Singer, The (see Arthur Tracy)

1 **Street Reporter** (12/21/39) WWRL

1 **Strength Of America, The** (10/21/47) Mut

1 **Strengthen The Arm Of Liberty** (2/12/49) NBC

Strictly Business (with Lawson Zerbe and Shirley Booth) (5/31/40 - 8/23/40) Bl, Fri, 8 pm

Strictly From Dixie (with hosts, Helena Home and John Hicks; also Henry Levine Orchestra)
(1941) NBC, 15m
(1954) ABC

Strictly Personal (11/42 - 6/29/44) Gotham Silk, Mut (with Pegeen Fitzgerald)
11/42 - 12/42, 3t, 10m, 1:35 pm
10/5/43 - 6/29/44, 2t, 5m, 11:55 am

1 **Strike It Lucky** (3/5/49) CBS

11 **Strike It Rich** (6/29/47 - 12/27/57)
6/29/47 - 2/20/49, Sus; Ludens as of 11/2/47, CBS, Sun
1949 - 50, Sus, CBS, Sun
4/30/50 - 12/27/57, Colgate, NBC, 5t

1 **Strike Me Pink** (1936) film sound track

2 **Strike Up The Band** (1940) Air trailer, film sound track

String Ensemble (7/8/45 - 9/30/45) ABC, Sun, 15m, 8 pm

1 **String Serenade, A** (10/7/51 - 4/26/53) CBS, Sun

1 **String Silhouettes** (7/3/49) NBC

String Symphony (with Frank Black)
(4/28/35 - 12/14/41) (various days and times including:)
4/28/35 - 9/22/35, Bl, Sun, 8 pm
4/7/37 - 10/6/37, Bl, Wed, 9 pm
10/29/39 - 3/31/40, NBC, Sun, 2 pm
12/15/40 - 12/14/41, NBC, Sun, various times

1 **Strings For Meditation** (6/7/44) NBC

Strings That Sing (3/23/40 - 9/14/40) NBC, Sat, 15m, 12 noon also Sun, 15m and 30m

Strings With Wings (see I Sustain The Wings)

Stringtime With Walberg Brown
(12/16/39 - 7/6/40) CBS, Sat, 10 am

1 **Strip, The** (1951) film sound track

11 **Stroke Of Fate** (10/4/53 - 12/27/53) NBC, Sun

Strollers, The (15m) (1938)

Stu Erwin Show, The (6/11/45 - 9/24/45) Ballantine, CBS, Mon, 10:30 pm

Stuart Erwin Show, The (see Stu Erwin)

Stuart Foster (with Alfredo Antonini) (12/20/56 - 5/2/57) CBS, Thu, 25m, 10:05 pm

2 **Studebaker Champions, The** (with Richard Himber Orchestra from 6/13/34 often Joey Nash) (1929 - 5/31/37) (on overlapping times)
1929 - 1/25/31 (with Jean Goldkette Orchestra), NBC, Sun
6/13/34 - 9/18/34, CBS, Tue, 9:30 pm
10/6/34 - 4/27/35, CBS, Sat, 60m, 9:30 pm
also 7/9/34 - 6/24/35, NBC, Mon, 30m, 8 pm
5/3/35 - 6/26/36, CBS, Fri, 10 pm; NBC, Fri, 9 pm as of 5/1/3
6/29/36 - 5/31/37, NBC, Mon, 9:30 pm; 10 pm as of 3/8/37, also syndicated

1 **Student Tour** (1934) film sound track

1 **Students Abroad** (12/30/53) UNESCO Radio

2 **Studies In Public Issues** (Wartime) Syn

58 **Studio One** (with Fletcher Markle) (4/22/47 - 7/27/48) CBS, Tue, 60m, 9:30 pm
also 10/30/50, CBS
and 10/12/67, Voice Of America

Studio Party (with Deems Taylor and Sigmund Romberg) (9/17/35 - 6/15/36) Swift, NBC
9/17/35 - 1/28/36, Tue, 10 pm
3/16/36 - 6/15/36, Swift, Mon, 9:30 pm

Studio Seven (with Jack and Loretta Clemens) (10/1/35 - 3/27/36) Blue Coal, NBC, 3t (Tue & Thu), 15m, 11:15 am

1 **Studio X** (12/8/41) WEAF

1 **Stuff Smith Trio** (World transcription)

Stump The Authors (with Sidney Mason) (6/16/46 - 1/5/47) ABC, Sun, 4 pm; 7:30 pm as of 10/20/46

1 **Style Show** (1930) Syn

1 **Style Talk** (Pre-war) Syn

1 **Submarine Warfare In The Atlantic** (10/25/42) Mut

2 **Success Session** (6/13/39, 10/23/39) Mut

Success Story (1/11/56 - 3/28/56) Mut, Wed, 15m, 9:15 pm

1 **Suffer The Little Children** (11/21/46) Mut

Sugar and Bunny (1/8/35 - 4/11/35) NBC, 2t, 15m, 5:30 pm

1 **Sugar Ray Robinson vs. Jake Lamotta** (2/23/45) Mut

Suit Yourself (6/12/45 - 9/18/45) Bl, Tue, 10:30 pm

1 **Sullivan Years, The** (10/17/71) CBS-TV

1 **Summary Of Prime Minister Chamberlain's Statement To Parliament** (3/31/39) BBC

1 **Summary Of Prime Minister Churchill's Statement** (6/4/40) BBC

1 **Summary Of The British Plan For Partial Release** (9/21/44) BBC

1 **Summary Of The King's and Queen's Activities** (6/8/39) CBS

1 **Summary Of The Supreme Soviet** (8/29/39) USSR

1 **Summer Concert** (Syn)

Summer Cruise (also American Cruise) (with Dick Powell, Frances Langford, Lud Gluskin Orchestra)
(7/4/41 - 8/29/41) CBS, Fri, 8 pm
(1952) (with host, Johnny Andrews; also Marilyn Ross, Ralph Norman Orchestra)
(1952) ABC

Summer In St. Louis (on many summers including:)
7/8/49 - 8/26/49, CBS, Fri, 60m, 8 pm
7/5/53 - 9/27/53, CBS, Sun, 6:30 pm (summer replacement for Our Miss Brooks)
7/4/54 - 9/5/54, CBS, Sun, 6:30 pm
6/5/55 - 8/21/55, CBS, Sun, 6:30 pm
7/8/56 - 9/2/56, CBS, Sun, 25m, 9:05 pm
6/23/57 - 9/8/57, CBS, Sun, 25m, 2:05 pm

1 **Summer Is For A Good Time** (1951) Syn

1 **Summer Night and Voices From The Air** (1925)

1 **Summer Of Judgment: The Watergate Hearings** (7/27/83) PBS-TV

Summer Pastime (see Tommy Dorsey)

Summer Promenade (7/20/36 - 9/14/36) CBS, Mon, 1:30 pm

1 **Summer Radio Picnic With The Kraft Family, A** (6/24/79) NBC

1 **Summer Recipe** (9/30/56) Syn

Summer Serenade (7/14/45 - 8/25/45) ABC, Sat, 8 pm
(7/19/48 - 8/31/48) ABC, Tue, 15m, 10:45 pm
(7/18/55 - 9/16/55 (with Guy Lombardo and Jim Coy) NBC, 5t, 7 pm

Summer Session (5/15/38 - 6/19/38) CBS, Sun, 8:30 pm)

1 **Summer Show, The** (6/13/54) CBS

Summer Stars (with Oscar Bradley Orchestra and Harry von Zell)
(7/4/37 - 9/26/37) Gulf, CBS, Sun, 7:30 pm

1 **Summer Stock** (1950) film sound track

Summer Theater (with Pat O'Brien and Virginia Bruce) (5/30/48 - 9/26/48) NBC, Sun, 7:30 pm (summer replacement for Phil Harris)

1 **Summerfest '79** (8/18/79) PBS-TV

Summerfield Bandstand (with various cast members of The Great Gildersleeve) (6/11/47 - 9/3/47) Kraft, NBC (summer replacement of The Great Gildersleeve)

1 **Summit At Glassboro** (6/22/67) KYW

1 **Summit Conference Coverage** (12/9/87 - 12/11/87) NBC-TV

Sumner Welles (also called Time For Decision) (10/11/44 - 1/31/45) Waltham Watch, Mut, Wed, 15m, 10 pm

1 **Sun Valley Serenade** (1941) film sound track

Sunbrite Smile Parade (with Ransom Sherman) (9/30/38 - 9/21/39) Bl, Fri; NBC & Bl, Thu as of 3/2/39

Sunday Afternoon At Home (1/12/36 - 3/29/36) Olson Rug, Mut, Sun, 15m, 5:30 pm

Sunday Afternoon In Rosedale (see Uncle Ezra)

1 **Sunday Afternoon With David Ross** (8/20/44)

Sunday At Home (with host, Jan Murray; also Frank Stevens, Elliot Lawrence Orchestra) (1/17/54 - 3/21/54) NBC, Sun, 8:30 pm

Sunday At Seth Parker's (see Seth Parker)

Sunday At The Chase (7/18/48 - 9/19/48) CBS, Sun, 5:30 pm

Sunday Bright Spot (with Jack Pettis Orchestra) (9/27/31 - 3/20/32) Investors Syndicate, NBC, Sun, 15m, 2:15 pm

1 **Sunday Digest** (1943) Mut

Sunday Dinner At Aunt Fanny's (with Fran Allison) (6/5/38 - 9/17/39) NBC, Sun

Sunday Down South (see Way Down South)

Sunday Drivers (directed by Arthur Fields and Fred Hall) (5/10/36 - 1/26/41) Sus, NBC, Sun

1 **Sunday Evening Party (Party Time)** (with Phil Davis Orchestra, Louise Carlyle) (7/29/45 - 1/19/47) Hires, ABC, Sun, 6 pm

Sunday Evenings At Home (with Geraldine Farrar and Frank Black) (1933) American Radiator, 60m

Sunday Forum (with Dr. Ralph Sockman) (1928 - 36+) Bl, Sun (summers) (summer replacement for National Radio Pulpit)

Sunday Gathering (1950 - 55) General Foods, CBS, Sun, 30m - 45m

1 **Sunday Hour, The** (Syn)

Sunday In Manhattan (1/1/39 - 2/19/39) Mut, Sun, 9 pm

Sunday Matinee Of The Air (with Vic Arden Orchestra, Beatrice Mable) (10/16/32 - 5/21/33) Jo-Cur, CBS, Sun, 15m, 2:15 pm

Sunday Morning at Aunt Susan's (with Elaine Ivans) (3/18/34 - 1/9/38) CBS, Sun, 30m, 60m

3 **Sunday Morning Serenade** (7/24/48, 9/16/51) NBC, WMAQ

Sunday Night Concert (6/9/40 - 9/22/40) Bl, Sun, 8 pm

Sunday Night Music Hall (with Al Datz Orchestra) (1955) ABC

Sunday Night Party (see Saturday Night Party)

Sunday Night Serenade (with Kitty Kallen; Francis Craig Orchestra) (1940) CBS

Sunday On N-K Ranch (see Curt Massey)

Sunday Overseas Pickup (1933 - 40) CBS (also see European War Roundup; The War This Week; The World This Week)

1 **Sunday Players, The** (Syn)

1 **Sunday Serenade** (1939) WWRL

1 **Sunday Serenade Of Song** (2/18/43) WFBR

Sunday Strings (with Ralph Norman, conductor) (6/2/46 - 3/9/47) ABC, Sun, 12:30 pm

Sunday Symphonette (7/9/39 - 9/17/39) NBC, Sun, 1:30 pm

Sunday Theater

Sunday Toastchee Time (see Edward McHugh)

1 **Sunday With Murrow** (3/27/49) CBS

5 **Sundial** (9/21/39, 4/7/49) WJSV, WTOP

Sundial Bonnie Ladies (1/14/32 - 7/15/32) Sundial shoes, Bl, Wed, 15m, 7:15 pm

Sunkist Musical Cocktail
(2/4/31 - 5/20/31) Sunkist, CBS, Wed, 8:30 pm

Sunkist Time (with Bill Goodwin) (1938)

2 **Sunny Meadows Radio Show, The** (1929) Syn

Sunny Melodies (10/9/36 - 7/7/41) CBS, 15m
10/9/36 - 4/23/37, Fri, 8:30 am
5/8/39 - 8/8/39, Tue, 9:15 am (not always in New York)
5/5/41 - 7/7/4l (with Stuart Stevens) Mon, 9:30 am

1 **Sunny Side Of The Atom, The** (6/30/47) CBS

Sunny Skylar (7/26/43 - 2/2/45) Mut, various days, 15m

1 **Sunny and Other Jerome Kern Musicals** (1941) Air trailer

3 **Sunoco Three Star Extra**
(9/29/47 - 5/28/65) Sunoco, NBC, Ray Henley, 15m

1 **Sunrise Salute** (6/30/41)

Sunset Dreams (see The Morin Sisters)

Sunset Harmonies (with John Fogarty and Sarah Jordan) (1/7/32 - 3/24/32) Sunsweet prunes, NBC, Thu, 15m, 3:15 pm

Sunset Serenade (see Glenn Miller)

4 **Sunset Village** (directed by Olan Soulé) (1936) 15m (Audition)

1 **Sunshine Inn** (11/3/39) (Audition) 15m; with Zazu Pitts

1 **Sunshine Sammy** (11/14/28) Synchro-disc

Sunshine Sue (6/8/53 - 12/28/56) Corn Products, CBS
6/8/53 - 6/4/54, 5t, 5m, 4:15 pm; 15m as of 9/7/53; 3t as of 3/8/54
6/27/56 - 12/28/56, 3t (Wed - Fri) 5m, 3:30 pm

Super Noodle Show (see Space Adventures Of Super Noodle)

Superman (see The Adventures Of Superman)

1 **Superman's Christmas Adventure** (1941) Syn

2 **Supernaturally Yours** (2/24/47, 4/23/47) Mut

Superstition On The Air (with Ralph Bell) (6/6/48 - 9/5/48) ABC, Sun, 9:30 pm (summer replacement for Theater Guild Of The Air)

Supper Club (see Chesterfield Supper Club)

Surprise Package (with host, Jay Stewart) (3/6/50 - 7/7/50) ABC, 5t, 4 pm

Surprise Party (with Stu Wilson)
(7/2/46 - 12/26/47) G. Washington Coffee, CBS, 2t, 3 pm (also see Kay Kyser's Orchestra)

11 **Surprise Serenade** (with hosts, Don Gordon and Ed Davies; also Joseph Gallichio Orchestra; Hugh Downs
(9/12/48 - 1/26/53) NBC, Sun, 5 pm

1 **Survivors, The** (12/21/52) NBC

704 **Suspense** (6/17/42 - 9/30/62) CBS; there were 945 performances
6/17/42 - 9/30/42, Sus, Wed, 9:30 pm
10/27/42 - 8/10/43, Sus, Tue, 9:30 pm; 10 pm as of 6/15/43
8/21/43 - 8/28/43, Sus, Sat 7:30 pm
9/2/43 - 10/7/43, Sus, Thu, 10:30 pm
10/12/43 - 11/30/43, Sus, Tue, 10 pm
12/2/43 - 11/20/47, Roma Wines, Thu, 8 pm
11/28/47 - 12/26/47, Sus, Fri, 9:30 pm
1/3/48 - 5/15/48, Sus, Sat, 60m, 8 pm
7/8/48 - 6/30/49; 9/1/49 - 6/29/50; 8/31/50 - 6/28/51, Autolite, Thu, 9 pm
8/27/51 - 6/9/52; 9/15/52 - 6/8/53; 9/14/53 - 6/7/54, Autolite, Mon, 8 pm
6/15/54 - 8/10/54, Sus, Tue, 9:30 pm
9/30/54 - 2/17/55, Sus, Thu, 8 pm
2/22/55 - 10/4/55, Sus, Tue, 8 pm
10/11/55 - 7/3/56, Sus, Tue, 8:30 pm
7/11/56 - 9/5/56, Sus, Wed, 8:30 pm
9/25/56 - 10/30/56, Sus, Tue, 8:30 pm
11/4/56 - 11/16/58, Multi, Sun, 4:30 pm
11/23/58 - 11/27/60, Multi, Sun, 5:30 pm
6/25/61 - 9/30/62, Multi, Sun, 6:30 pm

Suspicion (1930s) 15m)

1 **Suzy** (1936) Air trailer

1 **Swamp Caesar** (1935) Syn

1 **Swan CARE Drive** (6/13/49)

1 **Swanee River** (1939) film sound track

Swap Night (2/14/42 - 7/11/42) Bl, Sun, 8:30 pm

1 **Swartchild and Company** (Syn)

1 **Sweater Girl** (1942) Air trailer

31 **Sweeney and March** (with Bob Sweeney and Hal March) (7/5/46 - 10/1/48) Sus, CBS (most recent information from SPERDVAC)
7/5/46 - 11/2/46, Sat, 7 pm; started of as CBS - West coast; network as of 9/7/46
11/11/46 - 4/21/47, Mon, 10:30 pm
5/31/47 - 10/4/47, Sat, 8:30 pm
10/8/47 - 8/18/48, Wed
8/20/48 - 10/1/48, Sanka, Fri, 8:30 pm; 8 pm as of 9/10/48
(4/1/51 - 5/11/51) ABC, 5t, 15m, 2:35 pm

Sweeney and March Program, The (see Sweeney and March)

Sweeney and March Show, The (see Sweeney and March)

1 **Sweet Adeline** (with Una Merkle, Gale Gordon) (1949)
also (1935) Air trailer

1 **Sweet and Lowdown** (1944) film sound track

Sweet and Rhythmic (with Charles Dant Orchestra; Gordon Jenkins from 9/6/41)
(7/26/41 - 10/25/41) Bl, Sat, 10:30 pm

Sweet Land Of Liberty (see Luther-Layman Singers)

1 **Sweet Music** (1935) film sound track

Sweet River (with Ed Prentiss)
(10/4/43 - 7/21/44) Staley Cornstarch (from 1/3/44), Bl, 5t, 15m

Sweetest Love Songs Ever Sung (with Frank Munn) (5/25/36 - 8/3/37) Phillips (as of 1/4/37), Bl, Mon, 8:30 pm; Tue, 9:30 pm as of 4/27/37

Sweetheart Melodies (called Sweetheart Serenaders as of 12/7/32) (with Ruth Jordan; Harriet Lee)
(7/22/31 - 7/5/34) Sweetheart Soap, 15m
7/22/31 - 6/15/32; 9/14/32 - 1/11/33, Bl, Wed, 11:45 am
11/23/31 - 5/23/32, NBC, Mon, 5:30 pm
1/25/34 - 7/5/34, Bl, Thu, 10:30 am

1 **Sweetheart News** (11/18/41) WGAR

1 **Sweetheart Of The Campus** (1941) film sound track

1 **Sweetheart Time** (with Johnny White Orchestra, Marion Mann and Phil Kaler)
(3/18/45 - 12/8/46) Ivorene (until 6/9/46), Mut, Sun, 1:30 pm

1 **Sweethearts** (12/38) Air trailer

Sweethearts Of The Air (see Breen and DeRose)

1 **Swelling Tide Of Polio, The** (1/2/52) Syn

Swift Garden Program (1/31/32 - 5/8/32; 2/19/33 - 4/23/33; 2/18/34 - 4/22/34; 2/10/35 - 4/14/35) Swift Meats, Bl, Sun; NBC as of 2/19/33

Swift Hour (10/6/34 - 4/13/35) Swift, NBC
10/6/34 - 4/13/35, Sat, 60m
1935 - 36 (see Studio Party)

Swift Music (2/15/31 - 5/10/31) NBC, Sun, 3:30 pm

Swing and Sway Time (see Sammy Kaye)

Swing and Sway With Sammy Kaye (see Sammy Kaye)

1 **Swing High, Swing Low** (1937) Air trailer

Swing School (see Benny Goodman)

Swing Serenade (with Rakov Orchestra)
(1/29/38 - 2/11/39) Bl, Sat, 15m, 10:45 am; 10:30 am as of 1/21/39
also 1938 - 8/14/39, Bl, 3t, 15m, 8:30 am

Swing Shift Frolics (5/20/44 - 11/25/44) Bl, Sat
5/20/44 - 9/9/44, 1:30 pm
9/16/44 - 11/25/44, 15m, 12 noon

Swing Time At The Savoy (with Noble Sissle, Lucky Millinder Orchestra, Jackie Mabley) (7/28/48 - 8/25/48) NBC, Wed, 8 pm

Swing Unlimited (5/27/40 - 9/23/40) CBS, Mon, 15m, 4:30 pm

Swing With The Strings
(8/13/36 - 2/13/37) Hormel, CBS, Thu, 10:45 pm; Sat, 8 pm as of 9/19/36

1 **Swing's The Thing** (1/45 - 12/27/45) Brach, Mut, Thu, 10:30 pm

1 **Swingin 'N Sweet**

Swinging Sweethearts (see Frank Crumit and Julia Sanderson)

18 **Swingtime** (AFRS) 15m

1 **Swingtime In The Smokies**

1 **Swingtones (With Jumpin' Jacks), The** (Thesaurus transcription)

SWOP Night (with H. Allen Smith; Lew Valentine as of 6/13/42
(2/14/42 - 7/11/42) Bl, Sat, 8:30 pm

8 **Sy Oliver and His Orchestra**
(5/7/70 - 7/3/70) CBS

7 **Sylvan Levin Opera Concert, The**
(1949 - 1/28/51) Mut

Sylvanians, The (10/6/31 - 6/26/32) Sylvania, CBS, 2t (Sun & Tue) 15m, 6:30 pm; Sun, 7:45 pm as of 2/21/32

Sylvia Froos (7/24/34 - 10/13/34) CBS, Tue, 7:30 pm; Sat, 15m, 11 pm as of 8/11/34
(12/30/35 - 1/6/36) Bl, 2t (Mon & Fri) 15m, 7:45 pm

1 **Sylvia Marlowe and Richard Dyer-Bennet** (Lavender and New Lace) (also with Kay Lorraine)
(2/16/41 - 1/4/42) Red, Sun, 15m
(4/4/48 - 4/25/48) (Coffee Concerts) ABC, Sun, 8:30 am

Symphonic Adventure (1952 - 53) from Chicago; Sus, NBC, Sun/Sat, 90m

2 **Symphonic Echoes** (7/18/30) Synchro-discs, Syn

Symphonic Hour (4/21/40 - 11/24/40) Mut, Sun, 55m, 10:05 pm

Symphonic Strings (with Alfred Wallenstein) (9/7/37 - 1/27/46) Sus, Mut
9/7/37 - 3/1/38, Tue, 10:30 pm
1938 - 5/11/40, Sat
5/14/40 - 10/22/40, Tue, 8 pm
11/1/40 - 5/16/41, Fri, 8 pm
5/18/41 - 9/21/41, Sun, 6 pm; 10 pm as of 7/27/41
10/12/41 - 5/9/43, Sun, 7 pm
12/2/45 - 1/27/46, Sun, 15m, 2:45 pm

2 **Symphonic Swing By Szath-Myri** (Lang-Worth transcriptions)

1 **Symphonies For Youth** (with Alfred Wallenstein) (1/12/45 - 3/30/45) Bl, Sat, 45m, 1 pm
(12/3/49 - 4/28/56) Sus, Mut, Sat, 60m

2 **Symphonies Of The World** (1946) ABC, NBC

1 **Symphonies Under The Stars** (8/5/48) AFRS

1 **Symphony Hour** (6/12/39) WFBR

1 **Symphony In D For The Dodgers** (9/47) Mut

Symphony Of The Americas
(4/14/45 - 7/14/45) Mut, Sat, 8:30 pm

1 **Symphony Of The Birds** (4/24/55)

Syncopated Piece (from St. Louis)
(8/13/39 - 9/17/39) CBS, Sun, 4:30 pm
(6/29/41 - 8/10/41; 12/28/41 - 3/1/42) CBS, Sun, 12 noon
(3/16/52 - 6/15/52) Sus, CBS, Sun
(7/6/52 - 9/28/52) CBS, Sun, 6:30 pm (summer replacement for Our Miss Brooks)
(9/13/53 - 1/10/54) CBS, Sun, 1:30 pm

Syncopated Sermons (with Willard Robison and Deep River Orchestra)
(7/16/33 - 11/23/33) CBS, Thu, 10 pm

1 **Syncopation Piece** (5/1/49) CBS

1 **T Minus Four Years, Nine Months, and Thirty Days** (3/1/65) CBS-TV

2 **T-Man** (with Dennis O'Keefe)
(4/29/50 - 9/2/50) CBS, Sat, 8:30 pm

3 **T-Men** (1956) Syn

1 **T. Texas Tyler Show, The** (1/11/50) NBC

Tabloid Operetta (1932 - 2/23/33) Esso, CBS, Thu, 10 pm

1 **Tailspin Tommy** (9/5/41) CBS, Fri, 30m; also on for 15m

1 **Take A Break** (9/14/47) Syn
(3/12/49 - 6/4/49) Charles B. Silver Co., Mut, Sat, 15m, 10:45 am

Take A Card (with Wally Butterworth)
(4/28/43 - 10/20/43) Lehn & Fink, Mut, Wed, 8:30 pm

9 **Take A Chance** (unidentified recordings)

Take A Chorus (7/3/49 - 7/31/49) ABC, Sun, 5:30 pm

Take A Note (with Henry Morgan; see Ernie Fio Rito)

Take A Number (6/5/48 - 5/20/55) Mut
6/5/48 - 7/30/49, U S Tobacco, Sat, 5 pm; 8:30 pm as of 1/8/49
10/22/49 - 3/3/51; 6/30/51 - 1/5/52, Sus, Sat
12/10/51 - 2/1/52 (with Happy Felton), Sus, 5t
4/10/53 - 12/25/53, Multi, Fri, 8 pm
1/1/54 - 5/20/55, Sus, Fri, 8 pm

9 **Take A Record, Please** (AFRS origination)

Take A Word (In A Word) (with George Hogan and Carlton Warren)
(5/12/46 - 7/28/46) Mut, Sun, 15m, 1 pm

Take It Easy (with Ed Drew) (1940) CBS

3 **Take It Easy Time** (with Dick Willard; Landt Trio) (1/29/45 - 7/26/46) Van Camp, Mut, 3t, 15m, 11:30 am

Take It From There (8/15/46 - 10/31/46) ABC, Thu, 9:30 pm

10 **Take It Or Leave It** (4/21/40 - 9/3/50) Eversharp, Sun, 10 pm (developed into $64 Question)
4/21/40 - 9/7/47 (with Bob Hawk; Phil Baker as of 12/28/41), CBS; NBC from 8/3/47
9/14/47 - 7/24/49; 9/11/49 - 9/3/50 (with Garry Moore, Eddie Cantor as of 9/11/49; Jack Parr as of 6/11/50), NBC

1 **Take Off Of Bikini Atom Bomb Flyers** (6/30/46) Mut

1 **Take Off Of Swedish Plane** (10/6/36) WOR

1 **Take Off Of The Atom Bomb Plane** (6/30/46) Mut

Take These Notes (3/22/46 - 4/12/46) Mut, Fri, 15m, 10:15 pm

26 **Take Your Choice** (1946) Syn

Tale Of Today, A (see Princess Pat Players)

Talent Hunt (6/3/48 - 8/5/48) Mut, Thu, 8:30 pm

1 **Talent Jackpot** (3/11/48 - 10/28/48) Mut, Thu, 8 pm

Talent Search, Country Style (see Saturday Night, Country Style)

2 **Talent Theater, The** (Philip Morris, NBC) (7/3/45, 8/28/45) NBC

Talent, Ltd. (with Garry Moore and Rex Maupin Orchestra) (5/11/41 - 7/6/41) Bl, Sun, 3:30 pm

1 **Tales From Harlem** (1/7/38) WMCA, 15m

2 **Tales From Ivory Towers** (Pre-war) Syn, 15m

37 **Tales From The Diamond K** (1951) Syn

66 **Tales From The Reader's Digest** (with Boris Karloff) (10/8/62 - 10/31/66) 5 times a week for 3 minutes (15 minutes a week)

Tales Of Adventure (CBS) (1946)

1 **Tales Of Fatima, The** (with Basil Rathbone) (1/8/49 - 10/1/49) Fatima, CBS, Sat, 9:30 pm

Tales Of The Foreign Legion (written by Willis Cooper) (10/2/32 - 6/23/33) CBS (on previously in Midwest)
10/2/32 - 2/19/33, Sun, 5:30 pm; 10:30 pm as of 2/12/33
2/23/33 - 5/11/33, Thu, 10 pm
5/19/33 - 6/23/33, Fri, 4:30 pm

15 **Tales Of The Foreign Service** (6/7/46 - 10/25/46) NBC, Fri, 11:30 pm

Tales Of The Opera (1/13/37 - 3/24/37) Bl, Wed, 10:30 pm

76 **Tales Of The Texas Rangers** (with Joel McCrea) (7/8/50 - 9/14/52) NBC
7/8/50 - 8/26/50, General Mills, Sat, 9:30 pm (partial summer replacement of Dennis Day)
9/2/50 - 5/27/51; 9/30/51 - 9/14/52, Sus, Sat, 9:30 pm; Sun, 8:30 pm as of 10/8/50; 6 pm as of 9/30/51

Tales Of Time and Space (with Drusilla Campbell) (3/10/74 - 75)

1 **Tales Of Today's American Heroes** (7/9/45) WCPO

Tales Of Tomorrow (host was Raymond Edward Johnson) (1/1/53 - 4/9/53)
1/1/53 - 2/26/53, ABC Thu, 9 pm; 15 shows broadcast
3/5/53 - 4/9/53, CBS

Tales Of Willie Piper (see Willie Piper)

Talk Back (with Happy Felton) (10/2/50 - 5/11/51) American Tobacco from 7/2/51, ABC, 5t, 15m, 3:45 pm

Talk Your Way Out Of It (with Peter Donald) (3/30/49 - 6/10/49; 9/12/49 - 12/9/49) Quaker, ABC, 3t, 3 pm

Talkie Picture Time (1930 - 7/7/35) NBC
1930 - 7/30/31 (Rinso Talkie Time) Rinso, 2t, 15m, 5:30 pm
10/15/33 - 7/7/35 (Sally Of The Talkies) Luxor, Sun, 5:30 pm

2 **Talking Drums** (see Moon Over Africa) (1935) Syn

4 **Talking With David Frost** (1/3/92, 5/29/92, 9/25/92, 10/30/92) PBS-TV

1 **Taming Of The Shrew, The** (Pre-war) Syn

Tangee Musical Dreams (with Wally Maher) (6/14/32 - 12/20/32) Tangee, Bl, various days and times

Tangee Varieties (see Sammy Kaye)

Tapestry Musicale (see Leopold Spitalny)

Target Tomorrow

81 **Tarzan** (9/12/32 - 6/27/53)
9/12/32 - 3/5/34; 5/11/34 - 6/22/34; 1936 (Syn) WOR, New York, 3t; 231 episodes were syndicated from 9/12/32 through 3/5/34 (Tarzan Of The Apes). 286 episodes were syndicated. With James Pierce, Joanne Burroughs. 39 episodes were syndicated in 1934 (Tarzan and The Diamonds Of Ashair); 39 episodes were syndicated in 1936 (Tarzan and The Fires Of Tohr) with Carlton KaDell.
3/22/52 - 6/27/53 (with Lamont Johnson), Post Toasties, CBS, Sat (67 shows broadcast), also syndicated

1 **Tarzan, The King Of The Apes** (Syn)

Tastyeast Jesters (Breadwinners), The (also see The Happiness Boys; Original Tastyeast Jesters) (1930 - 33) (with Guy Bonham, Dwight Latham, Wamp Carlson; songs with mandolute accompaniment; Swedish stories with dialect) Bl, 15m, various days and times

Tastyeast Theater (7/1/34 - 10/30/34) Bl, Sun, 15m, 9:30 pm

Tattered Man (1/23/34 - 10/9/34) NBC, Tue, 5:30 pm (called The Nursery Rhyme; with Milton Cross from 2/13 - 5/1)

1 **Tax Instruction Book** (1954) Syn

1 **Tax Reforms: Other Views** (5/31/85) CBS-TV

Taxi (with Max Baer) (5/7/34 - 6/15/34) Goodrich, Bl, 3t, 15m, 7:45 pm

Taylor Grant (also see Headline Edition) (11/2/52 - 6/4/55) Old Gold, ABC, Sun,

18 **Taystee Breadwinner, The** (with Ben Selvin) (1934); see also The Happiness Boys, Syn

Tea At The Ritz (with Jerry Cooper and Margaret Santry) (12/2/35 - 1/31/36) Pompeian Company, CBS, 3t, 15m, 4:45 pm

1 **Tea For Two** (1950) film sound track

Tea Time At Morrell's (with Don McNeill) (9/3/36 - 5/28/37) Red Heart, NBC, Thu; Fri, 4 pm as of 11/6/36

Tea Time Tunes (with Ramona and The Three Jesters; Jack Shilkret Orchestra) (5/24/36 - 8/16/36) CBS, Sun, 4:30 pm

1 **Teaser** (1932) Syn

1 **Ted Black and His Orchestra** (1932) Syn

1 **Ted Brown Show, The** (1/18/47) WOR

Ted Drake, Guardian Of The Big Top (with Vince Harding) (6/20/49 - 9/16/49) Mut, 3t, 5 pm

3 **Ted Fio Rito and His Orchestra**
(4/28/37) CBS
(1939) film sound track
(8/42) CBS

1 **Ted Fio Rito and His Orchestra (Cocoanut Grove Dance Hour)** (1932) NBC

Ted Fio Rito Orchestra (1934) (see also Frigidaire Frolics)

5 **Ted Heath (and His Orchestra)** (World transcriptions)

8 **Ted Heath and His Orchestra** (World transcriptions)

Ted Husing (1935 - 8/24/45) CBS, 15m
1935 - 36 (see The Charioteers)
9/29/36 - 1/2/37, Atlantic, 3t (Tue, Thu, Fri), 7:15 pm
7/27/41 - 9/21/41 (Sports), CBS, Sun, 15m, 5:45 pm
6/22/43 - 10/5/43, (Sports) CBS, Tue, 15m, 10:45 pm
7/2/45 - 8/24/45, CBS, 5t, 15m, 7 pm

2 **Ted Husing Bandstand** (Syn) 15m

1 **Ted Lewis and His Orchestra** (CBS)

3 **Ted Lewis Show, The** (1934 - 35)
(1946) (CBS); Audition
(10/9/47 - 12/25/47) Mut, Thu, 8 pm
(1947 - 48) Syn

1 **Ted Lewis, The High Hatted Tragedian Of Song**

Ted Mack Family Hour (1/7/51 - 12/2/51) General Mills, ABC, Sun

Ted Malone (Ted Malone From England) (6/14/44 - 12/8/44) Bl, 3t, 15m, 10:15 pm (see also Between The Bookends)

1 **Ted Steele** (11/6/40) WABC

Ted Steele Orchestra (1939 - 5/2/43) Sus (see also Boy Meets Band)
1939 (Ted Steele's Novatones) NBC, 15m
12/15/39 - 2/9/40, Mut, Fri, 15m, 10:45 pm
11/19/40 - 5/27/41, CBS, Tue, 15m, 6:15 pm
7/2/41 - 9/24/41, Bl, Wed, 25m, 9:35 pm
also 7/19/41 - 2/7/42, Bl, Sat, 30m, 8 pm
2/28/43 - 5/2/43, Mut, Sun, 9:30 pm
(9/13/54 - 6/17/55) Mut, 5t, 1:30 pm
(1/23/56 - 9/14/56) Mut, 5t, 1:30 pm

10 **Ted Steele's Novatones** (12/16/41) Thesaurus, World transcriptions

Ted Straeter Orchestra (1942; see Jerry Wayne)

2 **Ted Weems and His Orchestra** (with Perry Como, Elmo Tanner)
(4/12/36 - 6/27/37; 9/26/37 - 11/28/37) Varady Of Vienna, Mut, Sun, 1:30 pm; 2:30 pm as of 9/26/37

1 **Teddy Powell and His Orchestra** (9/21/39) CBS

2 **Teddy Powell Orchestra** (Thesaurus transcriptions)

1 **Teddy Roosevelt Speaks Again** (7/8/37) Mut

Teddy Wilson (7/25/54 - 9/5/54) CBS, Sun, 15m, 4 pm

1 **Teddy Wilson and His Trio** (2/18/53) NBC

Teel Variety Hall (5/5/45 - 7/7/45) Teel, NBC, Sat, 8 pm

Teen Town (with Dick York)
(2/2/46 - 6/16/46) ABC, Sat, 10:30 am

Teenagers Unlimited (2/20/54 - 2/26/55) Mut, Sat, 55m, 5 pm

2 **Teentimer's Canteen** (Teentimer's Club as of 11/24/45) (with Johnny Desmond; John Conte, Gordon MacRae as of 11/23/46)
(8/25/45 - 12/25/48) Teen-Timers, Inc.,Sat
8/25/45 - 8/16/47, NBC, 10 pm; 11 pm as of 11/24/45
3/13/48 - 12/25/48, Mut, 11:30 pm

1 **Teetering Van Totters, The** (1935) Syn

1 **Tele-Kid Test** (7/29/50) WOR

Telephone Hour (see Bell Telephone Hour)

1 **Television Experiments** (7/22/46) WOR-TV

1 **Television Tower News Insert** (4/22/49) WOR

2 **Tell It Again** (with Marvin Miller)
(1/8/48 - 7/2/49) Sus, CBS, Sun, 1:30 pm; Sat, 10:30 am as of 4/30/49

1 **Tell Me A Story** (created by Carlton E. Morse) (1946) Audition

Tell Me Doctor (12/8/45 - 6/21/47) ABC, Sat, 15m

Tell Us Your Story (3/2/37 - 5/29/37) Ford, CBS, 3t (Tue, Thu, Sat) 15m, 2 pm

3 **Tell Your Neighbor** (with Walter Mason)
(1946 - 2/15/50) Mut, 5t, 15m (not in New York)

2 **Teller Of Hawaiian Tales, The** (Syn)

1 **Tello-Test** (4/2/45 - 2/16/51) Mut, 5t, 15m

1 **Temperance Lecture** (5/36) Syn

Tempest, The (1934) Bl, Mon

Temple Of Song (with Chicago a cappella Choir and Edward Davies)
(3/10/35 - 4/7/35) NBC, Sun, 25m, 11:35 pm
(4/14/35 - 7/14/35) Bl, Sun, 4:30 pm

1 **Ten Dancing Fingers** (11/1/38) Mut

Ten From Tokyo (7/14/45 - 9/8/45) CBS, Sat, 15m, 3:45 pm

1 **Ten From "Your Show Of Shows"** (8/31/75) ABC-TV

1 **Ten Troubled Years** (6/21/55) NBC

Ten Who Escaped Tojo (NBC) (1944)

54 **Ten-Two-Four Ranch (Time)** (with The Sons Of The Pioneers, Martha Mears)
(11/22/41 - 3/14/45) Syn, Dr. Pepper, 3t, 15m

2 **Tena and Tim** (with Peggy Beckmark)
(5/1/44 - 8/2/46) Cudahy, CBS, 5t, 15m; previously syndicated

Tennessee Ernie (see Tennessee Ernie Ford)

26 **Tennessee Ernie Ford**
(10/25/52 - 8/31/58) Multi
10/25/52 - 5/15/53, Gillette, ABC, 5t, 15m; 3t (Tue, Thu, Fri) as of 1/27/53)
3/8/54 - 12/29/55, CBS, 5t, 7 pm
6/2/58 - 8/31/58) Ford, CBS, 15m, 5t

Tennessee Ernie Ford Show, The (see Tennessee Ernie Ford)

Tennessee Ernie Show, The (see Tennessee Ernie Ford)

Tennessee Ernie Time (see Tennessee Ernie Ford)

1 **Tennessee Jamboree** (1949 - 50) Mut, 5t, 9:30 pm (not in New York)

6 **Tennessee Jed** (5/14/45 - 11/7/47) Tip Top (at least as of 8/10/45), ABC, 5t, 15m

2 **Tenth Anniversary Salute To Movie Radio Guide** (Syn)

13 **Tenth Man, The** (8/4/47 - 10/23/47) Syn

Terkel Time (with Studs Terkel, John Conrad) (1950) NBC

1 **Terrible Rain, The** (9/1/55) CBS

1 **Terror** (AFRTS)

Terror By Night (3/1/36 - 6/7/36) Sus, CBS, Sun, 10 pm; 10:30 pm from 3/22/36 - 3/29/36; 8:30 pm on 6/7/36

Terry Allen and The Three Sisters (with Terry Allen; Margie, Bea and Geri Ross)
(10/12/44 - 4/6/45) CBS, 5t, 15m, 5:30 pm

Terry and Ted (see The Adventures Of Terry and Ted)

26 **Terry and The Pirates** (11/1/37 - 6/30/48) 15m
11/1/37 - 6/1/38, Dari-Rich, NBC, 3t (Mon, Tue, Wed), 5:15 pm
9/26/38 - 3/22/39 - Dari-Rich, Bl, 3t (Mon, Tue, Wed), 5:15 pm
10/6/41 - 5/29/42, Libby, WGN (Midwest), 5t, 15m, (170 episodes broadcast)
1/4/43 - 4/30/43
8/25/47 - 6/30/48, (with Bill Fein as of 8/25/47) Quaker, Bl/ABC, 5t, 6 pm; 5 pm as of 5/29/44; 5:15 pm as of 8/25/47

Terry Regan (see Attorney At Law)

Terry's House Party (with Terry Pepin; Bobby Norris Orchestra)
(10/10/44 - 12/16/45) Bl, 5t, 15m, 1:15 pm; Fri as of 1/26/45

1 **Test Launching Of The Saturn V** (12/67) CBS

1 **Tex and Jinx** (called Hi Jinx until 10/7/49) (with Tex McCreary and Jinx Falkenberg)
(4/29/45 - 60s), mornings, mostly local, New York City (WEAF), 5t, 30m - 60m
also 7/2/47 - 9/24/47, 6/30/48 - 9/29/48, Ipana, NBC, Wed, 9 pm (summer replacement for Duffy's Tavern)

1 **Tex Baker's Ramblers** (1/16/37) WCNW

Tex Beneke (Bring Back The Bands) (with host Ray McKinley) 15m (On The Beam) (3/13/48 - 9/11/48) Mut, Sat, 1:30 pm

2 **Tex Beneke and His Orchestra** (7/9/54, 7/15/79) CBS, PBS-TV

5 **Tex Beneke Orchestra** (Thesaurus transcriptions)

1 **Tex Beneke Show, The** (Thesaurus transcription)

Tex Fletcher, Lonely Cowboy
(7/4/38 - 9/5/38) Mut, Mon, 15m, 10:30 am

1 **Tex Ritter Show, The** (Syn)

124 **Texaco Star Theater, The**
(10/5/38 - 6/15/49) hosts were:
10/5/38 - 11/2/38, Adolphe Menjou;
11/9/38 - 1/11/39, John Barrymore;
1/18/39, Eddie Cantor;
1/25/39 - 2/8/39, Ken Murray;
2/15/39 - 6/28/39; 9/13/39 - 6/26/40, John Barrymore
10/2/40 - 6/25/44 (see Fred Allen)
7/2/44 - 9/22/46 (see James Melton)
4/6/47 - 3/17/48 (see Tony Martin)
3/24/48 - 9/15/48 (see Gordon MacRae)
9/22/48 - 6/15/49 (see Milton Berle)

Texaco Town (see The Eddie Cantor Show)

3 **Texas Jim Lewis and His Lone Star Cowboys** (Standard transcriptions)

1 **Texas Jim Robertson** (3/18/39 - 9/20/47) Sat, 15m
3/18/39 - 10/26/40, NBC, 9 am
5/10/41 - 7/12/41, NBC, 9 am
7/15/41 - 9/26/41, Bl, 5t, 15m, 8:30 am
also 7/19/41 - 42, Bl, 8:30 am
11/9/46 - 3/15/47; 6/14/47 - 9/20/47, ABC, 12 noon

1 **Texas Rangers, The** (8/14/37 - 4/17/38) CBS, Sun, 11 am
(4/24/38 - 6/19/38) CBS, Sun, 5 pm
(3/18/39 - 6/24/39) CBS, Sat, 15m, 4 pm; 2:30 pm as of 5/6/39, also World syn

Textron Theater, The (see The Helen Hayes Theater)

1 **Thanks For Listening** (4/13/52) WMAQ

2 **Thanks For The Memory** (1938) Air trailer

Thanks For Tomorrow (with Mary Jane Higby)

1 **Thanks To America**

Thanks To The Yanks (with Bob Hawk) (10/31/42 - 6/23/44) Camel, CBS (see also Bob Hawk)
10/31/42 - 7/3/43, CBS, Sat, 7:30 pm
7/9/43 - 10/8/43, Fri, 10 pm
10/9/43 - 6/23/44, Sat, 7:30 pm

1 **Thanksgiving Special Program** (11/23/44) AFRS

2 **That Brewster Boy** (9/8/41 - 3/2/45) Quaker
9/8/41 - 3/2/42, Red, Mon, 9:30 pm
3/4/42 - 6/3/42, CBS, Wed, 7:30 pm
6/5/42 - 3/2/45, CBS, Fri, 9:30 pm; developed into Those Websters

7 **That Hammer Guy** (with Larry Haines) (1/6/53 - 10/5/53) Multi until 4/7/53, Mut, Tue, 8 pm; effective 2/24/53 called Mickey Spillane Mystery

1 **That Lady In Ermine** (1948) film sound track

11 **That Other Generation** (with Rudy Vallee; then Henry Morgan) (3/30/69 - 9/28/69) Syn

That They May Live (1/17/43 - 12/18/44) NBC
1/17/43 - 10/10/43, Sun, 12:30 pm
10/16/43 - 12/18/44, Sat, 1 pm

46 **That Was The Week That Was** (1/17/64 - 5/4/65) NBC-TV

1 **That Was The Year** (Syn) 15m, years covered are 1896 - 1934

1 **That Was The Year That Was** (12/26/76) NBC-TV

That's A Fact (with Gilbert Martyn) (10/1/42 - 6/10/43) Bl, 2t, 15m, 7:30 pm

That's A Good Idea (with Dave Vaille) (1945) CBS

That's A Good One (with Hope Emerson and Ralph Dumke; Ed Herlihy, announcer, John Gart (organist)
(9/12/43 - 12/5/43) Adam Hats, Bl, 15m, 8:15 pm
(1944 - 1945) Wilshire Motor Oil

That's A Hit (with Vivian Martin) NBC

That's Finnegan (see Phone Again, Finnegan)

2 **That's Life** (with Jay C. Flippen) (5/3/46 - 1/16/47) CBS
5/3/46 - 9/5/46, Thu, 10:30 pm; 10 pm as of 6/27/46
10/4/46 - 12/7/46, Fri, 5:30 pm
12/17/46 - 1/16/47, 2t, 4:30 pm

1 **That's My Pop** (with Hugh Herbert) (6/7/45 - 9/7/45) CBS, Sun, 7:30 pm (summer replacement for Kate Smith)

1 **That's Our Boy** (created by Carlton E. Morse) (8/26/50) Audition

4 **That's Rich** (with Stan Freberg; Alan Reed, Dawes Butler, Hal March)
(1/8/54 - 9/23/54) Sus, CBS
1/8/54 - 5/21/54, Fri
7/15/54 - 9/23/54, Thu, 9 pm

That's Show Biz (with Ken Murray) 60m

That's What I Said (with Ted Husing) (7/25/39 - 8/29/39) CBS, Tue, 15m, 7:15 pm (summer replacement for Jimmy Fidler)

Thatcher Colt (based on stories by Anthony Abbott)
(9/27/36 - 9/26/37) (with Hanley Stafford)
(1/9/38 - 4/3/38) (with Richard Gordon) Packer's Soap, NBC, Sun, 2:30 pm

89 **Theatre Five** (announcer - Fred Foy) (8/3/64 - 7/30/65) ABC, 5t (260 shows broadcast)

60 **Theatre Guild On The Air, The** (12/6/43 - 6/7/53) 60m
12/6/43 - 2/29/44 (Theater Guild Dramas) Sus, CBS, Tue
9/9/45 - 6/2/46; 9/8/46 - 6/29/47; 9/7/47 - 5/30/48; 9/12/48 - 6/5/49 (also called US Steel Hour) US Steel, ABC, Sun
9/11/49 - 6/4/50; 9/10/50 - 6/3/51; 9/9/51 - 6/1/52; 9/14/52 - 6/7/53, US Steel, NBC, Sun

Theatre Of Famous Radio Players (1945) Mut - West coast

Theatre Of Hits (AFRS)

Theatre Of Romance (see Romance)

Theatre Of Stars (2/22/53 - 5/24/53) CBS, Sun, 6 pm

29 **Theatre Royal** (with Laurence Olivier) (10/4/53 - 5/30/54) CBS, Radio Luxembourg
10/4/53 - 11/1/53, Sun, 9:30 pm
11/7/53 - 3/27/54, Sat, 8:30 pm; 7 pm as of 1/23/54
4/4/54 - 6/6/54, Sun, 9:30 pm, also syndicated

Theatre Time

3 **Theatre U.S.A.** (11/11/48 - 6/30/49) ABC,Thu; produced by ANTA (American National Theater and Academy)

1 **Theatre Workshop Group, The** (1949) Syn

Theatre X (1958 or 1959)

Then and Now (see Sears - Then and Now)

1 **Then Are The Children Free** (1947) Syn

1 **There Shall Be No Gestapo In America** (6/12/41) Mut

There Was A Woman (with Raymond Edward Johnson and Betty Caine)
(7/4/37 - 1/1/38) Bl, Sun, 5 pm
(1/8/38 - 10/2/38) Glass Containers, Bl, Sun, 1:30 pm; 5 pm as of 4/10/38

There's A Law Against It (1/20/39 - 6/7/39) Mut
1/20/39 - 3/10/39, Fri, 9:30 pm
3/29/39 - 6/7/39, Wed, 10 pm

1 **There's Always A Woman** (9/25/48) Mut

2 **There's Always The Guy** (with Sweeney and March) (10/44) American Vitamin Company, CBS

2 **There's Music In The Air** (with Donald Richards, Clark Dennis, Alfredo Antonini Orchestra) (6/13/50)
(1/16/53 - 9/25/53) CBS, Fri, 60m, 9 pm; 8:30 pm as of 8/7/53

1 **Thesaurus Audition Program** (Syn)

7 **These Are My People** (12/46) Syn

These Are Our Men (12/16/44 - 2/17/45) Parker Watches, NBC, Sat, 2 pm

1 **These The Humble** (Syn)

1 **They Call Me G.I. Joe** (also called They Call Me Joe) (7/29/44 - 10/7/44) NBC, Sat, 7 pm

1 **They Came Back** (11/3/43) BBC

1 **They Gave Him A Gun** (5/37) Air trailer

They Live Forever (with Berry Kroeger) (2/8/42 - 10/27/42) CBS
2/8/42 - 6/7/42; 7/26/42 - 10/18/42, Sun, 10:30 pm
10/27/42, Tue, 9:30 pm

1 **They Met The Boat** (10/9/49) ABC

2 **They Shall Be Heard** (9/19/46) Mut, auditions

They Stand Accused (with Jay Jostyn) (1943) Syn, 15m

Thin Man, The (see The Adventures Of The Thin Man)

1 **Things To Come** (1936) Air trailer

2 **Think** (ABC Radio Workshop) (1953) ABC

Think Fast (with Mason Gross) (5/29/49 - 5/7/50) Sus, ABC, Sun

1 **Think Fast Brother** (9/5/45) WOR

Thinking Makes It So (with Suzanne Silvercruys) (7/28/41 - 8/25/41) Bl, Mon, 15m, 11:30 am

1 **Thinking Man's Moon Coverage** (7/20/69) WKCR-FM

1 **Third Annual Rag Revival Reunion** (5/72) WBAI

Third Horseman, The (8/22/47 - 9/5/47) NBC, Fri, 9 pm (partial summer replacement for People Are Funny)

50 **Third Man, The** (The Lives Of Harry Lime) (with Orson Welles) (Syn) (1952); originally a BBC show (8/3/51 - 8/1/52)

1 **Thirsty Land, The** (9/27/55) UNESCO Radio

1 **Thirteen By Thornbough** (7/20/49)

2 **Thirteenth Juror, The** (with Vincent Price) (4/23/49, 8/20/53) NBC, Sat

Thirty Minutes In Hollywood (see George Jessel)

1 **Thirty Minutes To Go** (Wartime)

1 **Thirty Five Eventful Years** (5/4/57) WJR

This Amazing America (from Chicago; with Bob Brown, Roy Shield's Orchestra) (2/16/40 - 6/28/40) Greyhound, Bl, Fri, 8 pm; 9:30 pm as of 5/3/40

1 **This Amazing World** (Audition)

1 **This Atomic Age** (5/31/53) UNESCO Radio

This Changing World (7/3/44 - 12/29/44) Standard Brands, CBS, 5t, 15m; 10:30 am; replaced Open Door (see also Harrison Wood)

1 **This Day Is Ours** (11/7/38 - 3/29/40) Crisco, 5t, 15m
11/7/38 - 1/19/40, CBS
1/22/40 - 3/29/40, Bl

2 **This Fabulous World** (Syn)

1 **This Guitar Chose Freedom** (1959) Syn

94 **This I Believe** (11/4/51 - 6/3/55) CBS, 5t, 5m

This Is Adventure (narrated by Edwin C. Hill) (1/26/48 - 4/12/48) ABC, Mon, 10 pm

2 **This Is America** (Syn)

20 **This Is Bing Crosby** (see Bing Crosby)

This Is Bix (see Bix Beiderbecke)

This Is Britain

2 **This Is Broadway** (with Clifton Fadiman, Helen Hayes, Artie Shaw, Abe Burrows, George S. Kaufman; Ray Bloch Orchestra) (4/16/49 - 6/29/49) CBS, Wed, 60m; 9:30 pm

6 **This Is Civil Defense** (10/56) Syn

This Is Europe (7/22/51 - 10/14/51) Mut, Sun, 8 pm

This Is Farming (1/4/46 - 11/22/58) NBC - West, Sat, 15m
1/4/46 - 8/24/57, Skelly Oil, 8 pm
8/31/57 - 2/22/58, Massey-Harris-Ferguson, 8 pm
3/1/58 - 11/22/58, Behlen Mfg. Co., 7 pm

This Is For You (6/5/48 - 10/30/48) ABC, Sat, 10 am

1 **This Is Fort Dix** (with Tom Slater) (12/15/40 - 9/17/44) Sus, Mut, Sun

3 **This Is Halloran** (9/30/44 - 9/15/45) Mut

2 **This Is Holland** (1950) Syn

3 **This Is Hollywood** (1946) Syn

1 **This Is It** (6/6/44) Mut

33 **This Is Jazz** (with Rudi Blesh) (1/18/47) Audition
(2/8/47 - 10/4/47) Mut
2/8/47 - 4/7/47, Mon, 10 pm
4/19/47 - 10/4/47, Sat, 2:30 pm

This Is Judy Jones (with Mercedes McCambridge) (8/21/41 - 10/9/41) Bl, Thu

1 **This Is Life** (with Vincent Pelletier) (10/13/41 - 5/15/42) Hecker Products, Mut, 3t

5 **This Is My Best** (with Orson Welles as of 3/13/45)
(9/5/44 - 5/29/45; 9/18/45 - 5/28/46) Cresta Blanca, CBS, Tue, 9:30 pm

This Is My Land (8/31/40 - 9/14/40) CBS, Sat, 15m, 3:45 pm

17 **This Is My Story** (3/31/44 - 12/2/44) Forty Two Hair Oil, CBS, Sat
(10/20/55 - 12/29/56) NBC (possibly just WRCA, New York), Thu, 8:30 pm

2 **This Is New Jersey** (4/49) Syn

2 **This Is New York** (12/11/38 - 3/19/39) with Lyn Murray, Leith Stevens Orchestra) CBS, Sun, 60m, 8 pm (see also Danny O'Neil)
also 2/3/47, 15m

17 **This Is Nora Drake** (10/27/47 - 1/2/59) NBC, 5t, 15m
10/27/47 - 51, Toni
1951 - 1/2/59, Multi

1 **This Is O'Shea** (with Hy Averback and Jerry Hausner) (10/1/52) Audition

This Is Official (5/30/43 - 8/22/43) Bl, Sat, 1 pm

This Is Our America (7/3/40 - 8/28/40) Bl, Wed, 8 pm (Syn; written by Arch Oboler) (8/3/42 - 9/42)

53 **This Is Our Duty** (2/3/46 - 1/26/47) Syn also (3/19/74) WBAI

2 **This Is Our Enemy** (with Frank Lovejoy; narrated by Arnold Moss
(5/24/42 - 10/21/43) Mut
5/24/42 - 3/3/43, Sun, 10:30 pm
3/9/43 - 4/20/43, Tue, 9:30 pm
5/6/43 - 10/21/43, Thu, 8 pm

2 **This Is Our Heritage** (1/18/51) (Audition) (6/22/63) NBC-TV

4 **This Is Our Music** (Syn)

7 **This Is Paris** (6/3/36 - ?) (with Jacques Lenoir) Bl, Wed, 10 pm
(3/1/49 - 9/22/49) (with Maurice Chevalier) Mut, Thu, 10 pm

4 **This Is Poland** (1944, 1945) Syn

1 **This Is Polio** (1952) Syn

1 **This Is Radio** (8/3/40) Mut

This Is Show Business (see George Jessel)

2 **This Is South Africa** (Syn)

This Is The Army (with Ezra Stone) (see Pass In Review)

This Is The Life (10/5/41 - 12/21/41) CBS, Sun, 1:30 pm

This Is The Mrs. (with Rudy Vallee and Doris Day) (Audition) 11/20/47, Brewer's Yeast, ABC

This Is The Show (with Cliff Nazarro) (12/23/40 - 4/28/41) Bl, Mon, 7:30 pm (not always in New York)

1 **This Is The So-Called Robber, I Guess** (12/22/70) WGN

23 **This Is The Story** (with Madeleine Carroll) (1944) Mut
(4/12/48 - 1951) Syn

2 **This Is Turkey** (1952) Syn

2 **This Is War** (directed by Norman Corwin) (2/14/42 - 5/9/42) Sus, all networks, Sat, 7 pm

1 **This Is WCBS** (1/2/46) WCBS

1 **This Is Worth Fighting For** (Syn)

4 **This Is Your Air Force** (8/48) Syn

1 **This Is Your Country** (8/12/46) Mut

68 **This Is Your FBI** (4/6/45 - 1/30/53) ABC, Fri (409 shows broadcast)
4/6/45 - 12/19/52, Equitable Life
12/26/52 - 1/30/53, Sus

2 **This Is Your Home** (4/13/47, 11/8/53) KPO, KNBC

4 **This Is Your Life** (with Ralph Edwards) (11/9/48 - 5/30/50) Philip Morris
11/9/48 - 6/14/49, NBC, Tue, 8 pm
9/21/49 - 5/3/50, NBC, Wed
5/9/50 - 5/30/50, CBS, Tue, 9:30 pm
also 3/5/61, NBC-TV

1 **This Is Your Navy** (1946) Syn

10 **This Land We Defend** (1941) Syn

5 **This Life Is Mine** (with Betty Winkler) (3/22/43 - 8/24/45) Sus, CBS, 5t, 15m

1 **This Man...This Office** (8/14/80) pool feed

This Moving World (1942)

This Nation At War (5/26/42 - 11/16/43) narrated by Jim Backus; Bl,
5/26/42 - 9/22/42, Tue, 9:30 pm
12/8/42 - 11/16/43, Tue, 10:15 pm; 10:30 pm as of 1/11/43

1 **This New World Of Peace** (5/14/40) NBC

1 **This Our America** (6/4/39) Red

This Romantic Shop (11/8/49 - 12/12/49) Radio Offers Co., ABC, Tue, 15m, 3 pm

This Small Town (with Joan Banks) (9/30/40 - 4/25/41) Duz, NBC, 5t, 15m, 10 am

2 **This War** (with Major Leonard H. Nason) (11/6/39 - 2/27/40) Mut, Mon, 15m, 9:15 pm

6 **This Was News** (2/9/38 - 10/7/38) WHN, WLW

1 **This Was Our Love** (3/5/41) Mut

3 **This Way Please** (9/37) Air trailer, film sound track

2 **This We Have Done** (1943, 1944) Syn

1 **This Week Around Paris** (1/47) Syn

This Week Around the World (1947)

14 **This Week With David Brinkley** (8/15/82 - 6/25/95) ABC-TV

This Woman's Secret (1947 - 1951) General Mills, NBC, Regional

This Wonderful World (see Hayden Planetarium)

This, Our America (7/3/40 - 8/21/40) Bl, Wed, 8 pm

1 **Thomas Dewey Press Conference** (6/25/48) Mut

Thomas Edison Foundation Program (5/15/36 - 7/10/36) CBS, Fri, 1:45 pm

Thomas L. Thomas (see The New Borden Program)

Thompkins Corners (with George Frame Brown) (4/21/32 - 10/6/32) Post Toasties, Bl, Thu, 9:30 pm

2 **Thompson's Of America, The** (5/12/48, 5/14/48) CBS

Thornton Fisher (Sports Parade) (10/20/34 - 3/6/37) NBC, Sat, 15m, 6:45, 7 and 7:45 pm at different times; sponsored by Briggs until 9/28/35

1 **Those Good Old Days** (with Pat Bames, Hal Willard, Joe Rines Orchestra)
(5/14/42) Bl, audition
(8/7/42 - 7/8/44) Bl
8/7/42 - 1/15/43, Fri, 8:30 pm
2/4/43 - 8/12/43, Thu, 25m, 7:05 pm
12/5/43 - 12/26/43, Sun, 4 pm
4/22/44 - 7/8/44, Sat, 7 pm

Those Great Americans (see Lest We Forget)

10 **Those Happy Days** (6/24/70 - 8/27/70) CBS-TV

Those Happy Gilmans (with Bill Bouchey) (8/22/38 - 5/19/39) Kix, NBC & Bl, 5t, 15m

Those Mad Masters (see Mad Masters)

Those O'Malleys (10/22/35 - 4/23/36) Mut, 2t - 3t, 7:30 pm

Those Sensational Years
(4/17/47 - 9/14/47) ABC
4/17/47 - 5/22/47, Thu, 9:30 pm
7/20/47 - 9/14/47, Sun, 7:30 pm

Those We Love (with Nan Grey)
(1/4/38 - 4/1/45)
1/4/38 - 3/29/38, Ponds, Bl, Tue, 8 pm
4/4/38 - 3/27/39, Ponds, Bl, Mon, 8:30 pm
10/5/39 - 3/28/40, Royal Gelatin, NBC, Thu, 8:30 pm
9/16/40 - 6/23/41, Teel, CBS, Mon, 8 pm
7/1/42 - 9/23/42, Sal Hepatica, NBC, Wed, 9 pm (summer replacement for Eddie Cantor)
10/11/42 - 5/30/43, General Foods, CBS, Sun, 2 pm
6/6/43 - 10/3/43, General Foods, NBC, Sun, 7 pm (summer replacement for Jack Benny
10/10/43 - 6/22/44, General Foods, NBC, Sun, 2 pm
6/29/44 - 8/24/44, Maxwell House, NBC, Thu, 8 pm (summer replacement for Maxwell House Coffee Time)
10/8/44 - 4/1/45, NBC, Sun, 2 pm

1 **Those Websters** (with Willard Waterman, Gil Stratton) (3/9/45 - 8/22/48) Quaker
3/9/45 - 2/22/46, CBS, Fri, 9:30 pm
3/3/46 - 8/22/48, Mut, Sun, 6 pm

1 **Those Young Bryans** (3/25/56) NBC, audition

1 **Thousand and One Wives, A** (9/7/39) NBC

4 **Thousand Wives, A** (in Yiddish)

Threads Of Happiness (with Andre Kostelanetz Orchestra, David Ross)
(9/6/32 - 6/6/33) J & P Coates, CBS, Tue, 9:15 pm
(9/29/33 - 12/22/33) CBS, Fri, 9:15 pm

Three Bakers (with Frank Luther and Sylvia Froos)
(1930 - 7/29/31) CBS, Mon, 9 pm
(11/8/31 - 6/26/32) Fleischmann's Yeast, Bl, Sun, 7:30 pm

1 **Three Caballeros, The** (1944) Air trailer

Three Cheers (3/18/39 - 10/15/39) 15m
3/18/39 - 6/10/39, NBC, Sat, 5 pm
7/27/39 - 9/8/39, Bl, Fri, 7:30 pm
9/10/39 - 10/15/39, Bl, Sun, 5 pm

Three City Byline (with Hy Gardner, Sheilah Graham and Irv Kupcinet)
(7/14/53 - 5/7/54) ABC, 4t (Tue - Fri) 15m, 8 pm

Three Consoles (5/9/38 - 10/3/38), CBS, Mon, 2:30 pm (summer replacement of American School Of The Air)

Three Doctors, The (with Russel Pratt, Ransom Sherman and Joe Randolph
(1927 - 4/21/32) WMAQ; NBC from 12/14/31, various days and time

1 **Three European War Actualities** (1939)

Three For Adventure (with Jack Webb, Elliott Lewis, Barton Yarborough)

Three For The Money (with Bud Collyer) (6/26/48 - 9/25/48) Mut, Sat, 60m, 9 pm

1 **Three Hundred Party** (4/27/46) Mut

1 **Three Hundredth Anniversary Of Brooklyn** (6/11/46) WOR

Three Jesters (2/27/42 - 3/13/42) Bl, Fri, 15m, 7 pm

1 **Three Little Girls In Blue** (1946) Air trailer

1 **Three Marshalls, The** (4/23/39) Mut

1 **Three Musketeers, The** (1948)

1 **Three Of A Kind** (4/13/44) CBS, audition

1 **Three Rhythm Rascals** (Standard transcriptions)

Three Romeos (10/29/38 - 10/3/39) 15m
10/29/38 - 2/11/39, Bl, Sat, 10 am
5/30/39 - 10/3/39, NBC, Tue, 1: 15 pm

1 **Three Sailors and A Girl** (1953) film sound track

Three Scamps, The (3/17/34 - 1/2/36) NBC
3/17/34 - 9/1/34, Sat, 7 pm
11/7/35 - 1/2/36, Thu, 2:30 pm

Three Score and Five (with H. V. Kaltenborn) (7/26/56 - 9/6/56) NBC, Thu, 9:30 pm

Three Sheets To The Wind (with John Wayne and Helga Moray)
(2/15/42 - 7/5/42) NBC, Sun, 11:30 pm

Three Sisters (3/20/43 - 11/24/44) 15m
3/20/43 - 4/17/43, NBC, Sat, 10:45 am
8/16/43 - 9/6/43, CBS, Mon, 7:15 pm
5/1/44 - 10/11/44 (often with Jack Smith) CBS, 3t, 5:30 pm (from 10/12/44 see Terry Allen)

1 **Three Smart Girls** (1936) Exploitation disc

Three Star Extra (see Sunoco Three Star Extra)

7 **Three Suns** (World transcriptions)

4 **Three Suns and A Starlet, The** (1948) Syn

9 **Three Suns, The** (5/5/41 - 56) also called at times The Three Suns and A Starlet (various days and times including:
5/5/41 - 5/30/41, Sus, NBC, 5t, 15m
6/2/41 - 2/7/42, NBC, 6t, 15m
1951 - 52, Sus, ABC, Sat
8/17/52 - 10/12/52, ABC, Sun, 15m, 7:15 pm
1953 - 54, Sus, ABC, 2t
1955 - 56, Sus, ABC, 4t
also World transcriptions

Three Views Of The News (with Ben Grauer, Ed Thorgerson)
(7/20/47 - 8/24/47)

Three X Sisters (10/3/32 - 7/17/36) 15m
10/3/32 - 11/26/32, Tydol, CBS, 3t, 7:30 pm
3/3/33 - 35, Feen-A-Mint, Bl, 2t/5t
1935 - 7/17/36, NBC, 2t; Bl, Fri, 10m, 6:35 pm as of 6/5/36

1 **Three Years, Ten Facts** (5/43) Syn

Three-Quarter Time (with Freddie Rich Orchestra)
(10/14/39 - 12/23/39) Bl, Sat, 1:30 pm
Three-Ring Time
(3/8/43 - 12/20/43) Ballantine, CBS, Mon, 10:30 pm (also see Milton Berle)

Three-Thirds Of The Nation (with Connie Boswell) (4/22/42 - 6/24/42) Bl, Wed, 10 pm

1 **Threshold** (Syn)

1 **Thrill Hunter, The** (Syn)

2 **Thrill Of A Lifetime** (12/37) film sound track, air trailer

1 **Thrills** (ABC) Sun, 15m, 9 pm with Gayne Whitman, Union Oil, NBC

Thrills and Romance (also Chills and Romance) (1940 - 41) Bl, Sun, 15m, 10:30 am

1 **Thrills and Romance In This Amazing America** (10/12/41) Red

1 **Thrills From Great Operas (Thrills From The Opera)** (Pre-war) Syn

Thrills Of The Highway Patrol (see Highway Patrol)

2 **Thrills Of TomorrowFor Boys** (with A. C. Gilbert) (10/30/33 - ?) Mon

5 **Through The Iron Curtain** (11/17/46 - 1/12/47) CBS

Through The Looking Glass (with Frances Ingram) (1930 - 12/27/32) Ingram's Milkweed Cream, Bl, Tue, morning

1 **Through The Looking Glass and What Alice Found There** (10/15/65) Syn

3 **Through The Sport Glass** (1937) Syn

1 **Through The Years** (12/31/45) CBS/International

1 **Through The Years With WLW** (3/2/47) WLW

1 **Thumbs Up** (2/16/41) Mut

Thunder Over Paradise (with Laurette Fillbrandt) (7/24/39 - 2/28/41) Bl, 5t, 15m, 10 am

Thurston, The Magician (with Howard Thurston) (11/3/32 - 5/25/33) Swift, Bl, 2t (Thu & Fri), 15m, 8:45 pm

Thus We Live (see Harvey and Dell)

Thy Kingdom Come (with Ray Middleton) (11/27/54 - 6/11/55) NBC, Sat, 6:30 pm

Thy Neighbor's Voice (6/25/51 - 9/21/51) ABC, 5t, 25m, 5:30 pm; 30m, 12 noon as of 7/23/51

Tic Toc Revue (see Time To Shine with Barry McKinley)

Tide Show, The (see Jack Smith)

1 **Tidings Of Great Joy** (12/22/63) CBS

2 **Till The End Of Time** (Syn)

Tillie, The Toiler (with Caryl Smith) (4/11/42 - 10/10/42) CBS, Sat, 7:30 pm

Tim and Irene (with Tim Ryan and Irene Noblette) (1934 - 1/9/38)
1934 - 35, Bl, Tue
6/28/36 - 9/27/36, Jell-O, NBC, Sun, 7 pm; Bl as of 8/30/36 (summer replacement of Jack Benny)
4/18/37 - 1/9/38 (Fun In Swing Time), Admiration Shampoo, Mut, Sun, 6:30 pm; see also Royal Crown Revue

Tim Healy (see Captain Tim Healy)

Tim Tyler's Luck (Syn; 1936 - 37)

Timber Town

1 **Time and Her Life** (4/20/49) CBS

1 **Time Capsule** (with Art Van Horn) (6/22/52 - 9/24/53)
6/22/52 - 10/5/52, ABC, Sun, 7:30 pm
10/12/52 - 2/8/53, ABC, Sun, 10:30 pm
2/12/53 - 9/24/53, ABC, Thu, 9:30 pm

Time Flies (with Frank Hawks also with Allyn Joslyn) (9/25/36 - 12/18/36) Elgin, Mut, Fri, 8 pm

Time For Decision (see Sumner Welles)

Time For Defense (10/25/49 - 10/2/51) ABC
10/25/49 - 9/26/50, Tue, 10 pm
10/3/50 - 11/21/50, Tue, 8:30 pm
11/30/50 - 3/29/51, Thu, 10 pm
4/3/51 - 10/2/51, Tue, 10 pm

1 **Time For Love** (with Marlene Dietrich also Robert Readick) (1/15/53 - 5/27/54) CBS, Thu
1/15/53 - 5/28/53, Sus, 9 pm
9/3/53 - 5/27/54, Jergens, 9:30 pm

Time For Reason (see Lyman Bryson)

Time For Reason: About Radio (see Lyman Bryan)

Time For Thought (with Dr. Daniel Poling, others) (5/30/38 - 3/27/40) NBC, 5t, 15m, 12:30 pm

Time For Women (with Shelley Mydens) (1/2/46 - 47?) ABC, 5t, 15m

4 **Time Hill Frolic** (Syn)

1 **Time Is Now, The** (1947) Syn

1 **Time Machine, The**

Time Of Your Life, The (with Sheila Barrett and Graham McNamee) (10/3/37 - 12/26/37) Gruen, NBC, Sun

4 **Time Out** (1946) Syn

Time Out For Laughs (see Lou Holtz)

14 **Time Out With Allen Prescott** (1945, 1946) Syn

3 **Time To Keep, A** (1963, 1964, 1965)

1 **Time To Remember** (with Milton Bacon) (8/6/41, 4/16/45 - 1/10/47) CBS, 5t, 15m

1 **Time To Shine** (with Barry McKinley, John B. Gambling, Jean O'Neill) (5/17/37 - 11/8/37) Griffin, Bl, Mon, 7 pm (originally called Tic Toc Revue and Allwite Melody Revue) (see also Hal Kemp)

22 **Time To Sing With Lanny and Ginger Grey** (1946, 1947, 1948) Syn

Time To Smile (see Eddie Cantor)

Time To Take It Easy (3/9/40 - 6/1/40) CBS, Sat, 1:30 pm

Time Turns Back (4/7/36 - 5/26/36) Gruen, Mut, Tue, 15m, 7:45 pm

Time Views The News (6/5/44 - 7/27/45) Welch, Bl, 3t, 15m, 4:30 pm; 4 pm as of 12/11/44
(11/23/44 - 8/16/45) O'Cedar Corp., Bl, Thu, 15m; 2t from 2/20/45 - 5/16/45

1 **Time Was** (4/2/68) WFMU-FM

Time's A Wastin' (with Bud Collyer) (10/6/48 - 12/29/48) CBS, Wed, 10 pm

1 **Time, The Place, and The Girl, The** (1946) film sound track

Time, The Place, The Tune, The (1946 - 48) NBC
1946 - 4/19/47, Sat
1948 - summer, Fri

2 **Timely Farm Topics** (1945) Syn

1 **Times Square Lady** (1935) Air trailer

3 **Timex All Star Jazz Show** (12/30/57, 5/30/58, 11/10/58) CBS-TV

1 **Timex All Star Swing Festival** (11/29/72) NBC-TV

2 **Timid Soul, The** (with Billy Lynn) (10/12/41 - 3/15/42) Mut, Sun, 9:30 pm

Tin Pan Alley Of The Air (with Jack Owens until 6/9/45) (1/20/45 - 7/13/46) Leaf Gum, NBC, Sat, 15m, 5:45 pm

Tin Pan Alley Presents (4/19/38 - 7/19/38) CBS, Tue, 3 pm

Tin Pan Valley (3/30/52 - 8/16/52)
3/30/52 - 4/20/52, NBC, Sun, 10:30 pm
7/12/52 - 8/16/52, CBS, Sat, 10 pm

1 **Tiny Hill and His Hill-Toppers** (World transcription)

1 **Tiny Hill and The Hill-Toppers** (World transcription)

1 **Tiny Markle Show, The** (10/23/72) WNAB

Tish (6/6/32 - 8/31/32) Bl, Mon/Tue/Wed

Tish (with Betty Garde) (10/14/37 - 2/28/38) WPA, CBS, Thu; Wed, 9:30 pm as of 11/3/37; Mon, 8 pm as of 1/10/38, pm; a different series starting on Monday

Title Tales (with Sylvia Rhodes, Bert Farber) (1940) Mut

Tito Guizar (4/19/31 - 39) occasionally sponsored by Brillo, CBS, various days, 15m

1 **Tito Guizar and His Guitar** (NBC) Bromo Seltzer

1 **Tito Guizar and His Orchestra** (NBC) Bromo Seltzer

1 **Tito On Trial**

4 **TM Radio Program, The** (1976) Syn

To Be Perfectly Frank (see Frank Sinatra)

68 **To Have and To Hold** (8/4/75 - 11/5/75) Syn

To Live In Peace (4/6/46 - 1/18/47) Bl, Sat, 1 pm

To The Ladies (with Tito Guizar; Morton Downey as of 10/7/32) (1/1/32 - 12/23/32) Woodbury Soap, CBS, Fri, 15m, 9:30 pm; 30m, as of 9/6/32

1 **To The Moon and Beyond** (7/9/94) PBS-TV

1 **To The President** (written by Arch Oboler) (10/18/42 - 12/20/42) Bl, Sun, 12:30 pm

17 **To The Rear March** (AFRS)

4 **To You In America** (12/47) Syn

To Your Good Health (see Lyn Murray)

1 **Toast Of The Town, The** (1/11/52) CBS-TV

Toastchee Time (4/14/40 - 12/20/42) Lance Packing Company
4/14/40 - 7/10/40, NBC, Wed, 11 pm
8/9/42 - 12/20/42, Bl, Sun, 4:30 pm

1 **Toby Comes Home** (1949) Syn

Toby Reed's Hollywood Scrapbook (6/30/47 - 10/9/47) ABC, 5t, 15m, 4:30 pm; 2t as of 7/22/47, previously on a Pacific net for Gallenkamp Shoes

1 **Today and The World Of Tomorrow** (7/5/39) WWRL

Today and Yesterday (with Donald Voorhees Orchestra; Coburn Goodwin, narrator) (3/4/32 - 6/24/32) Dupont, CBS, Fri, 8:30 pm

1 **Today At Night** (7/5/75) NBC-TV

Today At The Duncans (with Mary and Frank Nelson; Dix Davis)
(11/2/42 - 7/30/43) California Fruit, CBS, 3t, 15m. 6:15 pm; Fri as of 2/5/43

1 **Today In Europe** (with William Shirer, Edward R. Murrow, Albert Warner, Robert Trout, others) (1939 - 40)

1 **Today Show, The** (4/24/64) NBC-TV

6 **Today's Children** (with Helen Kane) (9/11/33 - 6/2/50) NBC, 5t, 15m
9/11/33 - 12/31/37, Pillsbury
12/13/43 - 6/2/50, General Mills; this version replaced Lonely Women

1 **Today's Moderns** (11/28/47) Mut, audition

Today's Pioneer Women (with Ida Bailey Allen) (8/16/32 - 11/15/32) Pebeco, CBS, Tue, 15m, 11: 15 am

4 **Todd Grant Gets The Story** (1943) Syn

Todds, The (with Art and Dorothy Todd) (1947, 1948) 15m
1947 - summer, Cardinay, CBS, Tue
1948 - summer, Ben Hur Coffee, NBC, Fri

1 **Together...A New Beginning** (6/17/80) pool feed

Tokyo Calling (6/25/45 - 8/20/45) Bl, Mon, 10 pm

1 **Tokyo Flag Raising** (9/7/45) Mut

1 **Tokyo Rose** (9/20/45) Newsreel

1 **Tokyo Rose: Two Wars Later** (11/4/69) WBBM-TV

2 **Tom and Ward Laugh Club** (1933) Syn

1 **Tom Breneman's Laugh Parade** (8/8/45) Audition

43 **Tom Corbett, Space Cadet** (with Frankie Thomas) (1/1/52 - 7/3/52) Kellogg, ABC, 2t (Tue & Thu), 30m, also NBC-TV

1 **Tom Dixon Meets The Enemy** (10/4/42) Syn

Tom Farley's Dog Tales (15m)

Tom Glazer's Ballad Box (11/4/45 - 1/12/47) Bl, Sun, 15m, 8:15 - 8:30 am

Tom Howard (with Jeannie Lang, Harry Salter Orchestra) (3/10/33 - 7/28/33) NBC, Fri, 9 pm

17 **Tom Mix** (9/25/33 - 12/16/51) Ralston, 15m
9/25/33 - 3/19/34; 10/l/34 - 3/29/35; 9/30/35 - 3/30/36 (with Artells Dickson), NBC, 3t, 5:30 pm; 5:15 pm from 10/1/34 - 3/29/35
9/28/36 - 3/26/37, NBC, 5t, 5:15 pm
9/27/37 - 3/25/38; 9/26/38 - 3/31/39; 9/25/39 - 4/26/40; 9/29/41 - 3/27/42 (with Jack Holden, Bl, 5t, 5:45 pm
6/5/44 - 9/1/44, 2t (Wed & Fri) 5:30 pm (with Curley Bradley)
9/4/44 - 12/29/44, Mut, 5:30 pm
12/31/44 - 6/24/49, Mut, 5:45 pm; 3t (Tue, Thu & Fri) from 6/24/46 - 8/30/46
9/26/49 - 6/23/50 (starts as Curley Bradley Show), Mut, 3t, 25m, 5:30 pm
8/6/50 - 12/31/50 (The Singing Marshal; with Curley Bradley) Mut, Sun, 8 pm
6/11/51 - 9/7/51, Mut, 3t, 5:30 pm
10/21/51 - 12/16/51, Mut, Sun, 8 pm

Tom Mix Ralston Straightshooters, The (see Tom Mix)

Tom Powers Life Studies
(9/26/35 - 6/4/36) NBC, Thu, 15m
(11/19/40 - 5/15/41) Bl, 2t, 7:30 pm

1 **Tom Terris** (11/7/37 - 10/20/40) Sus, NBC, Sun, 15m (also called Vagabond Adventures, Letters From Abroad) started on WOR 4/17/32; called Vagabond Traveler)
(6/20/43 - 8/8/43) Bl, Sun, 15m, 10:15 pm

3 **Tom, Dick and Harry** (2/17/36 - 12/4/36) Fels Naptha, Mut, 3t, 15m, 10:45 am; 12:15 pm as of 3/2/36 (on locally on WGN into the 40s) (1949) Mut, also syn

Tom, Timmy and Mae (with Tom Glazer and Mae Questel) (9/17/49 - 6/10/50) NBC, Sat, 15m, 11:15 am; 9 am as of 10/29/49

Tommy Bartlett Time (8/23/47 - 48) ABC, Sat, 60m, 10 am; 9 am as of 11/1/47

2 **Tommy Carlyn and His Orchestra** (8/15/64, 7/31/66) CBS

Tommy Dorsey and Company (see Tommy Dorsey)

25 **Tommy Dorsey and His Orchestra** (see Tommy Dorsey)

1 **Tommy Dorsey and His Orchestra... Featuring Jimmy Dorsey** (1953) NBC

1 **Tommy Dorsey Audition** (5/6/47) Mut

46 **Tommy Dorsey Orchestra, The**
(1934 - 10/18/46) 1934, Chrysler, 15m
5/17/36 - 5/24/36, CBS, Sun, 7 pm
8/4/36 - 8/25/36, Ford V8, CBS, Tue, 9 pm (summer replacement of Fred Waring)
11/9/36 - 3/8/37, Raleigh and Kool, Bl, Mon, 9:30 pm (see Jack Pearl)
3/19/37 - 6/25/37, Raleigh and Kool, Bl, Fri, 10 pm (see Jack Pearl)
7/2/37 - 1/28/38, Raleigh and Kool (also with Jack Leonard, Morton Bowe), Bl, Fri, 10 pm; 9:30 pm as of 10/22/37
2/2/38 - 9/20/39, Raleigh, NBC, Wed, 8:30 pm
also 6/1/40 - 11/30/40, NBC, Sat, 55m, 5 pm
6/25/40 - 9/17/40 (Summer Pastime), Pepsodent, NBC, Tue, 10 pm (summer replacement for Bob Hope)
10/17/40 - 4/14/41 (Fame and Fortune) (Amateur Songwriters), Nature's Remedy, Bl, Thu, 8:30 pm
3/8/42 - 7/5/42 (Tommy Dorsey's Variety Show) Bl, Sun, 8 pm
also 6/16/42 - 9/8/42, Raleigh, NBC, Tue, 10:30 pm (summer replacement for Red Skelton)
9/16/42 - 9/8/43, Raleigh, NBC, Wed, 8:30 pm
also 3/12/43 - 3/26/43 (Fri)
6/3/45 - 9/30/45, NBC, RCA, Sun, 8:30 pm
also 7/22/45 - 11/25/45, NBC, Sun, 4:30 pm (partial summer replacement of Music America Loves Best)
3/20/46 - 8/7/46 (Endorsed By Dorsey; with Sy Oliver) Mut, Wed, 10 pm
5/17/46 - 7/12/46 (Tommy Dorsey's Playshop), Mut, Fri, 10 pm

Tommy Dorsey Orchestra, The (continued)
7/22/46 - 9/30/46 (Summer Playhouse), Mut, Mon, 10 pm
also 8/30/46 - 10/18/46, Mut, Fri, 8:30 pm
also 7/7/46 - 9/29/46, Tenderleaf Tea, NBC, Sun, 8:30 pm (summer replacement for Fred Allen)
1947 (Summer Serenade) from Casino Gardens, ABC; U.S. Navy (Your Navy Show), 15m; National Guard; with Rosemary Clooney, also band remotes, Standard transcriptions

Tommy Dorsey Playshop, The (see Tommy Dorsey)

Tommy Dorsey Show, The (see Tommy Dorsey)

1 **Tommy Dorsey, "That Sentimental Gentleman Of Swing"** (Lang-Worth transcription)

1 **Tommy Martin and His Orchestra** (1964) CBS

1 **Tommy Peluso and His Orchestra** (1949) NBC

1 **Tommy Purcell and His Orchestra** (12/31/65) CBS

2 **Tommy Riggs and Betty Lou** (with Tommy Riggs as Tommy and Betty Lou) (10/1/38 - 9/13/46) NBC
10/1/38 - 5/20/39 (Quaker Party), Quaker, Sat, 8 pm
9/4/39 - 3/25/40 (Quaker Variety Show), Quaker, Mon, 8 pm
7/7/42 - 9/29/42 (with Johnny Cash), Swan, CBS, Tue, 9 pm; replaced by Burns and Allen
10/9/42 - 10/1/43, NBC, Fri, 7:30 pm; 10 pm as of 1/29/43
5/10/46 - 9/13/46, Borden, CBS, Fri, 7:30 pm (summer replacement for Ginny Simms)

Tommy Riggs Show (see Tommy Riggs and Betty Lou)

1 **Tommy Taylor** (also Hello Sweetheart) (1/17/44 - 8/4/44) Gum Lab, NBC, 5t, 15m, 10:45 am

1 **Tommy Taylor and Taylor-Made Songs** (6/6/44) NBC

Tommy Tucker and His Orchestra (see Tommy Tucker Orchestra)

6 **Tommy Tucker Orchestra** (see Sing For Your Supper)
also 11/13/39 - 2/12/40, Mut, Mon, 5:30 pm
also 10/30/43 - 12/11/43, (Tommy Tucker's Topics) Bl, Sat, 5:30 pm (War Bond Matinee)
(1945) Mut, 15m, also Lang-Worth, Standard transcriptions

Tommy Tucker's Orchestra (see Tommy Tucker Orchestra)

7 **Tomorrow** (11/1/74 - 12/11/80) NBC-TV, Syn

1 **Tomorrow Calling** (10/30/48) KNX

1 **Tomorrow Will Be Ours** (4/43) Syn

1 **Tomorrow Won't Wait** (Syn)

1 **Tomorrow's Harvest** (11/27/47) CBS

Tomorrow's Headliners (7/2/36 - 7/23/36) CBS,Thu, 9 pm)

Tomorrow's Tops (with Margo Whiteman) (5/30/48 - 8/22/48) ABC, Mon, 9 pm

1 **Tomorrow's Washington** (9/21/44) WRC

Tone Pictures (6/23/40 - 2/1/42) Bl, Sun, 8:30 am

13 **Toni Arden Show, The** (Syn)

1 **Tonight At 9:30** (KPO; from San Francisco) (1/12/46 - 2/2/46+)

Tonight At Hoagy's (see Hoagy Carmichael)

1 **Tonight In Hollywood** (4/4/36, 1945) KMTR

Tonight On Broadway (with Connie Boswell, Ted Husing, Ken Roberts announcing, Ray Bloch Orchestra) (5/13/46 - 11/11/46) Eversharp, CBS, Mon, 10:30 pm

15 **Tonight Show, The** (9/17/54 - 10/11/71) NBC-TV

1 **Tonight's World News** (9/5/45)

Tony and Gus (with Mario Chamlee and George Frame Brown)
(4/29/35 - 9/27/35) General Foods, Bl, 5t, 15m, 7:15 pm

2 **Tony Awards, The** (3/28/48, 3/28/71) Mut, ABC-TV

1 **Tony Freeman and His Orchestra**

2 **Tony Martin** (1/1/41 - 3/17/48) (see also Andre Kostelanetz (Tune Up Time)
1/1/41 - 6/25/41 (with David Rose Orchestra), Woodbury, NBC, Wed, 15m, 8 pm
4/20/46 - 10/5/46 (Listen To A Love Song), Bourjois, CBS, Sat, 7:30 pm
3/30/47 - 1/4/48 (Texaco Star Theater) , Texaco, CBS, Sun, 9:30 pm
1/14/48 - 3/17/48 (Texaco Star Theater) CBS, Wed, 10:30 pm
(7/5/53 - 9/13/53) NBC, Sun, 8 pm

2 **Tony Martin Show, The** (1955)

Tony Morse (1946)

1 **Tony Mottola and His Rhythm Group** (Thesaurus transcription)

1 **Tony Mottola's Dance Rhythms** (SESAC transcription)

2 **Tony Pastor and His Orchestra** (3/20/40) NBC, Lang-Worth transcription

Tony Russell (4/27/36 - 12/1/36) Bl, 2t (Mon & Tue), 15m, 7:15 pm

Tony Won's Scrapbook (1930 - 4/5/42) 15m; also locally on WMAQ
1930 - 4/19/31, Sus, CBS, Sun
8/31 - 11/31, NBC
11/10/32 - 11/19/32, International Silver, CBS, 3t (Thu, Fri, Sat), 9:30 am
8/20/33 - 7/8/34 (The House By The Side Of The Road), Johnson Wax, CBS, 5t
9/2/34 - 7/21/35, Johnson Wax, NBC, Sun, 30m; 15m as of 6/23/35
9/27/37 - 3/25/38, Vicks, CBS, 3t, 10:30 am
10/13/40 - 4/10/41; 10/4/41 - 4/5/42, Hallmark, NBC, 3t (Sun, Tue, Thu); only Sun as of 1/1/42

1 **Too Many Cooks** (with Hal March and Mary Jane Croft) (7/3/50 - 8/21/50) CBS, Mon, 9 pm (half of summer replacement for Lux Radio Theater)

Tooth Fairy (created by Dick Orkin) 3m episodes; about 160 episodes broadcast

Top O' The Morning (7/6/35 - 11/16/35) CBS, Sat, 9 am

Top Guy, The (with J. Scott Smart) (10/17/51 - 5/28/53) ABC
10/17/51 - 10/24/52, Multi, ABC, Wed, 8:30 pm; Fri, 8 pm as of 7/11/52
11/6/52 - 5/28/53, Sus, Thu, 8:30 pm

2 **Top Hat** (1935) film sound track, air trailer

Top Hatters, The (2/3/36 - 3/23/36) NBC, Mon, 10m, 6:35 pm
(5/26/36 - 7/7/36) NBC, Tue, 15m, 5 pm

2 **Top Of The Evening** (with Sally Sweetland, Ted Malone, The King's Men) (3/13/44 - 6/6/45) Bl, 3t, 15m; (Mon, Tue, Wed as of 12/11/44)

1 **Top Of The World** (AFRS)

6 **Top Secret** (with Ilona Massey) (6/12/50 - 10/26/50) NBC
6/12/50 - 7/10/50, Mon, 10:30 pm
7/23/50 - 8/20/50, Sun, 9:30 pm
9/1, Fri 9/18 - 9/25, Mon 10/5 - 10/26, Thu, 10 pm

Top Secret Files (10/4/54 - 9/12/55) Multi, Mut, Mon, 8 pm

1 **Top Secrets Of The FBI** (11/12/47) Mut, audition

1 **Top Tunes Of The Week, The** (6/25/55)

Top Tunes With Trendler (with Robert Trendler Orchestra) 1949, Mut

82 **Tops In Sports** (10/19/60 - 1964) Syn

1 **Torch Hour, The** (with Franklyn MacConnack) (11/25/59) WGN

Torch Of Progress, The (with Dr. Edward Howard Griggs) (10/6/39 - 1/12/40) NBC, Fri, 15m, 6 pm

Torme Time (see Mel Torme)

1 **Tornado** (CBS)

Toronto Promenade Orchestra (5/12/38 - 10/2/41)
5/12/38 - 10/6/38, Bl, Thu, 60m, 9 pm; NBC as of 7/7/38
6/5/41 - 10/2/41, Bl,Thu, 10 pm

1 **Toscanini, The Man Behind The Legend** (with Ben Grauer) (9/24/66) NBC, 60m

1 **Total Eclipse Of The Sun** (6/8/37) CBS

Touchdown Tips (with Sam Hayes) (1946)

3 **Tour Of The City, A** (3/22/83 - 3/15/84) WPBH-FM

Tourist Adventure (with Irvin Talbot Orchestra) (2/22/34 - 4/11/34) Bl, Wed, 10:30 pm

Tours In Tone (6/7/38 - 10/11/38) CBS, Tue, 2 PM

1 **Toward The Light** (1946) Syn

Tower Playhouse (KVI, Seattle; written and directed by Jim French; led to Crisis) (7/25/72 - 9/19/72)

Tower Town Tempos (5/24/38 - 6/24/38) CBS, 3t, 15m, 12:15 pm

87 **Town and Country Time** (1953, 1954) Syn, 15m

1 **Town Crier, The** (with Alexander Woollcott) (9/15/30 - 1/6/38) CBS
9/15/30 - 12/12/30, Gruen, 2t (Mon, Fri), 15m, 7:15 pm
7/21/33 - 11/10/33, CBS, 2t (Wed & Fri), 15m, 10:30 pm
11/20/33 - 2/16/34, Sus, various days, 15m, 9:15.pm
10/7/34 - 3/31/35, Cream Of Wheat, Sun, 9 pm; 7 pm as of 1/6/35
10/6/35 - 12/29/35, Cream Of Wheat, Sun, 7 pm
1/7/37 - 1/6/38, Granger Tobacco, 2t, 15m, 7:30 pm

Town Hall Big Game Hunt (with Norman Prescott) (7/6/38 - 7/27/38) Ipana and Sal Hepatica, NBC, Wed, 9 pm (partial summer replacement of Fred Allen) see Town Hall Varieties

1 **Town Hall Interview** (1938) NBC/Syn

Town Hall Tonight (see Fred Allen)

Town Hall Varieties (with E Chase Taylor) (8/10/38 - 9/28/38) Ipana and Sal Hepatica, NBC, Wed, 9 pm; second part of summer replacement of Fred Allen

2 **Town Meeting** (10/29/92, 10/30/92) WZZM-TV

Town Meeting Of The Air (see America's Town Meeting)

1 **Town Meeting With President Clinton, A** (2/10/93) WXYZ-TV/C-SPAN

1 **Town Meeting: Tel Aviv** (8/21/49)

Town Topics (with Lois Long and Mark Wamow Orchestra) (10/1/35 - 1/19/36) CBS, Tue, 3 pm

Townsend Murder Mystery, The (with Thurston Hall; written by Octavius Roy Cohen) (2/14/33 - 6/17/33) Bl, 3t (Tue, Thu, Sat), 15m, 7:45 pm

1 **Trader Ginsberg** (1930) Synchro-disc

2 **Trailer Show, The** (9/13/37) Audition

1 **Traitor Within, The** (4/12/53) NBC

Trans-Atlantic Call (People To People) (2/7/43 - 4/12/53) CBS, Sun, 12 noon; 12:30 pm as of 6/13/43; heard in Great Britain and America
2/7/43 - 4/21/46, Sus
10/19/52 - 4/12/53 (America Calling) Riggio Tobacco, Sun, 4 pm

1 **Trans-Atlantic Murder Mystery** (Pre-war) Syn

Trans-Atlantic Quiz (with Alistair Cooke) (4/15/44 - 9/2/45) Bl/BBC
4/15/44 - 1/27/45, Sat, 15m, 11:30 am
2/13/45 - 5/8/45, Tue, 30m, 10 pm
5/16/45 - 5/23/45, Wed, 30m, 10 pm
6/4/45 - 6/18/45, Mon, 30m, 10 pm
6/28/45 - 8/2/45, Thu, 30m, 10 pm
8/5/45 - 9/2/45, Sun, 30m, 10 pm

1 **Transatlantically Yours** (9/25/45) CBS

1 **Transcribed and Live Announcement Plan For The Victory Loan** (6/44) Syn

1 **Transit Of Mercury** (11/11/40) WOR

1 **Translation Of Dr. Benes Speech** (10/5/38) Czechoslovakia

1 **Translation Of Mussolini's Speech** (9/18/38) Italy

1 **Translation of Daladier's Speech** (10/10/39) France

1 **Trash Is Cash** (with Walt Framer) (5/27/43) WOR

Travelin' Man (with Bill Adams) (7/1/46 - 9/19/46) NBC
7/1/46 - 8/19/46, Mon, 8 pm (summer replacement of Cavalcade Of America)
8/29/46 - 9/19/46, Thu, 10:30 pm

1 **Traveling Hoosier** (7/18/30) Syn, 15m

Travels Of Mary Ward, The (8/24/36 - 37) Montgomery Ward, 5t, 15m

Treasure Chest (see Boris Karloff's Treasure Chest; Horace Heidt)

6 **Treasure Hour Of Song,The** (with Alfredo Antonini Orchestra) (1/24/42 - 6/26/47) Conti, Mut
1/24/42 - 5/2/42 (with Josephine Tuminia) Sat, 8 pm
5/8/42 - 7/24/42 (with Lucia Albanese as of 5/22/42) Fri, 10 pm
1/20/43 - 6/10/43; 11/18/43 - 6/15/44; 11/23/44 - 5/31/45; 11/29/45 - 6/20/46; 11/28/46 - 6/26/47, Thu, 9:30 pm

Treasure House (see The World Is Yours)

Treasure Hunt (see Go, Get It)

Treasure Trails Of Songs (with Mary Briney, Dick Fulton) (7/23/39 - 10/5/41)
7/23/39 - 8/20/39; 9/10/39 - 10/1/39, Bl, Sun, 2:30 pm; 1:30 pm as of 9/10/39
5/12/40 - 10/6/40, Bl, Sun, 2 pm
5/4/41 - 10/5/41, Bl, Sun, 11:30 am

5 **Treasury Agent** (with Raymond Edward Johnson) (4/14/47 - 58)
4/14/47 - 7/14/47, Sus, ABC, Mon, 9 pm
7/21/47 - 9/22/47, ABC, Mon, 8:30 pm
10/2/47 - 10/23/47, ABC, Thu, 8 pm
1/11/48 - 6/6/48, ABC, Sun, 5 pm
10/12/54 - 58, Multi, Mut, Tue, 8 pm

5 **Treasury Bandstand** (7/14/45 - 8/10/52)
7/14/45 - 10/3/45, CBS, Sat, 5:30 pm
12/22/45 - 3/30/46, CBS, Sat, 2:30 pm
4/6/46 - 4/20/46, CBS, Sat, 4:30 pm
4/27/46 - 9/21/46, CBS, Sat, 2:30 pm; 3 pm as of 7/27/46
1/13/47 - 6/20/47, CBS, 5t, 30m, 5:30 pm
5/31/47 - 9/27/47, CBS, Sat, 3 pm
12/20/47 - 2/4/50, ABC, Sat, 4 pm
7/6/52 - 8/10/52 (with Tex Beneke), CBS, Sun, 6 pm

1 **Treasury Bond Rally** (11/11/45) Mut

5 **Treasury Briefs** (1945) Syn

3 **Treasury Department Song For Today** (6/12/44) Syn

1 **Treasury Hour, The** (7/2/41 - 9/24/41) see Millions For Defense) CBS
(9/30/41 - 12/23/41) Bendix Aviation, Bl, Tue, 60m, 8 pm (see also Lawrence Welk)

Treasury Of Music (1/24/53 - 2/21/53) NBC, Sat, 5 pm
(7/1/55 - 10/28/55) (with John Conte) ABC, Fri, 9:30 pm (1959)

Treasury Of Song (see Squibb)

Treasury Of Stars (9/1/54 - 10/6/54) NBC, Wed, 15m, 8 pm

Treasury Of Wisdom

213 **Treasury Salute** (1944 - 1945) Syn, 15m

1 **Treasury Salute, The** (Audition)

113 **Treasury Song For Today** (1944) Syn

500 **Treasury Song Parade** (3.5m) Syn

286 **Treasury Star Parade** (Syn) (4/11/42 - 2/11/44), Bl, 3t/2t, 15m, 4:30 pm

Treasury Tunes (1942)

1 **Treasury Varieties** (1/21/50) Mut

1 **Treaty: A Cautious Celebration, The** (3/26/79) NBC-TV

1 **Tree Grows In Brooklyn, A** (with John Larkin)
(7/8/49 - 9/30/49) NBC, Fri, 8:30 pm

Treet Time (with Buddy Clark) (2/24/41 - 2/20/42) Armour, CBS, 3t, 15m, 11 am

Tremaynes, The (with Mr. and Mrs. Les Tremayne) (7/30/49 - 9/24/49) Mut, Sat, 1:30 pm

Tremendous Triffies (with George Hicks) (10/8/55 - 9/9/56) CBS, Sat/Sun, 5m

1 **Trial Of Harry Morley, The** (10/4/42) Syn

2 **Trial Of Millie Norton, The** (Syn)

1 **Tribute To A Trooper** (6/17/48) WKBV

1 **Tribute To Babe Ruth** (4/27/47) Mut

1 **Tribute To Bing Crosby, A** (1/7/51) Liberty Broadcasting

1 **Tribute To Eddie Cantor** (10/11/64) ABC

1 **Tribute To Ernie Pyle** (4/18/45) Mut

1 **Tribute To Ethel Barrymore** (8/15/45) ABC

Tribute To Franklin Delano Roosevelt, A (Special 2-hour tribute following his death; on all networks) (4/12/45)

1 **Tribute To George Gershwin** (7/15/37) Mut

1 **Tribute To Glenn Miller** (6/5/45) WNEW

1 **Tribute To Irving Berlin** (8/3/38) CBS

1 **Tribute To Jimmy Dorsey, A** (1958) Syn

1 **Tribute To King George VI, A** (5/1/52) NBC

1 **Tribute To Lou Gehrig** (6/6/41) NBC

1 **Tribute To Lyndon B. Johnson** (1/22/73) NBC

1 **Tribute To Robert Frost, A** (1/29/63) NBC

1 **Tribute To Ross Columbo** (1964) KFRC

1 **Tribute To The Radio Industry** (11/30/40) Mut

10 **Tribute To..., A** (7/43 - 12/29/74) Syn, NBC, BBC, CBS, CBS-TV

1 **Tribute To...Sir Winston Churchill, A** (1/16/65) CBS

40 **Trilby** (Syn)

Triolians (10/7/34 - 12/30/34) Spartan Radio, Bl, Sun, 15m, 6:15 pm

1 **Trip To Mars, A** (3/58) Syn

Triple B Ranch (with Bob Smith) (3/8/47 - 5/28/49) NBC, Sat, 9 am

1 **Triumphant Hour, The** (3/28/48) Mut

2 **Trobriand The Adventurer** (Pre-war) Syn

1 **Trojan Women, The** (4/15/47) Mut

2 **Troman Harper, The Rumor Detective** (12/13/42 - 11/28/43) Bromo Quinine, Mut, Sun, 15m, 6:30 pm; 6:45 pm as of 2/28/43

Tromer's Troopers (see Monday Night Show)

1 **Tropic Holiday** (1939) Air trailer

Tropical Serenade (4/8/39 - 9/12/42) Mut (also see Don Arres)
4/8/39 - 10/21/39 (with Sagi Vela; Don Arres as of 6/17/39), Sat, 8 pm
10/19/40 - 2/15/41, Sat, 15m
5/10/41 - 7/12/41, Sat, 15m, 8:45 pm
12/19/41 - 1/9/42, Fri, 15m, 8:30 pm
7/3/42 - 9/12/42, Sat, 45m, 10: 15 pm

1 **Troubadors Male Quartette and Lou Raderman** (Lang-Worth transcription)

Troubadour and The Lady, The (11/22/41 - 12/20/41) Bl, Sat, 15m, 12:15 pm

Troubadours (10/4/33 - 3/14/34) Bristol Myers, NBC, Wed, 9 pm

Trouble House (with Anne Elstner) heard on Heinz Magazine Of The Air (9/2/36 - 8/24/37)

Trouble Is My Business (1951)

Trouble With Marriage, The (7/3/39 - 12/29/39) Procter & Gamble, Bl, 5t, 15m

1 **Truculent Turtle, The** (10/1/46) ABC

True Action Adventures

True Adventures (with Floyd Gibbons) (1/7/37 - 10/7/37) Colgate, CBS, Thu, 10 pm

65 **True Adventures Of Junior G-Men** (3/1/36 - 3/18/38) Mut, 5t, 15m, Syn

3 **True Confessions** (with Bess Johnson) (1944 - 1958) True Confessions Magazine, NBC, 5t
(1946) Mut

24 **True Detective Mysteries** (narrated by Jack Shuttleworth) (5/16/29 - 59) MacFadden Publications
5/16/29 - 5/8/30, CBS, Thu
9/8/36 - 8/31/37, Mut, Tue, 9:30 pm
4/5/38 - 3/24/39, Listerine, Mut, Tue, 30m; 15m from 1/39
4/29/44 - 6/24/44, Mut, Sat, 30m, 10:15 pm
10/1/44 - 3/11/45, Sus, Mut, Sun, 30m, 1:30 pm
1/20/46 - 53, O'Henry, Mut, Sun, 4:30 pm
1953 - 4/10/55, Sus, Mut, Sun
4/13/55 - 9/14/55, Mut, Wed, 8 pm
9/19/55 - 58, Mut, Mon, 8 pm
1958 - 59, Multi, Mut, Sun

1 **True Enemy, The** (El Verdadero Enemigo) Syn

1 **True Glory Of Thanksgiving, The** (11/46) Syn

1 **True Gospel, The** (7/27/48) WLOS

True Legal Dramas (on WGR in Buffalo from Jun through Nov, 1948, Sat, 6:15 pm (26 weeks); then syndicated to local bar associations in other states)

1 **True Life Stories** (Syn)

1 **True Or False** (1/3/38 - 2/4/56)
1/3/38 - 6/27/38, Williams Shaving Cream, Mut, Mon, 10 pm
7/4/38 - 8/7/39, Williams, Bl, Mon, 10 pm
8/14/39 - 7/1/40; 9/9/40 - 6/30/41; Williams, Bl, Mon, 8:30 pm
7/7/41 - 9/8/41, W. E. Young, Bl, Mon, 8:30 pm
9/15/41 - 6/28/43, Williams, Bl, Mon, 8:30 pm
2/7/48 - 4/30/49, Shotwell Mfg. Co., Mut, Sat, 5:30 pm
5/4/49 - 5/19/49, Mut, Thu, 8:30 pm
1/7/50 - 4/1/50, Anahist, Mut, Sat, 5 pm
4/8/50 - 1/20/51, Sus, Mut, Sat, 5 pm
1/16/53 - 10/9/53, Sus, Mut, Fri, 8:30 pm
7/17/54 - 7/16/55, Mut, Sat, 8 pm
12/17/55 - 2/4/56, Sus, Mut, Sat, 8 pm

True Romances (10/8/29 - 3/4/30) MacFadden Publications, CBS, Tue, 8:30 pm; Wed, 9 pm as of 12/24/29

True Stories (NBC) 1952

True Story Hour with Mary and Bob (with Nora Stirling) (1/26/32 - 6/28/32) True Story Magazine, NBC, Tue, 8 pm

True Story Theater Of The Air (with Henry Hull) (9/23/42 - 12/30/42) Howard Clothes, Mut, Wed, 8:30 pm

True Story Time (with Fulton Oursler) (5/23/39 - 10/3/39) Bl, Tue, 9:30 pm

True Tale Dramas (1935) 15m

1 **True To Life** (with Kaye Brinker) 8/27/39 - 5/19/40) Mut, 15m
8/27/39 - 9/17/39, Sun, 11: 15 pm
11/5/39 - 11/19/39, Sun, 12:30 pm
2/11/40 - 5/19/40, 2t - 3t, 10: 15 am; includes Sun, 9 pm
also 1943, film sound track

Truitts, The (with John Dehner) (6/11/50 - 9/20/51) NBC
6/11/50 - 9/10/50, Sun, 3 pm
7/5/51 - 9/20/51, Thu, 8 pm

1 **Truman Assassination Attempt** (11/1/50) CBS

1 **Truman Train, The** (10/21/48) Mut

1 **Trumpet Blows, The** (4/8/34) Air trailer

1 **Trumpet Serenade** (1942) film sound track

1 **Truth About Cancer, The** (1956) Syn

17 **Truth Or Consequences** (with Ralph Edwards) (3/23/40 - 9/12/56)
3/23/40 - 7/27/40, Ivory, CBS, Sat, 9:45 pm
8/17/40 - 6/27/42; 9/12/42 - 6/26/43; 8/28/43 - 7/15/44; 9/9/44 - 7/7/45; 9/8/45 - 7/6/46; 9/7/46 - 7/5/47; 9/6/47 - 6/26/48; 8/28/48 - 6/25/49; 8/27/49 - 6/24/50, Duz, NBC, Sat, 8:30 pm
9/5/50 - 5/29/51, Philip Morris, CBS, Tue, 9:30 pm
6/17/52 - 9/30/52, Pet Milk, NBC, Tue, 9:30 pm; (summer replacement for Fibber McGee & Molly)
9/18/52 - 6/18/53, Pet Milk, NBC, Thu, 9 pm
6/24/53 - 9/16/53, Pet Milk, NBC, Wed, 9:30 pm
9/24/43 - 4/15/54, Pet Milk, NBC, Thu, 9 pm
10/26/55 - 9/12/56, Multi, NBC, Wed, 8 pm

Try and Find Me (8/27/45 - 12/6/46) Southern Cotton Oil Co., CBS, 5t, 15m; ABC as of 3/11/46

Tuesday Night Party (see Al Jolson)

1 **Tums Hollywood Theater** (NBC) (9/18/51 - 3/11/52, Tums, NBC, Tue, 8:30 pm
also 12/17/52

Tums Show (see Frank Fay)

Tums Treasure Chest (see Horace Heidt)

1 **Tumult and The Shouting: His Finest Hour, The** (11/28/54) NBC

2 **Tune Detective, The** (with Sigmund Spaeth) (12/9/31 - 5/2/33) Bl, 15m
12/9/31 - 32, Wed
1932 - 5/2/33, Thu/Tue
(1/19/47 - 3/23/47 (Sigmund Spaeth's Music Quiz) Mut, Sun, 15m, 1:15 pm
also Thesaurus transcription

Tune Timers (7/19/41 - 8/30/41) NBC, Sat, 10m, 9:05 am

Tune Toppers, The (9/6/41 - 9/27/41) NBC, Sat, 15m, 10 am

Tune Twisters (3/28/35 - 4/18/35) Bl, Thu, 15m, 8:15 pm

Tune Types (4/3/39 - 6/19/39) Bl, Mon, 8:30 pm

Tune Up America (with Betty Rhodes and David Rose Orchestra) (3/4/42 - 5/6/42) Mut, Wed, 11:30 pm

Tune-Up Time (see Andre Kostelanetz)

Tunes From The Tropics (7/2/40 - 10/2/41) CBS, 15m
7/2/40 - 11/19/40, Tue
5/5/41 - 7/7/41, Mon, 9:15 am
7/10/41 - 10/2/41, Thu, 9:30 am

Turn Back The Clock (with Alice Remson and Bailey Axton) (11/21/37 - 1/21/40) Bl, Sun, 15m, 9 am
(8/4/55 - 9/29/55) Colonial Dames, NBC, Thu, 15m, 3:45 pm
(1958 - 60)

1 **Turn Back The Turntable** (7/30/48) NBC

1 **Turn Off The Moon** (5/37) Air trailer

10 **Turning Points** (11/5/48 - 2/21/49) Syn

1 **Turning Wheel, The** (3/1/52) NBC

1 **Twelve Biggest News Stories Of 1935, The** (12/35) Mut

1 **Twelve Crowded Months** (12/29/42) CBS

1 **Twelve Crowded Months of 1939** (12/39) CBS

1 **Twelve O'Clock News** (1/12/50)

1 **Twelve Players** (8/19/45 - 11/3/45) CBS, Sat (also 2/8/48 & 3/29/48, ABC, Mon, 8:30 pm)

1 **Twelve Players Present**

1 **Twentieth Century** (1934) Air trailer

Twentieth Century Concert Hall (12/6/53 - 4/11/54) CBS, Sun, 4 pm

1 **Twentieth Century International Radio Newsreel** (1939) Audition

2 **Twentieth Century International Radio Productions** (9/39) Auditions

1 **Twentieth Century Limited Insert** (9/14/48) WOR

1 **Twentieth Century Pilgrims** (11/23/44)

5 **Twentieth Century, The** (1957 - 12/64) CBS-TV

Twenty - One Stars (6/17/44 - 9/9/44) Bl, Sat, 3 pm

Twenty - Thousand Years In Sing Sing (with Lewis E. Lawes, Warden Of Sing Sing)
(1/22/33 - 4/21/39) Sloan's Liniment from 10/4/33
1/22/33 - 5/7/33, Bl, Sun, 9 pm
10/4/33 - 3/14/34; 9/19/34 - 4/17/35; 9/18/35 - 4/8/36, Bl, Wed; 9 pm; 9:30 pm as of 9/18/35
10/12/36 - 4/5/37, Bl, Mon, 9 pm
10/18/37 - 4/11/38 (Behind Prison Bars) Bl, Mon, 10 pm
10/21/38 - 4/21/39 (Criminal Case Histories With Warden Lewis E. Lawes) Bl, Fri, 8 pm

Twenty Fingers Of Harmony (with Mathilda and Irene Harding)
(11/14/31 - 32) Benrus, Bl, Sat, 15m, 10:45 pm

2 **Twenty Five Years Ago** (9/37) Syn

1 **Twenty Million Sweethearts** (1934) Air trailer

2 **Twenty One** (12/5/55, 3/11/56) NBC-TV

9 **Twenty Questions** (2/2/46 - 3/27/54) Mut
2/2/46 - 6/23/51, Ronson, Sat, 8 pm
6/30/51 - 9/27/52, Sus, Sat, 8 pm
10/4/52 - 6/27/53, Wildroot, Sat
7/4/53 - 12/29/53, Multi, Sat
1/2/54 - 3/27/54, Sus, Sat, 8 pm

1 **Twenty-Fifth Silver Trumpet, The** (3/47) WWL

25 **Twenty-First Precinct, The** (with Everett Sloane) (7/7/53 - 7/26/56) Sus, CBS
7/7/53 - 11/24/53, Tue, 9:30 pm
1/20/54 - 4/20/55, Wed, 8:30 pm
7/9/55 - 10/1/55, Sat, 8 pm
10/7/55 - 1/20/56 (with James Gregory), Fri, 8:30 pm
1/26/56 - 7/27/56 (with James Gregory; then Les Damon) Thu, 8:30 pm

1 **Twenty-Second Letter, The** (7/15/42 - 9/30/42) CBS, Wed, 10:30 pm

2 **Twenty-Twenty** (5/8/80, 5/29/92) ABC-TV

1 **Twilight Tales** (Syn)

1 **Twin Beds** (1942) Air trailer

Twin Stars (10/2/36 - 6/20/37) National Biscuit
10/2/36 - 3/26/37 (with Rosemarie Brancato and Helen Claire), Bl, Fri, 9:30 pm
4/4/37 - 6/20/37 (with Helen Broderick and Victor Moore), CBS, Sun, 8 pm

Twin Views Of The News (with Hy Gardner and Danton Walker)
(8/1/48 - 9/19/48) (Discuss Broadway) Mut, Sun, 15m, 10 pm
(5/1/49 - 6/21/52) Mut, Sat

1 **Two Daffodils, The** (with Ken Gillum and Duke Attenbury) (1931) 15m

Two For The Money (9/30/52 - 9/23/56) Old Gold
9/30/52 - 9/22/53, NBC, Tue, 10 pm
10/3/53 - 6/26/54, CBS, Sat
8/28/54 - 9/3/55, CBS, Sat
9/11/55 - 9/23/56, CBS, Sun

1 **Two For Tonight** (1935) film sound track

46 **Two Lives Have I** (Pre-war) Syn

1 **Two Men On A Raft** (1944) Syn

Two On A Clue (with Louise Fitch and Ned Wever) (10/2/44 - 1/4/46) General Foods, CBS, 5t, 15m, 2:15 pm; 2 pm as of 3/26/45

Two On A Shoestring (with Peggy Zinke) (10/17/38 - 12/16/38) Dioxogen Face Creme, Mut, 5t, 15m, 2 pm

Two Seats In The Balcony (with Harold Sanford Orchestra) (1/3/34 - 7/7/35) NBC, Wed, 2 pm

1 **Two Sleepy People** (8/18/47)

9 **Two Thousand Plus** (3/15/50 - 1/2/52) Sus, Mut
3/15/50 - 2/28/51, Wed, 9 pm
3/2/51 - 5/11/51, Fri, 9 pm
7/8/51 - 9/23/51, Sun, 2:30 pm
9/26/51 - 1/2/52, Wed, 9 pm

Two Ton Baker (1947 - 55) Sus, Mut; from Chicago, 5t, 15m

2 **Two Views Of The Cancer Fight** (1965) Syn

1 **Two Voices** (11/16/58) CBS

Two Westminster College Choirs (12/19/38 - 4/3/39) Bl, Mon, 9:30 pm

Two's Company (1949 - 50) NBC, 5t

Tydol Jubilee, The (with Paul Specht Orchestra, Three X Sisters)
(11/28/32 - 1/13/33) Tydol, CBS, 3t, 15m, 7:30 pm

Typical American Family, A (7/3/40 - 9/25/40) Bl, Wed, 15m, 2:15 pm (every other week)

29 **U.N. Album** (11/3/49 - 12/8/53) United Nations Radio

1 **U.N. Charter Day Program** (10/24/48) CBS

U.N. in Action, The (8/1/48 - 6/26/49; 9/18/49 - 12/18/49) CBS, Sun, 15m, 1:15pm

1 **U.N. Is My Beat, The** (6/53) Syn

116 **U.N. Story** (5/31/53 - 9/20/53) NBC, Sun, 15m, 11:45 am
also (1949 - 1954) Syn

1 **U.S. Army Band, The** (9/20/41) WHN

1 **U.S. Government Reports** (Pre-war) Syn

7 **U.S. Marine Band** (Syn)

1 **U.S. Naval Academy Graduation Ceremonies** (6/19/42) WFBR

1 **U.S. Naval Academy Graduation Exercises** (6/5/45) WFBR

2 **U.S. Navy Band Concert** (6/6/44, 6/7/44) CBS

8 **U.S.O. Campaign** (1947) Syn

1 **U.S.O. Farewell Program** (1/11/48) NBC

U.S. Steel Hour (see Theater Guild Of The Air)

1 **U.S. Wheat In 1942** (1942) Syn

1 **Ukulele Ike** (8/13/45) (see Cliff Edwards)

Una Mae Carlisle (2/24/51 - 10/6/51) ABC, Sat, 15m, 6:15 pm

Uncle Abe and David (with Parker Fennelly and Arthur Allen)
(1930 - 5/9/31) Goodrich, NBC, 4t, 15m

Uncle Charlie's Tent Show (with Charles Winninger)

6 **Uncle Don** (with Don Carney)
(9/28 - 2/9/49) mostly New York (WOR), 5t - 6t (including Sunday); then Sunday only as of 2/21/47 (8:45 am)
1939 - 40, Maltex, Mut
also 3/1/47 - 1/3/48 (Uncle Don's Record Party) Sat, 9:30 am

Uncle Don Reads The Comics (see Uncle Don)

Uncle Don Reads The Funnies (see Uncle Don)

11 **Uncle Ezra** (with Pat Barrett) (also called Uncle Ezra's Radio Station)
(10/19/34 - 6/28/41) started 5/4/34 on WLS, Chicago
(10/19/34 - 4/21/39) Alka-Seltzer, NBC, 15m
10/19/34 - 11/16/34, 3t (Sun, Wed & Fri), 7:30 pm
11/19/34 - 6/28/35, 3t, 7:45 pm
7/15/35 - 8/12/38, 3t, 7:15 pm
10/23/38 - 11/10/38, 3t (Sun, Tue, Thu)
11/15/38 - 4/21/39, 2t (Tue & Fri) 10:30 pm
also 10/23/38 - 4/16/39 (Sunday Afternoon In Rosedale), Alka - Seltzer, NBC, Sun, 30m, 5 pm
(7/13/40 - 6/28/41) Camel, NBC, Sat, 10 pm
also syndicated

Uncle Jim's Question Bee (with Jim McWilliams) (9/26/36 - 7/8/41)
9/26/36 - 12/16/39, George Washington Coffee, Bl, Sat, 7:30 pm
6/18/40 - 6/25/40, Spry, CBS, Tue, 8 pm (summer replacement of Big Town)
7/10/40 - 10/2/40, Spry, CBS, Wed, 8 pm (summer replacement of Big Town)
10/8/40 - 7/8/41 (with Bill Slater), Bl, Tue, 9 pm; 8:30 pm as of 11/12/40

Uncle Jimmy (with Jimmy W. Famum) 15m

4 **Uncle Joe's Curio Shop** (Baron Keyes) (1932) Syn

1 **Uncle Jonathan** (8/7/39 - 2/9/40) CBS
8/7/39 - 9/22/39, 3t, 15m, 6:30 pm
10/9/39 - 10/30/39, Mon, 15m, 6:15 pm
also 10/14/39 - 11/4/39, Sat, 15m, 10 pm
11/6/39 - 2/9/40, 5t, 10m, 3:35 pm

2 **Uncle Judge Ben** (by Carlton E. Morse) 5/26/51 (Audition)

Uncle Lou's Little Theater (with Lou Costello) 1947 (Audition)

1 **Uncle Ned's Squadron** (1950 - 54) WMAQ, Sat

Uncle Olie (11/9/31 - 2/5/32) Kreml, CBS, 3t, 15m, 5:30 pm

Uncle Remus (with Fred L. Jeske) (10m)

8 **Uncle Sam** (5/24/43 - 7/23/43) Syn

Uncle Sam Presents (see Glenn Miller)

14 **Uncle Sam Speaks** (5/17/43 - 7/19/43) Syn

1 **Uncle Stan, Your Journal Funny Paper Man** (2/9/46)

Uncle Walter's Doghouse (with Tom Wallace) (5/2/39 - 7/8/42) NBC
5/2/39 - 40, Raleigh, Tue, 10:30 pm
1940 - 4/22/41, Sus, Tue, 10:30 pm
5/2/41 - 2/6142, Raleigh, Fri, 9:30 pm
2/11/42 - 7/8/42, NBC, Wed, 8:30 pm

Uncle Wiggily (with Albert Goris)

1 **Unconquered** (1947) Air trailer

2 **Under Arrest** (with Craig McDonnell) (7/28/46 - 10/4/54) Mut (off and on)
7/28/46 - 9/1/46; 6/8/47 - 8/31/47; 6/6/48 - 9/5/48, Blue Coal, Sun, 5 pm (summer replacement for The Shadow)
11/7/48 - 51, Dictograph, Sun
1951 - 12/27/53, Sus, Sun
1/4/54 - 10/4/54, Sus, Mon

Under Western Skies (see Johnny Mack Brown)

Underwood Hour (see Voice Of America)

1 **Uneasy Street** (3/2/29) Synchro-disc

31 **Unexpected, The** (Syn) (1948) 15m; on Mut (4/11/48 - 7/25/48) Sun, 10:30 pm

14 **Unforseen, The** (1956) Syn

1 **Uninvited, The** (12/48) Syn

1 **Union In Space** (7/13/75) ABC-TV

Unit Ninety-Nine (6/18/57 - 10/1/57) ABC, Tue, 7:30 pm

1 **United Airlines Inaugural Service** (6/1/48) WFBR

1 **United China Relief** (4/13/42) Bl

1 **United Jewish Appeal Program** (12/8/55) CBS

1 **United Nations Conference** (4/25/45) NBC

2 **United Nations Conference On International Organizations** (5/45, 6/45) AFRS

1 **United Nations Conference Report** (5/8/45) Mut

1 **United Nations Cornerstone Ceremony** (10/4/49) Mut

1 **United Nations General Assembly** (11/29/47) United Nations Radio

1 **United Nations General Assembly Opening Session** (10/23/46) CBS

1 **United Nations Mass Meeting** (6/17/42) WFBR

1 **United Nations Organization Conference** (1946) United Nations Radio

1 **United Nations Rally** (Wartime) Syn

469 **United Nations Today, The** (11/29/47 - 5/1/53) United Nations Radio

1 **United Nations, The** (1Syn)

8 **United Nations: Status Of Women Interviews** (1948) Syn

United Or Not (6/12/50 - 10/1/51) ABC, Mon, 10 pm; 9 pm as of 1/22/51

20 **United Press Is On The Air** (3/41 - 7/11/41) Syn

3 **United States Army Band** (1941) Syn

1 **United States Drama** (6/29/39) Mut

6 **United States Government Reports** (Syn)

1 **United States Navy Band** (1941) Syn

1 **United States Treasury Christmas Program** (12/25/43) Syn

1 **United We Attack** (1942) Syn

1 **Unity In A Year Of Victory** (12/25/43) BBC

1 **Unity Viewpoint** (2/14/48) WMCA

Universal Rhythm (with Rex Chandler Orchestra; Frank Crumit)
(1/1/36 - 4/2/37) Ford, Bl, Wed; Fri, 9 pm as of 1/1/37
(4/17/37 - 6/12/37) (with Alec Templeton) CBS, Sat, 60m, 9 pm
(6/20/37 - 9/5/37) (with Alec Templeton) CBS, Sun, 60m, 9 pm

University Life Forum
(12/16/39 - 2/21/42) Mut, Sat
12/16/39 - 5/4/40, 1:30 pm
2/8/41 - 5/17/41, 5:30 pm
1/10/42 - 2/21/42) 3 pm

41 **University Of Chicago Round Table, The** (10/30/33 - 6/12/55) Sus, NBC, Sun; on Sat from 3/11/50 - 6/23/51; started 2/1/31 over WMAQ, Chicago

University Theater (see NBC University Theater)

Unlimited Horizons (11/1/40 - 7/4/43) often local New York until 1943
11/1/40 - 2/14/41, Bl, Fri, 11:30 pm
4/20/42 - 7/20/42, NBC, Mon, 11:30 pm
10/4/42 - 7/4/43, NBC, Sun, 11:30 pm

1 **UNRRA In The Far East** (Syn)

Unshackled (produced by Pacific Garden Mission) (9/23/50 - present)

2 **Unsolved Mysteries** (11/15/34 - 5/9/35) Ken-Rad Corporation, WLW, Thu, 8:30 pm CST (1936)
(also called Dr. Kenrad's Unsolved Mysteries) (with Stanley Peyton)
(1/15/49 - 12/18/49) Mut, 15m
1/15/49 - 2/5/49, Sat, 12:15 pm
3/20/49 - 12/18/49, Sun, 10:45 pm also syndicated

2 **Unsung Americans** (with Dr. Frank Kingdon) (12/5/39 - 3/21/40) Mut, 2t, 7:30 pm

6 **Unsung Victory** (1949) Syn

1 **Until I Come Back** (2/24/43)

1 **Untitled Jazz Program**

1 **Unto Death Hurrah!** (10/27/83) WPBH-FM

2 **Untouchables, The** (7/23/51, 7/30/51) WBBM

Unwanted (1934) (15m)

11 **Up and Down The Scales** (9/48) Syn

10 **Up For Parole** (3/10/50 - 12/8/50) CBS, Fri, 9 pm

2 **Up In Arms** (1944) Air trailers

1 **Update** (1/13/72) ABC

1 **Update: Czechoslovakia** (11/28/56) CBS

1 **Update: Hungary** (1956) CBS

6 **Upper Room Radio Parish, The** (1949) Syn, 15m

Upton Close (9/14/41 - 2/11/47)
9/14/41 - 42, NBC (The Far East)
1942 - 44, Lumberman Insurance, NBC
1944 - 45, Lumberman Insurance, Mut
8/20/46 - 2/11/47, Lumberman Ins, Mut

4 **Urbie Green and His Orchestra** (9/26/69 - 10/17/69) CBS

2 **Urbie Green and His Sextet** (1/24/69, 2/7/69) CBS

1 **Urbie Green Sextet, The** (3/14/69) CBS

1 **V-12 Dance Band** (5/16/45)

1 **V-Day Plus 365** (8/14/46) Syn

1 **V-Day Program** (1945) Syn

1 **V-E Anniversary** (5/8/65) CBS

6 **V-E Coverage** (5/8/45) Mut

1 **V-E Day Broadcast** (5/8/45) NBC

4 **V-E Day Coverage** (5/8/45) CBS

1 **V-E Day Special** (5/8/45) AFRS

1 **V-E Day Special Religious Broadcast** (5/16/45) Mut

1 **V-E Day...A Salute To The Coast Guard** (1945) Syn

1 **V-Home Campaign** (11/3/42) WBBM

1 **V-J Celebrations** (8/14/45) NBC

1 **V-J Day** (9/1/45) ABC

1 **V-J Day After Two Years** (8/14/47) Mut

14 **V. D. Radio Project** (1948) Syn

Vacation Parade

Vacation Serenade (with Dorothy Kirsten; then Rose Bampton as of 7/10/44 - Ben Grauer announcer)
(7/19/43 - 9/3/44) NBC
7/19/43 - 9/6/43, 7/10/44 - 9/3/44; Heinz, NBC, Mon, 10:30 pm (summer replacement for Information Please)

1 **Vacation Symphonies** (7/13/46) Mut

Vacation Time (with Pauline Frederick) (3/19/50 - 5/21/50) ABC, Sun, 3 pm

Vacation With Music (with Phil Brito, Ed Herlihy, Harry Sosnik Orchestra)
(8/2/46 - 9/13/46) NBC, Fri, 9 pm (summer replacement of People Are Funny)

1 **Vacationing In New York** (6/23/39) WOR

Vagabond Adventures (see Tom Terris)

Valentino (see Barry Valentino)

7 **Valiant Lady** (3/7/38 - 2/29/52) 5t, 15m
3/7/38 - 5/27/38, Gold Medal Flour and Bisquick, CBS, 1:45 pm
5/30/38 - 3/16/42, General Mills, NBC
3/17/42 - 8/23/46, General Mills, CBS
10/8/51 - 2/29/52, ABC

Vallee Varieties (see Rudy Vallee)

Valspar Orchestra (With Ted Lewis) (3/16/31 - 6/20/31) NBC, Sat, 7:30 pm

Valvoline Program (with Vincent Lopez Orchestra) (1930s)

1 **Van and Schenck** (3/4/29) Syn, 15m

Van Heusen Program (with Gus Van, Nat Brusiloff Orchestra) (4/8/32 - 7/1/32) Van Heusen CBS, Fri, 15m, 9:45 pm

2 **Vandeventer News, Fred**
(1/2/44 - 8/13/48) (1951 - 53) Mut

Vanette Fashion Previews (with Virginia Stewart) (1/14/39 -?) Vanette Hosiery Mills, Bl, Sat, 15m

Vanished Voices (9/30/35 - 3/25/36) Blue Coal, CBS, 2t (Mon & Wed)

Vanity Fair (5/25/33 - 1/5/34) NBC, Fri, 9:30 pm
(9/20/37 - 11/1/37) (with Cal Tinney and Sheilah Graham) Campana, Bl, Mon, 8:30 pm

8 **Variety Bandbox** (12/27/42 - 9/28/52) BBC

Variety Fair (with Holland Engle) (1946) Syn, 15m

2 **Variety Girl** (1947) film sound track, air trailer

Variety Hall (see Teel Variety Hall)

Variety Musicale (with Jerry Cooper, Ray Block Orchestra, others)
(10/11/42 - 9/21/45) Mut, Fri, 7:30 pm; other shows had the same title

1 **Variety Plaque** (12/29/39) WFBR

1 **Varsity Show** (1937) film sound track

Vass Family, The (1932 - 6/14/41) 15m (various days and times including:)
1932 - 9/11/37, NBC, Sat, 11:15 am
10/22/39 - 12/8/40, Bl, Sun, 15m, 1:15 pm
1/26/40 - 7/14/40, Bl, Fri, 10m, 12:15 pm,
12/14/40 - 6/14/41, Bl, Sat, 6:30 pm

Vaudeville (with Roger Bower)
(8/29/42 - 9/12/42) Mut, Sat, 8:30 pm

Vaudeville Theater (see Saturday Morning Vaudeville Theater)

1 **Vaughn de Leath Show, The**
(8/6/31 - 9/22/39) 15m (on various days, networks and times; on WEAF and WJZ in the 1920s)
8/6/31 - 33, CBS, 2t
1933 - 34, NBC, Tue
1934 - 35, NBC, Wed
1935 - 36, CBS, Mon
1936 - 37, NBC, 15m
4/2/38 - 1/7/39, Bl, Sat, 11 am
6/30/39 - 9/22/39, Mut, 3t, 15m, 1;45 pm (summer replacement of Voice Of Experience)

5 **Vaughn Monroe** (6/29/42 - 9/21/42) CBS, Mon, 7:30 pm (summer replacement for Blondie)
(7/4/46 - 9/26/46) Camel, NBC, Thu, 10 pm (summer replacement of Abbott and Costello)
(10/12/46 - 8/20/49; 9/25/49 - 8/25/51; 10/13/51 - 12/29/51; 1/5/52 - 7/5/52; 9/3/52 - 10/1/52 (NBC, Wed, 8 pm), 10/4/52 - 6/27/53; 10/5/53 - 4/5/54) Camel, CBS, Sat (except where noted), 7:30 pm; 8 pm as of 5/3/47; 9:30 pm as of 7/12/47; 7:30 pm as of 10/2/48 (also called Camel Caravan) with Sauter-Finegan Orchestra from 10/5/53

4 **Vaughn Monroe and His Orchestra**
(10/10/44, 12/13/45, 11/23/65) CBS, Lang-Worth transcriptions

Vaughn Monroe Show, The (see Vaughn Monroe)

Vaughn Monroe's Camel Caravan (see Vaughn Monroe)

Vee Lawnhurst and Johnny Seagle
(1/29/33 - 1934) NBC, Sun, 15m

Venida Program (with William Robyn, Emery Deutsch Orchestra)
(10/25/31 - 3/13/32) Venida Hair Nets, CBS, Sun, 15m, 1:45 pm

Vera Brodsky (3/31/35 - 2/25/45) CBS except where noted 3/31/35 - 6/30/35) (also called Ghost Stories; also with Harold Twiggs, Louis K. Anspacher), Van Heusen, Bl, Sun, 15m, 10:15 pm; 9:45 pm as of 6/2/35
12/9/39 - 4/13/40, Sat, 25m, 3:35 pm
6/15/40 - 7/7/40, Sat, 11:30 am
8/31/40 - 10/19/40, Sat, 2 pm
6/7/41 - 8/16/41, CBS, Sat, 25m, 3:30 pm
11/23/41 - 1/18/42, Sun, 25m, 11:05 am
5/10/42 - 6/21/42, CBS, Sun, 25m, 11:05 am
11/19/44 - 2/25/45, CBS, Sun, 15m, 11:15 pm

Vera Burton Show, The (with Walter Gross Orchestra) (1942) CBS

Vera Holly (2/23/46 - 9/29/46) Mut
2/23/46 - 3/16/46, Sat, 9:30 am
6/9/46 - 9/29/46, Sun, 3:30 pm

Vera Massey (7/22/45 - 1/12/47) Bl, Sun, 15m, 11:15 pm (see also Bob Johnson)

Vera Massey and Hal Horton
(7/29/46 - 11/2/46) Mut, Sat, 15m, 5:45 pm

Vera Scott (3/14/39 - 5/9/39) Bl, Tue, 15m, 1:45 pm (not always in New York)

Vera Vague Show, The (with Barbara Jo Allen) (1949) ABC, 15m

Vermont Lumberjacks (1930 - 3/28/31) Vermont Maid Syrup, Bl, 6t, 15m, 8:30 am
(9/28/31 - 3/31/32) Vermont Maid Syrup, NBC, 2t (Mon & Thu), 15m, 7 pm

8 **Vernon Crane's Storybook**
(5/7/39 - 7/14/40) NBC, Sun, 12 noon

4 **Vernon M. Spivey Institute, The** (3/57) WJJD

2 **Vernon M. Spivey Lectures, The**
(3/16/57, 4/14/57) WJJD

Veronica Wiggins and The Rondoleers

Very Private Enterprise, A

1 **Veteran Wireless Operators Association Dinner, The** (2/21/40) NBC/Mut

Veterans Aide (Advisor), The (called Salute To Veterans as of 2/14/48) (with Tyrrell Krum) (4/14/45 - 48) NBC, Sat, 15m

1 **Veterans Emergency Housing Programs** (1946) Syn

1 **Veterans Of Foreign Wars** (1948) Syn

1 **Veterans Of Foreign Wars Jubilee Show, The** (4/4/49) NBC

Vi and Velma Vernon (1942) NBC, 15m

148 **Vic and Sade** (with Art Van Harvey and Bemardine Flynn) (6/29/32 - 9/19/46) 5t, daytime, 15m except where noted
6/29/32 - 11/2/34, Sus, NBC
11/5/34 - 12/29/34; 4/3/36 - 10/13/39; 4/1/40 - 3/28/41, Crisco, Bl
11/5/34 - 5/27/38; 11/7/38 - 9/29/44, Crisco, NBC
also 4/6/37 - 9/21/37, NBC, Tue, 10:45 pm
also 5/30/38 - 11/4/38, Crisco, CBS, 5t, 15m, 1:15 pm
also 3/31/41 - 9/26/41, Mut, St, 8:30 am
12/29/41 - 9/17/43, Crisco, CBS

Vic and Sade (continued)
8/21/45 - 12/7/45, Crisco, CBS, 4t (Tue - Fri), 7:15 pm; 5t as of 9/10/45
6/27/46 - 9/19/46, Fitch, Mut, Thu, 30m, 8:30 pm; also 10/26/46

Vic Arden (1932 - 5/21/33) CBS, Sun, 15m, 2:15 pm

Vic Arden Orchestra (1/10/42 - 9/12/42) NBC, Sat, 11:30 am (see also America, The Free)

1 **Vic Berton and His Artistic Swing** (D&S transcription)

2 **Vic Damone Show, The** (with Sylvan Levin Orchestra) (2/18/47 - 7/1/47) Mut, Tue, 15m, 10:15 pm
also 3/18/50

5 **Vice President Al Gore** 12/1/93 - 1/11/94) C-SPAN

10 **Vice President Dan Quayle** (4/15/89 - 8/20/92) C-SPAN, WHO, ABC

5 **Vice President George Bush** (7/14/88 - 10/29/88) C-SPAN, WCBS

1 **Vice President George Bush and Senator Dan Quayle** (8/17/88) C-SPAN

1 **Vice President Gerald Ford** (12/3/73) pool feed

1 **Vice President Hubert Humphrey** (8/68)

1 **Vice President Mondale** (8/14/80) pool feed

1 **Vice President Richard Nixon** (1960) NBC/C-SPAN

2 **Vice President Rockefeller** (12/19/74, 11/6/75) pool feed

4 **Vice Presidential Debate** (10/15/76, 10/11/84, 10/5/88, 10/13/92) pool feed

Vick's Open House (10/7/34 - 3/20/38) Vick Chemical
1/1/35 - 3/26/35 (with Grace Moore), Bl, Tue, 9 pm
also 10/7/34 - 3/31/35 (with Donald Novis and Vera Van as of 1/6/35), CBS, Sun, 5 pm
9/16/35 - 3/9/36 (with Grace Moore), NBC, Mon, 9:30 pm
9/27/36 - 3/21/37 (with Nelson Eddy), CBS, Sun, 8 pm
9/26/37 - 3/20/38 (with Nelson Eddy), CBS, Sun, 7 pm

Vick's Tello Test (see Tello Test)

Vicki Chase (6/15/39 - 10/8/39) Bl
6/15/39 - 10/5/39 (with Tom Thomas) Thu, 8 pm
also 7/16/39 - 10/8/39, Sun, 7 pm

16 **Victor Borge Show, The** (3/8/43 - 6/1/51)
3/8/43 - 7/9/43, Bl, 5t, 15m, 7 pm
7/3/45 - 9/25/45 (with Benny Goodman), Johnson, NBC, Tue, 9:30 pm (summer replacement of Fibber McGee & Molly)
10/21/46 - 6/23/47 (The Victor Borge Show starring Benny Goodman), Socony Oil, NBC, Mon, 9:30 pm
1/1/51 - 6/1/51, Mut; 10/1/51 - 12/51, ABC; both 5m, 5:55 pm

1 **Victor Demonstration Record** (1932)

1 **Victor Herbert Memorial** (2/2/39) Mut

Victor Lindlahr (1/25/37 - 53) 15m
1/25/37 - 7/29/38, Journal Of Living, Mut, 3t/Tue, 30m, 12 noon
9/26/38 - 6/24/40, Mut, 3t, 12 noon
9/16/40 - 7/11/41, Sus, Mut, 3t
9/15/41 - 9/8/44, Sus, Mut, 5t
9/11/44 - 53, Serutan, Mut, 5t

3 **Victor Lusinchi** (11/16/39 - 4/20/40) Mut

Victor Talking Machine Hour (1/1/26 - 1929) various days and times

1 **Victorian Christmas** (12/13/49) BBC

1 **Victorious Living** (4/15/46) Syn

1 **Victory Belles** (12/12/42) KNX

1 **Victory Bond Show** (12/6/45)

1 **Victory Chest Program, The** (9/29/45) pool feed

2 **Victory F. O. B.** 9/23/44, 10/7/44) CBS

8 **Victory For America, Freedom For Italy** (Wartime) Syn

1 **Victory Front, The** (12/30/42) CBS

1 **Victory Hour, The** (10/25/42 - 5/25/43) Bl, Tue, 2:30 pm

1 **Victory Loan Programs** (1945) Syn

1 **Victory Loan Sports Figures** (10/6/45) Syn

2 **Victory Loan Spots** (12/45) Syn

Victory Parade (with Lionel Barrymore) (6/7/42 - 8/23/42) NBC, Sun, 7 pm; 6:30 pm as of 7/5/42 (partial summer replacements of Jack Benny and The Great Gildersleeve)

Victory Parade Of Spotlight Bands (see Spotlight Bands)

Victory Radio Auction (see Auction Gallery)

1 **Victory Report** (5/8/45) BBC

1 **Victory Thanksgiving Services** (5/8/45) Mut

1 **Victory Theatre, The** (with Cecil B. DeMille) (7/20/42 - 9/7/42) CBS, Mon, 9 pm (partial summer replacement of Lux Radio Theater)

2 **Victory View** (1940) Syn

Victory Volunteers (10/11/42 - 12/11/42) NBC, 5t, 15m, 10 am

Vienesse Ensemble (3/31/41 - 12/5/41) Bl, 5t, 15m, 11 am; 11:15 am as of 7/14/41

1 **Vienna** (1947) Syn

4 **Viennese Nights** (1933) Syn

1 **Vietnam Peace Parade** (1967)

1 **Vietnam: A War That Is Finished** (4/29/75) CBS-TV

1 **View From Space** (4/7/69) ABC-TV

Viewpoint USA (1/13/52 - 7/27/52) NBC, Sun, 11:30 pm

2 **Vigoro Garden Program** (Pre-war) Syn

1 **Viking** (7/4/76) ABC-TV

1 **Viking 1 and Viking 2 Reports** (6/18/76)

1 **Viking Mars Mission** (7/20/76) NBC-TV

1 **Villa Victoria Musicale** (5/5/45) WOR

4 **Village Green Four** (SESAC transcriptions)

Village Store (see Sealtest Village Store)

Vince Program (see Our Home On The Range)

Vince Williams (1948)

Vincent Lopez and His Orchestra (see Vincent Lopez Orchestra)

37 **Vincent Lopez Orchestra** (9/5/28 - 6/23/56) (on various days and times including:) (see also Pleasure Parade; Valvoline Program)
9/5/28 - 11/14/28, Kolster Radio, CBS, Wed, 10 pm
2/5/33 - 6/25/33, Bl, Sun, 30m, 10:15 pm
1934 - 35, Bl, 2t; also NBC, Fri
1935 - 36, CBS, Sat
10/3/36 - 6/26/37 (see Nash Program)
1937 - summer, CBS, Sun
1939 - summer, Bl, Thu, 10:30 pm
6/30/41 - 8/29/41, NBC, 3t - 5t, 1:15 pm
9/2/41 - 5/31/43, Sus, Bl, 2t - 4t
6/14/43 - 9/20/46, Sus, Mut, 6t, 30m, 1:30 pm; 15m as of 9/23/44
1946 - 56 (Luncheon With Lopez) Mut, 5t (not in New York)
10/11/48 - 12/6/48, NBC, Mon, 15m, 7:30 pm
6/6/51 - 1/10/54, ABC, Sat, 1:30 pm
11/27/54 - 6/23/56, ABC, Sat, 1:30 pm
6/26/55 - 10/26/55, ABC, Wed, 9:30 pm
also film sound tracks, Thesaurus transcriptions

1 **Vincent Valsante and His Orchestra** (1935)

Vincente Gomez (7/17/39 - 8/25/40) 15m
7/17/39 - 11/6/39, NBC, Mon, 6:30 pm
6/23/40 - 8/25/40, Bl, Sun, 3 pm

Violin Concerto Series (1/5/41 - 3/23/41) Mut, Sun, 7 pm

Virginia and Sam

1 **Virginia Baptist Home For The Aged Program** (1/16/48) Syn

Virginia Hayes (9/25/39 - 1/26/40) Bl, 5t, 15m, 1:15 pm

1 **Virginia Lane** (3/2/39) Bl, 15m

Virginia Lee and Sunbeam
(3/11/35 - 4/26/35) Bl, 3t, 15m, 1:30 pm
(4/29/35 - 7/8/35) Bl, 5t, 15m, 1:15 pm

Virginia Marvin (1947) (Audition) 15m

1 **Virginia Rounds Round Up Of World Wide News** (12/8/41) WEAF

Virginia Verrill (see Vocals By Verrill)

1 **Virginia: Pattern Of Resistance** (8/31/58) CBS

1 **Viscount Halifax** (7/22/40) BBC

1 **Vision Of Invasion** (5/11/44) Germany

1 **Visit To A Doll Factory, A** (12/8/38) WOR

1 **Visit To The Chinese Junk "Amoy," A** (9/18/37) WOR

Visiting America's Little House (see Little House Family)

Visiting Hour (with Ted Husing) (4/29/44 - 9/9/44) CBS, Sat, 3:30 pm

7 **Vistas Of Israel** (1951 - 8/57) Syn

1 **Visual Radio** (1974)

1 **Vita Fig Mush Quarter Hour, The** (Pre-war)

Vitality Personalities (with Freddie Rich Orchestra) (3/25/31 - 6/17/31; 8/12/31 - 3/9/32) Vitality Shoes, CBS, Wed, 15m, 10 pm

1 **Viteen Variety Show, The** (11/15/43) Michigan Radio Network

4 **Viva America** (1/20/44 - 12/23/44) CBS, Thu, 11:30 pm
(7/7/45 - 10/6/45) CBS, Sat, 8:30 pm; 8 pm as of 9/15/45
(6/16/46 - 8/25/46) CBS, Sun, 6:30 pm also CBS International

1 **Vivi Janiss** (6/27/46) Audition

Vivian Della Chiesa (7/14/35 - 4/9/39) (various days and times including:)
7/14/35 - 9/1/35 (with Billy Mills Orchestra), CBS, Sun, 7 pm
12/6/35 - 2/14/36, CBS, Fri, 4 pm
also 1/28/36 - 4/21/36, CBS, Tue, 4:30 pm
5/26/36 - 3/28/39, Bl, 2t, Tue, 15m, 6:45 pm/7:45 pm
1/8/39 - 4/9/39, 3:45 pm
1938 - 4/9/39, Sus, NBC, Sun, 15m

Vladimir Horowitz (6/14/52 - 5/2/53) NBC, Sat, 7:30 pm

Vocal Varieties (with The Smoothies and Jerry Cooper) (4/6/36 - 7/13/39) Tums (as of 1/28/37), NBC, 2t, 15m, 7:15 pm; 3t (Tue, Thu, Fri) as of 3/31/39

Vocals By Verrill (with Virginia Verrill) (1/6/36 - 6/5/37) CBS, various days and times, 15m

1 **Voice From Paris, The** (Pre-war) Syn

1 **Voice In The Night, A** (5/3/46 - 10/18/46) Mut, Fri, 8:30 pm; 8 pm as of 8/23/46

Voice Of A Nation (1948)

Voice Of America (with William Lyons Phelps) (11/30/33 - 4/26/34) Underwood, CBS, Thu, 8:30 pm (also called Underwood Hour)

2 **Voice Of Aviation** (Pre-war) Syn

1 **Voice Of Bert Howell, The** (4/21/46) Mut

1 **Voice Of Broadway, The** (with Dorothy Kilgallen) (4/5/41 - 12/24/44)
4/5/41 - 1/8/42, Johnson & Johnson, CBS, Sat, 15m, 11:30 am
also 8/19/41 - 9/22/42, CBS, Tue, 15m, 6:15 pm
9/10/44 - 12/24/44, Mut, Sun, 15m, 2:45 pm also 1/18/45

Voice Of Business (see It's Your Business)

2 **Voice Of China and Asia** (6/55) Syn

2 **Voice Of Defense** (5/41) Syn

4 **Voice Of Democracy Winners** (1948 - 1954) Syn

1 **Voice Of Eileen Farrell, The** (8/10/45) CBS

Voice Of Experience (with Dr. Marion Sayle Taylor) (4/24/33 - 9/44) 15m (heard locally earlier)
4/24/33 - 7/24/33, Kreml, CBS, 5t, 11 am
9/11/33 - 7/13/34, Kreml, CBS, 6t
9/10/34 - 5/24/36, Kreml, CBS, 6t
5/25/36 - 7/4/36; 8/29/36 - 5/21/37, Kremel, NBC, 6t
9/13/37 - 38, Lydia Pinkham, Mut, 5t
9/5/38 - 1/21/39, Lydia Pinkham, Mut, 3t, 1:45 pm, on Pacific net after 1939, Albers Brothers, NBC
3/6/44 - 9/44 (Syn - WHN, New York) 5t, 15m, 7:45 pm

26 **Voice Of Firestone, The** (with William Daly; Hugo Mariani; Alfred Wallenstein as of 1936; then Howard Barlow as of 1943)
(12/3/28 - 6/10/57) Firestone, Mon, 8:30 pm; 8 pm from 12/3/28 - 5/26/30
12/3/28 - 5/26/30; 9/7/31 - 8/29/32; 12/5/32 - 3/27/33; 12/4/33 - 6/7/54, NBC
6/14/54 - 6/10/57, ABC

1 **Voice Of Frank Sinatra, The** (6/15/58) BBC

10 **Voice Of Freedom, The** (3/15/43 - 5/10/43) Syn

Voice Of Hawaii (7/23/39 - 9/7/40) Bl, Sun
7/23/39 - 9/3/39, 10 pm
11/12/39 - 3/7/40, 8:30 pm
4/14/40 - 9/7/40, 5:30 pm

Voice Of Liberty (8/25/36 - 3/41) Liberty Magazine, Mut, 15m
8/25/36 - 11/17/36, Tue, 10 pm
1/41 - 3/41, 2t (Thu & Sat) 9 pm with Gabriel Heatter

1 **Voice Of New York, The** (6/16/42) WOR

Voice Of Niagara (with Francis Bowman) (10/17/36 - 4/10/37; 10/16/37 - 10/19/40) Carborundum Co., CBS, Sat, 7:30 pm (not in New York)

Voice Of One Thousand Shades (with Jack Kerr) (3/1/32 - 5/24/32) Pratt and Lambert, CBS, Tue, 15m, 10 pm

Voice Of Prophecy (10/4/42 - 5/27/56) Mut, Sun; ABC as of 6/19/49
(6/3/56 - ?) NBC, 9:30 am

1 **Voice Of Sir George Williams, The** (3/18/1895)

283 **Voice Of The Army** (5/8/44 - 7/26/50) Syn, 15m

1 **Voice Of The City, The** (1929) Synchro-disc

Voice Of The Crusaders (12/18/34 - 4/25/35) CBS, Tue & Thu, 15m, 10:45 pm

Voice Of The Dairy Farmer (3/21/43 - 7/21/46) American Dairy Assoc., Sun, 15m
3/21/43 - 6/13/43, Bl, 1:45 pm
7/18/43 - 7/21/46, NBC, 1:45 pm; 1 pm as of 10/10/43

Voice Of The Farm (with Everett Mitchell) (1938) Firestone

3 **Voice Of The Lithuanians, The** (10/15/36 - 11/3/36) WMBQ

Voice Of The People (with Jerry Belcher, Parks Johnson) (7/7/35 - 9/29/35) Bl, Sun, 7:30 pm (summer replacement for Joe Penner)
(10/6/35 - 2/2/36) Molle, NBC, Sun, 2:30 pm

Voice Of The Snake (with Van Mason)

Voice Of Vic Damone, The (see The Vic Damone Show)

1 **Voices And Events Of 1953, The** (1/1/54) NBC

1 **Voices and Events** (7/3/49 - 12/10/50) NBC
7/3/49 - 9/18/49, Sun, 5:30 pm (summer replacement for Harvest Of Stars)
4/2/50 - 5/7/50, Sun, 5 pm
8/12/50 - 9/2/50, Sat, 7 pm

2 **Voices Down The Wind** (1/8/45, 2/28/45) WGY

8 **Voices From Michigan's Past** (1976) WMUK-FM

1 **Voices From The Hollywood Past** (1958)

5 **Voices In The Headlines** (11/5/67 - 12/10/67) ABC (Fred Foy)

1 **Voices Of The Twentieth Century, The**

122 **Voices Of Vista** (1966 - 1968) Syn

2 **Voices Of Yesterday** (10/4/37) Mut, auditions

Voices That Live (10/1/49 - 9/10/50) ABC
10/1/49 - 3/18/50, Sat, 10 pm
also 12/11/49 - 4/9/50, Sun, 4 pm
4/16/50 - 9/10/50, Sun, 7 pm

1 **Vojta Benes** (9/26/38)

5 **Vox Pop** (7/7/35 - 5/19/48)
7/7/35 - 9/29/35 (also called Sidewalk Interviews from 10/13/36 - 1/12/37; with Parks Johnson, Jerry Belcher; Wally Butterworth replaced Belcher on 10/13/36), Fleischmann, NBC, Sun, 7:30 pm
10/13/35 - 1/19/36, Molle, NBC, Sun, 2:30 pm
1/28/36 - 9/13/38, Molle, NBC, Tue, 9 pm
10/1/38 - 9/23/39, Kentucky Club, NBC, Sat, 9 pm
10/5/39 - 6/26/41, Kentucky Club, CBS, Thu, 7:30 pm
8/4/41 - 4/22/46, Bromo-Seltzer CBS, Mon, 8 pm
also 8/8/41 - 9/26/41, Bromo-seltzer, Bl, Fri, 9 pm
8/27/46 - 5/20/47, Lipton, CBS, Tue, 9 pm
10/1/47 - 5/19/48, American Express, ABC, Wed, 8:30 pm

33 **Voyage Of The Scarlet Queen, The** (with Elliott Lewis) (7/3/47 - 2/25/48) Mut, Thu, 8:30 pm; 10 pm from 12/3/47 - 12/24/47
also 1/10/48 - 2/21/48, Mut, Sat, 9:30 am
also 2/2/47, Audition

1 **Voyage Of The Sun Boat** (1951) UNESCO Radio

1 **Voyager 1, Closest Encounter With Saturn** (11/13/80) PBS-TV

4 **Voyager 2, Saturn '81** (8/26/81 - 8/31/81) PBS-TV

1 **W. C. Fields On Radio** (7/5/69)

1 **W. L. MacKenzie King** (9/3/39) CBC

1 **W. P. A. Negro Radio Unit Of Southern California** (1941) Syn

1 **W2XOR FM Transmitter Dedication** (8/1/40) WOR/W2XOR

1 **W43B Salutes W71NY** (11/30/40) Yankee FM Network

1 **WAGE Dedication Show** (4/22/41) Mut

Waggoners, The (1947)

1 **Waiting People, The** (1955) Syn

1 **Waikiki Wedding** (1937) Air trailer

1 **Wake Island** (1942) Air trailer

241 **Wake Up America** (9/40 - 3/2/47)
9/40 - 5/41, Mut
9/28/41 - 7/11/43; 8/29/43 - 12/19/43, Sus, Sun, 60m; 45m as of 6/28/42, Bl/ABC

1 **Wake Up and Live** (1937) Air trailer

Wake Up and Smile (with Hal O'Holloron, Patsy Montana, Rex Maupin Orchestra) (1/19/46 - 4/13/46) Popular Home Products, ABC, Sat, 60m, 9 am
(7/26/47 - 8/16/47) ABC, Sat, 60m, 10 am

1 **Waking Giant, The** (10/4/48) ABC

Walberg Brown Strings
(6/23/35 - 10/15/39) CBS, Sun, 15m

1 **Walgreen Birthday Party, The** (6/10/45)

Walk A Mile (with Win Elliot)
(10/8/52 - 6/24/53; 10/7/53 - 6/30/54; 9/1/54 - 12/29/54) Camel, NBC, Wed, 8 pm
(6/2/52 - 8/25/52; 7/6/53 - 9/28/53) Camel, CBS, Mon, 10 pm

14 **Walk Softly, Peter Troy** (1962) South African, Syn

9 **Walker's Austex Castillians** (Pre-war) Syn

Walking Down Broadway (1944) (with Al Goodman)

1 **Walking My Baby Back Home** (1953) film sound track

Wallace Butterworth (2/10/34 - 4/5/35) Norwich Dental, CBS, 3t, 15m, 12:30 pm; 11:45 pm as of 1/21/35

26 **Wally Fowler and The Oak Ridge Quartet** (Syn)

1 **Walt Disney Interview** (12/15/66) ABC

Walt Disney Song Parade (10/19/41 - 42) Mut, Sun, 15m, 3:30 pm (not always in New York) Parker Pens

Walt Disney's Magic Kingdom
(12/5/55 - 4/13/56) ABC, 5t, 25m, 11:05 am

Walter Blaufuss Orchestra
(2/15/41 - 3/29/41) NBC, Sat, 15m, 11:30 am

Walter Cassell (11/30/42 - 6/11/43) Squibb, CBS, 5t, 15m, 6:30 pm

1 **Walter Cronkite** (11/15/90) C-SPAN

4 **Walter Cronkite Staff** (1967 - 1970)

1 **Walter Gross and His Orchestra**
(7/13/41 - 10/5/41) CBS, Sun, 4 pm

1 **Walter Huston Dramatic Readings** (World transcription)

7 **Walter Huston Dramatic Recitations** (World transcriptions)

1 **Walter Kiernan Commentary**
(1/1/45 - 12/20/48) Bl/ABC

Walter Logan's Musicale
(10/8/36 - 11/19/36) NBC, Thu, 15m, 2 pm
(5/14/39 - 10/29/39) NBC, Sun, 12 noon

1 **Walter Mondale** (7/19/84) pool feed

Walter O'Keefe (1929 - 11/10/37)
1929, Life Savers
1931, E. Fougera, Bl, Sat, 9:30 pm
9/8/32 - 12/12/32 (see Jack Pearl)
8/25/33 - 8/17/34, Nestles, Bl, Fri, 8 pm
10/2/34 - 6/27/35; 10/1/35 - 6/25/36, Camel, CBS, 2t (see Camel Caravan)
7/7/37 - 11/10/37, Ipana, NBC, Wed, 60m, 9 pm (summer replacement of Fred Allen)

Walter O'Keefe's Almanac (KHJ, Los Angeles) (11/25/62 - ?) 75m

2 **Walter O'Keefe's Americana** (5/6/53) Auditions, 15m

1 **Walter O'Keefe's Little Show** (12/2/46) CBS

Walter Pidgeon (see The Star and The Story)

1 **Walter Wanger's Vogues Of 1938** (1938) Air trailer

7 **Walter Winchell** (8/30/31- 3/3/57) Sun (except where noted), 15m (other commentators substituted for Winchell many summers)
8/30/31 - 1/5/32, CBS, Tue, 15m, 8:45 pm
12/4/32 - 7/13/47; 8/31/47 - 48 (Jergen's Journal) Jergens, Bl/ABC
1/2/49 - 7/17/49, Kaiser, ABC
9/1/49 - 3/16/52, Hudnut, ABC
10/12/52 - 7/5/53, Gruen, ABC
9/6/53 - 7/4/54, Multi, ABC
9/12/54 - 6/26/55, American Razor, ABC
also 9/18/55 - 3/3/57, Mut, 6 pm

Walter Winchell's Jergens Journal (see Walter Winchell)

22 **Waltz Time** (with Abe Lyman Orchestra) (9/27/33 - 7/16/48) Phillips, NBC, Wed, 8:30 pm; Fri, 9 pm as of 12/8/33; 9:30 pm from 10/5/45; 60m as of 7/2/48

1 **Wanamaker Mile** (5/5/38) Mut

1 **Wandering Minstrel, The** (5/18/45) WOR

1 **Wandering Troubadors** (7/18/30) Syn, 15m

Wanted (with Walter McGraw)
(7/7/50 - 9/29/50) NBC, Fri, 10 pm

1 **War and Crime** (9/23/42) Mut

1 **War and Then What?, The** (12/15/45) Mut

War Bond Matinee (1945) (with George Olsen Orchestra) (15m)

1 **War Bond Rally** (2/1/44) Mut

6 **War Correspondent** (1/10/42 - 4/11/42) Libby-Owens, NBC, Sat, 15m, 5:45 pm, also syndicated

War Front - Home Front
(9/4/50 - 9/22/52) Mut, Mon
9/4/50 - 2/26/51, 9:30 pm
5/28/51 - 9/17/51, 8 pm
10/24/51 - 9/22/52, 9:30 pm

1 **War In Korea, What Does It Mean?, A** (6/27/50) WOR-TV

War In The Air, The (10/23/40 - 2/12/41) Mut, Wed, 15m, 10:15 pm

1 **War Of The Worlds, The** (10/30/88) NPR

1 **War Production Board's Report On The War Production Drive, The** (3/17/42) NBC

1 **War Reports** (6/6/44) BBC

War This Week, The (see European News Roundup)

15 **War Town** (1945) Syn

Ward and Muzzy (10/9/35 - 3/27/36) Bl, Fri, 15m, 4:30 pm

Warden Lawes (see Twenty Thousand Years In Sing Sing; Crime Cases Of Warden Lawes)

7 **Warner Brothers Academy Theater** (4/3/38 - 6/26/38) Syn - Gruen, Sun

Warner Brothers Presents (60m)

1 **Warning Bell, The** (12/20/55) CBS

1 **Warren Commission Report, The** (9/27/64)

5 **Warren Covington and His Orchestra** (8/28/70 - 10/16/70) CBS

Warren Sweeney (9/14/44 - 2/1/45) CBS
(1947 - 49) Curtis Candy, CBS. Sat

Warriors Of Peace (3/31/46 - 10/5/47) ABC, Sun, 2 pm, 1 pm as of 6/8/47

Washington Calling (4/40 - 6/40) Bl, Tue, 7:30 pm (not in New York)
(10/6/40 - 11/24/40) NBC, Sun, 2 pm

Washington Merry-Go-Round
(10/1/35 - 9/2/40)
10/1/35 - 3/31/36, Gruen, Mut, 2t (Tue, Sat) 15m, 7:45 pm
7/8/40 - 9/2/40 (with Drew Pearson and Robert Allen), Bl, Mon, 8:30 pm (summer replacement for True Or False)

1 **Washington Newsroom Special, A** (7/71) WNET-TV

3 **Washington Scene**
(12/30/42, 2/16/43, 3/2/43) WWDC

1 **Washington Story, The**
(4/29/45 - 9/16/45) Bl, Sun
also 1949, Syn

1 **Washington U.S.A.** (8/21/54) CBS

Washington Variety Show
(12/12/39 - 1/23/40) Bl, Tue, 15m, 6:15 pm

1 **Washington Wives** (7/25/51) CBS, audition

Watch The Fun Go By (see Al Pearce)

5 **Watch Tower Bible and Tract Society** (1935) Syn

Watch Your Step (with Fields and Hall)
(2/24/40 - 1/4/41) NBC, Sat, 15m, 9:15am

1 **Watchers, The** (1960) CBS

2 **Watchman, The** (with Gene Lockhart) Auditions, 15m

1 **Watergate Coverup Trial, The** (12/5/75) PBS-TV

Waterloo Junction (5/14/39 - 10/15/39) Bl, Sun, 1 pm

Watson, Flotsom and Jetsam
(4/16/39 - 6/4/39) Bl, Sun, 6 pm

2 **Waverly Root** (8/25/39, 9/14/39) Mut

1 **Waverly Root and Victor Lusinchi** (7/17/40) Mut

Waves Of Melody (with Vic Arden Orchestra, Tom Brown)
(10/12/31- 7/20/32) Jo-Cur, Bl, various days and times

1 **Way Back Home** (1951) AFRS

160 **Way Down East** (with Agnes Moorehead and Van Heflin) (11/23/36 - 4/16/37) Mut, 5t, 15m, also syndicated

Way Down Home (7/10/38 - 9/11/38) NBC, Sun, 1:30 pm
also 9/26/37 - 11/14/37, NBC, Sun, 2:30 pm

Way Down South (with Peter Brescia Orchestra) (9/1/40 - 10/5/41) NBC, Sun

35 **Way It Was, The** (7/2/75 - 5/15/77) PBS-TV

1 **Way Of Life** (10/41) Syn

1 **Way, The** (4/30/49)

Wayfarin' Stranger, The (see Burl Ives)

Wayne and Dick (with Wayne West alone from 8/14/39) (3/13/39 - 12/4/39) Mut, Mon, 15m, 4:30 pm

Wayne and Shuster (with Johnny Wayne and Frank Shuster) (CBC - NBC)
(1946 - 53)

1 **Wayne Howell Show, The**
(3/7/49 - 2/3/50) NBC, 5t, 6:30 pm
(1/28/51 - 4/1/51) Doubleday, NBC, Sun, 10m, 5:15 pm
also 8/19/50

14 **Wayne King** (9/27/31 - 47) many programs overlap
9/27/31 - 4/8/34. Lady Esther, NBC, Sun; when sponsored by Lady Esther, programs often called Lady Esther Serenade (Gus Arnheim substituted 7/31/31 - 8/28/32)
3/30/32 - 6/1/32, NBC, Wed, 15m, 5:30 pm
10/11/32 - 8/25/38, NBC, Tue, 8 30 pm
2/6/33 - 12/14/33, NBC, Thu, 9:30 pm
10/9/33 - 4/8/34, Lady Esther, CBS, Mon, 10 pm
12/6/33 - 12/1/38, NBC, Wed, 8:30 pm
4/15/34 - 2/17/36, Lady Esther, CBS, 2t (Sun & Mon) 10 pm
3/15/36 - 7/19/36, Mut, Sun, 6:30 pm
2/24/36 - 10/3/38, Lady Esther, CBS, Mon, 10 pm
3/15/36 - 7/19/36, Mut, Sun, 6:30 pm
9/2/38 - 10/7/38, NBC, Fri, 10 pm
10/21/39 - 6/15/40, Halo, CBS, Sat, 8:30 pm
10/5/40 - 2/1/41, Cashmere, CBS, Sat, 8:30 pm
6/7/41 - 3/21/42, Luxor, CBS, Sat, 7:30 pm (not in New York)
6/3/45 - 9/23/45, Lucky Strike, NBC, Sun, 7 pm (summer replacement for Jack Benny)
6/14/46 - 9/6/46, CBS, Fri, 9:30 pm (summer replacement for Jimmy Durante)
1946 - 47, Syn - ZIV; 78 shows broadcast
also Thesaurus transcription
1952, WNBQ-TV

Wayne King Orchestra (see Wayne King)

Wayne King Orchestra and Choir (see Wayne King)

Wayne King Serenade (see Wayne King)

Wayne King Show, The (see Wayne King)

Wayne Morse (1957) 15m

24 **Ways Of Mankind** (1962) Syn

Wayside Cottage, The (also called House By The Side Of The Road) (with Vivian Ogden and William Adams)
(7/10/34 - 9/13/34) CBS, 2t, 15m (partial summer replacement for Just Plain Bill) (on locally in New York from 1929 - 1933)

Wayside Inn (2/4/31 - 5/5/31) Bl, Wed, 9 pm

1 **Wayside Pulpit, The** (11/1/53) WLOS

9 **Wayside Theatre, The** (10/2/38 - 5/19/39) The Chicago Motor Club, WBBM, Sun

3 **WCBS Christmas Show**
(12/24/47, 12/20/48, 12/49-not for broadcast) WCBS

2 **WCNW All Request Program**
(1/7/37, 1/13/37) WCNW

We Americans (with Walter Pitkin)
(10/26/35 - 12/7/35) CBS, Sat, 8 pm

1 **We Are Always Young** (with William Janney) (3/3/41 - 11/17/41) Mut, 6t, 15m

We Are Four (with Charles Flynn and Marjorie Hannan) (3/1/37 - 12/3/37) Libby, Mut, 5t, 15m; started on WGN in 9/9/35

1 **We Are Not Alone** (10/21/66) Goodrich Tires, ABC-TV

We Believe (6/7/42 - 9/20/42) NBC, Sun, 4:30 pm

1 **We Came In Peace For All Mankind**

2 **We Came This Way** (NBC University Theater Of The Air)
(10/6/44 - 10/4/45) NBC
10/6/44 - 2/16/45, Fri, 11:30pm
7/5/45 - 8/23/45, NBC, Thu, 10:30 pm (summer replacement for Rudy Vallee)
8/30/45 - 10/4/45, NBC, Thu, 11:30 pm
also 1/22/55, 2/19/55, WMAQ

1 **We Can Do It** (1950) Syn

1 **We Care** (with Douglas Fairbanks, Jr.)
(1/4/48 - 9/22/49) CARE, ABC, 15m
1/4/48 - 2/1/48; 5/18/48 - 6/21/48; 7/25/48 - 9/19/48, Sun, 10:45 pm
11/11/48 - 9/22/49, Thu, 10:30 pm

We Deliver The Goods (1944) (with Howard Culver) CBS, Sun

1 **We Have The Ships...Send Our G.I.s Home** (11/27/45) Mut

2 **We Hold These Truths** (12/15/41) pool feed
(12/16/91) American Public Radio

5 **We Love and Learn** (with Frank Lovejoy)
(4/6/42 - 3/23/51) 5t, 15m; began as The Twig Is Bent, a syndicated show,
3/23/41 - 4/3/42 4/6/42 - 3/31/44, General Foods, CBS
4/3/44 - 9/29/44, NBC, 5:15 pm
6/28/48 - 3/23/51, Sweetheart Soap, NBC (then changed to Woman In My House)

1 **We Point With Pride** (2/16/50) CBS, audition

We Present (8/6/41 - 10/8/41) NBC, Wed, 7:30 pm

1 **We Refuse To Die** (10/25/42)

3 **We Remember**
(12/9/50, 12/10/50, 12/30/50) NBC

1 **We Take You Back** (3/13/58) CBS

2 **We Take Your Word** (with Abe Burrows, Lyman Brown and John McCaffrey)
also (5/12/40) CBS
(9/2/49) Audition
(2/5/50 - 7/6/51) CBS
2/5/50 - 6/25/50, Sun, 10:30 pm
7/2/50 - 7/23/50, Sun, 9 pm
9/22/50 - 7/6/51, Fri, 10 pm

1 **We The Abbotts** (with John McIntire)
(10/14/40 - 4/3/42) Nucoa, 5t, 15m
10/7/40 - 5/30/41, CBS, 4:15 pm
6/2/41 - 4/3/42, NBC, 5:30 pm

6 **We The People** (10/4/36 - 1/25/51)
10/4/36 - 5/16/37, Calumet, Bl, Sun, 5 pm
10/7/37 - 5/12/38, Sanka, CBS, Thu, 7:30 pm
9/27/38 - 3/10/42, Sanka, CBS, Tue, 9 pm
4/26/42 - 5/17/47, Gulf, CBS, Sun, 7:30 pm; 10:30 pm as of 6/18/44
6/24/47 - 10/25/49, Gulf, CBS, Tue, 9 pm
11/4/49 - 9/22/50, Gulf, CBS, Fri, 8:30 pm
9/28/50 - 1/25/51, Gulf, NBC, Thu, 9:30 pm

1 **We Want A Touchdown** (with Red Barber) (1938, 9/28/39 - 11/2/39) Mut, Thu. 10:30 pm

We Went Back (1947) (60m)

1 **We're Not Dressing** (1934) film sound track

1 **We've Got Your Number**
(4/27/45) WOR, 4t, 15m
(12/8/45 - 4/13/46) Mut, Sat, 15m, 10:15 am

We, The Wives (with Chuck Acree)
(2/5/39 - 4/16/39) Farina, Mut, Sun, 4 pm
(10/22/39 - 3/31/40) Farina, NBC, Sun, 1 pm; 3:30 pm as of 11/26/39 (not in New York)

We, Who Dream (with Claire Niesen)
(3/17/44 - 10/13/44) Englander Co., CBS, Fri, 15m

1 **Weapon Of Tomorrow** (6/15/45) ABC/Bl

1 **Weary River** (Synchro-disc)

Weber and Fields (with Joe Weber and Lew Fields) (2/7/31 - 7/13/31) NBC, Sat, 8 pm; Mon, 15m, 8:15 pm as of 5/25/31

1 **Webley Edwards** (7/7/45) Mut

1 **Wedding Of Princess Elizabeth** (11/20/47) pool feed

1 **Wedding Of The Century, The** (7/29/81) Independent Network (TV) News

Wednesday Night Fights
(11/1/50 - 12/17/52) CBS, Wed, 45m, 10 pm

1 **Wednesday Review** (6/66) WNDT-TV

10 **Wednesday With You** (with Nora Martin)
(6/27/45 - 9/19/45) NBC, Wed, 9 pm (summer replacement for Eddie Cantor)

Weekday (with Mary Margaret McBride and Mike Wallace, others)
(1/9/56 - 8/3/56) NBC, 5t, various lengths of time

1 **Weekday Theatre** (11/8/57)

2 **Weekend** (10/11/53 - 6/5/55) NBC, Sun, 2 hours, 4 pm; 30m as of 5/8/55
also 2/7/76, 4/22/79, NBC-TV

Weekend Cruise (7/13/41 - 9/21/41) Bl, Sun, 3:30 pm

3 **Weekend Sound Flights '63** (1963) Syn

Weekend Whimsey (with Loulie Jean and Sylvia Marlowe)
(2/8/41 - 1/3/42) NBC, Sat
2/8/41 - 5/3/41, 9:30 am
5/10/41 - 6/28/41, 11:30 am
7/5/41 - 9/27/41, 4 pm
10/4/41 - 11/15/41, 5 pm
11/22/41 - 1/3/42, 4:30 pm

Weekly War Journal (1943 - 45) ABC

2 **Wehrmacht Hour, The**
(11/15/44, 11/22/44) O.W.I./ABSIE

75 **Weird Circle, The** (11/43 - 10/6/47) (Syn) Mut
11/43 - 45, Sun
1945 - 47, Fri
9/15/47 - 10/6/47, ABC, Mon, 10:30 pm

Welcome Lewis (see The Singing Bee)

1 **Welcome Neighbor** (with Dave Driscoll and Tom Wolf; from The World's Fair)
(3/15/39 - 10/20/39) Mut
3/15/39 - 6/7/39, Wed, 8:30 pm
6/28/39 - 8/2/39, Wed, 8 pm
8/11/39 - 10/20/39, Fri, 8 pm

1 **Welcome Stranger** (1947) Air trailer

Welcome To Hollywood
(1/16/50 - 7/6/51) ABC, 5t, 2 pm; 3 pm as of 1/8/51; 2:30 pm as of 5/14/51

2 **Welcome Travelers** (with Tommy Bartlett)
(6/30/47 - 9/24/54) Procter & Gamble, 5t
6/30/47 - 7/8/49, ABC
7/11/49 - 9/24/54, NBC

Welcome Valley (with Edgar Guest)
(5/19/32 - 12/29/36) Household Finance, Bl, Tue, 8:30 pm; for 5/19/32 -12/25/35 (see Musical Memories; developed into It Can Be Done)

1 **Welfare Council Of New York City**
(1/22/37) WCNW

Wendell Hall (1931 - 36) 15m (also see Community Sing)
1931 (The Pineapple Picador), NBC
1932 - 6/9/35, Fitch, NBC, Sun, 7:45 pm
6/25/35 - 10/10/35, Bl, 3t (Tue - Thu), 15m, 11:15 am
10/1/35 - 1936, Fitch, Bl, Tue, 10 pm

14 **Wendell Willkie** (5/15/40 - 10/26/42) Bl, WAAB, Mut, WIRE, WOR, WFBR

1 **Wendell Willkie Goes To Washington/Victory For Willkie** (1940)

1 **Wendell Willkie Memorial Plans**
(12/21/44) Mut

1 **Wendell Willkie Memorial Program**
(10/8/45) Mut

7 **Wendy Warren and The News** (with Florence Freeman)
(6/23/47 - 11/12/58) CBS, 5t, 15m
6/23/47 - 9/17/54, Maxwell House
9/20/54 - 11/12/58, Multi

1 **Werner's Orchestra** (1939)

2 **Wesley Tuttle and His Coon Hunters** (MacGregor transcriptions)

1 **West Point Story** (1950) film sound track

Westbrook Van Voorhis
(8/2/43 - 11/30/45) Bl

Western Caravan (with Tex Williams, Robert Armbruster Orchestra)
(6/25/50 - 10/29/50) NBC, Sun, 6:30 pm

Westerners, The (see Louise Massey)

Westinghouse Program, The (see John Charles Thomas)

1 **WEVD Weekly Friday Evening Service** (11/30/64) WEVD

1 **WFBR Christmas Serenade** (12/25/43) WFBR

1 **WFBR Handicap, The** (11/4/39) WFBR

1 **WFBR Jamboree** (6/24/39) WFBR

1 **WHAM Fiftieth Anniversary Show** (7/11/72) WHAM

1 **Wharf Angel** (3/11/34) Air trailer

2 **What Am I Offered?** (with Bob Dixon)
(6/21/47 - 3/6/48; 10/30/48 - 2/26/49) WOR, Sat, 15m

1 **What America Thinks: 1976** (12/27/76) NBC-TV

6 **What Are We Fighting For?**
(4/2/42 - 5/28/42) CBS

What Can I Do For Defense?
(5/18/41 - 6/7/41) CBS, Sun, 2 pm

1 **What Can The U. S. Do To Help Solve The Displaced Persons Problem?**
(5/49) Syn

1 **What Did We Learn From Apollo 13?**
(6/24/70) WRVR-FM

What Do You Think (1/41 - 8/41) Roma Wine, Mut, 2t (Mon & Fri), 15m, 11:15 pm; Sat, 20m, 1:30 pm as of May; 3t, 30m, 1:30 pm as of July (not in New York)

What Happened To Jane?
(8/4/31 - 12/31/31) NBC, 2t, 15m, 5:30 pm

1 **What Happens Now?** (11/5/49) WOR-TV

What Home Means For Me
(1/20/35 - 7/7/35) General Foods, NBC, Sun, 15m, 12:15 pm

What Makes You Tick? (6/6/48 - 3/31/51)
6/6/48 - 8/29/48, Helbros, Mut, Sun, 5:30 pm (summer replacement of Quick As A Flash)
9/20/48 - 7/8/49 (with John K McCaffery), Ivory, ABC, 5t, 15m; CBS as of 12/27/48
9/23/50 - 3/31/51 (with Gypsy Rose Lee), Sus, ABC, Sat, 9 pm

1 **What Price America?** (1/28/39 - 1/27/40) CBS, Sat

What Price Defense (with Theodore Granik) (11/14/41 - 42) Mut, Fri, 15m, 9:15 pm (not in New York)

1 **What Should Congress Do About High Prices?** (4/12/47)

1 **What Would You Do?** (with Ben Grauer) (1/26/40 - 7/17/40) Energine, Bl, Fri, 9:30 pm; Wed, 8:30 pm as of 4/24/40

What's Art To Me? (with Holger Cahill) (10/28/39 - 1/20/40) CBS, Sat, 6:30 pm

What's Cooking? (with Beulah Karney) (8/19/44 - 8/11/45) Chef Boy-Ar-Dee, Bl, Sat, 10:30 am

What's Doing Ladies? (1943 - 48) Bl/ABC, Multi, 5t

1 **What's Good For The Army?** (1943) Syn

6 **What's My Line?** (5/20/52 - 7/1/53)
5/20/52 - 8/26/52, Philip Morris, NBC, Tue, 10 pm; Wed, 8 pm as of 7/2/52
9/3/52 - 11/26/52, Philip Morris, CBS, Wed, 9:30 pm
12/3/52 - 7/1/53, Jules Montenier, CBS, Wed, 9:30 pm
also CBS-TV

What's My Name? (usually with Arlene Francis and Budd Hulick)
(3/25/38 - 7/30/49)
3/25/38 - 3/17/39, Philip Morris, Mut, Fri, 8 pm
7/5/39 - 9/27/39 (with Fred Uttal and Arlene Francis) NBC, Wed, 9 pm (summer replacement of Fred Allen)
11/4/39 - 9/27/40, Oxydol, NBC, Sat, 7 pm; Fri, 9:30 pm as of 3/1/40
7/6/41 - 8/31/41 (also with John Reed King), Chase and Sanborn, NBC, Sun, 8 pm (summer replacement of Charlie McCarthy)
1/6/42 - 6/30/42, Fleischmann, Mut, Tue, 8 pm
2/21/43 - 6/27/43 (also with Budd Hulick), Lydia Grey Cleansing Tissues, NBC, Sun, 10:30 pm
6/3/48 - 9/29/48, GE, ABC, Thu, 9 pm; Sat, 9:30 pm as of 6/12/48
2/5/49 - 7/30/49, Servel, ABC, Sat, 11:30 am; 12:30 pm as of 4/30/49

What's New At the Zoo? (with John Reed King)
(6/1/41 - 10/5/41) CBS, Sun, 11:30 am; 12 noon as of 8/31/41
(2/8/42 - 6/28/42) CBS, Sun, 1:35 pm

What's New In Music? (with Percy Faith and Donald Woods) (5/29/55 - 6/24/56) CBS, Sun, 60m, 1 pm

What's New in Sports? (1946) (15m)

What's New? (with Don Ameche)
(9/4/43 - 2/26/44) RCA, Bl, Sat, 60m, 7 pm

What's On Your Mind (with Maybelle Jennings) (10/20/36 - 12/3/36) Laco Products, CBS. 2t, 15m, 1:15 pm
also 1941, Planters, CBS - Pacific

What's Right With the UN? (1948) 15m

1 **What's The Answer** (11/9/50)

1 **What's The Good Word?** (10/7/45) Mut

1 **What's The Matter With Father?** (3/12/46) Audition

1 **What's The Name Of That Song?** (with Dud Williamson) (9/24/44 - 12/16/48) Mut, various days including:
9/24/44 - 7/8/45, Knox, Sun, 4:30 pm
1945 - 46, Sus, Sun/Sat, 10:30 pm
9/28/46 - 11/2/46, Mut, Sat, 5 pm
12/8/46 - 2/12/47, Sus, Wed, 9:30 pm
6/13/48 - 8/8/48, Sun, 3 pm
10/2/48 - 10/23/48, Sat, 9:30 pm
11/4/48 - 12/16/48, Thu, 8 pm

What's The Score (with Happy Felton) (1949)

1 **What's The Word** (3/29/49) Mut

What's With Herbert (NBC) 1950 with Phil Foster

1 **What's With Hubert?** (7/25/50) NBC, audition

2 **What's Your Idea?** (with Ted Fio Rito Orchestra; also Don McNeill; then Nelson Olmsted)
(3/2/41 - 5/4/41) Mars Candy, NBC, Sun, 6:30 pm (10/26/43 - 10/5/45) (with Imogene Wolcott) Mott, Mut, 3t, 15m, 11:45 am
(1945) (with Dud Williamson) Mott

What's Your War Job? (with Woody Herman and Anita O'Day)
(11/4/42 - 8/25/43) Bl, Wed, 25m, 7:05 pm

Whatcha Know, Joe (12/13/41 - 4/11/42) NBC, Sat, 2:30 pm

47 **Whatever Became Of...** (with Richard Lamparski)
(9/65 - 12/22/70) WBAI-FM, KPFA

1 **Whatever Happened To 1972?** (12/28/72) CBS-TV

1 **Wheat and The War** (1942) Syn

Wheatena Playhouse (Wuthering Heights, Alice Adams, The Citadel, Till We Meet Again, Of Human Bondage)
(9/30/40 - 3/28/41) Wheatena, NBC, 5t, 15m, 12 noon

Wheatenaville Sketches (with Raymond Knight and Alice Davenport)
(9/11/32 - 5/4/33) NBC, 5t (Sun - Thu), 15m, 7:15 pm

Wheatsworth Program (with King Kill Kare) (8/15/32 - 3/24/33) Wheatsworth Crackers, Bl, 3t, 15m

Wheel Of Chance (1/14/56 - 7/21/56) Mut, Sat, 25m, 11:30 pm

1 **Wheel Of Fortune, The** (7/11/55) Mut

4 **Wheeling Steel Company Family Broadcast, The** (12/39 - 12/7/41) Mut, Bl

1 **Whelan Drug Audition, The** (1/29/46)

13 **When A Girl Marries** (with Noel Mills; Mary Jane Higby from 12/39)
(5/29/39 - 8/30/57) 5t, 15m
5/29/39 - 8/22/41, Prudential, CBS, 2:45 pm; 12:15 pm as of 7/31/39
9/29/41 - 6/29/51, General Foods, NBC, 5 pm
7/2/51 - 9/21/51, ABC, 11:30 pm
9/24/51 - 3/28/52, General Foods, ABC, 11:15 am
11/18/52 - 5/29/53, Multi, ABC, 10:45 am
1/5/54 - 4/1/55, Carnation, ABC, 10:45 am
4/4/55 - 8/30/57, Multi, ABC

1 **When Johnny Comes Marching Home** (1943) film sound track

1 **When Radio Was All There Was** (3/18/74) WBAI-FM

1 **When Television Was Young** (4/28/77) CBS-TV

2 **When The West Was Young** (AFRTS origination)

When We Were Young (with Ruth Carhart, The Four Clubmen)
(4/29/39 - 5/27/39) CBS, Sat, 15, 12:15 pm

1 **Where Are They Now?**
(1/27/45 - 9/22/45) Mut, Sat, 3:30 pm

Where Are We? (with Budd Hulick)
(3/24/39 - 5/12/39) Philip Morris, Mut, Fri, 8 pm
(4/3/40 - 8/28/40) Philip Morris, Mut, Fri, 8:30 pm

Where Are You From? (with Dr. Henry Lee Smith) (9/4/40 - 7/30/41) Sus, Mut, Wed, 8 pm

Where Do We Stand? (with John Gunther and John W. Vandercook)
(2/14/43 - 2/20/44) Clark Gum, Bl, Sun, 5 pm

Where Have You Been? (with Horace Sutton and Emie Kovacs)
(12/9/54 - 4/28/55) NBC, Thu, 9:30 pm

1 **Where Is The Meat?** (10/11/46) Mut

1 **Where There's Life** (1947) Air trailer

3 **Where We Stand**
(1/4/59, 3/6/63, 5/17/72) CBS-TV

1 **Which Is To Say, Master** (CBS)

1 **Which Is Which?** (with Ken Murray)
(10/25/44 - 6/6/45) Old Gold, CBS, Wed, 9:30 pm

Which Way To Lasting Peace? (with Dr. James T. Shotwell) (1/27/40 - 4/27/40) CBS, Sat, 15m, 6:30 pm

While The City Sleeps (with Finney Briggs)
(1935 - 10/29/37) 15m 1935, Mut, 2t
3/1/36 - 9/27/36, Dari-Rich, NBC, 2t (Thu & Sun)
9/29/36 - 3/4/37, Dari-Rich, NBC, 2t, 5 pm
3/8/37 - 10/29/37, Dari-Rich, NBC, 3t, 5 pm

While There's Life (see John B. Kennedy)

2 **Whippoorwills With Georgia Brown, The** (Standard transcriptions)

1 **Whipsaw** (1935) Air trailer

Whirlgig (with Benny Rubin)
(4/1/36 - 4/15/36) Bl, Wed, 8:30 pm

2 **Whisper Men, The** (with Karl Swenson; then Joseph Curtin)
(9/8/45 - 2/2/46) Sus, Mut, Sat
9/8/45 - 10/6/45, 9:30 pm
10/13/45 - 11/3/45, 8:30 pm
12/22/45 - 1/5/46, 11:30 am
1/12/46 - 2/2/46, 8 pm

9 **Whisperer, The** (with Carleton Young)
(7/8/51 - 12/16/51) NBC, Sun, 5 pm

6 **Whispering Jack Smith**
(10/31/32 - 4/13/35) 15m
10/31/32 - 4/5/33, Musterole, CBS, 2t (Mon & Wed), 8 pm
9/11/34 - 4/13/35, Ironized Yeast, CBS, 3t (Tue, Thu, Sat), 7:15 pm; NBC as of 1/15/35
also 9/37, WOR/Syn

1 **Whispering Jack Smith and His Whispering Strings** (1937) Syn

Whispering Rhythm (4/8/40 - 6/3/40) Bl, Mon, 15m, 6:30 pm

15 **Whispering Streets** (3/3/52 - 11/25/60) 5t
3/3/52 - 54, General Mills, ABC
1954 - 59, Multi, ABC
1959 - 11/25/60, Multi, CBS

345 **Whistler, The** (with Gale Gordon) (Audition show); followed by Joseph Kearns (first season), Bill Forman except Everett Clark (7/3/46 - 9/25/46) summer replacement for Jack Carson; Bill Johnstone in HFC national version for 26 weeks from 3/24/48 - 9/29/48; Marvin Miller (announcer)
(5/16/42 - 7/31/55) CBS - Pacific except where indicated; sponsor was Signal Oil from 12/12/43 - 8/22/54
5/16/42 - 9/5/42, Sat
9/13/42 -4/18/43, Sun
1/3/43 - 3/28/43; 5/1/43 - 6/26/43, Sat
7/2/43 - 9/24/43, Fri
10/3/43 - 9/10/44, Sun
9/18/44 - 6/23/47, Mon including network
7/3/46 - 9/25/46, CBS, Mon, 8 pm (summer replacement of Jack Cason); The Whistler was also broadcast on Wednesday nights in 1946.
7/2/47 - 9/29/48, Household Finance (East) (with Everett Clark) Signal Oil (West) (with Bill Forman; Bill Johnstone in summer of 1948), CBS (Network), Wed, 10 pm (still broadcast on Pacific net on Mon until 6/23/47); during the summer of 1948, the HFC version and the Signal Oil version were broadcast with different casts and directors (William N. Robson for East Coast and George Allen for West Coast)
10/3/48 - 7/31/55, CBS - West coast, Sun, 9:30 pm (Lever Brothers from 2/6/55 - 7/31/55)
also 2/24/55 - 9/8/55, CBS - Pacific, Thu

1 **White Banners** (6/18/38) Mut

1 **White Cliffs, The** (10/13/40) Bl

5 **White Fires Of Inspiration** (1937, 1938, March, April/47) (with Lurene Tuttle and Ted Osbome) CBS, KOIN, Mon

1 **White House Christmas Tree Lighting Ceremony** (12/24/48) Mut

1 **White House Conversation: The President and Howard K. Smith** (3/22/71) ABC-TV

1 **White House Correspondent's Dinner** (3/4/44) NBC

1 **White House Jazz Festival** (6/17/78) NPR

1 **White House Story, The** (7/3/49) CBS

1 **White House Tapes: On To The Grand Jury, The** (1/19/74) CBS

1 **White House Tapes: The Nixon Decision, The** (10/23/73) CBS-TV

1 **White House Transcripts, The** (8/9/75) PBS-TV

White Rabbit Line (see Coast To Coast On A Bus)

1 **White Shirt Brigade, The** (11/6/43) WLAV

1 **White Woman** (11/33) Air trailer

2 **Whitehall 1212** (written by Wyllis Cooper)
(11/18/51 - 9/28/52) Sus, NBC, Sun, 10:30 pm; 5 pm as of 12/23/51; 5:30 pm as of 2/24/52

Whitman Sampler Program (with Jack Denny Orchestra, Evan Evans)
(10/27/32 - 12/23/32) Whitman Sampler, CBS, Thu, 15m, 8:45 pm

Whitney Ensemble (6/8/35 - 8/28/37) NBC, Sat

1 **Whittaker Chambers** (2/13/52) NBC

Whiz Quiz (with Johnny Olsen)
(9/11/48 - 12/4/48) Paul F. Beich Co., ABC, Sat, 8:30 pm

Who's In Town Tonight? (1940) 15m

Who Are You? (6/18/40 - 8/26/40) Mut, Mon, 8:30 pm

1 **Who Killed Michael Farmer?** (4/21/58) CBS

Who Knows? (3/16/40 - 8/29/41) Griffin, Mut, Sat, 15m, 8:30 pm; Mon, 10:15 pm as of 5/13/40; Fri, 10:15 pm as of 5/30/41

1 **Who Said That?** (with Robert Trout)
(7/2/48 - 8/22/50) NBC
7/2/48 - 9/24/48, Sus, Fri, 8:30 pm
1/2/49 - 4/17/49, Sun, 10:30 pm
7/2/50 - 8/22/50 (Radio playback of TV show) Tue, 8 pm (summer replacement for Cavalcade Of America)

1 **Who Speaks For Germany** (1/4/44) Mut

1 **Who's Boss** (9/52) Syn

1 **Who's Talking?** (WGN) audition

Who's Who, The Grove Tonic Two
(5/25/31 - 9/25/31) Grove Laboratories, CBS, 3t, 15m, 2:15 pm

1 **Who, What, When, Where and Why With Harry Reasoner** (8/22/67) CBS-TV

Who, What, When, Where? (with Francis Scott) (7/3/43 - 10/2/43) NBC, Sat, 10:30 pm

Who-Dun-It (with Bob Dixon and Santos Ortega) (5/30/48 - 7/4/48) CBS, Sun, 4:30 pm, on West coast since 1941, Albers Brothers

Whoa Oincus (6/5/35 - 11/20/35) CBS, Wed, 3:30 pm

1 **Whole Grand Family, The** (11/14/46) ABC

2 **Whole Town's Talking, The** (with Wilson Ames) (4/3/37, 6/11/37) Syn

1 **Whole Truth Gospel Radio Hour** (3/12/50) WIBG

1 **Whoopee** (1930) film sound track

1 **Whose Time Is Come** (Post-war) Syn

1 **Why Did Lenny Bruce Die?**

13 **Why Do You Worry?** (1948) Syn

1 **Why I Chose Not To Run** (12/28/69) CBS

Why, Aunt Alice (12/23/41 - 12/30/41) Bl, Tue, 8 pm

Wide Horizons (with Eddie Dowling)
(2/27/44 - 5/28/44) Boots Aircraft, Mut, Sun, 4 pm

Widow's Sons, The (with Lucille LaVerne) (12/8/35 - 12/13/36) NBC, Sun, 4 pm

1 **Wife Line** (5/3/71) WLOL

Wife Saver, The (with Allen Prescott)
(1932 - 9/29/46) 15m
1932 - 34, Sus, NBC, 3t
1934 - 35, NBC, Tue 1935 - 36, NBC, 2t
6/3/36 - 8/26/37, Sweetheart Soap, NBC, 2t (Wed & Fri), 11:45 am
also 1/13/37 - 1/12/38, Sweetheart Soap, CBS, 2t (Wed & Fri), 1:30 pm; Mon, 1:30 pm as of 4/26/37
10/21/38 - 2/10/39, Sweetheart Soap, NBC, Fri, 9:45 am
7/10/39 - 7/11/41, Sus, Bl, 5t
7/14/41- 2/26/43 (Prescott Presents) (also with Jimmy Lytell Orchestra) Bl, 5t, 30m, 3 pm
also 1/10/42 - 11/14/42 (Prescott Variety Show), Sus, NBC, Sat, 10:30 am
7/7/46 - 9/29/46 (Allen Prescott's Party) ABC, Sun, 5 pm; Allen Prescott on locally on WJZ, New York for many years

Wigglesworths, The (see Keeping Up With Wigglesworth)

1 **Wild Bill Davison and His Band** (World transcription)

3 **Wild Bill Elliot** (Syn) 15m

88 **Wild Bill Hickok** (with Guy Madison and Andy Devine) (5/27/51 - 2/12/56) Mut
5/27/51 - 12/30/51, Sun, 7 pm; 4:30 pm as of 10/21/51
1/4/52 - 6/6/52; 9/15/52 - 6/12/53; 9/14/53 - 6/11/54; 9/13/54 - 12/31/54, Kellogg, 3t, 25m, 5:30 pm
7/17/55 - 2/12/56, Sus, Sun, 5:30 pm

1 **Wild Harvest** (1947) Air trailer

1 **Wild Ones, The** (12/31/65) NBC

Wilderness Road (with Ray Collins)
(6/2/36 - 4/16/37) Sus, CBS, 5t, 15m, 5:45 pm
(6/26/44 - 5/11/45) CBS, 5t, 15m, 5:45 pm

Wildroot Chat (with Elizabeth May and Vee Lawnhurst) (1930 - 1/8/33) Wildroot, NBC, Wed, 15m, 10:30 am; Sun, 4:15 pm as of 7/24/32

Wiley Walker and Gene Sullivan Show, The (1939)

Wilfred Fleisher (5/19/45 - 4/13/46) ABC

16 **Will Bradley and His Jazz Octet** (SESAC transcriptions)

3 **Will Bradley and His Orchestra** (2/21/40, 3/15/40, 8/21/41) NBC

1 **Will Bradley Orchestra** (Lang-Worth transcription)

7 **Will Osborne and His Orchestra** (1937, 9/13/48 - 10/11/48) film sound track, NBC, Keystone transcription

1 **Will Osborne and His Slide Music** (10/4/48) NBC

2 **Will Osborne Orchestra** (Thesaurus transcriptions)

3 **Will Rogers** (The Gulf Headliners) (4/30/33 - 8/15/35) Gulf, Sun
4/30/33 - 7/8/34, Bl, 9 pm
1/6/35 - 8/15/35, CBS, 7:30 pm

1 **Will Rogers Jr.** (3/11/38) Voice Of Republican Spain

1 **Will Rogers Says...** (1934)

Will to Freedom, The (6/15/42 - 8/19/42) CBS, Mon, 10:30 pm

1 **Will Toward Peace, The** (5/8/45) Syn

2 **Willa Cather: A Look Of Remembrance** (5/83) NPR

1 **Willa Cather: Days Of Remembrance** (9/11/84) NPR

Willard Robison's Deep River Orchestra (6/9/35 - 10/6/35) NBC, Sun, 4 pm; Bl, 4 pm as of 9/8/35 Willard Tablet
(1937) Willard stomach Tablets, 15m

1 **Willard Tablet Program, The** (Syn)

William A. Brady (12/30/34 - 4/14/35) CBS, Sun, 15m, 10:30 pm

4 **William B. and Company** (4/11/76 - 9/19/76) Syn

1 **William Hillman and Bill Henry** (10/15/50) Mut

William Hillman (11/5/39 - 4/21/40) Bl, Sun, 10 pm

1 **William Jennings Bryan** (1916) reading

2 **William L. Shirer** (9/28/41 - 45) Sanka, CBS
(1945 - 47) J B Williams, CBS
(1947 - 4/10/49) Piedmont, Mut

William Lang (9/13/45 - 50) 15m
9/13/45 - 46, Semler, Mut, 2t (Tue & Fri)
1946 - 47, W. Wise, ABC, 2t
1949 - 50, Doubleday, Mut, Sun

2 **William Wirges Orchestra** (Thesaurus transcriptions)

1 **Willie Pep vs. Phil Teranova** (2/20/45) Mut

1 **Willie Piper** (with Dick Nelson; then William Redfield) (also called Tales Of Willie Piper) (10/20/46 - 5/27/48) ABC
10/20/46 - 1/19/47, Sus, Sun, 6:30 pm
4/13/47 - 6/29/47, Sun, 7 pm
9/4/47 - 5/27/48, GE, Thu, 9 pm

Willman and Clapper (9/25/41 - 12/18/41) Trimount Clothing, Bl, Thu, 15m, 9 pm

1 **Willy Gans At The Console** (Syn)

Willys - Overland Orchestra (with Harold Stokes Orchestra, Tom, Dick and Harry) (9/27/31 - 5/25/32) Willys, Bl, Sun, 15m, 7 pm; Wed, 8 pm as of 4/6/32

1 **Willys-Overland Dealer Announcements: Aero Willys "Phyllis"** (Syn)

2 **Wimbledon Tennis Tournament** (7/4/47, 7/5/47) BBC

1 **Win The Peace** (Wartime) Syn

Win Your Lady (with Betty Lou Gerson, Jim Ameche) (7/3/38 - 9/25/38) Woodbury, Bl, Sun, 9 pm (summer replacement for Hollywood Playhouse)

Win Your Spurs (NBC) (1952) (Audition) with Hoot Gibson

Win, Lose Or Draw (10/12/46 - 11/30/46) Mut, Sat, 15m, 1:30 pm
(9/29/51 - 12/1/51) Mut, Sat, 1:30 pm

2 **Win, Place Or Show** (8/27/45 - 10/1/45) ABC, Mon, 10:30pm
also 1946

Winchell Column Quiz (with Ben Grauer) (7/10/38 - 7/21/38) Jergens, Bl, Sun, 9:30 pm (summer replacement for Walter Winchell)

Windfall (with Happy Felton)

Windy City Revue (9/3/34 - 9/24/34) CBS, Mon, 8:30 pm

Windy City, The (with Lee Bennett and The Dinning Sisters) (1949) Mut

Wings For America (with Elissa Landi and Phillips Holmes) (7/5/40 - 9/6/40) Mut, Fri, 8 pm

Wings For The Martins (with Adelaide Klein and Ed Latimer)
(11/9/38 - 5/10/39) Bl, Wed, 9:30 pm

1 **Wings For Tomorrow** (4/21/45 - 7/21/45) Mut, Sat, 2 pm

Wings Of Destiny (10/11/40 - 2/6/42) Wings, NBC, Fri, 10 pm

Wings Of Healing (with Dr. Thomas Wyatt) (8/16/53 - 3/17/57) ABC, Sun, 2:30 pm

Wings Of Music (7/15/43 - 7/29/43) Jell-O, NBC, Thu, 8:30 pm (partial summer replacement of The Aldrich Family)

2 **Wings Of Song** (with Emil Coté) Syn

Wings On Watch (with Cliff Soubier) (6/2/41 - 9/23/41) Bl, 5t, 15m, 5:45 pm

Wings Over America (6/23/40 - 2/23/41) NBC, Sun, 12:30 pm

1 **Wings Over Jordan** (1/16/38 - 10/19/47) 4/24/38 - 3/11/45; 1/20/46 - 10/19/47, CBS, Sun

2 **Wings Over The West Coast** (11/30/44, 12/6/44) Mut - Don Lee

Wings To Victory (11/5/42 - 3/16/44) Bl, Thu

1 **Wingy Manone** (World transcription)

2 **Winner Take All** (6/14/46 - 2/1/52) Sus, CBS
6/14/46 - 4/25/47, 5t, 15m
4/28/47 - 6/23/47, CBS, Mon, 30m, 7:30 pm
10/6/47 - 10/1/48, Multi, CBS, 5t, 4:30 pm
also 7/4/48 - 9/26/48, Sun, 9 pm
10/16/48 - 1/1/49, Sat, 9 pm
2/6/49 - 8/26/49, Rayve, CBS, 5t, 4:30 pm
1/8/51 - 2/23/51, 5t, 15m, 3:15 pm
10/22/51- 2/1/52, 5t, 45m, 3:45 pm

Winners Circle, The (Audition) with Wendell Niles and Freddy Martin Orchestra

Winnie, The Pooh (9/27/33 - 12/20/33) NBC, Wed, 15m, 5:15 pm
(4/30/35 - 8/29/35) Bl, various days, 15m

Winnie, The Wave (with Chuck Easter, Criss Cross; big bands) (1946) 15m

1 **WINS News Conference** (4/20/80) WINS

46 **Winston Churchill** (10/1/39 - 3/25/53) BBC, Mut, WCBS-TV, CBS, pool feed

1 **Winston Churchill and Field Marshall Montgomery** (10/23/45) BBC

1 **Winston Churchill Interview** (1/5/53) WNYC

1 **Winston Churchill Press Conference Report** (3/23/49) WOR

Wisdom Of The Ages (with Janet Beecher and Olive Wyndham) (7/9/33 - 9/3/33) Bl, Sun, 7:30 pm

2 **Wise Handyman Program, The** (1948) WOR

Wise Man, The (1934 - 36) NBC, 3t, 15m
(10/23/37 - 2/25/39) NBC, Sat, 15m, 9 am
(3/4/39 - 3/30/40) NBC, Sat, 15m, 10 am (not in New York after that; continued until 11/40)
2/3/41 - 3/31/41) NBC, Mon, 15m, 1:15 pm

1 **Wishbone Party** (2/24/45) WHN

1 **Wishing Well** (12/15/44) BBC

1 **Wit's End** (6/9/48) WPTZ-TV audio

11 **Witch's Tale, The** (with Alonzo Deen Cole) (5/28/31 - 6/13/38) WOR and Mutual; times are New York (about 328 shows broadcast). Air Features syndicate (1933 - 34), also syndicated by Kruschen Salts in 1934, KECA, Los Angeles (1938 - 39). There was an Australian series (Grace Gibson Productions; 1939 - 45) used Alonzo Deen Cole's scripts and new scripts by E. Mason Wood
5/28/31 - 7/9/31, Thu, 10:15 pm
7/13/31 - 34, local on WOR, New York
10/15/34 - 3/5/37, various days in New York and other parts of the country
3/11/37 - 9/23/37, Thu, 10 pm
10/5/37 -11/9/37, Tue, 10:30 pm
12/30/37 - 2/10/38, Thu, 10 pm
3/8/38 - 4/18/38, Tue, 9:30 pm
4/25/38 - 6/13/38, Mon, 9:30 pm

Witching Hour (with John Dailey and Bess Johnson; written by Wyllis Cooper) (1/23/32 - 3/5/32) Breethem Breath Tablets, CBS, Sat, 15m, 5:30 pm

With Canada's Mounted (with Eustace Wyatt and Allyn Joslyn) (1/4/32 - 4/11/32) Canada Dry, Bl, Mon, 10 pm

1 **Witness!**

Witness, The (Syn) 15m

1 **Wittnauer Choraliers, The** (6/11/50) CBS

Wizard Of Odds, The (1949 - 54) (with Jay Stewart), NBC
6/15/53 - 6/4/54 (with Walter O'Keefe), Multi, CBS, 5t, 15m, 3:45 pm

3 **Wizard Of Oz, The** (with Nancy Kelly) (9/25/33 - 3/23/34) Jell-O, NBC, 3t, 15m, 5:45 pm

1 **WJZ Twenty Fifth Anniversary Show** (10/7/46) WJZ

1 **WKBF, Indianapolis Dedication Program** (8/31/33) NBC

1 **WLOS Barn Dance, The** (WLOS)

1 **WLW News** (8/17/41) WLW

9 **WLW Programs** (WLW)

1 **WLW Stock Company, The** (1946 - 1947) WLW

1 **WMAQ Radio Coverage Of The Richard Carpenter Case** (8/15/55) WMAQ

1 **WMAQ Station Break** (2/19/42) WMAQ

1 **WMAQ Twenty Fifth Anniversary Show** (4/13/47) WMAQ

1 **WMAQ...But Why?** (10/12/53) WMAQ

1 **WMBQ Announcements** (5/9/39) WMBQ

1 **WNEW Selling Briefs** (WNEW)

1 **WNYC Sixty Fifth Anniversary Broadcast** (7/8/89) WNYC-FM

Woman's Club (with Isabel Leighton; Eleanor Wilson McAdoo as of 7/15/46) (5/13/46 - 10/4/46) CBS, 5t, 15m, 5:15 pm

Woman From Nowhere, The (see Irene Rich)

5 **Woman In My House, The** (with Forrest Lewis and Janet Scott) (3/26/51 - 59) NBC, 5t, 15m
3/26/51 - 55, Sweetheart Soap
1955 - 57, Miles Laboratory
1957 - 59, Multi

4 **Woman In White, The** (1/3/38 - 5/28/48) 5t, 15m
1/3/38 - 9/27/40, Pillsbury, NBC
9/30/40 - 41, Carnay, CBS
1941 - 9/25/42, Oxydol, CBS
6/5/44 - 5/28/48, General Mills, NBC

2 **Woman Of America, A** (1/25/43 - 6/21/46) Ivory, NBC, 5t, 15m
1/25/43 - 9/24/43 (with Anne Seymour)
9/27/43 - 6/21/46 (Florence Freeman)

1 **Woman Of Courage** (7/17/39 - 7/10/42) Octagon & Crystal Soap, CBS, 5t, 15m

Woman Of The Year (with Bette Davis) (1/7/52 - 6/30/52; 9/29/52 - 12/22/52) Mut., Mon, 8 pm

Woman Of Tomorrow, The (with Nancy Booth Craig) (1938 - 10/30/42) Bl, 5t, 15m, 9:15 am; 9 am as of 5/15/39

1 **Woman Who Dyed Twice, The** (Syn)

1 **Woman's Club** (9/12/46) CBS

Woman's Exchange, The (3/18/46 - 12/27/46) ABC, 5t, 15m, 1:15 pm

Woman's Home Companion (with Jean Abbey) (1939)

Woman's Jury (see American Woman's Jury)

Woman's Life, A (7/16/45 - 11/30/45) Lever Brothers, CBS, 5t, 15m, 11:30 am

1 **Woman's Magazine Of The Air** (11/1/49) KNBC

Woman's Prison (8/18/52) Audition

Woman's Radio Review (5/11/31 - 10/23/36) NBC, 5t
5/11/31 - 32, 60m, 3 pm
1932 - 10/23/36, 30m

Woman's Story, A (1944) (Audition) Bl

1 **Woman's World , A**

Woman, The (with Lorna Farrell and Bryna Raeburn) (1946) Syn

Women In A Changing World (6/11/40 - 9/24/40) Bl, Tue, 15m, 1:30 pm

Women In The Making Of America (5/19/39 - 8/11/39) NBC, Fri

1 **Women In The News** (11/1/39) Mut

Women In The World Of Tomorrow (5/27/39 - 10/7/39) CBS, Sat, 15m, 12:15 pm

1 **Women In World Affairs** (1944) Syn

Women's Clubs (1/5/40 - 7/7/40) NBC, Fri, 15m, 1:30 pm
(11/26/40 - 5/3/41) NBC, Sat, 15m, 11:15 am (also see Federation Of Women's Clubs)

1 **Women, The** (1939) Air trailer

1 **Wonder Bar** (1934) Air trailer

Wonder Hour, The (with Rudolph Mangold Orchestra) (3/20/32 - 4/10/32) Minneapolis-Honeywell, CBS, Sun, 1:30 pm

1 **Wonder Man** (1945) Air trailer

8 **Wonder Of Vision, The** (Syn)

6 **Wonder Show, The** (with Jack Smart for two weeks; Orson Welles for rest of show; also starred Adele Ronson, Florence Halop
(8/9/36 - 11/15/36) Wonder Bread, Mut, Sun, 60m, 9 pm (see also Jack Haley 10/14/38 - 11/25/38)

Wonderful City (with Harry Wismer, Nat Brandwynne Orchestra)
(6/15/53 - 11/11/55) Multi, Mut, 25m
6/15/53 - 9/4/53, 5t, 1 pm
9/7/53 - 9/29/53, 5t, 2 pm
1/4/54 - 3/26/54, 5t, 11 am
7/17/54 - 7/9/55, Sat, 1:30 pm; 1 pm as of 1/23/55
8/8/55 - 11/11/55, 5t, 3:05 pm

1 **Wonderful World Of Animals, The** (Syn)

12 **Wonderland Of Vision, The** (1953 - 1954) Syn

1 **Woodbury Hollywood News** (10/20/46) ABC

1 **Woodbury Journal, The** (10/17/48) ABC

2 **Woodbury Soap Show, The** (5/28/34, 9/18/34) CBS

1 **Woodbury's Hollywood Playhouse** (5/29/40) NBC

1 **Wooden Fish, The** (1949) Syn

1 **Woody** (11/14/76) PBS-TV

2 **Woody Herman** (1964) PBS-TV, World transcription

13 **Woody Herman and His Orchestra** (1/7/40 - 9/61) NBC, CBS, CBS-TV, World transcription

4 **Woody Herman and The Third Herd** (1954) NBC, CBS

4 **Woody Herman Show, The** (3/26/42 - 8/31/47)
3/26/42 - 4/30/42, Mut, Thu, 8:30 pm
1944, Old Gold, Wed
10/13/45 - 7/6/46, Wildroot, ABC, Sat, 8 pm; Fri, 8 pm as of 1/25/46
7/13/47 - 8/31/47 (also with Peggy Lee) CBS, Sun, 4:30 pm National Guard:

Woody Woodpecker Show, The (1953) (with Mel Blanc) Mut, Sat

Wooley The Moth (3/7/35 - 6/20/35) Enoz Chemical Company, Bl, Thu, 15m, 5:15pm

4 **Woolworth Hour, The** (with Percy Faith Orchestra and host, Donald Woods) (6/5/55 - 12/29/57) Woolworth, CBS, Sun, 55m, 1:05 pm
(1/5/58 - 10/12/58) (The Best In Music) (with host Robert Alda, Ralph Storey) CBS, Sun, 55m, 1:15 pm

1 **WOR Diamond Jubilee** (2/28/82) WOR

1 **WOR Jukebox, The** (3/29/44) WOR

45 **WOR Newsreel** (8/15/44 - 8/27/45) WOR

1 **WOR Opera Concert, The** (12/12/48) WOR

1 **WOR Radio Mystery Theatre, The** (6/5/78) WOR

1 **WOR Salutes Channel Nine** (1/1/50) WOR

3 **WOR Summer Theatre, The** (8/13/42 - 9/3/42) WOR

WOR Symphony Orchestra (with Alfred Wallenstein) (9/27/38 - 2/21/39) Mut, Tue, 9:30 pm

2 **WOR Twenty Fifth Anniversary Broadcast** (9/22/47) WOR

1 **WOR Workshop** (2/26/48) WOR

Word Detective (with Basil Rathbone) (Syn)

Word Dramas (with Thomas Conrad Sawyer) (8/28/39 - 12/25/39) Mut, Mon, 15m

1 **Word From The People** (4/24/45) CBS

1 **Word Game, The** (with Max Eastman) (4/20/38 - 9/38) WABC, Wed, 9:30 pm

1 **Word Of Life** (6/26/43)

Word Stories (with Dr. Joseph Shipley) (10/26/47 - 12/7/47) Mut, Sun, 15m, 1:15 pm

Word To The Wise (1/27/35 - 9/22/35) Better Speech Institute, Sun, 15m
1/27/35 - 4/7/35, Bl, 11:45 am
4/14/35 - 7/21/35, Bl, 2 pm
7/28/35 - 9/22/35, NBC, 2 pm

Words and Music (with Harvey Hays) (1931 - 6/24/45) NBC, Sun, 15m
also 2/15/37 - 8/28/41, 3t - 5t
also 7/29/39 - 9/23/39, Sat, 1:30 pm
also see Fred Waring

Words and Music By Joan Brooks (see Joan Brooks)

51 **Words At War** (6/24/43 - 10/3/44) NBC
6/24/43 - 7/1/43, Thu, 8 pm
7/10/43 - 8/14/43, Sat, 8:30 pm (summer replacement for Truth Or Consequences)
8/19/43 - 10/3/44, Thu, 11:30 pm; Tue as of 10/5/43 including:
6/27/44 - 10/3/44 (with Carl Van Doren), Johnson, NBC, Tue, 9:30 pm (summer replacement for Fibber McGee & Molly)
10/10/44 - 6/5/45, Tue, 11:30 pm

1 **Words Of Romance** (1945) WIND

20 **Words With Music** (Wartime) AFRS, 15m

Words Without Music (directed by Norman Corwin) (1/1/39 - 7/2/39) CBS, Sun, 5 pm; 2:30 pm as of 2/19/39; 4 pm as of 5/28/39

1 **Workshop For War** (3/11/44) WBBM

World Adventurer's Club, The (see Adventurer's Club)

World and You, The (10/31/55 - 4/13/56) ABC, 5t, 8 pm

World Church, The (with Rev. O. L. Jaggers) (10/10/54 - 2/6/55) ABC, Sun, 6:30 pm

World Dances (with Lud Gluskin; called Fiesta as of 1/23/37)
(5/8/36 - 2/6/37) CBS
5/8/36 - 11/22/36) Sun, 8 pm
11/28/36 - 2/6/37, Sat, 10:30 pm

1 **World Events** (3/4/38) Mut

1 **World Food Crisis** (4/19/46) Mut

World From The Country (1947) (15m)

World Front (6/6/43 - 5/23/48) Bunte Brothers, NBC, Sun, 12 noon

World In Action, The

1 **World In Depth, The** (5/21/66) Mut

3 **World In Review, The** (1930, 1931, 3/29/39) Syn

1 **World In Sound, The** (1965)

1 **World In Sound...1966, The** (1966) AP Broadcast News

3 **World Is Yours, The** (6/14/36 - 5/2/42) Sus, Bl, Sun except 12/7/40 - 9/13/41. Sat, 5 pm; NBC as of 10/25/36 (first broadcast as Treasure House)

1 **World Jazz Series** (8/20/60) CBS

1 **World Music Festival** (1956) CBS

1 **World News** (3/4/38) Mut

1 **World News Parade** (3/28/43) NBC

5 **World News Roundup, The** (3/13/38) still on the air, CBS

74 **World News Today** (1940 - 9/23/45) Admiral as of 5/14/42, CBS (Also see CBS World News Roundup)

1 **World News Tonight** (6/22/41) CBS

1 **World Of Disney, The** (6/12/64) NBC-TV

8 **World Of F. Scott Fitzgerald, The** (6/8/79, 11/81, 12/81) NPR, 60m

12 **World Of Folk Music, The** (Syn)

World Of Jazz (1956) (with John S. Wilson and George Simon)

2 **World Of Music, A** (Syn)

1 **World Of Religion, The** (6/5/69) CBS

2 **World Of Rosalind Marlowe, The** (5/15/46) (Audition) with Lurene Tuttle

World Of Science (with George Viereck) (2/15/36 - 3/7/36) Bl, Sat, 10:30 pm

2 **World Of Song** (4/16/44 - 11/19/44) Sherwin-Williams, Bl, Sun, 4:30 pm (summer replacement of Metropolitan Opera Auditions)

3 **World Security Workshop** (11/14/46 - 8/1/47) Sus, ABC, Thu, 10 pm

16 **World Series Game** (10/8/37 - 10/10/51) Mut

4 **World Series Preview** (9/30/41, 9/28/44, 9/29/45, 9/13/46) Mut

1 **World Series Repeat** (10/9/49) Mut

World This Week, The (1940)

20 **World Today, The** (4/3/40 - 6/5/67) CBS, Mut

World Tonight, The (1940)

World Tourist, The (12/17/55 - 4/28/56) ABC, Sat, 10m, 12:05 pm

World Traveler, The (see American Travel Guide)

1 **World War II**

World We Live In, The (4/2/54 - 2/25/55) ABC, Fri, 9:30 pm

5 **World Without End** (12/21/48) Syn

World's Best Dramas, The
(5/8/41 - 5/15/41) Bl, Thu, 8:30 pm
(7/7/41 - 9/28/41) Bl, Mon, 8 pm

2 **World's Fair Band, The** (7/7/40 - 9/22/40) Bl, Sun, 7:30 pm

1 **World's Fair Closing Night** (10/27/40) WOR

4 **World's Fair Holiday** (1965) Syn

1 **World's Fair Song** (8/25/39)

74 **World's Great Novels, The**
(10/14/44 - 2/17/45) NBC University Of The Air, NBC, Sat, 7 pm
(2/23/45 - 5/31/46; 11/1/46 - 7/23/48) Sus, NBC, Fri, 11:30 pm
(for 7/6/45 - 9/7/45 see American Story Teller (developed into NBC University Theater)

1 **World's Greatest Mother, The** (5/8/49) Mut

World's Greatest Short Stories (see Nelson Olmsted)

1 **World's Greatest Showman, The** (11/63) NBC-TV

1 **World's Greatest Stories, The** (see Nelson Olmsted) also CBS

World's Most Honored Flights, The (with Captain Eddie Rickenbacker)
(2/3/46 - 6/2/46) Mut, Sun, 3:30 pm

8 **Wormwood Forest** (1/8/49 - 4/30/49) NBC, Sat, 15m, 5:15pm

Worry Clinic (3/2/36 - 4/29/36) General Mills, Mut, 5t (Wed & Fri) 15m
(6/3/36 - 7/24/36) CBS, 2t (Wed & Fri) 15m WOR Summer Theater (with Peter Donald)
(7/16/42 - 9/10/42) WOR, New York, Thu, 9:30 pm

2 **WPA American Folk Singers Of Boston** (1941) Syn

1 **WPA Opera Company** (1941) Syn

2 **WPA Swing Version Of The Mikado** (3/8/39, 5/1/39) WOR

2 **WPA War Service Band** (1/11/42, 8/15/42) WNYC

1 **Wrap Up** (5/17/72) WMCA

1 **WREN Barn Dance** (WREN)

1 **Wright Mood For Dancing, The** (1/52) WKY

1 **Wrigley Christmas Party** (12/25/48) CBS

1 **WTIC 11:00 P.M. News** (12/10/50) WTIC

Wuthering Heights (see Wheatena Playhouse)

1 **WWRL Microphone Test** (1939) WWRL

1 **WWRL Sign-Ons** (1939) WWRL

1 **Wynn Show, The** (NBC) Audition

Wythe Williams (8/4/40 - 9/7/41) Peter Paul, Mut, Sun, 7:45 pm
(9/3/40 - 9/11/41) American Razor, Mut, 2t, 8pm

153 **X Minus One** (4/24/55 - 1/9/58) Street and Smith, NBC; occasionally sponsored by Bromo Quinine, Pabst Beer
4/24/55 - 6/5/55, Sun, 8 pm
7/7/55 - 11/10/55, Thu, 8 pm; 9 pm as of 7/28/55
11/16/55 - 3/28/56, Wed, 8 pm; 9:30 pm as of 1/4/56
4/3/56 - 9/11/56, Tue, 8:30 pm; 8 pm as of 7/3/56
9/26/56 - 4/24/57, Wed, 9 pm
6/20/57 - 1/9/58, Thu, 8 pm and
1/17/73 (amateurish revival)

4 **Xavier Cugat and His Orchestra** (World, Associated, Thesaurus transcriptions)

6 **Xavier Cugat and Orchestra** (Thesaurus transcriptions)

7 **Xavier Cugat Orchestra** (Thesaurus transcriptions)

8 **Xavier Cugat Show, The**
(10/30/33 - 9/22/48)
10/30/33 - 6/1/34, Sus, NBC, 5t, 6 pm
10/15/34 - 35, Sus, NBC, 5t, 15m
7/1/39 - 9/7/39, Mut, Sat, 15m, 12:45 pm
1/9/41 - 1/1/42 (Cugat Rumba Revue as of 6/19/41), Camel, NBC, Thu
1/6/42 - 7/7/42 (Rumba Revue) Camel, Bl, Tue, 8 pm
7/10/42 - 7/2/43 (see Camel Caravan)
9/4/43 - 11/27/43, Dubonnet, Bl, Sat, 11 am
12/1/43 - 7/26/44, Dubonnet, Mut, Wed, 8:30 pm
8/3/47 - 9/7/47, Eversharp, CBS, Sun, 10 pm
7/7/48 - 9/22/48, ABC, Wed, 8 pm

1 **Yacht Club Boys, The** (1934) film sound track

1 **Yamashita Surrender** (9/2/45) Mut

13 **Yank Bandstand** (1944/1945) AFRS, 15m

15 **Yank Swing Session** (Wartime) AFRS origination

Yank, The Army Weekly
(11/25/44 - 12/9/44) NBC, Sat, 1 pm

1 **Yankee Clipper** (2/24/39) WFBR

Yankee Doodle Goes To Town
(9/2/40 - 9/23/40) Mut, Mon, 15m, 3:30 pm

Yankee Doodle Minstrels
(11/21/42 - 12/12/42) ABC, Sat, 10 pm

Yankee Doodle Quiz (with Ted Malone)
(5/8/43 - 7/1/44) Sus, Bl
5/8/43 - 5/15/43, Sat, 7:30 pm
9/3/43 - 9/10/43, Fri, 8:30 pm
1/8/44 - 7/1/44, Sat, 10 am

Yankee Yarns (with Alton Blackington)
(1944 - 52) 15m

Yanks In The Orient (10/1/44 - 7/15/45) Bl, Sun, 15m, 11:15 pm

Yardley Program (with Beatrice Herford)
(2/21/32 - 5/8/32) Yardley, Bl, Sun, 2 pm

19 **Yarns For Yanks** (AFRS) 15m

1 **Yazoo City Asks The President** (6/21/77) ABC-TV

1 **Ye Olde Tyme Minstrel Show** (Syn)

1 **Year Apart: 1973, A** (1/13/74) NBC-TV

1 **Year End Review: A Dinner At Howard K. Smith's** (12/28/66) ABC-TV

1 **Year End Summary** (1/68) CBS-TV

1 **Year Gone By: The Arts and Sciences In 1958, The** (12/28/68) CBS-TV

1 **Year In, Year Out** (12/67) ABC-TV

1 **Year It Began, The**

1 **Year Out - Year In** (12/26/65) ABC-TV

1 **Year The Walls Came Down, The**
(12/30/72) ABC-TV

1 **Years Of Anguish, Day Of Peace**
(1/27/73) ABC-TV

1 **Years Of Confrontation** (12/23/62) ABC-TV

8 **Years Of Crisis** (1/2/55 - 12/63) CBS, CBS-TV

1 **Years Of Lightning, Day Of Drums** (film sound track)

1 **Years Of Our Faith** (1/2/54) Syn

Yeast Foamers Orchestra (1929 - 4/8/35) Yeast Foam, Bl
1929 - 3/4/31, various days
3/1/31 - 4/22/34 (with Jan Garber from 1933), Sun
4/30/34 - 4/8/35 (with Jan Garber), Mon, 8 pm

Yella Pessl (6/9/40 - 10/13/40) CBS, Sun, 15m, 11:15 am

1 **Yes Or No** (6/25/44) Mut

1 **Yes, Mr. Walker** (Syn)

1 **Yessirree...It's Mr. B!** (1953) Syn

Yesterday and Today (with Blue Barron Orchestra, Alec Templeton) (1942) NBC

Yesterday's Children (with Dorothy Gordon) (11/24/39 - 5/24/40) Bl, Fri, 7:30 pm

1 **Yesterdays** (7/29/40) Mut

3 **Yiddish Swing Program** (with The Barry Sisters, Gil Mack and Pat Spencer)
(1941) WHN
(1946 - 47) Manischewitz, Sun

You (with Gilbert Seldes)
(4/26/36 - 8/16/36) NBC, Sun, 2 pm

You and Alcohol (11/12/46 - 2/4/47) CBS, Tue, 6:15 pm

1 **You and Japan** (9/24/49) CBS

14 **You and The Atom** (7/22/46 - 8/16/46) CBS, 5t, 15m, 11:15 pm
also 9/21/50, WOR-TV

You and The War (7/13/42 - 8/28/42) NBC, 5t, 15m, 5:30 pm

8 **You and The World** (11/2/48 - 1/9/53) Sus, CBS, 5t, 15m, Stuart Novins

You and Your Government
(6/18/35 - 9/24/35) NBC, Tue, 15m, 6:45 pm

13 **You and Your Security** (1949) Syn

You And... (11/2/48 - 12/21/48) CBS, Tue, 15m, 6:15 pm

6 **You Are The Jury** (Syn)

67 **You Are There** (called CBS Is There until 4/25/48) (7/7/47 - 6/12/49) Sus, CBS
7/7/47 - 8/18/47, Mon
12/7/47 - 7/4/48; 8/22/48 - 6/12/49, Sun
(2/19/50 - 3/26/50) Sun, 2 pm

244 **You Bet Your Life** (with Groucho Marx)
(10/27/47 - 9/19/56)
10/27/47 - 4/28/48; 9/22/48 - 5/25/49; 10/5/49 - 12/28/49, Elgin, ABC, Mon, 8 pm; Wed, 9:30 pm as of 12/31/47; CBS, Wed as of 10/5/49
1/4/50 - 6/28/50, DeSoto, CBS, Wed, 9 pm
10/4/50 - 6/27/51; 10/3/51 - 9/19/56, DeSoto, NBC, Wed, 9 pm

You Can Be An Actor (ABC) 15m, 2/6/46 (Audition)

1 **You Can Be An Angel** (1/16/50) Syn

1 **You Can Change The World** (Syn)

18 **You Can't Beat The Dutch** (1944/1945) Syn

24 **You Can't Do Business With Hitler** (1942 - 43) Office Of War Information, Syn, 15m

2 **You Can't Have Everything** (film sound track, air trailer)

1 **You Can't Take It With You** (with Everett Sloane)
(8/27/44 - 11/19/44) Emerson Radio, Mut, Sun, 5 pm
(5/13/51 - 11/16/51) (with Walter Brennan) NBC
5/13/51 - 9/30/51, Sun, 6 pm
10/5/51 - 11/16/51, Fri, 9:30 pm

You Decide (4/27/41 - 8/24/41) CBS, Sun, 1:30 pm

1 **You Have Seen Its Shadow** (Post-war) Syn

1 **You Have To Go Out** (8/4/47) Syn

You Know What? (with Joe Kelly) 15m (Auditions)

You Make The News (11/22/45 - 5/16/46) Mut, Thu, 10 pm

1 **You Only Live Once** (6/13/47) CBS

You Said It (see Monday Night Show)

1 **You Tell 'Em Club** (with Tom Slater) (8/19/43 - 10/21/43) Mut, Thu, 9:30 pm

1 **You Were Meant To Be A Star** (6/10/45) Mut

64 **You Were There** (Red Cross) (10/8/53 - 9/11/55) Sun, 15m, Syn

1 **You Win** (1953) Audition

1 **You'd Be Surprised** (1944) Air trailer

1 **You'll Never Get Rich** (1942) Air trailer

You're In The Act (with Nils T. Granlund) (3/4/46 - 6/7/46) CBS, 5t, 3 pm

You're In The Army Now (with Wyllis Cooper) (11/18/40 - 3/31/41) Bl, Mon, 9 pm

1 **You're Telling Me** (4/1/34) Air trailer

You're The Expert (with Fred Uttal; Del Sharbutt announcer) (7/7/41 - 8/1/41) Campbell, CBS, 5t, 15m, 2:30 pm

1 **You're The One** (1941) film sound track

1 **Young America Wants To Help** (4/27/41) Mut

Young At Heart (12/4/47) Audition

1 **Young Book Reviewers, The** (12/6/47) WMCA

10 **Young Doctor Malone**
(11/20/39 - 11/25/60) 5t, 15m
11/20/39 - 4/26/40, Bran Flakes, Bl
4/29/40 - 1/5/45, General Foods, CBS
also 8/31/42 - 1/1/43, Procter & Gamble, NBC
4/2/45 - 6/24/55, Procter & Gamble, CBS
7/19/55 - 11/25/60, Multi, CBS

Young Hickory (9/29/36 - 3/4/37) Bl, 3t (Tue - Thu), 15m

Young Ideas (6/29/41 - 8/24/41) CBS, Sun, 5 pm

12 **Young Love** (with Jimmy Lydon, Janet Waldo) (4/30/49) Audition
(7/4/49 - 5/13/50) CBS
7/4/49 - 8/22/49, Mon, 8:30 pm (summer replacement for Arthur Godfrey's Talent Scouts)
11/25/49 - 1/13/50, Ford, CBS, Fri, 9:30 pm
2/4/50 - 5/13/50, Ford, CBS, Sat, 7 pm

1 **Young Man With A Band**
(8/14/39 - 2/9/40) Columbia Records, CBS, Fri, 10:30 pm (summer replacement for Believe It Or Not)

Young People's Church Of The Air (10/40 - 4/41; 10/41 - 6/20/48) Mut, Sun, 30m (not in New York)

Young People's Concerts (with New York Philharmonic Orchestra)
(1938 - 41) CBS, Sat, 60m, 11 am (on periodically)

Young People's Conference (with Rev. Daniel Poling) (1926 - ?) NBC

28 **Young Widder Brown** (with Florence Freeman; with Wendy Drew as of 1/18/54)
(6/6/38 - 6/22/56) NBC, 5t, 15m
6/6/38 - 9/23/38, Sus
9/26/38 - 6/22/56, Bayer

Younger Generation, The (1945) (Syn)

Your Adventurers (1/7/37 - 9/30/37) Colgate, CBS, Thu, 10 pm

3 **Your Air Force** (9/48)

18 **Your All Time Hit Parade**
(2/12/43 - 9/24/44) Lucky Strike, NBC
2/12/43 - 6/2/44, Fri, 8:30 pm
6/11/44 - 9/24/44, Sun, 7 pm (summer replacement for Jack Benny)

Your America (1/8/44 - 9/30/45) Union Pacific
1/8/44 - 10/6/44, NBC, Sat, 5 pm
10/15/44 - 9/30/45, Mut, Sun, 4 pm

1 **Your Army Service Forces** (7/12/44) Mut

Your Better Tomorrow
(11/2/55 - 4/13/56) ABC, 3t, Wed - Fri, 8:30 pm

Your Bible Story Hour

Your Blind Date (with Connie Haines, Frances Scully) (4/20/42 - 7/6/42) Bl, Mon, 25m, 9 pm: 9:30 pm as of 5/18/42 (began as West Coast Show)

4 **Your Business Reporter**
(4/14/48 - 5/5/48) Syn

Your Child (1929 - 5/26/36) Sus, NBC, Tue, 15m; also see Angelo Patri

6 **Your Child and Religion**
(12/30/45 - 4/14/46) WMCA, Associated Broadcasting System

Your Children and Your Schools
(3/22/47 - 6/7/47) ABC, Sat, 15m, 12 noon

Your Date With Don Norman
(3/16/42 - 8/28/42) Mut, 5t, 15m, 1:45 pm

Your Dream Has Come True (with Ian Keith) (10/27/40 - 4/27/41) Quaker, NBC, Sun, 5:30 pm

Your English (2/17/35 - 4/19/36; 10/18/36 - 1/10/37) Bl, Sun, 11:45 am; 3 pm as of 4/14/35

1 **Your Esso Reporter** (10/8/45) WJZ

1 **Your Family and Mine** (with Bill Adams and Raymond Edward Johnson)
(4/25/38 - 4/26/40) Sealtest, 5t, 15m
4/25/38 - 4/28/39, NBC, 5:15 pm
5/1/39 - 4/26/40, CBS, 2:30 pm

1 **Your Family Doctor** (4/9/42) WOR

1 **Your Family Quiz Club** (4/4/49) WOR

Your Farm Reporter (9/26/38 - 6/23/39) Goodyear, Bl, 15m, 1:15 pm

1 **Your Favorite Melodies** (1/29/49) WOR

1 **Your Garden** (3/21/44) WOR

1 **Your Girl Friend** (Audition)

1 **Your Gospel Singer** (12/8/41) Red

Your Happy Birthday (with "Tiny" Ruffner and Jimmy Dorsey Orchestra) (1/3/41 - 8/15/41) Spud and Twenty Grand Cigarettes, Bl, Fri, 9:30 pm

Your Health (see AMA Health Dramas)

100 **Your Hit Parade** (4/20/35 - 1/16/53) Lucky Strike
4/20/35 - 4/25/36, NBC, Sat, 60m, 8 pm
5/2/36 - 4/19/47, CBS, Sat, 45m; 30m, 10 pm as of 11/28/36; 45m as of 2/13/37; 45m, 9 pm as of 7/8/39
also 3/11/36 - 12/1/37, NBC, Wed, 60m, 10 pm; 30m as of 11/25/36; 45m as of 3/31/47
also 6/17/36 - 9/30/36, Bl, Wed, 60m, 10 pm
4/26/47 - 7/7/51; 9/6/51 - 6/26/52; 8/29/52 - 1/16/53, NBC, Sat, 30m; Thu, 10 pm as of 9/6/51; Fri, 8 pm as of 8/29/52 (continued on television until 4/24/59)

1 **Your Hit Parade On Parade**
(6/5/49 - 9/4/49) Lucky Strikes, CBS, Sun, 7 pm
(6/25/55 - 9/3/55) Lucky Strikes, CBS, Sat, 10:30 pm

Your Hollywood News Girl
(3/8/41 - 6/14/41) NBC, Sat, 15m, 1:15 pm

Your Hollywood Parade (see Hollywood Parade)

2 **Your Hollywood Radio Reporter** (1942) Syn

Your Home (Garden) and Mine (with Bryson Rash, Ruth Cross)
(2/27/37 - 9/4/37) CBS, Sat, 15m, 10 am

2 **Your Home and You** (Syn)

Your Home Beautiful (with Vicki Vola, Johnny Thompson and Betty Moore)
(3/1/47 - 5/24/52) Benjamin Moore, 15m
3/1/47 - 7/19/47; 3/6/48 - 5/29/48, ABC, Sat, 10 am
3/5/49 - 5/28/49, Mut, Sat, 10:30 am
3/4/50 - 5/27/50; 3/3/51- 5/26/51; 3/1/52 - 5/24/52, Mut, 11 am

Your Hope Chest (1947)

Your Host (with Leslie Bell Singers; CBC; 1951)

2 **Your Hymns and Mine** (1935) Syn

1 **Your Income Tax** (3/42)

Your Invitation To Music (4/30/50 - 9/24/50; 9/9/51 - 10/14/51; 5/4/52 - 10/12/52) CBS, Sun, 90m

Your Land and Mine (see Henry J. Taylor)

Your Lover (with Frank Luther) (1934) NBC, 2t (Tue & Fri), 4 pm

1 **Your Lucky Strike** (with Don Ameche) (12/6/48 - 3/4/49) Lucky Strike, CBS, 5t

Your Marine Corps (7/21/45 - 9/8/45) CBS, Sat, 3 pm

Your Marriage Club (with Haven MacQuarrie)
(1/31/40 - 6/19/40) Bl, Wed, 12 midnight; on West coast for several months before
(9/7/40 - 8/7/41) Wonder Bread, CBS, Sat, 7:30 pm; Thu as of 6/26/41

6 **Your Movietown Radio Theatre** (1948) Syn

7 **Your Navy Show** (1950) AFRS
(1952) Navy, Syn

Your Neck Of The Woods (with Carl Carmer) (5/31/37 - 9/27/37) CBS, Mon, 10:30 pm

Your Neighbors, The Haines
(8/13/40 - 10/1/40) Mut, Tue, 9:30 pm

Your News Parade (with Edwin C. Hill) (4/5/37 - 4/1/38) Lucky Strike, CBS, 5t, 15m, 12:15 pm

Your Number Please (4/25/42 - 6/13/42) NBC, Sat, 4:30 pm

Your Parlor Playhouse (5/9/37 - 6/20/37) Lovely Lady Beauty Aids, Mut, Sun, 10:30 pm

14 **Your Personal Problem Clinic** (1937) Syn

22 **Your Playhouse Of Favorites**
(1947 - 1949) Syn

3 **Your Quarter Hour Serenade** (Pre-war) Syn

Your Radio Reporter (10/10/43 - 4/8/45) NBC, Sun, 15m, 1 pm

Your Radio Theater (with Herbert Marshall) (10/11/55 - 1/10/56) Multi, NBC, Tue, 55m

11 **Your Rhythm Revue** (1953, 1954) 15m, Syn

2 **Your Richfield Reporter**
(4/12/45, 5/1/47) NBC - Pacific

1 **Your Ruppert Sports Reporter**
(12/25/46) WOR

1 **Your Saturday Dance Date** (5/29/50) NBC

Your Singin Secretary (1949) (with Evelyn Knight)

Your Song and Mine (with Thomas L. Thomas) (4/21/48 - 7/14/48; 9/15/48 - 12/29/48) Borden, CBS, Wed, 9 pm

1 **Your Sports Question Box** (1/25/47) ABC

28 **Your Star Time** (1952 - 1953) 15m, Syn

Your Story Hour (Syn)

Your Story Parade (15m)

Your Sunday Date (with Harold Stokes Orchestra) (4/24/38 - 9/11/38) Mut, Sun, 10:30 pm

1 **Your Sunshine Reporter** (9/21/39) WJSV

Your Symphony Scrapbook (1950 - 53) 15m, Sat

Your Tropical Trip (see Desi Arnaz)

Your True Adventures (see True Adventures)

Your United Nations (with Andrew Corder as of 11/26/46)
(10/1/46 - 5/6/47) NBC, Tue, 11:30 pm

Your Unseen Friend (with Maurice Joachim, Arlene Jackson)
(10/4/36 - 1/1/38) Personal Loan, CBS, Sun, 5: 30 pm; Tue, 10:30 pm as of 4/27/37; then Sat as of 10/2/37

1 **Your Voice Counts** (1/21/72) pool feed

14 **Your Voice Of America** (1951) Syn

1 **Your Weight In Gold** (6/8/44) (with Bud Collyer) Mut, Thu

Yours For A Song (also called Conti Castille Show) (with Kay Armen, Earl Wrightson) (11/19/48 - 5/13/49) Conti, Mut, Fri, 25m, 9:30 pm; 8:30 pm as of 1/28/49

1 **Yours Sincerely** (with Charles Collingwood) (4/28/46 - 2/23/47) CBS, Sun, 12:30 pm (also see Isham Jones)

619 **Yours Truly, Johnny Dollar**
(12/7/48) Audition
(2/11/49 - 9/30/62) Sus except where indicated, CBS
2/11/49 - 4/22/49, Fri, 10:30 pm (Charles Russell until 1/14/50)
10/1/49 - 1/14/50, Sat, 7 pm
2/3/50 - 3/3/50, Fri, 10 pm (Edmund O'Brien until 9/3/52)
3/7/50 - 5/30/50, Tue, 10 pm
6/8/50 - 8/31/50, Thu, 10 pm
9/30/50 - 6/16/51, Sat, 7 pm
6/20/51 - 9/26/51 , Wed, 9:30 pm (summer replacement for Bing Crosby as of 7/4/51)
10/6/51 - 1/12/52, Sat, 7 pm
7/2/52 - 9/3/52, Wed, 9 pm
11/28/52 - 3/6/53, Fri, 8:30 pm (John Lund until 9/19/54)
3/10/53 - 12/29/53, Wrigley, Tue, 9 pm
1/5/54 - 8/10/54, Wrigley, Tue, 9 pm also 1 Audition show; 8/29 with Gerald Mohr 9/5/54 - 9/19/54, Wrigley, Sun
10/3/55 -11/2/56, 5t, 15m, 8:15 pm; 9:15 pm as of 4/2/56 (Bob Bailey until 12/11/60)
11/11/56 - 12/29/57, Sun, 5:30 pm
1/5/58 - 12/25/60, Sun (Bob Bailey until 11/27/60; Bob Readick as of 12/4/60)
1/1/61 - 6/18/61, Sun (Bob Readick)
6/25/61 - 9/30/62, Sun (Mandel Kramer)

Youth Asks The Government
(9/30/47 - 12/21/48) Bl, Tue, 15m, 8 pm

Youth Brings You Music
(1/1/53 - 2/15/53) NBC, Sun, 15m, 3:15 pm

Youth In the Toils (3/4/40 - 7/15/40) Bl, Mon, 15m, 7:15 pm (Youth Tells Its Story as of 6/3/40)

Youth Matinee (1/1/32 - 4/3/32) Edna Wallace Hopper, Bl, Fri, 15m, 2:45 pm

Youth Meets Government
(2/4/39 - 6/10/39) NBC, Sat, 45m, 5:15 pm

1 **Youth On Parade** (with Dolphe Martin) (6/27/42 - 8/11/45) CBS, Sat, 10 am

Youth Opportunity Program (see Horace Heidt)

Youth Questions The Headlines
(10/22/39 - 12/18/39) Bl, Mon, 9:30 pm

Youth Speaks For Itself (1940) (15m)

1 **Youth Takes A Stand** (1946) Syn

5 **Youth Tells Its Story** (6/40) Syn

Youth Versus Age (with Cal Tinney; Paul Wing as of 1/27/40)
(6/6/39 - 4/20/40) Sloan's Liniment
6/6/39 - 10/3/39, NBC, Tue, 7:30 pm
10/14/39 - 1/20/40, Bl, Sun, 8:30 pm
1/27/40 - 4/20/40, NBC, Sat, 9 pm

Youth Wants To Know
(10/12/52 - 7/5/53) NBC, Sun, 1 pm

Yvette Sings (with Elsa Harris; also with Ben Grauer) (2/19/40 - 1/12/41) NBC, 15m
2/19/40 - 3/11/40, Mon, 6 pm
3/19/40 - 8/24/40, Tue, 6:30 pm
also 3/24/40 - 1/12/41 (with Blue Barron Orchestra), Sun
also 8/31/40 - 1/11/41, Sat, 7:30 pm

RURAL RADIO NETWORK, INC.
Ithaca, New York
Title
Date
Remarks:
Speed
Filter

3 **Zane Grey Show (Theater), The** (with Vic Perrin; then Don MacLaughlin) (9/23/47 - 3/6/48) Mut, Tue, 9:30 pm

2 **Zeke Manners** (1937 - 12/23/40) Mut, 15m
1937 - 38
6/29/40 - 8/3/40, Sat
1/18/40 - 12/23/40, Mon, 1:30 pm
also 1947, Sterling Drug, ABC

8 **Zeke Manners and His Gang** (1937 - 1938) Syn

Zenith Radio Foundation (with Olan Soule) (9/5/37 - 3/27/38) Zenith, CBS, Sun, 10 pm

Zero Hour (5/2/67) ABC-TV, WOR

Zero Hour, The (see The Hollywood Radio Theatre)

2 **Zero Hour, The** (8/14/44) JLP,

1 **Zerone Jesters, The**

Zerone Program (see Dupont Zerone Jesters)

1 **Ziegfeld Follies Of The Air, The** (with Eddie Dowling, Al Goodman Orchestra) (4/3/32 - 6/26/32) Chrysler, CBS, Sun, 8:30 pm; 10:30 pm as of 4/24/32
also 1/27/36
2/22/36 - 6/6/36) (with Fanny Brice, Patti Chapin) Palmolive, CBS, Sat, 60m 8 pm

1 **Ziegfeld Girl** (1940) Air trailer

2 **Ziggy Elman and His Orchestra** (Lang-Worth transcriptions)

Zorex Moth Chasers (4/25/32 - 6/24/32) Zorex Mothcakes, CBS, 3t

1 **9:34 A. M., May 5, 1961** (5/5/61)

10-2-4 Ranch (see Ten-Two-Four Ranch)

10-2-4 Time see Ten-Two-Four Time)

1 **50s...Moments To Remember, The** (12/31/82) PBS-TV

1 **$64,000 Question, The** (5/6/55) CBS-TV

1 **150th Anniversary Of The Inauguration Of George Washington, The** (4/30/39) Bl

1 **784 Days That Changed America** (6/17/82)

1 **880 Quiz Club, The** (8/27/42) WABC

1 **1929 Wishing You A Merry Christmas** (12/25/29) Don Lee

1 **1933 Musical Revue** (12/31/33) Air trailer

1 **1936 In Review** (1/1/37) Mut

1 **1937 In Review** (1/2/38) Mut

8 **1937 Shakespeare Festival** (3/12/37 - 8/30/37) CBS

1 **1939 In Review** (1/1/40) Mut

1 **1940 In Review** (12/29/40) Mut

1 **1941 In Review** (12/28/41) Mut

1 **1943 In Review** (12/28/43) Mut

1 **1944 In Review** (12/26/44) Mut

2 **1944 March Of Dimes Campaign, The** (1944) Syn

1 **1945 Christmas Seal Campaign** (1945) Syn

1 **1945 In Review** (12/45) Mut

1 **1946 In Review** (12/26/46) Mut

1 **1946 March Of Dimes, The** (1/14/46) Syn

1 **1947 March Of Dimes Campaign** (1947) Syn

1 **1947 March Of Dimes, The** (1/15/47) Syn

1 **1948 Christmas Seal Party** (1948) Syn

4 **1948 March Of Dimes Show, The** (1/4/48, 1/9/48, 1/15/48) Syn

1 **1948 March Of Dimes, The** (1948) Syn

6 **1949 March Of Dimes, The** (12/48, 1/14/49) Syn

1 **1949 Savings Bond Show** (5/16/49) ABC

3 **1950 March Of Dimes** (1950) Syn

2 **1950 March Of Dimes, The** (1/16/50) Syn

1 **1951 March Of Dimes** (1951) Syn

1 **1951 March Of Dimes Is On The Air, The** (1951) Syn

3 **1951 March Of Dimes On The Air, The** (1951) Syn

1 **1951 Packard Radio Spots** (1951) Syn

3 **1952 Heart Fund, The** (2/1/52) Syn

3 **1953 Heart Fund, The** (2/53) Syn

4 **1953 March Of Dimes On The Air** (1/2/53) Syn

4 **1954 Heart Fund, The** (2/54) Syn

3 **1954 March Of Dimes** (1/2/54) Syn

1 **1954 March Of Dimes Is On The Air With The Fabulous Dorseys, The** (1/2/54) Syn

3 **1954 March Of Dimes Is On The Air, The** (1/2/54) Syn

1 **1954 March Of Dimes On The Air** (1/2/54) Syn

4 **1955 March Of Dimes** (1/3/55) Syn

6 **1955 March Of Dimes Is On The Air, The** (1/3/55) Syn

2 **1955 March Of Dimes, The** (1/3/55) Syn

1 **1955 Pennsylvania Cancer Crusade, The** (1955) Syn

1 **1956 Easter Seal Parade Of Stars** (2/25/56) CBS

6 **1956 March Of Dimes Is On The Air, The** (1/3/56, 1/31/56)

1 **1957 Heart Fund, The** (2/18/57) Syn

5 **1957 March Of Dimes Galaxy Of Stars, The** (1/2/57) Syn

2 **1957 March Of Dimes Is On The Air, The** (1/2/57) Syn

1 **1957 March Of Dimes Presents The One and Only Judy, The** (1/2/57) Syn

1 **1958 March Of Dimes Carousel, The** (1/2/58) Syn

5 **1958 March Of Dimes Star Carousel, The** (1/2/58) Syn

6 **1959 Cancer Crusade Musical Interludes** (1959) Syn

11 **1960 Cancer Crusade** (1960) Syn

1 **1960: Jiminy Cricket!** (9/8/47) ABC

6 **1962 Cancer Crusade** (1960) Syn

1 **1962: A TV Album** (12/30/62) CBS-TV

1 **1963: A TV Album** (12/22/63) CBS-TV

1 **1968: Up Against The Establishment** (12/31/68) WNBC-TV

1 **1969...A Record Of The Year** (1969)

1 **1973: A Television Album** (12/30/73) WCBS-TV

1 **1974: A Television Album** (12/29/74) WCBS-TV

1 **1975: The World Turned Upside Down** (1/5/75) NBC-TV

1 **1976 - 1977. What Was...What Will Be** (1/2/77) ABC-TV

1 **7382 Days In Vietnam** (4/29/75) NBC-TV

Radio People

A listing of all the names appearing in the Radio Yesteryear database. The numbers to the left of each listing represent the number of different broadcasts on which the credit appears in our files. Check for alternate spellings and billings carefully. William Ackerman is not the same person as Willy Ackerman!

> ***We The People*** *(10/4/36 - 1/25/51) 10/4/36 - 5/16/37, Calumet, Bl, Sun, 5 pm 10/7/37 - 5/12/38, Sanka, CBS, Thu, 7:30 pm; 9/27/38 - 3/10/42, Sanka, CBS, Tue, 9 pm 4/26/42 - 5/17/47, Gulf, CBS, Sun, 7:30 pm; 10:30 pm as of 6/18/44; 6/24/47 - 10/25/49, Gulf, CBS, Tue, 9 pm 11/4/49 - 9/22/50, Gulf, CBS, Fri, 8:30 pm 9/28/50 - 1/25/51, Gulf, NBC, Thu, 9:30 pm*

1	A and P Gypsies, The
1	Aadland, Beverly
1	AAF Orchestra and Chorus, The
1	AAF Orchestra, The
8	AAFTC Band, The
3	Aaron, Abe
3	Aaron, Arthur
2	Aaron, Hank
2	Abas, Nathan
1	Abato, Jimmy
1	Abbas, Mahmoud
1	Abbey, George
1	Abbey, Jean
2	Abbey, Steven
2	Abbink, John
47	Abbott, Bud
1	Abbott, Chris
2	Abbott, Diane
1	Abbott, George
15	Abbott, Gregory
2	Abbott, John
11	ABC Symphony Orchestra, The
3	Abel, Carmen
2	Abel, Elie
1	Abel, Professor
22	Abel, Walter
1	Abelow, Sam
1	Abend, Hallett
7	Abernathy, Bill
1	Abernethy, Bob
1	Abidar, Achmed
4	Abigail and Buddy
1	Abodano, Hugo
1	Abraham, Spencer
1	Abrahamson, General
1	Abramovitz, Mrs.
1	Abrams, Carl
1	Abrams, Frank W.
1	Abrams, Jacques
1	Abrams, Michael
1	Abrams, Samuel J.
1	Abravanel (Maurice Abravanel and His Orchestra)
2	Abravanel, Maurice
163	Ace, Goodman
152	Ace, Jane
13	Acheson, Dean
1	Ackerman, Eugene
1	Ackerman, Forrest
1	Ackerman, William
1	Ackerman, Willy
34	Ackers (Andrew Ackers and His Orchestra)
1	Ackerston, Rose
1	Acuff (Roy Acuff and The Cumberland Valley Boys)
62	Acuff (Roy Acuff and The Smoky Mountain Boys)
6	Acuff, Roy
1	Acuna, Mario
1	Adair, Francis
1	Adair, Jean
4	Adair, John
1	Adair, Tom
1	Adami, Louis
1	Adams, Ben
93	Adams, Bill
2	Adams, Brenda
1	Adams, Brian
1	Adams, Casell
5	Adams, Cedric
1	Adams, Charlotte
3	Adams, Christine
1	Adams, Cleve F.
1	Adams, Don
1	Adams, Eddie
9	Adams, Edie
2	Adams, Fay
64	Adams, Franklin P.
1	Adams, Gini
22	Adams, Inge
6	Adams, J. Donald
1	Adams, Jack
1	Adams, James S.
1	Adams, James Truslow
3	Adams, Joey
3	Adams, John
1	Adams, Judge
11	Adams, Julie
1	Adams, Leslie
1	Adams, Lynn
5	Adams, Mary
291	Adams, Mason
3	Adams, Paul
3	Adams, Ray
8	Adams, Stanley
7	Adams, Wiley
2	Adams, William
13	Adamson, Edward
13	Adamson, Hans Christian
6	Adamson, Helene
2	Adderly, Cannonball
1	Addis and Croffutt
1	Addleman, Elizabeth
14	Addy, Wesley
1	Adelman, Jerry
1	Adelson, Philip
121	Adlam (Basil Adlam and His Orchestra)
1	Adlam (Basil Adlam and The Hollywood Music Hall Orchestra)
101	Adlam, Basil
1	Adler, Dick
3	Adler, Felix
1	Adler, Kurt
21	Adler, Larry
3	Adler, Lou
3	Adler, Luther
1	Adler, Stella
3	Adrian
1	Adrian, George
1	AFRS Trio, The
1	Agabashian, Freddie
4	Agar, Donald
2	Agar, Herbert
3	Agar, John
2	Agar, William
16	Agate Jr., James
1	Agay (Denes Agay and His Orchestra)
3	Agnello, Virginia
1	Agnew (Charles Agnew and His Orchestra)
3	Agnew (Charlie Agnew and His Orchestra)
6	Agnew, Spiro
1	Agostini, Lucio
8	Agronsky, Martin
1	Aharon, Sharona
42	Aherne, Brian
6	Aherne, Pat
1	Ahlert, Fred
1	Ahrens, Captain
1	Ahrens, Max
1	Aidman, Charles
1	Aids, Holly
1	Aiken, Conrad
1	Aiken, David
1	Aiken, Virgil
1	Ailey, Justin
1	Ainsley, Norman
3	Air Crew, The
6	Air Force (U. S. Air Force Band, The)
4	Air Force (U. S. Air Force Dance Orchestra, The)
1	Air Force (U. S. Air Force Orchestra, The)
10	Air Force (U. S. Air Force Symphony Orchestra, The)
3	Air Force Concert Orchestra, The
1	Air Force Dance Band, The
2	Air Force Symphony Orchestra, The
1	Airmen of Note, The
1	Airto
2	Akins, Zoe
1	Akst, Harry
1	Ala, Prince
6	Alamo, Tony
5	Alba, Florence
12	Albanese, Licia
1	Albany, Ed
1	Albee Sisters, The
1	Albee, Edward
1	Alber, Beverly
1	Alberg, Somer
9	Alberghetti, Anna Maria
4	Alberni, Luis
1	Albert, Billy
1	Albert, Carl
1	Albert, Don
31	Albert, Eddie
3	Albert, Grace
3	Albert, Lee
1	Albert, Margot
5	Albertson, Frank
1	Albertson, Grace
5	Albertson, Jack
2	Albertson, Mabel
1	Albrecht, Commander
1	Albtack, Johnny
1	Alcindor, Lew
2	Alcorn, Alvin
7	Alcott, Louisa May
1	Alda, Alan
5	Alda, Robert
2	Aldebert, Monique
1	Alden, Bob
7	Alden, Daisy
5	Alden, Glen
1	Alden, Gwen
1	Alden, Mary
1	Alden, Maurey
13	Alden, Norman
1	Alden, Owen
1	Alders, Lieutenant
1	Alderson, Joan
2	Aldrich, Arnold
1	Aldrich, C. Anderson
1	Aldrin, Buzz
1	Aldrin, Louise
2	Alessi, Sam
1	Alex, Lucille
104	Alexander (Jeff Alexander and His Orchestra)
1	Alexander (Jeff Alexander and His Orchestra and Chorus)
1	Alexander (Jeff Alexander Choir, The)
23	Alexander (Jeff Alexander Chorus, The)
1	Alexander (Meyer Alexander and His Orchestra)
5	Alexander (Van Alexander and His Orchestra)
1	Alexander (Van Alexander Trio, The)
1	Alexander Brothers, The
2	Alexander, A. B.
5	Alexander, A. L.
199	Alexander, Ben
2	Alexander, Darce
15	Alexander, Denise
1	Alexander, Dorn
1	Alexander, Franz
1	Alexander, Gail
2	Alexander, Harold
2	Alexander, Janet
4	Alexander, Jeff
362	Alexander, Joan
2	Alexander, Joe
1	Alexander, June
1	Alexander, Lamar
7	Alexander, Larry
1	Alexander, Martha
10	Alexander, Ruth
1	Alexander, Will
1	Alexayev, Kyril
16	Aley, Albert
1	Alfaro, Ricardo
1	Alford, Bobby
6	Ali, Muhammed
1	All American Jazz Band, The
1	All Angels Choir, The
1	All, Thelma
1	All-American Quintet, The
15	Alland, William
2	Allbritton, Louise
2	Allen (Don Allen and His Music)
1	Allen (Don Allen and His Orchestra)
1	Allen (Jackie Allen and Barbara)
1	Allen (Richard Allen and His Orchestra)
1	Allen (Steve Allen and His Orchestra)
3	Allen, Andrew
5	Allen, Arthur
53	Allen, Barbara Jo
19	Allen, Barclay

14 Allen, Bob
1 Allen, Brooke
1 Allen, Bunny
1 Allen, C. B.
12 Allen, Casey
8 Allen, Charme
9 Allen, David
2 Allen, Dayton
5 Allen, Dorothy
67 Allen, Edward
1 Allen, Everett
230 Allen, Fred
2 Allen, Frederick Lewis
2 Allen, George
191 Allen, George W.
2 Allen, Glen
1 Allen, Gloria
269 Allen, Gracie
1 Allen, Harriet
6 Allen, Herb
1 Allen, Herbie
2 Allen, Ida Bailey
1 Allen, Ivan
17 Allen, Jack
1 Allen, James
1 Allen, Jay
1 Allen, Jerry
1 Allen, Jimmy
1 Allen, Joe
3 Allen, John
1 Allen, Joseph P.
1 Allen, Judith
1 Allen, Kay
1 Allen, Kenny
1 Allen, Lester
3 Allen, Lewis
66 Allen, Lynn
62 Allen, Mel
1 Allen, Merritt P.
1 Allen, Michael
4 Allen, Patrick
3 Allen, Paul
1 Allen, Peggy
1 Allen, Peter
21 Allen, Ray
2 Allen, Red
14 Allen, Rex
1 Allen, Richard
1 Allen, Rita
2 Allen, Robert
1 Allen, Roy
38 Allen, Steve
1 Allen, Steven
1 Allen, Stuart
1 Allen, Sue
1 Allen, Ted
2 Allen, Terry
11 Allen, Vera
1 Allenby, Frank
9 Allenby, Peggy
1 Aller, Robert
1 Allers, Franz
7 Allesandro, Victor
1 Allgood, Sarah
3 Allison (Jack Allison Sextette, The)
10 Allison, Fran
25 Allison, Jone
1 Allister, Claude
99 Allman, Elvia
1 Allman, John
1 Allman, Lenore
22 Allyson, June
1 Almanac Singers, The
1 Almond, Joyce
52 Alpert, Elaine
1 Alpert, Mickey
2 Alpert, Pauline
11 Alpert, Trigger
1 Alsop, Joel
1 Alston, Walter
3 Alter, Louis
1 Altmeyer, Arthur J.
1 Altoff, Charlie
1 Altori, Franco
3 Altschuller, Modeste
1 Alvary, Lorenzo
1 Alvin, Lionel
3 Alvin, Raymond MacDonald
4 Amadon, Bill
1 Amalgamated Dance Orchestra, The
1 Amara, Lucine
2 Amaral, Nestor
1 Amazing Randi, The
2 Ambassadors, The
1 Ambler, Eric
1 Ambrose and His Orchestra
1 Ambrose, Anthony
108 Ameche, Don
132 Ameche, Jim
1 American Folk Singers Of Boston
1 American Horse, George
2 Ames (Wilson Ames and His Orchestra)
7 Ames Brothers, The
2 Ames, Adrian
2 Ames, April
1 Ames, Barbara
2 Ames, Carol
1 Ames, Ed
2 Ames, Florence
1 Ames, Judith
4 Ames, Leon
10 Ames, Marlene
1 Ames, Thomas
1 Amfitheatrof, Daniel
4 Amison, Willard
3 Amison, William
1 Amlon, Jack
4 Ammons, Albert
1 Ammons, Felix
9 Amoroso, Johnny
1 Amory, Cleveland
1 Amoury, Daisy
1 Amright, John
21 Amsterdam Chorus, The
19 Amsterdam, Morey
26 Amundsen, Albert
25 Anders, Bill
2 Anders, Glen
1 Anders, Irene
1 Anders, Laurie
1 Anders, Merry
2 Anders, Rudolph
4 Andersen, Hans Christian
1 Andersen, Stell
2 Anderson
2 Anderson (Leroy Anderson and His Orchestra)
6 Anderson (Leroy Anderson and His Pops Orchestra)
1 Anderson, Al Cat
1 Anderson, Allen
17 Anderson, Arthur
5 Anderson, Barbara
1 Anderson, Bill
12 Anderson, Bob
1 Anderson, Casey
1 Anderson, Catherine
1 Anderson, Charles
1 Anderson, Clinton
4 Anderson, Corny
14 Anderson, David
5 Anderson, Dick
1 Anderson, Don
1 Anderson, Earle
3 Anderson, Eddie
1 Anderson, Ernest
1 Anderson, Frederick Irving
5 Anderson, Ivy
1 Anderson, Jack
1 Anderson, Jimmy
26 Anderson, John
14 Anderson, Judith
1 Anderson, Lawrence
1 Anderson, Lee
2 Anderson, Leroy
2 Anderson, Les
23 Anderson, Marian
62 Anderson, Marjorie
30 Anderson, Mary
16 Anderson, Maxwell
1 Anderson, McKeeter
1 Anderson, Mel
1 Anderson, Nancy
4 Anderson, Orville
1 Anderson, Paul
5 Anderson, Poul
3 Anderson, Ray
5 Anderson, Robert
1 Anderson, Roger
1 Anderson, Roy
2 Anderson, Sherwood
5 Andes, Keith
1 Andrade, Ray
1 Andre, Eugene
21 Andre, Pierre
1 Andres, Brad
1 Andres, Irene
62 Andrews Sisters, The
3 Andrews, Bill
1 Andrews, Bob
10 Andrews, Cameron
2 Andrews, Charlie
6 Andrews, Clark
101 Andrews, Dana
2 Andrews, Donald
3 Andrews, Ellen
17 Andrews, Ernie
12 Andrews, Garth
7 Andrews, Helen
1 Andrews, Ira
1 Andrews, John Williams
4 Andrews, Julie
1 Andrews, Laverne
1 Andrews, Lillian
1 Andrews, Lois
1 Andrews, Mae E.
2 Andrews, Mary
1 Andrews, Maxine
1 Andrews, Nancy
1 Andrews, Roy Chapman
5 Andrews, Tige
2 Andrini Trio, The
1 Andrus, Nile
9 Angel, Buckley
8 Angel, Heather
3 Angel, Wilson
1 Angelela, Michael
1 Angeles, Muriel
1 Angell, Norman
1 Angels, The
1 Anglin, Jack
1 Angus, Bob
2 Anita
3 Anka, Paul
2 Ankrum, Morris
2 Ann, Mary
5 Ann-Margret
3 Annabella
1 Anne
1 Annette
20 Ansbro, George
4 Ansermet, Ernest
1 Anson, Bill
1 Anson, Bruce
1 Antheil, George
1 Anthony (Al Anthony and His Orchestra)
1 Anthony (Ray Anthony and His Orchestra and Chorus)
20 Anthony (Ray Anthony and His Orchestra)
1 Anthony (Thomas Anthony and His Orchestra)
1 Anthony Jr., Burl
1 Anthony, Al
1 Anthony, Allan C.
4 Anthony, Bob
1 Anthony, Christopher
12 Anthony, John J.
1 Anthony, Julie
1 Anthony, Ralph
4 Anthony, Ray
1 Antima, Theodore O.
1 Antoine, Don
8 Antoine, Josephine
2 Antoine, Tex
1 Anton, Anita
32 Antonini (Alfredo Antonini and His Orchestra)
8 Antonini (Alfredo Antonini Ensemble)
13 Antonini, Alfredo
1 Antoninni (Maestro Antoninni and His Starlight Orchestra)
2 Anyos, Tom
1 Apaka, Alfred
1 Apgar, Charles
16 Aplon, Boris
1 Appel, Don
1 Apple, R. W.
2 Appleby, Ray
1 Appleby, Robert
1 Appleton, Scott
3 Applewhite, Charlie
3 Appling, Luke
5 April, Albert
1 Arafat, Yasser
2 Arbogast, Bob
1 Arbory, Guy
1 Arcane, Gene
5 Arcaro, Eddie
1 Arcaro, Jimmy
1 Archer, Bill
1 Archer, Freddy
1 Archer, Gene
1 Archer, Gleason L.
2 Archer, Jerry
3 Archer, John
4 Archer, Jules
14 Archey, Jimmy
1 Archibald, James
1 Archibald, Joe
17 Arden (Victor Arden and His Orchestra)
21 Arden and Arden
1 Arden and Ohman
122 Arden, Eve
1 Arden, Jean
39 Arden, Toni
2 Arden, Victor
1 Arena, Alberto
30 Arent, Arthur
1 Arera, Serita
1 Arevsen, John
1 Argent, Arthur
2 Argus, Don
1 Arkenstires, David
2 Arky
5 Arlen, Harold
3 Arlen, Jerry
7 Arlen, Richard
1 Arlesberg, Arthur
4 Arline
81 Arlington, Charles
2 Arliss, Florence
2 Arliss, George
5 Arliss, Joan
18 Arlo
1 Armando, Ray
33 Armbruster (Robert Armbruster and His Orchestra)
1 Armbruster (Robert Armbruster and His Radio City Orchestra)
14 Armbruster, Cyril
197 Armbruster, Robert
98 Armed Forces Radio Service Orchestra, The
3 Armed Forces Radio String Quartet, The
1 Armen (Kay Armen and The Honeydreamers)
61 Armen, Kay
1 Armetta, Henry
1 Armey, Richard
1 Armitage, Harold
2 Armor, Richard
14 Arms, Russell
1 Armstead, Alair
1 Armstrong (Bob Armstrong and His Orchestra)
5 Armstrong (Louis Armstrong and His All-Stars)
7 Armstrong (Louis Armstrong and His Orchestra)
1 Armstrong, Alice
1 Armstrong, Audrey
1 Armstrong, Bill
1 Armstrong, Bruce

1 Armstrong, Edwin
65 Armstrong, Louis
2 Armstrong, Nancy Rupley
3 Armstrong, Neil
1 Armstrong, Paul
17 Armstrong, Robert
2 Army (370th Army Air Forces Band, The)
1 Army (378th Army Service Forces Band, The)
1 Army (447th Army Service Forces Orchestra, The)
2 Army (640th Army Air Forces Band, The)
2 Army (12th Infantry Band, The)
3 Army (67th Infantry Band, The)
1 Army (6th Field Artillery Band, The)
1 Army (Eighth Army Band, The)
1 Army (Fourth Army Invaders, The)
2 Army (Official Army Air Forces Band, The)
42 Army (U. S. Army Band and Chorus, The)
22 Army (U. S. Army Band Orchestra, The)
1 Army (U. S. Army Band, The)
1 Army (U. S. Army Choir, The)
1 Army (U. S. Army Field Band and Chorus, The)
1 Army (U. S. Army Field Band, The)
1 Army (U. S. Army Symphony Orchestra, The)
51 Army (United States Army Band, The)
1 Army Air Forces Band, The
4 Army Air Forces Orchestra, The
1 Army Blues, The
1 Army Ground Forces Symphonic Band, The
9 Army Of Stars Orchestra, The
1 Arn, Freddie
4 Arnaz (Desi Arnaz and His Orchestra)
3 Arnaz, Desi
1 Arndt, Frances
1 Arnell (Artie Arnell and His Orchestra)
33 Arnell, Amy
1 Arnell, Patricia
1 Arness, James
1 Arnett, Peter
11 Arnheim (Gus Arnheim and His Orchestra)
1 Arnheim, Gus
1 Arno (Victor Arno and His Orchestra)
1 Arnold
1 Arnold (Eddy Arnold and The Wranglers)
1 Arnold (Horace Arnold Quintet, The)
1 Arnold (Murray Arnold and His Orchestra)
3 Arnold Jr., Edward
3 Arnold, Betty
1 Arnold, C. R.
49 Arnold, Eddy
153 Arnold, Edward
1 Arnold, Elliott
1 Arnold, Gene
3 Arnold, Hap
4 Arnold, Jack
2 Arnold, James
1 Arnold, Jean
1 Arnold, Jesse
1 Arnold, Lee
16 Arnold, Murray
1 Arnold, Newton
1 Arnold, Paul
1 Arnold, Peter
1 Arnold, Thurmond
44 Arnold, Wade
1 Arns, Frances
1 Aronforth, Harold
64 Arquette, Cliff
1 Arr, Mary
1 Arr, Stephen
1 Arrau, Claudio
1 Arsher, Inez
1 Arthur, Beatrice
1 Arthur, Bob
5 Arthur, Eric
4 Arthur, Hartney
10 Arthur, Jack
10 Arthur, Jean
26 Arthur, Jon
1 Arthur, Louis
16 Arthur, Louise
1 Arthur, Michael
70 Arthur, Robert A.
1 Arthurs, Ted
5 Artist, Michael
3 Artzt (William Artzt and His Orchestra)
28 Arvan, Jan
1 Arvel, Paul
1 Asbury, Herbert
1 Asch, Sam
1 Asch, Sholom
3 Ascot, Rita
8 Ash, Marvin
1 Ash, Ralph
2 Ashburn, Richie
1 Ashby, Irvin
7 Ashdown, Isa
35 Ashe, Warren
1 Ashey, Shirley
1 Ashford, Nick
10 Ashkenazy, Irvin
1 Ashley, Arthur H.
3 Ashley, Bruce
2 Ashley, Ira
1 Ashley, Irving
1 Ashley, Shirley
2 Ashman, Jane
1 Ashton, Ruth
3 Ashworth, Lou
6 Ashworth, Mary
13 Asimov, Isaac
1 Askew, John
4 Askew, Reuben
1 Askins, Barbara
2 Asnass, George
8 Asner, Edward
1 Aspe, Pedro
4 Asper, Frank W.
3 Aspin, Les
2 Astaire, Adele
27 Astaire, Fred
2 Asthma
1 Asti, Lou
6 Astin, John
19 Astor, Mary
1 Astridge, Eddie
2 Aswell, James
16 Atchison, Tex
2 Ates, Roscoe
11 Atkins, Chet
48 Atkins, Jimmy
3 Atkins, Kenneth
5 Atkinson, Brooks
1 Atkinson, Hal
1 Atkinson, Henry A.
1 Atkinson, John
8 Atlee, Clement
3 Atterbury, Duke
1 Atwater, Lee
5 Atwell, Roy
3 Atwill, Lionel
1 Atwood, Frank
8 Aubele, Lois
5 Auberjonois, Rene
1 Auburn, Jack
6 Auchincloss, Gordon
3 Auden, W. H.
44 Audley, Eleanor
1 Audrey, Robert
11 Auer, Mischa
2 Auerbach, Arnold
83 Auerbach, Artie
2 Auerbach, Larry
3 August, Jacques
5 August, Jan
1 August, Selma
1 Ault, Dorothy
1 Aumann, George
3 Aumont, Jean Pierre
1 Aurandt (Richard Aurandt and His Orchestra)
196 Aurandt, Richard
2 Aurer, Lal Shan
3 Auslander, Joseph
27 Austen, Jane
1 Austin, Bunny
1 Austin, Don
8 Austin, Gene
1 Austin, Jerry
1 Austin, Lois
70 Austin, Warren
1 Austin, William
1 Australian Jazz Quartet, The
56 Autry, Gene
3 Avalon, Frankie
1 Avalon, Lynn
301 Averback, Hy
1 Averner, Maurice
1 Avery, Carl
5 Avery, Gaylord
1 Avery, Jane
1 Avery, Paul
4 Avery, Tol
2 Avery, Tom
2 Avilla, Al
1 Avins, Perry
1 Avon Comedy Four, The
1 Axelrod, David
1 Axis Sally
1 Axman, Fred
48 Axton, Bailey
2 Aye, Marion
1 Ayers, Jackie
1 Aylesworth, M. H.
1 Aymar, Jan
1 Aymar, Jane
1 Ayme, Marcel
1 Aynesworth, Hugh
2 Aynley, Lynn
2 Aynsley, Norman
29 Ayres (Mitchell Ayres and His Orchestra)
1 Ayres, Agnes
1 Ayres, Ann
29 Ayres, Lew
3 Ayres, Mitchell
1 Aziz, Tariq
1 Aznavour, Charles
1 Azusa College Acapella Choir
2 Azuza College Choir, The
3 Azuza Pacific College Choir, The
1 Bacon, Irving
3 Bacon, Lloyd
2 Bacon, Milton
4 Bacon, Roger
2 Baer (Buddy Baer and His Orchestra)
3 Baer, Bugs
1 Baer, Jackie
1 Baer, James
3 Baer, Max
680 Baer, Parley
1 Baer, Richard
1 Baez, Joan
3 Bagby, Charles
1 Bagby, George
1 Bagdasarian, Ross
3 Baggiore, Attilio
13 Bagni, Gwen
13 Bagni, John
1 Bagwell, Gertrude
1 Bahama, Yama
2 Bailey, Ann Howard
491 Bailey, Bob
3 Bailey, Buster
2 Bailey, Ed
11 Bailey, Jack
1 Bailey, Judson
13 Bailey, Mel
41 Bailey, Mildred

1 Babbe, Owen
2 Babbitt, Bruce
26 Babbitt, Harry
1 Babison (Harry Babison and His Orchestra)
1 Babson, Monty
39 Bacall, Lauren
1 Bacar, Harry
1 Bach Aria Group
2 Bacharach, Burt
12 Bacher, William A.
1 Back, Robert
13 Backes, Alice
7 Backman, Jules
27 Backus, Georgia
1 Backus, Henny K.
117 Backus, Jim
12 Bailey, Pearl
1 Baillie, Hugh
2 Bain, Bob
4 Bain, Donald
1 Baines, Al
21 Bainter, Fay
54 Baird, Eugenie
1 Baird, Janet
3 Baird, John
2 Baird, Pamela
1 Baker (Don Baker and His Orchestra)
2 Baker (Jack Baker and The Cadets)
2 Baker Street Irregulars, The
10 Baker, Art

1 Baker, Belle
1 Baker, Benny
1 Baker, Bob
1 Baker, Chet
2 Baker, Diane
1 Baker, Don
6 Baker, Fay
2 Baker, Florence
1 Baker, Fred
30 Baker, Gene
3 Baker, Graham
8 Baker, Gretta
1 Baker, Harry
2 Baker, Henry
9 Baker, Howard
2 Baker, Jack
4 Baker, James
1 Baker, Joe
6 Baker, John
1 Baker, Josephine
1 Baker, Kenneth
181 Baker, Kenny
3 Baker, La Verne
1 Baker, Mike
29 Baker, Phil
1 Baker, Ray
1 Baker, Sy
1 Baker, Tex
1 Baker, Two Ton
2 Baker, W. W.
2 Baker, Wee Bonnie
1 Bakewell, William
1 Balcom, Carroll Healy
1 Baldanzi, George
1 Baldelli, Ray
1 Balderston, J. L.
1 Baldoni, Tony
1 Baldus Jr., Bud
1 Baldus, Frederic
59 Baldwin, Bill
1 Baldwin, Bob
1 Baldwin, Charlie
2 Baldwin, Darrell
5 Baldwin, Dick
2 Baldwin, Faith
1 Baldwin, Hanson
1 Baldwin, Lord
1 Baldwin, Marie
2 Baldwin, Mel
1 Baldwin, Roger
1 Baldwin, Senator
1 Bales, Bill
1 Balfour, Honor
1 Balkan, Bernt
2 Balkman, Lois
1 Ball, Everett
1 Ball, George W.
5 Ball, Joseph
120 Ball, Lucille
1 Ball, Olive
1 Balladiers, The
2 Ballance, Bill
3 Ballantine (Eddie Ballantine and His Orchestra)
3 Ballantine, Dave
1 Ballantine, Frank
2 Ballard, Dave
4 Ballard, Kaye
1 Ballard, Les
1 Ballard, Pat
3 Ballew, Smith
2 Ballin, Bob
139 Ballinger, Art
1 Ballinger, Stuart
1 Ballou, Dick
2 Balon, Nanette
1 Balsey, Clive
4 Balter, Sam
1 Baltimore and Ohio Railroad Chorus, The
1 Baluso (Thomas Baluso and His Orchestra)
38 Balzer, George
4 Bamber, George
7 Bampton, Rose
1 Bancroft, Penny
3 Band Of America, The
4 Band Of The AAF Training Command, The
1 Band Of The Scots Guards, The
1 Band Of The Sixth Field Artillery, The
1 Banda, Francisco
1 Bane, Collins
198 Banghart, Kenneth
1 Bankhead, Rep.
51 Bankhead, Tallulah
2 Bankhead, William
1 Banks, Aaron
1 Banks, Bruce
87 Banks, Joan
1 Banks, Leslie
2 Banks, Raymond
1 Bannister, Harry
73 Bannon, Jim
6 Bannon, Julie
1 Baptist Hour Choir, The
1 Bar-Ilan, David
8 Bara, Nina
2 Bara, Theda
5 Baragrey, John
1 Baranski, Christine
1 Barber, Charlie
1 Barber, Oliver
36 Barber, Red
2 Barber, Russell
1 Barber, Tom
1 Barbi, Vincent
1 Barbier, George
1 Barbieri, Fedora
1 Barbirolli, John
2 Barbour (Dave Barbour and His Orchestra)
2 Barbour (Dave Barbour Four, The)
3 Barbour, Dave
3 Barbour, Don
3 Barbour, Ross
1 Barboza, Alberto
6 Barclay, George
21 Barclay, John
1 Barclay, Louise
176 Bard, Kathryn
2 Bardeen, William
1 Bardy, Emanuel
3 Barfield, Becky
64 Bargy (Roy Bargy and His Orchestra)
8 Bargy, Roy
16 Bari, Lynn
1 Barile, Nick
2 Barini, Mario
13 Barker, Albert
1 Barker, Blue Lou
8 Barker, Brad
28 Barker, Danny
10 Barker, Duckworth
4 Barker, Jess
1 Barker, Lex
1 Barker, Margaret
2 Barkin, Solomon
15 Barkley, Alben
1 Barkley, Betty
1 Barkley, Roger
1 Barkus, Helen
1 Barley, Ann
2 Barlick, Al
3 Barlow (Howard Barlow and His Orchestra)
1 Barlow (Howard Barlow and His Symphony Orchestra)
24 Barlow, Howard
1 Barlowe, Connie
10 Barnes (George Barnes Octet, The)
1 Barnes, Beth
1 Barnes, Beverly
11 Barnes, Binnie
1 Barnes, Dr.
5 Barnes, Forrest
2 Barnes, George
2 Barnes, Howard
1 Barnes, Irving
1 Barnes, Jay Foster
1 Barnes, Margaret Ayer
1 Barnes, Norman
40 Barnes, Pat
200 Barnes, Paul
29 Barnet (Charlie Barnet and His Orchestra)
7 Barnet, Charlie
2 Barnett (Arnie Barnett and His Orchestra)
1 Barnett, Albert E.
79 Barnett, Griff
1 Barnett, John
1 Barnett, Mary
1 Barnett, Reed
9 Barnett, S. H.
1 Barnett, Sonny
2 Barnett, Vince
1 Barney, Jay
1 Barnhardt, Jeffrey
3 Barnhart, Ralph
44 Barnouw, Erik
1 Barnum, H. B.
1 Barnum, Keith
1 Barnum, P. P.
2 Barnum, Pete
47 Baron (Paul Baron and His Orchestra)
1 Baron, Bob
1 Baron, Frank
1 Baron, Jack
1 Baron, Martha
7 Baron, Paul
2 Baron, Roger
1 Barr, Fred
1 Barr, Fred J.
2 Barr, George
1 Barr, William
1 Barracks Bag Players, The
1 Barrand, Paul
1 Barrett Sisters, The
1 Barrett, Bernice
2 Barrett, Edith
1 Barrett, Leslie
70 Barrett, Michael Ann
1 Barrett, Patricia
1 Barrett, Ray
1 Barrett, Robert
260 Barrett, Tony
4 Barrie, Betty
1 Barrie, Elaine
11 Barrie, James M.
1 Barrie, Lester
31 Barrie, Wendy
173 Barrier, Edgar
2 Barrio, Art
4 Barris, Harry
6 Barron (Blue Barron and His Orchestra)
1 Barrow, Virginia
1 Barrows, Cliff
5 Barry Sisters, The
1 Barry, Charles
5 Barry, Dave
1 Barry, David
5 Barry, Donald
2 Barry, Elaine
3 Barry, Eleanor
1 Barry, Felix
1 Barry, Gene
1 Barry, Gracie
5 Barry, Ivor
9 Barry, Jack
1 Barry, James
1 Barry, Jim
1 Barry, John
1 Barry, Ken
1 Barry, Mona
18 Barry, Peter
7 Barry, Philip
1 Barry, Vivian
51 Barry, Warren
1 Barrymore Jr., John
1 Barrymore, Diana
13 Barrymore, Ethel
40 Barrymore, John
191 Barrymore, Lionel
1 Bart, Jan
1 Bartell, Bab
5 Bartell, Freddy
500 Bartell, Harry
1 Bartell, Jean
1 Bartell, Mel
1 Barth, Charles
1 Barth, Diana
2 Barthelme, Donald
3 Barthelmess, Richard
11 Bartholomew, Freddie
4 Bartlett and Robinson
1 Bartlett, Ken
44 Bartlett, Marjorie
1 Bartlett, Richard
2 Bartlett, Tommy
2 Bartlett, Vernon
1 Bartok, Bela
1 Bartok, Ditta
1 Barton, Bruce
4 Barton, Dan
25 Barton, Eileen
37 Barton, Frank
3 Barton, Fred
3 Barton, Hal
6 Barton, Helen Townsend
1 Barton, Irene
1 Barton, James
4 Barton, Joan
1 Barton, Joe
1 Barton, June
1 Barton, Ken
1 Barton, Michael
7 Barton, Phil
2 Barton, Vera
1 Barton, William
1 Baruch, Mrs. Bernard
5 Basehart, Richard
79 Basie (Count Basie and His Orchestra)
27 Basie, Count
1 Basilevsky, Alexander
3 Basillio, Carmen
1 Basin Street Boys, The
6 Baskerville, David
1 Baskus, James
43 Basquette, James
1 Basquette, Lina
7 Bass, Leonard L.
3 Bassett, John A.
1 Bassett, William
1 Basso, Hamilton
2 Bast, Roy
1 Bastin, Charles
1 Bastion, James W.
4 Bat, Miles
2 Batchelder, Charles
2 Batchelder, John
1 Bates, Bill
1 Bates, Elizabeth
4 Bates, Florence
4 Bates, Fred
1 Bates, Granville
1 Bates, H. E.
175 Bates, Jeanne
1 Bates, Ken
3 Bates, Lulu
3 Bates, Ralph
1 Bates, Russell
1 Bathgate, Andy
27 Batista, Lloyd
1 Batten, Tony
1 Battle, John D.
2 Battle, John Tucker
1 Batts, M. P.
2 Baucon, Robert
1 Bauduc (Ray Bauduc and His Combo)
3 Bauduc, Ray
20 Bauer, Charita
1 Bauer, Elaine
2 Bauer, Hank
1 Bauer, Rosalie
5 Bauer, W. W.
2 Baugh, Sammy
23 Baukhage, H. R.
5 Baukum, Bill
2 Baukus, Max
1 Baul, Phil
2 Baum, Claire
1 Baum, Harold
1 Baum, L. Frank
1 Baum, Vicki
1 Baumgartner, Hank

8 Baumgartner, Herb
1 Baur, Franklyn
3 Bavaar, Tony
1 Bavaro (Bill Bavaro and His Raggediers)
2 Bavaro, Bill
1 Bavasi, Buzzy
1 Baver, Siegfried
1 Bax, Roger
5 Baxter (Les Baxter and His Orchestra)
1 Baxter (Les Baxter and The Voices Of The Orchestra)
11 Baxter, Alan
24 Baxter, Anne
3 Baxter, Frank
1 Baxter, Jane
1 Baxter, Jimmy
1 Baxter, Laura
1 Baxter, Les
2 Baxter, Tom
4 Baxter, Warner
1 Bay, Boots
1 Bay, Frances
1 Bay, Nee Da
3 Bayes, Gus
1 Bayh, Birch
1 Baylo, Denes
1 Baylor, Dave
3 Baylor, Elgin
1 Baytown Four, The
1 Bazaar, Joseph
2 BBC Symphony Orchestra, The
1 Beach Boys, The
2 Beach, Jim
1 Beach, Olive Mae
1 Beach, William
2 Beachcombers, The
1 Beaham III, Gordon
1 Beal, Joan
28 Beal, John
1 Beal, Kenny
1 Beal, Royal
8 Beal, William
1 Bealby, Vangie
1 Beale, Charles
1 Beale, Lewis
3 Bealen, Frank
1 Beall, Jack
112 Beals, Dick
1 Beals, Joseph
4 Bean, Alan
1 Bean, Floyd
2 Bean, Orson
1 Bean, Reginald
1 Bear, Richard
5 Beard, Betsy
1 Beard, Stanley
1 Beardon, Joseph
5 Beasley, Irene
2 Beatles, The
1 Beattie, Ed
13 Beatty, Clyde
1 Beatty, Harriet
1 Beatty, Jane
1 Beatty, Jim
14 Beatty, Lane
33 Beatty, Morgan
1 Beauchamp, Bud
1 Beaudine Jr., Maurice
2 Beaumont, Kathryn
1 Beaumont, Lorraine
2 Beavers, Louise
2 Beazley, Johnny
1 Bechet, Allen
15 Bechet, Sidney
1 Bechet, Warren
3 Bechtel, Harry
1 Beck, Barney
1 Beck, Dave
2 Beck, Eve
3 Beck, George
1 Beck, Hal
1203 Beck, Jackson
1 Beck, Josef
1 Beck, Reginald
1 Beck, Roger
2 Beckenback, Edwin
5 Becker, Barbara
1 Becker, Bob
1 Becker, Don
1 Becker, Lei
1 Becker, R.
25 Becker, Sandy
18 Beckett, Scotty
2 Beckley, Zoe
4 Beckner (Denny Beckner and His Orchestra)
1 Beckner, Denny
1 Beckner, Garry
1 Beddingfield, Sam
1 Bedelia, Bonnie
1 Bedell, Ruth
1 Bedford, Brian
1 Bednarik, Chuck
2 Bee, Molly
2 Beebe, Lucius
1 Beecham, Lady Thomas
2 Beecham, Thomas
5 Beecher, Janet
1 Beedey, Douglas
1 Beedle-Smith, General
267 Beemer, Brace
9 Beers, Bobby
7 Beers, Marvin
3 Beery Jr., Noah
3 Beery, Carol Ann
9 Beery, Noah
28 Beery, Wallace
2 Beeson, Eleanor
1 Beethoven String Quartet, The
1 Beetle
1 Begay, Andrew
9 Beggs, James
2 Begin, Menachem
140 Begley, Ed
1 Begon, Jack
1 Begtrup, Mrs. Bodil
2 Begue, John
13 Behrens, Bernard
3 Behrman, S. N.
1 Beisho, Allen
1 Beith, John Hay
3 Bekey, Ivan
9 Bel Geddes, Barbara
11 Belafonte, Harry
1 Belager, Lupe
1 Belaire, Malcolm
1 Belange, Paul
1 Belasco, David
33 Belasco, Leon
1 Belasco, Norman
1 Belcher, Jerry
1 Belding, Don
4 Belew, Leland
1 Belinson, Anthony
1 Bell (Graham Bell and His Australian Jazz Band)
3 Bell Orchestra, The
7 Bell Sisters, The
1 Bell Symphonic Orchestra, The
3 Bell Telephone Orchestra, The
1 Bell, Aaron
1 Bell, Chris
1 Bell, Dick
13 Bell, Don
2 Bell, Frederick
1 Bell, Jack
3 Bell, James
29 Bell, Joseph
3 Bell, Marion
2 Bell, Neil
1 Bell, Nicky
4 Bell, Orth
189 Bell, Ralph
1 Bell, Raymond
1 Bell, Steven
26 Bell, Ted
1 Bellabio, Dennis
1 Bellaire, Robert
1 Bellak, James Warner
2 Bellamann, H. H.
5 Bellamy, Albert
88 Bellamy, Ralph
1 Belle, La
1 Belle, Lulu
1 Bellinger, Admiral
1 Bellinger, Steve
1 Bellini, Mario
2 Bellis, Guy
1 Bellock, George
9 Bellson, Louis
1 Belmont, Terry
5 Belmore, Lionel
17 Beloin, Ed
1 Belova, Harry
1 Bemick, Ruth Vital
1 Bemmelmans, Ludwig
6 Ben Gurion, David
480 Benaderet, Bea
1 Benay, Vickie
2 Bench, Bob
2 Benchley, Nathaniel
25 Benchley, Robert
6 Bender, Charles E.
20 Bender, Dawn
1 Bender, Russell
157 Bendix, William
1 Benedes, Dick
1 Benedict, Brooks
2 Benedict, Eleanor
3 Benedict, Richard
19 Beneke (Tex Beneke and His Orchestra)
33 Beneke, Tex
3 Benes, Eduard
36 Benet, Stephen Vincent
1 Benike, Abe
1 Benkin, Dr.
6 Bennett, Arnold
1 Bennett, Bernice
4 Bennett, Betty
2 Bennett, Bruce
7 Bennett, Burton
1 Bennett, Charles
1 Bennett, Charlie
8 Bennett, Constance
1 Bennett, Frank
1 Bennett, Janey
1 Bennett, Jay
1 Bennett, Jean
38 Bennett, Joan
1 Bennett, John
13 Bennett, Julie
29 Bennett, Lee
1 Bennett, Louis
3 Bennett, Marjorie
2 Bennett, Mary
1 Bennett, Melba
2 Bennett, Nan
1 Bennett, R. B.
1 Bennett, Rain
1 Bennett, Richard
1 Bennett, Robert
1 Bennett, Robert Russell
1 Bennett, Russell
6 Bennett, Tom
22 Bennett, Tony
21 Bennett, Vern
1 Bennett, William
1 Benny The Fan
857 Benny, Jack
1 Benny, Joan
19 Benoff, Mac
128 Benson, Court
1 Benson, Ezra Taft
6 Benson, George
1 Benson, Joan
1 Benson, Kenny
2 Benson, Lorraine
1 Benson, Red
1 Benson, Walter
4 Benti, Joseph
3 Bentkover, Jack
1 Bentley, Bob
2 Bentley, E. C.
2 Bentley, Elizabeth
1 Bentley, Gladys
2 Bentley, June
1 Benton, Barbara
1 Benton, Mike
2 Benton, Nelson
16 Bentsen, Lloyd
2 Bentz, Robert
12 Benzell, Mimi
1 Beranus (Walter Beranus and His Lido Club Orchestra)
15 Berch, Jack
2 Berdahl, Archie
1 Berdoni, Don
1 Berens, Carl
1 Berenson, Carl
22 Berenson, Irving
11 Berg, Gertrude
1 Bergen Symphony Orchestra, The
1 Bergen, Bobby
2 Bergen, Candice
201 Bergen, Edgar
4 Bergen, Frances
8 Bergen, Polly
32 Berger, Jay
7 Berger, Sylvia
4 Berghart, Betty
9 Bergman, Alan
2 Bergman, Herbert John
36 Bergman, Ingrid
8 Bergman, Jules
1 Bergman, Lee
1 Bergman, Peter
1 Bergner, Elisabeth
1 Bergoff, Herbert
3 Berigan (Bunny Berigan and His Orchestra)
5 Berigan, Bunny
3 Berkeley, Busby
1 Berkova, Sondra
1 Berkovici, Conrad
5 Berkowitz, William
1 Berle, Adolph
92 Berle, Milton
1 Berle, Mrs. Milton
1 Berlin, Guy
15 Berlin, Irving
3 Berlin, Margaret
1 Berlin, Mrs. Irving
92 Berman, Albert
1 Berman, Ben Lucien
1 Berman, Bob
2 Berman, Edward H.
4 Berman, Ruth
2 Berman, Shelly
1 Bern, Brooke
1 Bernard (Jack Bernard and His Orchestra)
1 Bernard, Betty
1 Bernard, Butch
1 Bernard, Connie
38 Bernard, Don
2 Bernard, Paul
28 Bernard, Tommy
1 Bernard, William S.
1 Bernardi, Herschel
1 Bernatowicz, Dan
1 Berner, Charlotte
86 Berner, Sara
4 Bernhardt, Ernie
1 Bernhardt, Prince
2 Bernhardt, Sarah
1 Bernie (Ben Bernie and His Hotel Roosevelt Orchestra)
19 Bernie (Ben Bernie and His Orchestra)
2 Bernie, Al
14 Bernie, Ben
1 Bernie, Lee
43 Berns, Larry
1 Bernstein (Elmer Bernstein and His Orchestra)
1 Bernstein, Arthur
3 Bernstein, Carl
1 Bernstein, Kenneth
7 Bernstein, Leonard
2 Bernstein, Robert L.
2 Berra, Yogi
1 Berratin, General
11 Berrens, Frank
2 Berry, Charles
4 Berry, Chu
3 Berry, Chuck
1 Berry, Don
1 Berry, Eleanor

1 Berry, Ellen
1 Berry, Emmett
3 Berry, John
5 Berry, Ken
1 Berry, Milton H.
9 Berry, Norman
1 Berry, Peter
1 Berry, Raymond
1 Berry, Richard
1 Berry, Sidney
1 Bert, Gil
1 Berth, Jack
1 Berton (Vic Berton and His Artistic Swing)
5 Berton, Pierre
1 Bervridge, Bill
3 Berwick, Viola
4 Berwin, Bernice
1 Besley, Ted
1 Bessabera, Beatrice
3 Besse, Arthur
1 Besse, Ralph M.
1 Bessell, Hal
13 Besser, Joe
2 Besser, Wally
1 Bessier, Rudolph
12 Best, Edna
6 Best, Lois
2 Best, Marvin
1 Best, Robert
1 Best, Samuel M.
11 Bester, Alfred
3 Bester, Rolly
1 Bestoff, Virginia
20 Bestor (Don Bestor and His Orchestra)
2 Bestor, Don
1 Bestor, Wally
1 Beth (Mack Beth The Great and His Orchestra)
1 Bethune, Mary McLeon
22 Bettencort, Jose
4 Bettencourt (Frank Bettencourt and His Orchestra)
5 Bettencourt, Frank
1 Bettman, Iphigene
1 Betty
1 Beutel, Bill
1 Bevan, Billy
7 Bevarro (Phil Bevarro and His Orchestra)
2 Beverly
1 Beverly, Elaine
1 Beverly, Helen
1 Bevin, Bill
2 Bevin, Ernest
1 Bevins, Clem
3 Bey (Victor Bey and His Orchestra)
4 Bey, Turhan
3 Bey, Victor
1 Bezel, Tom
3 Bibb, Leon
1 Bibbers, Carlisle
1 Bible, Francis
1 Bibo, Irving
1 Biby, Mary Alice
12 Bickart, Sanford
1 Bickel, Art
1 Bickford
8 Bickford, Charles
3 Biddell, Roger T.
1 Biddle, George
2 Biden, Joseph
1 Bidwell, Percy W.
1 Bieler, Manfred
2 Bielman, Pete
1 Bienstock, Victor
2 Bierbauer, Charles
11 Bierce, Ambrose
3 Bierce, Jane
2 Bierman, Jack
2 Bierson, Lawrence
18 Bigard, Barney
4 Bigelow, Joe
3 Biggers, Earl Derr
1 Biggs, E. Power
3 Bigley, Isobel
1 Bigley, William
4 Bikel, Theodore
1 Bileck, Charlie
1 Billian, Ross
5 Billingham, John
2 Billings, Charles
1 Billings, Josh
1 Billingsley, Jackie
6 Billingsley, Sherman
54 Billsbury, Rye
2 Binder, Carroll
1 Bing, Geoffrey
2 Bing, Herman
1 Bing, Rudolph
1 Bingaman, Jeff
1 Bingham, Alfred
1 Bingham, Barry
2 Bingham, Jeff
24 Bingman, Frank
1 Binns, Ed
12 Binyon, Conrad
1 Birch, William N.
1 Bircher, Ralph
2 Bird, Larry
5 Birdbath, Dr. Horatio Q.
1 Birkhead, Leon M.
1 Birkson, Seymour
15 Birman, Len
1 Birnbaum, Louis
1 Birnbrier, Edmond
1 Birnell, Bonnie
1 Birney, Louis L.
4 Birquist (Whitey Birquist and His Orchestra)
38 Birquist (Whitey Birquist and The Homesteaders)
1 Birquist (Whitey Birquist and The NBC Ensemble)
11 Birquist (Whitey Birquist and The NBC Orchestra)
1 Birquist (Whitey Birquist and The Solitaires)
9 Birquist, Bernard
21 Birquist, Whitey
1 Bish, Charles
1 Bishop, Adelaide
1 Bishop, Ann
1 Bishop, Jim
5 Bishop, Joe
2 Bishop, Joey
1 Bishop, Julie
1 Bishop, Scott
2 Bishop, Sheldon Hale
1 Bishop, Ted
1 Bishop, William
1 Bisiroff, Michael
1 Bissell, Ben
2 Bissell, Bill
18 Bivens, Bill
3 Bivens, Jack
8 Bivona, Gus
1 Bixby, Bill
2 Bixby, Carl
1 Bixby, Jerome
3 Bjoerling, Jussi
1 Black (Frank Black and His Orchestra and Chorus)
23 Black (Frank Black and His Orchestra)
5 Black (Ted Black and His Orchestra)
3 Black and White
2 Black, A.G.
2 Black, Alan
1 Black, Betty
3 Black, Bill
1 Black, Buddy
3 Black, David
1 Black, Doris
1 Black, Edward A.
52 Black, Frank
6 Black, Governor
1 Black, Hilda
1 Black, Hugo
1 Black, Joe
2 Black, Valerie
15 Black, Walter
5 Blackburn, Arlene
5 Blackburn, Clarice
1 Blackburn, Tom
7 Blackmer, Sidney
39 Blackstone, Harry
1 Blackstone, Oran
9 Blackton (Jay Blackton and His Orchestra)
2 Blackton, Jay
1 Blackwell, Ewell
1 Blackwood Brothers, The
4 Blackwood, Algernon
1 Blade, Jimmy
6 Blaine, Jimmy
2 Blaine, Joan
1 Blaine, Judy
6 Blaine, Martin
20 Blaine, Vivian
1 Blaine, William
21 Blainey, Ed
1 Blair, Betsy
14 Blair, Frank
21 Blair, Henry
32 Blair, Janet
2 Blair, Jimmy
1 Blair, Judith
2 Blair, Stewart
1 Blair, William
1 Blake, Amanda
4 Blake, Cameron
2 Blake, Carter
3 Blake, Cici
3 Blake, Eubie
1 Blake, George
1 Blake, Larry
1 Blake, Leonard
9 Blake, Meredith
1 Blake, Nicholas
2 Blake, Pamela
2 Blake, Peggy
1 Blakey (Art Blakey All Stars)
2 Blakey (Art Blakey and The Jazz Messengers)
3 Blakely, Don
5 Blakely, Rubel
1 Blakeslee, Alton
3 Blakey, Art
318 Blanc, Mel
2 Blanchard, Doc
1 Bland, Lee
11 Blandick, Clara
1 Blanding, Claire
2 Blandon, Ned
3 Blandy, Admiral
2 Blandy, Vice Admiral
1 Blane, Ralph
7 Blane, Rose
4 Blank, Shirley
1 Blankenhorn, David
1 Blankford, Michael
1 Blanton, Floyd
2 Blanton, Jimmy
1 Blarda, George
1 Blast, Ingrid
2 Blattner, Bud
2 Blau, Faith
4 Blau, Raphael David
1 Blaufuss (Walter Blaufuss and His Orchestra)
1 Blaustein, Jacob
1 Blaustein, Julian
1 Blayhos, John
1 Blazedale, Walter
1 Bleasedale, Jack
1 Bledso, Jules
2 Blesh (Rudi Blesh's All-Star Stompers)
32 Blesh, Rudi
2 Bletcher, Billy
90 Bleyer (Archie Bleyer and His Orchestra)
1 Bleyer (Archie Bleyer Trio)
39 Bleyer, Archie
1 Blifer, John
1 Blileven, Gerard
1 Blileven, Mrs. Gerard
1 Blish, James
1 Bliss, Arthur
1 Bliss, Lucille
3 Bliss, Milt
49 Bliss, Ted
3 Blitzer, Wolf
3 Bliven, Bruce
1 Bloch (Ray Bloch and His Choir)
1 Bloch (Ray Bloch and His Dixieland All-Stars)
253 Bloch (Ray Bloch and His Orchestra)
1 Bloch, Hal
2 Bloch, Jesse
1 Bloch, Mildred
2 Bloch, Ray
1 Blochman, Lawrence
1 Block and Sully
1 Block, Admiral
1 Block, Bertram
169 Block, Martin
2 Block, Robert
1 Blocker, Dan
1 Blockie, Fritz
58 Blondell, Gloria
26 Blondell, Joan
1 Blood, Wallace
10 Bloodworth, Edward
1 Bloodworth, James
3 Bloom, Harold Jack
1 Bloor, William F.
9 Blore, Eric
1 Blow, Joe
3 Blowers, Johnny
1 Bloxom, Bill
2 Bluder, Patsy
5 Blue Coal Mammy, The
6 Blue Flames, The
25 Blue Jackets, The
4 Blue Jeans, The
1 Blue Jivers, The
7 Blue Notes, The
1 Blue Ribboneers, The
7 Blue, Ben
1 Blue, Monte
1 Bluestone (Harry Bluestone and The Air Force Orchestra)
3 Bluestone (Harry Bluestone and The Band Of The Armed Forces Training Command)
1 Bluestone, Harry
3 Blum, Audrey
1 Blum, Margot
1 Blume, Joseph
2 Blume, Sol
1 Blunt, Gabriel
1 Blute, Peter
1 Bluth, B. J.
1 Blyberg, Bob
2 Blyden, Larry
1 Blyforce, John
26 Blyth, Ann
7 Blythe, Betty
1 Boal, Pierre
4 Boardman, Nan
48 Boardman, True
9 Boataneers, The
1 Boatwright, McHenry
1 Bob-O-Links, The
11 Bobcats, The
1 Bober, Eva
2 Bobko
5 Bochner, Lloyd
1 Boden, Beryl
1 Bodine, Russ
1 Bodkin, A.L.
1 Bodra, Richard
1 Bodyguards, The
1 Boehm, Carla
1 Boehner, John
1 Boel, Pol
1 Bogarde, Dirk
66 Bogart, Humphrey
1 Boggess, Nancy
1 Boggs, Bill
1 Boggs, Frank
1 Boggs, Governor
1 Boggs, Lind
2 Boggs, Noel
36 Bogue, Merwyn
1 Bohn, Frank
1 Bokeman, Lois
1 Bolan, Patty

1 Boland, Arthur
17 Boland, Joseph
9 Boland, Mary
1 Boland, Shannon
1 Bolcomb, Bill
2 Boles, Jack
146 Boles, Jim
14 Boles, John
1 Boles, Mary Lee
1 Boley, Ann
14 Bolger, Ray
1 Bollinger, Anne
1 Bollits, Rick
1 Bolt, S. A.
1 Bolton, Guy
1 Bolton, Isabel
8 Bolton, Joseph
1 Bolton, Matthew
2 Bolton, Muriel Roy
1 Bolton, Patsy
1 Bolton, Whitney
1 Bombadiers, The
2 Bomberg, Robert
1 Bon (Angie Bon Trio, The)
9 Bon Bon
1 Bonano (Sharky Bonano and His Sharks Of Rhythm)
1 Bonanova, Fortunio
1 Bonaparte, Jerome Napoleon
3 Bond (Johnny Bond and His Red River Valley Boys)
1 Bond (Johnny Bond and The Cass County Boys)
1 Bond, Bill
2 Bond, Bryce
1 Bond, Derek
194 Bond, Ford
16 Bond, Johnny
1 Bond, Kit
3 Bond, Lillian
1 Bond, Lyle
10 Bond, Nelson
1 Bond, Ted
1 Bond, Vivian
1 Bond, Walter
11 Bond, Ward
11 Bondi, Beulah
1 Bonds, Bill
1 Bonds, Erbie
1 Bonds, Forrest
1 Bonell, Robert
1 Bonell, William
1 Bongiorno, Carlo
6 Bonier, David
1 Bonilla, Henry
1 Bonime (Josef Bonime and His Orchestra)
1 Bonker, Don
1 Bonnel, Lee
1 Bonney, Betty
18 Bonney, Gail
2 Bonnie Sisters, The
1 Bonowitz, Carl
1 Bonser, Allen
1 Booker T and The MGs
9 Boone County Buccaneers, The
2 Boone, David
46 Boone, F. E.
33 Boone, Pat
2 Boone, Richard
6 Boone, Robert
1 Boot, Jason
1 Booth, Bill
1 Booth, Carleton
1 Booth, Charles
1 Booth, Clayton
34 Booth, Shirley
1 Boothe, Clare
1 Boran, Arthur
2 Borden (Ray Borden and His Orchestra)
1 Borden, Betty
1 Borden, Marshall
1 Bordoni, Irene
1 Borenshein, Franz
8 Boretz, Alvin
1 Borgan, Bob
54 Borge, Victor
1 Borger, Bob
2 Borger, Gloria
1 Borghesa, G. A.
2 Borgnine, Ernest
2 Bori, Lucrezia
1 Boris, Anthony
2 Borman, Frank
1 Born (Hal Born and His Orchestra)
1 Born, Hal
1 Born, Ruth
1 Boroso, Jose
1 Bosch, Henry
6 Bose, Sterling
1 Boskin, Michael
2 Bosley, Tom
1 Bostik, Joe
1 Boston (State Symphony Of Boston, The)
14 Boston Pops, The
4 Boston Symphony Orchestra, The
8 Boswell Sisters, The
70 Boswell, Connie
1 Bosworth, Hobart
1 Bothwell, Johnny
6 Botkin (Perry Botkin and His Orchestra)
2 Botkin (Perry Botkin and Trio)
20 Botkin, Perry
7 Bottcher, Ed
1 Bottomly, Roland
6 Botzer, Alan
55 Boucher, Anthony
49 Bouchey, Bill
2 Boudreau, Frank
3 Boudreau, Lou
3 Boult, Adrian
20 Boulton, Milo
1 Bourbon, Diana
3 Bourgholtzer, Frank
4 Bourneuf, Phillip
2 Bovasso, Julie
1 Bovay, Peter
5 Bowe, Morton
1 Bowe, Peter
1 Bowen, Charles
3 Bowen, Elizabeth
8 Bower, Antoinette
1 Bower, Ray
18 Bower, Roger
1 Bowers, Dan
3 Bowers, Emma K.
1 Bowers, Kenny
1 Bowers, Richard
6 Bowers, Robert Hood
1 Bowers, Ruth
3 Bowersmith, Paula
17 Bowes, Edward
3 Bowes, Margie
2 Bowie, Michael
3 Bowles, Chester
1 Bowlly, Al
1 Bowman (John Bowman and His Orchestra)
1 Bowman, Dave
42 Bowman, Lee
2 Bowman, Roger
1 Bowser, Buddy
1 Bowyer, C. S.
1 Boxer, Barbara
1 Boxer, Ben Zion
1 Boyce, Alfred
1 Boyd Jr., William R.
2 Boyd, Bobby
1 Boyd, Bonnie
1 Boyd, Eugene
1 Boyd, Forrest
1 Boyd, Harry
1 Boyd, Henry
2 Boyd, James
1 Boyd, Ralph
1 Boyd, Shorty
1 Boyd, Stephen
117 Boyd, William
2 Boyer, Anita
47 Boyer, Charles
1 Boyer, Clete
2 Boyer, Ken
2 Boyer, Lucien
5 Boyer, Robert
2 Boyer, Tryon
1 Boyington, Gregory
2 Boylan, Buddy
6 Boyle, Betty
1 Boyle, Kay
1 Boys and Girls Of Manhattan, The
1 Boys Choir Of St. Phillips Church, The
2 Boys In The Back Room, The
2 Bracha, Illya
1 Bracken, Charles
19 Bracken, Eddie
2 Brackett, Charles
60 Bradbury, Ray
3 Braddock, James J.
3 Braden, Bernard
1 Braden, Miss
1 Braden, Spruille
1 Braden, Stu
1 Bradford, Johnny
2 Bradford, Louise
1 Bradford, Ronald
13 Bradley (Oscar Bradley and His Orchestra)
1 Bradley (Oscar Bradley Orchestra, The)
4 Bradley (Owen Bradley and His Orchestra)
16 Bradley (Will Bradley and His Jazz Octet)
6 Bradley (Will Bradley and His Orchestra)
1 Bradley, Anne
4 Bradley, Betty
1 Bradley, Bill
14 Bradley, Curley
1 Bradley, Ed
1 Bradley, Harry
1 Bradley, Jack
2 Bradley, Jim
1 Bradley, Joe
21 Bradley, Omar
2 Bradley, Oscar
1 Bradley, Steve
187 Bradley, Truman
4 Bradley, Will
2 Bradne, Olympe
3 Bradshaw (Tiny Bradshaw and His Orchestra)
1 Bradshaw, Terry
2 Bradshaw, Tiny
1 Brady, Alice
4 Brady, Ben
2 Brady, Ed
1 Brady, June
1 Brady, Nicholas
49 Brady, Pat
2 Brady, Ruth
1 Brady, Scott
1 Brady, Stuart
1 Brady, William A.
1 Braff (Ruby Braff-George Barnes Quartet, The)
1 Bragen, Bobby
17 Braham, Horace
1 Brained, Lefty
1 Braislin, Johnny
1 Bramlet, Leon
2 Branca, Ralph
1 Branch, John
3 Branch, Judy
1 Branch, William
1 Brand, Elsa
1 Brand, Jack
1 Brand, Max
15 Brand, Oscar
1 Brand, Stewart
8 Brand, Vance
1 Brandhorst, Henry
3 Brando, Marlon
1 Brandon (Harry Brandon and His Orchestra)
2 Brandon (Henry Brandon and His Orchestra)
4 Brandon, Dorothy
1 Brandon, Henry
1 Brandon, Joan
1 Brandon, Martha
2 Brands, Celia
1 Brandt, Bill
80 Brandt, Mel
2 Brandwynne (Nat Brandwynne and His Orchestra)
4 Brandwynne, Nat
1 Brandy, Harold
5 Brann, Gilbert
2 Brann, Ruth
1 Brannigan, Bill
1 Brannon, Charles Franklin
1 Branstadter, Eddie
2 Brant, Loppy
1 Brant, R. N.
12 Brasfield, Rod
1 Brasis, Algard
6 Brass, Ralph
3 Brasselle, Keefe
1 Brastov, Sasha
1 Braud, Wellman
3 Braun, Peter Leonhard
1 Bravender, Susan
3 Braxton, Robin
1 Bray, Dick
1 Braytenbaugh, Dick
36 Brayton, Margaret
1 Breaux, John
1 Brecher, Earl
57 Brecher, Irving
15 Brecher, Jack
2 Breckenridge, Betty
1 Brecker Brothers, The
1 Breckinridge, Henry
1 Bredt, James
1 Breechen, Harry
15 Breen, Bobby
4 Breen, May Singhi
4 Breen, Richard
2 Brees, Buddy
1 Breese (Lou Breese and His Breezy Rhythm)
6 Breese, Sidney
2 Breeze, Edmund C.
2 Bregman (Buddy Bregman and His Orchestra)
1 Bregman, Adolph
2 Brel, Jacques
21 Bremner, Muriel
4 Brendler, Charles
8 Breneman, Tom
1 Brennan, Patrick
2 Brennan, Pete
1 Brennan, Terry
20 Brennan, Walter
2 Brenner, Ray
1 Brenner, Sarah
3 Brennerman, Aldine
1 Brenson, Cheer
6 Brent, Carol
1 Brent, Evelyn
18 Brent, George
38 Brent, Rhoda
7 Brent, Romney
6 Bresee, Frank
1 Bresher, Ewald T.
1 Breslin, Howard
2 Breslin, Jimmy
2 Bressart, Felix
1 Brested Jr., James H.
2 Brett, Harris
2 Brett, Robin
1 Brett, Rufus
1 Bretton, Donna
17 Breuer, Harry
4 Breur, Betty
1 Breverton, Vivian
1 Brewer, David
1 Brewer, Fred
1 Brewer, Harriet
4 Brewer, Jameson
11 Brewer, Teresa
1 Brewster (Ralph Brewster Singers, The)
6 Brewster, John
1 Brewster, June

2 Brewster, Margaret
1 Brewster, Neal
1 Breyer, Stephen
5 Brian Sisters, The
28 Brian, David
56 Brian, Donald
2 Brian, Warren
1 Briand, Guy
1 Briar, Denise
123 Brice, Fanny
1 Brice, Ronald
1 Bricken, Carl
1 Bricker, Carlton
1 Bricker, Governor
1 Bricker, Sanford
7 Brickhouse, Jack
1 Bricknell, George
6 Bridges, Lloyd
1 Bridges, Lorraine
1 Bridges, Stiles
1 Bridges, Victor
2 Brierly, Art
1 Briggs, Bunny
30 Briggs, Don
6 Briggs, Geoffrey
3 Briggs, Harlan
1 Briggs, Jack
1 Briggs, Lillian
2 Brigham, Connie
1 Bright, Carol
1 Bright, Helen
7 Bright, Joyce
1 Bright, Patricia
2 Brindle, Carl
1 Briney, Martha
1 Briney, Mary Martha
74 Bring (Lou Bring and His Orchestra)
2 Bring, Lou
1 Brink, Robert
3 Brink, William
5 Brinker, Kay
34 Brinkley, David
2 Brinkley, Don
5 Brinkley, Jack
4 Brinkley, John
1 Brinkmeyer, Bill
1 Brinsbach, Joe
1 Briskin, Samuel J.
2 Brisson, Carl
1 Bristol, Lee H.
1 Britain, Dewey
24 Brito, Phil
3 Britt, Elton
5 Britt, Jim
6 Britten, Benjamin
14 Britton, Barbara
2 Broadbent, George
1 Broadly, Ken
1 Broadway Parade Orchestra and Chorus, The
1 Brock, M. C.
1 Brock, Mary
3 Brock, William
1 Brocka, Elia
1 Brockhausen, M. C.
5 Brockner, Gary
2 Brockwell, Bette
5 Broder, David
1 Broderick, Helen
1 Brodin, Peggy
3 Brodsky, Vera
1 Brody, Don
1 Brody, Leslie
1 Brody, Stuart
70 Broekman (David Broekman and His Orchestra)
3 Broekman (David Broekman and His Orchestra and Chorus)
75 Broekman (David Broekman and The Treasury Ensemble)
261 Broekman (David Broekman and The Treasury Orchestra)
12 Broekman (David Broekman and The Treasury Orchestra and Chorus)
1 Broekman Glee Club, The
2 Broekman, David
1 Brogan, D. W.
2 Brogan, Ron
1 Brogiatti, Gloria
12 Brokaw, Tom
80 Brokenshire, Norman
1 Bromberg, Conrad
1 Bromberg, J. Edward
1 Brome, Charlie
7 Bromfield, Louis
15 Bronte, Charlotte
11 Bronte, Emily
1 Brook, Bob
3 Brook, Clive
1 Brook, Nick
1 Brook, Pamela
1 Brooke, Hillary
1 Brooke, Tyler
1 Brookhurst, Clara
1 Brooklyn Symphony Orchestra, The
1 Brookmire, Bob
4 Brooks (Randy Brooks and His Orchestra)
1 Brooks Jr., Shelton
1 Brooks, Bill
1 Brooks, Colin
1 Brooks, Congressman
2 Brooks, David
1 Brooks, Dorothy
1 Brooks, Dudley
1 Brooks, Foster
2 Brooks, Geraldine
1 Brooks, Hadda
2 Brooks, Jacqueline
8 Brooks, Joan
2 Brooks, John
9 Brooks, Larry
2 Brooks, Lee
4 Brooks, Mel
2 Brooks, Norman
4 Brooks, Phyllis
5 Brooks, Randy
1 Brooks, Ruth
1 Brooks, Senator
1 Brooks, Shelton
1 Broome, G. Calvin
2 Brophy, Ed
1 Brossard, Edgar B.
1 Brother Joe Of The Mission Sisters
1 Brothers, Joyce
3 Broun, Heywood
1 Broun, Heywood Hale
1 Browder, Earl
1 Brower (Cecil Brower and His Kilocycle Cowboys)
1 Brower, Gerald C.
1 Brown (Gene Brown and The Debonaires)
1 Brown (Ken Brown and Sal)
112 Brown (Les Brown and His Orchestra)
1 Brown (Wally Brown and His Orchestra)
1 Brown and LaVelle
1 Brown Jr., Joe
32 Brown Jr., Oscar
2 Brown, Ada
4 Brown, Anne
1 Brown, Jr., Arthur
1 Brown, Bam
1 Brown, Barbara
1 Brown, Barton
2 Brown, Beverly
1 Brown, Bill
3 Brown, Bob
1 Brown, Brad
30 Brown, Cecil
1 Brown, Charlie
1 Brown, Clarence Gatemouth
1 Brown, Cleo
1 Brown, Colonel
1 Brown, Commander
1 Brown, Dave
1 Brown, David
5 Brown, Dick
1 Brown, Dolores
11 Brown, Donald
3 Brown, Dorothy
2 Brown, Eddie
1 Brown, Francis
2 Brown, Fred
6 Brown, Frederick
1 Brown, Gate Mouth
1 Brown, George
1 Brown, H. Rap
1 Brown, Hank
1 Brown, Harold
2 Brown, Harry
1 Brown, Harry Joe
2 Brown, Harvey O.
40 Brown, Himan
1 Brown, Janet
2 Brown, Jerry
11 Brown, Jimmy
1 Brown, Joe
16 Brown, Joe E.
321 Brown, John
5 Brown, John Mason
6 Brown, Johnny Mack
1 Brown, Josephine
4 Brown, June
2 Brown, Katherine Brinker
1 Brown, Kay
1 Brown, Kimmy
4 Brown, Lawrence
7 Brown, Les
1 Brown, Lew
1 Brown, Mallory
1 Brown, Mary
12 Brown, Maurice
1 Brown, Mel
1 Brown, Michael
12 Brown, Milton
1 Brown, Monroe
1 Brown, Nellie
1 Brown, Nickodemus
3 Brown, Pamela
1 Brown, Paul
1 Brown, Phillip
1 Brown, Porter Emerson
4 Brown, Ray
5 Brown, Robert
1 Brown, Roland
1 Brown, Ruth
4 Brown, Stumpy
4 Brown, Sweet Georgia
7 Brown, Ted
1 Brown, Tina
12 Brown, Tom
1 Brown, Tony
1 Brown, Val
15 Brown, Vanessa
3 Brown, Vernon
24 Brown, Wally
1 Brown, Warren
1 Brown, William
1 Brown, Willie
1 Brown, Winnie
1 Browne, Jerry
1 Brownell, Betty
8 Brownell, Bill
13 Browning, Doug
2 Browning, Reid
1 Browning, Robert
2 Browning, Rod
1 Browning, Ronald K.
1 Browning, Ted
2 Brownlee, John
1 Brownless, Sheila
1 Brownlow, James A.
2 Brox Sisters, The
14 Brubeck (Dave Brubeck Quartet, The)
1 Brubeck, Darius
7 Brubeck, Dave
1 Bruce, Betty
47 Bruce, Bob
8 Bruce, Carol
1 Bruce, Chet
6 Bruce, David
3 Bruce, Eddie
9 Bruce, Edwin
1 Bruce, Katherine
1 Bruce, Lenny
3 Bruce, Lydia
2 Bruce, Marion
2 Bruce, Michael
11 Bruce, Millie
73 Bruce, Nigel
9 Bruce, Robert
37 Bruce, Virginia
1 Bruckner, Herman
1 Brudell, Betty
2 Bruder, Clarence
3 Bruder, Patsy
1 Bruer (Ford Bruer and His Orchestra)
3 Bruer (Harry Breuer and The Clefdwellers)
2 Bruer (Harry Breuer's Novelty Orchestra)
1 Bruer Jr., George
7 Bruff, Larry
1 Bruman, Henry
2 Brumby, Bob
1 Brundage, Avery
22 Brundage, Hugh
2 Brune, James N.
1 Bruner, Jerome S.
1 Bruner, Jeff
2 Brunis (George Brunis and His Orchestra)
13 Brunis, George
73 Bruno Zirato Jr.
1 Bruno, Hal
1 Brusher, Julian
7 Brusiloff (Nat Brusiloff and His Orchestra)
2 Brustal, Beaumont
665 Bryan, Arthur Q.
1 Bryan, Donald
8 Bryan, George
2 Bryan, Jane
1 Bryan, Joyce
1 Bryan, Julien
2 Bryan, Marvin
1 Bryan, Mary
1 Bryan, Walter
2 Bryan, William Jennings
2 Bryan, Wright
1 Bryant (Jilly Bryant Singers, The)
1 Bryant (Ray Bryant Trio)
4 Bryant (Slim Bryant and His Wildcats)
1 Bryant (Slim Bryant Trio, The)
11 Bryant, Anita
3 Bryant, Jeffrey
1 Bryant, Nana
1 Bryant, Nelson
1 Bryant, Nina
32 Bryce, Edward
1 Bryden, William
1 Brylowski, Alexander
7 Brynner, Yul
14 Bryson, Lyman
1 Bua, Gene
1 Bubbles, John
3 Bubeck, Harry
4 Buccaneers, The
3 Buchanan, Edgar
1 Buchanan, Edward
1 Buchanan, Elsa
3 Buchanan, Jack
1 Buchanan, John
1 Buchanan, Pat
5 Buchanan, Robert
1 Buchanan, Scott
2 Buchanan, Stuart
1 Buchet, Frankie
2 Buchman, Frank
4 Buchwald, Art
1 Buchwold, Charlotte
1 Buck and Bubbles
1 Buck, Ashley
1 Buck, Baumont
1 Buck, Charles
54 Buck, Cousin Louis
2 Buck, Frank
7 Buck, Gene
1 Buck, J. L. Blair
6 Buck, Pearl S.
1 Buckingham Choir, The

27 Buckley (Emerson Buckley and His Orchestra)
4 Buckley Jr., William F.
1 Buckley, Charles
12 Buckley, Emerson
1 Buckley, F. R.
4 Buckley, Floyd
2 Buckley, James
1 Buckley, Tim
1 Buckmaster, Henrietta
1 Buckner, Buck
1 Buckner, Robert
1 Bud, Mr.
1 Budd, Julie
1 Budrys, Algis
6 Buey, John
3 Buffalo Bills, The
13 Buffington, Sam
15 Buffum, Ray
1 Bugas, John Steven
42 Buka, Donald
4 Bulifant, Joyce
1 Bull, Frank
2 Bull, Howard W.
1 Bull, John
1 Bullet, William C.
1 Bullock, Hiram
2 Bullock, Turner
3 Bulwer-Lytton, Edward
4 Bumpers, Dale
21 Bunce, Alan
20 Bunche, Ralph
2 Bundy, Jack
2 Bundy, Jonathan
1 Bundy, Wayne
1 Bunker, Ellsworth
1 Bunn, Teddy
3 Bunning, Jim
1 Bunting, Ken
1 Buono, Nick
1 Burbridge, Margaret
1 Burchard, John E.
1 Burden, Jimmy
31 Burdett, Winston
29 Burdick, Hal
1 Burdick, Robert
2 Burdon, Hugh
1 Burford, Annette
1 Burfridge, Annette
2 Burge, Harry
1 Burge, Stuart
1 Burger, Gloria
1 Burger, Gordon
1 Burger, Harris
1 Burger, Tony
3 Burger, Warren
1 Burgess, Betty
1 Burgess, Gelett
1 Burgess, Kay
14 Burke (Sonny Burke and His Orchestra)
33 Burke, Billie
7 Burke, Bonnie
8 Burke, Don
1 Burke, Edward
4 Burke, Georgia
1 Burke, Golen
1 Burke, Jack
2 Burke, James
2 Burke, Jim
5 Burke, Johnny
3 Burke, Kenneth
27 Burke, Larry
1 Burke, Ray
1 Burke, Sonny
9 Burke, Walter
1 Burkey, Ralph
1 Burkh, Inge
1 Burkhardt, Betty
1 Burkhardt, Richard
12 Burleson, Bob
2 Burley, Dan
25 Burley, Viola
1 Burling, George F.
1 Burna, Phillips
1 Burnbriar, Edmund
1 Burnett (Johnny Burnett Trio, The)
1 Burnett, A.
4 Burnett, Carol
8 Burnett, Frances Hodgson
37 Burnett, Murray
1 Burnette (Johnny Burnette Trio)
7 Burnette, Smiley
1 Burney, Al
1 Burns (Bobby Burns and His Orchestra)
1 Burns (Freddy Burns and His Rancho Boys)
1 Burns (Martin Burns and The Irish Blackbirds)
3 Burns (Ralph Burns and His Orchestra)
8 Burns, Al
1 Burns, Bill
78 Burns, Bob
1 Burns, Davie
1 Burns, E. J.
2 Burns, Eveline M.
287 Burns, George
1 Burns, Glen
1 Burns, Helen Jean
1 Burns, James
5 Burns, Katherine
1 Burns, Robert
26 Burns, Ronnie
21 Burns, Stanley
4 Burns, William
22 Burr, Anne
1 Burr, Lonnie
3 Burr, Peter
131 Burr, Raymond
1 Burr, Robert
1 Burrell, Jimmy
4 Burrell, Kenny
13 Burrell, Lloyd
2 Burris, Glenn
1 Burris, Neal
2 Burroughs, Eric
38 Burroughs, Joan
1 Burrow, Admiral
33 Burrows, Abe
1 Burrows, E. G.
3 Burt, Clyde
78 Burt, Frank
1 Burt, Kim
4 Burtis, Eric
8 Burton, Corey
1 Burton, Frank
3 Burton, Harold
16 Burton, James
2 Burton, John
1 Burton, Laverne
1 Burton, Lillian
2 Burton, Max
6 Burton, Pat
3 Burton, Richard
1 Burton, Robert
1 Burton, Roland
9 Burton, Sarah
1 Burzon, Melanie
4 Bush (Lou Bush and His Orchestra)
9 Bush, Barbara
202 Bush, George
1 Bush, George Prescott
3 Bush, James
1 Bush, Margaret
1 Bushelo, John
1 Bushkin (Joe Bushkin and His Orchestra and Chorus)
1 Bushkin (Joe Bushkin and His Swinging Strings)
1 Bushkin (Joe Bushkin Trio)
18 Bushkin, Joe
30 Bushman, Francis X.
1 Bushman, Mrs. Francis X.
1 Busse (Henry Busse and His Montmartre Orchestra)
9 Busse (Henry Busse and His Orchestra)
3 Busse, Henry
1 Butcher, Jesse
4 Buterra (Sam Buterra and The Witnesses)
4 Butler, Carl
7 Butler, Champ
1 Butler, Davis
66 Butler, Daws
4 Butler, Frank
1 Butler, Henry
1 Butler, John
2 Butler, Kid
5 Butler, Lois
2 Butler, Nicholas Murray
2 Butler, Patrick
1 Butler, Sally
3 Butler, Samuel
1 Butram, Jack
1 Butterfield (Billy Butterfield and His Orchestra)
1 Butterfield (Billy Butterfield Quintet, The)
25 Butterfield, Billy
1 Butterfield, Catherine
1 Butterfield, Charles
2 Butterfield, Erskine
342 Butterfield, Herb
1 Butterfield, Robert
5 Butterworth, Charles
1 Butti, Carlo
1 Buttler, Louis
1 Button, Betty
3 Buttons, Red
39 Buttram, Pat
1 Buxton, Frank
182 Buyeff, Lillian
1 Buzaine, Alonzo
1 Byas, Don
1 Byers, Bernice
1 Byers, Carl C.
24 Byers, Catherine
1 Bygraves, Max
7 Byington, Spring
2 Byrd, Billy
1 Byrd, Charlie
1 Byrd, Harry F.
5 Byrd, Jerry
1 Byrd, Ralph
2 Byrd, Richard
12 Byrd, Robert
1 Byrers, J.
19 Byrne, Brian J.
11 Byrne, John
1 Byrne, Pauline
1 Byrne, Peter J.
1 Byrnes, Marion
1 Byron, Arthur
2 Byron, Brook
3 Byron, Dick
4 Byron, Edward A.
32 Byron, George
3 Byron, Lord
1 Byron, Lorna
1 Byron, Mildred
1 Byron, Waldo
2 Byron, Walter
13 Byron, Ward

WDBO
ORLANDO, FLORIDA
78 - 33 1/3 RPM
STARTS INSIDE
ORDER NO.
PART
C
Recorded
By

2 Cabibbo, Joseph
1 Cables, George
1 Cabot (Tony Cabot Octet, The)
1 Cabot, Blake
2 Cabot, Bruce
9 Cabot, Sebastian
63 Cacavas (John Cacavas and His Orchestra)
22 Cacavas (John Cacavas Orchestra and Chorus)
1 Cacavas, John
29 Caceres, Ernie
1 Cactus Kids, The
13 Cadillac Choral Symphony, The
2 Cadillacs, The
12 Cady, Frank
1 Caesar, Arthur
5 Caesar, George
2 Caesar, Irving
2 Caesar, Sid
33 Cagney, James
11 Cagney, Jeanne
2 Cahill, Jack
3 Cahn, Sammy
1 Cahoot (Hank Cahoot Trio, The)
1 Caidin, Martin
7 Caillou, Alan
1 Cain, James
1 Cain, Mary
2 Caine, Betty
1 Caine, Michael
1 Caine, Whitford
11 Cairman, Michael
68 Cairn, Bill
1 Calder, Crane
6 Calder, King
2 Caldwell, Erskine
16 Caldwell, Hank
1 Caldwell, James
1 Caldwell, Nate
3 Caldwell, Orville R.
2 Calender, Red
24 Calhern, Louis
4 Calhoun, Rory
2 Cali, John
1 California (Northern California Symphony Orchestra)
2 California (Northern California WPA Symphony Orchestra)
2 California (Southern California Light Opera Orchestra and Chorus)
1 California (Southern California Mexican Typica Orchestra)
1 California (Southern California Symphony Orchestra)

4 California (Southern California WPA Symphony Orchestra)
1 Californians, The
7 Caliver, Ambrose
2 Calker (Darrell Calker and His Swing-Phonics)
1 Call, Asa V.
2 Callaghan, James
2 Callahan, Steven R.
1 Callas, Maria
1 Calleia, Joseph
1 Callejo, Cecilia
1 Callender (Red Callender Trio, The)
1 Calloway (Cab Calloway and His Cabbaliers)
4 Calloway (Cab Calloway and His Cotton Club Orchestra)
15 Calloway (Cab Calloway and His Orchestra)
21 Calloway, Cab
19 Calmer, Ned
2 Caluba, Will
120 Calvert, Charles
5 Calvert, William
2 Calvet, Corinne
2 Calvin, Harry
2 Calvin, Rosemary
1 Calyspo Boys, The
1 Camaguay, Van
1 Camara (Toots Camarata and His Orchestra)
1 Camarata and His Orchestra
1 Camargo, Felice
131 Camargo, Ralph
2 Cambridge, Godfrey
1 Cameron, Alan
2 Cameron, Charles S.
1 Cameron, Don
4 Cameron, John
1 Cameron, Lehman
1 Cameron, Louise
1 Cameron, Pat
1 Cameron, Phil
6 Cameron, Robert
3 Cameron, Rod
1 Camey, Charles
1 Camillan, Stephen
1 Camon, Bruce
1 Camp Lee Soldiers Chorus, The
1 Camp McAllister Bunter Abend, The
1 Camp Upton Dance Band, The
1 Camp, Charles L.
1 Campanella, Frank
7 Campanella, Joseph
3 Campanella, Roy
24 Campbell Jr., John
1 Campbell, Allen
2 Campbell, Anthony
5 Campbell, Archie
1 Campbell, Bill
1 Campbell, Bob
1 Campbell, Chris
4 Campbell, Colin
1 Campbell, Cullen
8 Campbell, Dave
3 Campbell, Donald
1 Campbell, Ellen
1 Campbell, Frances
2 Campbell, Guy
1 Campbell, H.
1 Campbell, Harry
5 Campbell, Jim
1 Campbell, John
1 Campbell, Louise
4 Campbell, Naomi
1 Campbell, Patrick
7 Campbell, Patsy
2 Campbell, Peter
1 Campbell, Rick
1 Campbell, Ted
1 Campbell, Thomas
1 Campbell, Tom
1 Campion, Thomas
9 Campo, Del
1 Campus Freshman, The
1 Campus Kids, The
1 Camries, Marvin
1 Camroy, Michael
1 Canaday, Al
1 Canaras, Johnny
1 Canby, Henry Sidell
41 Candido, Candy
1 Candy and Coco
1 Candy Kids, The
1 Caneely, Marla
3 Canel, Pat
1 Canelli, Martin
1 Canfield, Cass
6 Canfield, Homer
1 Caniff, Milton
1 Cannon, Billy
1 Cannon, Bruce
1 Cannon, General
3 Cannon, Jimmy
1 Cannon, John
7 Canon, Blanche
1 Canon, Maureen
2 Canon, Stuart
34 Canova, Judy
9 Cantelli, Guido
2 Canterbury Chorus, The
94 Cantor, Charlie
221 Cantor, Eddie
2 Cantor, Ida
1 Canutt, Yakima
1 Capazzola, Antonio
56 Capell, Peter
6 Capiello, Sam
1 Capote, Truman
2 Capp, Al
1 Capper, Senator
1 Capps, Jimmy
4 Capra, Frank
1 Capri Sisters, The
1 Caprine, Ken
1 Capstaff, Albert
4 Captain Stubby and The Buccaneers
1 Carbo, Joseph
7 Carbonell, Kenny
2 Card, Katherine
2 Card, Ken
1 Carden, Huey
1 Cardinal, Edward V.
4 Cardoni, Tony
1 Cardy, John
1 Carew, Peter
1 Carew, Thomas
2 Carey, Christopher
1 Carey, Dick
5 Carey, Harry
1 Carey, Harvey
1 Carey, Hugh
1 Carey, James
2 Carey, James B.
22 Carey, MacDonald
9 Carey, Mutt
1 Carey, Norman
1 Carignon, Jean
5 Carillo, Inez
1 Cariner, Carl
1 Carioca, Joe
1 Carl, Candy
24 Carle (Frankie Carle and His Orchestra)
13 Carle, Frankie
1 Carley, Paul
1 Carlin, Dorothy
7 Carlisle (Russ Carlisle and His Orchestra)
1 Carlisle, Bill
1 Carlisle, Carl
2 Carlisle, Charles
4 Carlisle, Kitty
3 Carlisle, Mary
6 Carlisle, Russ
2 Carlisle, Una Mae
5 Carlisles, The
14 Carlon, Fran
1 Carlson, Dean
2 Carlson, Dick
1 Carlson, Ernest
3 Carlson, Frankie
1 Carlson, Harry
2 Carlson, John Roy
3 Carlson, Joseph
2 Carlson, Lewis
2 Carlson, Richard
1 Carlton (Dick Carlton and His Orchestra)
1 Carlton (Maurice Carlton and His Orchestra)
1 Carlton, Catherine
2 Carlton, Dean
1 Carlton, Dick
1 Carlton, Don
1 Carlton, Jean
1 Carlton, Maurice
1 Carlton, Nina
1 Carlton, Pierce
1 Carlton, Sam
1 Carlton, Tony
8 Carlton, Tory
1 Carlyle, Aileen
24 Carlyle, Louise
3 Carlyn (Tommy Carlyn and His Orchestra)
1 Carmel, Daniel D.
6 Carmene
2 Carmer, Carl
46 Carmichael, Hoagy
1 Carmichael, Leonard
3 Carmine, Betty
1 Carn, Lillian
1 Carnahan, Walter H.
1 Carnation Concert Orchestra, The
4 Carnegie, Dale
3 Carnegie, Tom
1 Carnes, Cecil
1 Carney, Alan
82 Carney, Art
1 Carney, B.W.
7 Carney, Don
2 Carney, Fred
6 Carney, Harry
1 Carney, Otis
1 Carol, Shirley
1 Carol, Sue
3 Carollers, The
1 Caron, Leslie
3 Carothers, Neil
5 Carpenter (Ike Carpenter and His Orchestra)
115 Carpenter, Bill
1 Carpenter, Carlton
16 Carpenter, Cliff
1 Carpenter, Imogene
1 Carpenter, Jim
739 Carpenter, Ken
18 Carpenter, Thelma
1 Carr
1 Carr (Joe Fingers Carr and His Ragtime Band)
1 Carr, Charlotte
1 Carr, David
1 Carr, Frank
2 Carr, Gerald
9 Carr, Jack
2 Carr, Joe Fingers
27 Carr, John Dickson
4 Carr, Joyce
1 Carr, Leon
1 Carr, Marion
36 Carr, Nancy
1 Carr, Phil
8 Carr, Richard
1 Carr, Tom
2 Carr, Vicki
1 Carr, William G.
14 Carradine, John
1 Carrigan, John
8 Carrillo, Leo
8 Carrington, Elaine
5 Carrington, Jack
1 Carroll (Helen Carroll and The Satisfiers)
4 Carroll Jr., Bob
3 Carroll Sisters, The
1 Carroll, Al
30 Carroll, Bob
10 Carroll, Carolyn
3 Carroll, Carroll
2 Carroll, Charles
2 Carroll, Christina
4 Carroll, Diahann
2 Carroll, Estelle
1 Carroll, Frances
25 Carroll, Gene
25 Carroll, Georgia
3 Carroll, Helen
1 Carroll, Irene
1 Carroll, Ivan
33 Carroll, Jack
3 Carroll, Jean
60 Carroll, Jimmy
1 Carroll, Joan
5 Carroll, John
2 Carroll, Judy
1 Carroll, Leo G.
5 Carroll, Lewis
10 Carroll, Lily Ann
44 Carroll, Madeleine
2 Carroll, Marilyn
4 Carroll, Marvin
1 Carroll, Pat
1 Carroll, Ray
1 Carroll, Rita
2 Carroll, Robert
1 Carroll, Roger
2 Carroll, Ruth
2 Carroll, Sherry
2 Carroll, Vinette
1 Carron, Suzanne
1 Carruth, Charles
1 Carskadon, Thomas R.
4 Carson, Cathy
1 Carson, Frank
65 Carson, Jack
3 Carson, Jean
14 Carson, Johnny
47 Carson, Ken
3 Carson, Lee
1 Carson, Martha
64 Carson, Mindy
13 Carson, Paul
1 Carson, Rita Jean
3 Carson, Robert
1 Carson, Saul
58 Carstensen, Verne
1 Carston, Lee
9 Carter (Benny Carter and His Orchestra)
1 Carter (Benny Carter's All Stars)
1 Carter (Betty Carter Trio, The)
2 Carter Family, The
1 Carter Sisters, The
3 Carter, Ann
1 Carter, Ben
1 Carter, Benjamin
6 Carter, Benny
2 Carter, Betty
1 Carter, Bob
1 Carter, Cassie
1 Carter, Desmond
1 Carter, E. E.
1 Carter, Eliot
5 Carter, Fred
11 Carter, Gaylord
1 Carter, Harold
1 Carter, Helena
5 Carter, Jack
1 Carter, Janice
146 Carter, Jimmy
6 Carter, John
3 Carter, June
1 Carter, Maureen
1 Carter, Nick
1 Carter, Paul
6 Carter, Paulina
1 Carter, Ralph
1 Carter, Ray
3 Carter, Ron
5 Carter, Rosalynn
1 Carter, Tammy
1 Carter, Violet Bonhomme
1 Carther, William
1 Carton, Sam
2 Cartosi, Frank R.
6 Cartulsey, Frank
1 Cartwright, Angela

2 Cartwright, E. M.
1 Cartwright, Lowell
1 Cartwright, Veronica
2 Caruso, Anthony
32 Caruso, Carl
1 Carver, Eddie
2 Carver, George Washington
3 Carver, Lynn
1 Carvette, Gordon
1 Casadesus, Gaby
9 Casadesus, Robert
1 Casani, Kane
1 Casanova and His Tsagon
1 Cascas, Anna
43 Case (Russ Case and His Orchestra)
1 Case, Evelyn
1 Case, Francis
35 Case, Nelson
1 Case, Russ
1 Casella, Albert
9 Casey, Al
8 Casey, Bob
1 Casey, Clark
1 Casey, Tom
1 Cash, Clayton
28 Cash, Jimmy
2 Cash, Johnny
1 Cashman, Ed
2 Casino, Del
2 Caspary, Vera
1 Casper, Billy
1 Casper, David
27 Cass County Boys, The
2 Cassabon, John
1 Cassady (Al Cassady and His Orchestra)
1 Cassals, Pablo
1 Cassanavee, Don
2 Cassar, Barbara
3 Cassel, Walter
11 Cassell, Clancey
1 Cassell, Sally
4 Cassell, Sid
1 Cassella, Alfred
1 Casseloan
1 Cassely, Richard
1 Cassey (Chuck Cassey Singers, The)
1 Cassey, Chuck
1 Cassidy, Bruce
9 Cassidy, Henry
1 Cassidy, Jack
2 Cassidy, Jim
1 Cassidy, Tom
1 Cassity, Jimmy
1 Castaneta, Grace
2 Castelnuovo-Tedesco, Mario
5 Castillo, Carmen
61 Castillo, Del
4 Castle (Lee Castle and The Jimmy Dorsey Orchestra)
1 Castle (Walter Castle and His Orchestra)
1 Castle, Adele
1 Castle, Bill
1 Castle, Elaine
2 Castle, Irene
9 Castle, Jimmy
3 Castle, Lee
2 Castle, Peter
2 Castlelaw, Chet
1 Castleman, Jeff
1 Castro, Juan Jose
1 Catalino and His Rhumbas
4 Catell, Clyde
17 Cates (George Cates and His Orchestra)
11 Cates (Opie Cates and His Orchestra)
13 Cates, Opie
2 Cathcart (Jack Cathcart and His Orchestra)
8 Cathcart, Dick
1 Cather, Willa
1 Catlaw, Lewis
18 Catlett, Sid
20 Catlett, Walter
1 Cats N' Jammers, The
2 Caudle, Roy
4 Caulder, Beth
1 Caulder, Richard
1 Cauldwell, Ernest C.
2 Caulfield, Betty
25 Caulfield, Joan
1 Causo, Marion
1 Cavalcade Orchestra, The
2 Cavaliers, The
14 Cavallaro, Carmen
13 Cavallero (Carmen Cavallaro and His Orchestra)
2 Cavallo (Jimmy Cavallo and The House Rockers)
1 Cavanaugh (Dave Cavanaugh and His Orchestra)
1 Cavanaugh (Dave Cavanaugh Quintet, The)
64 Cavanaugh (Page Cavanaugh Trio, The)
6 Cavanaugh, Page
1 Cavanaugh, Paul
1 Cavaretta, Phil
1 Cave, Hugh
1 Cave, Richard
7 Cavell, Butch
1 Cavenaugh, John J.
26 Cavendish, Constance
2 Caveness, Pamela
5 Cavett, Dick
1 Caygill, Susanne
1 CBC String Orchestra, The
1 CBS Jump Band, The
4 CBS Symphony Orchestra, The
1 Cecil, Lawrence H.
1 Cedar, John
1 Cedarholm, Doris
1 Celebreese, Anthony
9 Celler, Emanuel
1 Cellini, Renato
1 Cello, Theodore
17 Cenedella, Robert
10 Cerf, Bennett
7 Cernan, Eugene
1 Cerv, Bob
8 Cervantes, Miguel de
2 Cesana, Renzo
1 Chacksfield (Frank Chacksfield and His Orchestra)
1 Chadwick, Dionne
2 Chadwick, Robert
1 Chafin, Patty
5 Chain, Hugh
1 Chalmers, Alice
2 Chalmers, Helen
1 Chalmers, Rita
3 Chalmers, Thomas
2 Chamberlain (Roy Chamberlain and His Orchestra)
1 Chamberlain, George Andrew
1 Chamberlain, John
15 Chamberlain, Neville
9 Chambers, Bill
1 Chambers, Dickie
1 Chambers, Henderson
1 Chambers, Jo Ellen
7 Chambers, Roy
1 Chambers, Shirley
3 Chambers, Wheaton
2 Chambers, Whittaker
3 Champion, Gower
3 Champion, Marge
1 Champman, Eric
50 Chan, Charles
1 Chan, Sou
1 Chance, Dean
1 Chance, Lightnin'
26 Chancellor, John
1 Chandlee, Richard
2 Chandler, A.B.
1 Chandler, Chick
1 Chandler, David
2 Chandler, Doug
2 Chandler, Eddie
2 Chandler, Freddy
5 Chandler, Fredericka
13 Chandler, Gloria
2 Chandler, Happy
1 Chandler, Helen
176 Chandler, Jeff
1 Chandler, Karen
1 Chandler, Mimi
98 Chandler, Raymond
2 Chandler, Richard
1 Chandler, Robin
2 Chandor and His Gypsy Orchestra
7 Chaney, Frances
1 Changing Scene, The
5 Channing, Carol
3 Chapel Singers, The
1 Chapin, Billy
1 Chapin, Howard
3 Chapin, Michael
3 Chaplin, Charlie
13 Chaplin, W. W.
7 Chapman, John
4 Chapman, Marguerite
7 Chapman, Pattee
1 Chappell, C. R.
150 Chappell, Ernest
1 Chappell, Rick
124 Charioteers, The
2 Charisse, Cyd
12 Charles (Ray Charles Singers, The)
3 Charles, Henry
1 Charles, Lewis
74 Charles, Milton
2 Charles, Ray
1 Charleston Symphony Orchestra, The
2 Charlesworth, Clifford
1 Charlesworth, John
9 Charlesworth, Tom
1 Charlie and His Orchestra
1 Charlita
1 Charlotta
2 Charlotte
2 Charmley, Gloria
4 Charney, Jordan
1 Charo
1 Charters, Spencer
1 Chartok, Melanie
4 Chase (Bruce Chase and His Orchestra)
1 Chase, Barrie
1 Chase, Bordon
2 Chase, Connie
2 Chase, Eddie
11 Chase, Ilka
30 Chase, Steven
3 Chase, Stuart
1 Chase, Sylvia
1 Chase, Vicki
2 Chassay, Roger
1 Chatter, Lotta
7 Chatterton, Larry
4 Chatterton, Ruth
1 Chauveau, Yvonne
2 Chavez, Carlos
1 Chavez, Raoul
2 Cheatham, Doc
1 Cheerio
3 Cheerleaders, The
1 Cheers, The
1 Cheever, John
1 Cheever, Martha
1 Chef, Walter
8 Chekhov, Anton
1 Chenault, James
1 Chenery, William L.
7 Cheney, Dick
1 Cheney, Jack
1 Chenkman, Edgar
1 Cher
1 Cherne, Gail
4 Cherne, Leo
1 Cherrington, Ben M.
1 Cherry Sisters, The
3 Cherry, Don
1 Cherry, R. H.
2 Cheshire, Pappy
1 Cheskin (David Cheskin and His Orchestra)
6 Chesney, Diana
1 Chesney, Joel
1 Chessman, Caryl
11 Chester (Bob Chester and His Orchestra)
2 Chester, Bob
1 Chesterfield Swingerettes, The
1 Chesterton, G. K.
1 Chestnut, Ike
21 Chevalier, Maurice
1 Chevell, Ken
16 Chevigny, Hector
66 Chevillat, Dick
1 Chianovsky, George
1 Chicago Opera Company, The
1 Chicago Symphony Orchestra, The
1 Chico and His Orchestra
1 Chiffons, The
1 Childre, Lew
2 Children's Orchestra
1 Childress, Alvin
1 Childs, Billy
1 Chiles, George
4 Chiles, Lawton
1 Chimes, Michael
1 Chipman, Eric
1 Chiquita
1 Chiquito
2 Chisholm, Robert
6 Chittison (Herman Chittison Trio, The)
40 Chittison, Herman
2 Choate, Bill
34 Choate, Helen
1 Choir Of The Sistine Chapel, The
1 Choir, Eva Jesse
1 Choir, Trumpet
3 Chomsky, David
1 Chong, Peter
2 Choralaires, The
1 Choralites, The
17 Chordettes, The
2 Chorlian, Edward
1 Chorney, Alec
1 Chorus Of Stars, The
1 Chorus Of The Great Lakes Naval Training Station, The
1 Chorus Of The International Ladies Garment Workers Union, The
2 Chorus Of The Jewish Institute Of Religion, The
2 Chorus Of The School Of Sacred Music
4 Chorus Of The School Of Sacred Music-Hebrew Union College, The
2 Christakos, Dean
21 Christian, Bobby
1 Christian, Charlie
31 Christian, Helen
1 Christian, Larry
2 Christian, Linda
1 Christian, Ralph
8 Christians, Mady
1 Christianson, Gary
1 Christianson, George B.
1 Christianson, Marjorie
2 Christianson, Reed
6 Christie, Agatha
3 Christie, Audrey
1 Christie, Robert
51 Christine, Virginia
1 Christmas, Eric
1 Christopher, Joe
5 Christopher, Karen
2 Christopher, Kay
1 Christopher, Warren
2 Christy (Ken Christy Chorus)
20 Christy, June
226 Christy, Ken
1 Chrysler, Dick
1 Chu, Sam

1 Chukin, Phil
2 Church In The Wildwood Choir
1 Church In The Wildwood Choir and Orchestra
1 Church, Francis P.
2 Church, Frank
2 Churchill, Kenneth
2 Churchill, Mrs. Winston
3 Churchill, Sarah
2 Churchill, Savannah
6 Churchill, Stewart
75 Churchill, Winston
1 Chute, B.J.
1 Ciannelli, Eduardo
1 Ciano, Count
1 Ciatto, John
1 Ciffone, Don
33 Circle A Wranglers, The
2 Circle, Alan
1 Cities Service Band, The
1 Cities Service Chorus, The
1 Cities Service Orchestra, The
1 Clair, Rene
1 Claire, Bernice
1 Claire, Debby
2 Claire, Dorothy
17 Claire, Helen
1 Claire, Ina
44 Claire, Marion
1 Claire, Willis
1 Clancey, Jim
16 Claney, Howard
1 Claney, Tom
1 Claridge (Gay Claridge and His Orchestra)
1 Clark (Dave Clark Five, The)
1 Clark Candy Chorus, The
12 Clark Sisters, The
2 Clark, Angela
5 Clark, Barrett J.
1 Clark, Bennett
3 Clark, Betty
1 Clark, Blair
1 Clark, Blake
3 Clark, Bob
1 Clark, Bobby
35 Clark, Buddy
1 Clark, Carlyn
24 Clark, Cliff
61 Clark, Cottonseed
23 Clark, Dane
1 Clark, Dick
51 Clark, Don
2 Clark, Evans
34 Clark, Everett
1 Clark, Frank
1 Clark, Frank J.
2 Clark, Fred
156 Clark, Fred G.
4 Clark, Gene Emmet
2 Clark, George
1 Clark, Gordon
4 Clark, Harry
4 Clark, Herbert
2 Clark, Jeff
1 Clark, John
2 Clark, John L.
1 Clark, Joseph
4 Clark, Lillian
492 Clark, Lon
1 Clark, Marguerite
55 Clark, Marian
1 Clark, Marjorie
4 Clark, Mark
1 Clark, Michelle
5 Clark, Petula
18 Clark, Phillip
2 Clark, Roy
1 Clark, Ruth
1 Clark, Tom
2 Clark, W. Kenneth
4 Clark, Wallace
1 Clark, Walter Van Tilber
1 Clark, William
2 Clark, William Kendall
2 Clarke, Arthur C.
1 Clarke, Lloyd
3 Clarke, Mae
5 Clarke, Robert
2 Clary, Robert
1 Clason, Ben
1 Classeti, Ben
1 Claxton, William
2 Clay, Jeffrey
2 Clay, Lucius
1 Clayberger, Katherine
1 Claybourne, Phil
2 Clayton, Bob
1 Clayton, Buck
1 Clayton, Gloria
2 Clayton, Jan
3 Clayton, Lou
1 Clayton, Mary
1 Clayton, Nancy
1 Clayton, Norman
18 Clayton, Patty
2 Clayton, Ruth
2 Clayton, William L.
1 Cleary, Jack
94 Cleary, Leo
1 Cleave, Mary
12 Clebanoff, Herman
1 Cleffs, Clifford
2 Cleftones, The
1 Clem
4 Clem, Bill
2 Clemens, Loretta
1 Clemente, Elvita
1 Clemente, Roberto
1 Clements, Stanley
2 Clemons, Larry
3 Cleva, Fausto
12 Cleveland Symphony Orchestra, The
1 Cleveland, Gerald
12 Cleveland, Nancy
1 Cleveland, Nancy J.
1 Click, Mary
1 Clicquot Club Eskimos, The
1 Cliff, Oliver
4 Clifford (Bill Clifford and His Orchestra)
1 Clifford, Bill
5 Clift, Montgomery
1 Clifton, Bill
2 Clifton, Mark
2 Clinch Mountain Clan, The
4 Cline, Patsy
5 Cline, Richard
1 Clinger, William
3 Clinker, Zeno
11 Clinton (Larry Clinton and His Orchestra)
216 Clinton, Bill
1 Clinton, Chelsea
8 Clinton, Hillary Rodham
1 Clinton, Larry
11 Clinton, Mildred
1 Clipper, P. M.
1 Clive, Madeline
1 Cloche, Maurice
5 Clooney, Betty
4 Clooney, Nick
100 Clooney, Rosemary
1 Close, Glenn
16 Close, Upton
1 Close, Virginia
1 Close, Woody
3 Clouden, Nina
6 Cloutier (Norman Cloutier and His Orchestra)
2 Cloutier, Norman
2 Clovers, The
1 Clucas, Richard
4 Cluney, Clark
68 Clunis, Tom
9 Clute, Chester
61 Clyde, Andy
2 Coakley (Jack Coakley and His Orchestra)
1 Coakley (Tom Coakley and His Orchestra)
1 Coast Artillery Swing Five, The
5 Coast Guard (Eleventh Naval District Coast Guard Band, The)
2 Coast Guard (U. S. Coast Guard Band, The)
1 Coast Guard (U. S. Coast Guard Quartet, The)
14 Coast Guard Cutters Dance Band, The
1 Coates, Josephine
2 Coates, Mike
2 Coates, Paul
1 Coats, Albert
2 Coats, Daniel
1 Cobb, Arnette
1 Cobb, Buff
4 Cobb, David
1 Cobb, Hubbard
4 Cobb, Irvin S.
10 Cobb, Lee J.
3 Cobb, Ty
1 Cobbs, Susan Parker
1 Cober, Dick
2 Cobina Wright Jr.
1 Coburn, Bill
22 Coburn, Charles
1 Coca, Imogene
1 Cochette, Marina
1 Cochise, Nino
1 Cochran, Donna
1 Cochran, Hamilton
1 Cochran, Jacqueline
11 Cochran, John
9 Cochran, Joseph
1 Cochran, Mike
7 Cochran, Ron
6 Cochran, Steve
1 Cochran, Thad
1 Cochran, William
1 Cocks, Dorothy
2 Codin, Ron
1 Codmore, William
1 Cody, Iron Eyes
1 Cody, Pop
1 Coe, Don
1 Coe, Jerry
2 Coe, Socker
4 Coelho, Tony
3 Coffee, John M.
4 Coffer, Jerry
3 Coffin, Haskell
12 Coffin, Tristram
1 Coffin, Vincent
1 Cogan (Harry Cogan and His Orchestra)
3 Coghlan Jr., Frank
2 Coghlan, Phyllis
1 Cohan Jr., George M.
14 Cohan, George M.
16 Cohan, Phil
1 Cohen, Art
5 Cohen, Benjamin
1 Cohen, Bill
1 Cohen, Mickey
10 Cohen, Phillip
1 Cohen, Robert
1 Cohn, Al
5 Cohn, Roy
1 Coke, Harriet Burger
1 Colavito, Rocky
55 Colbert, Claudette
1 Colby, Anita
2 Colby, Bainbridge
1 Colby, Frank
1 Colby, Gene
1 Colby, Jean
1 Colby, Marion
1 Colder, Richard
2 Cole (Buddy Cole and His Men)
2 Cole (Buddy Cole and His Orchestra)
35 Cole (Nat King Cole Trio, The)
1 Cole (Ronnie Cole Trio, The)
1 Cole Jr., Marshall
1 Cole, Ann
47 Cole, Buddy
1 Cole, Buff
6 Cole, Cozy
1 Cole, Dennis
3 Cole, Fred B.
1 Cole, Idaho
2 Cole, Ken
63 Cole, Nat King
1 Cole, Polly
10 Cole, Robert
1 Cole, Sandra
2 Cole, Sylvia
1 Cole, Ted
1 Colean, Miles L.
1 Colebrook, Coral
1 Colegiate Chorale, The
1 Coleman (Cy Coleman and His Trio)
3 Coleman (Emil Coleman and His Orchestra)
1 Coleman, Bill
2 Coleman, Booth
1 Coleman, Carol
13 Coleman, Charles
7 Coleman, Cy
1 Coleman, Denardo
1 Coleman, Herbert
3 Coleman, Jerry
2 Coleman, Keith
3 Coleman, Nancy
1 Coleman, Ornet
1 Coleman, Robert
2 Coleman, Ron
1 Coleman, Rosemary
1 Coleman, William A.
2 Coleridge, Samuel Taylor
1 Coleridge-McInnes, Hugh J.
18 Coles, Stedman
2 Colin, Larry
1 Colla-Negri, Adelyn
1 Colladoy, Raymond
3 Colleen, Madeline
2 College (Carl College and His Orchestra)
1 Coller, Ralph
5 Collier, Bob
2 Collier, Constance
1 Collier, Greg
1 Collier, John
2 Collier, Lois
1 Collin, Edward
59 Collingwood, Charles
1 Collins (Craig Collins and Ames)
1 Collins, Addison
6 Collins, Al
2 Collins, Al Jazzbeaux
1 Collins, Cardiss
1 Collins, Carlene
1 Collins, Charles Elster
8 Collins, Colleen
58 Collins, Dorothy
1 Collins, Elliott
222 Collins, Fred
1 Collins, Governor
5 Collins, Howard
4 Collins, Jim
3 Collins, Libby
1 Collins, Marion
4 Collins, Michael
1 Collins, Nancy
1 Collins, Pat
1 Collins, Patricia
3 Collins, Peter
1 Collins, Phillip
99 Collins, Ray
2 Collins, Reid
3 Collins, Sid
36 Collins, Ted
125 Collins, Tom
15 Collins, Wilkie
1 Collison, John
1 Collyer, Bill
1292 Collyer, Bud
2 Collyer, John
1 Colman, Bill
158 Colman, Ronald
1 Colmans, Edward
1 Colonials, The
104 Colonna, Jerry
1 Colspan (Adolph Colspan and His Orchestra)
2 Colter, Beth
1 Colter, John Lee
7 Colton, Kingsley

4 Coltrane, Suzy
3 Columbia Band, The
1 Columbia Concert Orchestra, The
2 Columbia Orchestra, The
36 Columbia String Orchestra, The
2 Columbia Symphony Orchestra, The
3 Columbo, Lee
12 Columbo, Russ
13 Colvig, Pinto
7 Colvig, Vance
1 Comacho, President
2 Combs, Fuzzy
3 Combs, George Hamilton
3 Comden, Betty
3 Comer, Adila
2 Comer, Twyler
1 Comfort, Ron
1 Cominsky, Joe
1 Commonwealth Symphony and State Chorus Of Boston
88 Como, Perry
2 Compaignons de La Chanson, Les
1 Comprubi, Jose
2 Compton, Ann
1 Compton, Carl
1 Compton, Francis
1 Compton, Lewis
14 Compton, Walter
1 Compton, Wilson
2 Comstock (Frank Comstock and His Orchestra)
1 Comstock, Bill
1 Comstock, Bob
2 Conant, James B.
2 Conant, Wes
1 Conants, Lee
1 Concepcion (Cesar Concepcion and His Orchestra)
21 Concert Hall Orchestra, The
3 Concertgebouw Orchestra Of Amsterdam, The
1 Concords, The
1 Condoli, Connie
2 Condoli, Pete
2 Condon (Eddie Condon and His Orchestra)
53 Condon, Eddie
2 Condon, Maurie
1 Condon, Michael
1 Confers, Gloria
1 Confers, Jimmy
1 Confrey, Zez
1 Conga, Gwen
1 Congden, Barney
2 Conger, Juli
1 Congers
1 Coniff (Ray Coniff and His Orchestra and Chorus)
6 Coniff (Ray Coniff and His Orchestra)
1 Coniff, Ray
1 Conigliaro, Tony
1 Conkle, E. P.
17 Conklin, Gene
1 Conklin, Grace
12 Conklin, Peggy
4 Conkling, George
1 Conlan, Dave
1 Conlan, Paul
2 Conley, Gene
1 Conley, James
1 Conley, Truman W.
6 Conlon (Jud Conlon Choristers, The)
1 Conlon (Jud Conlon's Chorus)
106 Conlon (Jud Conlon's Rhythmaires)
1 Conlon, Jud
1 Conlon, Pat
6 Conn (Lenny Conn and His Orchestra)
10 Conn, Al J.
5 Conn, Billy
1 Conn, Harry
1 Conn, Lenny
1 Conn, Marv
4 Connell, Richard
14 Connelly, Marc
13 Conner, Nadine
7 Conners, Chris
1 Connery, Sean
2 Connolly, Donald H.
5 Connolly, Eugene
3 Connolly, James
37 Connolly, Joe
3 Connolly, John
1 Connolly, Marc
2 Connolly, Tom
4 Connolly, Vincent
8 Connolly, Walter
1 Connor (Jack Connor Trio, The)
1 Connor, Helen
2 Connor, Herbert
65 Connor, Whitfield
1 Connors, Chuck
4 Connors, Frankie
1 Conover, Harry
5 Conover, Hugh
20 Conover, Willis
1 Conrad, Allen
1 Conrad, Con
1 Conrad, Hugh
2 Conrad, Jack
12 Conrad, John
15 Conrad, Joseph
8 Conrad, Paul
6 Conrad, Pete
751 Conrad, William
369 Conried, Hans
1 Conroy, John
1 Conry, Bob
1 Consentino, Nicholas
8 Considine, Bob
13 Considine, John
1 Consolo, Betina
1 Constance, Hector
1 Constance, Joan
259 Conte, John
17 Conte, Richard
2 Conte, Robert
1 Conte, Ruth
2 Continental Trio, The
1 Continentals Quartet and Chorus, The
2 Contino, Dick
1 Converse, Curt
1 Conway, Delson
2 Conway, Jack
1 Conway, Jim
1 Conway, John
2 Conway, Joseph
4 Conway, Julie
4 Conway, Stuart
11 Conway, Tom
1 Conway, Vincent
1 Conwill, Allan
1 Cooch, Arthur T. Quiller
1 Coogan
4 Coogan, Jackie
5 Coogan, Richard
1 Cook Painter Boys, The
1 Cook, Alton
2 Cook, Billy
1 Cook, Bob
1 Cook, Carol
8 Cook, Charles L.
3 Cook, Donald
1 Cook, Fred
1 Cook, Gerald
2 Cook, Harry
3 Cook, Henry
4 Cook, Lou
2 Cook, Lynn
1 Cook, Mark
1 Cook, Merrill
2 Cook, Perry
2 Cook, Phil
2 Cook, Rupert Croft
2 Cook, Shorty
1 Cook, Sidney
93 Cook, Tommy
1 Cook, Tony
2 Cook, Vernon
16 Cooke, Alistair
13 Cooke, Dwight
1 Cooke, Terrence
1 Cooksie, Curtis
1 Cool (Danny Cool and His Velvet Rhythm)
12 Cool, Gomer
10 Cool, Harry
1 Cooley, Harold
3 Cooley, Howard
1 Cooley, Lee
23 Cooley, Spade
2 Cooley, Wayne
2 Coolidge, Calvin
1 Coolidge, Phil
1 Coonaraswamy, Ananda
4 Cooney, George
12 Coons, Johnny
1 Cooper
1 Cooper (Mel Cooper and His Orchestra)
2 Cooper, Albert Duff
2 Cooper, Alex
1 Cooper, Alice
1 Cooper, Anthony Campbell
32 Cooper, Ben
1 Cooper, Buster
1 Cooper, Curt
3 Cooper, Ed
1 Cooper, Edward
9 Cooper, Edwin
3 Cooper, Frank
33 Cooper, Gary
1 Cooper, Giles
1 Cooper, Gordon
29 Cooper, Jackie
56 Cooper, James Fenimore
14 Cooper, Jerry
1 Cooper, Joel
1 Cooper, John Sherman
2 Cooper, Kemball
1 Cooper, Ken
1 Cooper, Lillian Kimball
1 Cooper, Marion
2 Cooper, Ralph
1 Cooper, Robert L.
2 Cooper, Stoney
3 Cooper, Wilma Lee
90 Cooper, Wyllis
1 Coopman, Jean Pierre
2 Coote, Robert
1 Coots, J. Fred
5 Copas, Cowboy
1 Copasetics, The
1 Cope, Gary
2 Copeland, Alan
3 Copeland, Dr.
71 Copeland, Joan
18 Copeland, Maurice
1 Copeland, Nick
1 Copen, Grace
1 Copinger, John M.
2 Coppel, Lester
1 Corasco, Carlos
1 Corbett, Leonora
39 Corbett, Lois
1 Corbin, Charles
1 Corbin, Virginia
1 Corby, Ellen
2 Corcoran, Bob
7 Corcoran, Corky
1 Corcoran, Red
1 Corcoran, Thomas J.
1 Corday, Don
1 Corday, Marcel
1 Corday, Sandra
13 Corday, Ted
23 Cordell, Cathleen
1 Cordell, Malcolm McCaw
5 Cordell, Roy
1 Cordic, Reg
2 Cordner, Blaine
1 Cordon, Norman
1 Cordova, George
1 Cordova, Victoria
1 Cordovan, Kathy
3 Corea, Chick
1 Corelli, Franco
5 Corey, Gertrude
3 Corey, Irwin
1 Corey, Jack
51 Corey, Jeff
38 Corey, Jill
1 Corey, Steven
9 Corey, Wendell
2 Corio, Ann
1 Corley, Bob
2 Corley, Cynthia
1 Cornell, Alice
10 Cornell, Don
3 Cornell, Gerald
6 Cornell, Katharine
3 Cornell, Lillian
1 Cornett, Alice
8 Corning, Tip
5 Cornwall, J. Spencer
33 Cornwell, Arden
261 Correll, Charles
1 Corri, Adrienne
1 Corrigan, Ray Crash
3 Corrigan, Douglas
1 Corsey, Ferris
1 Corson, George
1 Cortez, Leon
2 Cortez, Ricardo
2 Cortland, Jerome
10 Corum, Bill
1 Corwin, Edward Samuel
148 Corwin, Norman
2 Cosby, Bill
3 Cosell, Howard
2 Coslow, Sam
1 Coslowe (Lou Coslowe and His Orchestra)
53 Coslowe, Lou
1 Cosma, Tibor
1 Cosmopolitan Singers, The
1 Cossack (Don Cossack Chorus, The)
1 Cossack (Don Cossacks, The)
1 Cossert, Valerie
1 Costa, Carmella
1 Costa, Don
4 Costa, Mary
2 Costello, Anne
4 Costello, Bill
1 Costello, Dolores
2 Costello, Frank
1 Costello, Helene
57 Costello, Jack
5 Costello, Kay
15 Costello, Lois
47 Costello, Lou
1 Costello, Pat
1 Coster, Henry
2 Coster, John
1 Costigan, Tom
7 Cote (Emil Cote Serenaders)
2 Cote (Emil Cote Serenaders, The)
2 Cote, Emil
4 Cotner (Carl Cotner and His Orchestra)
5 Cotner, Carl
203 Cotsworth, Staats
1 Cott, Ted
1 Cotten, Grace
1 Cotten, Jimmy
78 Cotten, Joseph
2 Cottenham, Tom Lincoln
1 Cottingham, Ruth
1 Cottle, Josephine
1 Cottler, Irv
5 Cotton, Carolina
4 Cotton, Larry
1 Cotton, R. T.
6 Cottrell, Leonard
39 Coughlin, Charles
2 Coulet, Helen
38 Coulouris, George
1 Country Cousins, The
96 Courage, Alexander
1 Courage, Sandy
1 Courrier, Isabelle
1 Court, Eileen

1 Courtley, Steven
4 Courtney (Del Courtney and His Orchestra)
1 Courtney, Charles
18 Courtney, Diane
1 Courtney, Inez
1 Courtney, Jean
1 Courtright, Jorga
9 Coury, Milly
1 Cousellor, Hans Olav
2 Cousins, Bob
1 Cousins, Jeff
1 Cousins, Margaret
1 Cousins, Micky
5 Cousins, Norman
2 Cousteau, Jacques
3 Cousy, Bob
1 Couzzens, James Gould
1 Cover, Carl
2 Coverdell, Paul
10 Covington (Warren Covington and His Orchestra)
1 Covington (Warren Covington and The Commanders)
1 Covington, Clark
4 Covington, Warren
1 Cowan, Harry
7 Cowan, Jean
3 Cowan, Jerome
6 Cowan, John
9 Cowan, Louis G.
21 Coward, Noel
1 Cowen, Sata
3 Cowings, Patricia
16 Cowl, Jane
6 Cowlan, Bert
1 Cowles, Gardner
1 Cowlin, John
1 Cowling, Sam
2 Cox
1 Cox, Archibald
9 Cox, Betty
2 Cox, Christopher
1 Cox, Gene
3 Cox, George Harmon
1 Cox, Kenneth
2 Cox, Slim
2 Cox, Wally
1 Coxon, Jimmy
1 Coyne, Lelia
1 Cozlinko, William
1 Crabbe, Alfred Leland
4 Crabbe, Buster
178 Crabtree, Paul
1 Craft, Harold
1 Craft, Morty
1 Craig, Bob
6 Craig, Catherine
3 Craig, Don
2 Craig, Francis
1 Craig, Gloria
2 Craig, Helen
8 Craig, James
3 Craig, John
2 Craig, Larry
1 Craig, Nancy
1 Craig, Nick
1 Craig, Rena
1 Craig, Rita
1 Craig, Tony
2 Craig, Walter
1 Craigar, Lawrence
5 Craige, John Houston
2 Craigo, Bill
1 Craigor (Manny Craigor and His Orchestra)
1 Craigor, Manny
1 Crain, Burton
12 Crain, Jeanne
8 Cramer, Floyd
1 Cramer, Jerome
1 Cramer, Lee
1 Cramer, Norman R.
1 Cramoy, Michael
1 Crandall, Joan
56 Crandall, P. C.
37 Crandall, Perry
1 Crandall, Russ
2 Crane, Dolores
1 Crane, Hugh
2 Crane, Maurice
2 Crane, Philip
8 Crane, Stephen
8 Crane, Vernon
1 Cranford, Eugene
7 Cranston, Alan
1 Cranston, Claudia
23 Cranston, Joe
4 Cranston, Joel
4 Cranston, Joseph
1 Crater, Burnham
1 Craven, Cicely
7 Craven, Frank
1 Craven, John
1 Cravens, Catherine
11 Crawford, Broderick
1 Crawford, Fred
3 Crawford, Harvey
15 Crawford, Jesse
1 Crawford, Jimmy
22 Crawford, Joan
2 Crawford, Kitty
1 Crawford, Lester
1 Crawford, Thelma
1 Crawl, Irene
1 Crawson, Jack
6 Crazy Orchestra, The
7 Crazy Trio, The
1 Crear, General
1 Creatore, Guiseppe
2 Creed, Don
9 Creekmore, Lloyd
1 Creel, George
1 Creel, Hurley G.
1 Cregar, Bert
9 Cregar, Laird
1 Creighton, Sally
215 Crenna, Richard
1 Crenshaw, Virgil S.
1 Cressoy, Pierre
1 Creston, Paul
35 Crew Chiefs, The
6 Crew Cuts, The
1 Crim, Mort
2 Cripine, Ken
4 Crippen
4 Crippen, Robert
1 Crippen, Roger
1 Cripps, Stafford
1 Criscuono, Eduardo
1 Crismond, Serge
20 Crisp, Donald
1 Crisp, Ray
1 Crist, Phil
5 Crocker, Emerson
1 Crockett, Gene
1 Croft, Larry
173 Croft, Mary Jane
1 Croft, Patty
14 Cromer, Tex
1 Cromwell, Jean
1 Cromwell, John
1 Cromwell, Richard
1 Cromwell, Robert
5 Cronin, Joe
79 Cronkite, Walter
12 Cronman, Harry
19 Cronin, A.J.
25 Cronyn, Hume
5 Crook, George
17 Crooks, Richard
1 Croonaders, The
23 Crosby (Bob Crosby and His All-Stars)
1 Crosby (Bob Crosby and His Dixieland Band)
1 Crosby (Bob Crosby and His Dixieland Jamboree)
24 Crosby (Bob Crosby and His Orchestra)
7 Crosby (Bob Crosby and The Bobcats)
1 Crosby Brothers, The
1 Crosby Sr., Mrs. H. L.
667 Crosby, Bing
124 Crosby, Bob
5 Crosby, Catherine
2 Crosby, David
5 Crosby, Dennis
3 Crosby, Dixie Lee
2 Crosby, Everett S.
40 Crosby, Gary
1 Crosby, Howard
3 Crosby, John
1 Crosby, Larry
41 Crosby, Lindsay
162 Crosby, Lou
1 Crosby, Norm
6 Crosby, Phillip
4 Crosby, Virginia
20 Crosby, Wade
1 Crosetti, Frank
1 Crosley Melody Maids, The
2 Crosley, Lester
1 Crosley, Powell
9 Cross, Glenn
174 Cross, Milton
1 Cross, Netwon
2 Crossen, Ken
1 Crothers (Scatman Crothers and His Orchestra)
7 Crouse, Russell
1 Crow, John
1 Crow, Nathan
1 Crowder, Charles
6 Crowder, Constance
1 Crowder, Leslie
1 Crowell, Robert
6 Crowlbein, Julius
1 Crowle, Nathan
13 Crowley, Dale
2 Crowley, Jim
2 Crowley, Lawrence
176 Crowley, Matt
2 Crowley, Pat
1 Crown Prince Olaf
1 Crowther, Jeffrey
1 Croy, Homer
1 Cruisinberry, Jane
1 Crum, Bartley
1 Crumb, Richard
8 Crumit, Frank
1 Crump, Russ
1 Crumpler, Chester
4 Crutcher, Jack
13 Crutcher, Robert Riley
224 Crutchfield, Les
4 Cruz, Albert
2 Cruz, Claudia
2 Cryer, Katherine
1 Crystal, Jim
1 Crystals, The
1 Csisbatron Group, The
78 Cubberly, Dan
1 Cuccinello, Tony
1 Cudahy, Grace
2 Cudahy, John
49 Cugat (Xavier Cugat and His Orchestra)
8 Cugat, Xavier
1 Cukor, George
1 Culbertson, Ely
1 Culbertson, Joyce
3 Culbertson, Phillip
39 Cullen, Bill
2 Cullen, James
2 Culler, Dick
1 Cullin, James J.
1 Cullis, Winifred
1 Cullum (Jim Cullum's Happy Jazz Band)
1 Culp, Robert
1 Culver, Dick
150 Culver, Howard
1 Cumagai, Ben
1 Cummings, Alan
2 Cummings, Constance
41 Cummings, Irving
1 Cummings, Ralph
25 Cummings, Robert
2 Cummings, Vicki
1 Cummins (Bernie Cummins and His Orchestra)
1 Cuni, Jean
1 Cunningham, Air Marshall
2 Cunningham, Allan
1 Cunningham, Bob
3 Cunningham, Joe
2 Cunningham, Owen
1 Cunningham, Paul
1 Cunningham, Scott
1 Cunningham, Warren
1 Cunningham, Zama
2 Cuomo, Mario
1 Cure, Vilma
2 Curlan, Arthur
1 Curley, Len
19 Curley, Leo
1 Curlin, Don
1 Curly Fox and Texas Ruby
2 Curran, Edward
1 Curran, Henry
1 Curran, Joseph
1 Curren, Jack
1 Curry, Brainard
56 Curry, Hugh
1 Curry, Louise
1 Curt, Larry
17 Curtin, Joseph
2 Curtis, Alan
1 Curtis, Bill
6 Curtis, Burton B.
1 Curtis, Donald
2 Curtis, Harold
1 Curtis, Howard J.
2 Curtis, Jack
13 Curtis, Keene
3 Curtis, Ken
2 Curtis, King
3 Curtis, Margaret
2 Curtis, Myrt
6 Curtis, Tony
1 Curtis, Wally
4 Curtiz, Michael
1 Curtwright, Jay
1 Curtwright, Jorja
2 Curwood, James Oliver
3 Cury, Ivan
1 Curzi, Cesare
1 Curzon, Clifford
1 Cusak, Anja
1 Cushing, George
1 Cushing, Richard
1 Cushner, Mary Beth
1 Cusick, Fred
1 Custer, Joe James
1 Cuter, Jean
2 Cutrer, T. Tommy
3 Cutshall, Cutty
1 Cutshaw, H.
8 Cutting, Dick
1 Cutting, Phil
1 Cuviello, Mike
1 Cuzzi, Jeff
2 Cvetic, Matt
1 Cyr, Johnny

2 D'Agostino, Charles
1 D'Amato, Alfonse
1 D'Amica, Joe
1 D'Amico (Hank D'Amico and His Orchestra)
1 D'Amico, Atilo
3 D'Amico, Hank
4 D'Aquino, Iva Toguri
4 D'Arcy, Jeanne
1 D'Arcy, Roy
1 D'Artega
1 D'Artega (D'Artega and His All Girl Orchestra)
4 D'Artega (D'Artega and His Orchestra)
3 D'Orsay, Fifi
1 D'Orsay, Marcelle
1 Da Costa, Morton
32 Da Silva, Howard
11 Dabney, Augusta
20 Dae, Donna
1 Dagen, Ken
1 Dagenais, Gil
1 Daggen, Johnny
3 Dagmar
6 Dahl, Arlene
6 Dahlstead, Dresser
1 Daigneau, Ken
1 Dailey (Pete Dailey and His Chicagoans)
1 Dailey (Pete Dailey and His Orchestra)
3 Dailey, Carroll C.
18 Dailey, Dan
1 Dailey, Howard P.
1 Dailey, Ted
1 Daily, Clot
1 Dairy Maids, The
1 Daisy
6 Daladier, Edouard
1 Dalair, Edgar P.
1 Dalair, Ingrid
2 Dalbert, Suzanne
9 Dale (Ted Dale and His Orchestra)
1 Dale (Ted Dale and The Carnation Orchestra)
20 Dale, Alan
8 Dale, Carlotta
5 Dale, Dick
1 Dale, Irene
2 Dale, Jim
1 Dale, Len
1 Dale, Phil
6 Dale, Ted
1 Dale-Moore, Shirley
1 Daley, Albert
1 Daley, Bill
38 Daley, Cass
1 Daley, Richard
1 Dali, Salvador
2 Dall, John
1 Dallas, Danny
1 Dalton (James Dalton and His Orchestra)
6 Dalton, Doris
1 Dalton, Doug
1 Dalton, James
2 Daly, Charles
1 Daly, Frank
135 Daly, John
1 Daly, Lorraine
1 Dalyrimple, Jean
1 Damari, Shoshana
22 Dame, Donald
3 Damon, Jerry
41 Damon, Les
19 Damone, Vic
6 Damrosch, Walter
1 Dan, Nick
11 Dana, Richard
1 Danch, Bill
2 Dandridge, Dorothy
25 Dandridge, Ruby
1 Dane, Andrew
1 Dane, Barbara
1 Dane, Clemence
3 Dane, Frank
1 Dane, Jeff
1 Danford, Charles
1 Danforth, John
2 Dangerfield, Rodney
1 Dania, Ken
1 Daniel Quartet, The
2 Daniel, Clifton
2 Daniel, Oliver
1 Daniel, W. Leo
1 Daniela, Lee
1 Danielian, N. R.
3 Daniell, Henry
15 Daniels (Elliot Daniels and His Orchestra)
13 Daniels, Anthony
6 Daniels, Bebe
3 Daniels, Billy
34 Daniels, Cecil
1 Daniels, Dorothy
4 Daniels, Elliot
6 Daniels, Fats
5 Daniels, Harold
1 Daniels, Leslie
1 Daniels, Lou
1 Daniels, Termite
4 Daniels, Tom
1 Daniels, Tommy
1 Daniels, William
1 Dankmeijer, Emil
2 Dankworth, Johnny
238 Dann, Sam
7 Dann, Victoria
1 Danny and The Juniors
60 Dant (Charles Dant and His Orchestra)
8 Dant, Charles
3 Dantine, Helmut
1 Danton, Bob
3 Danton, Joan
5 Danton, Ray
32 Danzig, Frank
4 Danzig, Jerry
1 Dappy Rhythm Boys
2 Darby (Ken Darby Choir, The)
16 Darby (Ken Darby Chorus, The)
4 Darby (Ken Darby Singers, The)
19 Darby, Ken
1 Darby, Marge
1 Darby, Natalie
3 Darcel, Denise
1 Darcy, Don
1 Darcy, Emery
2 Darcy, John
3 Darcy, Thomas F.
1 Dare, Darlene
2 Dare, Dorothy
1 Dare, Irene
1 Darian, Anita
6 Darin, Bobby
3 Dark, Alvin
1 Darktown Quartet, The
1 Darling, Denver
2 Darling, George
1 Darling, Jean
8 Darlington, Ed
1 Darlington, Erwin
1 Darlington, Mildred
1 Darlow, Bill
5 Darnay, Toni
1 Darnell, James
45 Darnell, Linda
1 Darowl, Al
7 Darrid, William
1 Darro, Frankie
1 Dartmouth Glee Club, The
5 Darwell, Jane
1 Darwin, Glen
1 Das, Taraknath
2 Daschle, Thomas
7 Dasso, Betty
1 Daunton, Nancy
1 Davenport, Doris
1 Davenport, Harry
1 Daves, Delmer
2 Davey, Jack
1 David, Bob
1 David, Eli
1 David, Freddy
1 David, John
1 Davidson, Carter
1 Davidson, Clinton
1 Davidson, Dewitt
1 Davidson, Joe
2 Davidson, John
1 Davidson, Lawrence
1 Davidson, Roy
1 Davie, Mrs. Preston
1 Davies, Brian
1 Davies, Bruce
2 Davies, Doug
13 Davies, Edward
1 Davies, Elaine
20 Davies, Gwen
1 Davies, Len
1 Davies, Lew
3 Davies, Marion
5 Davies, Marjorie
1 Davila, Charles
1 Davilla, Carlos
1 Davis (Chuck Davis and The Roundup Boys)
14 Davis (Dick Davis Chorus, The)
1 Davis (Dick Davis Glee Club, The)
1 Davis (Dix Davis Glee Club, The)
12 Davis (Phil Davis and His Orchestra)
1 Davis (Richard Davis Choir, The)
2 Davis (Saul Davis Trio, The)
10 Davis Jr., Sammy
1 Davis, Adelle
1 Davis, Agnes
1 Davis, Al
1 Davis, Allison
15 Davis, Beryl
49 Davis, Bette
5 Davis, Bob
18 Davis, Boyd
19 Davis, Charles
1 Davis, Cleo
7 Davis, Clive
22 Davis, Dix
6 Davis, Don
1 Davis, Earl
1 Davis, Ed
1 Davis, Eddie
6 Davis, Eddie Lockjaw
1 Davis, Ellabelle
105 Davis, Elmer
2 Davis, Esker
1 Davis, Frank
2 Davis, Gail
1 Davis, Glenn
1 Davis, Hal
1 Davis, Harriet Eager
1 Davis, Harry
50 Davis, Humphrey
1 Davis, James P.
36 Davis, Janette
1 Davis, Jim
1 Davis, Jimmy
44 Davis, Joan
1 Davis, Joe
5 Davis, Joel
1 Davis, John
2 Davis, Kay
1 Davis, Leighton
1 Davis, Lisa
1 Davis, Lucien
3 Davis, Luther
1 Davis, Mac
6 Davis, Malcolm
1 Davis, Meyer
1 Davis, Mike
1 Davis, Nathan
2 Davis, Norman H.
3 Davis, Ossie
1 Davis, Owen
3 Davis, Richard
13 Davis, Richard E.
1 Davis, Robert E.
5 Davis, Rufe
3 Davis, Ruth
2 Davis, Saville
1 Davis, Shelly
5 Davis, Skeeter
2 Davis, Stanley
1 Davis, Stringer
3 Davis, Sylvia
1 Davis, T. J.
1 Davis, Tom
3 Davis, Tommy
1 Davis, Watson
1 Davis, William H.
1 Davison (Wild Bill Davison and His Band)
1 Davison, Mrs. Henry P.
29 Davison, Wild Bill
6 Dawn (Dolly Dawn and The Manhattan Nighthawks)
1 Dawn, Alice
6 Dawn, Dolly
2 Dawn, Janice
1 Dawn, Maureen
1 Dawn-Busters Dixieland Band, The
6 Dawsha, Billy
1 Dawson (Mark Dawson and His Orchestra)
1 Dawson, Congressman
1 Dawson, Glory
18 Dawson, Hal K.
1 Dawson, Herb
1 Dawson, Joe
112 Dawson, John
1 Dawson, Liz
1 Dawson, Marion
1 Dawson, Mark
1 Dawson, Michael
2 Dawson, Nick
1 Dawson, Richard
7 Dawson, Ronald
4 Dawson, Sam

1 Dawson, William Levy
1 Day, Albert N.
1 Day, Clarence
412 Day, Dennis
1 Day, Donald
74 Day, Doris
6 Day, Everett
1 Day, Gordon
20 Day, Irene
1 Day, Jerry
1 Day, Jimmy
19 Day, Laraine
1 Day, Lazy Jim
2 Day, LeRoy
1 Dayan, Moishe
1 Daye, Marilyn
4 Days, Bill
1 Dayton, Ronny
1 De Angeles, Ralph
1 De Angeli, Marguerite
1 De Baer, General
15 de Balzac, Honore
1 de Bruine, N. A. C. Slotemaker
1 de Camp, L. Sprague
41 De Camp, Rosemary
5 De Carlo, Yvonne
3 De Castro Sisters, The
8 De Christ, Paul
14 De Cordoba, Pedro
4 de Cordova, Arturo
2 De Cordova, Frederick
113 de Corsia, Ted
4 De Forest, Lee
1 De Franco Family, The
23 De Franco, Buddy
1 de Frank, Eleanor
1 De Galindez, Jesus
6 De Gaulle, Charles
1 De Graysock, Fred
33 De Haven, Gloria
1 De Jong, L.
1 De Koven, Reginald
130 De Koven, Roger
1 de la Garza, John
1 De la Garza, Kiki
2 de la Torre, Rey
2 de La Fuente, Alfred
5 de Leath, Vaughn
2 De Leo, Don
1 De Los, Yana
2 De Lugg (Milton DeLugg Quartet, The)
1 De Lyon, Leo
57 De Marco Sisters, The
1 De Marnay, Terrance
1 De Marra, Ferdinand
21 de Maupassant, Guy
3 de Merimee, Prosper
1 De Mille, Agnes
1 De Mille, William C.
1 De Paul, Gene
1 De Pauw (Leonard De Pauw Chorus, The)
6 De Pauw, Leonard
1 de Puglia, Dolores
4 de Ropp, Stephen
5 de Rose, Peter
2 de Saint Exupery, Antoine
8 De Sales, Francis
2 de Seversky, Alexander
5 De Soto, Johnny
1 de Spain, Edna
1 De Sylva, B.G.
1 de Toth, Andre
1 De Vincenzi, Donald
26 De Vito, Buddy
117 De Vol (Frank De Vol and His Orchestra)
2 De Vol, Frank
2 De Vore Sisters, The
1 De Vries, Peter
5 De Vry, Guy
3 de Wilde, Brandon
3 de Wilde, Brandon
3 De Witt, John
1 de Witt, Marie
3 De Wolfe, Billy
2 Deacon, Richard
1 Dean (Jimmie Dean and His Texas Wildcasts)
2 Dean (Jimmie Dean and His Trail Riders)
53 Dean (Jimmy Dean and His Texas Wildcats)
1 Dean, Barney
1 Dean, Charles
5 Dean, Dizzy
4 Dean, Eddie
1 Dean, Eileen
2 Dean, Faye
3 Dean, James
23 Dean, Jimmy
1 Dean, Man Moutain
3 Dean, Martha
2 Dean, Robert Anthony
1 Dean, Robert George
2 Dean, Vera Micheles
2 Dean, Viola
1 Dearborn, Ned
3 Dearenforth, Bob
1 Dearing, John
1 Deaver, Michael
1 Debank, Felix
2 DeBecker, Harold
2 Debit, Alan
3 Debonaires, The
1 Debry, T. Myron
2 Debus, Kurt
3 Debutantes, The
1 Decca Concert Orchestra, The
2 Decker, Henri
1 DeCoe, Darold D.
7 Decola, Felix
1 Deconcinni, Dennis
1 Deday, Kathleen
7 Dee, Frances
1 Dee, Jerry
10 Dee, Ruby
1 Deems, Harold
1 Deeney, Robert
2 Deep River Boys, The
1 Deering, Diane
6 Deering, Olive
2 Deese, John
6 DeFelita, Frank
1 Defoe, Daniel
1 Defoe, Dr.
6 Defore, Don
2 DeFranco (Buddy DeFranco Quartet, The)
1 Degnan, Dwight
631 Dehner, John
2 Deighton, Marga Ann
1 Deke, Michael
9 Dekker, Albert
1 del Mar, Vina
1 del Rey, Lester
5 Del Rio, Dolores
78 del Valle, Jaime
1 Del Vayo, J. Alvarez
1 Delafield, Ann
2 Delaney, Robert Mills
12 Delano, Gwen
1 Delano, Nick
2 DeLeon, Tommy
1 Delivet, Louis
1 Dell Trio, The
2 Dell, Alfred
2 Dell, Claudia
4 Dell, Dorothy
1 Dell, Jeffrey
1 Dell, Joseph
1 Dell, Judy
1 Dell, Myrna
1 Dell, Walton
12 Della Chiesa, Vivienne
139 Delmar, Kenny
1 Delmore Brothers, The
1 Delory (Al Delory and His Orchestra)
1 DeLouise, Dom
44 Delta Rhythm Boys, The
1 DeLugg (Milton DeLugg and His Trio)
2 DeLugg (Milton DeLugg and The NBC Orchestra)
1 DeLugg (Milton DeLugg's Accordion and Quartet)
17 DeLugg, Milton
15 Demarest, William
2 Demaret, Jimmy
1 Demas, Lou
2 Demby, Emanuel
323 DeMille, Cecil B.
18 Demling, Bill
1 Demling, Frank
4 Demmick, Marshall
1 Demming, Alan
1 Demoploye, Stavros
1 Demott, Jed
9 Dempsey, Jack
1 den Doolard, A.
2 Denbeau, Jacques
1 Dendrick, Richard
1 DeNel, Doris
1 Denham, Reginald
3 Denker, Henry
1 Denning, Dolores
1 Denning, Ellen
2 Denning, Glen
1 Denning, Mark
62 Denning, Richard
1 Dennis (Johnny Dennis and His Ranchos)
1 Dennis Sisters, The
1 Dennis, Alan
13 Dennis, Clark
2 Dennis, Ginny
1 Dennis, Lawrence
1 Dennis, Marion
14 Dennis, Matt
1 Dennis, Paul
1 Dennis, Rex
1 Dennis, Robert C.
1 Dennis, Ruth
1 Dennis, Sandy
3 Dennison, Leslie
13 Dennison, Merrill
18 Denny Jr., George V.
2 Denny, Barbara
3 Denny, Reginald
1 Denny, Rex
1 Denny, Roger
1 Denove, Jack
2 Denton, Crahan
10 Denton, Robert
1 Denver, Bob
1 Denver, John
1 Dereis, Joe
2 Derek, John
18 Derman, Lou
2 Derita, Joe
1 Derr, Clifford
1 Derr, John
1 Derran, Darla
1 Derrick, Butler
2 Derwin (Hal Derwin and His Orchestra)
9 Derwin, Hal
1 Desmond (Johnny Desmond with Manhattan Nighthawks)
1 Desmond (Paul Desmond Quartet, The)
4 Desmond, Connie
70 Desmond, Johnny
18 Desmond, Mary Frances
1 Desmond, Paul
1 deSola Poole, David
8 Desvernine, Raoul E.
1 Detterman, Ted
4 Dettin, Bob
1 Deutsch (Emery Deutsch and His Orchestra)
1 Deutsch, Adolph
1 Deutsch, Helen
1 Devene, George
1 DeVere, Cliff
2 Devers, General
200 Devine, Andy
4 Devine, Art
1 Devine, Charles
1 Devine, David
97 Devine, Jerry
7 Devitt, Alan
1 Devlin, Rick
1 Devon, Lee
1 Devoto, Bernard
2 Devron, George
64 Devry, Mike
1 Dewey, Phil
17 Dewey, Thomas
1 Dewhurst, Colleen
1 Dewhurst, J. Frederick
1 DeWitt, Faye
1 Dewitt, George
1 DeWitt, Gordon Schuyler
7 DeWitt, Jacqueline
10 Di Angelo, Carlo
13 Di Maggio, Joe
152 Di Santis, Joe
2 Diamond (Leo Diamond Harmonaires)
1 Diamond (Leo Diamond Harmonaires, The)
1 Diamond (Lou Diamond and His Orchestra)
13 Diamond, Anne
154 Diamond, Don
4 Diamond, Leo
1 Diamond, Neil
11 Diamond, Selma
1 Diane
2 Diaz, Franklin Chang
2 Dibbs, Kay
1 Dice, Robert
3 Dick, Phillip K.
1 Dickens Sisters, The
142 Dickens, Charles
7 Dickens, Jimmy
1 Dickens, John
1 Dickenson, Bookie
30 Dickenson, Jean
1 Dickenson, Richard
2 Dickenson, Shirley
14 Dickenson, Vic
2 Dickerson, Nancy
15 Dickey, Annamary
1 Dickey, Jay
1 Dickey, Joe
1 Dickey, Mary Lou
1 Dickie, Bill
2 Dickies Hometowners, The
2 Dickinson, Angie
3 Dickson, Gloria
2 Dickson, Gordon R.
3 Dickson, H. Vernon
1 Dickson, Jesse
1 Dickson, Tom
1 Dicky Doo and The Don'ts
1 Diehl, Bill
1 Diehl, John
3 Dieterle, William
29 Dietrich, Marlene
1 Dietz, David
1 Dietz, Howard
50 Dietz, John
1 Dietzer, Edward Roderick
6 Digges, Dudley
1 Dilka, Mike
1 Dill, Howard
1 Dill, Marshall
3 Dillard, Bill
2 Dillard, Dorothy
4 Diller, Phyllis
1 Dillon, Mary Earheart
1 Dillon, Paul
3 Dillon, Tom
1 Dilse, Mary
16 Dimbleby, Richard
1 Dimetrie, James
5 Dimetrie, Jim
1 Dimsdale, Shirley
1 Dine, Norman
1 Dinehart, Alan
37 Dinelli, Mel
5 Dingle, Charles
1 Dinken, Herm
1 Dinken, Stepahnie
12 Dinning Sisters, The
2 Dinning, Lou
1 Dinsdale, Jack
2 Dionne Quintuplets, The
1 Dipsy Doodlers, The
3 Director, Joyce
6 Director, Stanley

1 Dirkey, Frank B.
13 Dirksen, Everett
2 Disatel, Van
1 Dishy, Bob
13 Disney, Walt
3 Disque, Jr., Brice
3 DiSolis, Solito
1 DiStefano, Giuseppe
103 Ditmars, Ivan
1 Ditter, J. William
1 Divino, Ray
1 Diviveck, Harvey
1 Dix, Dorothy
2 Dix, Richard
1 Dix, Tommy
1 Dixie Jubilee Singers, The
2 Dixieland All Stars, The
1 Dixieland Band
1 Dixieland Jazz Band, The
1 Dixielanders, The
15 Dixon, Bob
1 Dixon, Del
1 Dixon, Donald
1 Dixon, Jean
1 Dixon, Jeanne
1 Dixon, Joe
1 Dixon, John Paul
3 Dixon, Lee
1 Dixon, Peter
1 Dixon, Pierson
3 Dixon, Redge
1 Dixon, Samuel
1 Dixon, Sidney
1 Dixon, Tim
1 Dixon, Tina
4 Dixon, Tom
1 Dmytryk, Ed
1 Doar, Charles
7 Doar, Graham
1 Dobey, Duncan
1 Dobie, J. Frank
510 Dobkin, Lawrence
1 Dobkin, Toby Blue
2 Dobson, James
2 Dockey, Robert
3 Doctor, Lloyd
1 Docusen, Bernard
1 Dodd, Christopher
1 Dodd, Estelle
5 Dodd, Jimmy
26 Dodds, Baby
11 Dodge Orchestra, The
1 Dodge, Cleveland E.
1 Dodge, David
1 Dodge, Dora E.
1 Dodge, Estelle
1 Dodge, Mary Mapes
1 Dodgers Quartet, The
3 Dodson, Owen
9 Dodsworth, John
1 Doenitz
6 Doerner (George Doerner and His Orchestra)
1 Doerr (Clyde Doerr's Saxophone Trio)
2 Doerr, Bobby
1 Doggett (Bill Doggett Trio, The)
1 Doherty, Duffy
1 Doherty, Loreen
75 Dolan (Robert Emmett Dolan and His Orchestra)
1 Dolan, Don
1 Dolan, Jimmy
2 Dolan, Michael
20 Dole, Robert
2 Dolenz, George
1 Dolin (Max Dolin and His Grenadiers)
1 Dolin (Max Dolin and His Orchestra)
6 Dolinsky, Meyer
2 Domenici, Peter
1 Domian, Lana
1 Domino, Fats
1 Doms, Peter
1 Don Juans, The
2 Don Lee-KHJ Orchestra and Singers, The
4 Donahue (Al Donahue and His Orchestra)
3 Donahue (Sam Donahue and His Navy Band)
4 Donahue (Sam Donahue and His Orchestra)
1 Donahue (Sam Donahue and The AFRS Swing Wing)
1 Donahue, Al
1 Donahue, Dr.
1 Donahue, Mary Jane
3 Donahue, Sam
1 Donahue, Thomas
186 Donald, Peter
6 Donaldson, Dan
1 Donaldson, Don
8 Donaldson, Earl
1 Donaldson, Lou
10 Donaldson, Sam
8 Donaldson, Ted
1 Donaldson, Tom
1 Donaldson, Walter
1 Donat, Robert
5 Donath, Ludwig
1 Donato (Eduardo Donato and His Orchestra)
1 Donato, Anthony
1 Donato, Tony
5 Donegal, Lord
5 Donegan, Dorothy
55 Donlevy, Brian
4 Donn (Lou Donn and His Orchestra)
1 Donn, Carol
1 Donnell, Horace
2 Donnell, Jeff
1 Donnelly, Andy
1 Donnelly, James
3 Donnelly, Robert
1 Donnelly, Ruth
3 Donnenfeld, Harry
1 Donner, David W.
1 Donohue Jr., Jay Ray
1 Donohue, Joe
1 Donohue, Phil
1 Donohue, Vincent
1 Donovan, General
17 Donovan, Greg
12 Donovan, Hobart
1 Donovan, Nancy
1 Doodletown Pipers, The
1 Dooley, Eddie
1 Dooley, Larry
1 Doolittle, Don
9 Doolittle, Jimmy
3 Doolittle, Mrs. Jimmy
4 Doran, Ann
1 Doran, Jim
1 Doran, Mary
2 Dorati, Antal
8 Doremus, John
1 Dorenmont, Fredrich
2 Dorey, Ray
7 Dorfman, Sid
1 Dorgen, Byron
1 Dorian Sisters, The
1 Dorin, Bobby
2 Dorin, Phoebe
1 Doring Sisters, The
4 Dorman, Paul
1 Dorn, Larry
2 Dorn, Phillip
2 Dorris, Red
1 Dors, Diana
26 Dorsey (Jimmy Dorsey and His Orchestra)
1 Dorsey (Tommy and Jimmy Dorsey Orchestra, The)
99 Dorsey (Tommy Dorsey and His Orchestra)
3 Dorsey (Tommy Dorsey Orchestra, The)
18 Dorsey Brothers Orchestra, The
3 Dorsey, Betty
1 Dorsey, Howard
11 Dorsey, Jimmy
84 Dorsey, Tommy
3 Dos Passos, John
1 Dosh, Joe
6 Dostoyevsky, Fyodor
1 Dotheidi, Hazel
1 Doty, John
1 Doty, Judith
46 Doud, Ann
72 Doud, Gil
1 Doue, John
1 Dougherty (Stan Dougherty and His Orchestra)
3 Dougherty, Eddie
1 Dougherty, Julia
1 Dougherty, Maria
1 Douglas
1 Douglas, Carol
1 Douglas, Chad
16 Douglas, Don
1 Douglas, Emily Taft
4 Douglas, Glenn
3 Douglas, Helen Gahagan
167 Douglas, Hugh
8 Douglas, Jack
17 Douglas, Kirk
27 Douglas, Larry
2 Douglas, Linda
5 Douglas, Lloyd C.
1 Douglas, Louis
34 Douglas, Melvyn
6 Douglas, Michael
1 Douglas, Milton
1 Douglas, Mr.
1 Douglas, Mrs. Kirk
2 Douglas, Nancy
33 Douglas, Paul
1 Douglas, Robert
26 Douglas, Sharon
13 Douglas, Susan
1 Douglas, Tom
4 Douglas, William O.
1 Douglas-Howe, Alec
1 Dovells, The
1 Dover, Jane
3 Dow, Peggy
4 Dowd, Don
1 Dowing, Tom
15 Dowling, Eddie
2 Dowling, Janet
37 Down, Margaret
3 Downe, Saxy
1 Downes, Olan
1 Downey, James
47 Downey, Morton
1 Downey, Sheridan
1 Downey, Vernon
2 Downing, David
2 Downing, Francis
4 Downs, Armand
22 Downs, Bill
3 Downs, Cathy
1 Downs, Edward Gray
63 Downs, Hugh
1 Downs, James
9 Downs, Johnny
2 Downs, William Henry
2 Doxie, Devona
65 Doyle, Arthur Conan
2 Doyle, Bobby
17 Doyle, Jim
1 Doyle, Jimmy
10 Doyle, Len
1 Doyle, Maxine
1 Doyle, Rear Admiral
1 Doyle, Walter B.
83 Dragon (Carmen Dragon and His Orchestra)
31 Dragon, Carmen
36 Dragonette, Jessica
1 Drake, Alan
28 Drake, Alfred
4 Drake, Betsy
1 Drake, Bill
1 Drake, Charles
7 Drake, Drexel
1 Drake, Edwin
3 Drake, Frances
5 Drake, Galen
4 Drake, Gordon
1 Drake, Jack
1 Drake, Johnny
4 Drake, Pauline
10 Drake, Tom
2 Draney, John
7 Draper, Margaret
2 Draper, Rusty
1 Drason, Danny
1 Drayton, Grace
7 Dream Choristers, The
1 Dreamtones, The
3 Drees, Jack
6 Dreier, Alex
4 Dreiser, Theodore
7 Dressen, Charlie
1 Dresser, Louise
40 Dressler, Eric
3 Drew, Barry
1 Drew, Charlie
6 Drew, Doris
9 Drew, Ellen
1 Drew, Frances
2 Drew, Helene
1 Drew, James
7 Drew, Roland
1 Drew, Wendy
3 Dreyfus, Michael
1 Dreyfus, Theodore
4 Drifters, The
8 Driggs, Collins
1 Drinkwater, John
1 Driscoll, Alfred
4 Driscoll, Bobby
20 Driscoll, Dave
1 Driscoll, Dick
3 Driscoll, John
1 Driver, Neil
1 Dropsie, Herb
5 Dru, Joanne
1 Drucker, Stanley
1 Drum, Howard
1 Drummond, Jane
1 Drummond, Jim
1 Druskin, Beatrice
1 Druskin, Robert
1 Drusky, Bob
3 Drusky, Roy
1 Druyan, Ann
11 Dryanforth, Harold
413 Dryden, Robert
6 Dryer, Bernard
1 Dryer, Marlo
2 Dryer, Sherman H.
1 Dryfus, Robert
2 Drysdale, Don
1 Du Klu, Walter
11 du Maurier, Daphne
41 Du Maurier, George
1 Du Maurier, Gerald
1 Du Pont, Pierre
78 Du Val, Joseph
1 Dubin, Al
1 Dubinsky, David
1 Dubois, Geraldine
22 Dubois, Rachel Davis
3 Dubov, Joe
133 Dubov, Paul
1 Dubridge, Lee A.
10 Duchin (Eddie Duchin and His Orchestra)
17 Duchin, Eddie
4 Duchin, Peter
1 Duddy (Lyn Duddy Chorus, The)
20 Dudley, Bernard
2 Dudley, Clara
7 Dudley, Dick
1 Dudley, Jimmy
6 Dudley, Paul
1 Duff, Brian
1 Duff, Harry
181 Duff, Howard
1 Duff, Irene
1 Duff, Robin
8 Duffield, Brainard
2 Duffield, Mark
1 Duffy, Al
3 Duffy, Jack
17 Duffy, John

6 Dugan, Patti
1 Dugan, Tom
3 Dugdale, Charlie
8 Duggan, Andrew
5 Duhamel, Maurice
1 Dujour, Madame
1 Dukakis, Kitty
14 Dukakis, Michael
7 Dukas, James
53 Duke Of Paducah, The
2 Duke Of Windsor, The
1 Duke University Glee Club, The
1 Duke, Charles
1 Duke, Marylin
2 Duke, Michael
5 Duke, Patty
5 Duke, Paul
4 Duke, Vernon
2 Dukes Of Dixieland, The
1 Dukes, Cora
42 Dukorn, Leo
1 Dulany, Howard
1 Dulcina
4 Dullea, Keir
1 Dulles, Allen W.
17 Dulles, John Foster
1 Dulo, Ginger
97 Dumas, Alexandre
1 Dumas, Helene
6 Dumbrille, Douglas
6 Dumke, Ralph
2 Dumont (Oscar Dumont and His Orchestra)
1 Dumont, Alan B.
2 Dumont, Helen
4 Dumont, Margaret
1 Dumont, Oscar
1 Dunbar, Bonnie
2 Dunbar, Dixie
15 Dunbar, Russ
1 Duncan (Slim Duncan and His Texas Tornadoes)
1 Duncan Sisters, The
6 Duncan, Alistair
1 Duncan, Archie
1 Duncan, Buddy
2 Duncan, Hank
5 Duncan, Herb
1 Duncan, Molly Jo
1 Duncan, Pamela
1 Duncan, Richard M.
1 Duncan, Slim
6 Duncan, Todd
2 Dunham (Sonny Dunham and His Orchestra)
4 Dunham, Dick
1 Dunham, Eddie
6 Dunham, Edwin
1 Dunham, Sonny
8 Duning (George Duning and His Orchestra)
1 Duning, George
1 Dunjavoy, Roshan
73 Dunkel, John
1 Dunkin, Phillip
16 Dunlap, Patricia
1 Dunlop Jr., Orrin E.
2 Dunlop, Patricia
3 Dunn, Arty
1 Dunn, Elizabeth
1 Dunn, J. Kyuang
12 Dunn, James
2 Dunn, James C.
26 Dunn, Michael
1 Dunn, Richard
1 Dunn, Ron
3 Dunn, Sam
2 Dunn, Tom
8 Dunn, William J.
7 Dunne, Eddie
64 Dunne, Irene
1 Dunne, J. Malcolm
6 Dunne, James A.
2 Dunne, John
31 Dunne, Steve
11 Dunninger
2 Dunnock, Mildred
1 Dunnock, Richard
31 Dunphy, Don
1 Dunphy, Ralph
3 Dunsany, Lord
1 Dunstedter (Eddie Dunstedter and His Orchestra)
160 Dunstedter, Eddie
1 Dunton, Marjorie
7 DuPage, Richard
1 Dupar, Barbara
3 Dupont Company Chorus, The
1 Dupont Speed Blenders, The
1 Dupont, Pete
10 Duprez, June
1 Duprez, Minnie
1 Durand, Charles
1 Durant, Will
188 Durante, Jimmy
1 Durante, Margie
24 Durbin, Deanna
2 Durelle, Jeannie
2 Duren, Ryne
1 Durenberger, David
1 Durham, Bobby
25 Durham, Richard
19 Durocher, Leo
1 Durr
1 Durrance, T.
1 Durso, Joe
2 Durston, Gigi
2 Durwin, Clarence
7 Duryea, Dan
2 Dutch Swing College Band
1 Dutch, Helen
2 Duthie, George
1 Dutra, Olin
13 DuVal, David
1 Duvall, O. P.
1 Dvonch, Fred
10 Dvorak, Ann
2 Dwan, Robert
1 Dwyer, Jerry
3 Dwyer, Marlo
1 Dwyer, Virginia
2 Dyal, Palmer
1 Dyce, Hamilton
8 Dyer, Dick
3 Dyer, Eddie
1 Dyer-Bennet, Richard
1 Dykes, Bobby
1 Dykes, Jimmy
1 Dylan, Bob
2 Dylan, Tom
1 Dysart, Richard
2 d'Estang, Valery Giscard

1 Eager, Edward
45 Eagles, James
2 Eagleton, Clyde
52 Eames, Hamilton
1 Eammond, Earl
2 Eamon, Joseph
1 Earhart, Amelia
1 Earhart, Amy Otis
1 Earhorn, Phillip
1 Earl, Lawrence
14 Early, Stan
12 Earnshaw, Harry A.
1 Earthine, James
8 East, Ed
1 East, George
1 Eastland, Richard
2 Eastman Rochester Pops Orchestra, The
2 Eastman Symphonic Wind Ensemble, The
17 Eastman, Carl
2 Eastman, George
1 Eastman, Mary
2 Eastman, Max
2 Easton, Harvey
1 Easton, Jane
1 Easton, Joan
7 Easton, Robert
1 Easton, Ruth
1 Easy Riders Trio, The
1 Eaton, Colin
2 Eaton, Evelyn
1 Eaton, Jack
1 Eaton, Mrs. Rex
2 Eaton, Richard
1 Eaton, Victoria
1 Eauje, Pierre
1 Eaves, Margaret
29 Eban, Abba
1 Ebel, Earl
2 Eberle (Ray Eberle and His Orchestra)
41 Eberle, Ray
13 Eberly, Bob
3 Eberman (Buddy Eberman and His Orchestra)
1 Ebersole, Huston
1 Ebert, Paul
1 Ebert, Roger
6 Ebsen, Buddy
4 Eby, Kermit
2 Eckenoff, Ivan
1 Eckersly, Peter
1 Eckert, Dennis
1 Eckhardt (George Eckhardt and His Ambassadors)
9 Eckhart, Agnes
1 Eckland, Erlin
6 Eckles, Randolph
3 Eckstine (Billy Eckstine and His Orchestra)
13 Eckstine, Billy
1 Ed, Ernie
1 Ed, Kaye
1 Edberg, James
1 Eddington, May
4 Eddy, Bob
69 Eddy, Nelson
4 Eddy, Ralph
1 Eddy, Sherwood
1 Eddy, Val
1 Edelman, Erv
1 Eden, Alice
14 Eden, Anthony
2 Eden, Ursula
1 Eden, W. G.
4 Edgar, Leon
1 Edge, Bob
3 Edgely, Lesley
1 Edington, D. H.
2 Edison, Harry Sweets
2 Edison, John
1 Edison, Thomas
2 Edkins, Alden
4 Edmond, Irwin
3 Edmonds, Walter
1 Edmondson, Ray
1 Edmonson, Bill
1 Edwards
151 Edwards (George Edwards Players, The)
16 Edwards Jr., Jack
19 Edwards, Alyn
1 Edwards, Amelia
1 Edwards, Bill
88 Edwards, Blake
1 Edwards, Bob
1 Edwards, Buddy
18 Edwards, Cliff
87 Edwards, Douglas
51 Edwards, George
109 Edwards, Jack
1 Edwards, James
93 Edwards, Joan
1 Edwards, Joe
1 Edwards, Lee
1 Edwards, Leslie
1 Edwards, Marty
1 Edwards, Mrs. Gus
56 Edwards, Ralph
254 Edwards, Sam
64 Edwards, Webley
1 Egan, Edward
8 Egan, Leo
1 Egbert, Joe
1 Egger, Jack
1 Eggerth, Marta
3 Eggleston, Edward
10 Egleston, Charles
3 Egner, Red
1 Ehlers, Dorothy
1 Ehrenberger, J.
1 Ehrlenborn, Ray
14 Ehrlich, Max
1 Ehron, Emily
15 Eichelberger, Clark
1 Eichmann, Adolph
1 Eichner, Bernard
5 Eid, Leif
1 Eidell, Eddy
2 Eigen, Jack
1 Eikenberry, Jill
128 Eiler, Barbara
7 Eiler, Virginia
3 Eilers, Sally
6 Einstein, Albert
8 Einstein, Harry
1 Einvick, Will
1 Einz, Arlene
1 Eisen, Marshall
3 Eisen, Sammy
1 Eisen, Steve
4 Eisenbach, Robert
1 Eisenberg, Walter
1 Eisenhower, David
64 Eisenhower, Dwight
1 Eisenhower, Julie Nixon
2 Eisenhower, Milton
4 Eisinger, Jo
3 Eisler (Hans Eisler and His Orchestra)
2 Elachi, Charles
2 Elder, Don
20 Elders, Harry
1 Eldon, J. Warren
1 Eldridge (Roy Eldridge and His Orchestra)
1 Eldridge, Don
17 Eldridge, Florence
20 Eldridge, Roy

3 Eldridge, Tom
1 Eleanor
3 Elgart (Les and Larry Elgart and Their Orchestra)
7 Elgart (Les and Larry Elgart Orchestra, The)
10 Elgart (Les Elgart and His Orchestra)
1 Elgart, Les
1 Elgin, Frank
1 Elias, Alex
1 Elias, Irv
1 Eligibles, The
3 Elinson, Irving
89 Eliot, George Fielding
2 Eliot, T. S.
3 Eliott, Bill
2 Elizondo, Hector
1 Elkin, Stanley
1 Elkins, Jeannie
11 Elkins, Samuel
1 Ellas, Andy and Forest Wood
7 Ellen, Jean
1 Ellender, Allen J.
1 Ellgood, Percival George
2 Ellingston, John R.
9 Ellington (Duke Ellington and His Famous Orchestra)
102 Ellington (Duke Ellington and His Orchestra)
74 Ellington (Ray Ellington Quartet, The)
61 Ellington, Duke
3 Ellington, Jean
1 Ellington, Judy
1 Ellington, Ken
3 Ellington, Marie
5 Ellington, Mercer
1 Elliot
1 Elliot, Barron
1 Elliot, Don
3 Elliot, George
1 Elliot, Georgia
1 Elliot, Harold
1 Elliot, Harriet
1 Elliot, Lee
1 Elliot, Madge
46 Elliot, Patricia
2 Elliot, Roger
13 Elliot, Stephen
1 Elliot, Walter
16 Elliot, Win
1 Elliott Brothers, The
1 Elliott, Bill
354 Elliott, Bob
16 Elliott, Bruce
5 Elliott, Dick
1 Elliott, June
180 Elliott, Larry
2 Elliott, Melvin
1 Elliott, Scott
279 Elliotte, John
1 Ellis
4 Ellis (Seger Ellis and His Orchestra)
64 Ellis, Anita
98 Ellis, Antony
17 Ellis, Bobby
59 Ellis, David
1 Ellis, Dellie
2 Ellis, Edward
441 Ellis, Georgia
15 Ellis, H. Emory
2 Ellis, Harry
135 Ellis, Herb
1 Ellis, Jean
1 Ellis, Jimmy
1 Ellis, Junie
8 Ellis, Maurice
1 Ellis, Patricia
1 Ellis, Peggy Ann
1 Ellis, Ray
4 Ellis, Seger
14 Ellis, Steve
4 Ellis, Suzanne
1 Elliscue, Nelson
1 Ellison, Curley
1 Ellison, Dick
1 Ellison, Irving
1 Ellison, Lynn
1 Ellison, Wilmer
1 Elm City Four, The
1 Elman (Ziggy Elman and His Air Force Band)
6 Elman (Ziggy Elman and His Orchestra)
1 Elman (Ziggy Elman and The Long Beach Air Transport Orchestra)
8 Elman, Dave
1 Elman, Irving
1 Elman, Lotte
1 Elman, Mischa
33 Elman, Ziggy
2 Elmassion, Zaruhi
19 Eloise
1 Elon, Jean
3 Elson, Bob
1 Elson, Elizabeth
1 Elson, Sam
1 Elstner, Anne
7 Elstrom, Sidney
1 Elton, David
1 Eltzer, Frank B.
1 Elvira
2 Elyn, Mark
4 Elzy, Ruby
4 Emerick, Bob
1 Emerson
2 Emerson, Ann
2 Emerson, Charles
40 Emerson, Ed
1 Emerson, Elsie May
12 Emerson, Faye
9 Emerson, Hope
4 Emerson, Joe
1 Emerson, Ralph Waldo
4 Emerson, Waldo
4 Emery, Bob
1 Emery, De Witt
4 Emery, John
1 Emily, Carl
1 Emke, Edith
1 Emlin, Robert
1 Emma, Sweet
1 Emmett, Catherine
12 Emory, Carl
3 Emory, Russ
1 Empire Builders, The
1 Empire Chamber Trio, The
1 Emthwaite, Harlan
1 Encores, The
14 Enders, Robert J.
4 Endfield, Cyril
3 Engberg, Dick
1 Engel (Lehman Engel and His Orchestra and Chorus)
2 Engel (Lehman Engel and His Orchestra)
1 Engel, Curly
1 Engel, Irving
7 Engel, Lehman
1 Engel, Owen
1 Engel, Roy
11 Engle, Cliff
1 Engle, Holland
4 Engle, Joe
35 Englebach, Dee
2 Engleby, Ronald
1 Englehardt, Joseph
1 Englehardt, Nicholas L.
1 Englehart, Frederick
1 Engler, John
1 English Singers, The
1 English, Richard
1 Englund, George
1 Englund, Pat
2 Enis, Joe
1 Enloe, Nell Howard
2 Enlow, Grayson
24 Ennis (Skinnay Ennis and His Orchestra)
1 Ennis (Skinnay Ennis and The Santa Anita Ordnance Training Center Band)
2 Ennis, Ethel
1 Ennis, John
1 Ennis, Leroy
23 Ennis, Skinnay
2 Enright, Dan
1 Enrique, Luis
1 Enroth, Dick
4 Envick, William
1 Epsom, Donna
1 Epstein, Abraham
2 Epstein, Jerome
2 Erdman, Richard
1 Erdmann, John
1 Erede, Alberto
102 Eric, Elspeth
1 Erickson, Charles
15 Erickson, Leif
161 Erickson, Louise
1 Erickson, Stephen
1 Ericson, John
1 Erlenborn, Ray
1 Erns, Morris
1 Ernst, Bud
1 Ernst, Morris
1 Errair, Ken
2 Errol, Leon
1 Errol, Ralph
1 Erskine, Carl
7 Erskine, Eileen
2 Erskine, Laurie York
5 Erskine, Marilyn
1 Ervine, St. John
2 Erwin (Pee Wee Erwin and His Dixieland Band)
1 Erwin, George
1 Erwin, Harry
3 Erwin, Pee Wee
1 Erwin, Sam
1 Erwin, Stan
20 Erwin, Stu
27 Erwin, Trudy
1 Erwin, William
1 Escortiers, The
2 Escorts and Betty, The
6 Eshelman, Miriam
1 Eskin, David B.
1 Esler, Fred
1 Esman, Harry
1 Esmee Of Paris
3 Esmond, Carl
3 Esmond, Jill
1 Esmond, Karl
1 Esposito, Larry
1 Essen, Bill
2 Este, Louis
1 Estelita
2 Esterbrook, Howard
1 Estes, John
1 Estes, Milton
3 Estes, Roy
2 Estey, Louis
68 Estherman, Laura
1 Eton Boys, The
2 Etterer, Bernard
10 Etting, Ruth
2 Ettlinger, Don
1 Eubanks, David
1 Eulilius, Betty
2 Eureka Brass Band, The
1 Euripedes
2 Eustace, Elizabeth
1 Evan, Carl
1 Evangelista, Alfredo
1 Evanich, Peggy
1 Evans (Lee Evans and His Orchestra)
1 Evans Quartet, The
2 Evans, Bergen
6 Evans, Bill
1 Evans, Bob
12 Evans, C. P.
1 Evans, Chick
2 Evans, Connie
96 Evans, Dale
1 Evans, Douglas
2 Evans, Harold
1 Evans, Harry
1 Evans, Herbert
1 Evans, Herschel
4 Evans, Joan
1 Evans, John
1 Evans, Judith
1 Evans, Lee
1 Evans, Lou Red
1 Evans, Luther
5 Evans, Madge
1 Evans, Mark
11 Evans, Maurice
1 Evans, Michael
5 Evans, Nancy
1 Evans, Ray
1 Evans, Red
1 Evans, Redd
2 Evans, Reynolds
5 Evans, Richard
2 Evans, Ronald
1 Evans, Sandy
1 Evans, Warren
3 Evans, Wilbur
1 Evanston, Edith
1 Eveling, Stan
48 Evelyn and Her Magic Violin
9 Evelyn, Judith
25 Everett, Ethel
1 Everett, John
1 Everett, Michael
6 Everett, William
2 Everly Brothers, The
1 Evert, Herbert
1 Evert, Michael
1 Every, Bert
1 Ewald, Carl
1 Ewbank, Weeb
1 Ewell, Don
1 Ewing Sisters, The
11 Ewing, Bill
1 Ewing, Jean
1 Ewing, Jolane
1 Exon, James
1 Eytan, Walter
2 Eythe, William
2 Ezra and His Beverly Hillbillies

WMT
CEDAR RAPIDS, IOWA
600 K.C.
PROGRAM No.
PART No.
TITLE
F
DATE
START OUTSIDE
33 1/3 RPM
N.A.B. RECORDING CHARACTERISTICS

1 Fabian
1 Fabian, John
4 Fabray, Nanette
1 Fabritious, Johann
1 Faddis, John
91 Fadiman, Clifton
14 Fadiman, Edwin
1 Faget, Max
1 Fagnant, Frenchy
2 Fahl, Franz
1 Fain (Elmer Fain and His Orchestra)
1 Fain, Sammy
2 Fair, Lois
1 Fair, Wynne
38 Fairbanks Jr., Douglas
4 Fairbanks, Douglas
1 Fairbanks, Joan
28 Fairchild (Cookie Fairchild and His Orchestra)
1 Fairchild (Cookie Fairchild and The Treasury Orchestra)
10 Fairchild, Henry Pratt
1 Fairchild, Ken
1 Fairchild, Mildred
13 Fairchild, Morgan
1 Faircloth, Lauch
1 Fairfax (Joan Fairfax and Her All Girl Orchestra)
1 Faith (Larry Faith and His Orchestra)
1 Faith (Percy Faith and Buddy Cole Orchestra, The)
48 Faith (Percy Faith and His Orchestra)
5 Faith, Percy
1 Falcone, Gino
1 Falconer, Martha
1 Falk, Edna
1 Falk, Peter
16 Falkenburg, Jinx
1 Falker, Lisell
1 Fall, Ellen
1 Faller, Kevin
1 Fallhaber, Robert
1 Fallon, Joey
1 Fallon, Larry
32 Falstaff Singers, The
1 Falwell, Jerry
10 Fanelli, Al
2 Fant, Roy
1 Farah, Elizabeth
3 Farber (Bert Farber and His Orchestra)
2 Farber, Bert
1 Farber, Frank
27 Farber, Jerry
1 Farina, Richard
2 Farley, Ed
11 Farley, James
1 Farley, John
7 Farley, Morgan
2 Farley, Scott
4 Farley, Tom
1 Farlow, John
39 Farm and Home Quartet, The
1 Farmer, C. B.
2 Farmer, Frances
7 Farmer, Malvin
2 Farmhands, The
3 Farmhurst, Gene
1 Farney, Dick
1 Farno, Roland
2 Farnon (Robert Farnon and His Orchestra)
5 Farnum, William
1 Faron, Harry
4 Faron, Jack
1 Farquhar, Elizabeth
2 Farquhar, Robert
6 Farr, Carl
14 Farr, Hugh
1 Farrago, Ladislas
90 Farrar, Stanley
2 Farrar, Stewart
1 Farrell (Skip Farrell and His Chorus)
6 Farrell, Bill
1 Farrell, Brian
23 Farrell, Charles
24 Farrell, Eileen
3 Farrell, Frank
5 Farrell, Glenda
8 Farrell, Jerri
1 Farrell, Louis
37 Farrell, Skip
1 Farrell, Virginia
5 Farren, Harry D.
24 Farrington, Fielden
1 Farris, Timothy
1 Farrow, Norman
2 Fascinato (Jack Fascinato and His Orchestra)
1 Fass, Donald
6 Fass, George
6 Fass, Gertrude
1 Fass, Julius
1 Fassett, Jim
2 Fasshauer (Carl Fasshauer and The Homesteaders)
4 Fast, Howard
1 Fates, Gil
10 Fatool, Nick
22 Faulkner, George
1 Faulkner, Jeanne
1 Faulkner, Perry
4 Faulkner, William
2 Faust, Gil
1 Favor, Edwin M.
7 Favorite Four, The
1 Fawcett, Eric
1 Fawcett, Fran
1 Fawcett, Frank
1 Fawcett, Hudson
7 Fay, Frank
1 Fay, Jack
141 Faye, Alice
3 Faye, Francis
1 Faye, Joey
2 Faylen, Frank
2 Fazah, Adib
1 Fazenda, Louise
1 Fazio, George
1 Fazio, Vick
3 Fazola, Irving
1 Fearson, Arthur
6 Feather, Leonard
5 Featherstone, Jimmy
1 Fedderson, Don Lee
1 Feder, D. D.
1 Federal Symphony Of New York
1 Federspiel, Per
1 Fedor, Otto
12 Fee, John
1 Feeley, Billy
3 Feeney, Jack
1 Feeney, John
1 Feiffer, Jules
4 Fein, Irving
1 Fein, William
10 Feins, Bernard
1 Feiser, James L.
12 Feld, Fritz
2 Feld, Morey
1 Feldberry, Eric
2 Feldman, Fred
1 Feldman, Gladys
1 Feldman, Sherlock
1 Felice (Ernie Felice and His Orchestra)
1 Felice (Ernie Felice Quartet)
2 Felice (Ernie Felice Quartet, The)
1 Felice, Tony
2 Felix, Richard
8 Feller, Bob
1 Fellers, Bonner
1 Fellon, Rick
3 Fellows, Edith
1 Felton, Happy
28 Felton, Norman
308 Felton, Verna
2 Felun, Ray
1 Fen, Ake
1 Fencler, Harlan
125 Fennelly, Parker
420 Fenneman, George
1 Fenton, Frank
1 Fenton, Leslie
2 Fenwick, Ellen
2 Feola, Tony
16 Ferber, Edna
1 Ferdinando (Felix Ferdinando and His Orchestra)
1 Ferguson (Maynard Ferguson and His Orchestra)
2 Ferguson, Dorothy
9 Ferguson, Franklin
1 Ferguson, Gilbert
1 Ferguson, Harry
3 Ferguson, Homer
1 Ferguson, Maynard
6 Ferguson, Ray
1 Fernandez
14 Fernandez, Peter
4 Ferone, George
2 Ferotti, George
1 Ferozi
1 Ferranda, Michael
73 Ferrante and Teicher
1 Ferrar, Dorothy
1 Ferrar, Jean
1 Ferrar, Larson
1 Ferrar, Sam
2 Ferraro, Geraldine
1 Ferrer, Joe
20 Ferrer, José
5 Ferrer, Mel
15 Ferrin, Frank
1 Ferris, Allan
1 Ferris, Don
1 Ferris, Eugene B.
1 Ferris, John
1 Ferris, Walter
2 Fertig, Lawrence
2 Fessier, Michael
1 Fetchit, Stepin
1 Feud, Charlie
11 Feuer, Cy
1 Fickert, Sandy
40 Fickett, Homer
1 Ficking, Gloria
1 Ficking, Skip
1 Fiddlers Five, The
20 Fidler, Jimmy
2 Fiedler (Arthur Fiedler and His Orchestra)
12 Fiedler (Arthur Fiedler and The Boston Pops Orchestra)
11 Fiedler, Arthur
2 Fiedler, Johnny
7 Field, Betty
4 Field, Bryan
1 Field, Charles K.
1 Field, Daniel
4 Field, George
1 Field, Joan
247 Field, Norman
3 Field, Rachel
2 Field, Stanley
3 Field, Virginia
1 Field, Walker T.
14 Fielding (Jerry Fielding and His Orchestra)
2 Fielding, Henry
10 Fielding, Jerry
1 Fielding, Ray
1 Fields (Herbie Fields and His Reception Center Orchestra)
1 Fields (Herbie Fields and His Septet)
1 Fields (Irving Fields and His Orchestra)
1 Fields (Irving Fields Trio)
2 Fields (Irving Fields Trio, The)
1 Fields (Shep Fields and His New Music)
16 Fields (Shep Fields and His Orchestra)
9 Fields (Shep Fields and His Rippling Rhythm Orchestra)
2 Fields and Hall Mountaineers
7 Fields, Benny
1 Fields, Billy
1 Fields, Dorothy
31 Fields, Eddie
9 Fields, Estelle
1 Fields, George
13 Fields, Gracie
1 Fields, Harry
1 Fields, Herbert
1 Fields, Ray
4 Fields, Shep
6 Fields, Sidney
29 Fields, W. C.
53 Fifield Jr., James W.
2 Fifield, William
1 Fifth Dimension, The
1 Filarski, Michael
1 Filene, Madeleine
12 Fillbrandt, Laurette
1 Fillmore, Hildegard
1 Fillmore, Russell
1 Fillson, Betty
1 Fimmel, Richard
4 Fina (Jack Fina and His Orchestra)
1 Fina (Jack Fina and His Waldorf Astoria Orchestra)
10 Fina, Jack
1 Finch, Dee
1 Findell, Jack
2 Findley, I. A.
85 Fine, Morton
4 Fine, Sylvia
2 Finer, Herman
3 Fink, Jack
3 Fink, Jack Anson
2 Fink, Julian
1 Finkle, William
1 Finletter, Thomas K.
3 Finley, Stuart

1 Finn, Cleland
1 Finn, Gloria
1 Finn, Jonathan
1 Finn, W. G.
1 Finston (Nat Finston and His Orchestra)
1 Finston, Nathaniel
3 Fio Rito (Ernie Fio Rito and His Orchestra)
38 Fio Rito (Ted Fio Rito and His Orchestra)
3 Fire Chief Double Quartet, The
9 Fire Chief Quartet, The
6 Firehouse Five Plus Two, The
2 Firestone Jr., Harvey
2 Firestone Orchestra, The
3 Firestone Symphony Orchestra, The
2 Firestone, Beryl
47 Firestone, Eddie
1 Firestone, Harvey
2 First Piano Quartet, The
1 Firth, George
3 Fischer (Carl Fischer and His Orchestra)
3 Fischer, Carl
2 Fischer, Dorothy
2 Fischer, Gloria
6 Fischer, Louis
2 Fischer, Shug
1 Fish, Hamilton
2 Fish, Richard
1 Fishbein, Dr.
1 Fishburn, Alan M.
2 Fisher (Buddy Fisher and His Orchestra)
1 Fisher (Mark Fisher and His Orchestra)
4 Fisher, Albert
1 Fisher, Austin M.
1 Fisher, Anna
1 Fisher, Bob
1 Fisher, Charlie
2 Fisher, Cy
1 Fisher, Dorothy Canfield
197 Fisher, Eddie
62 Fisher, George
2 Fisher, Ham
1 Fisher, John
2 Fisher, Maggie
1 Fisher, Marvin
1 Fisher, Singapore Joe
1 Fisher, Steve
1 Fisher, Walter
1 Fisher, William
2 Fishface, Senator Frankenstein
1 Fishman, Harvey
1 Fitch, Louise
8 Fitz, Kathleen
1 Fitzell, Jim
6 Fitzgerald (Ella Fitzgerald and Her Orchestra)
16 Fitzgerald, Barry
4 Fitzgerald, Ed
35 Fitzgerald, Ella
7 Fitzgerald, F. Scott
12 Fitzgerald, Geraldine
1 Fitzgerald, Katherine
2 Fitzgerald, Neil
3 Fitzgerald, Pegeen
22 Fitzmaurice, Michael
1 Fitzmaurice, Pamela
2 Fitzpatrick (Eddie Fitzpatrick and His Orchestra)
2 Fitzpatrick, Eddie
1 Fitzpatrick, Jimmy
1 Fitzpatrick, Joe
1 Fitzpatrick, Leo
2 Fitzwater, Marlin
6 Five Jones Boys, The
2 Five Kaydettes, The
2 Five Keys, The
2 Five Of A Kind
2 Fix, David
1 Fjellbu, Dean Arne
1 Flagg, James Montgomery
1 Flaherty, Pat
1 Flairs, The
1 Flambeck, Herb
1 Flame, Rosemary
3 Flamingos, The
25 Flanagan (Ralph Flanagan and His Orchestra)
3 Flanagan, Alvin
6 Flanagan, Bill
1 Flanagan, Bob
6 Flanagan, Edward
1 Flanders, Senator
5 Flannery, Harry
1 Flannery, Mike
1 Flares, The
9 Flato (Lud Flato and His Orchestra)
2 Flatow, Fred
1 Flatow, Ira
2 Flatt and Scruggs
5 Flatt, Lester
2 Flaum, Irving
1 Flavin, Jim
1 Flavin, Martin
1 Flavorettes, The
1 Fleigers, Serge
2 Fleischer, Max
1 Fleischer, Nat
1 Fleischer, Richard
2 Fleischer, Wilbur
1 Fleischman, Harry
2 Fleming, Alexander
1 Fleming, Arthur S.
1 Fleming, Catherine
9 Fleming, Denna F.
5 Fleming, Ed
2 Fleming, Frank
1 Fleming, Harold M.
13 Fleming, James
2 Fleming, June
10 Fleming, Rhonda
1 Fleming, Tom
3 Fleming, Van
1 Flemming, Robert
1 Fletcher, Billy
4 Fletcher, Bramwell
1 Fletcher, Granville
10 Fletcher, James
12 Fletcher, Jim
9 Fletcher, Lester
29 Fletcher, Lucille
1 Fletcher, R. V.
1 Fletcher, Tex
1 Flexner, James Thomas
3 Flick, Patsy
1 Flint, Helen
2 Flint, Kelly
12 Flippen, Jay C.
1 Flood, Dick
1 Flood, Maxine
2 Florea, Louise
2 Floren, Myron
1 Florie, Heidi
1 Florsham, Mary
1 Flory, Harry
1 Flower, Clem
1 Flowerday, Fred
1 Flowers, Harriet
5 Flowers, Pat
2 Floyd, Henry
1 Fly, James L.
1 Flynn, Art
155 Flynn, Bernardine
1 Flynn, Bess
5 Flynn, Charles
14 Flynn, Errol
1 Flynn, Fahey
1 Flynn, Howard
1 Flynn, John P.
26 Flynn, John T.
1 Flynn, Paul
1 Flynn, Shelia
13 Foch, Nina
1 Fogarty (Howard Fogarty and His Orchestra)
6 Fogel, George L.
1 Fogel, Jerry
5 Foggy Mountain Boys, The
1 Foggy River Boys, The
2 Fokker, John
2 Folde, Andrew
1 Foley (Red Foley and The Cumberland Valley Boys)
1 Foley, Raymond
25 Foley, Red
11 Foley, Thomas
2 Folger, Byron K.
1 Folger, Samuel Hopkins
23 Folia, Marty
1 Follieta, Thomas
1 Folsom, Marion
52 Fonda, Henry
1 Fonda, James
1 Fonda, Jane
2 Fong, Benson
1 Fonseca, Lew
1 Fontaine, Eddie
7 Fontaine, Frank
26 Fontaine, Joan
1 Fontaine, William
19 Fontane Sisters, The
18 Fontane, Leo
14 Fontanne, Lynn
2 Foote, Bradbury
22 Foote, Bruce
1 Foote, Herbert
1 Foote, Issac
1 Foote, Ruth
5 Foran, Dick
42 Foray, June
2 Forbes, Archibald
6 Forbes, Brenda
60 Forbes, Don
1 Forbes, Katherine
1 Forbes, Louis
1 Forbes, Mark
1 Forbes, Mary
2 Forbes, Muriel
12 Forbes, Murray
4 Forbes, Ralph
1 Forbes, Scott
1 Ford II, Henry
1 Ford Symphony Orchestra and Chorus, The
4 Ford Symphony Orchestra, The
3 Ford, Art
2 Ford, Betty
2 Ford, Billy
3 Ford, Corey
1 Ford, Don
3 Ford, George
1 Ford, George B.
80 Ford, Gerald
18 Ford, Glenn
27 Ford, Jan
1 Ford, Janie
1 Ford, Jeannie
3 Ford, John
1 Ford, Karen
53 Ford, Mary
23 Ford, Paul
2 Ford, Ruth
31 Ford, Senator
49 Ford, Tennessee Ernie
2 Ford, Wallace
5 Ford, Whitey
1 Forde, Agnes
2 Foreman, Carl
1 Foreman, Laura
1 Foreman, William
2 Forest, Frank
1 Forest, William
3 Forester, C. S.
3 Forestier, Francois
297 Forman, Bill
2 Forman, Ed
1 Forman, Elaine
1 Forman, Harrison
1 Formby, George
2 Forney, Robert
2 Forrest, Bob
60 Forrest, Helen
1 Forrest, Jimmy
3 Forrest, Sally
2 Forrest, Steve
6 Forrestal, James
42 Forrester (David Forrester and His Orchestra)
1 Forrester, David
42 Forrester, Howdy
22 Forrester, Ross
4 Forrester, Will
1 Forsina, David
4 Forster, E. M.
1 Forster, Marylou
5 Forster, Peter
5 Forsythe, Eugene
6 Forsythe, John
1 Fort Dix Glee Club, The
1 Fort Oachuca Band, The
2 Fortas, Abe
58 Forte, Joe
1 Forte, Tommy
39 Fortina, Carl
3 Fortunato, Chris
1 Forty Niners, The
1 Forward, Bill
1 Forward, Bob
2 Fosdick, Harry Emerson
3 Fosdick, Raymond
30 Fosler, Dean
1 Fosney, Madame
1 Foss, Joe
21 Foster (Chuck Foster and His Orchestra)
5 Foster (Stuart Foster and The Sentimentalists)
1 Foster Trio, The
4 Foster, Alan
1 Foster, B.O.
4 Foster, Cedric
7 Foster, Chuck
2 Foster, Clarence
1 Foster, Donald
14 Foster, George
1 Foster, Gloria
2 Foster, Jack
2 Foster, Kay
6 Foster, Lee
1 Foster, Lloyd E.
1 Foster, Malcolm
2 Foster, Margaret
1 Foster, Mary Lou
1 Foster, Norman
4 Foster, Phil
1 Foster, Phoebe
30 Foster, Pops
25 Foster, Preston
10 Foster, Ray
5 Foster, Roger
1 Foster, Sally
41 Foster, Stuart
4 Foster, Susanna
1 Foster, Will A.
1 Fostieri, Americo
2 Fostini, John
5 Fotine (Larry Fotine and His Orchestra)
1 Fountain (Pete Fountain and His Jazz Band)
5 Fountain, Pete
1 Fountainaires, The
3 Four Aces, The
4 Four Blazes, The
1 Four Blue Flames, The
3 Four Bobettes, The
1 Four Boys, The
1 Four Brothers, The
12 Four Chicks and Chuck
3 Four Clubmen, The
1 Four Country Boys, The
1 Four DeLovelies, The
1 Four Domatics, The
2 Four Esquires, The
2 Four Fellows, The
11 Four Freshmen, The
1 Four Gardeners Quartet, The
1 Four Guys, The
6 Four Hits and A Miss
8 Four Hits, The
1 Four Honors, The
1 Four Horsemen of Notre Dame, The
1 Four Jills, The
1 Four Kings, The
13 Four Knights, The
13 Four Lads, The
2 Four Norton Sisters, The

20 Four Notes, The
2 Four Pitch-hikers, The
1 Four Playboys, The
6 Four Pops, The
7 Four Preps, The
1 Four Reasons, The
1 Four Renegades, The
1 Four Serenaders, The
1 Four Sisters, The
1 Four Spirits Of Rhythm, The
2 Four Vagabonds, The
2 Four Vees, The
1 Four Wilsonettes, The
1 Fourquard, Christian
1 Fourth, Muriel
2 Fourtissimos, The
1 Foutrell, Jacques
8 Fowle, Farnsworth
1 Fowler (Wally Fowlers's Oak Ridge Quartet)
1 Fowler, Art
1 Fowler, Bertram
3 Fowler, Frosty
3 Fowler, Gene
43 Fowler, Keith
26 Fowler, Wally
1 Fowler, White
1 Fox (Roy Fox and His Orchestra)
1 Fox, Bob
1 Fox, Charles
2 Fox, Curley
1 Fox, Finest
8 Fox, Frank
8 Fox, Fred
10 Fox, Gibson Scott
1 Fox, Janet
1 Fox, Melvin
4 Fox, Roy
1 Fox, Scott
1 Fox, Sidney
1 Fox, Sonny
1 Fox, Stuart
1 Fox, Terry Curtis
3 Foxx, Redd
2 Foy (Dick Foy and His Orchestra)
3 Foy Jr., Eddie
1 Foy, Brian
198 Foy, Fred
1 Foy, Pat
1 Frame, Fred
2 Framer, Walt
5 France, Anatole
1 France, Rosalind
2 Francescati, Zino
2 Franchi, Sergio
16 Francine
1 Francis, Al
36 Francis, Arlene
1 Francis, Clarence
10 Francis, Connie
1 Francis, Dorothy
22 Francis, Eugene
36 Francis, Ivor
1 Francis, Josephine Young
14 Francis, Kay
1 Francis, Marion
1 Francis, May
2 Francis, Norma
1 Francis, Paula
1 Francis, Thomas P.
1 Francois, Stephen M.
1 Frank, Alan
1 Frank, Barry
36 Frank, Carl
1 Frank, Clint
8 Frank, Joe
4 Frank, John
2 Frank, Marilyn
5 Frank, Pete
1 Franke, Paul
3 Frankel, Doris
14 Frankel, Harry
3 Frankel, Max
2 Franken, Rose
2 Frankenstein, Richard T.
1 Franklin, Aretha
1 Franklin, Chester
28 Franklin, Harold
2 Franklin, Jay
2 Franklin, Joan
3 Franklin, Joe
1 Franklin, Lynn
5 Franklin, Maurice
3 Franklin, Nancy
6 Franklin, Paul
2 Franklin, Robert
1 Franklin, Sidney
1 Franklin, Steve
2 Franklin, William
1 Franks, Maurice R.
1 Franson, Tom
1 Franum, Edward
5 Franz, Joe
1 Franzella Quintette, The
4 Franzella, Sal
1 Fraser, Cy
2 Fraser, Gordon
4 Fraser, Jackson
8 Fraser, Monte
1 Frasey, William
1 Frasier, John
16 Frawley, William
7 Frazee, Harry
3 Frazee, Jane
1 Frazier, Joe
1 Frazier, Lynn
1 Freams, George
1 Freberg, Donna
2 Freberg, Donovan
36 Freberg, Stan
1 Freddie
1 Freddycats, The
4 Frederick, Pauline
1 Frederick, Tommy
1 Fredericks, Carlton
1 Fredericks, Dirk
5 Fredericks, Don
1 Free, Marion
5 Freed (Alan Freed Band, The)
30 Freed, Alan
1 Freed, Isadore
1 Freed, Martin
1 Freedom Singers, The
1 Freeland, Don
1 Freeman (Bud Freeman and His Summa Cum Laude Orchestra)
6 Freeman (Stan Freeman and His Jazz Quartet)
3 Freeman (Tony Freeman and His Orchestra)
1 Freeman, Ben Peter
9 Freeman, Bud
1 Freeman, Charles
1 Freeman, David
1 Freeman, Devry
1 Freeman, Everett
1 Freeman, Florence
10 Freeman, Mona
1 Freeman, Russ
7 Freeman, Stan
2 Freeman, Ticker
1 Freeman, Tony
1 Freeman, Vaughn
1 Freeman, Wayne
193 Frees, Paul
1 Freitag, Dorothea
1 Freitag, Robert
1 French (Albert Papa French and The Original Tuxedo Jazz Band)
2 French, Bevan
1 French, H.
3 French, Jim
1 French, Ken
1 French, Pat
1 French, Webster
1 Frenoy (Lorenzo Frenoy Trio, The)
1 Fresell, Bob
1 Freshi, Judge
3 Freshman Trio, The
20 Fresnell Jr., Robert
11 Frey, Fran
1 Frick
1 Frick, Alice
8 Frick, Ford
14 Friday, Pat
2 Fridell, Ron
1 Friebus, Florida
1 Fried, Arthur
1 Fried, Joseph
18 Friedburg, Billy
86 Friedkin, David
2 Friedley, Vinton
1 Friedman, Arnold
1 Friedman, Bill
1 Friedman, Herbert
5 Friedman, Jacob
1 Friedman, Michael
1 Friedman, Morris
2 Friedman, Morton
2 Friedman, Thomas
23 Frieman, Louis
2 Friend, Bob
3 Friend, Phillip
1 Friendly Four, The
2 Friendly, Fred
1 Frierson, Reverta
1 Frihagen, Anders
1 Friley, Jeannie
1 Friley, Vernon
2 Friml (Rudolph Friml Jr. and His Orchestra)
4 Friml Jr., Rudolph
2 Friml, Rudolph
6 Frisch, Frank
4 Frisco, Joe
1 Frist, Bill
1 Fritz, Gilbert
1 Fritzell, Jim
1 Frizzell, Bernard
4 Frizzell, Lefty
1 Frizzelle, Dan Paul
3 Froeba (Frank Froeba and His Backroom Boys)
1 Frohman, Daniel
1 Froman (Lou Froman and His Orchestra)
26 Froman, Jane
1 Froos, Sylvia
7 Frosch, Robert
36 Frost, Alice
16 Frost, David
1 Frost, Martin
1 Frost, Michael
3 Frost, Robert
1 Frotkin, Fred
6 Froug, William
1 Fruit Jar Drinkers, The
8 Fry, Gilbert
4 Frye, Don
3 Frye, Leon
2 Fuentes, Carlos
1 Fuji, Yasuko
1 Fulani, Lenora
3 Fulbright, William
85 Fuller, Barbara
3 Fuller, Bill
14 Fuller, Charles E.
1 Fuller, Curtis
1 Fuller, Ed
1 Fuller, Elspeth
1 Fuller, Frances
6 Fuller, Jack
2 Fuller, James
1 Fuller, Lester
1 Fuller, Margaret
13 Fuller, Mrs. Charles E.
1 Fuller, Peggy
1 Fuller, Sammy
2 Fullerton, Gordon
1 Fullmer, Gene
1 Fulton, Art
2 Fulton, Bob
1 Fulton, George L.
6 Fulton, Jack
2 Fulton, Lou
1 Funicello, Annette
2 Funk G-Men, The
1 Funk, Dr.
1 Funk, Mary Ruth
6 Funt, Allen
4 Funt, Julian
1 Fuqua, Dan
1 Fuquay, Steven
3 Furillo, Carl
2 Furman (Clarence Furman and His Orchestra)
1 Furman, Clarence
2 Furnace, J. C.
5 Furness, Betty
1 Furneval, J. S.
26 Fussell, Sarah
1 Futran, Herb
1 Fyfe, Maxwell

2 G-Noters, The
1 Gaarde, Oliver
1 Gabbard, Rusty
65 Gabel, Martin
1 Gabely, Bill
33 Gable, Clark
1 Gable, June
2 Gabor, Eva
1 Gabor, Jan
1 Gabor, Zsa Zsa
1 Gaboriau, Emile
1 Gabriel, Cathy
2 Gabriel, Iris
13 Gabrielson, Frank
3 Gabrielson, Ira N.
1 Gabrilovich, Oscar
9 Gaeth, Arthur
1 Gage (Ben Gage and The Singing People)
12 Gage, Ben
1 Gahagan, Andrew J.
1 Gaines, Harris
37 Gaines, Ruben
2 Gainford, Rod
2 Gainot, Creole George
8 Gair, Sondra
2 Gaitskill, Hugh
1 Gala Lads, The
7 Galbraith, John
1 Galbraith, John Kenneth
1 Gale, Jeanne
1 Gale, Jerry
2 Gale, Sunny
2 Gale, Warren
1 Galeck, Denise
1 Galen, Betty
49 Galen, Frank
16 Galen, Hetty
8 Galente, Al
2 Galento, Tony
4 Galidoro, Al
1 Gallagher, Brian
25 Gallagher, Donald
3 Gallagher, Frank
1 Gallagher, Helen
1 Gallagher, James
2 Gallagher, Patty
1 Gallagher, Roger
1 Gallagher, Skeets
27 Gallaher, Eddie
1 Gallant, Gladys
1 Gallatin, Harry
1 Gallery, Daniel V.
1 Galley Sisters, The
1 Galli, Ray
2 Galliard (Slim Galliard Trio)
5 Galliard (Slim Galliard Trio, The)
4 Galliard, Slim
4 Galliart, Mel
6 Gallicchio (Joseph Gallicchio and His Orchestra)
1 Gallicchio (Joseph Gallicchio and The Homesteaders)
62 Gallicchio (Joseph Gallicchio and The NBC Orchestra)
1 Gallicchio, John
101 Gallicchio, Joseph
3 Gallicchio, Mike
1 Gallichio, Patsy
6 Gallico, Paul
1 Gallo, Gene
147 Gallop, Frank
2 Galloway, Hunter
7 Gallup, George
1 Galouye, Daniel
6 Galsworthy, John
1 Gam, Rita
6 Gambling, John
3 Gambling, John A.
2 Gambling, John B.
3 Gambling, John R.
1 Gambling, Mrs. John
1 Gambone, Frank
2 Game, Mildred
1 Games, Horace
53 Gammill, Noreen
1 Gamow, George
2 Gampell, Chris
1 Gandhi, Indira
1 Gandhi, Mohandas
2 Ganio, Felix
1 Gannett, Charles
2 Gannett, Frank
1 Gannett, Louis
3 Gannon, Frank
1 Gans, George
1 Gans, Wiily
1 Gant, Barbara
24 Gapin, Ken
11 Garagank, Pierre
30 Garagank, Rene
3 Garagiola, Joe
25 Garber (Jan Garber and His Orchestra)
3 Garber, Jan
5 Garbo, Greta
20 Garde, Betty
1 Garden, Mary Stewart
1 Garden, Stanley
1 Gardenia, Vincent
216 Gardiner, Don
17 Gardiner, Reginald
1 Gardner (Dick Gardner and His Hotcha Club Orchestra)
1 Gardner (Dick Gardner and His Orchestra)
10 Gardner, Ava
1 Gardner, Burleigh
318 Gardner, Ed
9 Gardner, Erle Stanley
1 Gardner, Freddy
5 Gardner, Hy
1 Gardner, Jack
1 Gardner, John
27 Gardner, Kenny
1 Gardner, Lou
1 Gardner, Mel
18 Gardner, Peggy
46 Garfield, John
6 Gargan, Ed
40 Gargan, William
1 Garina, Guy
1 Garis, John
1 Garisto (Lou Garisto and The Metropolitan Jazz Quartet)
1 Garland (Hank Garland and The Garland Four)
1 Garland, Beverly
9 Garland, Ed
7 Garland, Hank
121 Garland, Judy
1 Garland, Leonore
4 Garland, Margaret
1 Garland, Sue
1 Garman, George
5 Garn, Jake
1 Garner (Errol Garner Trio, The)
2 Garner, Darlene
8 Garner, Erroll
1 Garner, John
1 Garner, Pam
6 Garner, Peggy Ann
2 Garnett, John
2 Garnett, Tay
1 Garo, Don
1 Garrett, Ansell
4 Garrett, Betty
1 Garrett, Bobby
1 Garrett, Eve
1 Garrett, Michael
5 Garrett, Patsy
1 Garrick, Douglas
1 Garrigus, Fred
5 Garriot, Owen
1 Garris, John
6 Garrison, Garnet
1 Garrison, Greg
1 Garrison, Jim
1 Garrison, Paul
34 Garroway, Dave
1 Garry, Linda
1 Garry, Vivian
20 Garson, Greer
2 Garson, Henry
2 Gart (John Gart and His Orchestra)
71 Gart, John
2 Garth, David
1 Garver, Lori
1 Garvey, Lou
39 Gary, Arthur
2 Gary, John
1 Gary, Robert
1 Gary, Sam
4 Garza, Ava
1 Gasavius, Hans Bernt
3 Gaskell, Elizabeth Cleghorn
1 Gasner, John
1 Gasparre (Dick Gasparre and His Orchestra)
7 Gass, Sir Frederick
1 Gast, Harold
1 Gast, Paul
3 Gately, William
2 Gates (Dick Gates and His Orchestra)
2 Gates (Dick Gates and His Polish Orchestra)
5 Gates, Connie
1 Gates, Curtis
1 Gates, Frieda
2 Gates, John
3 Gates, Nancy
2 Gateson, Marjorie
1 Gatlin (Larry Gatlin and The Gatlin Brothers)
1 Gatlin, Don
1 Gaul, George
2 Gault, Galan
1 Gauthet, David
3 Gautier, Theophile
1 Gavillan, Kid
6 Gaxton, William
3 Gay Rancheros, The
1 Gay, Charles
1 Gay, Chester
56 Gay, Connie B.
2 Gaye, Betsy
1 Gaye, Leslie
1 Gaye, Shirley
2 Gaye, William
1 Gayer, Anne-Marie
1 Gayla, Penny
1 Gayle (Al Gayle and His Biltmore Orchestra)
3 Gayle, Diana
1 Gayle, Jeannie
3 Gayle, Nancy
1 Gayle, Warren
2 Gaylord, Chester
2 Gaylord, Ruth
1 Gaylord, Slim
1 Gayn, Mark
9 Gaynor, Janet
1 Gaynor, Mitzi
1 Gaynotes, The
3 Gazzara, Ben
1 Gearhart, Maureen
1 Gearson, Vidiers
1 Geary, Elwood
1 Gebert, Gordon
2 Geddis, Helen
1 Gedis, Esther
1 Gedney, Gloria
1 Gee, Sho
1 Geer, Louella
27 Geer, Will
1 Geezenslaws, The
1 Geffin, Joy
2 Gehrig, Lou
1 Gehrig, Mrs. Lou
68 Geiger, Milton
1 Gelb, Philip
1 Gelbart, Larry
74 Geldry, Max
1 Geller (Harry Geller and His Orchestra)
1 Geller, Harry
1 Gellman, Barton
4 Gelman, Michael
51 Gendeaux, Adrian
6 Gendron, Henri
12 Gene and Charley
1 Gene and Glenn
1 Gene, Elinor
4 Genevieve
1 Gennaro, Peter
1 Gentile, Don
1 Gentile, Jim
1 Gentile, Lois
2 Gentry, Art
1 Gentry, Fred
1 George, Carl
1 George, Catherine
1 George, David Lloyd
4 George, Earl
3 George, Florence
3 George, Grace
1 George, Jack
2 George, Senator
3 George, Walter
1 Georgette
1 Gephard, Bill
13 Gephardt, Richard
2 Gerald, Helen
1 Gerard, Adele
3 Gerard, Barney
1 Gerard, Bernard
16 Gerard, Hal
1 Gerard, John
8 Gerard, Ken
1 Gerard, Lester Ann
10 Gerard, Merwyn
1 Gerard, Ralph Waldo
1 Geray, Steve
2 Gerbandy, Premier
2 Gerber, Dan
1 Gerber, Joe
1 Gerdes, Ron
1 Gergen, David
1 German, Frank

136 Goodwin, Bill
1 Goodwin, Charles
2 Goodwin, Eileen
1 Goodwin, Hal
10 Goodwin, Sid
9 Gorbachev, Mikhail
1 Gorbachev, Raisa
9 Gorcey, Leo
1 Gordanker, Leon
1 Gordie, Joe
1 Gordon
2 Gordon (Claude Gordon and His Orchestra)
2 Gordon (Gray Gordon and His Orchestra)
1 Gordon String Quartet, The
32 Gordon, Al
28 Gordon, Anita
83 Gordon, Bert
48 Gordon, Bill
2 Gordon, Brad
2 Gordon, C. Henry
24 Gordon, Clarke
2 Gordon, Claude
1 Gordon, Claudia
4 Gordon, Dexter
17 Gordon, Don
2 Gordon, Dorothy
5 Gordon, Elsie Mae
2 Gordon, G. Swain
895 Gordon, Gale
13 Gordon, Gavin
1 Gordon, George
42 Gordon, Gloria
1 Gordon, Grant
1 Gordon, Gus
1 Gordon, Gypsy
1 Gordon, Harold
1 Gordon, Huntley
1 Gordon, Jack
14 Gordon, James Craig
75 Gordon, Joyce
1 Gordon, King
1 Gordon, Larry
1 Gordon, Mack
1 Gordon, Marjorie
4 Gordon, Mary
1 Gordon, Michael
2 Gordon, Paul
1 Gordon, Phil
4 Gordon, Richard
1 Gordon, Russ
2 Gordon, Ruth
1 Gordon, Sam
8 Gordon, Shirley
1 Gordon, Sid
1 Gordon, Stanley
10 Gordon, Virginia
1 Gordon, William
1 Gordy, Berry
35 Gore, Albert
3 Gore, Tipper
1 Goren, Michael
27 Gorin, Igor
36 Goring, Marius
2 Goris, Jan-Albert
3 Gorlay, Doug
1 Gorman, Gene
1 Gorman, Inez
1 Gorman, Ruth
2 Gorman, Tom
13 Gorme, Eydie
1 Gorner (Joseph Gorner and The Ensemble)
1 Gorno, Giacinto
260 Gosden, Freeman
7 Gosfield, Maurice
1 Gosho, Henry
1 Gosling, Alan
1 Goss (Joss Goss and His London Singers)
51 Goss, Frank
3 Goss, James
1 Goss, Noel
1 Goss, Porter
2 Gotchman, Lem
1 Gotham Quartet, The
1 Gotham, Grace
2 Gothard, David
1 Gottlieb, Eddie
2 Gottlieb, Joseph
1 Gottlieb, Rosa
1 Gottschalk, Louis
12 Gottschalk, Norman
1 Gough, Lewis L.
30 Gould (Morton Gould and His Orchestra)
2 Gould, Billy
1 Gould, Elliot
3 Gould, Frank
1 Gould, Glen
30 Gould, Gordon
1 Gould, Harold
1 Gould, Kenneth
18 Gould, Lawrence
1 Gould, Leslie
11 Gould, Mitzi
11 Gould, Morton
33 Gould, Sandra
1 Gould, Wilhelmina
1 Gould, Will
2 Goulding, Edmund
2 Goulding, Phil
346 Goulding, Ray
2 Goulding, Ted
7 Goulet, Robert
1 Goupil, Augie
1 Gowans, Brad
30 Gowdy, Curt
1 Grabbey, Eugene
46 Grable, Betty
1 Grace, Janet
1 Graden, Joe
2 Gradenwitz, Peter
3 Grady, Rhoda
1 Grady, William
20 Graf, Louis
3 Grafton, Gloria
6 Graham, Billy
8 Graham, Bob
1 Graham, Charles
2 Graham, Donald
97 Graham, Frank
10 Graham, Fred
5 Graham, Hilda
2 Graham, Joe
2 Graham, June
3 Graham, Kenneth
1 Graham, Lee
2 Graham, Margo
2 Graham, Otto
1 Graham, Rita
1 Graham, Ross
2 Graham, Roy
5 Graham, Sheila
43 Graham, Tim
2 Graham, Virginia
3 Graham, William
2 Grahame, Gloria
23 Grainger, Percy
1 Grainger, Sharon
3 Gramlich, George
10 Gramling, Oliver
1 Gramm, Phil
4 Grammer, Billy
1 Grammer, Bobby
1 Grand Duchess Marie
1 Grand Opera Chorus and Orchestra Of Los Angeles
17 Grandby, Joseph
2 Grande, Joe
3 Granden, Thomas
1 Grandma Moses
1 Grandy, Roy
4 Grange, Red
1 Granger, Ken
1 Granger, Lester
2 Granger, Stewart
1 Granick, Harry
2 Granik, Theodore
1 Granky, Joseph
2 Grant (Bob Grant and His Orchestra)
2 Grant, Allen
26 Grant, Bernard
2 Grant, Bill
1 Grant, Billy
50 Grant, Cary
2 Grant, Cathy
1 Grant, Coot
1 Grant, Douglas
1 Grant, Earl
7 Grant, Gloria
5 Grant, Gogi
2 Grant, Helen
1 Grant, Jeanne
2 Grant, Loren
9 Grant, Peter
1 Grant, Ray
1 Grant, Rhoda
4 Grant, Taylor
14 Granville, Bonita
1 Grapewin, Charlie
5 Grappelly, Stephane
1 Grapperhouse, Bob
9 Graser, Earle
1 Grashio, Samuel
20 Grass, Cliff
1 Grassen, Arv
1 Grassley, Charles
1 Grasso, Eddie
1 Grateful Dead, The
1 Gratke, Charles
266 Grauer, Ben
1 Grauman, Sid
7 Grauso, Joe
1 Graves, B. I.
6 Graves, Ernest
1 Graves, Harry
1 Graves, Russell
2 Gray (Glen Gray and His Orchestra)
33 Gray (Glen Gray and The Casa Loma Orchestra)
53 Gray (Jerry Gray and His Orchestra)
1 Gray, Al
1 Gray, Alexander
1 Gray, Arthur L.
15 Gray, Barry
24 Gray, Billy
1 Gray, Bob
3 Gray, Buddy
1 Gray, Carl
6 Gray, Coleen
1 Gray, Dick
2 Gray, Dolores
1 Gray, George W.
1 Gray, Gilda
2 Gray, Glen
3 Gray, Gordon
4 Gray, Jerry
2 Gray, Mack
7 Gray, Maxine
1 Gray, Michael
6 Gray, Phil
7 Gray, Robert
6 Gray, Tony
1 Gray, Wade
8 Gray, William
3 Grayco, Helen
11 Grayson, Carl
1 Grayson, Harry
1 Grayson, Jack
10 Grayson, Kathryn
36 Grayson, Mitchell
1 Grayson, Paul
2 Grayson, Shirley
1 Grayton, Bernard
1 Graziano, Rocky
1 Great Lakes Band, The
1 Great Lakes Naval Training Command Band, The
1 Great Lakes Orchestra, The
1 Great Lakes Salon Orchestra, The
5 Greaza, Walter
1 Greco, Buddy
3 Greco, Johnny
1 Greco, Stephen
3 Greeley (George Greeley and His Orchestra)
1 Greeley, George
34 Green (Bernard Green and His Orchestra)
20 Green (Johnny Green and His Orchestra)
4 Green (Larry Green and His Orchestra)
12 Green (Marie Green and Her Merry Men)
3 Green (Phil Green and His Orchestra)
4 Green (Urbie Green and His Orchestra)
3 Green (Urbie Green and His Sextet)
2 Green (Urbie Green Sextet, The)
1 Green Brothers Orchestra
1 Green Brothers, The
2 Green, Abel
3 Green, Adolph
1 Green, Amy
1 Green, Angela
5 Green, Austin
10 Green, Bernard
282 Green, Bill
3 Green, Billy M.
2 Green, Bob
2 Green, Charlie
1 Green, Clara
69 Green, Denis
80 Green, Eddie
1 Green, Eugene
1 Green, F. L.
2 Green, Fred
1 Green, Harry
1 Green, Howard J.
1 Green, Ivan
1 Green, Jackie
1 Green, Jay
3 Green, Joe
16 Green, John L.
15 Green, Johnny
1 Green, Larry
8 Green, Marie
2 Green, Martin
1 Green, Milton
12 Green, Mitzi
13 Green, Morton
2 Green, Norma
1 Green, Oscar
1 Green, Patterson
2 Green, Paul
21 Green, Phillip Leonard
4 Green, Ray
1 Green, Rena K.
3 Green, Richard
5 Green, Robert L.
1 Green, Robert S.
1 Green, Thelma
4 Green, Urbie
1 Green, Vern
7 Green, William
4 Greenberg, Hank
4 Greenberg, Kenneth
1 Greene, Carlton
9 Greene, Graham
25 Greene, Lorne
2 Greene, Rosaline
1 Greene, Shecky
1 Greenfield, Felix
1 Greenhouse, Johnny
22 Greenhouse, Martha
2 Greenleaf, John
74 Greenslade, Wallace
1 Greenspan, Alan
20 Greenspan, Bud
1 Greenspan, Jeanette
37 Greenstreet, Sydney
1 Greenwald, Marilyn
4 Greenwood, Charlotte
1 Greenwood, Joan
3 Greer, Frances
2 Greer, Howard
9 Greer, Jo Ann
1 Greer, Joe
2 Greer, Sonny
1 Greet, Cabbel
3 Gregg, Judd
726 Gregg, Virginia
1 Gregory, David
1 Gregory, Fran
1 Gregory, Frederic
3 Gregory, Jay
1 Gregory, John
1 Gregory, Kay

7 Gregory, Maya
1 Gregory, Paul
1 Grenediers Quartet, The
1 Grenier, Hilda
1 Grensabach, Joe
1 Grequtt, Helen
1 Gresham, Edith
1 Gress (Louis Gress and His Orchestra)
4 Grew, Joseph
1 Grewat, Dorothy
3 Grey, Bill
1 Grey, Carolyn
1 Grey, Dorothy
1 Grey, Dorrie Ann
1 Grey, Earl
4 Grey, Ginger
2 Grey, Gloria
1 Grey, Jane
1 Grey, Jerry
2 Grey, Joel
4 Grey, Lanny
2 Grey, Linda
4 Grey, Nan
36 Grey, Sam
1 Grey, Sylvia
1 Grey, Virginia
1 Greyhall, Nick
1 Gribbs, Marty
1 Gridley, Dan
2 Grieg, Edvard
7 Grier (Jimmie Grier and His Orchestra)
2 Grier (Jimmy Grier and His Coast Guard Band)
13 Grier (Jimmy Grier and His Orchestra)
3 Grier, Jimmy
2 Grier, Roosevelt
2 Grieves, Bill
1 Griff, Vander
1 Griffen, Bobby
1 Griffen, Gerald
2 Griffen, Ken
1 Griffies, Ethel
1 Griffin, Alexander R.
3 Griffin, Charles
2 Griffin, Chris
2 Griffin, Gerald
1 Griffin, Howard
1 Griffin, John
1 Griffin, Johnny
19 Griffin, Ken
30 Griffin, Merv
41 Griffin, Robert
1 Griffis
186 Griffis, William
33 Griffith, Andy
3 Griffith, Clark
1 Griffith, Cliff
1 Griffith, D. W.
2 Griffith, E. H.
2 Griffith, Eddie
1 Griffith, Edward H.
1 Griffith, Homer
2 Griffith, James
2 Griffith, Les
2 Griffith, Paul
1 Griffith, Rex
1 Griffith, Wayne
1 Griggs, Harold
41 Griggs, John
1 Grigsby, Doris
1 Grill, Katherine
2 Grim, George
1 Grimaldi, Joe
1 Grimard, Francois
32 Grimes, Fred
110 Grimes, Jack
1 Grimes, Mae
38 Grimes, Tammy
2 Grimm, Jolly Joe
1 Griner, Carolyn
1 Grinnell, John
61 Griskie, Bill
1 Grisman, David
4 Grissom, Jimmy
1 Griswold, Lawrence
3 Groat, Dick
19 Grobe, Albert
1 Grobely, John
1 Groer, Anne
6 Grofe (Ferde Grofe and His Orchestra)
3 Grofe, Ferde
1 Gromeck, Steve
2 Gromyko, Andrei
1 Groom, Peter
1 Groom, Stanley
1 Gropius, Walter
3 Gross (Walter Gross and His Orchestra)
2 Gross, Alan
1 Gross, Ben
20 Gross, Ernest
1 Gross, Gil
2 Gross, Milt
1 Gross, Terry
6 Gross, Walter
1 Grosse, Lloyd
1 Grossman, Gary
1 Grossman, Roz
12 Grossman, Suzanne
1 Grossman, Ted
1 Grove, George
5 Grover, John
3 Groves, Leslie
1 Growan, Bill
1 Growsmith, Lawrence
2 Groza, Lou
4 Gruen Choir, The
2 Gruenberg, Axel
1 Gruenberg, Sidonie M.
1 Gruenther, Alfred
1 Grunbaum, Benjamin H.
1 Grundfest, Warren
3 Grundy, Doris
1 Gruner, Carl
3 Guadalajara Trio, The
1 Guare, John
1 Guarnieri (Johnny Guarnieri and His Orchestra)
1 Guarnieri (Johnny Guarnieri Quartet, The)
38 Guarnieri (Johnny Guarnieri Quintet, The)
2 Guarnieri (Johnny Guarnieri Trio, The)
1 Guarnieri, Isabel
269 Guarnieri, Johnny
1 Guastaferro, Angelo
2 Gudel, Gene
8 Guedel, John
1 Guenther, Jack
7 Guenther, John
1 Guerra, Frank
1 Guest, Eddie
2 Guest, Edgar A.
1 Guffy, Joseph F.
1 Guida, Michael
1 Guild Choristers, The
1 Guild, Lurelle
1 Guild, Nancy
2 Guildsmen Septet, The
1 Guilfoyle, Kieren
3 Guilfoyle, Paul
1 Guinan, Texas
4 Guiness, Abram S.
1 Guinn, Ralph
2 Guinn, Wyman
2 Guinness, Alec
1 Guise, Whit
17 Guizar, Tito
1 Gulden Serenaders, The
30 Gulfspray Gang, The
1 Gulkins, Sam
1 Gulliver, Mrs. Stanley
1 Gummere, Richard M.
2 Gunder, Hank
1 Gunn, Earl
14 Gunn, George
5 Gunn, James E.
6 Gunn, John Martin
10 Gunnison, Royal Arch
2 Gunsky, Maurice
2 Gunter, Hardrock
1 Gurgli, John
2 Gurie, Sigrid
1 Gurnett, Donald
1 Gurney, Jr., A.R.
1 Gursky, Herbert
2 Gusman, Charles
1 Gustafson, John
1 Guthrie, A.B.
1 Guthrie, Arlo
1 Guthrie, Fred
1 Guthrie, Karen
6 Guthrie, Woody
1 Gutierrez, Vincente
1 Gutman, Harry
1 Guzman, Rodney
16 Gwenn, Edmund
32 Gwynne, Fred
1 Gyohten, Toyoo

25 Haag, Robert
22 Haake, Alfred P.
1 Haas, Hugo
1 Haber, Paul
4 Hackady, Hal
1 Hackady, Jerry
13 Hacker, Louis M.
5 Hackes, Peter
7 Hackett (Bobby Hackett and His Orchestra)
5 Hackett (Bobby Hackett Quartet, The)
2 Hackett (Bobby Hackett Quintet, The)
1 Hackett, Albert
44 Hackett, Bobby
2 Hackett, Buddy
1 Hackett, Ernie
1 Hackett, Gilbert
2 Hackett, Joan
1 Hackett, Rita
1 Hackman, Bobby
1 Haddas, Moses
1 Hadden, Marie
1 Haden, Sara
10 Hadley, Reed
3 Haenschaen (Gus Haenschaen All-String Orchestra, The)
41 Haenschen (Gustave Haenschen and His Orchestra)
1 Haenschen, Gustave
6 Hafter, Robert
1 Hagadorn, Herman
1 Hagen (Earl Hagen and His Orchestra)
1 Hagen (Earle Hagen and His Orchestra)
1 Hagen, Chet
1 Hagen, Earl
3 Hagen, Harry
2 Hagen, Jean
1 Hagen, Paul
2 Hagen, Uta
1 Hager, Joan
1 Hager, Walter
2 Haggard, H. Rider
2 Haggart (Bob Haggart Septet, The
38 Haggart, Bob
1 Haggerty, James
3 Hahn, Bob
2 Haig, Alexander
1 Haight, Louis
33 Haile, Pennington
1 Haim, Paul Ben
9 Haines, Bob
84 Haines, Connie
1 Haines, Henry
1 Haines, Hilda
1 Haines, Jackie
207 Haines, Larry
1 Haines, Mr.
1 Haines, Roy
2 Haines, William
4 Hairston, Jester
3 Haise, Fred
1 Halas, George
2 Haldeman, H. R.
2 Haldemann, Edward
11 Hale, Alan
5 Hale, Arthur
3 Hale, Barbara
2 Hale, Diana
3 Hale, Edward Everett
2 Hale, Frank
2 Hale, Jim
1 Hale, Laura
2 Hale, Lionel
1 Hale, Monte
1 Hale, Nathan
1 Hale, Ramsay
1 Halee, Roy
1 Haleloke
1 Haler, Fred K.
4 Haley (Bill Haley and The Comets)
1 Haley, Herb
52 Haley, Jack
16 Haley, Marianne
3 Halifax, Edward
1 Hall (George Hall and His Hotel Taft Orchestra)
3 Hall (George Hall and His Orchestra)
1 Hall (Homer Hall Chorus, The)

1 Hall (Juanita Hall Choir, The)
2 Hall (Juanita Hall Singers, The)
6 Hall Negro Quartette
9 Hall, Al
1 Hall, Albert H.
2 Hall, Alexander
3 Hall, Arthur
3 Hall, Bob
1 Hall, Bruce
1 Hall, Buddy
12 Hall, Charles
4 Hall, Cliff
1 Hall, Dickie
1 Hall, Dorothy
13 Hall, Edmond
1 Hall, Fred
1 Hall, G. Leslie
1 Hall, George
1 Hall, Grayson
1 Hall, Harry
8 Hall, Henry Noble
1 Hall, Hillary
1 Hall, Holworthy
2 Hall, Homer
3 Hall, Howard
1 Hall, James
1 Hall, James Norman
1 Hall, Joe
3 Hall, Jonathan
6 Hall, Juanita
1 Hall, Lou
1 Hall, Miss Frank
1 Hall, Mort
1 Hall, Nelson
5 Hall, Porter
3 Hall, Radcliff
1 Hall, Randy
6 Hall, Richard
2 Hall, Wanda
2 Hall, Wendell
3 Hall, Wilson
2 Halle, Muriel
2 Halleck, Charles
3 Hallet (Mal Hallet and His Orchestra)
1 Hallet, Richard Matthew
1 Halley, Rudolph
2 Halliday, Brett
1 Halliday, Johnny
1 Halloran (Jack Halloran Quartet, The)
1 Halloran Band, The
12 Halop, Billy
24 Halop, Florence
2 Halperin, Martin
6 Halpern, Richard
1 Halsey, George
2 Halsey, William
1 Halton, Charles
1 Halton, Matthew
1 Hambro, Cato
2 Hambro, Lenny
1 Hamburg, Joan
1 Hamby, Grady H.
1 Hamey, Roy
13 Hamill, Mark
1 Hamilton (Johnny Hamilton Quintet)
7 Hamilton IV, George
2 Hamilton Quartet, The
1 Hamilton, Arthur
39 Hamilton, Bill
1 Hamilton, Bob
2 Hamilton, Chico
1 Hamilton, Clayton
1 Hamilton, David
1 Hamilton, Dorothy
1 Hamilton, Edith
46 Hamilton, Gene
1 Hamilton, George
1 Hamilton, Jeffrey
1 Hamilton, Jim
1 Hamilton, Jimmy
1 Hamilton, John
1 Hamilton, Johnny
1 Hamilton, Kim
5 Hamilton, Lee
1 Hamilton, Lynn
4 Hamilton, Margaret
132 Hamilton, Mark
1 Hamilton, Millie
4 Hamilton, Neil
2 Hamilton, Patrick
25 Hamilton, Richard
1 Hamilton, Roy
1 Hamilton, Suzanne
1 Hamilton, Thomas J.
1 Hamilton, Tom
1 Hamilton, Wes A.
13 Hamilton, William
1 Hamlet, Jim
1 Hamlin (Edward Francis Hamlin and His Orchestra)
1 Hamlin, Harry
1 Hamlisch, Marvin
1 Hammack (Bobby Hammack Quartet, The)
8 Hammarskjold, Dag
1 Hammer, Alfred
1 Hammerman, Dan
14 Hammerstein, Oscar
18 Hammett, Dashiell
1 Hammill, Marjorie
1 Hammond Jr., Harry S.
1 Hammond Jr., John
2 Hammond, Billy
2 Hammond, Bob
178 Hammond, Earl
2 Hammond, Helen
3 Hammond, John
2 Hammond, Laurence
2 Hammond, Marie
3 Hammond, Paul
4 Hamner, Earl
4 Hamp (Charles W. Hamp and The Rhythm Rascals)
3 Hampbell, Stuart
11 Hampden, Burford
38 Hampden, Walter
18 Hampton (Lionel Hampton and His Orchestra)
1 Hampton (Lionel Hampton Quartet)
5 Hampton, Bill
37 Hampton, Lionel
1 Hampton, Louis
5 Hampton, Steve
1 Hampton, Wade B.
1 Hanc, Josef
57 Hancock, Don
2 Hancock, Herbie
1 Hancock, John
3 Hancock, Wiley
1 Handley, Harvey
1 Handy, Captain
1 Handy, John
1 Handy, Owens
4 Handy, W. C.
1 Hane, William
2 Haney, Al
4 Haney, Betty Jean
2 Haney, Fred
1 Haney, James
1 Haney, Lewis H.
1 Hangen, Welles
2 Hankey, Mel
1 Hankins, James
1 Hanks, Tom
1 Hanley, Fred
1 Hanley, Jean
1 Hanley, Joyce
111 Hanley, Tom
22 Hanlon, Tom
1 Hanna, Philip S.
1 Hannah, Bob
5 Hannah, Phil
1 Hannah, Roland
1 Hannam, Alberta
1 Hannes, Andy
67 Hannes, Art
20 Hannon, Bob
3 Hannon, Marjorie
1 Hannum, Ken
1 Hanou, Michael A.
4 Hanrahan, Bill
1 Hanselrole, Phillip
1 Hansen, Gladys
1 Hanser, Richard
1 Hanshaw, Annette
1 Hanson, Alvin H.
2 Hanson, Howard
1 Hanson, Kenneth
1 Hanson, Phyllis
1 Hants, Kenneth G.
1 Hapman, Eric
1 Happytimers, The
3 Harbach, Otto
5 Harbord, Carl
1 Harbord, James G.
1 Harbour, Dennis
1 Harburg, E. Y.
1 Harcourt, John
1 Harcourt, Richard
1 Harden (Harry Harden and His Orchestra)
2 Harden, Sergeant
1 Harden-Branch, C. H.
1 Harder, Mel
1 Harding (Harvey Harding and His Orchestra)
2 Harding College Chorus
1 Harding Student Chorus
4 Harding, Ann
3 Harding, Dick
1 Harding, Earl
1 Harding, Gilbert
4 Harding, Harvey
1 Harding, Joe
1 Harding, Michael
1 Harding, Ray
2 Harding, Vince
18 Hardwicke, Cedric
1 Hardy, Cherry
1 Hardy, Gordon
1 Hardy, Joe
4 Hardy, Oliver
1 Hardy, Sherry
15 Hardy, Thomas
25 Hare, Ernie
4 Hare, Marilyn
5 Hare, Will
32 Harford, Alec
10 Harford, Betty
29 Hargis, Tom
9 Hargrave, William
1 Hargrove, Marion
1 Haritoonian, Joseph
3 Hark, Mildred
1 Harker, Ed
3 Harkin, Tom
2 Harkins, Jim
13 Harkness, Richard
1 Harlene (Lee Harlene and His Orchestra)
3 Harlin, Lee
7 Harlow, Jean
1 Harmatones, The
3 Harmer, Shirley
1 Harmon, Bill
2 Harmon, Charles
1 Harmon, Francis S.
17 Harmon, Jennifer
1 Harmon, Jim
2 Harmon, Larry
1 Harmon, Steve
7 Harmon, Tommy
2 Harmonaires, The
1 Harmonica Rascals, The
1 Harmount, Thomas
2 Harnell (Joe Harnell Quartet, The)
1 Harp, Tom
24 Harpell, Bill
6 Harper, Betty
1 Harper, Billy
1 Harper, Brunette
1 Harper, Fowler
1 Harper, James
2 Harper, Janice
1 Harper, Maurice
1 Harper, Pat
1 Harper, Phil
24 Harper, Redd
1 Harper, Sabrina
3 Harper, Toni
1 Harper, Troman
1 Harpers, The
7 Harrell, Charles
113 Harrice, Cy
2 Harridge, Will
4 Harriet, Eleanor
1 Harrigan, Anetta
1 Harrigan, Jack
1 Harrigan, Neda
1 Harrigan, William
3 Harriman, Averell
1 Harriman, Florence J.
1 Harrington (Bob Harrington and His Orchestra)
2 Harrington, Bill
1 Harrington, Fred
1 Harrington, Hamtree
18 Harrington, Mary Lou
1 Harrington, Mickey
1 Harrington, Oliver
2 Harrington, Pat
2 Harriot, Elinor
1 Harris (Albert Harris and His Orchestra)
192 Harris (Phil Harris and His Orchestra)
1 Harris Jr., Joel Chandler
1 Harris, Abraham L.
1 Harris, Ace
36 Harris, Albert
1 Harris, Anthony
16 Harris, Arlene
1 Harris, Betty
2 Harris, Bill
1 Harris, Billy
2 Harris, Bob
2 Harris, Bucky
1 Harris, Chetwin
1 Harris, Cybil
4 Harris, Dave
1 Harris, Don
1 Harris, E. A. Gene
2 Harris, Eddie
1 Harris, Frank
2 Harris, Gary
1 Harris, Gertrude
1 Harris, Holly
18 Harris, Howard
1 Harris, Joan
6 Harris, Joe
1 Harris, Johanna
5 Harris, Joyce
4 Harris, Julie
1 Harris, Mark
1 Harris, Mary
10 Harris, Murray G.
1 Harris, Nancy
11 Harris, Nick
1 Harris, Percy
335 Harris, Phil
2 Harris, Radie
26 Harris, Robert
1 Harris, Roy
1 Harris, S. R.
3 Harris, Seymour E.
1 Harris, Sidney J.
143 Harris, Stacy
1 Harris, Sybil
1 Harris, Terry
3 Harris, Theresa
1 Harris, Walter
3 Harris, William
1 Harris, Winifred
2 Harrison, Adele
1 Harrison, Barton
1 Harrison, Betty
1 Harrison, Chester
2 Harrison, Earl
1 Harrison, Guy Fraser
1 Harrison, Harry
1 Harrison, Hazel
1 Harrison, Nell
13 Harrison, Paul
1 Harrison, R. W.
10 Harrison, Rex
1 Harrison, Sam
2 Harrison, Wallace
1 Harron, Alexander

3 Harron, Don
2 Harrower, Elizabeth
7 Harsch, Joseph C.
1 Harshaw, Margaret
1 Hart, Alfred Gaylord
4 Hart, Bertha
1 Hart, Charles Spencer
1 Hart, Clyde
2 Hart, Ed
1 Hart, Elizabeth
18 Hart, Gary
3 Hart, Gloria
1 Hart, Henry H.
31 Hart, John
1 Hart, Lorenz
1 Hart, Maurice
11 Hart, Moss
1 Hart, Oliver James
1 Hart, Richard
2 Harte, Bret
2 Hartley, Fred A.
3 Hartley, Jack
1 Hartley, Mariette
1 Hartley, Ray
1 Hartman, Grace
1 Hartman, Henrietta
2 Hartman, Johnny
1 Hartman, Paul
6 Hartman, Ray
1 Hartnett, Gabby
53 Hartrich, Edwin
3 Hartsfield, Henry
3 Hartz, Jim
1 Hartz, Phoebe
92 Hartzell, Clarence
3 Hartzell, Lois
1 Harven, Jane
8 Harvey, Don
3 Harvey, Ed
3 Harvey, Georgette
4 Harvey, Jack
3 Harvey, James
11 Harvey, Jane
1 Harvey, Joan
5 Harvey, John
35 Harvey, Ken
1 Harvey, Mrs. John
3 Harvey, Paul
1 Harvey, Trevor
3 Harvey, W. F.
1 Harwell, Ernie
1 Haryout, Clifford
94 Haskell, Jack
1 Haskins, George
16 Haskins, Virginia
1 Hasler, Frederick E.
5 Hasso, Signe
1 Haster, Robert
1 Hastert, Dennis
1 Hastey, Jack
62 Hastings, Bob
2 Hastings, Donald
1 Hastings, Hudson B.
1 Hasty, John Eugene
1 Hat, Paul K.
25 Hatch (Wilbur Hatch and His Orchestra)
2 Hatch, Carl
2 Hatch, Orrin
446 Hatch, Wilbur
2 Hatcher, Eric
2 Hatcher, Mary
1 Hatchet, Starling
2 Hatfield, Guy
3 Hatfield, Hurd
1 Hatfield, Lansing
3 Hatfield, Mark
1 Hatfield, Toni Terry
23 Hathaway, Charles
1 Hathaway, Donny
1 Hathaway, Henry
1 Hatos, Steve
1 Hatsfield Jr., Henry W.
5 Hattie, Hilo
1 Hatton
1 Hatton, Raymond
1 Hauck
42 Hauser, Dwight
150 Hausner, Jerry
1 Hausner, Lawrence
1 Haven, Marie
1 Havens, Bob
1 Havens, Richie
1 Havenschauffler, Robert
10 Haver, June
1 Havergirst, Robert J.
3 Havier, Alex
14 Havoc, June
22 Havrilla, Alois
5 Hawk, Bob
1 Hawk, Mildred
1 Hawke, Robert
2 Hawkins (Coleman Hawkins and His Orchestra)
8 Hawkins (Erskine Hawkins and His Orchestra)
1 Hawkins, Augustus
2 Hawkins, Blanche
14 Hawkins, Coleman
3 Hawkins, Dolores
1 Hawkins, Doretta
2 Hawkins, Erskine
2 Hawkins, Harry C.
3 Hawkins, Hawkshaw
1 Hawkins, John
8 Hawkins, Odie
2 Hawkins, Stuart
1 Hawkins, William
2 Hawley, Adelaide
1 Hawley, Paul R.
1 Hawley, Steve
1 Haworth, C. V.
1 Haworth, Jill
1 Hawthorne, Harry
11 Hawthorne, Jim
12 Hawthorne, Nathaniel
20 Hay, Bill
1 Hay, Bob
2 Hay, George
1 Hay, George A. F.
1 Hay, John
1 Hayakawa, S. I.
1 Haycock, Robert
1 Haycox, Ernest
3 Hayden, Julie
1 Hayden, Kenneth
1 Hayden, Russell
1 Hayden, Steven
2 Haydn, Everett
6 Haydn, Richard
1 Haydon, Louise
13 Hayes, Arthur Garfield
5 Hayes, Bill
6 Hayes, Bruce
7 Hayes, Clancy
3 Hayes, Doug
14 Hayes, Gabby
1 Hayes, George
1 Hayes, Harry
3 Hayes, Harvey
63 Hayes, Helen
1 Hayes, Isaac
1 Hayes, J. Robert
2 Hayes, Jack
16 Hayes, John Michael
1 Hayes, Johnny
45 Hayes, Larry
2 Hayes, Linda
2 Hayes, Michael
33 Hayes, Peter Lind
6 Hayes, Richard
4 Hayes, Sam
1 Hayes, Virginia
1 Hayes, William A.
2 Hayman (Richard Hayman and His Orchestra)
1 Hayman, Art
6 Hayman, Richard
1 Haymes, Bob
2 Haymes, Cyril
70 Haymes, Dick
1 Haynes, Daniel L.
1 Haynes, Eldridge
2 Haynes, William
13 Hays, Arthur Garfield
1 Hays, Edward L.
1 Hays, Ted
4 Hays, Will
4 Hayton (Lennie Hayton and His Orchestra)
1 Hayton, Lennie
1 Hayward, Bob
2 Hayward, Jim
2 Hayward, Louis
3 Hayward, Michael
17 Hayward, Susan
7 Hayward, Thomas
1 Hayworth, J. D.
23 Hayworth, Rita
21 Hayworth, Vinton
18 Hazam, Louis
1 Hazard, Henry B.
1 Hazen, Pat
3 Hazlitt, Henry
1 Heacock, Larry
1 Head, Dr.
3 Head, Edith
1 Head, James
1 Head, Walter D.
2 Headlock, Jim
2 Healy, Dan
1 Healy, Denis
1 Healy, Frank
6 Healy, Mary
1 Healy, Michael
4 Healy, Peggy
3 Healy, Ted
1 Healy, Tim
2 Hearn, Chick
61 Hearn, Sam
1 Hearst, Patricia
1 Heartbeats, The
2 Hearth, Donald
1 Heater, Claude
13 Heath (Ted Heath and His Orchestra)
1 Heath, Alice
3 Heath, Ann
8 Heath, Gordon
1 Heath, Horton
2 Heath, Louise
3 Heath, Mary
2 Heath, Porter
1 Heath, Rex
1 Heath, Ted
1 Heatherton (Ray Heatherton and His Orchestra)
1 Heatherton, Joey
25 Heatherton, Ray
25 Heatter, Gabriel
1 Hebert
1 Hecht, Albert
16 Hecht, Ben
25 Hecht, Homer
2 Hecht, Joshua
75 Hecht, Paul
1 Heckart, Eileen
1 Heckman, Helene
2 Hecksher (Ernie Hecksher and His Orchestra)
4 Hector, Charles R.
3 Hedager, Ted
1 Hedge, Jim
1 Hedge, Ray
1 Hedgepeth, John
1 Hedges, William S.
1 Hedgwood, Bobby
1 Hedren, Tippi
1 Heemstra, Charlie
2 Heer, Ewald
1 Heese, Paul
3 Heflin, Frances
36 Heflin, Van
2 Hefti (Neal Hefti and His Orchestra and Chorus)
1 Hefti (Neal Hefti and His Orchestra)
1 Hefti, Neal
1 Hegelin, John
1 Hegland, Fred
1 Hehn, Joe
7 Heidt (Horace Heidt and His Musical Knights)
8 Heidt (Horace Heidt and His Orchestra)
6 Heidt, Horace
1 Heidtones, The
22 Heifetz, Jascha
1 Heilbron, Fritz
1 Heimstra, Rowena
1 Heindorf, Ray
1 Heinerman, Edna
15 Heinlein, Robert
1 Heinritz, Stuart
1 Heintzen, Tommy
1 Heinz, H. J.
1 Heisinger, J. H.
1 Heiss, Carol
38 Helburn, Theresa
1 Helemi, Alphonse
4 Helfer, Al
1 Helgeson, Joseph
1 Hellenan, Vivian
3 Heller, Jackie
6 Hellinger, Mark
1 Hellman, Lillian
1 Hellman, William
1 Hellwig, Ed
2 Helm, Fay
2 Helm, Harvey
1 Helms, Bobby
2 Helms, Don
1 Helms, Paul H.
1 Helmvite, Nils
1 Helwig, James
1 Hembrook, George
13 Hemingway, Ernest
54 Hemingway, Frank
1 Hemphill, Ralph
3 Hemus, Percy
3 Henderson (Fletcher Henderson and His Orchestra)
1 Henderson (Fletcher Henderson and His Sextet)
20 Henderson (Skitch Henderson and His Orchestra)
1 Henderson, Bob
1 Henderson, Charles
1 Henderson, Dave
1 Henderson, Eddie
1 Henderson, Ernest
2 Henderson, Fletcher
5 Henderson, Florence
1 Henderson, Horace
2 Henderson, James
1 Henderson, John
1 Henderson, Larry
4 Henderson, Leon
7 Henderson, Mary
1 Henderson, Pamela
1 Henderson, Ray
61 Henderson, Skitch
1 Hendle, Walter
1 Hendricks (John Hendricks and Company)
1 Hendricks (Lambert Hendricks and Ross)
1 Hendricks, Cheryl
1 Hendricks, Cornelia
1 Hendricks, Joe
2 Hendricks, John
12 Hendricks, Ray
1 Hendricks, Stanley
3 Hendrickson, Al
7 Hendrickson, Fred
3 Hendrickson, Rod
1 Hendrix, Marcella
1 Hendrix, Tommy
7 Hendrix, Wanda
1 Hendry, Tommy
1 Hener, Donna
7 Henie, Sonja
1 Henley, Dody
3 Henley, Ray
1 Henley, William Ernest
1 Henline, Butch
1 Hennant, Skip
2 Hennessey, Harry
3 Hennessey, Mitzi
1 Henney, Henry
1 Henney, Robert
7 Henning, Linda Kay

1 Henning, Pat
15 Henning, Paul
1 Hennings, Josephine
11 Henreid, Paul
1 Henri-Spaak, Paul
12 Henry, Bill
1 Henry, Buck
1 Henry, Charlotte
1 Henry, Don
1 Henry, G. A.
1 Henry, Helen
1 Henry, Jack
1 Henry, Joseph
1 Henry, Norm
12 Henry, O.
2 Henry, Robert S.
1 Henry, Sherrye
1 Henry, William E.
1 Henschel, Charles
1 Henschel, Harry
1 Henshaw, Gail
1 Hensley, Harold
4 Hepburn, Audrey
12 Hepburn, Katharine
1 Hepburn, Premier
2 Herbeck (Ray Herbeck and His Orchestra)
1 Herbeck, Ray
1 Herbert (Victor Herbert and His Orchestra)
2 Herbert, A. J.
1 Herbert, A. P.
1 Herbert, Charles
2 Herbert, Dick
5 Herbert, F. Hugh
7 Herbert, Hugh
3 Herbert, Ralph
5 Herbert, Victor
152 Herbert, Wilms
1 Hergeshimer, Joseph
158 Herlihy, Ed
1 Herlihy, Walter
6 Herman (Jules Herman and His Orchestra)
3 Herman (Lenny Herman Quintet, The)
50 Herman (Woody Herman and His Orchestra)
1 Herman (Woody Herman and His Septette)
1 Herman (Woody Herman and The Fourth Herd)
19 Herman (Woody Herman and The Third Herd)
1 Herman (Woody Herman and The Thundering Herd)
1 Herman (Woody Herman and The Young Thundering Herd)
1 Herman's Hermits
1 Herman, Babe
3 Herman, Cleve
1 Herman, Fred
2 Herman, George
1 Herman, Jules
4 Herman, Lenny
1 Herman, Lou
1 Herman, M. C.
4 Herman, Milton
1 Herman, Pat
1 Herman, Ralph
38 Herman, Woody
1 Hermanaires, The
4 Hern, Arthur
1 Hern, Pepe
1 Hernandez (Juano Hernandez and His Cotton Club Choir)
2 Hernandez, Josita
1 Hernandez, Juan José
14 Hernandez, Juano
1 Hernandez, Peter
1 Hernandez, Rene
1 Herne, Lafcadio
1 Herper (Hal Herper and His Orchestra)
1 Herrick, Genevieve Forbes
87 Herrmann, Bernard
52 Herron (Joel Herron and His Orchestra)
1 Herron, E.
1 Herron, H.
8 Herron, Joel
1 Hersey, John
1 Hersfeld, Helen
30 Hershey, Anne
1 Hershey, Colonel
40 Hershfield, Harry
20 Hersholt, Jean
1 Hershon, Jack
1 Hershon, Jeannie
6 Hersley, Doris
6 Hersley, Frank
2 Herter, Christian
20 Herth (Milt Herth Trio, The)
2 Herth, Milt
2 Hertosig, Frank
1 Hertz, Barbara
1 Hertzinger, Carl
1 Herzog, Earl
3 Hess, Myra
2 Hess, Rudolph
3 Hess, Seymour
4 Hess, Sol
1 Hessler, Fred
4 Hester, Harriet
17 Heston, Charlton
1 Heston, Lilla
1 Hetzell Jr., Ralph
1 Hewitt, Admiral
41 Hewitt, Alan
1 Hewitt, Julie
29 Hewitt, Virginia
2 Hewson, Isabel Manning
1 Heyden, Conrad
3 Heydt, Louis Jean
1 Heyerdahl, Thor
1 Heyes, Doug
1 Heyman, Joseph
3 Heywood (Eddie Heywood and His Orchestra)
3 Heywood (Eddie Heywood Sextette, The)
2 Heywood (Eddie Heywood Trio, The)
4 Heywood, Eddie
1 Heywood, Louis
1 Heywood, Michael
14 Hi Lo Jack and The Dame
9 Hi-Lo's, The
14 Hibbler, Al
7 Hibbs, Al
1 Hichens, Robert
25 Hickcocks, Andrew
1 Hickerson, Jay
1 Hickey, Margaret
1 Hickman, Dwayne
1 Hickman, Emily
1 Hickman, Henry
1 Hickman, Herman
2 Hickman, Jim
3 Hickman, John
1 Hickory Singers, The
1 Hicks, Bobby
1 Hicks, Clay
80 Hicks, George
5 Hicks, Granville
9 Hicks, John
1 Hicks, Lowell
3 Hicks, Russell
1 Hielman, Harry
384 Hiestand, Bud
1 Higby, Hiram
2 Higby, Kirby
56 Higby, Mary Jane
1 Higgenbotham, Dr.
3 Higginbotham, J. C.
1 Higgins, Billy
2 Highet, Gilbert
1 Higinbotham, William A.
1 Higley, Philo
19 Hiken, Nat
2 Hildebrand, W. N.
37 Hildegarde
2 Hilgenberg, Katherine
1 Hill (Tiny Hill and His Double Shuffle Beat)
2 Hill (Tiny Hill and His Hilltoppers)
1 Hill (Tiny Hill and His Orchestra)
1 Hill (Tiny Hill and His Shuffle Beat)
2 Hill Jr., Al
1 Hill Jr., James
4 Hill, Bertha Chippie
2 Hill, Betty
2 Hill, Bill
5 Hill, Dick
2 Hill, Eddie
31 Hill, Edwin C.
1 Hill, Fanny
1 Hill, Fred
2 Hill, Goldie
2 Hill, Irene
1 Hill, Jackie
1 Hill, James
1 Hill, Jess
12 Hill, John Ramsay
1 Hill, Lanford
3 Hill, Lister
1 Hill, Max
1 Hill, Mildred
1 Hill, Mrs. Edgar R.
58 Hill, Ramsay
1 Hill, Russell
38 Hill, Sammie
1 Hill, Stanley
7 Hill, Steven
1 Hill, Tiny
69 Hilliard, Harriet
1 Hilliard, William
1 Hillman, Bill
12 Hillman, Don Stewart
1 Hillman, Sidney
8 Hillman, William
2 Hilly, Bob
1 Hillyer, Mary
1 Hilsberg, Alexander
1 Hilton, Ann
71 Hilton, James
2 Hilton, Paul
1 Himan, Earl
14 Himber (Richard Himber and His Orchestra)
2 Himber (Richard Himber and His Studebaker Champions)
2 Himber (Richard Himber and The Ritz Carlton Orchestra)
1 Himes, Stephen
1 Himmelbaum, Monty
2 Hinaman, Eda
2 Hincke, Mel
1 Hindemith
1 Hinds, Billy
1 Hindshaw, Carl
2 Hine and Her Hawaiians
1 Hine, Gregory
1 Hiner, Marjorie
1 Hines (Earl Fatha Hines and His Grand Terrace Orchestra)
3 Hines (Earl Fatha Hines and His Orchestra)
1 Hines (Roy Hines Group)
1 Hines, Bill
68 Hines, Drex
13 Hines, Earl Fatha
5 Hines, Jerome
1 Hink and Dink
1 Hinkel, George
2 Hinkel, Wilda
1 Hinman, Joline
3 Hinners, Noel
1 Hinrichs, Albert F.
7 Hinton, Milt
1 Hinton, Sam
2 Hipsher, Harold
86 Hire, David
1 Hirsch (Bert Hirsch and His Orchestra)
16 Hirsch (Bert Hirsch's Novelty Dance Orchestra)
25 Hirsch, Bert
1 Hirsch, Elroy
3 Hirt (Al Hirt and His Orchestra)
1 Hirt, Al
3 Hiss, Alger
1 Hissey, Jimmy
25 Hit Paraders, The
8 Hitchcock, Alfred
1 Hitchcock, Ardith
3 Hitchcock, Keith
1 Hitchcock, Raymond
9 Hite, Bob
15 Hite, Jean
60 Hite, Kathleen
1 Hite, Les
1 Hite, Winifred
39 Hitler, Adolf
1 Hitt, Fred
1 Hitz, Elsie
55 Hix, John
4 Hixon (Jimmy Hixon and The Teenagers)
3 Hixon, Jimmy
1 Hixson (Leonard Hixon and His Alameda Coast Guard Station Band)
1 Hlass, Jerry
1 Hmansky
1 Ho, Jonathan
2 Hoagland (Everett Hoagland and His Orchestra)
1 Hoale, Don
1 Hoar, Joseph P.
1 Hobart, Garrett
1 Hobart, Rose
1 Hobbes, Halliwell
1 Hobbs, Bill
1 Hobbs, Bud
10 Hobbs, Carleton
1 Hobbs, Mark L.
1 Hobbs, Peter
1 Hobish, John
1 Hobson, Irene
1 Hock, Robert
1 Hocker, Ed
2 Hodapp, William
9 Hodes, Art
41 Hodge, Al
1 Hodge, George
1 Hodge, Hal
1 Hodge, Herbert
2 Hodge, Ken
1 Hodges, Charles
4 Hodges, Eddie
1 Hodges, General
6 Hodges, Gil
10 Hodges, Johnny
8 Hodges, Joy
2 Hodges, Margaret
1 Hodges, Paul
3 Hodges, Russ
32 Hodiak, John
2 Hodiak, Katrina Baxter
2 Hodja, Milan
1 Hoehler, Fred
8 Hoey, Dennis
1 Hoey, Jane M.
15 Hoff (Carl Hoff and His Orchestra)
1 Hoff (Carl Hoff and The Treasury Orchestra)
1 Hoff (Sid Hoff and His Orchestra)
4 Hoff, Carl
1 Hoffa, James
105 Hoffa, Portland
4 Hoffer, Bob
1 Hoffman, Clare E.
1 Hoffman, Dustin
1 Hoffman, Elwood
1 Hoffman, Governor
1 Hoffman, Harold
3 Hoffman, Herbert
1 Hoffman, Jack
68 Hoffman, Jane
1 Hoffman, Jeane
1 Hoffman, Jeff
2 Hoffman, Oswald
2 Hoffman, Paul G.
1 Hoffman, Richard
2 Hoffman, Samuel

1 Hoffman, Sidney
1 Hoffnagle, Ed
1 Hoffsmith, Fred
1 Hofling, Mark
4 Hofmann, Josef
1 Hogan, Anne
2 Hogan, Ben
2 Hogan, Bob
2 Hogan, Claire
2 Hogan, Dick
1 Hogan, Eddie
1 Hogan, George
1 Hogan, John
2 Hogan, Louanne
1 Hogg, James
1 Hogg, Quentin
1 Hogue, Richard
3 Hohl, Arthur
29 Holbrook, John
1 Holbrook, Stuart
1 Holcomb, Grant
1 Holcomb, Harry
4 Holcombe, Arthur
2 Holden, Carl
1 Holden, Charles
1 Holden, Donald
2 Holden, Eddie
14 Holden, Fay
6 Holden, Gloria
4 Holden, Jack
1 Holden, Jane
1 Holden, Peter
1 Holden, Thomas S.
35 Holden, William
1 Holder, Barbara
2 Holder, Owen
15 Holdren, Judd
1 Holdridge, Herbert C.
1 Hole, Darrell
5 Hole, Jonathan
18 Holiday, Billie
2 Holiday, Frank
25 Holiday, Gloria
1 Holiday, Mary
2 Holidays, The
5 Holiner, Mann
1 Holland Symphony Orchestra, The
48 Holland, Bert
2 Holland, Charles
22 Holland, Charlotte
4 Holland, Cliff
6 Holland, Gerald
11 Holland, Gladys
1 Holland, Greg
2 Holland, Joseph
1 Holland, Kenneth
1 Holland, Lou
6 Holland, Peanuts
4 Holland, Richard
45 Holland, Tom
1 Hollander, Alfred
1 Hollander, Lorin
2 Hollenbeck, Bill
27 Hollenbeck, Don
1 Holles, Everett
12 Holliday, Judy
1 Hollies, The
5 Holliman, Earl
7 Hollings, Ernest
1 Hollingsworth, Sam
1 Hollis, Morgan
1 Hollister, Carol
2 Holloway, Gene
1 Holloway, Harry
136 Holloway, Jean
2 Holloway, Stanley
17 Holloway, Sterling
2 Holly, Herb
2 Holly, Major
13 Holly, Vera
1 Hollywood Blazes, The
2 Hollywood Four Blazes, The
1 Hollywood Playboys, The
1 Hollywood Pops Orchestra, The
23 Holm, Celeste
1 Holman (Bill Holman and His Orchestra)
1 Holman, Eddie
1 Holman, Helen Fisher
3 Holman, John
2 Holman, Libby
1 Holmes (Herbie Holmes and His Orchestra)
1 Holmes (Leroy Holmes and His Orchestra)
1 Holmes, Bill
2 Holmes, Bruce
1 Holmes, Charles
1 Holmes, Chester W.
2 Holmes, Elsie
1 Holmes, Helen
1 Holmes, John
1 Holmes, Jonathan
1 Holmes, Julius C.
1 Holmes, Leroy
3 Holmes, Marian
1 Holmes, Ralston S.
5 Holmes, Taylor
63 Holmes, Wendell
7 Holt, Alan
1 Holt, Carl
1 Holt, Hamilton
4 Holt, Jack
1 Holt, Jennifer
3 Holt, Jonathan
1 Holt, Memo
1 Holt, Rackham
1 Holt, Rusty
2 Holt, Tim
1 Holt, Will
51 Holtman, John
1 Holton, Bob
3 Holton, James L.
14 Holtz, Lou
1 Holtzer, Lou
96 Holtzman, Arthur
2 Holtzman, Mrs. Arthur
12 Home Harmonizers, The
9 Homeier, Skip
2 Homer and Jethro
1 Homestead Steel Works Male Chorus, The
9 Homesteaders, The
5 Hometowners, The
7 Homolka, Oscar
10 Honey and The Bees
1 Honey, A. Winfield
13 Honeydreamers, The
1 Hong, James
1 Honte, Joseph
1 Hood, Alan
2 Hood, Darla
1 Hood, Robin
2 Hood, Thomas
2 Hook, Charles R.
2 Hookey, Bobby
2 Hooks, Lance
1 Hooks, Robert
3 Hooley, Jack
12 Hooper, Larry
7 Hoople, Henry
20 Hoosier Hot Shots, The
1 Hoover, Calvin B.
23 Hoover, Herbert
6 Hoover, J. Edgar
328 Hope, Bob
2 Hope, Clifford
2 Hope, Dolores
1 Hope, George
2 Hope, Nancy
1 Hopkin, Willa
5 Hopkins (Claude Hopkins and His Orchestra)
7 Hopkins, Arthur
15 Hopkins, Barry
2 Hopkins, Claude
1 Hopkins, Earl
1 Hopkins, Ernest M.
1 Hopkins, Harry
4 Hopkins, Jewel
11 Hopkins, Miriam
3 Hopkins, Neil
1 Hopkins, Pauline
4 Hopkins, Polly
2 Hopp, Johnny
1 Hopper, De Wolf
14 Hopper, Hedda
1 Horkheimer, Jack
8 Horlick (Harry Horlick and His Orchestra)
1 Horlick (Harry Horlick and The A and P Gypsies)
1 Horn, Steve
1 Horn, William
42 Horne, Lena
11 Horne, Lou
2 Horne, Marilyn
1 Horne, Robert I.
1 Horning, William
2 Hornsby, Rogers
2 Hornung, Paul
3 Horowitz, Norman
2 Horowitz, Vladimir
2 Horszowski, Mieczyslaw
2 Horton (Johnny Horton and The Four B's)
1 Horton, Dr.
43 Horton, Edward Everett
2 Horton, Lee
4 Horton, Robert
98 Horton, Russell
1 Hoschman
1 Hoshell, Marjorie
4 Hoskins, Percy
1 Hoskins, Ray
9 Hosley, Pat
1 Hotchkiss, Preston
28 Hottelet, Richard C.
1 Hottle, Althea
1 Houdini, Beatrice
1 Houghton, Bill
1 Houghton, Norris
2 Houk, Ralph
1 Houle, Cyril
1 House, Billy
1 House, Edwin M.
1 House, Karen Elliott
4 Household, Geoffrey
1 Housely, Patricia
2 Houseman, A. E.
2 Houseman, John
1 Houston, Ann
5 Houston, Bob
6 Houston, Dolly
1 Houston, Don
1 Houston, Happy
1 Houston, Jessie
138 Houston, Lou
1 Houston, Phillip
1 Houston, Thelma
1 Houton, Ernest Albert
1 Houton, Steve
1 Hovde, Bryn J.
1 Hovick, Louise
15 Howard (Eddy Howard and His Orchestra)
1 Howard (Hal Howard and His Orchestra)
1 Howard Quartet, The
1 Howard University Players, The
1 Howard University Women's Glee Club, The
3 Howard, Alan
2 Howard, Bill
8 Howard, Bob
1 Howard, Charlotte
2 Howard, Cliff
30 Howard, Cy
16 Howard, Eddy
1 Howard, Elaine
4 Howard, Elston
4 Howard, Frank
30 Howard, Fred
1 Howard, Fria
5 Howard, Gene
5 Howard, George
3 Howard, Henry
1 Howard, Irving
3 Howard, Jack
1 Howard, James
1 Howard, Jan
4 Howard, Joe
2 Howard, Joe E.
6 Howard, John
12 Howard, Leslie
2 Howard, Leslie Ruth
1 Howard, Lorette
1 Howard, Michael
1 Howard, Nora
1 Howard, Ralph
4 Howard, Shirley
3 Howard, Sidney
1 Howard, Terry
1 Howard, Tod
33 Howard, Tom
1 Howard, Trevor
2 Howard, Virginia
1 Howard, Wed
1 Howard, William K.
3 Howard, Willie
3 Howard, Wyatt
2 Howe, Dorothy
1 Howe, Gordie
10 Howe, Louise Hill
2 Howe, Pete
28 Howe, Quincy
2 Howe, Virginia
2 Howell, Bert
26 Howell, Cliff
1 Howell, Edward
6 Howell, Gene
11 Howell, Wayne
5 Howells, William Dean
1 Howland, Marty
1 Howrani, Raja
2 Hoyer, Stennie
5 Hoyer, Tom
2 Hoysrot, John
1 Hoyt, Alan
1 Hoyt, Catherine
17 Hoyt, John
1 Huang, Robert T.
1 Hubbard (Freddie Hubbard and The Quintet)
1 Hubbard, Alan
3 Hubbard, Freddie
24 Hubbard, Irene
1 Hubbard, Ivan
16 Hubbard, John
1 Hubbard, L. Ron
1 Hubbell, Jack
57 Huber, Ethel
15 Huber, Harold
1 Huberman, Bronislaw
1 Hubert, Rene
1 Hubler, Ethel
7 Hucko, Peanuts
14 Hudes, Ted
1 Hudkins, Keith
1 Hudson (Dean Hudson and His Orchestra)
1 Hudson, Beverly
2 Hudson, Bill
2 Hudson, Dean
1 Hudson, Jean
2 Hudson, John Everett
1 Hudson, Mary
2 Hudson, Rochelle
4 Hudson, Rock
2 Hudson, Sid
1 Hudson, Tom
1 Hudson, W. H.
3 Huey, Richard
1 Huey, William Bradford
1 Huff, Donald
1 Huff, Sam
2 Hug, Armand
2 Hugely, Archie
1 Hugenot, Harry
1 Huggins, Bill
1 Huggins, Charles B.
1 Huggins, Miller
2 Hughes, Arthur
1 Hughes, Buddy
1 Hughes, Charles Evans
7 Hughes, Don
3 Hughes, Donald
3 Hughes, Dorothy
1 Hughes, Ernie
1 Hughes, Floy Margaret
17 Hughes, Glenn
36 Hughes, Gordon
1 Hughes, Harold

9 Hughes, Howard
2 Hughes, J. Anthony
3 Hughes, John B.
1 Hughes, John W.
3 Hughes, Langston
8 Hughes, Marjorie
13 Hughes, Marvin
90 Hughes, Paul
1 Hughes, Randy
2 Hughes, Richard
4 Hughes, Robin
5 Hughes, Rupert
21 Hughes, Rush
98 Hughes, Russell
1 Hughes, Spike
9 Hughes, Tony
1 Hughes, Walter
11 Hugo, Victor
10 Hulick, Budd
2 Hull, Cordell
2 Hull, E. M.
1 Hull, Helen Rose
46 Hull, Henry
1 Hull, Howard
2 Hull, Ira L.
3 Hull, Josephine
1 Hull, Richard
1 Hull, Shelly
68 Hull, Warren
3 Hulman, Tony
1 Hum and Strum
2 Humberland, Jim
59 Hume, Benita
1 Hume, Britt
1 Hume, Julius
5 Humes, Helen
1 Hummel, Elfie
1 Hummel, Hazel
1 Hummell (Mark Hummell and His Orchestra)
1 Hummerlund, Jim
70 Hummert, Anne
53 Hummert, Frank
3 Hummingbirds, The
1 Humphrey, Boyd
6 Humphrey, Harry
14 Humphrey, Hubert
1 Humphrey, Hugh
1 Humphrey, Muriel
1 Humphrey, Percy
8 Humphrey, Stetson
1 Humphries, Cecil
1 Humphries, Grace
1 Humphries, Joe
1 Humphries, Peter
1 Hunley, Rod
1 Hunnington, Ann
1 Hunt (Pee Wee Hunt and His 12th Street Rag Band)
1 Hunt (Pee Wee Hunt and His Dixieland Band)
4 Hunt (Pee Wee Hunt and His Orchestra)
1 Hunt Jr., James
1 Hunt, A. M.
2 Hunt, Albert
1 Hunt, Annette
8 Hunt, Frazier
5 Hunt, Gary
1 Hunt, Hugh
2 Hunt, Joel
2 Hunt, John
1 Hunt, Lee
1 Hunt, Leroy
1 Hunt, Lois
1 Hunt, Marjorie
21 Hunt, Marsha
1 Hunt, Mildred
1 Hunt, Pauline
9 Hunt, Pee Wee
2 Hunter, Alberta
1 Hunter, Ben
3 Hunter, Ben S.
2 Hunter, G. B.
3 Hunter, Gloria
1 Hunter, Howard
1 Hunter, Ian
2 Hunter, Ivory Joe
1 Hunter, Jack
3 Hunter, Jeffrey
5 Hunter, Joyce
2 Hunter, Kenneth
16 Hunter, Kim
60 Hunter, Mary
3 Hunter, Pinky
3 Hunter, Ralph
1 Hunter, Tab
38 Huntley, Chet
2 Huntoon, Carolyn
1 Hurd, Richard
1 Hurdle, Jack
2 Hurlburt, Glen
7 Hurlburt, Jim
3 Hurleigh, Gene
9 Hurleigh, Robert F.
1 Hurley, Ambassador
13 Hurley, Eugene
1 Hurlick, Phil
1 Hurok, Sol
9 Hurst, Fannie
2 Hurt, Earl
69 Hurt, Marlin
17 Husing, Ted
1 Husky Song Squad, The
1 Husky, Betty
11 Husky, Ferlin
1 Hussein, Saddam
19 Hussey, Ruth
7 Hustead, Don
1 Huston, George
1 Huston, Jane
5 Huston, John
1 Huston, Josephine
60 Huston, Walter
1 Hutch, Glen
2 Hutchins, Daryl
1 Hutchins, Robert M.
1 Hutchinson, Charles
2 Hutchinson, Fred
10 Hutchinson, Josephine
1 Hutchinson, Karen
1 Hutchinson, Leslie
3 Hutchinson, Neil
1 Hutchinson, Susan
1 Hutchison, Kay Bailey
42 Hutto, Max
1 Hutton (Ina Ray Hutton and Her Melodears)
2 Hutton (Ina Ray Hutton and Her Orchestra)
1 Hutton (Marion Hutton and The Modernaires)
26 Hutton, Betty
1 Hutton, Graham
3 Hutton, Ina Ray
30 Hutton, June
44 Hutton, Marion
3 Hutton, Robert
7 Huxley, Aldous
1 Huzzack, Jane
1 Hyams, Marjorie
1 Hyatt, Helen
1 Hyde, James
1 Hyden, Bob
2 Hyer, Martha
3 Hyers, Frankie
1 Hyland, Dick
3 Hylton (Jack Hylton and His Orchestra)
1 Hyman (Dick Hyman and His Orchestra)
6 Hyman, Dick
1 Hymer, Warren

1 Ian and Sylvia
1 Ian, Janis
7 Ibsen, Henrik
5 Ickes, Harold
1 Ickes, John
36 Idelson, Billy
1 Ignatius, David
2 Ijams, George E.
1 Ikes, Gene
1 Illinois Jacquet Sextette, The
2 Imhoff, Marc
5 Impelliteri, Vincent
1 Imperial Quartet, The
2 Indianapolis Symphony Orchestra, The
1 Inge, William
5 Ingebretsen, James C.
1 Ingelus, Dorothy
1 Ingersol, Mr.
1 Ingersoll, Admiral
3 Ingersoll, Andrew
1 Ingham, Travis
1 Ingle (Red Ingle's Natural Seven)
11 Ingle, Red
1 Ingmann, Jorge
1 Ingraham, Admiral
4 Ingraham, Gail
5 Ingraham, Harry
4 Ingram, Michael
2 Ingram, Rex
2 Inhofe, James
18 Ink Spots, The
1 Inman, Autry
1 Inman, Bob
1 Innis, William
1 Interliggi, Joseph
1 Interludes, The
1 International All-Stars, The
1 International Sweethearts Of Rhythm, The
1 International Symphony Orchestra, The
2 Ipana Troubadors, The
1 Ipolitov, Carmela
2 Ippolito, John
1 Ireland, Anthony
3 Ireland, John
1 Ireland, Ray
4 Irish, Jack
1 Irish, Ned
6 Irish, William
2 Irvin Twins, The
1 Irving, Adelaide
1 Irving, Bob
32 Irving, Charles
1 Irving, Paul
2 Irving, Peter
3 Irving, Roy
9 Irving, Washington
1 Irwin (Pee Wee Irwin and His Orchestra)
1 Irwin, Bill
1 Irwin, Boyd
27 Irwin, Carol
1 Irwin, Dennis
4 Irwin, Francis
1 Irwin, Pee Wee
1 Isaac B. Singer
4 Isaacs, Charles
4 Isaacs, Harold
1 Isby, Glenda
2 Ise, Rein
2 Isherwood, Christopher
2 Isinger, Joe
1 Isliff, Alfred
1 Israel, Bob
16 Israel, Charles E.
1 Issachsen, Captain
1 Iturbi, Amparo
1 Iturbi, Impalla
19 Iturbi, Jose
2 Ivan, Rosalind
3 Ives, Ann
84 Ives, Burl
1 Ives, Jack
11 Ives, John
2 Ives, Ray
1 Ivey, Dana
2 Ivins, Perry
1 Izzo, Bernard

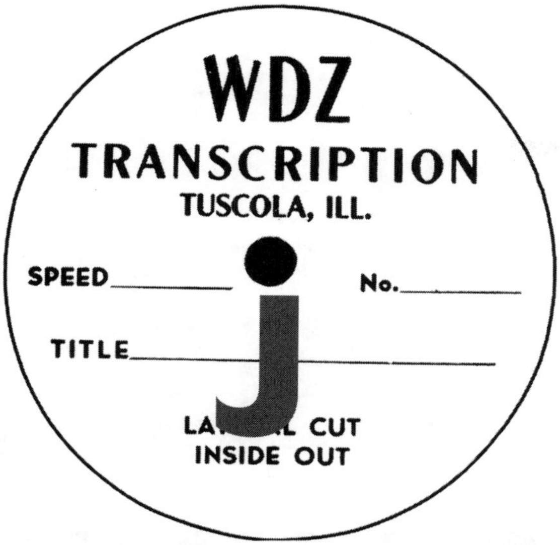
WDZ
TRANSCRIPTION
TUSCOLA, ILL.
SPEED
No.
TITLE
J
CUT
INSIDE OUT

1 Jack, Arlene
1 Jack, Beau
7 Jack, Colonel
1 Jack, King
4 Jack, Stephen
41 Jackey, Frederick
2 Jacks, The
1 Jackson (Chubby Jackson-Bill Harris Herd, The)
5 Jackson (Harry Jackson and His Orchestra)
1 Jackson (Jack Jackson and His Orchestra)
1 Jackson (Tommy Jackson and The Tennessee Travelers)
17 Jackson, Alan
1 Jackson, Arnold
1 Jackson, Avon
1 Jackson, Bill
2 Jackson, Bob
1 Jackson, Charles
1 Jackson, Cherlene
1 Jackson, Christine
4 Jackson, Chubby
3 Jackson, Chuck
1 Jackson, Cliff
1 Jackson, Cornwell
8 Jackson, Eddie
1 Jackson, Frank
2 Jackson, Glenda
29 Jackson, Hal
2 Jackson, Harry
2 Jackson, Helen Hunt
170 Jackson, Jay
14 Jackson, Jesse
1 Jackson, Jimmy
2 Jackson, Joanne
1 Jackson, Ken
2 Jackson, King
1 Jackson, Larry
1 Jackson, Leo
7 Jackson, Mahalia
1 Jackson, Mayor
1 Jackson, Mike
1 Jackson, Riley
1 Jackson, Roy
2 Jackson, Sherry
1 Jackson, Shirley
2 Jackson, Shot
3 Jackson, Stonewall
11 Jackson, Tommy
8 Jackson, Virginia
1 Jackson, William E.
1 Jackson-Harris Herd, The
1 Jacob, Betty
1 Jacob, Norman
2 Jacobi (Elliot Jacobi and His Orchestra)
1 Jacobi, Elliot
1 Jacobi, Henry
3 Jacobi, Lou
1 Jacobs, Betty
1 Jacobs, Charles
1 Jacobs, Harry
2 Jacobs, Harvey
2 Jacobs, Jacob
2 Jacobs, Jerome
5 Jacobs, John
24 Jacobs, Johnny
7 Jacobs, Joseph
2 Jacobs, Marguerite
1 Jacobs, Mr.
10 Jacobs, Ruth
2 Jacobs, Seaman
1 Jacobs, Sheldon
1 Jacobs, Thornwall
2 Jacobs, W. W.
1 Jacobson, Art
11 Jacobson, Arthur
1 Jacobson, Lou
2 Jacoby, Bill
1 Jacoby, Frank
4 Jacoby, Neil H.
1 Jacoby, Ronnie
12 Jacquet, Illinois
1 Jadin, Colonel
2 Jaeckel, Richard
1 Jaffe (Fred Jaffe Singers, The)
1 Jaffe, Bernard
8 Jaffe, Sam
2 Jaffee, Ben
30 Jaffrey, Tom
1 Jager, Harry A.
17 Jagger, Dean
1 Jahns (Al Jahns and His Orchestra)
1 Jakobowski, Walter
1 James (Harry James and His New Jazz Band)
150 James (Harry James and His Orchestra)
3 James (Jimmy James and His Orchestra)
1 James, Ann
1 James, Barney
2 James, Betty
125 James, Bill
1 James, Brian
2 James, Buddy
15 James, Dennis
21 James, Edward
3 James, Etta
1 James, Gigi
3 James, Grover
56 James, Harry
9 James, Henry
39 James, Hugh
7 James, Ida
2 James, Jason
2 James, Jimmy
1 James, Jinny
4 James, John
19 James, Jonelle
17 James, Joni
7 James, Lee
2 James, Marquis
1 James, Montague R.
16 James, Owen
1 James, Pauline
1 James, Skip
7 James, Sonny
1 James, Stafford
1 James, Vicki
1 James, Vincent
50 Jameson, House
4 Jamison, Anne
3 Jampel, Carl
1 Jan and Dean
2 Janiero, Tony
1 Janis, Byron
1 Janis, Deane
3 Janis, Elsie
1 Janis, Irene
191 Janney, Leon
2 Janney, William
104 Janniss, Vivi
2 Janocheck, William
17 Janover, Dick
2 Jansen, Elsa
3 Janssen, Warner
1 Janta, Aleksander
1 January, Lois
3 Jarman, Claude
1 Jarmon, Joe
2 Jarmyn, Jill
1 Jarrett, Art
6 Jarvis, Al
1 Jarvis, Cal
1 Jarvis, Carol
1 Jarvis, Sidney
1 Jaslow, Frank
1 Jason, Jack
1 Jason, Pamela
1 Jason, Rick
4 Jastrow, Robert
1 Jaworski, Leon
1 Jay (Morty Jay and The Showmen)
1 Jay and The Americans
1 Jay, Joey
5 Jay, Lester
2 Jay, Miriam
1 Jay, Victor
1 Jaynes, Betty
1 Jazz Jesters, The
5 Jean, Gloria
1 Jean, Norma
26 Jeanette
1 Jeanine
3 Jeanne
7 Jeannie
1 Jebb, Gladwyn
1 Jefferson, Carter
1 Jeffords, James
3 Jeffrey, Howard
1 Jeffrey, June
4 Jeffreys, Allen
1 Jeffries, Fran
16 Jeffries, Herb
1 Jeffries, James J.
2 Jeffries, Jimmie
1 Jeffries, Phillip
16 Jellison, Bob
1 Jemail, Jimmy
1 Jenkins
1 Jenkins (Gordon Jenkins and His Orchestra and Chorus)
66 Jenkins (Gordon Jenkins and His Orchestra)
1 Jenkins, Abe
1 Jenkins, Alice
8 Jenkins, Allen
2 Jenkins, Ed
34 Jenkins, Gordon
1 Jenkins, Harriet
1 Jenkins, Leroy
1 Jenkins, Shorty
3 Jenks, Frank
1 Jenks, Frederic
2 Jenks, Hugh
5 Jennings, Al
7 Jennings, Jack
1 Jennings, Patricia
7 Jennings, Peter
37 Jennings, Robert G.
1 Jennings, Waylon
2 Jenorio, Rosita
1 Jensen, Jackie
2 Jensen, Ken
1 Jenson, Franklin
1 Jenson, John
9 Jepson, Helen
2 Jeracki, Robert
1 Jergens, Adele
1 Jeritza, Maria
11 Jerome (Henry Jerome and His Orchestra)
1 Jerome (Jerry Jerome and His Orchestra)
51 Jerome, Edwin
1 Jerome, Helene
1 Jerome, Mrs. Bill
1 Jerome, Stuart
7 Jerrold, Helen
1 Jerrold, Peter
85 Jessel, George
1 Jessel, John
6 Jessup, Richard
1 Jessye (Eva Jessye Choir, The)
15 Jesters, The
1 Jethro
1 Jeva, Tomara
1 Jewell, Bruce
34 Jewell, Isabel
2 Jewell, James
9 Jewett, Ted
1 Jewison, Norman
2 Jo, Damita
1 Job, Richard
1 Jobe, Sidney
1 Jobert, Michel
1 Jobim, Antonio Carlos
1 Jobs, Steven
1 Joe and Eddie
1 Joel, Mary Lee
1 Joel, Peter
15 Joels, Merrill E.
1 Joey and Chuck
1 Johann, Zita
1 Johanneson, Grant
2 John Paul II
1 John, Ruth
10 Johnny
9 Johnny and Jack
5 Johnsen, Waldemar
1 Johnson
12 Johnson (Arnold Johnson and His Orchestra)
2 Johnson (C. P. Johnson and His Orchestra)
7 Johnson (Hall Johnson Choir, The)
1 Johnson (J. J. Johnson Quintet, The)
1 Johnson Choir, The
6 Johnson Negro Choir
1 Johnson Sisters, The
1 Johnson, A. J.
3 Johnson, Arnold
2 Johnson, Bess
2 Johnson, Betty
3 Johnson, Bill
1 Johnson, Billy
3 Johnson, Bunk
1 Johnson, C. S.
3 Johnson, Carl
8 Johnson, Chic
1 Johnson, Chuck
1 Johnson, D. H.
3 Johnson, Doug
3 Johnson, Earl J.
2 Johnson, Earl S.
1 Johnson, Edna
2 Johnson, Edward
3 Johnson, Erskine
1 Johnson, Fess
1 Johnson, Frank
1 Johnson, Ginny
1 Johnson, Hardesty
1 Johnson, Harry
4 Johnson, Hugh
1 Johnson, I. C.
2 Johnson, J. J.
2 Johnson, J. Rosamond
1 Johnson, James C.
13 Johnson, James P.
9 Johnson, Jason
3 Johnson, Jay

25 Johnson, Joanne
2 Johnson, Joe
2 Johnson, Johnny
3 Johnson, Judy
1 Johnson, Kay
122 Johnson, Lamont
1 Johnson, Lee
1 Johnson, Lem
1 Johnson, Leon W.
3 Johnson, Luther A.
28 Johnson, Lyndon
1 Johnson, Mark
1 Johnson, Maxine
1 Johnson, Mrs. Raymond Edward
2 Johnson, Owen
4 Johnson, Parks
2 Johnson, Paul
4 Johnson, Pete
1 Johnson, Pitch
1 Johnson, R. E.
3 Johnson, Rafer
1 Johnson, Ray
128 Johnson, Raymond Edward
2 Johnson, Richard
15 Johnson, Rita
1 Johnson, Robert
1 Johnson, Robert E.
9 Johnson, Rome
1 Johnson, S. C.
1 Johnson, Samuel
1 Johnson, Ted
2 Johnson, Thomas
1 Johnson, Tom
9 Johnson, Torrence
33 Johnson, Van
3 Johnson, Walter
1 Johnson, William
1 Johnston (Merle Johnston and His Saxophone Quartet)
1 Johnston, Albert
1 Johnston, Alva
1 Johnston, Bennett
2 Johnston, Carolyn
1 Johnston, Dippy
1 Johnston, Don
1 Johnston, Eric A.
16 Johnston, Johnny
1 Johnston, May
1 Johnston, Redge
4 Johnstone, Bob
406 Johnstone, Jack
10 Johnstone, Johanna
388 Johnstone, William
111 Jolley, Norman
6 Jollos, Inge
1 Jolly, Lawrence
170 Jolson, Al
1 Jonas, Paul
1 Jonay, Roberta
2 Jones (Isham Jones and His Orchestra)
1 Jones (Jo Jones Trio, The)
2 Jones (Jonah Jones and His Orchestra)
1 Jones (Jonah Jones and His Quartet)
2 Jones (Jonah Jones Quartet, The)
2 Jones (Jonah Jones Quintet, The)
2 Jones (Spike Jones and His Orchestra)
82 Jones (Spike Jones and The City Slickers)
1 Jones (Spike Jones' Other Orchestra)
1 Jones (Thad Jones Orchestra, The)
26 Jones, Alan
1 Jones, Arch Dale
2 Jones, Bettina
5 Jones, Bill
25 Jones, Billy
81 Jones, Bob
3 Jones, Buck
1 Jones, Bud
2 Jones, Carolyn
2 Jones, Casey
2 Jones, Dale
1 Jones, David
1 Jones, David Dallas
6 Jones, Dickie
1 Jones, Dill
1 Jones, Elvin
2 Jones, Frank
1 Jones, Frankie
1 Jones, Fred
15 Jones, G. Stanley
1 Jones, George Washington
4 Jones, Ginger
8 Jones, Grandpa
10 Jones, Grover
9 Jones, Hank
2 Jones, Isham
1 Jones, J. Franklin
5 Jones, Jack
1 Jones, James Earl
3 Jones, Jennifer
1 Jones, Jim
1 Jones, Jimmy
3 Jones, Jo
12 Jones, Jonah
4 Jones, Kay Cee
1 Jones, Kenneth L.
1 Jones, Lloyd
2 Jones, Marcia Mae
1 Jones, Nowell
1 Jones, Paul
2 Jones, Paul Whitson
12 Jones, Peter
1 Jones, Preston
1 Jones, Robert T.
1 Jones, Rodney
1 Jones, Rufus
4 Jones, Shirley
12 Jones, Simon
7 Jones, Spike
6 Jones, Stan
1 Jones, Thad
1 Jones, W. Alton
1 Jones, Walton
3 Jordan (Louis Jordan and His Orchestra)
3 Jordan (Louis Jordan and His Tympani Five)
1 Jordan, Anthony
1 Jordan, Benjamin
1 Jordan, Ed
2 Jordan, Fats
1 Jordan, Jerry
609 Jordan, Jim
2 Jordan, Jimmy
4 Jordan, Jo-ann
1 Jordan, John J.
2 Jordan, Lee
4 Jordan, Louis
580 Jordan, Marian
6 Jordan, Max
1 Jordan, Mickey
3 Jordan, Owen
1 Jordan, Phillip
1 Jordan, R.
3 Jordan, Ricky
2 Jordan, Russ
1 Jordan, Taft
1 Jordan, Ted
1 Jordan, Top
2 Jordan, Will
30 Jordanaires, The
1 Jorge, Rene
1 Jorgensen, Christine
1 Jorgenson, Arthur
10 Jorgenson, Fred
60 Jory, Victor
40 Josefsberg, Milt
1 Joseph, Franz
1 Joseph, Harry
1 Joseph, Irving
1 Joseph, Jackie
9 Josephy, Alvin
7 Joslyn, Allyn
41 Jostyn, Jay
1 Jou-Jerryville, Jacques
1 Joudry, Patricia
3 Jourdan, Louis
2 Jovy, Felix
35 Joy, Dick
1 Joy, Leatrice
3 Joy, Nicholas
1 Joyce, Barbara
1 Joyce, Brenda
1 Joyce, Dorothy
1 Joyce, Father
1 Joyce, James
9 Joyce, Patricia
1 Joyce, Peggy Hopkins
3 Joyce, William
1 Joyce, Willie
39 Jubalaires, The
1 Jubilee All Stars, The
1 Jubilee Singers, The
1 Judd, Walter H.
1 Judge, Arline
3 Judson, Paul
2 Judy Ann and Zeke
21 Juhran, Bob
1 Julian, Arthur
95 Julian, Joseph
1 Jumpin' Bill and All The Carlisles
13 Jumpin' Jacks, The
1 June, Jimee
1 Jungleers, The
1 Junier, Katherine
20 Junkin, Harry W.
1 Jurado, Katie
1 Juran, Joseph M.
4 Juran, McKay
20 Jurgens (Dick Jurgens and His Orchestra)
1 Jurgenson, Karen
1 Juriff, Mark
5 Jurist, Edward
1 Jurnigan, W. H.
131 Juster, Evie
4 Justine, Bill
2 Juve, Jorgen

1 K. C. and The Sunshine Band
51 KaDell, Carlton
1 KaDell, Jean
2 Kaempffert, Waldemar
2 Kafka, Franz
18 Kagan, Ben
1 Kahn (Roger Wolfe Kahn and His Orchestra)
1 Kahn, Grace
1 Kahn, Gus
1 Kahn, Herman
5 Kahn, Judy
3 Kahn, Milton P.
1 Kai-Shek, Chiang
6 Kai-Shek, Madame Chiang
1 Kain, Jackie
3 Kaiser, Henry J.
1 Kalama, Ben
1 Kalb, Bernard
10 Kalb, Marvin
1 Kale, Jimmy
1 Kalen, Samuel
1 Kalenyi, Edward
1 Kaleolani (Alvin Kaleolani and Trio)
48 Kaliban, Bob
1 Kalinski, Mr.
1 Kalischer, Peter
50 Kallen, Kitty
1 Kalmar, Bert
2 Kalmus, Bea
103 Kaltenborn, H. V.
1 Kaltenborn, Mrs.
1 Kaltenmeyer, Professor
2 Kamen, Milt
1 Kaminker, George
29 Kaminsky, Max
1 Kampfert, Dirk
1 Kampfert, Mortimore
1 Kandahl, Torolv
215 Kane, Byron
1 Kane, Catherine
1 Kane, Charles
4 Kane, Eddie
1 Kane, Edward
19 Kane, Frank
1 Kane, Georgia
3 Kane, Helen
1 Kane, Henry
1 Kane, Jan
1 Kane, Jimmy
2 Kane, Joel
31 Kane, John
1 Kane, Kitty
3 Kane, Michael
2 Kane, Sugar
2 Kane, Whitford
1 Kanigher, Robert
1 Kanin, Garson
26 Kanner (Hal Kanner's Little Band)
1 Kansas City Nighthawks, The
1 Kansas City Philharmonic, The
1 Kantor, Hal
2 Kantor, MacKinlay
1 Kapek, Carel
1 Kaplan, Adele
10 Kaplan, Marvin
1 Kaplan, Mildred
3 Kaplan, Nate
3 Kaplow, Herb
1 Kapp, Anthony
1 Kappel, William
2 Kapps, Jack
9 Kapryan, Walter
1 Karacker, George
50 Karas, Anton
2 Karen, Anna
1 Karen, Barbara

1 Karen, Suzanne
2 Karenko, Maria
1 Karker, Morris
1 Karloff, Bogart
101 Karloff, Boris
1 Karmin, Monroe
2 Karns, Mary Jane
10 Karns, Roscoe
1 Karol, Milton
1 Karski, Jan
3 Kasem, Casey
3 Kasher, Charles D.
1 Kasich, John
1 Kasik, John
1 Kasiloff, Skitch
1 Kasper, Fred
6 Kassell (Art Kassell and His Orchestra)
2 Kassell, Art
1 Kasser, Eddie
2 Kasten (Louis Kasten and His Orchestra)
10 Kathleen
4 Katims (Milton Katims and His Orchestra)
5 Katims, Milton
1 Katsuky, Julius
5 Katy, Frank
2 Katy, Hugh
1 Katz (Mickey Katz and His Orchestra)
1 Katz, Anna
9 Katz, Bernard
3 Katz, Mickey
1 Katz, Peter
2 Katzman (Lou Katzman and His Orchestra)
15 Katzman, Sam
4 Kauf, Dewitt
18 Kaufman, George S.
1 Kaufman, Harry
3 Kaufman, Irving
3 Kaufman, Millard
1 Kaufman, Murray
2 Kavelin (Al Kavelin and His Orchestra)
1 Kavelin Trio, The
1 Kay (Herbie Kay and His Orchestra)
1 Kay (Mary Kay Trio, The)
26 Kay, Beatrice
6 Kay, Carol
1 Kay, Joan
1 Kay, Lambdin
7 Kaydettes, The
43 Kaye (Sammy Kaye and His Orchestra)
1 Kaye Choir, The
1 Kaye, A. P.
1 Kaye, Alma
91 Kaye, Danny
17 Kaye, Geraldine
1 Kaye, Harriet
1 Kaye, Jack
1 Kaye, Marion
6 Kaye, Milton
1 Kaye, Milton Bernard
1 Kaye, Pat
16 Kaye, Sammy
1 Kaye, Sidney
2 Kaye, Stubby
2 Kaye, Tommy
2 Kaye, Virginia
1 Kayersling, Leon H.
3 Kaylor, Bill
3 Kazan, Elia
1 Kazan, Nicholas
1 Kazin, Alfred
2 Kazotkis, Teddy
66 Keach, Stacy
1 Keagy, Grace
3 Kean, Jane
1 Kean, Robert Emmet
1 Keane, Bertrand
34 Keane, Gerald
2 Keane, John
1 Keane, Leonore
142 Keane, Teri
1 Kearn, Otto
1 Kearney, Mark
1 Kearns, James
491 Kearns, Joseph
1 Kearns, Kathleen
1 Kears, Helen
1 Kearse, Timothy
1 Keating, Frank
177 Keating, Larry
1 Keating, Rex
2 Keaton, Buster
1 Keats, John
2 Keats, Steven
1 Keboe, Ray
3 Keddy, Grace
3 Keech, Kelvin
1 Keegan, Hugh
1 Keegan, Junie
2 Keel, Howard
1 Keel, Lee
1 Keeler, Marjorie
10 Keeler, Ruby
24 Keen, Earl
1 Keen, Hal
1 Keen, Judy
2 Keen, Linda
4 Keen, Malcolm
1 Keen, Mrs. Hal
1 Keenan, Ann
1 Keenan, Joe
1 Keene Sisters, The
2 Keene, Joseph
1 Keene, Sidney
2 Keene, Tom
29 Keene, William
1 Keener, Ward
2 Kefauver, Estes
2 Kehr, LaVerne
134 Keighley, William
2 Keil, Jack
1 Keil, Klaus
1 Keilor, Garrison
1 Keitel
1 Keith, Ben
1 Keith, Donna
1 Keith, Ian
11 Keith, Richard
440 Kelk, Jackie
1 Kell (Reginald Kell and His Orchestra)
2 Kellaway, Cecil
1 Keller, Catherine
1 Keller, Charlie
8 Keller, James
4 Keller, Jerry
1 Keller, Suzanne
1 Kellerman, Annette
1 Kellin, Mike
2 Kellino, Pamela
4 Kellner (Leon Kellner and His Orchestra)
2 Kellogg, Cecil
2 Kellogg, Ray
1 Kelly Jr., Paula
6 Kelly, Al
1 Kelly, Betsy
1 Kelly, Betty
3 Kelly, Bill
1 Kelly, Charles
2 Kelly, DeForest
1 Kelly, Dr.
1 Kelly, Emmett
35 Kelly, Gene
1 Kelly, George
1 Kelly, Grace
1 Kelly, Jim
68 Kelly, Joe
1 Kelly, Laura
3 Kelly, Mark
1 Kelly, Mary
14 Kelly, Nancy
5 Kelly, Pat
1 Kelly, Patrick J.
10 Kelly, Patsy
6 Kelly, Paul
16 Kelly, Paula
1 Kelly, Penny
1 Kelly, Rock
3 Kelly, Rosemary
1 Kelly, Russ
1 Kelly, T. J.
1 Kelly, Tom
6 Kelly, Welborn
1 Kelly, William P.
3 Kelsey, Bill
2 Kelsey, Jack
2 Kelton, Carlton
24 Kelton, Pert
1 Kelvin, Rosemary
1 Kemmer, Andrew J.
166 Kemmer, Ed
1 Kemp (Hal Kemp and His Hotel Astor Orchestra)
9 Kemp (Hal Kemp and His Orchestra)
1 Kemp, Elaine
1 Kemp, Hal
3 Kemp, Harold
1 Kemp, Hugh
5 Kemp, Jack
1 Kemper, Art
4 Kemper, Charles
95 Kemper, Ray
4 Kemper, Ronnie
3 Kemple, Karen
1 Kendal, Jimmy
15 Kendall, Cy
1 Kendall, Fred
1 Kendall, Norma
1 Kendrick (Merle Kendrick and His Orchestra)
7 Kendrick, Alexander
2 Kendrick, Baynard
1 Kendrick, Merle
1 Kendrick, Richard
3 Kennedy, Arthur
1 Kennedy, Bill
6 Kennedy, Bob
1 Kennedy, Caroline
1 Kennedy, Charles Rand
1 Kennedy, Charlie
3 Kennedy, Dale
1 Kennedy, Edgar
12 Kennedy, Edward
6 Kennedy, George
2 Kennedy, J. Richard
29 Kennedy, John
12 Kennedy, John B.
232 Kennedy, John Milton
2 Kennedy, Joseph
1 Kennedy, Katherine
2 Kennedy, Lucy
1 Kennedy, Raymond
14 Kennedy, Reed
6 Kennedy, Robert
2 Kennedy, Robert W.
2 Kenneth, Keith
8 Kenney, Beverly
1 Kenney, George C.
1 Kenney, Richard
2 Kennison, Lois
2 Kenny, Charles
1 Kenny, Elizabeth
3 Kenny, Nick
15 Kent, Alan
2 Kent, Barbara
15 Kent, Crawford
2 Kent, Edgar
5 Kent, Elaine
1 Kent, Fred I.
1 Kent, Lenny
2 Kent, Marshall
4 Kent, Mona
13 Kent, Priscilla
1 Kent, Susan
1 Kent, Walter
2 Kentish, Elizabeth
63 Kenton (Stan Kenton and His Orchestra)
9 Kenton, Stan
7 Kenworthy, Wayne
1 Kenyatta, Robin
1 Kenyon, Bernice
1 Kenyon, Chris
2 Kenyon, Dorothy
2 Kenyon, Gloria
1 Kenyon, Theta
1 Kerig, Walter
2 Kerker, William
1 Kerkhoven, August
5 Kerman, Bernice
16 Kerman, David
1 Kern, David
3 Kern, Grace
3 Kern, Herb
1 Kern, James V.
13 Kern, Jerome
1 Kerouac, Jack
8 Kerr, Deborah
2 Kerr, John
1 Kerr, Laura
1 Kerr, LaVerne
4 Kerr, Lawrence
1 Kerr, Robert S.
5 Kerr, Walter
4 Kerrigan, J. M.
1 Kerrington, Jack
1 Kerry, Lois
1 Kerwin, Jerome G.
8 Kerwin, Joseph
1 Kesey, Carlton
1 Kessell, Barney
1 Kessell (Barney Kessell Trio)
1 Kessler, Dave
1 Kessler, Don
1 Kessler, Henry
1 Kessler, Lou
1 Kessner, Dick
2 Kestenbaum, Meyer
1 Kester, Karne
1 Ketchum, Omar B.
5 Kettering, Charles F.
1 Key, William
11 Keyes, Evelyn
1 Keyes, Katherine
1 Keyes, Kenneth S.
2 Keynotes, The
2 Keys, Robert H.
1 Keyworth, George
2 Khruschev, Nikita
1 Kibbee, Gordon
6 Kibbee, Guy
2 Kibbee, Louis
1 Kibbee, Lucille
1 Kidd, John
1 Kidoodlers, The
1 Kieland, Frances
69 Kieran, John
2 Kiernan, Walter
1 Kiest, William R.
1 Kilauea, Jack
2 Kilbride, Percy
10 Kilburn, Terry
1 Kilday, Paul J.
1 Kildy, Dale
1 Kilenyi, Edward
5 Kiley, Richard
12 Kilgallen, Dorothy
1 Kilgore, Harley M.
1 Kilgore, Harry
1 Killen, Buddy
5 Killiam, Paul
1 Killian (Al Killian and His Band)
3 Killian, Victor
1 Killoway, Brian
57 Kilpack, Bennett
1 Kilpatrick, John Reed
4 Kilty, Jack
1 Kimball, Molly
1 Kimball, Ward
1 Kimber, Mary
1 Kimberly, Kim
1 Kimble, George H. T.
68 Kimbrell, Charles
1 Kimbro, Edward
23 Kimbro, Kyle
1 Kimmons, Anthony
1 Kinard, William
1 Kindwall, Josef
1 Kine, Peter B.
2 Kinelao, Dan
4 Kiner, Ralph
30 King (Henry King and His Orchestra)
5 King (Pee Wee King and His Golden West Cowboys)

1 King (Pee Wee King and His Orchestra)
2 King (Pete King and His Orchestra)
1 King (Wayne King and His Orchestra and Choir)
15 King (Wayne King and His Orchestra)
2 King Edward
1 King Family, The
36 King George VI
4 King Haakon VII
1 King Leopold
10 King Moses
1 King Of Yugoslavia, The
1 King Paul I
30 King Sisters, The
4 King, Al
5 King, Alan
1 King, Alexander
2 King, Alice
4 King, B. B.
1 King, Ben E.
1 King, Bonnie
5 King, Buddy
1 King, Cameron
3 King, Charles
1 King, Charles Scott
1 King, Coretta Scott
39 King, Del
3 King, Dennis
1 King, Dudley
90 King, Edward
3 King, Ernest
1 King, Frances
2 King, Gene
1 King, George
4 King, Henry
1 King, Jack
4 King, James C.
6 King, Jean
6 King, Jean Paul
44 King, Joe
1 King, John
10 King, John F. W.
51 King, John Reed
2 King, Judy
19 King, Larry
1 King, Lila
2 King, Linda
3 King, Louis
1 King, Louise
1 King, Mabel
1 King, Malcolm
2 King, Martha
1 King, Martin Luther
13 King, Marty Clark
1 King, Mary
1 King, Morris
1 King, Pat
4 King, Pee Wee
15 King, Peggy
13 King, Perry
2 King, Richard
1 King, Saunders
1 King, Sonny
1 King, Stan
3 King, Stephen
5 King, Ted
4 King, Teddy
1 King, Wally
15 King, Walter
4 King, Wayne
3 King, William MacKenzie
1 King, Wright
1 King, Yvonne
8 Kingdon, Frank
1 Kingman, Eddie
1 Kings, Charles
3 Kingsbury, Chet
1 Kingsford, Guy
6 Kingsford, Walter
1 Kingsley, Guy
2 Kingsley, J. Donald
1 Kingsley, Michael
5 Kingsley, Sidney
14 Kingslow, Janice
13 Kingston Trio, The
1 Kingston, Adrian
1 Kingston, G. B.
1 Kingston, Leonore
534 King's Men, The
1 Kinnamon, Larry
1 Kinnelly, Martin
1 Kinney, Nina Mae
158 Kinoy, Ernest
20 Kinsella, Walter
1 Kinslow, Janice
10 Kipling, Rudyard
2 Kipnis, Alexander
1 Kipp, Emily
1 Kirberry, Ralph
3 Kirby (John Kirby and His Orchestra)
1 Kirby (John Kirby Group, The)
1 Kirby (John Kirby Sextet, The)
25 Kirby, Durward
5 Kirby, Gene
2 Kirby, George
1 Kirby, Jean
1 Kirby, John
11 Kirby, Kleve
2 Kirby, Paul
1 Kirchwey, Freda
6 Kirk (Andy Kirk and His Orchestra)
1 Kirk (Buddy Kirk and His Orchestra)
1 Kirk (Buddy Kirk and His Orchestra)
1 Kirk, Admiral
1 Kirk, Bob
1 Kirk, Ed
1 Kirk, Eddie
3 Kirk, Grayson
5 Kirk, Lisa
1 Kirk, Mrs.
1 Kirk, Paul
1 Kirk, Phyllis
2 Kirk, Rahsaan Roland
1 Kirk, Red
5 Kirkeby, Ed
1 Kirkland, Alexander
1 Kirkland, Bill
1 Kirkland, Lane
1 Kirkland, Muriel
2 Kirkland, Patricia
2 Kirkman, Muriel
2 Kirkpatrick, Carol
48 Kirkpatrick, Jess
1 Kirkpatrick, Ted
2 Kirkum, Joe
97 Kirkwood, Jack
1 Kirkwood, James
1 Kirkwood, Lil
1 Kirsten, Bob
50 Kirsten, Dorothy
1 Kissel, Arthur
4 Kissinger, Henry
5 Kitchell, Alma
5 Kitt, Eartha
1 Kjellin, Alf
1 Klacsmann, Joseph J.
1 Klaffland, Avery
1 Klaus, Hans
7 Klavan, Gene
1 Klee, Harry
77 Klee, Lawrence
3 Kleeb, Bill
55 Kleeb, Helen
1 Kleiber, Erich
21 Klein, Adelaide
1 Klein, Art
1 Klein, Bill
1 Klein, Edward E.
1 Klein, Hannah
8 Klein, Harold
10 Klein, Harrison
1 Klein, L. Roy
3 Klein, Larry
24 Klein, Manny
1 Klein, Officer
1 Klein, Stuart
3 Kleinknecht, Kenneth
1 Klemperer, Otto
3 Kline, Norman
1 Klinger Sisters, The
1 Klotsche, J. Martin
1 Klug, Scott
17 Kluge, George
1 Klumpner, Wandra
1 Klutznick, Phillip
2 KMBC Texas Rangers, The
2 Knapp, Bud
16 Knickerbocker Four, The
1 Knickerbocker Little Symphony
8 Knickerbocker, H. R.
1 Knickerbocker, Suzy
2 Kniffen, Donald
1 Knight (Gladys Knight and The Pips)
8 Knight (June Knight and The Sixty Piece All-Girl Orchestra)
2 Knight (Norvell Knight and His Orchestra)
5 Knight, Bill
2 Knight, Eric
54 Knight, Evelyn
28 Knight, Felix
98 Knight, Frank
1 Knight, Fuzzy
1 Knight, Goodwin
1 Knight, John
1 Knight, Kathleen Moore
1 Knight, Lloyd
1 Knight, Norvell
1 Knight, Paul
6 Knight, Raymond
1 Knight, Russell
2 Knight, Ruth Adams
11 Knight, Vic
1 Knights, The
1 Knobeloch, Walter
1 Knots, James
1 Knott, Del
1 Knotts, Don
2 Knowland, William F.
1 Knowles, Patrick
1 Knox, Dorothy
7 Knox, Frank
4 Knox, Harrison
1 Knoxin, Gerald
2 Knudson, Martin
1 Knudson, Thurston
1 Knudson, William
2 Knutson, Peggy
1 Koblinsky, Chet
3 Koch, Edward
1 Koch, Helen
3 Koch, Howard
1 Kock, Berwin
1 Koerner, Ben
56 Kogan, David
2 Kogen (Harry Kogen and His Orchestra)
4 Kogen (Harry Kogen and The Homesteaders)
2 Kogen (Harry Kogen and The Treasury Orchestra)
7 Kogen, Edward
1 Kogen, Harry
26 Kohl, Arthur
1 Kohl, Helmut
8 Kohlhase, Charles
1 Koier, Kay
2 KOIN Orchestra, The
1 Kol Israel Orchestra, The
1 Kolb, Clarence
142 Kollmar, Richard
13 Kondolf, George
1 Kondracki, Morton
14 Koppel, Ted
1 Koppelman, Lou
2 Koralites, The
1 Korean Children's Choir, The
9 Korjus, Miliza
1 Korman, Harvey
2 Korman, Seymour
9 Korn Kobblers, The
2 Kornbluth, C. M.
3 Korngold, Erich
1 Korvin, Charles
1 Kosleck, Martin
1 Kosmahi, Henry
1 Kosman, Joseph
1 Kosover, Mordecai
2 Koss, Sid
28 Kostelanetz (Andre Kostelanetz and His Orchestra)
2 Kostelanetz, Andre
2 Koto, Yaphet
1 Koues, Helen
2 Koufax, Sandy
241 Koury, Rex
4 Kousnetzova, Anna
3 Kovacs, Ernie
116 Kovacs, Bela
1 Kozyrov, Andrei
2 Kraal, Heidi
1 Kraft Choral Club Of Chicago, The
8 Kraft Choral Club, The
2 Kraft Choristers, The
12 Kraft, Arthur
1 Kraft, Chris
11 Kraft, Christopher
6 Kraft, Hy
3 Kraft, James L.
1 Kraft, Randy
3 Kramer, Bill
1 Kramer, Floyd
3 Kramer, Harry
2 Kramer, Jack
2 Kramer, James
196 Kramer, Mandel
1 Kramer, Milton
1 Kramer, Norman
1 Kramer, Phil
3 Kramer, Stanley
3 Kramer, Wright
2 Kranes, David
5 Kranz, Eugene
1 Kranz, Leon
1 Kraus, Milton
1 Krauss, Harriet
13 Kreisler, Fritz
1 Kreml, Franklin
1 Krentz, Bill
2 Krentz, Milton E.
1 Kress (Carl Kress and His Orchestra)
4 Kress, Carl
2 Kreuger, Kurt
1 Krier, Gary
1 Krimigis, Stamatios
94 Kroeger, Berry
8 Kroenke, Carl
1 Krone, Robert
1 Kronenberger, Lewis
2 Krueger (Bennie Krueger and His Orchestra)
3 Krueger, Dick
7 Krueger, Maynard
1 Krug, J. A.
3 Kruger, Alma
26 Kruger, Otto
148 Krugman, Lou
1 Krumgold, Joe
4 Krumschmidt, E. A.
24 Krupa (Gene Krupa and His Orchestra)
2 Krupa (Gene Krupa Quartet, The)
1 Krupa (Gene Krupa Trio, The)
47 Krupa, Gene
2 Krupp, Roger
390 Kruschen, Jack
3 Kruschen, Miriam
4 Kubasov, Valeri
2 Kubek, Tony
1 Kuhn (Dick Kuhn and His Orchestra)
1 Kuhn, Mickey
4 Kullman, Charles
1 Kunan, James Simon
4 Kuney, Jack
2 Kupcinet, Irv
6 Kupfer, Curt
3 Kupperman, Joel

1 Kur, Bob
9 Kuralt, Charles
1 Kurer, Wilma
1 Kurjack, Ed
1 Kurtch, Frances
1 Kurtz, Frank
1 Kurtz, Margo
1 Kuruzu, Ambassador
1 Kusack, Andzia
2 Kushner, Victor
2 Kusske, Amy
1 Kutovoy, Evgeny
1 Kwan, Nancy
1 Kwo, Helena
1 Kyl, Jon
5 Kyle, Alastair
1 Kyle, Billy
1 Kynion, Kaye
47 Kyser (Kay Kyser and His Orchestra)
42 Kyser, Kay
2 Kyte, Benny

7 Lacossette, Henry
1 LaCost, Francis
1 LaCurto, James
95 Ladd, Alan
1 Ladd, Carl Edwin
1 Ladd, Ed
3 Ladd, Hank
1 Ladd, Marion
3 LaDell Sisters, The
2 Laderoot, Joseph
1 Lads Of Enchantment, The
1 Ladwig, Alan
1 Lady Reading
1 Laeser, Dick
2 Lafferty, Fran
1 Lafferty, Perry
1 Lafitte, Jean
1 Lafleur, Joy
1 LaFoucheus, Marie Helene
21 LaFrandre, Jack
28 Lahr, Bert
4 Laidler, Harry

2 La Barr, Eugene
36 La Centra, Peg
1 La Farge, Oliver
2 La Follette, Philip
12 La Frano, Tony
45 La Guardia, Fiorello
3 La Mar, Edwin
1 La Marche, Maurice
1 La Neri, Madame
15 La Rosa, Julius
1 La Salle (Dick La Salle and His Orchestra)
39 La Valle (Paul La Valle and His Orchestra)
1 La Valle (Paul La Valle and The Band Of America)
13 La Valle, Paul
1 La Velle, Maurice
1 Laabs, Chet
1 Labarca, Amanda
1 LaBelle, Rupert
1 LaBua, Jack
1 Lacey (Butch Lacey String Consort, The)
1 Lacey, Robert
5 Lachman, Mort

2 Laine, Cleo
29 Laine, Frankie
1 Laing, John
1 Laird, Jack
1 Laird, Melvin
1 Laird, Mom Ann
3 Laird, Pat
1 Lake (Bonnie Lake and Her Bachelors)
23 Lake, Arthur
5 Lake, Bonnie
8 Lake, Florence
13 Lake, John
1 Lake, Stewart M.
16 Lake, Veronica
1 Lakin, R. B.
1 LaLanne, Jack
1 Lalli, Mario
51 Lally, William
1 Lamar and Corro
2 LaMar, Lewis
1 LaMarr, Eddie
10 Lamarr, Hedy
2 LaMarr, Nappy
2 Lamas, Fernando

1 Lamb, Bob
5 Lamb, Brian
3 Lamb, Gil
1 Lamb, Harold
1 Lambert, Edward
1 Lambert, Kent C.
1 Lamberton, Harry
1 Lambright, Rosemary
1 Lambs Quartet, The
1 Lamer, Jackie
1 LaMer, Monique
1 Lamere, Charles
1 Lames, Charles J.
33 Lamkin, Phil
1 Lammermeyer, Marie
5 Lamond, Don
2 Lamont, Corliss
1 Lamont, Marcie
1 Lamott, Willis
3 LaMotta, Jake
58 Lamour, Dorothy
47 Lamparski, Richard
19 Lampell, Millard
1 Lampert, Diane
1 Lamson, Peggy
14 Lancaster, Burt
1 Lancaster, Pope
1 Lance, Mary Louise
11 Lanchester, Elsa
2 Land, E. W.
2 Land, Emory S.
2 Landay, Jerry
1 Landers, Muriel
7 Landi, Elissa
11 Landis, Carole
1 Landis, Fred
1 Landis, Gail
3 Landis, Jessie Royce
5 Landon, Alf
1 Landon, Hope
1 Landon, Ray
1 Landon, Thomas
1 Landry, James
1 Landt Trio and White, The
12 Landt Trio, The
2 Landt, Carl
2 Lane (Ken Lane and The Hit Paraders)
14 Lane (Ken Lane Chorus, The)
2 Lane (Ken Lane Singers, The)
2 Lane Jr., Tom
1 Lane Sisters, The
7 Lane, Abbe
1 Lane, Alan Rocky
1 Lane, Amanda
2 Lane, Burton
1 Lane, Dave
18 Lane, Dick
2 Lane, Francine
3 Lane, Gloria
1 Lane, Kathleen
9 Lane, Ken
7 Lane, Lillian
3 Lane, Lola
1 Lane, Lonnie
1 Lane, Marjorie
1 Lane, Mark
1 Lane, Mary
1 Lane, Muriel

4 Lane, Phyllis
6 Lane, Priscilla
1 Lane, Red
1 Lane, Rose Wilder
4 Lane, Rosemary
1 Lane, Ruby
1 Lane, Shirley
3 Lane, Tommy
1 Lane, Ward
9 Lane, Zella
2 Lanferty, Lillian
1 Lanfield, Sidney
2 Lang (Cliff Lang and His Orchestra)
3 Lang, Eddie
1 Lang, Fred
1 Lang, Fritz
117 Lang, Harry
1 Lang, Jeannie
95 Lang, John
1 Lang, Judy
2 Lang, Ned
1 Lang, Phyllis
1 Lang, Ralph
2 Lang, Sally
4 Lang, Vicki
2 Lang, Walter
20 Lang, William
7 Lang-Worth Concert Orchestra
5 Lang-Worth Foursome, The
6 Lang-Worth Gauchos, The
7 Lang-Worth Gypsy Orchestra
1 Lang-Worth Gypsy Trio, The
1 Lang-Worth Hillbillies
4 Lang-Worth Military Band, The
5 Lang-Worth Mixed Quartette
2 Lang-Worth Mixed Quintette and Organ
4 Lang-Worth Singing Saxophones, The
4 Lang-Worth Specialty Orchestra
4 Lang-Worth Swing Orchestra, The
12 Langan, Glenn
1 Langden, Dorothy
1 Lange, Halvard M.
3 Langel, Robert
3 Langer, Hans
147 Langford, Frances
1 Langford, Robert
1 Langlois, Cy
41 Langner, Lawrence
3 Langton, Paul
1 Langtry, Hugh
1 Lanham, Ray
5 Lanin (Lester Lanin and His Orchestra)
1 Lanin, Sam
10 Lansbury, Angela
2 Lansing, Hal
1 Lansing, Johnny
69 Lansing, Mary
2 Lansing, Robert
9 Lanson, Snooky
2 Lansworth, Jean
2 Lansworth, Lew X.

28 Lanza, Mario
1 Lapchik, Joe
1 Lapham, Roger
2 LaPonti, Jacque
1 Larangeira, Crispin
9 Larch, John
9 Lardner, Ring
1 Largo, Key
1 Lark, John
1 Larkin (Ellis Larkin Trio, The)
3 Larkin, Ellis
29 Larkin, John
1 Larkin, Linda
1 LaRocca (Roxy LaRocca and His Rockettes)
2 LaRoche, Mary
1 LaRocque, Rod
1 Larogo, Mike
1 LaRouche, Lyndon
1 Larrabee, S. J. Louise
10 Larson, Bobby
1 Larson, Don
1 Larson, Douglas
2 Larson, Gerry
4 Larson, Hank
1 Larson, Howard
2 Larson, Jack
2 Larson, Jerri
1 Larson, Juliana
1 Larson, Libby
1 Larson, Priscilla
1 Larson, Ray
4 LaRue, Jack
1 LaRue, Ralph
1 Lasalva, Vince
1 LaShell and Hickey
1 Lashof, Carol
1 Lasker, Frank
4 Lasky, Jesse
1 Lass, Lou
5 Lassie
1 Lasso, Raphael V.
1 Last, Ruth
2 Laszo, Alexander
1 Latham, Cynthia
1 Latham, Elizabeth
3 Latham, Gary
4 Latham, Jack
10 Latham, Joe
1 Latham, Mrs. Wales
1 Lathrop, Barbara
1 Lathrop, Jack
34 Latimer, Ed
1 Latouch, Jean
4 Latouche, John
2 Latour, Charles
1 Latour, Nick
1 Lattimore, Owen
1 Latting, Bob
1 Laub, Morris
854 Lauck, Chester
5 Lauder, Harry
78 Laughton, Charles
1 Laughton, Gail
2 Laurent, Stephen
6 Laurel, Stan
2 Lauren, Jane
33 Laurie Jr., Joe

4 Laurie, Piper
1 Lausay, Eduardo
1 Lausen, John
1 Laushe, Frank
4 Lautenberg, Frank
3 Lava, William
1 Lavangetto, Cookie
1 Lavella, Tony
24 Lavere, Charles
4 LaVey, Gloria
1 Law, Gordon
1 Law, Vernon
3 Law, Warner
2 Lawes, Lewis E.
1 Lawford, Mary
10 Lawford, Peter
1 Lawler, Sherman
5 Lawrence (Elliot Lawrence and His Orchestra)
1 Lawrence Quartet, The
1 Lawrence, Arthur
1 Lawrence, Barbara
30 Lawrence, Bill
5 Lawrence, Carol
77 Lawrence, Charlotte
7 Lawrence, D. H.
1 Lawrence, Doug
4 Lawrence, Elizabeth
4 Lawrence, Elliot
19 Lawrence, Gertrude
7 Lawrence, Greg
3 Lawrence, Harry
2 Lawrence, Jane
1 Lawrence, Jay
42 Lawrence, Jerome
1 Lawrence, Jody
1 Lawrence, John
1 Lawrence, Lee
3 Lawrence, Marjorie
6 Lawrence, Mark
3 Lawrence, Martin
5 Lawrence, Morton
2 Lawrence, Paula
1 Lawrence, Phillip
44 Lawrence, Raymond
5 Lawrence, Robert
79 Lawrence, Steve
2 Lawrence, Ted
1 Lawrence, Vicki
1 Lawrence, W. A.
10 Lawrence, William
1 Lawrey, Ted
1 Laws, Hubert
1 Laws, Ronnie
4 Lawson, Yank
37 Lawton, Alma
2 Lawton, Kenneth
1 Layne, Bobby
1 Layne, Evelyn
1 Layton, Gerry
2 Layton, Jean
12 Lazar, Bill
1 Lazar, Jack
1 Lazarus, Irna
14 Lazer, Joan
6 Lazer, Peter
15 Lazito, James
1 Lazo, Hector
1 Le Fanu, Sheridan
4 Le Gallienne, Eva
1 Leach, Albert
1 Leach, Jim
1 Leach, Ken
1 Leach, Margaret
1 Leacock, Stephen
6 Leadbelly
88 Leader, Anton M.
1 Leader, George
1 Leaf, Ann
1 Leaf, Earl
2 Leahy, Frank
1 Leahy, Patrick
2 Leahy, William
1 Lear, David
1 Lear, Norman
1 Leary, Ford
1 Leatherneck Swingeroos, The
1 Leatherwood, Ray
10 Leaton, Anne
1 Leavitt, Mike
1 LeBaron, Eddie
1 LeBaron, William
2 Lebine, Clem
2 LeCroy Sisters, The
3 Lederberg, Joshua
1 Lederer, Charles
1 Lederer, Francis
1 Ledoux, Claudine
19 LeDoux, Leone
4 Lee, Anna
1 Lee, Barbara
1 Lee, Beauregard
3 Lee, Bert
2 Lee, Betty
1 Lee, Bill
3 Lee, Bob
3 Lee, Brenda
4 Lee, Burr
49 Lee, Canada
1 Lee, Carolyn
1 Lee, Charles
9 Lee, Chester M.
1 Lee, Clark
23 Lee, Earl
1 Lee, Gary
1 Lee, General
1 Lee, Georgia
3 Lee, Gypsy Rose
1 Lee, Hosh
8 Lee, Irvin
2 Lee, Irving
3 Lee, Irving J.
1 Lee, Isiah
2 Lee, Jack
1 Lee, James
1 Lee, Jenny
1 Lee, Jessica
40 Lee, Johnny
2 Lee, Karen
5 Lee, Katie
7 Lee, Lillian
2 Lee, Linda
1 Lee, Lois
2 Lee, Loretta
1 Lee, Lorraine
5 Lee, Madaline
1 Lee, Margo
18 Lee, Marjorie
2 Lee, Mary
1 Lee, Norma
156 Lee, Peggy
1 Lee, Penny
4 Lee, Pinky
2 Lee, R. E.
6 Lee, Ralph
41 Lee, Robert E.
3 Lee, Roberta
1 Lee, Stan
5 Lee, Sylvia
2 Lee, Terry
1 Lee, Thomas
1 Lee, Tommy
1 Lee, W. F.
1 Lee, Wayne
1 Leech, Bill
4 Leech, Nancy
6 Leeds, Andrea
1 Leeds, Howard
203 Leeds, Peter
4 Leeds, Phil
1 Leeds, Steve
1 Leeds, Thelma
2 Leeman, Cliff
1 Leemans, Tuffy
1 Leestma, Dave
1 Lefarge, Christopher
7 LeFevre, Ned
6 Leff, Henry
109 Lefferts, George
566 LeGrand, Richard
2 Lehar, Franz
9 Lehman, Herbert
1 Lehman, Irving
3 Lehman, Lotte
4 Lehr, Lew
4 Lehrer, Jim
5 Leiber, Fritz
1 Leiber, Leslie
1 Leiberman, Elias
17 Leibert, Richard
1 Leicester, William
1 Leigh Jr., Bernie
10 Leigh, Janet
5 Leigh, Vivien
1 Leighton, Charles
2 Leighton, Isabel
2 Leinsdorf, Erich
9 Leinster, Murray
9 Leisen, Mitchell
1 Leitel, Hazel
1 Leith, Marvin
1 LeMay, Curtis
1 Lemew, Fred
13 Lemke, Connie
3 Lemmon, Jack
2 Lemmon, Martin F.
2 Lemmon, Walter S.
2 Lemon, Bob
135 Lemond, Bob
5 Lenard, Grace
9 Lenay, Will
1 Lenihan, Winifred
11 Lennon Sisters, The
2 Lennon, John
1 Lennon, Roy
1 Leno, Charles
1 Lenoir, William
2 Lenox, Elizabeth
79 Lenrow, Bernard
2 Leo, Arnold G.
1 Leon, Bene
1 Leon, Danny
2 Leonard, Benny
5 Leonard, Bill
1 Leonard, Bob
8 Leonard, Gene
2 Leonard, Jack
2 Leonard, Jack E.
1 Leonard, James
12 Leonard, Jimmy
1 Leonard, Lee
3 Leonard, Leroy
1 Leonard, Mrs. James
11 Leonard, Queenie
4 Leonard, Richard
1 Leonard, Roy
84 Leonard, Sheldon
5 Leonard, Tony
1 Leonardi (Leo Leonardi and The Warner Brothers Orchestra)
3 Leonardi (Leon Leonardi and His Orchestra)
1 Leonardi, Leonid
3 Leone, Richard
5 Leonetti, Tommy
1 Leoni, Danny
4 Leonov, Alexei
5 Lepage, Al
1 Lerioux, Harriet
1 Lerner and Lowe
2 Lerner, Alan Jay
1 Lerner, Isiah
4 Lerner, Max
1 Leroux, Gaston
3 Leroy, Baby
1 LeRoy, Grace
1 LeRoy, Hal
1 Leroy, Harvey
1 LeRoy, Mervyn
2 Lesan, David
8 Lesberg, Jack
8 Lescoulie, Jack
1 Lesk, Lorraine
1 Lesley, Chuck
2 Leslie, Al
4 Leslie, Aleen
1 Leslie, Bob
8 Leslie, Joan
3 Leslie, Laura
280 Leslie, Phil
1 Lesser, Milton
1 Lessig, Joe
1 Lester, Bill
1 Lester, Buddy
2 Lester, Cedric
6 Lester, Jack
14 Lester, Jerry
8 Lester, Selig
62 Lesueur, Larry
1 Letelier, Claudio
5 Lettermen, The
124 Levant, Oscar
7 Levene, Sam
4 Levenson, Sam
2 Levenstein, Aaron
1 Lever, Les
1 Levere, Tony
1 Levey (Harold Levey and His Orchestra)
39 Levey, Harold
25 Levin (Sylvan Levin and His Orchestra)
2 Levin, Carl
1 Levin, Gene
1 Levin, Gilbert
1 Levin, Herman
23 Levin, Sylvan
1 Levine, Arthur
3 Levine, Henry
13 Levine (Henry Levine Octet)
10 Levine, Irving R.
1 Levine, Joel
2 Levine, Joseph
1 Levine, Mel
1 Levine, Mike
1 Levine, Mr.
1 Levinsky, King
1 Levinson, Ellis
1 Levinson, Joe
34 Levinson, Leonard L.
12 Levitow (Bernhard Levitow's Salon Orchestra)
1 Levitsky, Mischa
1 Levitt (Rod Levitt and His Orchestra)
69 Levitt, Gene
1 Levitties, Samuel W.
4 Levy, Ben
2 Levy, Ben W.
8 Levy, David
5 Levy, Estelle
1 Levy, Joann
9 Levy, Parke
5 Levy, Ralph
1 Lewald, James
3 Lewerth, Margaret
2 Lewin, Charles
1 Lewin, Edmond
1 Lewin, Phillip
1 Lewin, Walter
1 Lewis (Benny Lewis and His Orchestra)
1 Lewis (Fran Lewis and Her Guys)
1 Lewis (James Lewis Elkins and His Choir)
1 Lewis (Johnny Lewis and His Orchestra)
1 Lewis (Ramsey Lewis Trio)
2 Lewis (Ramsey Lewis Trio, The)
13 Lewis (Ted Lewis and His Orchestra)
4 Lewis (Texas Jim Lewis and His Lone Star Cowboys)
1 Lewis and Doty
40 Lewis Jr., Fulton
1 Lewis Jr., J. C.
32 Lewis, Abby
55 Lewis, Al
1 Lewis, Anthony
1 Lewis, Archie
1 Lewis, Arnold
2 Lewis, Arthur
1 Lewis, Brenda
2 Lewis, Catherine Handy
236 Lewis, Cathy
1 Lewis, Charles
1 Lewis, Chuck
2 Lewis, David
1 Lewis, Dean
5 Lewis, Diana
2 Lewis, Don

3 Lewis, Dorothea J.
10 Lewis, Dorothy
1 Lewis, Draper
1 Lewis, Edwin
552 Lewis, Elliott
196 Lewis, Forrest
2 Lewis, Frederick
1 Lewis, George
1 Lewis, Harrington
2 Lewis, Helen
1 Lewis, Herbert Clyde
1 Lewis, Herbie
10 Lewis, Ira
1 Lewis, J. Frederick
10 Lewis, Jack
1 Lewis, Jack Weir
46 Lewis, Jerry
34 Lewis, Jerry D.
1 Lewis, Jimmy
3 Lewis, Joe E.
1 Lewis, John
3 Lewis, John L.
1 Lewis, Judy
1 Lewis, Julius
1 Lewis, Leopold
6 Lewis, Lester
1 Lewis, Louise
1 Lewis, M. G.
1 Lewis, Margaret
1 Lewis, Marjorie
1 Lewis, Martin
1 Lewis, Maxine
5 Lewis, Meade Lux
1 Lewis, Mel
6 Lewis, Milton
1 Lewis, Mitchell
21 Lewis, Monica
6 Lewis, Mort
2 Lewis, Naomi
8 Lewis, Philip
1 Lewis, R. R.
3 Lewis, Ralph
7 Lewis, Ray
1 Lewis, Reginald
13 Lewis, Richard
7 Lewis, Robert
23 Lewis, Robert Q.
1 Lewis, Samuel
1 Lewis, Sidney
18 Lewis, Sinclair
11 Lewis, Ted
2 Lewis, Texas Jim
2 Lewis, Therese
1 Lewis, Tom
1 Lewis, Victor
57 Lewis, Warren
1 Lewis, William Mather
3 Ley, Willy
3 Leyden (Norman Leyden and His Orchestra)
1 Leyden, Bill
1 Leyssen, Father
1 Leyton (Bernie Leyton and His Orchestra)
1 Leyton, Bernie
1 Lezberg, Irwin
20 Liberace
2 Liberace (George Liberace and His Orchestra)
3 Liberace, George
1 Lidell, Barney
2 Lido, Bob
65 Lie, Trygve
13 Lieberfeld, Daniel
1 Lieberman, Joseph
4 Lieberson, Goddard
1 Liebert (Bill Leibert and His Orchestra)
3 Liebert (Billy Liebert and His Orchestra)
1 Liebowitz, Sam
1 Liebowitz, Samuel
1 Lieper, Henry Smith
5 Lierley, Charles
1 Lifshin, Morris
1 Lifson, Tol
2 Liggens (Joe Liggens and The Honeydrippers)
1 Liggett, Bob
2 Light (Ben Light Trio, The)
2 Light (Enoch Light and His Orchestra)
3 Light Crust Doughboys, The
1 Light, Benny
8 Light, David
1 Light, Judith
5 Light, Robert
1 Lightner, Fred
1 Lightner, Freddy
1 Lightsey, Kirk
1 Lilburn, James
13 Lillie, Beatrice
1 Lillie, Charles
3 Lillienthal, David
2 Lilly (Joseph Lilly and His Orchestra)
36 Lilly (Joseph Lilly Chorus, The)
3 Lilly, Joseph
3 Lilo
4 Limelighters, The
1 Limerick, Kay
1 Linard, Herbert
1 Lincoln, Dan
1 Lincoln, James F.
1 Lind, Don
2 Lind, Helen
2 Lind, Jenny
1 Lind, Sherwin
9 Lindbergh, Charles
1 Linde, Mary
2 Lindell, John
3 Lindeman, Mitch
1 Lindemann, Edward C.
3 Linden, Eric
1 Linden, Hal
2 Linden, Joyce
1 Linden, Lou
4 Linden, Nat S.
1 Linderman, Lindy
1 Lindfors, Viveca
1 Lindholm, Lou
2 Lindley, Ernest
1 Lindsay, Alice
15 Lindsay, Howard
2 Lindsay, John
5 Lindsay, Margaret
1 Lindsay, Vachel
8 Lindsey (Mort Lindsey and His Orchestra)
1 Lindsey, Jake
1 Lindsey, Ruth
30 Lindsley, Charles Frederick
25 Lindsley, Frederick
1 Lindstrom, Robert
1 Lindy, Betty
17 Liner, Sammy
1 Lingren, Anna
2 Link, Walter
33 Linkletter, Art
1 Linn, James Weaver
1 Linton, M. Albert
1 Lintzer, William
1 Linville, Joanne
3 Linwood, Lucille
1 Lipp, Frederick J.
1 Lipp, Noah
28 Lippert, Robert
1 Lippin, Max
1 Lippman, Walter
45 Lipscott, Alan
66 Lipton, Bill
5 Lipton, James
4 Lipton, Martha
2 Lisa, Anna
5 Liss, Joseph
2 Liss, Julian
112 Liss, Ronald
3 Liss, Ted
2 List, Margie
1 Listener, John
1 Liszt
2 Liszt, Eugene
1 Litow (Joseph Litow and His Orchestra)
1 Litowski, Hazel
1 Little (Big Tiny Little and His Orchestra)
1 Little (Little Jack Little and His Orchestra)
37 Little Jr., Herbert
1 Little Richard
1 Little, Ben
2 Little, Big Tiny
13 Little, Jack
9 Little, Little Jack
3 Little, Lou
2 Little, Rich
1 Littlefield, Lucien
1 Littlefield, Robert
1 Litvanoff, Maxim
1 Litz, A. Walton
2 Liu, B. A.
1 Livingston, Jay
1 Livingston, Robert
1 Livingstone (Jerry Livingstone and His Orchestra)
2 Livingstone, Bob
9 Livingstone, Charles D.
473 Livingstone, Mary
1 Livitsky, Bill
2 Lizak, Ruth
1 Lizer, William F.
1 Llewellyn, Carl
1 Llewellyn, Richard
1 Lloyd (Charlie Lloyd and His Quartet)
1 Lloyd, Alma
19 Lloyd, Doris
1 Lloyd, Frank
5 Lloyd, Harold
11 Lloyd, Jack
2 Lloyd, Mandred
9 Lloyd, Norman
9 Lloyd, Rita
10 Lloyd, Selwyn
11 Lloyd, Ted
1 Lochner, Louis
1 Locke, Katherine
1 Locke, Newton
3 Locke, Ralph
40 Lockhart, Gene
14 Lockhart, June
20 Lockhart, Kathleen
1 Lockman
2 Lockner, Louis P.
1 Lockser, Judy
1 Lockwood, Alexander
1 Lockwood, Allen
1 Lockwood, Margaret
12 Loder, John
4 Lodge, Henry Cabot
3 Lodge, John
58 Loeb, Marx B.
1 Loeb, Phillip
4 Loesser, Bud
3 Loesser, Frank
1 Lofton, Bob
1 Lofton, Cripple Clarence
1 Lofton, Mrs. Bob
1 Loftus, Cecilia
18 Logan, Ella
3 Logan, Janet
1 Logan, Joshua
1 Logan, Linda
1 Logerwell, Carmelita
1 Loggerman, John K.
11 Loghran, Dick
1 Login, Allan
4 Lohr, Lenox
1 Lolly Sisters, The
1 Lomas, Marie
5 Lomax, Alan
15 Lomax, Stan
15 Lombard, Carole
1 Lombardi, Vince
40 Lombardo (Guy Lombardo and His Orchestra)
28 Lombardo (Guy Lombardo and The Royal Canadians)
1 Lombardo Trio, The
7 Lombardo, Carmen
27 Lombardo, Guy
1 Lombardo, Leibert
2 Lombardo, Rosemarie
1 Lombardo, Victor
8 Lon, Alice
1 Loncock, Leon
1 London Symphony Orchestra, The
2 London, Bob
1 London, George
3 London, Jack
2 London, Jerry
4 London, Julie
1 Lone Star Quartet, The
1 Loneman, Amy
1 Long
15 Long (Johnny Long and His Orchestra)
1 Long Beach Band Of The Air Transport Command, The
2 Long, Avon
1 Long, Breckinridge
3 Long, Huey
2 Long, James
1 Long, Janis
2 Long, Johnny
1 Long, Lillian
1 Long, Lois
2 Long, Richard
2 Long, Ronald
1 Long, Sarah Hass
2 Long, Stuart
1 Long, Yvonne
7 Longfellow, Henry Wadsworth
1 Longines Choraliers, The
88 Longines Symphonette, The
1 Longley, Jim
1 Longmeyer, Adele
1 Lonigan, Lester
1 Lonsdale, Frederick
3 Lonzo and Oscar
1 Loo, Paul
1 Loo, Richard
2 Lopat, Ed
52 Lopez (Vincent Lopez and His Orchestra)
5 Lopez, Al
1 Lopez, Nico
1 Lopez, Trini
12 Lopez, Vincent
5 Lor, Denise
1 Lord Haw Haw
1 Lord Marley
3 Lord, Bobby
1 Lord, Eric
1 Lord, Jack
2 Lord, Mindred
1 Lord, Mrs. Oswald
2 Lord, Pauline
5 Lord, Phillip
37 Lord, Phillips H.
19 Lorde, Athena
1 Lorden, Herb
1 Lorell, Lucille
1 Lorentz, Pare
1 Lorenz, John
1 Loretta, Dee
1 Lorge, Irvine
3 Lorimer, Louise
1 Lorimer, M.
1 Loring, Ann
3 Loring, Eric
1 Loring, Gloria
5 Loring, Lynn
1 Lorraine
13 Lorraine, Kay
51 Lorre, Peter
120 Lorring, Joan
1 Lortz, Richard
1 Los Angeles County Band, The
1 Los Angeles Dance Band
1 Los Angeles Folklore Choir
19 Los Angeles Philharmonic Symphonic Orchestra, The
1 Los Angles Philharmonic, The
1 Loschke, Paul
11 Losey, Joseph
7 Lotis, Dennis

1 Lotsie, Norma
1 Lotwick, Al
1 Lou, Betty
1 Loughlin, David
1 Loughrane, Basil
1 Louis, Jean
21 Louis, Joe
1 Louis, Louise
6 Louise
13 Louise, Anita
3 Louise, Jean
1 Louisville Symphony, The
1 Loundes, Belac
5 Lousma, Jack
2 Louvin Brothers, The
2 Louvin, Charlie
1 Louvin, Ira
86 Love, Andrew C.
1 Love, Bob
1 Love, Dorothy
1 Love, Edmund G.
3 Love, Freddy Careless
1 Love, Helen
1 Love, Jeannine
3 Love, Montague
1 Lovecraft, H. P.
262 Lovejoy, Frank
32 Lovejoy, Joan
1 Lovelace, Linda
2 Lovell, Bernard
3 Lovell, James
1 Lovell, Leigh
3 Lovell, Marilyn
5 Lovett, Dorothy
1 Lovett, Walter
1 Lovring, John
1 Lovring, Mrs. John
2 Low, George M.
1 Lowe, Billy
3 Lowe, Don
8 Lowe, Edmund
15 Lowe, Jim
4 Lowe, Mark
5 Lowe, Mundell
1 Lowell (Gene Lowell and His Orchestra)
1 Lowell, Eugene
1 Lowens, Kurt
1 Lowenthal, Eugene
1 Lowenthal, Stuart
1 Lowery, Aden
1 Lowery, Bob
9 Lowery, Fred
2 Lowery, Patricia
1 Lowrie, Commander
2 Lowther, Betty
95 Lowther, George
1 Lowy, Otto
2 Loxo, Nels
26 Loy, Myrna
1 Luberschutz and Neminoff
24 Lubin (Harry Lubin and His Orchestra)
1 Lubin, Isadore
70 Lubin, Lou
1 Lubin, Peggy
3 Lubitsch, Ernst
29 Luboff (Norman Luboff Choir, The)
6 Luboff, Norman
1 Lucas (Clyde Lucas and His Orchestra)
1 Lucas, Donny
1 Lucas, Edward J.
13 Lucas, George
1 Lucas, Jerry
1 Lucas, John Meredyth
2 Lucas, Nick
3 Lucas, Rupert
3 Lucas, Tommy
2 Lucas, William
1 Luce, Clare Boothe
2 Luckman, Sid
1 Ludden, Allen
61 Luddy, Barbara
1 Ludeen, Ernest
1 Ludlow (Godfrey Ludlow and Male Trio)
39 Ludlow, Ben
3 Ludlow, Godfrey
1 Ludlow, Wanda
3 Ludlum, Kennedy
1 Ludoff, Paul
1 Ludwig, Emil
4 Luftig, Don
1 Lugar (Joseph Lugar and The WLW Orchestra)
3 Lugar, Richard
6 Lugosi, Bela
1 Luine, Charles L.
1 Lukas, Edwin J.
43 Lukas, Paul
3 Luke, Keye
12 Lulu Belle and Scotty
2 Lum, Henry
13 Lunceford (Jimmy Lunceford and His Orchestra)
1 Lunceford, Jimmy
11 Lund, Art
101 Lund, John
1 Lund, Lucille
2 Lund, Roy
1 Lund, Vin
2 Lundgren, Dan
10 Lundigan, William
1 Lundin, Bruce
2 Lundine, Stan
1 Lundquist, Charles
1 Lundy, Lonnie
52 Lung, Charlie
4 Lunney, Glynn
2 Lunsford, Beverly
15 Lunt, Alfred
48 Lupino, Ida
1 Lurch, John
1 Luscher, Marie Louise
1 Lusgarten, Edgar
1 Lush, Tillie
4 Lusinchi, Victor
3 Lutcher, Nellie
7 Luther, Frank
1 Luther, Herbert G.
6 Luther, Paul
1 Lutz, Harley L.
18 Lydon, Jimmy
1 Lyle, John E.
5 Lyman (Abe Lyman and His Californians)
34 Lyman (Abe Lyman and His Orchestra)
3 Lyman, Abe
5 Lymon (Frankie Lymon and The Teenagers)
1 Lynch, Bill
4 Lynch, Christopher
54 Lynch, Ken
82 Lynch, Peg
1 Lynch, Richard
1 Lynch, Theodora
1 Lynde, Paul
2 Lynn, Bambi
2 Lynn, Betty
1 Lynn, Billy
17 Lynn, Diana
1 Lynn, Edward
4 Lynn, Helen
2 Lynn, Imogene
10 Lynn, Jeffrey
4 Lynn, Judy
2 Lynn, Lennie
1 Lynn, Lorna
1 Lynn, Mary
17 Lynn, Rita
13 Lynn, Roberta
4 Lynn, Vera
1 Lynne, Gloria
8 Lynne, Phyllis
4 Lynne, Virginia Safford
5 Lyon, Ben
114 Lyon, Charles
1 Lyon, Earl
1 Lyon, Helen
1 Lyon, Jack
1 Lyon, Jane
1 Lyon, Jean
14 Lyon, Peter
6 Lyon, Priscilla
1 Lyon, Therese
3 Lyoness, Charles
1 Lyons (Al Lyons and His Orchestra)
1 Lyons T. Carr
1 Lyons, A.
2 Lyons, Bobby
1 Lyons, Cliff
1 Lyons, George
1 Lyons, James J.
1 Lyons, Ken
1 Lyons, Leonard
2 Lyons, Molly
1 Lyons, Mrs. Leonard
7 Lyons, Roger
1 Lyons, Ruth
2 Lyric Singers, The
5 Lytell (Jimmy Lytell and His Delta Eight)
11 Lytell (Jimmy Lytell and His Orchestra)
6 Lytell, Bert
208 Lyttle Sisters, The
34 Lytton, Herb

WBT
Jefferson Standard Broadcasting Company
AM FM TV
AIR DATE AND TIME:
ORIG. DATE AND TIME:
TITLE
M
PART
78
"PIONEER STATION OF THE SOUTH"
CHARLOTTE, N. C.

1 Ma, John T.
1 Maas, Warren
1 Mabel, Terrence
1 MacAdoo, Eleanor
8 MacAllaster, Ian
2 MacArthur, Bill
6 MacArthur, Charles
31 MacArthur, Douglas
2 MacArthur, Lawrence
1 MacAuley, Ed
189 MacCormack, Franklyn
1 MacCracken, Henry Noble
2 MacDonald, Anthony
1 MacDonald, Arch
3 MacDonald, Dan
1 MacDonald, Don
4 MacDonald, Donald
5 MacDonald, Ed
26 MacDonald, Edmond
1 MacDonald, Edward
1 MacDonald, Fred
1 MacDonald, George
2 MacDonald, George M.
1 MacDonald, Gil
36 MacDonald, Jeanette
1 MacDonald, Jim
3 MacDonald, Margaret
1 MacDonald, Mary
1 MacDonald, Ray
543 Macdonnell, Norman
1 MacDoran, Pete
3 MacDougal, Gil
4 MacDougall, Ranald
1 MacDowell, Charles
1 Macelli, Joe
2 Macey, Jerry
1 MacFarland Twins Orchestra, The
5 MacFarlane, Ian Ross
1 MacFerrin, Robert
1 MacGordon, Elsie
577 MacGregor, C. P.
56 MacGregor, Evelyn
74 MacGregor, Jock
1 MacGregor, Kathy
22 MacGregor, Kenneth
12 MacHarrie, Lindsay
2 Machen, Eddie
1 Machito
1 Machold, Earle J.
1 Macias, Raton
2 Mack (Cactus Mack and His Saddle Tramps)
1 Mack (Cecil Mack Mixed Choir, The)
2 Mack, Connie
26 Mack, Dick
1 Mack, Ed
8 Mack, Floyd
102 Mack, Gilbert
16 Mack, Helen
15 Mack, Nila
1 Mack, Ted
1 Mack, Tommy
1 Mack, Warner
2 Mack, Willard
84 MacKaye, Fred
75 MacKenzie, Gisele
3 MacKenzie, Robert
2 MacKenzie, Will
2 MacLain, Roland
1 MacLaine, Shirley
4 MacLane, Barton
23 MacLaughlin, Don
1 MacLean, Douglas
1 MacLean, Jack
1 MacLean, Jodie
3 MacLean, Katherine
28 MacLeish, Archibald
3 MacLeish, Rod
6 MacMahon, Aline
1 MacMannus, Mary Ann
1 MacMillan, Harold
1 MacMitchell, Leslie
75 MacMurray, Fred
3 MacNeil, Robert
2 Macon, Gilda
1 Macon, Uncle Dave
13 MacPhail, Douglas
5 MacQuarrie, Haven
1 MacQuarrie, Marie

8 MacRae, Carmen
5 MacRae, Ellen
130 MacRae, Gordon
1 MacRae, Meredith
2 MacRae, Sheila
2 MacTaggart, Malcolm
6 MacTavish, Meggin
1 MacWalters, Virginia
1 Macy, Bill
1 Macy, Jerry
6 Madden, Donald
1 Madden, J. Warren
1 Madder, Jean
2 Maddox, Daphne
2 Maddox, Gaynor
3 Maddox, Rose
1 Maderos, Julio
9 Madigan, Betty
2 Madison, Buddy
1 Madison, E. A.
89 Madison, Guy
1 Madison, Noah
1 Madison, Noel
1 Madison, Ruth
6 Madison Singers
2 Madrigal Singers Of New York
17 Madriguera (Enric Madriguera and His Orchestra)
2 Madriguera, Enric
2 Mael, Merrill
4 Magistrelli, Mark
1 Maglie, Sal
1 Magnante (Charles Magnante Quintet, The)
4 Magnante Charles Magnante Trio, The)
5 Magnante, Charles
5 Magner, Martin
1 Magruder, Peyton
1 Mahal, Taj
1 Mahar, Bernie
5 Maharis, George
234 Maher, Wally
1 Mahl, David
2 Mahoney
2 Mahr, Beverly
14 Mahr, Bill
1 Mailey, Bob
6 Main, Marjorie
1 Mains, Dick
4 Maio, Gia
4 Maitland, Arthur
2 Maitland, Jules
6 Maitland, Patrick
12 Majestic Orchestra, The
1 Major Minor and Marion
1 Major, John
1 Major, Olive
1 Makeba, Miriam
1 Mala, Jane
2 Malbin, Elaine
1 Malcolm, Artie
1 Malconian, Jasmin
4 Malden, Karl
1 Malek, Charles
6 Malik, Jacob
1 Malkin, Mike
1 Mall, Harry E.
1 Mallard, Oscar Ian
1 Mallet, Jane
1 Malley, William
9 Mallie, Ted
3 Mallory, Boots
1 Mallow, Gina
2 Mallow, John
1 Malloy, Gardner
1 Malloy, Mary
20 Malneck (Matty Malneck and His Orchestra)
3 Malneck, Matty
2 Malone, Ben
3 Malone, Dorothy
12 Malone, Dumont
47 Malone, Joel
2 Malone, Paul B.
15 Malone, Pick
9 Malone, Ted
1 Maloney, Jim
48 Maloney, Martin
2 Maloney, Russell
1 Maloney, Senator
4 Maltby (Richard Maltby and His Orchestra)
2 Maltby, Richard
3 Malten, William
1 Maltz, Albert
10 Malvin, Artie
3 Mamet, David
1 Mamiaux, Al
17 Mamorsky, Morris
1 Mance (Junior Mance Trio, The)
1 Manchester, William
1 Mancini (Thomas Mancini and His Ensemble)
1 Mancini, Henry
1 Manda, Frederick
1 Mandela, Nelson
3 Mandeville, Betty
1 Manes, Artie
2 Maney, Richard
1 Mangano, Mickey
1 Manger, Ted
8 Manhattan Concert Band
1 Manhattan Madcaps
2 Manhattan Nighthawks, The
3 Manheim, Hett
1 Manhoff, Arnold
4 Manhoff, Bill
1 Manieri, Michael
2 Manke, John
2 Mankiewicz, Joseph
6 Manlove, Dudley
1 Mann (Herbie Mann and His Octet)
1 Mann (Herbie Mann Jazz Ensemble, The)
1 Mann (Herbie Mann Sextette, The)
1 Mann (Herbie Mann Trio, The)
1 Mann, Abby
1 Mann, Adrian
2 Mann, Alfred E.
16 Mann, Arthur
1 Mann, Erica
21 Mann, Gloria
2 Mann, Herbie
3 Mann, Jack
3 Mann, Jerry
1 Mann, Marion
1 Mann, Michael
17 Mann, Paul
15 Mann, Peggy
3 Mann, Thomas
1 Manne, Freddie
8 Manne, Shelley
1 Manners, Joyce
9 Manners, Lucille
3 Manners, Zeke
1 Manning, Bishop
2 Manning, Bob
1 Manning, Dick
3 Manning, Irene
16 Manning, Jack
1 Manning, Joan
30 Manning, Knox
1 Manning, Marie
8 Manning, Paul
1 Manning, Paul D. V.
1 Manning, Tom
1 Manoff, Richard
2 Manone (Wingy Manone and His Orchestra)
6 Manone, Wingy
1 Manor House Foursome, The
2 Manor House Quintet, The
1 Mansar, Nicholas
1 Mansefield, Joseph
1 Mansfield, Eric
2 Mansfield, J. F.
2 Mansfield, Jayne
3 Mansfield, Marion
4 Mansfield, Mike
1 Mansfield, Ronnie
1 Manski, Inge
1 Mansoer, Mohammed
1 Manson (Matty Manson and His Orchestra)
9 Manson, Allen
12 Manson, Charlotte
1 Manson, Eddie
2 Manson, Ellen
6 Mantel, Burns
6 Mantle, Mickey
3 Manton, Maria
1 Manton, Raymond
3 Mantovani and His Orchestra
1 Manululu, Rass
2 Manville, Butler
2 Maples, Richard
1 Mara, Adele
1 Marais and Miranda, Joseph
2 Marais, Joseph
4 Maran, Stephen
2 Marand, Pat
1 Mararosa (Dodo Mararosa and His All-Stars)
2 Marble, Alice
21 Marble, Harry
1 Marcantonio, Congressman
10 Marcell, Lou
1 Marcelli (Rico Marcelli and His Orchestra)
2 Marcellino (Muzzy Marcellino and His Orchestra)
4 Marcellino, Muzzy
69 March, Fredric
85 March, Hal
1 March, Howard
5 March, Lori
1 March, Maxine
1 March, William
1 Marchand, Nancy
1 Marciano, Lena
4 Marciano, Rocky
1 Marconi, Guglielmo
2 Marcos, Ferdinand
1 Marcos, Imelda
1 Marcus, Gerald
33 Marcus, Larry
1 Marcus, Mark
2 Marcus, Mary
1 Marcy, Helen
4 Marden, Adrienne
1 Margan, Bruce
28 Margetts, Monty
16 Margo
2 Margotson, Arthur
1 Margulies, Fred
1 Margulies, Stanley
3 Margulis, Lynn
2 Marian
2 Marianne
1 Marie
10 Marie, Rose
7 Marin, Eda Reis
32 Marine (U. S. Marine Band, The)
1 Mariners Quartet, The
25 Mariners, The
1 Marion, Charles R.
49 Marion, Ira
1 Marion, Joseph
3 Marion, Marty
2 Marion, Paul
2 Maris, Roger
4 Mark, Hans
1 Mark, Herman
1 Markell, Hazel
1 Markels (Mike Markels and His Orchestra)
1 Markey, Enid
209 Markham, Emerson
2 Markham, Steve
40 Markim, Al
125 Markle, Fletcher
1 Markle, Robert
11 Markle, Steven
1 Markle, Tiny
1 Marks, Garnett
1 Marks, Gerald
44 Marks, Hilliard
3 Marks, Larry
17 Marks, Sherman
1 Marley, John
1 Marlowe (Charles Marlowe Octet, The)
1 Marlowe, Charles
1 Marlowe, Faye
3 Marlowe, Hugh
1 Marlowe, Jan
1 Marlowe, Jane
1 Marlowe, Jennifer
1 Marlowe, June
1 Marlowe, Kathy
1 Marlowe, Lucy
2 Marlowe, Marion
3 Marlowe, Mary
1 Marlowe, Nancy
1 Marlowe, Nora
2 Marlowe, Sylvia
1 Marlowe, Van
1 Marmarosa (Dodo Marmarosa Trio, The)
1 Marmarosa, Dodo
1 Marmola Baritone, The
5 Marquand, John P.
1 Marquand, Rube
5 Marquis, Arnold
8 Marquist, Mal
171 Marr, Edward
2 Marr, James
1 Marr, Randy
1 Marrine, Joe
1 Marriot, John
1 Marrow, Esther
7 Marrow, Macklin
1 Marryatt, Frederick
2 Marsach, Maurice
1 Marsala (Joe Marsala Quartet)
7 Marsala, Joe
1 Marschak, Jacob
1 Marsden, John
2 Marsh, Anthony
6 Marsh, Audrey
1 Marsh, Bea
1 Marsh, Benjamin C.
1 Marsh, Carol
1 Marsh, Daniel L.
1 Marsh, Joan
16 Marsh, Myra
6 Marsh, Scotty
2 Marsh, Trudy
2 Marsh, Warren
1 Marshall
2 Marshall (Jack Marshall and His Orchestra)
6 Marshall, Alan
39 Marshall, Armina
33 Marshall, Brenda
2 Marshall, Catherine
2 Marshall, Clarence
1 Marshall, Connie
2 Marshall, Dave
3 Marshall, Dolores
1 Marshall, Don
806 Marshall, E. G.
15 Marshall, George
127 Marshall, Herbert
2 Marshall, Howard
2 Marshall, Ian
1 Marshall, James
16 Marshall, Jerry
1 Marshall, Lois
1 Marshall, Mary
1 Marshall, Peggy
5 Marshall, Peter
3 Marshall, Robert
8 Marshall, Sanford
8 Marshall, Sidney
1 Marshall, T. H.
2 Marshall, Theresa
1 Marshall, Tully
3 Marshall, William
1 Marshaloff, Boris
1 Marson, Albert
32 Marson, Truda
1 Martel, Jan
9 Martell (Paul Martell and His Orchestra)
3 Martell, Bill
4 Martell, Curt
1 Martell, Doug

17 Martell, Fred
6 Martell, June
2 Martell, Louise
7 Martelli, Tony
12 Marterie (Ralph Marterie and His Orchestra)
2 Marterie, Ralph
1 Martin (Dude Martin and His Orchestra)
92 Martin (Freddy Martin and His Orchestra)
1 Martin (Hugh Martin Singers, The)
1 Martin (Nick Martin and His Orchestra)
1 Martin (Paul Martin's Velvetones)
1 Martin (Tommy Martin and His Orchestra)
1 Martin Jr., George
3 Martin Jr., James S.
46 Martin Men, The
1 Martin, Ben
1 Martin, Benny
1 Martin, Betty
26 Martin, Bill
1 Martin, Billy
1 Martin, Blackie
9 Martin, Bob
4 Martin, Bruce
4 Martin, Charles
49 Martin, Dean
1 Martin, Dick
2 Martin, Dude
1 Martin, Edward
1 Martin, Edwin
1 Martin, Ernest
1 Martin, Eugene
53 Martin, Frank
15 Martin, Freddy
1 Martin, Gene
3 Martin, George
2 Martin, Gilbert
1 Martin, Gunnar
3 Martin, Harry
4 Martin, Helen
5 Martin, Hugh
443 Martin, Ian
1 Martin, Isabel
1 Martin, Jack
1 Martin, Jan
2 Martin, Janis
1 Martin, Jerry
3 Martin, Joe
1 Martin, Johnny
3 Martin, Joseph
3 Martin, Judy
1 Martin, Kenneth
6 Martin, Kenny
1 Martin, Kingsley
1 Martin, Luray
1 Martin, Lynn
2 Martin, Marion
51 Martin, Mary
2 Martin, Moira
2 Martin, Murphy
1 Martin, Nan
6 Martin, Nancy
49 Martin, Nora
1 Martin, Odell
2 Martin, Pat
2 Martin, Peter
1 Martin, Richard
1 Martin, Robert Dale
1 Martin, Robert P.
21 Martin, Ross
1 Martin, Ruth
2 Martin, Stanley
1 Martin, Tommy
70 Martin, Tony
1 Martin, Virginia
8 Martin, Vivian
2 Martinelli, Giovanni
1 Martinet, Charles
4 Martinez, Chucho
1 Martinez, Pete
2 Martinez, Raoul
5 Martinez, Willie
1 Martingales, The
2 Martini, Nino
4 Martino, Al
9 Martins, The
1 Martyr, Westin
1 Marvin, Ed
4 Marvin, Edgar
1 Marvin, John
1 Marvin, Ken
2 Marvin, Lee
128 Marvin, Tony
1 Marvintile, Helen
1 Marx (Chico Marx and His Orchestra)
9 Marx Brothers, The
6 Marx, Chico
315 Marx, Groucho
5 Marx, Harpo
4 Marx, Melinda
1 Marx, Mrs. Groucho
1 Mary-Jean and Betty
1 Maryvale, Jack
5 Masaryk, Jan
1 Masefield, John
1 Mashek, John
1 Mashel, John
1 Mashulsi, J. P.
1 Mason, Allan
4 Mason, Bill
1 Mason, Ed
3 Mason, Esther
1 Mason, Harry
5 Mason, Iris
14 Mason, James
2 Mason, Jana
1 Mason, Jimmy
2 Mason, Linda
1 Mason, Marion
2 Mason, Mary
1 Mason, Nancy
5 Mason, Pamela
1 Mason, Paula
1 Mason, Reginald
13 Mason, Sidney
20 Mason, Sully
1 Mason, Van Wyck
3 Mason, Walter
9 Mason, William
2 Massen, Osa
3 Masserman, Jules
3 Massey (Louise Massey and The Westerners)
3 Massey, Alan
59 Massey, Curt
9 Massey, Ilona
2 Massey, Louise
64 Massey, Raymond
1 Massey, Vera
1 Master Gardeners, The
2 Master Radio Canaries, The
14 Masters (Frankie Masters and His Orchestra)
2 Masters, Frankie
11 Masters, Monte
12 Masters, Natalie
1 Masterson, Carol
10 Masterson, Paul
1 Masterson, William E.
1 Mastisse, Catherine
2 Mastren (Carmen Mastren and His Orchestra)
4 Mastren, Carmen
1 Masur, Richard
12 Masursky, Harold
1 Matelin, Arthur
1 Mathenson, Don Paul
1 Mather, Aubrey
127 Mather, Jack
1 Mather, Jim
6 Mather, John
1 Matheson, Murray
5 Matheson, Richard
1 Matheson, Thora
1 Mathewson, Christie
1 Mathias, Anna
2 Mathias, Ernie
5 Mathis, George
2 Mathis, Joe
12 Mathis, Johnny
2 Mathis, Rose Lee
5 Mathison, Mervin
2 Matlock (Matty Matlock and His Orchestra)
19 Matlock, Matty
1 Matranga, Gene
1 Matson, Dennis
1 Matson, Ollie
2 Matsui, Robert
1 Matthau, Walter
2 Matthew, Edward
1 Matthews (Dave Matthews and His Orchestra)
4 Matthews (Sal Matthews and His Orchestra)
1 Matthews, Ann Elstner
2 Matthews, Bob
11 Matthews, Carmen
7 Matthews, Charles
1 Matthews, Chris
2 Matthews, Edward
5 Matthews, George
97 Matthews, Grace
2 Matthews, Herbert
12 Matthews, James
113 Matthews, Junius
4 Matthews, Leah
2 Matthews, Lester
1 Matthews, Tom
1 Matthey, Nicholas
4 Mattingly, Ken
1 Mattison, Ruth
1 Matty, Lou
22 Mature, Victor
1 Mauch, Gene
1 Maude, Beatrice
2 Maude, Marjorie
7 Mauer, Bob
9 Maugham, Somerset
1 Mauldin, Bill
5 Maupin (Rex Maupin and His Orchestra)
1 Maupin, Rex
1 Maurey, Nicole
1 Maurulis, Nick
1 Mawk, Bob
94 Max, Edwin
1 Max, Hans
3 Maxey, Virginia
1 Maxie, Paul
2 Maxim, Joey
3 Maxine
1 Maxon, Mr.
7 Maxted (Billy Maxted and His Manhattan Jazz Band)
15 Maxted (Billy Maxted and His Orchestra)
4 Maxted (Billy Maxted Band, The)
3 Maxted, Billy
3 Maxwell, Bobby
3 Maxwell, Charles
8 Maxwell, Elsa
5 Maxwell, Frank
1 Maxwell, Jimmy
63 Maxwell, Marilyn
6 Maxwell, Marvel
3 Maxwell, Officer
1 Maxwell, Phillip
7 Maxwell, Richard
44 Maxwell, Robert
13 Maxwell, Roberta
1 Maxwell, Sandy
2 Maxwell, Ted
1 Maxworthy, Tony
36 May (Billy May and His Orchestra)
1 May, Benjamin
15 May, Billy
1 May, Congressman
9 May, Elaine
1 May, Ellery
1 May, Herbert
2 Maybelle, Big
1 Maybelle, Mother
1 Maye, Marilyn
19 Mayehoff, Eddie
3 Mayer, Fred
1 Mayer, John
122 Mayer, Ken
8 Mayer, Louis B.
1 Mayer, Walter
1 Mayes, Monica
3 Mayfair, Mitzi
1 Mayfield, Curtis
1 Mayhew, Jack
1 Mayland, Patrick Murphy
37 Maynard, Ken
1 Mayne, Charles
3 Maynor, Dorothy
1 Mayo, Archie
1 Mayo, Margaret
1 Mayo, Mary
17 Mayo, Virginia
1 Mayo, Waldo
4 Mays, Willie
3 Maytho, Fred
2 Mazaroski, Bill
1 Mazda, Mary
2 Mazurki, Mike
14 McAfee, Johnny
3 McAllister, Bud
1 McAnnally, Robert
1 McArdle, Dorothy
1 McArthur, William
2 McAuliffe, Christa
2 McAvity, Thomas A.
12 McBirney, James H.
6 McBride, Jack
1 McBride, Jean
5 McBride, Mary Margaret
1 McBridge, Jack
2 McCabe, Leo
1 McCabe, Peter
4 McCafferty, Joe
1 McCaffrey, John
1 McCain, John
1 McCall Sisters, The
1 McCall, Andre
2 McCall, Daryl
1 McCall, Frank
22 McCall, Joan
1 McCall, Peggy
1 McCall, Robert
1 McCalla, Irish
74 McCallion, James
8 McCallister, Lon
1 McCallum, John
1 McCallum, Mary
1 McCally, Jack
103 McCambridge, Mercedes
1 McCance, Larry
4 McCandless, Bruce
2 McCann, Larry
3 McCann, Patricia
15 McCann, Robert C. C.
1 McCannon, Bess
1 McCardigan, Joyce
4 McCarey, Leo
1 McCarry, Larry
3 McCarthy, Charles F.
12 McCarthy, Clem
1 McCarthy, Dorothy
2 McCarthy, Eugene
18 McCarthy, Frank
1 McCarthy, Jack
1 McCarthy, James
1 McCarthy, Jay P.
14 McCarthy, Joseph
23 McCarthy, Kevin
1 McCarthy, Linwood
1 McCarthy, Mary
1 McCarthy, Tom
1 McCartney, Forrest
1 McCarty, Mary
1 McChesney, Brunson
2 McClellan, John
1 McClelland, Gene
1 McClelland, Jack
1 McCliment, Jack F.
4 McClintock, William J.
2 McClory, Sean
1 McCloskey, Robert
1 McCloud, Artie
1 McCloud, Mrs. Robert
1 McCloud, Robert
3 McClure, James
1 McClurg, Edie
1 McCluskey, George

25 McCluskey, Joyce
1 McClusky, Blair
2 McClusky, Howard
1 McCollum, Bill
1 McConal, John Bunky
1 McConnell, Dorothy
30 McConnell, Ed
20 McConnell, Lulu
31 McConnell, Mary
1 McConnell, Mitch
3 McConnor, Vincent
8 McCoo, Arthur
1 McCool
1 McCord, Bill
1 McCormack, Joe
8 McCormack, John
1 McCormack, Patrick
1 McCormick
1 McCormick, Ann O'Hare
1 McCormick, Joe
2 McCormick, John
30 McCormick, Myron
1 McCormick, Peter
52 McCormick, Robert
5 McCormick, Stephen
1 McCorrigan, Rosie
2 McCosker, Al
2 McCoy (Clyde McCoy and His Orchestra)
7 McCoy (Herman McCoy Singers, The)
1 McCoy, Bud
1 McCoy, Clyde
1 McCoy, Gene
2 McCoy, Herman
27 McCoy, Jack
1 McCoy, Jo Ann
3 McCoy, Sid
1 McCracken, Henry
5 McCracken, Richard
1 McCrary, Karen
9 McCrary, Tex
1 McCray, Bill
85 McCrea, Joel
5 McCrea, Margaret
1 McCroy, Helen
1 McCullar, Ron
1 McCullough, Clay
497 McCullough, Dan
1 McCullough, Jim
4 McCullough, Mickey
1 McCullough, Paul
8 McCullough, Ruth
1 McCullum, Warren
1 McCune (Bill McCune and His Orchestra)
1 McCusick, Vincent L.
1 McDaney (Jack McDaney and His Orchestra)
15 McDaniel, Hattie
1 McDaniels, Jimmy
1 McDaniels, Sam
2 McDermott, Michael J.
1 McDivott, Leland
1 McDonald, David J.
1 McDonald, Ed
1 McDonald, Elaine
3 McDonald, Grace
1 McDonald, James G.
3 McDonald, Jimmy
7 McDonald, Marie
1 McDonald, Tommy
16 McDonnell, Craig
1 McDonnell, Kyle
1 McDonough, Dick
1 McDonough, John
8 McDonough, Richard
2 McDonough, Richard P.
1 McDonough, Vince
1 McDougall, Douglas
1 McDowall, Don
18 McDowall, Roddy
7 McDowell, Virginia
9 McEachern (Murray McEachern and His Orchestra)
3 McEachern (Murray McEachern and The AFRS Swing Band)
5 McEachern, Murray
2 McElhone, Eloise
2 McElroy, Chief
1 McElroy, Jack
1 McElroy, Leo
1 McElroy, Maude
3 McElroy, Michael
2 McElroy, Robert
1 McFadden, Bernarr
1 McFadden, Harry
1 McFarland (Gary McFarland and His Jazz Orchestra)
1 McFarland Twins and Their Orchestra, The
1 McFarland, Earl
1 McGaha, Charles P.
1 McGarity, Joe
7 McGarity, Lou
1 McGarrity, Everett
1 McGarry, Mack
1 McGear, Pat
2 McGee (Howard McGee Sextet, The)
1 McGee (Howard McGee Sextette)
1 McGee Jr., John Gillespie
1 McGee, Dorothy H.
1 McGee, Foghorn
13 McGee, Frank
1 McGee, John
150 McGeehan, Pat
1 McGeorge, James
2 McGhee, Brownie
1 McGhee, Granville
1 McGifford, John
53 McGill, Earle
1 McGill, Jerry
1 McGill, Maury
2 McGinn, Jim
1 McGinn, John
13 McGinnis (Eddie McGinnis and His Orchestra)
1 McGinnis, Pat
1 McGivern, Johnny
2 McGloughlin, Dan
2 McGlynn, Frank
1 McGlynn, Stoney
1 McGoldrick, Donald
1 McGonnigal, Bob
1 McGory, Mary
8 McGovern, George
53 McGovern, John
1 McGovern, Johnny
7 McGovern, Mary
1 McGovern, William
1 McGowan, Bill
1 McGowan, Tom G.
1 McGraff, Byron
1 McGrath, Earl
1 McGrath, Frank
1 McGrath, John
25 McGrath, Paul
20 McGraw, Charles
1 McGraw, Mrs. John
9 McGraw, Walter
1 McGregor, Chummy
1 McGregor, Marjorie
1 McGrew, Ted
1 McGuffey, Drake
1 McGuire (Mac McGuire and His Harmony Rangers)
1 McGuire (Mac McGuire and His Tennessee Mountaineers)
6 McGuire Sisters, The
4 McGuire, Bobby
36 McGuire, Dorothy
6 McGuire, Harp
1 McGuire, Marcy
1 McGurk, Charmine
1 McHenry
1 McHugh, Edward
10 McHugh, Frank
7 McHugh, Jimmy
163 McIntire, John
1 McIntosh, J. T.
4 McIntosh, Ray
1 McIntosh, Stuart
6 McIntyre (Hal McIntyre and His Orchestra)
1 McIntyre, Frank
1 McIntyre, Hal
2 McIntyre, Leila Hyams
1 McIntyre, O.
1 McIntyre, Russ
2 McIver (Alan McIver and His Orchestra)
2 McIver, John
1 McKay, John
1 McKay, Margaret
1 McKay, Scott
1 McKaye, Carolyn
1 McKaye, David
1 McKaye, Milton
1 McKean, Jeannie
5 McKeckney, James
5 McKee, Bob
12 McKee, Elmore
1 McKee, Frederick C.
32 McKee, Tom
1 McKell, Peggy O'Kelly
1 McKenna, Dave
4 McKenna, Jean
6 McKenna, Kate
1 McKenty, Jack
8 McKenzie, Fay
1 McKenzie, Joyce
238 McKenzie, Murdo
10 McKenzie, Red
1 McKeon, Richard
1 McKimmon, Jennie
1 McKinley (Barry McKinley and His Orchestra)
22 McKinley (Ray McKinley and His Orchestra)
2 McKinley (Ray McKinley and The Glenn Miller Orchestra)
1 McKinley (Ray McKinley Quintet, The)
6 McKinley, Barry
1 McKinley, Chuck
1 McKinley, Larry
134 McKinley, Ray
2 McKinney, Ed
1 McKinney, Ruth
1 McKinney, Walton
16 McKinnon, Dal
1 McKinstry, Ray
18 McKnight, Dick
2 McKnight, John
7 McKnight, Tom
1 McKuen, Catherine
1 McKuen, Leo
1 McKuen, Rod
1 McKuen, Vance
7 McLaglen, Victor
6 McLaren, Ian
1 McLarty, Thomas Mack
1 McLaughlin, Pete
1 McLaughly, Oscar
1 McLean, Lowell
3 McLeay, Jeanette
1 McLendon, Gordon
1 McLeod, Bentley
4 McLeod, Keith
24 McLeod, Mercer
1 McLeod, Norman
1 McLeod, Peter
1 McLoughlin, Bob
1 McLoughlin, Jean
1 McMahon, Brien
1 McMahon, David
5 McMahon, Ed
1 McMahon, Eileen
2 McMahon, Smilin' Frank
1 McMann, Bryan
1 McMann, Patsy
1 McManus, George
1 McManus, Jeannie
1 McManus, Ken
11 McManus, Marian
2 McMartin, Lorraine
2 McMechen, June
19 McMichaels, Flo
1 McMillan, Alex
1 McMillan, Donald
74 McMillan, Gloria
2 McMillan, Wheeler
5 McMorrow, William
1 McMullan, Nell
2 McMurtry, Tom
1 McNair
1 McNair, Barbara
1 McNair, Harley F.
3 McNally, Stephen
2 McNamara, Nora
2 McNamara, Robert
49 McNamee, Graham
2 McNary, Charles
1 McNatt, Deacon
35 McNaughton, Harry
625 McNear, Howard
1 McNeely, Jim
14 McNeill, Don
1 McNider, Hanford
2 McNierney, General
1 McNinch, Frank R.
1 McNish, A. G.
3 McNulty, Dorothy
6 McNutt, Paul
2 McPartland, Marian
1 McPeake Family, The
1 McPhail, Jimmy
2 McPhail, Larry
2 McPhatter, Clyde
1 McPherson (Charles McPherson Quartet, The)
1 McPherson, Stuart
2 McPugh, Marjorie
2 McQuade, John
1 McQueen, Alexander
32 McQueen, Butterfly
3 McQueen, Noel
2 McQuinn, Harry
1 McRay, Norman
1 McReynolds, Bob
3 McShann (Jay McShann and His Orchestra)
1 McShann (Jay McShann Trio, The)
1 McShann, Jay
1 McSherry, William
3 McSkiving, Mary
1 McTaggart, Bud
1 McTell, Penny
1 McTighe, Harry
7 McVane, John
3 McVea (Jack McVea and His All-Stars)
2 McVea, Jack
28 McVeagh, Eve
1 McVey, Father
1 McVey, Pat
30 McVey, Paul
98 McVey, Tyler
1 McWethy, John
1 McWilliams, Jim
1 Meacham, Monty
3 Mead, Margaret
1 Mead, Sidney
1 Meade, Julia
4 Meade, Martha
6 Meader, Phil
49 Meadow, Herb
1 Meadow, Leon
1 Meadowcroft, Enid Lamont
38 Meadows, Audrey
3 Meadows, Jayne
1 Meakin (Jack Meakin and His Orchestra)
605 Meakin, Jack
3 Meany, George
1 Meara, Ann
1 Meara, Lol Chan
1 Meara, Martha
81 Mears, Martha
1 Medberry, John P.
5 Medford, Harold
1 Medoff, Jack
1 Medwick, Joe
1 Meecham, Malcolm
38 Meeder, William
3 Meehan, Don
1 Meehan, James
4 Meek, Donald
3 Meeker, Ralph
1 Meerbach, Alexander

1 Meese, George
1 Mehegan, Peter
1 Meidell, Gert
1 Meighan, Jack
1 Meighan, James
1 Meighan, Louis
12 Meiser, Edith
1 Meister, Sylvia
1 Meitner, Lisa
3 Mel-Tones, The
2 Melachrino (George Melachrino and His Orchestra)
2 Melachrino, George
1 Melba, Thomas
2 Melcher, John
1 Melcher, Martin
26 Melchior, Lauritz
2 Melis, José
1 Melland, Frank
4 Mellolarks, The
1 Mellon, Paul
1 Melloreenees, The
1 Mellow, Frank
5 Melody Choristers, The
1 Melody Girls, The
12 Melody Maids, The
40 Melomen, The
1 Melotin, Al
1 Melton (Harry Melton Choir, The)
1 Melton, Frank
77 Melton, James
1 Melton, Sid
1 Melton, William
1 Meltzer, Bernard
2 Melville, Alan
15 Melville, Herman
1 Melvin (Harold Melvin and The Blue Notes)
4 Melvin, Allan
2 Melvin, Susan
1 Melzer, Bernard D.
4 Memory Four Quartet, The
2 Men Of Melody, The
1 Menafee, Seldon
2 Mencken, H. L.
1 Mendel, Joseph
1 Mendell, Vladimir
2 Mendell, Wendell
1 Mendelssohn, Felix
2 Mendes, Pierre
2 Mendez, Jim
15 Mendez, Rafael
5 Mendick, Charles
2 Mendis, Asoka
4 Menefee, Selden C.
2 Mengelberg, Willem
46 Menjou, Adolphe
3 Menken, Helen
101 Menken, Shepard
7 Menuhin, Yehudi
1 Menzies, Robert
1 Mera, Lauschan
1 Merbold, Ulf
1 Mercedes
2 Mercer Mary Ann
1 Mercer, Frances
112 Mercer, Johnny
32 Mercer, Tommy
80 Meredith, Brian
48 Meredith, Burgess
1 Meredith, Don
1 Meredith, Dorothy
1 Meredith, Elaine
4 Meredith, George
1 Meredith, Iris
2 Meredith, Jay
2 Meredith, Jim
37 Meredith, Lucille
1 Mergenheimer, Joseph
1 Meriden, Elaine
1 Merino, Jo
3 Merivale, Phillip
60 Merkel, Una
1 Merkin, Barry
2 Merklin, Ed
4 Merlin, Barbara
44 Merlin, Jan
11 Merlin, John
1 Merlin, Mary
12 Merlin, Milton
42 Merman, Ethel
7 Mermon, Joe
5 Merrick (Mahlon Merrick and His Orchestra)
1 Merrick, Joseph
16 Merrick, Mahlon
2 Merrick, William
2 Merrill, Bob
1 Merrill, Danny
1 Merrill, Dick
16 Merrill, Gary
3 Merrill, Howard
1 Merrill, Jean
10 Merrill, Joan
1 Merrill, Ken
233 Merrill, Lou
1 Merrill, Mona
59 Merrill, Robert
6 Merriman, Nan
1 Merringh, P. W.
1 Merrion, Paul
23 Merry Macs, The
17 Merryfield, Mary
1 Merryvale, Bernard
2 Merryvale, Jack
2 Merryvale, John
2 Mervin, William
1 Meskill, Catherine
1 Mess, James
1 Messer, R. E.
2 Messey, Bob
5 Messick, Don
23 Messina, Frankie
1 Messner (Johnny Messner and His Music Box Band)
7 Messner (Johnny Messner and His Orchestra)
8 Messner, Johnny
290 Meston, John
2 Metcalfe, Eddie
2 Metropolis, Dimitri
1 Metropolitan Jazz Quartet, The
19 Metz, Stuart
1 Metz, Zachary
2 Metzenbaum, Howard
1 Mexican Symphony Orchestra, The
1 Meyer (Carl Meyer's Trained Canines)
1 Meyer (Gus Meyer's Orchestra)
1 Meyer, Harry
2 Meyer, Larry
3 Meyer, Marjorie
1 Meyer, Ray
1 Meyer, Virginia
1 Meyers, Alonzo
4 Meyers, Bill
6 Meyers, Dale D.
2 Meyers, Dickie
1 Meyers, Francis J.
1 Meyers, Gustavus
2 Meyers, Joseph O.
1 Meyers, Kenny
1 Meyers, Pauline
1 Meyers, Stan
6 Meyers, Ted
1 Meyerson, Alonzo
1 Meyerson, Harvey
2 Meyner, Dorothy
3 Mezzrow, Mezz
1 Mich, Dan
7 Michael, Frank
1 Michael, Franz
83 Michael, Jay
2 Michael, Joyce
2 Michael, Mary
2 Michael, Robert
2 Michael, Sondra
1 Michaels, David
1 Michaels, Pat
3 Michaels, Tony
2 Michalopoulos, Andre
2 Miche, Gertrude
1 Michel, Robert
26 Michelson, Charles
13 Michelson, Dr.
1 Michener, Carroll K.
1 Michener, James
2 Michie, Lola
1 Mickelson, Sig
1 Mickey Mouse Grand Opera Company, The
2 Mickey, Alan
3 Middleman, Robert
2 Middleton, Bob
1 Middleton, Faith
15 Middleton, Ray
7 Middleton, Velma
1 Midgely, Lesley
1 Midler, Bette
1 Miehle, Bob
1 Miessner, John
1 Mighty Clouds Of Joy, The
1 Mikulski, Barbara
3 Milan, Mike
2 Milani, Chef
1 Milano, Bright
15 Milano, Frank
1 Milano, Si
1 Milanov, Zinka
1 Miles, Bill
1 Miles, Ginger
1 Miles, Jackie
1 Miles, Lillian
1 Miles, Linda
1 Miles, Phillip
7 Miles, Phyllis
1 Miles, Vera
1 Milestone, Lewis
1 Miljan, John
1 Milk, Marvin
1 Milland, Lynn
45 Milland, Ray
47 Millar, Lee
1 Millard, John
3 Millay, Edna St. Vincent
3 Millender (Lucky Millender and His Orchestra)
1 Miller (Albert Miller and Choir)
1 Miller (Glenn Miller and His American Band Of The AEF)
45 Miller (Glenn Miller and His Orchestra)
6 Miller (Glenn Miller and The AAFTC Orchestra)
19 Miller (Glenn Miller and The Band Of The AAF Training Command)
2 Miller (Glenn Miller and The Band Of The AEF)
2 Miller (Glenn Miller Modernaires With Paula Kelly, The)
41 Miller (Glenn Miller Orchestra, The)
2 Miller (Hap Miller and His Orchestra)
15 Miller (Irving Miller and His Orchestra)
7 Miller (Jack Miller and His Orchestra)
1 Miller (Max Miller Trio, The)
1 Miller (Mitch Miller and His Gang)
5 Miller (Mitch Miller and His Orchestra and Chorus)
4 Miller (Mitch Miller and His Orchestra)
1 Miller (Mitch Miller Singers, The)
3 Miller (Ray Miller and His Orchestra)
20 Miller (Victor Miller and His Orchestra)
15 Miller Jr., Walter
1 Miller, Admiral
2 Miller, Albert G.
1 Miller, Alice
1 Miller, Alice Duer
8 Miller, Ann
15 Miller, Arthur
1 Miller, Barbara
2 Miller, Bill
10 Miller, Bob
3 Miller, Brewster S
3 Miller, Brian
1 Miller, Corrine
1 Miller, Dan
3 Miller, Eddie
1 Miller, Emma Guffey
1 Miller, Flournoy
1 Miller, Floyd
2 Miller, Frank
1 Miller, General
4 Miller, Gladys
17 Miller, Glenn
1 Miller, Harvey
1 Miller, Helen
3 Miller, Howard
12 Miller, Irving
12 Miller, Jack
1 Miller, Jason
1 Miller, Jimmy
1 Miller, Johnny
1 Miller, Julius
1 Miller, Justin
4 Miller, Kay
1 Miller, Marcus
2 Miller, Marcy
2 Miller, Margaret
2 Miller, Marilyn
1 Miller, Martha
468 Miller, Marvin
1 Miller, Mary
1 Miller, Mary Jean
1 Miller, Max
1 Miller, Melina
3 Miller, Merle
2 Miller, Michael
5 Miller, Milana
1 Miller, Mildred
9 Miller, Mitch
1 Miller, Patsy Ruth
1 Miller, Paul
2 Miller, Punch
1 Miller, Robert
1 Miller, Robert M.
89 Miller, Sidney
24 Miller, Sigmund
8 Miller, Susan
1 Miller, Vernon
2 Miller, William
74 Milligan, Spike
1 Milliken, William M.
542 Mills (Billy Mills and His Orchestra)
37 Mills (Felix Mills and His Orchestra)
39 Mills Brothers, The
21 Mills, Billy
1 Mills, Burly
1 Mills, Byron
1 Mills, Edward
4 Mills, Edwin
37 Mills, Felix
1 Mills, George R.
1 Mills, Jackie
2 Mills, John
5 Mills, Juliet
1 Mills, Noel
2 Mills, Rod
2 Mills, Stephanie
18 Mills, Thomas
4 Mills, Warren
1 Milm, Ella
1 Milne, A. A.
3 Milner, Martin
43 Milo, Henry
1 Milo, Melisa
1 Milos, Jana
1 Milsap, Ronnie
4 Milstein, Nathan
1 Milton (Harry Milton and His Choir)
2 Milton, Jack
30 Milton, Paul
1 Mims, Holly
1 Minard, Ken
2 Mince, Johnny
2 Mindel, Joseph

1 Mindszenty, Jozsef
1 Mineo, Sal
3 Miner, Ellis
102 Miner, Jan
1 Miner, Worthington
2 Minevitch (Borrah Minevitch and The Harmonica Rascals)
1 Minevitch, Borrah
1 Mingus (Charles Mingus Quintet, The)
1 Mingus, Charlie
1 Minneapolis Symphony Orchestra, The
3 Minnelli, Liza
1 Minnick, Maurice
1 Minow, Newton
1 Minton, Robert
1 Miranda
1 Miranda, Aurora
23 Miranda, Carmen
1 Miranda, Isa
1 Mirandy, Dora
1 Misener, Sanford
6 Miss Audrey
1 Mitchell (Bob Mitchell Boys Choir, The)
10 Mitchell (Robert Mitchell Boys Choir, The)
1 Mitchell (Roy Mitchell Singers, The)
1 Mitchell, Abbie
6 Mitchell, Albert
1 Mitchell, Andrea
68 Mitchell, Bob
8 Mitchell, Broadus
4 Mitchell, Cameron
11 Mitchell, Dolly
53 Mitchell, Everett
2 Mitchell, Franklin
11 Mitchell, George
1 Mitchell, Greg
3 Mitchell, Guy
22 Mitchell, Harry
1 Mitchell, Helen S.
1 Mitchell, Howard
2 Mitchell, Jack
6 Mitchell, James
1 Mitchell, James P.
1 Mitchell, Johnny
1 Mitchell, Joni
7 Mitchell, Les
1 Mitchell, Leslie
1 Mitchell, Madeline
1 Mitchell, Maurice B.
3 Mitchell, Millard
2 Mitchell, Perry
1 Mitchell, President
70 Mitchell, Robert
314 Mitchell, Shirley
1 Mitchell, Sidney
1 Mitchell, Sue
1 Mitchell, Terry
29 Mitchell, Thomas
1 Mitchum, John
9 Mitchum, Robert
1 Mix, Mrs. Tom
2 Mix, Tom
1 Mixer, Robert
1 Mixin, Danny
1 Mize, John
2 Mock, Alice
1 Mock, Bobby
1 Modarelli, Antonio
3 Modern Choir, The
7 Modern Jazz Quartet, The
2 Modern Melody Trio, The
6 Modern Rhythm Ensemble Of Boston
65 Modernaires, The
1 Modiste, Silva
1 Moffett, Judy
1 Mogel, Len
1 Moger, Art
1 Moger, Stan
1 Mohr, George
263 Mohr, Gerald
1 Mohr, Matt
1 Moira, Robert
4 Molasses and January
3 Mole (Miff Mole and His Orchestra)
29 Mole, Miff
2 Moliere
2 Molinari, Bernardino
2 Molinari, Susan
1 Mollar (Bob Mollar and His Orchestra)
3 Molotov, V. M.
1 Moman, Virginia
8 Monahan, Dickie
1 Monahan, Frank
1 Monash, Paul
1 Mondale, Mrs. Walter
29 Mondale, Walter
1 Mondello, Toots
2 Mone, Monty
1 Monhank, George
1 Monica, Corbett
1 Monk, Thelonius
32 Monks, James
1 Monroe (Ronny Monroe and His Orchestra)
24 Monroe (Vaughn Monroe and His Orchestra)
4 Monroe, Bill
1 Monroe, Charles
6 Monroe, Lucy
6 Monroe, Marilyn
1 Monroe, Paul
1 Monroe, Sam
40 Monroe, Vaughn
1 Montague, C. E.
3 Montalban, Ricardo
3 Montana Slim
10 Montana, Monty
1 Monte, Eric
99 Montell, Doug
4 Montesavaj, William
1 Montez, Maria
11 Montgomery, Bernard
3 Montgomery, Douglass
7 Montgomery, George
1 Montgomery, Jerry
2 Montgomery, Ralph
56 Montgomery, Robert
1 Montgomery, Sonny
1 Montoya, Larry
1 Montserrat, Nicholas
1 Montsos, John
1 Monzell, Specs
2 Monzoni, Alessandro
3 Moody, Frank
1 Moody, Helen Wills
2 Moody, James
156 Moody, Ralph
1 Moon, Bob
1 Moon, Jake
1 Moon, Winifred
5 Moonbeam Trio, The
18 Mooney (Art Mooney and His Orchestra)
1 Mooney (Harold Mooney and His Orchestra)
2 Mooney (Joe Mooney Quartette, The)
2 Mooney, Art
2 Mooney, Joe
5 Moonglows, The
2 Moonier, Charlotte
3 Moonlight Serenaders, The
5 Moonmaids, The
2 Moonmen, The
4 Moorad, George
1 Moore (Billy Moore Trio, The)
1 Moore (Carl Deacon Moore and His Wah Wah Music)
1 Moore (Phil Moore and His Orchestra)
1 Moore (Phil Moore Four, The)
2 Moore, Ann
1 Moore, Archie
2 Moore, Bill
1 Moore, Bob
1 Moore, Carl
152 Moore, Clayton
1 Moore, Clement Clarke
1 Moore, Cleo
1 Moore, Colleen
7 Moore, Constance
1 Moore, Curley
1 Moore, Dan
2 Moore, Dennis
1 Moore, Dickie
1 Moore, Earl B.
1 Moore, Frank
2 Moore, Freddy
102 Moore, Garry
8 Moore, Grace
1 Moore, H. F. S.
1 Moore, Harris Campbell
2 Moore, Irving
3 Moore, Jesse
9 Moore, John
1 Moore, Kent
1 Moore, Mabel
6 Moore, Mary Tyler
4 Moore, Maver
1 Moore, Melba
1 Moore, Mrs. Harris Campbell
1 Moore, Mrs. Thomas
5 Moore, Nancy
1 Moore, Patrick
2 Moore, Phil
3 Moore, Robert
152 Moore, Sam
6 Moore, Terry
3 Moore, Tim
6 Moore, Tom
50 Moore, Victor
200 Moorehead, Agnes
1 Moorehead, Jean
4 Moorewood, William
1 Morabito, Linda
1 Morales, Richie
1 Moramoto, Claudia
1 Moran (Jose Moran and His Orchestra)
1 Moran and Mack
33 Moran, Betty
2 Moran, George
1 Moran, Jackie
1 Moran, Jim
2 Moran, Lois
1 Moran, Pat
2 Moran, Patsy
2 Moran, Polly
1 Moran, Robert
1 Moran, Warren
1 Morath, Anna Maude
7 Morath, Max
101 Moraweck, Lucien
1 Moray, Ann
4 Moray, Helga
1 More, Chauncey
4 Morea, Robert
1 Moreheim, Joe
1 Moreland, Joanna
4 Moreland, Mantan
2 Moreland, Peg
1 Morely, Ed
1 Morely, Felix
3 Morely, John
3 Moreno (Buddy Moreno and His Orchestra)
239 Moreno, Amerigo
28 Moreno, Buddy
1 Moreno, Pete
1 Moreno, Rita
3 Morgan
1 Morgan (George Morgan and His Candy Kids)
3 Morgan (Mal Morgan Trio, The)
82 Morgan (Russ Morgan and His Orchestra)
1 Morgan Brothers, The
1 Morgan, Al
1 Morgan, Alan
2 Morgan, Andrew
2 Morgan, Betty
1 Morgan, Billy
12 Morgan, Brewster
1 Morgan, Charles
10 Morgan, Claudia
10 Morgan, Dan
14 Morgan, Dennis
6 Morgan, Dick
1 Morgan, Ed
1 Morgan, Eddie
3 Morgan, Edward P.
7 Morgan, Elizabeth
22 Morgan, Ellen
111 Morgan, Frank
10 Morgan, Freddie
1 Morgan, General
14 Morgan, George
3 Morgan, Harry
9 Morgan, Helen
121 Morgan, Henry
5 Morgan, Jack
149 Morgan, Jane
9 Morgan, Jaye P.
1 Morgan, Jim
1 Morgan, Joan
2 Morgan, Johnny
1 Morgan, Joy Elmer
1 Morgan, June
1 Morgan, Mac
17 Morgan, Marian
3 Morgan, Michele
1 Morgan, Officer
1 Morgan, Patty
1 Morgan, Paula
1 Morgan, Polly
15 Morgan, Ralph
18 Morgan, Ray
1 Morgan, Richard
3 Morgan, Robert
3 Morgan, Robin
38 Morgan, Russ
2 Morgan, Tommy
1 Morgan, Warren
5 Morganaires, The
1 Morganthau Jr., Mrs. Henry
1 Morganthau, Hans
8 Morganthau, Henry
1 Morhan, Jean
2 Morheim, Gerald
1 Moriale (Pepe Moriale Trio, The)
1 Morin Sisters, The
1 Moring, Bill
2 Moring, Kansas
1 Morise, Andre
10 Morley, Christopher
2 Morley, Karen
1 Morley, Robert
8 Mormon Tabernacle Choir, The
1 Morn, William
1 Morner, Stanley
4 Moross, Joe
1 Morra, Edgar Ansel
1 Morris (Johnny Morris and His Orchestra)
2 Morris (Philip Morris Songsters, The)
1 Morris Sisters, The
1 Morris, Al
4 Morris, Ben
21 Morris, Chester
1 Morris, Curt
1 Morris, Gouverneur
1 Morris, Greg
2 Morris, Howard
2 Morris, Joe Alex
1 Morris, John
8 Morris, Lester
1 Morris, McKay
2 Morris, Newbold
4 Morris, Phyllis
1 Morris, Phyllis Christine
1 Morris, Ray
3 Morris, Roland
1 Morris, Tony
10 Morris, Wayne
2 Morris, William
1 Morrison (Ralph Morrison and His Orchestra)
33 Morrison, Anne
165 Morrison, Bret
1 Morrison, Charles
9 Morrison, Chester
2 Morrison, David
50 Morrison, Donald

4 Morrison, Herbert
4 Morrison, Jack
1 Morrison, John
6 Morrison, Patricia
1 Morrison, Phil
2 Morrison, Philip
1 Morrison, Ralph
4 Morrow (Buddy Morrow and His Night Train Orchestra)
8 Morrow (Buddy Morrow and His Orchestra)
254 Morrow, Bill
1 Morrow, Bruce
4 Morrow, Buddy
1 Morrow, Don
2 Morrow, Doretta
1 Morrow, Jackie
8 Morrow, Jeff
1 Morrow, Kay
1 Morrow, Ken
1 Morrow, Larry
5 Morrow, Liza
1 Morrow, Mary Jane
1 Morrow, Tommy
1 Morrow, Walter
1 Morse, Alice
11 Morse, Barry
94 Morse, Carlton E.
16 Morse, Ella Mae
1 Morse, Jack
1 Morse, Jean
1 Morse, Ralph
7 Morse, Robert
1 Morse, Stanley
1 Morse, Tilda
1 Morse, True D.
2 Morse, Wayne
1 Morstad, Pete
1 Mortimer, John
6 Morton, Benny
2 Morton, Bob
2 Morton, Bruce
12 Morton, Gregory
4 Morton, Jelly Roll
1 Morton, Nancy Kenna
1 Morton (Ray Morton and His Orchestra)
7 Morton, Robert
4 Morwood, William
1 Moscona, Nicola
1 Mose, Estelle
1 Moseby, Eileen
1 Moseman, Joan
2 Moseman, John
1 Moser, Carol
31 Moser, James
1 Moses, Charles
1 Moses, Kingsley
3 Moses, Robert
37 Mosher, Bob
2 Mosley, Donald
6 Mosley, Sidney
2 Mosley, Walter
1 Mosner, Marianne
1 Moss
1 Moss, Albert
149 Moss, Arnold
1 Moss, Carl
1 Moss, Garland
1 Moss, Hilda
1 Moss, Jack
4 Moss, Leslie Bates
3 Moss, Llewellyn
1 Moss, Lloyd
1 Moss, Marjorie
1 Moss, Mary Dean
6 Moss, Stella
1 Mossen, Richard
41 Mosser, Helen
133 Mosser, Mike
1 Most, Abe
1 Most, Johnny
5 Mostel, Zero
4 Moten, Etta
1 Motley, Albert
1 Mottola (Tony Mottola and His Rhythm Group)
1 Mottola (Tony Mottola Group, The)
2 Mottola (Tony Mottola Quartet, The)
3 Mottola (Tony Mottola Trio, The)
1 Mottola (Tony Mottola's Dance Rhythms)
43 Mottola, Tony
1 Motz, Lloyd
20 Mountain, Charles
1 Mountbatten, Louis
1 Mouquin Salon Orchestra, The
1 Mouquin, Louis H. F.
1 Mousheng, Lin
1 Movshon, George
5 Mowbray, Alan
2 Mowery, Jean
5 Mowery, Joan
7 Moyers, Bill
4 Moylan Sisters, The
221 Moyles, Jack
10 Moynahan, Daniel
1 Mudaliar, A. Ramaswamy
10 Mudd, Roger
1 Mudd, Rose Ellen
1 Muddle, MacIntosh
3 Mudie, Leonard
2 Mueller
12 Mueller, Merrill
1 Mugler, John P.
2 Muir, Billy
1 Muir, Ellen
1 Muir, Gavin
4 Muir, Jean
1 Muir, Malcolm
3 Mulay (Johnny Mulay and His Orchestra)
3 Mulay, Johnny
1 Mulcay, Jimmy
1 Mulcay, Mildred
1 Muldowny, John Humphrey
1 Mulgroo, George
2 Mulholland, Ross
1 Mullavey, Greg
1 Mullen, Charles
1 Mullen, Christopher
3 Mullen, Virginia
1 Mullendore, W. C.
1 Muller, Norbert
3 Muller, Romeo
1 Muller, Steven
4 Mullican, Moon
7 Mulligan, Gerry
2 Mulligan, Richard
1 Mullin, Joe
11 Mulliner, Betty
2 Mulroney, Brian
1 Mulvey, Paul
1 Mulvey, Timothy
5 Munch, Charles
1 Mundhay, George
1 Mundorf, Bertram
3 Mundt, Carl
1 Mundt, Carl E.
1 Mundy (Jimmy Mundy and His Orchestra)
22 Muni, Paul
19 Munier, Ferdinand
30 Munn, Frank
1 Munro, H. H.
35 Munsel, Patrice
2 Munshin, Jules
11 Munson, Ona
2 Munzak, Marcus
2 Mura, Corina
1 Murad (Jerry Murad's Harmonicats)
12 Murcott, Joel
53 Murdock, Kermit
1 Murphin, Jane
1 Murphy (Buddy Murphy and His Orchestra)
2 Murphy (Johnny Murphy and His Orchestra)
1 Murphy (Turk Murphy's San Francisco Jazz Band)
8 Murphy Sisters, The
6 Murphy, Audie
48 Murphy, Bob
1 Murphy, Charles
1 Murphy, Dean
1 Murphy, Eugene P.
54 Murphy, George
1 Murphy, Honore
13 Murphy, Horace
2 Murphy, James
1 Murphy, Joe
2 Murphy, Mark
1 Murphy, Norm
1 Murphy, Pat
2 Murphy, Robert D.
3 Murphy, Rose Chi Chi
8 Murphy, Rosemary
1 Murphy, Senator
1 Murphy, Turk
12 Murphy, William J.
117 Murray (Lyn Murray and His Orchestra)
2 Murray (Lyn Murray and The Hit Paraders)
1 Murray (Lyn Murray and The Squibb Orchestra)
1 Murray (Lyn Murray Choir)
5 Murray (Lyn Murray Chorus, The)
1 Murray (Lyn Murray Quartet, The)
20 Murray (Lyn Murray Singers, The)
1 Murray (Lyn Murray's Four Clubmen)
3 Murray The K
2 Murray, Arthur
3 Murray, Billy
8 Murray, Bonnie
8 Murray, Bruce
1 Murray, Charles
1 Murray, Edith
1 Murray, Feg
2 Murray, George
1 Murray, Gilbert
16 Murray, Hugh K.
1 Murray, James E.
6 Murray, Jan
15 Murray, Jimmy
1 Murray, John
1 Murray, John Fenton
5 Murray, Johnny
21 Murray, Ken
51 Murray, Lyn
1 Murray, Mae
1 Murray, Phillip
2 Murray, Roseanne
6 Murray, Ross
9 Murray, Wynn
200 Murrow, Edward R.
1 Murrow, Mrs. Edward R.
2 Murtaugh, Danny
2 Murtha, John
9 Muse, Clarence
1 Muse, Herb
2 Muse, Margaret
3 Musgrave, Story
1 Mushotzky, Richard
8 Musial, Stan
3 Music Builders Orchestra, The
2 Music Maids and Hal, The
3 Music Maids and Lee, The
8 Music Maids and Phil, The
55 Music Maids, The
2 Music Of Manhattan, The
1 Musical Millmen, The
2 Musical Steelmakers, The
1 Musicland Serenaders, The
1 Musicmakers, The
5 Muskie, Edmund
1 Musmano, Michael
1 Musser, Myron
7 Musso, Vido
9 Mussolini, Benito
1 Mussulli, Boots
3 Mutch, Thomas
2 Myers, Carmel
1 Myers, Lisa
1 Myers, Marty
1 Myers, Marvel
1 Myerson, Bess
1 Myra
5 Myrdal, Gunnar
1 Myron, Mary
14 Mystic Knights Of The Sea Quartet, The

WKBW
BUFFALO
BROADCASTING
CORPORATION
PROGRAM
LATERAL
RECORDING
DATE
USE
FILTER
INSIDE START
PREPARED FO
RAND BUILDING
BUFFALO 3, N. Y.

1 Nabokov, Vladimir
1 Nabors, Jim
1 Nabukoff, Nicholas
7 Nagel (Freddy Nagel and His Orchestra)
1 Nagel, Anne
81 Nagel, Conrad
1 Nagel, Freddy
1 Nair, Jack
1 Nairne, Chet
56 Naish, J. Carrol
1 Nakamura, Henry
1 Nakana, Lane
1 Nakavichi, Joseph
1 Namath, Joe
2 Nance, Andy
11 Nance, Ray
1 Naney, Bill
1 Nantz, Elwood C
4 Napier, Alan
19 Napoleon (Phil Napoleon and His Memphis Five)
1 Napoleon, Phil
4 Napoleon, Teddy
1 Nardone, Vince
8 Narz, Jack
1 Nash (Lavinia Nash Singers, The)
1 Nash, Chaya
4 Nash, Clarence
1 Nash, Eleanor
1 Nash, Joey
3 Nash, Johnny
3 Nash, Mary
3 Nash, Ogden
2 Nash, Ted
1 Nash, Walter
3 Nason, Leonard
1 Natalie
1 Nathan, John
9 Nathan, Robert
5 Nathan, Robert Roy
2 Nathan, Theodore R.
2 National Champion Hillbillies, The
1 National Lutheran Chorus, The
1 National Symphony Orchestra, The
5 Natwick, Mildred
1 Naughton, Bill
5 Naugle, John
1 Naval Academy Band, The
1 Navy (U. S. Navy Band and Chorus, The)
7 Navy (U. S. Navy Band, The)
1 Naylor, Jerry
1 Naysmith, Otler
24 Nazarro, Cliff
1 Nazimova, Alla
5 NBC Chicago Orchestra, The
6 NBC Concert Orchestra, The
1 NBC Dance Orchestra, The
2 NBC Hollywood Orchestra, The
1 NBC Minstrels, The
106 NBC Orchestra, The
5 NBC String Orchestra, The
148 NBC Symphony Orchestra, The
4 Neagle, Anna
1 Neagles, Helen
1 Neal Sisters, The
1 Neal, David
1 Neal, Floyd
1 Neal, John
4 Neal, Patricia
1 Neal, Roy
1 Neal, Tom
1 Nealy, Henry
2 Near, Jack
1 Neary, Mrs. Edward
1 Neblett, Johnnie
1 Neday, Kathleen
1 Needles, William
1 Neely, Henry
1 Neering, Vivian
2 Negley, Harrison
1 Negro Art Singers, The
5 Negro Melody Singers Of New York
1 Negulesco, Jean
2 Nehru, Jawaharlal
1 Neighbor Boys, The
3 Neighborbors (Paul Neighbors and His Orchestra)
4 Neill, Larry
2 Neill, Noel
1 Neilon, John
1 Neilson, Howard
2 Neilson, Marv
1 Neilson, Patty
1 Neilson, William Allen
1 Nelligan, Mrs. H. Paul
1 Nelson
1 Nelson (Oliver Nelson and His Orchestra)
9 Nelson (Ozzie Nelson and His Orchestra)
2 Nelson, Barbara
3 Nelson, Barry
1 Nelson, Bill
2 Nelson, Bud
1 Nelson, Byron
1 Nelson, Charles
1 Nelson, Claire
17 Nelson, David
5 Nelson, Ed
5 Nelson, Felix
348 Nelson, Frank
1 Nelson, Freud A.
2 Nelson, Gaye
2 Nelson, Gene
2 Nelson, George
3 Nelson, Harriet
3 Nelson, Harry
3 Nelson, Herbert
1 Nelson, Herbert U.
1 Nelson, Ivan
4 Nelson, Jack
2 Nelson, John
1 Nelson, Lindsey
1 Nelson, Lori
1 Nelson, Martin
1 Nelson, Mrs.
55 Nelson, Ozzie
1 Nelson, Phillip
1 Nelson, Ralph
1 Nelson, Ray
2 Nelson, Richard
15 Nelson, Ricky
3 Nelson, Sam
1 Nelson, Sergeant
8 Nelson, Skip
1 Nelson, Stan
1 Nelson, Steady
1 Nelson, Walter M.
1 Nelson, Wynn
2 Nelsonics, The
1 Nero, Paul
3 Nero, Peter
1 Nesbitt, Cathleen
1 Nesbitt, E.
44 Nesbitt, John
1 Nesbitt, Norman
1 Ness, Elliot
1 Ness, Norman
2 Nessler, Jack
9 Nessler, Joel
6 Nestor-Chayres, Nestor
1 Netherton, Clyde
1 Nett, Bud
7 Nettleton, Lois
30 Neufelt, Erno
1 Neugebauer, Marcia
46 Neuman, E. Jack
1 Nevard, Billie
1 Nevil, Charles
1 Neville, Robert
1 Nevin, Frances
1 Nevins, Allan
6 New Christy Minstrels, The
1 New Jersey Opera Company, The
4 New Lost City Ramblers, The
1 New Orleans Classic Ragtime Band
1 New Orleans Ragtime Band
1 New York (Philharmonic Symphony Orchestra Of New York, The)
1 New York City Band, The
1 New York City Police Glee Club, The
1 New York City Symphonic Orchestra
2 New York City Symphony Orchestra, The
3 New York Civic Orchestra
1 New York Civic Symphony
1 New York Musical Choir, The
28 New York Philharmonic, The
1 New York Pro Musica, The
1 New York State Symphonic Band, The
1 New Yorkers, The
1 Newberger, Elizabeth
1 Newbold, John
1 Newburn, Ray
3 Newcombe, Don
8 Newell, James
1 Newell, Michael
1 Newell, Skip
3 Newhouser, Hal
1 Newkirk, Bob
6 Newland, John
1 Newman (Joe Newman and His All-Stars)
3 Newman (Ruby Newman and His Orchestra)
7 Newman, Alfred
1 Newman, Arthur
1 Newman, Charlie
14 Newman, Edwin
1 Newman, Hank
5 Newman, Jimmy
4 Newman, Lionel
3 Newman, Martin
2 Newman, Nancy
1 Newman, Paul
4 Newman, Phyllis
16 Newman, Robert
8 Newman, Sidney
68 Newman, Stephen
24 Newman, Walter
1 Newmar, Julie
2 Newsome, Gil
1 Newson, Phil
1 Newton (Frankie Newton and His Orchestra)
1 Newton, Adele
10 Newton, Ernest
2 Newton, Ken
1 Newton, Mary
1 Newton, Patricia
2 Newton, Richard
2 Newton, Robert
3 Newton, Walt
3 Newton, Wayne
1 Newton-John, Olivia
4 Ney, Richard
1 Niblick, Johnny
4 Nicholas Brothers, The
26 Nicholas, Albert
2 Nicholls, Ann
1 Nicholls, D. F.
1 Nicholls, Don
6 Nicholls, Joy
2 Nicholls, Marion
2 Nicholls, Rusty
2 Nicholls, Ted
1 Nichols (Red Nichols and His New Pennies)
22 Nichols (Red Nichols and The Five Pennies)
3 Nichols, Barbara
1 Nichols, Beverly
1 Nichols, Bobby
1 Nichols, Jack
2 Nichols, Joan
2 Nichols, Leslie
1 Nichols, Meredith
1 Nichols, Michelle
9 Nichols, Mike
18 Nichols, Red
1 Nichols, Sherman
1 Nicholson, Dave
2 Nicholson, Harold
5 Nicholson, Kenyon
1 Nick, Carol
1 Nicklaus, Jack
2 Nickles, Don
3 Nicks, William
1 Nicogossian, Arnold
1 Nicol, James
1 Nicolaysen, Ragnar
2 Nicole, James W.
39 Niece, George
1 Nielsen, Leslie
7 Niesen, Claire
23 Niesen, Gertrude
1 Nietze, Paul
2 Nighthawks, The
1 Nightingale, Earl
1 Nightingale, Florence
1 Nigling, Jack
2 Niglis, Betty
1 Nigut, Bill
1 Niles, Jacquelin
127 Niles, Ken
226 Niles, Wendell
5 Nilsson Twins, The
47 Nilsson, Norma Jean
8 Nimitz, Chester
2 Nimoy, Leonard
1 Nina and Rosa
3 Nina, Gypsy
1 Nipres, Janet
28 Niss, Stanley
9 Nissim, Renso
18 Niven, David
1 Nixon, Marion
1 Nixon, Pat
125 Nixon, Richard

1 Nixon, Russ
3 Nizer, Louis
298 Noa, Julian
1 Noarse, Alan
9 Nobels, Charlie
10 Noble (Leighton Noble and His Orchestra)
56 Noble (Ray Noble and His Orchestra)
1 Noble and King
1 Noble, Aimee
3 Noble, Al
1 Noble, Charles
12 Noble, Dick
1 Noble, Gil
1 Noble, Harry
2 Noble, Larry
9 Noble, Leighton
66 Noble, Ray
1 Noble, Rommy
1 Noble, Wendell
2 Noblemen, The
1 Noblick, Cal
23 Noel, Dick
1 Nofziger, Ray
1 Nola, Frank J.
2 Nolan (Bob Nolan and The Sons Of The Pioneers)
79 Nolan, Bob
187 Nolan, Jeanette
4 Nolan, Jimmy
29 Nolan, Lloyd
1 Nolan, Lorenzo
1 Noland, Doris
2 Nolde, O. Frederick
1 Nolt, Evelyn
1 Nomellini, Leo
1 Noodleman, Leslie
1 Noonan, Stan
1 Noonan, Tom
1 Noone (Jimmy Noone and His Orchestra)
9 Noone, Jimmy
2 Nordberg, William
1 Nordic Choral Ensemble Of Duluth
27 Nordine, Ken
1 Nordquist, Ingeborg
2 Norma
3 Norman (Ralph Norman and His Orchestra)
1 Norman, Adele
4 Norman, Betty
1 Norman, Cathy
1 Norman, Fred
25 Norman, Gene
1 Norman, James
1 Norman, Lou Lee
20 Norman, Lucille
3 Norman, Lulie-Jean
1 Norman, Maidy
12 Norman, Nancy
1 Norman, Ralph
5 Norman, Teddy
25 Norrell, Henry
2 Norris (Bobby Norris and His Orchestra)
1 Norris, Eddie
1 Norris, Helen
3 Norris, Henry
2 Norris, Kathleen
2 Norris, Marianna
2 Norsemen, The
1 North Carolina Agricultural and Technical College Chorus, The
4 North, Clyde
1 North, Gretchen
1 North, Jessica Nelson
1 North, Mary
5 North, Noel
67 North, Robert
1 North, Sheree
6 Northerners, The
1 Norton Sisters, The
1 Norton, Betty
23 Norton, Cliff
2 Norton, Coe
3 Norton, Edgar
1 Norton, Jacques
1 Norton, Kay
1 Norton, Robert
1 Norvo (Red Norvo and His Orchestra)
1 Norvo (Red Norvo Quintet)
2 Norvo (Red Norvo Sextet, The)
4 Norvo (Red Norvo Trio, The)
35 Norvo, Red
2 Nosco, Henri
25 Nosserman, Dick
1 Noteworthies, The
1 Nourse, Alan E.
1 Nova, Lou
3 Novack (Frank Novack and His Orchestra)
1 Novack, Kathy
1 Novak, Bob
2 Novak, Kim
1 Novak, Robert
1 Novarro Sisters, The
1 Novarro, Ramon
2 Novatime Trio, The
2 Novatna, Jamilla
2 Noveliers, The
1 Novello, Al
177 Novello, Jay
2 Novick (Doc Novick and His Orchestra)
7 Novick (Nat Novick and His Orchestra)
13 Novins, Stuart
35 Novis, Donald
1 Novis, Julietta
1 Novotna, Jarmila
22 Noyce, Harold
5 Noyes, Alfred
1 Noyes, Betty
1 Noyes, Crosby
1 Nudell, Sam
1 Nugent, Edward
4 Nugent, Elliott
1 Nugent, Paul
2 Nugent, Richard
2 Nunn, Larry
1 Nunn, Ralph
1 Nunn, Sam
1 Nussbaum, Adam
142 Nusser, James
1 Nye, Bob
1 Nye, Carol
4 Nye, Gerald
12 Nye, Louis
6 Nyland, Ralph
2 Nype, Russell

1 O'Brien, Adrian
1 O'Brien, Daniel T.
13 O'Brien, Dottie
59 O'Brien, Edmond
4 O'Brien, Fitzjames
1 O'Brien, Gene
1 O'Brien, George
1 O'Brien, Gloria
2 O'Brien, Hugh
1 O'Brien, Jack
1 O'Brien, Jimmy
1 O'Brien, Lawrence
1 O'Brien, Lois
1 O'Brien, Louise
32 O'Brien, Margaret
3 O'Brien, Marissa
50 O'Brien, Pat
1 O'Brien, Perry
3 O'Brien, Robert
2 O'Brien, Stacy
2 O'Brien, Tim
1 O'Brien, Tom
19 O'Brien, Virginia
2 O'Brien-Moore, Erin
1 O'Bryant, William T.
1 O'Carlin, Michael
47 O'Connell, Helen
1 O'Connell, Patrick A.
20 O'Connor, Basil
4 O'Connor, Bill
2 O'Connor, Bob
1 O'Connor, Carroll
5 O'Connor, Dick
12 O'Connor, Donald
1 O'Connor, Everett
9 O'Connor, Giles
1 O'Connor, Glynnis
1 O'Connor, Governor
1 O'Connor, Hugh
1 O'Connor, Johnson
10 O'Connor, Maureen
5 O'Connor, Norman
2 O'Connor, Pat
1 O'Connor, Robert
276 O'Connor, Rod
3 O'Connor, Una
1 O'Dare, Tony
12 O'Day, Anita
12 O'Day, Michael
2 O'Day, Molly
3 O'Dell, C. R.
1 O'Dell, Day
3 O'Dell, Edna
3 O'Demus, Nick
1 O'Dell, Kerry
1 O'Donald, Spec
6 O'Donnell, Gene
5 O'Donovan, Finn
5 O'Driscoll, Martha
1 O'Duffy, Michael
1 O'Dwyer
1 O'Dwyer, Marr
3 O'Dwyer, Mayor
1 O'Fallon, Sean
1 O'Grady, John
1 O'Hara, Betty
1 O'Hara, Hamilton
1 O'Hara, Jeffrey
2 O'Hara, John
17 O'Hara, Maureen
2 O'Harran, Dick
2 O'Hearn, Walter
43 O'Herlihy, Dan
15 O'Keefe, Dennis
2 O'Keefe, John
4 O'Keefe, Lester
23 O'Keefe, Walter
2 O'Keefe, Winston
1 O'Malley, Jack
6 O'Malley, John
10 O'Malley, Neal
21 O'Malley, Pat
2 O'Malley, Rex
1 O'Malley, Walter
1 O'Mara, Kathy
2 O'Moore, Marion
6 O'Neal, Frederick
1 O'Neal, Margaret W.
2 O'Neal, Patrick
3 O'Neil, Danny
1 O'Neil, Henry
1 O'Neil, Kitty
2 O'Neill Jr., Eugene
6 O'Neill, Ann
3 O'Neill, Barbara
2 O'Neill, Charles
2 O'Neill, Dolores
4 O'Neill, Eugene
2 O'Neill, Gerard
1 O'Neill, Holly
3 O'Neill, Jean
1 O'Neill, Margaret
9 O'Neill, Thomas
1 O'Rearden, Conal
1 O'Reilly
3 O'Reilly, Jack
1 O'Shaughnessy, Dick
1 O'Shea, Eddie
14 O'Shea, Michael
6 O'Shea, Patsy
23 O'Sullivan, Maureen
55 O'Sullivan, Terry
1 O'Toole, Jim
4 O'Toole, Ollie
26 Oak Ridge Quartet, The
3 Oakar, Mary Rose
1 Oakes, Theresa
19 Oakie, Jack
1 Oakley, Don
1 Oakun, Louis
1 Oarsborn, Chuck
1 Oats, Edward
1 Ober, Emil
1 Oberg, James
14 Oberon, Merle
4 Obie, David
139 Oboler, Arch
1 Ocean
2 Oceans, Julie
1 Ochs, Ed
1 Ochs, Phil
113 Ocko, Dan
1 Octavius Roy Cohen
1 Odee, Jerry
2 Odetta
3 Odetts, Clifford
1 Odist, Michael
1 Odom, James B.
10 Ogg, Jimmy
16 Ogg, Sammy
1 Ogilvie, Governor
1 Ogilvie, Jack
1 Ohmae, Kenichi
2 Ohman (Phil Ohman and His Orchestra)
1 Ohman, Phil
8 Oklahoma City Symphony, The
3 Oland, Cliff
3 Old Hickory Singers, The
1 Oldfield, Barney
78 Oldham, Vera
4 Oldsburg, Arthur
1 Oliphant, Marshall
1 Oliphant, Professor
2 Oliveira (Luis Oliveira and His Orchestra)

2 Oliver (Eddie Oliver and His Orchestra)
23 Oliver (Sy Oliver and His Orchestra)
1 Oliver Twisters, The
1 Oliver, Edith
5 Oliver, Edna May
1 Oliver, Shirley
2 Oliver, Shirling
5 Oliver, Susan
10 Oliver, Sy
1 Olivera, José
34 Olivia De Havilland
35 Olivier, Laurence
1 Olmos, Edward James
21 Olmquist, Dean
1 Olmquist, Ed
48 Olmsted, Nelson
1 Olsen (George Olsen and His Music)
9 Olsen (George Olsen and His Orchestra)
1 Olsen, Edward J.
2 Olsen, Haave
11 Olsen, Ole
6 Olsen, Robert
2 Olsen, Verne
1 Olsen, Vernon
2 Olson, Bob
1 Olson, Culbert L.
2 Olson, Johnny
2 Olson, Margaret
3 Olson, Nancy
13 Olympian Quartet
1 Omeron, Carl
1 Onion, Pearl
1 Onions, Oliver
3 Ono, Hiroshi
1 Onyx Trio, The
2 Ophuls, Max
1 Oppenheim, E. Phillips
1 Oppenheim, Irene
1 Oppenheim, Jill
6 Oppenheimer, Jess
2 Oppenheimer, Robert
1 Opper, Frederick B.
1 Opperman Jr., George
1 Orbach, Jerry
1 Ord, Berly
1 Ordasi, Carlotta
1 Ordley, Alan
2 Orek, David
1 Orenti, Rose
4 Original Dixieland Jazz Band, The
2 Orkin, Dick
1 Orlando, Tony
1 Orlock, John
7 Ormandy, Eugene
1 Ormont, Dave
1 Orn, Wallace
1 Oro, John
1 Orr, Angeline
8 Orr, Corinne
1 Orr, Mary
2 Orrick, Don
10 Orrison, Jack
141 Ortega, Santos
6 Orten (Irving Orten and His Orchestra)
1 Orton, Della Louise
5 Orton, Irv
2 Orwell, George
2 Ory (Kid Ory and His Creole Jazz Band)
1 Ory (Kid Ory and His Dixieland Band)
1 Ory (Kid Ory and His Orchestra)
11 Ory, Kid
167 Osborn, Lyn
14 Osborne (Will Osborne and His Orchestra)
2 Osborne Brothers, The
1 Osborne, Ben
4 Osborne, Mary
1 Osborne, Paul
9 Osborne, Reynold
103 Osborne, Ted
1 Osborne, Thomas
11 Osborne, Will
1 Oscarwald, Phoebe
2 Osgood, Charlene
1 Osgood, Charles
1 Osgood, Cornelia
1 Osgood, Nancy
1 Osgood, Parlenia
2 Osman, David
1 Osmond, Donny
2 Osmond, Marie
3 Osser (Glenn Osser and His Orchestra)
62 Osser, Glenn
1 Ossman, Orson Broderick
1 Ossman, Steve David
1 Ostby, Gunnar
1 Oster, Leah
1 Osterwald, Mimi
3 Ostroff, Manning
1 Ostrovsky, Chaim
1 Ostrowski, John
28 Oswald, Bashful Brother
2 Oswald, Lee Harvey
1 Othman, Fred
1 Othmer, Donald F.
2 Otis, Don
2 Ott, Mel
1 Ottenheimer, Albert M.
1 Ottinger, Lawrence
5 Ottley, Hilda
17 Ottley, Roi
6 Otto, Walter
2 Oursler, Fulton
1 Oursler, Will
3 Ousley, Gilbert
1 Ouspenskaya, Maria
5 Outland, George E.
3 Outland, Henry
1 Overmeyer, Robert
1 Overstreet, Benaro
2 Overstreet, Harry
1 Overton, Ken
3 Owen, Bill
4 Owen, David
69 Owen, Elwyn
15 Owen, Ethel
1 Owen, Forrest
1 Owen, Francine
1 Owen, Laura Lee
2 Owen, Paul
5 Owen, Reginald
2 Owen, Tobias
33 Owen, Tudor
5 Owens (Harry Owens and His Orchestra)
4 Owens (Harry Owens and His Royal Hawaiians)
1 Owens, Buck
3 Owens, Fran
1 Owens, Gary
1 Owens, Harry
2 Owens, Jack
6 Owens, Jesse
2 Owens, Jimmy
9 Owens, Ray
4 Owens, Roy
1 Owings, Harold
2 Oxford, Earl
1 Oxley, J. Leonard
1 Oxnam, G. Bromley
1 Ozal, President
1 Ozark Mountain Boys, The

WJR
THE GOODWILL STATION
DETROIT 2, MICHIGAN
START
SPEED
DATE
P
PART

1 Paar, Harold
19 Paar, Jack
1 Pacelli, Frank
1 Pachling, Frank
1 Pacific Bible College Choir, The
2 Pack, Freddy
2 Packard, Eleanor
1 Packard, Reynolds
1 Paddock, Stephen
2 Padelford, Norman J.
3 Paderewski, Ignace
1 Padgett, Dan
15 Padgett, Pat
1 Padilla, Leopold
1 Padrick, Ben
1 Pafko, Andy
1 Paganinni
1 Pagano, Joe
1 Page (Larry Page and His Orchestra)
1 Page, Bill
1 Page, Bradley
5 Page, Gale
2 Page, Geraldine
9 Page, Hot Lips
32 Page, Patti
14 Page, Richard
1 Page, Susan
1 Pages Of Melody, The
6 Paget, Debra
1 Pagnol, Marcel
28 Paige (Raymond Paige and His Orchestra)
1 Paige, Helen
7 Paige, Janis
2 Paige, Raymond
2 Paige, Robert
1 Paige, Satchell
1 Paine, Ruth
5 Paine, Thomas
1 Painton, Frederick
1 Paitch (Marty Paitch and His Orchestra)
1 Paitch (Marty Paitch Septette, The)
42 Paiva, Nestor
1 Pal, George
1 Palance, Jack
1 Palangi, Carl
1 Paley, Edwin
1 Paley, Mrs. William
11 Paley, William S.
2 Palladino, Vincenzo
1 Pallette, Eugene
4 Palmer (Jimmy Palmer and His Orchestra)
1 Palmer Brothers, The
1 Palmer, Arnold
5 Palmer, Betsy
22 Palmer, Bud
2 Palmer, Byron
1 Palmer, Earl
3 Palmer, Effie
4 Palmer, Eileen
1 Palmer, Gloria
2 Palmer, Greta
1 Palmer, Hilda
2 Palmer, Jack
1 Palmer, Jimmy
5 Palmer, Lilli
9 Palmer, Maria
2 Palmer, Mary Virginia
1 Palmer, Olive
2 Palmer, Patti
1 Palmer, Roberta
2 Palmer, Stuart
10 Palmieri, Remo
1 Palyi, Melchior
1 Pamularo, Al
4 Pan American Orchestra, The
1 Pancho and His Orchestra
78 Pandit, Korla
1 Panetta, Leon
1 Panette, Jacqueline
7 Pangborn, Franklin
1 Panier, Ralph
4 Panitz, Sol
4 Pannell, Bill
1 Paolino, Joe
27 Pap and The Jug Band
1 Papandreou, Andreas
1 Papashvily, George
1 Papashvily, Helen
11 Papp, Frank
4 Papp, Mary
2 Pappas, Ike
2 Paradiso, Carl
16 Paratzo, Gene
1 Paray, Paul
29 Pardo, Don
1 Parent, Lionel
1 Parenti and Jackson
1 Parenti, Tony
19 Paris (Norman Paris Trio, The)
2 Paris Sisters, The
88 Paris, Frank
2 Paris, Norman
1 Parish, Bob
2 Parish, Mitchell
15 Parish, Tony
1 Park, Gene
1 Park, Gwen
2 Park, Natalie
4 Parker (Andy Parker and The Plainsmen)
2 Parker, Andy
1 Parker, Bill
1 Parker, Buddy
5 Parker, Cecilia
6 Parker, Charlie
2 Parker, Dee
1 Parker, Dolores
12 Parker, Dorothy
1 Parker, Dr.
5 Parker, Eleanor
2 Parker, Evelyn
2 Parker, Fess
74 Parker, Frank
9 Parker, Franklyn
3 Parker, Gibson
1 Parker, Glen
2 Parker, Jack
1 Parker, Jackie
6 Parker, Jean
1 Parker, Jess
2 Parker, Joe
1 Parker, Johnny
1 Parker, June
1 Parker, Kay

31 Parker, Lew
1 Parker, Mother
3 Parker, Phyllis
1 Parker, Pigmeat
1 Parker, Pinky
1 Parker, Ralph
1 Parker, Robert
123 Parker, Rollon
1 Parker, Sarah
2 Parker, Virginia
3 Parker, Warren
1 Parker, Woody
6 Parkhurst, Douglas
15 Parks, Bert
8 Parks, Larry
2 Parks, Robert
15 Parkyakarkus
1 Parmentier, C. A. J.
2 Parnell, Emory
1 Parnell, Eva
2 Parnell, Henry
1 Parr, Grant
2 Parran, Thomas
1 Parrish, Frank
2 Parrish, Helen
5 Parrish, Judith
1 Parrish, Leslie
1 Parrish, Wayne W.
6 Parsons, Jim
1 Parsons, Joe
1 Parsons, Johnnie
1 Parsons, Kate
13 Parsons, Louella
1 Parsons, Robert
1 Partch, Virgil
1 Partridge, Bellamy
12 Pascal, Greg
1 Pascal, Milton
2 Pasco, Francis
2 Passarelli, Art
1 Pasternak (Joseph Pasternak and The Orchestra)
2 Pasternak, Joseph
4 Pastor (Tony Pastor and His All-Stars)
26 Pastor (Tony Pastor and His Orchestra)
1 Pastor (Tony Pastor and Sons and Orchestra)
4 Pastor, Guy
2 Pastor, Stubby
14 Pastor, Tony
2 Pastrano, Willie
1 Patch, General
1 Patchelli, Frankie
1 Pate, Lionel
1 Paterson, Lanca
1 Patillo, Linda
1 Patman, Wight
4 Patmore, Derek
1 Patri, Angelo
1 Patrick, Dorothy
21 Patrick, Gail
4 Patrick, Gil
1 Patrick, Hugh
1 Patrick, John
7 Patrick, Lee
1 Patrick, Muzz
26 Patrick, Pat
2 Patrick, Roger
2 Patrick, Van
1 Patten, Jack
4 Patten, Luana
1 Patterson Jr., S. J.
8 Patterson, Elizabeth
2 Patterson, Flora
3 Patterson, Floyd
1 Patterson, Holyard
1 Patterson, Joan
1 Patterson, Ken
1 Patterson, Marnie
1 Patterson, Nina
3 Patterson, Robert
1 Patterson, Russell
1 Patterson, W. A.
1 Patterson, Walter
1 Patti, Irene
4 Patton, George
2 Patton, James
1 Patton, Lowell
10 Patton, Mary
1 Paturea, Allen
1 Paul (Ed Paul and His Orchestra)
3 Paul (Eddie Paul and His Orchestra)
50 Paul (Les Paul Trio, The)
64 Paul, Charles
1 Paul, Dolores
2 Paul, Edgerton
1 Paul, Elliot
126 Paul, Les
1 Paul, Marilyn
2 Paul, Norman
37 Paul, Ralph
1 Paul, Richard
1 Paul, Ron
45 Paul, Sidney
1 Paul, Smokey
5 Paulee, Mona
1 Paulette Sisters, The
1 Pauley, Jane
1 Paulist Boys Choir, The
4 Paull, Jarna
1 Pauls, Dix
1 Pavalones, Clem
3 Pawley, Edward
3 Paxinou, Katina
1 Paxon, Bill
4 Paxton (George Paxton and His Orchestra)
1 Paxton, Theodore
4 Paxton, Tom
1 Payne, Benny
21 Payne, Bruce
1 Payne, Catherine
1 Payne, Darwin
23 Payne, John
2 Payne, Les
4 Payne, Sally
162 Payne, Virginia
1 Payne, Walter
1 Payton, Louella
10 Peabody, Eddie
1 Peace, Dan
1 Peaches and Herb
1 Peale, Mrs. Norman Vincent
1 Peale, Norman
11 Peale, Norman Vincent
11 Peale, Richard
21 Pearce, Al
1 Pearce, Eric
2 Pearce, Mildred
4 Pearl (Ray Pearl and His Orchestra)
2 Pearl, Arnold
5 Pearl, Bert
23 Pearl, Cousin Minnie
2 Pearl, Hal
11 Pearl, Jack
1 Pearl, Maury
1 Pearson, Albie
1 Pearson, Anthony
4 Pearson, Beatrice
1 Pearson, Ben
6 Pearson, Drew
1 Pearson, Eleanor
29 Pearson, Fort
92 Pearson, GeGe
1 Pearson, Hugo
23 Pearson, Leon
11 Pearson, Lester
1 Pearson, Louise Randall
1 Pearson, Mort
1 Pearson, T. Gilbert
105 Pearson, Ted
505 Peary, Harold
1 Pease, Jim
12 Peattie, Yvonne
1 Pechman, Joseph
1 Peck, Bill
4 Peck, Charles
1 Peck, Ed
1 Peck, Geraldine
32 Peck, Gregory
1 Peck, Robert
1 Peckelow, Sam
1 Pecson, Elorima
1 Peddap, Michael
4 Pederson, Kenneth
1 Pederson, Tommy
1 Peel, June
50 Peerce, Jan
1 Peers, Leon
1 Peeze, Sharon
1 Pegoskin, S. Lee
1 Pektos, Mihri
1 Pell (Dave Pell and The Dave Pell Singers)
2 Pell, Dave
1 Pellegrin, Frank
3 Pelletier, Louis
15 Pelletier, Vincent
4 Pelletier, Wilfred
2 Peluso (Thomas Peluso and His Orchestra)
2 Peluso, Thomas
1 Pemberton, Brock
9 Pembroke, George
3 Penario, Joe
3 Pendleton, Andrew
1 Pendleton, Gaylord
1 Pendleton, James
4 Pendleton, Nat
4 Pendleton, Steve
2 Penguins, The
17 Penman, Charles
1 Penman, Lee
1 Penn, Leo
1 Penn, Robert
1 Pennario, Leonard
1 Pennel, John
6 Pennell, Bill
12 Pennell, Elizabeth
15 Penner, Joe
1 Pennington, Lee
1 Penny (Hank Penny and His Western Dance Band)
2 Penny, Edmund
6 Penny, Frank
1 Pentecost, Hugh
2 Pep, Willie
1 Peppard, George
2 Pepper Uppers, The
1 Pepper, Art
4 Pepper, Claude
4 Pepper, Jack
2 Pepple, Sidney
2 Pepsi Cola Concert Band, The
2 Percival, John
1 Percy, Edward
1 Percy, Senator
4 Perelman, S. J.
1 Pererra, Tony
1 Peres, Shimon
1 Peretti, Hugo
1 Peretz, Issac Roll
1 Perez (Chui Perez and His Argentine Tango Orchestra)
1 Perez, Jose
7 Perkins, Albert
1 Perkins, Frances
1 Perkins, Jack
1 Perkins, Lew
1 Perkins, Osgood
1 Perkins, Porter J.
8 Perkins, Ray
9 Perkins, Richard
1 Perkins, Ron
2 Perkins, Tony
1 Perkoff, Stuart
1 Perlman, Itzahk
22 Perot, H. Ross
1 Perot, Margot
1 Perranowski, Ron
4 Perrier (Mishel Perrier and His Orchestra)
14 Perrier, Mishel
2 Perrin, Curley
6 Perrin, Lloyd
1 Perrin, Mack
2 Perrin, Nat
1 Perrin, Ruth
40 Perrin, Sam
469 Perrin, Vic
54 Perrott, Ruth
5 Perry (Al Kealoha Perry and His Orchestra)
3 Perry, Betty
11 Perry, Bill
8 Perry, Charles
18 Perry, David
1 Perry, Frank
1 Perry, Fred
1 Perry, Jack
1 Perry, Joan
1 Perry, Katherine
1 Perry, Phyllis
1 Perry, Ronnie
1 Perry, Vincent
6 Perryman, Lloyd
1 Persen, Kristen A.
2 Pershing, John J.
1 Pershing, Yvonne
1 Persina, David
5 Persoff, Nehemiah
1 Person (Houston Person Quartet)
5 Persons, Fern
3 Peske, Johnny
1 Peskin, Dina
1 Petain, Henri
1 Petardi, Bernie
13 Petch, Gladys
8 Peter Paul and Mary
2 Peter, Muffet
2 Peters Sisters, The
1 Peters, Bernadette
21 Peters, Brock
1 Peters, Cortez
1 Peters, Don
5 Peters, Jean
1 Peters, Joan
36 Peters, Ken
3 Peters, Laurie
1 Peters, Loraine
5 Peters, Paul
1 Peters, Roberta
1 Peters, Rollo
8 Peters, Susan
1 Peters, Tim
1 Peters, Tommy
2 Peterson
1 Peterson (Dick Peterson and His Vibratones)
1 Peterson (Oscar Peterson and His Orchestra)
3 Peterson (Oscar Peterson Trio, The)
1 Peterson (Tommy Peterson and His Orchestra)
1 Peterson Brothers, The
16 Peterson, Arthur
1 Peterson, Ben
1 Peterson, Carol
1 Peterson, Carolyn C.
1 Peterson, Chuck
3 Peterson, Curt
1 Peterson, Donald
1 Peterson, Dorothy
11 Peterson, Elmer
16 Peterson, Howard
1 Peterson, L. E.
1 Peterson, Larry
1 Peterson, Len
3 Peterson, Lenka
2 Peterson, Melinda
1 Peterson, Nan
2 Peterson, Oscar
1 Peterson, Ralph Howard
3 Peterson, Rod
1 Peterson, Roger Tory
1 Petrach, Rudolph
1 Petrash, Don
1 Petrie, Bob
1 Petrie, Charlie
92 Petrie, George
80 Petrie, Howard
6 Petrillo (Cesar Petrillo and His Orchestra)
1 Petrillo, James
6 Petrone, Rocco
14 Petruzzi, Jack
8 Petticini, Richard George

2 Pettiford (Oscar Pettiford Trio, The)
8 Pettiford, Oscar
1 Pettijohn, Lynnjoy
1 Pettijohn, Otho
7 Pettingill, Samuel B.
2 Pettis, Kenneth
1 Pettit, Ed
1 Petty (Emil Petty and His Orchestra)
2 Petty, Frank
3 Peyton, Patrick
14 Pfeffer, David
3 Pfoeffer, Bob
1 Phelan, Frank
1 Phelan, Pat
1 Phelps Jr., A. A.
5 Phelps, Eleanor
1 Phelps, Jackie
1 Phelps, Robert
1 Phen, Robert
1 Philadelphia Navy Yard Band
4 Philadelphia Orchestra, The
1 Philharmonic Club Orchestra, The
1 Philharmonic Trio, The
1 Phillipe, Andre
11 Phillips, Arthur
290 Phillips, Barney
2 Phillips, Bernard
1 Phillips, Dickie
1 Phillips, Esther
2 Phillips, Flip
1 Phillips, George T.
3 Phillips, Howard
1 Phillips, James
2 Phillips, Judson
1 Phillips, Kate
2 Phillips, Margaret
1 Phillips, Marie
1 Phillips, Mary
42 Phillips, Paul
2 Phillips, Peter
1 Phillips, Ruth
1 Phillips, Steven
1 Phillips, Stu
1 Phinney, William
1 Phisher, Bill
3 Piaf, Edith
77 Piastro, Mishel
5 Piatagorsky, Gregor
10 Piazza, Marguerite
4 Pichel, Irving
10 Pickens Sisters, The
22 Pickens, Jane
51 Picker, Sylvia
1 Pickering, William
1 Pickett, Andy
10 Pickford, Mary
1 Pickles, Dorothy
1 Picon, Molly
38 Pidgeon, Walter
1 Pieck, Ludwig
101 Pied Pipers, The
1 Pieran, Bob
1 Pierce (Nat Pierce Frankie Kapp Juggernaut Big Band, The)
1 Pierce (Ross Pierce and His Orchestra)
1 Pierce (Webb Pierce and His Wandering Boys)
1 Pierce, Alan
1 Pierce, Ann
1 Pierce, Betty
1 Pierce, Billie
1 Pierce, Dee Dee
39 Pierce, James
1 Pierce, Leon
2 Pierce, Madeleine
87 Pierce, Paul
18 Pierce, Sam
1 Pierce, Waldo
7 Pierce, Webb
8 Pierce, William F.
2 Pierlot, Premier
1 Pierney, Duncan
6 Pierpoint, Robert
1 Pierson, Arthur
1 Pietermaat, Reiner
1 Pigley, William
1 Pillar (Max Pillar and His Orchestra)
6 Pilot, Bernice
7 Pinafores, The
1 Pinario, Joe
19 Pinchon, Ed
1 Pinchot, Rosamon
1 Pinckney, Ann
1 Pine, Phillip
1 Pineapple, Johnny
3 Pinero, Arthur Wing
2 Pingatore, Mike
1 Pink, Louis H.
34 Pinkard, Fred
1 Pinkham, R. L.
1 Pinkley, Virgil
1 Pinto Pete
1 Pinto Pete and His Ranch Boys
22 Pinza, Ezio
105 Pious, Minerva
1 Piper, H. Beam
4 Piper, Penny
1 Piper, Theresa
1 Pirandello
4 Pironne, George
1 Pisner, Marvin
2 Pitkin, Walter
2 Pitney, Gene
37 Pitoniak, Ann
5 Pitt (Merle Pitt and His Orchestra)
2 Pittendry, Ken
1 Pittenger, L. A.
13 Pittman, Frank
1 Pitts, Derek
25 Pitts, ZaSu
1 Pittsburgh Painters Orchestra, The
5 Pittsburgh Painters, The
1 Pittsburgh Symphony Orchestra, The
1 Pius XI
2 Pius XII
1 Pizarro II, Juan
2 Plainsmen, The
1 Plambeck, Herb
2 Plato
1 Platt, Bob
2 Platt, Dick
1 Platt, Ed
1 Platt, Joseph B.
3 Platters, The
6 Platts, Alma
1 Playboy Quartet, The
4 Playboys, The
2 Playfair, Wendy
1 Playtonics, The
1 Pleasure Sisters, The
2 Pledger, Doug
1 Plotkin, Abraham
4 Plotnikoff, Eugene
1 Plummer, Don Eugene
3 Plummer, Gene
1 Plumsen, George
1 Plunkett, Walter
1 Podell, David L.
8 Podmore, William
47 Poe, Edgar Allan
15 Poe, James
2 Pogge, Oscar C.
2 Pogue, William
12 Pohl, Frederick
1 Pointon, Loretta
1 Poitier, Sidney
3 Pola, Eddie
1 Poland, Bob
8 Polari, David
2 Poleman, Horace I.
1 Polen, Lou
115 Polen, Nat
6 Polesie, Herb
1 Poletti, Lieutenant Governor
1 Police Department Band
1 Polimini, Anthony
1 Poling, Daniel A.
1 Polk, C. Audrey
1 Polk, George
8 Polk, Gordon
8 Polk, Lucy Ann
1 Polk, Mrs. George
39 Polk, Vernon
1 Polka Dots, The
5 Pollack (Ben Pollack and His Pick-A-Rib Boys)
2 Pollack (Ben Pollack Dixieland Band)
5 Pollack, Ben
2 Pollack, Bob
8 Pollack, Channing
3 Pollack, James
1 Pollack, John
1 Pollack, Lou
3 Pollack, Louis
1 Polombo, Albert
1 Polton, Bob
1 Polton, Lionel
1 Pomerantz, Charlie
1 Pomeroy, Hugh R.
1 Pompano, Dr.
1 Pond, Frederick L.
1 Pond, Geoffrey
1 Poney, Brian
1 Ponnamperuma, Cyril
2 Pons, Beatrice
1 Pons, Dorothea
24 Pons, Lily
2 Ponselle, Rosa
3 Pool, Sam
8 Poole, Bob
1 Poole, L. F.
1 Pope, Arthur Upham
1 Pope, Dale
1 Pope, Gene
1 Pope, Joseph
1 Pope, Marshall
1 Pope, Patty
1 Pope, Tony
1 Popkin, Zelda
2 Poppele, J. R.
1 Poptie (Frans Poptie and His Quintet)
1 Poretta, Frank
1 Porter (Ray Porter's Esquires)
3 Porter, Bob
1 Porter, Catherine
1 Porter, Catherine Ann
1 Porter, Cole
15 Porter, Del
2 Porter, Garrett
1 Porter, Judy
3 Porter, Katherine Anne
1 Porter, Paul A.
12 Porter, Ray
1 Porter, Roy
8 Porter, Stan
1 Porterfield, Jane
1 Portman, Robert
1 Posey, Roland
2 Posner, Henry
1 Posner, Joseph
1 Posner, Lewis S.
2 Posner, Vladimir
1 Possum Hunters, The
1 Post Jr., William
77 Post, Clayton
2 Post, G. Worthington
1 Post, M. D.
2 Post, Thomas
17 Post, Tom
1 Potatoe Bugs, The
1 Potofski
1 Potter, Andrew
1 Potter, Andy
1 Potter, C. J.
5 Potter, Dale
3 Potter, Hank
1 Potter, Peter
1 Potts, Mary
1 Potts, Willis
2 Pound, Ezra
4 Powell (Andy Powell and His Orchestra)
5 Powell (Teddy Powell and His Orchestra)
1 Powell, Adam Clayton
1 Powell, Art
1 Powell, Bud
4 Powell, Colin
209 Powell, Dick
1 Powell, Edward
1 Powell, Elaine
12 Powell, Eleanor
19 Powell, Ginnie
2 Powell, James
29 Powell, Jane
3 Powell, Jody
1 Powell, Ken
2 Powell, Luther
1 Powell, Madelein
8 Powell, Mel
2 Powell, Richard
18 Powell, Specs
1 Powell, Teddy
1 Powell, Victor
36 Powell, William
1 Powells, Beatrice
1 Power, Margaret
1 Power, Paul Scully
35 Power, Tyrone
4 Powers, Charles
1 Powers, Francis J.
1 Powers, Gary
1 Powers, Harry
1 Powers, Jimmy
2 Powers, John
2 Powers, John Robert
2 Powers, Leona
3 Powers, Mala
1 Powers, Patty
1 Powers, Peggy
1 Powers, Robert
1 Powers, Ron
1 Powers, Tom
2 Prado, Prez
3 Prager, Manny
2 Prager, Sammy
1 Prager, Stanley
1 Pramoj, M. R. Seni
2 Pratt, Dallas
5 Pratt, Fletcher
1 Pratt, William B.
1 Prayers, The
1 Preisser, June
2 Premice, Josephine
4 Preminger, Otto
1 Prenderbill, Maybelle
19 Prentiss, Ed
37 Prescott, Allen
3 Prescott, Bob
1 Prescott, Elsie
10 Prescott, Norman
1 Prescott, Orville
1 Preservation Hall Band
3 Presley, Elvis
1 Presley, Vernon
1 Pressler, Larry
5 Pressman, Gabe
2 Pressman, Lee
1 Preston
4 Preston, Joey
7 Preston, Kathy
18 Preston, Robert
3 Preston, Walter
1 Previn (Andre Previn and His Orchestra)
4 Previn (Andre Previn Trio, The)
1 Previn (Charles Previn and His Orchestra)
12 Previn, Andre
1 Previn, Charles
2 Previtali, Fernando
1 Price (Jesse Price and His Quartet)
2 Price (Ray Price and His Cherokee Cowboys)
1 Price, Alberta
9 Price, Barbara
1 Price, Bob
8 Price, Byron
1 Price, Donald
1 Price, Eugenie
5 Price, Georgie
1 Price, Gerald

1 Price, Gwilym A.
42 Price, John
1 Price, Julie
1 Price, Lee
2 Price, Leontyne
1 Price, Peter
1 Price, Precious
4 Price, Ray
8 Price, Roger
1 Price, Tony
141 Price, Vincent
2 Price, William
1 Prichard, Peter
1 Priddy, Jerry
1 Prideaux, James
6 Priest, Natalie
4 Priestly, J. B.
1 Priestly, Harriet
1 Pright, Pat
2 Prim, Arthur
13 Prima (Louis Prima and His Orchestra)
19 Prima, Louis
1 Primavera, Joseph
13 Prime, Harry
2 Primeaux, Gary
1 Primrose, William
1 Prince Felix
1 Prince Phillip
1 Prince, Bob
2 Prince, Eileen
6 Prince, Frank
1 Prince, Jack
1 Prince, John
9 Prince, William
7 Princess Elizabeth
1 Princess Juliana
2 Princess Martha
1 Princess Tsahai
1 Princey, Carl
1 Pringle, Don
1 Pringle, Eileen
1 Pringle, William
2 Prinz, Rosemary
1 Prinze, Freddie
1 Pripps (Eddie Pripps and His Orchestra)
1 Pritt, D. N.
1 Probinson, Martin
2 Probst, George
1 Probst, Leonard
1 Procope, Russell
8 Proctor, Bernard J.
3 Proctor, Phillip
1 Prodi, Romano
2 Professor Koleslaw
1 Project Nine, The
2 Prophet, Johnny
2 Proust, Peter
2 Prouty, Olive Higgins
1 Prowse, Juliet
2 Proxmire, William
43 Prud'Homme, Cameron
1 Prue, Jeannie
2 Pruitt, Carl
5 Pruitt, Louise
5 Pryor (Larry Pryor and His Blue Coal Orchestra)
1 Pryor, Arthur
35 Pryor, Don
1 Pryor, John
1 Pryor, Margerie
9 Pryor, Nick
93 Pryor, Roger
2 Puckett (Gary Puckett and The Union Gap)
22 Pudney, Earle
1 Puente (Tito Puente and His Orchestra)
1 Puga, Maria Christina
16 Pugh, Jess
3 Pugh, Madelyn
1 Pulley, B. S.
15 Pultz, Neal
1 Purcell (Tommy Purcell and His Orchestra)
2 Purcell, Bob
1 Purcell, Keith
20 Purdum, Herb
1 Purdum, R. B.
1 Purdy, Richard
3 Pursell, Gene
1 Pursely, Johnny
1 Pursuit, Dan
2 Purvis, Ian
1 Purvis, Melvyn
3 Pushkin, Alexander
1 Putman, Terry
37 Putnam, George
6 Putnam, George Carson
4 Putter, Peter
3 Putterman, David
1 Pyatt, Keith
3 Pyle, Ernie
1 Pyne, Joe

CBS
WHIO
DAYTON, OHIO
START OUTSIDE
SPEED
Q

3 Quaide, William
1 Qualen, John
1 Quarrels, Donald A.
3 Quartararo, Florence
1 Quattrochi, Frank
1 Quayle, Anthony
30 Quayle, Dan
2 Quayle, Marilyn
1 Quayle, Marjorie
1 Queen
9 Queen Elizabeth
2 Queen Juliana
5 Queen Wilhelmina
1 Queen's Maids, The
4 Queen, Ellery
1 Queener, Charlie
5 Queller, Eve
1 Quello, Olga
1 Quentin, Patrick
2 Questel, Mae
1 Queston, Paul
1 Quick, Robert
1 Quigley, Juanita
5 Quigley, Quig
6 Quillan, Joe
2 Quillen, John
1 Quine, Richard
2 Quinlan, Roberta
2 Quinn, Alfred
3 Quinn, Anthony
52 Quinn, Bill
1 Quinn, Bob
4 Quinn, Carmel
344 Quinn, Don
1 Quinn, Grace
1 Quinn, Joe
1 Quinn, Mary C.
1 Quinn, Pat
1 Quinn, Thomas
3 Quinn, William
1 Quinnan, Dorothy
1 Quinnan, Dorothy Cheney
2 Quintet Of The Hot Club Of France, The
1 Quirter, Bill

DATE RECORDED
SERIAL NO.
NOT TO BE USED FOR BROADCAST PURPOSES
PROGRAM TIME
MIN. SEC.
THIS IS A
LATERAL
USE ACETATE RECORD NEEDLES
WGN
LATERAL
33⅓
START INSIDE
RECORDING
TITLE
R
441 NORTH MICHIGAN AVENUE
CHICAGO

1 R and H Boys, The
1 Raaf, Vici
1 Raber, Paul J.
1 Rabey, Derek
1 Rabin, Jonathan
3 Rabin, Michael
2 Rabin, Yitzhak
3 Rabiner, Charles
1 Rabinowitz, Harry
1 Rabson, Edward
4 Raby, John
2 Rachel and Oswald
1 Radatz, Dick
1 Radcliff, William J.
26 Radcliffe, Virginia
1 Raddis, Leslie
1 Radee, John
1 Rader, Alan
1 Rader, Charles
1 Raderman, Lou
1 Radieaux, Robert
1 Radio Arte Quartet, The
1 Radio Pakistan Orchestra, The
8 Radio Rogues, The
5 Radmilovich, Milton
9 Raeburn (Boyd Raeburn and His Orchestra)
1 Raeburn, Boyd
292 Raeburn, Bryna
1 Raeburn, John
1 Rael (Jack Rael and His Orchestra)
1 Rafaelson, Samuel
1 Rafall, Paul
1 Raffaelli, Angelo
2 Rafferty, Chips
1 Rafferty, James
13 Raffetto, Michael
1 Rafitte, Ken
23 Raft, George
1 Ragaway, Martin
3 Ragge, Ed
1 Raggediers, The
3 Ragland, Rags
1 Rahe, Jergen
11 Raht, Katharine
1 Raimondi, Lillian
3 Rainbow Ranch Boys, The
4 Raine, Jennifer
1 Raine, Larry
1 Raine, Lorrie
9 Rainer, Luise
4 Raines, Ella
5 Rainger, Ralph
32 Rains, Claude
1 Rains, Jack
1 Rains, Ted
1 Rait, Bob
1 Rait, George
3 Raitt, John
1 Rajcsanyi, Peter
1 Rake, Kitty
1 Ralston, Bill
1 Ralston, Robert
2 Ralston, Vera
5 Rambeau, Marjorie
1 Ramblers, The
16 Ramirez, Carlos
1 Ramon, John
10 Ramona
2 Ramona and Her Men Of Music
1 Rampino, Michael
5 Ramsay, Helen
4 Ramsay, Wally
1 Ramsby, George
3 Ramsey, Jim
1 Ramsey, John
1 Ramsey, Mrs. John
1 Ranaudo, Rick
1 Ranch Boys, The
1 Rand, Dick
1 Rand, Edwin
4 Rand, Kelly
1 Rand, Sally
1 Rand, Sidney
1 Randall (Gordie Randall and His Orchestra)
1 Randall, Bill
1 Randall, Brooks
1 Randall, Charles
1 Randall, Doc
4 Randall, Earl
1 Randall, Edwin
1 Randall, George

2 Randall, Meg
2 Randall, Tommy
10 Randall, Tony
1 Randazzo, Teddy
1 Randel, Elinor
1 Randell, Ron
1 Randolph, A. Phillip
29 Randolph, Amanda
1 Randolph, Dexter
17 Randolph, Don
171 Randolph, Isabel
2 Randolph, Jack
1 Randolph, Jennings
4 Randolph, John
32 Randolph, Joyce
549 Randolph, Lillian
2 Randolph, Mary
32 Randolph, William
1 Randow, Carl
1 Randy and The Rainbows
1 Raney, Sue
2 Raney, William S.
4 Rangel, Charles
1 Rankin, Jeanette
8 Rankin, Peter
1 Ransome, Glen
1 Ransome, Jo Ann
1 Ransome, Norman
1 Ransome, Steven
1 Ransome, Susan
1 Ranucci, Anthony
1 Rao, Benegal
1 Raphael, Gerianne
1 Rapp (Barney Rapp and His New Englanders)
1 Rapp, Barney
1 Rapp, Bill
12 Rapp, Phil
2 Rapp, William Jordan
2 Rarick (John Rarick and His Orchestra)
1 Raschi, Vic
4 Rash, Bryson
13 Raskyn, Sam
2 Rasofsky, Yuri
1 Raspodino, Fred
2 Rath, Bill
125 Rathbone, Basil
1 Rathbone, Cynthia
27 Rather, Dan
1 Ratner, Herbert
14 Ratoff, Gregory
2 Rattigan, Officer
2 Rattigan, Terence
1 Ratto, Sidney
1 Ratzjczak, Anthony
1 Rauch, Fred R.
6 Ravazza (Carl Ravazza and His Orchestra)
6 Ravazza, Carl
1 Ravel (Arthur Ravel and His Orchestra)
7 Ravenal, Florence
1 Ravenscroft, Therell
7 Ravetch, Irving
1 Rawlings, E. J.
2 Rawlings, Marjorie
1 Rawlings, Ray
52 Rawlinson, Herbert
2 Rawls, Lou
47 Rawson, Ron
1 Raxon (David Raxon and His Orchestra)
2 Ray, Alan
1 Ray, Harry
1 Ray, Irmay
1 Ray, J. Franklin
2 Ray, Joan
2 Ray, John
7 Ray, Johnny
28 Ray, Lea
1 Ray, Oscar
1 Ray, Paula
1 Ray, Rita
3 Rayburn, Gene
1 Rayburn, Noel
7 Rayburn, Sam
2 Raye, Dorothy
1 Raye, Edna
1 Raye, Frank
1 Raye, Gene
41 Raye, Martha
1 Raymer, Erwin
1 Raymond, Allen
4 Raymond, Bill
9 Raymond, Gene
6 Raymond, John
2 Raymond, Mary
1 Raymond, Royal
1 Raymond, Sid
1 Raynes, Bill
1 Razaff, Andy
1 Razumny, Mikhail
1 Rea, Peggy
1 Reade, Charles
3 Reader, Gordon
56 Readick, Frank
55 Readick, Robert
1 Readick, Tommy
1 Reagan, Bernice
1 Reagan, Eleanor
6 Reagan, Nancy
1 Reagan, Neal
492 Reagan, Ronald
1 Reagan, Thomas
1 Reardon, Caspar
1 Reardon, Deems
3 Reardon, Marjorie
1 Reardon, Patricia
1 Reardon, Tim
9 Reasoner, Harry
2 Reber, Carl
15 Rebner, Edward
1 Rechichar, Bert
1 Rector, Thomas
1 Red River Dave
1 Red, Irvin
29 Redd, Robert L.
1 Reddy, Helen
20 Reddy, Tom
1 Redeker, Bill
1 Redfield, Robert
195 Redfield, William
20 Redgrave, Michael
1 Redisch, William
4 Redman (Don Redman and His Orchestra)
1 Redman, Dick
1 Redman, Don
1 Redman, George
2 Redstone, David
1 Redwig, Rod
1 Reece, Jimmy
244 Reed, Alan
3 Reed, Dale
1 Reed, Dan
18 Reed, Donna
1 Reed, Hal
1 Reed, Israel
1 Reed, James
1 Reed, Jared
1 Reed, Jimmy
1 Reed, Kay
1 Reed, Larry
2 Reed, Leonard
4 Reed, Lewis
1 Reed, Paul
1 Reed, Philip
4 Reed, Robert
3 Reed, Roland
5 Reed, Russ
1 Reed, Stanley
3 Reed, Susan
61 Reed, Toby
1 Reed, Veronica
1 Reed, Vivian
2 Reed, Walter
1 Reeg, Leonard
2 Reese, Amos
1 Reese, Anise
2 Reese, Bob
1 Reese, Chairman
1 Reese, Curt
7 Reese, Della
1 Reese, Dorothy
1 Reese, Emma
3 Reese, Ginny
1 Reese, Joy
7 Reese, Peewee
1 Reetz, Arthur
1 Reeve, William
1 Reeves (Reet Veet Reeves and His Orchestra)
2 Reeves, Betty
1 Reeves, Del
91 Reeves, George
14 Reeves, Jim
8 Reeves, John
2 Regal Caballeros, The
1 Regal Pale Orchestra, The
1 Regan, Donald
2 Regan, Kirk
18 Regan, Phil
6 Regeant, Rex
4 Regent, Robert
1 Reggiani, Hilda
1 Reggie, Betty
3 Regot, Henri
33 Reichman (Joe Reichman and His Orchestra)
2 Reichman, Joe
2 Reid (Don Reid and His Orchestra)
1 Reid, Bob
1 Reid, Carl Benton
1 Reid, Daniel A.
6 Reid, Don
1 Reid, Dorothy
1 Reid, Eleanora
1 Reid, Ellen
58 Reid, Elliott
1 Reid, Frances
1 Reid, Helen
4 Reid, Ione
1 Reid, Irene
2 Reid, Joyce
1 Reid, Kate
3 Reid, Leslie
10 Reid, Lucille
1 Reid, Mark
1 Reid, Nancy
1 Reid, Russ
7 Reid, Ted
1 Reid, Whitelaw
1 Reid, William
1 Reig, Harriet
4 Reig, Howard
1 Reiger, John
1 Reikert, Nick
1 Reilly, Henry J.
2 Reimers, Ed
7 Reiner, Carl
2 Reiner, Fritz
3 Reines, Bernard
2 Reinhardt, Django
33 Reinheart, Alice
7 Reinheart, Max
2 Reinmann, John
1 Reis (Reis and Dunn)
14 Reis, Irving
1 Reisenberg, Nadia
3 Reisenfeld (Hugo Riesenfeld and His Orchestra)
3 Reisman (Joe Reisman and His Orchestra)
4 Reisman (Leo Reisman and His Orchestra)
1 Reisman, Stan
2 Remey, Ethel
1 Remington, Mr.
1 Renaldo, Tito
1 Renaud, Artmund
3 Rendon, Jay
1 Rene
17 Rene (Henri Rene and His Orchestra)
5 Rennie, Hedley
3 Rennie, Michael
3 Renthal, Sidney
1 Renwick, Kay
2 Replogle, Elizabeth
2 Repp, Ellen
146 Repp, Guy
7 Reser (Harry Reser and His Orchestra)
1 Reser, Peter
2 Resnick, Judy
1 Resnick, Paul
1 Resnick, Regina
3 Resnick, Sid
9 Ressler, Elmira
1 Reston Jr., James
2 Reston, James
4 Retray, Peter
2 Rettenberg, Milton
1 Reuben, Rabbi
1 Reuther, Walter
6 Revelers, The
2 Revell, Nellie
1 Revell, Roger
6 Revere, Anne
2 Revuers, The
10 Rey (Alvino Rey and His Orchestra)
10 Rey, Alvino
1 Reyes (Chuy Reyes and His Orchestra)
12 Reynard (Jacques Reynard and His Orchestra)
3 Reynard, Ken
9 Reynaud, Paul
1 Reynolds (Tommy Reynolds and His Orchestra)
9 Reynolds, Abe
1 Reynolds, Al
1 Reynolds, Allie
1 Reynolds, Audrey
1 Reynolds, Blake
14 Reynolds, Brad
10 Reynolds, Debbie
5 Reynolds, Frank
2 Reynolds, Gene
11 Reynolds, Marjorie
33 Reynolds, Quentin
1 Reynolds, Texas Bob
1 Reynolds, Tony
1 Rezek, Terry
1 Rhinehart, Mary Roberts
2 Rhoads, Dusty
6 Rhodes, Betty
4 Rhodes, Betty Jane
1 Rhodes, Charlotte
2 Rhodes, Cornelius P.
2 Rhodes, Erik
1 Rhodes, Genevieve
1 Rhodes, Homer
1 Rhodes, Jane
4 Rhodes, John
1 Rhubarb Red and His Rubes
145 Rhymer, Paul
4 Rhymer, Virgil
6 Rhythm Boys, The
4 Rhythm Five, The
8 Rhythm Girls, The
1 Rhythm Kings, The
13 Rhythm Makers Orchestra
1 Rhythm Makers, The
1 Rhythm Rascals, The
2 Rhythm Riders, The
60 Rhythmaires, The
1 Rhythmettes, The
1 Ribicoff, Abraham
2 Ricardi, Enrico
1 Ricardi, William
2 Ricci, Ruggiero
1 Rice, Bob
9 Rice, Craig
2 Rice, Del
2 Rice, Edward
3 Rice, Edward A.
5 Rice, Elmer
4 Rice, Florence
21 Rice, Grantland
1 Rice, Herbert
3 Rice, Marjorie
138 Rice, Rosemary
1 Rice, Warner G.
7 Rich (Buddy Rich and His Orchestra)
1 Rich (Buddy Rich Quartet, The)
37 Rich (Freddie Rich and His Orchestra)
38 Rich, Buddy
1 Rich, Freddie

1 Rich, Irene
2 Rich, John
5 Rich, Vernon
1 Richards (Dal Richards and His Orchestra)
1 Richards Jr., Danny
1 Richards, Ann
1 Richards, Beverly
42 Richards, Carol
1 Richards, Dal
2 Richards, Donald
1 Richards, Emil
9 Richards, Frank
6 Richards, Grant
1 Richards, Harriet
1 Richards, Johnny
1 Richards, Lloyd
44 Richards, Paul
1 Richards, R.
47 Richards, Robert L.
1 Richards, Shirley
1 Richards, Susan
7 Richards, Sylvia
1 Richards, Trudy
1 Richards, Vincent
1 Richards, Walter Hank
3 Richardson, Bobby
1 Richardson, Doc
2 Richardson, Elliot
1 Richardson, Emery
1 Richardson, Hamilton
1 Richardson, Louise
33 Richardson, Ralph
1 Richardson, Robert S.
1 Richardson, Rod
9 Richardson, Stanley
1 Richberg, Donald R.
2 Richie Jr., Andy T.
1 Richman (Harry Richman and His Orchestra)
2 Richman (Harry Richman and The Dodge Orchestra)
41 Richman, Harry
17 Richman, Marion
7 Richmond, June
2 Richmond, Marian
1 Richmond, Russell B.
1 Richter, Dr.
1 Richter, Pat
2 Rickaby, Ruth
21 Rickenbacker, Eddie
1 Rickenbacker, Mrs. Eddie
2 Rickey, Branch
23 Rickles, Don
3 Rickman, Bob
1 Rickman, Doug
1 Rickover, Hyman
1 Ricky, Paul
15 Ricou, Lionel
2 Riddell, Betty
1 Ridder, Maggie
40 Riddle (Nelson Riddle and His Orchestra)
1 Riddle, Almeda
41 Riddle, Jimmy
2 Riddle, Nelson
1 Riddle, Tab
6 Riddlers, The
2 Ride, Sally
1 Ridenauer, Dr.
1 Ridenouer, Rex
1 Rider, Al
1 Rider, Lee
3 Riders Of The Purple Sage, The
1 Ridge, Thomas
2 Ridgely, John
2 Ridges, Stanley
2 Ridgeway, Matthew
1 Riegel, Dan
3 Riegel, Don
1 Rieman, Roger
1 Rieseberg, Harry
1 Riesel, Victor
1 Rifkin, Sam
1 Rifus, Harry
1 Rigal, Delia
1 Riggs, Bobby
1 Riggs, Dudley
39 Riggs, Glenn
78 Riggs, L. A. Speed
1 Riggs, Lynn
6 Riggs, Tommy
1 Righter, Carrol
3 Rigney, Bill
2 Riker, Frank
1 Riley, Arthur
2 Riley, Dick
1 Riley, Helen
1 Riley, Hugh
1 Riley, Jack
1 Riley, Jeannie C.
1 Riley, John
1 Riley, Margaret
2 Riley, Mike
2 Riley, Walter
3 Riley, William
5 Rinard, Florence
1 Rine, Hal
7 Rines, Joe
1 Ring, Teddy
1 Ringle, Don
1 Ringwold, Roy
1 Ringwold, Rudolph
3 Rinker, Al
1 Rio, Rita
322 Rio, Rosa
1 Rios, Elvira
1 Rios, Rosita
1 Ripley
3 Ripley, Betty
106 Ripley, Joe
22 Ripley, Robert
8 Rippe, Bill
3 Risdon, Elizabeth
3 Risdon, Henry M.
1 Risener, Ruth
2 Risman, Hope
25 Riss, Dan
1 Rissling, Bob
8 Rita
6 Ritchard, Cyril
1 Ritchie, Jean
1 Ritner Twins, The
1 Ritter, Dick
18 Ritter, Tex
80 Ritter, Thelma
12 Ritz Brothers, The
1 Riva, Maria
1 Rivera, Chita
1 Rivers, Jack
1 Rivers, Joan
1 Rivers, Sam
2 Rivers, Tony
1 Rivett, Roan
1 Rizzo, Florita
8 Rizzuto, Phil
3 Roach Jr., Hal
3 Roach, Hal
5 Roach, Max
21 Roark, Jack
1 Roark, Robert
5 Robard, John
1 Robards, Jason
2 Robb, Charles
1 Robb, Gordon
1 Robb, Harvey
2 Robb, Inez
204 Robb, Marylee
1 Robbins, Alan
144 Robbins, Fred
3 Robbins, Gail
3 Robbins, Isabel
1 Robbins, Jack
2 Robbins, James
1 Robbins, June
9 Robbins, Marty
1 Robbins, Mildred
1 Robbins, Norma
1 Robel (Jolly Jack Robel and His Orchestra)
1 Rober, Richard
1 Robert, Albert
10 Robert, John
2 Roberti, Lyda
1 Roberts (Cal Robert's Swingers)
2 Roberts, Andy
3 Roberts, Barry
2 Roberts, Betty Jo
3 Roberts, Beverly
2 Roberts, Clete
3 Roberts, Cokie
2 Roberts, Dave
2 Roberts, Dick
25 Roberts, Ed
1 Roberts, Elizabeth Maddox
2 Roberts, Eric
1 Roberts, George
1 Roberts, Henry
2 Roberts, Jane
9 Roberts, Joan
266 Roberts, Ken
3 Roberts, Leona
1 Roberts, Leslie
2 Roberts, Lloyd
1 Roberts, Lucky
8 Roberts, Lynn
2 Roberts, Margaret
1 Roberts, Mary
1 Roberts, Mimi
1 Roberts, Mrs. Oral
1 Roberts, Needham
7 Roberts, Oral
4 Roberts, Paul
7 Roberts, Peter
8 Roberts, Steve
1 Roberts, Steven
42 Roberts, Tony
1 Roberts, Tracy
2 Roberts, Wallace
1 Roberts, Zelma
1 Robertson Jr., Ben
18 Robertson, Arnold
1 Robertson, Bill
1 Robertson, Dick
3 Robertson, Don
1 Robertson, Ed
4 Robertson, Eddie
1 Robertson, Elizabeth
24 Robertson, General
138 Robertson, Larry
1 Robertson, Lou
1 Robertson, Oscar
2 Robertson, Pat
1 Robertson, Ralph
1 Robertson, Robert
24 Robertson, Steven
2 Robertson, Stuart
1 Robertson, Texas Jim
28 Robertson, Walter M.
7 Robeson, Paul
2 Robin Sisters, The
4 Robin, Leo
3 Robins, The
3 Robinson
4 Robinson (Carson Robison and His Buckaroos)
1 Robinson (Carson Robison and His C. R. Ranch Boys)
1 Robinson (Smokey Robinson and The Miracles)
1 Robinson, Ann
30 Robinson, Bartlett
10 Robinson, Bill Bojangles
1 Robinson, Brooks
1 Robinson, Dewey
7 Robinson, Earl
84 Robinson, Edward G.
1 Robinson, Fava
4 Robinson, Florence
93 Robinson, Frances
1 Robinson, Frank
3 Robinson, Frank M.
1 Robinson, Henry Morton
2 Robinson, Hubbel
42 Robinson, Jack
4 Robinson, Jackie
1 Robinson, Jim
69 Robinson, John
21 Robinson, Larry
1 Robinson, Lee
1 Robinson, Lennon
1 Robinson, Lisa
1 Robinson, Marvin
1 Robinson, Maurice
2 Robinson, Mayor
1 Robinson, Mrs. Edward G.
1 Robinson, Paul
4 Robinson, Prescott
1 Robinson, Rad
1 Robinson, Rudie
2 Robinson, Sugar Ray
1 Robinson, Virginia
1 Robinson, William E.
1 Robison, Carson
3 Robson, Flora
1 Robson, Mark
6 Robson, May
179 Robson, William N.
2 Roby, Art
2 Roby, Vic
6 Rocco, Maurice
1 Roche String Quartet, The
1 Roche, Mary
1 Rochelle, Claire
391 Rochester
1 Rochester Philharmonic Orchestra, The
4 Rochester Pops Orchestra, The
1 Rochester Symphony Orchestra, The
1 Rock (Jack Rock and The Yacht Club Boys)
23 Rock, George
1 Rock, Warren
1 Rockefeller, Jay
1 Rockefeller, John D.
11 Rockefeller, Nelson
1 Rocket Richard
1 Rockland, Ross
6 Rockwell, Bob
5 Rockwell, Doc
1 Rockwell, R. J.
6 Rockwell, Rocky
1 Rockwood, Jerry
1 Rod, Phillip
1 Rodan, Luis
1 Rodd, Marcia
9 Roddenberry, Gene
2 Rodding, W. Stewart
1 Rodeheaver, Homer
1 Rodell, Dolores
1 Rodendorf Sisters, The
3 Rodgers (Rodgers and Hammerstein)
1 Rodgers (Rodgers and Hart)
13 Rodgers, Richard
1 Rodier, Renee
2 Rodin (Gil Rodin and His Orchestra)
1 Rodin, Mel
2 Rodino, Peter
4 Rodman, Howard
1 Rodman, Nan
63 Rodman, Victor
15 Rodney, Don
1 Rodriguez, Adeline
1 Rodriguez, Joseph C.
7 Rodriguez, Willie
8 Rodzinski, Artur
1 Roe, Esther
1 Roe, Margo
1 Roe, Raymond
1 Roed, Elsa Margaretta
1 Roemheld, Hans
1 Rogan, James
1 Rogel, Albert S.
2 Roger (Roger Roger and His Orchestra)
1 Roger (Eddie Roger and His Orchestra)
1 Rogers
1 Rogers (Billie Rogers and Her Orchestra)
2 Rogers (Shorty Rogers and His Orchestra)
1 Rogers Jr., James
31 Rogers Jr., Will
2 Rogers, Al
13 Rogers, Barbara Ellen
20 Rogers, Bill
2 Rogers, Billie
4 Rogers, Buddy

2 Rogers, Charles Buddy
14 Rogers, Clyde
1 Rogers, Dick
1 Rogers, Don
1 Rogers, Earl
1 Rogers, Edward
3 Rogers, Eileen
49 Rogers, Ginger
3 Rogers, Grace
1 Rogers, Howard Emmet
3 Rogers, Jean
4 Rogers, Jimmy
2 Rogers, Kenny
7 Rogers, King
1 Rogers, Lee
1 Rogers, Leila
1 Rogers, Mark
1 Rogers, Marshall
1 Rogers, Mary
5 Rogers, Roc
2 Rogers, Roswell
103 Rogers, Roy
4 Rogers, Roz
2 Rogers, Rusty
2 Rogers, Shorty
4 Rogers, Smokey Joe
1 Rogers, Tim
5 Rogers, Timmy
7 Rogers, Will
1 Rogerson, Bruce
9 Roget, Betty
1 Roggero, Margaret
1 Rogofsky, Howard
3 Rohde, Ruth Bryan
3 Roland, Alex
2 Roland, Helen
8 Roland, Henry
1 Roland, John
9 Roland, Ralph
1 Rolando, Juan
7 Rolfe (B. A. Rolfe and His Orchestra)
1 Rolfe (B. A. Rolfe and The D'Artega Orchestra)
2 Rolfe, B. A.
4 Rolfe, Eric
1 Rolfe, Frederick
1 Rolfe, John
1 Rolfe, Red
56 Rolfe, Sam
1 Rolfin, John
1 Rolli, Nino
1 Rollini (Adrian Rollini and His Ensemble)
1 Rollini (Adrian Rollini Quartet)
7 Rollini (Adrian Rollini Trio, The)
18 Rollini, Adrian
2 Rollini, Art
1 Rollins, Herbert
1 Rollins, Hugh
1 Rollins, Sonny
1 Rolls (Jimmy Rolls Trio, The)
14 Roman, Larry
1 Roman, Nancy
4 Roman, Ruth
1 Romandi, Dion
5 Romano (Tony Romano and His Orchestra)
3 Romano, Emilio
1 Romano, Johnny
10 Romano, Michael
22 Romano, Tony
3 Romanoff, Michael
33 Romay, Lina
8 Romberg (Sigmund Romberg and His Orchestra)
7 Romberg, Sigmund
2 Rome, Betty
1 Rome, Harold
13 Romero, Cesar
2 Rommel, Ed
2 Romney, George
30 Romulo, Carlos
1 Ronald, James
4 Rondaliers, The
3 Rondall, Marie
1 Rondo (Don Rondo and The Sy Oliver Band)
1 Rondo, Don
1 Ronettes, The
2 Roney, Jack
5 Ronsley, Ina
4 Ronson, Adele
1 Rook, Susan
1 Rooney Jr., Pat
1 Rooney, Andy
1 Rooney, Anne
1 Rooney, Art
1 Rooney, John
69 Rooney, Mickey
1 Roos, Bob
93 Roos, Jeanine
1 Roosevelt Jr., Franklin
2 Roosevelt Jr., Theodore
66 Roosevelt, Eleanor
5 Roosevelt, Elliot
184 Roosevelt, Franklin
1 Roosevelt, Henry
2 Roosevelt, Sarah Delano
2 Roosevelt, Theodore
7 Root, Elizabeth
2 Root, Waverly
2 Roper, Elmo
2 Roper, John
3 Rorick, Isabel Scott
4 Rosa, Nita
1 Rosch, John
1 Roscoe, Joseph
107 Rose (David Rose and His Orchestra)
3 Rose (David Rose and The Savings Bonds Orchestra)
1 Rose, Arnold
2 Rose, Billy
1 Rose, Bob
24 Rose, David
1 Rose, Donald
2 Rose, James
2 Rose, Jane
1 Rose, Jewel
1 Rose, Leonard
141 Rose, Norman
12 Rose, Oscar
5 Rose, Ralph
7 Rose, Sy
14 Rosenbloom, Maxie
2 Rosenblum, Louis
1 Rosendhal, Jeffrey
1 Rosenfeld, Alvin
1 Rosenfeld, Big Joe
1 Rosengarten (Bob Rosengarten and His Orchestra)
2 Rosengarten, Bobby
1 Rosenthal, Abe
1 Rosenthal, Leazar David
1 Rosenwald, Francis
1 Rosier, Joseph
6 Roskol, Joseph
1 Ross (Arnold Ross Quartet)
1 Ross (Bill Ross and His Orchestra)
1 Ross (Edmundo Ross and His Rhumba Band)
1 Ross (Jim Ross and His Orchestra)
1 Ross (Ross and Hunt)
1 Ross Sisters, The
7 Ross, Anthony
6 Ross, Arthur
2 Ross, Barney
1 Ross, Betsy
15 Ross, Bob
2 Ross, Bud
3 Ross, Candy
27 Ross, Clarice A.
1 Ross, Clark
41 Ross, David
2 Ross, David H.
2 Ross, Dean
490 Ross, Earle
1 Ross, Francisco
1 Ross, Frankie
1 Ross, Freddie
1 Ross, Hank
1 Ross, Helen
3 Ross, Howard
2 Ross, Jerry
1 Ross, Joey
1 Ross, John C.
1 Ross, Johnny
39 Ross, Lanny
1 Ross, Lou
1 Ross, Marion
4 Ross, Merrill
3 Ross, Miles
1 Ross, Murray
1 Ross, Nancy Wilson
1 Ross, Norma Jean
2 Ross, Norman
3 Ross, Roy
29 Ross, Shirley
1 Ross, Terry
1 Ross, Winston
2 Rosselli, Frederico
1 Rossen, Robert
1 Rossi, Steve
1 Rossner, Carl
75 Rost, Elaine
4 Rostand, Edmond
4 Rostang (Hubert Rostang Sextette, The)
1 Rosten, Leo
5 Rosten, Norman
6 Rostenkowski, Dan
1 Rostow, Walt
31 Rote, Kyle
1 Roth (Al Roth and His Orchestra)
2 Roth (Alan Roth and His Orchestra)
1 Roth (Alan Roth Chorus, The)
1 Roth (Alan Roth Singers, The)
1 Roth (Allen Roth and His Orchestra and Chorus)
12 Roth (Allen Roth and His Orchestra)
1 Roth (Lillian Roth and Her Piano Boys)
2 Roth Quartet, The
1 Roth, Allen
1 Roth, Almon E.
1 Roth, Armand E.
1 Roth, Betty
1 Roth, Eric
1 Roth, Guy
1 Roth, Howard
4 Roth, Lillian
2 Roth, William
1 Rothchild, Richard
1 Rothman, Archie
1 Rotie, James Arthur
1 Rotile, Francesca
2 Roundtree, Luther
5 Roundup Boys, The
2 Rounseville, Robert
10 Rourke, Jack
1 Rousch, Ed
1 Rousseau, Pat
1 Rousseau, Theodore
18 Rousseau, William P.
2 Rouvaun
8 Rover Boys, The
1 Rovero, Joseph
3 Rowan and Martin
4 Rowan, Eloise
1 Rowan, Joe
1 Rowan, Louis
433 Rowan, Roy
1 Rowda, Willa
11 Rowe, Genevieve
1 Rowe, Patricia
3 Rowe, Red
2 Rowe, Ruth
1 Rowell, David N.
1 Rowels, Jimmy
1 Rowland, Adele
26 Rowland, Jada
15 Rowland, Luther
28 Rowland, Ralph
3 Roy (Harry Roy and His Orchestra)
9 Roy, Billy
10 Roy, Cecil
1 Roy, Harry
1 Roy, Jerry
1 Roy, Lisa
25 Roy, Michael
1 Roy, Renne
1 Roy, Subodh Chandra
1 Roy, William
1 Royack, Annette
3 Royal Air Force (Orchestra Of The Royal Air Force, The)
1 Royal Teens, The
1 Royal, John F.
1 Royal, Kenneth
1 Royal, William
2 Royce, Riza
5 Royle, Selena
9 Roza, Lita
2 Rozelle (Dick Rozelle and His Swing Quartette)
1 Rozsa, Miklos
3 Ruark, Barbara
1 Rub, Christian
2 Rubell, Norman
1 Rubin (Stan Rubin and His Tigertown Five)
59 Rubin, Benny
1 Rubin, Betty
2 Rubin, Gene
12 Rubin, Jack
1 Rubin, Rennie
2 Rubine, Irving
1 Rubini (Jan Rubini and His Orchestra)
1 Rubini, Maria
5 Rubinoff (David Rubinoff and His Orchestra)
28 Rubinoff, David
1 Rubinoff, Jay
9 Rubinstein, Artur
1 Rubinstein, John
8 Rubinstein, Sholom
3 Ruby, Harry
9 Ruby, Martin
2 Ruby, Texas
9 Rucker, Allen W.
1 Rudd, Charles
1 Rudder, Bill
1 Rudey, Richard
2 Rudie, Evelyn
1 Rudier, Robert
8 Rudley, Herb
1 Rudolfski, John
2 Rudolph, Wilma
1 Rudy (Ernie Rudy and His Orchestra)
1 Rue, Joe
1 Ruffin, Bobby
10 Ruffner, Tiny
1 Ruffner, William
1 Rugel, Yvette
33 Ruggles, Charles
1 Ruggles, Jack
1 Ruggles, Wesley
2 Rugolo (Pete Rugolo and His Orchestra)
1 Ruhel, Joe
197 Ruick, Melville
1 Ruiz, Martin
14 Rukeyser, Merryle Stanley
1 Rumann, Sig
1 Ruml, Beardsley
2 Rundquist, Kenneth
62 Runyon, Damon
2 Runyon, Jim
1 Ruppert, Jacob
2 Ruric, Peter
56 Rush, Art
3 Rush, Barbara
14 Rush, Celeste
1 Rush, Tom
1 Rushdie, Salman
1 Rusher, Williams A.
27 Rushing, Jimmy
1 Rushmore, Howard
1 Rushton, Joe
1 Rusk, Dean
1 Rusk, Howard
1 Ruskin, Shimon

3 Rusoff, Lou
2 Russ, Elmer
1 Russell
1 Russell (Don Russell and His Orchestra)
1 Russell (Hank Russell and His Rangesingers)
12 Russell (Henry Russell and His Orchestra)
39 Russell, Andy
1 Russell, Ann
5 Russell, Bertrand
5 Russell, Bob
25 Russell, Charles
8 Russell, Connie
3 Russell, Cordy
1 Russell, Dakota
1 Russell, Dan
1 Russell, Della
2 Russell, Don
102 Russell, Frank
7 Russell, Gilbert
2 Russell, Grace
2 Russell, Harold
1 Russell, Helen
44 Russell, Henry
1 Russell, Jack
15 Russell, Jane
1 Russell, Janet
5 Russell, John
4 Russell, Johnny
1 Russell, Joseph
1 Russell, Larry
2 Russell, Lee
2 Russell, Madeline
1 Russell, Marion
1 Russell, Mark
2 Russell, Max
7 Russell, Pamela
40 Russell, Pee Wee
1 Russell, Richard
1 Russell, Robin
41 Russell, Rosalind
8 Russell, Todd
1 Russell, Waldo
1 Russell, William F.
5 Russert, Tim
4 Russin, Babe
1 Russo and The Samba Kings
1 Russo, Andy
1 Russolini, Anna
1 Rust, David
1 Rusty and Doug
16 Ruth, Babe
1 Ruth, Claire
25 Rutherford, Ann
5 Rutherford, Judge
1 Rutherford, Margaret
1 Rutland, Carey
1 Rutledge, Ann
1 Rutledge, Patricia
82 Ruysdael, Basil
9 Ryan, Ann
1 Ryan, Babs
3 Ryan, Bill
8 Ryan, Dennis
103 Ryan, Dick
5 Ryan, Edward
2 Ryan, Fiddlin' Buck
17 Ryan, Irene
1 Ryan, Jim
1 Ryan, Joe
6 Ryan, Mary
1 Ryan, Mauren Roden
3 Ryan, Patricia
5 Ryan, Peggy
1 Ryan, Quinn
1 Ryan, Richard
11 Ryan, Robert
13 Ryan, Tommy
1 Ryan, Valerie
2 Ryan, Vic
3 Rydell, Bobby
2 Ryder, Alfred
1 Ryder, Clock
3 Ryder, Ruth Ann
2 Ryeson, Donald S.
2 Ryeson, Martin
61 Ryf, Robert
1 Rythmettes, The

1 Sabins Jr., Floyd
4 Sablon, Jean
2 Sabor, Al
1 Sabronksy, William
2 Sabu
1 Sach, Erna
1 Sachs, Alexander
13 Sachs, Ann
1 Sachs, Eddie
1 Sachs, Henry
18 Sack (Albert Sack and His Orchestra)
3 Sack, Albert
2 Sadat, Anwar
11 Saddle Kings, The
3 Saddleman, William S.
1 Saddler (Johnny Saddler and The Tennessee Mountain Boys)
1 Saddler, Sandy
10 Sadenberg, Ted
4 Saerchinger, Cesar
1 Safer, Morley
1 Saffell
1 Safir, James L.
2 Safire, William
20 Safranski (Eddie Safranski and His Orchestra)
2 Safranski (Eddie Safranski Quintet, The)
10 Safranski, Eddie
14 Sagan, Carl
7 Sagerquist (Eric Sagerquist and His Orchestra)
1 Sahl, John
1 Sahl, Mort
2 Saidenberg (Dan Saidenberg and His Orchestra)
1 Sailor Boy's Octet, The
1 Sain, Johnny
1 Saint Brenden's Boys Choir, The
1 Saint, Edward
1 Saint, Eva Marie
1 Saints, The
1 Sakall, S. Z.
3 Saki
1 Salata, Val
1 Saldue
2 Salerno, Sam
1 Sales, Richard
3 Sales, Soupy
3 Salinger, Pierre
2 Salisbury, Harrison
1 Salisbury, Morse
1 Salon Swing Ensemble, The
1 Salt Lake Tabernacle Choir, The
1 Salter (Harry Salter and His All-Army Band)
10 Salter (Harry Salter and His Orchestra)
1 Salter (Harry Salter and The New York Port Of Embarkation Orchestra)
1 Salter, Arthur
4 Salter, Dorothy
3 Salter, Harry
1 Saltman, Charles
2 Saltman, Paul
2 Saltonstall, Leverett
1 Saltzman, Ed
1 Saltzman, Edward
5 Salvey, Alberto
1 Salvo, Len
2 Samos, John
2 Samoza, President
4 Sample, James
1 Sampson, George
1 Samuel, Maurice
1 Samuel, Viscount
2 Samuels, Joel
1 San Francisco All-Stars, The
8 San Juan, Olga
1 San Pietro (Joseph San Pietro and His Castillians)
1 San Ramon, Jesus
2 Sand, Leonard
1 Sand, Rebecca
1 Sanda, Paul
22 Sandburg, Carl
2 Sandeford, Charles
1 Sanderfer, Tony
1 Sanders (Coon-Sanders Nighthawks, The)
1 Sanders (Joe Sanders and His Orchestra)
1 Sanders, Annette
2 Sanders, Dennis
1 Sanders, Dick
7 Sanders, George
2 Sanders, Hugh
1 Sanders, Joe
1 Sanders, Pharoah
1 Sanders, Red
2 Sanders, Richard
1 Sanders, Tad
2 Sanders, Terry
7 Sanderson, Julia
1 Sandler and Young
1 Sandler, Harold
1 Sandrich, Mark
2 Sands (Pat Sands and His Vigilantes)
1 Sands, Billy
3 Sands, Dorothy
114 Sandville, Richard
1 Sanella (Andy Sanella and His Orchestra)
2 Sanford, Erskine
2 Sanford, Harold
1 Sanford, Herb
1 Sanford, John
1 Sanford, Susan
2 Sanford, Terry
1 Sanford, Virginia
1 Sanger, Margaret
14 Sangster, Margaret
3 Sannella, Andy
2 Sansbury, Hope
8 Sant, Kimball S.
1 Santarpia, Dominick
1 Santayana, George
18 Santelmann, William F.
1 Santon, Bob
2 Santon, Bobby
1 Santoni, Rennie
1 Santoro, Olivio
2 Santorum, Rick
2 Sapir, Cliff
1 Saputo, Frank
1 Sarah and Sassafras
1 Sarak, Ivan
1 Sarasate
1 Sarasen, Gene
2 Sargent, Anne
4 Sargent, Kenny
14 Sargent, Nannette
1 Sargent, Noel
1 Sarion, Alex
7 Sarnoff, David
5 Sarnoff, Dorothy
2 Saroyan, William
1 Sartre, Jean-Paul
6 Sasser, James
1 Satin, Bobby
17 Satisfiers, The
1 Satterfield, Bob
1 Satterly, Bruce
1 Saudek, Robert
1 Sauer, George
4 Saul, John
1 Saul, Margaret
8 Saul, Oscar
1 Saunders (Herman Saunders Trio, The)
89 Saunders, Bill
1 Saunders, Del
1 Saunders, Emma
3 Saunders, Felicia
21 Saunders, Frank
2 Saunders, George
1 Saunders, Herb
1 Saunders, Herman
11 Saunders, Jimmy
1 Saunders, Mary Jane
3 Saunders, Woody
1 Sauter (Eddie Sauter and His Orchestra)
1 Sauter, James E.
14 Sauter-Finegan Orchestra, The
1 Savage, Guy
1 Savage, Milo
2 Savage, Paul
1 Savage, Susan
2 Savalas, Telly
1 Savants, The
1 Savin, Sheriff
1 Savin, Thomas G.
2 Savinas, Joe
1 Savino, Joseph
2 Savitsky, Fabian
12 Savitt (Jan Savitt and His Orchestra)
4 Savitt (Jan Savitt and His Top Hatters)
1 Savitt, Jan
1 Savitz, Aaron
3 Savo, Jimmy
5 Savoy, Harry
1 Savoy, Peter
2 Sawyer, Diane
8 Sawyer, Hal
1 Sawyer, Ross
2 Sawyer, Stan
1 Saxon, Dave
6 Saxon, Lon
2 Saxon, Luther
1 Saxon, Lyle
5 Saxon, O. Glen
1 Saxon, Rise
1 Saxophone Eight, The

1 Saxophone Sextette Of Boston
2 Saxton, Jim
1 Saxton, Johnny
7 Sayao, Bidu
1 Sayers, Dora
5 Sayers, Dorothy L.
1 Sayers, Jo Ann
1 Sayle, Richard
1 Saypole, Irving
1 Sayre, Mrs. Raymond
1 Scabb, George
1 Scandinavian Male Chorus
2 Scanlon, Joe
1 Scanlon, Walter
17 Scardino, Don
2 Schacht, Al
2 Schackley, George
1 Schact
5 Schacter, George
11 Schaden, Chuck
13 Schaefer (Lloyd Schaefer and His Orchestra)
1 Schaefer, Lloyd
1 Schaeffer, Al
2 Schaeffer, Isiah
2 Schaeffer, John
4 Schallert, William
1 Schapp, Dick
1 Scharat, Bruton
87 Scharf (Walter Scharf and His Orchestra)
2 Scharf, Walter
1 Scharftsman, Elliot
2 Schary, Dore
1 Scheerer, Maude
1 Scheffing, Bob
1 Scheider, William H.
1 Scheidler, Hal
1 Schellenbarger, Samuel
1 Schenck, Joe
2 Schenkel, Chris
1 Schenkel, David
1 Scherer, Bernard
4 Scherer, Lee
1 Scherer, Len
3 Scherer, Ray
1 Scherman, Thomas
1 Schermerhorn, James
1 Schertzer, Hymie
2 Schick, William
1 Schieber, Etta
6 Schieffer, Bob
2 Schiff, Mary
1 Schifrin, Lalo
12 Schildkraut, Joseph
1 Schiller (Gunter Schiller and The New England Conservatory Ensemble)
2 Schilling, Gus
1 Schilling, John
2 Schilperoort, Peter
1 Schipp, Dave
3 Schirmer (Joe Schirmer Trio)
1 Schirmer, Hazel
9 Schirra, Wally
1 Schlay, Earl
1 Schlesinger Jr., Arthur D.
3 Schlessinger, Arthur
2 Schlessinger, Sanford
1 Schlessinger, Sidney
2 Schlick, Frederick
1 Schlosser, Herb
2 Schlott, John
2 Schmeling, Max
1 Schmidt, Al
3 Schmidt, Carl
2 Schmidt, E. Robert
6 Schmidt, Harrison
1 Schmidt, Helmut
1 Schmidt, Joseph
1 Schmidt, Lucien
1 Schmidt, Ray
8 Schmidt, Reinhold
1 Schmitz, James H.
1 Schmuck, Mr.
46 Schnabel, Stefan
2 Schnay, Thelma
2 Schneider
1 Schneider, Alexander
1 Schneider, Howard
1 Schneider, Julian
1 Schneider, Moe
1 Schneider, Paul
8 Schneider, William
1 Schneider, William A.
6 Schoen (Vic Schoen and His Orchestra)
1 Schoen, Kenneth
1 Schoen, Vic
8 Schoenbrun, David
1 Schoendiest, Red
1 Schoenfeld, Bernard
1 Schofield, Lemuel B.
1 Scholar, Michael
1 School, Victoria
1 Schoolman, Ralph
1 Schoor, Gene
1 Schope, Henry
1 Schorn, Kenneth
7 Schorr, Daniel
1 Schoskis, Michael
1 Schottland, Charles I.
1 Schovers, Gerard
1 Schraeder, Marion
45 Schrager, Rudy
1 Schrager, Stanley
1 Schram, Ken
4 Schramm (Rudolph Schramm and His Orchestra)
5 Schramm, John C.
36 Schramm, Rudolph
1 Schrapps, Ernest
12 Schroeder, Gene
1 Schroeder, Pat
3 Schroff, Brody
1 Schub, Max
1 Schuber
1 Schubert Group, The
14 Schubert, Bernard L.
3 Schubert, Paul
3 Schueller, Whistling John
1 Schulberg, Bud
3 Schuler, Annie Caroline
2 Schuller, John
1 Schulman, Arnold
1 Schulman, Max
1 Schultes, Steve
4 Schultz, George
11 Schultz, Sigrid
1 Schultz, Steve
1 Schumann (Walter Schumann and Chorus)
1 Schumann, Earl
1 Schumann, Henrietta
1 Schumann, Roy
111 Schumann, Walter
11 Schumann-Heink, Ernestine
2 Schuster, Joseph
1 Schuur, Diane
17 Schuyler, Sonny
2 Schwab Jr., Laurence
1 Schwab, Art
1 Schwab, Lawrence
12 Schwartow, William
24 Schwartz, Al
1 Schwartz, Alvin
3 Schwartz, Arthur
1 Schwartz, Dave
1 Schwartz, Ed
1 Schwartz, Helen
1 Schwartz, Herman
1 Schwartz, Jack
1 Schwartz, Jean
1 Schwartz, Monty
23 Schwartz, Sherwood
1 Schwartz, Tiny
3 Schwartz, Tony
1 Schwartz, William
1 Schwartzkopf, Steve
2 Schwarzkopf, Norman
1 Schwedler, Karl
3 Schweickert, Russell
2 Schweig, Erwin
2 Schwellenbach, Louis
1 Science, Albert
4 Scobey (Bob Scobey and His Frisco Jazz Band)
2 Scobey, Bob
1 Scofield, Lew
1 Scofield, Muriel
1 Scoggin, Margaret C.
12 Scooler, Zvee
1 Scopa, Joe
55 Scott (Raymond Scott and His Orchestra)
12 Scott (Raymond Scott Quintet, The)
1 Scott (Shirley Scott Trio, The)
1 Scott (Tony Scott Quartet, The)
6 Scott, Adele
1 Scott, Alan
6 Scott, Alexander
1 Scott, Allen
1 Scott, Arlene
9 Scott, Ashmead
1 Scott, Bonnie
11 Scott, Bud
1 Scott, Carlisle
2 Scott, David
1 Scott, David R.
1 Scott, Dick
16 Scott, Dorothy
3 Scott, Douglas
2 Scott, Elizabeth
3 Scott, Evelyn
3 Scott, Frances
3 Scott, Fred
2 Scott, George C.
1 Scott, Gordon
8 Scott, Hazel
1 Scott, Helmut
31 Scott, Janet
9 Scott, John
1 Scott, Kirk
1 Scott, Laurina
1 Scott, Linda
8 Scott, Lizabeth
1 Scott, Lorraine
5 Scott, Lurene
3 Scott, Mabel
1 Scott, Marion
24 Scott, Martha
1 Scott, Mary
2 Scott, Nathan
1 Scott, Norman
1 Scott, Peter
3 Scott, Ralph
10 Scott, Randolph
1 Scott, Randy
3 Scott, Raymond
1 Scott, Robert
2 Scott, Sandra
1 Scott, Sidna
11 Scott, Tom
12 Scott, Walter
3 Scott, Will
128 Scott, Willard
13 Scott, Zachary
1 Scotti, Vito
51 Scourby, Alexander
1 Scouten, Rex
1 Scoville, John W.
1 Scowcroft, Brent
1 Scranton, William
31 Scribner, Jimmy
6 Scruggs, Earl
1 Scubby, John
1 Scully, Frances
2 Scully, Vin
1 Seaborg, Glen
2 Seabrook, Gay
1 Seabrooks, Bernie
11 Seabury, Inez
1 Seaga
2 Seagle Mixed Quartet, The
1 Seagle, John
1 Seale, Alfred
1 Seale, Nancy
1 Sealy, Jack
1 Seaman, Henry F.
1 Searle, Jackie
1 Searock, Grace
3 Sears (Jerry Sears and His Music In Miniature)
1 Sears (Jerry Sears and His Orchestra)
1 Sears Orchestra
1 Sears, Al
1 Sears, Florine
1 Sears, Ken
1 Sears, William B.
1 Seashore, Robert H.
2 Seaton, George
1 Seavey, Hollis
6 Sebastian (George Sebastian and His Orchestra)
6 Sebastian, George
4 Sebastian, John
1 Sebrell, W. H.
1 Secaucus, Dr.
1 Seckler, Curly
74 Secombe, Harry
52 Sedan, Rolfe
3 Sederholm, Doris
1 Sedges, John
1 Sedgewick, Anne
3 Sedgewick, Arthur
1 See, Frank
1 Seeay, James
1 Seeds, Russell
1 Seef, Nathaniel
1 Seeger, Elizabeth
7 Seeger, Pete
176 Seel, Charles
5 Seeley, Blossom
1 Seely, Doug
3 Seff, Richard
58 Segal, Eli
2 Segal, Manny
19 Segal, Robert
1 Segal, Vivienne
2 Segal, Zelig R.
4 Segovia, Andres
2 Seiberling Singers, The
1 Seiberling, J. P.
1 Seiff, Alvin
1 Seigel, Morton
1 Seis-Inquart
4 Seiter, William
1 Seittel, Tasha
1 Seitz, George B.
1 Seiver, Roy
2 Selassie, Haile
1 Selby, David
1 Selby, Frank
39 Selby, Sarah
1 Seldes, George
28 Seldes, Gilbert
140 Seldes, Marian
29 Selinsky, Vladimir
1 Selko, Herb
74 Sellers, Peter
1 Sellers, Preston
1 Sellers, Virginia
1 Sellings, Arthur
1 Sellins, Marie
1 Seltzer, Arthur
1 Seltzer, Scotty
1 Selusky String Quartet, The
4 Selvin (Ben Selvin and His Cocktail Orchestra)
20 Selvin (Ben Selvin and His Orchestra)
1 Selvin, Ben
1 Selwart, Tonio
1 Selwyn, Edgar
1 Selznick Recording Orchestra, The
1 Selznick Studio Orchestra
1 Selznick, David
1 Selznick, Irene
13 Semmler, Alexander
1 Semon, Maxine
4 Semon, Primrose
2 Sennett, Mack
27 Sentimentalists, The
1 Serafini (Al Serafini and His Orchestra)
1 Serasini, Gerard
1 Serendipity Singers, The
1 Sergal, Alan
1 Sergeant, Brent

2 Sergio, Lisa
1 Serino, Domenico
1 Serious, Henry
2 Serkin, Rudolph
70 Serling, Rod
1 Sesno, Frank
2 Seuss, Dr.
79 Sevareid, Eric
1 Seven Senders, The
1 Sever, Tom
1 Severe, Cliff
2 Severinsen, Doc
1 Severn, Billy
2 Severn, Clifford
1 Seward, Floyd A.
3 Sewell, Bud
60 Sextette From Hunger, The
7 Seymore, John
59 Seymour, Anne
1 Seymour, Arthur G.
7 Seymour, Bill
225 Seymour, Dan
1 Seymour, Jane
2 Seymour, Joe
1 Shaara, Michael
2 Shackleton, Robert
5 Shackley, George
1 Shackner, Alan
4 Shadel, Bill
11 Shady Valley Folks, The
1 Shaffer, Paul
2 Shaindlin (Jack Shaindlin and His March Of Time Orchestra)
43 Shakespeare, William
1 Shalikashvili, John
1 Shalit, Gene
3 Shamblin, Eldon
1 Shand, Texas Terry
1 Shandmira, Lal
1 Shane, Denny
1 Shanks, Edward
1 Shanley, Bob
2 Shannon, Dick
1 Shannon, Ginger
1 Shannon, James
9 Shannon, Paul
2 Shannon, Ray
1 Shapely, Bob
1 Shapiro, Artie
1 Shapiro, Debby
1 Shapiro, Milton
1 Shapiro, Mr.
1 Shapiro, Sam
2 Shapiro, Stanley
1 Shapiro, Ted
5 Shapley, Harlow
340 Sharbutt, Del
1 Shard, Jerry
1 Sharkey, Jack
1 Sharkley, Marion
1 Sharky, Parky
1 Sharnitiski, Dick
1 Sharon, Leo
4 Sharon, Steve
1 Sharp, Albert
3 Sharp, Don W.
1 Sharp, Elliot
8 Sharp, Lester
2 Sharp, Phil
1 Sharp, Raymond
3 Sharpe, Malcomb
2 Sharpfer, Bob
1 Sharshug, George
1 Shatlov, Senator
2 Shatner, William
53 Shavers, Charlie
1 Shavers, Ernie
24 Shaw (Artie Shaw and His Orchestra)
2 Shaw (Artie Shaw and The Gramercy Five)
1 Shaw (Georgie Shaw and His Orchestra)
13 Shaw (Robert Shaw Chorale, The)
1 Shaw (Robert Shaw Male Chorus, The)
1 Shaw (Shaw and Lee)
1 Shaw (Woody Shaw Ensemble)
1 Shaw, Al
1 Shaw, Alan
13 Shaw, Artie
8 Shaw, Arvell
1 Shaw, Ben
10 Shaw, Bernard
4 Shaw, Bill
4 Shaw, C. Montague
1 Shaw, Carey
11 Shaw, Charles
1 Shaw, David
8 Shaw, George Bernard
2 Shaw, Gordon
8 Shaw, Hollis
4 Shaw, Irwin
1 Shaw, J. Howland
1 Shaw, John
4 Shaw, Martha
6 Shaw, Robert
1 Shaw, Stan
2 Shaw, Tom
1 Shaw, Victoria
11 Shaw, Walter
2 Shaw, Wini
1 Shaw, Woody
1 Shawhan, Stan
41 Shay, Dorothy
3 Shay, John
3 Shay, Patricia
2 Shayne, Lee
2 Shayne, Robert
1 Shayne, Ruth
1 Shayon, Monya
50 Shayon, Robert Lewis
1 Shea, Allen
1 Shea, Beverly
1 Shea, Father
3 Shea, George Beverly
1 Shea, Gilly
138 Shea, Joan
1 Shea, Margaret
2 Shearer, Harry
9 Shearer, Norma
6 Shearin, Lee
8 Shearing (George Shearing Quintet)
22 Shearing (George Shearing Quintet, The)
1 Shearing, Diana
5 Shearing, George
20 Shears, Jerry
13 Sheckley, Robert
1 Sheehan, Jim
7 Sheehan, John
4 Sheehan, Vincent
1 Sheeley, Leonard
7 Sheen, Fulton
1 Sheer, Harry
1 Sheets, Gene
1 Sheets, Payson
1 Sheffield, Charlotte
4 Sheffield, Reginald
1 Sheft (Bert Sheft and The United States Maritime Service Orchestra)
1 Sheiner, David
1 Shelby, K. W.
1 Shelby, Richard
28 Sheldon (Earl Sheldon and His Orchestra)
1 Sheldon, Bert
6 Sheldon, Herb
4 Sheldon, James
9 Sheldon, Jerome
6 Sheldon, Walt
1 Shelley, Carole
1 Shelley, Jack
3 Shelley, Joshua
7 Shelley, Mary
10 Shelley, Norman
2 Shelley, Percy
1 Shelley, William
1 Shelly, Bob
2 Shelly, David
1 Shelton, Ann
32 Shelton, George
2 Shelton, Marla
2 Shelton, Vaughn
1 Shenton, Bob
1 Shep Brothers, The
8 Shepard, Alan
1 Shepard, Bob
14 Shepard, Jean
3 Shepard, Joan
36 Shephard, Ann
1 Shepherd, Bob
2 Shepherd, Coulson
14 Shepherd, Jean
1 Sheppard, Harry
10 Sherdeman, Ted
2 Sherer, Leonard
9 Sheridan, Ann
1 Sheridan, Frank
12 Sheridan, Nancy
2 Sherill, Joya
4 Sherman, Alan
1 Sherman, Allie
4 Sherman, Billy
1 Sherman, Eleanor
1 Sherman, Floyd
12 Sherman, Hiram
1 Sherman, John
2 Sherman, Lenny
1 Sherman, Louis L.
1 Sherman, Lowell
2 Sherman, Paul
43 Sherman, Ransom
1 Sherman, Ray
1 Sherman, Roy
1 Sherman, Solly
1 Sherman, Val
1 Sherman, Vincent
1 Sherman, Winthrop
44 Shermet, Hazel
1 Sherock (Shorty Sherock and His Orchestra)
1 Sherock, Shorty
7 Sherrill, Joya
4 Sherrill, Wray
37 Sherrin, Ukie
19 Sherry, Bob
1 Sherry, Eleanor
1 Shertler, Ron
9 Sherwood (Bobby Sherwood and His Orchestra)
2 Sherwood (Bobby Sherwood Trio, The)
1 Sherwood, Bob
6 Sherwood, Bobby
3 Sherwood, Gale
1 Sherwood, Lorraine
2 Sherwood, Madeline
13 Sherwood, Robert
2 Sherwood, Sherry
2 Shevardnadze, Eduard
1 Shiel, R. J.
20 Shield, Roy
1 Shield (Roy Shield and His Demolition Crew)
14 Shield (Roy Shield and His Orchestra)
62 Shields, Frederick
10 Shields, Helen
22 Shields, Jimmy
3 Shields, Nancy
2 Shielman, Joan
1 Shilkret (Nathaniel Shilkret and His Orchestra)
1 Shilkret, Nathaniel
2 Shiner, Claude
46 Ship, Ruben
2 Shipley, Bill
1 Shipley, Joseph
1 Shipman, Mel
62 Shipp, Mary
3 Shipp, Walter
1 Shirelles, The
46 Shirer, William L.
34 Shirley, Alfred
5 Shirley, Anne
1 Shirley, Bill
1 Shirley, Donna
1 Shirley, Mildred
62 Shirley, Tom
6 Shishkin, Boris
1 Shlessinger, Stan
1 Shockley, Marian
1 Shoemaker, Eugene
1 Shoemaker, Willie
1 Shoffner, Del
1 Shook, Jack
2 Shor, Toots
337 Shore, Dinah
1 Shore, Sal
2 Shores, Byron
6 Shores, Richard
3 Short, Bobby
3 Short, Don
1 Short, Nicholas
1 Shortcuts, The
1 Shorthill, Richard
7 Shorty's Hillbillies
1 Shoskus, Mike
1 Shostakovich, Dimitri
7 Shotwell, James T.
1 Shous, James D.
1 Show, Danny
1 Showmen, The
1 Shrewsberry, David
1 Shrine, Alexander
12 Shriner, Herb
1 Shube, Lou
1 Shufford, Helen
3 Shuken, Phil
1 Shula, Al
1 Shultz (Steve Shultz and His Orchestra)
1 Shumsky, Oscar
1 Shuster, Joe
2 Shute, Nevil
2 Shutta, Ethel
1 Sibley, William A. L.
1 Sickle, Norm
38 Sidell, Amy
1 Sidelman, Cantor
13 Sides, Tony
1 Sidewinders, The
2 Sidner, Earl
2 Sidney, George
7 Sidney, Sylvia
1 Sidney, T. J.
2 Sieck, Robert
1 Siefert, Martin
1 Siegel, Donald
2 Siegel, Jerry
4 Siegel, John
1 Siegal, Marc
5 Siegel, Morris H.
1 Siem, Kaare
1 Sientz, John B.
2 Siepi, Cesare
1 Sigmeister, Eli
1 Signorelli, Frank
4 Sikora, Al
1 Sikorski, Igor
1 Sikorsky, General
18 Silan, Bert
1 Sill Jr., Joseph
1 Sills, Dotty
1 Silva, Simone
4 Silver Masked Tenor, The
9 Silver, Abba Hillel
2 Silver, Charles H.
44 Silver, Douglas
39 Silver, Jeffrey
4 Silver, Jerry
28 Silver, Joe
1 Silver, Ken
2 Silver, Stanley
1 Silvera, Frank
5 Silverberg, Robert
175 Silverheels, Jay
1 Silverman, Leonard
1 Silvermaster, Nathan
4 Silvers (Louis Silvers and His Orchestra)
1 Silvers Family, The
1 Silvers, Chubby
1 Silvers, Leon
370 Silvers, Louis
1 Silvers, Mrs. Phil
15 Silvers, Phil
1 Silvers, Shirley
1 Silvers, Sid
1 Silvestri, Ken
9 Simak, Clifford

2 Simeon, Harry
1 Simeone (Harry Simeone Chorale)
2 Simeone (Harry Simeone Chorale, The)
1 Simes, Eugene
1 Simes, Harold
1 Simiskey, Lada
1 Simmons, Addison
3 Simmons, Dick
1 Simmons, Harwood
2 Simmons, Jean
21 Simmons, Richard Allen
2 Simmons, Robert
2 Simmons, William
3 Simms, Frank
80 Simms, Ginny
6 Simms, Hilda
4 Simms, Lu Ann
1 Simon, Abbey
1 Simon, Al
1 Simon, Caroline K.
2 Simon, George
1 Simon, Maury
4 Simon, Paul
1 Simon, Robert
1 Simon, S. Sylvan
1 Simon, Scott
3 Simon, Simone
1 Simone, Lisa
2 Simone, Nina
2 Simons, Constance
1 Simons, Henry C.
2 Simpson, Alan
1 Simpson, C. P.
1 Simpson, Carole
2 Simpson, General
15 Simpson, Gloria Ann
2 Simpson, Ivan
1 Simpson, Jack
1 Simpson, Kenneth
1 Simpson, Leo
1 Simpson, Mary Lou
1 Simpson, Robert
3 Simpson, Russell
1 Simpson, Valerie
1 Simpson, W. C.
1 Sims (Zoot Sims Sextet, The)
2 Sims, Alan
1 Sims, Bob
5 Sims, Hal
2 Sims, Jay
2 Sims, Ray
6 Sims, Zoot
26 Sinatra (Ray Sinatra and His Orchestra)
266 Sinatra, Frank
2 Sinatra, Nancy
1 Sinclair, Arthur
2 Sinclair, Betty
1 Sinclair, Leonard
2 Sinclair, Lister
2 Sinclair, Mary
1 Sinclair, Peter
2 Sinclair, Ronald
1 Sinful Seven, The
3 Sing Band, The
1 Sing, Kitty
4 Singer, Campbell
12 Singer, Carol
1 Singer, Curt
66 Singer, Ray
1 Singer, Richard
1 Singer, Russell E.
7 Singer, Stubby
11 Singer, Stuffy
1 Singh, Anup
16 Singin' Sam
3 Singing Americans, The
1 Singing Bob
1 Singing Chefs, The
1 Singing Cowboy, The
2 Singing Millmen, The
1 Singing People, The
13 Singing Sergeants, The
1 Singing Strings, The
1 Singing Waves Platoon, The
203 Singiser, Frank
1 Singleton, Don
75 Singleton, Doris
2 Singleton, Dorothy
16 Singleton, Penny
12 Singleton, Zutty
2 Siodmak, Curt
3 Siodmak, Robert
1 Sipes, Larry
9 Sir Lancelot
6 Siracusa, Joe
1 Sisler, Dick
2 Sissle, Noble
1 Sisson, James
1 Sisti
1 Sitterley, Eugene
3 Six Hits and A Miss
1 Six, Jack
1 Sizoo, Joseph
3 Skelly, Hal
200 Skelton, Red
1 Skidmore, Hubert
1 Skiera, Peter
4 Skiles, Marlin
1 Skill, Adrian
29 Skinner, Cornelia Otis
1 Skinner, George
1 Skinner, Samuel
1 Skipton, Marjorie
3 Skipworth, Alison
1 Sklam, Stuart
1 Sklar, George
9 Sklar, Michael
1 Sklar, Rick
1 Skolovksy, Zadel
4 Skolsky, Sidney
2 Skowron, Bill
4 Skrivanek (Eddie Skrivanek and His Guardsmen)
47 Skrivanek (Eddie Skrivanek and His Orchestra)
1 Skrivanek (Eddie Skrivanek Sextette, The)
24 Skrivanek, Eddie
1 Skulnik, Menasha
8 Skylarks, The
1 Skylighters, The
2 Skyliners, The
1 Skyriders, The
1 Slack (Freddy Slack and His Orchestra)
1 Slade, Alan
5 Slagle, John
1 Slam and Bam
1 Slate Brothers, The
4 Slate, Chuck
1 Slate, Orrin
18 Slater, Bill
17 Slater, Ruth
9 Slater, Tom
1 Slatkin (Felix Slatkin and His Orchestra)
2 Slatkin, Felix
1 Slatkin, Leonard
1 Slattery, Edward
1 Slattery, Jack
2 Slattery, Joe
1 Slaughter, Enos
1 Slava, Myra
1 Slayman (Don Slayman and His Magic Fiddle)
9 Slayton, Donald
1 Sled, James
1 Sleeper, Martha
47 Slesar, Henry
8 Slezak, Walter
1 Slight, David
1 Slim
1 Slim and Shep
2 Slim and Slam
1 Slipher, Elizabeth
1 Sloan, Arnold
1 Sloan, Bill
2 Sloan, Carol
1 Sloan, Donald
13 Sloane, Allan
174 Sloane, Everett
14 Sloane, Robert
29 Slocum Jr., Bill
4 Slocum Jr., William
32 Slon, Sidney
2 Slot, John
1 Sly and The Family Stone
1 Small (Mary Small and The Modernaires)
15 Small, Mary
1 Smalle (Ed Smalle and His Seven Voices)
1 Smalle (Ed Smalle and The Seven G's)
1 Smalle, Ed
1 Smallens, Alexander
11 Smart Set, The
15 Smart, J. Scott
2 Smedley, Agnes
1 Smiley and Kitty
1 Smiley, Bessie
1 Smite, Jack
1 Smith (Billy Smith's Comedettes)
17 Smith (Howard Smith and His Orchestra)
1 Smith (Howard Smith Trio, The)
1 Smith (Johnny Smith Quartet)
1 Smith (Johnny Smith Trio)
1 Smith (Lonnie Liston Smith and The Cosmic Echoes)
1 Smith (Miles Smith and His Orchestra)
1 Smith (Paul Smith and His Orchestra)
2 Smith (Paul Smith Trio, The)
2 Smith (Something Smith and The Redheads)
1 Smith (Stuff Smith and His Orchestra)
3 Smith (Stuff Smith Trio, The)
5 Smith and Dale
1 Smith Dobson Trio, The
33 Smith Twins, The
3 Smith, Al
1 Smith, Al Roy
1 Smith, Albert
11 Smith, Alexis
1 Smith, Alice
1 Smith, Alson J.
2 Smith, Arthur
2 Smith, Aubrey
1 Smith, Barclay
1 Smith, Ben
2 Smith, Bernie
2 Smith, Bessie
2 Smith, Betty
35 Smith, Bill
1 Smith, Blaine
6 Smith, Bob
7 Smith, Bradford
1 Smith, Bronc
2 Smith, Bruce
6 Smith, Buddy
1 Smith, Burley
10 Smith, C. Aubrey
1 Smith, Carey
7 Smith, Carl
2 Smith, Carleton
3 Smith, Carlton
2 Smith, Carol
3 Smith, Carrie
1 Smith, Cathy
12 Smith, Charles
1 Smith, Connie
1 Smith, Cotton John
2 Smith, Cyril
1 Smith, Dale
2 Smith, David
1 Smith, Derek
1 Smith, Dick
1 Smith, Dody
1 Smith, Doris
1 Smith, Douglas A.
2 Smith, Earl
1 Smith, Edgar
4 Smith, Effie
1 Smith, Elwood
28 Smith, Ethel
1 Smith, Evelyn
2 Smith, F. Mark
2 Smith, Frank
3 Smith, Fred
1 Smith, G. Albert
1 Smith, Gar
1 Smith, Gary
1 Smith, George
1 Smith, Gerald
4 Smith, Glenn
1 Smith, Gwinifred
1 Smith, H. Allen
1 Smith, Hal
1 Smith, Harrison
2 Smith, Harry
23 Smith, Howard
38 Smith, Howard K.
2 Smith, Humbert
1 Smith, Ian
139 Smith, Jack
1 Smith, James
1 Smith, Jerry
1 Smith, Jesse Evans
1 Smith, Joe
11 Smith, Joe Bates
2 Smith, John T.
62 Smith, Kate
11 Smith, Keely
1 Smith, Ken
1 Smith, Kenneth
14 Smith, Kent
1 Smith, Lamar
2 Smith, Larry
1 Smith, Lee
25 Smith, Leonard
1 Smith, Les
1 Smith, Lillian
3 Smith, Lois
2 Smith, Lowell
1 Smith, Malcolm
2 Smith, Marcylin
5 Smith, Mark
1 Smith, Mary
1 Smith, Mary Jane
11 Smith, Muriel
1 Smith, Naomi
1 Smith, O. C.
2 Smith, O. L.
2 Smith, Patrick
1 Smith, Paul
1 Smith, Paul Gerard
1 Smith, Phil
4 Smith, R. T.
1 Smith, Ralph
4 Smith, Red
1 Smith, Rep.
4 Smith, Richard
1 Smith, Richard Norton
17 Smith, Robert
6 Smith, Robert D.
4 Smith, Robert T.
1 Smith, Roy
2 Smith, S. Mark
1 Smith, Sam
1 Smith, Selma
17 Smith, Sidney
5 Smith, Stuff
6 Smith, T. V.
1 Smith, Ted
1 Smith, Thelma
1 Smith, Thomas
5 Smith, Thomas Freebairn
2 Smith, Tommy
175 Smith, Verne
1 Smith, Virginia Cox
1 Smith, Viva
1 Smith, Wallace
1 Smith, Wanda
9 Smith, Whispering Jack
2 Smith, Willie Bobo
19 Smith, Willie The Lion
28 Smith, Wonderful
1 Smoky Mountain Boys, The
6 Smolen, Jay
5 Smolen, Vivian
1 Smollen, Mark
1 Smoot, George
1 Smoothies, The

1 Smothers Brothers, The
1 Smuts, Jan
4 Smythe, J. Anthony
1 Smythe, Robert E.
2 Snarey, Bill
2 Snay, John
1 Snead, Sam
1 Sneed, Norm
1 Snell, John
1 Snell, Matt
1 Snider, Betsy
7 Snider, Duke
2 Snider, Howard
1 Snider, Joseph L.
4 Snow (Hank Snow and His Rainbow Ranch Boys)
1 Snow, Charles
1 Snow, Elena
18 Snow, Hank
1 Snow, Harry
2 Snow, Jimmy
1 Snow, William
1 Snowden, Commander
89 Snowden, Eric
2 Snowden, Ward Washington
1 Snowflakes, The
3 Snyder (Bill Snyder and His Orchestra)
1 Snyder, Conway W.
1 Snyder, J. Buhl
2 Snyder, John
1 Snyder, Robert
7 Snyder, Tom
1 Sobol, Louis
3 Soderberg, Robert
3 Soderblom, Laurence
16 Soderstrom, Emil
2 Sodja, Joe
9 Soffen, Gerald
1 Sohl, Jerry
1 Soja, Joe
20 Sokolov, Nikolai
1 Sokolsky, Eric
34 Sokolsky, George E.
2 Solarz, Steven
1 Solenstein, Margaret
1 Soleri, David
3 Solidaires, The
1 Solomon, Eisner
1 Solomon, Gerald
1 Solomon, Leo
1 Solomonson, Vincent
1 Solow, Larry
1 Somer, Hilda
26 Somerville, Warren
1 Sommer (Earl Sommer and The Musical Steelmakers)
9 Sommer, Edith
5 Sommers, Jimsey
7 Sommers, Joanie
1 Sommes, Brian
5 Sondergaard, Gail
40 Sondergaard, Hester
1 Sondheim, Stephen
2 Song Chefs, The
1 Song Liberty Orchestra, The
17 Song Spinners, The
1 Songs Of Good Cheer Chorus, The
3 Songsmiths, The
1 Songsters, The
1 Sonicson, C. L.
1 Sonnenberg, Nellie
1 Sonny and Cher
1 Sons and Daughters Of The Pioneers, The
139 Sons Of The Pioneers, The
1 Sons Of The South, The
1 Sons Of The Western Soil, The
1 Soo, Jack
1 Soong, President
2 Sophocles
12 Sorel, George
202 Sorel, Guy
1 Soren, Tabitha
4 Sorenson, Nefi
3 Sorey, Vincent
6 Sorin, Louis
1 Sorokin, Pitirim
92 Sosnik (Harry Sosnik and His Orchestra)
29 Sosnik (Harry Sosnik and The Defense Bonds Orchestra)
1 Sosnik (Harry Sosnik and The Guest Star Orchestra)
155 Sosnik (Harry Sosnik and The Savings Bonds Orchestra)
4 Sosnik, Harry
9 Sotcamp, Jack
53 Sothern, Ann
1 Soubier, Cliff
1 Souchon, Edmund
7 Soule, George
153 Soule, Olan
1 Soule, Oscar F.
3 South (Eddie South and His International Orchestra)
1 South (Eddie South and His Orchestra)
1 South (Eddie South Trio)
2 South, Eddie
3 Southern Singers, The
9 Southern, Jeri
2 Southernaires, The
3 Southland Harmony Quartet, The
1 Southland Singers Of Boston
1 Southworth, Dorothy Faye
1 Souza, Kenneth A.
8 Sovine, Red
1 Sox, John
4 Spaatz, General
1 Spaatz, Mrs.
2 Spaeth, Robert
14 Spaeth, Sigmund
2 Spahn, Warren
1 Spahr, Walter
3 Spangenberg, Edwin
4 Spanier (Muggsy Spanier and His Dixieland Band)
1 Spanier, Frances
25 Spanier, Muggsy
4 Spaninger, Hilton
2 Spann, Al
1 Spann, Guy
2 Spann, Helen
1 Spano, Joe
1 Sparbaro, Tony
5 Spargrove, William
9 Sparklers, The
6 Sparkman, John
2 Sparks, Hale
25 Sparks, Jeff
13 Sparks, Ned
1 Sparkwell, Bill
2 Sparr (Paul Sparr and His Orchestra)
1 Sparrow, Alan
5 Spaulding, Albert
1 Spaulding, Charles
2 Spaulding, Jean
5 Spaull, Guy
1 Speaker, Tris
1 Speaks, Margaret
7 Spear (Sammy Spear and His Orchestra)
1 Spear, Bernard
1 Spears, Al
1 Spears, Billie Jo
5 Spears, Les
1 Spector, Arlen
1 Speed, James
2 Speer, F. A.
1 Speiden, Norman
10 Spellman, Francis
1 Spellman, Jerry
1 Spelman, Marian
4 Spelvin, George
2 Spencer (Earl Spencer and His Orchestra)
1 Spencer (Kenneth Spencer and The Paulist Choir)
1 Spencer, Barbara
1 Spencer, Johnny
2 Spencer, Kenneth
2 Spencer, Larry
1 Spencer, Milt
1 Spencer, William H.
1 Spenser, Norman
1 Spenser, Susan
10 Spenser, Tim
2 Sperling, Jack
3 Spewack, Bella
2 Spewack, Samuel
2 Spicer, Sandra
1 Spicer, Willie
1 Spicher, Buddy
1 Spiegel, Marvin
1 Spier, Carlos
185 Spier, William
4 Spigelgass, Leonard
1 Spilhaus, Atherton
1 Spina, Helen
1 Spinks, Leon
2 Spinrad, Hyron
4 Spitalny (H. Leopold Spitalny and His Orchestra)
1 Spitalny (Maurice Spitalny and His Orchestra)
45 Spitalny (Phil Spitalny and His All-Girl Orchestra)
7 Spitalny (Phil Spitalny and His All-Girl Orchestra and Choir)
1 Spitalny (Phil Spitalny and His Hotel Pennsylvania Orchestra)
3 Spitalny (Phil Spitalny and His Orchestra)
2 Spitalny, H. Leopold
2 Spitalny, Jimmy
2 Spitalny, Phil
1 Spitz, Mark
1 Spitzenberg, Wilbur
27 Spivak (Charlie Spivak and His Orchestra)
2 Spivak, Charlie
2 Spivak, Eli
2 Spivak, Lawrence
7 Spivey, Vernon M.
1 Spivey, Victoria
2 Spizer, Chuck
2 Splawn, James
1 Spock, Benjamin
152 Sportsmen, The
1 Sprague, Robert C.
1 Sprague, Ruth
1 Spratt, John
1 Spreckles, Geraldine
1 Spriegle, William R.
4 Spriggins, Deuce
2 Spring, Helen
1 Springfield, Dusty
1 Sprintzen, Nathaniel
1 Spross, Fred
1 Spruance, Don
1 Squibb Chorus, The
1 Squire, Christy
1 Squire, Louise
1 Squires, Dave
1 Squires, The
1 St. Angel, Michael
2 St. Aubrey, June
2 St. Carr, Regen
1 St. Clair, Cyrus
1 St. Clair, Dick
2 St. Clair, James
2 St. Clair, Leonard
1 St. Clair, Malcolm
9 St. Germaine, Kay
1 St. James, Christopher
1 St. John, Jill
18 St. John, Robert
1 St. Joseph, Ella
1 St. Joseph, Ellis
1 St. Louis Carol Association, The
1 St. Luke's Chorus, The
1 St. Marie, Buffie
1 St. Marie, Buffie
24 Stabile (Dick Stabile and His Orchestra)
1 Stabile (Joe Stabile and His Orchestra)
4 Stabile (Joe Stabile and The Air Transport Command Band)
6 Stabile, Dick
1 Stack, Edward
7 Stack, Robert
2 Stackhouse, Robert
2 Stacy (Jess Stacy Trio)
15 Stacy, Jess
1 Stadium Concerts Orchestra, The
1 Stadler, Connie
9 Stadler, Glen
1 Staehle, Robert
1 Staffen, Jack
3 Stafford, Anna
1 Stafford, Gail
1 Stafford, General
1 Stafford, Grace
9 Stafford, Gray
423 Stafford, Hanley
96 Stafford, Jo
7 Stafford, Tom
1 Stagg, Tommy
5 Stahl, Leslie
3 Stalin, Joseph
2 Stallane, Bjorn
1 Stallard, Tracy
1 Stalling, David
1 Stamberg, Susan
2 Stanborn, Lynn U.
4 Stander, Arthur
33 Stander, Lionel
1 Standing, Guy
1 Standing, Windham
1 Standley, William N.
1 Stanford, John
93 Stang, Arnold
2 Stankey, Eddie
2 Stanley (Bob Stanley and His Orchestra)
4 Stanley (Robert Stanley and His Orchestra)
3 Stanley Jr., Aileen
2 Stanley, Aileen
1 Stanley, Bert
99 Stanley, Don
1 Stanley, Ed
1 Stanley, Ernie
1 Stanley, Glen
1 Stanley, Henry
11 Stanley, John
1 Stanley, Louis
2 Stanley, Lyle
7 Stanley, Peggy
6 Stanley, Robert
1 Stansbury, Helen
1 Stanton (Dell Stanton Trio, The)
2 Stanton, Bill
4 Stanton, Bob
1 Stanton, Dakota
2 Stanton, Ernie
4 Stanton, Frank
18 Stanton, Jack
1 Stanton, Savalle
1 Stanton, Val
38 Stanwyck, Barbara
9 Stapleton, Eddie
2 Stapleton, Maureen
1 Stapley, Richard
1 Star Dreamers, The
1 Star Kings, The
3 Star, Ben
1 Star, Jimmy
2 Stardusters, The
74 Stark (Wally Stark and His Orchestra)
1 Stark, Admiral
34 Stark, Charles
2 Stark, Dolly
2 Stark, Hal
2 Stark, Harold
1 Stark, J. C.
1 Stark, Mrs.
1 Stark, Pete
23 Stark, Richard
1 Stark, Sally
7 Stark, Sheldon

1 Starkman, Molly
27 Starlighters, The
2 Starling, David
1 Starmer, Garrett
1 Starr, Freda
1 Starr, Jimmy
6 Starr, Josephine
9 Starr, Judy
42 Starr, Kay
7 Starr, Louis E.
1 Starrett, Vincent
1 Stase (William Stase and His Orchestra)
1 Stase, William
10 Stassen, Harold
4 Staton (Merrill Staton Voices, The)
2 Stauffer, Joseph R.
11 Stavisky, Lotte
2 Stavridi, Val
19 Steber, Eleanor
4 Steed, Phillip
3 Steel Sisters, The
1 Steel, Barry
3 Steel, Charles
3 Steel, Johannes
2 Steel, Karen
1 Steel, Tommy
14 Steel, Vernon
1 Steelberg, Wesley R.
32 Steele (Ted Steele and His Novatones)
11 Steele (Ted Steele and His Orchestra)
20 Steele, John
8 Steele, Ted
2 Steele, Wilbur Daniel
1 Steers, Lou
32 Stehli, Edgar
1 Steifer, Dorothy
1 Steigenberg, Edward K.
1 Stein, Geraldine
1 Stein, Gertrude
2 Stein, Lewis
1 Stein, Lou
1 Stein, Sol
4 Steinbeck, John
1 Steinberg, Wilheim
3 Steindel, Walter
1 Steinem, Gloria
69 Steiner, Frederick
1 Steiner, Max
1 Steinert, Alex
5 Steinhouse, Herbert
2 Steinkraus, Herman
1 Stellman, Maxine
1 Stempel, Herb
1 Stendahl
8 Stengel, Casey
1 Stenger, Dick
3 Stenyee, Gloria
11 Stephan, Bud
1 Stephanie, Diane
2 Stephenson, Carl
2 Stephenson, Henry
1 Stephenson, James
1 Stephenson, Vilhilma
1 Sterling, Bill
2 Sterling, Ethel
1 Sterling, Georgie
1 Sterling, Jack
3 Sterling, Jan
15 Sterling, Len
4 Sterling, Nora
20 Sterling, Phil
2 Sterling, Robert
1 Sterling, Stuart
206 Stern, Bill
2 Stern, Hank
6 Stern, Isaac
1 Stern, James
1 Stern, Lawrence
4 Stern, Leonard
2 Stern, Martin
2 Sterney (George Sterney and His Orchestra)
12 Sternhagen, Frances
2 Sterrett, Anne
7 Stettinius Jr., Edward R.
1 Steumann, Edward
7 Stevens (Leith Stevens and His Orchestra)
1 Stevens (Ray Stevens and His Orchestra)
1 Stevens (Roy Stevens and His Orchestra)
6 Stevens, Bob
1 Stevens, Carlyle
1 Stevens, Charles
1 Stevens, Christie
1 Stevens, Chuck
5 Stevens, Craig
1 Stevens, Cy
1 Stevens, Diana
38 Stevens, Ed
1 Stevens, Gary
2 Stevens, George
1 Stevens, Gloria
1 Stevens, Haig
2 Stevens, Hal
1 Stevens, Harvey
1 Stevens, Jack
20 Stevens, James
1 Stevens, Jenny
4 Stevens, Julie
4 Stevens, K. T.
2 Stevens, Kay
6 Stevens, Ken
30 Stevens, Larry
102 Stevens, Leith
6 Stevens, Lynn
1 Stevens, Manny
8 Stevens, Mark
12 Stevens, Naomi
1 Stevens, Norm
3 Stevens, Phil
1 Stevens, Purley
1 Stevens, Ray
32 Stevens, Rise
1 Stevens, Robert
1 Stevens, Robin
1 Stevens, Si
2 Stevens, Ted
2 Stevens, Terry
1 Stevens, Vicki
5 Stevens, Warren
15 Stevenson, Adlai
3 Stevenson, Allan
43 Stevenson, Bob
1 Stevenson, Edward F.
1 Stevenson, George
2 Stevenson, James
62 Stevenson, John
1 Stevenson, Margot
1 Stevenson, Martin
39 Stevenson, Robert Louis
1 Stevenson, Robert P.
1 Steward, Herb
1 Stewart (Nick Stewart and His Orchestra)
1 Stewart (Rex Stewart and His Orchestra)
1 Stewart, Mary Ann
4 Stewart Sisters, The
1 Stewart, Al
1 Stewart, Arthur
2 Stewart, Bill
1 Stewart, Blanche
2 Stewart, Bob
4 Stewart, Buddy
1 Stewart, Carol
2 Stewart, Charles
2 Stewart, Eleanor
1 Stewart, Franklin
2 Stewart, Gene
5 Stewart, George
9 Stewart, Gloria
10 Stewart, Harry
1 Stewart, Ian
1 Stewart, James
1 Stewart, James Garfield
4 Stewart, Jan
1 Stewart, Janet
37 Stewart, Jay
1 Stewart, Jerry
136 Stewart, Jimmy
9 Stewart, Kay
17 Stewart, Larry
2 Stewart, Laura
1 Stewart, Lisa
1 Stewart, Lori
9 Stewart, Martha
1 Stewart, Maxine
1 Stewart, Newell
1 Stewart, Nick
13 Stewart, Paul
1 Stewart, Paula
3 Stewart, Randy
5 Stewart, Redd
3 Stewart, Rex
2 Stewart, Robert
11 Stewart, Sally
3 Stewart, Sandy
5 Stewart, Slam
2 Stewart, Sophie
1 Stewart, Streator
1 Stewart, Virginia
2 Stidger, William L.
1 Stiedry, Fritz
2 Stiller and Meara
2 Stiller, Jerry
1 Stillman, Calvin
30 Stillwell, Edna
7 Stillwell, Jack
1 Stillwell, Joseph W.
1 Stilwell, Joseph
4 Stimson, Henry
1 Stires, David Ogden
2 Stitt, Sonny
1 Stock, Ron
3 Stockdale, James
2 Stocker, Walter
2 Stockton, Norman
7 Stockwell, Dean
3 Stockwell, Harry
1 Stoddard, Dick
1 Stoddard, Haila
1 Stoddard, Mrs.
1 Stoffa, Andy
1 Stoker, Bill
10 Stoker, Bram
2 Stokes (Harold Stokes and His Orchestra)
7 Stokes Jr., Walter W.
126 Stokes, Ed
1 Stokes, Harold
2 Stokes, Leonard
3 Stokes, Peggy
1 Stokes, William S.
4 Stokowski (Leopold Stokowski and His Symphony Orchestra)
9 Stokowski, Leopold
1 Stolberg, Benjamin
1 Stolchek, Bernice
2 Stoll (George Stoll and His Orchestra)
2 Stoll (Georgie Stoll and His Orchestra)
1 Stollars, Marguerite
2 Stoloff (Morris Stoloff and His Orchestra)
1 Stolz, John
5 Stone (Cliffie Stone and His Home Town Jamboree Gang)
1 Stone (Eddie Stone and His Orchestra)
1 Stone (Kirby Stone Company, The)
1 Stone (Kirby Stone Four, The)
28 Stone, Anne
170 Stone, Bob
21 Stone, Butch
2 Stone, Cliffie
1 Stone, Cynthia
4 Stone, Eddie
8 Stone, Edward
5 Stone, Edward C.
36 Stone, Ezra
1 Stone, Fred
43 Stone, Gene
21 Stone, George
20 Stone, Harlan
10 Stone, Harold
1 Stone, Harvey
4 Stone, Irving
2 Stone, Jeannie
1 Stone, Leland
22 Stone, Lewis
1 Stone, Martin
1 Stone, Marvin
5 Stone, Paula
1 Stone, Phil
1 Stoneham, Horace
1 Stoner, Frank
1 Stonesiter, John
8 Stopak, Joseph
1 Stoppard, Tom
1 Storch, Larry
190 Stordahl (Axel Stordahl and His Orchestra)
1 Storey (Lou Storey Quintet)
27 Storm, Gale
25 Storm, John
1 Stoska, Polnya
18 Stout, Rex
1 Stove, Constance
2 Stover, Smokey
4 Stowaways, The
1 Stowe, Leland
1 Strable, Thelma
5 Stracke, Win
3 Stradivari Orchestra, The
6 Straeter (Ted Straeter and His Orchestra)
2 Straeter, Ted
1 Straight (Charlie Straight and His Orchestra)
6 Straight, Beatrice
1 Strait, Clarence
2 Strand (Manny Strand and His Band)
1 Strand, Paul
2 Strange, Bill
1 Strange, Billy
2 Strange, Robert
5 Strasberg, Susan
1 Strasser, Otto
57 Stratton, Chester
99 Stratton, Gil
1 Strauss, Anna Lord
2 Strauss, Johann
1 Strauss, Nathan
6 Strauss, Robert
6 Strauss, Sandy
1 Strauss, Victor
1 Stravinsky, Igor
4 Strayhorn, Billy
1 Strecker, Edward A.
6 Street, David
2 Street, James
1 Street, Mrs. Jesse
1 Strete, Craig
1 Stribling, T. S.
12 Strickland, Amzie
1 Striker
12 Striker, Fran
1 Strindberg, August
5 Stringbean
1 Stringer, Lou
1 Stringer, Robert
1 Stritch, Elaine
1 Strom, Robert
7 Stromberg, Hunt
1 Strong (Benny Strong and His Orchestra)
28 Strong (Bob Strong and His Orchestra)
2 Strong, Austin
2 Strong, Benny
6 Strong, Bob
1 Strong, Jim
4 Strong, Judson
8 Stroud Twins, The
1 Stroud, Marie
2 Strout, Dick
9 Strudwick, Shepperd
1 Strum (Cal Strum and His Rhythm Rangers)
1 Strut, Gloria
3 Struther, Jan
1 Strutton, Will
1 Stuart, Anne
1 Stuart, Bill
1 Stuart, Larry
1 Stuart, Mary
1 Stuart, Miriam

1 Stuarti, Enzo
1 Stubbs, Eddie
1 Stubbs, Sandy
1 Stuckey, Nat
26 Studebaker, Hugh
2 Studebaker, John W.
58 Studer, Hal
1 Stuhlinger, Ernst
1 Sturc, Ernest
2 Sturgeon, Bob
6 Sturgeon, Theodore
3 Sturges, Preston
3 Styne, Jule
2 Suber, Ray
1 Suchy, John
1 Suckling, John
28 Sudrow, Lyle
1 Sudy, Joe
49 Sues (Leonard Sues and His Orchestra)
3 Sues, Leonard
1 Sugar and Spice
1 Sugarfoot Four, The
1 Suggs, Eric
2 Sugudi, Hugo
1 Suisse, Dana
1 Suitcase Six, The
1 Suiter
10 Sullavan, Margaret
1 Sullivan (Joe Sullivan Quartet)
2 Sullivan, A. M.
1 Sullivan, Arthur
25 Sullivan, Barry
5 Sullivan, Brian
3 Sullivan, Catherine
2 Sullivan, Danny
1 Sullivan, Derry
20 Sullivan, Ed
3 Sullivan, Frank
6 Sullivan, Fred
18 Sullivan, Jeri
13 Sullivan, Joe
3 Sullivan, John L.
1 Sullivan, Joseph
1 Sullivan, Katharine
1 Sullivan, Lee
1 Sullivan, Louis
19 Sullivan, Maxine
3 Sullivan, Norman
2 Sullivan, Pat
5 Sullivan, Paul
2 Sullivan, Roger
1 Sully, Eva
2 Sumac, Yma
1 Summerland, John
2 Summers, Bill
1 Summers, Brooke
1 Summers, Carol
2 Summers, Colleen
20 Summers, Hope
5 Summers, Jay
1 Summers, Jocelyn
1 Summers, Lydia
6 Summerville, Kerwin
2 Summerville, Slim
1 Sumner, Gil
1 Sunberg, Clinton
1 Sunbrock, Larry
2 Sunday Players, The
4 Sunderland, Nan
1 Sundown
1 Sung, Dr.
1 Sunset Riders, The
1 Sunset Trio, The
2 Sunshine Girls, The
1 Sunshine Sue
1 Suntones, The
1 Surfriders, The
3 Surrey, Berne
1 Susa, Leone
4 Susann, Jacqueline
1 Susie
1 Sussex, James
1 Sutcliff, Sick
1 Sutherland, James
1 Sutiff, Bill
1 Sutman, Ralph W.
1 Sutter, Betty
40 Sutter, Daniel
1 Sutter, Peggy
1 Sutterfield, Bill
1 Suttler, Luis
69 Sutton, Dolores
1 Sutton, Ellen
2 Sutton, John
2 Sutton, Kay
34 Sutton, Paul
13 Sutton, Ralph
2 Suzuki, Pat
1 Sved, Alexander
3 Svedrovski, Henry
1 Swain, Charles
2 Swain, Susan
1 Swan, Buddy
1 Swan, Ed
9 Swanee River Boys, The
1 Swanhholm, Setz
1 Swanson, Andrew
13 Swanson, Gloria
9 Swanson, Ruth
8 Swantet, The
40 Swanton, Harold
1 Swantones, The
14 Swart, Howard
1 Swart, Lawrence
29 Swarthout, Gladys
1 Swarts, George
1 Swartz, Dave
6 Swayze, John Cameron
1 Swearingen, John
1 Sweeney and March Choral Society, The
2 Sweeney, Bill
75 Sweeney, Bob
1 Sweeney, Budd
1 Sweeney, Frank
1 Sweeney, Fred
92 Sweeney, Warren
1 Sweet, Blanche
2 Sweet, Jeff
3 Sweet, Paul
13 Sweeten (Claude Sweeten and His Orchestra)
81 Sweeten, Claude
1 Sweetheart, Sally
7 Sweetland, Lee
1 Sweetland, Sally
10 Sweets, William
2 Sweetser, Arthur
1 Sweikert, Bob
3 Swenson, Al
119 Swenson, Karl
2 Swersky, Sid
2 Swett, Ira
1 Swift, Allen
2 Swift, Jack
7 Swift, Jonathan
2 Swing Choir, The
1 Swing Four, The
34 Swing, Raymond Gram
4 Swing Wing, The
1 Swingin' Gates, The
1 Swinging Strings, The
1 Swingle, Kay
1 Swingle, Ozzie
1 Swingle, Ward
1 Swingmasters, The
1 Swingtones, The
5 Swire, Sidney
3 Swope, Herbert Bayard
2 Swope, Jr., Herbert
1 Swore and Good
1 Sykes
1 Sykes, Bobby
3 Sykes, Ethel
1 Sykes, Judge
1 Sykes, Wally
1 Sylte Sisters, The
1 Sylvera, Frank
26 Sylvern (Henry Sylvern and His Orchestra)
17 Sylvern, Henry
20 Sylvester, John
1 Sylvester, Joshua
1 Sylvester, Robert
2 Symington, Stuart
1 Symphonettes, The
1 Symphonic Swing Orchestra, The
2 Symphony Sid
6 Syms, Sylvia
1 Synge, John
1 Synnott, Stephens
2 Szabo, Gabor
1 Szalai, Kenneth
3 Szathmary, Irving
1 Szazlo, Michael
7 Szell, George
4 Szigeti, Joseph

CBS
KNX
33⅓—OUTSIDE START
DATE
PART
T
RECO[...]D BY
RADIO RECORDERS
7000 SANTA MONICA BLVD.
HOLLYWOOD 38, CALIFORNIA

7 Tabbard, Bill
1 Tabioni, Frank
25 Tabori, Kristoffer
44 Tackaberry, John
4 Tackner, Edith
2 Tadoose, George
1 Tafarella, Joe
5 Taft, Charles P.
12 Taft, Robert
2 Taggart, Elon
1 Tagliavini, Ferruccio
1 Taie, Lin
1 Tajo, Italo
1 Talbot (Irvin Talbot and His Orchestra)
1 Talbot, Godfrey
4 Talbot, James W.
3 Talbot, Lyle
2 Talbot, Slim
1 Talbot, William
1 Talbus, Frank
4 Talent, Ziggy
1 Tall, Steven
1 Tallman, Gil
75 Tallman, Robert
26 Talmadge, Norma
5 Tambo and Bones
9 Tamiroff, Akim
21 Tandy, Jessica
2 Tannen, Charles
27 Tannen, Eleanor
31 Tanner, Desmond
2 Tanner, Earl
10 Tanner, Elmo
1 Tanoway, Harry
5 Tanswell, Bertram
1 Taplin, Walter
1 Tapp, Mara
1 Tapscott, Carl
1 Taradash, Daniel
1 Taranik, James
1 Tarion, Leon
10 Tarkington, Booth
2 Tarloff, Frank
109 Tarplin, Maurice
1 Tarriers, The
1 Tarry, Suzette
1 Tarson, Elliot
1 Tarter, Jill
1 Tarteroff, Jerome
1 Tate, Buddy
1 Tate, Dorothy
3 Tate, Grady
3 Tate, Maggie
1 Tatum (Art Tatum and His Orchestra)
2 Tatum (Art Tatum Trio)
21 Tatum, Art
1 Tatum, Clifford
2 Tatum, Dee
59 Tatum, Jean
1 Taub, Sam
1 Tauber, Emma
1 Tauber, Richard
2 Taubman (Paul Taubman Trio, The)
1 Taubman, Howard
42 Taubman, Paul
1 Taurog, Norman
1 Tauzin, Billy
17 Tavaras, Ernie
1 Taxco, Ray
2 Taylor
6 Taylor (Billy Taylor Trio, The)
3 Taylor (Paul Taylor Choristers, The)
3 Taylor (Paul Taylor Chorus, The)
1 Taylor (Paul Taylor Douglas Airenaders, The)
10 Taylor (Sam The Man Taylor and His Orchestra)
2 Taylor Maids, The
1 Taylor, Baird
12 Taylor, Betty
1 Taylor, Beverly
12 Taylor, Billy
2 Taylor, Bruce
1 Taylor, Cathy
1 Taylor, Cecil
3 Taylor, Charles
1 Taylor, Coleridge
1 Taylor, Dan
5 Taylor, Davidson

75 Taylor, Deems
1 Taylor, Don
2 Taylor, Donald
1 Taylor, Eleanor
9 Taylor, Elizabeth
16 Taylor, F. Chase
8 Taylor, Forrest
2 Taylor, Gil
4 Taylor, Glen
1 Taylor, Grant
1 Taylor, Harold
6 Taylor, Henry
1 Taylor, Henry L.
1 Taylor, Ida
2 Taylor, Irene
1 Taylor, Jack
1 Taylor, Jane
6 Taylor, Jeanne
1 Taylor, Joan
1 Taylor, John
2 Taylor, Kent
1 Taylor, Larry
1 Taylor, Lawrence Edmond
1 Taylor, Libby
2 Taylor, Lucy
1 Taylor, Madeline
1 Taylor, Marjorie
5 Taylor, Mary
13 Taylor, Mary Lee
1 Taylor, Maxwell
1 Taylor, Montana
3 Taylor, Peggy
7 Taylor, Reese
46 Taylor, Robert
3 Taylor, Sam
3 Taylor, Tom
5 Taylor, Tommy
1 Taylor, Vaughn
1 Taylor, Walter
1 Taylor, Wayne C.
1 Taylor, William
11 Tazewell, Charles
1 Tazewell, James
2 Teagarden (Jack Teagarden and His New Orchestra)
16 Teagarden (Jack Teagarden and His Orchestra)
3 Teagarden, Charlie
56 Teagarden, Jack
2 Teagarden, Norma
1 Teague, Charles C.
1 Teague, Richard
1 Teaman, Ann
7 Tearle, Conway
17 Teasdale, Verree
1 Tebaldi, Renata
3 Tebbetts, Birdie
2 Tedder, Arthur
2 Tedrow, Henrietta
83 Tedrow, Irene
1 Teenagers, The
1 Teeter, Robert
7 Teichmann, Howard
30 Teitel, Carol
1 Teitle, Irving
6 Tell, Gladys
2 Teller, Edward
4 Temple, Alvina
1 Temple, Brooke
1 Temple, Fred
1 Temple, George
1 Temple, Pick
29 Temple, Shirley
35 Templeton, Alec
1 Templeton, Alice
2 Templeton, Patrick
1 Tempo, Nino
1 Temptations, The
1 Ten Harmonaires, The
7 Tenn, William
4 Tennessee Mountain Boys, The
2 Tennessee Plowboys, The
12 Tennyson, Jean
17 Tennyson, Scott
1 Tepa, J.
7 Tepperman, Emil
1 Teranova, Phil
1 Terazzo, Gene
1 Terhune, Albert Payson
6 Terkel, Studs
2 Terlhet, Hildegarde
1 Terr (Max Terr's Choral Group)
1 Terr, Max
1 Terrell, Danny
3 Terrell, Fha
1 Terrille, Rich
1 Terriss, Mildred
27 Terriss, Tom
2 Terry (Clark Terry Quintet, The)
12 Terry (Dave Terry and His Orchestra)
1 Terry (Dave Terry and The U.S.M.S. Orchestra)
1 Terry (David Terry and His Orchestra)
4 Terry, Clark
2 Terry, Don
1 Terry, Doug
1 Terry, Frank
5 Terry, Gordon
79 Terry, Joy
1 Terry, Margaret
2 Terry, Megan
3 Terry, Phillip
1 Terry, Ralph
2 Terry, Sonny
1 Terry, Vince
8 Terwilliger, Daryl
2 Terzian, Yervant
1 Testardi, Louis
661 Tetley, Walter
7 Tetzel, Joan
1 Texaco Chorus, The
3 Texaco Singers, The
1 Texas Rangers, The
7 Thackery, William Makepeace
1 Thagard
3 Thais, Jean
1 Thale, June Bryde
2 Thant, U
1 Tharpe, Rosetta
1 That Snappy Saxophone Eight
1 Thatcher, Dior
1 Thatcher, Heather
11 Thatcher, Leora
2 Thatcher, Lynn
1 Thatcher, Margaret
4 Thatcher, Torin
6 Thaxter, Phyllis
1 Thayer, Tiffany
3 Theatre Of Stars Orchestra, The
7 Thebom, Blanche
3 Theodore, Brother
7 Theodore, Paul
1 Theon, John
14 Thibault, Conrad
1 Thiele (Bob Thiele and His New Happy Times Orchestra)
1 Thielemans, Toots
1 Thienel, Charles
1 Thieu, President
1 Thigh, Edward
1 Thinnes, Roy
1 Thole, John
1 Thom, Randy
1 Thom, Sharon
1 Thomas (Don Thomas and His Symphonic Swing Orchestra)
1 Thomas, Alan
1 Thomas, Albert
1 Thomas, Albert D.
39 Thomas, Ann
2 Thomas, Bill
2 Thomas, Bob
1 Thomas, Clarence
38 Thomas, Danny
1 Thomas, Duff
1 Thomas, Dylan
4 Thomas, Elbert
3 Thomas, Elmer
1 Thomas, Elton D.
2 Thomas, Evan
19 Thomas, Frank
21 Thomas, Frank
43 Thomas, Jr., Frank
1 Thomas, Frazier
1 Thomas, George
3 Thomas, Gilbert
3 Thomas, Gretchen
1 Thomas, Hal
1 Thomas, Helen
12 Thomas, Hugh
1 Thomas, J. Parnell
5 Thomas, Jack
2 Thomas, Jay
3 Thomas, Joe
14 Thomas, John
34 Thomas, John Charles
3 Thomas, Johnny
1 Thomas, Leon
30 Thomas, Lowell
1 Thomas, Marlo
1 Thomas, Miles
1 Thomas, Millard
20 Thomas, Norman
3 Thomas, Olive
1 Thomas, Pam
1 Thomas, Patty
4 Thomas, Peter
3 Thomas, Phil
8 Thomas, Phillips
1 Thomas, R. J.
1 Thomas, Rose Fay
1 Thomas, Ruth
10 Thomas, Shirley
1 Thomas, Sybil
2 Thomas, Terry
27 Thomas, Thomas L.
1 Thomas, Tony
1 Thomas, Winfred Vaughn
1 Thomason, S. E.
2 Thome, Pitt
1 Thompson
1 Thompson (Hank Thompson and His Orchestra)
1 Thompson (Hank Thompson and The Brasos Valley Boys)
1 Thompson (Kay Thompson Singers, The)
1 Thompson (Lang Thompson and His Orchestra)
1 Thompson Jr., Frank
12 Thompson, B. J.
1 Thompson, Bess
443 Thompson, Bill
1 Thompson, Bob
4 Thompson, Bobby
21 Thompson, D. J.
6 Thompson, David
1 Thompson, Dick
3 Thompson, Don
3 Thompson, Dorothy
23 Thompson, Duane
1 Thompson, Frank
1 Thompson, Fred
1 Thompson, George
1 Thompson, Gwen
1 Thompson, Hank
1 Thompson, Hans
1 Thompson, Howard J.
2 Thompson, Hugh
1 Thompson, Jack
1 Thompson, James
2 Thompson, Janie
1 Thompson, John
6 Thompson, Johnny
16 Thompson, Kay
1 Thompson, Lawrence
4 Thompson, Lenore
1 Thompson, Les
2 Thompson, Marshall
1 Thompson, Milton
11 Thompson, Palmer
2 Thompson, Paul
1 Thompson, Proctor
1 Thompson, R. F.
1 Thompson, Rex
5 Thompson, Robert
1 Thompson, Sadie
1 Thompson, Sue
1 Thompson, Sylvia
1 Thompson, Tommy
1 Thompson, V. J.
2 Thompson, Virgil
1 Thompson, Wayne
19 Thomson, Barry
1 Thomson, Sedge
1 Thor, Jerome
150 Thor, Larry
1 Thorber, Usten
2 Thorgersen, Ed
3 Thorn, Brian
1 Thorn, Susan
1 Thorn, W. L.
2 Thornbough, Don
1 Thornburgh, Dick
20 Thorne, Richard
1 Thorne, Susan
20 Thornhill (Claude Thornhill and His Orchestra)
1 Thornhill, C. E.
4 Thornhill, Claude
1 Thornley, George H.
1 Thornly, Gordon
8 Thornton, Gladys
1 Thornton, Thomas
3 Thornton, William
2 Thorpe, Jim
1 Thorpe, Virginia
1 Thorsness, Cliff
2 Thorson, Karen
186 Thorson, Russell
1 Thorson, Sally
2 Thrasher Sisters, The
1 Three Aces, The
10 Three Ambassadors, The
1 Three Banjo Kings, The
1 Three Barons, The
2 Three Beaus and A Peep
2 Three Berries, The
1 Three Blue Keys, The
1 Three Chocolates, The
2 Three Chuckles, The
3 Three D's, The
1 Three Debutantes, The
3 Three Flames, The
1 Three Graces, The
1 Three Jacks, The
1 Three Jokers, The
1 Three Little Words, The
1 Three Marshalls, The
2 Three Merry Men, The
2 Three Radio Rogues, The
1 Three Rhythm Rascals
2 Three Roberts Boys, The
1 Three Scamps, The
5 Three Sisters, The
1 Three Sun Bonnet Girls, The
32 Three Suns, The
1 Three Toppers, The
1 Three Treys and A Queen
5 Three Two-Timers, The
2 Threlkeld, Richard
1 Thumball, Loretta
9 Thurber, James
1 Tibbett Jr., Lawrence
27 Tibbett, Lawrence
1 Tibbetts, Clark
17 Tice, Olen
1 Tidelow, Joseph
1 Tiedi, Alexander
21 Tierney, Gene
1 Tierney, Harry
1 Tierney, Lawrence
1 Tiffin, Pamela
1 Tighe, Elaine
1 Tighe, Larry
1 Tilbury, Zeffie
2 Tilden, Bill
13 Tilden, Weslan
7 Tile, Ted
1 Tilford, Shelby
1 Tillis, Mel
1 Tillish, Ingabord
2 Tillman, Floyd
7 Tillman, John
1 Tillstrom, Burr

1 Tilton, Alice
1 Tilton, George
7 Tilton, Liz
1 Tilton, Marilyn
105 Tilton, Martha
4 Tim and Irene
1 Timberley, H. R.
1 Timmons, Jimmy
1 Timperley, Harold
1 Tiner, McCoy
4 Tines, Gwen
1 Tingwell, Charles
2 Tinney, Cal
1 Tinney, Larry
1 Tinsley, Charlotte
1 Tinsley, Jack
1 Tiny, Colonel
4 Tiomkin, Dimitri
1 Tip Tap Toe
1 Tiplady, George
1 Tippett, Wayne
1 Tirebiter, George
1 Tito
1 Tito, Rocco
2 Tittle, Y. A.
1 Titus, Dave
1 Titus, Davis
5 Tizol, Juan
2 Tjader, Cal
1 Toberg, Kirsten
3 Tobias, Channing
1 Tobias, Charles
8 Tobias, George
1 Tobias, Harry
2 Tobiason, Dick
1 Tobin (Harry Tobin and His Orchestra)
13 Tobin, Ann
1 Tobin, Dan
1 Tobin, Joe
5 Tobin, Lou
4 Tobin, Ruth
1 Toby
1 Toby, Ken
1 Toby, Mark
2 Todd (Tommy Todd Trio, The)
3 Todd, Ann
2 Todd, Arthur
28 Todd, Dick
1 Todd, Dot
3 Todd, Elizabeth
220 Todd, John
3 Todd, Mabel
1 Todd, Mike
1 Todd, Richard
3 Todd, Tommy
7 Todman, Bill
1 Toffler, Alvin
3 Tokar, Norman
2 Tokyo Rose
23 Tolan, Michael
2 Toler, Sidney
1 Toler, Stephanie
26 Tolkien, J. R. R.
1 Tolley, Howard
1 Tolliver, Toby
1 Toloucious, Otto
1 Tolson, Robert
10 Tolstoy, Leo
6 Tom Dick and Harry
1 Tombes, Andrew
2 Tomlin (Pinky Tomlin and His Orchestra)
1 Tomlin, Lily
5 Tomlin, Pinky
5 Tomlinson, Edward
1 Tomlinson, H. M.
1 Tomlinson, Tommy
12 Tommy, T.
1 Tompkins, Ellsworth
1 Tompkins, Jane
13 Tompkins, Joan
1 Tompkins, Junior
1 Toms, Nick
1 Tomseth, Victor
32 Tone, Franchot
1 Tone, Jeff
2 Tones, Joe
2 Tong, Phillip
16 Tonkin, Phil
3 Toomey, Regis
3 Toon, Brian
1 Toppers, The
2 Topping, Dan
1 Topping, Seymour
41 Torch, Sidney
1 Toren, Marta
1 Torgeson
10 Torme (Mel Torme and The Meltones)
57 Torme, Mel
2 Tornabene, Russ
1 Torre, Joe
2 Torrence, David
1 Tors, Ivan
95 Toscanini, Arturo
1 Tossick, Frank
2 Totie, John
26 Totter, Audrey
2 Tough, Davey
9 Tours (Frank Tours and His Orchestra)
6 Tours, Frank
8 Tourtellotte, Wesley
1 Touten, James W.
2 Tower, John
1 Towers, Constance
84 Towers, Harry Alan
3 Towers, Robert
1 Towers, Susan
2 Town and Country Four, The
19 Town Criers, The
4 Town Hall Quartet, The
1 Towne (George Towne and His Orchestra)
2 Towne, Gene
1 Towne, Joyce
2 Towne, Rosella
1 Townes, Vince
1 Townman, Robert
2 Townsend, Barbara
5 Townsend, Dallas
1 Townsend, Francis
1 Townsend, Jewell
1 Townsend, M. Clifford
3 Townsend, Vincent
1 Townsmen Quartet, The
2 Toynbee, Arnold
2 Tozair, Frederick
1 Tozin, Maurice
6 Tozzi, George
1 Trace (Al Trace and His Orchestra)
1 Tracher, Ernest
6 Tracy, Arthur
3 Tracy, Emerson
47 Tracy, Lee
1 Tracy, Mrs. Spencer
20 Tracy, Spencer
21 Tracy, Sterling
46 Tracy, William
2 Trafficante, Marie
5 Trammel, Niles
1 Trapp Family Singers, The
1 Trappe, Arthur
1 Trask (Clyde Trask and His Orchestra)
24 Traubel, Helen
1 Travalena, Fred
2 Travers (Ted Travers and His Orchestra)
1 Travers, Lawrence
1 Travers, Patricia
1 Travis
3 Travis, Frank
15 Travis, Merle
1 Travis, Tony
1 Traynor (Tommy Traynor and The Crewchiefs)
2 Traynor, Tom
8 Traynor, Tommy
96 Treacher, Arthur
7 Treadway, Charlotte
1 Tredway, William
1 Tree, Toni
1 Trefil, James
5 Trella, Mark
156 Tremayne, Les
8 Trendle, George W.
1 Trendler (Bob Trendler and His Orchestra)
3 Trendler (Robert Trendler and His Orchestra)
1 Trendler (Robert Trendler and His Orchestra and Chorus)
34 Trendler, Robert
2 Trenent (Billy Trenent Orchestra)
1 Trenet, Charles
1 Trenier, Claude
1 Treniers, The
2 Trenner, Don
1 Trent, Bruce
1 Trent, Elaine
19 Trent, Sybil
1 Tresh, Tom
1 Trevell, George
1 Trevino, Lee
1 Treviramus, G.
47 Trevor, Claire
1 Trevor, Edward
1 Trewartha, Glenn T.
3 Trilling, Diana
5 Trio Los Panchos
4 Tripp, Paul
1 Trombka, Jacob
387 Trotter (John Scott Trotter and His Orchestra)
3 Trotter, John Scott
2 Troubador, The
1 Troubadors Male Quartette
1 Troup (Bobby Troup and His Quartet)
2 Troup (Bobby Troup Trio, The)
14 Troup, Bobby
66 Trout, Dink
2 Trout, Paul Dizzy
147 Trout, Robert
1 Troutman, George
1 Trowbridge, Charles
3 Troxl (Mark Troxl and His Orchestra)
1 Troy, Helen
1 Truax, Anne
1 Truex, Ernest
1 Truex, James
1 Truitt, Henry
6 Truly, Richard
1 Truman, Faith
171 Truman, Harry
6 Truman, Margaret
1 Truman, Paula
5 Truman, Rafe
3 Trumbauer (Frankie Trumbauer and His Orchestra)
1 Trumbauer (Frankie Trumbauer's Swing Seven)
3 Trumbauer, Frankie
2 Trumbo, Dalton
1 Trumpeter, Lanfrey
1 Truscutt, General
1 Tsongas, Paul
6 Tsweig, Esther
3 Tubb (Ernest Tubb and His Texas Troubadors)
23 Tubb, Ernest
2 Tubb, Justin
1 Tubeman, Raymond
1 Tuberd, Marcello
2 Tucker (Bobby Tucker Singers, The)
8 Tucker (Orrin Tucker and His Orchestra)
41 Tucker (Tommy Tucker and His Orchestra)
1 Tucker, Arnold
5 Tucker, Forrest
1 Tucker, George
5 Tucker, Happy Jack
1 Tucker, John
6 Tucker, Orrin
1 Tucker, Ray
8 Tucker, Richard
1 Tucker, Richard T.
15 Tucker, Sophie
1 Tucker, William
1 Tucson Boys Choir, The
1 Tudor, Fred
1 Tudor, George
1 Tudor, Godrey
3 Tudor, Jean
120 Tufeld, Dick
4 Tufte, Esther Van Waggoner
16 Tufts, Sonny
50 Tully, Tom
2 Tuminia, Josephine
13 Tundberg, Carl A.
14 Tundberg, William
1 Tune Jugglers, The
39 Tune Twirlers, The
19 Tune Twisters, The
34 Tunick, Irve
7 Tunney, Gene
329 Tupper, Howard
1 Turcott, Ron
1 Turing, Clark
1 Turlington, Edgar
1 Turnbull, Glen
2 Turnbull, Johnny
8 Turner (Billy Turner and His Orchestra)
1 Turner, Admiral
1 Turner, Catherine
5 Turner, Claramae
1 Turner, Clarance
1 Turner, Fred
1 Turner, Gil
11 Turner, Grant
1 Turner, Happy Jack
1 Turner, Harold Milton
1 Turner, Jill
1 Turner, Joe
17 Turner, Lana
1 Turner, Lillian
2 Turner, Nancy
1 Turner, Ray
1 Turner, Roscoe
1 Turpin (Bea Turpin and Her Eight Jills Of Jive)
1 Turrell, Charles
3 Turrell, Jenny
1 Turtelov, Arthur
1 Tuscany, Bill
5 Tuskegee Institute Choir, The
1 Tuthill, Betsy
2 Tuttle (Wesley Tuttle and His Coon Hunters)
469 Tuttle, Lurene
1 Tuttle, Marilyn
2 Tuttle, Roger
2 Tuttle, Wesley
25 Twain, Mark
1 Twanley, Mack
3 Tweed, Tommy
2 Twelvetrees, Helen
4 Twerp, Joe
3 Twice, Jonathan
1 Twin Tones, The
2 Twining, Nathan
2 Twiss, Buddy
2 Two Bees and A Honey
1 Two Black Jacks, The
1 Two Counts and A Countess
1 Two Hits and A Miss
1 Two Wives, The
1 Two-Timers, The
1 Two-Tones, The
16 Twombley, Gene
1 Twombley, Matt
2 Tyler (T. Texas Tyler and His Band)
4 Tyler, Betty Jane
3 Tyler, Beverly
1 Tyler, Harry
2 Tyler, Jack
1 Tyler, June
1 Tyler, Steven
2 Tyler, T. Texas
1 Tyler, William
1 Tyler, Willie
1 Tymes, The
2 Tyner, Evelyn

1 Tyre, Marjorie
1 Tyres, John
26 Tyson, Cecily
5 Tyson, Charles
1 Tyson, Joan

5 U.S.S. Helena Band, The
2 Udall, Morris
7 Uggams, Leslie
2 Ulanov (Barry Ulanov's All-Star Modern Jazz Musicians)
1 Ulin, Harris
1 Ullman, Blanche Firth
9 Uncle Bill
2 Uncle Ezra
1 Underwood, Agnes
3 Underwood, Cecil
1 Underwood, Jeffrey
1 Unger, Arthur
3 Unitas, Johnny
1 United Scandinavian Male Chorus, The
1 Unsen, Dale
2 Untermeyer, Louis
1 Upham, Charles M.
1 Upson, Dean
1 Upton, Fred
1 Upton, John R.
3 Upton, Julian
1 Uptowners, The
1 Urey, Francis
2 Urey, Harold
1 Urquahrt, Charles
2 Ursha, Elizabeth
1 Urthine, James
3 Usher, Billy
1 Ussleton, Billy
5 Ustinov, Peter
2 Usyli, Gaston
3 Utley, Clifton
3 Utley, Garrick
1 Utsman, Thomas
28 Uttal, Fred
2 Utvich, Michael
1 Uzcudun, Paolino

1 Vaccarro, Brenda
2 Vagabonds, The
1 Vail, Virginia
4 Vaille, Dave
1 Vaine, Vivian
1 Valdez (Miguelito Valdez and His Orchestra)
7 Valdez, Miguelito
1 Valdez, Nino
12 Vale, Jerry
1 Vale, Rita
1 Valence, Alma
5 Valente, Caterina
1 Valenti (Vic Valenti and His Orchestra)
1 Valenti, Jack
1 Valenti, Lily
1 Valentine (Kid Thomas Valentine Preservation Hall Band)
7 Valentine, Dick
1 Valentine, John
1 Valentine, Judy
1 Valentine, Lew
1 Valentine, Lili
1 Valentine, Nancy
2 Valentines, The
4 Valentino, Barry
6 Valentino, Francesco
1 Valentino, Rudolph
1 Valenty, Lili
2 Valeriani, Richard
1 Valeur, Robert
7 Valitis, Jonas
2 Vallard, Paul
6 Vallee (Rudy Vallee and His Orchestra)
7 Vallee (Rudy Vallee and The Connecticut Yankees)
1 Vallee, Felix
107 Vallee, Rudy
2 Valli
12 Valli, June
1 Vallin, Jerry
5 Vallin, Rick
1 Valochek, Andrew J.
5 Valsante (Vincent Valsante and His Orchestra)
1 Valtin, Jan
2 Van Allen, James
1 Van and Schenck
1 Van Antwerp, Albert
1 van Berkel, Jacob
2 Van Brocklin, Norm
11 Van Cleave, Nathan
11 Van Damme (Art Van Damme Quintet)
33 Van Damme (Art Van Damme Quintet, The)
8 Van Deventer, Fred
1 van Dias, Arnold
17 Van Doren, Carl
3 Van Doren, Charles
1 Van Doren, Mamie
4 Van Doren, Mark
2 Van Dorn (George Van Dorn and His Orchestra)
1 Van Druton, John
1 Van Dusen, Albert C.
1 Van Dusen, Henry P.
2 Van Dusen, James
1 Van Dyk, Billy
1 Van Dyke, Dick
1 Van Dyke, Henry
12 Van Dyke, James
1 Van Dyke, Jerry
1 Van Dyke, W. S.
2 Van Emburgh, Hurl
2 Van Eps, George
1 Van Fleet, James
1 Van Gorder, George
33 Van Hartesfeldt, Fran
153 Van Harvey, Art
3 Van Heusen, Jimmy
3 van Hoogstraten, Willem
8 Van Horn, Art
1 Van Horne (Randy Van Horne and The Swing Choir)
1 Van Horne, Harriet
1 Van Kirk, Mary
1 Van Kleffens, Eelco
1 Van Lose, Audrey
1 Van Niece, Frederick
1 Van Patten, Dick
1 Van Patten, Joyce
2 Van Riper, Hart
163 Van Rooten, Luis
1 Van Scott, Glory
1 Van Sickle, John
40 Van Steeden (Peter Van Steeden and His Orchestra)
2 Van Steeden, Peter
1 van Straten, N. L. W.
1 Van Vooren, Monique
37 Van Voorhis, Westbrook
1 Van Wagoner, Murray D.
1 Van White, Carolyn
2 Van Zandt, James E.
1 Van Zant, Dorothy
1 Van, Bobby
5 Van, Gloria
5 Van, Gus
1 Van, Lyle
1 Van, Rex
1 Van, Solly
1 Van, Stan
1 Van, Vera
1 Vance, Jack
1 Vance, Roger
12 Vanda, Charles
2 Vandas (Emil Vandas and His Orchestra)
1 Vandenberg, Arthur
1 Vandenberg, Arthur H.
1 Vandenberg, Berta
3 Vandenberg, Hoyt
19 Vander Pyl, Jean
1 Vanderbilt, Alfred
16 Vandercook, John
1 Vanderkellin, Ron
1 Vandermost, Gail
1 Vandertbilt, Amy
6 Vandover, Bud
1 Vanelli, Richard
2 Vanini (Caesar Joe Vanini and His Highway Five)
1 Vannier, Michael
6 Vanocur, Sander
1 Vantveer, Pete
8 Varden, Evelyn
34 Varden, Norma
1 Vardi, Immanuel
1 Vargas, Pedro
1 Varnoux, Roland
1 Varsity Eight, The
2 Vase, Gus
1 Vasquez, Jimmy
1 Vass Family, The
17 Vaughan, Sarah
13 Vaughn (Billy Vaughn and His Orchestra)
2 Vaughn (Denny Vaughn and His Orchestra)
42 Vaughn, Beryl
2 Vaughn, Denny
1 Vaughn, Frankie
3 Vaughn, Juanita
1 Vaughn, Miles W.
7 Vaughn, Walter
1 Vaughn, William
1 Veal, Doris
1 Veccioni, Caspare
1 Veeck, Bill
2 Veedy, George
1 Vega (Celsa Vega Boys, The)
1 Vega (Celsa Vega Quartet, The)
1 Vega (Celsa Vega Quintet, The)
1 Vega, Celsa
2 Veidt, Conrad
1 Veith, Bob
1 Velasco, Jack
13 Velasco, John
1 Velayati, Ali Akbar
2 Velez, Lupe
2 Velone, Nanette
1 Veloz, Frank
1 Veltman, J. H. F.
2 Venable, Evelyn
1 Venback, Joe
1 Venick, Nell
1 Venning, Michael
2 Ventura (Charlie Ventura and His Combo)
3 Ventura, Betty
8 Ventura, Charlie
3 Ventura, Nino
1 Venturi, Ken
14 Venuta, Benay
3 Venuti (Joe Venuti and His Orchestra)
4 Venuti (Joe Venuti and The Blue Five)
41 Venuti, Joe
13 Vera-Ellen
1 Verbeloff, Joe
14 Verdera, Claire
4 Verdon, Gwen
2 Vereen, Ben
1 Vermillion, Charles
5 Vermilyea, Harold
8 Verne, Jules
1 Vernier, Lisa
1 Vernon, Jackie
1 Vernon, Louis
1 Vernon, Mickey
5 Vernon, Whit

2 VerPlanck, Marlene
28 Verrill, Virginia
3 Vester, Gil
1 Vi and Vilma
1 Vibration Society, The
1 Vichegonov, Lubomir
1 Vick, Bruno
2 Vickers, John
1 Vickers, Martha
1 Vickery, Howard L.
1 Victor Orchestra, The
1 Victor, Brevard
1 Victor, Buddy
1 Victor, Charles
52 Victor, David
1 Victor, Frankie
7 Victor, Johnny
2 Victor, Paula
1 Victor, Sally
1 Victorians, The
1 Victory All-Star Orchestra, The
1 Victory War Chest Orchestra, The
1 Vidor, King
1 Vienna Symphony Orchestra, The
1 Viennese Street Ensemble, The
1 Vigastaff, Knight
1 Vigoda, Abe
167 Vigran, Herb
4 Village Green Four, The
1 Villar, Lawrence
1 Villard, Oswald Garrison
1 Villars, M. Henry
11 Villerts, Rick
1 Villiars, Doreen
1 Vince, Frankie
1 Vincent
1 Vincent (Gene Vincent and The Blue Caps)
1 Vincent (Gene Vincent and The Blue Chips)
1 Vincent, Bob
9 Vincent, Chick
3 Vincent, Dorrie
2 Vincent, G. Robert
1 Vincent, Hal
1 Vincent, Helen
1 Vincent, June
1 Vincent, Pete
4 Vincent, Robert C.
2 Vincent, Romo
1 Vines, Ben
1 Vines, Florence
8 Vines, Lee
1 Viney, Henry
1 Vining, Elizabeth Gray
1 Vinson, Eddie Cleanhead
1 Vinson, Frederick
4 Vinson, Owen
25 Vinton, Arthur
1 Vinton, Bobby
2 Viola (Al Viola Quintet, The)
1 Viola, Al
1 Virdier, Christine
6 Virdier, William
1 Virgin, Chets
1 Virtue, Archie
24 Vishinsky, Andrei

1 Visser, Paul
1 Vita Ray Quartet, The
3 Vitale, Joseph
1 Vitaphone Orchestra, The
1 Vitez, Joan
10 Vito, Edward
9 Vittes, Louis
1 Viva America Orchestra, The
12 Vivian
33 Vlas Datsenko, Alexander
1 Vliet, R. G.
1 Vodonya, Natalie
1 Voeller, Will
1 Vogel, Paul
2 Vogler, Robert
2 Voices Four, The
1 Voices Of Walter Schumann, The
1 Voices Three, The
1 Voigt, Karsten
1 Voitikov, Boris
31 Vola, Vicki
3 Volkman, Lois
3 Voltaire
5 von Braun, Wernher
62 Von Eltz, Theodore
1 Von Freeman Quartet
1 von Furstenburg, Betsy
2 Von Hallberg (Sven Von Hallberg's Oriental Orchestra)
2 Von Loon, Henrik Willem
5 von Puttkamer, Jesco
5 Von Ribbentrop, Joachim
13 Von Seggerne, Orville
1 Von Selten, Dave
4 Von Stroheim, Erich
3 von Tiesenhausen, George
1 Von Tilzer, Albert
408 Von Zell, Harry
51 Vonn, Veola
1 Vonnegut Jr., Kurt
18 Voorhees (Donald Voorhees and His Orchestra)
243 Voorhees, Donald
4 Voran, Arthur
1 Vordenberg, Wes
2 Vornholt, John
2 Voss, Carl
2 Votrian, Peter
16 Voutsas, George
1 Vox, Martha
1 Vucanovich, Barbara

WADC
AKRON, OHIO
RECORDING STUDIOS
INSIDE START
OUTSIDE START
SPEED 33⅓ R.P.M.
SPEED 78 R.P.M.
W
AKRON'S PIONEER STATION

2 W.P.A. War Service Band
1 W65H Ensemble, The
1 WAAC Band, The
88 Wade, Ernestine
9 Wade, Gerald
2 Wade, Johnny
1 Wade, Justin
30 Wade, Stuart
5 Wadleigh, Ellen
1 Wadsen, Tommy
1 Wadsworth, Carolyn
30 Wager, Michael
1 Waggoner, Lyle
5 Wagner (Roger Wagner Chorale, The)
1 Wagner, Albert
2 Wagner, Conrad
1 Wagner, Helen
1 Wagner, Honus
68 Wagner, Irene
1 Wagner, Karl Edward
4 Wagner, Murray
1 Wagner, Ouida
1 Wagner, Richard
8 Wagner, Robert
8 Wagoner, Porter
1 Waikiki Girls, The
57 Wain, Bea
4 Wainright, Jonathan
2 Wakely (Jimmy Wakely and His Orchestra)
2 Wakely (Jimmy Wakely and His Rodeo Boys)
1 Wakely (Jimmy Wakely and His Rough Riders)
3 Wakely, Arthur
1 Wakely, Gwen
31 Wakely, Jimmy
1 Wakeman, Frederick
1 Walburn, Patrick
9 Walburn, Raymond
1 Wald, Jerry
133 Wald, John
2 Wald, Melvin
1 Wald, Virginia
2 Waldecker, Frank
2 Waldeman, Herman
4 Waldon, Ben
1 Walden Pell II

1 Walden, Roy
1 Walders, Sam
4 Waldman, Louis
2 Waldman, Marian
82 Waldo, Janet
1 Waldorf, Lynn
12 Waldrop, Robert
1 Wales, Martin
1 Walker, Al Rube
7 Walker, Arlene
1 Walker, Art
2 Walker, Billy
1 Walker, Bob
2 Walker, Charles
1 Walker, Cindy
1 Walker, Clifford
1 Walker, Clint
27 Walker, Danton
3 Walker, Dixie
1 Walker, Doak
15 Walker, Dusty
3 Walker, Harry
3 Walker, Helen
9 Walker, Jimmy
3 Walker, Joe
3 Walker, June
1 Walker, Kirby
1 Walker, Mickey
4 Walker, Nancy
2 Walker, Pax
1 Walker, Postmaster General
1 Walker, Ray
8 Walker, Robert
1 Walker, Sherman
5 Walker, Sidney
1 Walker, Terry
1 Walker, Wayne
8 Wall, Lucille
1 Wall, Steve
2 Wallace
8 Wallace, Alice
1 Wallace, Andrea
1 Wallace, Babe
1 Wallace, Bill
6 Wallace, Chris
2 Wallace, F. L.
2 Wallace, Francis

2 Wallace, Fred S.
1 Wallace, Glenn
6 Wallace, Guy
9 Wallace, Henry
1 Wallace, Irving
68 Wallace, Mike
24 Wallace, Regina
3 Wallace, Richard
1 Wallace, Sylvia
1 Wallace, Ted
1 Wallace, Timmy
14 Wallach, Eli
2 Wallach, George
1 Wallenstein (Alfred Wallenstein and His Orchestra)
27 Wallenstein, Alfred
1 Waller (Fats Waller and His Orchestra)
1 Waller (Fats Waller Band, The)
1 Waller (Fats Waller's Original Band)
7 Waller, Eddie
11 Waller, Fats
332 Wallington, Jimmy
3 Wallis, Hal
17 Walliser, Blair
1 Wallop, Malcolm
1 Walpole, Hugh
1 Walsh (Jimmy Walsh and His Orchestra)
2 Walsh, Dan
7 Walsh, Gene
170 Walsh, George
2 Walsh, Henry
12 Walsh, J. Raymond
4 Walsh, Mary Jane
1 Walsh, Raoul
1 Walsh, Thomas
2 Walston, Ray
1 Walston, Robert
1 Walstrom, Harry
1 Walstrom, Martha
1 Walter, Bob
6 Walter, Bruno
11 Walter, Cy
1 Walter, Felix
1 Walter, Jerry
5 Walter, Jessica
1 Walter, Patricia
1 Walter, Wilmer
1 Walters, Alan
13 Walters, Barbara
1 Walters, Howard
4 Walters, Joe
4 Walters, Lee
2 Walters, Teddy
1 Walters, Vernon
1 Waltham, Florence
2 Walton, Cedar
1 Walton, Charles
19 Walton, Eloise
6 Walton, Jayne
3 Walton, Sidney
1 Walworth, Dorothy
6 Wanamaker, Sam
2 Wandalevska, Wanda
1 Wandering Boys, The
11 Wang, Eugene
1 Wang, Yoeh E.
2 Wanger, Walter

1 Warburton, Charles
1 Ward (Billy Ward and The Dominoes)
1 Ward and Peters
4 Ward, Al
17 Ward, Albert
1 Ward, Arch
1 Ward, Arthur
2 Ward, Colleen
1 Ward, Dave
6 Ward, Don
1 Ward, F. Champion
2 Ward, Frank
2 Ward, George
15 Ward, Helen
13 Ward, Jack
1 Ward, Jeff
7 Ward, John
1 Ward, Mary Jane
1 Ward, Michael
1 Ward, Palmer
2 Ward, Penelope
6 Ward, Perry
1 Ward, Richard
1 Ward, Rodger
1 Ward, Russ
3 Ward, Shirley
4 Wardell, Billy
1 Warden, George
1 Warden, Marvin
20 Ware, Harlan
2 Ware, J. Douglas
10 Ware, Linda
11 Warenskjold, Dorothy
5 Warfield, William
2 Waring (Fred Waring and His Chorus)
33 Waring (Fred Waring and His Orchestra)
73 Waring (Fred Waring and The Pennsylvanians)
1 Waring (Fred Waring Chorus, The)
2 Waring (Fred Waring Glee Club, The)
1 Waring, Don
1 Waring, Ellen
8 Waring, Fred
7 Waring, Richard
2 Waring, Tom
1 Warn, Helen
1 Warner Brothers Orchestra, The
2 Warner Jr., Jack
36 Warner, Albert
1 Warner, Albert L.
60 Warner, Gertrude
2 Warner, H. B.
5 Warner, Henry
5 Warner, Jack
1 Warner, John
1 Warner, Margaret
1 Warner, Mark
1 Warner, Richard
1 Warner, Ted
1 Warnow (Mark Warnow and His Carnegie Hall Orchestra)
251 Warnow (Mark Warnow and His Orchestra)
40 Warnow, Mark
3 Warren, Ann
5 Warren, Annette
1 Warren, Avra
23 Warren, Bob
3 Warren, Carl
16 Warren, Charles
1 Warren, Constance
19 Warren, Earl
1 Warren, Elton J.
27 Warren, Fran
2 Warren, Frank
2 Warren, Gil
2 Warren, Harry
1 Warren, Helen
3 Warren, Janet
1 Warren, Julia
1 Warren, Katherine
10 Warren, Leonard
2 Warren, Marty
1 Warren, Paul
3 Warren, Robert Penn
1 Warren, Salstein
1 Warren, Stu
1 Warren, Sue
10 Warrick, Ruth
2 Warrington (Johnny Warrington and His Orchestra)
1 Wartenbaker, Thomas
1 Warwich, Keith
2 Warwick, Dionne
1 Warwick, James W.
4 Warwick, Robert
23 Washburn (Country Washburn and His Orchestra)
2 Washburn, Beverly
16 Washburn, Country
2 Washburn, Mona
4 Washburn, Sonny
1 Washington Jr., Grover
1 Washington, Booker T.
9 Washington, Dinah
2 Washington, Don
1 Washington, Harold
1 Washington, John
1 Washington, Kenny
1 Washington, Ned
1 Washington, W. Selden
1 Wassell, Corydon
1 Watch, Mary
281 Waterman, Willard
1 Waters Jr., Lewis W.
18 Waters, Ethel
1 Waters, Frank
1 Waters, Lou
2 Waters, Muddy
1 Waters, Ozie
1 Watkins, James
1 Watkins, Kermit
4 Watkins, Linda
1 Watkins, Tony
1 Watson Sisters, The
1 Watson, A. J.
2 Watson, Allan
1 Watson, Betty Jean
1 Watson, Del
2 Watson, Douglas
2 Watson, Duke
2 Watson, Ernie
1 Watson, Judith
2 Watson, Leo
3 Watson, Lucille
1 Watson, Robert
1 Watson, Susan
3 Watson, Thomas
4 Watt, Billie Lou
1 Watt, Billy Lou
1 Watt, Constance
1 Watt, George
1 Watt, James
1 Watt, Robert J.
5 Watt, Stan
1 Watters (Lu Watters' Yerba Jazz Band)
1 Watters, Lu
1 Watts, Bill
1 Watts, Bob
1 Watts, Frederick
2 Watts, J. C.
1 Watts, Richard
2 Waugh, Evelyn
1 Waves Singing Platoon, The
2 Waxman, Franz
1 Waxman, Percy
46 Waxman, Stan
1 Wayne (Jerry Wayne and The Dell Trio)
6 Wayne, Anthony
17 Wayne, Artie
3 Wayne, Bill
3 Wayne, Charlie
1 Wayne, Christina
7 Wayne, David
2 Wayne, Elizabeth
14 Wayne, Frances
1 Wayne, Fred
64 Wayne, Jerry
9 Wayne, John
1 Wayne, Justina
2 Wayne, Ken
16 Wayne, Milton
3 Wayne, Roger
1 Wayne, Shirley
1 Wayne, Steve
1 Weathers, Joyce
5 Weatherwax, Rudd
1 Weaver, Dennis
32 Weaver, Doodles
1 Weaver, Hank
1 Weaver, Harry M.
1 Weaver, Marjorie
2 Weaver, Pat
2 Weavers, The
2 Webb (Chick Webb and His Orchestra)
1 Webb, Alan
1 Webb, Arthur
1 Webb, Chick
13 Webb, Clifton
1 Webb, Del
1 Webb, Floyd
1 Webb, Gene
394 Webb, Jack
32 Webb, Jane
3 Webb, Jean
7 Webb, Jilla
1 Webb, Jim
4 Webb, June
6 Webb, Louis
1 Webb, Mary
1 Webb, Maurice
3 Webb, Spider
1 Webb, Theodore
1 Webber, Fred
124 Webber, Peggy
1 Weber
1 Weber (Fred Weber and His Orchestra)
1 Weber (Henry Weber and His Orchestra)
4 Weber and Fields
1 Weber, Charles
1 Weber, Dick
64 Weber, Henry
4 Weber, Joan
68 Weber, Karl
2 Weber, Kay
1 Weber, Vivian
1 Webster (Ralph Webster and His Orchestra)
5 Webster, Ben
1 Webster, Carol
27 Webster, Charles
2 Webster, Gene
9 Webster, Harvey C.
1 Webster, Hush
1 Webster, Jean
7 Webster, Margaret
5 Webster, Maurie
2 Webster, William
3 Wedlock, Hugh
4 Weed (Buddy Weed Quartet, The)
4 Weed (Buddy Weed Septet, The)
2 Weed (Buddy Weed Trio, The)
2 Weed, Buddy
1 Weed, Russ
16 Weede, Robert
1 Weegee
12 Weeks (Anson Weeks and His Orchestra)
17 Weeks, Barbara
1 Weeks, Dave
2 Weeks, Edward
1 Weeks, Hartfield
1 Weem, Mr.
16 Weems (Ted Weems and His Orchestra)
1 Weems, Ted
1 Weible, Walter L.
1 Weidler, Jimmy
8 Weidler, Virginia
1 Weigand, Dennis
9 Weigle, John
97 Weihe, Fred
1 Weil, Alice
1 Weiland, Charles H.
1 Weilbacher, Mike
7 Weiler, Edward
4 Weill, Kurt
2 Wein, George
4 Weinberger, Caspar
2 Weinberger, Ilse
2 Weingart, Owen
6 Weingarten, Victor
1 Weinhouse, Irwin
4 Weinred, Nat
1 Weinrodt, Les
6 Weinstock, Jack
1 Weisgall, Hugo
1 Weiss, Bob
1 Weiss, Dick
1 Weiss, George
1 Weiss, Howard
1 Weiss, Johnny
9 Weiss, Rube
1 Weiss, Rudolph
6 Weiss, Sid
3 Weissmuller, Johnny
28 Weist, Dwight
1 Weist, Paul
2 Weitlemann, Whitey
7 Weitz, Paul
3 Welch, Emma Lou
4 Welch, Joseph
1 Welch, Lauren
3 Welch, Nelson
7 Welch, Niles
26 Welch, William
4 Welcome, Buddy
1 Welden, Ben
1 Weldman, Sonny
1 Weldon, Joan
1 Weldon, Martin
1 Welitsch, Alexander
111 Welk (Lawrence Welk and His Orchestra)
4 Welk, Lawrence
6 Wellborn, Charles
1 Welles, Christina
13 Welles, Halsted
325 Welles, Orson
3 Welles, Sumner
1 Wellington (Larry Wellington and The Travelers)
1 Wellington, Jack
4 Wellington, Larry
1 Wellman, Charlie
1 Wellman, Paul
1 Wellman, William
1 Wells Jr., William K.
1 Wells, Bill
2 Wells, Bob
1 Wells, Dick
8 Wells, Frank
28 Wells, H. G.
2 Wells, Jacqueline
10 Wells, Kitty
19 Wells, Linton
1 Wells, Maurice
5 Wells, Sarajane
11 Wells, Virginia
1 Wells, Zetta Carveth
1 Welsh, George
1 Welsh, Homer
1 Welsh, Howard
1 Welsh, Jean
1 Welshel, John
2 Welty, Glenn
1 Wench, Harold
2 Wendell, Bill
1 Wendlin, Ozzie
3 Wentworth
1 Wentworth, Barbara
3 Wentworth, Florence
70 Wentworth, Martha
1 Wenworth, Zi
1 Werblin, Sonny
1 Wergeland, Arild
1 Werker, Alfred
1 Werlewis, Jack
1 Werner's Orchestra
2 Werner, Max
2 Werner, Michael
1 Werner, Roy

3 Werris, Snag
1 Wershba, Joe
2 Wersky, Sidney S.
1 Wert, George F.
1 Wertz, Vic
1 Weslake
1 Wesler, Bernard
18 Wesley, Jay
1 Wessick, Gaylord
12 Wesson, Dick
4 Wesson, Gene
27 West (Alvy West and His Orchestra)
1 West and Lexey
1 West Coasters, The
1 West, Andrew
1 West, Brooks
1 West, Don
2 West, Dottie
1 West, Dr.
1 West, Ira
1 West, James
1 West, John
16 West, Mae
1 West, Mal
1 West, Norris
77 West, Paul
1 West, Rebecca
1 West, Ted
1 Westbrook, Helen
8 Westendorf, Bernard
3 Westerfield, James
1 Westernaires, The
1 Westerners Quartet, The
4 Westerners, The
1 Westin, Doris
1 Westley, Helen
1 Westmore, Betty
1 Westmore, Ern
2 Westmore, Wally
95 Weston (Paul Weston and His Orchestra)
2 Weston, Cliff
1 Weston, Kris
3 Weston, Paul
1 Weston, Ruth
2 Westover, Jim
1 Westover, Russ
1 Westphal, James
2 Westrum, Wes
3 Wetmore, Joan
14 Wettling, George
1 Wetzel, Ray
24 Wever, Ned
1 Wexler, Jerry
1 Wexler, Julius
1 Wexler, Nate
1 Weyrich, Paul
1 WGN Octet, The
2 WGN Orchestra, The
11 Whalen, Grover
1 Whalen, Monica
15 Wharton, Edith
1 What Four, The
13 Wheatley, Joan
166 Whedon, John
81 Wheel, Patricia
12 Wheeler, Bert
6 Wheeler, Burton K.
2 Wheeler, Country Joe
3 Wheeler, George
1 Wheeler, Jack
2 Wheeler, Jackson
1 Wheeler, Onie
1 Wheeler, Romney
1 Wheelus, Captain
1 Whelan, Arlene
1 Whelan, Joanne
1 Whelan, Michael
1 Whelan, Tom
4 Whipper, Leigh
1 Whipple (Doc Whipple and His Orchestra)
33 Whipple, Doc
1 Whipple, Sheldon
2 Whippoorwills With Georgia Brown, The
31 Whipporwills, The
2 Whitcomb, Richard
1 Whitcup, Leonard
1 White (Johnny White Quartet, The)
1 White (Johnny White Quintet)
1 White Guard, The
2 White Jr., Josh
1 White Jr., Lynn Townsend
76 White Jr., Walter
1 White, Albert
1 White, Alice
276 White, Andy
2 White, Betty
1 White, Bob
1 White, Bobby
1 White, Ethel Lena
1 White, Frances
4 White, Francia
10 White, Frederick
1 White, Gilbert
1 White, Graham McNamee
1 White, Jack
1 White, Jane
11 White, Jesse
2 White, Johnny
16 White, Josh
5 White, Kenneth
1 White, Kitty
2 White, Lasses
1 White, Lawrence
30 White, Lee
1 White, Lester
44 White, Lew
1 White, Llewellan
1 White, Mike
1 White, Mrs. Burton H.
1 White, Patrick
4 White, Paul
1 White, Portia
2 White, Robert A.
1 White, Senator
3 White, Theodore
1 White, Una
1 White, Valerie
1 White, Vernon C.
1 White, W. C.
1 White, W. L.
12 White, Walter
4 White, Warren
1 White, William L.
1 Whitehall Four, The
17 Whitehouse, David
1 Whiteman (Paul Whiteman and His Concert Orchestra)
1 Whiteman (Paul Whiteman and His Orchestra and Chorus)
75 Whiteman (Paul Whiteman and His Orchestra)
1 Whiteman (Paul Whiteman and The Blue Network Concert Orchestra)
6 Whiteman, Loyce
37 Whiteman, Paul
1 Whitesall, J. Roger
2 Whiteside, Arthur
1 Whitever, Catherine
148 Whitfield, Anne
26 Whitfield, Bobby
1 Whitfield, Edward
30 Whiting, Barbara
1 Whiting, Jack
119 Whiting, Margaret
19 Whitley, June
1 Whitman, Christine
76 Whitman, Ernest
70 Whitman, Gayne
2 Whitman, Stanley
1 Whitman, Stuart
2 Whitman, Walt
2 Whitmore, James
1 Whitmore, Jean
1 Whitney and Kramer
1 Whitney, Barbara
1 Whitney, Bill
1 Whitney, Carroll
1 Whitney, Claire
2 Whitney, Douglas
1 Whitney, Eleanor
19 Whitney, Lynn
1 Whitney, Phyllis
1 Whitney, Robert
5 Whitney, Susan
2 Whitson, Dorothy
3 Whittaker, Daniel
1 Whittaker, John
1 Whittemore and Scott
1 Whittier, John Greenleaf
1 Whittifield, Cecil
11 Whitty, Dame May
1 Whoopee John and His Orchestra
6 Whorf, Richard
1 Wibel, A. M.
1 Wick, Bruno
4 Wickard, Claude
7 Wicker, Ireene
2 Wicker, Tom
7 Wickes, Mary
1 Wickey, Gould
13 Wickman (Dick Wickman and His Orchestra)
1 Wickman, Thelma
1 Wicksell, Benjamin H.
1 Widemeyer, General
1 Widen, Ron
16 Widener, Alabama Jim
2 Widener, Jimmy
2 Widman, Ralph
53 Widmark, Richard
2 Widmer, Harriet
225 Widom, Bud
1 Wiedoeft, Rudy
1 Wiener, Willard
1 Wiffletree, Jughead
1 Wiggens, Veronica
2 Wiggins, Chuck
21 Wiggins, Roy
1 Wigginton, Dick
1 Wilbert, William
4 Wilbur (Jimmy Wilbur and His Swingtette)
2 Wilbur, Bob
4 Wilbur, Elizabeth
9 Wilburn Brothers, The
2 Wilburn, Doyle
2 Wilburn, Teddy
2 Wilcher, Louise
1 Wilcox, Ella W.
837 Wilcox, Harlow
1 Wilcox, Johnny
5 Wilcox, Pamela
4 Wilcoxon, Henry
6 Wild, Earl
1 Wild Ones, The
1 Wilde Twins, The
23 Wilde, Cornel
12 Wilde, Oscar
6 Wilder, Billy
2 Wilder, Honeychile
1 Wilder, Joe
1 Wilder, Margaret Buhl
1 Wilder, Robert
7 Wilder, Thornton
1 Wildhack, Robert
1 Wildinson, Jean
1 Wildiss, William
1 Wildon, Richard
10 Wile (George Wile and His Orchestra)
1 Wile, Paul
1 Wile, Phyllis
2 Wile, Richard
2 Wiley, Alexander
1 Wiley, Fletcher
42 Wiley, Howard
1 Wiley, Katherine
22 Wiley, Lee
1 Wiley, Max
1 Wilhelm, Hoyt
2 Wilhelm, Jim
2 Wilk, Max
1 Wilkenson, Ellen
1 Wilkenson, Marty
1 Wilkenson, Ralph
1 Wilkerson, Harriet
85 Wilkerson, Martha
1 Wilkerson, Marty
19 Wilkes, Charles
1 Wilkes, Patty
3 Wilkins, Ford
1 Wilkins, Marion
2 Wilkins, Roy
1 Wilkinson, Garnett C.
2 Wilkinson, Kate
6 Will, George
1 Will, Robert
4 Willard and His Orchestra
1 Willard, Dick
1 Willard, Forrest
9 Willard, George
1 Willard, Hal
12 Willard, Horace
4 Willard, James
1 Willard, Jess
2 William, David
33 William, Warren
1 Williams (Billy Williams Quartet, The)
4 Williams (Cootie Williams and His Orchestra)
2 Williams (Griff Williams and His Orchestra)
1 Williams (Hank Williams and His Drifting Cowboys)
1 Williams (Mary Lou Williams Trio, The)
2 Williams (Otis Williams and The Charms)
1 Williams (Roger Williams and His Orchestra)
3 Williams (Tex Williams and His Band)
6 Williams Brothers, The
1 Williams III, Clarence
3 Williams, Albert N.
93 Williams, Andy
17 Williams, Anne
1 Williams, Ben Ames
1 Williams, Bert
9 Williams, Bill
17 Williams, Billie
6 Williams, Bob
8 Williams, Bonnie Lou
1 Williams, Brian
1 Williams, Buddy
1 Williams, Buster
2 Williams, Camilla
1 Williams, Cara
1 Williams, Charlie
1 Williams, Chester
3 Williams, Chili
6 Williams, Cootie
1 Williams, Dick
1 Williams, Dolores
2 Williams, Don
1 Williams, Douglas
1 Williams, Eddie
2 Williams, Elaine
3 Williams, Emlyn
11 Williams, Esther
4 Williams, Florence
1 Williams, Frances
1 Williams, Gene
2 Williams, George
4 Williams, Gladys
1 Williams, Grady
7 Williams, Gwen
8 Williams, Hank
1 Williams, Hannah
2 Williams, Hugh
3 Williams, Ike
1 Williams, Jack
1 Williams, Jackie
1 Williams, James
2 Williams, Jan
4 Williams, Janet
1 Williams, Jay
1 Williams, Jean
31 Williams, Joe
4 Williams, Johnny
5 Williams, Ken
1 Williams, Kenny
2 Williams, Lawrence
1 Williams, Marian
1 Williams, Mary
8 Williams, Mary Lou

1 Williams, Melva
1 Williams, Midge
1 Williams, Milton
1 Williams, Pat
1 Williams, Paul B.
1 Williams, Paul L.
13 Williams, Rhoda
1 Williams, Rita
3 Williams, Roger
1 Williams, Rosa
1 Williams, Rosetta
1 Williams, Russell Harrington
3 Williams, Spencer
1 Williams, Stan
1 Williams, Taylor
2 Williams, Ted
2 Williams, Tennessee
26 Williams, Tex
1 Williams, Tony
1 Williams, Vince
2 Williams, Whiting
1 Williams, Wilfred
12 Williams, William B.
1 Williams, Wye
2 Williamson, Jack
1 Williamson, M. A.
2 Williamson, Mel
111 Willing (Foy Willing and The Riders Of The Purple Sage)
1 Willing, Foy
15 Willis (Guy Willis and The Oklahoma Wranglers)
3 Willis Brothers, The
2 Willis, Chuck
2 Willis, Frank
2 Willis, Gordon
1 Willis, Larry
1 Willis, Maury
1 Willis, Paul S.
1 Willis, Richard
12 Willkie, Earl
22 Willkie, Wendell
9 Willock, Dave
7 Wills (Bob Wills and The Texas Playboys)
1 Wills Jr., Lou
3 Wills, Chill
1 Wills, Colin
1 Wills, David
1 Wills, Gary
1 Wills, Peter
164 Willson (Meredith Willson and His Orchestra)
1 Willson (Meredith Willson and The BBC Variety Orchestra)
1 Willson, M. L.
83 Willson, Meredith
1 Wilmot, Bertha
1 Wilmot, Jerry
1 Wilner, Norman
1 Wilsey, Mary
1 Wilshire, J. C.
4 Wilson (Gerald Wilson and His Orchestra)
2 Wilson (Ken Wilson and The Ensemble)
1 Wilson (Teddy Wilson and His Orchestra)
3 Wilson (Teddy Wilson and His Trio)
2 Wilson (Teddy Wilson Sextette, The)
1 Wilson (Teddy Wilson Trio, The)
1 Wilson, Alan
1 Wilson, Andy
7 Wilson, Art
1 Wilson, Bert
1 Wilson, Betty
8 Wilson, Billy
1 Wilson, Brian
10 Wilson, Buster
4 Wilson, Carey
1 Wilson, Cedric
2 Wilson, Charles
1 Wilson, Charles E.
1 Wilson, Charles Morrow
1 Wilson, Charlie
2 Wilson, Danny
1 Wilson, David
1 Wilson, Desmond
1 Wilson, Doghouse Jake
643 Wilson, Don
3 Wilson, Dooley
4 Wilson, Earl
8 Wilson, Eileen
3 Wilson, Ethel
1 Wilson, Faye
4 Wilson, Flip
28 Wilson, Frank
2 Wilson, Gerald
2 Wilson, Gill Robb
2 Wilson, Hal
2 Wilson, Harold
2 Wilson, Howard
41 Wilson, J. Donald
2 Wilson, Jack
39 Wilson, Jack C.
1 Wilson, Jackie
1 Wilson, James
1 Wilson, James J.
28 Wilson, Jane
1 Wilson, Jean
4 Wilson, John C.
3 Wilson, Julie
263 Wilson, Ken
1 Wilson, Kid Sox
1 Wilson, Lois
2 Wilson, Lyle
34 Wilson, Marie
1 Wilson, Mary Lou
1 Wilson, Max
3 Wilson, Muriel
4 Wilson, Nancy
1 Wilson, P. K.
2 Wilson, Pete
2 Wilson, Rail
25 Wilson, Ray
1 Wilson, Reed
12 Wilson, Richard
51 Wilson, Teddy
30 Wilson, Ward
2 Wilson, Woodrow
1 Wilson, Woody
1 Wilt, Fred
1 Wilton, Eric
6 Winchell, Paul
20 Winchell, Walter
1 Winckel, Hans
4 Windheim, Marek
5 Winding (Kai Winding and His Sextet)
2 Winding, Kai
2 Windler, Milton
2 Windsor, Betty
1 Windsor, Joy
1 Windsor, Kathleen
6 Windsor, Marie
17 Wingate, John
2 Winget, Charles
1 Winkle, M.
9 Winkler, Betty
5 Winkler, Bobby
15 Winninger, Charles
3 Winselberg, Simon
1 Winslow, C. E. A.
1 Winslow, Paul
183 Winslowe, Paula
38 Winsor, Roy
59 Winstanley, Ernie
5 Winston, Irene
1 Winter, David
1 Winter, Johnny
1 Winter, Louise
1 Winter, Norman
1 Winter, Ray
1 Winter, William
12 Winterhalter (Hugo Winterhalter and His Orchestra)
3 Winterhalter, Hugo
1 Winternitz, Milton C.
1 Winters, Hal
2 Winters, Jerry
1 Winters, John
1 Winters, Jonathan
1 Winters, Kay
1 Winters, Lawrence
19 Winters, Marion
37 Winters, Roland
5 Winters, Shelley
4 Winwood, Estelle
1 Wire
2 Wirges (Bill Wirges Orchestra)
23 Wirges, Bill
2 Wirtz, Willard
1 Wisdom, Diane
1 Wise, Buddy
2 Wise, Chubby
1 Wise, Stubby
1 Wise, Wes
2 Wiseman (Mac Wiseman and His Country Boys)
2 Wiseman, Joseph
8 Wiseman, Mac
1 Wisener, Jerome
1 Wiser, Milton
28 Wishengrad, Morton
52 Wismer, Harry
6 Wisoff, Milt
5 Wissler, Rudy
1 Wissoner, Lawrence
1 Witell, Josephine
1 Withers, Googie
2 Withers, Grant
6 Withers, Jane
3 Withers, William
3 Witherspoon, Cora
1 Witherspoon, Jimmy
1 Witkowski (Anthony Witkowski and His Polish Swing Orchestra)
1 Witkowski (Anthony Witkowski and The Brooklyn Knights)
5 Witkowski, Anthony
1 Witt, Catherine
1 Witt, Peter
1 Wittemore and Lowe
32 Witten, Louis A.
1 Wittenberg, Edward
1 Wittnauer Choraliers, The
1 Witty, Don
1 WMAQ Orchestra, The
1 WNUR Studio Orchestra, The
2 Wodehouse, P. G.
2 Wogan, Robert
1 Wok, Anderson
6 Wolcott, Florence
2 Wolcott, Jersey Joe
1 Wolcott, Judith
2 Woldum, Roy
5 Wolf, Bob
1 Wolf, Ed
1 Wolf, Perry
1 Wolf, Sanford
1 Wolf, Walter
1 Wolfe, Bud
1 Wolfe, Daniel
6 Wolfe, David
1 Wolfe, Hal
1 Wolfe, Hugo
10 Wolfe, Ian
1 Wolfe, J. E.
2 Wolfe, Jeanette
6 Wolfe, John
1 Wolfe, Johnny
1 Wolfe, Marion
28 Wolfe, Miriam
4 Wolfe, Thomas
1 Wolfe, Tom
2 Wolfe, Winifred
22 Wolff, Nat
1 Wolfman, Lois
1 Wolfser, Maurice
23 Wolfson, Martin
2 Wolfson, Victor
1 Woll, Matthew
1 Wollheim, Donald
1 Wollheim, Donald A.
8 Wolman, Leo
1 Wolper, David
2 Wolverton, Bill
1 Womble, Pee Wee
1 Wonder, Stevie
1 Wong, Anderson
1 Wong, Anna May
20 Wong, Barbara Jean
1 Wong, David
1 Wong, Jade Snow
1 Wons, Tony
4 Wood (Donna Wood and Her Don Juans)
5 Wood, Allen
48 Wood, Barry
1 Wood, Brent
6 Wood, Britt
4 Wood, Del
3 Wood, Dick
1 Wood, Donna
1 Wood, Douglas
3 Wood, Gloria
4 Wood, Helen
9 Wood, Keith
5 Wood, Kirk
1 Wood, Margie
4 Wood, Natalie
1 Wood, Nell
5 Wood, Peggy
1 Wood, Robin
1 Wood, Trudy
1 Woodard, Harold
4 Woodard, Woody
2 Woodbury (By Woodbury and His Orchestra)
5 Woodcock, George
1 Wooden, Eric
1 Woodgate, Bruce
2 Woodman, Ruth
1 Woodring
6 Woodruff, Judy
6 Woods, Buck
76 Woods, Charles
1 Woods, Chris
1 Woods, Dennis
10 Woods, Donald
10 Woods, Eileen
1 Woods, Glade
1 Woods, Harriet
2 Woods, Harrison
1 Woods, Illene
2 Woods, Jean
3 Woods, Johnny
45 Woods, Lesley
1 Woods, Mark
1 Woods, Percy
1 Woods, Phil
3 Woods, Roy
1 Woods, Ruby
4 Woods, Tighe
1 Woods, Tuliki
1 Woodson, Billy
60 Woodson, William
3 Woodward, Bob
16 Woodward, Luther E.
1 Woodward, Stanley
3 Woodward, Van
1 Wooley, Sheb
5 Woolf, Charles
1 Woolfe, Virginia
11 Woollcott, Alexander
3 Woollen, Dick
34 Woolley, Monty
25 Woolrich, Cornell
1 Woolson, L. I.
1 Wooten, C. Richard
2 Wooten, Elizabeth
2 Wooten, Serita
3 WOR Symphony Orchestra, The
1 Wordsworth, Richard
1 World Light Opera Company, The
1 World Mixed Chorus, The
2 World's Fair Band, The
1 World's Fair Glee Club, The
3 World's Greatest Jazz Band, The
5 Worley, Jo Anne
17 Worlock, Frederic
1 Wormser, Ann
1 Wormser, Jack

1 Worth (Frank Worth and His Orchestra and Chorus)
7 Worth (Frank Worth and His Orchestra)
118 Worth, Frank
2 Worth, Harry
6 Worth, Irene
4 Worth, Louis
1 Worth, Martin
3 Worth, Petey
1 Worthen, Tom
1 Worthing, Craig
1 Worthy, Joseph
3 Wouk, Herman
2 WPA American Folk Singers Of Boston
1 WPA Negro Radio Unit Of Southern California
1 Wrangell, Phyllis
11 Wray, Fay
1 Wren, McCadja
1 Wren, Percival
1 Wrench, Evelyn
7 Wright, Arthur
417 Wright, Ben
2 Wright, Bill
3 Wright, Bob
4 Wright, Edythe
1 Wright, Elizabeth McFadden
1 Wright, Floyd
3 Wright, Frank Lloyd
20 Wright, George
1 Wright, George W.
1 Wright, Holly
1 Wright, Irving S.
12 Wright, Jim
3 Wright, Jimmy
1 Wright, John Richard
1 Wright, Johnny
4 Wright, Judith
4 Wright, Ken
3 Wright, Lee
1 Wright, Lois
29 Wright, Martha
1 Wright, Marvin
1 Wright, Mickey
2 Wright, Monte D.
1 Wright, Naomi
1 Wright, Oliver
3 Wright, Peter
4 Wright, Quincy
1 Wright, Richard
2 Wright, Robert
6 Wright, Teresa
122 Wright, Will
1 Wright, Wynn
1 Wrightsman, Stanley
38 Wrightson, Earl
1 Wrigley, Ben
2 Wrublik, Donald
2 Wunder, Elizabeth
20 Wyatt, Eustace
6 Wyatt, Jane
1 Wyatt, Jim
1 Wyatt, William
1 Wyble, Jimmy
1 Wyfield, William
1 Wyler, Gretchen
3 Wyler, William
1 Wylie, Evan
4 Wylie, I. A. R.
1 Wylie, Max
2 Wylie, Philip
46 Wyman, Jane
4 Wyman, Mel
1 Wyman, Rita
1 Wymark, Olwen
1 Wynant, John G.
1 Wynn, Bessie
44 Wynn, Dick
56 Wynn, Ed
32 Wynn, Keenan
18 Wynn, Nan
1 Wyss, Johann

1 X, Malcolm

11 Yacht Club Boys, The
1 Yacobson, Lou
1 Yaffee, Ben
1 Yaged, Sol
1 Yale Glee Club, The
2 Yamaguchi, Shirley
1 Yamashita, General
1 Yamata, Romi
1 Yaner, Milton
1 Yankovic (Frankie Yankovic and His Orchestra)
4 Yankovic, Frank
1 Yankovsky, Paul
260 Yarborough, Barton
1 Yarborough, Cale
1 Yarborough, Glenn
1 Yardley, John F.
3 Yarnell, Duane
1 Yarnell, Harry E.
1 Yarnell, Wayne
1 Yarrow, Don
1 Yarrow, Kenneth
1 Yashima, Taro
1 Ybarra, T. R.
3 Yeager, Chuck
5 Yellin (Gleb Yellin's Gypsy Orchestra)
1 Yellin, Gleb
1 Yeltsin, Boris
1 Yen, Frances
1 Yen, Ren Ye
1 Yendell, William R.
1 Yeng, Ren Ying
24 Yeo, Erwin
3 Yeomans, Donald
3 Yerby, Frank
1 Yessner, George
1 Yiddish Swing Orchestra, The
2 Yiddish Swingtet, The
4 Ymone, Diane
4 Yogi, Maharishi Mahesh
1 York, Alvin
6 York, Cal
2 York, Dick
16 Yorke, Ruth
1 Yost, Carol
1 Yost, Walter
2 Youmans, Scott
2 Youmans, Vincent
2 Young
1 Young (Faron Young and His Deputies)
1 Young (John Young Trio)
90 Young (Victor Young and His Orchestra)
1 Young Americans, The
1 Young Mary Ann
1 Young People's Choir Of The Abyssinian Baptist Church, The
1 Young Tuxedo Jazz Band, The
22 Young, Agnes
72 Young, Alan
4 Young, Arthur
3 Young, Babe
9 Young, Bob
100 Young, Carleton
1 Young, Carlton G.
1 Young, Charles
1 Young, Chic
4 Young, Christopher
1 Young, Clara Kimball
1 Young, Cy
1 Young, Dan
11 Young, David
3 Young, Don
1 Young, Doug
1 Young, Douglas
5 Young, Eve
69 Young, Faron
2 Young, George
3 Young, Harold
1 Young, Hollis
2 Young, J. Arthur
3 Young, James R.
1 Young, Janet
3 Young, Jean
1 Young, Jimmy
3 Young, Joe
3 Young, John
1 Young, John M.
9 Young, Larry
1 Young, Lee
4 Young, Lester
53 Young, Loretta
1 Young, Lorna
2 Young, Lymon
1 Young, Margaret
14 Young, Marshall
3 Young, Norman
1 Young, Paddy
2 Young, Richard
142 Young, Robert
34 Young, Roland
5 Young, Russ
3 Young, Stanley
3 Young, Stewart
1 Young, Thomas
3 Young, Trummy
1 Young, Vansuela
9 Young, Victor
14 Younger, Beverly
2 Younger, Joan
1 Younger, Kenneth
14 Youngman, Henny
3 Your Father's Moustache Banjo Band
24 Yourman, Alice
1 Yudkov, Alvin
2 Yukel, Joe
2 Yurka, Blanche
1 Yutang, Lin
4 Yvette
1 Yvonne, Rosalind

5 Zabach, Florian
1 Zacharias, Ellis M.
11 Zachery, George
3 Zaharias, Babe Didrikson
2 Zahn, Paula
1 Zale, Tony
1 Zamble, Bernard
1 Zamma, Florette
2 Zampieri, Guiseppe
1 Zandell, Bernard
2 Zanelli, Ralph
4 Zanuck, Darryl
2 Zaputo, Frankie
1 Zaret, Hy
2 Zatkin, Nathan
1 Zato, Sammy
1 Zayde, Jacob
1 Zayde, Jascha
1 Zeal, Bob
1 Zeckendorf, William
1 Zeer, Isadore
1 Zeiland, Van
1 Zekins, Joe
18 Zelinka, Sid
1 Zellers, John
1 Zeno, Ronnie
13 Zentner (Si Zentner and His Orchestra)
2 Zentner, Si
1 Zerbe, Anthony
141 Zerbe, Lawson
1 Zernicke, Willim
1 Zerone Jesters, The
1 Ziaszki, Dick
1 Ziazski, Michael
1 Ziegfeld Chorus, The
1 Ziegfeld, Florenz
1 Ziegler, Carl
1 Ziff, George Kingsley
2 Ziff, William B.
2 Zimbalist Jr., Efrem
1 Zimbalist Sr., Efrem
1 Zimberkin, Noel
1 Zimmer, Don
8 Zimmer, Lee
1 Zimmer, Norma
1 Zimmermaids, The
216 Zimmerman (Harry Zimmerman and His Orchestra)
11 Zimmerman (Harry Zimmerman and The Voices Of Romance)
6 Zimmerman (Harry Zimmerman Chorus, The)
1 Zimmerman, Ed
42 Zimmerman, Harry
35 Zink, Al
1 Zinkey, Peggy
1 Zinn, Maurice
1 Zinneman, Fred
73 Zirato Jr., Bruno
3 Zito, Jimmy
1 Zivic, Fritzie
1 Zoff, Otto
1 Zola, Emile
70 Zoller, John
1 Zomar, Karl
1 Zon, Cecil
1 Zoppi, Tony
1 Zorin, Valerian
4 Zorina, Vera
1 Zousmer, Jesse
10 Zucco, George
24 Zuckert, William
1 Zucksmith, Leon
1 Zugsmith, Albert
4 Zukor, Adolph
1 Zupke, Bob

AIR CHEK
• • GOTTSCHALK PROCESS • •
ELECTRICAL TRANSCRIPTION
USE FIBRE NEEDLE ONLY
Radio Station
Date
Part No.
Name of Program
The Man Who Saved Radio
ELECTRO-VOX, Inc.
BENDIX BLDG. 1206 MAPLE AVE
LOS ANGELES, CALIF

It was the best of times, it was the worst of times. It was 1942 and we were at war. Radio was at its zenith (no pun intended) but about to get even better. Although I fought the Axis mostly from my crib, Dave Goldin and radio were connected from the beginning.

It wasn't until many years later that I found a copy of the birth announcement that Buddy and Alberta Goldin sent out to proclaim their blessed event. Imagine my surprise to find that the stork pictured on the card was a radio announcer! He is shown interrupting the regular programming of station "B-A-B-Y" with a special bulletin, a new addition to the program schedule! Perhaps my parents had a premonition of the interest that would occupy my thoughts for the next five decades.

It Pays To Be Ignorant *(with Tom Howard) (6/25/42 - 9/26/51) 6/25/42 - 11/26/42, Mut, Thu, 8 pm; 3/29/43 - 2/28/44, Sus, Mut, Mon, 7:30 pm 2/25/44 - 1/25/46; 5/3/46 - 2/6/48, Philip Morris, CBS, Fri, 9 pm; 10 pm as of 9/20/46 ; 2/28/48 - 7/17/49, Sus, CBS, Sat; Sun as of 1/8/49 (on 3/13/49?) ; 7/25/49 - 9/13/49, Sus, CBS, Tue, 9:30 pm; 7/5/50 - 9/27/50, Chrysler, CBS, Wed, 9 pm; 7/4/51-9/26/51, DeSoto, NBC, Wed, 9 pm (summer replacement for You Bet Your Life)*

According to legend, when I was still very young, my mother took me to the banks of the Harlem River (there being no branch of the Styx nearby, the Harlem made an acceptable substitute). Holding me by one heel, she dipped me into the crystal clear waters in order that I might achieve invulnerabilty in broadcasting. Unfortunately, I choked on what used to be called an "Orchard Beach Whitefish" and swallowed some of the water flowing past the Bronx. The result was a heavy New York accent that doomed my career in front of a microphone and no doubt preserved the jobs of Don Wilson, Ken Niles and Bill Goodwin.

We all remember our first kiss, our first car, our first radio (don't we?). Mine was an Emerson model #547A which was a cheap plastic set with a satisfying glow in my darkened bedroom. My grandmother had a DeWald model #A501 in her living room that I listened to frequently (Nana would be shocked to know that this radio, made of a very collectible plastic called Catalin, was worth about $750 today!).

I'd like to brag about the many happy hours I spent listening to Jack Benny, Tom Mix, The Lone Ranger and Suspense during the years these shows were in their prime. The truth is that we had one of those new "television" sets and I spent a considerable amount of time watching Captain Video, Winky Dink and You, and the WATV test pattern from Newark, New Jersey while waiting for Uncle Fred and "Junior Frolics" to begin. What radio I did listen to was mostly from WQXR, the classical music AM station (at the time) in New York. Among the shows I best remember, and that had a lasting influence on me as a broadcaster, was "Cocktail Time" with Duncan Pierney. The show ran Monday to Friday from 5:00 in the afternoon to 7:00 P.M. I wasn't even sure what a cocktail was, but the program was sponsored by an unending roster of Manhattan's finest restaurants, caviar merchants and importers of French aperitifs. Duncan Pierney was obviously the New York sophisticate, as knowledgeable about whether the appetizers at a certain restaurant featured fresh snails or merely canned ones in a butter/garlic sauce, as he was about which side of the vineyard a certain "presumptuous" bordeaux called home. I therefore became a gourmand.

One night a week, "Nights In Latin America," hosted by Pru Devon, would come over the Emerson. It was sponsored by Panagra Airlines (which not-too-surprisingly flew to South America) and featured the kind of music favored by guanaco herders on the Argentine pampas and selections played on Bolivian panpipes. I therefore became a world traveler and eventually got to Patagonia in search of the reality behind that show, and to learn what nights in Latin America were really like.

Weekday evenings at 8:00 P.M. was the big show of WQXR's schedule. It was "Symphony Hall" and usually consisted of one or two works of the standard repertory, presented on records. I became a lover of renaissance and classical music. The closest I came to a kid show was "Big Jon and Sparkie" ("No School Today") which I heard over WJZ in New York. Fifty years later, I still have a cocker spaniel named "Sparky IV."

As I grew older and learned to read (or at least look at the pictures), I became seriously influenced by a comic book character. Actually, it was a whole family of characters called "The Marvel Family." In a direct copy of "Superman," Fawcett Publications created Billy Batson, his sister Mary and his "crippled" pal Freddy Freeman, Jr. (there were no handicapped zones back then, if you walked with crutches, you were "crippled"). Given super-human powers by an ancient Egyptian sorcerer (who lived in a subway tunnel!), Billy would utter the sorcerer's name ("Shazam") and turn into Captain Marvel. Over the years, I named two cocker spaniels "Shazam," but no matter how many times I would call them, the lightning bolt changing me into a costumed superhero never arrived (it wasn't a total loss, the spaniels were very affectionate). Your homework is to remember what ancient heroes Shazam's acronymic title represented. Captain Marvel's main appeal for me was the profession of his not-so-secret identity, Billy Batson. Billy worked for a man named Sterling Morris, a portly older gent (he must have been at least 50!), who ran radio station WHIZ in a large city (there is a real station with WHIZ call letters in Zanesville, Ohio, I felt I had to visit this place as soon as I was old enough to drive). Zanesville, home of the world's only "Y" bridge, was a nice place, but Sterling Morris was not on staff. Billy was known as "the boy newscaster," and that's where my fantasies took me. After all, who wanted to be a crippled newsboy like Freddy Freeman, Jr. when you could read the news on radio! The adventures of Billy Batson, after saying the name of "Shazam" and turning into Captain Marvel, fueled my imagination as to the wonders possible with radio.

As I grew older, I found myself discovering the pleasures to be found collecting 78 rpm records and later radio transcriptions. My friends were discovering girls. I taught myself code (poorly) and became a "ham" operator, WA2BRD and later WB1EZA.

Strangely enough, the first "real" broadcast I ever made was from Radio Moscow! It was in 1957 on a program called "Moscow Mailbag." I mailed a tape of myself talking about tape recording. The show's host played the tape over the Radio Moscow world-wide shortwave service. This was pretty nifty, listening to myself on the 25 meter band over my Zenith Transoceanic (a "portable" set built like an anvil, but weighing more). I suppose my fate as "the man who saved radio" was by now written in stone, but I didn't yet realize it. Let me make clear that "saving radio" refers to collecting the media's programming, and should not be considered in the sense of "salvation" or "rescue of the industry."

My graduation from Stuyvesant High put me in the record business. The event made the front page of the New York Times when a riot broke out in the Greenwich Village theatre where the ceremonies were taking place. I put together a 7 minute documentary (cribbed from local telecasts), cut 45 rpm records at a small studio at 42nd street at 6th Avenue, and mailed a flyer to all the graduating class as listed in the yearbook. I was now in the mail order business too.

My radio career at New York University wasn't as contentious as Professor Segal remembers it. I was introduced however, to calculus and girls at the same time. No contest. I got a Bachelor Of Science degree in "Radio Production" from NYU (probably one of the last to do so), all the other students were majoring in film or television and just taking a few radio courses. I am still surprised that a major university was teaching the practice of producing good broadcasts at a time there was no "creative" radio being done in the U.S. My real radio education came from the college station (WNYU) which first put me in front of a microphone in 1961 with a program called "Varsity Drag" (I played 78s) and in 1962 with a program called "Radio Yesteryear." This gave me the opportunity to learn good radio from bad radio...by being bad.

With young hormones raging (for radio, there are no steamy sex scenes in this book), I dropped out of NYU for a job at a real station in Alaska. KSEW was a 250 watter on Baronof Island in the southeast panhandle of the state. Alaska had been a state for about three years. Sitka, Alaska was the home of a junior college, a pulp mill, a Coast Guard base, many Alaskan brown bears and not much else. There were no roads in or out, the ferry to Prince Rupert, B.C. ran twice a week and you could fly in only on the daily PB-Y amphibian sea plane (there was no airport). Now this is a setting for small town radio! I was on the air 48 hours a week. I also operated the transmitter, wrote advertising copy (mostly copied from the Sitka Yellow Pages, all 20 of them) and sold time on the station. As a time salesman, I once asked the station manager why we had no cigarette or beer commercials as did most other stations (both were acceptable back then). My boss told me of the time he visited a station rep in New York to ask the same question. The ad executive replied, "When we want to reach a market of 5000 people, we put up a notice in the elevator."

Part of my job at KSEW was an afternoon DJ show for the kids called "Totem Jamboree." Earlier in the day, the station offered programming in the Tlingit language (pronounced "Clink´-it"), as a service to the tribe of indians who lived on Baronof Island. I came on right afterwards, broadcasting to this huge and receptive audience, sounding like "Radio Free Bronx." However, in all the time I worked there, I never heard a disparaging word about the Harlem River caressing my tonsils. Perhaps my listeners thought we were still transmitting in Tlingit.

Jobs at WVIP in Mt. Kisco, New York and WHBI-FM in Newark, New Jersey taught me more about the realities of small time radio. A short stretch at WOR television taught me I liked radio better. When I got my "first phone ticket," I decided to stay firmly on the other end of the mike and become an operating engineer (Ken Carpenter breathed a sigh of relief). After teaching broadcast electronics at a private school in New York City, I got my big break in network radio. I went to work for the NBC radio network and WNBC-AM/FM in New York and learned about big-time radio. The most important thing I learned (unfortunately too late) was to keep my big mouth shut. During a periodic cutback (which we were told to expect), I was dismissed along with 66 other engineers on the same day. So much for the New York labor market for radio engineers! Finally landing a spot at the Mutual Broadcasting System, I found my NABET card (National Association Of Broadcast Employees and Technicians) from NBC was worthless, so I had to join IATSE (International Alliance Of Theatrical and Stage Employees). When I left Mutual (just about a year before they closed their New York studios) for CBS, I then had to join IBEW local 1212 (International Brotherhood Of Electrical Workers). It seemed one more job and I could play pinochle with my union cards!

The nice thing about working for a radio network (besides slightly higher wages than KSEW could offer) is that it was real radio. It may not have been the radio of "Suspense" and "The Fred Allen Show," but I did interview famous people. I did real band remotes twice a week, I was at the control board while Muhammed Ali was knocking out everyone in sight (and made $20 in overtime too!), I was in the studio when Apollo 11 first touched down on the moon, I did

"Music Til Dawn" (an all-night classical music show with Bob Hall, a one time "Green Hornet"). Godfrey was still on the air, I ran the board while Ed McMahon did "Monitor" on the weekends, Lowell Thomas knew me by name, Morgan Beatty bounced up and down in front of me while reading the news, Long John Nebel and I tolerated each other on the overnight talk show and George Hamilton Combs taught me what a "class act" was all about. In short, I was right where I wanted to be...a part of radio.

While all this was going on in 1968, I started producing records of old radio shows. Starting with a joint project involving the Mutual Broadcasting System, The Longines Symphonette and my small-but-growing archive, my second project was a resounding success. It was called "Themes Like Old Times" and was merely the openings of 90 famous programs segued together. Initially sold to a book club, the record was picked up by a small record label in California and distributed by Dot-Decca. "Themes Like Old Times" eventually rose to #23 on the Variety chart of LP record sales, ahead of the latest Beatles release at one point for several weeks (whatever became of them?). A comedy album of "W.C. Fields and Charlie McCarthy On Radio" that I did for Columbia never rose higher than 198 on the charts, but was nominated for a Grammy award. Not bad for a beginner! Radiola Records, my own label, went on to be nominated for six Grammies, winning the award only once in 1981 ("Best Dramatic and Spoken Word Record"). The next year, they eliminated the category.

My experiences with Columbia, Dot-Decca and others in the record industry led me to the conclusion that this business was filled with knaves and jackals, and so to maintain control over my own product, I began Radiola Records in 1970. It was the first record label devoted to radio broadcasts. "Radio Yesteryear," the parent company, had switched from being a show on a college station to a mom-and-pop mail order company by 1965. We incorporated in 1967 and were the first to offer radio broadcasts for sale. I continued running the company on an absentee basis while I was working in network radio, but finally the economic realities of being my own boss put an end to my network radio career. After 33 years running Radio Yesteryear, I've decided that leaving CBS was financially the right thing to do...but I still miss real radio. Being called "The Man Who Saved Radio" is a big responsibilty. The job is daunting and I feel unequal to the task, but it certainly is fun trying to meet the challenge. For example, my good friend Pierre Fermat once told me about a huge collection of transcriptions from the 1920s that he found, but left the directions about where they were kept on a page of his book, saying "I have discovered a marvelous batch of transcriptions which this margin is too narrow to contain." That was the last ever I heard from him!

Can you imagine getting paid to listen to and work with all these great radio recordings? The memories of the famous broadcasts I worked on and the creative, intelligent and talented people I worked with (there were some bastards too) make my radio career a most pleasant part of my life.

Now that I'm semi-retired, what of the future? In addition to continuing to "save radio," I plan to occasionally put down my script and step back from the microphone, say the name of "Shazam," and if that lightning bolt finally strikes, "it will be my sacred duty to defend the poor and helpless, right wrongs and crush evil everywhere."

Hello Everybody this is station
B-A-B-Y with a special bulletin

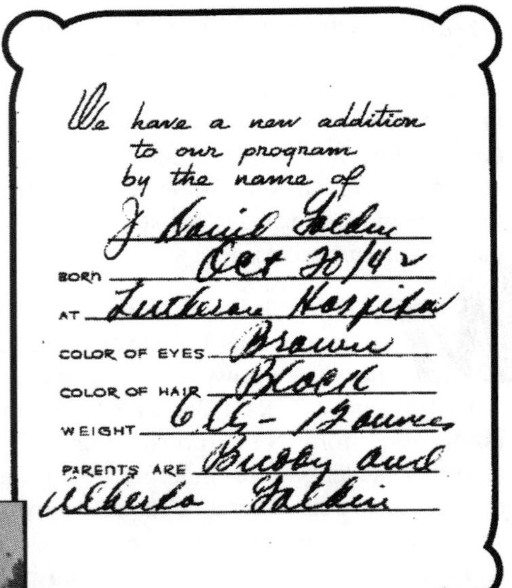

SIGN ON.
My actual birth announcement as mailed to my Uncle Harvey and others I can't stand, late in 1942. My father spent the next three years on a battleship in the Pacific, single-handedly sinking the Japanese Navy.

Reproduced for historical purposes only with thanks to J.S. Liebowitz, President of National Periodical Publications, Inc,.

IN THE PUBLIC INTEREST, CONVENIENCE AND NECESSITY.
Oct. 1961. My first stint in front of a microphone, WNYU in the Bronx. Fellow broadcasters will recognize the Shure mike and the Altec "Birdcage," the Magnacord PT-6 and a Berlant Concertone on the far wall. The console (seen from behind) was reportedly used as an authentic prop during the filming of "Jurassic Park."

Photo by Bernstock.

TROUBLE WEST OF DENVER.
On the air in Alaska. August 1963. Behind me is an example of Tlingit folk art, ahead of me was a better job.

Photo by Birt Hilson.

INCREASED RADIATED POWER.
Sept. 1965. Long John Nebel liked me about as much as I liked him, but his was the only all-night show in town where the guests claimed to have been in flying saucers and had the ability to levitate. The photo was taken at NBC Studio 5B (30 Rock Plaza) from where "Monitor" originated on the weekends. The glass behind us is where Radio City tours went by almost continuously, forcing one and all to wear neckties (except Long John).

MUTUAL...
YOUR NETWORK FOR NEWS.
September 1967. My first day on the job for Mutual Broadcasting, my first assignment: lug a 40 lb. Ampex 601 plus mike, cans, cables and connectors to the Overseas Press Club. The purpose was to interview an ex-Vice President who had recently lost an election for Governor of California. Eighteen minutes into the interview, I discovered a short in my mike cable and that the tape was blank. "I'll have to remember that," he said. The photo is reproduced from a magazine published by the Overseas Press Club.

It's Richard Nixon's turn before the microphone for talk in the Williams Room.

TONIGHT'S GUEST STAR.
August 1974. A chance to watch, interview, listen to and have lunch with a radio immortal. You'll never guess who picked up the check at lunch.

YOU MUST REMEMBER THIS...
A band remote from exotic "Rick's Cafe Americain" in beautiful downtown Casablanca. "Of all the gin joints in all the towns in all the world, she walks into mine! What's that you're playing?" (Just kidding...it's a Warner Brothers movie set.)

TRANSCRIBED FOR PRESENTATION AT A MORE CONVENIENT TIME.
January 1974. Far from the chaos and confusion of network radio, I settled into the peace and tranquility of owning my own company, meeting the payroll and dealing with customers.

A WORD FROM OUR SPONSOR.
I love doing trade shows. You get to travel to many exotic cities, but never leave the convention center. You get to stand on your feet all day and chat with such interesting people. At least in radio you get to sit down!

RETURN TO THE SCENE OF THE CRIME.
February 1998, taken at the CBS net studios on W. 57th Street in New York. The same Ampex 354s were still in use! The Otari deck, the console and the cart machines were new. The IBM tab card reader had been replaced by a slightly more sophisticated computer. It was my first visit in 27 years and only two people actually remembered me. Have I changed that much?
Sic transit gloria radio!

Photo by Gary Scherer.